The Routledge
Wc

The Routledge Handbook of World Englishes constitutes a comprehensive introduction to the study of world Englishes, drawing on the expertise of leading authors within the field.

The handbook is structured in six sections covering historical perspectives, core issues and topics and new debates which together provide a thorough overview of the field, taking into account the new directions in which the discipline is heading.

Among the key themes covered are the development of English as a lingua franca among speakers for whom English is a common but not first language, the parallel development of English as a medium of instruction in educational institutions throughout the world and the role of English as the international language of scholarship and scholarly publishing, as well as the development of computer-mediated Englishes, including cyberprose. The handbook also includes a substantial introduction from the editor.

The Routledge Handbook of World Englishes is the ideal resource for postgraduate students of applied linguistics as well as those in related degrees such as applied English language and TESOL/TEFL.

Andy Kirkpatrick is Professor of Linguistics at Griffith University, Australia.

Routledge Handbooks in Applied Linguistics

Routledge Handbooks in Applied Linguistics provide comprehensive overviews of the key topics in applied linguistics. All entries for the handbooks are specially commissioned and written by leading scholars in the field. Clear, accessible and carefully edited *Routledge Handbooks in Applied Linguistics* are the ideal resource for both advanced undergraduates and postgraduate students.

The Routledge Handbook of Forensic Linguistics
Edited by Malcolm Coulthard and Alison Johnson

The Routledge Handbook of Corpus Linguistics
Edited by Anne O'Keeffe and Mike McCarthy

The Routledge Handbook of World Englishes
Edited by Andy Kirkpatrick

The Routledge Handbook of Applied Linguistics
Edited by James Simpson

The Routledge Handbook of Discourse Analysis
Edited by James Paul Gee and Michael Handford

The Routledge Handbook of Second Language Acquisition
Edited by Susan Gass and Alison Mackey

The Routledge Handbook of Language and Intercultural Communication
Edited by Jane Jackson

The Routledge Handbook of Language Testing
Edited by Glenn Fulcher and Fred Davidson

The Routledge Handbook of Multilingualism
Edited by Marilyn Martin-Jones, Adrian Blackledge and Angela Creese

The Routledge Handbook of Translation Studies
Edited by Carmen Millán-Varela and Francesca Bartrina

The Routledge Handbook of World Englishes

Edited by
Andy Kirkpatrick

Routledge
Taylor & Francis Group

LONDON AND NEW YORK

First published 2010
by Routledge

First published in paperback 2012
by Routledge
2 Park Square, Milton Park, Abingdon, Oxon OX14 4RN

Simultaneously published in the USA and Canada
by Routledge
711 Third Avenue, New York, NY 10017

Routledge is an imprint of the Taylor & Francis Group, an informa business

British Library Cataloguing in Publication Data
A catalogue record for this book is available from the British Library

Library of Congress Cataloging in Publication Data
The Routledge handbook of world Englishes / edited by Andy Kirkpatrick.
    p. cm. – (Routledge handbooks in applied linguistics)
  1. English language–Variation–English-speaking countries. 2. English language–Variation–Foreign countries. 3. English language–Dialects. I. Kirkpatrick, Andy.
  PE1066.R68 2012
  427–dc23
            2012016347

ISBN: 978-0-415-47039-1 (hbk)
ISBN: 978-0-415-62264-6 (pbk)
ISBN: 978-0-203-84932-3 (ebk)

Typeset in Times New Roman
by Taylor & Francis Books

MIX
Paper from
responsible sources
FSC® C004839
www.fsc.org

Printed and bound in Great Britain by
TJ International Ltd, Padstow, Cornwall

Contents

Figures

Maps

Tables

Contributors

Rebecca Black is an assistant professor of Language, Literacy, and Technology in the Department of Education at the University of California, Irvine. She received her PhD from the University of Wisconsin, Madison in 2006. Her research interests centre on how youth, particularly English language learners, are using new technologies to learn, create and communicate. Her publications include a recent book, *Adolescents and Online Fan Fiction*.

Kingsley Bolton is Chair Professor of English and Head of the English Department at the City University of Hong Kong. Professor Bolton was Elected President of the International Association of World Englishes (IAWE) 2003–4. He is an editorial board member of the journals *English World-Wide*, *Journal of English Linguistics* and *World Englishes*, and co-editor of the Cambridge University Press journal *English Today*.

David Britain is Professor of Modern English Linguistics at the University of Bern in Switzerland, having previously worked in the Department of Linguistics at Victoria University of Wellington in New Zealand (1991–3) and in the Department of Language and Linguistics at the University of Essex in England (1993–2009). He has edited *Language in the British Isles* (Cambridge University Press, 2007).

Kate Burridge is Professor of Linguistics at Monash University. Her main research interests are on grammatical change in Germanic languages, Pennsylvania German, linguistic taboo and the structure and history of English. She is a regular presenter of language segments on ABC radio and television.

Yen-Lin Chou is a PhD student in the Department of Education at the University of California, Irvine, specializing in Language, Literacy and Technology. Her research interests include discourse analysis, computer-mediated communication and second language learning and teaching.

Daniel R. Davis is Associate Professor of Linguistics at the University of Michigan-Dearborn. He studied linguistics and Celtic languages at Harvard and Oxford universities. His publications include *The History of World Englishes: North America* (edited, 8 vols, 2003). He is editor of the journal *World Englishes* (Wiley-Blackwell) and President of the International Association of World Englishes (IAWE).

David Deterding is an Associate Professor at the University of Brunei Darussalam. His book *Singapore English* was published by Edinburgh University Press in 2007, and he has papers on the pronunciation of various Englishes in a wide range of international journals.

Gerard J. Docherty is Professor of Phonetics at Newcastle University in the north-east of England. His research is focused on determining how the phonetic performance of speakers is shaped by the various dimensions (physical, linguistic, cognitive and social) of spoken communication, with a view to developing theories which account for the systematic properties of speech in its social context. He has recently undertaken a number of projects looking at the production and perception of sociophonetic properties of speech across a number of varieties of English.

Adriana González holds a doctorate in linguistics (TESOL) from the State University of New York at Stony Brook. She is an Associate Professor in the undergraduate and graduate programs in foreign language teacher education at the School of Languages of the Universidad de Antioquia in Medellín, Colombia. She is the current secretary of the Colombian Association of English Teachers (ASOCOPI).

Ha Jin left China for the United States in 1985 and began to write in English after the Tiananmen incident in 1989. To date he has published three volumes of poetry, four books of short fiction, five novels and a book of essays, all in English. His works have received several awards, including the National Book Award (1999) and the PEN/Faulkner Award (2000 and 2005), and have been translated into more than thirty languages. He teaches fiction writing and literature at Boston University.

Azirah Hashim is a Professor in the English Language Department, Faculty of Languages and Linguistics, University of Malaya. Her research interests include Language and Law, Discourse of Advertising and English in Malaysia and in the Region.

Raymond Hickey studied for his MA in Trinity College, Dublin, and did his PhD at Kiel, Germany, in 1980. He completed his second doctorate (German Habilitation) in Bonn in 1985 and has held professorial appointments at four German universities (Bonn, Munich, Bayreuth, Essen). His main research interests are computer corpus processing, extraterritorial varieties of English (especially Irish English), Dublin English and general questions of language contact, shift and change.

Andy Kirkpatrick is Chair Professor of English as an International Language at the Hong Kong Institute of Education and Director of the Institute's Research Centre into Language Education and Acquisition in Multilingual Societies (www.ied.edu.hk/rcleams). His most recent book is *English as a Lingua Franca in ASEAN: The Multilingual Model*, published (2010) by Hong Kong University Press.

Bernd Kortmann is Full Professor of English Language and Linguistics at the University of Freiburg, Germany. His publications include four monographs, six edited volumes, a two-volume handbook-cum-CD-ROM on the phonology and morphosyntax of the varieties of English around the world (2004), and about eighty articles and reviews in journals and collective volumes. His main research interest over the last decade has been the grammar of non-standard varieties of English around the world, especially from a typological perspective.

William A. Kretzschmar, Jr. teaches English and Linguistics as Harry and Jane Willson Professor in Humanities at the University of Georgia. His major publications include *The Linguistics of Speech* (Cambridge, 2009), and *The Oxford Dictionary of Pronunciation for Current English* (Oxford, 2001) He is the editor of the American Linguistic Atlas Project, the oldest and largest national research project to survey how people speak differently in different parts of the country.

Stephen Levey is Assistant Professor of Linguistics at the University of Ottawa. His research deals with variation in contemporary English, focusing on linguistic variability in urban settings, as well as the language of children and adolescents.

David C.S. Li is Professor in the English Department of the Hong Kong Institute of Education. His research interests are mainly related to the study of social aspects of language learning and use in multilingual settings. He has published in three main areas: World Englishes and perceptions of 'Hongkong English', code-switching in Hong Kong and Taiwan, and EFL learners' difficulties and error-correction strategies.

Low Ee Ling is concurrently Associate Professor at the English Language and Literature Academic Group and Associate Dean of Programme and Student Development at the National Institute of Education, Singapore. Her research interests are in acoustic phonetics and features-based studies on world varieties of English, English language teacher education and teacher education in general.

Margaret Maclagan is Associate Professor of Communication Disorders at the University of Canterbury. Her research interests include sound change over time in New Zealand English and the Maori language. She is a member of the Origins of New Zealand English (ONZE) and Maori and New Zealand English (MAONZE) research groups.

James McLellan is a Lecturer in Sociolinguistics and Applied Linguistics at the University of Waikato, Hamilton, Aotearoa (New Zealand). He previously taught at secondary and tertiary levels in Malaysia (1978–84) and in Brunei Darussalam (1986–2002). His research interests include Malay–English codeswitching, language maintenance and shift in Borneo, language policy in education and Southeast Asian varieties of English.

Ahmar Mahboob is a Senior Lecturer in the Department of Linguistics at the University of Sydney. His research interests include educational linguistics, teacher education, minority languages (in South Asia), language policy development, NNEST studies, pidgin and creole languages, pragmatics and World Englishes. He is the co-editor of *Questioning Linguistics* (2008) with Naomi Knight; *Studies in Applied Linguistics* *and Language Learning* (2009) with Caroline Lipovsky; *Appliable Linguistics: Texts, Contexts, and Meanings* (in press for 2010) with Naomi Knight.

Isabel Pefianco Martin is Associate Professor and Coordinator for Research at the School of Humanities, Ateneo de Manila University. She was Chair of the English Department from 1998 to 2004, President of the Linguistic Society of the Philippines (LSP) from 2006 to 2008, and Secretary of the American Studies Association of the Philippines (ASAP) in 2006.

Joyce T. Mathangwane is an Associate Professor of Language and Linguistics in the Department of English, University of Botswana. She has published widely in the areas of Bantu phonology and morphology, sociolinguistics, comparative linguistics and onomastics.

Anna Mauranen is Professor of English at the University of Helsinki. Her current major research interests are English as a lingua franca, corpus linguistics and modelling spoken language. Her publications focus on spoken language, corpus linguistics, contrastive rhetoric, translation and academic discourses. She is Director of the ELFA project, which has compiled a 1-million word corpus of academic ELF (the ELFA corpus).

Dushyanthi Mendis is a Senior Lecturer at the Department of English, University of Colombo, Sri Lanka. She has a PhD in Linguistics from the University of Michigan, Ann Arbor, and her research interests are sociolinguistics, corpus linguistics and discourse analysis. She is currently involved in compiling the International Corpus of English – Sri Lanka (ICE-SL), in collaboration with the University of Giessen, Germany.

Andrew Moody is an Associate Professor of Linguistics in the English Department at the University of Macau, where he teaches sociolinguistics at both the undergraduate and graduate levels. His research interests include the development of varieties of World Englishes and the role of English in popular culture, especially within Asia. Currently he is editing, together with Jamie Shinhee Lee, a collection of essays for Hong Kong University Press entitled *English in Asian Pop Culture*.

Joybrato Mukherjee is Full Professor of English Linguistics at Justus Liebig University, Giessen (Germany). His research interests include applied linguistics and corpus linguistics, English lexico-grammar and syntax, South Asian varieties of English and English as a world language.

Catherine Nickerson is an Associate Professor at Zayed University in the United Arab Emirates. She has lived in India, the United States, the Netherlands and the United Kingdom. She has been teaching and researching the use of English as an international business language for the past fifteen years.

Tope Omoniyi is the Chair of Sociolinguistics in the School of Arts, Roehampton University, in London. He is also a poet and the author of *Farting Presidents and Other Poems* (Kraft Books, 2001). His poems have also appeared in journals in Nigeria (*ANA Review*), Singapore (*AWARE*), Malaysia (*Tenggara* and *The Gombak Review*), USA (Quill Books and *Anthropology and Humanism*), UK (*The Unruly Sun*), seven Forward Press anthologies, and in Sweden (*Nordic African Institute Newsletter*). In 1985, he won a runner-up prize in the National Anti-Apartheid Poetry Competition in Nigeria and in 2001 he received a honourable mention in the *Anthropology and Humanism* Annual Poetry Competition. The poems published in *African Writing On-line* are from a yet-to-be published collection titled *Word-o-graphs*, a series of pictures in verse form of the poet's response to some of the places he has been.

Alastair Pennycook is Professor of Language Studies at the University of Technology Sydney. He is interested in how we understand language in relation to globalization, colonial history, identity, popular culture and pedagogy. His many publications include *Critical Applied Linguistics: A Critical Introduction* (Lawrence Erlbaum, 2001) and *Global Englishes and Transcultural Flows* (Routledge, 2007). His new book *Language as a Local Practice* (Routledge) is due for publication in 2010.

Carmen Pérez-Llantada is a Senior Lecturer of English at the University of Zaragoza, Spain. She is interested in genre-based, pragmatic and rhetorical analyses of academic speech and writing. With G.R. Ferguson (University of Sheffield), she co-edited *English as a GloCalisation Phenomenon: Observations from a Linguistic Microcosm* (2006).

Zoya Proshina is currently Professor in Department of Theory of FLT, School of Foreign Languages and Area Studies, Lomonosov Moscow State University (Moscow, Russia), where she teaches EFL, the WE paradigm, cross-cultural communication, translation and interpretation theory and practice. She is currently President (2010–12) of the International Association of World Englishes.

Harshana Rambukwella completed his PhD on representations of nationalism in Sri Lankan writing at the University of Hong Kong in 2008. He is now Honorary Assistant Professor at the School of English, University of Hong Kong. Harshana's research interests are postcolonial literatures in English and the role of historical narratives in community and national identity formation.

Edgar W. Schneider holds the Chair of English Linguistics at the University of Regensburg, Germany. He has written and edited several books and published widely on the dialectology, sociolinguistics, history, semantics and world-wide varieties of English. He edits the scholarly journal *English World-Wide* and an associated book series.

Barbara Seidlhofer is Professor of English and Applied Linguistics at the University of Vienna, Austria. She is the founding director of the Vienna–Oxford International Corpus of English (VOICE).

Farzad Sharifian is an Associate Professor and the Director of the Language and Society Centre within the School of Languages, Cultures and Linguistics, Monash University, Australia. He is also the Convenor of the academic program of English as an International Language at Monash University. He has a wide range of research interests including cultural linguistics, pragmatics, English as an International Language, World Englishes, language and politics, and intercultural communication. He is the editor of *English as an International Language* (2009, Multilingual Matters).

Hazel Simmons-McDonald is Pro-Vice Chancellor and Principal of the Open Campus of the University of the West Indies, a post she has held from 2007. She is Professor of Applied Linguistics and her primary research interests are second language acquisition and literacy development in creole contexts. She served for several years as the Secretary-Treasurer of the Society for Caribbean Linguistics, as Vice President for one year, and as President in 2008–9.

Augustin Simo Bobda holds several academic and professional qualifications from Cameroon, Great Britain and America. He is Professor of English Language and Linguistics and Head of the Department of English at the Higher Teaching Training College (Ecole Normale Supérieure) of the University of Yaounde I. He is the author of over seventy journal articles, book chapters, edited volumes, textbooks and monographs on various aspects of English language, linguistics, sociolinguistics and applied linguistics.

Birgit Smieja is a lecturer at the University of Koblenz-Landau in the Department of English, teaching English to students aiming at becoming teachers for primary school. She has published and co-authored several books in the area of sociolinguistics with a focus on Africa.

John M. Swales is Professor Emeritus of Linguistics at the University of Michigan, where he was also Director of the English Language Institute from 1985 to 2001. Books that appeared in 2009 include two small textbooks (with Chris Feak) on aspects of advanced academic literacy (*Abstracts and the Writing of Abstracts* and *Telling a Research Story*) and *Incidents in an Educational Life: A Memoir (Of Sorts)*, all published by the University of Michigan Press.

Eszter Szenes is a PhD candidate in the Department of Linguistics at the University of Sydney. She graduated as a Master of Arts in English Language and Literature and TESOL in 2005 in Budapest, Hungary. Her research interests include Systemic Functional Linguistics, academic literacy, World Englishes, NNEST studies and Critical Applied Linguistics.

Yuko Takeshita is Professor in the Faculty of Social Sciences, Toyo Eiwa University. As a founding member and a board member of the Japanese Association for Asian Englishes, she has focused on intercultural communication between Thai and Japanese people. She has been an editor of *Asian Englishes*, has worked as a researcher for the Education Ministry and as the director of a municipal Board of Education.

Brian Tomlinson is a Visiting Professor at Leeds Metropolitan University and the Founder and President of MATSDA (the international Materials Development Association). He has worked in Indonesia, Japan, Nigeria, Oman, Singapore, Vanuatu and Zambia and has published numerous books and articles on materials development for language learning, on language through literature, on language awareness and on English as an international language.

T. Ruanni F. Tupas is Senior Lecturer, Centre for English Language Communication (CELC), National University of Singapore (NUS). He is the 2009 recipient of the

Andrew Gonzalez Distinguished Professorial Chair in Linguistics and Language Education awarded by the Linguistic Society of the Philippines, and a 2008 National Book Award Finalist for the edited volume *(Re)Making Society: The Politics of Language, Discourse and Identity in the Philippines* (University of the Philippines Press, 2007).

Mark Warschauer is Professor of Education and Informatics at the University of California, Irvine, and director of the Digital Learning Lab at the university. He also directs the university's PhD in Education program, which includes a specialization in Language, Literacy and Technology. His books include *Laptops and Literacy: Learning in the Wireless Classroom* (Teachers College Press, 2006); *Technology and Social Inclusion: Rethinking the Digital Divide* (MIT Press, 2004).

Hans-Georg Wolf is Associate Professor in the School of English at the University of Hong Kong, and currently also holds the Chair for Development and Variation of the English Language at the University of Potsdam. His research interests include sociolinguistics (in particular World Englishes), cognitive linguistics and intercultural pragmatics.

Xu Zhichang is Assistant Professor in the English Department of the Hong Kong Institute of Education. His current research interests include teaching English in multilingual settings, Chinese English (CE) studies, language and cross-cultural education, blended learning and teaching, developing academic literacy, and teacher training. He is currently working on *Chinese English: Features and Implications* for the Open University of Hong Kong Press.

Abbreviations

1s	first-person singular pronoun
1pi	first-person plural inclusive pronoun
1pe	first-person plural exclusive pronoun
3s	third-person singular pronoun
3p	third-person plural pronoun
<	comes from
>	becomes
*	reconstructed or unattested form
AAVE	African American Vernacular English
AbE	(Australian) Aboriginal English
ABBR	abbreviation
AppE	Appalachian English
AusCs	Australian Creoles
AusVE	Australian Vernacular English
AV	active verb
BahE	Bahamian English
BelC	Belizean Creole
BlSAfE	Black South African English
ButlE	Butler English (India)
CamE	Cameroon English
CamP	Cameroon Pidgin
ChcE	Chicano English
CollAmE	Colloquial American English
CollAusE	Colloquial Australian English
CollBrE	Colloquial British English
DEM	demonstrative
DM	discourse particle/marker
EAfE	East African English
FijE	Fiji English
FUT	future

GhE	Ghanaian English
GhP	Ghanaian Pidgin
Gmc	Germanic
HawC	Hawaii Creole
HKE	Hong Kong English
IMP	imperative
INT	interrogative particle/marker
IndE	Indian English
InSAfE	Indian South African English
IrE	Irish English
IsSE US	South Eastern American English enclave dialects
JamC	Jamaican Creole
JamE	Jamaican English
Lat	Latin
MalE	Malaysian English
Mid	English Midlands
Nfk	Norfolk
NfldE	Newfoundland English
NigP	Nigerian Pidgin
NIrE	Northern Irish English
NZE	New Zealand English
OzE	Ozarks English
PakE	Pakistani English
PASS	passive
PhilE	Philippines English
POSS	possessive
RDP	reduplication
REL	relative
ScE	Scottish English
SgE	Singapore English
ScH	Scottish Highlands
SolP	Solomon Islands Pidgin
SurC	Suriname Creoles
Tob/TrnC	Tobagonian/Trinidadian Creole
TP	Tok Pisin, New Guinea Pidgin, Neomelanesian
WelE	Welsh English
WhSAfE	White South African English
N	North
EA	East Anglia
SW	Southwest
SE	Southeast

Introduction

Andy Kirkpatrick

It is commonly accepted that there are now many more people who speak English as a second or later language than there are native speakers of it. In China alone, some estimate that there are as many learners of English (some 350 million) as there are native speakers of it (Xu, this volume). This means that the great majority of the world's English users are multilinguals. As Graddol (2006: 114) has pointed out, this extraordinary increase in the number of English speakers in today's world means that the position and prestige previously associated with being a native speaker of English is becoming questioned. Furthermore, the monolingual speaker of English is likely to be at a considerable disadvantage in today's multilingual world, especially when so many of the multilinguals have English as one of their languages.

The spread of English – where 'spread implies adaptation and non-conformity' (Widdowson 1997: 140) – has seen the development of many different varieties of English. Many of these newer varieties of English developed in places which were colonized by English-speaking colonizers, primarily from Great Britain, but also from the United States of America, as was the case in the Philippines, for example. New varieties developed in these countries and some of these later became institutionalized. Thus we can now talk about the different varieties of English across many parts of the world, including many African countries, in the subcontinent, across Asia and in the Caribbean. We can also talk about the different varieties of English which exist *within* each country where English has become institutionalized.

Varieties of English are not restricted to these postcolonial settings, of course. There remains an extraordinary range of varieties and variation within the traditional homes of English. Great Britain is host to a large number of distinctive vernaculars of English, from Doric in the north east of Scotland to West Country in Devon and Cornwall. The United States is also home to a wide range of English vernaculars, as are the other 'settlement' colonies (Mufwene 2001) such as Australia and New Zealand, where local varieties of English spoken by Australian Aborigines and New Zealand Maori add to the mix.

Kachru, the scholar who could be called the founding father of World Englishes as a discipline, classified the various types of Englishes using a circles analogy (Kachru 1992). This classification is adopted or discussed by a number of contributors to this volume, and Schneider (Chapter 21) gives a useful summary. Kachru called the Eng-lishes of Great Britain, the United States and settlement colonies in general, 'inner circle' varieties. The new Englishes that developed in these settlement colonies depen-ded more on the speech of the settlers themselves, although the speech and languages of the indigenous inhabitants naturally had – and continue to have – some influence. The Englishes which developed in the trade or exploitation colonies, such as those in Africa and Asia, were naturally more influenced by the languages of the indigenous peo-ples, simply because there was much more contact between the colonizers and the locals and because the locals usually represented the overwhelming majority of the population. Kachru classified these Englishes as 'outer circle' varieties. The third 'circle' of Eng-lishes which Kachru identified belonged to the 'expanding circle'. These were found in countries where English was traditionally learned as a foreign language and in which English played little or no administrative or institutional role. As Kachru himself has pointed out, however, it is in these expanding circle countries where the development of English has been most pronounced in recent years. For example, as China's eco-nomic and political influence spreads, so has the role of English increased in importance for many educated Chinese within China. As argued by several contributors to this Handbook, it seems likely that new varieties of English will develop in at least some of the countries which were classified as belonging to the expanding circle.

In addition to these regional varieties of English, there is also a range of Englishes whose roles and features are determined by their function. These include, for example, the Englishes of businesses and computer-mediated Englishes. They include the Eng-lishes of academia and of pop culture. And, as Pennycook reminds us in the final chapter of this Handbook, we are also seeing the emergence of 'translingua franca English' whereby 'new' English speakers draw on linguistic resources which are not determined by national boundaries.

The very number of different varieties of English – both 'traditional' and 'new' – coupled with the extraordinary increase in the use of English as the international lingua franca among English-speaking multilinguals, means that the publication of this *Handbook of World Englishes* is timely. The Handbook aims to provide the general reader and student with an overview of recent developments and debates in this rapidly expanding field. It should be stressed, however, that no Handbook of World Englishes could ever be complete. There are simply too many Englishes and varieties of these to be covered in a single volume. Instead, this Handbook will provide an overview and description of a selected number of Englishes, regional, national, functional and international, along with a review of recent trends, debates and the implications of these new developments for the future of English.

The Handbook is divided into six sections, namely 'Historical perspectives and tradi-tional Englishes', 'Regional varieties and the "New" Englishes', 'Emerging trends and themes', 'Contemporary contexts and functions', 'Debates and pedagogical implications' and 'The future'.

Section I: Historical perspectives and traditional Englishes

Section I comprises eight chapters. In 'Standardized English: the history of the earlier circles', Daniel Davis presents a richly illustrated historical survey of the major effects of linguistic change on the standardized forms of English and shows that the standar-dized forms of inner circle Englishes are themselves hybrid forms. In this sense, therefore, they are comparable to new varieties of English. There never was a 'pure' English. All varieties of English have been shaped by contact with other languages. He argues that an 'awareness of the hybrid origins of standardized inner circle Englishes can help speakers and linguists to contextualize and contain the defensive language ideologies of that circle'. Chapters 2 and 3 describe grammatical and phonological variation in contemporary British Englishes. 'Grammatical variation in the contemporary spoken English of England' (David Britain) shows that standard British English is a 'minority dialect' and describes a wide variety of non-standard features across a range of English vernaculars. Britain concludes that 'diversity reigns' and that non-standard forms are the rule rather than the exception. In Chapter 3, 'Phonological innovation in contemporary spoken British English', Gerry Docherty provides examples of phonological variation across a number of vernaculars, but argues that, while our knowledge of phonological variation has increased, 'we are still some way short of a comprehensive understanding of the dynamics of phonological innovation and change'.

Chapters 4 to 8 provide descriptions of the Englishes of Ireland, the United States, Canada, Australia and New Zealand respectively. In Chapter 4, 'The Englishes of Ireland: emergence and transportation', Ray Hickey stresses that Irish English comprises a number of varieties and traces the historical development of these Englishes in Ireland. He also describes the transportation of Irish English overseas and illustrates how it has influenced Englishes in other parts of the world. For example, he shows that the Newfoundland usages of '*ye*' for plural and the structures, '*he's after spilling the beer*' and '*that place do be really busy*' can all be traced to Irish influence. 'The development of Standard American English' (William Kretzschmar) traces the development of American English and the emergence of Standard American English (SAE). In this, Noah Webster was pivotal and his *American Spelling Book* had sold more than 5 million copies by 1831. This far outsold Webster's more famous *American Dictionary of the English Language*. Kretzschmar concludes that what is really important about SAE 'is the perception that it exists, reflecting an attitude towards language and standards that Webster originally sold to Americans and which our schools still promote today'. In Chapter 6, 'The Englishes of Canada', Stephen Levey argues that Canadian English does not constitute a uniform variety, as frequently claimed, but is characterized by diversity, but that this has not yet been adequately investigated. He provides examples to show that diversity is an integral part of the Canadian linguistic landscape.

Chapters 7 and 8 take the reader to the southern hemisphere. 'English in Australia' (Kate Burridge) begins with the early story of Australian English and then describes and illustrates a selection of the distinctive features of Australian English. She also describes and illustrates a number of distinctive cultural and discourse features of Australian English, pointing out that the current Australian attachment of the 'vernacular' can be traced back to the linguistic habits of the early settlers. She quotes a 1911 commentator:

> But, in addition to this lack of good-breeding and the gross mispronunciation of common English words, the Australian interlards his conversation with large quantities of slang, which make him frequently unintelligible to the visitor.

Chapter 7 concludes with a discussion about the respective roles of the indigenous and migrant communities upon the development of Englishes in Australia and the possible influence of Americanization. The final chapter of Section I is 'The Englishes of New Zealand' and Margaret Maclagan points out that New Zealand English is unique among inner circle Englishes in that 'recorded evidence is available for its entire history'. The chapter traces the historical development of New Zealand English and includes sections on the Maori language, Maori English and Pasifika English. Maclagan also offers illustrations of the use of various Englishes in literature, as in this example from Alan Duff's novel *Once Were Warriors*:

> Fear on the associate's face. Real fear. Like he's walked into a nightmare and only just realised it. Nig feeling sorry for him, Okay lettem fight, the scared fulla agreein. The Brown givinim a wicked smile: Thas cool, man. Make it in half an hour; give my boys time ta warm up. Chuckling at the scared dude. C'mon, boys. pulling his three dogs away. Y'c'n have ya suppa in half an hour. Laughing.

Section II: Regional varieties and the 'new' Englishes

The eleven chapters of Section II provide descriptions and discussions of the features and roles of English in a variety of different geographical regions. Some of these varieties (e.g. Chapters 9, 10, 11, 12, 13, 15 and 18) have developed in postcolonial settings and can be considered 'outer circle' varieties. Others, however (e.g. Chapters 15, 16, 17 and 19), have developed in settings where English was traditionally learned as a foreign language and would have been considered as belonging to the 'expanding circle'. As the authors of these chapters point out, however, the role of English in each country has developed to a remarkable degree in the past decade or so, so that English is now more than simply a 'foreign' language in these countries.

Chapter 9, 'The development of the English language in India' (Joybrato Mukherjee) describes the development of English in India using Schneider's evolutionary model (itself the topic of Chapter 21). Mukherjee also provides examples of a selection of linguistic features of standard Indian English and discusses their causes or origins, arguing that many of the innovations have been caused, not by L1 interference, but by 'nativized semantico-structural analogy'. For example, the new verb of Indian English 'de-confirm' is created by analogy from a verb like 'destabilize'. The author concludes that Indian English can be classified as a semi-autonomous variety which has been extremely important in identity construction, especially in the field of creative writing. The subcontinent is also the topic of Chapter 10, 'Sri Lankan Englishes'. The authors, Dushyanthi Mendis and Harshana Rambukwella, quote Meyler (2007: x–xi) to help outline the complexity of the Englishes of Sri Lanka:

> Even within a small country like Sri Lanka, and even within the relatively tiny English-speaking community, there are several sub-varieties of Sri Lankan English. Sinhalese, Tamils, Muslims and Burghers speak different varieties; Christians, Buddhists, Hindus and Muslims have their own vocabularies; the older generation speak a different language from the younger generation; and the wealthy Colombo elite (who tend to speak English as their first language) speak a different variety from the wider community (who are more likely to learn it as a second language).

The authors also report the confusion in Sri Lanka over the belief that English is an official language, and point out that this is not the case, as the Constitution terms it a 'link' language, a supposedly 'neutral' language to be used to link the Sinhalese majority and the Tamil minority. But, as the authors show, it is actually far more than simply a link language, being the language of the Supreme Court, among other things. The chapter considers the current status and role of English in Sri Lanka and concludes with illustrations from Sri Lankan creative writing in English.

The focus shifts to Africa for Chapters 11 and 12. In Chapter 11, 'East and West African Englishes: differences and commonalities', Hans-Georg Wolf provides an overview and comparison of the development of Englishes in East and West Africa and argues that 'British colonial policy contributed significantly to the sociolinguistic and, indirectly, even to the structural similarities and differences these varieties exhibit'. Wolf also cautions, however, that despite the similarities, the Englishes of West Africa are more hetero-geneous than those of East Africa, and need to be seen in their own right. Examples from Cameroon, Nigerian, Ghanaian, Liberian, Sierra Leonian and Gambian English are pro-vided. The chapter concludes with a discussion on 'cultural conceptualizations' and a call for more research into cultural conceptualizations of World Englishes in general. In Chapter 12, 'The development of English in Botswana: language policy and education', Birgit Smieja and Joyce Mathangwane describe the multilingual situation within Bots-wana and the role English plays within this multilingual nation. The authors critically evaluate Botswana's national language policy and show that English is privileged at the expense of local languages. Nevertheless, they conclude that, even though a Botswana variety of English has developed, of which they provide examples, English presents little threat to the main language of the nation, Setswana.

Chapters 13, 14, 15 and 16 consider the development of Englishes in East and South East Asia. 'English in Singapore and Malaysia: differences and similarities' is the title of Chapter 13, and Low Ee Ling first provides a brief comparative history of the development of English in these two neighbouring countries. She shows that, despite many historical similarities, the roles of English in Malaysia and Singapore have been and remain quite different. She then compares and contrasts a selection of linguistic features from the standard varieties of Singaporean and Malaysian Englishes and, in conclusion, predicts that the two varieties will continue to diverge, especially given the Malaysian government's recent decision to replace English with Malay as the medium of instruction in primary and secondary schools.

In Chapter 14, 'Periphery ELT: the policy and practice of English teaching in the Philippines', Isabel Martin discusses the place of English in the Philippines from the perspective of its past as an American colony. 'Throughout the American colonial period, English was systematically promoted as the language that would "civilize" the Filipi-nos.' Evidence that the colonial influence remains is that the school English curriculum remains largely based on American authors, despite the large quantity of excellent local creative writing in English. The author then goes on to challenge a number of accepted myths concerning the superior status of American English in the Filipino context. She concludes with some lines from the Filipino poet Amador T. Daguio:

Though I may speak the English language,
Let me tell you: I am a Filipino,
I stand for that which make my nation,
The virtues of the country where I was born.
I may have traces of the American,
Be deceived not: Spain has, too, her traces in me,
But my songs are those of my race.

Chapter 15, 'East Asian Englishes: Japan and Korea' (Yuko Takeshita) compares and contrasts the development and status of English in Japan and Korea and provides examples of linguistic features of these varieties. She recounts the controversies surrounding the recent proposals to make English an official language in both countries and describes the extraordinary lengths that Koreans are prepared to go to in order to ensure their children learn English. These range from extended periods of overseas travel to lingual surgery. Takeshita predicts that 'Cultural, financial and personal sacrifices will inevitably continue to be made in this search for "better" English'. In this context, she argues that this task would be made both easier and more equitable if the stakeholders concerned would accept Korean and Japanese varieties of English as models, rather than insisting on a native-speaker model.

Chapter 16, 'Chinese English: a future power?' (Xu Zhichang), reviews the debate surrounding the definitions of Chinese English (CE), and then provides a detailed linguistic description of CE. His discussion is illustrated by an extensive selection of distinct lexical, syntactic and discourse features of CE, including an account of the importance of 'home town discourse' in Chinese communication. He concludes that, with an estimated 350 million Chinese currently learning English, CE 'shall become a major variety of English, and a powerful member of the World Englishes family'.

'Slavic Englishes: education or culture?' (Zoya Proshina) is the title of Chapter 17. Proshina first describes the current sociolinguistic situation in Russia, especially with regard to the status and role of English in education, on the one hand, and in popular culture, on the other. Many pop music lyrics and the names of bands are either in English or in some form of code-mixed Russian and English. A new wave of émigré Russian authors has also given rise to a new generation of Russian writers writing in English. Among the examples provided by Proshina is this excerpt from a novel by Ulinich:

> She needed to discuss the upcoming Winter Pageant. The first-grade girls, the teacher explained, would play Snowflake Fairies … twirling tutus, flying blond braids, and flushed pink faces, against which Grandfather Frost and Snegurochka were to display their benevolence.

Proshina then illustrates the distinctive linguistic and pragmatic features of Russian English. Some features of what she calls 'Rushlish', a basilectal less educated variety of Russian English, are also provided and include *dishvoska* ('dishwasher') and the adding of Russian suffixes to mark plurals as in *shoesy* and *childrenyata*.

In Chapter 18, 'West Indian Englishes: an introduction to literature written in selected varieties', Hazel Simmons-McDonald first describes the emergence of Caribbean creoles and reviews various definitions of the term 'creole', citing Roberts (1988: 110) in this context:

> The traditional and most tenacious interpretations of the word 'Creole' itself accord a crucial role to the child … However, most theories explicitly or implicitly regard the initial formative period of West Indian language as second-language learning by West African speakers with then a second stage which involved first-language learning by children born into a slave society.

She then discusses how West Indian poets and writers have exploited and adopted vernacular and standard varieties of English in their writing, using excerpts from the works of the Jamaican poet Edward Baugh and the St Lucian playwright Derek Walcott to illustrate this. She concludes the chapter by suggesting that 'The significant contribution of West Indian writers to the international recognition and acceptance of creoles and creole-influenced vernaculars as "alternative English varieties" presents a compelling medium through which the full potential of these languages can be appreciated'.

Chapter 19, 'English and English teaching in Colombia: tensions and possibilities in the expanding circle', concludes Section II. Here, Adriana Gonzalez first provides a general picture of the status of English in Columbia and then describes a wide selection of the linguistic features of Islander, the English-based creole spoken on the islands of San Andres and Providencia. She then moves on to discuss the rapid expansion of English in mainland Colombia and shows that the increasing use of English in higher education is but one cause of this heightened demand. The tensions of the chapter's title include the notion of bilingualism in Colombia being restricted to Spanish–English bilingualism, as though proficiency in indigenous languages was not worth considering. She concludes by urging the adoption of a far more critical approach to English and English language teaching in Colombia.

Section III: Emerging trends and themes

The six chapters that comprise Section III all deal with some aspect of an emerging trend or theme in the field of World Englishes. No topic has caused as much controversy in recent times as the role and definition of English as a lingua franca, and in Chapter 20, 'Lingua franca English: the European context', Barbara Seidlhofer queries the discrepancy between the official promotion of multilingualism in Europe on the one hand and the obvious, but often ignored, fact that English is becoming increasingly important as Europe's lingua franca. She asks, 'Why are official communications and websites suggesting that there is a fully functional multilingualism in EU institutions, while, unofficially, one learns from the people involved that this is simply not the case?' She then goes on to point out that English is, in fact, the *de facto* lingua franca of Europe and argues that if this indisputable fact were officially acknowledged, it could have extremely important implications for European language policy. These include perceiving English as a lingua franca as 'a co-existent and non-competitive addition to the learner/user's linguistic repertoire' rather than as the language spoken by native speakers of English. In this way, she argues, the threat of English is diminished. It is simply a lingua franca used by most Europeans and can exist alongside other languages.

The next three chapters, Chapters 21, 22 and 23, look at emerging patterns in World Englishes from different perspectives. In Chapter 21, 'Developmental patterns of English: similar or different?', Edgar Schneider starts by reviewing 'the historical processes by which English came to be spoken in new lands, and the sociolinguistic settings which determine its uses today'. He then moves on to examine the linguistic features of new varieties of English and proposes a number of linguistic processes that influence these, from koinéization – the emergence of a 'middle of the road' variety – to structural nativization and the adaption of indigenous forms. A discussion of various developmental frameworks for new varieties of English comprises the third part of the chapter and this includes a presentation of Schneider's own 'dynamic' model. In conclusion, he cautions that 'the outcome of the task of establishing similarities and differences between

World Englishes in terms of their evolutionary patterns and properties needs to be critically assessed'.

Chapter 22, 'Variation across Englishes: phonology' (David Deterding) compares and contrasts the pronunciation of three outer circle Englishes, namely Indian, Nigerian and Singaporean. Deterding also compares these with other outer circle varieties of English and finally considers the implications of these systems of pronunciation for mutual intelligibility. He concludes that it seems likely that patterns of pronunciation found in a wide range of outer circle Englishes will have a substantial influence on the way that the language evolves in the future, 'so even if these patterns do not constitute a world standard that is adopted by everyone, they will at least become increasingly accepted as one possible standard'.

Chapter 23, 'Variation across Englishes: syntax' (Bernd Kortmann) is the companion chapter to Chapter 22 (and both are companion chapters to Chapters 2 and 3). The core of Kortmann's chapter comprises a survey of grammatical (morphosyntactic) variation alongside a critical discussion of the likely causes of such variation. He draws on data from 46 varieties of English and presents a list of the most likely candidates to be classified as the most common linguistic features across all these varieties. In the discussion of the most likely causes of the shared and distinctive features in these varieties, he argues that

> variety type – and not geography – is of primary importance, at least when we look at large-scale patterns, profiles and coding strategies in morphosyntax. It is to be expected that the impact of geography is stronger in phonology, in the lexicon and in phraseology.

A common characteristic of many new varieties of English is the use of code-mixing and this is the topic of Chapter 24, 'Mixed codes, or varieties of English?', in which James McLellan first points out that it is a truism that speakers of World Englishes 'have access to other languages in the linguistic ecosystem of their national or local community'. Drawing on data from Brunei online discussion forums, McLellan illustrates how multilingual speakers of English and varieties of Malay use and mix these languages in different ways, sometimes using only one of the languages and, at other times, mixing them in significantly different ways. He argues that these multilingual speakers are linguistically highly sophisticated and have 'a continuum of code choices', one of which is represented by equal language alternation, in which both English and Malay play an equal role.

The final chapter in this section is 'Semantics and pragmatic conceptualizations within an emerging variety: Persian English' (Farzad Sharifian). The chapter presents a semantic–pragmatic account of Persian English and includes a description of selected Persian cultural values. One such is *târof*, which is realized linguistically through the use of "ostensible" invitations, repeated rejection of offers, insisting on making offers, hesitation in making requests, giving frequent compliments, hesitation in making complaints, etc. Often, a combination of these occurs, in varying degrees, within one conversation. The major aim of *târof* is to negotiate and lubricate social relationships. Sharifian argues that the study of World Englishes needs to include studies of distinctive cultural values such as these in order to establish 'metacultural competence' in speakers of World Englishes, and for researchers to construct comparative cultural maps to help in intercultural communication through English.

Section IV: Contemporary contexts and functions

The first two chapters of Section IV are by creative writers for whom English is an additional language. In Chapter 26, 'In defence of foreignness', the Chinese novelist Ha Jin discusses the obstacles faced by creative writers for whom English is not a given but an acquisition. He considers in detail the linguistic struggles and work of Conrad, 'the founding figure of this literary tradition', and of Nabokov, 'its acme', and records the criticism Edmund Wilson made of Nabokov's use of English. Two of the major technical challenges facing such writers are how to present non-native speakers' Englishes and how to present their mother tongues in English. Ha Jin describes how he himself has attempted to meet these challenges and recounts how Updike referred to some expressions from Ha Jin's novel, *A Free Life*, as 'small solecisms', a comment the Chinese media reported widely, as Updike is revered in China. But, as Ha Jin points out, 'the Chinese who knew English could not see what was wrong with them' and goes on to give examples of these so-called solecisms. He sides with Achebe over the debate of the use of English to describe the African writer's experience and concludes,

> Indeed, the frontiers of English verge on foreign territories, and therefore we cannot help but sound foreign to native ears, but the frontiers are the only proper places where we can claim our existence and make our contributions to this language.

In Chapter 27, 'Writing in English(es)', the Nigerian poet Tope Omoniyi provides his perspective on the creative use of English by writers from outside the inner circle. He describes his own journey to becoming a poet and the tensions and contradictions he encountered as he tried to use different languages and different varieties of English to find his voice. Using illustrations from the works of a number of writers, including his own, he concludes that they and he use 'multivariety Englishes' and, foreshadowing the point made by Pennycook in the final chapter of the Handbook, warns that 'it may be unwise to attempt to identify writers using nation-state tags when the reality they live and express in contemporary times is a global one'.

In Chapter 28, 'Online Englishes', Mark Warschauer, Rebecca Black and Yen-Lin Chou first review the exponential growth in online communication over the last decade and explain the ways in which online communication differs from other forms of interaction. While English remains the predominant language of online communication, fears that the internet represented the 'ultimate act of intellectual colonialism' (Specter 1996: 1) have subsided now that the net has become much more multilingual and that mixed-language messaging is common. The authors review recent research on different forms of online communication, from email to blogs and wikis, and show that 'there are many varieties and genres of online English'. They illustrate the linguistic features of different and innovative forms of the Englishes used in online communication, but argue that several of these forms have historical precedents. They distinguish between blogs (new forms of expressing voice) and wikis (new forms of sharing and producing knowledge) and note that research comparing the accuracy of Wikipedia and the *Encyclopædia Britannica* indicate that Wikipedia is only marginally less accurate than the *Encyclopædia*. Linguistically, Wikipedia uses a formal standard style of language which is also comparable to the style found in the *Encyclopædia*.

'The Englishes of Business' is the topic of Chapter 29, and Catherine Nickerson provides an overview of a wide range of studies into the use of English as a language of business in inner, outer and expanding circle settings, while also showing that, in many settings, people representing all three circles are frequently involved. Nickerson thus also reviews recent research into the use of English as a business lingua franca (BELF). She argues that the use of English in business, almost by definition, transcends national and cultural barriers. 'It is used as a first language for some speakers in business, but for millions, perhaps billions more, it is used either as a business lingua franca or as an international business language.' Business English is no longer the sole preserve of inner circle speakers. For the great majority, Business English is 'a neutral and shared communication code which allows them to get their work done ... they neither associate it with the inner circle varieties of English, nor do they try to reproduce them'.

Closely linked to business is advertising, and 'Englishes in advertising' is the title of Chapter 30. Azirah Hashim summarizes international research into the topic and then illustrates her chapter with examples of print and radio advertisements used in Malaysia. She discusses how certain languages are used to advertise certain products, and how a mix of languages is also often used to attract the attention of listeners and readers. In the Malaysian context, this means that advertisements may well combine the use of Standard English, the local variety of English and one or more of the local languages. The use of a particular language is often determined by the role the speaker is playing in the respective advertisement.

Chapter 31, 'The Englishes of popular cultures' (Andrew Moody), argues that much can be learned from a study of the way English is used in popular culture, even though its use in such settings is neither 'spontaneous' nor 'naturally occurring', the usual criteria for the sociolinguistic study of language use. Moody makes a distinction between the English *of* popular culture and English *in* popular culture, arguing that most work to date has focused on English *in* popular culture and that this work does not consider the influence the respective genres of pop culture may have on the language. The study of the English *of* popular culture, on the other hand, sees 'the language variety as a specialized genre-specific variety that belongs to the pop culture. In these types of studies, the language variety is owned and regulated by the popular culture apart from the larger speech community.' Moody also points out that the media of popular culture are often inextricably linked and thus characterized by intertextuality. Popular culture also mixes languages and crosses boundaries, so transnationalism is another of its key characteristics. Popular culture thus allows new forms of Englishes to travel across different cultures and within different popular cultures.

Kingsley Bolton's chapter, '"Thank you for calling": Asian Englishes and "native-like" performance in Asian call centres' concludes Section IV. In his study of a major call centre in the Philippines and through the analysis of recordings of call centre interactions, he seeks to answer the following questions: (1) What expectations do employers have of native-like performance from their staff? (2) How is such performance defined (and judged) by employers? (3) What is the profile of successful call centre agents (in terms of language background, education, etc.)? (4) What strategies do agents use to pass as native users of the language? and (5) What are the characteristics of successful versus unsuccessful communication in such contexts? In exploring answers to these questions, Bolton also shows how an international operation which exemplifies the globalizing world affects 'lives lived locally'. In this way, research of this type 'can uncover individual local experiences and linguistic practices that reveal fresh new insights into World Englishes as well as the locally negotiated dynamics of language and globalization'.

Section V: Debates and pedagogical implications

The chapters in this section all address the implications of the presence of so many varieties of English for specific aspects of pedagogy and scholarship. In Chapter 33 'Which norms in everyday practice – and why?', Ruanni Tupas argues that this question must be answered from the perspective of classroom practice. The extent to which teachers and students have the freedom or power to decide upon which norm to adopt is crucial. Tupas reports on two empirical studies, one of which was conducted in the Philippines and one in Singapore. He found that, while English language teachers were happy to accept the World Englishes paradigm and embrace the notion of different varieties of English and different norms and standards, in reality they were constrained in their choices, as they felt compelled to teach the 'standard'. He quotes one teacher as saying:

> This is my job and this is my duty … I have to tell them this is wrong in terms of grammar but when I talk to a student from China, for example, of course we don't use grammatical structures all the time. In that sense our purpose is communication as long as we can communicate with each other, we complete the exchange … But when it comes to the norm, I tell them this is the norm. And this is the structure and we have to follow.

Tupas thus concludes that 'if we want to empower teachers and learners with particular models of English, we must let these models emerge from the communities of teachers and learners themselves, where education is inextricably linked with local cultures, literacies, and politics'.

This theme is continued in Chapter 34, the title of which is 'Construing meaning in World Englishes', but the focus moves from the school to the university setting. The two authors, Ahmar Mahboob and Eszter Szenes, use a tool developed from systemic functional linguistics to analyse essays written by three students, one an Australian student of Sri Lankan heritage, one a Singaporean student of Indian background and the third an Australian citizen, also with an Indian background. They found that the three students used similar linguistic resources to create the texts, but used different linguistic resources to project their identities and perspectives. They conclude that, while the study of World Englishes has usefully focused on geographical regions, there is now a need for these studies to become broader in scope, so that they analyse and describe the 'uses' of English in specific contexts.

Chapter 35, 'Which test of which English and why?' (Brian Tomlinson) critically evaluates a number of well-known English language tests and the commonly accepted reasons for testing. In answer to the question, 'Which English should students be tested in?' Tomlinson replies, 'The varieties which the learners are likely to need to communicate in'. At present, however, most public examinations and tests of English evaluate a student's knowledge of standard British or American English. Tomlinson points out that many students will fail such tests, even though they have a good command of a local variety of English. The second part of the chapter presents an in-depth discussion of testing criteria and concludes with a list of eight criteria, which, if adopted, would ensure that tests of English were valid, reliable and fair.

In Chapter 36, 'When does an unconventional form become an innovation?', David Li first points out several illogicalities of the grammatical system of English, providing several illustrations of this. He terms these 'sources of learner-unfriendliness'. He also shows that generalizations and analogies drawn from these illogicalities are a frequent source of learner error, but that, with the increasing development of new varieties of English, many of these so-called errors are becoming increasingly common, and that realizations of these 'errors' can often be found on respectable internet sites. In conclusion, he argues that

> research in World Englishes and other related paradigms for over two decades … has made a very strong case for the legitimacy of non-standard features found in the Englishes of ESL users who use English for intra-ethnic communication. The fine line between errors and innovations has been challenged.

The discussion of the role of standards and norms is also evident in Chapter 37, 'Academic Englishes: a standardized knowledge?' The authors, Anna Mauranen, Carmen Pérez-Llantada and John Swales, open their chapter with the following statement: 'It is a fact universally acknowledged that English has emerged in recent decades as the premier vehicle for the communication of scholarship, research and advanced post-graduate training.' But, as they also point out, the rise of English in this context has been the subject of contentious debate over several years. After some 'initial considerations', one of which is the importance of studying spoken academic English as well as written academic English, the authors stress how complex and multifaceted academic English is. For example, along with cross-linguistic and cross-cultural issues, there are also differences in the academic Englishes of British and American users, as well as between the way men and women use academic speech and writing. The nature of academic speech is now better understood with the compilation of new corpora, including the Michigan Corpus of Academic Spoken English (MICASE) and the corpus of English as an academic lingua franca, the ELFA corpus. In considering whether all academics will need to adopt an inner circle style of academic speech, they suggest that this is unlikely as, in certain contexts, native-speaker styles of academic speech do not always travel well. They conclude that both globalizing and localizing tendencies can be discerned. On the one hand, there are the powerful centralizing forces of major publishing houses which 'strongly privilege the use of English … and control … the forms of that language', while on the other hand, English as a lingua franca appears 'alive and well'.

In the final chapter of Section V, 'Cameroon: which language, when and why?', Augustin Simo Bobda discusses the choice of which languages to use in education. This question is one that confronts stakeholders and ministries of education around the world, and here Simo Bobda discusses it in the context of a number of African nations but with a specific focus on Cameroon, where the language issues are complex, not least because of Cameroon's history of being a colony of both Britain and France. One legacy of this is that French and English are still used as media of instruction, even for the early years of primary school. And, while Pidgin English has been promoted by certain academics, its acceptance is hampered by several obstacles, including its lack of prestige among many locals and its lack of penetration into the northern regions of the country, where Fufulde is used as the lingua franca. His view is that, while Cameroon's adoption of colonial languages as media of instruction make Cameroon an extreme case, as a whole Africa has maintained its colonial languages to the detriment of local languages. His conclusion is that 'it is hard to predict that the colonial languages will concede a significant portion of their ground to the local languages in the near future'.

Section VI: The future

The sole chapter of Section VI is Chapter 39, 'The future of Englishes: one, many or none', and Alastair Pennycook argues that 'Whether the future of English ... should be seen in terms of the continuation of English, the plurality of Englishes, or the demise of English, depends equally on global economic and political changes and theoretical approaches to how we think about language.' He speculates on alternative histories and their potential linguistic outcomes to show that the current position of English is dependent on a particular set of historical circumstances and thus that its future position is neither guaranteed nor inevitable. Furthermore, in order to see how English may change in future, Pennycook proposes a new way of looking at language itself. Instead of retaining a focus on the centrality of nation-states in the study of Englishes, we need a better understanding of 'the way different language ideologies construct English locally'. The study of English is not just a matter of linguistic variation, but one which includes cultural and ideological difference. We therefore now need to think of English outside nationalistic frameworks and 'to take on board current understandings of translingual practices across communities, other than those defined along national criteria'. A 'translingua franca English' includes all uses of English. These include the use of hybrid and 'multivocal' languages. In this context, Pennycook introduces Maher's notion of 'metroethnicity', which is 'a reconstruction of ethnicity: a hybridized "street" ethnicity deployed by a cross-section of people with ethnic or mainstream backgrounds who are oriented towards cultural hybridity, cultural/ethnic tolerance and a multicultural lifestyle in friendships, music, the arts, eating and dress' (Maher 2005: 83). The crucial question is not so much about the plurality of Englishes as about the language ideologies that underpin them.

Conclusion

The contributions to the Handbook both demonstrate and illustrate the plurality of Englishes in today's world. Not only are there an increasing number of national and regional varieties of English developing across the world, but English, in some form or another, is being increasingly used across a wide range of functions, from professional and formal to personal and 'popular'. One common trend that can be discerned across all these Englishes is that they are created via some form of mixing. They are all the result of some form of linguistic and cultural contact. A second common trend is that the great majority of English speakers are now native speakers of languages other than English. We have moved beyond a postcolonial period and are entering a post-Anglophone period, where it is likely that the multilingual speaker of English will soon be determining its future and providing classroom models, rather than the native speaker of an inner circle variety. I hope this Handbook will provide readers with clear and stimulating descriptions and discussions of how these many Englishes are developing, while at the same time providing plenty of food for thought and debate.

References

Graddol, D. (2006) *English Next*, London: The British Council.

Kachru, B.B. (1985) 'Standards, codification and sociolinguistic realism', in R. Quirk and H.G. Widdowson (eds) *English in the World: Teaching and Learning the Language and Literatures*, Cambridge: Cambridge University Press for the British Council.

Kachru, B.B. (ed.) (1992) *The Other Tongue: English Across Cultures*, Urbana, Chicago: University of Illinois Press.

Maher, J. (2005) 'Metroethnicity, language, and the principle of cool', *International Journal of the Sociology of Language*, 175/176: 83–102.

Meyler, M. (2007) *A Dictionary of Sri Lankan English*, Colombo: Michael Meyler.

Mufwene, S. (2001) *The Ecology of Language*, Cambridge: Cambridge University Press.

Roberts, P. (1988) *West Indians and their Language*, Cambridge: Cambridge University Press.

Specter, M. (1996) 'Computer speak: world, wide, web: 3 English words', *New York Times* (online edition), 14 April 1996. Available http://query.nytimes.com/gst/fullpage.html?res=9E0DE2DA1139F9 37A25757C0A960958260 (accessed 24 December 2008).

Widdowson, Henry (1997) 'EIL, ESL, EFL: global issues and local interests', *World Englishes*, 16 (1): 135–46.

Section I

Historical perspectives and 'traditional' Englishes

Standardized English

The history of the earlier circles

Daniel R. Davis

Introduction

Before the three circles

Kachru (1992: 356) describes the Three Circles Model of the sociolinguistic profile of English as consisting of 'three concentric circles', representing, 'the types of spread, the patterns of acquisition, and the functional allocation of English in diverse cultural contexts'. McArthur (1998: 97), substituting the description 'contiguous ovals' for 'concentric circles', draws attention to the 'smaller unlabelled ovals belonging presumably to the past'. The purpose of this chapter is to give a brief history of those earlier ovals or circles, bearing in mind that Kachru's model enables a contextualization that has both historical and present-day sociolinguistic significance (Kachru 2008: 568). The smaller unlabelled circles signify earlier forms of English in time, or they signify sociolinguistic profiles or ideologies of English inspired by those earlier forms, but written on today's map (see Milroy 2002: 9–12 on language history as a legitimizing ideology). As Kachru states:

> The inner circle is *inner* with reference to the origin and spread of the language, and the outer is *outer* with reference to geographical expansion of the language – the historical stages in the initiatives to locate the English language beyond the traditional English-speaking Britain; the motivations, strategies, and agencies involved in the spread of English; the methodologies involved in the acquisition of the language; and the *depth* in terms of social penetration of the English language to expand its functional range in various domains, including those of administration, education, political discourses, literary creativity, and media.
>
> (Kachru 2008: 568).

It is fundamental to Kachru's model that the historical contexts of the movement of English have an effect on the sociolinguistic manifestation of World Englishes today.

Table 1.1 Periodization of the history of the English language

Date	Period initiated	Defining event
3000 BCE	Proto-Germanic	Grimm's Law (sound change)
449 CE	Old English	Anglo-Saxon invasion of Britain
1066 CE	Middle English	Norman Conquest of England
1476 CE	Early Modern English	First printing press in England
1776 CE	Modern English	First colonial transfer of sovereignty (USA)
1997 CE	?	Last colonial transfer of sovereignty (Hong Kong)

Source: Based on Hogg *et al.* 1992–2001.

Periodization

A useful periodization of English, based on Hogg *et al.* (1992–2001) and Ringe (2006) is given in Table 1.1.

Curzan (forthcoming) reviews the question of periodization, in particular the debate over balance between internal (linguistic) versus external (social and historical) criteria. It is clear that the periodization adopted in the *Cambridge History* is based loosely on external events which held significance for the later development of the language.

Proto-Germanic period

Grimm's Law (the first consonant shift)

Old English, in common with Gothic, Old Norse, and Old High German, descends from Proto-Germanic, which itself descends from Proto-Indo-European. The Indo-European language family includes not only the Germanic languages, but also Sanskrit and the Indic languages, Persian, Greek, Latin and the Romance languages, the Celtic languages, Armenian, Albanian, Lithuanian, and the Slavic languages (useful charts appear in Morris 1969; Arlotto 1972: 107; Mallory 1989: 15). Proto-Germanic is the hypothetical parent language reconstructed on the basis of the earliest surviving texts in the Germanic daughter languages; Proto-Indo-European is the hypothetical parent language reconstructed on the basis of the earliest surviving texts in all of the Indo-European languages. Grimm's Law (the first Germanic sound shift) separates the Germanic languages from the other branches of Indo-European. It was identified by Rasmus Rask as early as 1810 and given popular form by Jakob Grimm in 1822 (Collinge 1995: 203). A set of regular correspondences, one of which occurred between /p/ in Latin, Greek, and Sanskrit, an absence ('zero') in Old Irish, and a fricative /f/ in Gothic, Old English, and Old High German, was identified. For example, Sanskrit *pitár*, Greek πατήρ [pater], and Latin *pater* have a /p/ where Old Irish *athir* lacks the /p/, and where /f/ occurs in Gothic *fadar*, Old English *fæder*, Old High German *fater*, Old Norse *faðir* (all related or cognate words for 'father,' Buck 1933: 121; Bammesberger 1992: 35; Ringe 2006: 79). The correspondence p:f is regular in that it can be expected to occur in more than one example, so, taking the word meaning 'foot,' we see Sanskrit *pāt*, Greek πούς [pous], Latin *pēs*, (Old Irish is left out as the word for 'foot' is not related, see Buck 1949: 243–4), Gothic *fōtus*, Old English *fōt*, Old High German *fuoz*, and Old Norse *fótr* (Buck 1933: 121; Robinson 1992: 6; Ringe 2006: 94). By hypothesizing a parent language from which all of these languages descended, and by suggesting that all 'p's become 'f's (p > f) within one dialect area of that parent language, a linguistic history can be told, tracing the development of one parent language, Proto- (meaning: hypothetical) Indo-European, through different sound changes in different regions, to result in differentiated daughter languages. When p > f, the daughter language Proto-Germanic came into being. Other sound changes within the Proto-Germanic language gave rise to the daughter Germanic languages (Gothic, Old English, etc.) in turn. These 'granddaughter' languages (and their daughters following on) still show evidence of the p > f change that separated their mother, Proto-Germanic, from her mother, Proto-Indo-European. Nearly all of the consonants of non-loanwords in all of the older and present-day Germanic languages are the output of Grimm's Law and so show its effect. In Modern English these include voiceless fricatives /f, θ, h, hʷ/ (and also, in special cases covered by Verner's Law, voiced fricatives /v, ð/), voiceless stops /p, t, k, kʷ/, and voiced stops /b, d, g/. The history of how a language breaks up into a family of related languages can be told in terms of a sequence of regular sound changes, and that the sound changes involved in Grimm's Law mark the divergence of the Germanic languages from the rest of the Indo-European family.

The concept of regular sound change enables historians of the language to comment on the direction and in some cases timing of word borrowing. The sound change p > f in Germanic languages suggests that the word *father* 'male parent' has existed in English from the present day back through Early Modern, Middle and Old English, and Proto-Germanic to the time in which the p > f change occurred. By contrast, the word *paternal* 'pertaining to the male parent' must have been borrowed from Latin into English some time after the sound change p > f was no longer in operation (otherwise one would expect *paternal* to have undergone p > f to produce *faternal). Borrowing, supported by sound change, can be used as a form of historical evidence for contact between speakers of different languages, placed alongside archaeological and social historical evidence to allow the external or social history of the language to be told.

Language and social contact in the Germanic period

Archaeological and linguistic evidence places the early speakers of Germanic languages in Denmark and southern Sweden as late as 500 BCE and perhaps as early as 2000 BCE. Roman historical records at the beginning of the Christian Era (roughly 100 BCE to 100 CE) locate the Germanic tribes east of the Rhine and south of Denmark (Mallory 1989: 85; Robinson 1992: 16–17), indicating the spread of the Germanic peoples and various types of contact (including trade and warfare) with the Romans. This can be seen in early borrowings from Germanic into Latin and the reverse: Lat *sāpō* 'soap' < Gmc saip(i)ōn (Buck 1949: 453); Gmc *kaup- (seen in OE *cēap* 'bargain, price', OHG *kouf,* ModE *cheap* 'inexpensive') < Lat. *caupō* 'merchant, small trader, innkeeper' (Serjeantson 1935: 291; Hoad 1986: 72; Ringe 2006: 296).

Kastovsky (1992: 301–2, using Serjeantson 1935: 271–7) estimates that there are approximately 170 loanwords from Latin to Germanic during this period, showing Roman influence in commerce, agriculture, building, military and legal institutions, and household items. These early loanwords are identified through the existence of corresponding forms in other Germanic languages (implying early borrowing) or by their phonological shape (showing the effect of the earlier sound changes in Old English, or not showing the effect of later changes in Vulgar Latin). Further examples (cited in their

OE form) include: *stræt* 'paved road' (ModE *street*), *coper* 'copper', *purpur* 'purple', *socc* 'shoe, sock', *candel* 'candle', *butere* 'butter', *wīn* 'wine', *cupp(e)* 'cup', *panne* 'pan', *cycene* 'kitchen', *pipor, piper* 'pepper', and *plante* 'plant'.

Old English 449–1066

Social history and its linguistic effects

The Roman Empire in Britain 43–410 CE

At the time of Julius Caesar's attempted invasion during the Gallic War (55–54 BCE), southern Britain was inhabited by speakers of the Brythonic or Brittonic branch of Celtic, distributed in tribal or ethnic regional kingdoms much like the Celts in Gaul (modern France). Starting in 43 CE the Romans conquered this area, created fortifications and towns, and ruled Britain as a colony for 360 years. During this time several hundred loanwords entered into British and Irish from Latin (Henry Lewis 1980: 31, 38, 45; Kenneth Jackson 1953: 76, 227, 412). Examples include: British *pont 'bridge' (seen in Modern Welsh *pont*) < L. *pons, pontis*, and British *eclēsia 'church' (seen in ModW *eglwys*, Cornish *eglos*, Old Irish *eclais* [egliʃ], and the British place-name *Eccles*) < L. *ecclēsia*.

The settlement of the Angles, Saxons, and Jutes 449 CE

As the Roman Empire declined in the fifth century CE, Irish and Scots from Ireland, and Picts from modern Scotland began to raid Romano-British settlements south of Hadrian's Wall. The Romano-British ruler Vortigern (etymologically in British this name can be analysed as 'over-lord', suggesting that it may have been a title) enlisted the help of Germanic mercenaries who, seeing the weakness of the British, began to occupy lands in the east of Britain, following the river valleys inland and moving from east to west during the next 250 years. The Romano-British town and villa-(rural estate-)based economy collapsed, and the British Celts were subjugated or were pushed to the west. They resisted, but ultimately were able to defend only isolated regions in the west: the corners and upland areas of Cornwall, Wales, Cumbria (the north-western corner of present-day England: that is, the Lake District), and southern Scotland. Some Britons fled to Gaul, settling in what is now Brittany in modern France. British thus grew into three separate languages, Welsh, Cornish and Breton (Jackson 1953: 194–219; Russell 2007: 188–9). As the Germanic tribes pushed west, political power coalesced into seven kingdoms known as the Heptarchy: Wessex, Essex, Sussex, Kent, East Anglia, Mercia and Northumbria. Of these, Kent, Northumbria (625–75 CE), Mercia (650–825 CE) and Wessex (800–1050 CE) held varying degrees and successively greater degrees of prominence and influence throughout the Old English period (Toon 1992: 416), and this had an indirect effect on the development, recognition and literary productivity of the dialects of Old English.

Contact with the British Celts

English place-name evidence shows that there was some contact between the Britons and the Germanic invaders. Jackson divides Britain into four areas with progressively greater survival of Celtic river names, reflecting the extent to which the British-speaking population survived at the time of conquest (Jackson 1953: 228–30). Earlier theories of genocide or total depopulation are no longer supported (Jackson 1953: 229; Filppula *et al.* 2008: 14). Nevertheless, fewer than ten words were borrowed from British into Old English, and the only four uncontested are: *binn* 'manger', *brocc* 'badger', *cumb* 'valley' and *luh* 'sea, pool' (Kastovsky 1992: 318; Coates 2007: 177). Schrijver (2007) argues that the borrowings from Latin into British occurred in the Highland areas during Roman rule, and that south-eastern Britain was populated by Latin speakers by the time of the Anglo-Saxon invasion. This hypothesis explains the larger number of Latin as opposed to Celtic loanwords, as the Germanic settlers moving from east to west came into contact with Romano-British Latin speakers in the first instance. Tristram (2004) re-examines the evidence for contact between the British and the Anglo-Saxons, and following White (2002, 2003) suggests that significant numbers of British speakers may have survived in the south west and north, and over generations acquired a grammatically modified, low-prestige form of Old English. This would not have appeared in the written record, for which more conservative, high-prestige dialects were used. When the high-prestige form of Old English was submerged after the Norman Conquest, some of these British Celtic-derived (the progressive aspect in the south west) or Celtic-influenced features (invariable case and gender inflection of nouns, pronouns, adjectives and the definite article, starting in the north) survived and spread in the various regional dialects of Middle English. Filppula (2008) considers the history of this question, and identifies four syntactic features present in the Celtic languages, in Celtic Englishes, and in English in general, which are not present in other Germanic languages: the internal possessor construction (*He's got a nasty wound on **his** head*), the periphrastic use of *do*, progressive *-ing* aspect, and cleft constructions (*It's father who did it*). The body of evidence and the debate over it is reviewed extensively in Filppula *et al.* (2008); a polemical version is popularized in McWhorter (2008).

Latin loanwords in Old English

Old English continued the Germanic tradition of adopting loanwords from Latin. Those borrowed during the period of settlement (450–650 CE) show the influence of early Old English sound changes. Sound changes are not always able to provide a basis for clearly dating these terms and distinguishing them from the first group. Serjeantson's list gives 112 loanwords from this period, including some words from the semantic field or discourse area of religion (Serjeantson 1935: 277–81). Examples are: *pægel* 'pail', *pere* 'pear', *trūht* 'trout', *nunne* 'nun', and *sætern-(dæg)* 'Saturday'.

After St Augustine's mission to the English in 597 CE, English kings, followed by their subjects, converted to Christianity. Latin was the language of the Roman Catholic Church and was used as the language of religious services and in the administration of church affairs. Monasteries were founded, and the schools attached to them promoted the study and copying of biblical and other Latin texts (Baugh and Cable 2002: 84). The British and Irish Celts had converted earlier, and the influence of Irish missionaries can be seen in the insular half-uncial script adopted in the English monasteries, and in the linguistic form of the word *cross*, which, though subject to debate, shows the effect of the Irish sound change ks > s (Hogg 1992a: 11; Kastovsky 1992: 319). This led to a fairly large number of borrowings into English from Latin, often influenced by written forms and thus closer to classical Latin when compared with earlier loanwords. This

21

tendency was reinforced by the monastic reforms of the tenth century (Kastovsky 1992: 307; Baugh and Cable 2002: 87–90). The important economic role of the monasteries as major landholders and as introducers of agricultural improvements is also seen in these words. Serjeantson (1935: 281–8) lists 244 terms, in discourse fields similar to earlier borrowing, but with a greater number relating to religion. Some of the words borrowed in this third period are: -*spendan* 'spend', *purs* 'purse', *cōc*, *cōcere* 'cook', *crēda* 'creed', *paradīs* 'paradise', and *scōl* 'school'.

Contact with Old Norse

From the eighth through tenth centuries CE social and political conditions in Scandinavia encouraged sea raiders or Vikings to set out on long voyages in search of wealth and power (Loyn 1977: 9–30). The Vikings attacked and eventually settled in numerous coastal, island and river locations in the Baltic, the North Sea and the Atlantic, including Russia, the British Isles, France, Iceland and Greenland (Baugh and Cable 2002: 92). They appeared in England in 787 CE and sacked Lindisfarne monastery in 793 CE. During the ninth century Danes began settling in the east and Norwegians in the west. A Danish army threatened to conquer the entire country, but was defeated by the English king Alfred at Eddington in Wiltshire. In the Treaty of Wedmore (reported variously as 878 or 886 CE) Alfred and the Danish leader Guthrum established the Danelaw: an area in the north and east of England in which the Danes and Norwegians could settle, and within which the law had a Scandinavian basis. Danish settlers took up unoccupied land in the midst of the earlier Anglian population in this area. (See Strang 1970: 319; Wakelin 1988: 69–70.) Later attacks ultimately led to a period of Danish rule in all of England under Canute and his son from 1016 to 1042 (Kastovsky 1992: 325).

Lexical borrowing from Old Norse began during the Old English period, with 30 words appearing before 1020 CE (*hūsbōnda* 'householder, husband', *feolaga* 'fellow', *lagu* 'law', *ūtlaga* 'outlaw', *wrang* 'wrong') and another 30 by 1150 CE (*cnīf* 'knife', *dīegan* 'to die', *hittan* 'to meet with' (ModE *hit*), *tacan* 'touch, take'). Many of these pertain to the law and the sea (Serjeantson 1935: 63–70). A large number of loanwords from Old Norse (between 400 and 1000) appeared during the Middle English period: *anger, bag, cake, dirt, flat, fog, happy, ill, leg, low, neck, odd, raise, seem, silver, skin, sky, want, window* (Burnley 1992: 421). Kastovsky (1992: 327–8) points out that, 'Borrowings of the type encountered here normally presuppose either a fair amount of mutual intelligibility or relatively widespread bilingualism, and a considerable period of coexistence of the two languages involved.' Thomason and Kaufman (1988: 274) draw attention to a 'sizable but lesser amount of grammatical influence'. These dialects later played a key role in the development of a standardized form of English, accounting for the third plural personal pronoun *they*, *them* and *their* replacing the Old English forms, and possibly involved in the development and spread of present third singular verbal inflection -*s* replacing -*eth* (Nielsen 1998: 183–4). Modern non-standard dialects of English in these areas show even greater influence, retaining Scandinavian forms such as *kirk* 'church' < ON *kirkja*, *laik* 'play' < ON *leika*, and *lop* 'flea' < ON *hloppa* (Wakelin 1988: 77–84).

Grammatical features

Old English was still to some extent a case-inflected language. Readers who have experience of Sanskrit, Greek or Latin will understand this, as will those who have studied

Modern German. In a case-inflected language, number and the grammatical function of the noun phrase in the sentence is indicated by some form of morphological marking, such as an inflectional ending, on the noun or associated adjectives or determiners. The names of the cases are drawn from Latin, and include nominative (the ending typically used for the subject function), accusative (typically for the direct object function), genitive (typically for the possessor), dative (typically for the indirect object and for the object of most prepositions in Old English). Individual cases frequently identify more than one grammatical function in a language, and the functions identified by a parti-cular case vary from language to language. For example, accusative case marks the direct object (*hē ofslōg **þone aldorman** 'He killed **the mayor**'*), but also for an adverb denoting extent of space or time (*þā sǣton hīē **þone winter** æt Cwātbrycge* 'they then stayed **that winter** at Bridgenorth'), and for the object of a preposition implying movement (Quirk *et al.* 1994: 60–1). A further challenge for learners is that a particular noun belongs to a specific declension; that is, it exhibits a patterned set of endings. For example, the nouns *stān* 'stone' and *cyning* 'king' have the inflection *-as* in nominative and accusative plural, whereas *lufu* 'love' and *talu* 'tale' have the forms *lufa* and *tala* in nominative and accusative plural.

Within a declension there are overlaps in the patterning: the nominative and accusa-tive singular are frequently identical. When this happens the accompanying determiner (masculine accusative singular demonstrative *þone* in the above two examples) may help to identify the grammatical function of the noun phrase. However, as Hogg (1992b: 133) states, the increasing similarity of various case endings throughout the Old Eng-lish period emphasizes the extent to which late Old English was dependent on other means (word order and prepositions) to indicate subject and object. The overall struc-ture of the Old English case system strongly resembles Modern German: determiners and pronouns rather than noun markers seem to bear the functional load of identifying case (Hogg 2002: 18). In addition, certain inflectional forms (such as plural *-as* declen-sion) began to expand at the expense of forms in other declensions. Remnants of the displaced declensions survive in Middle and Modern English, as can be seen in the plural forms of Modern English irregular nouns (*child/children*, *sheep/sheep*, *foot/feet*). Most grammatical survivals from Old English undergo regularization in later forms of English (both standardized and non-standardized varieties, with regularization more advanced in non-standard varieties). The survivors become grammatical peeves or sticking points within the ideology of the prescriptive grammatical tradition.

Middle English 1066–1476

Social history and its linguistic effects

English submerged

The Norman Conquest of Britain in 1066 CE is the traditional date for the beginning of the Middle English period. William, Duke of Normandy (in modern France), took advantage of a period of social chaos following the death of Edward the Confessor and the elec-tion of Harold to the English throne, to advance his own claim. He and his followers invaded England, defeated Harold at the Battle of Hastings in Sussex, and re-established the feudal hierarchy with a predominance of Anglo Norman (French) speakers in the upper classes. Stenton (1943: 548–9, 618) attributes the Norman success to their ability to fight on horseback, to their rapid construction of motte-and-bailey earthwork fortifications to secure territory against revolt, and to William's insistence that his followers observe the pre-existing framework of feudal rights and obligations, in the lands with which he rewarded their service. Berndt (1969: 370–7) states that there was no mass immigration from France, estimating that at most 10 per cent of the population of England was of French origin. In some towns there were sizeable communities of Normans, but this was nowhere greater than 50 per cent in any community. There were more French in the clergy and in the land-holding nobility, particularly among the most powerful.

As a result of the conquest England became a trilingual society, with Latin as the language of official records (displacing Old English), French as the language of royalty and the upper nobility, and English as the language of the lower classes, particularly the peasants. All three languages were used in the Roman Catholic Church, with French spoken by many clergymen, Latin used as the language of the liturgy, and English used to communicate with the mass of worshippers. The growing towns and cities were also multilingual, with the number of French speakers varying but not greater than half of the speakers. During the twelfth century CE French was used in literature, but at the same time there are indications that English was becoming a household language for some members of the upper classes. By the thirteenth century this seems to have been the norm. At this time a central dialect of French enjoyed prestige as an additional language among the nobility, and Norman French (or 'Anglo-Norman') acquired a provincial reputation (Smith 1992: 48–52; Burnley 1992: 423–8). Kibbee (1991) gives an authoritative and detailed discussion of the role of French and the distribution of French speakers at different periods.

The re-emergence of English

Traditionally, the re-emergence of English is treated in the context of social developments of the 1300s. However, it might be revealing in the context of World Englishes to see that this re-emergence took place after more than two hundred years of Norman attempts to control the marginalized Celtic societies of the British Isles. Having achieved the conquest of England in 1066, and the enumeration of this conquest in the Domesday Book of 1086, the Normans extended their field of operation to Wales, Ireland and Scotland. In each of these operations, soldiers and settlers were drawn from England, Wales and Flanders in Belgium. Each resulted in diglossic societies with English and Celtic languages in some kind of equilibrium. The central events of the fourteenth century no doubt influenced the status of the English language on the Celtic periphery, but the reverse, that events on the periphery may well have influenced the status of the English language in England, deserves further attention.

During the fourteenth century the status of French and English changed. John Trevisa's commentary suggests that, following first outbreak of the bubonic plague (in 1348–50), French lost prestige and English gained prestige in education and in the upper classes (Smith 1992: 52–3, citing Leith 1983: 30 and Sisam 1921: 149). The Black Death caused the death of up to one-third of the population, and created a labour shortage, leading to the gradual emancipation of serfs, the development of paid labour, and the growth of a middle class populated by increasing numbers of English speakers. At the same time, the experience of fighting in France against the French during the Hundred Years War (1337–1453) made the Anglo-Norman nobility more aware of their

Englishness. This process had begun earlier, when Anglo-Norman lords were forced to choose between their English and French lands, owing to the English king John's refusal to swear fealty (as Duke of Normandy) to Philip, King of France. Parliament opened in English in 1362 (Kibbee 1991: 58–62; Baugh and Cable 2002: 128, 141–8).

French loanwords into Middle English

There are at least 1,000 loanwords from French into Middle English. As was the case with Scandinavian loanwords, there is a small trickle of words at first during a lag period of several centuries, followed by a flood of loanwords. The difference is that the social domain of Old Norse loanwords, that of everyday life, suggests a degree of social equality between Old English and Old Norse, whereas the French loanwords in Middle English are associated with institutional power and high culture. *Castle* was borrowed before the conquest; others that follow have to do with politics (*were* 'war', *pais* 'peace', *iustise* 'justice') and religion (*miracle, messe* 'mass', *clerc* 'educated person, cleric', see Burnley 1992: 429–30). In the early loanwords Norman French *c* appears, where later borrowings from Central French have *ch (catch* versus *chase)*; *w* appears for later *gu (warrant* versus *guarantee)*. Textbooks (Millward 1996: 199–200; Brinton and Arnovick 2006: 237) follow Serjeantson (1935) in dividing these into discourse fields including social relationships and ranks (*parentage, aunt, cousin, duke*), household and furnishings (*chair, table, lamp, couch, mirror, towel, blanket*), food and eating (*dinner, supper, fry, plate, salad, fruit, beef, pork*), fashion (*fashion, dress, button, jewel*), sports and entertainment (*tournament, dance, chess, fool, prize, tennis, audience, entertain, recreation*), the arts (*art, painting, colour, music, poet, story*), education (*study, science, university, grammar, test, pen, pencil, paper*), medicine (*medicine, surgeon, pain, disease, cure, poison*), government (*government, city, village, office, rule, court, police, tax, mayor, citizen*), law (*judge, jury, appeal, punish, prison, crime, innocent, just*), religion (*chapel, religion, confession, pray, faith, divine, salvation*), the military (*enemy, battle, peace, force, capture, attack, army, navy, soldier, captain, march*) and economic organization and trades (*grocer, tailor, mason*). Everyday or general words borrowed include *age, catch, chance, change, close, enter, face, flower, fresh, hello, hurt, large, letter, move, pay, people, please, poor, rock, save, search, sign, square, sure, touch, try, turn* and *use*. These discourse fields reflect those domains in which French was used, and in which, when the shift to English came, French vocabulary was borrowed because of its prestige and other identity associations within those domains. The situation is in some respects comparable to code mixing of English-origin words in Cantonese in informal situations in Hong Kong during the period preceding the return to Chinese sovereignty: as Luke (1998: 157) states, 'Cantonese–English language mixing in Hong Kong is not merely a way of talking about new experiences, but, perhaps more importantly, the linguistic reflection of how different groups in society respond to these new objects, institutions, and experiences.' Li (2002: 84) elaborates on Luke's model, 'orientational mixing allows for dynamic manipulation, or "display", of the speaker's social identities and distance vis-à-vis the interlocutor(s)'.

Loss of inflectional endings in Middle English

The most striking grammatical feature of Middle English is the loss of inflectional cases. This happened during the early part of the Middle English period when the sound

25

change termed 'reduction' occurred. Unstressed /a/, /o/, /u/, and /e/ merged and were 'reduced' to /ə/; then word-final and medial /ə/ were lost. As a result, most noun endings were reduced to those of the modern system (singular zero, possessive *-(e)s*, and plural *-(e)s*), and these were generalized to nouns from other declensions, with some competition from the *-en* plural from the Old English weak declension, seen in *children*, *oxen*, but also *shoon* or *shoen* 'shoes'). A more fixed word order, and extensive use of prepositional constructions, developed with these changes. The subject came to occupy the first position in the sentence (making nominative case marking redundant), the direct object came to occupy the position after the verb (in place of accusative case marking), and the preposition *to* came to mark the indirect object, in place of dative marking. The preposition *of* marked non-possessive genitive relationships (Lass 1992: 103–16; Brinton and Arnovick 2006: 266–9, 271–2 and 286–9). Adjective marking was greatly simplified, and the definite article was reduced to a single invariable form.

Strong verbs began to undergo regularization to weak endings, and thus appear with strong and weak forms (*halp* beside *helped*) (Millward 1996: 175–8). The inflectional endings for verbs were reorganized differently in different dialects, as can be seen in the present indicative plural *-es* in northern dialects, *-e(n)* or *-es* in Midland dialects, and *-eth* (as expected from OE) in southern dialects (Brinton and Arnovick 2006: 284). Compared to this level of variation, modern English variability in third singular present *-s* seems much less significant, but must be viewed in the light of the normativity that has accompanied standardization. The same holds true for the surviving irregular forms, which often undergo some form of levelling in non-standardized dialects and varieties.

Early Modern English 1476–1776

Social history and its linguistic effects

Centralization of political power

The Early Modern period of the English language can be assigned to certain events marking the end of the Middle Ages in England and the British Isles. In politics, the Tudor dynasty emerged from the Wars of the Roses, marked by the defeat of Richard III by the Welsh-descended Henry Tudor at Bosworth Field in 1485. In general the Tudors favoured and strengthened the central authority of the monarchy and supporting institutions at the expense of the feudal nobility; this led to increased power for the House of Commons in parliament, representing the urban merchants and rural gentry (smaller landowners).

Printing

While the strength of the Tudors clearly led to political centralization, the more important event, from a linguistic perspective, was the establishment of the printing press in England, in 1476 CE. William Caxton set up his press in Chancery Lane, in the City of Westminster (next to London), in close proximity to Chancery (later the Public Records Office). Texts, which up to this point had been copied by hand, could be produced quickly, and in much larger numbers. This increased the potential audience for books, but forced printers, translators and authors to confront the problem of dialect variation.

In order to sell the largest possible number of books, printers tended to choose the most common or understandable of several variant forms. This form was then reproduced in hundreds of copies of a book. Over time this contributed to the standardization of the written form of English (Bex 1996: 32–4; Graddol and Leith 1996: 139–41; Harris and Taylor 1997: 87–92).

Chancery, law and administration

The location of Caxton's press on Chancery Lane suggests a link between the forms he adopted and the standardizing practices of the scribes recording government records. Samuels (1969: 407) identifies four 'types of language that are less obviously dialectal, and … thus cast light on the probable sources of the written standard English that appears in the fifteenth century'. The fourth of these is the 'Chancery Standard' found in 'a flood of government documents that starts in the years following 1430' (411). Nielsen (2005: 131–50) explains that clerks were carefully trained and that Chancery documents were sent throughout England in large numbers. There are disagreements over the details: the role of Chancery is amplified in a series of papers by Fisher (1996) to an extent that is questioned by Benskin (2004). Rissanen (2000), tracing four variables in the Helsinki Corpus, finds that in the case of future modal auxiliaries (*shall* vs *will*), the legal records' preference for *shall* is outweighed by increasing preference for *will* in the speech-like genres. A preference for compound adverbs (*hereby, therefore*) in legal and administrative texts is eventually overturned in favour of prepositional phrases more generally. On the other hand, *provided that* seems to have spread from law texts to other genres, and legal texts led the way in relying on *not … any* as opposed to double negative *not … no*.

The City of London

Keene (2000) reviews the role played by the City of London in the development of Standard English from 1100 to 1700. Though geographically on the margins of Europe, London was by far the largest city in the British Isles and was a centre of local, regional and international commerce, manufacture and immigration from other parts of Britain.

> London is likely to have had an influence on the emergence of Standard English not primarily as a site of government and power but rather as an engine of communication and exchange … Key processes to consider would include the establishment of fellowship, trust and norms which fostered understanding and an ability quickly to conclude deals in acknowledged and repeatable ways.
>
> (Keene 2000: 111)

The wealth generated in these exchanges led to the further growth of the middle class. On the one hand, immigration from other parts of Britain enabled dialect items to enter the feature pool of standardizing English. On the other, competition within and insecurity about the social hierarchy encouraged selection and codification (Knowles 1997: 128–9).

The Reformation

In the Protestant Reformation (1517 CE), factions (later denominations) broke off from the Roman Catholic Church in Germany, England and other countries, while in most

27

cases retaining an official monopoly of religious practice under the authority of local and national leaders. Barber (1976: 71) explains that, in England, the debate between advocates and opponents of the Reformation occurred in English, as authors wanted to reach the widest possible audience. Vernacular translations of the Bible and the liturgy were authorized and used at home and in religious services. The language of these translations had prestige and exposure, providing a consistent prose model and source of idiom and style (Millward 1996: 225; Knowles 1997: 94–100).

Expansion of vocabulary

Nevalainen (1999: 350–2, citing Wermser 1976: 40) indicates that 'borrowing is by far the most common method of enriching the lexicon in Early Modern English'. Thousands of words were borrowed during this time, ranging between 40 per cent and 53 per cent of all new words. By contrast, Cannon (1987) shows that borrowing is less than 10 per cent of the new words in American English from 1963 to 1981.

Latin is the primary source language for loans into Early Modern English, ranging from 45 per cent to 60 per cent except during the first quarter of the eighteenth century, when the percentage dropped to 37.9 per cent (Görlach 1991: 166, citing Wermser 1976: 45). Over half of the loanwords from 1560 to 1670 come from Latin, and these are primarily learned and specialist terminology, reflecting both the Renaissance interest in Roman and Greek culture, and the growth of science (Nevalainen 1999: 364–5; Leith *et al.* 2007: 79–96). Barber (1976: 169–72, with examples supplemented by Serjeantson 1935: 264–5) identifies sciences of medicine (*cadaver, delirium, virus*), anatomy (*appendix, vertebra*), biology (*fungus, pollen, species*), physics (*spectrum, vacuum*), and mathematics (*area, multiplicand, radius*), as well as religion (*relapse*), grammar (*copula*), rhetoric (*caesura*), logic (*data, tenet*), philosophy (*crux, query, transcendental*), fine arts (*literati*), classical civilization (*gorgon, rostrum, toga*), public affairs (*militia, veto*) and geography (*aborigines, peninsula*) as major fields for Latin loanwords. Glosses are omitted to save space, and there is some overlap that can only be decided by careful examination of the initial borrowing context (for example, *virus* could be medicine or biology). More general loanwords given in Barber (1976: 172) include *relaxation, invitation, relevant, investigate, commemorate* and *officiate.*

Görlach (1991: 166, citing Wermser 1976: 45) states that French loanwords range between 20 and 40 per cent of the loanwords in any given 15-year period from 1510 to 1724, second only to Latin. Italian (1–14 per cent), Spanish (1–3 per cent), Dutch (1–3 per cent) each contribute small percentages, while the rest of European languages (2–7 per cent) are comparable to overseas loans (0.3–7 per cent). Görlach (1991: 167–8) characterizes the social context of the French loanwords: French occurred commonly in certain documents until the seventeenth century; knowledge of French was common among the nobility, and even more common in Scotland; large numbers of French and Flemish Protestants emigrated to England after the Edict of Nantes (protecting French Protestants) was revoked in 1685; and there was a surge of popularity for French when English royalists returned to England at the restoration of the monarchy in 1660. The loanwords reflect the status of French as a marker of membership in an educated elite. The phonology of these loanwords bears greater resemblance to the source forms, in comparison to earlier borrowings from French: Earlier *fine*, now [faɪn] show the effect of the Great Vowel Shift (discussed further below), while later *machine* [məʃin] does not. Other more Anglicized loans nevertheless reflect changes that had occurred in

French at the time of borrowing (Nevalainen 1999: 369, citing Skeat 1970: 12–13). The loanwords fall into the domains of military (*colonel, cartridge, platoon, terrain, espionage*), navy (*pilot*), diplomacy (*envoy*), commerce (*indigo, gauze*), social terms (*bourgeois, naïve, class, etiquette*), arts (*crayon, memoir, nuance*), fashion (*dishabille, rouge, corduroy*), games, dancing (*ballet*), food (*fricassee, casserole, liqueur*), medicine (*migraine*) and geography (*glacier, avalanche*). Most of these examples are from Serjeantson (1935: 160–5, supplemented by Nevalainen 1999: 370).

Greek loans, often via Latin, pertain to classical civilization (*alphabet, bathos*) and scientific terminology (*crisis, meteorology, coma*). Italian loans are for the most part via French, and include domains of trade (*traffic, bankrupt*), literature, music, architecture and other arts (*carnival, cupola, sonnet, piano*). Spanish loanwords include trade (*anchovy, lime, cargo*), military (*armada*) and some cultural loans (*sierra, guitar*), particularly those connected with the Americas (*cannibal, potato, alligator, tobacco, vanilla*). Dutch loans fall within domains of seafaring (*yacht, cruise, jib*) and trade (*dock, excise, dollar, snuff*) but include terms from other discourse areas and of more general use (*knapsack, easel, sketch, drill, skate*). Portuguese loanwords reflect Portuguese trade and colonization in Asia and Brazil (*banana, molasses, teak, veranda, palaver*). German loans include *lobby, hamster, zinc, quartz, iceberg, nickel*; both *steppe* and *mammoth* are Russian loans. 'Overseas' source languages, primarily relating to the expanding trade networks of the fifteenth through eighteenth centuries, include Turkish (*horde, jackal, yogurt*), Persian (*turban, divan, bazaar, caravan*) and Arabic (*algebra, arsenal, jar, civet, tamarind, tarragon, alcohol, albacore, couscous, sherbet, albatross*). Contact with African languages introduced *zebra, baobab* and *chimpanzee*. Hindi, Urdu and Tamil were the source of words including *typhoon, toddy, cot, bungalow, dungaree* and *shampoo*. Other source languages are Malay, Chinese, Japanese and native American languages (Nevalainen 1999: 374–6). It can be seen from these brief lists that many of the words from Arabic entered English via other languages, including French, Spanish, Italian and Turkish (this had been going on since the Old English period but seems to increase in the Early Modern English period). In selecting from others' lists I have deliberately avoided terms evoking cultural stereotypes (such as *assassin*) and have tried to include everyday words from a wide range of social activities. These lists conceal the method (identifying source forms and sound changes in source and borrowing languages), but also raise the problems of lexical attrition, meaning changes and, most of all, borrowing into developing local varieties in new overseas contexts versus related but not identical borrowing into the standardizing metropolitan variety/ies.

The Great Vowel Shift

The most important change demarcating the Middle English from the Early Modern English was the Great Vowel Shift. Although recent views take the position that this is a number of sound changes taking place during the period 1400–1700, it is convenient to summarize these under the general term Great Vowel Shift. In phonetic terms, the tongue height for long vowels was raised, and high long vowels were diphthongized (see Table 1.2).

The Great Vowel Shift accounts for a number of irregularities and inconsistencies troubling English speakers, learners and readers to this day. It explains why children learning to read in English have to learn qualitatively different long and short

Table 1.2 The Great Vowel Shift

	1400	1550	1640	Later
Bite	iː	ɛi (əi)	ɛi (əi)	aɪ [əɪ]
Meet	eː	iː	iː	iː
Meat	ɛː	ɛː	e(ː)	iː
Mate	aː	aː/æː	ɛː.	eɪ
Out	uː	ɔu (əu)	ɔu (əu)	aʊ [əʊ]
Boot	oː	uː	uː	uː
Boat	ɔː	ɔː	oː	oʊ/ɛʊ

Source: Based on Lass 1999b: 85, with additions.

Notes: X/Y = X or Y in some dialects or varieties
X (Y) = X or Y according to some accounts
X [Y] = X with allophone Y in some environments

pronunciations of vowel symbols, for example, long *ā* pronounced [eɪ] versus short *ă* pronounced [æ], and rules such as 'The long vowel says its name'. It explains some of the haphazardness of English spelling, since this began to assume an increasingly fixed form while the vowel shift was underway. It explains why learners of English have to memorize or ignore morphophonological alternations such as south [saʊθ] versus southern [sʌðərn]. It explains some of the regional and social variation encountered throughout the English-speaking world, in forms such as *root* (pronounced with [uː] or [ʊ]) and *route* ([uː] or [aʊ]). Brinton and Arnovick (2006: 309–11) give three examples of varieties in which some aspects of the vowel shift were not realized: Scottish English, which retains [u] in *mouse*; Irish English, which retains [e] in *tea*; and Canadian (and some dialects of the United States) in which ME [i] and [u] are not fully lowered to [ai] and [aʊ], but in some environments are [əi] and [əʊ]. Smith (2004) explores northern versus southern versions of the vowel shift, and clarifies sociolinguistic context and actuation.

In theory, the Great Vowel Shift should permit dating of loanwords, with those words borrowed earlier undergoing the shift (as in the example of *fine* and *machine* above). In practice, this is not so clear. For example, the word *route* 'way, course' appears as a borrowing from Anglo-Norman in the thirteenth century; the modern British and American pronunciation [ruːt] can only be explained as a re-borrowing from French after the Great Vowel Shift had diphthongized /uː/ to /au/ (Hoad 1986: 409). The currently spreading and standardizing American pronunciation [raʊt] must be either a spelling pronunciation (influenced by *out*, *shout*, etc.) or possibly was borrowed from French into a particular British regional dialect before that dialect had undergone the Great Vowel Shift, then the output of which appeared after transportation to America. It can be seen that the vowel shift is of limited utility in the face of the expansion of literacy, and the dialect mixing that must have accompanied standardization, as the survival and standardization of the [eɪ] pronunciation of *great* and *steak* (next to *eat* and *freak* with [iː]) suggest.

Grammatical developments in Early Modern English

Three major grammatical developments listed by Lass (1999a: 11) are: the replacement of third singular present *-(e)th* by *-(e)s*; the loss of the *-(e)n* marker of verb plurals and infinitives; and the displacement of second singular personal pronouns *thou, thee, thy, thine* with the second plural *ye* (later *you*), *you, your, yours*. In syntax do-support is gradually restricted to negative, interrogative and emphatic clauses, and the progressive is developed.

Early Modern English allowed a great deal of grammatical variation that was later proscribed within the grammatical tradition. Brinton and Arnovick (2006: 327–54) give a host of examples drawn from Shakespeare, indicating variation which modern prescriptivists would find unacceptable but which in many cases still occurs in one variety or another. One out of many examples shows pronominal case variation: here object case appearing in the subject: *And damn'd be **him** that first cries, 'Hold, enough!'* (*Macbeth*).

Conclusion

This chapter emphasizes the earlier periods at the expense of the later periods, committing precisely the error that Jim Milroy (2007: 32–3) warns of. In part this is necessary, as an introduction to the history of standardized varieties in the context of World Englishes must make clear the multiplicity of linguistic sources, the patchwork nature of language structure, and political character of ideologies shaping and regularizing language and our perception of it, then as much as now. Also, the comfortable methods of philology, as applied to the earlier periods, cease to give reassurance in the sociolinguistic, cultural and political complexity of the modern world. It may be that we have too much evidence to generalize away from variation, or it may be that, in their increased size and complexity, modern language communities have outgrown methods that were developed to make sense of language change occurring in societies with a predominance of relatively small and isolated agricultural communities.

At the same time as forces of standardization came into focus and were brought to bear on the language, English entered on the world stage as explorers, fishermen, merchants, pirates and settlers engaged in a world-wide economic, political and cultural expansion. The resulting ideologies are examined in Bailey (1991). As imperial expansion transformed those societies drawn or forced into a relationship with Britain, the industrialization which drove it transformed British society itself (Briggs 1983: 158–224). 'Standard English' experienced a corresponding redefinition and reinstitutionalization as language ideologies developed, spread and receded (see Crowley 1989, 1991, and 1996). New words, including loanwords, reflect the growth of certain areas of life as we have seen them in the earlier periods or circles of English. What is needed for a full historical understanding of World Englishes is an analysis of the centre developing in response to developments on the periphery. This is true in each period of English we have examined, and remains true in the modern period. This period is given extensive coverage in Görlach (1990), Mugglestone (1995), Bailey (1996), Romaine (1998), Beal (2004) and Mair (2006).

English has always been heterogeneous and has always involved extensive language contact. As Bailey (2006: 334) says, 'English is (and has been) one language among many.' Kirkpatrick (2007: 6) states, 'After all, other languages preceded English in England and the British varieties of English have certainly been influenced by local languages and cultures. The same can be said of American and Australian varieties of English.' The language has responded to social conditions and ideologies emerging from economic

and technological developments, prompting the adoption of successive cultural identities. This heterogeneity is obscured by the historically inaccurate use of the term
Anglo Englishes as a shorthand for inner circle Englishes. Reducing the characterization
of these multiple identities and sources to this term is to impose homogeneity on these
heterogeneous experiences, and even to confer a historical legitimacy upon their ideologies. It risks missing the point: the standardized metropolitan varieties of the inner
circle are themselves World Englishes. They, their compatriot non-standardized varieties, and the varieties of the outer and expanding circles have been shaped by many of
the same social, political and linguistic processes in the near and distant past. However,
the inner circle standardized varieties are accompanied by a set of ideologies which
emerged in response to those processes, and which serve to control access to privileged
varietal functions. The paradigm of World Englishes, and the linguists associated with
it, continue to confront a world in which, to paraphrase Orwell, all varieties are created
equal, but some varieties are more equal than others.

Summary

This chapter introduces major effects of linguistic change found in standardized forms
of the English language, and looks at contributing historical circumstances. Language
contact is shown to have influenced the lexical development of the language from the
earliest period. Loanwords from Latin, Old Norse and Old French are examined, and
the possibility of Celtic influence on grammar is considered. Later changes include the
loss of inflectional endings at the beginning of the Middle English period, and the sound
changes collectively termed the Great Vowel Shift. Historical factors influencing standardization during the Early Modern period are examined. Awareness of the hybrid origins
of standardized inner circle Englishes can help speakers and linguists to contextualize
and contain the defensive language ideologies of that circle.

Suggestions for further reading

Hogg, R.M., Blake, N.F., Lass, R., Romaine, S., Burchfield, R.W. and Algeo, J. (1992–2001) *The
    Cambridge History of the English Language*, Cambridge; New York: Cambridge University Press.
    (Authoritative and thorough, although historical and sociolinguistic context take second place to
    language description.)
Mesthrie, R. (2006) 'World Englishes and the multilingual history of English', *World Englishes*, 25
    (3–4): 381–90. (A useful application of current sociolinguistic thought to the multilingual origins of
    English.)
Milroy, J. (2007) 'The history of English', in D. Britain (ed.) *Language in the British Isles*, Cam-
    bridge: Cambridge University Press. (A concise and balanced overview of major structural changes
    and sociolinguistic considerations in the history of English.)
Mufwene, S.S. (2001) *The Ecology of Language Evolution*, Cambridge: Cambridge University Press.
    (A valuable theorization of the language change in traditional and non-traditional sociolinguistic
    contexts, with numerous illustrations from the history of English and other languages.)
Smith, J.J. (1996) *An Historical Study of English: Function, Form and Change*, London: Routledge.
    (Well-referenced and critical consideration of historical linguistic theory and method as it pertains
    to the sociolinguistic and structural development of English. Benefits from non-traditional examples
    and an extremely useful annotated bibliography.)

References

Arlotto, A. (1972) *Introduction to Historical Linguistics*, New York: Houghton Mifflin.

Bailey, R.W. (1991) *Images of English: A Cultural History of the Language*, Ann Arbor: University of Michigan Press.

——(1996) *Nineteenth-century English*, Ann Arbor: University of Michigan Press.

——(2006) 'English among the languages', in L. Mugglestone (ed.) *The Oxford History of English*, Oxford: Oxford University Press.

Bammesberger, A. (1992) 'The place of English in Germanic and Indo-European', in R.M. Hogg (ed.) *The Cambridge History of the English Language, Volume I: The Beginnings to 1066*, Cambridge: Cambridge University Press.

Barber, C.L. (1976) *Early Modern English*, London: Deutsch.

Baugh, A.C. and Cable, T. (2002) *A History of the English Language*, Upper Saddle River, NJ: Prentice Hall.

Beal, J.C. (2004) *English in Modern Times, 1700–1945*, London: Arnold.

Benskin, M. (2004) 'Chancery Standard', in C. Kay, C. Hough, and I. Wotherspoon (eds) *New Perspectives on English Historical Linguistics. Selected Papers from 12 ICEHL, Glasgow, 21–26 August 2002, Volume II: Lexis and Transmission*, Amsterdam, Philadelphia: John Benjamins.

Berndt, R. (1969) 'The linguistic situation in England from the Norman Conquest to the loss of Normandy (1066–1204)', in R. Lass (ed.) *Approaches to English Historical Linguistics: An Anthology*, New York: Holt, Rinehart and Winston.

Bex, T. (1996) *Variety in Written English: Texts in Society: Societies in Text*, London: Routledge.

Briggs, A. (1983) *A Social History of England*, New York: Viking Press.

Brinton, L.J. and Arnovick, L.K. (2006) *The English Language: A Linguistic History*, Don Mills, Ontario: Oxford University Press.

Buck, C.D. (1933) *Comparative Grammar of Greek and Latin*, Chicago: University of Chicago Press.

——(1949) *A Dictionary of Selected Synonyms in the Principal Indo-European Languages; A Contribution to the History of Ideas*, Chicago: University of Chicago Press.

Burnley, D. (1992) 'Lexis and semantics', in N. Blake (ed.) *The Cambridge History of the English Language, Volume II: 1066–1476*, Cambridge: Cambridge University Press.

Cannon, G.H. (1987) *Historical Change and English Word-formation: Recent Vocabulary*, New York: P. Lang.

Coates, R. (2007) 'Invisible Britons: the view from linguistics', in N.J. Higham (ed.) *Britons in Anglo-Saxon England*, Woodbridge, Suffolk: Boydell Press.

Collinge, N.E. (1995) 'History of historical linguistics', in E.F.K. Koerner and R.E. Asher (eds) *Concise History of the Language Sciences: From the Sumerians to the Cognitivists*, Oxford: Pergamon.

Crowley, T. (1989) *Standard English and the Politics of Language*, Urbana: University of Illinois Press.

——(1991) *Proper English? Readings in Language, History, and Cultural Identity*, London; New York: Routledge.

——(1996) *Language in History: Theories and Texts*, London; New York: Routledge.

Curzan, A. (forthcoming) 'Periodization in the history of English', in L. Brinton and A. Bergs (eds) *Historical English Linguistics*, Berlin; New York: Mouton de Gruyter.

Filppula, M. (2008) 'The Celtic hypothesis hasn't gone away: new perspectives on old debates', in M. Dossena, R. Dury and M. Gotti (eds) *English Historical Linguistics 2006, Volume III: Geo-historical Variation in English*, Amsterdam: John Benjamins.

Filppula, M., Klemola, J. and Paulasto, H. (2008) *English and Celtic in Contact*, New York: Routledge.

Fisher, J.H. (1996) *The Emergence of Standard English*, Lexington: University Press of Kentucky.

Görlach, M. (1990) *Studies in the History of the English Language*, Heidelberg: Winter.

——(1991) *Introduction to Early Modern English*, Cambridge: Cambridge University Press.

Graddol, D. and Leith, D. (1996) 'Modernity and English as a national language', in D. Graddol, D. Leith and J. Swan (eds) *English: History, Diversity, and Change*, London and Milton Keynes: Routledge and Open University.

Harris, R. and Taylor, T.J. (1997) *The Western Tradition from Socrates to Saussure*, London: Routledge.

Higham, N.J. (2007) *Britons in Anglo-Saxon England*, Woodbridge: Boydell Press.

Hoad, T.F. (1986) *The Concise Oxford Dictionary of English Etymology*, Oxford: Oxford University Press.

Hogg, R.M. (1992a) 'Introduction', in R.M. Hogg (ed.) *The Cambridge History of the English Language, Volume I: The Beginnings to 1066*, Cambridge: Cambridge University Press.

——(1992b) 'Phonology and Morphology', in R.M. Hogg (ed.) *The Cambridge History of the English Language, Volume I: The Beginnings to 1066*, Cambridge: Cambridge University Press.

——(2002) *An Introduction to Old English*, Oxford: Oxford University Press.

Hogg, R.M., Blake, N.F., Lass, R., Romaine, S., Burchfield, R.W. and Algeo, J. (1992–2001) *The Cambridge History of the English Language*, Cambridge; New York: Cambridge University Press.

Jackson, K. (1953) *Language and History in Early Britain: A Chronological Survey of the Brittonic Languages, First to Twelfth Century AD*, Cambridge: Harvard University Press.

Kachru, B.B. (1992) 'Teaching world Englishes', in B. Kachru (ed.) *The Other Tongue: English across Cultures*, Urbana: University of Illinois Press.

——(2008) 'World Englishes in world contexts', in H. Momma and M. Matto (eds) *A Companion to the History of the English Language*, Chichester, UK: Wiley-Blackwell.

Kastovsky, D. (1992) 'Semantics and vocabulary', in R.M. Hogg (ed.) *The Cambridge History of the English Language, Volume I: The Beginnings to 1066*, Cambridge: Cambridge University Press.

Keene, D. (2000) 'Metropolitan values: migration, mobility and cultural norms, London 1100–1700', in L. Wright (ed.) *The Development of Standard English 1300–1800: Theories, Descriptions, Conflicts*, Cambridge: Cambridge University Press.

Kibbee, D.A. (1991) *For to Speke Frenche Trewely: The French Language in England, 1000–1600: Its Status, Description, and Instruction*, Amsterdam: John Benjamins.

Kirkpatrick, A. (2007) *World Englishes: Implications for International Communication and English Language Teaching*, Cambridge: Cambridge University Press.

Knowles, G. (1997) *A Cultural History of the English Language*, London: Arnold.

Koerner, E.F.K. and Asher, R.E. (1995) *Concise History of the Language Sciences: From the Sumerians to the Cognitivists*, Oxford: Pergamon.

Lass, R. (1992) 'Phonology and morphology', in N. Blake (ed.) *The Cambridge History of the English Language, Volume II: 1066–1476*, Cambridge: Cambridge University Press.

——(1999a) 'Introduction', in R. Lass (ed.) *The Cambridge History of the English Language, Volume III: 1476–1776*, Cambridge: Cambridge University Press.

——(1999b) 'Phonology and morphology', in R. Lass (ed.) *The Cambridge History of the English Language, Volume III: 1476–1776*, Cambridge: Cambridge University Press.

Leith, D. (1983) *A Social History of English*, London: Routledge and Kegan Paul.

Leith, D., Graddol, D. and Jackson, L. (2007) 'Modernity and English as a national language', in D. Graddol, D. Leith, J. Swann, M. Rhys and J. Gillen (eds) *Changing English*, Abingdon and Milton Keynes: Routledge and Open University.

Lewis, H. (1980) *Yr Elfen Ladin yn yr Iaith Gymraeg*, repr. edn, Caerdydd: Gwasg Prifysgol Cymru.

Li, D.C.S. (2002) 'Cantonese–English code-switching research in Hong Kong: a survey of recent research', in K. Bolton (ed.) *Hong Kong English: Autonomy and Creativity*, Hong Kong: Hong Kong University Press.

Loyn, H.R. (1977) *The Vikings in Britain*, New York: St Martin's Press.

Luke, K.K. (1998) 'Why two languages might be better than one: motivations of language mixing in Hong Kong', in M.C. Pennington (ed.) *Language in Hong Kong at Century's End*, Hong Kong: Hong Kong University Press.

McArthur, T. (1998) *The English Languages*, Cambridge: Cambridge University Press.

McWhorter, J.H. (2008) *Our Magnificent Bastard Tongue: The Untold History of English*, New York: Gotham Books.

Mair, C. (2006) *Twentieth-century English: History, Variation, and Standardization*, Cambridge: Cambridge University Press.

Mallory, J.P. (1989) *In Search of the Indo-Europeans: Language, Archaeology and Myth*, London: Thames and Hudson.

Millward, C.M. (1996) *A Biography of the English Language*, Fort Worth, Texas: Harcourt Brace College Publishers.

Milroy, J. (2000) 'Historical description and the ideology of the standard language', in L. Wright (ed.) *The Development of Standard English, 1300–1800: Theories, Descriptions, Conflicts*, Cambridge, England: Cambridge University Press.

——(2002) 'The legitimate language: giving a history to English', in R. Watts and P. Trudgill (eds) *Alternative Histories of English*, London: Routledge.

——(2007) 'The history of English', in D. Britain (ed.) *Language in the British Isles*, Cambridge: Cambridge University Press.

Morris, W. (1969) *The American Heritage Dictionary of the English Language*, New York: American Heritage Publishing.

Mugglestone, L. (1995) *'Talking Proper': The Rise of Accent as Social Symbol*, Oxford: Clarendon.

Nevalainen, T. (1999) 'Early Modern English lexis and semantics', in R. Lass (ed.) *The Cambridge History of the English Language, Volume III: 1476–1776*, Cambridge: Cambridge University Press.

Nielsen, H.F. (1998) *The Continental Backgrounds of English and its Insular Development until 1154*, Odense: Odense University Press.

——(2005) *From Dialect to Standard: English in England 1154–1776*, Odense: University Press of Southern Denmark.

Quirk, R., Wrenn, C.L. and Deskis, S.E. (1994) *An Old English Grammar*, DeKalb: Northern Illinois University Press.

Ringe, D.A. (2006) *A Linguistic History of English*, Oxford: Oxford University Press.

Rissanen, M. (2000) 'Standardisation and the language of early statutes', in L. Wright (ed.) *The Development of Standard English 1300–1800: Theories, Descriptions, Conflicts*, Cambridge: Cambridge University Press.

Robinson, O.W. (1992) *Old English and its Closest Relatives: A Survey of the Earliest Germanic Languages*, Stanford, CA: Stanford University Press.

Romaine, S. (1998) *The Cambridge History of the English Language, Volume 4: 1776–1997*, Cambridge: Cambridge University Press.

Russell, P. (2007) 'The history of the Celtic languages in the British Isles', in D. Britain (ed.) *Language in the British Isles*, Cambridge: Cambridge University Press.

Samuels, M.L. (1969) 'Some applications of Middle English dialectology', in R. Lass (ed.) *Approaches to English Historical Linguistics: An Anthology*, New York: Holt, Rinehart and Winston.

Schrijver, P. (2007) 'What Britons spoke around 400 AD', in N.J. Higham (ed.) *Britons in Anglo-Saxon England*, Woodbridge, Suffolk: Boydell Press.

Serjeantson, M.S. (1935) *A History of Foreign Words in English*, London: Routledge and Kegan Paul.

Sisam, K. (1921) *Fourteenth Century Verse and Prose*, Oxford: Clarendon.

Skeat, W.W. (1970) *Principles of English Etymology*, College Park, MD: McGrath.

Smith, J.J. (1992) 'The use of English: language contact, dialect variation, and written standardization during the Middle English period', in T.W. Machan, C.T. Scott and S. Romaine (eds) *English in its Social Contexts: Essays in Historical Sociolinguistics*, New York: Oxford University Press.

——(2004) 'Phonological space and the actuation of the Great Vowel Shift in Scotland and Northern England', in M. Dossena and R. Lass (eds) *Methods and Data in English Historical Dialectology* (Linguistic Insights 16), Bern: Peter Lang.

Stenton, F.M. (1943) *Anglo-Saxon England*, Oxford: Clarendon.

Strang, B.M.H. (1970) *A History of English*, London: Methuen.

Thomason, S.G. and Kaufman, T. (1988) *Language Contact, Creolization, and Genetic Linguistics*, Berkeley: University of California Press.

Toon, T.E. (1992) 'Old English dialects', in R.M. Hogg (ed.) *The Cambridge History of the English Language, Volume I: The Beginnings to 1066*, Cambridge: Cambridge University Press.

Tristram, H.L.C. (2004) 'Diglossia in Anglo-Saxon England, or what was spoken Old English like?', *Studia Anglica Posnaniensia: An International Review of English Studies*, 40: 87–110.

Wakelin, M.F. (1988) *The Archaeology of English*, London: Batsford.

Watts, R.J. and Trudgill, P. (2002) *Alternative Histories of English*, London: Routledge.

Wermser, R. (1976) *Statistische Studien zur Entwicklung des englischen Wortschatzes*, Bern: Francke.

White, D. (2002) 'Explaining the innovations of Middle English: what, where, and why?', in M. Filppula, J. Klemola and H. Pitkänen (eds) *The Celtic Roots of English*, Joensuu Finland: University of Joensuu, Faculty of Humanities.

——(2003) 'Brittonic influence in the reduction of Middle English nominal morphology', in H.L.C. Tristram (ed.) *The Celtic Englishes III*, Heidelberg: Universitätsverlag C. Winter.

2

Grammatical variation in the contemporary spoken English of England

David Britain

Introduction

Standard English is a minority dialect in England. Surveys of speech communities across the country over the past few decades have consistently found a majority of the population of whichever geographically based speech community is under investigation using at least some non-standard dialect forms. The first person to guestimate what proportion of the population of the UK spoke Standard English was Trudgill (1974). He suggested that just 12 per cent of the population spoke it (and therefore around 49 million people didn't). He later (2002: 171) presented a case to justify this figure. His survey of the speech of Norwich in eastern England was based, as was common then, but unusual in social dialectological work today, on a random sample of the Norwich speech community, using the electoral register as the sampling frame. Given that only 12 per cent of his random sample had no non-standard grammatical features, he suggested that this was a fair estimate of the figure nationally too. He recognized that there would possibly have been a (small) sampling error and that some towns and cities (he suggested Bath and Cheltenham) would likely have more standard speakers than that proportion and others (Hull and Glasgow) were likely to have many fewer.

Few have scrutinized this claim in any detail, but the nearest we have to a contemporary figure is a 1995 report by Dick Hudson and Jason Holmes on the use of non-standard grammatical features found among school children in four locations across the country (the south west, London, Merseyside and Tyneside). The authors make it clear that the recordings were expressly made to find out about the children's (semi)formal speech, rather than about their everyday informal vernacular that tends to be the prime focus of social dialectological research.

> The children were recorded in situations likely to encourage their use of standard rather than non-standard English and the focus of the study was the extent to which they did use standard forms in these situations … [the recordings] were made in school situations likely to have inclined pupils more towards the use of standard than to non-standard forms. The pupils were for the most part speaking

in the presence of an unfamiliar adult whom they knew to be a teacher, and they were carrying out specific spoken language tasks.

(Hudson and Holmes 1995: 3–5)

Despite this formality, and given only five to ten minutes of speech was collected from each child, they found that 61 per cent of the 11 year olds and 77 per cent of the 15 year olds used non-standard forms at some point (1995: 10). Given the formal contexts in which the data were being collected, and the likelihood that their informal speech is even more likely to contain non-standardness, Trudgill's 1974 figure of 88 per cent non-standard speakers is probably not wildly inaccurate even today. The figures also suggest that exposure to formal education does not necessarily increase levels of Standard English usage – 15 year olds used *less* Standard English than 11 year olds in this survey.

Supporting this evidence of robust non-standardness is the work of a number of social dialectologists who have consistently found significant levels of non-standardness in detailed variationist research – two notable examples for work on grammatical variation include Jenny Cheshire's work, mostly on southern England – Reading (Cheshire 1981, 1982, 2005, 2007; Cheshire and Ouhalla 1997), Milton Keynes (Cheshire *et al.* 2005), London (Cheshire and Fox 2007, 2009; Cheshire *et al.* 2007) – but including variationist work on Hull in northern England (Cheshire 2007; Cheshire *et al.* 2005) as well as national surveys (Cheshire *et al.* 1989, 1993) and Sali Tagliamonte's work predominantly on northern English communities, but some comparative work from the south west of England too (e.g. Tagliamonte 1998, 2002a, 2002b; Godfrey and Tagliamonte 1999; Tagliamonte and Hudson 1999; Tagliamonte and Ito 2002; Tagliamonte and Smith 2002; Tagliamonte and Roeder 2009). Cheshire *et al.*'s *Survey of British Dialect Grammar* (1989, 1993) also focused on school children and found a large number of non-standard forms to be reported in more than four out of every five questionnaires. The suggestion that there is perhaps a common core of non-standard forms that are used by a majority of people in the country, and that don't appear to be regionally restricted, is supported by Cheshire *et al.*'s survey as well as other work (Hughes and Trudgill 1979; Hudson and Holmes 1995). This common core appears to include the following:

- *them* as a demonstrative;
- absence of plural marking on nouns of measurement;
- *never* as a past tense negator;
- regularized reflexive pronouns;
- *there's*/*there was* with notional plural subjects;
- present participles using the preterite rather than continuous forms;
- adverbs without -*ly*;
- *ain't*/*in't*;
- non-standard *was*.

These features will all be discussed in more detail below. Surveys such as those of Cheshire *et al.* and Hudson and Holmes have also been useful in shedding some light on the actual geographical distribution of some grammatical non-standard variants. Some, that had been assumed to be common across the country, were, according to these surveys, restricted to certain parts of the country, or found in much higher proportions in some areas than others – this set includes, perhaps surprisingly, negative concord (see below), reported at much lower levels in the north than in the south. Similarly, recent work on the Freiburg Corpus of English Dialects (FRED), a collection of transcripts of oral history recordings from around the country, has also enabled comparative work on the robust grammatical variation (and the geographical distribution of that variation) found across England and the rest of the British Isles (e.g. Kortmann 2004; Kortmann *et al.* 2004).

So England (and the remainder of the British Isles even more so) should not be seen as a homogeneous, largely standard-speaking speech community that contrasts with the largely non-standard Englishes spoken elsewhere. It too is highly diverse and variable, and it's probably fair to say that it is a good deal more variable, from a grammatical point of view, than many of the other inner circle Englishes spoken outside of the British Isles. A large proportion of its speakers too suffer from potential discrimination on the basis of their habitual use of non-standard varieties and from the standard ideologies that permeate the society in which they live. The remainder of this chapter provides a survey of the most well-documented characteristics of this grammatical variability.

Here, then, I present some coverage of the studies that have been conducted into variation in specific parts of the grammar of non-standard dialects spoken in England in the past few decades. Space limitations mean this cannot be an exhaustive survey, but readers can find other, often more detailed reports in Edwards *et al.* (1984), Milroy and Milroy (1993), Kortmann *et al.* (2004) and Britain (2007).

Studies of variation

Present tense verbs

Perhaps the most commonly found non-standard variability in the present tense verbal system concerns the scope of -*s* marking. In some varieties, predominantly those in the south west of England, but also in parts of northern England, -*s* is variably applied across the whole verbal paradigm and is not restricted to third-person singular contexts, as in (1) (e.g. Cheshire 1982; Ihalainen 1985; Edwards 1993; Godfrey and Tagliamonte 1999; Shorrocks 1999).

 1   We eats there most Sundays

This generalized -*s* marking appears to be linguistically constrained in two ways. The first is the so-called Northern Subject Rule, according to which -*s* is favoured after noun phrases and non-adjacent pronouns, but disfavoured after adjacent pronouns. The second is the 'following clause constraint' reported by Cheshire and Ouhalla (1997) in their work on the large town of Reading. Here, if (a) the subject is *not* third-person singular, and (b) the complement of the verb is a clause or a heavy noun phrase, -*s* is *not* found, as in (2) and (3):

 2   I bet the landlord hates it (cf. *I bets the landlord hates it)
 3   They think he's gone totally mad (cf. *they thinks he's gone totally mad)

Such verbal marking in these varieties is almost certainly on the decline (cf. Cheshire 1982 and Godfrey and Tagliamonte 1999). The latter also report that -*s* marking is most often found in third singular contexts (1999: 100), perhaps indicating a gradual shift towards a more standard-like paradigm (1999: 106).

On the other hand, in East Anglia present tense verbs traditionally lack any verbal marking at all, even in third-person singular contexts (Trudgill 1974, 2004; Peitsara 1996; Kingston 2000; Spurling 2004; Duffer 2008), as in (4):

4   She love going up the city

As in the south west with generic -s, however, this non-standard form appears to be undergoing attrition. Duffer (2008), Kingston (2000) and Spurling (2004) all find zero on the decline across apparent time in rural and urban Norfolk and Suffolk, though the attrition seems to be more marked, perhaps surprisingly, in rural parts of the region. Zero marking is also occasionally found in third-person singular contexts in the south west, since, as mentioned above, -s marking is variable right across the paradigm there (Godfrey and Tagliamonte 1999).

Present tense of BE

Despite the claim by Edwards *et al.* (1984: 19) that 'virtually all dialects simplify the conjugation of *to be*', there have been very few empirical reports of simplification, and no quantitative studies, beyond a wealth of discussion about the use of singular forms in plural existential contexts (see below). Ihalainen (1985: 65) and Piercy (forthcoming) report the use of non-first person singular cliticized *'m* in Somerset and Dorset respectively, but both show that these forms are only attached to pronoun subjects and not to full NPs (see (5) below). Britain (2002: 25–6) reports the use of *bes* in the East Anglian Fens signalling habitual durative aspect, as in (6):

5   You put a big notice on your door saying *you'm* a blood donor (Piercy forthcoming)
6   Stephen says she bes in the Wisbech Arms a lot

Piercy (forthcoming) reports invariant *be* as in (7) from Dorset:

7   so I be Dorset born and bred (Piercy forthcoming)

The use of *is*, or much more usually *'s*, in plural existentials is an extremely widely reported phenomenon (e.g. Cheshire 1982; Ojanen 1982; Petyt 1985; Peitsara 1988; Cheshire *et al.* 1989; Hudson and Holmes 1995 (who report it as the most used non-standard grammatical form in their survey); Anderwald 2004b; Beal 2004; Piercy forthcoming), as in (8):

8   there's crumbs all over the floor

Periphrastic do/did

In the south west of England, an unstressed periphrastic *do/did* is found as in (9) and (10) below (Ihalainen 1994; Klemola 1994; Megan Jones 2002; Kortmann 2002; Wagner 2004; Piercy forthcoming), with Klemola (1994) showing, on the basis of an analysis of the Survey of English Dialects and its fieldworker notebooks, that periphrastic *did* was more geographically restricted than *do*.

9 In autumn, cider becomes too strong and that do wake 'ee up a bit (Megan Jones 2002: 120)

10 She did jump on the pigs back and he did take her to school (Piercy forthcoming)

Present participles

A number of studies (e.g. Hudson and Holmes 1995: 20) report the use of the preterite rather than the progressive in present participles, as in (11):

11 I'm *sat* at a desk all day and I don't even have a window

Hughes and Trudgill (1979) and Beal (2004) also point to the regional variation in the use of different participle forms after the verbs *need* and *want*. Hughes and Trudgill report the progressive after *need* in the south of England and after both *need* and *want* in the Midlands and the north (1979: 21), but Beal reports the preterite after *need* and *want* in the north east (2004: 135).

Past tense verbs

General descriptions of regional varieties of English in England always point to the very significant differences between the past tense systems used in the non-standard dialects and that used in the standard variety (Cheshire 1982; Ojanen 1982; Petyt 1985; Cheshire *et al.* 1989, 1993; Edwards 1993; Hudson and Holmes 1995; Shorrocks 1999: 130–49; Stenström *et al.* 2002; Anderwald 2004b: 179–81, 183–4; Beal 2004; Trudgill 2004; Wagner 2004; Hughes *et al.* 2005; Watts 2006; Piercy forthcoming). There is a wide range of different past tense paradigms used across non-standard varieties spoken in England, but we can point to the following common patterns:

(a) Past tense forms that are weak in the non-standard variety but strong in Standard English (e.g. I grow, I growed, I've growed; I draw, I drawed, I've drawed).

(b) Preterite forms that are strong in the non-standard variety but weak in Standard English (e.g. East Anglian *owe*, *snow* becoming /uː/ and /snuː/ (Trudgill 2003: 52–3)).

(c) Past participle = preterite (e.g. I do, I done, I've done; I write, I writ, I've writ; I fall, I fell, I've fell; I take, I took, I've took, I begin, I begun, I've begun).

(d) Present = preterite = past participle (e.g. I come, I come, I've come).

A number of studies (Hughes and Trudgill 1979; Cheshire 1982; Cheshire *et al.* 1989) point to the difference in non-standard varieties between the past tense of full verb and auxiliary *do* as in (12):

12 You done it, did you?

Past tense BE

Non-standard paradigms of past *BE* are well reported in England (Cheshire 1982; Cheshire *et al.* 1989, 1993; Hudson and Holmes 1995; Tagliamonte 1998, 2002a;

Shorrocks 1999; Anderwald 2002, 2003, 2004a; Britain 2002; Stenström *et al.* 2002; Moore 2003; Levey 2007; Cheshire and Fox 2009; Vasko 2010).

Despite the dominant pattern of non-standard past *BE* marking *outside* England showing a system favouring *was* across the paradigm, studies in England, however, have largely found one of two different constellations of past *BE* forms. The first, and the system that is perhaps dominant in the southern half of the country, levels to *was* in the positive paradigm and *weren't* in the negative (Cheshire 1982; Tagliamonte 1998; Anderwald 2002, 2003; Britain 2002; Khan 2006; Levey 2007; Cheshire and Fox 2009; Vasko 2010), as in (13) and (14):

13   she weren't very steady on her feet, was she?
14   the youngsters was drinking outside the shop, weren't they?

A number of these studies from the south of England (e.g. Britain 2002; Levey 2007) find levelling to *weren't* at higher levels than levelling to *was*. Tagliamonte (1998), Anderwald (2002) and Cheshire and Fox (2009) all find that *weren't* levelling seems to be more common in tags than in main clauses.

The other pattern common in England shows levelling to *were* in positive contexts (Petyt 1985; Shorrocks 1999; Anderwald 2002, 2003; Britain 2002; Moore 2003; Beal 2004; Vasko 2010). Many of these show that levelled *were* is found in an area concentrated in the north west (parts of southern and western Yorkshire, Derbyshire, the north-west Midlands and southern Lancashire). Both Britain (2002) and Vasko (2010) find *were* levelling among older speakers in Cambridgeshire and the Fens in the east of England, though it is now becoming much rarer.

The use of *was* after plural existentials, as in (15), is reported widely (Ojanen 1982; Ihalainen 1985; Peitsara 1988; Cheshire *et al.* 1989, 1993; Tagliamonte 1998; Britain 2002; Vasko 2010), as it is in most (all?) L1 Anglophone speech communities:

15   there was piles of rotten apples everywhere

Perfective aspect

Standard English uses auxiliary *have* to construct the perfect tense, as in (16), but in the East Midlands and western parts of East Anglia, it is still possible to hear forms of *be* used as the auxiliary instead (see Ojanen 1982: 118–19, 143, 164; Peitsara and Vasko 2002; Britain 2003: 205), as in (17):

16   they've heard all sorts of rumours about him
17   I'm been strawberrying at Wisbech

Modal verbs

The little research here on non-standard varieties concerns either the distribution of double modals (usually in the form of reports rather than detailed empirical investigations – e.g. Milroy and Milroy 1993; Beal 2004) or comparisons between the functions of the modals in different varieties. Trousdale (2003) demonstrates that in the north east of England, unlike in Standard English, each modal verb tends to carry either epistemic modality or root modality but not both. So, for example, epistemic possibility in Tyneside is expressed with *might* and root possibility and permission with *can* (2003: 275). *Must* tends to carry epistemic modality in Tyneside rather than root necessity, for which *have got to* or *should* are used.

Quotative verbs

The system by which reported speech is marked in English dialect grammars has been in considerable flux in the past few decades. The rapid rise of *BE like* (as in (18)) as a global English quotative has been demonstrated in most Anglophone countries, and England is no exception (see Tagliamonte and Hudson 1999; Stenström *et al.* 2002; Baker *et al.* 2006; Buchstaller 2006; Levey 2006; Robles 2007).

18   and she was like 'no way, get out of here!'

The speed at which *BE like* has spread, and the variable geographical patterns in its use across England are demonstrated by a comparison of studies at different times over the past twenty years. Stenström *et al.* (2002), on the basis of the COLT corpus of London teenage speech collected in the early 1990s, find very low levels of *BE like* (accounting for less than 1 per cent of their quotatives). Buchstaller's work on corpora from Derby and Newcastle, collected in the early to mid 1990s, finds *BE like* somewhat higher, at 4.5 per cent (Buchstaller 2006: 8); Tagliamonte and Hudson's (1999: 158) York corpus collected in the mid to late 1990s showed 18 per cent *BE like*, and Richards' (2008) work on a suburb of Leeds found 23 per cent of tokens in data collected in 2005 were realized as *BE like*. Robles (2007), investigating a corpus of data collected in Colchester in south-east England from the late 1990s to 2005, finds *BE like* accounting for a third of all examples of quotatives. Baker *et al.* (2006) found *BE like* at over 60 per cent, but here only younger speakers were considered. Quotative *go*, as in (19), too, appears to be a feature in flux, appearing at higher levels among young people in Buchstaller's analyses (2006: 12).

19   and Helen went 'aaaaarrrgh'

While much of the literature is focusing on the diffusion and the social and linguistic embedding of the global variants *BE like* and *go*, Cheshire and Fox (2007) unearthed an apparently new local variant in London, namely *this is* SUBJECT, as in (20) and (21):

20   This is them 'What area are you from? What part?'
21   This is my mum 'What are you doing? I was in the queue before you'

Imperatives

Few studies report variation in imperatives. Trudgill (2004) and Peitsara (1996) note that in East Anglia, the second-person pronoun is usually explicit in imperative forms (see (22) below), even when strengthened by the verb *do* (23):

22   Sit you down!
23   Do you shut up!

Negation

Negative concord

The use of two or more negatives in a clause (as in 24) where Standard English requires just one is such a frequently occurring feature of the world's Englishes that Chambers (2004) labels it a vernacular universal.

24 I didn't do nothing!

It is reported in studies from across England (Cheshire 1982; Edwards 1993; Milroy and Milroy 1993; Hughes and Trudgill 1996; Shorrocks 1999; Anderwald 2002, 2004b; Stenström *et al.* 2002; Moore 2003; Beal 2004; Trudgill 2004; Wagner 2004; Beal and Corrigan 2005). Cheshire *et al.* (1989: 205) found, in their Survey of British Dialect Grammar, that multiple negation was reported more in the south than in the north of England, a geographical distribution largely confirmed by Anderwald (2002: 105, 2004b: 187) on the basis of an analysis of data from the British National Corpus (BNC).

Negation of auxiliaries and modals

This is one of the more substantially studied features of the dialect grammar of England and a site of considerable diversity, given that:

(a) negation can lead the auxiliary to be contracted ('auxiliary (AUX) contraction'), as in (25):

25 he's not been feeling very well

(b) the negator itself can be contracted ('negator (NEG) contraction'), as in (26):

26 she isn't feeling very well

(c) there is a wide range of regional variants of negated forms, as in (27) and (28):

27 she canna run any more
28 she divven't do it

(d) a number of types of 'secondary contraction' exist as in (29) and (30):

29 The band ain't [ɐɪnʔ] gonna come
30 they in't [ɪnʔ] gonna come either

(e) there is variation in the negation of *do*, i.e. *doesn't* and *don't* (31):

31 it don't seem to matter

A number of studies (Cheshire 1982; Tagliamonte and Smith 2002) of AUX versus NEG contraction of *BE* and *HAVE* have drawn attention to Hughes and Trudgill's

(1979) claim that AUX contraction, as in (25) above, is more common 'the further north one goes' (1979: 20). Hughes and Trudgill's claim (1979: 21), however, referred solely to speakers of *Standard* English, and did not include negation of *BE*. For negated *BE*, there is common agreement that AUX contraction is substantially more common that NEG contraction both in the south and the north of the country (Hughes and Trudgill 1979; Cheshire 1982: 52; Anderwald 2002: 76; Tagliamonte and Smith 2002: 270; Amos *et al.* 2007). Both Anderwald (2002: 78) and Tagliamonte and Smith (2002: 272), considering data from the Midlands, find much lower levels of AUX contraction of *BE*, suggesting that perhaps the Midlands form a buffer zone of lower levels of AUX contraction between regions to the north and south with much higher levels.

For negated *HAVE*, both Tagliamonte and Smith (2002: 268) and Amos *et al.* (2007) show extremely low levels of AUX contraction across England. For negated *WILL*, AUX contraction is either negligible, or, in Tagliamonte and Smith's (2002: 268) work near Durham, very high, approaching levels found in southern Scotland and Northern Ireland. If we put aside other forms, to be discussed below, then, we have a system within which BE and HAVE tend to be negated differently: *she's not feeling well* (AUX contraction with BE) but *she hasn't felt well* (NEG contraction with HAVE).

Secondary contractions of negative contracted forms – variants such as ain't [ɐɪnʔ – æɪnʔ], in't [ɪnʔ], een't [iːnʔ], etc. disturb this neat pattern, however. *Ain't* (and the other secondary contractions) can be used to negate copula *BE* (as in 32), auxiliary *BE* (as in 33) and auxiliary *HAVE* (as in 34):

32 It ain't my book
33 We ain't coming yet
34 They ain't seen him for ages

These forms are extremely widely reported (e.g. Cheshire 1982; Ojanen 1982; Petyt 1985; Cheshire *et al.* 1989, 1993; Edwards 1993; Hudson and Holmes 1995; Viereck 1997; Shorrocks 1999; Anderwald 2002, 2003, 2004b; Stenström *et al.* 2002; Beal 2004; Trudgill 2004; Amos *et al.* 2007), though Tagliamonte and Smith find very few examples in their data from a number of sites in both northern and southern England (2002: 262). Amos *et al.* (2007) found that East Anglia seemed to be the focal point for high levels of secondary contractions, where they represented over 20 per cent of all tokens of auxiliary HAVE and over 15 per cent of auxiliary and copula BE negation in Ipswich (Suffolk) and Mersea (near Colchester in Essex) and a very high 89 per cent and 96 per cent of all tokens for HAVE and BE respectively in Wisbech (Cambridgeshire).

Few studies distinguish between different forms of secondary contraction. Anderwald (2002) shows that *in't* [ɪnʔ] (as opposed to ain't [ɐɪnʔ – æɪnʔ]) is concentrated in London, the Midlands and the north west. She reports *in't* as being absent in East Anglia (2002: 130, 131), yet Trudgill (2004) claims this to be the dominant East Anglian form, and Amos *et al.* (2007) show it to be by far the dominant secondary contraction in Wisbech (Cambridgeshire) (where secondary contractions represent the almost categorical negation strategy). Viereck (1997: 251) reports *hain't* for East Anglian negated auxiliary *HAVE* and Ojanen (1982) reports *een't* [iːnʔ] for southern Cambridgeshire. Amos *et al.* (2007) find these as well as *en't* [ɛnʔ], *heen't* [hiːnʔ] and others. Cheshire (1981) shows evidence of a functional distinction between *ain't* and *in't* in Reading, with *in't* being the form of choice in tag questions, especially what she calls 'aggressive tags' which demonstrate some sort of hostility or divergence by the speaker towards the hearer.

A number of regional negated forms have been reported, such as -na (see 27 above), from parts of the west and north-west Midlands (e.g. Viereck 1997: 761, 763), Scottish-type -nae forms such as *dinnae* (for *don't*) and *cannae* (for *can't*) reported for Berwick-upon-Tweed in the far north east (Pichler and Watt 2006), and *divvent* (for *don't*) reported across the north east (Beal 2004; Pichler and Watt 2006; Rowe 2007), (28) above. Anderwald (2004a: 55) reports *amn't* for first-person singular negated BE (see also Broadbent 2009) in parts of the north-west Midlands in the Survey of English Dialects (SED) data, but it is not clear if it still survives.

Don't for third-person singular *doesn't*, as in (31), is widely reported (e.g. Cheshire 1982; Ojanen 1982; Cheshire *et al.* 1989, 1993; Hudson and Holmes 1995; Kingston 2000; Stenström *et al.* 2002; Anderwald 2003, 2004b). Anderwald (2003) compares the geographical distribution of *don't* in the data from the Survey of English Dialects (where she finds *don't* largely restricted to the south and Midlands) and the British National Corpus in which she finds that *don't* is 'present in practically every dialect area throughout Great Britain' and has been 'spreading from the south over the last few decades' (2003: 515). Kingston (2000: 56), however, finds that whilst *don't* is the dominant form among older and middle-aged people in rural Suffolk, it is being replaced by *doesn't* among younger, especially female speakers.

'Never' as a negator

A number of studies report *never* being used as a negator with definite time reference as in (35) (Cheshire 1982; Cheshire *et al.* 1989, 1993; Edwards 1993; Hudson and Holmes 1995; Viereck 1997; Stenström *et al.* 2002; Anderwald 2004b; Beal 2004):

35 I met her last week and she never told me about that!

Adverbs

Many varieties of English in England show variation with respect to whether adverbs append the inflection -*ly* or not (Hughes and Trudgill 1979). Inflectionless forms, as in (36) and (37) below, are reported from right across the country (Cheshire 1982; Ojanen 1982; Cheshire *et al.* 1989, 1993; Edwards 1993; Hudson and Holmes 1995; Shorrocks 1999; Stenström *et al.* 2002; Tagliamonte and Ito 2002; Anderwald 2004b; Beal 2004; Wagner 2004; Watts 2006):

36 Come quick!
37 It happened real fast

Tagliamonte and Ito (2002), in the most detailed empirical investigation of this phenomenon, showed a sharp decline in York English in the use of inflectionless forms across apparent time, but this decline is almost totally accounted for by the decline in the use of adverbial *real* as opposed to *really* in intensifiers. The use of zero marked adverbs otherwise showed a much shallower decline in apparent time, though there was a strong tendency for all zero marked forms to be found especially in the speech of male working-class speakers (2002: 252–3).

A number of researchers have investigated adverbial intensification of the kind that Tagliamonte and Ito noted for *real* (Hudson and Holmes 1995; Stenström *et al.* 2002). Hudson and Holmes (1995: 14) note that the use of the adverb *dead* as an intensifier was one of the few grammatical features found predominantly on Merseyside in their survey. Stenström *et al.* (2002: 151) show that *real* as an intensifier as in (37) above, is used most by *middle*-class speakers in their London corpus – showing a radically different social stratification of the feature than in York. They also show that intensifiers *right* as in (38) and *well* as in (39) were also predominantly middle-class forms:

38   I was *right* pissed off with that
39   And I thought she was *well* hard, sticking up for herself like that

Prepositions

Both Shorrocks (1999) and Vasko (2005) report a wide range of non-standard prepositional usages in their analyses of Bolton and southern Cambridgeshire respectively. Cheshire *et al.* (1993) report that the use of a simple preposition where Standard English has a complex one, as in (40), and the use of a complex preposition where Standard English has a simple one, as in (41), both tend to be features of southern varieties of English (1993: 77):

40   I'm going up my friend's house
41   He knocked his hat off of his head

Watts (2006) discusses variation in the omission and reduction of *to* in Cheshire and southern Lancashire, contrasting Cheshire, where *to* is often completely omitted by working-class speakers as in (42) (2006: 322) with neighbouring Lancashire and Greater Manchester where it is reduced to some form of glottal stricture or devoicing of the final consonant of the preceding word (Shorrocks 1999):

42   my dad needs to go the opticians (Watts 2006: 323)

Despite historical evidence that it was once more grammatically widespread, Watts only finds omission after the verb *go* in her Wilmslow data. In other contexts, reduction or assimilation is found. Ojanen/Vasko (Ojanen 1982: 252; Vasko 2005: 168–74) finds similar deletion in southern Cambridgeshire.

Plurality

Many non-standard varieties do not overtly mark plurality on a number of (especially measurement) nouns (Hughes and Trudgill 1979; Ojanen 1982; Petyt 1985; Cheshire *et al.* 1989, 1993; Edwards 1993; Peitsara 1996; Shorrocks 1999; Anderwald 2004b; Beal 2004; Trudgill 2004; Wagner 2004; Watts 2006), as in (43), (44) and (45) below:

43   that's five mile from the farm
44   I need ten foot of rope
45   three pound of tomatoes, please!

Pronouns

Personal pronouns

A number of non-standard forms are considered here: the use of distinct second-person plural subject pronouns, as in (46); the use of 'gendered pronouns' as in (47) and (48); 'pronoun exchange' as in (49) and (50), and the use of dummy *that* instead of *it* as in (51):

46 Yous'll have plenty of time for that
47 He have been a good watch
48 The little cottage up here, he's semi detached and he was put on the market for 350,000 (Piercy forthcoming)
49 He wanted he to go on milking the cows (Piercy forthcoming)
50 Us don't think naught about things like that (Wagner 2004: 158)
51 Come in quick – that's raining

A few studies report the use of *youse* as a plural form of *you* in some varieties (46 above). Beal notes its presence in Tyneside, Liverpool and Manchester (2004: 118) (see also Cheshire *et al.* 1993: 81), and Stenström *et al.* (2002) find it in London. Beal discusses both the possibility that this form may have its origins in Ireland as well as the continued existence in the traditional dialects of many parts of northern England (with the exception of Liverpool and Tyneside) of *thou* and *thee*. Trudgill (2003) shows that in East Anglia, *you ... together* can be used as the plural form of the second person, as in (52):

52 Come you on together!

Dialectologists of the south west of England have long recognized the existence there of 'pronoun exchange' whereby subject personal pronouns are used in non-subject positions and the reverse (see Ihalainen 1994; Wagner 2004; Piercy forthcoming) (see (49) and (50) above). Wagner (2004: 157–9) claims that 'with a frequency of occurrence of about 1% ... pronoun exchange seems to be all but dead in its former heartlands' (2004: 159). Piercy (forthcoming) finds pronoun exchange alive but rare in rural south Dorset. In addition, the use of the subject pronoun in non-subject position kind was once found in Essex (Trudgill 2003, 2004), and is still found in Tyneside (Beal 2004: 117–18).

Gendered pronouns are 'instances of pronouns which are marked for masculine or feminine gender but which refer to inanimate count nouns' (Wagner 2004: 159, see also Ihalainen 1994; Piercy forthcoming) as in (47) and (48) above. Wagner (2004) and Piercy (forthcoming) concur that these forms are now 'rare', but 'by no means dead' (Wagner 2004: 163).

In East Anglia, *that* is often found in place of Standard English *it* as in (51) above (Peitsara 1996; Trudgill 2003, 2004), a feature that is still robustly in evidence across the social and age spectrum.

Possessive pronouns

One obsolescing non-standard form reported in some varieties is the use of -(e)n forms, such as *hisn*, *hern*, *ourn* and *yourn*. Trudgill (1999: 90–1) reports that these seem to be most common in the Midlands and the south and south east (excluding the south west and East Anglia). Such forms are found at low levels among older speakers in the Cambridgeshire Fens.

In East Anglia, possessive pronouns can be used to refer to someone's house (Peitsara 1996: 293; Trudgill 2003: 61) as in (53):

53   Do you want to come round mine later?

Petyt (1985: 190) reports the use of *us* as a possessive pronoun in West Yorkshire (see also Beal 2004), as in (54):

54   We all take us cars to work nowadays

Reflexive pronouns

Possessive pronouns are often used to form reflexive ones in non-standard varieties in England, as in (55) and 56), marking them apart from the standard system which uses both object and possessive pronouns:

55   John bought hisself a Wii
56   The fans did theirselves no good at all

This is reported by, for example, Hughes and Trudgill (1979), Edwards (1993), Hudson and Holmes (1995), Shorrocks (1999), Stenström *et al.* (2002), Trudgill (2003), Anderwald (2004b), Beal (2004), Wagner (2004), Watts (2006) and Piercy (forthcoming).

Relative pronouns

Variation is endemic in the relativization system in English (see, for example, Hughes and Trudgill 1979: 17–18; Ihalainen 1985; Cheshire *et al.* 1989, 1993, 2007; Edwards 1993; Shorrocks 1999; Trudgill 1999, 2003, 2004; Stenström *et al.* 2002; Tagliamonte 2002b; Anderwald 2004b; Beal 2004; Wagner 2004; Watts 2006). The range of relative pronouns used in Standard English overlaps with those used in the non-standard varieties of England (e.g. *who, which, that,* Ø) but both have forms not used in the other (e.g. *whom, what, as*), and the forms they share often differ from each other, and differ across the non-standard varieties, in terms of their relative frequency in different syntactic environments. Important in determining relativizer choice is whether the antecedent noun plays a subject (57a–c) or object (58a–d) role in the relative clause and whether the gender of the antecedent is human, or non-human but animate or inanimate.

57(a)   Becky shouted at the bloke what spilt his drink on her dress
57(b)   Becky shouted at the bloke who spilt his drink on her dress
57(c)   Becky shouted at the bloke that spilt his drink on her dress
58(a)   That's the dog what he found injured on the side of the road
58(b)   That's the dog which he found injured on the side of the road
58(c)   That's the dog that he found injured on the side of the road
58(d)   That's the dog he found injured on the side of the road

49

A number of studies have looked in more detail at the relativization strategies in local dialects of English in England (see Britain 2007 for a detailed overview of these studies).

In subject position, *that* is the dominant form across the country, except in northern East Anglia which prefers *what* (see Cheshire *et al.* 2007; Poussa 1994). Ø, too, although rarely the most frequently occurring subject relativizer, is common in many of the country's dialects, especially in existentials, such as (59), and clefts, such as (60):

59   there's not many people like getting up at stupid o'clock to go to work
60   it's a small bungalow they moved to

Ø is the dominant form in object position, regardless of antecedent animacy. *That* is also very common in object position, except, again, in East Anglia, where it is a marginal minority form in Peitsara's (2002a) Suffolk data and barely present in any of the other East Anglian studies. In Cheshire *et al.*'s (2007) study of the Fens and London, *that* accounted for just 5 per cent of object relativizers in the Fens but 60 per cent of such tokens in London. Poussa (1994: 424) finds very little *that* in Norfolk and speculates about how far the area of '*that*lessness' extends, and whether it is simply an East Anglian phenomenon.

The two relativizers that occur only in non-standard varieties, *what* and *as*, seem to be experiencing somewhat different fates. *As* appears obsolescent. Peitsara (2002a) finds that relativizer *as* is rarely used in her Suffolk data, as do Ojanen (1982) for Cambridgeshire, and Cheshire *et al.* (2007) for the East Anglian Fens. It seems to be found at its highest levels in the south west (see Peitsara 2002a: 180). *What* appears to still be quite robust, however, accounting for more than 10 per cent of the relativizers in the south west and East Anglian corpora in Herrmann's research (2003), as a dominant form in both subject and object position in Reading (Cheshire 1982) and is used heavily in East Anglia (Ojanen 1982; Poussa 1994; Peitsara 2002a; Cheshire *et al.* 2007). Cheshire *et al.* (2007) find that *what* is the most used form in both subject and object relatives in the Fens. Herrmann (2003: 138) claims that *what* is spreading: 'from its southeastern (East Anglia including Essex) heartland' and 'has been radiating out through the adjoining Midlands and the Home Counties, especially London, to the Southwest and, eventually, to the North'. She adds, furthermore, that although *what* originated in East Anglia, it is not thriving there now because of stigmatization (2003: 141). Braddy (2009) finds that *what* is in sharp decline in East Anglia. In a study of the Essex village of Coggeshall, she finds dramatic shift over apparent time from a system where *what* was dominant (among older speakers in the village) to one in which, like in London (Cheshire *et al.* 2007), younger speakers very much prefer *that* while *what* has disappeared.

Further north and in the south west, however, *what* is barely used. Tagliamonte claims that '*what* is virtually non-existent' (2002b: 154), 'the sheer lack of WH-words … is astounding' (2002b: 163). *Wh-* forms were barely used in object positions at all in her research. An analysis of *who* in subject position across apparent time in her York corpus showed it to be used least among younger (under 35 years) and less well-educated speakers, whilst *that* was more common among the young. Given that *wh-* forms had been considered to be steadily *entering* the system, Tagliamonte adds that 'linguistic change in the English relative marker system may be like a pendulum swinging back in the opposite direction' (2002b: 164).

Pronominal word order

Kirk (1985: 135) discusses, on the basis of information from the Survey of English Dialects, the regional distribution of word order variation in clauses with both a direct and indirect object pronoun, with (61), (62) and (63) all possible in dialects of England. He found that Verb + DO + to IO (61) was reported as the dominant vernacular form only in the south west, Verb + DO + IO (62) in the Midlands, Lancashire and parts of the south east, with Verb + IO + DO (63) dominant in the north and East Anglia.

61   Give it to me
62   Give it me
63   Give me it

Demonstratives

A number of dialects in England show non-standard forms in the demonstrative system. The use of *them* as a distal plural demonstrative is extremely common (Hughes and Trudgill 1979; Cheshire 1982; Cheshire *et al.* 1989, 1993; Edwards 1993; Hudson and Holmes 1995; Shorrocks 1999; Stenström *et al.* 2002; Anderwald 2004b; Wagner 2004; Piercy forthcoming), as in (64).

64   Can you see them birds sitting in that hedge?

Both Cheshire *et al.* (1989: 194) and Hudson and Holmes (1995: 14) find that *them* is one of the most commonly found non-standard grammatical features in England. A number of varieties also report *this here*, *these here*, *that there* and *them there* used as demonstratives (e.g. Wagner 2004: 164 for the south west; Shorrocks 1999: 51 for Bolton in the north west; Trudgill 2003: 62 for Norfolk).

Wagner (2004) reports that *thik* [ðɪk] as a demonstrative has 'all but died out' in the south west (2004: 164), and Kortmann (2002) reports *they* used as the distal plural form in Somerset. Piercy (forthcoming) finds both present in rural south Dorset among older speakers, (65) and (66) respectively:

65   thik two boys, they got left standing there (Piercy forthcoming)
66   the one thing about it in they days (Piercy forthcoming)

Comparison

A good number of varieties spoken in England have 'double comparison' and use *both* the inflectional ending (*-er* for comparatives and *-est* for superlatives) *and* the appropriate analytic marker (*more* or *most*), as in (67) and (68), where in Standard English only one would be found (e.g. Ojanen 1982: 211; Edwards 1993: 231; Hudson and Holmes 1995: 20; Stenström *et al.* 2002: 134):

67   it's more fuller than what it was last week
68   the most wonderfulest holiday she's ever had

Definite and indefinite articles

A well-known phenomenon from across the north of England is so-called Definite Article Reduction, whereby *the* is reduced to [t] or [ʔ] (see Mark Jones 1999 for a discussion of regional variation in pronunciation, and also Petyt 1985; Ihalainen 1994; Shorrocks 1999; Mark Jones 2002; Rupp and Page-Verhoeff 2005; Tagliamonte and Roeder 2009), as in (69):

69 They had a baby, and as soon as *t' baby* arrived he got jealous (Rupp and Page-Verhoeff 2005)

Fox (2007), in a study of language use among a friendship group of adolescents of white and Bangladeshi ethnicity in the East End of London, finds that allomorphy both of the definite and indefinite articles is being rapidly eroded. Both articles are sensitive, in Standard English, to whether the sound after the article is a vowel or a consonant, as in (70) and (71). Fox finds, however, that the prevocalic variants are undergoing attrition, as in (72), with *a* being used before vowels in 74 per cent of all possible cases among the Bangladeshi boys in her sample, and [ðə] before vowels in 81 per cent of cases:

70 an apple, a pear
71 the [ði] apple, the [ðə] pear
72 a apple, the [ðəʔ] apple

This phenomenon has been found sporadically in a number of traditional dialects (see, for example, Ojanen 1982: 126; Peitsara 1996: 288; Britain 2003: 203 in East Anglia; Shorrocks 1999: 45 for the north west; Wagner 2004: 155 and Piercy forthcoming, for the south west) but given that these reports are from areas well away from London, it appears Fox's dramatic findings represent a diffusing innovation, possibly from within the ethnic minority community (see also Britain and Fox 2009; Gabrielatos *et al.* in press).

Conjunctions

A small number of studies report the use of non-standard conjunctions (e.g. Peitsara 1996; Shorrocks 1999; Trudgill 2003, 2004). The East Anglian research by both Trudgill and Peitsara discusses what the latter labels 'consecutive conjunctions' (1996: 300), such as (73) and (74):

73 Don't go near that dog *do* he'll bite you
74 Will you tidy your room *time* I get tea ready?

Question tags

Studies carried out in the south east of England (Stenström *et al.* 2002; Fox 2007 – see also Hudson and Holmes 1995; Anderwald 2004b) have noted the increasing use of the invariant tag *innit?* as in (75):

75 You told mum yesterday, innit? (Stenström *et al.* 2002: 169)

Stenström *et al.*'s analysis (2002) based on their corpus of London adolescent speech looks at *innit* alongside other tags such as *yeah?* and *right?* They find that *innit?* is largely used by working-class, ethnic minority females (2002: 187, 188, 189), with *yeah?* used most by adolescent middle-class males and *right?* (which they found was as popular as *innit?*), like *innit?*, used most by working-class ethnic minority adolescents. Cheshire and Fox (2009: 25) report the use of invariant *weren't it?* as a tag in London.

Conclusion

Diversity reigns, then, if we take a holistic view of the grammatical structures used in the varieties spoken in England. In conclusion, we can point to a number of themes that this review of grammatical diversity has raised. First, and to reiterate the point made at the start of the chapter, every corner of the country demonstrates a wide range of grammatically non-standard forms, reminding us that such forms are the rule rather than the exception in spoken English English – research has shown that there appears to be a common core of non-standard elements found very widely across the country, alongside more local grammatical forms. Second, there do, nevertheless seem to be some areas of the country that stand out as demonstrating a particularly distinctive constellation of non-standard grammatical forms: the south west, East Anglia and the north east, for example, have been particularly prominent and this is only partly because they have been relatively well described from a grammatical point of view (though the contemporary south west, particularly, is much less well described from a phonological perspective; see Piercy forthcoming). Third, and following on from the above, there are huge gaps in our knowledge of the present-day grammars of varieties in England, both from a sociogeographical perspective – which non-standard grammatical forms are used in place X, and by what sort of speakers there? – and a linguistic one – what is the linguistic conditioning of the grammatical non-standardness? Much of what we do know from some parts of the country comes from rather traditional and now almost certainly outdated sources. Considerable amounts of recent sociolinguistic and variationist work have shed light on phonetic and phonological variation, especially in the north of England, but our understanding of current grammatical variation has by no means kept up with this phonological work. It is likely that such research, if conducted, would unearth further diversity, as well as provide us with an update on the continued survival (or not) of some of the traditional grammatical variants reported in older dialectological research. Fourth, as some traditional grammatical forms have died, or are dying, others have been born – this review has highlighted a number of features which are either relatively recent arrivals to L1 English in England (such as quotative *BE like* and *this is me*), and other forms which appear to have been rejuvenated (e.g. lack of allomorphy in the article system). Central to many but not all of these are the innovating role played by the country's minority ethnic communities. Research such as that carried out in London (e.g. Cheshire and Fox 2007, 2009; Fox 2007) and Birmingham (Khan 2006) has showcased the important role that these communities are playing not just in creating and adopting new grammatical forms, but also in diffusing them to the local white populations with whom they have contact. Further research is needed from different parts of the country to enable us to fully understand the scope of these innovating communities. Despite the immediacy and proximity of the hegemonic standard, then, and despite the fact that some non-standard grammatical features appear obsolescent, geography, demography and ethnicity have combined to ensure that robust non-standardness remains pervasive in England.

Suggestions for further reading

Kortmann, B., Burridge, K., Mesthrie, R., Schneider, E. and Upton, C. (2004) *A Handbook of Varieties of English: Volume 2: Morphology and Syntax*, Berlin: Mouton de Gruyter. (The most thorough and detailed examination of grammatical variation across the dialects of England, this volume has separate chapters on the north, the south west, the south east and East Anglia (though, sadly, no coverage of the Midlands).)

Cheshire, J. (2005) 'Syntactic variation and beyond: gender and social class variation in the use of discourse-new markers', *Journal of Sociolinguistics*, 9: 479–508. (This very important paper by Jenny Cheshire explores variation from a somewhat different perspective from most variationist work, examining the different grammatical strategies that perform similar *functions* in the spoken language, rather than simply analysing, as most such research has done, variant grammatical *forms*. She finds that the social stratification of variable grammatical structures is deeply embedded in the grammar of spoken discourse, and suggests that in order to locate this social patterning, 'it may be necessary to … [take] as the starting point of an analysis the function of a specific syntactic construction rather than the form, and then explore the full range of other linguistic forms that speakers use to fulfil the same function' (Cheshire 2005: 500). This work opens up the potential for further research in other speech communities and on other grammatical functions to unearth hitherto unknown connections between social and grammatical structure.)

Cheshire, J. and Fox, S. (2009) '*Was/Were* variation: a perspective from London', *Language Variation and Change*, 21: 1–38.

Tagliamonte, S. and Smith, J. (2002) '"Either it isn't or it's not": NEG/AUX contraction in British dialects', *English World-Wide*, 23: 251–81. (These two papers, the former considering a multi-ethnic neighbourhood of London, the latter a study of multiple locations in northern and south-western England (as well as places in Scotland and Ireland) both represent exemplary clear accounts of the analytical methods used to study one specific grammatical variable in detail, ways to present the results of quantitative analyses of that variable, as well as theoretical interpretations of the findings of the analyses.)

References

Amos, J., Braña-Straw, M., Britain, D., Grainger, H., Piercy, C., Rigby, A., Ryfa, J. and Tipton, P. (2007) 'It's not up north but it's down south, ain't it? A regional examination of auxiliary versus negator contraction', paper presented at UKLVC6, Lancaster, September.

Anderwald, L. (2002) *Negation in Non-standard British English: Gaps, Regularizations, Asymmetries*, London: Routledge.

——(2003) 'Non-standard English and typological principles: the case of negation', in G. Rohdenburg and B. Mondorf (eds) *Determinants of Grammatical Variation in English*, Berlin: Mouton de Gruyter, pp. 508–29.

——(2004a) 'Local markedness as a heuristic tool in dialectology: the case of "amn't"', in B. Kortmann (ed.) *Dialectology Meets Typology: Dialect Grammar from a Cross-linguistic Perspective*, Berlin: Mouton de Gruyter, pp. 47–67.

——(2004b) 'The varieties of English spoken in the southeast of England: morphology and syntax', in B. Kortmann, K. Burridge, R. Mesthrie, E. Schneider and C. Upton (eds) *A Handbook of Varieties of English: Morphology and Syntax*, Berlin: Mouton de Gruyter, pp. 175–95.

Baker, Z., Cockeram, D., Danks, E., Durham, M., Haddican, B. and Tyler, L. (2006) 'The expansion of BE LIKE: real time evidence from England', paper presented at NWAV35, Ohio State University.

Beal, J. (2004) 'English dialects in the North of England: morphology and syntax', in B. Kortmann, K. Burridge, R. Mesthrie, E. Schneider and C. Upton (eds) *A Handbook of Varieties of English: Morphology and Syntax*, Berlin: Mouton de Gruyter, pp. 114–41.

Beal, J. and Corrigan, K. (2005) '"No, nay, never": negation in Tyneside English', in Y. Iyeiri (ed.) *Aspects of Negation in English*, Kyoto: University of Kyoto Press, pp. 139–57.

Braddy, M. (2009) 'Dialect levelling in Coggeshall: a village what's seen more than a foo changes', unpublished undergraduate dissertation, University of Essex.

Britain, D. (2002) 'Diffusion, levelling, simplification and reallocation in past tense BE in the English Fens', *Journal of Sociolinguistics*, 6: 16–43.

——(2003) 'Exploring the importance of the outlier in sociolinguistic dialectology', in D. Britain and J. Cheshire (eds.) *Social Dialectology*, Amsterdam: John Benjamins, pp. 191–208.

——(2007) 'Grammatical variation in England', in D. Britain (ed.) *Language in the British Isles*, Cambridge: Cambridge University Press, pp. 75–104.

Britain, D. and Fox, S. (2009) 'The regularisation of the hiatus resolution system in British English: a contact-induced "vernacular universal"?' in M. Filppula, J. Klemola and H. Paulasto (eds) *Vernacular Universals and Language Contacts: Evidence from Varieties of English and Beyond*, London: Routledge, pp. 177–205.

Broadbent, J. (2009) 'The *amn't gap: the view from West Yorkshire', *Journal of Linguistics*, 45: 251–84.

Buchstaller, I. (2006) 'Diagnostics of age-graded linguistic behaviour: the case of the quotative system', *Journal of Sociolinguistics*, 10: 3–30.

Chambers, J.K. (2004) 'Dynamic typology and vernacular universals', in B. Kortmann (ed.) *Dialectology Meets Typology: Dialect Grammar from a Cross-linguistic Perspective*, Berlin: Mouton de Gruyter, pp. 127–45.

Cheshire, J. (1981) 'Variation in the use of *ain't* in an urban British dialect', *Language in Society*, 10: 365–81.

——(1982) *Variation in an English Dialect*, Cambridge: Cambridge University Press.

——(2005) 'Syntactic variation and beyond: gender and social class variation in the use of discourse-new markers', *Journal of Sociolinguistics*, 9: 479–508.

——(2007) 'Discourse variation, grammaticalisation and stuff like that', *Journal of Sociolinguistics*, 11: 155–93.

Cheshire, J. and Fox, S. (2007) 'Innovation in the quotative system of London adolescents: The emergence of *this is me*', paper presented at NWAV-36, University of Pennsylvania, October.

——(2009) '*Was/Were* variation: a perspective from London', *Language Variation and Change*, 21: 1–38.

Cheshire, J. and Ouhalla, J. (1997) 'Grammatical constraints on variation', paper presented at UKLVC1, University of Reading.

Cheshire, J., Edwards, V. and Whittle, P. (1989) 'Urban British dialect grammar: the question of dialect levelling', *English World-Wide*, 10: 185–225.

——(1993) 'Non-standard English and dialect levelling', in J. Milroy and L. Milroy (eds) *Real English: The Grammar of English Dialects in the British Isles*, London: Longman, pp. 53–96.

Cheshire, J., Kerswill, P. and Williams, A. (2005) 'Phonology, grammar and discourse in dialect convergence', in P. Auer, F. Hinskens and P. Kerswill (eds) *Dialect Change: Convergence and Divergence in European Languages*, Cambridge: Cambridge University Press, pp. 135–70.

Cheshire, J., Fox, S. and Britain, D. (2007) 'Relatives from the South', paper presented at UKLVC6, Lancaster, September.

Duffer, L. (2008) 'Dialect attrition in Gorleston, Norfolk', unpublished BA dissertation, University of Essex.

Edwards, V. (1993) 'The grammar of Southern British English', in J. Milroy and L. Milroy (eds) *Real English: The Grammar of English Dialects in the British Isles*, London: Longman, pp. 214–38.

Edwards, V., Trudgill, P. and Weltens, B. (1984) *The Grammar of English Dialect: A Survey of Research: A Report to the ESRC Education and Human Development Committee*, London: ESRC.

Fox, S. (2007) 'The demise of "Cockneys"? Language change in London's "traditional" East End', unpublished PhD dissertation, University of Essex.

Gabrielatos, C., Torgersen, E., Hoffmann, S. and Fox, S. (in press) 'A corpus-based sociolinguistic study of indefinite article forms in London English', *Journal of English Linguistics*.

Godfrey, E. and Tagliamonte, S. (1999) 'Another piece of the verbal -s story: evidence from Devon in Southwest England', *Language Variation and Change*, 11: 87–121.

Herrmann, T. (2003) 'Relative clauses in dialects of English: a typological approach', unpublished PhD dissertation, Albert-Ludwigs-Universität Freiburg.

Hudson, R. and Holmes, J. (1995) *Children's Use of Spoken Standard English*, London: School Curriculum and Assessment Authority.

Hughes, A. and Trudgill, P. (1979) *English Accents and Dialects: An Introduction to Social and Regional Varieties of English in the British Isles*, London: Arnold.

Hughes, A., Trudgill, P. and Watt, D. (2005) *English Accents and Dialects: An Introduction to Social and Regional Varieties of English in the British Isles*, London: Hodder Arnold.

Ihalainen, O. (1985) 'Synchronic variation and linguistic change: evidence from British English dialects', in R. Eaton, O. Fischer, W. Koopman and F. Van der Leek (eds) *Papers from the 4th International Conference on English Historical Linguistics*, Amsterdam: John Benjamins, pp. 61–72.

——(1994) 'The dialects of England since 1776', in R. Burchfield (ed.) *The Cambridge History of the English Language, Vol. 5. English in Britain and Overseas: Origins and Development*, Cambridge: Cambridge University Press, pp. 197–274.

Jones, Mark (1999) 'The phonology of definite article reduction', in C. Upton and K. Wales (eds) *Dialectal Variation in English*, special issue of *Leeds Studies in English*, 30: 103–21.

——(2002) 'The origin of definite article reduction in northern English dialects: evidence from dialect allomorphy', *English Language and Linguistics*, 6: 325–45.

Jones, Megan (2002) '"You do get queer, see. She do get queer.": Non-standard periphrastic DO in Somerset English', *University of Pennsylvania Working Papers in Linguistics*, 8 (3): 117–32.

Khan, A. (2006) 'A sociolinguistic study of the Birmingham dialect: variation and change', unpublished PhD dissertation, University of Lancaster.

Kingston, M. (2000) 'Dialects in danger: rural dialect attrition in the East Anglian county of Suffolk', unpublished MA dissertation, University of Essex.

Kirk, J. (1985) 'Linguistic atlases and grammar: the investigation and description of regional variation in English syntax', in J. Kirk, S. Sanderson and J. Widdowson (eds) *Studies in Linguistic Geography*, London: Croom Helm, pp. 130–56.

Klemola, J. (1994) 'Periphrastic DO in south-western dialects of British English: a reassessment', *Dialectologia et geolinguistica*, 2: 33–51.

Kortmann, B. (2002) 'New prospects for the study of English dialect syntax: impetus from syntactic theory and language typology', in S. Barbiers, L. Cornips and S. van der Kleij (eds) *Syntactic Microvariation*, Amsterdam: Meertens Institute Electronic Publications in Linguistics, pp. 185–213.

——(ed.) (2004) *Dialectology Meets Typology: Dialect Grammar from a Cross-linguistic Perspective*, Berlin: Mouton de Gruyter.

Kortmann, B., Burridge, K., Mesthrie, R., Schneider, E. and Upton, C. (2004) *A Handbook of Varieties of English: Volume 2: Morphology and Syntax*, Berlin: Mouton de Gruyter.

Kortmann, B., Herrmann, T., Pietsch, L. and Wagner, S. (2005) *A Comparative Grammar of British English Dialects: Agreement, Gender, Relative Clauses*, Berlin: Mouton de Gruyter.

Levey, S. (2006) 'Visiting London relatives', *English World-Wide*, 27: 45–70.

——(2007) 'The next generation: aspects of grammatical variation in the speech of some London preadolescents', unpublished PhD dissertation, Queen Mary, University of London.

Milroy, J. and Milroy, L. (eds) (1993) *Real English: The Grammar of English Dialects in the British Isles*, London: Longman.

Moore, E. (2003) 'Learning style and identity: a sociolinguistic analysis of a Bolton high school', unpublished PhD dissertation, University of Manchester.

Ojanen, A.-L. (1982) 'A syntax of the Cambridgeshire dialect', unpublished Licentiate dissertation, University of Helsinki.

Peitsara, K. (1988) 'On existential sentences in the dialect of Suffolk', *Neuphilologische Mitteilungen*, 89: 72–89.

——(1996) 'Studies on the structure of the Suffolk dialect', in J. Klemola, M. Kytö and M. Rissanen (eds) *Speech Past and Present: Studies in English Dialectology in Memory of Ossi Ihalainen*, Frankfurt am Main: Peter Lang, pp. 284–307.

——(2002) 'Relativizers in the Suffolk dialect', in P. Poussa (ed.) *Relativisation on the North Sea Littoral*, Munich: Lincom Europa, pp. 167–80.

Peitsara, K. and Vasko, A.-L. (2002) 'The *Helsinki Dialect Corpus*: characteristics of speech and aspects of variation', *Helsinki English Studies: The Electronic Journal of the Department of English at the University of Helsinki*, 2.

Petyt, K. (1985) *Dialect and Accent in Industrial West Yorkshire*, Amsterdam: John Benjamins.

Pichler, H. and Watt, D. (2006) '"We're all Scottish really": investigating the tension between claimed identity and linguistic behaviour in Berwick-upon-Tweed', manuscript. Online. Available www. abdn.ac.uk/langling/resources/Berwick.ppt (last accessed September 2009).

Piercy, C. (forthcoming) 'One /a/ or two? the phonetics, phonology and sociolinguistics of change in the TRAP and BATH vowels in the South-West of England', unpublished PhD dissertation, University of Essex.

Poussa, P. (1994) 'Norfolk relatives (Broadland)', in W. Viereck (ed.) *Regionalsprachliche Variation, Umgangs- und Standardsprachen: Verhandlungen des Internationalen Dialektologenkongresses: Band 3*, Stuttgart: Franz Steiner Verlag, pp. 418–26.

Richards, H. (2008) 'Mechanisms, motivations and outcomes of change in Morley (Leeds) English', unpublished PhD dissertation, University of York.

Robles, J. (2007) 'The diffusion of quotative Like: grammaticalization and social usefulness', paper presented at the Annual Meeting of the Intenational Communication Association, San Francisco, May.

Rowe, C. (2007) 'He divn't gan tiv a college ti di that, man! A study of do (and to) in Tyneside English', *Language Sciences*, 29: 360–71.

Rupp, L. and Page-Verhoeff, J. (2005) 'Pragmatic and historical aspects of Definite Article Reduction in northern English dialects', *English World-Wide*, 26: 325–46.

Shorrocks, G. (1999) *A Grammar of the Dialect of the Bolton Area. Part II: Morphology and Syntax*, Frankfurt am Main: Peter Lang.

Spurling, J. (2004) 'Traditional feature loss in Ipswich: dialect attrition in the East Anglian county of Suffolk', unpublished BA dissertation, University of Essex.

Stenström, A-B., Andersen, G. and Hasund, I. (2002) *Trends in Teenage Talk: Corpus Compilation, Analysis and Findings*, Amsterdam: John Benjamins.

Tagliamonte, S. (1998) 'Was/were variation across the generations: view from the city of York', *Language Variation and Change*, 10: 153–92.

——(2002a) 'Comparative sociolinguistics', in J.K. Chambers, P. Trudgill and N. Schilling-Estes (eds) *The Handbook of Language Variation and Change*, Oxford: Blackwell, pp. 729–63.

——(2002b) 'Variation and change in the British relative marker system', in P. Poussa (ed.) *Relativisation on the North Sea Littoral*, Munich: Lincom Europa, pp. 147–65.

Tagliamonte, S. and Hudson, R. (1999) 'Be like et al beyond America: the quotative system in British and Canadian youth', *Journal of Sociolinguistics*, 3: 147–72.

Tagliamonte, S. and Ito, R. (2002) 'Think really different: continuity and specialization in the English dual form adverbs', *Journal of Sociolinguistics*, 6: 236–66.

Tagliamonte, S. and Roeder, R. (2009) 'Variation in the English definite article: socio-historical linguistics in t'speech community', *Journal of Sociolinguistics*, 13: 435–71.

Tagliamonte, S. and Smith, J. (2002) '"Either it isn't or it's not": NEG/AUX contraction in British dialects', *English World-Wide*, 23: 251–81.

Trousdale, G. (2003) 'Simplification and redistribution: an account of modal verb usage in Tyneside English', *English World-Wide*, 24: 271–84.

Trudgill, P. (1974) *The Social Differentiation of English in Norwich*, Cambridge: Cambridge University Press.

——(1995) 'Grammaticalisation and social structure: non-standard conjunction formation in East Anglian English', in F. Palmer (ed.) *Grammar and Semantics*, Cambridge: Cambridge University Press, pp. 136–47.

——(1999) *The Dialects of England* (2nd edition), Oxford: Blackwell.

——(2002) 'The sociolinguistics of modern RP', in P. Trudgill (ed.) *Sociolinguistic Variation and Change*, Edinburgh: Edinburgh University Press, pp. 171–80.

——(2003) *The Norfolk Dialect*, Cromer: Poppyland.

——(2004) 'The dialect of East Anglia: morphology and syntax', in B. Kortmann, K. Burridge, R. Mesthrie, E. Schneider and C. Upton (eds) *A Handbook of Varieties of English: Morphology and Syntax*, Berlin: Mouton de Gruyter, pp. 142–53.

Vasko, A.-L. (2005) *Up Cambridge: Prepositional Locative Expressions in Dialect Speech: A Corpus-based Study of the Cambridgeshire Dialect*, Helsinki: Société Néophilologique.

——(2010) 'Past tense *Be*: old and new variants', in B. Heselwood and C. Upton (eds) *Proceedings of Methods XIII: Papers from the Thirteenth International Conference on Dialectology, 2008*, Frankfurt am Main: Peter Lang.

Viereck, W. (1997) 'On negation in dialectal English', in R. Hickey and S. Puppel (eds) *Language History and Linguistic Modelling: A Festschrift for Jacek Fisiak on his 60th Birthday: Volume II: Linguistic Modelling*, Berlin: Mouton de Gruyter, pp. 759–67.

Wagner, S. (2004) 'English dialects in the Southwest: morphology and syntax', in B. Kortmann, K. Burridge, R. Mesthrie, E. Schneider and C. Upton (eds) *A Handbook of Varieties of English: Morphology and Syntax*, Berlin: Mouton de Gruyter, pp. 154–74.

Watts, E. (2006) 'Mobility-induced dialect contact: a sociolinguistic investigation of speech variation in Wilmslow, Cheshire', unpublished PhD dissertation, University of Essex.

3

Phonological innovation in contemporary spoken British English

Gerard J. Docherty

Introduction

Misunderstandings as the result of an erroneous interpretation of the phonetic characteristics of an utterance are commonly discussed in the context of second-language
learners (e.g. Best and Tyler 2007), but, arguably, less so where they arise as a result of
variation within the native language (Labov 1994; Bond 1999). So, for example, the
present author (a native speaker of English who has lived his entire life in either England or Scotland) recently stopped in his tracks when 'Cheese Day' was the mistaken
interpretation which he made of a UK undergraduate student's realization of the word
'Tuesday' (in this case, the immediate context did not provide the necessary dis-
ambiguation until about ten seconds after the misinterpretation had been made). The
principal cause of this 'slip of the ear' was the sheer auditory distance between the
front and unrounded vowel quality produced by the speaker in the first syllable of that
utterance (as is now regularly the case for speakers of his age – see below) and the
author's phonological representation of the same vowel in the target word, such that, in
this particular instance, the target vowel /u/ was perceptually assimilated to /i/. The
misperception, of course, was enhanced by the realization of the initial /tj/ consonantal
sequence as a palato-alveolar affricate [ʧ] identical to that found at the onset of *cheese*.
And this instance was a striking reminder that even for native speakers of widely
spoken varieties of English, ongoing phonological change can lead to significant issues
regarding intelligibility, even in the case where the listener is attuned to and has regularly encountered this type of realizational variant in English and is familiar with its
association with a relatively younger generation of speakers.

If phonological innovations can lead to misinterpretations such as this for (even reasonably well-informed) speakers of varieties of English which are in social/geo-
graphical proximity, then it is arguably all the more likely that they will be a more
significant challenge for speakers of other varieties of English either as an L1 or L2
who have not had exposure to the innovative phonetic realizations of the variety concerned. With this in mind, the aim of this chapter is to paint in broad strokes some of
the key dimensions of innovation and change in patterns of pronunciation of British

English. By necessity the coverage is selective and the chapter does not provide in-depth accounts of the various features discussed. In presenting this overview, I do not focus on one particular variety, nor do I attempt to provide coverage of all of the interesting variability observable within UK varieties of English. Rather, the material is designed to draw readers' attention to a selection of features which are distinctive, and in many cases relatively recent innovations present across speakers of a number of UK varieties, and particularly so in the speech of the younger generations.

For further details of many of the features described below, readers are referred to the recent volumes by Britain (2007) and Kortmann and Schneider (2004), to the somewhat less recent collection by Foulkes and Docherty (1999), and to the descriptions provided by Hughes *et al.* (2005 – especially the overview presented in Chapter 4), as well as to a range of individual studies which are specified below. Readers are also referred to the excellent online resources providing stream-able samples of a wide range of contemporary UK English accents, perhaps the most notable of which are the BBC Voices project (www.bbc.co.uk/voices/) and the British Library 'Sounds Familiar' archive (www.bl.uk/learning/langlit/sounds/index.html).

Factors associated with variation and change

Prior to tackling some of the salient phonological innovations within contemporary varieties of UK English, it is instructive to pause on what appear to be the factors associated with the trajectories of change identified in recent studies of UK accents. A key observation is that, across the British Isles, there has been (and continues to be) a tangible reduction in the use of a number of localized and strongly marked variants. For example, in the north east of England the traditional realization of /r/ as a voiced uvular fricative or approximant, the so-call Northumbrian 'burr', has now almost completely disappeared, being now confined to a geographically constrained sub-set of elderly speakers (Beal 2004). Likewise, in the realization of the Tyneside NURSE[1] vowel, the previously frequently encountered [ɔ] variant now appears to be strongly in decline and tied to a relatively restricted set of lexical items (Maguire 2008). The consequence of changes such as these is that across the UK there is now, at least in some respects, a greater degree of accentual homogeneity than was previously the case – a process which is typically referred to as 'dialect levelling' (Trudgill 1986; Kerswill 2003), and which appears to have built up momentum over the past twenty to thirty years.[2]

Sociolinguists (e.g. Kerswill 2001, 2003; Britain 2002; Kerswill and Williams 2002) converge on the view that dialect levelling has arisen as a result of the increase in social mobility across recent generations (in turn driven to a large degree by changes to patterns of employment and an altering of the social and economic equilibria between urban and rural populations) which has weakened the social ties believed to underpin strongly localized varieties, and which has increasingly brought people into contact with others who have different accentual characteristics. While there is some controversy in the literature (e.g. Britain and Trudgill 1999; Kerswill 2002) about the ways in which accents interact when they come into contact in this way, there seems no doubt that one of the likely consequences is a degree of convergence. A very clear case of this has been tracked within the UK in recent years through Kerswill *et al.*'s (e.g. Kerswill and Williams 2000, 2005) study of phonological variation in the new town of Milton Keynes, located about 45 miles north of London, which demonstrates the development of new accentual characteristics and norms as the result of co-locating over a relatively short period of time populations of speakers with differing accents and socioeconomic backgrounds.

But it is important to note that greater accentual homogeneity in the UK context does *not* mean that speakers are converging on a single standard, and likewise does not mean that accentual innovation has ceased to take place. Evidence from recent studies points to regional differentiation in respect of levelled varieties; for example, Watt and Milroy (1999) and Watt (2002) show that levelling in speakers of Tyneside English can be analysed as the adoption of a levelled variety with distinctively northern characteristics, contrasting in many respects with the features identified by various investigators (e.g. Przedlacka 2002; Altendorf 2003) as characteristic of the so-called 'Estuary English' levelled variety which is widely encountered over large parts of the south-east quadrant of England. But note too that the extent of levelling is very much a function of speech style, with many investigators reporting a higher frequency of more localized variants being found in more informal styles and contexts (for example, as shown for Newcastle by Docherty *et al.* 1997; Watt 2000; and for Glasgow by Stuart-Smith 1999). And of course, where the factors which have driven levelling have not been so powerful, marked local varieties and realizational variants still flourish, as shown by Llamas' (2001) study of Middlesbrough and Williams and Kerswill's (1999) work on Hull, locations where speakers continue to show significant divergence from neighbouring varieties driven in part by demographic and socioeconomic factors, but also by prominent local ideologies which lead traditional accent features to act as strong conveyers of local identity.

Crucially, while it is true to say that some traditional accent features are indeed disappearing, levelling is perhaps best thought of (Trudgill 1986) as a process which is defined relative to a previous state characterized by the presence of a variety of localized marked forms (some of which had a prominent role in the definition of local identities). It should not be read as meaning that diversity and innovation are not strongly present within contemporary varieties. Clearly the social and demographic factors which have delivered substantial levelling in recent decades continue to evolve (e.g. Champion 2008, 2009) and in doing so create conditions conducive to new patterns of phonological innovation and change. For example, recent work by *inter alia* Heselwood and McChrystal (2000), Torgersen *et al.* (2006), Fox (2007), Khattab (2007), Lambert *et al.* (2007), Cheshire *et al.* (2008) points to the role of the steadily (and in some places rapidly) shifting ethnic mix within the major urban centres in the UK as a relatively new driver of phonological innovation (and there is clear evidence of this factor shaping other areas of language use – e.g. Rampton 2005).

Finally, in this section, the current status of Received Pronunciation (RP) warrants a mention, especially as this continues to be the variety which acts as the frame of reference provided in the instruction of English in many parts of the world, and it is the variety of UK English which is described in greatest detail, due perhaps to landmark publications such as Gimson (1980), but also to smaller-scale but detailed studies such as Bauer (1985), Deterding (1997), Fabricius (2002a, 2002b, 2007) and Hawkins and Midgely (2005). It seems clear that the social perturbations mentioned above have also led to a shifting of the ideologies associated with different UK varieties, and, as a consequence, the prestige which for a very long period of time was associated with RP has significantly dissipated (Kerswill 2001, 2007). Of course, one reflection of this is precisely the fact referred to above that dialect levelling does not involve gravitation to a single prestige variety (i.e. speakers are not abandoning their localized marked variants in order to take up RP-like realizations). More prosaically, this evolution of ideology is reflected in the readiness with which different varieties are now encountered through national media channels such as the BBC, and in the almost inevitable resistance to this change evidenced in recurrent articles in the press regretting the passing of the prestigious ideology formerly associated with RP (e.g. Henderson 2007).

While it is not difficult to find speakers of RP almost anywhere in England (probably least difficult in the south east of the country), there is no doubt that it is undergoing changes, some of which are discussed below, and in its own way appears to be participating in the levelling process described above, although from a very different starting point than the traditional, localized accent features. An interesting perspective on this can be gained from Harrington and colleagues' analysis of the phonetic characteristics of the UK monarch over fifty years' recordings of the annual Christmas Day Queen's Speech (Harrington *et al.* 2000, 2005). Not only did this study provide a unique real-time account of variation in an individual's speech performance, it also shed light on how even a particularly conservative variety of RP had evolved over five decades (focusing in particular on shifts in vowel quality), albeit that the Queen's phonological patterning remains somewhat conservative, not evincing to any significant extent the key innovative features described below (unlike the speech of younger members of the UK Royal Family).

English in the UK

In the following section of this chapter, I now draw attention to key innovative aspects of phonological patterning within British varieties of English. As mentioned above, this section does not attempt to give full descriptions of specific varieties (the references which are cited provide ample descriptions of this sort), but focuses instead on features that are particularly characteristic across many (but by no means *all*) contemporary spoken varieties, and particularly for younger generations of speakers. I deal in the first instance with consonantal variation before moving on to discuss vowels and some aspects of prosody.

Realization of /t/

A remarkable number of the interesting innovations in consonantal realization in UK varieties of English are focused on /t/. Perhaps most notably, many studies over recent decades have tracked the spread of glottal variants of /t/ and have clarified the social, geographical and linguistic factors which govern their occurrence (Docherty and Foulkes 2005 provide a full list of references, including Andrésen 1968; Roach 1973; Trudgill 1974; Wells 1982; Docherty *et al.* 1997; Docherty and Foulkes 1999; Fabricius 2000, 2002b; Przedlacka 2002). There are two types of glottal variant identifiable in contemporary varieties; *glottal replacement* (referred to by some authors as *glottaling*), where a glottal stop is produced in contexts where a [t] would be expected to occur in a citation form realization; and glottal *reinforcement* (also referred to as *glottalization*), where a glottal stop is produced as a double-articulation at the same time as the [t] oral occlusion. While both variants are usually referred to as involving the production of a glottal stop, in fact the little instrumental phonetic research that has been carried out on these realizations (e.g. Docherty and Foulkes 1999 on speakers from Newcastle and Derby) suggests that the glottal articulation often involves little more than a brief interval of laryngealized voice quality[3] as a result of a momentary adjustment of the tension of the vocal folds, and it is not unusual for a complete and sustained glottal occlusion to be absent.

The studies referred to above provide a thorough analysis of the conditions in which the two different types of glottal variant can be found across a number of different varieties of UK English. But for the purposes of the present chapter, it is perhaps most valuable to draw attention to the findings which point to a significant increase in the extent to which speakers across many parts of the UK are deploying the glottaled [ʔ] variant in two particular environments; in word-final pre-consonantal position (e.g. *get this*) and perhaps most strikingly in intervocalic position both word-medially (as in *water*) and word-finally (as in *get off*). For example, in a study comparing Reading, Milton Keynes and Hull carried out in the mid 1990s, Williams and Kerswill (1999: 147) note that 'glottal replacement of non-initial /t/ is the norm among young working class people in all three towns', and that the frequency of occurrence is greater in younger than in older speakers. In a study of Derby carried out at approximately the same time, Docherty and Foulkes (1999) noted substantial use of glottal variants by younger speakers and much less by their sample of older speakers (but with no class or gender differences). And glottaling of word-medial /t/ is regularly cited as a key characteristic of the so-called 'Estuary English' varieties of English (e.g. Przedlacka 2002; Altendorf 2003). Fabricius' (2002b) study of /t/-glottaling in RP brings out another aspect of this ongoing development, namely its sensitivity to speech style, finding that there were much lower frequencies of occurrence in a reading passage as opposed to an unscripted interview.

Of all of the innovations in UK varieties of English, the glottaling of /t/ in intervocalic position, especially word-medially, is arguably the most salient. This salience is partly phonetic in origin (the phonetic distance between a fully occluded [t] and a momentary laryngealization at the interface of two vowels is, by any measure, quite substantial, lending these variants significant auditory prominence), but it also relates to the social value which is attached to variants concerned. As discussed in detail by Fabricius (2002b), t-glottaling has become almost emblematic of the ideological shifts which have dissipated the status of RP (a variety which is not conventionally associated with intervocalic t-glottaling). Thus, in expressing their resistance to these shifts, commentators regularly alight on t-glottaling as the example of an 'undesirable' innovation in the speech of younger people (e.g. Norman 2001 – of course, this negative evaluation is not necessarily shared by the younger generation of speakers, in whose speech performance t-glottaling abounds). Another dimension to this is the interpretation given in the media to the use of t-glottaling by certain public personae that, in doing so, they are somehow trying to reach out to or display solidarity with the large part of the (especially younger) population for whom this is an increasingly typical and (as mentioned above) prominent speech characteristic; the former prime minister, Tony Blair, was often discussed in this respect – see, for example, Lyall (1998); de Burgh (2008).

But variation in /t/ is not restricted to the occurrence of glottal variants. Recent studies suggest that there is now fairly widespread use of a voiced variant. In the survey of regional varieties in Foulkes and Docherty (1999), this was reported in overviews from Newcastle (Watt and Milroy 1999), Glasgow (Stuart-Smith 1999), London (Tollfree 1999) and Sandwell in the West Midlands (Mathisen 1999). In some cases this is described as being a tap articulation ([ɾ]), but in others the description given suggests

63

[d] or [ʈ]. Stuart-Smith (1999) notes that in Glasgow the environment which is most regularly associated with this variant (as an alternative to glottaling) is word-final intervocalic position with a preceding short vowel as in *lot of* or *get off*, and a similar environment was found to be a productive locus for voiced variants of /t/ in Newcastle by Docherty *et al.* (1997). There are parallels between the environments identified for this voiced /t/ variant and those which trigger the so-called 't-to-r rule' applying to some speakers of a number of regional varieties of UK English, where /t/ is realized as a voiced approximant [ɹ] (Carr 1991; Docherty *et al.* 1997; Broadbent 2008). But, as with t-to-r, what remains to be investigated more systematically is the extent to which the occurrence of voiced /t/ is constrained to certain high frequency lexical items such as *got*, *lot*, *let*, *get*, *not*, *what*, *that*, *bit*, *it*, and to what extent it is subject to social, stylistic and prosodic factors.

A further innovation in the realization of /t/ which is beginning to come to light as the result of increased research on regional British varieties is the use of lenited or pre-aspirated variants. While fricated and affricated variants of /t/ have for a long time been primarily associated with the Merseyside variety of English (Knowles 1978; Honey-bone 2001; Sangster 2001; Watson 2006), in recent years, studies on the eastern side of the country have pointed to the existence of a range of other variants which appear to result from either a weakening of the oral occlusion for /t/ or a relatively early abduction of the vocal folds at the end of a preceding vowel, or possibly both. In Newcastle, there is evidence (Docherty and Foulkes 1999; Docherty 2008) pointing to a range of realizations of /t/ in word-final pre-pausal position including pre-aspiration, preceding vowel weakening, pre-affrication, frication. These can be found in combination or in isolation, and are most strongly associated with the speech of young female speakers (although not exclusively so). Subsequent work in Middlesbrough (Llamas 2001; Jones and Llamas 2003, 2008) has revealed a similar pattern of realization. Contrary to the situation for t-glottaling, this is an aspect of /t/ variation which appears to have been established without being explicitly noted by investigators working impressionistically, and, even in the areas where these 'weakened' variants are frequently used, they do not appear to carry any of the ideological 'baggage' associated with glottaling (in this light, it is also interesting to note the findings of Gordeeva and Scobbie (2004) of what they refer to as 'non-normative pre-aspiration' of fricatives in Scottish English).

Other key aspects of the realization of /t/ which should be factored into any overview of variation in UK varieties of English include the deletion of /t/ (and /d/ too, of course) in word-final consonant sequences such as *lost boy*, *mist came* or *walked purposefully,* and the palatalization of /t/ preceding /j/ as in *tune* or *Tuesday.* The factors associated with t/d deletion are amply documented in Tagliamonte and Temple's (2005) study of a corpus of York speakers who point to differences in the conditioning factors that apply in that variety of English, namely the relatively low influence of the word's morphological class, compared to those which are typically invoked for -t/-d deletion in USA English (e.g. Guy 1991). The realization of /t/ as [ʧ] (and of /d/as [ʤ]) before a /j/ (in fact, most likely, the coalescence of /t/ and /j/ into a single complex segment) has been long recognized as a feature of less conservative UK varieties of English (Wells 1982), but in recent years has been highlighted as one of the features most characteristic of Estuary English (although this is a feature which is a well-established and widespread feature of informal and formal speech throughout the UK). It is also relevant to mention here a further aspect of palatalization which characterizes many contemporary UK varieties, namely the realization of /s/ as [ʃ] before a /tr/ consonant as in *street*, *strange*, *structure*, etc.

TH-fronting

A close second to t-glottaling as the most frequent object of topical comment on the topic of UK English pronunciation is TH-fronting; i.e. the realization of /θ/ and /ð/ as the corresponding labiodental fricatives [f] and [v]. While this is a long-standing feature of London vernacular (Kerswill 2003), and has been closely associated with the levelled 'Estuary English' varieties prevalent within the south-east quadrant of England, there is now ample evidence (mapped in detail by Kerswill 2003) that TH-fronting is present in many of the urban centres of England and Scotland, most particularly in informal speech styles (Wells 1982; Stuart-Smith and Timmins 2006). It appears to be primarily a feature of younger generations of speakers (outside of the south east, Kerswill (2003) attributes it to speakers born post 1970 so it remains to be seen whether this age-based difference will continue to be the case), and reports suggest that it may not be equally present across male and female speakers; for example, in their study of Milton Keynes, Reading and Hull, Williams and Kerswill (1999) found quite high levels of TH-fronting in both sexes, but higher frequency in boys' realizations. Research has also highlighted a range of factors which are conducive to TH-fronting. A number of studies report that word-initial /ð/ is resistant to TH-fronting (Wells 1982: 328; Docherty and Foulkes 1999; Williams and Kerswill 1999); i.e. in a small set of high-frequency function words such as *this* and *that*, and in some varieties of English it is not unusual to encounter a plosive realization of word-initial /ð/ in words such as these (Wells 1982: 329; Tollfree 1999 for the London vernacular, Docherty and Foulkes (1999) for Derby). Stuart-Smith and Timmins (2006) found that the highest frequency of TH-fronting occurred word-finally, and the lowest word-medially, Clark's (2009) study of TH-fronting in informal conversations of adolescent members of a West Fife pipe band yielded effects of syllable position (TH-fronting more likely in syllable coda position) and lexical category (ordinals and place-names more likely to retain the dental realization), and found that the presence of a labiodental earlier in a word seems to predispose a fronted realization of a subsequent dental. Further work is needed to establish how widespread these factors are across different UK varieties.

Labial /r/ and rhoticity

In the not too distant past, the realization of /r/ as a labiodental approximant [ʋ], when it persisted beyond the age at which it was developmentally typical, was often characterized as a disorder of speech articulation (Foulkes and Docherty 2000) and would not infrequently lead to a referral for speech and language therapy. However, over the past two or three decades, for younger-generation speakers of many contemporary UK varieties of English, the situation has substantially changed with labiodental realizations of /r/ now being very common and generally no longer evaluated negatively or as some form of speech production disorder. What is perhaps most striking is that, unlike the situation applying to other changes over the same period, this seems to have happened largely without overt resistance or comment on the part of members of the speech communities concerned. This process of change is described in more detail by Foulkes and Docherty (2000), and is perhaps most strikingly exemplified by Trudgill's (1999) observation that in his 1968 survey of phonological variation in Norwich (Trudgill 1974) [ʋ] was 'idiosyncratic', whereas in a later 1983 study (reported in Trudgill 1988) labiodental variants were found to be present in over 30 per cent of the speaker sample born between 1959 and 1973.

More generally, as pointed by Hughes *et al.* (2005), rhoticity (the realization of /r/ in syllable-coda position either pre-pausally or pre-consonantally) is one of the key dimensions along which varieties of English (across the globe, not just in the UK) can be distinguished. Within the UK, rhoticity is most typically associated with the varieties of Scotland and Northern Ireland, and with the south-western quadrant of England. There is also a small enclave of rhotic varieties in the north west of England around the towns of Blackburn and Burnley. In general, though, Hughes *et al.* point to a gradual retreat of rhoticity within England, most likely due to the factors underpinning dialect levelling more generally, referred to above. What may well be the beginnings of a shift of this sort have also been observed in the archetypally rhotic varieties of English spoken in Scotland (Romaine 1978; Stuart-Smith 2007). Recent experimental phonetic studies of the realization of coda /r/ in speakers of Scottish English (e.g. Scobbie *et al.* 1999; Stuart-Smith 2007) point to a good deal of variability in the realization of /r/ (including for some speakers variants with a very notable uvular or pharyngeal quality), and also highlight a good deal of inter-rater variability in identifying when coda /r/ was present or not, suggesting that for some speakers of Scottish English derhoticization (the gradual progression of an accent from being rhotic to non-rhotic) may be further advanced than was previously thought simply because it has been difficult to identify impressionistically.

Vowels

The configuration of the vowel space and its alignment to the lexical stock of English provides arguably the most important and systematic basis for differentiating varieties of English (Wells 1982; Hughes *et al.* 2005), and the analysis of these differences has been enormously facilitated by referring them to the 'lexical sets' devised by Wells (1982) for capturing cross-accent vowel differences. For example, varieties can be classified in multiple dimensions by how they are positioned vis-à-vis the BATH–TRAP lexical sets (a front vowel akin to [a] for both in many, especially, northern varieties, in contrast to an [ɑ]–[a] split in many others), the realization of the STRUT lexical set (as a central and relatively open [ʌ] vowel or with a quality which overlaps substantially with that for the FOOT set), or by whether they have a single realization for the FOOT and GOOSE lexical sets (as is typically reported for Scottish varieties) as opposed to differentiating these in some way, most commonly via a [ʊ]–[u] split (although see below for more on these particular realizations). Many of these differences are deeply rooted and, no less so today than in the past, many carry very significant social value (e.g. within England, the fusion of the BATH–TRAP sets has strong ideological associations with 'northern-ness'), and they are accentual features that speakers will readily demonstrate an awareness of if asked.

Research carried out in more recent years, however, has pointed to a number of innovations in the realization of vowel contrasts occurring across varieties which would, on other grounds, be characterized as quite different from a vocalic point of view. While it is not within the remit of this chapter to explore the causes of such changes, they would seem to be at least in part a reflex of the more general process of dialect levelling commented on above, although investigators (e.g. Kerswill *et al.* 2008) are also keen to use these changes as a means of testing the phonology-internal factors which are claimed by Labov (1994) to be strong drivers of changes to vowel systems over time.

Perhaps the most striking of these is the fronting of the GOOSE and GOAT vowels by younger generations of speakers. Putting to one side those varieties where GOOSE is already fused with FOOT (and already has quite a central and close quality, as is generally the case in Scottish varieties), there are widespread reports of moderate to substantial fronting of GOOSE together with the production of much less marked lip-rounding/protrusion; e.g. Tollfree (1999) reports [ʉ] for London, Williams and Kerswill (1999) observe [ʏ:] or even [y:] for Reading and Milton Keynes, Trudgill (1999) reports a central diphthong [ʉ̈ʉ] for Norwich with gradually increasing lip-rounding, and Docherty and Foulkes (1999) report [ʉ:] and [ɪ:] for Derby. These findings are confirmed in instrumental studies by Bauer (1985), Deterding (1997), Harrington *et al.* (2008) and Hawkins and Midgeley (2005). And of course it is this particular innovation which underpins the misinterpretation cited at the very start of this chapter. With GOAT, the key innovatory elements do not apply to those varieties which prefer a monophthongal [o:] realization (e.g. Scotland, north of England), but in the southern half of England there is a more fronted quality and a lessening or complete absence of lip-rounding during the latter half of the diphthong. For example, Williams and Kerswill (1999) note the use of [əʏ] in Reading and Milton Keynes, and in the latter location they observe a more open variant [ɐɪ] in the speech of younger female speakers; Docherty and Foulkes (1999) report [əʉ], [əɪ], and [ɐʉ] for younger generation and older middle-class speakers in Derby.

The STRUT lexical set has received a considerable amount of attention from investigators, particularly for those varieties which retain a STRUT–FOOT split. Bauer's (1985) acoustic study of RP speakers suggested that STRUT was well established as a 'central-to-front' vowel as opposed to the back quality with which it was previously associated, a finding which was confirmed by Hawkins and Midgley (2005), and for Milton Keynes speakers by Williams and Kerswill (1999). In similar vein, other investigators (Docherty and Foulkes 1999; Watt and Milroy 1999; and Hughes *et al.* 2005) note that in northern English varieties it is not unusual to hear a vowel akin to [ə] or even slightly fronter than this. More recently, however, Torgersen *et al.*'s (2006: 261) study of vowel variation in a range of London speakers notes that younger speakers have 'back and raised STRUT vowels' pointing to convergence on this type of realization across the south-east quadrant of England.

Other vocalic features which reports suggest are widely present across a number of contemporary varieties include the tensing of unstressed /ɪ/ (referred to by Wells 1982 as HAPPY-tensing) by which the unstressed vowels in words such as *happy, city, pretty* are realized with [i] as opposed to [ɪ] (this change has been commented on as an ongoing change for a number of decades, but it does now appear to be strongly established across the southern half of England), the fronting, centralizing and loss of lip-rounding of the FOOT lexical set (Tollfree 1999 for London; Hawkins and Midgley 2005 for RP; Williams and Kerswill 1999 for Milton Keynes and Reading), and the convergence of the vocalic realizations of the CURE lexical set towards that for NORTH (Docherty and Foulkes 1999; Tollfree 1999; Williams and Kerswill 1999) such that, at least for younger speakers of many varieties in England, the most frequent realization of words like *cure, poor, tour* is with a monophthongal [ɔ] vowel as opposed to a diphthong akin to [ʊə] (thus ensuring that pairs like *paw/poor* are homophonous).[4]

One vowel feature which does not receive a great deal of detailed discussion in the literature but which seems to be widespread is the realization of the FLEECE vowel with an onset glide from a slightly centralized starting point (reported by Tollfree 1999 for London; Williams and Kerswill 1999 for Milton Keynes, Reading and Hull; Trudgill 1999 for Norwich; Mathisen 1999 for Sandwell; Stoddart *et al.* 1999 for Sheffield; and Docherty and Foulkes 1999 for Derby).

While the examples given above relate to innovations which can be encountered across a number of urban varieties of UK English, it is important to bear in mind that, notwithstanding the factors which are promoting levelling, there is a wealth of more localized vowel features still to be found in different varieties of English and which appear to be well entrenched. For example, alongside the BATH–TRAP realization referred to above, other key indicators of 'northern-ness' seem to be monophthongal realizations ([o:] and [e:]) for the GOAT and FACE lexical sets encountered routinely across the northern half of the UK (Watt and Milroy 1999; Watt 2002). And many geographically more localized varieties are almost defined by certain specific characteristics of vowel realizations; e.g. [ɔ:] for GOAT in Hull, [aʊ] or [ɔʊ] for the same set in the West Midlands (Mathisen 1999), open monophthongs for PRICE and MOUTH in urban centres in Yorkshire (Stoddart *et al.* 1999).

Aspects of prosody

While over the past couple of decades there has been something of a surge in work focused on segmental variation and change within varieties of British English, the same cannot be said for work on prosody (but the UK is no exception in this respect). So, for example, while there are sporadic reports of interesting cross-dialectal variation in the rhythmic and temporal properties of speech (e.g. Mees and Collins 1999; Scobbie *et al.* 1999), there has been no systematic study of the dimensions along which such variability can be found or about whether the patterns of variability which undoubtedly do exist are stable.

Likewise, while there are well-established and highly informative accounts of the phonetics and phonology of intonation within English (O'Connor and Arnold 1973; Cruttenden 1997), these are largely not drawn from a systematic analysis of large-scale corpora of natural spoken interaction and so (almost inevitably, and avowedly) fall short of capturing the full richness of intonational variation within UK varieties of English. That this is the case was amply illustrated in the late 1990s by the Intonational Variation in English (IViE) project (Grabe *et al.* 2000, 2004; Grabe 2004). Focusing on seven varieties of English from the British Isles (London, Cambridge, Leeds, Bradford, Newcastle, Belfast and Dublin), this project revealed

> extensive variation in the intonation [learners of English] might hear from native speakers, within and across dialects ... they need to be aware that variation in the southern 'standard' is as high or higher than in northern varieties of English spoken in the British Isles. In other words, the standard variety is no more uniform than non-standard varieties.
>
> (Grabe *et al.* 2004: 331)

Differences across the varieties investigated included the pitch contours associated with statements and questions (e.g. the regular presence of a 'nuclear rise-plateau' contour in Newcastle and Belfast speakers but not observed in the Cambridge speakers), but as the above quotation indicates, the intra-variety variability encountered within this study was substantial. Other studies focusing on variety-specific aspects of intonation are few in number (e.g. Cruttenden's 2001 study of women from Salford in Greater Manchester, Bilton 1982 on Hull, and Local *et al.* (1986) on Newcastle), but they do lend weight to the IvIE project's key finding of extensive inter- and intra-variety variation.

What none of this work has done, however, is to identify any particular trajectories of change with regard to patterns of intonation within UK English (not surprisingly, given that there were very few previous studies capable of providing a benchmark). Nevertheless, one intonational feature which does appear to have established a foothold in the performance of some speakers of British English is the use of a rising pitch contour in declarative contexts (such as statements and other expressions of certainty) where, for the varieties concerned, a falling contour would be more conventionally deployed (Fletcher *et al.* 2004). This pattern of realization has been assigned diverse labels, including 'High Rising Tone' (or 'Tune' or 'Terminal'), 'Australian Questioning Intonation' and 'uptalk', and has been the object of speculative debate in the press regarding its origins (Bradbury 1996; Norman 2001); as with t-glottaling it has been treated as something of a symbol of the 'decline' of contemporary spoken English by those who are concerned about such changes. With similar phonetic characteristics to analogous patterns found in antipodean varieties of English and in the USA, it has been claimed that this particular pitch contour is chiefly associated with the speech performance of upwardly mobile 'New Yuppies' (Cruttenden 1997: 130), but since there has been very little systematic study of this (Fletcher *et al.* 2004), it is difficult to state its distribution with certainty or to gauge whether it is spreading across a broader set of speakers. Cruttenden (1997: 129) notes that its usage, very much a feature of informal conversational interaction, seems to be associated with the conveyance of new information while at the same time being 'deliberately non-assertive and checking that you are following me'. It is important to differentiate this relatively recent innovation in British English (in the 1990s, according to Cruttenden) from the rising pitch contours which are a longstanding and routine characteristic of declarative utterances in certain varieties of English such as Newcastle, Liverpool, Glasgow and Belfast.

Prospects

As is evident from the references cited above, our knowledge and understanding of the evolving phonological characteristics of varieties of British English have developed very substantially over the past twenty years or so. Nevertheless, we are still some way short of a comprehensive understanding of the dynamics of phonological innovation and change and how sound patterning plays out in conversational interaction as a means of indexing individual and social characteristics (Foulkes and Docherty 2006). In particular, within the UK context, there is scope for much further investigation of how the full range of social factors which characterize a speech community are associated with phonological variation within that community; for example, there is a need to discover much more about how children become attuned to the sociophonetic properties of their native variety (Foulkes *et al.* 2005; Khattab and Roberts forthcoming), the extent to which individual identity is a driver for the adoption (or not) of innovative variants, and, as pointed out above, research to date has only skimmed the surface of the role played by ethnic identity within a country where (at least in the large urban centres) the ethnic mix continues to evolve and is a strong shaper of the social dynamics characterizing communities.

It is also important that more work is carried out on how and to what extent speakers shift their patterns of speech across different speech styles. Differences between word-list style and unscripted conversation have been widely reported, but style-shifting is not only about the degree of formality associated with a sample of speech. More interestingly, perhaps, it is closely related to how individuals orientate themselves to particular interactional situations and the extent to which this is a conscious process. And style-shifting is also closely tied to reigning language ideologies and the prestige (either overt or covert) which is associated with particular types of realization. We do indeed have a good idea of what the key dimensions of style-shifting might be (see, for example, papers in Eckert and Rickford 2001) but there have been relatively few studies to show how these translate into the variable performance of individual speakers (examples of such work are studies by Podesva *et al.* 2002 and Drager 2009).

Finally, the increase in recent years in the application of quantitative instrumental phonetic methods to the analysis of groups of speakers and individuals has provided new insights and is very likely to continue to do so (see contributions to Di Paolo and Yaeger-Dror forthcoming). One key contribution made by these techniques is that they have brought to light aspects of variation which simply would not have been evident had the researchers been relying on an impressionistic record (e.g. the findings mentioned above re: derhoticization, pre-aspirated variants of /t/, and the characteristics of 'labial-r'), thereby painting a broader picture of the extent of such innovation and variation across a sample of speakers. Acoustic phonetic analysis is perhaps the method with the greatest potential in this respect as it is non-invasive and can to a large degree be applied automatically to large tagged corpora, thereby quickly generating very substantial datasets. Indeed, the issue for researchers is perhaps now less about how to apply such techniques, and more about how to design and annotate corpora of natural speech recordings which are expandable over time and which provide good coverage of the relevant social and linguistic contextual factors which need to be tracked (see Fromont and Hay 2008 for discussion of how these issues have been addressed in the development of the ONZE corpus, which lays down a very clear benchmark for other researchers).

Acknowledgements

I'd like to thank Paul Foulkes, Dom Watt, Jennifer Nycz and Damien Hall for their comments on a draft of this chapter.

Notes

1 Note that in describing variation in the phonetic realization of vowels, use is made here of the lexical sets presented by Wells (1982) as a good basis for capturing the key vocalic features of different accents of English. Each lexical set is represented by a keyword in upper case (e.g. NURSE) which stands for a set of lexical items (e.g. *nurse*, *work*, *purse*, *curd*, etc.) which tend to share a particular vowel realization albeit that the precise quality of vowel realization may vary across accents.

2 In this chapter, the term *accent* is used to denote the phonological dimension along which varieties can differ, whereas *dialect* is used to refer to the wider set of dimensions across which varieties may differ (e.g. lexical, syntactic and phonological).

3 Laryngealized voice quality is a particular form of vibration of the vocal folds caused by adjusting the tension of the vocal folds such that they vibrate rather more slowly than usual and with higher

irregularity. If prolonged, laryngealization is heard as creaky voice (also known as vocal fry). See Ladefoged and Maddieson (1996) for further details.

4 Note that the realization of these vowels in rhotic varieties will be quite different as a result of the retention of the coda /r/, and that in the northern half of England strong diphthongal forms are still well established, albeit subject to quite a bit of social variation.

Suggestions for further reading

Britain, D. (ed.) (2007) *Language in the British Isles*, Cambridge: Cambridge University Press.
Foulkes, P. and Docherty, G.J. (eds) (1999) *Urban Voices: Accent studies in the British Isles*, London: Arnold.
Hughes, A., Trudgill, P. and Watt, D. (2005) *English Accents and Dialects: an Introduction to Social and Regional Varieties of English in the British Isles* (4th edition), London: Hodder Arnold/New York: Oxford University Press.
Kortmann, B. and Schneider, E. (eds) (2004) *A Handbook of Varieties of English*, Berlin: Mouton de Gruyter.

References

Altendorf, U. (2003) *Estuary English: Levelling at the Interface of RP and South-eastern British English*, Tübingen: Gunter Narr Verlag.
Andrésen, B.S. (1968) *Pre-glottalization in English Standard Pronunciation*, Oslo: Norwegian Universities Press.
Bauer, L. (1985) 'Tracing phonetic change in the received pronunciation of British English', *Journal of Phonetics*, 13: 61–81.
Beal, J. (2004) 'The phonology of English dialects in the north of England', in B. Kortmann (ed.) *A Handbook of Varieties of English*, Berlin: Mouton de Gruyter.
Best, C.T. and Tyler, M.D. (2007) 'Nonnative and second-language speech perception: commonalities and complementarities', in M. Munro and O.-S. Bohn (eds) *Second Language Speech Learning*, Amsterdam: John Benjamins, pp. 13–34.
Bilton, L. (1982) 'A note on Hull intonation', *Journal of the International Phonetic Association*, 12: 30–5.
Bond, Z.S. (1999) *Slips of the Ear: Errors in the Perception of Casual Conversation*, San Diego: Academic Press.
Bradbury, M. (1996) 'It's goodbye Memsahib, hello Sheila', *Daily Mail*, 20 March.
Britain, D. (2002) 'Phoenix from the ashes? The death, contact and birth of dialects in England', *Essex Research Reports in Linguistics*, 41: 42–73.
——(ed.) (2007) *Language in the British Isles*, Cambridge: Cambridge University Press.
Britain, D. and Trudgill, P. (1999) 'Migration, new-dialect formation and sociolinguistic refunctionalisation: reallocation as an outcome of dialect contact', *Transactions of the Philological Society*, 97: 245–56.
Broadbent, J. (2008) 't-to-r in West Yorkshire English', *English Language and Linguistics*, 12: 141–68.
Carr, P. (1991) 'Lexical properties of postlexical rules: postlexical derived environment and the Elsewhere Condition', *Lingua*, 85: 255–68.
Champion, A. (2008) 'The changing nature of urban and rural areas in the UK and other European countries' (Report #UN/POP/EGM-URB/2008/07). Online. Available www.un.org/esa/population/meetings/EGM_PopDist/P07_Champion.pdf (accessed 21 February 2010).
——(2009) 'Population change in England since 1981: is an "urban renaissance" really underway?' *Geocarrefour*, 83: 79–86.
Cheshire, J., Fox, S., Kerswill, P. and Torgersen, E. (2008) 'Ethnicity as the motor of dialect change: innovation and levelling in London', *Sociolinguistica*, 22: 1–23.

Clark, L. (2009) 'Variation, change and the usage-based approach', unpublished PhD dissertation, University of Edinburgh.

Cruttenden, A. (1997) *Intonation* (2nd edition), Cambridge: Cambridge University Press.

——(2001) 'Mancunian intonation and intonational representation', *Phonetica*, 58: 53–80.

de Burgh, L. (2008) 'Is Miliband morphing into Blair? A voice coach writes … ', *Guardian*, 23 September.

Deterding, D. (1997) 'The formants of monophthong vowels in Standard Southern British English pronunciation', *Journal of the International Phonetic Association*, 27: 47–55.

Di Paolo, M. and Yaeger-Dror, M. (eds) (forthcoming) *Best Practices in Sociophonetics*, London: Routledge.

Docherty, G.J. (2008) 'Speech in its natural habitat: accounting for social factors in phonetic variability', in J. Cole and J.I. Hualde (eds) *Laboratory Phonology, IX*, Berlin: Mouton de Gruyter, pp. 1–35.

Docherty, G.J. and Foulkes, P. (1999) 'Instrumental phonetics and phonological variation: case studies from Newcastle upon Tyne and Derby', in P. Foulkes and G.J. Docherty (eds) *Urban Voices: Accent Studies in the British Isles*, London: Arnold, pp. 47–71.

——(2005) 'Glottal variants of /t/ in the Tyneside variety of English', in William J. Hardcastle and Janet Mackenzie Beck (eds) *A Figure of Speech: A Festschrift for John Laver*, Mahwah, NJ: Lawrence Erlbaum, pp. 173–99.

Docherty, G.J., Foulkes, P., Milroy, J., Milroy, L. and Walshaw, D. (1997) 'Descriptive adequacy in phonology: a variationist perspective', *Journal of Linguistics*, 33: 275–310.

Drager, K. (2009) 'A sociophonetic ethnography of Selwyn Girls' High', unpublished PhD dissertation, University of Canterbury, New Zealand.

Eckert, P. and Rickford, J. (ed.) (2001) *Style and Sociolinguistic Variation*, Cambridge: Cambridge University Press.

Fabricius, A. (2000) 'T-glottaling between stigma and prestige: a sociolinguistic study of modern RP', unpublished PhD thesis, Copenhagen Business School.

——(2002a) 'Weak vowels in modern RP: an acoustic study of happY-tensing and KIT/schwa shift', *Language Variation and Change*, 14: 211–37.

——(2002b) 'Ongoing change in modern RP: evidence for the disappearing stigma of t-glottalling', *English World-wide*, 23: 115–36.

——(2007) 'Variation and change in the TRAP and STRUT vowels of RP: a real time comparison of five acoustic data sets', *Journal of the International Phonetic Association*, 37: 293–320.

Fletcher, J., Grabe, E. and Warren, P. (2004) 'Intonational variation in four dialects of English: the high rising tune', in Sun-Ah Jun (ed.) *Prosodic Typology. The Phonology of Intonation and Phrasing*, Oxford: Oxford University Press.

Foulkes, P. and Docherty, G.J. (eds) (1999) *Urban Voices: Accent Studies in the British Isles*, London: Arnold.

——(2000) 'Another chapter in the story of /r/: "labiodental" variants in British English', *Journal of Sociolinguistics*, 4: 30–59.

——(2006) 'The social life of phonetics and phonology', *Journal of Phonetics* 34: 409–38.

Foulkes, P., Docherty, G.J. and Watt, D. (2005) 'Phonological variation in child-directed speech', *Language*, 81: 177–206.

Fox, S. (2007) 'The demise of Cockneys? Language change in London's traditional East End', unpublished PhD thesis, University of Essex.

Fromont, R. and Hay, J. (2008) 'ONZE Miner: Development of a browser-based research tool', *Corpora*, 3: 173–93.

Gimson, A.C. (1980) *An Introduction to the Pronunciation of English* (3rd edition), London: Arnold.

Gordeeva, O. and Scobbie, J.M. (2004) 'Non-normative preaspiration of voiceless fricatives in Scottish English: a comparison with Swedish preaspiration', Colloquium of the British Association of Academic Phoneticians, University of Cambridge, 24–26 March.

Grabe, E. (2004) 'Intonational variation in urban dialects of English spoken in the British Isles', in P. Gilles and J. Peters (eds) *Regional Variation in Intonation*, Linguistische Arbeiten, Tübingen, Niemeyer, pp. 9–31.

Grabe, E., Post, B., Nolan, F., and Farrar, K. (2000) 'Pitch accent realisation in four varieties of British English', *Journal of Phonetics*, 28: 161–85.

Grabe, E., Kochanski, G. and Coleman, J. (2004) 'The intonation of native accent varieties in the British Isles – potential for miscommunication?' in K. Dziubalska-Kołaczyk and J. Przedlacka (eds) *English Pronunciation Models: A Changing Scene* (Linguistic Insights Series), Oxford: Peter Lang, pp. 311–37.

Guy, G. (1991) 'Explanation in variable phonology: an exponential model of morphological constraints', *Language Variation and Change*, 3: 1–22.

Harrington, J., Palethorpe, S. and Watson, C.I. (2000) 'Does the Queen speak the Queen's English?' *Nature* 408: 927–8.

——(2005) 'Deepening or lessening the divide between diphthongs? An analysis of the Queen's annual Christmas broadcasts', in W.J. Hardcastle and J. Beck (eds) *The Gift of Speech (Festschrift for John Laver)*, Erlbaum, pp. 227–61.

Harrington, J., Kleber, F. and Reubold, U. (2008) 'Compensation for coarticulation, /u/-fronting, and sound change in Standard Southern British: an acoustic and perceptual study', *Journal of the Acoustical Society of America*, 123: 2825–35.

Hawkins, S. and Midgley, J. (2005) 'Formant frequencies of RP monophthongs in four age groups of speakers', *Journal of the International Phonetic Association*, 35: 183–99.

Henderson, M. (2007) 'The English are losing their voice', *Daily Telegraph*, 15 September 2007. Online. Available www.telegraph.co.uk/comment/3642688/The-English-are-losing-their-voice.html (last accessed 23 September 2009).

Heselwood, B. and McChrystal, L. (2000) 'Gender, accent features and voicing in Panjabi–English bilingual children', *Leeds Working Papers in Linguistics and Phonetics* 8: 45–70.

Honeybone, P. (2001) 'Lenition inhibition in Liverpool English', *English Language and Linguistics*, 5: 213–49.

Hughes, A., Trudgill, P. and Watt, D. (2005) *English Accents and Dialects: an Introduction to Social and Regional Varieties of English in the British Isles* (4th edition), London: Hodder Arnold/New York: Oxford University Press.

Jones, M. and Llamas, C. (2003) 'Fricated pre-aspirated /t/ in Middlesbrough English: an acoustic study', *Proceedings of the 15th International Congress of Phonetic Sciences*, Barcelona: UAB, pp. 123–35.

——(2008) 'Fricated realisations of /t/ in Dublin and Middlesbrough English: an acoustic analysis of plosive frication and surface fricative contrasts', *English Language and Linguistics*, 12 (3): 419–43.

Kerswill, P. (2001) 'Mobility, meritocracy and dialect levelling: the fading (and phasing) out of Received Pronunciation', in P. Rajamäe and K. Vogelberg (eds) *British Studies in the New Millennium: The Challenge of the Grassroots*, Tartu: University of Tartu, pp. 45–58.

——(2002) 'Koineization and accommodation', in J.K. Chambers, P. Trudgill and N. Schilling-Estes (eds) *The Handbook of Language Variation and Change*, Oxford: Blackwell, pp. 669–702.

——(2003) 'Dialect levelling and geographical diffusion in British English', in D. Britain and J. Cheshire (eds) *Social Dialectology. In Honour of Peter Trudgill*, Amsterdam: John Benjamins, pp. 223–43.

——(2007) 'RP, Standard English and the standard/non-standard relationship', in D. Britain (ed.) *Language in the British Isles* (2nd edition), Cambridge: Cambridge University Press.

Kerswill, Paul and Williams, Ann (2000) 'Creating a new town koine: children and language change in Milton Keynes', *Language in Society* 29: 65–115.

——(2002) 'Dialect recognition and speech community focusing in new and old towns in England: the effects of dialect levelling, demography and social networks', in Daniel Long and Dennis Preston (eds) *A Handbook of Perceptual Dialectology*, Vol. 2, Amsterdam: John Benjamins, pp. 178–207.

——(2005) 'New towns and koineisation: linguistic and social correlates', *Linguistics*, 43 (5): 1023–48.

Kerswill, P., Torgersen, E. and Fox, S. (2008) 'Reversing "drift": innovation and diffusion in the London diphthong system', *Language Variation and Change*, 20: 451–91.

Khan, A. (2007) 'A sociolinguistic study of Birmingham English: language variation and change in a multi-ethnic British community', unpublished PhD, University of Lancaster.

Khattab, G. (2007) 'Variation in vowel production by English–Arabic bilinguals', in J. Cole and J. Hualde (eds) *Laboratory Phonology 9*, Berlin: Mouton de Gruyter, pp. 383–410.

Khattab, G. and Roberts, J. (forthcoming) 'Working with children', in M. Di Paolo and M. Yaeger-Dror (eds) *Best Practices in Sociophonetics*, London: Routledge.

Knowles, G. (1978) 'The nature of phonological variables in Scouse', in P. Trudgill (ed.) *Sociolinguistic Patterns in British English*, London: Arnold, pp. 80–90.

Kortmann, B. and Schneider, E. (eds) (2004) *A Handbook of Varieties of English*, Berlin: Mouton de Gruyter.

Labov, W. (1994) *Principles of Linguistic Change. Vol.1: Internal Factors*, Oxford: Blackwell.

Ladefoged, P. and Maddieson, I. (1996) *The Sounds of the World's Languages*, Oxford: Blackwell.

Lambert, K., Farhana, A. and Stuart-Smith, J. (2007) 'Investigating British Asian accents: studies from Glasgow', in J. Trouvain and W. J. Barry (eds) *Proceedings of the 16th International Congress of the ICPhS*, Saarbrücken: Universität des Saarlandes, pp. 1509–12.

Llamas, C. (2001) 'Language variation and innovation in Teesside English', unpublished PhD dissertation, University of Leeds.

Local, J.K., Kelly, J. and Wells, W.H.G. (1986) 'Towards a phonology of conversation: turntaking in Tyneside English', *Journal of Linguistics*, 22: 411–37.

Lyall, S. (1998) 'London journal; Britons prick up their ears: Blair's a li'l peculiar', *New York Times*, 18 June.

Maguire, W. (2008) 'What is a merger, and can it be reversed? The origin, status and reversal of the "NURSE–NORTH Merger" in Tyneside English', unpublished PhD dissertation, University of Newcastle upon Tyne.

Mathisen, A.G. (1999) 'Sandwell, West Midlands: ambiguous perspectives on gender patterns and models of change', in P. Foulkes and G.J. Docherty (eds) *Urban Voices: Accent Studies in the British Isles*, London: Arnold, pp. 107–23.

Mees, I.M. and Collins, B. (1999) 'Cardiff: a real-time study of glottalisation', in P. Foulkes and G.J. Docherty (eds) *Urban Voices*, London: Arnold, pp. 185–202.

Norman, P. (2001) 'What would 'Enry 'Iggins make of our Slop English?' *Daily Mail*, 2 March.

O'Connor, J. and Arnold, G. (1973) *Intonation of Colloquial English* (2nd edition), London: Longman.

Podesva, R., Roberts, S.J., and Campbell-Kibler, K. (2002) 'Sharing resources and indexing meanings in the production of gay styles', in K. Campbell-Kibler, R.J. Podesva, S.J. Roberts and A. Wong (eds) *Language and Sexuality: Contesting Meaning in Theory and Practice*, Stanford: CSLI Publications, pp. 175–89.

Przedlacka, J. (2002) *Estuary English? A Sociophonetic Study of Teenage Speech in the Home Counties*, Oxford: Peter Lang.

Rampton, B. (2005) *Crossing: Language and Ethnicity Among Adolescents* (2nd edition), Manchester: St Jerome Press.

Roach, P. (1973) 'Glottalization of English /p/, /t/, /k/ and /tʃ/ – a re-examination', *Journal of the International Phonetic Association*, 3: 10–21.

Romaine, S. (1978) 'Post-vocalic /r/ in Scottish English: sound change in progress?' in P. Trudgill (ed.) *Sociolinguistic Patterns in British English*, London: Arnold, pp. 144–58.

Sangster, C. (2001) 'Lenition of alveolar stops in Liverpool English', *Journal of Sociolinguistics*, 5: 401–12.

Scobbie, J.M., Hewlett, N. and Turk, A.E. (1999) 'Standard English in Edinburgh and Glasgow: the Scottish Vowel Length Rule revealed', in P. Foulkes and G.J. Docherty (eds) *Urban Voices: Accent Studies in the British Isles*, London: Arnold, pp. 230–45.

Stoddart, J., Upton, C. and Widdowson, J.D.A. (1999) 'Sheffield dialect in the 1990s: revisiting the concept of NORMs', in P. Foulkes and G.J. Docherty (eds) *Urban Voices: Accent Studies in the British Isles*, London: Arnold, pp. 72–89.

Stuart-Smith, J. (1999) 'Glasgow: accent and voice quality', in P. Foulkes and G.J. Docherty (eds) *Urban Voices: Accent Studies in the British Isles*, London: Arnold, pp. 201–22.

——(2007) 'A sociophonetic investigation of postvocalic /r/ in Glaswegian adolescents', *Proceedings of the XVIth International Congress of Phonetic Sciences*, Saarbrücken: Universität des Saarlandes.

Stuart-Smith, J. and Timmins, C. (2006) '"Tell her to shut her moof": the role of the lexicon in TH-fronting in Glaswegian', in G. Caie, C. Hough and I. Wotherspoon (eds) *The Power of Words*, Amsterdam: Rodopi, pp. 171–83.

Tagliamonte, S. and Temple, R. (2005) 'New perspectives on an ol' variable: (t,d) in British English', *Language Variation and Change*, 17: 281–302.

Tollfree, L. (1999) 'South-east London English: discrete versus continuous modelling of consonantal reduction', in P. Foulkes and G.J. Docherty (eds) *Urban Voices: Accent studies in the British Isles*, London: Arnold, pp. 163–84.

Torgersen, E., Kerswill, P. and Fox, S. (2006) 'Ethnicity as a source of changes in the London vowel system', in F. Hinskens (ed.) *Language Variation – European Perspectives. Selected Papers from the Third International Conference on Language Variation in Europe (ICLaVE3)*, Amsterdam: John Benjamins, pp. 249–63.

Trudgill, P. (1974) *The Social Differentiation of English in Norwich*, (Cambridge Studies in Linguistics 13) Cambridge: Cambridge University Press.

——(1986) *Dialects in Contact*, Oxford: Blackwell.

——(1988) 'Norwich revisited: recent linguistic changes in an English urban dialect', *English World-Wide*, 9:1–33.

——(1999) 'Norwich: endogenous and exogenous linguistic change', in Paul Foulkes and Gerard J. Docherty (eds) *Urban Voices*, London: Arnold, pp. 124–40.

Watson, K. (2006) 'Phonological resistance and innovation in the North-West of England', *English Today*, 22: 55–61.

Watt, D. (2002) '"I don't speak with a Geordie accent, I speak, like, the northern accent": contact-induced levelling in the Tyneside vowel system', *Journal of Sociolinguistics*, 6: 44–63.

——(2000) 'Phonetic parallels between the close-mid vowels of Tyneside English: are they internally or externally motivated?' *Language Variation and Change*, 12: 69–101.

Watt, D. and Milroy, L. (1999) 'Variation in three Tyneside vowels: is this dialect levelling?' in P. Foulkes and G.J. Docherty (eds) *Urban Voices: Accent Studies in the British Isles*, London: Arnold, pp. 25–46.

Wells, J.C. (1982) *Accents of English* (3 volumes), Cambridge: Cambridge University Press.

Williams, A. and Kerswill, P. (1999) 'Dialect levelling: continuity vs change in Milton Keynes, Reading and Hull', in P. Foulkes and G.J. Docherty (eds) *Urban Voices: Accent Studies in the British Isles*, London: Arnold, pp. 141–62.

4

The Englishes of Ireland

Emergence and transportation

Raymond Hickey

Introduction

Any treatment of the English language in Ireland must start from the recognition of a wide range of varieties throughout the country. There are varieties on the east coast which go back to the late twelfth century. In the north of Ireland, there was a significant Scots input in the seventeenth century. In the south west and west of the country, there are largely rural varieties which still show the effect of structural transfer from Irish during the period of the main language shift between the seventeenth and nineteenth century. The different forms of English in Ireland can be considered from the point of view of the structural characteristics which they share and through which they form a linguistic area across the island of Ireland (Hickey 1999a, 2004a). They can also be considered in terms of their distinguishing features which derive from their different historical roots and the particular demographic circumstances under which they took root in Ireland. The latter view is what justifies the term 'Englishes' in the title of this chapter. And, in the context of the present volume, the plural form of English has additional justification. This book is about the different forms of English which are found throughout the world and so the primary standpoint is one of diversity. There is a further reason for stressing differences among the varieties of English in Ireland: these diverse varieties were transported during the colonial period between the early seventeenth and the late nineteenth centuries (Hickey 2004d) and so provided specific input to emerging English at a number of overseas locations as far apart as Newfoundland (Hickey 2002) and Australia (Hickey 2007: 414–17).

The coming of English to Ireland

The most cursory glance at the history of Irish English reveals that it is divided into two periods. The first period starts in the late twelfth century with the arrival of the first English-speaking settlers and finishes around 1600 when the second period opens. The main event which justifies this periodization is the renewed and vigorous planting of

English in Ireland at the beginning of the seventeenth century. One must understand that during the first period the Old English – as this group is called in the Irish context – came increasingly under the influence of the Irish. The Anglo-Normans who were the military leaders during the initial settlement had been completely absorbed by the Irish by the end of the fifteenth century. The progressive Gaelicization led the English to attempt planting the Irish countryside in order to reinforce the English presence there (Palmer 2000). This was by and large a failure and it was only with James I that successful planting of (Lowland Scottish and English) settlers in the north of the country tipped the linguistic balance in favour of English in the north. The south of the country was subject to further plantations along with the banishment of the native Irish to the west during the Cromwellian period, so that by the end of the seventeenth century Irish was in a weak position from which it was never to recover. During the seventeenth century new forms of English were brought to Ireland, Scots in the north and West/North Midland varieties in the south (where there had been a predominantly West Midland and southwest input in the first period). The renewed Anglicization in the seventeenth century led to the view, held above all by Alan Bliss (see Bliss 1977, 1984), that the forms of English from the first period were completely supplanted by the varieties introduced at the beginning of the modern period. However, this is not true. On the east coast, in Dublin and other locations down to Waterford in the south east, there is a definite continuation of south-west English features which stem from the imported varieties of the first period (Hickey 2001).

The medieval period

The documentary record of medieval Irish English is confined for all intents and purposes to the collection of 16 poems of Irish provenance in BM Harley 913 which are known collectively as the *Kildare Poems* (Heuser 1904; Lucas 1995) after one of the poems in which the author identifies himself as from the county of Kildare to the south west of Dublin. The collection probably dates from the early fourteenth century. The language of these poems is of a general west midland to southern character. There are many features which can be traced to the influence of Irish phonology (Hickey 1993). It is a moot point whether the *Kildare Poems* were written by native speakers of Irish using English as an H-language in a diglossic situation and whether indeed the set was written by one or more individuals.

The early modern period

Apart from the *Kildare Poems* and other minor pieces of verse (see McIntosh and Samuels 1968 for a detailed list), there are attestations of English in the first period among the municipal records of various towns in Ireland (Kallen 1994: 150–6), especially along the east coast from Waterford through Dublin and up as far as Carrickfergus, north of present-day Belfast. But such documents are not linguistically revealing. However, at the end of the sixteenth century attestations of Irish English begin to appear which are deliberate representations of the variety of the time. These are frequently in the guise of literary parody of the Irish by English authors. The anonymous play *Captain Thomas Stukeley* (1596/1605) is the first in a long line of plays in which the Irish are parodied. Later, a figure of fun – the stage Irishman – was to be added, establishing a tradition of literary parody that lasted well into the twentieth century

77

(Bliss 1976, 1979; Sullivan 1980). The value of these written representations of Irish English for reconstructing the language of the time has been much questioned and it is true that little if any detail can be extracted from these sources. In addition most of the satirical pieces were written by Englishmen so that one is dealing with an external perception of Irish English at the time. Nonetheless, this material can be useful in determining what features at the beginning of the early modern period were salient and hence picked up by non-Irish writers.

Satirical writings are not the only source of Irish English, however. There are some writers, especially in the nineteenth century, who seriously attempt to indicate colloquial speech of their time. The first of these is probably Maria Edgeworth, whose novel *Castle Rackrent* (1801) is generally regarded as the first regional novel in English and was much admired by Sir Walter Scott. Other writers one could mention in this context are William Carlton and the Banim brothers (see the collection and discussion in Hickey 2003a).

Scots input to Northern Ireland

The succession of James VI of Scotland (1566–1625) as James I (1603–25) to the English throne led to the establishment of the Stuart monarchy. After the defeated Irish lords left Ulster in 1607, James I moved quickly and their lands were escheated. The government decided to initiate the plantation of Ulster along the lines of the Munster plantation in the late sixteenth century. This time, however, the land was reserved for Scots settlers, encouraged by their compatriot James I, together with Englishmen, mostly from the North Midlands and north of England (Adams 1958: 61ff. and 1967: 69ff.). Because of the union of the crowns in 1603, the Scottish were allowed to settle in Ireland without difficulty. Settlers were a mixture of private individuals along with royal officials (servitors) and some 'deserving' Irish, i.e. those loyal to the crown during the Nine Years War (1594–1603). The plantation settlements were to form the basis for the demographic split of the country. Due to the Scottish and English background of these immigrants the division of Ireland came to be as much linguistic as political and confessional.

The Scottish undertakers tended to have smaller estates than the English, probably because they were not in as financially robust a position as the latter (Robinson 1994 [1984]: 79). The settlers from Lowland Scotland received the slightly less profitable lands because their average incomes were somewhat below those of the corresponding English undertakers. Furthermore, their estates were scattered across the escheated land. Additional factors for the demographic development of Ulster are important here: in 1610 many landless Irish, who were supposed to move to estates administered by the church or by officials, were given a stay of eviction. Initially, this was because undertakers had not yet arrived in Ulster. But when they did, tenancies were granted to the Irish because these were willing to pay higher rents. Indeed, by 1628 this situation was given official recognition by a ruling which allowed undertakers to keep native tenants on maximally a quarter of their portions at double the normal rent. There was much competition between Irish, English and Scottish settlers, with the Irish generally having to be content with poorer, more marginal land, such as the Sperrin Mountains of central Tyrone, while others, for whatever reason, remained to work under Scottish/English owners.

The success of the Ulster plantation was relative: the numbers envisaged by the English administration did not always reach the targets set nor did the landlords always have the capital to carry through the agricultural and urban projects which the government had envisaged. Many of the companies retained Irish tenants (against the wishes of the English crown) and there were conspiracies against the English, notably in 1615.

The plantation of Ulster is regarded in works on Irish history, e.g. Canny (2001) and Foster (1988), as the major event at the beginning of the early modern period. There are differences in the assessment of both its significance and value. The major grievance which it triggered stemmed from the banishment of local Irish to poorer, more marginal lands in Ulster with the fertile lowlands left in English or Scottish hands.

The uneven spread of the Scots across Ulster meant that the regions where Ulster Scots was spoken did not encompass the entire province, and nowadays these are no

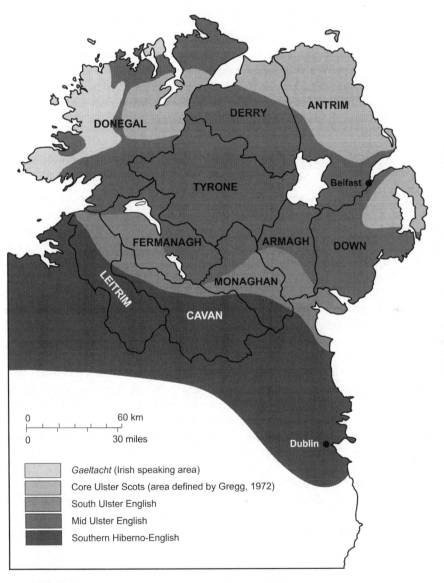

Map 4.1 Ulster dialects

longer contiguous because of a reduction of their size. The remaining areas are, however, regions of historical settlement. Three are located on the northern periphery from the north west through the north east to the south east of Ulster, hence the term 'Coastal Crescent' or 'Northern Crescent'. (See Map 4.1.)

The number of speakers of Ulster Scots today is difficult to estimate, especially because there is no clear demarcation between Ulster Scots and English-based varieties. Furthermore, the difference between it and more general forms of English in Ulster has been overlain by the strong antithesis of urban and rural speech in contemporary Ulster. The optimistic figure of 100,000 which is offered, not uncritically, by Montgomery and Gregg (1997: 213) may serve as a general orientation but nothing more precise is available.

The lexicography of Ulster Scots has been served by a large number of academic articles dealing with specific lexical items or word fields (see relevant section in Hickey 2002). A dictionary in popular style is available in James Fenton's *The Hamely Tongue. A Personal Record of Ulster-Scots in County Antrim* (2000 [1995]). Loreto Todd's *Words Apart. A Dictionary of Northern Irish English* (1990) is medium in size and coverage. A more academic work – with a broader brief – is the *Concise Ulster Dictionary* (1996) edited by Caroline Macafee. Most of the items concern farming and rural life in general, but regional vocabulary for parts of the body, clothing and terms for individuals is also recorded.

Language shift in Ireland

No censuses before 1851 gave data on speakers of Irish and English (after that date one can draw a reasonably accurate picture of the decline of Irish). Adams (1965) is a useful attempt to nonetheless produce a linguistic cartography of Ireland at the beginning of the early modern period. The upshot of this situation is that there is no reliable data on the language shift which began in earnest in the early seventeenth century and which had been all but completed by the late nineteenth century. This has meant that statements about the shift have been about what one assumes must have happened rather than on the facts revealed in historical documents. Nonetheless, the external history of this shift shows what the overall conditions were and allows some general statements in this respect. The first point to note about the shift from Irish to English is that in rural areas there was little or no education for the native Irish, the romanticized hedge schools (Dowling 1968 [1935]) notwithstanding. So it is clear that the Irish learned English from other Irish who already knew some, perhaps through contact with those urban Irish who were English speakers, especially on the east coast and through contact with the English planters and their employees. This latter group plays no recognizable role in the development of Irish English, i.e. there is no planter Irish English, probably because this group was numerically insignificant, despite their importance as a trigger in the language shift process. What one can assume for the seventeenth and eighteenth centuries in rural Ireland is a functional bilingualism in which the Irish learned some English as adults from their dealings with English speakers. By the early nineteenth century, the importance of English for advancement in social life was being pointed out repeatedly, by no less a figure than Daniel O'Connell, the most important political leader before Charles Parnell.

The fact that the majority of the Irish acquired English in an unguided manner as adults had consequences for the nature of Irish English. Bliss (1977) pointed out that this fact is responsible for both the common malapropisms and the unconventional word stress found in Irish English. However, the stress pattern in verbs with final long vowels, e.g. *distribute* [dɪstrɪˈbjuːt], *educate* [ɛdjuˈkeːt], can also be due to English input, particularly as non-initial stress is only a feature of southern Irish and so influence due to contact with Irish could only be posited for the south of Ireland.

Another point concerning the language shift in Ireland is that it was relatively long, spanning at least three centuries from 1600 to 1900 for most of the country. The scenario for language shift is one where lexical transfer into English is unlikely, or at least unlikely to become established in any nascent supra-regional variety of English in Ireland. After all, English was the prestige language and the use of Irish words would not have been desirable, given the high awareness of the lexicon as an open class. This statement refers to Irish lexical elements in present-day English in Ireland. In some written works, and historically in varieties close to Irish, there were more Irish words and idioms; on the latter, see Odlin (1991).

For phonology and syntax the matter is quite different. Speakers who learn a language as adults retain the pronunciation of their native language and have difficulty with segments which are unknown to them. A simple case of this would be the use of stops (dental or sometimes alveolar, depending on region) in the THIN and THIS lexical sets in Irish English. A more subtle case would be the lenition of stops in Irish English, e.g. *cat* [kæt̪], which while systemically completely different from lenition in Irish could be the result of a phonological directive applied by the Irish learning English to lenite elements in positions of maximal sonority.

In syntax there are many features which either have a single source in Irish or at least have converged with English regional input to produce stable structures in later Irish English. To begin with, one must bear in mind that adult speakers learning a second language, especially in an unguided situation, search for equivalents to the grammatical categories they know from their native language. The less they know and use the second language, the more obvious this search is. A case in point would involve the habitual in Irish. This is a prominent aspectual category in the language and generally available by using a special form of the verb 'be' and a non-finite form of the lexical verb in question *Bíonn sí ag léamh (gach maidin)* [is she at reading (every morning)]. There is no one-to-one correspondence to this in English, formally and semantically, so what appears to have happened (Hickey 1995, 1997) is that the Irish availed of the afunctional *do* of declarative sentences which was still present in English at the time of renewed plantation in the early seventeenth century (especially if one considers that the input was largely from the West Midlands) to produce an equivalent to the habitual in Irish. This use of an English structure in a language contact situation to reach an equivalent to an existing grammatical category in Irish depends crucially on a distinction between the existence of a category and its exponence. The difference in exponence (the actual form used) between the habitual in Irish and Irish English has often led scholars to either dismiss Irish as a source for this in Irish English or to produce unlikely equations to link up the category in both languages formally. But if one separates the presence of a category in a grammar from its exponence then one can recognize more clearly the search for equivalence which the Irish must have undertaken in acquiring English and can understand the process of availing of means in English, present but afunctional, i.e. declarative *do*, to realize an existing category in their native language. This habitual category in Irish English, usually expressed by *do* + *be* + V-*ing* as in *She does be worrying about the children*, may well have been carried to the Anglophone Caribbean by Irish deportees and indentured labourers in the seventeenth century (see the arguments for and against this in Hickey 2004b, 2004c).

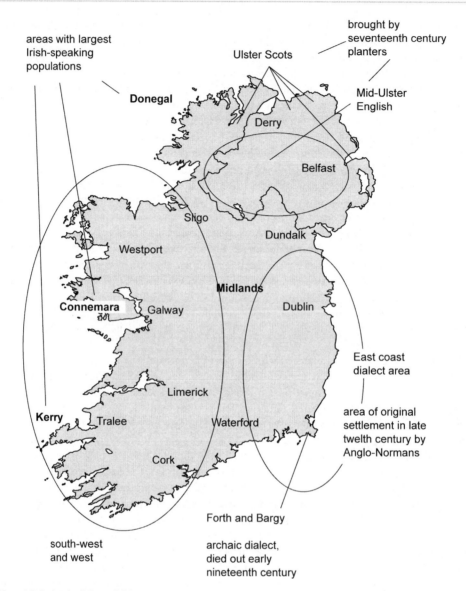

Map 4.2 Ireland: dialect divisions

Dublin English

Present-day Ireland shows a large demographic concentration in the Dublin metropolitan area with over one-third of the population of the Republic living there. This is the urban area which was first to experience the economic boom which set in during the early 1990s and it is here that the major instance of language change – the shift in pronunciation – appeared first. To understand the workings of this shift, one must realize that in the late 1980s and 1990s the city of Dublin, as the capital of the Republic of Ireland, underwent an unprecedented expansion in population size and in relative prosperity

82

Table 4.1 Summary of the Dublin Vowel Shift from the 1990s

(a) retraction of diphthongs with a low or back starting point

time	[taɪm]	→	[tɒɪm]
toy	[tɒɪ]	→	[tɔɪ], [toɪ]

(b) raising of low back vowels

cot	[kɒt̪]	→	[kɔt̪]
caught	[kɒːt̪]	→	[kɔːt̪], [koːt̪]

Raising

```
                 oɪ           oː
                 ↑            ↑
                 ɔɪ     ɔ     ɔː
                 ↑      ↑     ↑
                 ɒɪ     ɒ     ɒː
```

Retraction   aɪ   →   ɑɪ

with a great increase in international connections to and from the metropolis. The in-migrants to the city, who arrived there chiefly to avail themselves of the job opportunities resulting from the economic boom, formed a group of socially mobile speakers, no longer attached to local communities, and their section of the city's population has been a key locus for language change. The change which arose in the last two decades of the twentieth century was reactive in nature: fashionable speakers began to move away in their speech from their perception of popular Dublin English, a classic case of dissociation in an urban setting (Hickey 2000). This dissociation was realized phonetically by a reversal of the unrounding and lowering of vowels typical of Dublin English hitherto. The reversal was systematic in nature with a raising and rounding of low back vowels and the raising of the /i/ diphthong representing the most salient elements of the change (Hickey 1999b). These vowel changes are displayed in tabular form above. In addition, one has a fronting of the onset for the MOUTH vowel, the appearance of a velarized, syllable-final [ɫ] in words like FIELD and a retroflex [ɽ] for the older velarized [ɹ]. See Table 4.1.

The vowel and consonant changes in Dublin English in the decade before the new millennium spread very quickly throughout the rest of the country, especially with younger females, so that any speakers who do not speak the vernacular of their locality will have the vowel shift and the consonantal changes which emanated from Dublin. This means that a new variety of supra-regional Irish English (for the Republic of Ireland) has established itself and will become increasingly dominant as the numbers of speakers with the older supra-regional variety, dating from before the shifts of the 1990s, become less and less. For more information on this complex, see the detailed discussions in Hickey (2005).

The transportation of Irish English

For at least the last 1,500 years, the Irish have left Ireland to settle abroad more or less permanently. The emigration from the island which took place during the colonial period (1600–1900) was generally motivated by the desire to escape unfavourable circumstances in Ireland or the emigration was orchestrated by the English authorities, the latter being the case with deportation. There are two occasions when significant groups of Irish were deported to overseas locations and exercised an influence on a variety during its formative years. The first was in the south-east Caribbean, notably on Barbados (and later on Montserrat), where Irish were deported in the 1650s by Oliver Cromwell. The second was in Australia where deportations of Irish took place in the early days of the country, i.e. in the decades immediately following the initial settlement of 1788 in the Sydney area.

Another type of emigration has to do with religious intolerance, whether perceived or actual. During the eighteenth century the tension between Presbyterians of Scottish origin in Ulster and the mainstream Anglican Church over the demands of the latter that the former take an oath and sacramental test resulted in an increasing desire to emigrate (along with economic pressure), in this case to North America (see below).

A further reason which one might readily imagine to be the cause of emigration is economic necessity. This kind of emigration is what later came to characterize the movement of very large numbers of Irish to Britain, Canada and above all to the United States in the nineteenth century, but it was also a strong contributory factor with the Ulster Scots in the eighteenth century. (See Map 4.3.)

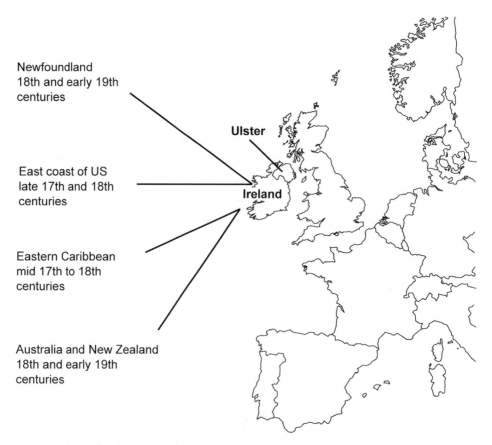

Newfoundland
18th and early 19th
centuries

Ulster

East coast of US
late 17th and 18th
centuries

Ireland

Eastern Caribbean
mid 17th to 18th
centuries

Australia and New Zealand
18th and early 19th
centuries

Map 4.3 Spread of English from Ireland

The Irish in Britain

There is a long history of Irish emigrants in Britain, reaching back almost as far as that of the English in Ireland (from the late twelfth century onwards). But mass emigration only set in during the nineteenth century. And similar to the pattern of emigration to the United States in the late nineteenth and early twentieth centuries (see below) the Irish congregated in areas where labour for industries like mining was wanting (O'Connor 1972; MacRaild 1999). It is estimated that by 1841 nearly 2 per cent of the population of England was born in Ireland (Dudley Edwards 2005 [1973]: 147). In Wales the percentage was much less but there was a concentration in Swansea and Cardiff, cities which have always had connections with counterpart cities on the south coast of Ireland, like Cork (O'Leary 2000). In Scotland the figures were much higher: 4.8 per cent of the population there was Irish-born and again these lived chiefly in the large cities – Glasgow and Edinburgh – which have a tradition of accepting migrant labour from Ulster.

As with the United States, the key period for the rise in the Irish sector of the population is the late 1840s. Between the censuses of 1841 and 1851 there was a jump from 49,000 to 734,000 Irish-born in Britain. This increase led to much friction between the English and Irish, especially as the Irish were frequently starving and diseased, and in 1852, for instance, there were anti-Catholic, i.e. anti-Irish, riots in Stockport.

Merseyside

The areas of Britain which absorbed most Irish were Merseyside and its hinterland of Cheshire in the south and Lancashire in the north. The reason for this is obvious: the port of Liverpool is directly opposite Dublin and there was a constant ship service between the two cities.

The local dialect of Liverpool is Scouse and it is characteristic of its speakers to show a degree of fricativization of /p, t, k/ in weakening environments such as in word-final position (Knowles 1978). Scholars such as Wells (1982) generally ascribe this to an independent development in Scouse. But one could also postulate that this is a relic of a former situation in Irish English. It is agreed that the Scouse fricativization is typical of that section of the community which is directly derived from Irish immigrants. Furthermore, the Irish immigration into the Merseyside area took place chiefly in the first half of the nineteenth century. This was a period in which Irish in Ireland was relatively strong. Furthermore, the Irish who were forced to emigrate were the economically disadvantaged, which is tantamount to saying that they were Irish speakers or poor bilinguals. The latter group would of course have spoken a variety of English which was strongly affected by their native Irish and would thus have been likely to show lenition as a transfer phenomenon.

If this is the case, then why is general lenition of all stops not a characteristic of modern Irish English? The explanation could be as follows. In the course of the nineteenth century, the position of English strengthened as that of Irish was weakened. With this increased influence the least resistant idiosyncratic features of Irish English – lenition of labials and velars – can be taken to have been replaced by more standard pronunciations. In addition, one can mention that the lenition of labials would have caused homophony as in word pairs like *cup* and *cuff*.

The generalized lenition in Scouse may well be a remnant of a wider and more regular distribution of lenition from Irish English which has been maintained, albeit recessively, in this transported variety of Irish English (see Hickey 1996 for a fuller discussion).

Tyneside

An area of England which falls outside the common pattern of poor rural immigration from Ireland is Tyneside. Here the Irish belonged to a higher social class and the influence of their speech has been general in Newcastle, as opposed to Merseyside where, in Liverpool, it was largely restricted to the Catholic working-class population. House (1954: 47) in Beal (1993: 189) notes: 'In 1851, Newcastle, the most cosmopolitan of the north-eastern towns, had one person in every ten born in Ireland.' The possible convergent influence of Irish English in Tyneside is noticeable in a number of grammatical parallels: for instance, it is the only variety of British English which shows *ye* as the second-person pronoun in England (Upton and Widdowson 1996: 66f.), an obvious parallel with Irish English (though conceivably a survival from older forms of English as it is present in Scotland as well). Other parallels are the use of epistemic *must* in the negative (Beal 1993: 197). The use of singular inflection with third-person plural verbs: *Her sisters is quite near* (Beal 1993: 194) is a feature both of northern English in general and of colloquial Irish English of the east coast, including Dublin. Failure of negative attraction is also attested for Tyneside English, e.g. *Everyone didn't want to hear them*, for *Nobody wanted to hear them*, as is *never* as a negative with singular time reference (Beal 1993: 198).

Some of the features are reminiscent of Northern Irish English, e.g. the use of double modals (not found in the south of Ireland and only very rarely in the north nowadays), especially in the negative in urban Tyneside, e.g. *they mustn't could have made any today* (Beal 1993: 195). This is also true of the use of a past participle after *need*, e.g. *My hair needs washed* for *My hair needs washing* (Beal 1993: 200). With these features one may be dealing with a geographical continuum including Tyneside and Scotland. Indeed, the use of a past participle after *need* would seem to have been taken to Northern Ireland by Scots settlers.

Not all the specific features of Tyneside speech point to possible Irish influence, e.g. the use of *for to* + infinitive is a common dialectal feature in the British Isles, as is the use of *them* as a demonstrative pronoun (*I like them books*, Beal 1993: 207) and of course the use of singular nouns after numerals (*I lived there for ten year*, Beal 1993: 209). Items from phonology where convergence with Irish English input may have been operative are the following: (i) retention of word-initial /h-/, (ii) retention of /hw/, [ʍ], e.g. *which* [ʍɪtʃ].

Ulster Scots in the United States

Where religious circumstances led to a search for a better way of life abroad, one has emigration from Ireland. The earliest cases of this stem from the period immediately after the Reformation and its adoption by the English crown (early sixteenth century). After this many Catholics sought refuge on the Catholic continent, for instance in France, Spain and the area of later Belgium.

The situation in Ulster of the early seventeenth century was characterized by a combination of economic and religious factors. The religious motivation was rooted in such demands as the sacramental test which, according to *An Address of Protestant Dissenting Ministers to the King* (1729), was found by Ulster Presbyterians to be 'so very grievous that they have in great numbers transported themselves to the American Plantations for the sake of that liberty and ease which they are denied in their native country' (Bardon 1996: 94). But there is consensus among historians today (Miller 1985; Foster 1988: 215f.; Bardon 1996) that economic reasons were probably more important: the increase in rents and tithes along with the prospect of paying little rent and no tithes or taxes in America. Added to this were food shortages due to failures of crops, resulting in famine in 1728/9 and most severely in 1741. Foster (1988: 216) stresses that the nature of Ulster trade facilitated emigration: the ships which carried flax seed from America were able to carry emigrants on the outward journey. Up to 1720, the prime destination was New England and this then shifted somewhat southwards, to Pennsylvania (from where the Irish frequently pushed further south, Algeo 2001a: 13f.; Montgomery 2001: 126) and later to South Carolina. The rate of emigration depended on the situation in Ireland. In the late 1720s, in the 1760s and in the early 1770s, there were peaks of emigration which coincided with economic difficulties triggered by crop failure or destruction in Ireland (Montgomery 2000: 244f.).

The option of emigration in the eighteenth century was open more to Protestants than to Catholics. The latter would equally have had substantial motivation for emigrating; after all, the Penal Laws, which discriminated against Catholics in public life, were in force from at least the mid seventeenth to the end of the eighteenth century. But emigration did not take place to the same extent with Catholics (the overwhelming majority for the eighteenth century were Protestants). It could be postulated that the Catholics lacked the financial means for a move to the New World. However, the Protestants who left were not necessarily in a financially better position – indeed, many were indentured labourers who thus obtained a free passage. Foster (1988) assumes that the Protestants were more ready to move and subdue new land (as their forefathers, who came from Scotland, had done in Ulster to begin with). The Protestant communities were separate from the Catholics and more closely knit. They were furthermore involved in linen production so that the cargo boats used for emigration would have been in Protestant hands.

The Ulster Scots emigration (Wood and Blethen 1997) is not only important because of its early date but because it established a pattern of exodus to America which, apart from Merseyside and to a much lesser extent Tyneside, became the chief destination of Irish emigration in the northern hemisphere (Miller and Wagner 1994). Estimates suggest that throughout the eighteenth century emigration ran at about 4,000 a year and totalled over a quarter of a million in this century alone (Duffy 1997: 90f.).

The Catholic dimension to Irish emigration

Although the reasons for Irish people to leave the country became more economic after the seventeenth century, the role of the church in the Irish diaspora should not be underestimated. The Catholic Church had a definite stance vis-à-vis emigration and used to send clergy to cater for Irish emigrants and attempted furthermore to regulate such essential social services as education.

Parallel to economically motivated emigration, there was missionary activity overseas. This began in Africa – in Liberia at the behest of the then Pope Gregory XVI – in 1842, along with missionaries from the major European colonizing nations in the scramble for Africa: France, Belgium, Holland and Germany. Despite the obvious Irish presence in this phase of African settlement, there is no discernible influence of Irish speech on any form of English in Africa. In South Africa, the numbers of immigrants from Ireland were under 1 per cent (mainly in the area of Grahamstown, north east of Port Elizabeth) and hence insignificant for the development of English there, although the level of education, and hence the social position, of these immigrants was generally high.

The deportation of Irish convicts to Australia began in 1791 (Dudley Edwards 2005 [1973]: 143) and within a decade there were over 2,000 of them. By 1836, there were over 21,000 Catholics and only half of them were convicts by this stage. In 1835, a Catholic bishop was appointed. During the rest of the century, the orientation of the Catholic Church in Australia towards a homeland of which immigrants had no direct experience diminished.

Of all countries which absorbed Irish immigrants, it was the United States which bore the lion's share. The figure for the entire period of emigration to America is likely to be something in the region of 6–7 million (Montgomery 2001: 90) with two peaks, one in the eighteenth century with Ulster Scots settlers (see above) and the second in the mid nineteenth century, the latter continuing at least to the end of that century. The greatest numbers of Irish emigrants went in the years of the Great Famine (at its height in 1848–9) and immediately afterwards, with a reduction towards the end of the century (Dudley Edwards 2005 [1973]: 149).

For the years 1847 to 1854, there were more than 100,000 immigrants per year. These Irish show a markedly different settlement pattern compared to their northern compatriots who left in the previous century. Whereas the Ulster Scots settled in Pennsylvania and South Carolina, the Catholic Irish, from the mid nineteenth century onwards, stayed in the urban centres of the eastern United Status accounting for the sizeable Irish populations in cities like New York and Boston (Montgomery 2000: 245; Algeo 2001a: 27). The reason for this switch from a rural way of life in the homeland to an urban one abroad is obvious: the memories of rural poverty and deprivation, the fear of a repetition of famine, were so strong as to deter the Irish from pushing further into the rural Midwest, as opposed to, say, the Scandinavian or Ukrainian immigrants of the nineteenth century or the Germans in Pennsylvania in the eighteenth century.

The desire to break with a background of poverty explains why the Irish abandoned their native language. It was associated with backwardness and distress, and even in Ireland the leaders of the Catholics – such as Daniel O'Connell – were advocating by the beginning of the nineteenth century that the Irish switch to English as only with this language was there any hope of social betterment.

Diminished tolerance and their own desire to assimilate rapidly meant that virtually no trace of nineteenth-century Irish English was left in the English spoken in the eastern United States where the later Irish immigrants settled (but see Laferriere 1986 for possible traces in Boston English). In addition, this emigration was quite late, and further removed from the formative years of American English than the earlier Ulster Scots movement to the New World. Nonetheless, there may be some lexical elements from Irish in American English, such as *dig* 'grasp' < Irish *tuigim* 'understand', *phoney* 'bogus' < Irish *fáinne* 'ring' (putatively traced to the Irish practice of selling false jewellery) or *so long* 'goodbye' < Irish *slán* > where the transition from [s] to a velarized [ɫ] would suggest an extra syllable to English speakers.

Canada

The Irish emigration to Canada must be divided clearly into two sections. The first concerns those Irish who settled in Newfoundland and the second those who moved to mainland Canada, chiefly to the province of Ontario, the southern part of which was contained in what was then called Upper Canada.

The oldest emigration is that to Newfoundland; it goes back to seasonal migration for fishing with later settlement in the eighteenth and early nineteenth centuries and is a special case (Hickey 2002). The second layer is that of nineteenth-century immigrants who travelled up the St Lawrence River to reach inland Canada. There was further diffusion from there into the northern United States. The numbers of these immigrants are much less for Canada, only a fifth (upwards of 300,000 for the entire nineteenth century) of the numbers which went to the United States. But seen relatively, this is nonetheless significant and some scholars maintain that elements of Irish speech are still discernible in the English of the Ottawa Valley (Pringle and Padolsky 1981, 1983).

Newfoundland

The Newfoundland settlement of Canada is unique in the history of extraterritorial English. The initial impetus was the discovery of the abundant fishing grounds off the shores of Newfoundland, the continental shelf known as the Great Banks. Irish and West Country English fisherman began plying across the Atlantic in the seventeenth century in a pattern of seasonal migration which took them to Newfoundland to fish in the summer months. The English ships traditionally put in at southern Irish ports such Waterford, Dungarvan, Youghal and Cork to collect supplies for the long transatlantic journey. Knowledge of this movement by the Irish led to their participation in the seasonal migration. Later in the eighteenth century, and up to the third decade of the nineteenth century, several thousand Irish, chiefly from the city and county of Waterford (Mannion 1977), settled permanently in Newfoundland, thus founding the Irish community there (Clarke 1997) which together with the West Country community forms the two Anglophone sections of Newfoundland to this day (these two groups are still distinguishable linguistically). Newfoundland became a largely self-governing colony in 1855 and as late as 1949 joined Canada as its tenth province.

Among the features found in the English of this area which can be traced to Ireland is the use of *ye* for 'you'-PL (which could be a case of convergence with dialectal English), the perfective construction with *after* and present participle, as in *He's after spilling the beer*, and the use of an habitual with an uninflected form of *do* plus *be*. Although Clarke (1997: 287) notes that the positive use of this is unusual in general Newfoundland English today – her example is *That place do be really busy* – it is found in areas settled by south-eastern Irish. This observation correlates with usage in conservative vernacular forms of south-eastern Irish English today (Hickey 2001: 13) and is clearly suggestive of an historical link.

There are also phonological items from Irish-based Newfoundland English which parallel features in south-eastern Irish English, such as the use of stops for dental fricatives, syllable-final /r/, the weakening of word-final, post-vocalic *t*, the low degree of distinctiveness between /ai/ and /i/ (cf. *bile* vs *boil*), if present at all, and the use of an epenthetic vowel to break a cluster of liquid and nasal as in *film* [fɪləm]. There are also reports of lexical items of putative Irish origin such as *sleeveen* 'rascal', *pishogue* 'superstition', *crubeen* 'cooked pig's foot', etc. (Kirwin 1993: 76f., 2001). For a detailed discussion of these and similar features of Newfoundland English, see Clarke (2004) and Hickey (2002).

Mainland Canada

Mainland Canada was also settled by Irish. Here the Irish were among the earliest immigrants and so formed a 'charter group' and enjoyed a relatively privileged status in early

Canadian society. By the 1860s the Irish were the largest section of the English-speaking population in Canada and constituted some 40 per cent of the British Isles immigrants in the newly founded Canadian Confederation. In mainland Canada the Irish came both from the north and south of the country, but there was a preponderance of Protestants (some two-thirds in the nineteenth and twentieth centuries), as opposed to the situation in Newfoundland where the Irish community was almost entirely Catholic.

The Protestants in Canada had a considerable impact on public life. They bolstered the loyalist tradition which formed the base of Anglophone Canada. In the Canadian context, the term 'loyalist' refers to that section of the American population which left the Thirteen Colonies after the American Revolution of 1776, moving northwards to Canadian territory outside American influence where they were free to demonstrate their loyalty to the English crown. As these Irish Protestants were of Ulster origin, they also maintained their tradition of organization in the Orange Order, which was an important voluntary organization in Canada.

In mainland Canada, the Irish dispersed fairly evenly throughout the country, even if there is a preponderence in Ontario and in the Ottawa Valley. There is nothing like the heavy concentration of Scotch-Irish in Appalachia (Montgomery 1989) or that of later, post-Famine Irish in the urban centres of the north-eastern United States such as New York and Boston.

The influence of nineteenth-century immigration on Canadian English is not as evident as in Newfoundland. Nonetheless, one should mention one feature which Canadian English has in common with the English in the north of Ireland (Gregg 1973): what is known in linguistic literature as 'Canadian Raising' (Chambers 1973). The essence of this phenomenon is a more central starting point for the diphthongs /ai/ and /au/ before a voiceless consonant than before the corresponding voiced one: *house, lout* [həʊs, ləʊt] but *houses, loud* [hauzɪz, laud].

The Caribbean

Although the Caribbean is an area which is not immediately associated with Irish influence, the initial Anglophone settlement of the area, in the so-called 'Homestead Phase', did involve considerable Irish input. The island of Barbados was the earliest to be settled by the British (Holm 1994), as of 1627, and Cromwell in the early 1650s had a sizeable number of Irish deported as indentured labourers. This input to Barbados is important to Caribbean English for two reasons. The first is that it was very early and so there was Irish input during the formative years of English there (before the large-scale importation of slaves from West Africa). The second reason is that the island of Barbados quickly became overpopulated and speakers of Barbadian English moved from there to other locations in the Caribbean, and indeed to coastal South Carolina and Georgia, i.e. to the region where Gullah was later spoken (Hancock 1980; Littlefield 1981).

The views of linguists on possible Irish influence on the genesis of English varieties in the Caribbean vary considerably. Wells (1980) is dismissive of Irish influence on the pronunciation of English on Montserrat. Rickford (1986) is a well-known article in which he postulates that southern Irish input to the Caribbean had an influence on the expression of habitual aspect in varieties of English there, especially because *do + be* is the preferred mode for the habitual in the south of Ireland. This matter is actually quite complex and Rickford's view has been challenged by Montgomery and Kirk (1996).

Australia

Anglophone settlement in Australia began in 1788 and in the 80 years up to 1868 various individuals were deported there from both Britain and Ireland. The Irish section of the population ranged somewhere between 20 and 30 per cent. Given the sizeable number of Irish among the original settlers of Australia, one would expect an influence on the formation of Australian English commensurate with their numbers. But the features traceable to Irish input are few and tenuous: for instance, the use of shwa for a short unstressed vowel in inflectional endings, e.g. *naked* British Eng: [ˈneikɪd], Australian Eng: [ˈnɛikəd] or the use of epistemic *must* in the negative, e.g. *He mustn't be in the office today*, 'He can't be in the office today' (possibly due to Scottish influence as well). Another candidate for Irish influence could be the retention of initial /h/, e.g. *hat, humour, home* all with [h-]. This sound has disappeared in urban vernaculars in Britain and its continuing existence in Australian English could be due to Irish influence.

The low prestige of the Irish sector of the early Australian community is probably the chief reason for the lack of influence on later Australian English (the same holds for New Zealand as well). This lack of influence presupposes that the Irish community was easily identifiable and so easily avoidable in speech. It can be assumed that the language of rural immigrants from Ireland in the later eighteenth and during the nineteenth century was a clearly identifiable contact variety of Irish English, and so its features would have been avoided by the remainder of the English-speaking Australian (or New Zealand) population. A feature of Australian English like negative epistemic *must* resulted from regularization across the positive and negative, which the Irish had already carried out, and could have been adopted easily by the Australians they were in contact with.

Another fact which may be indicative of the status of early Irish settlers in Australia is that the inflected form of *you* for the plural, *youse*, is found in vernacular usage in Australia. This form is definitely of Irish origin (see Hickey 2003b for a detailed discussion) and was probably adopted by the English in Australia through contact with the Irish, but on a level, outside formal usage, which was characteristic of Irish English in the early years of this country.

Conclusion

The history of English in Ireland has provided material for linguistic discussion, and continues to do so, because of the long-term interaction between Irish and English and because of the different types of regional input. It is a measure of the maturity of the field that recently all subareas have been covered by significant publications and that the arguments for various standpoints, especially the relative weight accorded to contact versus retention (Filppula 1999, 2003), are based on strictly linguistic arguments and show a balanced consideration of both sources. Avenues which remain to be explored do exist, most noticeably contemporary urban Irish English and non-native varieties used by immigrants, the most likely locus of linguistic change in years to come.

Suggestions for further reading

Corrigan, Karen (2010) *Irish English, Volume 1: Northern Ireland*, Edinburgh: Edinburgh University Press.

Filppula, Markku (1999) *The Grammar of Irish English: Language in Hibernian Style*, London: Routledge.

Hickey, Raymond (2002) *A Source Book for Irish English*, Amsterdam: John Benjamins.
——(2004a) *A Sound Atlas of Irish English*, Berlin: Mouton de Gruyter.
——(ed.) (2004b) *Legacies of Colonial English*, Cambridge: Cambridge University Press.
——(2005) *Dublin English. Evolution and Change*, Amsterdam: John Benjamins.
——(2007) *Irish English. History and Present-day Forms*, Cambridge: Cambridge University Press.

References

Adams, George Brendan (1958) 'The emergence of Ulster as a distinct dialect area', *Ulster Folklife*, 4: 61–73.
——(1965) 'Materials for a language map of 17th century Ireland', *Ulster Dialect Archive Bulletin*, 4: 15–30.
——(1967) 'Northern England as a source of Ulster dialects', *Ulster Folklife*, 13: 69–74.
Algeo, John (2001a) 'External history', in John Algeo (ed.) *English in North America. Cambridge History of the English Language, Vol. 6*, Cambridge: Cambridge University Press, pp. 1–58.
——(ed.) (2001b) *English in North America. Cambridge History of the English Language, Vol. 6*, Cambridge: Cambridge University Press.
Allen, Harold B. and Linn, Michael D. (eds) (1986) *Dialect and Language Variation*, Orlando: Academic Press.
Bardon, Jonathan (1996) *A Shorter Illustrated History of Ulster*, Belfast: Blackstaff Press.
Beal, Joan C. (1993) 'The grammar of Tyneside and Northumbrian English', in James Milroy and Lesley Milroy (eds) *Real English: The Grammar of the English Dialects in the British Isles* (Real Language Series), London: Longman, pp. 187–213.
Bliss, Alan J. (1976) 'The English language in early modern Ireland', in Theodore W. Moody, Francis X. Martin and Francis J. Byrne (eds) *A New History of Ireland. Vol. III: Early Modern Ireland (1534–1691)*, Oxford: Clarendon Press, pp. 546–60.
——(1977) 'The emergence of modern English dialects in Ireland', in Diarmuid Ó Muirithe (ed.) *The English Language in Ireland*, Cork: Mercier, pp. 7–19.
——(1979) *Spoken English in Ireland 1600–1740. Twenty-seven Representative Texts Assembled and Analysed*, Dublin: Cadenus Press.
——(1984) 'English in the south of Ireland', in Peter Trudgill (ed.) *Language in the British Isles*, Cambridge: Cambridge University Press, pp. 135–51.
Burchfield, Robert (ed.) (1994) *English in Britain and Overseas. Origins and Development. The Cambridge History of the English Language. Vol. 5*, Cambridge: Oxford University Press.
Canny, Nicholas (2001) *Making Ireland British 1580–1650*, Oxford: Oxford University Press.
Chambers, J.K. (1973) 'Canadian raising', *Canadian Journal of Linguistics*, 18: 113–35.
Clarke, Sandra (1997) 'The role of Irish English in the formation of New World Englishes. The case from Newfoundland', in Jeffrey L. Kallen (ed.) *Focus on Ireland*, Amsterdam: John Benjamins, pp. 207–25.
——(2004) 'The legacy of British and Irish English in Newfoundland', in Raymond Hickey (ed.) *Legacies of Colonial English*, Cambridge: Cambridge University Press, pp. 242–61.
Dowling, Patrick J. (1968 [1935]) *The Hedge Schools of Ireland* (revised edition), London: Longmans.
Dudley Edwards, Ruth with Hourican, Bridget (2005 [1973]) *An Atlas of Irish History*, London: Routledge.
Duffy, Sean, Newark, P., Brogan, C., Massey, P. and Smith, P. (eds) (1997) *An Atlas of Irish History*. Dublin: Gill and Macmillan.
Fenton, James (2000 [1995]) *The Hamely Tongue. A Personal Record of Ulster-Scots in County Antrim* (2nd edition), Newtownards: Ulster-Scots Academic Press.
Filppula, Markku (1999) *The Grammar of Irish English. Language in Hibernian Style*, London: Routledge.
——(2003) 'The quest for the most "parsimonious" explanations: endogeny vs contact revisited', in Raymond Hickey (ed.) *Motives for Language Change*, Cambridge: Cambridge University Press, pp. 161–73.

Foster, Roy F. (1988) *Modern Ireland 1600–1972*, Harmondsworth: Penguin.

Gregg, Robert J. (1973) 'The diphthongs ə and ɑ in Scottish, Scotch-Irish and Canadian English', *Canadian Journal of Linguistics*, 18: 136–45.

Hancock, Ian (1980) 'Gullah and Barbadian: origins and relationships', *American Speech*, 55: 17–35.

Henry, Alison, Ball, Martin and MacAliskey, Margaret (eds) (1996) *Papers from the International Conference on Language in Ireland. Belfast Working Papers in Language and Linguistics*, Belfast: University of Ulster.

Heuser, Wilhelm (1904) *Die Kildare-Gedichte. Die ältesten mittelenglischen Denkmäler in anglo-irischer Überlieferung* [The Kildare Poems. The Oldest Middle English Documents Attested in Anglo-Irish] (Bonner Beiträge zur Anglistik [Bonn Contributions to English Studies, Vol. 14]), Bonn: Hanstein.

Hickey, Raymond (1993) 'The beginnings of Irish English', *Folia Linguistica Historica*, 14: 213–38.

——(1995) 'An assessment of language contact in the development of Irish English', in Jacek Fisiak (ed.) *Language Contact under Contact Conditions*, Berlin: Mouton de Gruyter, pp. 109–30.

——(1996) 'Lenition in Irish English', in Alison Henry, Martin Ball and Margaret MacAliskey (eds) *Papers from the International Conference on Language in Ireland. Belfast Working Papers in Language and Linguistics*, Belfast: University of Ulster, pp. 173–93.

——(1997) 'Arguments for creolisation in Irish English', in R. Hickey and S. Puppel (eds) *Language History and Linguistic Modelling. A Festschrift for Jacek Fisiak on his 60th Birthday*, Berlin: Mouton de Gruyter, pp. 969–1038.

——(1999a) 'Dublin English: current changes and their motivation', in P. Foulkes and G.J. Docherty (eds) *Urban Voices: Accent studies in the British Isles*, London: Arnold, pp. 265–81.

——(1999b) 'Ireland as a linguistic area', in James P. Mallory (ed.) *Language in Ulster*. special issue of *Ulster Folklife*, 45: 36–53.

——(2000) 'Dissociation as a form of language change', *European Journal of English Studies*, 4 (3): 303–15.

——(2001) 'The south-east of Ireland. A neglected region of dialect study', in J.M. Kirk and D. Ó Baoill (eds) *Language Links: The Languages of Scotland and Ireland* (Belfast Studies in Language, Culture and Politics 2), Belfast: Queens University, pp. 1–22.

——(2002) 'The Atlantic Edge. The relationship between Irish English and Newfoundland English', *English World-Wide*, 23 (2): 281–314.

——(2003a) *Corpus Presenter. Processing Software for Language Analysis. Including a Corpus of Irish English*, Amsterdam: John Benjamins.

——(2003b) 'Rectifying a standard deficiency. Pronominal distinctions in varieties of English', in Irma Taavitsainen and Andreas H. Jucker (eds) *Diachronic Perspectives on Address Term Systems* (Pragmatics and Beyond, New Series, 107), Amsterdam: John Benjamins, pp. 345–74.

——(2003c) 'A corpus of Irish English', in Raymond Hickey, *Corpus Presenter. Processing Software for Language Analysis. Including a Corpus of Irish English*, Amsterdam: John Benjamins.

——(ed.) (2003d) *Motives for Language Change*, Cambridge: Cambridge University Press.

——(2004a) *A Sound Atlas of Irish English*, Berlin and New York: Mouton de Gruyter.

——(2004b) 'English dialect input to the Caribbean' in Raymond Hickey (ed.) *Legacies of Colonial English*, Cambridge: Cambridge University Press, pp. 326–59.

——(2004c) 'Development and diffusion of Irish English' in Raymond Hickey (ed.) *Legacies of Colonial English*, Cambridge: Cambridge University Press, pp. 82–117.

——(ed.) (2004d) *Legacies of Colonial English*, Cambridge: Cambridge University Press.

——(2005) *Dublin English. Evolution and Change*, Amsterdam: John Benjamins.

——(2007) *Irish English. History and Present-day Forms*, Cambridge: Cambridge University Press.

Holm, John (1994) 'English in the Caribbean', in Robert Burchfield (ed.) *English in Britain and Overseas. Origins and Development. The Cambridge History of the English Language. Vol. 5*, Cambridge: Cambridge University Press, pp. 328–81.

House, John W. (1954) *North Eastern England. Population Movements and the Landscape since the Early Nineteenth Century*, Newcastle: Department of Geography, King's College.

Kallen, Jeffrey L. (1994) 'English in Ireland', in Robert Burchfield (ed.) *English in Britain and Overseas. Origins and Development. The Cambridge History of the English Language. Vol. 5*, Cambridge: Cambridge University Press, pp. 148–96.

——(ed.) (1997) *Focus on Ireland*, Amsterdam: John Benjamins.

Kirwin, William J. (1993) 'The planting of Anglo-Irish in Newfoundland', in S. Clarke (ed.) *Focus on Canada* (Varieties of English around the World, General Series, Vol. 11), Amsterdam: John Benjamins, pp. 65–84.

——(2001) 'Newfoundland English', in John Algeo (ed.) *English in North America. Cambridge History of the English Language, Vol. 6*, Cambridge: Cambridge University Press, pp. 441–55.

Knowles, Gerald O. (1978) 'The nature of phonological variables in Scouse', in P. Trudgill (ed.) *Sociolinguistic Patterns in British English*, London: Edward Arnold, pp. 80–90.

Laferriere, Martha (1986) 'Ethnicity in phonological variation and change', in Harold B. Allen and Michael D. Linn (eds) *Dialect and Language Variation*, Orlando: Academic Press, pp. 428–45.

Littlefield, Daniel C. (1981) *Rice and Slaves: Ethnicity and the Slave Trade in Colonial South Carolina*, Baton Rouge: Louisiana State University Press.

Lucas, Angela (ed.) (1995) *Anglo-Irish Poems of the Middle Ages*, Dublin: Columba Press.

Macafee, Caroline (ed.) (1996) *A Concise Ulster Dictionary*, Oxford: Oxford University Press.

McIntosh, Agnus and Samuels, Michael (1968) 'Prolegomena to a study of medieval Anglo-Irish', *Medium Ævum*, 37: 1–11.

MacRaild, Donald H. (1999) *Irish Migrants in Modern Britain 1750–1922*, Basingstoke, Hampshire: Macmillan.

Mannion, John J. (ed.) (1977) *The Peopling of Newfoundland. Essays in Historical Geography*, St John's: Memorial University of Newfoundland.

Miller, Kerby (1985) *Emigrants and Exiles: Ireland and the Irish Exodus to North America*, Oxford: Oxford University Press.

Miller, Kerby and Wagner, Paul (1994) *Out of Ireland. The Story of Irish Emigration to America*, London: Aurum Press.

Milroy, James and Milroy, Lesley (eds) (1993) *Real English. The Grammar of the English Dialects in the British Isles* (Real Language Series), London: Longman.

Montgomery, Michael (1989) 'Exploring the roots of Appalachian English', *English World-Wide*, 10: 227–78.

——(2000) 'The Celtic element in American English', in H.L.C. Tristram (ed.) *The Celtic Englishes II*, Heidelberg: Carl Winter, pp. 231–64.

——(2001) 'British and Irish antecedents', in John Algeo (ed.) *English in North America. Cambridge History of the English Language, Vol. 6*, Cambridge: Cambridge University Press, pp. 86–153.

Montgomery, Michael and Gregg, Robert (1997) 'The Scots language in Ulster', in C. Jones (ed.) *The Edinburgh History of the Scots Language*, Edinburgh: Edinburgh University Press, pp. 569–622.

Montgomery, Michael and Kirk, John M. (1996) 'The origin of the habitual verb *be* in American Black English: Irish, English or what?', in Alison Henry, Martin Ball and Margaret MacAliskey (eds) *Papers from the International Conference on Language in Ireland. Belfast Working Papers in Language and Linguistics*, Belfast: University of Ulster, pp. 308–34.

Moody, Theodore W., Martin, Francis X. and Byrne, Francis J. (1976) *A New History of Ireland. Vol. III: Early Modern Ireland (1534–1691)*, Oxford: Clarendon Press.

Ó Muirithe, Diarmuid (ed.) (1977) *The English Language in Ireland*, Cork: Mercier.

O'Connor, Kevin (1972) *The Irish in Britain*, London: Sidgwick and Jackson.

Odlin, Terence (1991) 'Irish English idioms and language transfer', *English World-Wide*, 12 (2): 175–93.

O'Leary, Paul (2000) *Immigration and Integration. The Irish in Wales, 1798–1922*, Cardiff: University of Wales Press.

Palmer, Patricia (2000) *Language and Conquest in Early Modern Ireland. English Renaissance Literature and Elizabethan Imperial Expansion*, Cambridge: Cambridge University Press.

Pringle, Ian and Padolsky, Enoch (1981) 'The Irish heritage of the English of the Ottawa Valley', *English Studies in Canada*, 7: 338–52.

——(1983) 'The linguistic survey of the Ottawa Valley', *American Speech*, 58: 325–44.

Rickford, John R. (1986) 'Social contact and linguistic diffusion: Hiberno-English and New World Black English', *Language*, 62: 245–90.

Robinson, Philip (1994 [1984]) *The Plantation of Ulster. British Settlement in an Irish Landscape, 1600–1670*, Belfast: Ulster Historical Foundation.

Sullivan, James (1980) 'The validity of literary dialect: evidence from the theatrical portrayal of Hiberno-English', *Language and Society*, 9: 195–219.

Taavitsainen, Irma and Jucker, Andreas H. (eds) (2003) *Diachronic Perspectives on Address Term Systems* (Pragmatics and Beyond, New Series, 107), Amsterdam: John Benjamins.

Trudgill, Peter (ed.) (1984) *Language in the British Isles*, Cambridge: Cambridge University Press.

Upton, Clive and Widdowson, John D. (1996) *An Atlas of English Dialects*, Oxford: Oxford University Press.

Wells, John C. (1980) 'The brogue that isn't', *Journal of the International Phonetic Association*, 10: 74–9.

——(1982) *Accents of English* (3 volumes), Cambridge: Cambridge University Press.

Wood, Curtis and Blethen, Tyler (eds) (1997) *Ulster and North America: Transatlantic Perspectives on the Scotch–Irish*, Tuscaloosa: University of Alabama Press.

5

The development of Standard American English

William A. Kretzschmar, Jr

Introduction

American English holds a prominent place among world varieties of the language, and yet Americans do not all speak English in the same way. American English shows differences from place to place and from social group to social group, at every level of scale. We can, however, still make useful distinctions between American English (here distinguished from Canadian English, the subject of its own chapter) and other world varieties by referring to Standard American English (SAE), a generalization at the national level of scale abstracted from the speech of educated Americans. This chapter describes the development of SAE in two ways, first with discussion of the emergence of American English as a variety in its own right, and then with discussion of how SAE differs from other varieties of American English and from other world varieties.

The emergence of American English

North American settlement by English speakers began in the seventeenth century, amounting at that time to about 150,000 migrants from all parts of Britain (Bailyn 1986). Earlier European incursions in the New World were not without consequences: the Spanish had brought European diseases for which the Native Americans had no resistance, and the native population had seriously declined before the English arrived; no doubt English germs contributed further (e.g. Smith 1994: 259). Dobyns (1983) has estimated that up to 95 per cent of the aboriginal population in the eastern region was lost by these means, a loss rate of 20:1. More conservative estimates suggest loss rates on the order of 6.47:1 and 4.86:1 in the south east (Smith 1994: 269), but even these indicate that about 80 per cent or more of the aboriginal population was lost. The survivors were displaced as they fled in attempts to avoid epidemic disease, and this involved the abandonment of some traditional settlement areas (Smith 1994: 265–7, 271–2). The American poet William Carlos Williams has imaginatively treated another effect of European settlement in North America – its violence – in his book *In the*

American Grain (1925; see also Smith 1994: 264). These two characteristics of European settlement – disease and violence – created the pattern of replacement of the native population, rather than integration with it, that would continue long thereafter, even when Europeans encountered substantial populations of Native Americans (see Schneider 2007 and this volume for the contextualization of this tendency with regard to other new Englishes).

The settlers themselves were not immune to disease or other pathways to mortality. Sir Walter Raleigh's first North American colony, Roanoke, disappeared without trace. The Jamestown and Mayflower colonists suffered tremendous mortality rates. Half of the Pilgrims died during the first winter in Plymouth Plantation (pilgrims.net/plymouth/history), and two-thirds of Jamestown settlers died during the bad winter of 1609 (jefferson.village.virginia.edu/vcdh/jamestown/). During the seventeenth century, child mortality in the Chesapeake region was 50 per cent before the age of 20 (Bailyn 1986: 100). Many of these people had already migrated to London before taking ship for America. Keene reports that 'Most adult Londoners were born outside the city: in the eighteenth century the outsiders may have been as many as two-thirds of the total' (Keene 2000: 109). Mortality there, too, was high, owing to poor sanitation practices. When we combine the massive migration to London with emigration to North America we find that North American emigration accounted for as much as 70 per cent of English population increase during the seventeenth century, and a majority of those people came to North America through London (Bailyn 1986: 40).

Despite the high mortality rates, English settlers continued to flood to the colonies, whether willingly or not (about 50,000 English criminals were transported to North America in the eighteenth century). And other Europeans came, too, including large numbers of Germans from the Palatinate starting in 1709. Thousands of Africans were brought involuntarily to the colonies after 1680. These non-English groups were not spread randomly through the English-speaking population. A mixture of populations was the rule during early settlement, not the creation of large separate-language communities. Philadelphia and New York City were major ports of entry, and new immigrants often spent considerable time there before leaving for the interior (Bailyn 1986: 53). The delay was not always good for them: as in London, poor sanitation and crowded conditions led to high mortality rates. Bailyn (1986: 59–60) notes that Philadelphia hosted a large number of German immigrants, while New York City hosted more Scots and Scotch-Irish, yet overall he reports that:

> The population that spread inland from coastal nodes to form new communities was a composite of ethnic and religious groups – Germans, French, Swiss, Scotch, Scotch-Irish, English, Caribbean islanders, Africans, Afro-Americans – carrying with them different cultural baggage ... There was no single 'American' pattern of family and community organization. There were many patterns, reflecting the variety of human sources from which the population had been recruited and the swiftly changing, fluid situations in which the people lived.

Bailyn's account contrasts sharply with David Fischer's influential book, *Albion's Seed* (1989), whose section titles like 'East Anglia to Massachusetts' and 'The South of England to Virginia' give the impression that British regional culture was transplanted whole to North America. Fischer's statement that 'On Smith and Tangier islands ... immigrants from the far south west of Britain founded a culture which still preserves the dialect of seventeenth century Cornwall and Devon' (1989: 784) is simply wrong. No Americans anywhere today preserve in its entirety Shakespeare's English or any other regional British variety from the seventeenth century, because no language fails to change over time (unless, like Classical Latin, it remains fossilized in books without a living population of speakers). While there were certainly cultural influences from Old World regions, mortality and continuing immigration during early settlement created a dynamic demographic situation out of which American culture, and American English, would eventually emerge. These were not just continuations of Old World culture.

The effect of early general replacement of the native population by English settlers, and of the continuous change in the immigrant population owing to mortality and new migrants, was to create a new 'complex system' of speech interactions. Such complex systems were originally described in the physical and biological sciences, but they also occur in the social sciences, as for instance in economics. Kretzschmar (2009) demonstrates how complex systems constitute speech. In brief, complexity science shows how order, here American speech, emerges from massive numbers of random interactions among the elements in the complex system, rather than from simple causes. For our purposes, we know that there were massive numbers of exchanges of linguistic tokens – whether words or pronunciation or grammar – deployed by human agents, the speakers thrown together in America. In the early American environment, the immigrants all contributed their own resources of speech as they tried to talk to their neighbours. Given the preponderance of early English settlement, it is no surprise that English words and pronunciation and grammar came to constitute the majority of the tokens in the new order that emerged. It is also no surprise that substantial numbers of tokens, whether words or pronunciation and grammatical influences, also emerged in the new order from non-English sources, whether Native American languages or the languages of foreign places (see Marckwardt 1958 for contributions from various languages to American English, particularly the lexicon). Moreover, since complex systems by their nature have the property of scaling, somewhat different words, pronunciation and grammar emerged in the new order in different colonies and in different settlements.

Right from the beginning, it was also possible to see differences between the speech of different colonies, but also to make generalizations about how American English at the 'national' level of scale might differ from British English. The common explanation by linguists for what happened to language in America is 'language contact', and the words 'language contact' can lead us to expect that somehow languages came into contact with each other, in the same way that Fischer proposed that whole cultures came to the New World. However, again, it is speakers as individuals who came into contact and, in terms of complex systems, they acted as human agents who used the linguistic features that worked best for them and, over time, features self-organized out of these interactions into what we recognize as a new American variety. The order that emerged at the national level of scale was not exactly the same as what emerged in any single locality or colony and yet, owing to the scaling property of complex systems, neither was it just an abstraction that avoided any special characteristics of any individual colony, nor was it just a kind of average of speech from lower levels of scale, often called 'colonial levelling' or 'koinéization'. An American English distinct from anything found in Britain began to emerge almost immediately from the speech interactions in the new and fluid populations of speakers.

Schneider's 2007 *Postcolonial English* discusses the emergence of new varieties of English in former colonies world-wide. His description of the histories of English in a number of places, including the United States, shows that the emergence of these postcolonial varieties does seem to follow a similar trajectory. His 'Dynamic Model' suggests five phases in the evolution of such varieties: foundation of the colony, stabilization around the outside norm, nativization, formation of an internal norm, and diversification. American English began to form by self-organization out of the complex system of linguistic interactions in the new colonies, a process that continues to this day and explains how we can have different, changing American English voices in different places and social settings. 'Stabilization around the outside norm' represents the fact that, in every colony, a variety of English emerged as the everyday language of the founding population of settlers (see McDavid 1958: 483; Zelinsky 1993; and Mufwene 2001: Chapter 2 and 3, for the influence of original settlement populations, the Doctrine of First Effective Settlement, and the Founder Principle respectively). In Zelinsky's words, 'the specific characteristics of the first group able to effect a viable, self-perpetuating society are of crucial significance for the later social and cultural geography of the area, no matter how tiny the initial band of settlers may have been' (1993: 13–14). 'Nativization' began immediately in one sense, as settlers in every locality had to adopt words to describe local flora, fauna and places. These were often terms taken from Native Americans, as recorded, for example, in Thomas Harriot's *Briefe and True Report of the New Found Land of Virginia* (1588, cited in Bailey 2004: 4–5), which was based on Raleigh's failed Roanoke colony. The perception of nativization began in the eighteenth century, as British and American writers noted differences between the English of the Old and New World. John Witherspoon, for instance, commented in 1781 that (cited in Mathews 1931: 16)

the vulgar in America speak much better than the vulgar in Great-Britain, for a very obvious reason, viz. that being much more unsettled, and moving frequently from place to place, they are not so liable to local peculiarities either in accent or phraseology. There is a greater difference in dialect between one county and another in Britain, than there is between one state and another in America.

Schneider cites no fewer than four other eighteenth-century writers who comment on the uniformity of American English (2007: 269–70). He says elsewhere that

in the course of time speakers will mutually adjust their pronunciation and lexical usage to facilitate understanding – a process generally known as 'koinéization', the emergence of a relatively homogeneous 'middle-of-the-road' variety.

(Schneider 2007: 35)

However, the period comments he cited do more to distinguish American English from British English than they testify to any actual koinéization. The strongly marked regional dialects of Britain were not maintained in America (*pace* Fischer), and the population mixture noted by Witherspoon did not so much create a uniform koiné as it limited the degree of noticeable difference from locality to locality and from state to state. Still, the American situation was clearly different from Britain, as all the commentators tell us.

Schneider's 'diversification' was already underway, if not yet strongly marked. Witherspoon also noted verbal differences between different regions, such as the word *chunks* for 'firewood' in the middle colonies, and *tote* for 'carry' in the southern states. Emergent

99

regionalisms also appear in the writing of Anne Royall, a travel and society writer. Already in 1831 she illustrated spoken differences between Tennessee, Virginia (modern West Virginia), Pennsylvania and 'Yankee' territory (cited in Mathews 1931: 95). Some features that we associate yet today with those regions were present then, such as r-lessness and other matters of pronunciation, lexical choices like *chunks* and *tote*, and also grammatical choices like *hadn't ought*. As predicted by Hans Kurath (1949: 2) and Raven McDavid (1958: 499), controlled experiments on survey research data have demonstrated that migration patterns spread local features inland from focal cities on the coast (Kretzschmar 1996). Such east-to-west migration created the regional similarities in broad bands across the eastern half of the country, described as the Northern, Midland and Southern dialect regions (Kurath 1949; Kurath and McDavid 1961). While more recent descriptions by William Labov and others make claims for a Western dialect region (Labov 1991), relatively recent settlement and low population density in the west tend to undercut the consistency and coherence of any regional similarities there. And diversification has never stopped: the complex system of speech in America continues to operate, and new kinds of order in American English continue to emerge. Labov (1991) and Labov *et al.* (2005) describe what they consider to be ongoing sound changes called the Northern Cities Shift and the Southern Shift along with Western Merger. These large-scale descriptions are accompanied by smaller-scale changes in local and social settings such that:

> In spite of the intense exposure of the American population to a national media with a convergent network standard of pronunciation, sound change continues actively in all urban dialects that have been studied, so that the local accents of Boston, New York, Philadelphia, Atlanta, Buffalo, Detroit, Chicago and San Francisco are more different from each other than at any time in the past.
>
> (Labov and Ash 1997: 508)

Continuing diversification is a predictable consequence of the fact that speech, language in use, is a complex system.

The twentieth century brought demographic changes which in turn changed the conditions for diversification. Primary settlement of the country by homesteading was already complete, and demographic change thus occurred by internal migration and immigration to already-settled areas. In the first half of the century, southerners moved in great numbers to the north and west. In the second half of the century, northerners often moved away from the Rust Belt for work in new industries in the south. These population movements often created speech islands in the regions to which the migrants travelled, such as African-American or southern white neighbourhoods in northern cities. Similar islands have been created in many cities of twentieth-century immigrants from other countries, so that neighbourhoods in many cities may have a strong ethnic flavour and even preserve ancestral languages (such as, stereotypically, Polish in Chicago, Chinese in San Francisco, and many languages in New York City).

More important, however, was an essential change after World War II in the urban demographic pattern from residential neighbourhoods within cities to the model of an urban core surrounded by suburbs. Suburban housing changed the spoken interactions of the community, because people no longer lived with the people they worked with (see Milroy 1992). Moreover, American suburbs cater to different economic groups because of similar housing prices in different developments, so people of different economic means mingle less on a daily basis than they used to. Weak ties tend to promote the transmission of features from group to group, not the maintenance of strongly marked features within a population group. At the same time, late twentieth-century improvements in transportation (highways, airlines) created a super-regional marketplace for the highly educated. Traditionally, Americans at all levels of society tended to remain in the regions where they were born, so that all social strata could share regional speech habits. Now, the most highly educated segment of the population is mobile nationally, which has led to the idea that highly educated speech should not sound regional. Highly educated speakers in formal settings tend to suppress their regional features (Milroy and Milroy 1999), to the extent that they have them in the first place, owing to suburban housing patterns that separate them from less-mobile economic groups. The typical speech of national news broadcasters is a symptom, not a cause, of this situation.

Labov and Ash (1997) highlight a twentieth-century change in the conditions for the American complex system of speech, in that speakers not in the highly educated group are better able to maintain different regional and social features in their speech, while the highly educated have less access to local and regional speech, and among themselves often tend to suppress whatever such features they have. The term 'General American' has sometimes been used as a proxy for the English of highly educated Americans, because the label gives the impression that there is something 'general', or common, or popular, about it. Actually, just the reverse is true. Highly educated speakers remain a small minority of the population, and rather than sharing characteristics of speech as the term 'general' implies, their speech actually tends to be more mixed in its characteristics than the more strongly differentiated regional and social varieties of the less-mobile working-class and middle-class speakers described by Labov and Ash.

The emergence of Standard American English

Standard American English (SAE) is not a product of the same process that creates and continues to change regional and social varieties of American English and, at a larger scale, American English itself, in that it can be distinguished from British English and other World Englishes. Regional and social varieties and the American variety as a whole derive from the massive number of interactions in English conducted by members of regional and social groups, and, at the top level of scale, by all participants in American culture. SAE, on the other hand, is an institutional construct. It has no native speakers. It is, however, a fact of life for American speakers in formal settings, especially in the educational system.

There is some irony in the fact that James Milroy's lead essay in the excellent volume entitled *The Development of Standard English 1300–1800* (Wright 2000) locates the main impetus behind the idea of Standard English in the nineteenth century, in other words, after the period described in the title. Milroy connects standard ideology with growing nationalism at that time, and the 'promotion of the national language as a symbol of national unity and national pride' (Milroy 2000: 15), not only in England but elsewhere in northern Europe. In consequence, he argues, 'historicisation' reflected nineteenth-century (and later modern and contemporary) standard ideology back on to the history of English – all the way back to its origins with Hengest and Horsa in c. AD 449, and even beyond that to its precursor Germanic languages – so that the contemporary standard language appeared to be an inevitable endpoint of the historical development of the language (Milroy 1992: 125–9). Milroy recognized the division in Victorian scholarship between the study of rural dialects on the one hand, and the development of notions of purism and a focus on educated speech on the other. The latter movement leads to the expectation that the standard language will be uniform in structure and so tends to work against variability and change. It also mainly treats the written language, instead of the more highly variable use of language in speech (2000: 13–14). Standard languages, therefore, can be associated with the language of capital cities, not because the speech of the capital city provides a natural model for a national language, but because the political and social importance of the capital confers national status to written language originating in the capital. In Britain, 'the Queen's English' is another way of designating, not the actual speech of the Royal Family, but instead the socially preferred 'language of a great empire' (Milroy 2000: 16). Thus, as Laura Wright's introduction to the book in which Milroy's essay appeared states: 'Far from answering the questions "what is Standard English and where did it come from?", this volume demonstrates that Standard English is a complex issue however one looks at it' (Wright 2000: 6). Standard English is not to be taken for granted as some sort of default form of the language, and neither should it be brushed aside as unreal. Standard English, in both Britain and America, arises from particular historical circumstances and processes of thought.

SAE began with Noah Webster. Webster was interested in the creation of a specifically American variety of English, a national language for a new country:

> The author wishes to promote the honor and prosperity of the confederated republics of America ... This country must in some future time be distinguished by the superiority of her literary improvements, as she is already by the liberality of her civil and ecclesiastical constitutions. Europe is grown old in folly, corruption and tyranny. For America in her infancy to adopt the maxims of the Old World would be to stamp the wrinkles of decrepit old age upon the bloom of youth, and to plant the seeds of decay in a vigorous constitution.
>
> (written in 1783, cited in Commager 1958: 1)

As clearly expressed in this passage, and neatly characterized by Commager, 'The driving force in Webster, the compulsion that explains all particular expressions of his ambitions and his energies, was nationalism' (Commager 1958: 5). Again as Milroy suggested, the uniformity of a standard language was especially desirable in America. Commager explains (1958: 7):

> But if nationalism was to work in the United States – and in 1800 that was still very much an open question – it would have to get along without the Monarchy, the Church, the Military, and the many other institutions that provided common denominators abroad, and work with more democratic ingredients and build on popular support. It would have to frustrate those class and religious and racial divisions which were potentially so dangerous; it would have to overcome differences not merely of accent but of language itself. The United States, dedicated to the unprecedented experiment of republicanism in a vast territory, a heterogeneous population, and a classless society, could not afford differences of accent or of language.

As we have seen, variation in language naturally self-organizes out of a radically mixed population in a complex system. Thus, regional and social varieties of English were inevitable developments in the United States. A uniform standard, however, was then and still remains a politically attractive idea. That there were fewer differences between the speech of American states than there were differences between British counties might well have been taken as evidence at the time that a standard language was actually developing in the speech of America. Such a notion is as much an example of wishful thinking now as it was then, and usually promoted by those with some academic or political agenda.

Webster and prescriptive texts

The development of SAE nonetheless took place, if not naturally in the complex system from which American regional varieties emerged, then by Webster's salesmanship. John Adams did lead an unsuccessful attempt to create an American Academy on the model of the Académie Française (see Mathews 1931: 39–43), and Webster himself helped to create a Philological Society, but Commager again states the crucial fact: 'The Academy was never born; the Society withered and died; but they were not necessary. Webster's books did their work' (1958: 8). Webster was nothing if not a salesman. A footnote (dated March 1818) in the preface of the 1831 edition of *The American Spelling Book* claimed that sales to that point 'amount to more than FIVE MILLIONS of copies, and they are annually increasing' (1962 [1831]: 15). Webster wrote that his book had become 'the principal elementary book in the United States. In a great part of the northern States, it is the only book of the kind used; it is much used in the middle and southern States; and its annual sales indicate a large and increasing demand' (1831/ 1962: 15). The justice of his claim is shown by Mathews' estimate that *The American Spelling Book* had sold 50 million copies by 1865 (1931: 45), and Pyles' estimate that over 100 million copies were sold before it was replaced by other books (1952: 98). More famous than *The American Spelling Book* but less successful in sales was Webster's *American Dictionary of the English Language* (1825). Pyles reports that 'Unfortunately Webster, who was extremely good at the promotion of his books ... was not a very good man of business' (1952: 98). Webster had sold the rights to *The American Spelling Book* and thus did not accrue royalties on most of the millions sold, and he had to borrow money to finance both the first and second editions of the *American Dictionary* so that they, in Pyles' words, 'did not pile up much of a profit' (1952: 120). Still, the success of Webster's promotional efforts created one of the most successful textbooks of all time and made his name, in America at least, synonymous with the dictionary. Pyles did not like him, as this description shows: 'Webster was smug, self-assured, and pugnacious in his pedantry as in his Puritanism and his patriotism: the dour, thin-lipped, jut-jawed righteousness of his later portraits seems always to have been characteristic of him' (1952: 94). But he still offered the following summary assessment (1952: 123):

> It has been remarked that Webster may have taught us how to spell but taught us nothing else. With this it is difficult to agree. Webster was certainly one of the most influential commentators upon language who ever lived. More than any other single person, he shaped the course of American English, for he supplied us with the schoolmaster's authority which we needed for linguistic self-confidence. He

was largely responsible for the dissemination in this country of an attitude toward language that prevails to this day, even among the rank and file of our people – an attitude which, while it is by no means exclusively American, is yet notably so.

SAE is Webster's legacy, not primarily for the particular features of American spelling he advocated, but rather for the association of language with nationalism, uniformity, moral virtues and authority, especially within the school setting.

An edition from 1880, now called *The Elementary Spelling Book,* can serve to illustrate SAE a hundred years after the book's first appearance, to show how a simple textbook became an industry in itself without losing the core values it started with. The book is a revised edition of one first published in 1857, by the G. & C. Merriam company, which had bought rights to Webster's dictionary and still publishes its descendants. This edition was actually published by the American Book Company, a prominent textbook publisher, presumably under license. The title page boasts that the text is 'AN IMPROVEMENT ON THE AMERICAN SPELLING BOOK. THE CHEAPEST, THE BEST, AND THE MOST EXTENSIVELY USED SPELLING BOOK EVER PUBLISHED' (caps in the original). The advertising language and the corporate publication history tell us, not just about sales, but about the institutionalization of the product, not just about SAE as the possession of the socially advanced, but about its democratic status. Family ties are still present as well. Its preface is by Webster's son, William (dated as from 1866, fourteen years earlier), and indicates that:

> The pronunciation here given is that which is sanctioned by the most general usage of educated people, both in the United States and England. There are a few words in both countries whose pronunciation is not settled beyond dispute. In cases of this kind, the Editor has leaned to regular analogies as furnishing the best rule of decision.
>
> (1880: 6)

This passage marks a change from Noah Webster's undoubted nationalism, and also discounts differences between American and British pronunciation. The 1831 edition, itself a revision, had simply referred to 'the most accurate rules of pronunciation, and the most general usage of speaking' (1831/1962: 16). At the same time that the 1831 edition headed all of its pages with 'An Easy Standard of Pronunciation', its preface further asserted that 'A perfect standard of pronunciation, in a living language, is not to be expected; and when the best English dictionaries differ from each other … where are we to seek for undisputed rules? And how can we arrive at perfect uniformity?' (ibid.) What seems clear is that Webster and his revisers through numerous editions were interested in uniformity, authority and the rules of English, even though they recognized variation in actual practice. It is interesting to note that grammar was not a large part of the system. The 1831 edition tells us that the abridged grammar originally included in the book had been omitted, along with the geographical tables, because 'Geography and Grammar are sciences that require distinct treatises' and 'It is believed to be more useful to confine this work to its proper objects, the teaching of the first elements of language, spelling and reading' (ibid.). The 1880 edition merely says that it will provide 'the distinctions of the parts of speech, and thus anticipate, in some degree, the knowledge of grammar' (1880: 5–6). Authoritative treatment of grammar was not yet part of the American paradigm for elementary language teaching in these books.

After the front matter, the pronunciation key (for teachers), and presentation of the alphabet, the main content of the 1880 edition is presented in 152 tables. Many of these consist of words deemed to belong to a 'class' (e.g. one syllable, two syllables accented on the first, three syllables accented on the second, etc.), in which the spelling and syllabification of the words is accompanied by diacritical marks to indicate pronunciation. The earliest tables consist of single syllables, some of which are words in their own spelling (*hē, shē*). Others are only syllables (*hī, pī*), considered valuable for later word formation. Many tables also contain example sentences, including very short ones in the early tables and more complex ones later. Their aim was to teach reading and enliven class: 'These lessons will serve to substitute variety for the dull monotony of spelling, show the practical use of words in significant sentences, and thus enable the learner the better to understand them' (1880: 6). As the sentences get longer they begin to have useful content, such as 'The world turns round in a day' (Table 25) or 'The best paper is made of linen rags' (Table 26). Moral lessons were also popular, such as 'A rude girl will romp in the street' and 'Bad boys love to rob the nests of birds' (Table 25), or 'I love the young lady that shows me how to read' and 'The Holy Bible is the book of God' (Table 26). Each sentence for a table tells its own story, as in this miscellany that starts Table 33:

> Strong drink will debase a man.
> Hard shells incase clams and oysters.
> Men inflate balloons with gas, which is lighter than common air.
> Teachers like to see their pupils polite to each other.
> Idle men often delay till to-morrow things that should be done to-day.
> Good men obey the laws of God.

Earlier editions had postponed introducing sentences till later in the book, but when introduced, they were even more explicitly religious and moral (1831/1962: Table 13):

> Lesson I
> No man may put off the law of God:
> My joy is in his law all day.
> O may I not go in the way of sin!
> Let me not go in the way of ill men.

> Lesson II
> A bad man is a foe to the law:
> It is his joy to do ill.
> All men go out of the way.
> Who can say he has no sin?

Some of the later lessons in both the early and later editions are Aesop's fables, presented with illustrations and clear morals. Thus Webster and his revisers created SAE out of nationalism, and linked it explicitly with moral and religious teachings presented as reading instruction. The legacy in America of *The American Spelling Book* is an ideology of standard spelling and pronunciation, if not complete uniformity in either, as an expression of morality and patriotism.

Characteristics of SAE

'Spelling reform was only part of Webster's agenda for perfecting English, but it was to be the most effective part' (Bailey 1991: 189). Webster's spellings clearly differentiate SAE from other world varieties. His successful changes come in four classes (following Pyles 1952: 112):

> dropping of final *k* after *c* in words of more than one syllable (e.g. *music* for *musick*)
> uniform use of *-or* for *-our* in words of more than one syllable (e.g. *honor* for *honour*)
> uniform use of *-er* for *-re* (e.g. *theater* for *theatre*)
> *-se* for *-ce* in *defense, offense, pretense* but not in *fence*

Other prominent changes include replacement of *-que* with *-k* in words like *cheque/ check*, *masque/mask*, and removal of doubled consonants as in *programme/program*, *waggon/wagon*. Many other of Webster's proposed changes have not succeeded, such as simplification of *-ine, -ive, -ite* to *-in, -ive, -it* (e.g. *definite/definit*). Some changes were partially successful, such as *f* for older *ph* in *fantasy* but not *phantom*. Some were hit and miss: SAE has *draft* for *draught* and *plowman* for *ploughman*, while many other *-augh-* and *-ough-* spellings survive. We still have *island* instead of Webster's *iland*. Some American spelling changes arose after Webster, such as *tho* for *though*, *thru* for *through*, *catalog* for *catalogue*, and *judgment* for *judgement*, promoted by spelling reformers through educational associations and newspapers in the late nineteenth century. Occasional changes continued to be adopted, such as the 1950s *lite* for *light* (especially as an adjective with food products) and *nite/tonite* for *night/tonight*. Given the relatively small number of characteristic spelling differences like these, and despite the continued emphasis on spelling in American schools and communities (see Kretzschmar 2009: 14–15), Americans are no better spellers in general than speakers of other varieties of English. Winners of American spelling bees are often the children of immigrants who appear to have taken the lessons of American education more to heart than children from families with longer histories in the country.

As for pronunciation, SAE is best defined as the avoidance of pronunciations associated with particular regions or social groups. Hans Kurath and Raven McDavid described the vowels of four regional patterns of American pronunciation (1961, based on data from about two decades earlier):

> Type I: Upstate New York, Eastern Pennsylvania, and the South Midland
> Type II: Metropolitan New York, the Upper South, and the Lower South
> Type III: Eastern New England
> Type IV: Western Pennsylvania

These areas mainly recapitulate the Northern, Midland and Southern dialect regions described by Kurath from lexical evidence (1949). Upstate New York corresponds to what many have called the Inland Northern region (now the area of Labov's Northern Cities Shift), which continues across the northern tier of states as far as the Mississippi River. Eastern Pennsylvania and the South Midland corresponds to settlement through Philadelphia and moving south through the Shenandoah River Valley to the Cumberland Gap in Tennessee, spreading westward as far as the Ozark Mountains in Arkansas. The term 'Appalachian English' is applied to the eastern portions of this pattern, and the term 'Upland Southern' is often used to describe the entire pattern. The inclusion of both Inland Northern and Upland Southern in the same phonological pattern does not support the simple north/south division of American English dialects long assumed by many Americans, a generalization that has always had more to do with cultural differences and the American Civil War than with language. Similarly, by breaking up the north/south division, Metropolitan New York is included in the same phonological pattern with the Upper (Virginia) and Lower (South Carolina/Georgia) South. The lowland southern pattern extended across the southern states in lands suitable for plantation-style agriculture, as opposed to those suitable for small farming, as in the uplands and other marginal agricultural areas. Although it was a major port of entry in the nineteenth century, New York City historically was cut off from early regional extension by the Dutch settlements of downstate New York and northern New Jersey. Like New York City, eastern New England was cut off from immediate westward extension, this time by mountains. On the other hand, western Pennsylvania was a gateway to western expansion because it allowed access to the Ohio River at Pittsburgh, at a time when cross-country travel was much easier by water than by land.

All of these sets held the high and central front vowels and the high back vowels in common with some variation in the low vowels (Table 5.1).

The vowels of *sun*, *law*, *crop*, *boil* are variable between the major regions. The same patterns exist today, with the American west generally following the pattern for Western Pennsylvania. Discussion of Labov's Northern Cities Shift, the Southern Shift and Western Merger has focused on working-class and lower middle-class speakers, and so their relation to SAE is not well established, though some educated speakers, perhaps a great many in the northern cities and west, do participate in these patterns. The contemporary situation for SAE pronunciation is that the most highly educated speakers in formal settings tend to suppress any linguistic features that they recognize as regionally or socially identifiable ('marked' features). Educated participants in the Northern Cities Shift and Western Merger most often do not know that their pronunciation is recognizable by speakers from other regions. This is why it is ironic that Northern Cities Shifters often have the highest degree of linguistic self-confidence, as they strongly believe that they are SAE speakers, but people from other regions hear them as having a distinct accent. Because of the common suppression of marked features in formal educated circles, many educated speakers think that language variation in America is decreasing. On the other hand, however, the economically stratified suburban residential pattern promotes the continued existence and even expansion of local varieties, albeit that these varieties retain fewer strongly marked characteristics than were maintained in the previous era of stronger, denser ties in local social networks. The linkage between demographic trends and education remains the most important consideration

Table *5.1* American English Vowels

crib [ɪ]		*wood* [ʊ]
three [i]		*tooth* [u]
ten [ɛ]		*sun* [ə]
eight [ei]		*road* [ou]
bag [æ]	*crop* [ɑ]	*law* [ɔ]
five [ai]	*down* [au]	*boil* [ɔi]

Source: Adapted from Kurath and McDavid 1961: 6 with IPA symbols used in Upton *et al.* 2001.

for SAE: those who go the furthest in the educational system have the greatest invest-ment in SAE. Of course, some educated speakers will deliberately go against the trend and use regional speech characteristics, while others with less education will choose to try and suppress their regional features.

As for particular pronunciation features, the low-back vowels are historically unstable in American English. The *Don/Dawn* merger is characteristic of western Pennsylvania and the west, but also of eastern New England, where one also hears the fronted pro-nunciation of *crop* with [a].There is evidence that the merger has occurred differently in different areas, so that some may prefer *Don/Dawn* with [ɑ] while others prefer it with [ɔ]. SAE differs from mainstream British English in that it still has [ə] as the vowel of *love* and does not raise it towards [ʊ] as heard, for instance, in the Beatles' 'All you need is love'. The vowel in *roof, root* (but not *foot*) alternates between [u, ʊ], with [ʊ] more common in the northern US. New England preserves the [a] pronunciation in words of the *half, glass, class*, and these pronunciations are sometimes heard from educated speakers in other regions of the country. This may well be a historical con-sequence of Webster's *Spelling Book*, which offered New England pronunciations as standard. Educated speakers in the south commonly pronounce the diphthong in *five* with a weakened glide, and in many areas there is gradation in glide reduction by environment, such as increasing reduction in the series *rye, rice, ride. Marry, merry, Mary* are homophones for most SAE speakers. The vowels in unstressed final syllables like *-ed, -ness*, and others vary between [ɪ~ə] even though the spelling may not indicate it, as in the promotional rhyme 'all in for Michigan'. The most noteworthy SAE con-sonantal practice in contrast to other world varieties is the pronunciation of intervocalic *t* with voicing, so that *latter/ladder* are homonyms for educated Americans. The palatal glide /j/ remains in words like *cure, music*, but is frequently deleted in others like *Tuesday, coupon*. Postvocalic /l/ is often vocalized by educated speakers. These differ-ences are enough to create a distinctive American accent among world varieties of English. Finally, SAE pronunciation has different stress patterns from British English. SAE pronunciation tends to preserve secondary stress, and thus has more fully realized vowels than British English in words like *secretary, laboratory.* SAE therefore has a rhythm different from British and other World English varieties.

SAE grammar and lexicon do differ from those of British English and other world varieties, but the advent of corpus linguistics has made the differences difficult to represent in a list. Typical lexical and grammatical differences are quite familiar, such as Amer-ican/British *trunk/boot, windshield/windscreen, truck/lorry, elevator/lift, apartment/flat, toilet/loo, traffic circle/roundabout, try to sell/flog, government is/government are, in the hospital/in hospital, have gotten/have got, may have done so/may have done.* On the other hand, most real differences travel under the radar. For example, Americans have a *post office* but do not *post* letters as they do in Britain; then again, Americans *mail* letters and the British do not, while of course the *mail* exists in Britain as well as America, at least as a noun. When Stubbs' corpus analysis of the word *surgery* in British English is replicated for American English, only two of the four possible senses are present, 'medical procedure' and branch of 'medicine' but not 'doctor's office' and 'doctor's office hours' (Kretzschmar 2009: 152). Collocations are present at different frequencies in British and American English: *banks* in British English often have some-thing to do with fishing, but not so much in America (not at all in the 1960s Brown Corpus and the 1990s Frown Corpus consulted for Kretzschmar 2009). It turns out that even homely coordinating conjunctions like *and* occur at statistically significantly different rates in corpus analysis of British English and American English (Kretzschmar 2009: 166). Given a corpus approach, it is fair to say that every word in the language is likely to be different in British English versus American English, and every grammatical construction different as well, because every word and every construction will be used at somewhat different rates and with somewhat different collocations in the two varieties. Thus the problem with a list of differences: it would have to include the entire dictionary and the entire grammar.

Some English words will never be well represented in SAE. Because SAE is an institutional construct typically used by educated people in relatively formal circumstances, words from the street, including terms of abuse, common words regarding sex and sexual behaviour, popular words of the moment, or specialized cultural terms, will appear less often in SAE. So, too, will certain real but dispreferred grammatical constructions. Thus, multiple negation, *ain't* and many other verb forms, double modals like *might could*, and regional forms like *y'all*, appear much less frequently in SAE than in common everyday speech and writing. Still, a corpus approach would find that all of these forms and constructions are indeed found, although relatively rarely, in the speech or texts of SAE. The same is also true of the pronunciations noted above; speakers may try to suppress marked features when they are trying to use SAE, but they are never entirely successful and so even marked features occur at measurable rates of occurrence in spoken SAE.

Instead of noting what people actually say and write in SAE, then, another approach to defining SAE is to consider the lists of prescriptions in usage manuals, such as multiple negation or *ain't*. William Labov defined the standard in just this way (1972: 225): 'For many generations, American school teachers have devoted themselves to correcting a small number of nonstandard English rules to their standard equivalents, under the impression that they were teaching logic.' In his famous essay called 'The logic of non-standard English', Labov was trying to promote the idea that, when African-American children did not produce SAE in school, they did not have a language deficit but instead were using a different variety. Labov was right about the deficit/difference problem, but the real issue is more complex than a simple contrast between parallel systems. Grammatical prescriptions have become an issue in elementary education only relatively recently, as we have seen. Inclusion of prescriptive grammar in the basic curriculum means teaching children to suppress features of their home varieties in favour of an unmarked feature used in SAE. Labov's 'correcting a small number of English rules to their standard equivalents' in the school is thus a different problem for children using different varieties, because the kinds and number of 'corrections' needed will be different in every school. To demonstrate this point, we need only understand that there have been a very large number of usage prescriptions proposed in usage manuals, and that only a small number of prescriptions are the same between all the manuals. Chapman (2009) conducted a survey of such prescriptions in the usage manuals of the last century, and found that over 13,000 prescriptions had been proposed over the years. However, more than half were found in only one usage manual, and there were only 1,174 'core' prescriptions, with core being classified as having been mentioned in at least half of the usage manuals. This suggests that while there are some popular usage prescriptions that might be taken to define SAE as the set that teachers often 'correct', the number of them is quite small in comparison to the number of complaints that usage mavens have levelled against speakers and writers. Chapman found that, in the current century (2000–7), 3,785 new prescriptions had been proposed in usage manuals, while 1,470 previous prescriptions did not appear; and that fewer than 20 per cent of the recent entries were 'core'. SAE grammar is much like SAE pronunciation, in that users of SAE actually employ their home varieties, but try to suppress those features that they have noticed or have been taught to consider unacceptable. Unfortunately, people who want to use SAE do not have a well-defined set of rules, but instead must negotiate suppression of an unpredictable number of usages proscribed by different authorities.

Conclusion

Chapman's survey reminds us that what is really more important about SAE is the perception that it exists, reflecting an attitude towards language and standards that Webster originally sold to Americans and which our schools still promote today. Many educated Americans strongly support the authority of the school and continue Webster's advocacy of SAE uniformity. However, SAE has no fixed relation to any American regional or social variety, other than the article of faith that, for national and moral purposes, the standard variety of the home language of Americans ought to be taught in school. What users of English world-wide recognize as SAE cannot be successfully codified, phonologically, lexically or syntactically. It is not a variety that has emerged from any particular population and then been accepted as a standard. Instead, what users of English world-wide typically recognize as SAE more properly consists of a selection of features of American English at the national level, such as tendencies towards rhoticity and the preservation of secondary stress, features which emerge from the continuing operation of the complex system of speech in America. SAE may be an idealized institutional construct rather than a variety on the same terms as American regional and social varieties, but that does not make it any less real as a problem to be confronted by Americans and other speakers of English.

Suggestions for further reading

The North American volume of *The Cambridge History of the English Language* (Algeo 2001) provides a good reference volume covering many aspects of American English, as does the more recent American (and Caribbean) volume of the Mouton de Gruyter *Varieties of English* (Schneider 2008).

A current textbook on American English is Wolfram and Schilling-Estes' *American English: Dialects and Variation* (1998; 2nd edition 2005), which has a strong socio-linguistic viewpoint and less coverage than some readers may want of the history and current status of American English. Gunnel Tottie has prepared an American English textbook for a non-native readership, *An Introduction to American English* (2002). The classic textbooks in the field are Pyles' *Words and Ways in American English* (1952), Francis' *Structure of American English* (1958) and Marckwardt's *American English* (1958).

Recent American demographic changes are treated in Zelinsky (1993). The linguistic effects on speech in local areas are best described in terms made famous in socio-linguistics by James and Leslie Milroy: suburban social networks are characterized by weak ties as the density and multiplexity of linguistic interactions have decreased. See

J. Milroy (1992) and the earlier L. Milroy (1987) which describes the Belfast study in more detail. An alternative account of language in American neighbourhoods is offered by Labov (2001). Eckert (2000) provides an account of language relations in an American high school.

Comprehensive recent lexicographical resources for American English can be found in the *New Oxford American Dictionary* (2001) and in Upton *et al.* (2001). The third edition (online) of the *Oxford English Dictionary* contains significantly better coverage of North America than earlier editions.

References

Algeo, John (ed.) (2001) *The Cambridge History of the English Language. Vol. 6: North America*, Cambridge: Cambridge University Press.

Bailey, Richard (1991) *Images of English*, Ann Arbor: University of Michigan Press.

——(2004) 'American English: its origins and history', in E. Finegan and J. Rickford (eds) *Language in the USA* (2nd edition), Cambridge: Cambridge University Press, pp. 1–17.

Bailyn, Bernard (1986) *The Peopling of British North America*, New York: Vintage.

Chapman, Don (2009) 'Lost battles and the wrong end of the canon: attrition among usage prescriptions', paper presented at SHEL 6, Banff.

Commager, Henry Steele (1958) 'Noah Webster 1758–1958, schoolmaster to America', *Saturday Review* 41 (18 October): 10–12, 66–7 (reprinted 1962, in *Noah Webster's American Spelling Book* (Classics in Education 17), New York: Teachers College, Columbia University, pp. 1–12).

Dobyns, Henry (1983) *Their Number Become Thinned: Native American Population Dynamics in Eastern North America*, Knoxville: University of Tennessee Press.

Eckert, Penelope (2000) *Linguistic Variation as Social Practice*, Oxford: Blackwell.

Fischer, David H. (1989) *Albion's Seed*, Oxford: Oxford University Press.

Francis, W. Nelson (1958) *Structure of American English*, New York: Ronald.

Keene, Derek (2000) 'Metropolitan Values: Migration, Mobility and Cultural Norms: London 1100–1700', in Laura Wright (ed.) *The Development of Standard English 1300–1800*, Cambridge: Cambridge University Press, pp. 93–114.

Kretzschmar, William A., Jr (1996) 'Foundations of American English', in E. Schneider (ed.) *Focus on USA*, Philadelphia: John Benjamins, pp. 25–50.

——(2009) *The Linguistics of Speech*, Cambridge: Cambridge University Press.

Kurath, Hans (1949) *A Word Geography of the Eastern United States*, Ann Arbor: University of Michigan Press.

Kurath, Hans, and McDavid, Raven I., Jr (1961) *The Pronunciation of English in the Atlantic States*, Ann Arbor: University of Michigan Press (reprinted 1982, Tuscaloosa: University of Alabama Press).

Labov, William (1972) 'The logic of non-standard English', in *Language in the Inner City*, Philadelphia: University of Pennsylvania Press, pp. 201–40.

——(1991) 'The three dialects of English', in P. Eckert (ed.) *New Ways of Analyzing Sound Change*, Orlando: Academic Press, pp. 1–44.

——(2001) *Principles of Linguistic Change: Social Factors*, Oxford: Blackwell.

Labov, William and Ash, Sharon (1997) 'Understanding Birmingham', in C. Bernstein, T. Nunnally and R. Sabino (eds) *Language Variety in the South Revisited*, Tuscaloosa: University of Alabama Press, pp. 508–73.

Labov, William, Ash, Sharon and Boberg, Charles (2005) *Atlas of North American English: Phonetics, Phonology and Sound Change*, Berlin: Mouton de Gruyter.

McDavid, Raven (1958) 'The dialects of American English', in N. Francis (ed.) *The Structure of American English*, New York: Ronald, pp. 480–543, 580–5.

Marckwardt, Albert (1958) *American English*, New York: Oxford University Press.

Mathews, Mitford (1931) *The Beginnings of American English*, Chicago: University of Chicago Press.

Milroy, James (1992) *Linguistic Variation and Change*, Oxford: Blackwell.

——(2000) 'The ideology of the standard language', in Laura Wright (ed.) *The Development of Standard English 1300–1800*, Cambridge: Cambridge University Press, pp. 11–28.

Milroy, James and Milroy, Lesley (1999) *Authority in Language* (3rd edition), London: Routledge.

Milroy, Lesley (1987) *Language and Social Networks* (2nd edition), Oxford: Blackwell.

Mufwene, Salikoko (2001) *The Ecology of Language Evolution*, Cambridge: Cambridge University Press.

Pyles, Thomas (1952) *Words and Ways of American English*, New York: Random House.

Schneider, Edgar (2007) *Postcolonial English: Varieties around the World*, Cambridge: Cambridge University Press.

——(ed.) (2008) *Varieties of English. Vol. 2: The Americas and the Caribbean*, Berlin: Mouton de Gruyter.

Smith, Martin (1994) 'Aboriginal depopulation in the postcontact southeast', in C. Hudson and C. Tesser (eds) *The Forgotten Centuries: Indians and Europeans in the American South, 1521–1704*, Athens: University of Georgia Press, pp. 257–75.

Tottie, Gunnel (2002) *An Introduction to American English*, Oxford: Blackwell.

Upton, Clive, Kretzschmar, William A., Jr, and Konopka, Rafal (2001) *Oxford Dictionary of Pronunciation for Current English*, Oxford: Oxford University Press.

Webster, Noah (1962 [1831]) *Noah Webster's American Spelling Book* (Classics in Education 17), New York: Teachers College, Columbia University.

——(1880) *The Elementary Spelling Book*, New York: American Book Company.

Williams, William Carlos (1925) *In the American Grain*, Norfolk, CT: New Directions.

Wolfram, Walt and Schilling-Estes, Natalie (1998) *American English: Dialects and Variation*, Oxford: Blackwell (2nd edition 2005).

Wright, Laura (ed.) (2000) *The Development of Standard English 1300–1800*, Cambridge: Cambridge University Press.

Zelinsky, Wilbur (1993) *The Cultural Geography of the United States* (revised edition), Englewood Cliffs, NJ: Prentice Hall.

6

The Englishes of Canada

Stephen Levey

Introduction

An abiding theme in much of the contemporary literature on Canadian English is that it remains one of the least empirically documented major varieties of English (Allen 1980: 36; Clarke 1993: vii; Halford 1996: 4; Brinton and Fee 2001: 424). Frequently depicted as a composite of British and American English speech patterns owing to the formative influence of these varieties on its development (De Wolf 1990: 3), it is now viewed as an autonomous national variety engaged in its own trajectory of evolution (Bailey 1982: 152; Chambers 1991: 92; Brinton and Fee 2001: 422; Avery *et al.* 2006: 103). The existence of a number of publications dedicated to prescribing (or furnishing guidance on) matters of usage such as the *Canadian Oxford Dictionary* (Barber 2004) and the *Guide to Canadian English Usage* (Fee and McAlpine 2007) bears testimony to its status as an endonormative variety of English. Nevertheless, perusal of the literature on Canadian English suggests that its future as an autonomous variety remains precarious owing to the perceived trend in increasing convergence on American norms (Chambers 1991, 2004; Woods 1999 [1979]).

In spite of a good deal of scholarly interest in the putative encroachment of contemporary American norms on Canadian English, fuelled in no small part by the geographical proximity of the majority of the Canadian population to the US border, much of the evidence adduced in favour of Americanization is based on isolated phonological or lexical items retrieved from questionnaire surveys, rather than systematic investigation of the inherent variability embedded in natural speech data. Empirical examination of the spoken language has approached the issue of Americanization more cautiously, noting that orientation towards American norms is habitually invoked without necessarily considering the linguistic constraints and social meanings associated with variant usage in a Canadian context (Clarke 2006; Halford 2008).

Another prevalent – but insufficiently explored – assumption about Canadian English is the extent to which its alleged uniformity spanning a vast geographical area (Avis 1973: 62; Davison 1987: 122; Chambers 1991, 1998a; Brinton and Fee 2001: 422) remains an accurate characterization, or the result of a 'scholarly fiction' (Bailey 1982:

113

151). Chambers' (1998a: 253) oft-cited claim that urban middle-class Canadian English is virtually 'indistinguishable from one end of the country to the other' epitomizes the orthodox position espousing relative homogeneity, based largely on mainland phonological evidence (Dollinger 2008: 13–15).

Although the characterization of Canadian English as linguistically homogeneous remains prevalent in the literature, technological advances in the study of speech are beginning to elucidate the presence of diversity where earlier methodologies have largely detected uniformity. Valuable evidence has emerged from the use of advanced acoustic experimental methods, yielding more nuanced accounts of phonetic and phonological variation in contemporary speech (see e.g. Hagiwara 2006).

Claims about the uniformity of Canadian English must be additionally tempered by the dearth of corpus-based studies of sufficient empirical depth targeting natural speech data. Particularly pertinent is the fact that, until recently, most of the linguistic research on Canadian English was conducted within the framework of traditional dialectology rather than from a sociolinguistic perspective (Chambers 1991: 90). Thanks to the recent construction of extensive corpora of vernacular speech, the traditional and longstanding preoccupation with investigating lexical and phonological variability is now being steadily redressed by variationist studies of morphosyntactic and discourse features (see e.g. Poplack 2000; Tagliamonte 2005, 2006; Poplack *et al.* 2006; Walker 2007). These topics have hitherto received considerably less attention in the scholarly literature (Brinton and Fee 2001: 431).

The utility of a variationist approach (e.g. Weinreich *et al.* 1968; Labov 1972) resides in its capacity to uncover the underlying constraints on inherent variability, permitting the degree, directionality and social embeddedness of linguistic change to be accurately ascertained (Poplack and Tagliamonte 2001). In the ensuing sections, I illustrate how this methodological framework has contributed to more refined structural characterizations of varieties of Canadian English.

Sociohistorical context

Early migration patterns and the emergence of Canadian English

Canadian English has its roots in successive waves of migration. The early 1760s witnessed an influx of migrants, mostly originating from New England colonies, who arrived in present-day Nova Scotia and New Brunswick, many of them taking over land that had formerly belonged to French-speaking Acadians who had been expelled by the British government (Boberg 2008a: 146).

A significant wave of immigration was precipitated by the American Revolution, resulting in the arrival of many thousands of Loyalists (alternatively designated 'United Empire Loyalists') by 1783. Their anti-revolutionary sentiments and attendant loyalty to the British crown inspired migrations to several regions in Canada, including Nova Scotia, New Brunswick, the Eastern Townships of Quebec, and parts of Ontario. The subsequent arrival of the 'Late Loyalists' after 1783, who came in search of free land and British governmental aid (Dollinger 2008: 66), swelled the number of original settlers, diversifying the existing dialectal mix which had emerged as a result of the arrival of migrants from diverse locations including coastal New England, Vermont, New York, New Jersey and Pennsylvania.

The demographic constitution of this early migratory phase is claimed to have played a pivotal role in establishing the 'bedrock' of Canadian speech patterns by virtue of the Founder Principle, according to which speech patterns of early dominant population groups maintain a selective advantage over those associated with later arrivals, who adapt to local vernacular norms rather than imposing their own (Mufwene 2000: 240). This claim is not uncontroversial, particularly in light of the fact that after the war of 1812, British governmental policy, responding to American hostilities and fuelled by anxiety about latent pro-American republicanism in Canada, was directed towards actively recruiting British settlers as a mitigating measure, resulting in substantial immigration from Ireland, England and Scotland – and the concomitant incursion of regional British speech patterns – during the nineteenth century. The role of the founding population (as opposed to later 'dialect swamping' associated with British immigration) in the formation of Canadian English is briefly addressed below (see 'Linguistic heterogeneity and the roots of Canadian English').

Migration patterns in the late nineteenth and twentieth centuries

An additional migratory wave towards the end of the nineteenth century and continuing into the twentieth century augmented the number of British immigrants in Canada, and saw the arrival of thousands of Scottish and Irish immigrants (see Hickey, this volume), as well as settlers from diverse European locales including Germany, Italy, Scandinavia and the Ukraine (Chambers 1998a: 264). Post-war immigration involving Germans, Greeks, Chinese, Portuguese, Ukrainians and Italians, in addition to other nationalities, diversified the linguistic physiognomy of Canada's major urban centres, and witnessed the proliferation of second language varieties of Canadian English (Chambers 1998a: 266; and see 'Ethnicity and linguistic variation in Canadian English', below).

Linguistic heterogeneity and the roots of Canadian English

Although the majority of Anglophone communities in Canada have their linguistic roots in American ancestral varieties, the extent to which transplanted British speech patterns have intimately shaped the trajectory of Canadian English, beyond their apparent influence on specific enclave communities, remains a contentious and unresolved issue (Dollinger 2008; Trudgill 2006). Proponents of the early entrenchment of ancestral American speech patterns in Canada tend to minimize the linguistic impact of nineteenth-century British immigration on the subsequent evolution of Canadian English, arguing that British settlers arrived too late to have had any profound effect on the phonology and grammar of early Canadian English (Avis 1973; Chambers 1998a: 262; Brinton and Fee 2001: 425; Chambers 2008:14). Concessions are made, however, for communities where British immigrants were founding members, such as Cape Breton in Nova Scotia, and the Ottawa Valley and Peterborough County in Ontario, where regional British linguistic influence is reported to endure.

Nevertheless, Loyalist-base theories of the origins of Canadian English have not been accepted uncritically (see e.g. Scargill 1957). Trudgill (2006: 282), for example, has foregrounded dialect mixing resulting from different combinations of American *and* British input as a crucial component in the crystallization of Canadian English. Recent work by Dollinger (2008) widens the debate by examining the role of 'drift' (i.e. parallel developments in several varieties) as well as internally generated innovations in the emergence of Canadian English.

Variation and change

Phonological variation and change

Canadian English: a phonologically distinctive variety?

Canadian English has been conventionally classified as belonging to the relatively uniform North American 'Third Dialect' area, which also encompasses New England, western Pennsylvania and the western United States. Research to date, however, has identified a number of vocalic features which, if not entirely distinctive, are at least emblematic of Canadian English.

A recently documented vowel shift that has had important ramifications regarding the place of Canadian English within the overall taxonomy of North American dialects concerns the retraction and lowering of /æ/ in the direction of central open /a/, and the lowering of /ɪ/ to /ɛ/, and /ɛ/ to the slot occupied by /æ/, as schematized in Figure 6.1 (Clarke *et al.* 1995: 212).

The motivation for what is now known as the Canadian Shift, reported to be spear-headed by females (Clarke *et al.* 1995: 216), appears to reside in the low-back merger (shared with a few American regional varieties) of /ɒ/ and /ɔ:/, resulting in homophonous pairs such as *cot* and *caught, don* and *dawn,* etc.

Follow-up studies building on the seminal findings of Clarke *et al.* (1995) verify that the Canadian Shift is a pan-Canadian development, at least as far as the speech of the younger generation is concerned, although it is not necessarily advancing at the same rate in all regions, and there is some resistance to it in areas isolated from major urban centres (Boberg 2008b: 136–8).

Canadian Raising is another well-known feature of Canadian English, and is widely professed to be its most distinctive trait (Chambers 1998a: 262; Brinton and Fee 2001: 426; Boberg 2008b: 138). The term 'Canadian Raising' is used to describe the pronunciation

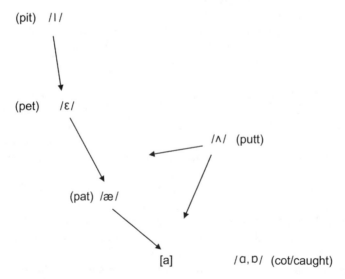

Figure 6.1 Schematization of the Canadian Shift.

of the diphthongs /au/ and /ai/ realized with higher nuclei (approximately [ʌʊ] and [ʌɪ], with some regional variation in the articulation of the raised allophone) before voiceless codas, resulting in contrasting vowel sounds in pairs such as *house/houses* and *knife/knives*. Diachronic research into the origins of this phenomenon, exploiting archived dialect databases, indicates that it has been entrenched in Canadian speech for well over a century, with early indications of its existence in Ontarian speech dating from the mid nineteenth century (Chambers 2006: 111). Opinion is divided on the nature of its precise origins: Trudgill (2006) pursues an explanation based on the structural reallocation of variants embedded in the primordial mix of transplanted dialects in the early history of Canadian English, while Bailey (1982: 155) considers it to be a distinctive Canadian development.

The term 'Canadian Raising' has generated some confusion, leading to the erroneous belief that the phenomenon it designates is exclusive to Canada, when it is not. Analogous allophonic processes, not always affecting both /ai/ and /au/, are attested in non-Canadian varieties, including Martha's Vineyard (off the coast of Massachusetts), Michigan, North Dakota, Minnesota, the Fens (England), as well as Tristan da Cunha and the Falkland Islands, to name but a few locations (Moreton and Thomas 2007), although the precise nature of the processes involved is by no means identical across all varieties.

Evidence of sporadic non-raising in contexts where raising is expected to occur was construed in earlier studies as a harbinger of the eventual demise of Canadian Raising, although there is little indication that it has become markedly less productive. Contemporary surveys reveal it to be a robust and relatively uniform feature of mainland Canadian English (Boberg 2008b: 139), corroborating Chambers' (2006: 115) recent assertion that 'it is intact and unscathed, albeit slightly altered in the phonetics of the onset vowel for the /aw/ diphthong'.

Regional variation

The recently compiled *Atlas of North American English* (Labov *et al.* 2006) reveals a number of salient regional divisions in Canadian English. The largest regional division comprises an expansive area stretching from Vancouver in the west to the Anglophone community of Montreal in the east. Atlantic Canada (including the Maritime provinces and Newfoundland) lies outside the confines of this inland zone. Within the latter, further divisions serve to delimit an inner core encompassing Edmonton in the north west to Toronto in the south east (Boberg 2008b: 131). These divisions are established on the basis of a number of coinciding phonetic isoglosses derived from acoustic measurement of several vocalic variables including (but not limited to) the low-back merger of /ɒ/ and /ɔː/, the Canadian Shift, and Canadian Raising detailed above.

Within this very broad regional delimitation, further studies have yielded preliminary evidence of a more refined picture of regional phonetic differentiation. Based on a series of acoustic analyses of vocalic variables in the speech of undergraduate students from across Canada, Boberg (2008b) suggests that the tripartite regional division put forward in the *Atlas of North American English* can be further decomposed into six major regions: British Columbia, the Prairies, Ontario, Quebec (Montreal), the Maritimes, and Newfoundland. While corroborating the pervasiveness of certain regional patterns described in the *Atlas of North American English*, such as the conditioned merger of /æ/, /ɛ/ /eɪ/ before intervocalic /r/ (e.g. in *marry, merry* and *Mary*), Boberg's (2008b: 143) study hones earlier findings by showing, for example, that the fronting of /ɑːr/ (e.g. in *start, dark*, etc.) is one of the strongest regional indicators of Canadian

English, with Ontario and Atlantic Canada exhibiting more advanced values than either the West or Quebec.

A synthesis of these findings shows that while regional phonetic differences may not be of the same magnitude as those found within the United States or the British Isles, subtle phonetic particularities in the English spoken in Ottawa and Toronto, and in Calgary or Vancouver hint at some degree of regional diversity in urban speech patterns (Boberg 2008b: 150).

The 'Americanization' of Canadian speech

A ubiquitous theme in sociolinguistic research on Canadian English concerns the perceived shift from Canadian autonomy to North American heteronomy (Chambers 1991: 93), catalysed by the putative incursion of American norms into Canadian speech. Staple examples routinely cited in support of this scenario include the use of the /i:/ variant in *leisure* as well as the use of /sk/ in *schedule*. The variable deletion of the palatal glide in stressed syllables after coronals (*news, tune, dew*) resulting in variants such as [nu:z] versus [nju:z], is another apparent manifestation of the same process which is reportedly aligning Canadian speech patterns with contiguous American ones (Clarke 1993).

Yet closer inspection reveals that these promiscuous assumptions are not entirely unproblematic. First, as Halford (2008: 26) notes, the social mechanisms by which such features (and their underlying constraints) diffuse across national borders are little discussed beyond the commonplace, but vague, notion that the mass media may be somehow responsible. Second, such inferences are often predicated on comparisons drawn with some ill-defined or idealized normative variety of Canadian English. As Chambers (1998b: 18) points out, glideless pronunciations in words such as *news* and *student* appear to have been majority variants in Canadian English for at least the past several decades, suggesting that they are by no means the product of recent contact-induced change.

Even admitting that there has been a decrease in the use of glided pronunciations over successive generations (Clarke 2006: 232), any appreciable increase in glideless variants may simply be the product of independent parallel trends in glide deletion that are widely attested in other varieties of English (Halford 2008). Moreover, Clarke's (2006) analysis of glide retention in media usage, supplemented by data culled from a number of sociolinguistic studies, points to a complex interplay of social and linguistic constraints governing variant choice in Canadian English. Specifically, Clarke (2006: 244) notes that within Canada, glided and glideless pronunciations may index different social meanings for different members of the same speech community, militating against the idea that in selecting glideless variants, Canadians are simply targeting American English as an external prestige variety.

Lexical variation and change

Lexical borrowings from indigenous languages

One of the most evident ways in which the lexical stock of Canadian English has diversified and expanded is by accruing new items to designate topographical and biological (flora and fauna) aspects of the environment in which it is spoken (Trudgill 2006). Borrowing from indigenous languages is one resource that has been mined in the process of lexical expansion: *kayak, anorak, husky* and *mukluk* (a type of knee-high boot) come from Inuktitut, whereas *chipmunk, moose* and *muskeg* (a type of organic bog) originate in other aboriginal (First Nations) languages such as Ojibwe and Cree (Fee 1992: 182). Toponyms such as *Quebec* and *Canada* are also claimed to be of aboriginal provenance, with the latter often (but not incontestably) traced to Iroquoian *kanata* meaning 'settlement' or 'community'. Several borrowings, such as *Eskimo, caribou* and *toboggan*, have now diffused into world-wide varieties of English (Bailey 1982: 138).

Lexical change

Lexical obsolescence and renewal have figured prominently in discussions of change in contemporary Canadian English. A widely cited example involves variation in the terms used to designate a 'long upholstered seat' (Chambers 1995: 157), encompassing forms such as *couch, chesterfield* and *sofa*, as well as minor contenders such as *davenport, settee, lounge* and *divan*. The term *chesterfield*, an erstwhile Canadian shibboleth (Chambers 1998b:7), has been receding in the course of the past several decades to the point where it is now principally associated with older speakers, contrasting with *couch*, which is largely preferred by the younger generation.

Regional lexical variability

Notwithstanding the fact that the lexical replacement of items such as *chesterfield* by *couch* is often mentioned as a further instance of the infiltration of American norms into Canadian English (Chambers 1998b: 11), a recent large-scale study aimed at developing a taxonomy of lexical differentiation in Canada established that Canadian dialect regions 'have more in common with one another than any of them has with the United States' (Boberg 2005: 53). Furthermore, no Canadian region appears to manifest lexical traits that can be characterized as more distinctively 'American' than any other. Using sets of related lexical items known to exhibit regional preferences (e.g. *pop, soda, soft drink*, etc., for a 'carbonated beverage') in order to quantify and rank regional lexical distinctiveness, Boberg (2005) identifies six major regional divisions in Canada (mirroring the regional taxonomy established for phonetic differentiation detailed in 'Regional variation' above): the West, Ontario, Montreal, New Brunswick–Nova Scotia, Prince Edward Island and Newfoundland (Boberg 2005: 40). Montreal ranks as the most lexically distinct region in Canada, where distinctive lexical items include *trio* for a 'sandwich-fries-drink combo meal', and *chalet* for a 'summer cottage' (Boberg 2005: 36). Another region evincing a marked degree of lexical distinctiveness is Newfoundland, where lexical preferences comprise *exercise book* for 'notebook' and *bar* for 'candy bar' or 'chocolate bar' (Boberg 2005: 37). Other regions bound by common historical and cultural backgrounds, such as the prairie provinces (Alberta, Saskatchewan and Manitoba), are less sharply demarcated from one another and, with British Columbia, constitute a relatively uniform area characterized by minimal interregional lexical variability.

Morphosyntactic variation and change

Early approaches

The study of morphosyntactic variation in Canadian English has received substantially less attention than either phonology or lexis (Dollinger 2008: 46). Without any national

119

survey of regional differences in morphosyntactic variation (Dollinger 2008: 33), the standard inference, based on extant information, is that there is little which is distinctive about the morphosyntax of Canadian English either within Canada (barring certain enclave varieties described below), or between Canadian and other varieties of English (Brinton and Fee 2001: 431).

Much of the literature dealing with morphosyntactic features displays a marked concern with documenting either the recessiveness of regionally circumscribed constructions such as *he complains a lot any more*, where 'positive' *any more* can be semantically glossed as 'nowadays' (Brinton and Fee 2001: 432), or morphological alternations in past temporal contexts, such as *she has drunk* versus *she has drank*; preterite *sneaked* versus *snuck*; and *dived* versus *dove* (De Wolf 1990; Chambers 1998b).

Early studies of morphosyntactic differentiation (e.g. De Wolf 1990), relying mainly on frequency data generated by postal surveys, uncovered evidence of social and regional variation in the use of structural variants such as *have you/have you got/ do you have?* Regional and social differences in usage are also implicated in the competition between *sneaked/snuck* and *dived/dove*. De Wolf (1990) discusses differences in the social embeddedness of *sneaked/snuck* variation in Ottawa and Vancouver, and observes that *snuck* is overwhelmingly preferred by the young in both cities. Chambers (1998b: 23–4) documents a similar age-related change in the use of *snuck*, and dates acceleration in its use to the 1940s. The rise of *dove* over *dived*, a long-standing variable in Canadian English (Chambers 1998b: 19), has followed a similar trajectory of change, which appears to have been well advanced by the 1930s (Chambers 1998b: 21).

Variationist studies of grammatical sub-systems

More recent corpus-based research on morphosyntactic variation transcends earlier approaches by focusing not simply on the variants themselves, but on the broader grammatical sub-systems in which competing forms are embedded, as well as situating variability in a diachronic and broader cross-varietal perspective.

Two examples of morphosyntactic variation and change in Canadian English exemplifying longitudinal processes of grammatical reorganization concern the stative-possessive system (1–3) (Tagliamonte 2006; Yoshizumi 2006), and deontic modality (4–7) (Tagliamonte and D'Arcy 2007a).

1   We *have* family in Toronto and around there. (QEC/031: 1003)
2   And she*'s got* three sons. (QEC/037: 452)
3   I still *got* my feet don't I? (QEC/066: 899)
4   So it's pretty understood on both sides what one *must* do to get the other's attention, you know. (3/D/m17)
5   Things change. And you *have to* change with it or you become an old lump. (N/®/f/49)
6   We told her owner, 'You*'ve got to* get control of that dog. You*'ve got to* get a license.' (I/®/f/49)
7   It's very bizarre. You just *gotta* go for the experience. (N/ə/m/26)

> (examples 1–3 cited in Yoshizumi (2006: 1);
> examples 4–7 cited in Tagliamonte and D'Arcy (2007a: 48))

Both Tagliamonte (2006) and Yoshizumi (2006) document the ascendancy of stative-possessive *have* in Toronto English and Quebec City English respectively. The newer variants in the stative-possessive system, *have got* and *got*, are marginal, particularly among the younger generation. This trajectory of change diverges from British English, which shows indications of a reduction in the frequency of possessive *have* in apparent-time. Tagliamonte (2006: 317) also adduces evidence suggesting that the frequency of possessive *have* in Canadian English exceeds rates in American English, a finding which runs counter to claims in the literature that Canadian English is a conservative variety (Chambers 1998a: 253; 1998b: 5).

Turning to deontic modal usage, research conducted by Tagliamonte and D'Arcy (2007a) reveals that *have to* outranks other exponents of deontic modality in Toronto English. Competing forms of varying antiquity, including *must*, the historically oldest variant, and *(have) got to* are comparatively infrequent. Diachronic evidence of gradient change in the modal system in Early Ontario English testifies to the early rise of *have to*, which appears to have been inherited from precursor Loyalist speech varieties (Dollinger 2006: 296). The ascendancy of modal *have to* in contemporary Canadian English dovetails more generally with a North American trend characterized by the specialization of *have to* across the deontic domain (Tagliamonte and D'Arcy 2007a: 72).

Discourse-pragmatic variation and change

The quotative system

In contemporary Canadian English, variation in the use of a number of competing forms to introduce reported speech, interior monologue or non-lexicalized sounds constitutes a vigorous area of change which has witnessed the dramatic rise of quotative *be like* (e.g. *she's like*, 'You look really familiar') within a relatively compressed time frame.

The evolution of *be like* has been carefully documented in Canadian English (Tagliamonte and Hudson 1999; Tagliamonte and D'Arcy 2004, 2007b), revealing a remarkable trajectory of change characterized by a fourfold increase between 1995 and 2002 alone (Tagliamonte and D'Arcy 2004), establishing it as the primary quotative variant in the speech of contemporary Canadian youth. (See Figure 6.2.)

Recent research by Tagliamonte and D'Arcy (2007b) confirms that *be like* is essentially an under-40s phenomenon, with older speakers preferring the longstanding *say* variant.

Discourse LIKE

Claimed to be rapidly diffusing in urban centres throughout the English-speaking world (D'Arcy 2005; Tagliamonte 2005), the use of *like* as a discourse marker is reported to be a ubiquitous feature of the vernacular of Canadian youth, as illustrated in (8)–(9) (cited in D'Arcy 2007: 392):

8 *Like* Carrie's *like* a little *like* out of it but *like* she's the funniest. *Like* she's a space-cadet. (3/f/18)
9 Well you just cut out *like* a girl figure and a boy figure and then you'd cut out *like* a dress or a skirt or a coat, and *like* you'd colour it. (N/f/75)

121

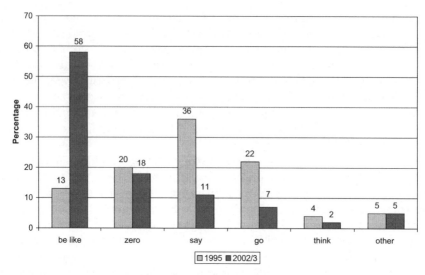

Figure 6.2 Comparison of the distribution of major quotative variants used by Canadian youth, 1995 and 2002/03.
Source: After Tagliamonte and D'Arcy 2004: 502.

Popular ideologies correlating the use of *like* with juvenile inarticulacy are based on the mistaken assumption that it is a haphazard, random insertion, or meaningless filler (D'Arcy 2007: 386). When these ideologies are confronted with the facts of actual usage, a more complex picture emerges: *like* is predominantly associated neither with syntactic planning difficulties nor with lexical indecision (D'Arcy 2005), but appears to play a role in indicating textual relations between sequentially dependent units of discourse (Schiffrin 1987), as well as marking focus, or the speaker's epistemic stance towards an utterance (D'Arcy 2008: 130).

Ground-breaking research conducted on the occurrence of *like* in Canadian English (D'Arcy 2005) indicates that despite its evident positional mobility, its distribution is subject to systematic syntactic constraints. It has also been demonstrated that while younger speakers are in the vanguard with respect to frequency of use, discourse *like* is by no means confined to the younger generation, and is encountered in the vernacular of older speakers, albeit at different rates. Crucially, D'Arcy (2005) establishes that there are systematic, incremental modifications in the use of *like* across successive generations, indicating that it is a change in progress rather than an age-graded feature exclusively propagated by the adolescent sub-section of the population.

Canadian eh

The most stereotypical discourse-pragmatic feature of Canadian English is the particle *eh* (Brinton and Fee 2001: 432), as in *nice day, eh?* (Gold and Tremblay 2006: 249). Qualified by some researchers as 'a marker of both the Canadian English dialect and of Canadian national identity' (Gold and Tremblay 2006: 247), it has been depicted as emblematic of Canadian speech since at least the 1950s (Avis 1967). Notwithstanding its characterization as a quintessentially Canadian feature, *eh* is also attested in Channel Island English, New Zealand English, as well as several other varieties (Avis 1972), although Gold (2008: 141) maintains that it is used more frequently and in a broader range of contexts in Canadian English than in other English varieties.

In spite of recent claims that *eh* continues to expand in use (Gold and Tremblay 2006), there are indications that this particle is declining in frequency in contemporary speech, at least among the younger generation. An apparent-time analysis of the frequency of utterance-final tags across different age cohorts carried out by Tagliamonte (2006: 325) revealed that speakers below the age of 30 used *eh* far less often than older speakers, preferring instead the form *right*, and to a lesser extent, two other variants, *whatever* and *so*, both of which appear to be on the increase.

Regional and enclave varieties

Although homogeneity is claimed to be an active force in Canadian English (Davison 1987: 122), Chambers (1991: 63) notes the existence of enclaves of other accents and dialects in non-urban regions. Several rural and relatively isolated communities are repositories of non-standard grammatical and phonological features which are 'by-products of the sociolinguistically peripheral status of the speech communities in which they are used' (Poplack *et al.* 2002: 87).

Newfoundland

The union of Newfoundland with the rest of Canada was accomplished only in 1949, prior to which time it existed as an independent British dominion. As one of the earliest British colonies in the New World, with a settlement history stretching back several centuries, its highly localized founder population, drawn largely from south-west England and south-east Ireland, remained relatively homogeneous and resistant to external influence until quite recently (Clarke 2008a). Geographical and sociocultural insularity, coupled with economic vicissitudes discouraging substantial in-migration, and the persistence of sparsely populated communities characterized by dense social networks, have favoured the maintenance of linguistic remnants inherited from precursor source varieties.

Notable phonological features of Newfoundland Vernacular English include the variable use of the alveolar stops [t] and [d] or the affricates [tθ] and [tð] for the interdental fricatives /θ/ and /ð/, yielding pronunciations such as *tin* for *thin*, and *den* for *then* (Clarke 1991: 110). Other consonantal variables that are legacies of its linguistic heritage, such as syllable-initial fricative voicing (e.g. *fan* pronounced as *van* and *said* pronounced as *zaid*), a traditional feature of rural dialects in south-west England, are now highly recessive (Clarke 2008a: 176). Divergence from extensive mainland patterns is evidenced by the infrequency of Canadian Raising (Boberg 2008b: 151), especially in the case of the MOUTH set, with many speakers using a raised mid-open vowel in the PRICE and MOUTH classes regardless of the nature of the following phonological segment (Clarke 2008a: 164).

Relic grammatical features inherited from earlier input varieties are also attested. As in other varieties, use of these features tends to be socially stratified, with working-class rural residents employing non-standard grammatical variants more often than members of higher socioeconomic groups. Examples of conservative features which have their vernacular roots in England and Ireland include the variable use of the suffix -*s* throughout the present-tense paradigm to express habituality (10); the use of *be* to encode habitual and sometimes durative aspect (11); non-standard morphological exponents of the present perfect, including the use of auxiliary *be* rather than *have* (12), and the *after* + *VERB* + *ing* construction (13), attested in contemporary Hiberno English, but not restricted to 'hot news' functions (i.e. the representation of recent events) in Newfoundland Vernacular English; and the use of 'pronoun exchange' (i.e. the use of subject personal pronouns in non-subject positions) (14), the latter being another feature found in traditional dialects of south-west England. Other grammatical features inherited from earlier varieties of English include the use of the *for to* construction in infinitival complements (15); and the retention of morphological irregularities in contexts of past temporal reference (16).

10   I *gets* sick when I *takes* aspirin or anything like that
11   It *bees* some cold here in the winter
12   *You're* come again
13   I'm *after havin'* eleven rabbits eaten [by dogs] this last three months
14   I had to give *dey* ['they' = 'oats'] to de hens, once a day
15   I managed *for to* do it
16   It *riz* (rose) up good

(examples 10–11 cited in Clarke 1999: 332;
examples 12–16 cited in Clarke 2008b: 495–6, 503, 505)

It is unclear whether these traits will persist into the future in view of the fact that Newfoundland speech appears to be succumbing to assimilatory pressures exerted by exogenous mainland norms. Clarke's (1991) examination of quantitative trends in the speech of the capital city, St John's, revealed that upper-class females were converging on supralocal norms, particularly in formal contextual styles. These shifting trends suggest that Newfoundland English, sometimes characterized as an autonomous variety (e.g. Chambers 1991: 92), is becoming increasingly heteronomous with respect to mainland Canadian English.

Enclaves of African-American English in Nova Scotia

Detailed investigation of sociolinguistically isolated speech communities on the east coast of Nova Scotia populated by the descendants of black Loyalists and refugee former slaves who fled the United States at the end of the eighteenth and beginning of the nineteenth centuries has furnished compelling new insights into the highly polemical origins of African-American Vernacular English (AAVE) (Poplack 2000; Poplack and Tagliamonte 2001).

These communities have retained a selective number of linguistic features which have disappeared from more mainstream varieties, including variable past tense marking (17); variable plural marking (18); and non-standard negation (19):

17   No. I got a few spankings when I shouldn't have-supposed to do. And they spankø me for that, but, nothing serious. (GYE/077/71)

(cited in Poplack 2006: 461)

18   The man had two trunk*s*. Two trunkø full of all kind of gold and silver and everything. Two trunkø, big trunk*s*. Full of gold and silver. (ANSE/30/1323)

(cited in Poplack *et al.* 2000: 73)

19 Didn't nobody say nothing about it. (ANSE/038/523)

(cited in Howe and Walker 2000: 110)

Drawing on speech from the oldest members of these communities taken to be representative of Early African-American English, and using the combined methods of historical comparative linguistics and variationist sociolinguistics, research targeting these communities has been instrumental in marshalling a range of evidence countering the longstanding belief that contemporary varieties of AAVE have their genesis in an ancestral plantation creole. An alternative explanation – and one which is supported by a considerable amount of statistically validated evidence – maintains that characteristic features of Early AAE are reflexes of vernacular patterns rooted in earlier varieties of English.

A pivotal component of the Nova Scotian research enterprise centres on assiduous comparisons of the grammatical constraints operating on select features in black varieties with those found in the speech of a geographically adjacent rural British-origin community (as well as other British-origin varieties). Systematic analysis of a series of grammatical variables revealed that features such as zero-marked verbs in past temporal reference contexts (see example 17 above), cited in earlier studies as evidence of the vestigial retention of creole tense-aspect distinctions in AAVE, were constrained by a similar array of linguistic constraints (e.g. phonological environment and verbal aspect) operating in both black *and* white vernacular varieties. The detection of highly structured similarities in the underlying grammatical conditioning of exponents of core tense-aspect categories in black and white vernacular speech, as well as robust parallels across these enclave varieties in the rates and conditioning of variability associated with a number of other linguistic features (Poplack 2000), has played a crucial role in establishing the existence of genetic relationships between African-American varieties spoken in Nova Scotia and British-origin non-standard vernaculars.

Canadian English in contact with other languages

The impact of multilingualism on Canadian English

A notable sociolinguistic characteristic of contemporary Canada is its officially bilingual status. Following the Official Languages Acts of 1969 and 1988, Canada's linguistic duality is enshrined in law. According to the 2006 census, approximately 58 per cent of the Canadians claim English as their mother tongue, with Francophone speakers constituting 22 per cent of Canadian population (Statistics Canada 2007: 5). The proportion of mother-tongue Anglophones and Francophones has fluctuated over the past decade, primarily as a result of the steady growth in the allophone population claiming a primary language other than English or French, concomitant with increased immigration since the mid 1980s. (See Figure 6.3.)

The relationship between English and French

According to a widely espoused assumption in the scholarly literature, English has had an indelible influence on Canadian French. Bailey (1982: 166), for example, claims that Canadian French has been 'invaded by loan words, calques, and artifacts of English

125

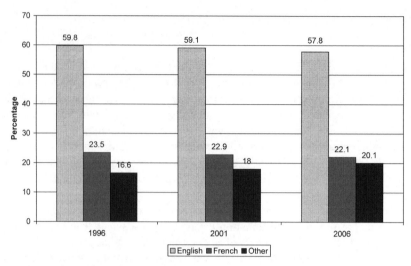

Figure 6.3 Comparison of population by mother tongue (1996–2006).
Source: Figures abstracted from *Statistics Canada* 2007: 5.

phonology'. Similar observations are made by Howard (2007: 8), who remarks that 'the use of anglicisms is one important aspect of Quebec French which gives it a quality of a variety of French which is in some way less standard than other international varieties'. Certainly, it is not difficult to enumerate examples of anglicisms in Canadian French such as *chum, fun, gang, tougher* 'tough out', *coper* 'cope', *afforder* 'afford', *firer* 'to fire', which exhibit varying degrees of phonological integration (Poplack *et al.* 1988). Likewise, in the province of Quebec, where the proportion of mother-tongue Anglophones varies markedly, ranging from 17.6 per cent in Montreal (Statistics Canada 2007) to less than 2 per cent in Quebec City (Poplack *et al.* 2006: 187), claims have been made about the receptiveness of Quebec English to French loanwords (Brinton and Fee 2001: 438). Gallicisms reported to be on the rise in Quebec English include *dépanneur* 'corner shop', *autoroute* 'highway', *caisse/caisse populaire* 'credit union', *poutine* 'French fries with melted cheese curds and gravy', *stage* 'apprenticeship/internship' (Boberg 2005: 43; Brinton and Fee 2001: 438–9; Poplack *et al.* 2006: 186). Grammatical constructions such as the preference for *different from* in Quebec English as opposed to the variant *different than* (reported to be especially frequent in other vernacular varieties of North American English), are adduced as further evidence of possible transfer effects from French (cf. French *différent de*; Chambers and Heisler 1999: 31). These examples, and others like them, are commonly invoked to qualify the uniqueness of Quebec English, which is believed to be the result of its isolated status within a French-speaking majority (Chambers and Heisler 1999: 46).

In spite of reports that geographical isolation and intimate contact with French are fostering the preservation of a highly distinct variety of English in Quebec (Brinton and Fee 2001: 425; Boberg 2005: 37), empirically accountable quantitative studies have neither corroborated *extensive* influence of French on (Quebec) English, nor English on Quebec French (see Poplack and Levey in press). Although borrowings from French have augmented the lexical resources of Quebec English (and vice versa), claims made in the literature about the extent of lexical borrowing and its presumed structural ramifications are often based on anecdotal observations or the examination of written sources (Poplack *et al.* 2006). When the number of borrowings in natural speech data is contextualized in terms of both the lexical stock of the host linguistic system and the productivity of borrowed forms in community repertoires, their impact is greatly attenuated. Thus, English-origin words represent under 1 per cent (0.83 per cent) of the total verbal output of Canadian French speakers examined by Poplack *et al.* (1988: 57). And this finding is replicated with regard to French borrowings in Quebec English: Poplack *et al.* (2006: 207) report that French lexical items have infiltrated Quebec English only to a very negligible extent, and are used with full speaker awareness.

Similarly, in spite of protracted contact between French and English, and high levels of bilingual proficiency among many speakers – conditions which are commonly invoked in the literature as being highly propitious to contact-induced change – evidence of grammatical convergence between the two languages in stable bilingual contexts remains empirically unsubstantiated (Poplack and Levey in press).

Ethnicity and linguistic variation in Canadian English

Bailey's (1982: 165) remark that there is 'little in Canadian English that reflects the languages of the many thousands of non-Anglophones who have come to Canada as immigrants' has come under renewed scrutiny in the wake of a small number of studies exploring ethnolectal variation in major Canadian urban centres.

Boberg (2004) investigates phonetic differentiation in the realization of vocalic variables in the speech of Montrealers with native or native-like proficiency in English drawn from Irish, Italian and Jewish heritage backgrounds. The most salient ethnic differences uncovered by acoustic analysis concern the system of back upgliding vowels, with /u:/ appearing further back for Italians, while /ou/ appears to be pronounced lower and further forward for Jews (Boberg 2004: 551–2). Other ethnically affiliated differences involve allophonic conditioning of /æ/ before nasals, which is higher and further forward for Irish-heritage speakers, as well as significantly lower realization of allophones of /au/ before nasal consonants for Italian-heritage speakers vis-à-vis other ethnic groups.

Research focusing on the Chinese and Italian communities in Toronto has extended the study of ethnolectal variation to other variables. Hoffman and Walker (in press) explore ethnic differences in the use of a stable variable, *-t/d* deletion in word-final consonant clusters (e.g. *tol'* for *told*), as well as participation by ethnic groups in the Canadian Shift.

Inspection of the patterning of linguistic constraints on variability in *-t/d* deletion revealed contrastive effects across different groups, with first-generation Italians and Chinese informants manifesting conditioning dissimilar to the British-descent control group. On the other hand, while the second- and third-generation Italians and Chinese informants fluctuated in overall rates of *-t/d* deletion, the linguistic conditioning of variation was largely comparable with that of the British-descent control group. With regard to engagement in the Canadian Shift, first-generation Chinese informants were not found to participate in ongoing change. Retraction of /æ/ by first-generation Italians, while superficially indicating participation in aspects of the Canadian Shift, may alternatively reflect transfer effects from Italian, which has no low front vowel. By contrast, both second- and third-generation Italians engage in the Canadian Shift, as do younger Chinese speakers, although at comparatively lower rates.

A synthesis of the Toronto findings suggests that language transfer effects do not vigorously persist beyond the first generation, although Hoffman and Walker (in press) surmise that vestiges of heritage language influence may be strategically conscripted by younger speakers to index ethnic identity.

Conclusion

There are currently a number of lacunae in research on Canadian English. Chief among these are the dearth of accounts dealing with the early history of Canadian English, and the shortage of corpus-based studies of spontaneous speech data representative of different regional varieties.

Brinton and Fee (2001: 426) lament the paucity of diachronic studies that address the evolution of Canadian English. In this regard, the recent construction of an electronic corpus of pre-Confederation Canadian English (Dollinger 2008) spanning the period 1776–1849 is a valuable adjunct to existing historical resources, and sheds important light on the basic – but as yet unresolved – issue concerning the point at which Canadian English emerged as a focused variety. Many other such studies would enable contemporary patterns of variation to be more clearly situated in a historical context, and would help to establish appropriate diachronic baselines for comparing trajectories of change across postcolonial Englishes. Comparative endeavours of this nature have featured in recent investigations into the transatlantic links between varieties of English, focusing in particular on the input of regional British and Irish dialects to the formation of New World vernaculars in Canada and elsewhere (Clarke 1999).

From a synchronic perspective, the extension of corpus-based approaches to the analysis of a wider range of communities, both urban and rural, would broaden the existing empirical base, and open up avenues for addressing the impact of space (as well as other external factors such as social class, age and sex) on regional diversity. Recent research (Tagliamonte and Denis 2008), focusing on the spatial diffusion of grammatical changes from Toronto to outlying communities of varying sizes and degrees of remoteness, confirms that linguistic differences between communities are intimately related to differential rates of participation in current mainstream developments. These findings add to a burgeoning body of evidence indicating that diversity is an integral, yet insufficiently explored, component of the Canadian linguistic landscape.

Suggestions for further reading

Ahrens, R. and Antor, H. (eds) (2008) *Focus on Canadian English*, special issue of *Anglistik* 19 (2). (A special edition encompassing a wide range of topics including lexical and phonological variation, as well as topics related to language contact.)

Avery, P., D'Arcy, A. and Rice, K. (eds) (2006) *Canadian English in the Global Context*, special issue of *Canadian Journal of Linguistics* 51 (2/3). (A special edition dedicated to Canadian English providing an up-to-date survey; notable for the information it includes on morphosyntactic and discourse-pragmatic variation.)

Dollinger, S. (2008) *New-Dialect Formation in Canada: Evidence from the English Modal Auxiliaries*, Amsterdam: John Benjamins. (A ground-breaking study of the early history of Canadian English.)

Poplack, S. and Tagliamonte, S. (2001) *African American English in the Diaspora*, Oxford: Blackwell. (An exemplary study of enclave varieties conducted from a variationist perspective.)

References

Allen, H. B. (1980) 'Review of W.A. Avis and A.M. Kinloch (eds) "Writings on Canadian English, 1792–1975: an annotated bibliography"', *Journal of English Linguistics*, 14: 36–9.

Avery, P., D'Arcy, A. and Rice, K. (2006) 'Introduction', *Canadian Journal of Linguistics*, 51: 99–104.

Avis, W.S. (1967) *A Dictionary of Canadian English on Historical Principles*, Toronto: Gage.

——(1972) ' So eh? Is Canadian, eh?' *Canadian Journal of Linguistics*, 17: 89–104.

——(1973) 'The English language in Canada', in T. Sebeok (ed.) *Current Trends in Linguistics, Vol. 10(1)*, The Hague: Mouton, pp. 40–74.

Bailey, R. (1982) 'The English language in Canada', in R. Bailey and M. Görlach (eds) *English as a World Language*, Ann Arbor: University of Michigan Press, pp. 134–76.

Barber, K. (ed.) (2004) *Canadian Oxford Dictionary* (2nd edition), Toronto: Oxford University Press.

Boberg, C. (2004) 'Ethnic patterns in the phonetics of Montreal English', *Journal of Sociolinguistics*, 8: 538–68.

——(2005) 'The North American Regional Vocabulary Survey: new variables and methods in the study of North American English', *American Speech*, 80: 22–60.

——(2008a) 'English in Canada: phonology', in E.W. Schneider (ed.) *Varieties of English Vol. 2: The Americas and the Caribbean*, Berlin: Mouton de Gruyter, pp. 144–60.

——(2008b) 'Regional phonetic differentiation in standard Canadian English', *Journal of English Linguistics*, 36: 129–54.

Brinton, L. and Fee, M. (2001) 'Canadian English', in J. Algeo (ed.) *The Cambridge History of the English Language Vol. VI: English in North America*, Cambridge: Cambridge University Press, pp. 422–40.

Chambers, J. (1991) 'Canada', in J. Cheshire (ed.) *English around the World: Sociolinguistic Perspectives*, Cambridge: Cambridge University Press, pp. 89–107.

——(1995) 'The Canada–US border as a vanishing isogloss: the evidence of chesterfield', *Journal of English Linguistics*, 23: 155–66.

——(1998a) 'English: Canadian varieties', in J. Edwards (ed.) *Language in Canada*, Cambridge: Cambridge University Press, pp. 252–72.

——(1998b) 'Social embedding of changes in progress', *Journal of English Linguistics*, 26: 5–36

——(2004) 'Canadian dainty: the rise and decline of Briticisms in Canada', in R. Hickey (ed.) *Legacies of Colonial English: A Study of Transplanted Dialects*, Cambridge: Cambridge University Press, pp. 224–41.

——(2006) 'Canadian Raising: retrospect and prospect,' *Canadian Journal of Linguistics*, 51: 105–18.

——(2008) 'The tangled garden: relics and vestiges in Canadian English', *Anglistik*, 19: 7–21.

Chambers, J. and Heisler, T. (1999) 'Dialect topography of Quebec City English', *Canadian Journal of Linguistics*, 44: 23–48.

Clarke, S. (1991) 'Phonological variation and recent language change in St John's English', in J. Cheshire (ed.) *English around the World: Sociolinguistic Perspectives*, Cambridge: Cambridge University Press, pp. 108–22.

——(1993) 'Introduction', in S. Clarke (ed.) *Focus on Canada* (Varieties of English around the World G11), Amsterdam: John Benjamins, pp. vii–xi.

——(1999) 'The search for origins: habitual aspect and Newfoundland vernacular English', *Journal of English Linguistics*, 27: 328–40.

——(2006) 'Nooz or nyooz? The complex construction of Canadian identity', *Canadian Journal of Linguistics*, 51: 225–46.

——(2008a) 'Newfoundland English: phonology', in E.W. Schneider (ed.) *Varieties of English Vol. 2: The Americas and the Caribbean*, Berlin: Mouton de Gruyter, pp. 161–80.

——(2008b) 'Newfoundland English: morphology and syntax', in E.W. Schneider (ed.) *Varieties of English Vol. 2: The Americas and the Caribbean*, Berlin: Mouton de Gruyter, pp. 492–509.

Clarke, S., Elms, F. and Youssef, A. (1995) 'The third dialect of English: some Canadian evidence', *Language Variation and Change*, 7: 209–28.

D'Arcy, A. (2005) '*Like*: syntax and development', unpublished PhD thesis, University of Toronto.
——(2007) 'LIKE and language ideology: disentangling fact from fiction', *American Speech*, 82: 386–419.
——(2008) 'Canadian English as a window to the rise of *like* in discourse', *Anglistik*, 19: 125–40.
Davison, J. (1987) 'On saying /aw/ in Victoria', *Toronto Working Papers in Linguistics*, 7: 109–22.
De Wolf, G.D. (1990) 'Social and regional differences in grammatical usage in Canadian English: Ottawa and Vancouver', *American Speech*, 65: 3–32.
Dollinger, S. (2006) 'The modal auxiliaries *have to* and *must* in the Corpus of Early Ontario English: gradient change and colonial lag', *Canadian Journal of Linguistics*, 51: 287–308.
——(2008) *New-Dialect Formation in Canada: Evidence from the English Modal Auxiliaries*, Amsterdam: John Benjamins.
Fee, M. (1992) 'Canadian English', in T. McArthur (ed.) *The Oxford Companion to the English Language*, Oxford: Oxford University Press, pp. 179–83.
Fee, M. and McAlpine, J. (2007) *Guide to Canadian English Usage* (2nd edition), Toronto: Oxford University Press.
Gold, E. (2008) 'Canadian *eh*? From *eh* to zed', *Anglistik*, 19: 141–56.
Gold, E. and Tremblay, M. (2006) 'Eh? and hein? Discourse particles or national icons', *Canadian Journal of Linguistics*, 51: 247–64.
Hagiwara, R. (2006) 'Vowel production in Winnipeg', *Canadian Journal of Linguistics*, 51: 127–41.
Halford, B.K. (1996) *Talk Units. The Structure of Spoken Canadian English*, Tübingen: Narr.
——(2008) 'Americanization, globalization, or vernacularization of Canadian English', *Anglistik*, 19: 23–42.
Hoffman, M. and Walker, J.A. (in press) 'Ethnolects and the city: ethnicity and linguistic variation in Toronto English', to appear in *Language Variation and Change*.
Howard, M. (2007) 'Language in Canada: a brief overview', in M. Howard (ed.) *Language Issues in Canada: Multidisciplinary Perspectives*, Newcastle: Cambridge Scholars Publishing, pp. 1–23.
Howe, D.M. and Walker, J.A. (2000) 'Negation and the creole-origins hypothesis: evidence from Early African American English', in S. Poplack (ed.) *The English History of African American English*, Oxford: Blackwell, pp. 109–40.
Labov, W. (1972) *Language in the Inner City*, Philadelphia: University of Pennsylvania Press.
Labov, W., Ash, S. and Boberg, C. (2006) *The Atlas of North American English: Phonetics, Phonology and Sound Change*, Berlin: Mouton de Gruyter.
Moreton, E. and Thomas, E. (2007) 'Origins of Canadian Raising in voiceless-coda effects: a case of phonologization', in J. Cole and J. I. Hualde (eds) *Papers in Laboratory Phonology 9*, Berlin: Mouton de Gruyter, pp. 37–64.
Mufwene, S. (2000) 'Some sociohistorical inferences about the development of African American English', in S. Poplack (ed.) *The English History of African American English*, Oxford: Blackwell, pp. 233–63.
Poplack, S. (ed.) (2000) *The English History of African American English*, Oxford: Blackwell.
——(2006) 'How English became African American English', in A. van Kemenade and B. Los (eds) *The Handbook of the History of English*, Oxford: Blackwell, pp. 452–76.
Poplack, S. and Levey, S. (in press) 'Contact-induced grammatical change: a cautionary tale', in P. Auer and J. Schmidt (eds) *Language and Space: An International Handbook of Linguistic Variation*, Berlin: Mouton de Gruyter.
Poplack, S. and Tagliamonte, S. (2001) *African American English in the Diaspora*, Oxford: Blackwell.
Poplack, S., Sankoff, D. and Miller, C. (1988) 'The social correlates and linguistic processes of lexical borrowing and assimilation', *Linguistics*, 26: 47–104.
Poplack, S., Tagliamonte, S. and Eze, E. (2000) 'Reconstructing the source of Early African American English: a comparative study of English and creole', in S. Poplack (ed.) *The English History of African American English*, Oxford: Blackwell, pp. 73–105.
Poplack, S., Van Herk, G. and Harvie, D. (2002) 'Deformed in the dialects: an alternative history of non-standard English', in R. Watts and P. Trudgill (eds) *Alternative Histories of English*, London: Routledge, pp. 87–110.

Poplack, S., Walker, J.A. and Malcolmson, R. (2006) 'An English "like no other"? Language contact and change in Quebec', *Canadian Journal of Linguistics*, 51: 185–213.

Scargill, M.H. (1957) 'Sources of Canadian English', *Journal of English and Germanic Philology*, 56: 611–14.

Schiffrin, D. (1987) *Discourse Markers*, Cambridge: Cambridge University Press.

Statistics Canada (2007) *The Evolving Linguistic Portrait, 2006 Census*, Ottawa: Minister of Industry.

Tagliamonte, S. (2005) 'So who? Like how? Just what? Discourse markers in the conversations of young Canadians', *Journal of Pragmatics*, 37: 1896–915.

——(2006) 'So cool, right? Canadian English entering the 21st century', *Canadian Journal of Linguistics*, 51: 309–31.

Tagliamonte, S. and Hudson, R. (1999) 'Be like et al. beyond America: the quotative system in British and Canadian youth', *Journal of Sociolinguistics*, 3: 147–72.

Tagliamonte, S. and D'Arcy, A. (2004) 'He's like, she's like: the quotative system in Canadian youth', *Journal of Sociolinguistics*, 8: 493–514.

——(2007a) 'The modals of obligation/necessity in Canadian perspective', *English World-Wide*, 28: 47–87.

——(2007b) 'Frequency and variation in the community grammar: tracking a new change through the generations', *Language Variation and Change*, 19: 199–217.

Tagliamonte, S. and Denis, D. (2008) 'From community to community: transmission and diffusion in Canadian English', paper presented at NWAV 37, Houston, Texas, USA, 6–9 November.

Trudgill, P. (2006) 'Dialect mixture versus monogenesis in colonial varieties: the inevitability of Canadian English', *Canadian Journal of Linguistics*, 51: 265–86.

Walker, J.A. (2007) 'There's bears back there: plural existentials and vernacular universals in (Quebec) English', *English World-Wide*, 28: 147–66.

Weinreich, U., Labov, W. and Herzog, M. (1968) 'Empirical foundations for a theory of language change', in W. Lehmann and Y. Malkiel (eds) *Directions for Historical Linguistics: A Symposium*, Austin: University of Texas Press, pp. 95–195.

Woods, H.B. (1999 [1979]) *The Ottawa Survey of Canadian English*, Kingston: Queen's University.

Yoshizumi, Y. (2006) 'She's got a thing there: the variation of stative possessives in Quebec City English', unpublished MA memoir, University of Ottawa.

7

English in Australia

Kate Burridge

The early story of Australian English

> There is a continuity in the story of Australian English back to 1788 and possibly beyond.
>
> (Mitchell 2003: 126)

Towards the end of the eighteenth century, the population of the British Isles was around 15 million. As many as one-third of the people spoke their own Celtic languages and little or no English. Regional diversity thrived and those who spoke English often spoke, not the standard language, but their own dialects – and linguistic differences at this time could be striking. This is roughly the linguistic situation, when exploration southwards established the first English-speaking settlers in the Antipodes. For Australia, the date coincides with the arrival of Captain Cook in 1770 and the establishment in 1788 of the first British penal colony in Sydney (New South Wales). Isolated coastal settlements then sprang up in Van Diemen's Land (now Tasmania), Victoria, Queensland, South Australia and Western Australia. The individual histories of these early colonies were all very different, and there were constant fluctuations and changes; nonetheless, Table 7.1 gives some idea of the population mix in one colony in these early times (Yallop 2003: 131).

The evolution of Australian English (AusE) can best be explained through the process of koinéization. When the contact dialects from the British Isles came together in those early years, the blending of features produced a new compromise dialect. The original mix comprised varieties from south-east England, Ireland and Scotland (in order of strength of input), with London English standing out as dominant (cf. Yallop 2003 on the distribution of convict origins). Trudgill (2004) identifies a number of stages in the dialect's formation: Stage I (the speech of the first settlers, showing rudimentary levelling and elimination of minority features); Stage II (the speech of first generation of native-born settlers, characterized by considerable inter- and intra-speaker variability) and Stage III (the speech of second generation of native-born settlers, with mixing, levelling, unmarking and reallocation producing an identifiable stable new dialect). Schneider (2007) also proposes that there is a shared underlying process driving the formation of the postcolonial Englishes. He identifies a sequence of five stages that characterize the

Table 7.1 Population of New South Wales based on 1828 census figures

Type	Number
Convicts	15, 668
Ex-convicts (pardoned or freed)	7, 530
Adults born free	3, 503
Adults arrived free	4, 121
Children under 12	5, 780

development of transplanted varieties such as AusE: Phase 1 (foundation – dialect mixture and koinéization); Phase 2 (exonormative stabilization – a 'British-plus' identity for the English-speaking residents); Phase 3 (nativization – the emergence of local patterns); Phase 4 (endonormative stabilization – 'Australian self-confidence' and codification) and Phase 5 (differentiation – the birth of new dialects). (See Burridge in press for a discussion of the early processes that created AusE, particularly the survival techniques of those linguistic features that went on to thrive in the new variety.)

AusE is remarkably homogeneous for a country that is some thirty times the size of Britain. Its unity is the result of the original dialect mixing and levelling, and the transience of the settlers in those early years. The mobility of the population was surprisingly high given the remoteness and distance of the settlements. With New South Wales as the point of departure, travel was largely by sea, and the swift spread kept the language uniform. Moreover, rapid pastoral expansion and numerous gold rushes all around the continent meant that any emerging regional distinctiveness was soon diluted by floods of new arrivals. However, as identified in the final phase of Schneider's model, fragmentation typically follows the period of uniformity and stability. Later in this chapter, we look at Indigenous variation (present in earlier phases) and also the emerging regional and ethnic dialects of AusE.

The distinctiveness of Australian English

AusE is one of the inner circle Englishes, but distinctive nonetheless from the other native national varieties. Collins and Peters (2004) compare AusE morphosyntax with New Zealand English and the two northern hemisphere standards and examine the case for endonormativity; in other words, the extent to which AusE is 'consolidating its own norms as an independent national standard' (2004: 608). They identify 'small but significant developments' in AusE grammar that supports the notion of an Australian Standard – justified also by a distinctive lexicon and lexical morphology (see below). The appearance of Australian style manuals (e.g. Peters' *Cambridge Australian English Style Guide*) and markedly Australian dictionaries (e.g. *The Macquarie Dictionary* and those published by Oxford University Press) have also helped to establish a distinctive standard for Australia. No longer does the country look to British norms and standards for linguistic guidance, as was previously the case.

Lexical features

The lexicon has incorporated little from Indigenous languages, a story often repeated in places where English has taken roots (cf. Schneider 2007: 36). Borrowed expressions

133

have been largely driven by need and include cultural terms (*boomerang, corroboree, waddy*), flora and fauna (*jarrah, kookaburra, mallee*) and around one-third of Australia's place-names (cf. Dixon *et al*. 1992; Moore 2008).

Many eighteenth- and nineteenth-century British regionalisms thrived in Australia and are now considered among the quintessential expressions of English 'downunder' (even if they no longer form part of speakers' active vocabulary): *billy* 'makeshift container for boiling water' (< Scotland); *fossick* 'to rummage' (< Cornwall); *fair dinkum* 'authentic, genuine' (< Derbyshire – and not, as popular belief has it, from a Cantonese expression meaning 'real gold'); *stone the crows* 'expression of surprise' (< London Cockney); *cobber* 'mate' (< Suffolk). The language of the original convicts (so-called 'flash language') provides the source of many Australianisms: *swag* 'stolen apparel' > 'collection of legitimate belongings (usually rolled in a blanket)'; *lurk* 'dodge, racket' > 'job, occupation'. The expression *bloody* (the so-called 'great Australian adjective') is described in Grose (1783/1811) as 'a favourite word used by thieves in swearing' and remains a favourite today. Some expressions derive from early contact with American English: *squatter* 'one who settles upon land without legal title' > 'respectable pastoralist'; *bush* 'woods, forest' > 'the country as distinct from the town'; *bushranger* 'woodsman' > 'criminal who hides in the bush'. The influx of Americans to the goldfields from the 1850s provided additional colloquialisms.

Vocabulary is linked to culture in obvious ways and often provides windows into a speech community's values and attitudes. AusE has a number of lexical items that have no easy equivalents in national varieties elsewhere (e.g. *cultural cringe* 'the feeling that other countries are better'). Many expressions are recognizably symbolic of the Anglo-Australian self-image, showing values such as 'laid-backness', fairness and community spirit: *whinge* 'to complain, gripe'; *battler* 'persistent struggler against heavy odds'; *bludger* 'one who lives off the efforts of others'; *she's apples/she'll be right/no worries* 'everything is under control' (note the female pronoun here, typical of male vernacular expressions); *fair-go* 'the fair treatment to which everyone is entitled'; *tall poppy* 'a high achiever or overly ambitious person who generates envy and derision' (note, tall poppies do not include sporting heroes); *dob in* 'betray, inform against'; *wet blanket* 'person dampening the ardour of others'; *The Yarts* 'high brow culture such as ballet, opera' (cf. Seal 1999; Wierzbicka 1991, 1992).

An earmark of the AusE lexicon is the rich system of nominal derivation that produces forms like: *Telly chef Brian Turner cooks a delicious grilled brekkie* (*The Sun*, 12 February 2009). Other examples include:

> *barbie* (barbecue); *bickie* (biscuit); *blowie* (blow fly); *Chrissie* (Christmas); *compo* (workers' compensation pay); *cozzie* (swimming costume); *demo* (demonstration); *garbo* (garbage or rubbish collector); *metho* (methylated spirits); *mozzie* (mosquito); *mushie* (mushroom); *muso* (musician); *pokies* (poker machines or coin-operated gambling machines); *rego* (car registration); *rellie/rello* (relative); *sickie* (sick day or a day taken off work while pretending to be ill); *sunnies* (sunglasses); *Tassie* (Tasmania); *truckie* (truck driver); *wharfie* (dockworker)

Words are shortened to one syllable (with the exception of *anotherie* 'another one') and either *-i* or *-o* is added. The endings have sometimes been described as diminutives; in other words, fondling endings to indicate a positive, warm or simply friendly attitude to something or someone. (Compare the diminutive *-s* ending on words like *cuddles* and pet names like *Susykins*.) While such endings do appear on proper names and can be affectionate (as in *Robbo*, *Susy*), the vast majority are not – *journo* or *polli* are not terms of endearment for journalists and politicians.

Wierzbicka (1992) describes the abbreviated words as the linguistic enactment of Anglo-Australian values such as informality, mateship, good humour, egalitarianism and anti-intellectualism (1992: 387). Over the years, other functions have also been suggested (cf. Simpson 2004). None have as yet satisfactorily accounted for the difference between the *-i* and *-o* suffixes. Many *-o* and *-i* words appear in similar contexts (e.g. occupations). There are *wharfies* and *truckies* but not *wharfos* and *truckos*; *garbos* and *musos* but not *garbies* and *musies*. There are notable gaps. Someone who builds a house is neither a *buildo* nor a *buildie*. Clearly, there is more to learn about this feature of vernacular AusE.

Despite the relative regional uniformity of AusE, there are some lexical differences. A medium-size glass of beer (approx 285 ml) in Melbourne is a *pot*, in Sydney a *middy*, in Adelaide a *schooner* and in Alice Springs a *ten*. The guttering along the roof is called *spouting* in Victoria and Tasmania, *guttering* elsewhere. *Swimming costume* is used Australia-wide, alongside regionalisms like *bathers* in the southern states, *swimmers* and *cozzies* in New South Wales and *togs* in Queensland and the south-eastern mainland. There are also expressions that appear confined to specific locations: *hook turn* 'a right-hand turn made from the left side of the road when the green light becomes red' (a peculiarly Melbourne driving manoeuvre). (See Bryant 1997 and more recently Moore 2008: Ch. 12 on regional variation.)

Phonological features

Generally speaking, it is possible to classify AusE into three overall varieties – Broad, General and Cultivated. These labels are not meant to be judgemental but simply represent a convenient three-way division along a continuum of broadness (originally identified by Mitchell and Delbridge 1965). More recently, Horvath (1985) has added another category, Ethnic Broad, to encompass the Migrant Englishes (see later discussion). The Broad variety (known colloquially as 'Strine') is the most distinctly AusE accent and is the one most familiar to other English speakers because it is associated with iconic Australian television and film personalities such as Steve Irwin ('The Crocodile Hunter') and Paul Hogan ('Crocodile Dundee').

The three varieties are distinguished largely on the basis of allophonic variation in the vowel phonemes and the use of one variety over another is governed by a complex of different factors, but principally education, gender identification and location (urban versus rural). Some of these varieties are characterized by distinctive grammar as well. For example, those falling closer to the Broad end strongly correlate with non-standard grammatical features.

The most reliable indicators of broadness are found in the following five vowels and these are often used to distinguish the different varieties. Table 7.2 gives some idea of the range of variation that exists. (For a fuller account, see descriptions in Mitchell and Delbridge 1965; Horvath 1985, 2004; Cox 2006.)

In moving from the Cultivated end to the Broad end, vowels become longer and more drawn out. The broader varieties have 'slower' diphthongs (indicated here by ˈ); this means that the first element is longer. Diphthongs also tend to be 'wider'; this means that the distance between the endpoints of the diphthongs is greater.

Table 7.2 Allophonic variation in five of the vowel phonemes of AusE

		Cultivated	*General*	*Broad*	*Ethnic Broad*
/i/	beat	[i]/[ɪi]	[əɪ]	[əˈɪ]	[əˈɪ]
/eɪ/	bait	[ɛɪ]/[eɪ]	[ʌɪ]	[ʌˈɪ]	[aˈɪ]
/oʊ/	boat	[oʊ/ɒʊ]	[ʌʊ]	[ʌˈʊ]	[aˈʊ]
/aɪ/	bite	[aɪ]	[aɪ/ɒɪ]	[ɒɪ]	[ɒɪ]
/aʊ/	bout	[aʊ]	[æʊ]	[æˈʊ]	[ɛʊ]

So-called 'Ockers' (slang for speakers of Strine) are rare these days. Many are avoiding the Broad end of the spectrum in favour of the middle-ground General accent. This has the advantage of being a distinctly Australian accent, but avoids the stigma that broadness has for some people. At the same time, however, speakers are also avoiding the Cultivated end. Put simply, talking 'posh' doesn't have the same prestige it once had and Australian reactions towards R(eceived) P(ronunciation) and the cultivated forms of AusE are now often hostile (or amused). As in other parts of the English-speaking world, people are trying to speak more 'down to earth', wishing to avoid the crème de la crème connotations of cultivated accents. Solidarity and 'down-to-earthness' are winning out over status and the trend is very clearly towards General Australian, as evident in the accents of international celebrities such as The Wiggles, Nicole Kidman and Kylie Minogue. TV and radio announcers have also moved right away from the BBC-inspired accents that used once to dominate. It is telling that when the new Managing Director of the A(ustralian) B(roadcasting) C(orporation), Brian Johns, took over in 1995, he is quoted as saying, 'We don't want an outdated accent' (by which he would have meant the local 'cultivated' accents closest to RP; cf. Bradley and Bradley 2001: 275). Australianness in an accent is not such a bad thing any more and observations like the following are dated.

> the common speech of the Commonwealth of Australia represents the most brutal maltreatment which has ever been inflicted upon the language that is the mother tongue of the great English nations.
>
> (William Churchill 1911: 17)

> The Australian accent has frequently been described by travellers, but none have done justice to its abominations. Many unobservant persons, shuddering through three or four months' experience, have left Australia saying that the people of the island continent use the dialect of the East End of London. This is a gross injustice to poor Whitechapel. Neither the coster of to-day, nor the old-time Cockney of the days of Dickens, would be guilty of uttering the uncouth vowel sounds I have heard habitually used by all classes in Australia.
>
> (Valerie Desmond 1911: 15–16)

The following are some additional distinctive features of the AusE accent.

Consonants

■ AusE is non-rhotic; in other words, there is no post-vocalic /r/. It shows 'linking /r/' (*beer in*), as well as 'intrusive /r/' (*idea-r-of it*).

▨ The vocalization of /l/ is extremely widespread and produced by speakers of all accent varieties. With this change, the /l/ is pronounced much like the back vowel /u/, possibly also rounded or labialized (*milk* [mɪuk], *pickle* [pɪku], *pill* [pɪu]).

▨ Commonplace are syllabic nasals and laterals (e.g. *button*, *puddle*).

▨ The general weakening of stops is widespread in the community. Between vowels (e.g. *thirteen*, *city*, *get it*), /t/ tends to be tapped and also before syllabic /l/ and /n/ (as in *petal* and *mitten*). Final stops tend to be unreleased (e.g. *bit*, *bid*). There is also a tendency to glottalize /t/, especially in pre-consonantal position (e.g. *not now*, *butler*). Increasingly, fricated /tˢ/ can be heard, especially in pre-pausal position (e.g. *That's a beautiful hat* [hætˢ]). (Cf. Tollfree 2001 on /t/ weakening.)

▨ Yods (/j/) tend not to be dropped after coronals before /u/ (*news* [njuz]), although there is considerable variation (e.g. [njud]/~[nud]). There is also coalescence of /tj/, /dj/, /sj/, /zj/ to /tʃ/, /dʃ/, /ʃ/, /ʒ/ (e.g. *tune*, *dune*, *assume*, *presume*). There is also variation ([əˈsjum]~[əˈʃum]), although palatal versions are more likely in unstressed syllables (*educate* [ˈɛdʒəkeɪt]).

▨ H-deletion is common in unstressed (function) words, such as *him* and *her*, but in content words (e.g. *helmet*, *happen*) it remains stigmatized and tends to occur more at the Broad end of the accent spectrum (more usually in male speech).

▨ Substitution of /f/ for /θ/ ([fɪŋk] for *think*) and /v/ for /ð/ ([mʌvə] for *mother*) is more widespread than is usually acknowledged.

▨ The four quantifying pronouns *something*, *everything*, *nothing* and *anything* commonly show the substitution of /ŋk/ for /ŋ/, especially among Broad speakers.

Vowels

▨ There is rounding of /ɜ/, as in *bird*.

▨ Some Broad speakers produce monophthong variants for the centring diphthongs (e.g. *near* /ɪ: / and *square* /ɛ:/).

▨ The schwa vowel /ə/ is realized in a range of unstressed contexts; for example, *rabbIT*, *boxES*, *commA*.

▨ One of the most characteristic features of falling diphthongs in Australia is the monophthongal [ɔ:] pronunciation for words such as *poor*, *moor*, *sure* and *tour*). (Note, if the [ʊə] glide occurs, it is generally following /j/, as in *cure*.)

Popular claims that people can identify someone's place of origin purely on the basis of how s/he speaks are exaggerated. As suggested earlier, accent differences are still not particularly striking. More likely, they are a matter of statistical tendency, with a certain pronunciation occurring more in one place than another. For example, speakers from Hobart and Melbourne are more likely to say *graph* with [æ]. Sydney and Brisbane speakers are more likely to pronounce the word with [a], and Adelaide and Perth speakers even more likely. However, as Bradley (1991) has shown, this is complex variation and the vowels do not occur uniformly across all words which could poten-tially have the same vowel; for example, many speakers in Melbourne say *c[æ]stle* but *gr[a]sp* and *contr[a]st*. The words that participate in this variation have [nasal + obstruent] or [fricative] following the vowel and Table 7.3 gives an idea of the lexical variation that exists between states.

Table 7.3 Percentage of [æ] in state capitals

Lexical Item	Hobart	Melbourne	Brisbane	Sydney	Adelaide
GRAPH	100	70	44	30	14
CHANCE	100	40	15	100	14
DEMAND	90	22	22	50	0
DANCE	90	65	89	93	14
CASTLE	40	70	67	0	14
GRASP	10	11	11	30	0
CONTRAST	0	0	0	9	29

Source: Based on Bradley 1991.

There are complex social and stylistic factors involved here and these also vary from city to city. The [a] variant tends to be more formal and belongs to a higher sociolect, especially for words with [nasal + obstruent]. Those speakers who attended a private (non-government) school are more likely to say *d[a]nce* and *pl[a]nt* and, if the situation is a more formal one, the likelihood of [a] is even greater. Everyone is likely to sing *adv[a]nce* in the national anthem ('Advance Australia Fair'), even if it is not their normal vowel in this word or in others (Bradley 2004: 647).

It is to be expected that regional differences will become increasingly more obvious. All it requires are three ingredients – time, physical/social distance and the processes of linguistic change. English-speaking settlement in Australia is recent (not yet 300 years), certainly not long in terms of language change. Yet the distances between Australian cities are considerable and regional chauvinism, as evident in the sort of strong rivalry between places like Sydney and Melbourne, is a major incentive for people to start highlighting their distinctiveness linguistically. The combination of these factors will inevitably give rise to more regional variation and the fact that there is no single prestige regional variety of the language in the country also means that, if groups want to be defined regionally, varieties are freer to go their separate ways. The separation of urban and rural communities looks to be inspiring some of the richest regional diversity. Between city and bush, there are some significant differences in terms of vocabulary, and particularly with respect to speed and also broadness of accent. For example, people in Melbourne tend to speak faster than those of the same socioeconomic background in surrounding rural areas. There is also a greater proportion of Broad speakers in the bush (cf. Bradley 2004).

The following are examples of changes involving the vowel systems of capital cities (cf. Cox and Palethorpe 2001, 2004; Bradley 2004; Horvath 2004; Clyne *et al.* 2006):

- The vowel in words such as *school* and *pool* tends to be more rounded in Adelaide than in other capitals, but here too there is much overlap between regional and social variation.
- There is vowel merging underway in pre-lateral environments. Melbourne and Brisbane share with New Zealand a neutralization of the [ɛ] and [æ] vowels before laterals. For many younger speakers, the words *shell* and *shall* are indistinguishable.
- Speakers in Hobart and Sydney are showing a merger of [i] and [ɪ], and also [u] and [ʊ] before laterals, with the tense vowels collapsing into the corresponding lax vowels; hence the words *deal* and *dill*; *fool* and *full* are not distinguished.

- In Melbourne there is evidence of a lowering of the vowel in words like *dress* to [æ] and an advancing of the vowel in words like *north* to a front variant of [ɔ].
- Melbourne speakers are lowering and retracting the vowel in words like *trap* towards [ɑ] (but not as far as in northern English or Scottish English).

There remains much work to be done on the emerging regional variation in AusE pronunciation. To date, only small parts of the country have been surveyed (largely on the eastern coast) and only a handful of regional differences have been noted.

Prosodic features

A striking prosodic feature of AusE varieties is the high rising contour on declarative clauses, especially common in narratives and descriptions. It goes by various names, but more usually High Rising Tone/Terminal (HRT) and Australian Questioning Intonation. Consider the following extract from a transcript of two teenage girls (M and B) talking about movies. The arrow (⇑) in M's speech indicates where the rising tones have occurred.

M: Oh were you there last night when we were watching ... [MTV]?
B: [Yeah]
M: and inside the house there's what's called a panic room ⇑
B: [mmm]
M: [so if] anything happens like ... there's like if someone tries to rob them or something, they run into the panic room ⇑ and lock themselves in the panic room, it's got like cameras all round the house, and ... no one can get into the panic room once the door's shut and stuff ⇑
B: And so the whole movie is about them ... being in the panic room \
M: Yeah but the thing is that the robbers that've come in ⇑ what they want is in the panic room with the people ⇑ what they want is in the panic room ⇑
B: oh =

(Recorded and transcribed by Debbie de Laps, December 2007; Burridge *et al.* 2009: 167–9 has the whole transcript)

Although this sort of questioning intonation is also found in North America and Britain, it has been stereotyped (and often stigmatized) as a distinctive pattern of AusE since the early 1960s when people first became aware of it. Although HRT is used by speakers of all ages and backgrounds, it is more prevalent in younger speakers, especially teenage working-class females (Horvath 2004: 639). Popular image also links HRT to young girls, and this is something that would encourage some males to move away from this usage – cultural stereotyping is a powerful influence on linguistic behaviour.

Early accounts of this phenomenon suggest that it was a marker of insecurity. However, as researchers now point out, the intonation pattern more usually occurs in the construction of extended turns and has a variety of functions to do with regulating conversational interaction and politeness. 'It elicits feedback from one's audience, checks to see if they understand what is being said, and secures their assent for an extended turn at talk for the speaker' (Guy and Vonwiller 1989: 33).

HRT appears to be on the increase. Fletcher and Loakes (2006a, 2006b), for example, examine the conversational data of 10 and 17 (respectively) females from Melbourne and surrounding rural districts in the eastern state of Victoria. Their studies confirm that uptalk is characteristic of the floor-holding intonational tunes of adolescents in south-eastern Australia and more abundantly so than was reported in Horvath (1985). They find little difference between rural and urban findings in this regard.

Grammatical features

This section focuses on those features that are genuinely AusE and those that are used either more or less frequently in this as opposed to other varieties. Particularly in focus are non-standard vernacular features. (See Szmrecsanyi and Kortmann 2009 for a discussion of grammatical structures that are common to vernaculars around the English-speaking world.) In Australia, these attributes tend to be more prevalent in rural areas, although it is difficult to talk about regionally defined variation in this case without appealing to social aspects. Basically, the higher up the social scale, the closer the speakers tend to be to the standard language; non-standard traits are more characteristic of the lower socioeconomic classes.

Pronouns

Colloquial AusE has the plural second-person pronoun forms that have become ubiquitous in the English-speaking world; namely, *yous* and *you guys* (***Yous'd*** *worked on it*).

A striking feature of vernacular Australian (most notably that spoken in Tasmania) is the appearance of gender marking on both animate and inanimate nouns (Pawley 2004). Items of food and drink, for instance, are feminine: *I put '****er*** [= the bottle of beer] *down that bloody quick that I blew the top off '****er***. *And* [he] *took '****er*** [= leg of lamb] *in and put '****er*** *on the plate.*

As elsewhere, *whom* is continuing to decline in favour of *who* in all varieties. It is stylistically highly marked and considered very formal.

AusE shows an overwhelming preference for oblique personal pronouns over the nominative following *than* (*He's bigger than* ***me***.) Preference for the accusative also extends to pronouns preceding the gerund participle (*He was angry at* ***me*** *scoring a goal*). These features are commonplace for standard speakers.

There are also non-standard pronoun forms more typical of vernacular varieties; for example, *them* in place of demonstrative *those* (*one of* ***them*** *things*); *me* in place of possessive *my* (*He's* ***me*** *youngest*); object forms in reflexive pronouns (*I thought to* ***meself***); object forms in coordinated pronouns (***Me*** *and Fred / Fred and* ***me*** *are coming too*; ***Me*** *and* ***her*** *were the last to go*); *us* in place of *me*, especially after verbs of giving and receiving (*Give* ***us*** *a light for me pipe*).

Nouns and noun phrases

A feature of vernacular AusE is the use of the adjective *old ~ ol'* before definite common nouns and personal names to refer to characters that are particularly salient in a narrative (*And on the corner was this* ***ol'*** *mountain duck with some little fellas, y'know*; cf. Pawley 2004).

Also commonplace in the vernacular varieties are doubly marked comparatives and superlatives (***most*** *rottenest*).

Verbs and verb phrases

AusE is showing the extended uses of the progressive that appear elsewhere; for example, in combination with stative verbs, such as *hear* and *think*.

Widespread use of the present perfect to simple past contexts of use, where other varieties prefer the simple past (*Then she's broken her leg*; cf. Ritz and Engel 2008).

Vernacular forms of AusE show *have*-deletion (*I ø only been there a couple of times*).

The use of the 'mandative subjunctive' is enjoying the same revival evident in America and Britain (*I insist that he be on time*).

AusE shows an increasing use of *of* in place of *have* after (preterite) modal verb forms *could*, *should* and *would* (*I would of waited*).

In Antipodean usage generally, only vestiges of *shall* usage remain, as more and more modal *will* encroaches on its territory, including first-person interrogatives (***Will** I call a taxi?*).

AusE follows the world-wide trend for *may* and *might* to be unmarked for tense. Both now indicate past possibility and hypothetical possibility (*I think he **might/may** come*).

Epistemic *mustn't* appears on the increase (*he **mustn't** have arrived yet* 'he can't have arrived yet').

AusE mirrors trends reported elsewhere for marginal modals, sharing with American usage a preference for *do*-support for *have (to), need (to), dare (to)* (*He **doesn't** need to leave*).

The omission of auxiliary *have* in vernacular varieties has meant that both *better* and *gotta* are showing modal-like behaviour (*we **better** go*; *you **gotta** do it*). This usage is considered colloquial and is rarely encountered in writing.

Trends suggest a growing use of the *get*-passive in writing and in speech, although it is still considered to be more informal than the *be* version (*He **got** arrested*).

As elsewhere, AusE shows the ongoing regularization processes that have been affecting strong verbs since Old English times. This levelling is particularly evident in the shift of strong verbs over to the weak (*show-showed-showed*) and the collapse of the preterite and past participle forms; in particular, past forms such as *came*, *did* and *saw* are being replaced by participle forms *come*, *done* and *seen* (e.g. *Me Mum seen it*). Occasionally the past form replaces the participle (*Someone might 'a **took** 'em*).

Vernacular varieties show invariant past tense forms for the verb *be* where *was* is used for all persons and for both singular and plural subjects (*You **was** late again*; *'Course they **was***). The use of invariant *is* (*Things **is** going crook*) appears to be in decline.

Singular marking in existentials with plural subjects is widespread among all speakers, especially in the contracted form (*There's fairies at the bottom of my garden*).

Speech shows an increased use of *gotten*, especially in intransitive constructions (*She's **gotten** really angry*).

Negation

Vernacular varieties have invariant *don't* in place of standard *doesn't* (*'E **don't** run away with it, y'see*), and also *aint* as an all-purpose negative auxiliary for *be* and *have*. Double negation is commonplace in vernacular speech, especially involving indeterminates (*I **never** said **nothing***). The use of *never* as a general negator in place of auxiliary plus *not* is also widespread (*You **never** opened it* 'You didn't open it').

Interrogatives

As elsewhere, AusE speakers can pose yes–no questions by rising intonation (*So, you want to become a benthic geologist?*).

Increasingly in evidence (also for standard speakers) is the invariant negative tag *isn't* (*You're going home soon, **isn't it**?*).

Composite sentences

Relative clauses with zero marking for subjects is widespread in the vernacular (*I knew a girl ø worked in an office down the street*).

The 'linking' relative clause is typical of speech (*[...] unless you get 88 **which** some universities are not going to give those marks*; cf. Reid 1997). These relatives elaborate on a stretch of discourse, often reiterating earlier information.

Distinctive cultural and discourse features

Australians have always regarded their colloquial idiom as being a significant part of their cultural identity. The standard language is more global in nature and many AusE speakers see their colloquialisms, nicknames, diminutives, swearing and insults to be important indicators of their Australianness and expressions of cherished ideals such as friendliness, nonchalance, mateship, egalitarianism and anti-authoritarianism (Wierzbicka 1992; Seal 1999; Stollznow 2004). This attachment to the vernacular can be traced back to the earliest settlements of English speakers. The language of convicts and free settlers alike was largely derived from the slang and dialect vocabularies of Britain. The 'vulgar' language of London and the industrial Midlands, the cant of convicts, the slang of seamen, whalers and gold-diggers contributed significantly to the linguistic melting pot in those early years. As Edward Wakefield wrote back in 1829:

> Hence, bearing in mind that our lowest class brought with it a peculiar language, and is constantly supplied with fresh corruption, you will understand why pure English is not, and is not likely to become, the language of the colony. This is not a very serious evil; and I mention it only to elucidate what follows.
>
> (Wakefield 1829: 106–7)

These sentiments were echoed in Desmond's condemnations of AusE:

> But, in addition to this lack of good-breeding and the gross mispronunciation of common English words, the Australian interlards his conversation with large quantities of slang, which make him frequently unintelligible to the visitor.
>
> (Desmond 1911: 20)

In the very early days, 'bad' language was an important way of fitting in and avoiding the label 'stranger' or 'new chum' (Gunn 1970: 51) and it continues to act as an in-group solidarity marker within a shared colloquial style. Allan and Burridge (2009) report that social swearing is the most usual type of swearing in the corpora they examined. A function of this 'bad language' is clearly stylistic – to spice up what is being said: to make it more vivid and memorable than straight-talking (or orthophemism). The following example comes from the Australian Corpus of English (ACE).

Don't phone me yet as I am having both my ears transplanted to my nuts so I can listen to you talk through your arse. (ACE S05 873)

Another, not unrelated aspect, is to display an attitude of emotional intensity towards what is being said or referred to.

Welfare, my arsehole. (ACE F10 1953)

Intensifiers such as *bloody* do not always convey an attitude of exasperation or disapproval, but may simply be a marker of excitement or exuberance. The following example comes from the Macquarie University talkback radio corpus (Australia-wide ABC and commercial radio stations; cf. Allan and Burridge 2009).

Did you hear about the new Irish Airways they just had they were allowed to come into Australia for the first time. Anyway they were flying into Perth n the conning tower there was a lotta cloud over the **bloody** skies n everything. N the conning tower called up he said Irish Airways Irish Airways he said you can't land yet we'll have to get you to circle round the airport so he says can you give me your height n position please. So the little Irish **bloody** pilot gets up n he says I'm five foot two n I'm sitting up the **bloody** front. (ART COMne2:[C5])

Though barely a taboo word in AusE, *bloody* still raises eyebrows in other parts of the English-speaking world, especially when it appears in the public arena. In 2006, Tourism Australia launched an international tourism campaign with a television advert showing images of everyday Australians set against a backdrop of famous landmarks and concluding with the ockerish Australian invitation *So where the bloody hell are you?* The ad managed to get itself banned from British TV and was censored in North America. (Cf. www.wherethebloodyhellareyou.com/)

Occasionally, expletives and taboo epithets are used so frequently that the expressions are bleached of their taboo quality and lose their standard force. The following example appears in the court case *Police v. Butler* (2003). The incident occurred outside the defendant's house at around 11.30 at night; he was intoxicated and is addressing the police and neighbours:

What the **fuck** are youse doing here. My **fuckin'** son had to get me out of bed. I can't believe youse are here. What the **fuck** are youse doing here?

I **fuckin'** know what this is about. It's about that **fuckin'** gas bottle. They can get **fucked**, I'm not paying them **fucking** nothing. They can get me our **fuckin'** bottle back [to the police about the neighbours].

We never had any **fuckin'** trouble till youse **fuckin'** moved here. **Youse** have **fuckin'** caused this trouble and called the **fuckin'** police on me [to the neighbours].
(*Police v. Butler* [2003] NSWLC 2 before Heilpern J, 14 June 2002)

In such examples, speakers use obscenities where others might use *like*, *well*, *you know*, and the like. This is not to suggest that such bleached swearwords are empty. Like other discourse particles, these expressions convey subtle nuances of meaning and can have complex effects on utterances. Wierzbicka (2002), for example, describes the various meanings of *bloody* in AusE and shows how they provide important clues to Australian attitudes and values.

Ethnic variation within Australia

> We are, after all, a microcosm of the world in its cultural diversity
>
> (Clyne 2005: 181)

There have been additional changes to AusE that go beyond breaking free of Britain and British norms and any discussion of the language must include mention of the bur-geoning socially defined variation in the country. Ethnicity is a crucial part of social identity – something that people want to demonstrate through their use of language – and multicultural Australia is seeing a flourishing of ethnocultural varieties or ethnolects.

Background

Well before English-speakers settled in Australia, the country was already linguistically diverse. The following shows the approximate numbers of Aboriginal dialects, languages and language families at the time of earliest European contact.

Language families	26–29
Languages	200–250
Dialects	500–700

(Figures based on Eagleson *et al*. 1982: 31)

As earlier described, the first English-speaking arrivals were largely prisoners, prison officers and their families. Free settlers came mainly from Britain and Ireland but didn't reach significant numbers until the mid nineteenth century. By the second half of this century the population had started to become more diverse. The gold rushes of the 1850s and the influx of large numbers of Chinese miners introduced a significant Asian presence for the first time. Statistics published by the Department of Immigration and Multicultural Affairs (DIMA) give the following breakdown for notable population groups born overseas at time of the Federation of the colonies (1901): United Kingdom (57.7 per cent); Ireland (21.5 per cent); Germany (4.5 per cent); China (3.5 per cent); New Zealand (3.0 per cent); Sweden (1.5 per cent). At this time the main languages (in addition to indigenous languages) were English, Welsh, Irish Gaelic, Scots Gaelic, German, French, Italian, Chinese and Scandinavian languages.

The introduction of the Immigration Restriction Act 1901 (excluding non-European migrants) had a negative impact on the levels of migration to Australia. DIMA statistics show that in 1947 only 9.8 per cent of the Australian population was born overseas. However, with immigration programs post World War II, the trend reversed and by 1954 the proportion of the Australian population born overseas had increased to 14.3 per cent. Most significant was the rise in immigrants from countries where English was not the first language. In 1901 the proportion of the overseas-born population from non-English-speaking countries was 17 per cent (of 857,576); in 1947 the numbers had risen to 20 per cent (of 744,187) and by 1954 to 44 per cent (of 1,286,466).

In more recent times, these figures have increased dramatically, clearly spurred on by the effects of globalization and economic development. Massive flows of people, including tourists, migrants and refugees have produced an intermixing of people and cultures that is unprecedented. At the time of the 2006 census, 4.4 million people (a quarter of Australia's population) were born overseas, with 47 per cent coming from Europe and 27 per cent from Asia. Some 80 per cent settled in major cities and, as new languages continue to arrive, these urban centres are seeing a constant expansion of multilingualism (Clyne 2009). This is having the effect of intensifying urban and rural differences.

Despite the multilingual and multicultural population in Australia, the pattern has been one of ongoing language attrition and shift to English (Clyne *et al.* 2001). For the Indigenous communities, this has involved wholesale extinction of many languages. Although around 145 of the original 200–250 languages remain today, according to the National Indigenous Languages Survey in 2005, 19 have more than 500 speakers, 45 between 10 and 50 speakers, and 67 fewer than 10 speakers. Even the remaining robust languages are under threat, despite vigorous efforts being made to maintain them. It has been estimated that the number of surviving languages might decline by as much as 50 per cent, as the most critically endangered languages lose their last speakers in the next 20–30 years.

Ethnic varieties of dominant languages can become potent markers of a group's identity, especially in the face of language attrition (cf. Giles 1979). As each of these language groups seeks to assert its own identity, different ethnic varieties of AusE start to take on symbolic significance, with migrant and Aboriginal features becoming an important means of signalling the group boundaries.

Migrant ethnolects

Horvath's 1985 study of Sydney speech indicated that Italian and Greek teenagers were choosing to distance themselves from the linguistic patterns of their parents, pre-sumably because Ethnic Broad had become so highly stigmatized and these speakers did not want to be typecast as working class and migrant. (For some time the variety had been providing lampooning fodder for comedians; e.g. media stereotypes like Con the Fruiterer, Effie and Wogboys.) Recent studies show that second-generation Aus-tralians of non-English-speaking background are developing an AusE of their own, different from the Ethnic Broad-accented English of their parents, but different also from General AusE. Cox and Palethorpe (2006), for example, describe the features of the new ethnolect that is used by Australian-born speakers of Lebanese background (so-called Lebanese AusE or Lebspeak). This is variation that is not necessarily the result of second language learning; in other words, these ethnolects cannot be described as foreign-accented AusE – many speakers now have English as their first language.

Interestingly, work by Warren (1999) suggests that the second generation may also adopt hyperdialectal elements of Ethnic Broad to use as an in-group code, a marker of non-Anglo ethnicity. This variety is a kind of stylized multiethnolect, a pan-ethnic variety, which Warren calls 'Wogspeak'.

> Some young people of the second generation adopt a distinctive accent and speech patterns which distinguish them both from their parents' values and from those of the Anglo host culture, in their search for 'a place to speak'.
>
> (Warren 1999: 89)

Aboriginal English and Aboriginal creoles

Not long after the arrival of the Europeans in Australia, there appeared pidgin varieties. These became increasingly important for contact, not only between Aboriginal speakers and English speakers, but also as a lingua franca between speakers of different Aboriginal languages. In areas where these pidgin varieties stabilized, creoles evolved (the Kimberley region, the Roper River area and parts of north Queensland). These various English-based creoles have much in common, but they also show some regional differences, depending on the Aboriginal languages represented in the community where the pidgin originated and also influences from other pidgins and creoles brought into Australia from the outside.

Aboriginal English (AbE) is an ethnolect that grew out of this original contact situation and is now maintained in Indigenous Australian communities across Australia. The interaction between AbE and creoles is complex. The varieties range from something that is virtually identical to Standard AusE in everything but accent (the 'acrolect') through to pure creole that is so remote from Standard AusE as to be mutually unintelligible (the 'basilect'). Midway between these two polar extremes is an array of speech varieties (or 'mesolects'). Generally speakers are able to move along the continuum and alter their speech to suit situation and audience.

In his description of the linguistic variation within the Aboriginal and Torres Strait Islander speech communities, Malcolm (2004a: 668) examines the educational implications, especially the need for a better integration of these Englishes into school learning.

> Although school systems are beginning to recognize the fact that creoles and Aboriginal English may be coherent linguistic systems, there is still a reluctance to allow them any significant place in the development of school literacy. It is assumed that literacy skills in St(andard) E(nglish) will be best acquired by concentrating only on that variety, despite research evidence of the relevance of home language to effective learning of standard varieties.

AbE differs from AusE at all linguistic levels, including pragmatics. In accent, there is a continuum from a 'heavy' or basilectal accent (close to the sound system of traditional Aboriginal languages) to a 'light' acrolectal accent (close to the sound system of AusE; cf. Harkins 2000; Malcolm 2004a). Lexical differences can be striking: some words are borrowed directly from Aboriginal languages (e.g. *gubba* 'white man'); familiar-looking English words can have quite different meanings (e.g. the future marker *got to/gotta*, *sorry business* 'ceremony associated with death'); some early English words are maintained (*gammon* 'joking, pretending', eighteenth-century cant). The opportunities for misunderstandings are considerable; cf. Sharifian (2008) on the different meanings of *sorry* in AbE and mainstream AusE. Miscommunication also arises from the differences in communication strategies. Aboriginal speakers' strategies for eliciting information are far more indirect than those of Anglo-Australians; silence also has an important role in Aboriginal communities and is frequently misinterpreted by outsiders (Eades 1994, 2000). Eades (1993, 1994, 1996) and Koch (1985) show that these differences can have serious implications in legal cases.

The grammar of AbE has many creole-like grammatical features that are sometimes very unEnglish-looking. There is, however, a lot of variation between speakers. The following examples (from Malcolm 2004b) illustrate some of the most distinctive features. Many of them are found in other non-standard dialects; some are shared with creoles:

- Omission of prepositions where they are required in the standard (*Afela going ø Back Beach* 'We're going to Back Beach'). Extreme varieties close to the creole end of the continuum also replace locative prepositions with *la* or *longa* (*We always go la ol' town* 'We always go to the old town').
- A range of different negative constructions, many shared with other non-standard varieties (*I **never** see **no** spirits*). The adverbs *not* and *nomore* commonly appear front of the verb for general negation (*Nail **not** float* 'The nail doesn't float').
- Widespread use of simplified tags such as *isn't it, init, ini, ana* and *na*. Another tag that AbE shares with other vernaculars is *eh*, as in *He can walk, **eh?***
- Substitution of relative particle *what* for *that* (*I got one mate **what** goes to a Catholic school*).
- Possession marked by juxtaposition (*That my Daddy car*). In those varieties most influenced by neighbouring creoles, the possessor follows the possessed and is connected with a marker like *belong* (*Gun **belong** to Hedley*).
- Extensive regularization of verb morphology in urban and rural varieties. The unmarked verb is frequently used for copula and auxiliary *be* (*I **be** cold*). Zero marking for third person is also usual for verbs in present tense (*He **get** wild* 'he gets/got wild'). As the last gloss illustrates, the verb can be unmarked for past tense, especially if past time is already established.
- Where past tense marking occurs, levelling of preterite and past participle verb forms for strong verbs (*seen, done, come, run* as past tense). There are also some irregular strong verb forms such as *brang* and *brung*. In regional and urban areas, doubly marked past tense forms are common (*camed, didn't stayed*). Occasionally the creole past tense marker *bin* (or *been*) is used (*We never **been** la court* 'We didn't go to court').
- Varieties spoken in remote communities show evidence of the creole transitive verb suffix *-em* or *-im* (*We see**im** buffalo got big horn* 'We saw a buffalo with big horns').
- An array of non-standard adverb-forming suffixes (e.g. *long-way, late-time*).
- Inconsistent marking for number. The plural inflection is often absent when plurality is obvious, either from context or via some other means (*Two **man** in a jeep* 'There are two men in a jeep'). Where plural does occur, irregular nouns may be doubly marked (*childr**ens***). Occasionally the creole plural marker *-mob* is used (*clean water-**mob*** 'lots of clean water').

In AbE discourse long loosely connected structures are the norm and there is little in the way of subordination. Clausal markers are often absent, as in *I bin go dere work* (with missing complementizer). This variety also has a type of verb-chaining construction where two main verbs are linked (with or without conjunction) to express both an activity and a motion that is closely associated with that activity (*They go there chargin on don't they*; *Nother mob go down long creek and go and drink water*). Another feature of AbE discourse is expressive word order. Especially striking is the repetition of phrases and sentences and speech exchanges full of highly topic-oriented structures such as left-dislocation (*The policeman he heard this banging*) and right-dislocation (*E got lots of trucks an cars, toy one*). While paratactic structures and expressive word order are typical of spontaneous spoken language generally, it is the relative frequency and the special combination of these features that make this variety different from others.

'Americanization' of AusE

Given the global presence of the United States and the inevitable loosening of ties between Britain and its former Antipodean colonies, it would be surprising if there were not some sort of linguistic steamrolling going on. There are identifiable American influences on teenage slang and, more generally on teenage culture; yet the impact elsewhere on the language is minimal. Despite this, news articles, letters to the editor and talkback calls on the radio continue to rail against 'ugly Americanisms' (many of which, in fact, are not Americanisms at all). The following extracts come from the many written complaints I have received on this matter:

> I have just heard your discourse on the Americanisation of English of ABC Wide Bay. I am one of the population who is *very much against* this phenomenon, particularly on the Australian Broadcasting Corporation … If the offenders are so enamoured of the American language that they have to inflict these words on the Australian listeners, they should be made redundant, emigrate to the United States of America, and go get paid by the American Broadcasting Commission.
>
> (Letter, 4 September 2008)

> People generally seem to be quite happy to let English deteriorate into a kind of abbreviated American juvenile dialect, but I'm not. I'll continue resist incorrect grammar and American English.
>
> (Email, 1 March 2008)

As is always the case, such lay concerns about language usage are not based on genuine linguistic worries, but reflect deeper and more general social judgements. Hostility towards American usage is born of linguistic insecurity in the face of a cultural, political and economic superpower; American English usage poses a threat to authentic 'downunder English' and is tabooed.

Conclusion

Australia, like New Zealand, has a relatively recent history of European settlement and English language development. Yet it is already quite distinct. The different mixes of original dialects that came in during the early years, as well as the physical separation from other English-speaking regions, have allowed this distinctiveness to flourish. Regional variation within Australia is still minor compared to other varieties, although with time local differences have been increasing. The separation of urban and rural communities currently looks to be inspiring the most notable regional diversity. Contact with languages other than English is seeing the rise, particularly in recent years, of new multicultural identities for AusE in the form of migrant ethnolects. Varieties of AbE and creoles have also been adding vibrant new socially relevant dimensions to these 'Extra-territorial Englishes' in Australia.

Suggestions for further reading

Australian Journal of Linguistics (2003) 23 (2). (Special issue devoted to the development of English in Australia.)

Fritz, Clemens W.A. (2007) *From English in Australia to Australian English, 1788–1900*, Frankfurt am Main: Peter Lang. (A corpus-based account of the evolution of English in Australia.)

Leitner, Gerhard (2004) *Australia's Many Voices: Ethnic Englishes, Indigenous and Migrant Languages. Policy and Education* and *Australia's Many Voices: Australian English – The National Language* (two volumes), Berlin: Mouton de Gruyter. (This presents a comprehensive survey of the Australian language habitat.)

Zion, Lawrie (2007) *The Sounds of Aus*, Australia: Film Finance Corporation Australia and Princess Pictures. (A generally available documentary on the Australian accent, presented by comedian John Clarke.)

Macquarie Dictionary Word Map. Online. Available www.abc.net.au/wordmap (A useful online mapping resource for lexical regionalisms.)

References

Allan, Keith and Burridge, Kate (2009) 'Swearing and taboo language in Australian English', in P. Peters, P. Collins and Adam Smith (eds) *Comparative Grammatical Studies in Australian and New Zealand English*, Amsterdam: John Benjamins.

Bradley, D. (1991) '/æ/ and /a:/ in Australian English', in J. Cheshire (ed) *English Around the World: Sociolinguistic Perspectives*, Cambridge: Cambridge University Press, pp. 227–34.

——(2004) 'Regional characteristics of Australian English: phonology', in E.W. Schneider, K. Burridge, B. Kortmann, R. Mesthrie and C. Upton (eds), *A Handbook of Varieties of English, Vol. 1: Phonology*, Berlin: Mouton de Gruyter, pp. 645–55.

Bradley, D. and Bradley, M. (2001) 'Changing attitudes to Australian English', in D. Blair and P. Collins (eds) *English in Australia*, Amsterdam: John Benjamins, pp. 271–85.

Bryant, P. (1997) 'A dialect survey of the lexicon of Australian English', *English World-wide*, 18 (2): 211–41.

Burridge, K. (in press) '"A peculiar language": the linguistic evidence for early Australian English', in R. Hickey (ed.) *Varieties in Writing: The Written Word as Linguistic Evidence*, Amsterdam: John Benjamins.

Burridge, K., Clyne, M. and de Laps, D. (2009) *Living Lingo (VCE English Language Units 3 and 4)*, Collingwood: Victorian Association for the Teaching of English.

Churchill, W. (1911) *Beach-la-Mar: The Jargon or Trade-speech of the Western Pacific*, Washington: Carnegie Institute of Washington Publication (No. 154).

Clyne, M. (2005) *Australia's Language Potential*, Sydney: University of New South Wales Press.

——(2009) 'What is urban and suburban about multilingualism in Australia', paper presented to the Inaugural Language and Society Centre Annual Roundtable, Monash University, 19 February.

Clyne, M., Eisikovits, E. and Tollfree, L. (2001) 'Ethnic varieties of Australian English', in D. Blair and P. Collins (eds) *English in Australia*, Amsterdam: John Benjamins, pp. 223–8.

Clyne, M., Fletcher, J., Loakes, D. and Tollfree, L. (2006) 'Australian English vowels: variation in young Melbourne English speakers', unpublished ms.

Collins, P. and Peters, P. (2004) 'Australian English: morphology and syntax', in B. Kortmann, K. Burridge, R. Mesthrie, E.W. Schneider and C. Upton (eds) *A Handbook of Varieties of English, Vol. 2: Morphology and Syntax*, Berlin: Mouton de Gruyter, pp. 593–611.

Cox, F.M. (2006) 'Australian English pronunciation into the 21st century', *Australian Journal of TESOL*, 21: 3–21.

Cox, F.M. and Palethorpe, S. (2001) 'The changing face of Australian English vowels', in D.B. Blair and P. Collins (eds) *Varieties of English Around the World: English in Australia*, Amsterdam: John Benjamins, pp. 17–44.

——(2004) 'The border effect: vowel differences across the NSW/Victorian border', in C. Moskovsky (ed.) *Proceedings of the 2003 Conference of the Australian Linguistics Society*, 1–14. Online. Available www.als.asn.au (accessed 26 February 2010).

——(2006) 'Some phonetic characteristics of Lebanese Australian English', paper presented to the Australian Linguistic Society Conference, University of Queensland, 7–9 July.

Desmond, Valerie (1911) *The Awful Australian*, Sydney: John Andrew.

Dixon, R.M.W., Moore, B., Ramson, W.S. and Thomas, M. (1992) *Australian Aboriginal Words in English: Their Origin and Meaning*, Melbourne: Oxford University Press Australia.

Eades, D. (1993) 'The case for Condren: Aboriginal English, pragmatics and the law', *Journal of Pragmatics*, 20: 141–62.

——(1994) 'A case of communicative clash: Aboriginal English and the legal system', in J. Gibbons (ed.) *Language and the Law*, London: Longman, pp. 234–64.

——(1996) 'Legal recognition of cultural differences in communication: the case of Robyn Kina', *Language and Communication*, 16: 215–27.

——(2000) 'I don't think it's an answer to the question: silencing Aboriginal witnesses in court', *Language in Society*, 29 (2): 161–96.

Eagleson, R.D., Kaldor, S. and Malcolm, I.G. (1982) *English and the Aboriginal Child*, Canberra: Curriculum Development Centre.

Fletcher, J. and Loakes, D. (2006a) 'Intonational variation in adolescent conversational speech: rural versus urban patterns', in R. Hoffman and H. Mixdorff (eds) *Speech Prosody*, Dresden: TUD Press.

——(2006b) 'Patterns of rising and falling in Australian English', in P. Warren and C.I. Watson (eds) *Proceedings of the 11th Australian International Conference on Speech Science and Technology 2006*, Auckland: University of Auckland, pp. 42–7.

Giles, H. (1979) 'Ethnicity markers in speech', in K.R. Scherer and H. Giles (eds) *Social Markers in Speech*, Cambridge: Cambridge University Press, pp. 251–89.

Grose, (Captain) F. (1783/1811) *Dictionary of the Vulgar Tongue*, London.

Gunn, J.S. (1970) 'Twentieth-century Australian idiom', in W.S. Ransom (ed.) *English Transported: Essays on Australasian English*, Canberra: Australian National University Press, pp. 49–67.

Guy, G. and Vonwiller, J. (1989) 'The high rising tone in Australian English', in P. Collins and D. Blair (eds), *Australian English: The Language of a New Society*, St Lucia: University of Queensland Press, pp. 21–34.

Harkins, J. (2000) 'Structure and meaning in Australian Aboriginal English', *Asian Englishes*, 3 (2): 60–81.

Horvath, B. (1985) *Variation in Australian English: The Sociolects of Sydney*, Cambridge: Cambridge University Press.

——(2004) 'Australian English: phonology', in E.W Schneider, K. Burridge, B. Kortmann, R. Mesthrie and C. Upton (eds) *A Handbook of Varieties of English, Vol. 1: Phonology*, Berlin: Mouton de Gruyter, pp. 625–44.

Koch, Harold (1985) 'Non-standard English in an Aboriginal land claim', in J.B. Pride (ed) *Cross-Cultural Encounters: Communication and Miscommunication*, Melbourne: River Seine, pp. 176–95.

Malcolm, I.G. (2004a) 'Australian creoles and Aboriginal English: phonology', in E.W. Schneider, K. Burridge, B. Kortmann, R. Mesthrie and C. Upton (eds) *A Handbook of Varieties of English, Vol. 1: Phonology*, Berlin: Mouton de Gruyter, pp. 656–70.

——(2004b) 'Australian creoles and Aboriginal English: morphology and syntax', in B. Kortmann, K. Burridge, R. Mesthrie, E.W. Schneider and C. Upton (eds) *A Handbook of Varieties of English, Vol. 2: Morphology and Syntax*, Berlin: Mouton de Gruyter, pp. 657–81.

Mitchell, A.G. (2003) 'The story of Australian English: users and environment', *Australian Journal of Linguistics*, 23 (2): 111–28.

Mitchell, A.G and Delbridge, A. (1965) *The Speech of Australian Adolescents*, Sydney: Angus and Robertson.

Moore, B. (2008) *Speaking our Language: The Story of Australian English*, Oxford: Oxford University Press.

Pawley, Andrew (2004) 'Australian vernacular English: some grammatical characteristics', in B. Kortmann, K. Burridge, R. Mesthrie, E. Schneider and C. Upton (eds) *A Handbook of Varieties of English, Vol. 2: Morphology and Syntax*, Berlin: Mouton de Gruyter, pp. 611–42.

Peters, P. (2005) *The Cambridge Australian English Style Guide*, Melbourne: Cambridge University Press.

Ramson, W.S. (ed.) (1988) *The Australian National Dictionary: A Dictionary of Australianisms on Historical Principles*, Melbourne: Oxford University Press.

Reid, J. (1997) 'Relatives and their relatives – relative clauses in conversational Australian English', unpublished PhD thesis, La Trobe University.

Ritz, M. and Engel, D. (2008) 'Vivid narrative use and the present perfect in spoken Australian English', *Linguistics*, 46 (1): 131–60.

Schneider, Edgar W. (2007) *Postcolonial English: Varieties around the World*, Cambridge: Cambridge University Press.

Seal, G. (1999) *The Lingo: Listening to Australian English*, Sydney: University of New South Wales Press.

Sharifian, Farzad (2008) 'Saying "Sorry" and being sorry', *Lingua Franca* (broadcast 19 July). Online. Available www.abc.net.au/rn/linguafranca/stories/2008/2305483.htm (accessed 21 September 2009).

Simpson, J. (2004) 'Hypocoristics in Australian English', in B. Kortmann, K. Burridge, R. Mesthrie, E. Schneider and C. Upton (eds) *A Handbook of Varieties of English, Vol. 2: Morphology and Syntax*, Berlin: Mouton de Gruyter, pp. 643–56.

Stollznow, K. (2004) 'Whinger! Wowser! Wanker! Aussie English: deprecatory language and the Australian ethos', in C. Moskovsky (ed.) *Proceedings of the 2003 Conference of the Australian Linguistics Society*, 1–14. Online. Available www.als.asn.au (accessed 26 February 2010).

Szmrecsanyi, B. and Kortmann, B. (2009) 'Vernacular universals and Angloversals in a typological perspective', in M. Filppula, J. Klemola and H. Paulasto (eds) *Vernacular Universals and Language Contacts: Evidence from Varieties of English and Beyond*, New York: Routledge, pp. 33–56.

The Australian Oxford Dictionary (1999) Melbourne: Oxford University Press.

The Macquarie Dictionary (2005) (4th edition), Macquarie Library, Macquarie University, NSW.

Tollfree, L. (2001) 'Variation and change in Australian English consonants: reduction of /t/', in D. Blair and P. Collins (eds) *English in Australia*, Amsterdam: John Benjamins, pp. 45–67.

Trudgill, P. (2004) *New-Dialect Formation: The Inevitability of Colonial Englishes*, Oxford: Oxford University Press.

Wakefield, Edward Gibbon (1829) 'A letter from Sydney: the principal town of Australasia', published by J. Cross (original from the New York Public Library; digitized 25 September 2007). Online. Available www.archive.org/details/aletterfromsydn00gouggoog (accessed 6 November 2009).

Warren, J. (1999) '"Wogspeak". Transformations of Australian English', *Journal of Australian Studies*, 62: 86–94.

Wierzbicka, A. (1991) *Cross-cultural Pragmatics: The Semantics of Human Interaction*, Berlin: Mouton de Gruyter.

——(1992) *Semantics, Culture, and Cognition: Universal Human Concepts in Culture-specific Configurations*, New York: Oxford University Press.

——(2002) 'Australian cultural scripts: *bloody* revisited', *Journal of Pragmatics*, 34: 1167–209.

Yallop, C. (2003) 'A.G. Mitchell and the development of Australian pronunciation', *Australian Journal of Linguistics*, 23 (2): 129–42.

8

The English(es) of New Zealand

Margaret Maclagan

Introduction

New Zealand English (NZE), like the other varieties of English discussed in the first section of this Handbook, falls into Kachru's category of 'inner circle' Englishes (Kachru 1992). NZE is the youngest of the inner circle Englishes, and is unique in that recorded evidence is available for its entire history. We are thus able to track the paths by which the English dialects brought by the early immigrants coalesced so that speakers born in the 1870s spoke a variety that is recognizable as NZE.

Historical background of NZ

New Zealand (NZ) is one of the most isolated countries in the world, with the closest country, Australia, being 1,600 km away. The indigenous people of NZ, the Maori, arrived in the country approximately 800 years ago from eastern Polynesia. The first European whalers and sealers arrived towards the end of the eighteenth century followed by a small steady stream of other Europeans (or *Pakeha* – the now widely used Maori term).

In 1840 the Treaty of Waitangi, signed by representatives of Queen Victoria and many Maori chiefs, gave Britain sovereignty over New Zealand; Maori ownership of land and traditional food resources were recognized and they were accorded the rights and privileges of British subjects. Although the treaty was not fully honoured, it still provides the basis of Maori/Pakeha relationships today. After the signing of the Treaty of Waitangi, the European population increased rapidly from 2,000 in 1840 to half a million in 1881, half of whom were New Zealand born. The Europeans quickly outnumbered Maori, whose numbers were greatly reduced by new diseases and by the use of muskets in inter-tribal warfare. By 1900, the Maori population had decreased to 46,000 and many people thought the race was dying out. However, since then the Maori population has gradually increased, numbering 565,329 in the 2006 census (14.6 per cent of the total NZ population) (Statistics New Zealand 2007a).

After 1840, the European settlers arrived in three major waves. The first wave formed five planned settlements organized by the New Zealand Company at Wellington, Nelson, New Plymouth, Otago and Canterbury. The next wave of immigrants arrived when gold was discovered in Central Otago. Thousands of miners poured into Otago and Westland, including many Irish who had been excluded by the New Zealand Company, and also some Chinese. The third wave of settlers arrived in the 1870s, when the government offered assisted passages. More than 100,000 people arrived through this scheme.

According to the 1871 census figures, most of the nineteenth-century immigrants to NZ came from the British Isles, with 51 per cent coming from England, mainly from the south east. The English migrants settled throughout the country, whereas the Irish (22 per cent) settled mainly in Auckland and on the west coast of the South Island and most Scots (27 per cent) went to Otago and Southland. Only 6.5 per cent were Australian born, but this figure greatly underestimates the influence of Australia on early NZ because there was a great deal of shipping traffic between the two countries, and many immigrants came to NZ via Australia. Immigration in the nineteenth century provided the melting pot in which NZE was created. Later immigration seems to have had relatively little effect on the New Zealand language.

In the latter part of the twentieth century, Pacific Islanders were encouraged to come to New Zealand, mainly to fill low-wage jobs. The term *Pasifika* is used in NZ to describe people of Pacific origins. In the 2006 census, 7.3 per cent of New Zealanders gave their ethnicity as one or other of the Pasifika groups. Asian immigrants also increased sharply since 1990, making up slightly more than 5 per cent of the total NZ population of 3,860,163 in 2006. By early in 2009, the NZ population had risen to just over 4 million (Statistics New Zealand 2007a, 2007b, 2007c). For more detailed information on NZ history, see Sinclair (1991) and King (2003); on the origins of early immigrants, see Gordon *et al.* (2004: Chapter 3).

Development of NZE

New Zealand is unusual in having recordings of people who were born in the country as early as the 1850s and were thus among the first generation of European people born in NZ. These recordings were collected between 1946 and 1948 by the Mobile Disc Recording Unit of the New Zealand Broadcasting Service and kept by Radio NZ Sound Archives (www.soundarchives.co.nz/). They form the basis of a research project on the Origins and Evolution of New Zealand English at the University of Canterbury (ONZE) which has studied the development of New Zealand English (see Gordon *et al.* 2004, 2007).

Speakers born in the 1850s and the early 1860s preserved the accents of their parents; some sound Scottish or Irish. Some speakers born in the late 1860s have mixed accents with some unusual sound combinations. Mr Malcolm Ritchie, for example, who was born in 1866 and whose parents came from Scotland, grew up in Cromwell on the Otago goldfields. He has Scottish features, including the aspirated [hw] pronunciation for words like *white*, but also has /h/-dropping on content words. The combination of aspiration on <wh> and /h/-dropping would not have occurred in British dialects at that time.

Characteristics of a NZ accent start to appear with speakers born in the 1870s. The ONZE project found that there were differences between speakers who lived in towns with mixed populations and people who lived in homogeneous settlements (Gordon *et al.*

2004). The earliest form of the New Zealand accent is found in South Island gold-mining towns made up of similar numbers of settlers from England, Scotland, Ireland and Australia. In close-by places settled primarily by people from Scotland, speakers continued to have Scottish features in their speech for several generations (see Trudgill *et al.* 2003).

Complaints about an emerging New Zealand accent (or 'colonial twang', as it was called) are found in writings from about 1900 and commentators then (and later) frequently claimed it was a transported form of the London dialect of Cockney (e.g. Wall 1951). This theory, and the later theory that New Zealand English was a variety transported from Australia, can be challenged on linguistic and demographic grounds (see Gordon *et al.* 2004: Chapter 4). The view of researchers today is that the New Zealand accent was formed within New Zealand in a relatively short space of time between 1870 and 1890.

The patterns found by the ONZE Project generally fit Trudgill's theories of New Dialect formation (Trudgill 2004). After an initial period of accommodation, there was a period of great variation both within individual speakers and between speakers. The final period of focusing occurred when the variation diminished and the eventual form of the dialect emerged.

Trudgill also developed a determinism theory for the origins of New Zealand English (Trudgill *et al.* 2000) which claims that the final outcome of the New Zealand accent was determined not by social influences but by settlement patterns. The reason that modern New Zealand English is most like the English of the south east of England is because most of the early settlers came from this area, so the accent was determined by the majority. Nevertheless, social factors affected the speed with which the accent emerged in specific places.

The earliest references to the New Zealand accent always involved children. It is significant that the time when the accent was developing coincided with the introduction of a national free compulsory primary education system, with the Education Act of 1877. Children from different backgrounds coming together in schools would have accelerated new dialect development.

Description of NZE

Phonology

Consonants

The NZE consonant inventory does not differ from that of other inner circle Englishes. Apart from a small area in the south of the South Island where there was originally a high proportion of Scottish settlers, NZE is non-rhotic. However both linking /r/, as in *car alarm*, and intrusive /r/ as *law r and order* occur commonly. Intrusive /r/ occurs after the THOUGHT vowel /ɔ/, and more recently with the MOUTH diphthong, /aʊ/. Phrases like *now and then* or *now is the hour*, that used to be pronounced with a linking /w/, are now often heard with an intrusive /r/, /naɹ ən ðen/.

/l/ is relatively dark, even in word initial position. In word final position and pre-consonantally, /l/ is regularly vocalized. Vocalized coda /l/ affects the previous vowel, so that contrasts that are available in other positions are neutralized before /l/. DRESS and TRAP do not contrast before /l/, so that *celery* and *salary* sound identical, as do the names *Ellen*, *Alan* and *Helen*. LOT and GOAT are not contrastive before /l/, so that *doll* and *dole* sound the same, and KIT and GOOSE are farther back before /l/ so that KIT, FOOT, GOOSE and THOUGHT may be distinguished by vowel length if at all. It is almost impossible to distinguish between single word productions of *fill*, *full*, *fool* and *fall* in NZE.

Intervocalic /t/ may be flapped in words like *butter* or phrases like *got it*. Final plosives can be glottally reinforced, but intervocalic voiceless plosives are not usually replaced by a glottal stop. TH-fronting, whereby /θ/ and /ð/ are realized as /f/ and /v/, is common among children and becoming more common among young adults, as is tr-affrication, whereby /tr/, /dr/, and /str/ become affricated, so that tree is [tʃɹi], *dream* is [dʒɹim] and *street* is [ʃtɹit]. However, the labio-dental /r/, [ʋ], that is common in Britain is not heard in NZ. NZE is an /h/-full variety of English, pronouncing /h/ in all content words (except some from French, like *honour*), including words like *herb* where American English speakers usually do not sound the /h/.

Vowels

The NZE accent is carried mainly by the vowels. Early complaints about the 'colonial twang' focused particularly on the diphthongs MOUTH and PRICE, followed quickly by FACE and GOAT. NZE has diphthong shift and glide weakening in these diphthongs (Wells 1982), so that PRICE is usually realized as [ɑə] or [ɔe] in a broader accent, FACE as [ae] or [ɒe] in a broader accent, and GOAT as [əʉ] or [ɐʉ] in a broader accent. MOUTH is losing its rounded second element, especially in closed syllables like *loud*, so that it is usually realized as [æə] or [ɛə] in broader NZE. The broader versions of these diphthongs are socially stigmatized and avoided especially by higher social class women.

Figure 8.1 shows the F1–F2 vowel space for ten NZ males and ten NZ females born around 1970. As in Australian English, the NURSE vowel /ɜ/, is raised and rounded in NZE, almost approaching [ö], START /a/ and STRUT /ʌ/ are distinguished by length, both being open and front of central [ɐ], and GOOSE is central [ʉ] except before /l/.

However, the short front vowels are very different from those of Australian English. The most distinctive of the front vowels is the KIT vowel, /ɪ/, which is centralized and lowered especially by the women. The most common pronunciation for KIT is [ə], with [ɐ] or even more open versions being heard from broader NZE speakers. The Australian and NZ pronunciations of the KIT vowel contrast greatly, with the phrase *fish and chips* being stereotypical. New Zealanders are caricatured as saying *fush and chups* and Australians, *feesh and cheeps*. DRESS and TRAP have raised over the development of NZE (Gordon *et al.* 2004) and, unlike the current trend in Australian English, both continue to raise. For the women in Figure 8.1, DRESS is almost as high as FLEECE, and the two vowels are no longer always distinguished by length (Maclagan and Hay 2007). FLEECE is, however, becoming more diphthongized. For some speakers in the ONZE corpora, DRESS is now higher and more front than FLEECE and has become the high front vowel.

GOOSE has centralized and THOUGHT /ɔ/ has raised so that THOUGHT is the high back vowel for NZE. In addition, THOUGHT usually has an off-glide so that it is realized as [ɔə], especially in open syllables as in *door*, *flaw*, but also in closed syllables like *flawed*.

The other distinguishing feature of the NZE vowel system is the ongoing merger of the NEAR /iə/ and SQUARE diphthongs /eə/. Most younger New Zealanders pronounce both

155

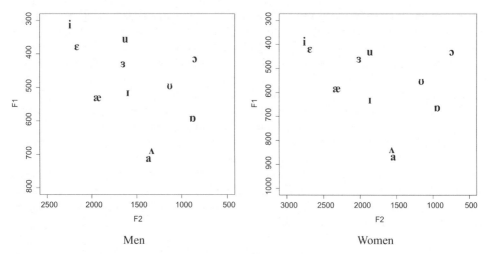

Men   Women

Figure 8.1 NZE vowel plots in Hz for 10 males and 10 females, born between 1970 and 1980.
Source: Maclagan and Hay 2007: 8.

diphthongs with a high start, effectively merging on NEAR. Some older speakers, especially women, use a more open start, and effectively merge the two diphthongs on SQUARE (Gordon and Maclagan 2001).

Syntax

It used to be believed that New Zealand syntax was indistinguishable from British English syntax. More recent studies suggest that this is not the case. The differences, however, are not categorical. Bauer states that 'it is usually the case that New Zealand English has the same constructions as British English, but uses them slightly differently, giving preference to different options' (1994: 399). Non-standard variation found in other mainstream English varieties can also be found in New Zealand syntax – *we seen it, I done it, he rung the bell, they come here yesterday.* Some of these forms are very common indeed, with young speakers in the ONZE corpus using *rung* rather than *rang* 50 per cent of the time for the simple past tense.

Bauer (1994: 400) lists differences between New Zealand English syntax and British syntax. These include a preference for *didn't used to* rather than *used not to*; a slight tendency to prefer singular concord with collective nouns; the use of *will* rather than *shall* in phrases like *Will I shut the door*; the transitive use of some verbs – *they farewelled their friends, we protested the decision.* Other examples include non-epistemic *must* in a negative sentence: *The bus mustn't be on time today* ('the bus is running late'), and the use of *anymore* with positive interrogatives: *Do they brew beer in Timaru anymore*? NZE uses *have* in cases where the simple past could be expected. This feature has been noticed for some time, as the following quote illustrates: 'Sanctions **have been imposed** by the UN thirteen years ago' (*Radio New Zealand News 12/79* – from Bauer 1989). It is becoming more prominent, especially in police bulletins or descriptions of criminal investigations. New Zealanders use an 'intrusive have' in descriptions of things that didn't happen, as in 'If I had **have** put it away properly, I wouldn't be in this mess now' and young people are often criticized for writing *should of* instead of *should have* as in *I should of done it earlier.*

156

Some American usages can be heard in New Zealand. These include *gotten* for *got*, *Sunday through Wednesday, we work on the weekend* and the deletion of *and* in numbers over 100.

Non-standard NZE can include the plural *yous*: *what are yous doing tomorrow?* and the use of *she* as a neutral pronoun: *she'll be right*, though this is usually in a few stereotyped phrases. The use of plural pronouns *they, them* as gender-neutral terms with singular nouns is increasing, in writing as well as speech.

Lexis

Most of the vocabulary used in NZE is common to English world-wide. Deverson (2000) estimates that only 5 per cent of NZE vocabulary is restricted to NZ. When Britain and the US have different terms for the same item, NZE often uses the British term. People wear *jerseys* rather than *sweaters* (though *sweatshirts* are common), two weeks are called a *fortnight* and cars run on *petrol* (if cars run on *gas* it's usually LPG – liquid petroleum gas). However, American terms are used as well as British terms. Cars have British *bonnets* and *boots*, but American *mufflers*, and there are American *trucks* and *station wagons* on NZ roads rather than British *lorries* and *estate cars*. Both *lift* and *elevator* or *torch* and *flashlight* are heard together with the pronunciation of *lieutenant* with *loo* in the first syllable and *schedule* with /sk/. Many items are shared with Australia, especially farming terms such as *the bush, paddock, creek* and the ubiquitous *mate*. Visitors often remark on the use of diminutives in -*ie*: *prezzie* for *present*, *cardie* for *cardigan*, *pozzie* for *position*.

The most distinctive feature of NZE vocabulary is the use of words borrowed from Maori. Many Maori words are used in newspapers without any gloss, to the initial confusion of visitors. *Hui* (meeting), *tangi* (funeral), *marae* (meeting place), *waka* (canoe), *kaumatua* (elder), *whakapapa* (genealogy), *whanau* (family) and *iwi* (tribe) to give a few examples, no longer need to be glossed for the general NZ public and *kia ora* is a common greeting, even among non-Maori. Maori does not have a plural affix, and the convention within NZ is not to put 's' on Maori plurals, as with 'non-Maori' in the previous sentence. Vowel length is phonemic in Maori, and is usually marked with a macron over the vowel, *Māori*, in Maori texts, but the usual convention is not to use macrons in English texts if the word is commonly used in NZE.

Discourse

The two notable features of NZE discourse are the use of High Rising Terminal intonation contours (HRTs) and the pragmatic particle *eh*. Non-New Zealanders can find it confusing if their question is answered with a statement with rising intonation. If the response to the question 'Where's the nearest gas station?' is 'There's a garage down the road and round the corner↑' where ↑ indicates a rising pitch, the questioner is likely to decide that the local doesn't actually know the answer and go off to ask someone else. Groups of HRTs often occur at the start of a narrative, presumably when the narrator is making sure that they have the listener's attention, and again round the resolution and evaluation. They seem to be a way of establishing rapport with the listener (see Holmes 1990). Initially it was noticed that young women were the most prolific users of HRTs, but HRTs are now used by both men and women of all ages. HRTs seem to be a particular feature of spoken Maori English.

157

The pragmatic particle *eh* is also a particular feature of Maori English speech, but it is used to some degree by many speakers of NZE. One possible origin is the all-purpose Maori tag question *ne*. NZ linguists tend to spell the particle *eh*, as in this chapter, but most young New Zealanders spell it *ay* or *aye*. A current anti-smoking advertisement, particularly aimed at young Maori, for example, includes the line 'Not a good look, aye.'

Social and regional variation

There is a popular myth that New Zealand is a classless society. However, linguistic research has shown clear social stratification in New Zealand English (e.g. Maclagan *et al.* 1999). Social class variation is mainly carried by the closing diphthongs MOUTH, PRICE, FACE and GOAT with people from the higher social groups avoiding the broader versions. In the past, higher-class New Zealand speakers used variants nearer to (but not the same as) British received pronunciation; lower-class speakers diverged strongly from RP. In more recent times the association with RP has been lost and social class variation is also represented in other ways such as use of a flapped 't' in *letter*, th-fronting, affrication of /tr/ or /dr/. Lower-class NZE is also marked by the use of non-standard syntax.

Lay people insist that there is clear regional variation in New Zealand, but so far (apart from in Southland) linguists have not found evidence of this. There are a few words associated with different regions: on the west coast of the South Island, for example, a grey woollen shirt worn in the bush is a *lammy*, and a miner's lunch is his *crib*. The name for 'h' is *haitch*. In the South Island a small strawberry container is a *pottle* or a *punnet* – in the North Island it is a *chip*. A rough unpaved road in the North Island is a *metal road*; in the South Island it is a *gravel road* or a *shingle road*.

There is only one distinctive regional dialect area in New Zealand, Southland in the south of the South Island of NZ, an area where the Scottish immigrant population has left its mark on pronunciation and lexis. NZE is non-rhotic but the Southland dialect is marked by variable rhoticity. Older rural speakers, especially men, may be rhotic after a range of vowels, but younger speakers usually only use post-vocalic /r/ after the NURSE vowel, as in *work*, and sometimes after *lett*ER as in *butter*. Southlanders follow Scottish usage and say *the cat wants fed* or *the plant needs watered*. Older terms like *ashet* for a serving plate, *sulky* for a child's pushchair or *soldering-bolt* for soldering iron are seldom heard today but Southlanders, still *lux their carpets* (from the brand name Electrolux), have *super heaters* rather than water heaters and eat *Belgian* (a type of luncheon sausage). The general NZ term for a holiday home is *bach* (from a bachelor's shack); in Southland they are known as *cribs.*

Laurie and Winifred Bauer studied names for playground games and found that the country could be split into three dialect regions. The clearest example was the chasing game, which was *tiggy* in the Northern region, *tag* in the Central region and *tig* in the Southern region (Bauer and Bauer 2002).

The Maori language

The Maori language is an Eastern Polynesian language, very closely related to Tahitian and the languages of the Cook Islands. Although there were various regional dialects in the nineteenth century, they were all mutually intelligible. Some few effects of these earlier dialects still linger but the comparative lack of variation in the Maori language around the country has been an advantage in the current revitalization efforts.

Until the end of the nineteenth century, all Maori spoke the Maori language. By the mid twentieth century, most Maori still spoke Maori, and most would have been bilingual in Maori and English. Maori was still passed on within the home and actively used on the marae, the tribal meeting place. Between 1950 and 1980, the majority of Maori moved from rural areas to live in cities (see Pool 1991) and connections with the home marae were lost. There was a dramatic shift to using English. Over a remarkably short time, the Maori language came close to being lost, with most young Maori in 1980 speaking only English. Benton (1991) carried out surveys in the 1970s and found that there were only approximately 60,000 fluent speakers of Maori, and most of them were middle-aged or elderly. Few children were being raised as speakers of the language.

These findings stimulated local efforts at language revitalization, with the best known being the *kohanga reo* (language nest) movement, where preschool children are taught by elders in a Maori-only environment. *Kura kaupapa Maori* (Maori immersion primary schools) soon followed and it is now possible for children to complete their entire education, including tertiary education, in the Maori language, though numbers decrease once children reach secondary school. Programmes were also devised for adult learners, and the number of people who claim to be able to speak 'some' Maori is now increasing, though the number who can hold a fluent conversation has actually remained static over the last two census periods (Bauer 2008). In the 2006 census, 131,613 people, or 23.7 per cent of the Maori population, indicated that they could hold a conversation about everyday topics. This rose to almost half (48.7 per cent) of people aged 65 or over and fell to 16 per cent of people aged under 15 years (Statistics New Zealand 2007b: 5).

Maori was established as an official language of New Zealand by the Maori Language Act (1987) which also set up the Maori Language Commission, Te Taura Whiri i te Reo Maori. One of the Commission's major operational principles for expanding Maori vocabulary is that new words should not be borrowings from English. See Harlow (1993) on attitudes towards adding new lexical items to the Maori language.

Maori has influenced the vocabulary of NZE as discussed above. There were two major waves of borrowing, when Europeans first came to NZ and borrowed names for natural features such as trees and birds, and then more recently since the 1980s, when borrowings include numerous social-cultural items such as those listed above under lexis (Macalister 2006). Maori has not influenced the pronunciation or grammar of NZE. Its other major influence, however, is in discourse with the pragmatic particle *eh*, described above, and a probable influence on the rhythm of NZE. Maori is described as mora-timed (Bauer 1981) with each short vowel and its preceding consonant taking approximately the same time interval. Inner circle Englishes are stress-timed with stressed syllables occurring at approximately equal time intervals. Outer circle Englishes like Singapore or Indian English are considerably more syllable-timed than most inner circle Englishes. NZE is less syllable-timed than Singapore or Indian English, but more syllable-timed than British English (Warren 1998). For more information on the Maori language see Bauer (1993) and Harlow (2007).

Maori English

Maori English is the fastest growing variety of NZE. Although comments about Maori English have been made since the 1960s, less than twenty years ago Benton (1991:

195) noted that 'the evidence for the existence of Maori English as a distinct and stable … variety of New Zealand English is at best tentative and ambiguous'. The main reason for the ongoing difficulties in adequately describing Maori English is that its features are all shared with mainstream NZE; it is the proportion of features rather than the specific features that identifies it. Maori English as described in the 1960s was usually spoken by people whose first language was Maori, and its phonology and grammar were clearly affected by features from that language. Most speakers of Maori English today are not fluent speakers of Maori, with many having minimal knowledge of the language. Maori comprise most of the speakers of Maori English, but non-Maori who live and/or work with Maori often speak it also. It is a solidarity marker and is sometimes called 'bro talk' (King 1999).

Maori English has few distinctive syntactic features, except, perhaps, a relatively high proportion of non-standard features such as past participles for past tense (e.g. *come* for *came*). Phonologically, Maori English is marked by very fronted GOOSE vowels, by monophthongization of diphthongs, especially FACE and GOAT, stopping and/ or affrication of /θ/ and /ð/ and devoicing of final /z/. There is increasing rhoticity, especially with the NURSE vowel, and a lack of linking and intrusive-/r/. Maori English speakers tend to use high numbers of HRTs and of the pragmatic particles *y'know* and *eh?* Their rhythm is considerably more syllable-timed than more mainstream NZE speakers (Szakay 2008) and they use kinship terms like *bro, cos* (cousin) and *sis*.

Just as lexical borrowing from English into Maori is currently rejected, so there is a tacit rejection of code-switching between English and Maori for young speakers. Older speakers, who are secure in their Maori language, code-switch freely, but younger ones do not. Older speakers will say 'But everybody worked … even *nga kuia* [the old women]' (Szaszy *et al.* 1993: 19), using Maori words with appropriate articles in English sentences or vice versa 'Ko matau te *generation* i mohio ki tenei kupu ki te "aroha" [We were the generation which knew this word "love"]' (ibid.: 28). English words can be given Maori endings as in 'kia *xray-ngia* taku turi [to have my knee x-rayed]' (ibid.: 106) where an English verb has been given a Maori passive ending, or there is switching between the languages as in 'Very seldom ka haere ki te kanikani [did I go to dances]' (ibid.: 36).

However, young people freely translate English syntactic constructions to create structures that would not be used by fluent Maori speakers (Harlow and McLellan 2008). For more information on Maori English, see Holmes (2005) and Maclagan *et al.* (2008).

Pasifika English

In the 2006 census, 7.3 per cent of the population (281,377 people) identified themselves as belonging to the Pacific nations that are usually grouped together as Pasifika. Of these Pasifika peoples, 67 per cent live in the Auckland region. Samoans form the largest group, followed, in descending order, by people from the Cook Islands, Tonga, Niue, Fiji, Tokelau and Tuvalu. The older generations usually speak their original language, but many of the younger generations do not. Some researchers consider that a distinct Pasifika variety of NZE is developing; others regard it as a variety of Maori English. Little research has yet been done on Pasifika English, though Stark (2008) found that Samoan, Tongan and Niuean speakers patterned together in terms of front vowel pronunciation, as did NZ Maori and Cook Islands Maori speakers. Pasifika words like *Palagi* (a white or non-Polynesian person), *lava-lava* (wrap-around skirt worn by both men and women), *taro* (a root vegetable, used like potato) and *umu* (an earth oven like a Maori *hangi*) are now well accepted into NZE and would not need to be glossed in a newspaper.

Written NZE

For many novels written by New Zealanders, it is the content rather than the language that is distinctively New Zealand. Place-names (such as *Auckland* or *Wellington*) or distinctive flora (such as *cabbage trees* or *kauri*) or fauna (birds such as *tui, kiwi* or *kakapo*) immediately mark a written text as coming from or referring to NZ, as does the use of NZ experiences such as *going flatting* (moving away from the family home into shared accommodation) or *the great OE* (overseas experience), both of which are rites of passage for young New Zealanders. Maori authenticity can be similarly added by using Maori concepts. In *Tu* (2004) Patricia Grace uses very few Maori words, but the main character constantly longs to go home to be under his mountain – when Maori introduce themselves, they always name the mountain and river with which their *iwi* (tribe) affiliates. All these features add to the authenticity of a work from the perspective of NZ readers, as in the following example from *The Burning Boy* where the place-names are fictitious (Gee 1990: 54):

> South through Darwood, past the meat-works, round two sides of Schwass's berry farm. The road ran straight through pea fields, then followed the curving south shore of the inlet. She saw plover in the fields and black-backed gulls and herons on the mudflats. Tar-seal gave way to metal. She drove up a valley in low hills, leaving dust as fluffy as whipped egg-whites behind her. John Toft's orchard lay at the head of the valley. Beyond it the road stopped. A padlocked gate and a clay forestry track went into pines.

By contrast, using the names of the two main islands without an article immediately marks the text as inauthentic to NZ readers. Phrases like *he went to North Island* or *they lived in South Island* can sometimes be found in novels not written by New Zealanders. When they are used as nouns, the two islands always take the definite article – *the North Island* and *the South Island* (also known as *the Mainland*, again with the article); they can only be used without the article adjectivally – *North Island towns* or *South Island wineries*.

Sometimes Maori English is represented in novels. In *Encounter* (Hilliard 1971) Paul, who is not Maori, is with a group of Maori in a pub:

> Paul knew things were not going his way. He said, 'Can't we just leave it at that then. Can I buy yous all a beer?'
> 'Why did you say *yous* all?'
> 'Look, are you having a drink or not?'
> 'Is it because you think that's a Maori way of talking? Are we supposed to fall in love with you because you suddenly start talking Maori English like we do – or like you suppose we do?'

(1971: 276)

In *Once Were Warriors* (1990) Alan Duff's main characters, who live in a very rough state housing area, do not know Maori, so that Beth is initially angry when speeches are made in Maori at her daughter's funeral.

> Beth not understanding. Not the language, not their insistence that she bring her child home [to the tribal marae] for proper farewell. Beth half resenting the male elders, their privileged position, their secret language that only they and a few others knew.
>
> (1990: 120)

All the major characters talk Maori English, with the proportion of non-standard features often representing the degree of drunkenness.

> Fear on the associate's face. Real fear. Like he's walked into a nightmare and only just realised it. Nig feeling sorry for him, Okay lettem fight, the scared fulla agreein. The Brown givinim a wicked smile: Thas cool, man. Make it in half an hour; give my boys time ta warm up. Chuckling at the scared dude. C'mon, boys. pulling his three dogs away. Y'c'n have ya suppa in half an hour. Laughing.
>
> (1990: 144)

The most distinctive feature of written NZE is the use of Maori words and phrases. Modern novels usually reflect the current prohibition on code-switching. In *Potiki*, Patricia Grace (1986) uses Maori terms for the *whare nui* (meeting house), the *whare kai* (dining room) and *urupa* (cemetery) and the recurring theme is that the people were not *pohara* (poor), but even the children do not code-switch. In *Whale Rider*, Witi Ihimaera (2003) uses Maori words which are now part of general NZE usage within English sentences as in '"Kia ora" she breathed as she gave me a hongi [touching noses in greeting]' (2003: 78), but Nanny Flowers uses either English or Maori: 'Enough of the loving! You and me are working girls! Haere mai! [come here] Kia tere! [hurry up]' (2003: 78). Koro addresses the whale totally in Maori. At first his words are glossed, 'Then, in the wind and the rain, Koro Apinana had approached the whale. "E te Tipua," he had called, "tena koe" [greetings, Supernatural Being]. Kua tae mai koe ki te mate? Ara, ki te ora.' There had been no reply to his question: 'Have you come to die or to live?' (2003: 113) but later no explanation is given.

> With a sudden heave and suck of sand the whale gained its equilibrium. Its eyes opened, and Koro Apirana saw the mana [prestige] and the wisdom of the ages shining like a sacred flame. The moko [tattoo] of the whale too seemed alive with unholy fire.
> *Ka ora tatou?* [Are we all well?]
> '"E te tipua," Koro Apirana said. "Ae, ka ora tatou [yes we are well]. Haere atu koe ki te moana. [Go to the sea]. Me huri koe ki te Ao o Tangaroa [Go to the world of Tangaroa (the god of the sea)].' The tractors began to pull the whale round.
>
> (2003: 119)

This section has necessarily been selective rather than comprehensive. However it does demonstrate the different ways in which a distinct NZ voice can be heard in literature.

Acknowledgements

I thank Jeanette King and Ray Harlow for help with the Maori and Maori English sections and Elizabeth Gordon and Boyd Davis for helpful comments.

Suggestions for further reading

Bauer, L. (1994) 'English in New Zealand', in Robert Burchfield (ed.) *English in Britain and Overseas: Origins and Development* (Volume 5 of *The Cambridge History of the English language*), Cambridge: Cambridge University Press. (This (see pp. 382–429) provides a good overview of NZE.)

Gordon, E, Campbell, L., Hay, J., Maclagan, M., Sudbury, A. and Trudgill, P. (2004) *New Zealand English: Its Origins and Evolution*, Cambridge: Cambridge University Press. (This provides a full account of the history and development of NZE, including a summary of early research on the variety.)

Hay, J., Maclagan, M. and Gordon, E. (2008) *New Zealand English*, Edinburgh: Edinburgh University Press. (This book is designed for a more general readership and provides a thorough overview of the current state of NZE together with a chapter on its origins and development. It also contains an annotated bibliography.)

For current details on the Maori language see Statistics New Zealand 2007b. The official statistics website is www.stats.govt.nz/. For a careful evaluation of the current health of the Maori language, see Bauer 2008.

References

Bauer, L. (1989) 'The verb have in New Zealand English', *English World-Wide*, 10 (1): 69–83.

—— (1994) 'English in New Zealand', in R. Burchfield (ed.) *The Cambridge History of the English Language, Vol. 5: English in Britain and Overseas: Origins and Development*, Cambridge: Cambridge University Press, pp. 382–429.

Bauer, Laurie and Bauer, Winifred (2002) 'The persistence of dialect areas', *Te Reo*, 45: 37–44.

Bauer, W. (1981) 'Hae.re vs. ha.e.re: a note', *Te Reo*, 24, 31–6.

——(1993) *Māori*, London and New York: Routledge.

——(2008) 'Is the health of te reo Māori improving?', *Te Reo*, 51: 33–73.

Benton, R. (1991) 'Māori English: a New Zealand myth?' in J. Cheshire (ed.) *English around the World*, Cambridge: Cambridge University Press, pp. 187–99.

Deverson, T. (2000) 'Handling New Zealand English lexis', in A. Bell and K. Kuiper (eds) *New Zealand English*, Wellington: Victoria University Press, pp. 23–39.

Duff, A. (1990) *Once Were Warriors*, Auckland: Random House.

Gee, M. (1990) *The Burning Boy*, Auckland: Viking (Penguin Books).

Gordon, E. and Maclagan, M.A. (2001) ' "Capturing a sound change": a real time study over 15 years of the NEAR/SQUARE diphthong merger in New Zealand English', *Australian Journal of Linguistics*, 21 (2): 215–38.

Gordon, E., Campbell, L., Hay, J., Maclagan, M., Sudbury, A. and Trudgill, P. (2004) *New Zealand English: Its Origins and Evolution*, Cambridge: Cambridge University Press.

Gordon, E., Maclagan, M.A. and Hay, J. (2007) 'The ONZE Corpus', in J.C. Beal, K.P. Corrigan and H. Moisl (eds) *Models and Methods in the Handling of Unconventional Digital Corpora, Vol. 2: Diachronic Corpora*, Basingstoke, Hampshire: Palgrave Macmillan, pp. 82–104.

Grace, P. (1986) *Potiki*, Auckland: Penguin Books.

——(2004) *Tu*, Auckland: Penguin.

Harlow, R. (1993) 'Lexical expansion in Maori', *Journal of the Polynesian Society*, 102 (1): 99–107.

——(2007) *Mäori: A Linguistic Introduction*, Cambridge: Cambridge University Press.

Harlow, R. and McLellan, J. (2008) 'Signposts on the way to, and back from, moribundity: comparing Mäori in Aotearoa and Bidayuh in Sarawak in terms of modernisation strategies,' paper presented at the International Conference on Moribund Languages and Cultures, Selangor, Malaysia, 14–15 October.

Hilliard, N. (1971) 'Encounter', *Landfall*, 99: 270–8.

Holmes, J. (1990) 'Hedges and boosters in New Zealand women's and men's speech', *Language and Communication*, 10 (3): 185–205.

——(2005) 'Using Māori English in New Zealand', *International Journal of the Sociology of Language*, 172: 91–115.

Ihimaera, W. (2003 [1987]) *Whale Rider*, Auckland: Reed Books.

Kachru, B. (1992) 'Teaching world Englishes,' in B. Kachru (ed.) *The Other Tongue, English Across Cultures* (2nd edition), Urbana: University Illinois Press, pp. 355–66.

King, J. (1999) 'Talking bro: Māori English in the university setting', *Te Reo*, 42: 19–38.

King, M. (2003) *The Penguin History of New Zealand*, Auckland: Penguin.

Macalister, J. (2006) 'The Māori presence in the New Zealand English lexicon, 1850–2000', *English World-Wide*, 27: 1–24.

Maclagan, M.A. and Hay, J. (2007) 'Getting *fed* up with our *feet*: contrast maintenance and the New Zealand English "short" front vowel shift', *Language Variation and Change*, 19 (1): 1–25.

Maclagan, M.A., Gordon, E. and Lewis, G. (1999) 'Women and sound change: conservative and innovative behaviour by the same speakers', *Language Variation and Change*, 11 (1): 19–41.

Maclagan, M., King, J. and Gillon, G. (2008) 'Māori English', *Clinical Phonetics and Linguistics*, 22 (8): 658–70

Pool, D.I. (1991) *Te iwi Māori: A New Zealand population past, present and projected*, Auckland: Auckland University Press.

Sinclair, K. (1991) *A History of New Zealand* (4th edition), Auckland: Penguin.

Stark, D. (2008) 'National and ethnic identity markers: New Zealand short front vowels in New Zealand Maori English and Pasifika Englishes', *English World-Wide*, 29 (2): 176–93.

Statistics New Zealand (2007a) *Profile of New Zealander Responses, Ethnicity Question: 2006 Census*, Wellington: New Zealand. Online. Available www.stats.govt.nz/census/default.htm (accessed 12 January 2009).

——(2007b) *QuickStats about Māori. Revised 27 March 2007. Census 2006/Tatauranga 2006*, Wellington: New Zealand. Online. Available www.stats.govt.nz/census/2006-census-data/quickstats-about-maori/2006-census-quickstats-about-maori-revised.htm?page=para011Master (accessed 8 January 2009).

——(2007c) *QuickStats about Pacific Peoples*. Online. Available www.stats.govt.nz/NR/rdonlyres/45BED 0E7-E709–4DCE-9B01–0C715EC050AE/0/quickstatsaboutpacificpeoples.pdf (accessed 13 January 2009).

Szakay, A. (2008) *Ethnic Dialect Identification in New Zealand – the Role of Prosodic Cues*, Saarbrücken: VDM Verlag Dr. Müller Aktiengesellschaft & Co. KG.

Szaszy, M., Rogers, A. and Simpson, M. (1993) *Te Timatanga, Tatau Tatau, Early Stories from Founding Members of the Māori Women's Welfare League*, Wellington: Bridget Williams Books.

Trudgill, P. (2004) *New Dialect Formation: The Inevitability of Colonial Englishes*, Edinburgh: Edinburgh University Press.

Trudgill, P., Gordon, E., Lewis, G. and Maclagan, M.A. (2000) 'Determinism in new-dialect formation and the genesis of New Zealand English', *Journal of Linguistics*, 36: 299–318.

Trudgill, P., Maclagan, M.A. and Lewis, G. (2003) 'Linguistic archaeology: the Scottish input to New Zealand phonology', *Journal of English Linguistics*, 31 (2*)*: 103–24.

Wall, A. (1951) 'The way I have come', radio broadcast talk. Christchurch, Radio NZ Sound Archives.

Warren, P. (1998) 'Timing patterns in New Zealand English rhythm', *Te Re*, 41: 80–93.

Wells, J.C. (1982) *Accents of English*, Cambridge: Cambridge University Press.

Section II
Regional varieties and the 'new' Englishes

9

The development of the English language in India

Joybrato Mukherjee

Introduction

Over the past 400 years, the English language – once transplanted to the Indian sub-continent as the language of the British colonizers – has developed into an integral part of the linguistic repertoire of India, with the pull towards English growing even stronger in the post-independence period. This process has been marked by the emergence of a distinctly Indian variety of English which fulfils a wide range of communicative functions in present-day India and which is a significant vehicle for Indian identity-construction for a relatively small but substantial and increasing part of the population. In fact, even according to conservative estimates the educated variety of Standard Indian English is used competently and regularly by c. 35 to 50 million Indians today – which makes Indian English the third largest variety of English world-wide in terms of numbers of speakers, outnumbered only by British and American English. The present chapter describes the development of English in India by (a) sketching out the various stages of the diachronic development of English in India from the early seventeenth century to the twenty-first century, (b) systematizing the characteristic features of present-day Indian English from a synchronic perspective, and (c) pointing out some prospects for future research.

Diachronic development: English in India 1600–2010

Describing the formation of Indian English: an evolutionary model

The development of a new variety of English in the Indian context is in many regards a prototypical example of the emergence of what Kachru (1985a) has labelled *institutionalized second-language varieties*, i.e. varieties of English in postcolonial settings which are based on educated speakers' use of English as an additional language for a wide range of institutionalized contexts (e.g. in administration, in the education system, in newspapers). In the following, the process of institutionalization will therefore be described along the lines of Schneider's (2003, 2007) dynamic model of the evolution of postcolonial Englishes – a model that is intended to capture the essentially uniform pattern of variety formation world-wide. The model is, in essence, based on two inter-related factors: (1) changing identity-constructions, and (2) changing interactions between two strands of population, namely the settlers (STL) and the indigenous population (IDG). The fundamental idea that combines the two factors is the following one: the more intense the contact and interaction between the local population and the colonizers becomes, the stronger is the effect on the sociocultural identity-construction of the two groups, which ultimately leads to the establishment of a new hybrid identity manifest-ing itself in a new variety of English: the IDG and STL '"strands" of development ... are interwoven like twisted threads' (Schneider 2003: 242). The two factors are held responsible for a universal evolutionary pattern in the formation of New Englishes consisting of five identifiable (but overlapping) stages (cf. Schneider, this volume):

Phase I – *Foundation*: In this initial phase, the English language is transported to a new (colonial) territory.

Phase II – *Exonormative stabilization*: There is a growing number of English settlers/ speakers in the new territory, but the language standards and norms are still determined by the input variety and are, thus, usually oriented towards British English.

Phase III – *Nativization*: The English language becomes an integral part of the local linguistic repertoire as there is a steady increase in the number of competent bilingual L2 speakers of English from the indigenous population.

Phase IV – *Endonormative stabilization*: After independence, English may be retained as a/an (co-)official language and a medium of communication for a more or less wide range of intra-national contexts (e.g. administration and the press, academia and education); in this phase a new variety of English emerges with generally accepted local standards and norms.

Phase V – *Differentiation*: Once a New English variety has become endonormatively stabilized, it may develop a wide range of regional and social dialects.

It has been shown in several applications of the model to the Indian context (cf. Mukherjee 2007; Schneider 2007) that the story of English in India over the past four centuries can indeed be told along the lines of phases I to IV, as will be shown in the following sections.

Foundation phase

The first Englishman to actually use English in India was Father Thomas Stephens, who came to India in 1579. The letters he sent home from Goa can be seen as the first items of 'Anglo–Indian literature' (cf. Ward and Waller 1916: 331). In 1600, a Royal Charter was granted to the East India Company, which led to the establishment of trade centres, and to a steadily growing influx of English merchants. They began to interact both with the Moghul emperors of various Indian states and with local Indians for reasons of trade. Besides trade, British missions were set up, their educational facilities attracting Indians who were also taught English in the missionary schools. Later, the British army also attracted many Indian soldiers (with a high proportion of Sikhs, a small religious minority based in Punjab). In the army, too, the English language spread quickly from the STL strand to the IDG strand. In spite of such pockets of early interaction between the two strands, however, for the first 150 years or so, the British colonizers and their descendants certainly continued to feel entirely British, while the local population regarded English as a clearly foreign language. In the mid eighteenth century, it became clear, however, that the British colonial rule would be in place for a longer period of time – and with it, the English language. The use of English in India, thus, became 'stabilized', but still 'exonormatively', i.e. on grounds of external (British) standards.

Exonormative stabilization

In the eighteenth century, the Moghul Empire in India gradually declined, resulting in a century-long struggle for mastery over India, fought between the British, the French, the Hindu Marathas and the Muslim leaders in the north and south of India. Britain became more and more engaged in the rivalries and conflicts on the subcontinent and established footholds in various coastal areas, especially on the west coast (the Bombay area) and the east coast (in Bengal). The victory of the British forces in the Battle of Plassey in 1757 marks the beginning of the British Empire in India as it established British administrative and political power over the provinces of Bengal and Bihar, the starting point for the colonization of the entire subcontinent over the next decades. The Regulating Act (1773), turning the East India Company into a British administrative body, and the East India Bill (1784), passing the control of the East India Company from the British parliament to Her Majesty's government, indicated the consolidation of British supremacy over India. One could thus view the second half of the eighteenth century as the beginning of the second phase in the evolution of Indian English, i.e. its exonormative stabilization.

Both the STL strand and the IDG strand were now fully aware that British presence in India was not to be a transient phenomenon and that, accordingly, the language of the new power would stay and become increasingly important: in the early nineteenth century, Britain controlled almost the entirety of India, either by direct rule or by setting up protectorates over Indian vassal states that were ruled by Indian princes. The growth of British power made more and more British people come to India. From the beginning of the nineteenth century onwards, many more missionaries arrived, spreading the English language among Indians, and many more Indians enrolled in the British-Indian army. Naturally, in this phase a range of local Indian words were absorbed by the English language that referred to items unique to the Indian context (e.g. *curry*, *bamboo*, *mango*, *veranda*). Despite the influx of Indianisms in the English language in India, the standards and norms of the English language in general – as it was used in the STL strand and taught to the IDG strand – remained British and, thus, exonormatively set.

In the late eighteenth and early nineteenth century, a relatively small but influential group among Indians became interested in Western and English education, culture and sciences. This was complemented by a growing interest among British linguists, philosophers and scientists in Indian traditions and expertise in their respective fields of research. Against this background, the colonial administration had to decide on what kind of language-educational policy to follow in India: should Indians be taught primarily in their local languages, or should there be an education system with English as the medium of instruction? While the Orientalists suggested that education for Indians should focus on Indian languages, literature and culture, the Anglicists viewed the English language as the more appropriate medium of instruction for two reasons: (1) English language and culture were regarded as more valuable than Indian languages (including Sanskrit); (2) the establishment of a bilingual elite among the Indians would help the British to stabilize their position as the supreme power over the subcontinent. In his famous *Minute on Indian Education* (1835), Thomas Macaulay made a strong plea for an English-medium education system for a new 'class of persons, Indian in blood and colour, but English in taste, in opinions, in morals, and in intellect'. Macaulay's ideas were officially accepted by the colonial administration so that soon afterwards an English-medium school system, especially designed for the education of the growing class of Indians to be appointed as members of the Indian civil service, was established. English became the sole language of instruction in secondary schools and also in the first universities in India, which were founded in Bombay (today: Mumbai), Calcutta (today: Kolkata) and Madras (today: Chennai).

Nativization

Macaulay's (1835) *Minute on Indian Education* marks the first step towards the beginning of nativization of the English language in India. It is in this phase that both the STL strand and the IDG strand construct a new identity and that the two strands become more and more intertwined in the process of the changing identity-construction. However, the creation of a new local identity – feasible as it may be – is not (yet) reflected in all spheres of the linguistic, social and political reality.

As for the IDG strand, English and European literature and culture infiltrated the Indian intelligentsia through the English-medium education system. What Macauley and others had not taken into account was that an 'Anglicist' education would also mean that Indians became familiar with Western ideas and ideals like democracy, enlightenment and self-determination, fuelling the struggle for independence (cf. Nehru 1946: 319).

In fact, a major factor in creating a pan-Indian freedom movement in the nineteenth century was the English language itself: against the background of the multilingual setting of India with its more than 600 local languages, the English language provided a welcome all-Indian communicative device that made it possible for Indian intellectuals from all over the subcontinent to jointly agitate against British rule and, thus, to form an all-Indian political identity. The growing acceptance of – and the increasingly positive attitude towards – the English language in India has a lot to do with the fact the 'English language contributed substantially in achieving national integration' (Rao 2003: 1).

Meanwhile, for the British people in India the subcontinent turned into a more and more Anglophone territory, making them feel less alien and – positively as well as negatively – at home in India. Thus, in the mid nineteenth century the STL strand and the IDG strand began to become intertwined: a local English-based identity emerged both among British settlers and among Indian locals, and the English language entered a long and tumultuous process of nativization, lasting for more than a century and marked by various political key events that intensified the ongoing nativization, the two most significant events being (a) the Great Revolt of 1857/8, triggered by the mutiny of the Indian army in Meerut and soon becoming a popular rebellion, and the final victory of the British army; (b) the proclamation of Queen Victoria as Empress of India in 1877, with an almost omnipotent Viceroy representing the British crown in India and reigning as an absolute monarch.

Sociolinguistically, these events firmly (re-)confirmed the status of English as the language of power and dominance. More British people came to India, and India turned from a colony *inter alia* to perhaps the most central part – the 'Jewel' – of the British Empire, with the British colonial power in turn viewing itself as an integral part of Indian politics and, more importantly, Indian identity.

From the mid eighteenth century onwards, a growing number of permanent residents of British origin came to stay in India, and many more Indians of the upper class and the higher middle class learned English – the only language that would guarantee access to, for example, highly estimated university education in England and to the Indian civil service in India. It is in this very period that the English language in India, at least as it was used by well-educated IDG users, began to change slowly but gradually towards a variety in its own right, marked not only by heavy lexical borrowing but also by phraseological and grammatical innovations (i.e. forms not found in the British English input variety, e.g. *England-returned, blessings-message*) and phonological changes (e.g. monophthongization of diphthongs such as /eɪ/ and /əʊ/): thus, the late nineteenth century marks the beginning of the emergence of 'educated' Indian English, i.e. a standardizing form of Indian English.

The process of nativization of English in India did not stop when India became independent in 1947. On the contrary, it may be viewed as a historical irony that the Constitution of the Republic of India, which was passed by the Constituent Assembly in 1949 and came into effect in 1950, had been written in English. Although the English language is not listed among the 18 official national and regional languages in the Indian Constitution, it is only the original English version of the Constitution that is legally binding even today (cf. Basu 1999: 391). However, since provisions were made in the Constitution for a replacement of English by Hindi (the mother tongue of approximately 35 per cent of the population of India) for all official purposes after 15 years, one could have expected that nativization would have stopped at some point after independence and that, as in some other former British colonies, the English language would have entered a process of fossilization or even 'de-nativization'. However, this has not happened. Rather, the English language has been transformed into an endonormatively stabilized variety of English in the post-independence period.

Endonormative stabilization

For a variety of English to enter the stage of endonormative stabilization there must be some sort of inner agreement in a speech community on the status and the usefulness of the English language. Thus, endonormative stabilization is usually a stage that can only be reached at some point after independence, as it is only then that the status and range of use of English can be (re-)negotiated without the interference from a colonial power.

It is difficult to pinpoint the precise beginning of this phase in the development of English in India. According to Schneider (2003, 2007), an 'Event X' – i.e. 'some exceptional, quasi-catastrophic political event' (Schneider 2003: 250) – usually marks the acceptance of an independent English-based identity, the transformation of English from a foreign to an indigenous language and, thus, the final emancipation from the historical input variety. It seems that the political events of the 1960s played a crucial role in this context. This was the time when according to the Indian Constitution English was to be replaced by Hindi altogether. The early 1960s were marked by an unprecedented escalation in the lingering conflict between northern parts of India, where Hindi was propagated as the only national language, and the southern parts, where many people forcefully rejected the idea of Hindi as the only national language because it was a non-native language for them. The language riots of the 1960s could be regarded as a language-political type of 'Event X', because they made the political parties readjust their stance on language policy and ensure the continuing use of the English language in India: the Official Language Act, passed in 1963 and amended in 1967, laid down that English continued to be used for official purposes alongside Hindi, and in 1976 official language rules were formulated to specify the various official communication situations at federal and state level in which Hindi and/or English were to be used. In the field of English language teaching, a compromise was found between Hindi-only proponents and supporters of English as the only official language of the Union, namely the three-language formula: according to this formula, Hindi, English and a regional language are taught in every state (cf. Biswas 2004). In states with Hindi as the regional mother tongue, a south Indian regional language is taught. Despite major problems and shortcomings, this formula has been at the heart of language policy in India in the education system over the past four decades (cf. Krishnaswami and Sriraman 1995). From the 1960s onwards, neither the status of English as the second official language of India (often labelled as *associate additional language* or *associate official language*, cf. Mehrotra 1998: 7) nor the wide range of communicative functions fulfilled by English has been under serious attack. On the contrary, the English language has steadily gained ground over the last forty years. From the 1960s onwards, the situation of the English language in India has, thus, been marked by features and factors typical of the emergence of an endonormatively stabilized variety:

- English has been retained in a wide range of communication situations, including administration and politics, education and academia, the press and book publications, and it has been increasingly used as a pan-Indian link language (cf. Mehrotra 1998: 7ff.).
- Additionally, the English language serves as the only official language in various contexts even at the federal level (most notably as the language of the Supreme Court) and as one of the official principal languages of four states and union territories (i.e. Chandigarh, Meghalaya, Mizoram, Pondicherry).
- Many Indian writers have adopted the English language as their communicative vehicle, including the highly esteemed and award-winning works of authors such as Upamanyu Chatterjee, Bharati Mukherjee, Arundhati Roy and Salman Rushdie. This has led Rushdie (1997: x) to the conclusion that '"Indo-Anglian" literature represents perhaps the most valuable contribution India has yet made to the world of books.'
- English has undergone a process of *structural nativization*, 'understood as the emergence of locally characteristic linguistic patterns' (Schneider 2007: 5f.). These patternings lead to deviations from the input variety of British English at the levels of pronunciation, lexis, grammar and style, and they have been increasingly accepted as features of a non-native variety of English in its own right, for which various labels have been coined, e.g. *Indian Varieties of English* (IVE) and *Educated Indian English* (EIE). The most commonly used (and most neutral) label is *Indian English* (IndE). The linguistic features on the various levels of description of the educated variant of Indian English will be summarized below.
- On grounds of the emerging acceptance of a local variety of English, attempts have been made to describe the Indian variety of English systematically and

empirically, including, for example, Kachru's (1983) qualitative work on the *Indianization* of English, which has exerted an enormous influence on the description of all second-language varieties of English, and a growing body of quantitative analyses on the basis of large and computerized corpora of Indian English (cf. e.g. Shastri 1992; Mukherjee and Hoffmann 2006; Schilk 2006).

- There have also been early attempts to codify the most salient features of Indian English pronunciation, lexis and grammar, most remarkably in Nihalani *et al.*'s (1979) handbook of usage and pronunciation, of which a more recent second edition is also available (cf. Nihalani *et al.* 2004). In this context, there is also a growing awareness that English language teaching in India can no longer be based on the fiction of a British English target model, but should focus on the educated local variant of English (compare, for example, Nihalani *et al.*'s (1979: 228) suggestion for an *Indian Recommended Pronunciation* (IRP) as a 'model to be prescribed for speakers of English in India').

Although Indian English can thus be viewed as a largely endonormatively stabilized variety in its own right, the present-day situation is also characterized by some remnants of the nativization phase. For example, one can still find many exponents of what Kachru (2005) has repeatedly labelled *linguistic schizophrenia*, i.e. the fact that many competent Indian users of English accept English as an integral part of their linguistic repertoire but at the same time reject the local variant of English at hand once they become aware of the differences between British and Indian English. In this context, the persistence of a 'complaint tradition', i.e. the 'stereotypical statement by conservative language observers that linguistic usage keeps deteriorating' (Schneider 2007: 50), should not go unmentioned (cf. e.g. D'souza 1997).

Differentiation?

There is general agreement that present-day Indian English has not entered the stage of differentiation (cf. Schilk 2006; Mukherjee 2007; Schneider 2007), since we cannot observe a systematic and widespread social and regional diversification of the new variety into stable and distinctive subvarieties as, for example, can be found in present-day American English. In fact, it may well be that differentiation is a stage that is bound to postcolonial settings in which English becomes the dominant first language of the majority of the population and does not remain an additional or second language for most speakers. This said, it needs to be stressed that English language use in India is marked by some degree of internal variation – but the variation is related to a much larger extent to different levels of language competence (i.e. to a *cline of bilingualism*, cf. Kachru 1983) and to the influence of different first languages (i.e. L1 interference) rather than to social and regional variables *per se*.

Synchronic manifestations: characteristic features of present-day Indian English

Having sketched out the historical development of the English language in the socio-cultural context of India from the seventeenth to the twenty-first century, some of the most salient local features that have emerged over the past centuries and that are characteristic of Indian English today will be summarized in the following. As in the diachronic synopsis in the preceding section, the focus will be on the standard and educated variant of Indian English as it is used by competent and regular users of English with an English-medium educational background. Before the features of present-day Standard Indian English are described, brief mention should be made of the two major factors that lead to variation within English usage in India and Indian English, namely the level of competence and the interference from regional L1s.

As in many other postcolonial contexts in which institutionalized second-language varieties of English have emerged, in India, too, only a relatively small part of the population in urban areas, from the upper and middle classes and with access to English-medium schools and universities, use the educated standard variant of English – it is this variant that is usually referred to as Indian English. It is useful to use the term *acrolect*, which is borrowed from creole studies, to refer to this 'high' variety linked to the top of the social and educational scale (as is done, for example, by Fernando (1989) in the Sri Lankan context). Many more people with different backgrounds of class and education have a markedly lower level of competence and proficiency in English and, thus, use different kinds of substandard varieties of English, which can be subsumed under the category of *mesolects*. The bottom of the gradient of competence is represented by a wide range of reduced and pidginized forms of English, so-called *basilects*, for which different labels have been used, e.g. *Baboo English*, *Broken English*, *Butler English* and *Kitchen English* (cf. Hosali 2008). Hosali (2000) provides a good synopsis of the reduced morphology and syntax of Butler English, understood as a pidgin English spoken, *inter alia*, by uneducated tourist guides all over India, market women selling goods to foreign tourists and local staff members from rural areas working in hotels, households and recreation centres. For example, in Butler English, articles, auxiliary verbs, prepositions and pronouns are very often omitted.

The most important factor that leads to variation within the educated variant of Indian English as the standard acrolectal variety is the regional background of the individual speaker and, linked to it, his/her specific first language. As Indian English is a largely non-native variety and, thus, typically a speaker's additional second (or third) language, there may be transfer effects from his/her first language on to English, either due to general features of certain language families (e.g. Indo-European languages in the north vs Dravidian languages in the south) or due to specific language features of individual Indian languages (e.g. Hindi vs Tamil). Regional differences are most prominent at the level of pronunciation; Gargesh (2008) provides a succinct overview of them. For example, while the vowel in *foot* is usually realized with a weakly rounded [ʏ] in Indian English, in some regions in north India (e.g. Bengal, Orissa, Rajasthan and Uttar Pradesh) it is also frequently produced as a long back [u:].

Features of Standard Indian English

In the following, the focus will be on Standard Indian English. What follows is an overview of some of the most salient local features and patternings at the various linguistic levels of analysis that can be routinely found in the acrolectal usage of educated Indian users all over the subcontinent.

Most innovations in Indian English and deviations from British English (BrE) can be found in vocabulary, and Nihalani *et al.*'s (1979/2004) dictionary documents many lexical items that are peculiar to Indian English. There are many loanwords that have been taken over from local languages, e.g. *bandh* (BrE *strike*), *challan* (BrE *bank receipt*), *coolie* (BrE *porter, luggage-carrier*), *crore* (BrE *10 million*), *goonda* (BrE *hooligan*), *lakh* (BrE *100,000*), *mela* (BrE *crowd*) and *swadeshi* (BrE *of one's own country*). Indian speakers have also created new lexical items and compounds made up of English material, as it were, e.g. *batch-mate* (BrE *class-mate*), *beer-bottle* (BrE *bottle of beer*), *to by-heart* (BrE *to learn by heart*), *inskirt* (BrE *petticoat*), *to off/on* (BrE *to switch off/ on*), *to prepone* (BrE *to bring forward in time*), *schoolgoer* (BrE *pupil/student*), *shoe- bite* (BrE *blister*). Lexical items that belong to the lexicon shared by Indian English and other varieties of English may be used in different ways in Indian English, both grammatically (e.g. *both* is admissible with the negative form of the verb in Indian English) and semantically (e.g. the use of *boy* for BrE *butler*). Some lexical items that have an archaic flavour in British English (e.g. *thrice*) are still used much more frequently in Indian English.

Indian English also deviates from native varieties at the morphological level, for example by extending the use of the suffix *-ee* (e.g. *affectee, awardee, recruitee*), the prefix *de-* (e.g. *de-confirm, de-friend, de-recognize*) and the zero-derivation of new verbs (e.g. *airline, public, slogan*).

Unlike vocabulary and word-formation, syntax tends to be quite stable in language change in general and in the emergence of varieties of English in particular (cf. Schneider 2000: 209). There are, however, some areas in which speakers of Indian English tend to deviate from British English grammar, for example with regard to article usage (e.g. BrE *a piece of chalk* → IndE also *a chalk*), invariant tag questions and question tags (e.g. *He has left, hasn't he?* → IndE also *He has left, isn't it?/ ... , no?*), the use of progressive forms with stative verbs (e.g. BrE *I simply don't understand* → IndE also *I am simply not understanding*) and the position of adverbs (e.g. BrE *I always drink coffee* → IndE also *Always I drink coffee*).

Recent corpus-based studies reveal that there are also innovations and new trends at the lexis–grammar interface in Indian English; however, the resulting differences between Indian English and British English usually are quantitative in nature and can thus only be described by analysing large amounts of natural data as included in large machine-readable text corpora. Schilk (2006), for example, shows by comparing various 1-million-word corpora of British and Indian English that particular collocations are very common in Indian English but untypical of British English (e.g. the word strings *illicit liquor, illicit den* and *illicit liquor den*). Olavarría de Ersson and Shaw (2003) and Mukherjee and Hoffmann (2006) use large web-derived newspaper corpora to describe differences between British and Indian English at the level of verb complementation, e.g. the use of so-called new ditransitives in Indian English (e.g. *gift, inform* and *put* in the double-object construction as in *she informed him the time*). Another interesting phenomenon at the lexis–grammar interface is the formation of new prepositional verbs such as *approach to, comprise of, discuss about, order for* and *visit to*, all of which are attested in the 1-million-word Indian component of the International Corpus of English (ICE), but not in the British component of ICE.

It should be noted that many of the innovations mentioned above, e.g. the extension of existing morphological rules of word-formation to new lexical items and the emergence of new ditransitive verbs and new prepositional verbs are not caused by L1 interference. Rather, they are triggered by what has been labelled *nativized semantico- structural analogy* in earlier work (cf. Mukherjee and Hoffmann 2006: 166f.). For example, Indian English speakers draw an analogy between the semantics of the combination of the prefix *de-* and the verbs *stabilize* (leading to *de-stabilize* with the opposite meaning of *stabilize*) and *confirm*, licensing new verbs such as *de-confirm* (with the opposite meaning of *confirm*). With regard to new ditransitives, Indian users of English draw an analogy between the ditransitive meaning of established ditransitive verbs such as *give* on the one hand and the similar semantics of *gift* on the other, which makes Indian speakers use the same complementation pattern (i.e. *gift someone something*). Similarly, new prepositional verbs can be viewed to be licensed by semantic and collocational patterns that already exist in the English language, as in the following example: IndE *discuss about* (verb) ← BrE *talk about* (verb) as a semantic template; *discussion* (noun) *about* as a collocational template (cf. Mukherjee 2009). Generally speaking, then, nativized semantico-structural analogy is a process by means of which non-native speakers of English as a second language introduce new forms and structures into the English language on grounds of semantic and formal templates that already exist in the English language system. These cases provide ample testimony to the fact that Indian English is a potentially norm-developing variety and that new forms and structures are often based on inherently creative and structurally innovative processes which are guided by an inner logic and not necessarily triggered by interference.

Perhaps the most transparent structural innovations of Indian English can be found in pronunciation because the phonological speech characteristics of an Indian speaker of English, typically embedded in a syllable-timed rhythm with the full realization of all stressed and unstressed syllables, are immediately apparent (cf. Shastri 1992: 263). For example, there is a very strong general tendency in Indian English to monophthongize diphthongs like /eɪ/ and /əʊ/ (e.g. *late, home*), to merge the two consonants /ʒ/ and /ʃ/ into /ʃ/ (e.g. *casual, division*), and to replace the dental fricatives /θ/ and /ð/ with /t/ and /d/ (e.g. *think, this*). Local features at the level of pronunciation can often be traced back to the influence exerted by the speaker's indigenous first language.

At the level of style, too, there are innovations in Indian English which cannot be found in the historical input variety. A very prominent example is the characteristic and culture-specific use of English in the discourse of matrimonial advertisements – a text-type which does not exist in Britain and other speech communities with English as a dominant native language.

Present-day Indian English as a semi-autonomous variety

Present-day Indian English is largely endonormatively stabilized, but some features of ongoing nativization can still be detected (especially the typical complaint tradition and the widespread linguistic schizophrenia, see above). What is more, while historically the English language has been subject to a process of acculturation and localization in the Indian context (resulting in structural nativization), today many users of English in India view a high competence in English not only as a key to upward social mobility within India, but also as a major vehicle to get access to international job markets (e.g. the United States). This international perspective in using English, which can also be found in various other Asian Englishes, has led Bolton (2008: 11) to hypothesize that the globalization of Asian industries and workforce might result in a 'reorientation of linguistic performance away from localized, intranational norms towards a "native-like" performance'. In fact, one could argue that the centrifugal forces that move Indian English further away from native Englishes, on the one hand, and centripetal forces that keep the norms of Indian English close to native Englishes for the sake of international intelligibility, on the other, are in a state of equilibrium, determining a *steady state* of progressive forces of language change and conservative forces of (native) norm persistence (cf. Mukherjee 2007).

It is in this context of the present steady-state situation of Indian English that the concept of Indian English as a *semi-autonomous variety* seems to be very appropriate. The notion of semi-autonomy captures three aspects of Indian English which have been pointed out repeatedly in a multitude of studies and which have, thus, been referred to in the description of Indian English in the preceding sections:

- Indian English is a variety based on – and including – the 'common core' (cf. Quirk *et al.* 1985: 16), which has been largely set by native speakers of English and which is not subject to spontaneous language change (e.g. inventory of function words, the core vocabulary and the core grammar of English).
- Indian English is an 'interference variety' (Quirk *et al.* 1972: 26), since many linguistic peculiarities that are characteristic of Indian English are based on interferences from Indian speakers' first languages (e.g. certain phoneme replacements and the trend towards syllable-timed rhythm).
- Indian English is a 'norm-developing' variety (Kachru 1985b: 17), characterized by a wide range of linguistic innovations, peculiarities and deviations from other varieties which have developed autonomously within Indian English and are not triggered by interference (e.g. the extension of morphological rules of word-formation and the emergence of new ditransitive verbs).

The creative function of Indian English

When assessing the degree to which the English language has become a tool for Indian identity-construction, it is of particular importance to take into account the increasing body of fiction in English written by Indian writers (see above). While it is true that Indian authors undeniably tend to write for an international audience (cf. Paul 2003: 362) and may thus be oriented towards exonormative standards (set by the largely native readership) to a much larger extent than the average Indian English speaker, the increasing acceptance of English as a means of literary creativity nevertheless indicates that English is no longer viewed as a foreign language by many writers – it is actively adopted as an appropriate vehicle for the literary encoding of genuinely Indian cultural experience and story-telling. The creative force and success of Indian authors over the past few decades has proven right the prediction of the famous Indian author Raja Rao (1938: vii) who, more than seventy years ago, envisaged the emergence of a distinctly Indian 'method of expression ... which will someday prove to be as distinctive and colourful as the Irish or the American'.

Conclusion and avenues for future research

In the present chapter, the historical development of English in India has been described from the beginnings of the colonization of the subcontinent to the postcolonial setting in which a new and endonormatively stabilized variety of English in its own right has emerged. It is marked by structural nativization at all linguistic levels, a wide range of communicative functions and an increasing acceptance as a vehicle for Indian identity-construction, culminating in a growing and rich body of Indian English fiction writing. Some of the most salient linguistic features of the educated variant of present-day Indian English have been described by giving examples from the areas of pronunciation, morphology and word-formation, lexicogrammar and syntax. Although there is a cline of competence and proficiency across users of English in India and a range of different L1 influences on Indian English, the acrolectal standard form of Indian English remains a relatively homogeneous variety of English.

In future research, the advent of large and machine-readable corpora of Indian English will certainly trigger off many more corpus-based quantitative studies, especially in those areas in which innovations in new Englishes are not of a categorial kind but manifest themselves in changing preferences and different frequencies of usage (e.g. in verb complementation). Apart from the empirical description of the formal features of English and the functions of English in the speech community, more research into speaker attitudes, issues of standardization and questions of norm development is needed. This is of particular importance for a wide range of practical fields of application, e.g. the production of new Indian English dictionaries and grammars and the design of socioculturally appropriate curricula for English language teaching in India.

Finally, more attention should be paid to the potential role of Indian English as a new lead variety for smaller neighbouring varieties in South Asia. Leitner (1992) hypothesizes that institutionalized second language varieties like Singapore English and Indian English may take the same path as Australian English and develop into *emergent epicentres*, i.e. reference varieties for their individual regions. In this context, both corpus-linguistic methods and sociolinguistic data should be utilized to provide a comprehensive picture of how individual second language varieties influence each other in postcolonial settings and to assess the epicentre hypothesis.

Suggestions for further reading

Kachru, B.B. (2005) *Asian Englishes: Beyond the Canon*, Hong Kong: Hong Kong University Press. (A comprehensive account of Asian Englishes with a focus on South Asia.)
Mehrotra, R.R. (1998) *Indian English: Texts and Interpretation*, Amsterdam: John Benjamins. (A wide range of Indian English texts and explanatory comments.)
Nihalani, P., Tongue, R., Hosali, P. and Crowther, J. (2004) *Indian and British English: A Handbook of Usage and Pronunciation* (2nd edition), Delhi: Oxford University Press. (The classic dictionary of Indian English.)
Rushdie, S. and West, E. (eds) (1997) *The Vintage Book of Indian Writing 1947–1997*, London: Vintage. (An impressive collection of Indian English fiction writing.)
Schneider, E.W. (2007) *Postcolonial English: Varieties around the World*, Cambridge: Cambridge University Press. (A description of World Englishes along the lines of an evolutionary five-stage model.)

References

Basu, D. (1999) *Introduction to the Constitution of India*, New Delhi: Prentice Hall of India.
Biswas, G. (2004) 'Language policy in Southeast Asia: a case study of India', in S. Mansoor, S. Meraj and A. Tahir (eds) *Language Policy, Planning, and Practice: A South Asian Perspective*, Oxford: Oxford University Press, pp. 106–11.

Bolton, K. (2008) 'English in Asia, Asian Englishes, and the issue of proficiency', *English Today*, 24: 3–12.

D'souza, J. (1997) 'Indian English: some myths, some realities', *English World-Wide*, 18: 91–105.

Fernando, S. (1989) 'Style range in Sri Lankan fiction: an analysis of four texts', *World Englishes*, 8 (2): 119–31.

Gargesh, R. (2008) 'Indian English: phonology', in R. Meshtrie (ed.) *Varieties of English, Vol. 4: Africa, South and Southeast Asia*, Berlin: Mouton de Gruyter, pp. 231–43.

Hosali, P. (2000) *Butler English: Form and Function*, New Delhi: BRPC.

——(2008) 'Butler English: morphology and syntax', in R. Meshtrie (ed.) *Varieties of English, Vol. 4: Africa, South and Southeast Asia*, Berlin: Mouton de Gruyter, pp. 563–77.

Kachru, B.B. (1983) *The Indianization of English: The English Language in India*, Delhi: Oxford University Press.

——(1985a) 'Institutionalized second-language varieties', in S. Greenbaum (ed.) *The English Language Today*, Oxford: Pergamon, pp. 211–26.

——(1985b) 'Standards, codification and sociolinguistic realism: the English language in the Outer Circle', in R. Quirk and H.G. Widdowson (eds) *English in the World: Teaching and Learning the Language and Literatures*, Cambridge: Cambridge University Press, pp. 11–30.

——(2005) *Asian Englishes: Beyond the Canon*, Hong Kong: Hong Kong University Press.

Krishnaswami, N. and Sriraman, T. (1995) 'English teaching in India: past, present and future', in R.K. Agnihotri and A.L. Khanna (eds) *English Language Teaching in India: Issues and Innovations*, New Delhi: Sage, pp. 37–57.

Leitner, G. (1992) 'English as a pluricentric language', in M. Clyne (ed.) *Pluricentric Languages: Differing Norms in Different Nations*, Berlin: Mouton de Gruyter, pp. 179–237.

Macaulay, T.B. (1835) 'Minute on Indian education', reproduced in H. Sharp (ed.) (1965) *Selections from Educational Records, Part I: 1781–1839*, Delhi: National Archives of India, pp. 107–17.

Mehrotra, R.R. (1998) *Indian English: Texts and Interpretation*, Amsterdam: John Benjamins.

Mukherjee, J. (2007) 'Steady states in the evolution of new Englishes: present-day Indian English as an equilibrium', *Journal of English Linguistics*, 35: 157–87.

——(2009) 'The lexicogrammar of present-day Indian English: corpus-based perspectives on structural nativisation', in U. Römer and R. Schulze (eds) *Exploring the Lexis–Grammar Interface*, Amsterdam: John Benjamins.

Mukherjee, J. and Hoffmann, S. (2006) 'Describing verb–complementational profiles of new Englishes: a pilot study of Indian English', *English World-Wide*, 27: 147–73.

Nehru, J. (1946) *The Discovery of India*, New Delhi: Oxford University Press.

Nihalani, P., Tongue, R.K. and Hosali, P. (1979) *Indian and British English: A Handbook of Usage and Pronunciation*, Delhi: Oxford University Press.

Nihalani, P.,Tongue, R.K., Hosali, P. and Crowther, J. (2004) *Indian and British English: A Handbook of Usage and Pronunciation* (2nd edition), Delhi: Oxford University Press.

Olavarría de Ersson, E.O. and Shaw, P. (2003) 'Verb complementation patterns in Indian Standard English', *English World-Wide*, 24: 137–61.

Paul, P. (2003) 'The Master's Language and its Indian Uses', in C. Mair (ed.) *The Politics of English as a World Language: New Horizons in Postcolonial Cultural Studies*, Amsterdam: Rodopi. 359–65.

Quirk, R., Greenbaum, S., Leech, G. and Svartvik, J. (1972) *A Grammar of Contemporary English*, London: Longman.

Quirk, R., Greenbaum, S., Leech, G. and Svartvik, J. (1985) *A Comprehensive Grammar of the English Language*, London: Longman.

Rao, B.V.R. (2003) *The Constitution and Language Politics of India*, New Delhi: BRPC.

Rao, R. (1938) *Kanthapura*, London: Allen and Unwin (second edition 1967).

Rushdie, S. (1997) 'Introduction', in S. Rushdie and E. West (eds) *The Vintage Book of Indian Writing 1947–1997*, London: Vintage, pp. ix–xxii.

Schilk, M. (2006) 'Collocations in Indian English: a corpus-based sample analysis', *Anglia*, 124: 276–316.

Schneider, E.W. (2000) 'Feature diffusion vs contact effects in the evolution of new Englishes: a typological case study of negation patterns', *English World-Wide*, 21: 201–30.

——(2003) 'The dynamics of new Englishes: from identity construction to dialect birth', *Language*, 79: 233–81.

——(2007) *Postcolonial English: Varieties around the World*, Cambridge: Cambridge University Press.

Shastri, S.V. (1992) 'Opaque and transparent features of Indian English', in G. Leitner (ed.) *New Directions in English Language Corpora: Methodology, Results, Software Developments*, Berlin: Mouton de Gruyter, pp. 263–75.

Ward, A.W. and Waller, A.R. (1916) *The Cambridge History of English Literature: Vol. XIV*, Cambridge: Cambridge University Press.

10

Sri Lankan Englishes

Dushyanthi Mendis and Harshana Rambukwella

Introduction

English in Sri Lanka dates back to British colonization at the beginning of the nineteenth century. In 1802, Sri Lanka, then known as Ceylon, was declared a Crown Colony with English as its official language. Although Sri Lanka gained independence from the British in 1948, English continued to function as the country's *de facto* official language until 1956, when Sinhala became the sole official language under the terms of the Official Language Act No. 33. Official recognition was not accorded to English again until 1987, when it was included in the chapter on language in the Constitution of Sri Lanka.

Attempting a description of English as it is used and spoken in Sri Lanka today is challenging because of the many complexities involved in terms of speakers, status and functions, dialectal variation and recognition and acceptance. As observed by Meyler (2007: x–xi):

> Even within a small country like Sri Lanka, and even within the relatively tiny English-speaking community, there are several sub-varieties of Sri Lankan English. Sinhalese, Tamils, Muslims and Burghers speak different varieties; Christians, Buddhists, Hindus and Muslims have their own vocabularies; the older generation speak a different language from the younger generation; and the wealthy Colombo elite (who tend to speak English as their first language) speak a different variety from the wider community (who are more likely to learn it as a second language).

In terms of speakers/users, Meyler makes an important observation here which has been consistently emphasized in the literature on Sri Lankan English (SLE) by reputed Sri Lankan scholars and academics, but which is often ignored or not clearly understood in descriptions that label SLE as a second-language variety – i.e. that English is used and spoken both as a first language and as a second/third language in Sri Lanka. In order to be both accurate and valid, any description of SLE as a regional variety must acknowledge and address the complexities arising from this contextual situation.

Second, there appears to be considerable confusion about the position of the English language in Sri Lanka in terms of status and policy. Several recent publications have reported that English is an official language in Sri Lanka, perhaps because of its strong presence, particularly in the nation's capital, in matters of official and state administration, in education and in the media. However, English is not an official language in Sri Lanka. The country's Constitution accords that status to only Sinhala and Tamil. Article 18 (3) in Chapter IV of the Constitution states that 'English shall be the link language'. While no elaboration follows as to what English is supposed to link, one can assume that, given the history of a 30-year conflict between the predominantly Sinhala-speaking majority and sections of the Tamil-speaking minority, English was chosen as a neutral medium of communication between the two communities.

In terms of use and functions, however, English in Sri Lanka is far more than a mere 'link'. It is still pervasive in many areas of officialdom, it is the language used in Sri Lanka's Supreme Court, it has a strong presence in the media and in advertising, it is making a comeback in the country's education system, and it is the undisputed language of choice in the private business and commercial sectors. In other words, its hegemonic grip on the country is still very evident.

Given the often contradictory tensions between description and use, and status and function, it is not surprising that definitions of SLE and its speakers have tended to be vague or simplistic, and often skirt a discussion of the complexities that have influenced and shaped the language into what it is today. Adding to the difficulties encountered in attempting a linguistic and functional description are the widely disparate attitudes prevalent about and towards SLE, ranging from outright rejection of its existence, through ambivalence, to the active encouragement of its use and institutionalization in education.

As in many other postcolonial nations, Sri Lanka too has a well-developed literary tradition in English. Tracing the trajectory of its development from the early twentieth century to the present reveals some of the attitudes of rejection, ambivalence and acceptance mentioned above expressed through choices of language, context and character. This demonstrates that to many of its speakers/users, SLE is not by any means a neutral code, but one that is vested with a meaning and symbolism that operates at many different conscious and subconscious levels.

In this chapter, we will attempt to deal with each of these complexities as comprehensively as possible. We will problematize hitherto unchallenged assumptions about SLE, discuss the findings and implications of recent empirical linguistic studies, and point to the difficulty of pigeon-holing an emergent and still-evolving code in order to make it fit into externally imposed models or typologies. Most multilingual South Asian societies were linguistically diverse and complex entities before the introduction of English and its imposition as the language of power and governance; today, in each of these entities, unique ethnic and cultural factors, both in conjunction and in opposition, have contributed to postcolonial frameworks that may have several commonalities but are also sufficiently diverse to resist easy categorization.

Speakers of Sri Lankan English

By 1940, as noted by C. Fernando (1996), English-speaking Sri Lankans, many of whom had completed their tertiary education in England, occupied leading positions in the government, in education and in the judiciary. In one of the earliest discussions on the

English language in Sri Lanka (1943), Passé observes, 'The small percentage of educated Ceylonese are "English educated"; they know English and for the most part they know it well' (Passé 1979: 16). By the middle of the twentieth century, therefore, a small but nevertheless significant minority of Sri Lankans for whom English was the first or at least the more dominant language was established in Sri Lanka.

The argument that English is still spoken as a first language in Sri Lanka today is based on several factors – method of acquisition, environment of acquisition and domains of use (most importantly, the home), level of proficiency, and the primary language of choice in interpersonal communication. Kandiah (1979: 86–7), referring to speakers of English who use it on a daily basis, notes that:

> The English that these habitual users of Lankan English 'pick up' in this very natural way as the first language of their thought, action and experience in these spheres would, in its spoken form be Lankan, not 'Standard English'.

Perhaps the most compelling argument for the existence of English as a first language in Sri Lanka comes from the country's Burgher community. The Burghers, who are of Eurasian descent, represent about 0.2 per cent of Sri Lanka's population. According to Roberts *et al.* (1989), English had become the mother tongue of many Burgher families as early as in the 1840s. C. Fernando (1996) reports that in the 1940s and 1950s the Burghers still regarded English as their mother tongue. More recently, Rajapakse (2008) cites interview data in which each of her Burgher informants (of three different age groups, representing three generations) unequivocally identified English as their mother tongue.

For a majority of speakers in Sri Lanka, however, English is a second or third language, used primarily for functional purposes. Also, all speakers of SLE today are bilingual, and some are trilingual (Kandiah 1981a; Gunesekera 2005; Meyler 2007). This widespread multilingualism should be placed in context beside the fact that, in Sri Lanka, the English language has been in close contact with Sinhala and Tamil for over two hundred years. This in turn has resulted in the evolution of linguistic features that make SLE distinct from its original input variety – i.e. British English – and continues to exert an influence in areas such as phonology, syntax, grammar and the lexicon.

The status and functions of English in Sri Lanka

Administration

The confusion that exists in relation to the constitutional status of English in Sri Lanka warrants some discussion. Article 22 of the Constitution, titled 'Languages of Administration' states:

(2) In any area where Sinhala is used as the language of administration, a person other than an official acting in his official capacity shall be entitled:
  a to receive communications from, and to communicate and transact business with, any official in his official capacity, in either Tamil or English;
  b if the law recognizes his right to inspect or to obtain copies of or extracts from any official register, record, publication or other document, to obtain a

copy of, or an extract from such register, record, publication or other document, or a translation thereof, as the case may be, in either Tamil or English;

c   where a document is executed by any official for the purpose of being issued to him, to obtain such document or a translation thereof, in either Tamil or English;

(3)   In any area where Tamil is used as the language of administration, a person other than an official acting in his official capacity shall be entitled to exercise the rights, and to obtain the services, referred to in sub paragraphs (a), (b) and (c) of paragraph (2) of this Article, in Sinhala or English.

In many respects, Article 22 stands in contrast to Article 18, which merely states that Sinhala and Tamil are the official languages and that English is the link language in Sri Lanka. First, Article 22 elaborates and spells out the functions of English as Article 18 (3) does not. Second, and perhaps more importantly, Article 22 accords English parity of status with Tamil and Sinhala as a language of administration under certain circumstances. It allows for the right of official communication and the obtaining of official documents in English in an area of the country where a language other than a speaker's mother tongue is the language of administration. Whether this actually happens in practice or not, it can certainly be read as the granting of some degree of official status or recognition to English.

The judiciary

A similar situation is found in Article 23 which specifies the languages of legislation in Sri Lanka: 'All laws and subordinate legislation shall be enacted or made and published in Sinhala and Tamil, together with a translation thereof in English.' Arguably, this may not accord parity of status to English with Sinhala and Tamil, but it does make an English translation a requirement. Sri Lanka's Constitution also spells out the languages that may be used in the country's courts in Article 24, and this is where the most obvious disparity can be seen between status and function. Article 24 (1) states,

> Sinhala and Tamil shall be the languages of the Courts throughout Sri Lanka and Sinhala shall be used as the language of the courts situated in all areas of Sri Lanka except those in any area where Tamil is the language of administration.

However, the language used in Sri Lanka's highest court – i.e. the Supreme Court – as well as quite frequently in the Court of Appeals, is English.

What these examples of the *de facto* status of English in administration and the judiciary clearly demonstrate is the strong presence the language has in important areas of governance in Sri Lanka, more than sixty years after independence from the British. This probably explains the fairly common perception that English is an official language in Sri Lanka, in spite of what the Constitution states in Article 18 (3). In a study conducted among 63 university students in Colombo, 9.3 per cent of the Sinhala students and 35.5 per cent of the Tamil students surveyed believed that English, along with Sinhala and Tamil, is an official language in Sri Lanka (Mendis 2002). A study by Raheem (2006), who surveyed a group of 20 academics who occupied decision-making positions in Sri Lanka's Open University, produced similar findings: 53 per cent of the Sinhala speakers and 40 per cent of the Tamil speakers believe that Sinhala, Tamil and English are all official languages in Sri Lanka. It remains to be seen if larger surveys and surveys of populations in sectors other than education will corroborate these results.

Education

The curriculum pertaining to the teaching of English in Sri Lanka's schools and several language policy decisions taken by universities in the country reveal a reintroduction of the language as a medium of instruction after about forty years of mother tongue education resulting from the Official Language Act No. 33 of 1956. Raheem and Devendra (2007) report that, by the early 1960s, the only university in the country at that time, the University of Ceylon, had begun changing the medium of instruction in its Faculty of Arts from English to Sinhala; C. Fernando (1996) states that by the end of the decade, English had been phased out of Sri Lanka's education system. However, the 1980s saw a new phenomenon – the appearance of privately managed 'International Schools' which were established as business enterprises, and which therefore did not come under the purview and dictates of the Ministry of Education, which would have meant adhering to the stipulation of mother tongue education as specified in the country's Constitution. The medium of instruction in these 'International Schools' is English, and this option has proved to be so popular that there are now English-medium pre-schools for children as young as three years.

The 1990s saw the introduction of government-sponsored interventions designed to strengthen the teaching of English in all state and private schools in which the medium of instruction was either Sinhala or Tamil. These interventions applied at all levels of the curriculum, from Grade 1 to Grade 13. Children were thus supposed to be exposed to English at a very early age. A policy of bilingual education came into practice in 2000, when English-medium instruction in science and mathematics subjects was introduced to selected schools at the secondary level (Grades 11 and 12). Around the same time, several of the faculties of arts and humanities in Sri Lanka's universities which had either Sinhala or Tamil as a medium of instruction started considering the possibility of moving towards English-medium instruction.

How successful the attempt at reintroducing English as a medium of instruction into the school system will be, and what effect it will have on the use and spread of English in Sri Lanka, is yet to be seen. Raheem and Devendra (2007) report on an initial dearth of teachers competent to teach in English, a lack of training provided for the new ESL initiatives introduced at the primary level in schools, and urban–rural disparities in terms of facilities and support for the new English language programmes. However, there does appear to be an increase in the use of English in interpersonal communication and in the domain of the home among young people in Sri Lanka, and this could very well be the result of a revitalization of English teaching in schools.

Interpersonal communication

Raheem's (2006) study of a group of university academics indicates an increase in the use of English among the informants' peers and children. More than half the group also reported that their language of choice would be English when talking to a superior. Although the study does not explain reasons for these choices, it is possible that an instrumental motivation underlies the use of English with children, while the use of English with a superior could be an acknowledgement of the prestige associated with knowing and using English in Sri Lanka. A more recent study by Künstler et al. (2009) of 122 participants also drawn mostly from Sri Lanka's education sectors reveals a correlation between age and the use of English in interpersonal communication. The

185

younger the respondents, the more likely they were to use English in general topics with friends. A possible reason for this is the use of English in email and text messaging, the latter having become an extremely popular and widespread method of communication in Sri Lanka. In fact, text messaging appears to have created a linguistic space in which even those who are not very proficient in English are not afraid to communicate, as the usual prescriptive rules pertaining to correctness of spelling and grammar rarely apply to this type of discourse (Mendis 2006).

Sri Lankan English (SLE): stability and evolution

SLE has been referred to as a language (Gunesekera 2005; Meyler 2007), a dialect (Parakrama 1995; Gunesekera 2005; D. Fernando 2007), both a language and a dialect (S. Fernando 1985: 2008) and 'an independent, distinctive and fully formulated linguistic organism' (Kandiah 1981a: 102). From a sociolinguistic point of view, SLE is all of these. It is a language in the sense of a superordinate term that can be used without reference to a dialect, whereas the term 'dialect' is meaningless unless it is implied that there is more than one dialect, or a language to which a dialect can be said to 'belong', as explained by Haugen (1966); however, as Haugen himself points out, in reality languages and dialects represent a dichotomy in a situation that is infinitely complex, and are thus best represented as a continuum rather than in contrast with or in opposition to each other. This is certainly the case with SLE, which is by no means a 'fixed' or static code with no dialectal variation. The term 'variety' is also applied to SLE, as is to be expected, from a New Englishes, World Englishes or Postcolonial Englishes perspective. This multiplicity of terminology, while sometimes confusing, is often necessary to convey all the connotations of a code that displays simultaneously the features of the input variety from which it derives its name as well as features which place it very firmly and without doubt in the sociolinguistic contexts from which it draws its current sustenance, and on which it depends for survival.

Much of the literature available up to now on the features of SLE has been largely impressionistic accounts not supported by representative samples of speakers or (in the case of phonology) instrumental acoustic analyses, or by corpus data that reflect syntactic and grammatical language in use across a range of genres. As Parakrama (1995: 34) observes:

> *all* the writing to date has been based on random examples and personal experience. Nothing like a large-scale sociolinguistic survey or a systematic study has been undertaken. As a result, the findings of linguists remain more impressionistic than necessary, and even the acceptability of the few cited examples are contested.

In 2007, however, a dictionary of Sri Lankan English was published, the compilation of which shows an attempt at using a corpus-based approach. Second, a corpus of Sri Lankan English (ICE-SL) is currently being compiled, as part of the larger International Corpus of English (ICE) project; about two-thirds of the written component of ICE-SL (130 text files) is now complete, and these data are beginning to provide insights into features of SLE in a number of written genres. The discussion that follows on the syntax, grammar and morphology of SLE will draw on these two databases.

Phonology

The phonology of SLE is an area in which a fair amount of work has been published, and there appears to be broad agreement on phonological features that mark SLE (Parakrama 1995; D. Fernando 2007). However, most of these studies have focused on features of a high prestige variety of SLE – i.e. the dialect used by speakers for whom SLE is the first language. S. Fernando (2008), whose recent study suggests that at least four different dialects of SLE can be distinguished on the basis of fairly systematic features of pronunciation, is a notable exception. However, empirical evidence is needed from speakers before these conclusions can be accepted.

The following list of phonological features is drawn from the early work of S. Fernando (1985) and the more recent observations of Meyler (2007), on the basis that the same or similar features being attested to after twenty years is a reasonable argument for relative stability. Before proceeding, however, a few points must be made. Fernando's 1985 list is much more comprehensive than Meyler's, and includes features that Fernando herself refers to as 'learner interlanguages' (1985: 53). Her differentiation between such features and those of a more 'standard' dialect of SLE is further support for the argument that SLE has more than one dialect. All of Meyler's observations, however, pertain to the high prestige variety of SLE, which he refers to as 'standard SLE'. The list that follows, therefore, is representative of features discernible in the high prestige variety of SLE.

1 Replacing of [ɛɪ] and [əu] in British English with the long vowels [eː] and [oː].
2 Replacing the voiced fricative [ð] with a voiced dental plosive [d̪] and the voiceless fricative [θ] with a voiceless dental plosive [t̪]. Fernando (1985) adds that alveolar plosives in British English take on a slightly retroflex articulation in SLE.
3 The use of a labiodental frictionless continuant [ʋ] for both [v] and [w] in word-initial position.
4 Devoicing of [z] in word initial, word final and intervocalic positions.
5 In the case of the inflectional suffix -ed, SLE uses [əd] instead of the British English [ɪd]. Fernando (1985) describes this as the feature of placing a neutral vowel [ə] in all unstressed vowels in final syllables of words.
6 Primary stress tends to be placed on the first syllable of a word, which Meyler (2007) contrasts with British English, in which he says the stress would typically be placed on the second syllable.

In addition to these features, Meyler (2007) lists many examples of variable (i.e. not systematic) pronunciation, pointing to the unstable nature of SLE phonology. One such example cited is the pronunciation of the syllable containing the letter 'i' in the words 'granite', 'marine' and 'binoculars'. Meyler reports the use of a diphthong [aɪ] in SLE in contrast to [i] or [ɪ] in British English; however, some speakers of SLE use the high front vowel [i] in *marine*. Similar variation is also found in the pronunciation of words such as 'direct' and 'finance'.

Syntax

A feature of SLE which it possibly shares with other South Asian varieties, but, according to Meyler (2007), not with British English, is a marked difference between speech and

187

writing. Several reasons can be posited for this, including an adherence to archaic written norms even to the extent of seeming 'dated and overly formal' (Meyler 2007: xiv) or a natural tendency on the part of speakers to maintain a distance between spoken and written codes as in the case of Sinhala and Tamil, both of which are languages with diglossic features. Unfortunately, this is another characteristic of SLE that has to remain unsubstantiated by data at present because of the lack of representative corpora for the purpose of comparison. However, some preliminary findings on syntactic patterns in speech have begun to appear. For instance, Rajapakse (2008), using a small corpus of speech data recorded in the homes of informants from Sri Lanka's Burgher community has been able to provide support for Kandiah's (1981b) observations of three syntactic structures he claims are characteristic of Sri Lankan English – ellipsis, focalization and topicalization.

Rajapakse (2008: 52) cites the following examples of ellipsis from the speech of her informants. The words omitted are given in brackets.

1 They hardly know that there's a community called Eurasians. Most of them have migrated. [There is] Just a handful here. (Male speaker, aged 65–90)
2 Where dressing is concerned also [there is] no place at all now. (Female speaker, aged 40–60)

Kandiah (1981b: 64) gives the following sentence as an example of what he means by focalization:

3 Before five o'clock, Nimal woke up.

Rajapakse's (2008: 53) speech data yields the following:

4 Now a Burgher is not heard of. (Female speaker, 65–90)
5 Today you can't say *no* who's a burgher and who's a Sinhalese. (Male speaker, 65–90)

Topicalization, interpreted by Rajapakse as the fronting of the topic of an utterance from Kandiah's sentence 'Kasy, I expect him to make an exciting contribution to Tamil studies' (1981b: 64) is evident in the following speech excerpts:

6 Today's Burghers I don't think that fun loving. (Female speaker, 18–35)
7 The British they treat us very shabbily. (Male speaker, 18–35)

(Rajapakse 2008: 53)

Since Rajapakse's data is admittedly limited in terms of a relatively small number of speakers from a single Sri Lankan speech community, these findings can only be considered as preliminary; they are, however, the first steps towards substantiating observations made about SLE before the advent of corpus-based techniques in analysing and describing language use.

Grammar

In his dictionary, Meyler (2007) lists several grammatical features of SLE which he claims are in contrast with British English in terms of either use, frequency or both. As not all of these features can be addressed in a work of a general nature, we have chosen to discuss phrasal verbs, an area of grammar that has recently come to the attention of both researchers and language teachers in Sri Lanka (D. Fernando 2007). Meyler highlights two differences between SLE and what he refers to as British Standard English (BSE) in terms of the verb particle – in some cases, a phrasal verb in BSE such as 'throw away' is used without a particle in SLE, as in 'Please don't throw my letter' (2007: xvii); in other cases, a particle is added in SLE which would not be found in BSE, as in 'She couldn't bear up the pain' (2007: xvii). A third feature of SLE is the existence of phrasal verbs with meanings not found in BSE, such as 'put on' meaning to gain weight, 'pass out' meaning to graduate (from a university or technical college) and 'come down' meaning to fail (an examination or test).

Not surprisingly, with such variety, phrasal verbs in SLE have become a heated topic of debate and not inconsiderable confusion in relation to their syntactic and semantic 'correctness'. For instance, while the use of 'put on' and 'pass out' are accepted in speech and in some informal written registers in the contexts of gaining weight and graduating from an institution, 'cope up' tends to be seen as an error. In one of the few studies conducted on perceptions of correctness of SLE lexico-grammar, D. Fernando (2007) surveyed 242 teachers of English from secondary schools in Sri Lanka and asked them to rate as correct or incorrect the use of a selection of phrasal verbs in sample sentences. Table 10.1 gives eight of these phrasal verbs, the contextual meaning of each as made clear in sample sentences, and the informants' responses in relation to correctness of use.

First, the percentages above illustrate a clear difference in the correctness ratings given to the first five phrasal verbs and the last three, which indicates that there is a collective sense of what is acceptable and not acceptable. Second, if the five phrasal verbs that received the highest percentages in terms of correctness are different in form and/or meaning from BSE, we can conclude that some parts of the grammar of SLE are evolving in directions that increase its distinctiveness from its input variety. As an example of such an evolving grammatical category, it will be interesting to see where 'cope up' will lie on a cline of acceptability in the future. A search of the 130-text ICE-SL sub-corpus produced two tokens of 'cope up', in the categories of Informational (popular) texts (W2B) and press editorials (W2E). The concordances are given below.

8   water is required. To **cope up** with the demand of the increasing population (W2B)
9   find it difficult to **cope up** with the hardships they have to endure (W2E)

Table 10.1 Phrasal verbs in SLE

Phrasal verb	Meaning in SLE	Rated correct
bear up	to endure	88%
come down	to fail (an examination)	79%
passed out	to graduate	78%
took it up	to accept	72%
go as	to be known as, to be called	71%
falls into	to meet, to intersect	43%
blew off	to explode	41%
got up	to wake up	36%

Clearly, 'cope up', whether considered correct or incorrect by language teachers and other prescriptivists, appears to be making inroads into certain written genres of SLE and could possibly be a phrasal verb that contributes to the distinctiveness of SLE at some future date.

Morphology and the lexicon

The lexicon of SLE is another area that has been subject to a fair amount of discussion, especially in relation to Sri Lankan creative writing in English (see, for instance, Canagarajah 1994; S. Fernando 1989). These studies have tended to focus on Sinhala, Tamil or Malay words which have been either borrowed or assimilated into SLE and which writers have used to convey a particular contextual ethos or Sri Lankan 'flavour' through their work. However, an examination of the vocabulary of colloquial SLE reveals processes more complex than straightforward borrowing in the coining or creating of 'new' lexical items.

For instance, SLE has many noun compounds which are unique to the Sri Lankan context, and which can be found in *A Dictionary of Sri Lankan English* (Meyler 2007) along with their meanings. Some of these are 'agency post office' (a private post office), 'border villages' (Sinhala villages bordering traditional Tamil areas in the Northern, Eastern and North Central Provinces), 'floor patient' (a patient in a hospital without a bed, who has to lie on the floor), 'jump seat' (a folding seat in the aisle of a bus) and 'line rooms' (estate labourers' accommodation). These compounds are the result of combining two English words, but others which are combinations of Sinhala and English words, such as 'boru part' (putting on airs) and 'peduru party' (an informal party usually with live traditional eastern music) also exist in SLE. As observed by Meyler, however, while such compounds are common features of colloquial SLE, they would not necessarily be considered acceptable in more formal written contexts.

A more creative morphological process is the application of English affixes to Sinhala words to form unusual and unique lexical items. Meyler refers to this process as one where non-English words are 'Anglicized' (2007: xv). For instance, the affix -fy is added to a Sinhala word/term to create a colloquial verb in SLE, such as 'rasthiyadufy' (to go to a lot of trouble and achieve nothing) or 'gnurugnurufy' (to moan or whinge). The same process is sometimes applied to an English word in a manner not permitted in British or American English, resulting in a colloquial SLE verb as in 'stingify'. The affix -ish is also sometimes employed to create 'new' words, as in the case of 'vomitish'.

If it can be shown that lexical items such as these are only found in speech data, the argument that there is a marked distinction between speech and writing in SLE would be strengthened considerably. A different and more difficult question to answer is whether lexical items which are a combination of an English and Sinhala/Tamil word or which have only an English suffix should be considered as part of the vocabulary of SLE. This can only be determined through wide-scale studies of acceptability and use which have unfortunately not yet been undertaken.

Sri Lankan English: myth or reality?

That English occupies a niche in Sri Lanka from which it cannot easily be dislodged is beyond dispute. However, there is far less agreement on what variety of English this is, or should be. There is still a belief among many speakers that the English spoken in Sri Lanka is British English. In a recent survey, Gunesekera (2005) found that a former president of Sri Lanka, the then leader of the opposition and several prominent ministers in the government believe that they speak British English. Furthermore, ironically, the English Language Teaching Unit of a university in Sri Lanka's Southern Province (known for its strong nationalistic ideologies) claims to teach RP (Received Pronunciation) in its ESL programme.

It should be noted that a lack of awareness of the distinctiveness of the language one speaks is not wholly unusual if the language has been acquired as a first language in the domain of the home, and if one does not have a point of comparison with a different variety. This is the case with grammar and syntax as comprehensive descriptions of British English are not easily available in Sri Lanka. The case of accent or pronunciation is different, as these features are discernible through the media, films and popular music. In fact, such an awareness is reflected in the responses to D. Fernando's (2007) study, in which 81 per cent of the respondents agreed that SLE refers to the accent of Sri Lankan speakers. One can argue therefore that an awareness of SLE as a variety distinct from British or American English is not entirely lacking.

When SLE is posited as a target or production norm, however, a more complex attitudinal picture emerges. In Künstler *et al.*'s study, when asked what kind of English is spoken in Sri Lanka, 62 per cent of the respondents selected the option 'Other variety of English' over RP or American English, with 30 per cent specifying this variety as 'Standard Sri Lankan English'; but when asked what kind of English they would like to speak, 50 per cent of the respondents selected RP, while only 40 per cent chose 'Other'. Similarly, in response to the question 'What kind of English do you think should be taught in schools?' 49 per cent said 'RP', 38 per cent said 'Other' and 6 per cent said 'RP and Other', pointing to a mismatch between the actual production form and the target norm the informants aim for (Künstler *et al.* 2009). Clearly, a situation of 'linguistic schizophrenia' (Kachru 1992: 60), not unusual with postcolonial Englishes, exists to some extent in Sri Lanka.

What does the future hold for English in Sri Lanka? Recent research indicates that the nationalistic ideologies of the 1960s and 1970s which rejected English (especially in education) have weakened (Mendis 2002; Raheem 2006). When asked about interpersonal communication, 97.5 per cent of the respondents of Künstler *et al.*'s study stated that they would like to speak English, and 75.4 per cent said they would be embarrassed if they had no English language skills. Based on these preliminary findings, Künstler *et al.* conclude that, overall, it seems fair to assume that in the future English will become even more firmly rooted in Sri Lankan society.

The final section of this chapter will discuss the use of English as a medium of creative expression in Sri Lanka. The discussion will show that some of the attitudes towards SLE described above, can be found, whether stated overtly or merely implicitly, in the history of Sri Lankan literature in English.

Sri Lankan writing in English

Creative writing in English has been a part of Sri Lankan literary culture since the late eighteenth century. In its early phases this writing was largely limited to the British expatriate community although a few Sri Lankan writers such as James de Alwis wrote

191

and published in the early nineteenth century. A more substantial body of English writing is evident in the first half of the twentieth century, with British writers such as Leonard Woolf and Sri Lankan writers such as R.L. Spittel and Lucian de Zilwa producing novels which received some critical acclaim. However, it is with the increasing output of writing in the post-independence period that Sri Lankan writing in English (SLWE) becomes identifiable as a distinctive postcolonial category.

There has been a steady increase in SLWE from the 1970s onwards with both resident and non-resident writers contributing to its regional and international profile. The Gratiaen Prize, which is awarded annually for the best creative work in English in Sri Lanka, and the State Literary Awards sponsored by the Sri Lankan government, which reserves a specific award for writing in English, give creative writing in English institutional recognition. The critical reception of SLWE, however, has been mixed. The conceptual and ideological debates attending to the choice of English as a medium of representation in non-Anglophone cultural contexts such as Africa and India have been largely absent in Sri Lanka. Sri Lankan writers, with the notable exception of Lakdasa Wikkramasinha (1941–78), have generally not engaged extensively with either the poetics or politics of writing in English. This in turn has led prominent Sri Lankan critics to view most SLWE as lacking a substantial connection to the larger political or cultural ethos it emerges from (Kandiah 1971, 1997; Canagarajah 1994). Both Kandiah and Canagarajah have argued that stylistic, and at times thematic, innovation when it appears has largely failed to capture what are understood to be 'local' realities.

Stylistic analyses have looked at how language use – whether it is the use of metaphor, words borrowed from Sinhala, Tamil or Malay, or experimentation with grammar – 'fits' the local reality it attempts to convey. Such analyses also often make a positive or negative evaluation of the writing based on its ability to be faithful to a local reality, i.e. how effective the writing has been in using English to convey a non-Anglophone ethos. However, such an approach can be highly subjective and at times tends to ignore how the paradigm of authenticity itself needs to be historicized. The localizing tendency in SLWE, and critical responses to it, cannot be understood in isolation from the strong cultural nationalist context that influenced it. Writers like Yasmine Gooneratne, James Goonewardene and Jean Arasanayagam who experimented with thematic and formal aspects of English writing in the 1970s and 1980s did so within a decolonizing framework where there was resentment towards English – precipitating a sense of beleaguerment among English writers.

Prior to the 1990s, when it was used in poetry or prose, SLE was a marker of a lack of education and a source of humour, with a variety of English close to the colonial standard used for the authorial/narrative voice in the text. While it is difficult to sustain a blanket claim that the Sri Lankan sociolinguistic landscape has altered radically, a greater fluidity in the use of SLE in general as a creative medium is evident in a number of recent publications. Also, we see that the inclusion of SLE does not necessarily serve the satirical purposes of earlier writers. Several recent novels suggest that thematically and linguistically Sri Lankan writers are relatively more attuned to the sociopolitical complexities of English in the country and at the same time use the language – i.e. SLE – unapologetically and with far less self-consciousness.

For instance, Manuka Wijesinghe's *Monsoons and Potholes* (2006) is a satirical text that interweaves a personal and familial coming-of-age narrative with sociopolitical commentary. Most of the dialogue in the novel occurs in SLE, which complements its urban middle-class social setting. But *Monsoons and Potholes* also confronts the hierarchies associated with different varieties of SLE. For instance the idea of 'goday' or rustic or unfashionable pronunciation associated with speakers of English as a second or third language is treated comically, but at the same time such attitudes are also critiqued overtly.

Monsoons and Potholes has two subaltern characters who are accorded a limited register of SLE. One of them is Dasa, a Sinhala boy from a village who works as a domestic for the narrator's family. Predictably, Dasa's attempts at speaking English evoke humour among the narrator's family. However, where an earlier novel would not have gone beyond the humour, Wijesinghe uses a dialogue between herself (as the narrator) and Dasa to critique this attitude.

[Dasa] 'Your friends told me I should come as a DJ to their parties.'
[Manuka] 'Don't talk nonsense, as if they would ask you to come to their parties? You can't even talk English.'
'My name is Dasa. I go to village school. I live in village big house where Mr Tissa's mother living [Manuka's paternal grandmother], I am … '
'Not like that. You don't speak English like a person from a Colombo school.' Dasa looked hurt.
'Okay, your English is good, but it is different to ours,' I tried to pacify him. I realized that what I had said wasn't very nice. We English speaking people had a sense of linguistic superiority. It was an idiotic sense of superiority but it was hard to eliminate.

(Wijesinghe 2006: 297)

Elmo Jayawardena's *Sam's Story* (2001) is a text that is less overtly concerned about issues of language than *Monsoons and Potholes*. Its central character, Sammy, is an intellectually challenged Sinhala villager whose quirky first-person perspective on contemporary Sri Lankan life forms the main narrative element of the novel. Seen through Sam's eyes the lifestyle of his upper-middle-class employers appears pampered and protected. For instance, the socioeconomic realities of war are made explicit in the following excerpt:

Our Boy [the master's son] knew very little about the war and what was going on. He only came here for holidays. To jump in the river and send his sky rockets, or row the red boat to build his arm muscles. This war had nothing to do with him. He was out of it, protected by who he was.
The sad part is my two little brothers didn't know about the war either. They certainly had nothing to do with it.
But then, they didn't have anyone to protect them …
That's why Jaya and Madiya went to this miserable war, one to die, the other to run and hide and be called a coward …

(Jayawardena 2001: 144)

As is evident, *Sam's Story* does not make a sustained attempt to 'localize' Sam's language but is arguably effective in conveying his perspective. What the text does, however, is to mark Sam's non-English-speaking identity by introducing some common mispronunciations of English words into his dialogue. Sam consistently pronounces the name of one of the pet dogs in the house, Brutus, as 'Bhurus', his master's favourite drink Scotch becomes 'is-scotch' and aeroplanes are 'aerobblanes'. All of these can be used to ridicule 'uneducated' speakers of English. But in the case of *Sam's Story,* because the dominant perspective is Sam's, the 'proper' pronunciation is rendered ironic instead:

> 'No no Sam, it is not Bhurus, it is BRUTUS.'
>
> She [the master's daughter] would make her eyes big and give this funny growl-ing sound; she called it rolling. She would start by tightening her mouth and extending her lips into a small round hole saying 'brrrrouuuuu' and go 'TUS' like breaking a stick …
>
> I never could get that funny sounding name. After a while she gave up. She stopped trying to correct me whenever I called my friend. I am not sure but I think she knew I was right. Once or twice I heard her ignoring her round mouth 'ooos' and stick breaking 'tusses' and calling my friend the way I did – Bhurus.
>
> Bhurus of course didn't mind. …
>
> When I said 'Bhurus, come, come,' he came. I think he liked my name better, Bhurus.
>
> (Jayawardena 2001: 8)

Sam's story illustrates that a non-Anglophone perspective can be sympathetically and effectively represented in English without major linguistic innovation. The self-irony built into the narrative facilitates a critical view of the linguistic and social practices of the English-speaking and/or affluent classes in the country without explicit concern about using English as the medium for such representation. Thus, the choice of English as a medium of creative expression no longer appears to raise the same fraught ideo-logical issues as it did a few decades ago. Syntactic and grammatical structures of SLE which were once stigmatized and used for comic effect are being appropriated by newer writers who use them with a remarkable lack of self-consciousness, and some-times even with pride, giving them a legitimacy that they previously lacked. It remains to be seen whether these recent trends in literature will in any way be instrumental in creating more awareness and eventually, more acceptance and recognition of SLE as a distinctive South Asian variety among its speakers.

Suggestions for further reading

Salgado, M. (2007) *Writing Sri Lanka: Literature, Resistance and the Politics of Place*, London: Routledge. (Salgado's text looks at a fairly representative selection of Sri Lankan writing in English (SLWE). Salgado critically interrogates how nationalist boundary-marking operates in SLWE and also provides readings of moments where Salgado believes texts/authors transcend such ethno-nationalist boundaries. It is an example of how SLWE now has a distinct profile within postcolonial writing – one large enough to warrant sustained study. It has a useful and extensive references list that can direct readers to more material on SLWE.)

Goonetilleke, D.C.R.A. (2005) *Sri Lankan English Literature and the Sri Lankan People, 1917–2003*, Colombo: Vijitha Yaapa Publications. (This is possibly the single most 'representative' work on Sri Lankan writing in English currently available. It contains chapters on a fairly extensive range of writers and traces the historical development of English writing in the country. Goonetilleke also attempts to position English writing in the context of writing in local languages, especially Sinhala.)

Coperahewa, S. (2009) 'The language planning situation in Sri Lanka', *Current Issues in Language Planning*, 10 (1): 69–150. (This monograph gives a fairly comprehensive historical introduction to the linguistic situation in Sri Lanka. It provides broad historical coverage on the development of local languages and the later introduction of English. Though the overall perspective is language policy planning there are substantial sections devoted to discussing the three main languages (Sinhala, Tamil and English) and their interrelationships. Data on literacy rates, distribution of linguistic groups within the country, etc., is also provided. It also has an extensive references section representing a large body of linguistic studies on Sri Lanka. It should serve as a good point of entry for those interested in the larger linguistic context of Sri Lanka.)

References

Canagarajah, A.S. (1994) 'Competing discourses in Sri Lankan English poetry', *World Englishes*, 13 (3): 361–76.

Constitution of the Democratic Socialist Republic of Sri Lanka (1978)

Fernando, C. (1996) 'The post-imperial status of English in Sri Lanka 1940–90. From first to second language', in J.A. Fishman, A.W. Conrad and A. Rubal-Lopez (eds) *Post-imperial English: Status Change in Former British and American Colonies, 1940–1990*, Berlin: Walter de Gruyter, pp. 485–511.

Fernando, D. (2007) 'Good English or Sri Lankan English? A study of English teachers' awareness of their own variety', unpublished MA thesis, University of Reading.

Fernando, S. (1985) 'Changes in Sri Lankan English as reflected in phonology', *University of Colombo Review*, 5: 41–53.

——(1989) 'Style range in Sri Lankan English fiction: an analysis of four texts', *World Englishes*, 8 (2): 119–31.

——(2008) 'When is a "hall" a "hole"?' in D. Fernando and D. Mendis (eds) *English for Equality, Employment and Empowerment* (selected papers from the 4th International Conference of the Sri Lanka English Language Teachers' Association), Colombo: SLELTA, pp. 71–81.

Gunesekera, M. (2005) *The Postcolonial Identity of Sri Lankan English*, Colombo: Katha Publishers.

Haugen, E. (1966) 'Dialect, language, nation', *American Anthropologist*, 68 (4): 922–35.

Jayawardena, E. (2001) *Sam's Story*, Colombo: Vijitha Yapa Publications.

Kachru, B. (1992) 'Models for non-native Englishes', in B. Kachru (ed.) *The Other Tongue: English Across Cultures*, Urbana, IL: University of Illinois Press, pp. 48–74.

Kandiah, T. (1971) 'New Ceylon English: *The Call of the Kirala*, a novel by James Goonawardene', *New Ceylon Writing*, 90–4.

——(1979) 'Disinherited Englishes: the case of Lankan English' (Part 1), *Navasilu*, 3: 75–89.

——(1981a) 'Disinherited Englishes: the case of Lankan English', (Part 2), *Navasilu*, 4: 92–113.

——(1981b) 'Lankan English schizoglossia', *English World-Wide*, 2 (1): 63–81.

——(1997) 'Towards a Lankan canon in English creative writing: subversions of postcolonialism and the resisting representations of Chitra Fernando's fictional voice', *Phoenix: Sri Lanka Journal of English in the Commonwealth*, 5 and 6: 47–72.

Künstler, V., Mendis, D. and Mukherjee, J. (2009) 'English in Sri Lanka: language functions and speaker attitudes', *International Journal of English Studies*, 20 (2): 57–74.

Mendis, D. (2002) 'Language planning and ethnicity: attitudes and perceptions from the education sector', *The Sri Lanka Journal of the Humanities*, XXVII and XXVIII: 161–84.

——(2006) 'Situating SMS (Short Message Service) discourse', *The Sri Lanka Journal of the Humanities*, XXXII (1 and 2): 125–34.

Meyler, M. (2007) *A Dictionary of Sri Lankan English*, Colombo: Michael Meyler.

Parakrama, A. (1995) *De-hegemonizing Language Standards*, London: Macmillan.

Passé, H.A. (1979 [1943]) 'The English language in Ceylon', *Navasilu*, 3: 12–20. Originally printed (1943) *University of Ceylon Review*, 1 (2).

Raheem, R. (2006) 'Configuring the mosaic: investigating language use and attitude in Sri Lanka' in R. Ratwatte and S. Herath (eds) *English in the Multilingual Environment* (selected papers from the 3rd International Conference of the Sri Lanka English Language Teachers' Association), Colombo: SLELTA, pp. 13–27.

Raheem, R. and Devendra, D. (2007) 'Changing times, changing attitudes. The history of English education in Sri Lanka' in Yeon Hee Choi and B. Spolsky (eds) *English Education in Asia: History and Policies*, Korea: Asia TEFL Book Series, pp. 181–203.

Rajapakse, A. (2008) 'A descriptive analysis of the language of the Burghers of Sri Lanka', in D. Fernando and D. Mendis (eds) *English for Equality, Employment and Empowerment* (selected papers from the 4th International Conference of the Sri Lanka English Language Teachers' Association), Colombo: SLELTA, pp. 48–58.

Roberts, M., Raheem, I. and Colin-Thome, P. (1989) *People Inbetween: The Burghers and the Middle Class in the Transformations within Sri Lanka, 1790s–1960s* (Vol. 1), Ratmalana: Sarvodaya Book Publishing Services.

Wijesinghe, M. (2006) *Monsoons and Potholes*, Colombo: Perera Hussein Publishing House.

11

East and West African Englishes

Differences and commonalities

Hans-Georg Wolf

Introduction

African English – that is, the second-language varieties of English spoken in Sub-Saharan Africa – can be divided into three distinct regional varieties: West African English, East African English and Southern African English. This chapter focuses on West African English (WAE) and East African English (EAE), while Southern African English, represented by English in Botswana, is dealt with in a separate chapter (Smieja and Mathangwane, this volume). Although all of the national varieties of WAE have a number of features in common, WAE is more heterogeneous than EAE. WAE comprises, moving from west to (south) east, Gambian English, Sierra Leonean English, Liberian English, Nigerian English and Cameroon English. While the varieties of WAE show more linguistic diversity amongst themselves, WAE is a geographically and notionally better delineated theoretical entity than EAE. In the so-called 'heartland' of EAE – Uganda, Kenya and Tanzania – a relatively homogenous variety is spoken. Yet the EAE varieties on the fringes are either not sufficiently described (e.g. the Englishes spoken in Somalia and Ethiopia – and for some initial findings on Sudanese English, see Peter 2003) or are part of a transition zone to Southern African English (especially Malawian English). The discussion of EAE will concentrate on the English spoken in the heartland.

This chapter is structured in the following way. First, the historical development of English in West and East Africa is briefly considered. It is argued that British colonial policy contributed significantly to the sociolinguistic and, indirectly, even to the structural similarities and differences these varieties exhibit. While colonial policy provided the political framework for the emergence of the regional and national varieties in question, a number of other factors contributed to their characteristics. These factors are introduced and exemplified. Then the discussion moves on to give a short overview of the two regional varieties and the national varieties of WAE. As already indicated, it is found that, although united by common linguistic features, WAE is far more heterogeneous than EAE, and the national varieties of WAE need to be seen in their own right. Focusing primarily on phonetic but also on lexical features, the section summarizes and contrasts the main diagnostic and distinctive features of the two regional varieties, and details the peculiarities of the national varieties of WAE. However, despite their structural differences, WAE and EAE are rooted in a shared 'African culture'. Another section introduces recent studies in which the expression of culture in African English is investigated from a cognitive sociolinguistic perspective, and conceptual and linguistic patterns common to both regional varieties in question, in contrast to American English and British English, are highlighted.

Historical background and reasons for the emergence of distinct West and East African varieties of English

Both East and West African English are rooted in colonialism. With the exception of Liberia, which was a settler colony of freed American slaves, all of the countries in which the varieties in question are spoken were British colonies. 'Colony' is a term broadly applied here, as it covers protectorates and League of Nations Mandates/UN Trusteeships. 'Indirect rule' is the usual label given to British colonial policy in Africa. This rule can be characterized as utilitarian, decentralized and socially distant from the colonial subjects. Unlike the French, for example, the British had no intention to assimilate or associate with the indigenous population in their African territories (for detailed discussions, see Wolf 2001: 66–99; Wolf 2008a). For linguistic and educational policy, this meant that, primarily for financial reasons, the British relied heavily on missions for the education of the locals. The missions, for the most part, were inclined to spread the gospel and to teach in the native languages. Furthermore, the British were rather possessive about their own language and very reluctant to provide, let alone encourage, education in English. Besides, in many places, especially the rural parts of the territories under their control, children did not receive education at all because of the unwillingness of the British to become financially involved. This educational policy had sociolinguistic consequences that persist until today. For practical purposes, the British administrations, and many mission societies, preferred the lingua francas that already existed in the territories under administration over English and the smaller African languages. In East Africa, the lingua franca was Swahili, which is still the overall dominating language in this region. In some parts of West Africa, for example the former Southern Cameroons and in Southern Nigeria, it was Pidgin English, or, in Sierra Leone, Krio. These varieties or languages – depending on whether one wants to classify them as varieties of English or as separate languages – are still predominant in the respective linguistic situations (cf. below). The same holds true for Haussa in Northern Nigeria. By and large, the British hands-off policy has led to a lower ratio of speakers of English in former British colonies, as compared to speakers of French in former French colonies. Though exact statistical figures for the countries in question are hard to come by, data from Cameroon – which has both a British and a French colonial legacy – indicates that the number of children who speak a standard form of Cameroon English in the Anglophone part is lower than the number of children who speak French in the Francophone part (see Wolf 2001: 72, 169–79).

The British non-involvement in educational matters, coupled with their refusal to teach English to the natives, in many instances helped the emergence of distinct national varieties, at least in West Africa (see below). Unlike in French colonies, there was no insistence on a metropolitan linguistic standard. The same laissez-faire policy was pursued in East Africa, yet EAE is, as indicated before, far more homogenous than

WAE (for a very general clustering of World Englishes in terms of features, see Schneider 2008). This difference calls for an explanation, although the various reasons cannot be discussed at length here. The idea that substrate influences alone can account for L2 variation is no longer tenable. Partially drawing from Abdulaziz (1991), Harris (1996), Simo Bobda (2003) and Peter (2008), I would like to suggest the following, to some extent overlapping, mix of factors to account for the differences between the two regional varieties in question: colonial input, geographic proximity, endonormative processes, attitudes and (functional) distribution of languages/language varieties.

An example of differentiating colonial input is the realization of the /ʌ/ or STRUT vowel of the Received Pronunciation (RP, the usual reference form) as predominantly /ɔ/ in WAE, as opposed to /a/ in EAE. The first sustained contacts of British merchants and sailors with the indigenous population in West Africa date back to the seventeenth century, 'when the vowel still had a rounded realisation in most British accents' (Simo Bobda 2003: 19; also see Harris 1996: 33–4). In East Africa, on the other hand, British settlers arrived in the nineteenth century, i.e. at a time when the STRUT vowel had already been fronted (Simo Bobda 2003: 19, also see Harris 1996: 33–4), with /a/ being the nearest phoneme from the phonetic inventory of the African languages.

Another important factor is geographical proximity or distance, and examples abound. Anglophone East and West Africa are separated by a vast geographical space and a linguistic barrier of Francophone countries. On the other hand, the varieties of English spoken in Cameroon and Nigeria – two adjacent countries – have several features in common (see below). The Anglophone part of Cameroon under League of Nations Mandate and later UN Trusteeship was practically administered as part of Nigeria, and Cameroonians had to go to Nigeria for a university education. Besides, many Igbo traders from Nigeria lived and were active in Cameroon (see Wolf 2001: Ch. 3). Hence, the realization of the /ɜː/ vowel for <er, ear, ir> as /ɛ/ is shared by speakers of English from Eastern Nigeria (the homeland of the Igbos) and Cameroon (Simo Bobda 2003: 31). Similarly, one finds the monophthongization of /aɪ/ to [ɛ], in words like *rice*, *like* and *time*, in both Sierra Leonean English and Liberian English, two otherwise quite distinct varieties. On the other side of the continent, Uganda, Kenya and Tanzania share common boundaries and the widespread use of Swahili (see below).

Endonormative processes lead to homogenization of a variety and to differentiation vis-à-vis other varieties. Such processes are due to the pressure of a national or regional norm, which is formed and perpetuated through the media, educational institutions and the demographic and sociopolitical weight of speech communities within a given society. In turn, this variety-internal norm is shaped through mother tongue influences, as well as orientation to and influences by extravarietal norms (cf. Simo Bobda 2003: 35; Peter 2008: 160–5). Gambian English is a good illustration of the way endo-normative processes have led to a relatively stable and uniform national variety. The most conspicuous features of Gambian English are the transformation of /ʃ/ to [s], as in [fis] *fish*, /ʒ/ to [z], as in [mɛzɔ] (*measure*) and /tʃ/ and /dʒ/ to [tç], [d(j)], or [d] respectively, as in [mɔtç] (*much*), [vilɛd(j)] (*village*), or [ɔrɛnj] (*orange*). These forms can be attributed to the fact that /ʃ/ and /ʒ/ are not part of the phonological systems of Mandingo and Wolof, the two dominant languages in The Gambia. Even speakers of Gambian English with an L1 in which these sounds exist (e.g. /tʃ/ in Fula) adapt to the national norm (see Peter *et al.* 2003). For the East African countries in question here, Abdulaziz (1991: 394) has noted common 'educational, socioeconomic, cultural and lin-guistic experiences' for most of the twentieth century. Under colonial rule, the British had unified various services and institutions across the three territories, including mass media and, for some time, tertiary education (Abdulaziz 1991: 394). These experiences led to a 'considerable levelling of differences caused by mother tongue interference', not only in terms of pronunciation (Abdulaziz 1991: 395).

A further factor contributing to the emergence of national differences and regional homogeneity in WAE and EAE is that of attitude, which includes the attitude of speakers towards their own variety and other varieties, and, in a wider sense, also the identification of members of a speech community with the speech community itself and its sociohistorical circumstances. Good cases in point are Ghanaian English and Liberian English. As the lists of contrasting features presented in the following section demonstrate, these two varieties are quite distinct. The works of Simo Bobda (e.g. 2000, 2003: 33–4) and others show that, within a generation, Ghanaian English has almost completely shed the perhaps most marked features of WAE, namely the production of [ɔ] for the /ʌ/ and /ɜ:/ vowels and for <or, our, ure> in post-tonic (RP) syllables. Ghanaian English has replaced /ɜ:/ by [ɛ]. It also has approximated /ʌ/ by /a/ and even gone beyond that, as a kind of hypercorrection, by having [ɛ] in some words (most prominently *study* and *just*). Post-tonic <or, our, ure> are likewise pronounced as [a]. These peculiarities (among others) could be explained by the Ghanaians' priding themselves in speaking a 'better English' than other West Africans (see e.g. Simo Bobda 2003: 33–4). Ghanaian authors (like Ahulu 1994: 26; Gyasi 1991: 26) highlight the importance of RP as a yardstick for Ghanaian speakers of English, regardless of the fact that this norm is hardly ever attainable. It is for the same attitudinal reason that among the varieties of West African Pidgin English (as spoken in Ghana, Nigeria, and Cameroon), the Ghanaian variety is held in lowest esteem by its speakers (Simo Bobda and Wolf 2003: 110). Further to the west, another good illustration for the role of attitudinal factors in the shaping of a distinct national variety is Liberian English. The connections of Liberia with the United States (see above) have reinforced the identification of Liberian speakers of English with American English in general, and, because of their unique historical experience, with their own peculiar kind of English vis-à-vis their Anglophone neighbours in particular. Liberian English is a mixture of American English and features that have developed through endonormative processes (see below). It is also part of this attitude that Liberians consider all forms of English, from pidginized to standard varieties, simply as 'English' and generally do not use labels like 'Broken' or 'Pidgin' to refer to basilectal forms (see Singler 1997: 205). The East Africans' attitude towards their English can be considered similar to that of the Ghanaians. Abdulaziz (1991: 395) reports, at least in an historical reference to educational contexts, a self-consciousness of East Africans towards the English they speak and a derision of forms not considered standard.

Last but not least, the functional distribution of languages or language varieties across countries and regions has an impact on how similar or dissimilar the varieties in question are. The Anglophone East African countries are united by the dominant role of Swahili in this region. It is the co-official language (together with English) of Kenya and Tanzania, and widely spoken in Uganda (where it is, *inter alia*, used by the security forces; Gordon 2005: Swahili). Given that Swahili functions as lingua franca throughout the region, English can be reserved for the higher domains, such as education, the media, and commerce, where a more or less uniform standard is expected. Also, because of the role of Swahili, pidginized forms of English never had the chance to develop in East Africa. In West Africa, on the other hand, a range of forms of

English exist. In the Anglophone part of Cameroon and in Southern Nigeria, Pidgin English predominates in the sociolinguistic situation (see Wolf 2001 and Igboanusi and Peter 2005), which in turn exerts considerable influence on the standard forms. Even in educated Nigerian or Cameroon English, one can often observe, for example, the use of *for* as locative preposition (as in *go for school*, *the rooms for the house*). Furthermore, in Nigeria, the Yoruba- and Igbo-influenced sub-variety spoken in the economically and demographically dominant south is spreading to the north, where a Haussa-influenced variety has been existing. If one language or language group dominates, such as Akan in Ghana and Mandingo in Gambia, one can expect more substrate influences on the national variety of English than in countries where the indigenous languages hold a 'balance of power' (also see above for the case of Gambia). Thus, one common, L1-induced feature observable in Ghanaian (Pidgin) English is an r/l-allophony (as in [blɛd] *bread*, and [brat] *blood*). In Sierra Leone, Krio is the L1 of only a small ethnic group, the Krios, but spoken by almost everyone in the country. Hence, features characteristic of Krio often occur in Sierra Leonean English, as the deletion of /h/ in initial position, as, e.g., in [ɔndrɛd] (*hundred*).

This section has outlined the colonial framework in which the regional and national varieties that are the topic of this chapter developed, and suggested some reasons for their similarities and differences. Some relevant linguistic features were also described. The following section will give a systematic overview of diagnostic and distinctive features of the individual varieties.

Linguistic features of East African and West African Englishes

The phonology and grammar of several – yet unfortunately not all – of the varieties discussed here have been concisely described in Kortmann and Schneider (2004). This section does not intend to simply replicate the findings given there and cannot be exhaustive in the description of each individual variety. The aim, rather, is to offer general clusters of phonological and lexical/discursive features that are minimally diagnostic and maximally distinctive vis-à-vis other varieties. The description of these clusters, on the one hand, goes back to distillations of the relevant literature but also to the author's exposure to thousands of speakers of African Englishes; these clusters have been confirmed and effectively applied in variety-identification. In other words, the features listed in the following are (a) representative of a prototypical speaker of a given variety (though WAE is an abstraction from the various national varieties), and (b) sufficient to identify and distinguish a variety. EAE and WAE are presented contrastively; the national varieties of WAE individually. The general features of WAE obtain in the national varieties, unless otherwise indicated. Besides, basically the same phonetic features are characteristic of the pidginized and creolized varieties, where they exist. No convincing account of the national varieties of EAE in terms of phonological and lexical specifics has been published so far, which may well be due to the homogeneity of EAE, as mentioned earlier. The lexical items are taken from a database, which forms the basis of a planned exclusive dictionary of West African English (see Peter and Wolf 2008). (See Table 11.1.)

A number of lexical items are exclusive to each regional variety. Words specific to EAE include *jembe* ('hoe'), *khansu* ('shirt'), *kyindi* ('maize beer'), *mandazi* ('wheat cake'), *matatu* ('collective taxi', 'mini bus'), *matoke* ('banana'), *maziwa* ('honey and

201

Table 11.1 Contrastive features of EAE and WAE

Feature (RP reference form for vowels)	East African English	West African English
/ɜː/	[a], occasionally [ε], especially in Tanzanian English, as in [wak] (*work*), [ban] (*burn*)	frequent occurrence of [ɔ], except for Ghanaian English, as in [wɔk] (*work*), [bɔn] (*burn*)
/ʌ/	[a]	[ɔ], except for Ghanaian English
post-tonic < our, or, ure, us, ous >	[a(s)], as in [nεba] (*neighbour*), [dɔkta] (*doctor*), [fjutʃa] (*future*), [dʒizas] (*Jesus*) and [sirias] (*serious*)	[ɔ(s)], except for Ghanaian English, as in [nεbɔ] (*neighbour*), [dɔktɔ] (*doctor*), [fjutʃɔ] (*future*), [dʒizɔs] (*Jesus*) and [siriɔs] (serious)
vocalization of /l/ in final Cl-clusters simplification of consonant clusters	to [o/ɔ], as in [pipol] (*people*), [baibɔl] (*Bible*) through vowel insertion, as in [milik] (*milk*), *and [ə]go*	to [u], as in [pipul] (*people*), [baibul] (*Bible*) through consonant deletion, as in [mik] (*milk*), *an' go*

milk'), *msungu* ('white person'), *panga* ('machete'), *ugali* (a corn dish). While the above-listed phonetic features unite the varieties of WAE, lexical items shared by all varieties of WAE are rare. *Dash* ('bribe, small gift') and *brown envelope* ('bribe') are among them, as well as *gari* ('flour made from cassava'), *fufu* ('pounded meal of cereal') and *juju* ('a charm' or 'practices related to witchcraft'). The latter three, however, are on their way to becoming part of the common core of English (cf. Peter and Wolf 2008: 232). There are practically no lexical items which can be found in both EAE and WAE but not in other varieties (though *nyama*, 'food', 'meat' exists in both Nigerian English and EAE).

Cameroon English

The easternmost national variety of WAE is Cameroon English. Table 11.2 shows the combination of phonetic features that is distinctive of this variety.

Because of the linguistic situation in Cameroon, where French and English are both official languages but the former dominates because of political and demographic factors, many lexemes exclusive to Cameroon English are derived from French, such as *gendarme* ('armed police') or *cahier* ('file'). Other popular items exclusive to Cameroon English are *erru* (a forest vegetable; the most exploited and commercialized vegetable in Cameroon), *ndole* (a dish made with bitter leaves, Cameroon's national dish) and *achu* ('pounded cocoyam paste').

Nigerian English

Given Nigeria's economic and demographic weight (it has the largest population of all African countries), Nigerian English is certainly the most prominent and perhaps even most influential variety of WAE. Typical features of Nigerian English are shown in Table 11.3, though not all are necessarily exhibited in the speech of a single speaker.

Given Nigeria's size and ethnic diversity, it comes as no surprise that Nigerian English has numerous nationally exclusive lexical items: for example, *draw soup* ('okra

Table 11.2 Distinctive features of Cameroon English

Feature (RP reference form for vowels)	Realization	Examples
/ɜː/	besides [ɔ], often and almost exclusively forms with [ɛ]	[tɛm] (term), [junivɛsiti] (university)
/eə/	monophthongization to [ɛ]	[wɛ] (where), [skwɛ] (square)
/aʊ/	occasionally monophthongization to [a]	[at] (out), [tan] (town)
final Cl-clusters	besides vocalization to [u], often forms with a schwa	[sɛtəl] (settle), [ɔŋkəl] (uncle)
weak final consonants	often tensed	[gut] (good), [dik] (dig)
/l/ in word-final position	often deleted	[sku] (school), [smɔ] (small)
<-ng> in monosyllabic words	[-ŋ]	[lɔŋ] (long), [briŋ] (bring)
<-ng> in -ing-forms	often as [-iŋ]	[dansiŋ] (dancing), [matʃiŋ] (marching)

Table 11.3 Distinctive features of Nigerian English

Feature (RP reference form for vowels)	Realization	Examples
/ɜː/	besides [ɔ], as [ɛ] and [a]	[pɛsən] (person), [tati] (thirty)
/eə/	as [iɛ], less frequently as [ia] and [ɛa] (though monophthongization to [ɛ] occasionally occurs with female and speech-conscious speakers)	[diɛ, dɛa] (there), [wia] (where)
/aʊ/	frequently monophthongized to [a]	[dan] (down), [əbat] (about)
initial (C)Cr-cluster	insertion of a schwa	[təri] (three), [stərit] (street)
/t/	dentalization	[it̪] (it), [wɔt̪] (what)
weak final consonants	often tensed	[bik] (big), [fut] (food)
/ks/-clusters	/k-/ frequently deleted	[sis] (six), [ɛsplɛn] (explain)
/l/ in word-final position often deleted	[nɔma] (normal), [tɛ] (tell)	
non-initial nasals	often deleted	[tais] (times), [naiti] (nineteen)
/h/	occasionally deleted in initial position and respective hypercorrection (mostly speakers from the south-west)	[ai] (high), [hɔp] (up)
/m, n/	occasional confusion	[dɛn] (them), [om] (own)
<-ng> in monosyllabic words (sing)	[-ŋg] or [-ŋk]	[strɔŋg] (strong), [siŋk] (sing)
<-ng> in -ing-forms	produced as [-in]	[rɔnin] (running), [slipin] (sleeping)
marked forms		[ajɔn] (iron), [bjud] (build), [bjudin] (building), [giɛl] (girl), [ɔjə] (oil), [pɔ] (poor), [pripa] (prepare), [taizi] (taxi), [tʃudrɛn] (children)

203

soup'), *molue* ('mini-bus', especially in Lagos), *oba* ('king', 'traditional ruler'), *oga* ('boss', big man'), *okada* ('commercial motorbike'), to name only a few. Nigerian English also has three conspicuous discourse markers, namely *na/now* (which some-times occurs in the speech of Cameroon English speakers as well) *sha* and *finish*. *Na* has various functions and conveys various attitudes; perhaps it is most frequently used to emphasize the informational content of an utterance, as in *it is big na, when you make soup na*. *Sha* has been defined as British English 'in short' (Igboanusi 2002: 249), and may convey an attitude of impatience, as in *sha I cannot explain*. *Finish* is used to signal the end of an enumeration or the end of the turn itself, as in *rice and yam, finish*; *went to visit my friend, finish*.

Ghanaian English

As indicated earlier, Ghanaian English diverges considerably from the common WAE prototype. The distinctive set of features is listed in Table 11.4.

Table 11.4 Distinctive features of Ghanaian English

Feature (RP reference form for vowels)	Realization	Examples
/ʌ/	mostly as [a]	[matʃ] (*much*), [bas] (*bus*)
/ɜ:/	regularly as [ɛ], rarely as [ɔ]	[wɛd] (*word*), [tSɛtʃ] (*church*)
/eə/	as [ɛ]	[tʃɛ] (*chair*), [dɛ] (*there*)
/aʊ/	occasionally monophthongized to [a]	[bran] (*brown*), [dan] (*down*)
post-tonic <our, or, ure, us>	as [a], occasionally as [ɛ]	[nɛba] (*neighbour*), [pasta] (*pastor*), [nɛtʃa] (*nature*), [mainas] (*minus*), [kalɛ] (*colour*)
/ə/ before word-final <-s> (mostly plural forms)	often as [ɛ]	[sistɛs] (*sisters*), [ɛldɛs] (*elders*)
/ə/ in <-able> words	as [a]	[itabəl] (*eatable*), [vɛdʒətabul] (*vegetable*)
final Cl-clusters	besides vocalization to [u], often forms with a schwa	[baisikəl] (*bicycle*), [sɛkəl] (*circle*)
/ə/ in <-ion> words	often as [i]	[nɛʃin] (*nation*), [mɛnʃin] (*mention*)
weak final consonants	often tensed	[haf] (*have*), [rit] (*read*)
/ks/-clusters	/k-/ occasionally deleted	[tris] (*tricks*), [bus] (*books*)
/l/ in word-final position	often deleted	[kapita] (*capital*), [sɛ] (*sell*)
nasals in medial and final position	often deleted	[tais] (*times*), [naiti] (*nineteen*)
/r/ and /l/	often allophonic	[loman] (*Roman*), [ripres] (*replace*)
marked forms		[ban] (*born*), [stɛdi] (*study*), [ɛs] (*us*), [dʒɛst] (*just*), [prabrɛm] (*problem*), [dʒab] (*job*)

Lexical items exclusive to Ghanaian English include *abenkwan* ('palm soup'), *abolo* ('baked or steamed maize dough'), *fugu* (a kind of smock), *komi* (a fufu-like food), *light soup* (usually pronounced [laisup], 'a soup containing neither palm nut oil nor groundnut paste'), *trokosi* (young virgin girls given to fetish priests as slaves).

Liberian English

Liberian English has the general features of WAE, but also a number of features that are unique within this regional variety. Liberian English shows a great deal of internal variation, both within the speech of any given speaker as well as variety-wise. However, even if speakers do not produce all the features covered in Table 11.5, their speech is usually unmistakably Liberian.

The following items are part of the exclusive lexical inventory of Liberian English: *bitter ball* (term for a local variety of eggplant), *bubble* ('amphetamines'), *dumboy* ('boiled cassava dough, squeezed into balls and dipped into palm oil soup'), *grona boy* ('street boy', 'young delinquent'), *jay-jay* (term for old Liberian dollar), *Kongors/Congoes* (the original settlers from America), *palm butter* ('fruit and oil of the oil palm', often as the basis for different sauces).

Table 11.5 Distinctive features of Liberian English

Feature (RP reference form for vowels)	Realization	Examples
/æ/	often as [æ] or [ɛ]	[ɔnəstæ] (*understand*), [mɛn] (*man*)
/ɜː/	besides [ɔ], often as [ɛ]	[bɛn] (*burn*), [lɛn] (*learn*)
[ɒ]	[ɑː]	[bɑːdɛ] (*body*), [gɑː] (*got*)
happY-vowel /i/	often as [ɛ]	[histɔrɛ] (*history*), [lɛdɛ] (*lady*)
/ə/	often as [ə], or [ɔ] in word-final position	[əmerəkɔ] (*America*), [brɔdɔ] (*brother*)
/aʊ/	often monophthongized to [a] or [ɔ]	[kɔntis] (*counties*), [na] (*now*)
/aɪ/	often monophthongized to [ɛ] or lengthened to [aː]	[rɛs] (*rice*), [daː] (die)
/ɔɪ/	often monophthongized to [ɔ]	[bɔ] (*boy*), [dʒɔn] (*join*)
final Cl-clusters	vocalized mostly to [o]	[nidol] (*needle*), [pipol] (*people*)
final consonants or consonant clusters	frequently deleted	[brɔ] (*brought*), [go] (*gold*)
intervocalic /-t-/	mostly weakened to [t̪]	[lɛt̪ɔ] (*later*), [fɔgɛt̪in] (*forgetting*)
/-ndV/, /-ntV/	frequent deletion of /d, t/	[ɛnɔ] (*enter*), [ɔnɔ] (*under*)
/r/	occasionally retroflex [ɻ], occasionally rhotic	[vɛɻɛ] (*very*), [ɔdəɻ] (*other*)
marked form		[ɛ] (*it*)

Table 11.6 Distinctive features of Sierra Leonean English

Feature (RP reference form for vowels)	Realization	Examples
/ɜː/	besides [ɔ], predominantly as [a]	[tam] (*term*), [lan] (*learn*)
/eə/	as [iɛ], [ia] and [ɛa]	[diɛ, dɛa] (*there*), [tʃia] (*chair*)
/h/	occasionally deleted	[abs] (*herbs*), [it] (*hit*)
/d/ in final Cd-clusters	often deleted	[daimɔn] (*diamond*), [fain] (*find*)
/l/ in word-final position	usually retained	[stil] (*still*), [fɔl] (*fall*)
/r/	velar-uvular /ʁ/, especially if Krio is L1	[bʁɔda] (*brother*), [ʁɔn] (*run*)

Sierra Leonean English

Sierra Leonean English is a fairly 'neutral' variety, i.e. it falls squarely within the general norm of WAE and has only few phonetic features which distinguish it from the other varieties. Some of these features can be traced to the influence of Krio, the lingua franca of Sierra Leone, spoken by nearly all inhabitants. Krio, in turn, shares some features with Nigerian English – most conspicuously perhaps the non-phonemic status of /h/ in Krio and the occasional deletion of /h/ in Nigerian English respectively. This correspondence is due to the fact that many of the freed slaves that were resettled in the Freetown area were Yoruba or of Yoruba descent. See Table 11.6.

Sierra Leonean English does have, however, a number of exclusive lexical items; frequently heard ones are: *Bondu/Bundu* ('a secret society for women'), *podapoda* ('mini bus'), *poyo* ('palm wine'), *omolankey* ('push cart'), *omole* ('locally brewed gin', 'alcoholic concoction').

Gambian English

Because of Gambia's size and population, Gambian English has the smallest number of speakers within WAE. However, this variety is just as stable and established as the other varieties of WAE. Although it also shares some features with Sierra Leonean English, the set shown in Table 11.7 makes Gambian English quite recognizable and distinctive.

Lexically, Gambian English can be identified by, *inter alia*, *domoda* ('meat in groundnut stew, usually served with rice'), *nawettan* ('off-season football tournament'), *superkanja* ('okra, fish or meat, palm oil, onions and pepper boiled together'), *yassa* (generic for various kinds of meat and fish prepared in a certain way).

This concludes the comparative survey of distinctive linguistic features of East and West African Englishes. The 'linguistic feature approach' adopted above is part of the traditional descriptivist take on World Englishes (cf. Wolf and Polzenhagen 2009: Chapter 1). Yet the description of African Englishes or World Englishes, for that matter, does not stop there. African Englishes and first-language varieties of English are embedded in different cultural contexts. In order to arrive at a fuller picture of a given variety, this cultural dimension – which includes far more than native terms as loan forms – needs to be captured as well (see also Sharifian, this volume). The following section will give an introduction to and a general summary of a recent attempt at the systematization of culture in African English.

Table 11.7 Distinctive features of Gambian English

Feature (RP reference form for vowels)	Realization	Examples
/ɜː/	besides [ɔ], as [a]	[ali] (*early*), [gal] (*girl*)
/æ/	occasionally as [ɛ]	[blɛk] (*black*), [fɛmili] (*family*)
/eə/	as [ɛa], less frequently as [ia] and [iɛ]	[dɛa] (*there*), [wia] (*where*)
/ʒ/, /ʃ/	often as [z], respectively as [s], and respective hypercorrection	[mɛzɔ] (*measure*), [sɔp] (*shop*), [brauʒa] (*browser*), [miʃ] (*miss*)
/dʒ/ and /tʃ/	transformed or simplified, especially to [dj], [dç] [d], [tç]	[djɔin] (*join*), [dçanuari] (*January*), [vilɛd] (*village*), [tçɔtç] (*church*)
/d/ in final Cd-clusters	often deleted	[frɛn] (*friend*), [stan] (*stand*)
/l/ in word-final position	usually retained [bɔl] (*ball*), [ɔl] (*all*)	
/r/	as apical trill	[raun] (*round*), [bridj] (*bridge*)
/v/	occasionally as bilabial [β]	[riβa] (*river*), [sɛβən] (*seven*)
marked forms		[gjiv] (*give*), [gjɛt] (*get*)

Cognitive sociolinguistic findings on African English

Until recently, culture in World Englishes was not adequately addressed from a linguistic perspective. Culture was seen as being either outside the scope of linguistic analysis proper or not rigorously and systematically analysed (see Wolf 2008b). However, advances in other fields of linguistics lend themselves to an incorporation into the World Englishes paradigm, for example Cognitive Sociolinguistics, a new branch of Cognitive Linguistics. Cognitive Sociolinguistics focuses on language variation and the role people's conceptions play in the constitution of sociocultural reality, and vice versa. Importantly, it calls for the use of computer corpora to study natural language. As such, Cognitive Sociolinguistics touches upon a major development in World Englishes, namely the International Corpus of English (ICE) project (see International Corpus of English, online). The various national sub-corpora are more or less identically designed to allow comparative research. The Cognitive Sociolinguistic study of culture in World Englishes, as conducted by Wolf and Polzenhagen, highlights three interrelated aspects: cultural keywords, culturally motivated collocational patterns and cultural conceptualizations. Wolf and Polzenhagen (2009) presents a detailed overview of this approach and a wide-ranging, corpus-based case study of the cultural model of community in African English. The singular form 'English' – as opposed to the use of 'Englishes' above – is significant, because the same cultural conceptualizations are found across Sub-Saharan Africa. To put it differently, in terms of a broader cognitive-cultural view, it is, at least on the basis of the current state of research, not warranted to speak of different African varieties in the context of cultural conceptualization.

Neither the theoretical and methodological framework nor the model itself can be described comprehensively here. Instead, in order to demonstrate how the analyses of cultural keywords, collocational patterns and conceptualizations (which, depending on the cultural standpoint of the interpreter, are conceptual metaphors or metonymies) form a coherent whole, a sample of each point, with a short explanation, shall be provided. The findings are partly extracted from Wolf and Polzenhagen (2009), to where the reader can turn for additional information and statistical details; the collocations were selected for this chapter. Available corpora of African English are the Corpus of English in Cameroon (CEC) – of which only unofficial copies exist – and the ICE East Africa (ICE-EA). These corpora were compared with a consolidated L1-corpus of English, FLOBFROWN, which represents the two major native varieties of English, namely British English (the FLOB corpus) and American English (the FROWN corpus). It was found that various terms relating to FAMILY and COMMUNITY – two closely related concepts in African culture – are significantly more frequent in the African corpora than in the Western reference corpus. Among these items are *family* and *community* themselves, as well as *kin* plus various compounded forms. Likewise, words indicating the continuation of family/community occur more frequently per 1 million words, so that words such as *offspring, marriage, parent, maternity* and *child*, and related forms of these words are more frequent. The fact that these terms are keywords points to the centrality of family/community in African culture. Furthermore, a look at collocations, i.e. of words that occur in textual proximity, is revealing. *Child* or *children* collocates with *community/communities/community's* only two times in FLOBFROWN (with a five words to the left and five words to the right search horizon), whereas it does so 23 times in the CEC and ICE-EA combined, which have about the same size as FLOBFROWN. Likewise, *community/communities/community's* collocates with *parents* only one time in FLOB-FROWN, while it does so with *parent(s)* 14 times in the CEC and ICE-EA combined. Importantly, in the combined CEC and ICE-EA, *community/communities/community's* collocate 21 times with *family/families/family's* and ten times with *society*, whereas in FLOBFROWN, one finds *community/communities/community's* collocating with *family/families* and *society/societies* only five times each.

The comparatively frequent collocations of *family, community* and *society* correspond to a prominent conceptualization in African English, that of COMMUNITY FOR KINSHIP or KINSHIP FOR COMMUNITY. The collocation of *community* and *society*, in turn, corresponds to the extension of this conceptualization to various social units and society at large. KINSHIP FOR COMMUNITY applies, for example, to villages and towns, as in

> The village was proud of its sons and daughters.
> She had buried her son, the village had buried its child.
> The chief is like a father of the town.
> Santa people whose son was a prime minister.

It also underlies references to countries or even Africa itself:

> Sons, Daughters or any other legal resident of The Land of Liberia.
> The health development of brothers and sisters in Cameroon.
> Tambo is one of the illustrious sons of Africa.
> That the two countries were brotherly nations, with the same ancestors.
> Soon, we will receive pictures taken with his brothers and sisters: Cameroonians, Nigerians, Ethiopians, Eritreans, Egyptians, black South Africans, Kenyans, Senegalese.

> (All examples taken from Wolf and Polzenhagen 2009: 78–9)

For the theoretical debate of variation in World Englishes, it is crucial to note that the linguistic material in the above data, with the exception of the names, is from the common core of English. In the field of lexis and semantics, variation comprises far more than terms for objects that do not exist in native varieties of English. Lexical frequency, regular textual co-occurrences and systematically related expressions generated by underlying conceptualizations indicate cultural variation on a broader scale. Arguably, description of difference, especially cultural difference, should not be an end in itself, but should serve intercultural understanding. The study of World Englishes, with the methodological toolbox of Cognitive Sociolinguistics, can make an important contribution to this endeavour.

Furthermore, the fact that cultural differences are reflected in African English is an argument against the 'English as a killer language' view (see Lucko 2003). The existence of L2-varieties of English does not necessarily imply the death of L1-culture; rather, this culture is carried over and expressed in various ways in the L2-varieties. Africans have made English their own.

Conclusion

This chapter looked at and compared East and West African English – two of the three broad regional L2-varieties of African English – from a variety of perspectives. First, the colonial context was considered from which these two Englishes grew. It was argued that hands-off British language and educational policy led to a stabilization of Pidgin English and Krio in the West African countries where these varieties were spoken, and was conducive to the development of distinct national varieties of English. In East Africa, on the other hand, this very policy confirmed the role of Swahili as a lingua franca and contributed to the emergence of a homogenous regional variety, lacking the pidginized forms one finds in West Africa. East and West African English are strikingly different in terms of internal variation, and this chapter attempted to provide some explanation for this phenomenon. The focus then shifted to variation in African Englishes themselves. Minimal sets of distinctive phonetic and lexical features were listed that distinguish East and West African English and the national varieties of WAE from each other.

Phonetic and lexical investigations are long-established topics of sociolinguistic research. Recent theoretical and methodological advances in other areas of linguistics, however, offer new ways to gain a different and new systematic insight, namely cultural–conceptual variation. Cognitive Sociolinguistics was introduced as one such advance; it combines, *inter alia*, corpus-linguistic methods and conceptual metaphor analysis, and allows for both quantitative and qualitative studies of semantic differences in language. At this level of enquiry, East and West African English were found to share cultural conceptualizations which are linguistically realized in their varieties. The methodical survey of culture in World Englishes has only begun (also see Sharifian, this volume); more World Englishes await this kind of examination.

Suggestions for further reading

Brutt-Griffler, J. (2002) *World English: A Study of its Development*, Clevedon: Multilingual Matters. (A survey of the spread of English from a sociopolitical perspective.)

Kirkpatrick, A. (2007) *World Englishes: Implications for International Communication and English Language Teaching*, Cambridge: Cambridge University Press. (A comprehensive discussion of educational issues of English in international contexts.)

Schneider, E.W. (2007) *Postcolonial English: Varieties around the World*, Cambridge: Cambridge University Press. (An analysis of the life cycle of postcolonial Englishes.)

References

Abdulaziz, M.H.H. (1991) 'East Africa (Tanzania and Kenya)', in C. Cheshire (ed.) *English around the World: Sociolinguistic Perspectives*, Cambridge: Cambridge University Press, pp. 391–401.

Ahulu, S. (1994) 'How Ghanaian is Ghanaian English?' *English Today*, 10: 25–9.

Corpus of English in Cameroon (CEC) (n.d.) Compiled as part of the International Corpus of English Project. Unfinished version.

Gordon, R.G., Jr (ed.) (2005) *Ethnologue: Languages of the World* (15th edition), Dallas: SIL International. Online. Available www.ethnologue.com (accessed 3 December 2008).

Gyasi, I.K. (1991) 'Aspects of English in Ghana', *English Today*, 7: 26–31.

Harris, J. (1996) 'On the trail of short "u"', *English World-Wide*, 17: 1–40.

Igboanusi, H. (2002) *A Dictionary of Nigerian English Usage*, Ibadan: Enicrownfit Publishers.

Igboanusi, H. and Peter, L. (2005) *Languages in Competition: The Struggle for Supremacy among Nigeria's Major Languages, English and Pidgin*, Frankfurt am Main: Peter Lang.

International Corpus of English (2008) Online. Available www.ucl.ac.uk/english-usage/ice/ (accessed 3 December 2008).

Kortmann, B. and Schneider, E.W. (eds) (2004) *A Handbook of Varieties of English: A Multimedia Reference Tool*, 2 vols, New York: Mouton de Gruyter.

Lucko, P. (2003) 'Is English a "killer language"?' in P. Lucko, L. Peter and H.-G. Wolf (eds) *Studies in African Varieties of English*, Frankfurt am Main: Peter Lang, pp. 151–65.

Mair, Christian (compiler) (1999) FROWN (The Freiburg BROWN Corpus of English) University of Freiburg, Germany. On *ICAME Collection of English Language Corpora* (2nd edition), CD-ROM, the HIT Centre, University of Bergen, Norway.

Mair, Christian and Hundt, Marianne (compilers) (1999) FLOB (The Freiburg LOB Corpus of English), University of Freiburg, Germany. On *ICAME Collection of English Language Corpora* (2nd edition), CD-ROM, the HIT Centre, University of Bergen, Norway.

Peter, L. (2003) 'English in Sudan', in P. Lucko, H.-G. Wolf and L. Peter (eds) *Studies in African Varieties of English*, Frankfurt am Main: Peter Lang, pp. 129–49.

——(2008) 'The quest for a standard: some notes on norms, usage and frequency patterns in Nigerian English', in P. Lucko, H.-G. Wolf and L. Peter (eds) *Studies in African Varieties of English*, Frankfurt am Main: Peter Lang, pp. 159–71.

Peter, L. and Wolf, H.-G. (2008) 'Compiling an exclusive dictionary of West African English: a report on work in progress', in A. Simo Bobda (ed.) *Explorations into Language Use in Africa* (Duisburg Papers on Research in Language and Culture 70), Frankfurt am Main: Peter Lang, pp. 221–34.

Peter, L., Wolf, H.-G. and Simo Bobda, A. (2003) 'An account of distinctive phonetic and lexical features of Gambian English', *English World-Wide*, 24 (1): 43–61.

Schneider, E.W. (2008) 'Clustering global Englishes automatically: neutral input, meaningful results', in H.-G. Wolf, P. Lucko and F. Polzenhagen (eds) *Focus on English: Linguistic Structure, Language Variation and Discursive Use. Studies in Honour of Peter Lucko*, Leipzig: Leipziger Universitätsverlag, pp. 51–63.

Simo Bobda, A. (2000) 'The uniqueness of Ghanaian English pronunciation in West Africa,' *Studies in the Linguistic Sciences*, 30 (2): 185–98.

——(2003) 'The formation of regional and national features in African English pronunciation: an exploration of some non-interference factors', *English World-Wide*, 24 (1): 17–42.

Simo Bobda, A. and Wolf, H.-G. (2003) 'Pidgin English in Cameroon in the new millennium', in P. Lucko, H.-G. Wolf and L. Peter (eds) *Studies in African Varieties of English*, Frankfurt am Main: Peter Lang, pp. 101–17.

Singler, J. (1997) 'The configuration of Liberia's Englishes', *World Englishes*, 16 (2): 205–31.

Wolf, H.-G. (2001) *English in Cameroon* (Contributions to the Sociology of Language 85), New York: Mouton de Gruyter.

——(2008a) 'British and French language and educational policies in the Mandate and Trusteeship Territories,' in C. Hutton and H.-G. Wolf (eds) *The History of Linguistics*, special issue of *Language Sciences*, 30 (5): 553–74.

——(2008b) 'A cognitive linguistic approach to the cultures of World Englishes: the emergence of a new model,' in G. Kristiansen and R. Dirven (eds) *Cognitive Sociolinguistics: Language Variation, Cultural Models, Social Systems* (Cognitive Linguistic Research 39), Berlin, New York: Mouton de Gruyter, pp. 353–85.

Wolf, H.-G. and Polzenhagen, F. (2009) *World Englishes: A Cognitive Sociolinguistic Approach* (Applications of Cognitive Linguistics 8), Berlin, New York: Mouton de Gruyter.

12

The development of English in Botswana

Language policy and education

Birgit Smieja and Joyce T. Mathangwane

Introduction

Located in the southern part of Africa and landlocked between South Africa, Namibia, Zambia, Zimbabwe and Angola, Botswana has developed into a strong democratically based nation surrounded by apartheid-stricken neighbours. Since its independence in 1966, after being a British protectorate for about eighty years and one of the poorest countries of the world, Botswana became a stable economic and political country remarkably quickly.[1]

Because of the colonial legacy, English still plays an important part in the country as the official language alongside the national language Setswana. The number of speakers of the two languages within the country is very different, however. Setswana is spoken by about 78.2 per cent of the population while English is spoken by only 2.2 per cent according to the 2001 census (Ministry of Labour and Home Affairs 2001). As we shall point out later in the chapter, however, these figures are seriously inaccurate, partly because of the way in which censuses are conducted in Botswana. For instance, the 2001 census was the first to have a question on language, and the question only asked for language use at home in the family context. Such a question would not reveal accurate numbers of English speakers (Chebanne and Nyati-Ramahobo 2003). But, as we shall see below, the number of English speakers is relatively small even though Botswana can be classified as an 'outer circle' country where English plays important institutional roles.

Since official sources concerning the number of English speakers and the development of English within Botswana are scarce, we have relied on a range of sources going back as far as the 1950s, which was when the real discussion around the language question started. Our main sources are books and articles written by renowned scholars who have conducted important research on the languages of Botswana during the last thirty years (Janson and Tsonope 1991; Sommer 1992; Hasselbring 1996, 2000a/b, 2001; Andersson and Janson 1997; Mathangwane and Gardner 1997, 1999; Nyati-Ramahobo 1999; Batibo and Mosaka 2000; Batibo *et al.* 2003; Smieja 2003; Bagwasi 2004; Batibo and Smieja 2006; Smieja and Batibo 2007; and Mathangwane 2008).

Following this introduction, the next section of the chapter describes the language situation in Botswana and the third section the language policy. The fourth section summarizes the historical development of English and the fifth section considers present-day English use in Botswana. The sixth section provides some examples of distinctive linguistic features of Botswana English and the seventh section concludes the chapter.

Language situation in Botswana

Like many African countries, Botswana is a multi-ethnic and multilingual country with more than 25 languages in use. These languages divide into three groups according to their linguistic affiliation. The Bantu language group represent the great majority, spoken by over 96 per cent of the population. This group comprises Setswana, Ikalanga, Sesubiya, Thimbukushu, Shiyeyi, Otjiherero, Shikgalagarhi, Setswapong, Sebirwa and Silozi. The second language group is the Khoesan family which, even though it comprises a large number of languages, is spoken by only about 3 per cent of the population. This group comprises languages such as Jul'hoan, Naro, !Xoo, IXaise, Danisi, Nama, IGana, Cara, Tshwa, Kua, IGui, Sasi, Hietshware, Ts'ixa, IAnda, Kxoe, Deti, Buga, Shuakwe, ǂKx'aul'ein, and ǂHuã. The third and smallest group comprise Afrikaans and English of the Indo-European family, with English primarily spoken as a second language.

When Botswana gained its independence in 1966, Setswana as the majority language was declared the national language, while English became the official language. Such a policy has meant many local languages have been restricted for use within their own communities. Only a few of these are taught in literacy classes, which are conducted by non-governmental organizations. As a result, many of these languages, especially those of the Khoesan group are dying.

The national language Setswana has assumed a semi-official status, with its use confined to certain domains, while English, the official language, has assumed a more prestigious role. For example, English is the language of instruction in schools from Standard Two to tertiary education, the language of parliamentary debates and administration.

As we have indicated above, it was not until the 2001 population census that a question eliciting data on language use at home was included. This question (Chebanne and Nyati-Ramahobo 2003: 3) was phrased thus:

> What language does ____ speak most often at home?
> 02   Setswana
> 03   English
> —— Other (specify)

This question would be unlikely to provide reliable and valid data on language use for reasons which include that it did not ask about ethnicity, and in answer to this question the respondents may have provided their first, second or third languages. Chebanne and Nyati-Ramahobo (2003) also note that the question inquired about a third person, and that the phrase 'most often' in the question eliminated any other languages spoken by the respondent. This means that today there is still no reliable data on language use in Botswana.

213

Table 12.1 Cross-border languages in Botswana

South Africa	**Afrikaans, English**, Sebirwa, Nama, Sindebele, Sepedi, Tsonga, Tswa, and **Setswana**
Namibia	**Afrikaans, English**, Otjiherero, !Kung, ǂX'aol'aĩ, Jul'hoan, Thimbukushu, Nama, Chikuhane, **Setswana**, !Xóõ, Khwe, Shiyeyi, Silozi
Zambia	Silozi, **English**, **Afrikaans**, Mbukushu, Sesubiya, Tonga
Zimbabwe	**Afrikaans, English**, Hiechware, Ikalanga, Silozi, Sindebele, Chishona (incl. Zezuru and Karanga), Tswa, **Setswana**, Nambya

Note: **Bold** = Languages spoken in South Africa, Namibia, Zimbabwe, Zambia and Botswana

The situation in Botswana compares to that of Cameroon (see Bobda, this volume) who notes that of the few population censuses conducted in that country, only the 2004 census – the results of which are still awaited – had two questions on language. Even then he adds that the politicians fear publishing such data, as it might exacerbate ethnic tensions since language distribution often indirectly refers to ethnic distribution. In Botswana, Setswana has always been considered a unifying language, with politicians ever ready to accuse anyone calling for the use of other local languages of being divisive and obstructing nation-building.

We also need to consider language use within the wider Southern African context. Just as in many other countries, some of Botswana's languages are spoken elsewhere, including in South Africa, Zimbabwe, Zambia and Namibia. These languages thus form a group of cross-border languages, facilitating interethnic communication. These cross-border languages are illustrated in Table 12.1.

Languages in bold characters are spoken in all five countries by a part of the population, i.e. Botswana, Namibia, South Africa, Zambia and Zimbabwe, and they are lingua francas across Southern Africa. These languages are Afrikaans, English and also Setswana.

Afrikaans is spoken by 6,300,000 people, the majority of whom live in South Africa. Nevertheless, it is also spoken in Namibia and Botswana (Grimes 1996; Gordon 2005). (However, the census data underlying this number of speakers is rather old, although it is the latest to date, i.e. the official census in Zimbabwe was done in 1969, in Namibia in 1991, in Botswana in 1993 and in South Africa in 1996.) Setswana is spoken by a total of 4,760,000 speakers (Wald 1994: 301; Gordon 2005), mainly in Botswana and South Africa. The role of English as an international language and its history in these countries explains the motive for promoting it.

Language policy of Botswana

When Botswana attained its independence in 1966, there was no clear policy on which language was to be the medium of instruction in the schools (Chebanne and Nyati-Ramahobo 2003). However, there was a general understanding that English was to be the medium of instruction. In the event, Setswana became the medium of instruction for the first two to three years of primary school (Chebanne and Nyati-Ramahobo 2003: 1) and thereafter English took over as medium of instruction up to tertiary level, with Setswana offered as a subject. In 1977, the National Commission of Education (Education for Kagisano) recommended that Setswana be used as the medium of instruction from Standard One to Standard Four, with English taking over from Standard Five up to tertiary education. The Revised National Policy on Education (RNPE) in 1994 recommended that 'English should be used as the medium of instruction from Standard 2' (Republic of Botswana 1994: 59). This policy, just as has always been the case, promoted the use of two languages, with English the official language and Setswana the national language. Ironically, in both cases, the Commission overlooked the importance of other local languages when making this recommendation. In this connection, Recommendation 32 of the 1994 Revised National Policy on Education reads:

> With regard to junior certificate curriculum … in addition each student should select a minimum of two and a maximum of three optional subjects. At least one of the subjects selected should be from each of the following groups of subjects … (ii) General studies: … third language (French and other local language)
> (Republic of Botswana 1994: 63)

This recommendation was later amended by Parliament by removing the phrase 'French and other local language'. However, the recommendation has never been implemented. In 2002, a team of consultants was engaged by the Ministry of Education (through the Curriculum Development Unit) to carry out a large-scale national study on the implementation of this recommendation. The aims of the study were to provide answers to the following questions (among others) for the Ministry of Education:

1 the number of people who speak the local languages
2 their development in terms of how many can be written
3 how much material has been published in each of the languages, and
4 the number of people who speak, write and can teach the languages.

(Batibo *et al.* 2003: ix)

The study was completed and the report submitted to the Curriculum Development Unit in 2003. To date, no action has been taken. As a result, the two languages English and Setswana remain the only languages officially recognized in Botswana.

Historical development of English in Botswana

It was not until the mid nineteenth century that English started to play an important role in Botswana. English was introduced to Botswana through missionaries and the colonial power from the middle of the nineteenth century onwards. Local colonial administration staff were taught English, as this was the medium for transmitting orders, and it was the language of the law and administration. Yet school education of the western model was education only for the royal elite, namely the *dikgosi* (chiefs) and their offspring.

The introduction of English as the language of administration and government has had little impact on the other languages used in Botswana. There was a slow transformation from a protectorate into the young and self-confident nation, which adopted Setswana as the national language from the start. At the beginning of the twentieth century, non-denominational schools (so called 'ward schools') (Tlou and Campbell 1984: 140) were started, often based on local initiative. English became an important part of the curriculum. According to 1946 census data only about 20 per cent of the total population of Botswana could read and write in Setswana, but far fewer had some proficiency in English (Andersson and Janson 1997: 170–1). This did not change even when English was declared the official language at independence in 1966. Since independence English has been taught for at least a couple of years to about 85 per cent of children (Andersson and Janson (1997: 171), and the duration of exposure to English through education and daily use has become longer with the change in policy in 1977 (Botswana Government 1977), which, as we have seen, stated that English be the medium of instruction from Standard Five up to tertiary education and with the 1994 Revised National Policy on Education, whereby English became the medium of instruction at Standard (secondary) Two. The reality may be different, though, because teachers find pupils fail to understand English that well at Standard Two and are forced to resort to Setswana. A teacher at one of the primary schools was quick to point out that this was one of the problems they faced especially during the first three years of primary schooling and which forced them to use Setswana for communication and learning to take place.

In the absence of reliable official statistics, only unreliable estimates can be made about the number and proficiency of English speakers. *The Cambridge Encyclopaedia of the English Language* (1995) estimates that there are about 620,000 English speakers in Botswana (i.e. about 40 per cent of the population) who speak English as their first or second language, although this does not say anything about their proficiency. Gordon (2005), based on the 1993 census and other publications (e.g. Hasselbring 1996, 2000a, 2000b; Andersson and Janson 1997; Central Statistics Office 1997a) estimates only 25–30 per cent of the Botswana population speak English. Bagwasi (2004: 212) gives the proportion as 35–40 per cent. Taking average school enrolment statistics from 1985 to 1995 (Central Statistics Office 1997b), adding an average number for 1966–99 and accounting for the numbers of early school leavers and drop-outs, suggests about 280,000–360,000 people may be able to understand and speak English at least to a certain degree, 'a certain degree' being defined as being able to understand important information given by the media or in school (Smieja 2003: 56).

The importance of English in Botswana is enshrined in its official status and functions: most official documents, reports and minutes of Parliament, decrees and legal documents are all issued in English, though some documents are produced in Setswana as well. Furthermore, English is dominant in the bank sector, industry and the media. English is thus the main written language, while Setswana is used far more often in speaking than in writing.

As a result of its official status in the country, English enjoys prestige. English is the language for upward social mobility, education and jobs.

Present-day English use in Botswana

In considering the use of language it is important to answer the question: 'Who speaks what language to whom and when?' (Fishman 1965: 67–88). In their study of diglossia Fishman (1966) and Ferguson (1959, 1964) investigated language use in different domains, classifying them into languages of high and low domains. High domains include government and administration, the legal system and police, science and technology, trade and industry, the media, secondary and tertiary education and health care; the low domains include (traditional) religious and community activities, cultural life, traditional customs, pre-primary and primary education, sports and leisure, agriculture, local media, local markets and domestic services, family, kinship and friendship networks. In the subsections below, we focus on the extent to which English is used in a selection of these domains.

Politics

Political rallies

English has always played a critical role in Botswana politics. Following Botswana's independence in 1966, both Setswana and English were used as media of communication. As already noted above, English is the official language in the country while Setswana is the national language. However, in the early years following independence, it was common to find politicians addressing political rallies in English, without much regard as to whether their audience understood the message or not. For example, Raditladi (2001) makes reference to a political rally he attended at one of the villages in the central part of the country (Mathangwane 2008). The rally was addressed by the then vice president of Botswana, who used words such as 'globalization', 'World Bank', 'IMF' without any consideration as to whether the audience understood them. This was no isolated incident (Mathangwane 2008: 33). It is common for politicians to address *kgotla* meetings in English without a Setswana interpreter. (A *kgotla* is the place or enclosure where the community assembles for any kind of business that is of importance to the community.) The reason behind this is the prestige associated with English and the belief that the speakers express themselves better when using English. It is common knowledge that some educated people often claim to be more articulate when using the English language, sometimes blaming the lack of developed terminology in the Setswana or other local languages for having to use English when discussing the economy and other 'modern' topics. As a result, code-switching is very common (see section on 'Language shift and code-switching', below).

Parliament

For the first twenty years after Botswana attained its independence in 1966, parliamentary debates were conducted only in English. This was irrespective of whether the elected Members of Parliament were proficient in the English language, as being proficient in English is not a criterion for entering politics. The linguistic situation changed in 1987, when Presidential Directive (Cab. 25/87) allowed the use of Setswana. Even then, exceptions were made so that the President's State of the Nation Address, the Budget Speech, Statements by Ministers are given in English. Bills, the Order Paper and the Hansard remain published in English, with a few copies made available in Setswana. Following the 1987 Directive, translators were employed to translate the Setswana portions of the parliamentary proceedings into the English language, evidence that Setswana remained subservient to English in the parliamentary domain (Mathangwane 2008). This practice continues to this day, even though some feel that this amounts to disempowering the national language, Setswana.

House of Chiefs ('Ntlo ya Dikgosi')

In addition to Parliament, Botswana has the House of Chiefs (*Ntlo ya Dikgosi*) whose membership comprises all the paramount chiefs (*dikgosi*) of the country's different tribal groups. Chieftainship is central to Batswana culture. Chiefs are mostly hereditary, although a few sub-chiefs are appointed from within the tribe. The role of both chiefs and sub-chiefs is to help maintain and restore order within the villages.

217

At independence, both Setswana and English were declared languages of the House of Chiefs. However, all proceedings have to be translated into English. English is also often the language used in important ceremonies such as the swearing-in ceremony of chiefs. It is important to note that a certain level of education is not a pre-requisite for being a chief, as the position is hereditary. Thus, the level of English proficiency of chiefs varies from poor to fluent. As a result, some have had problems with English during ceremonies (see *Mmegi* newspaper, 2 February 2007). Given the local cultural importance of the House of Chiefs, it is remarkable that English remains the preferred language.

Education

Botswana's education system is based on a 7 + 3 + 2 system, i.e. seven years of primary school, three years of junior secondary school and two years of senior secondary school. Since 1994, Setswana has been the medium of instruction for all the children at Standard One, with English taking over as the medium of instruction from Standard (secondary) Two up to tertiary education level. From Standard Two upwards, Setswana is taught as a subject (Revised National Policy on Education (RNPE) 1994). However, as noted above, in actual practice this may not be the case, since many of the children cannot follow the lessons when they are taught in English. Teachers thus use Setswana and English side by side as media of instruction. Code-switching between Setswana and English is a common and helpful pattern which fulfils a bridging function (see also 'Language shift and code-switching', below).

Table 12.2 demonstrates the importance of time in language learning. These figures were gathered in 1999 from 707 respondents throughout Botswana. In this survey respondents were asked about their acquisition of the different languages and were

Table 12.2 Knowledge of English by age of learning

English learnt at what age	Total respondents	Knowledge of English		
		Good	Medium	Bad
together with MT	3 (0.4 per cent)	3 (0.4 per cent)	—	—
3–5 years (before school)	48 (6.8 per cent)	30 (4.2 per cent)	11 (1.5 per cent)	7 (1.0 per cent)
6–9 years (lower primary)	428 (60.5 per cent)	198 (28.0 per cent)	174 (24.6 per cent)	56 (7.9 per cent)
10–13 years (higher primary)	165 (23.3 per cent)	72 (10.2 per cent)	62 (8.8 per cent)	31 (18.8 per cent)
14–18 years (secondary)	46 (6.5 per cent)	13 (1.8 per cent)	19 (2.7 per cent)	14 (2.0 per cent)
later than 18	17 (2.4 per cent)	—	5 (0.7 per cent)	12 (1.7 per cent)
TOTAL	707 (100 per cent)	316 (44.7 per cent)	271 (38.3 per cent)	120 (17.0 per cent)

Source: Smieja 2003: 175.

asked to judge their competence in these. The respondents' self-assessment of English and Setswana was then tested in a short interview. The data show that those respondents who had learned English in primary school or earlier claimed to possess satisfactory competence, while those who started using English more often at secondary school, i.e. between 14 and 18 years, admitted that their competence was considerably lower. Competence in the English language was at its lowest for those respondents who started learning English after the age of 18 or even later. Respondents reported that the earlier they started to learn English, the better they perceived their competence in the language.

One explanation for a child's success or failure in any subject-matter is the degree of literacy in the medium of instruction. The 1997 Central Statistics Office report (1997a: 28) states that 'it is believed that permanent literacy is only achieved after five years of formal education'. (The Central Statistics Office does not state what language they are referring to, but it is assumed that it is English.) In this respect, Cummins (1981) has argued that it takes a child one or two years to acquire context-embedded second-language fluency, but five to seven years or more to acquire context-reduced fluency. This means a child with conversational ability may appear ready to be instructed in a second language, yet not be cognitively or linguistically ready to understand the content. This is often the explanation of why children drop out of school.

The Education Policy of Botswana recognizes the important status of English as a global language. Hence, the recommendation of the 1993 Report of the National Commission on Education and the subsequent 1994 modification in the Revised National Policy on Education (RNPE). An advantage of this policy is that it has ensured Botswana's active participation in globalization. As a result, English-speaking Batswana are able to do business internationally and communicate effectively. Likewise, English-speaking Batswana students can study anywhere in the world where English is the language of instruction.

On the other hand, privileging one foreign language over the local languages has had negative consequences. English has become a national lingua franca and people who speak different local languages prefer English over those languages (Mathangwane 2008). Batswana do not see the need to learn and know each other's mother tongue because they can always fall back on either English or Setswana. As a result, the other languages are restricted to being used within their communities. The worst consequence is that many of these languages, especially those of the Khoesan family, are dying.

A further disadvantage is that students with poor English fail to enter degree programmes in the University of Botswana (UB). The normal basic requirement for entrance to undergraduate degree and diploma programmes in the only national university in the country is English Grade C in the Botswana General Certificate of Secondary Education (BGCSE). Entry into the science degree programmes requires a grade D or better in English language or equivalents (University of Botswana 2007: 10). Thus, the many students who attain poor results in English in the BGCSE examinations may not be admitted to the University of Botswana, even when they have excellent results in other subjects (Mathangwane 2008).

Home

English has become the dominant language in many middle- and upper-class households in urban Botswana. Children grow up speaking only English at the expense of their mother tongue (Bagwasi 2004: 215; Mathangwane 2008: 35). Parents who can afford it send their children to English-medium schools rather than to Tswana-medium schools or public schools, as these also have the reputation of being better schools. In these schools, the medium of instruction is English from pre-school upwards. Those who attend these schools grow up speaking English. Affluent English-speaking parents speak to their children in English. As a result, the number of middle- and upper-class children whose main language is English is on the increase.

Language distribution and language shift

A general picture of the language distribution across domains in Botswana is given in Table 12.3 (Smieja 2003). This shows the ambiguous status of the national language Setswana and shows that in general English does not play a big role in the family context. In the above study, people all over Botswana were observed and asked for their language use. Only the urban middle and upper class increasingly use English in the family context. The far bigger percentage of the population still lives under different conditions. Although the use of English in the family domain is increasing, if we look at all the social strata of society it is a slow process in general, which is faster in urban than in rural areas. The same language behaviour holds true for community activities and contact with relatives and friends.

The first change is noticeable when looking at the school domain where both English and Setswana are in use even though they are adapting dynamically to a complex situation. At primary school, especially during the first grades, Setswana is felt to be an important medium of instruction to ensure that children make a good start, with English being used more often in higher grades and throughout secondary school education. This is because the shift in medium of instruction from Setswana to English has taken place in Grade 2.

The domain of the mass media is also bilingual, although more information is given in English than in Setswana and code-switching is a frequent pattern of use. Small business and official communication on the local level take place in Setswana; big business, management discussions and government decisions on the higher level are communicated in English. It is obvious that the two languages are always in competition for usage, but we do not find English and another local language as an option in any of the domains. Setswana is used as the mediating choice.

The choice of languages for active use in situational contexts is not free, but often prescribed by governments or official bodies. This is socially conditioned diglossia. On the individual level there is indeed a personal choice to use one of the two (or more)

Table 12.3 General language distribution in selected domains in Botswana

Domain	English	Setswana	Minority languages
Home and family (L)		x	x
Social and cultural community activities (L)		x	x
Correspondence with relatives and friends (L)		x	x
School (H)	x	x	
Mass media (H)	x	x	
Business and commerce (H)	x	x	
Correspondence with government departments (H)	x	x	

languages in their active use (individual bilingualism), yet this choice is always directed to the dominant language (Dirven and Pütz 1993), which is English in the higher domains and Setswana in the lower domains.

Language shift and code-switching

'Language shift simply means that a community gives up a language completely in favour of another one … In language maintenance, the community collectively decides to continue using the language or languages it has traditionally used' (Fasold 1984: 213). Thus, language shift implies that a dominant language takes over a domain which was previously occupied by other (mostly ethnic) languages.

This language shift or language attrition (in different stages) is also a fact for some ethnic minority languages in Botswana with regard to the national lingua franca Setswana. Some speakers of ethnic languages, such as Deti, ǂHuã, Shiyeyi (Sommer 1992: 309, 402), Setswapong and Sebirwa (Smieja 2003), Ts'ixa, ǁGana, ǀGui, Sasi, Tshoa, Shuakwe, Phaleng, Kua, ǀXaise, and Ganadi (Batibo 1996, 1997) are on the verge of a total language shift towards Setswana.

Furthermore, Hasselbring (1996: 28) and Lukusa (2000: 58) show that intermarriage has an impact on the degree of language vitality. Lukusa (2000: 58) observes that 'intermarriage is the quickest way to ensure language shift'.

A further important factor for language shift is age. It is difficult to predict the future course which a language will take through usage, but young people's language use might indicate a general trend. There is ample proof for the shift of minority languages towards Setswana, but does this also hold true for English?

Some studies (Smieja 2003; Batibo 2004; Smieja and Batibo 2007) show that language shift from minority languages to Setswana and English is most common among younger people between the ages of 20 and 35. As we have seen, this includes the shift to a greater use of English as the main language, especially among the affluent. Respondents older than 35, however, do not show a strong shift to English, which may be due to the language and education policy on one hand, and to their schooling before or shortly after independence on the other hand.

Children who attend the private English-medium (elite) schools are exposed to a newly emerging variety of English

> influenced by American English and discotheque jargon. This variety, which is spoken in an accent and pronunciation that is neither Setswana nor English, is gaining prestige among peer groups and can be heard on a local radio station called RB2 or some television programmes.
>
> (Bagwasi 2004: 215)

This goes hand-in-hand with youth identity, which is often linked to language variety and, in Botswana, the specific use of Botswana English.

Therefore, a question of interest is the variety of English that is preferred by young Batswana. Most respondents of the 1999 survey (all of whom were senior secondary students) stated that Botswana has its own variety of English with a distinctive pronunciation, accent, intonation, speed of speech and vocabulary. The respondents were also asked which variety they liked best and which they understood best. Results are presented in Table 12.4 (Smieja 2003: 311).

Table 12.4 English variety liked and understood best

	Like best	*Understand best*
American English	32.9 per cent	3.8 per cent
British English	31.3 per cent	15.8 per cent
Botswana English	31.3 per cent	72.9 per cent
Others	4.5 per cent	7.5 per cent

Surprisingly, American English was liked best but understood the least. Possible reasons for their choice include: the respondents were senior secondary students and thus familiar with American culture and language; shortly before the research President Clinton had visited Botswana and his visit was widely covered in the press and had been discussed at school as well; South Africa provides most of Botswana's TV programmes, which mainly comprise American soap operas that reflect the American way of life. However, one-third of the respondents also indicated that they liked Botswana English best, and nearly three-quarters said that they understood it best. This shows clearly that the English language spoken in Botswana has distinctive features that are recognized and accepted. Examples of a selection of distinctive linguistic features of Botswana English will be given in the next section.

Code-switching, as a further factor in language shift, is observable in communication patterns of multilingual speakers and indicates language change or shift. In Botswana, code-switching can be heard in any shop, any administrative office, on the radio and even in political discourse in Parliament. (Parliamentarians presenting a bill, etc., do so in English by reading it). When they contribute to a discussion they basically do so in English, but 'there is some degree of code-mixing of Setswana and English in parliament. The code-mixing is such that Setswana is used informally for interruptions and private conversation' (Nyati-Ramahobo 1991:104). While there is a longstanding prejudice among older people, who feel that code-mixing results in deficient or improper speech, this prejudice is not apparent among the majority of the younger generation who have grown up with code-switching as a natural part of their everyday lives. The 1999 survey indicated that 90.3 per cent of the interviewees knew people who code-switched, although only 72.7 per cent said that they code-switched themselves sometimes. Not surprisingly Setswana and English are used in most combinations, i.e. up to 88.0 per cent (Smieja 2003: 231). The main reasons respondents gave for code-switching were: lack of appropriate vocabulary in one language (29.1 per cent); to accommodate to the conversational partner (23.2 per cent); to show that they are bicultural (16.5 per cent); to show off (16.5 per cent); and to exclude others from the conversation (14.3 per cent) (Smieja 2003: 237). Code-switching represents a systematic pattern of language use in all social domains in Botswana (Arua and Magocha 2000: 287), and in parliamentary debates, as pointed out above.

The acculturation of the Botswana variety of English

Several scholars have studied the English in Botswana (see Arua and Magocha 2000; Bagwasi 2006; Alimi 2007; Alimi and Bagwasi 2009, among others). Of particular interest is Bagwasi (2006: 114) who considers 'the relationship between the innovations in the Botswana variety of English with the social, cultural and historical factors involved in the contact between English and the local languages'. Bagwasi argues that when studying such innovations, studies should consider only those features that are a result of modification of the English language in order to express new meanings in the Botswana context. These are, in her view, those features which users can only fully understand by reference to the local culture.

The lexical examples in (a) below have been adopted from Bagwasi (2006: 117–18) and characterize those Setswana lexical items that form part of the Botswana variety of English. In (b) are examples of English words which are used in the Botswana context with culturally specific meanings; (c) gives some additional examples.

(a) *Kgotla*   'traditional meeting place'
    Kgosi   'chief'
    Pula   'Botswana currency note; rain or slogan for greeting'
    Omang   'identity card'
    Mohumagadi   'chief's wife'
    Bogwera   'boys' initiation school'
    Bojale   'girls' initiation school'

(b) *Deadwood*   'unproductive civil servant' (which meaning is less used by native speakers)
    Sharp   'okay/all right' (though considered slang by others)

(c) *Mma*   'madam, ma'am'
    Rra   'mister'
    Ntlo ya Dikgosi 'House of Chiefs'
    Mwali   'Bakalanga deity' (from Ikalanga, a local language)
    Wosana   'priest/priestess of Mwali'

Alimi and Bagwasi (2009) focused on identifying innovations peculiar to English in Botswana. In this study the items discussed divide into two broad categories of borrowing and semantic modification. Borrowings are those lexical items borrowed from Setswana into English because adequate translations in English cannot be found without losing their pragmatic force, while semantic modifications refers to meanings of English lexical items which are now adopted and adapted to express certain meanings (Alimi and Bagwasi 2009: 203). Examples include:

1 Borrowing
    mophato   'regiment' (of peers who went through initiation school together)
    matimela   'stray cattle'
    kgamelo   'referring to cattle-rearing practices unique to Setswana culture whereby a cattle owner puts some of his cattle in the custody of another and in return the custodian is entitled to milk'

2 Semantic modification (Alimi and Bagwasi 2009: 211)
    lands   'an open space used for cultivating grains' (semantic shift)

223

brigade   'vocational institutions where youth are trained in vocational skills such as building, carpentry, auto mechanics, etc.' (extended meaning)

Alimi (2007) considered the use of articles and modals in the writing of some Batswana students in the University of Botswana. This study indicates that there are systematic omissions, substitutions and insertions of the definite and indefinite articles as well as the recurrent use of the expression 'can be able'. Furthermore, the study found that the different forms of epistemic modality were confined to the use of 'could' where 'would' might be expected in other varieties. Complex verb phrases involving negation have their constituents reordered such that the negative operator 'not' consistently succeeded the perfective auxiliary (Alimi 2007: 209–22). Alimi cites these examples:

1 According to (*) Bible, it says thou shall not kill. [omission of 'the' article is indicated by (*): p. 213]
2 *(A)* word insult as a verb can not be divided into syllables unless stress marks are used. [substitution of article 'a' for 'the' is marked by parenthesis: p. 213]
3 John drank *(a)* very hot tea. [redundant use of an article is marked by parenthesis: p. 214]
4 Open classes do allow the formation of new meanings as we acquire new technology so that we *can be able* to name things that were not existing before. [the use of *can be able* for *is able*: p. 215]
5 If they had told Oedipus that they adopted him when he asked them, Oedipus *could have not decided* to run away from the oracle. [use of *could* for *would* and incorrect placement of *not*: p. 215]

Reading a Botswana newspaper or an English novel written by a Motswana, it is common to come across these words and usages.

Phonologically the most obvious feature of the Botswana variety of English lies with vowel sounds. Standard British English has 20 vowel sounds, comprising 12 pure vowels and eight diphthongs. By way of contrast, Setswana, the majority language of Botswana spoken by about 80 per cent of the population, has seven vowel sounds and this is a characteristic of other Bantu languages of the Sotho group. Other local languages of the Bantu family are characterized by having five vowel sounds. First-language influence means Botswana English has fewer vowel sounds than Standard British English. As is common with so many new varieties of English (see this volume), the lack of a distinction between the vowel sounds in the following pairs is common:

/iː, ɪ/ as in *heat* /hiːt/   and   *hit* /hɪt/
/aː, ʌ/ as in *heart* /haːt/   and   *hut* /hʌt/
/ɒ, ɔː/ as in *hot* /hɒt/   and   *hoard* /hɔːd/

In addition, vowel sounds with distinctive pronunciations include:

/əʊ/ as in *crow* /krəʊ/ pronounced as /krɔː/
/əʊ/ as in *show* /ʃəʊ/ pronounced as /ʃɔː/
/æ/ as *salad* /sæləd/ pronounced as /saːlaːd/
/ə/ as *salad* /sæləd/ pronounced as /saːlaːd/
/ɜː/ as in *bird* /bɜːd/ pronounced as /beːd/

Discussion and conclusion: view to the future of English in Botswana

Botswana does not differ very much from other African countries in that it privileges a European language at the expense of local languages. English certainly fulfils a prior-itized and privileged role and enjoys a high status in Botswana. Since English is a world language it is also felt to be the gatekeeper to modern technical developments, globalization and socioeconomic success. Therefore, English is considered the medium for upward social mobility. As a consequence, English dominates the education system past the primary level just as strongly as it did in colonial times. One result is a good command of English by a minority of wealthy young Batswana who are being trained for highly qualified jobs. Another result, however, is that the majority of Batswana are unable to master English as a second language (or even as a third), yet are required to learn all subjects through it from the age of 12. This is certainly a reason for high school drop-out rates when English becomes the medium of instruction. There thus remains a big gap between those who speak the socially exclusive and prestigious language English and those who do not.

Even though English is not really needed in many domains, the elite choose to use it in many of these domains. In addition, most jobs – even those that require few quali-fications – require the command of English. The dominant position of English is questioned, but generally speaking it is currently not viewed as a threat to Setswana. A Botswana variety of English has developed which reflects local culture and it is likely that Setswana and English will continue to co-exist. The co-existence of English and Setswana means that it is the smaller local languages that are under serious threat.

Suggestions for further reading

Andersson, L.-G. and Janson, T. (1997) *Languages in Botswana. Language Ecology in Southern Africa*, Gaborone: Longman Botswana. (This book remains an authority on the language situation of Botswana. Andersson and Janson not only discuss the languages of Botswana, but also cover their role in society, their history and estimations of the number of speakers.)

Bagwasi, M.M. (2006) 'A developing model of Botswana English', in A.E. Arua, M.M. Bagwasi, T. Sebina and B. Seboni (eds) *The Study and Use of English in Africa*, Newcastle, UK: Cambridge Scholars Press. (This article is an attempt at establishing a relationship between innovations in the Botswana variety of English. The paper argues that non-native varieties of English develop as a result of prolonged contact between local languages and English. Thus, a study of these varieties should take into consideration the duration as well as the history of the contact.)

Chebanne, A.M. and Nyati-Ramahobo, L. (2003) 'Language use and language knowledge in Botswana', paper delivered at the 2001 Population and Housing Census Dissemination Seminar, Gaborone, September 2003. (This paper addresses issues of language use and language knowledge in Botswana using the 2001 Botswana population census data in response to the one question on language use in the home.)

Mathangwane, J.T. (2008) 'English in Botswana: a blessing or a curse?' in M.M. Bagwasi, M. M. Alimi and P.J. Ebewo (eds) *English Language and Literature: Cross Cultural Currents*, New-castle upon Tyne, UK: Cambridge Scholars Publishing. (This article examines the use of English in Botswana to determine whether its dominance over the local languages in the country is a curse or a blessing. To achieve its goal, the paper uses illustrations from various events in Botswana to demonstrate this obsession with the English language even where other local languages would be appropriate.)

Nyati-Ramahobo, L. (1999) *The National Language – A Resource or a Problem?* Gaborone: Pula Press. (This book critically evaluates the Botswana language policy which has legitimized one language Setswana over others and the education policy. The author looks into the development of Botswana languages and discusses their present relationship to each other from the view of Setswana as the national language.)

Smieja, B. and Batibo, H.M. (2007) 'The effect of language policy on language attitudes: a case study of young Khoesan language speakers in Botswana', in C. Van der Walt (ed.) *Living through Languages: An African Tribute to René Dirven*, Stellenbosch: SUN Press. (The article presents the language situation of Botswana and discusses the situation of the Khoesan speakers in particular. The authors analyse their language attitudes in different domains in comparison with Setswana and English that seems to suffocate their languages, cultures and identities.)

Note

1 In the following it should be considered that according to the Bantu grammatical system, the country is characterized by the prefix *Bo-* as in *Botswana*, the people (plural) by *Ba-* as in *Batswana* (singular by *Mo-*, i.e. *Motswana*) and the language and culture by *Se-*, i.e. *Setswana*.

References

Alimi, M.M. (2007) 'English articles and modals in the writing of some Batswana students', *Language, Culture and Curriculum*, 20 (3): 209–22.

——(2008) 'English pronouns in the writing of some Batswana students', *Marang*, 18: 85–101.

Alimi, M.M. and Bagwasi, M.M. (2009) 'Aspects of culture and meaning in Botswana English', *Journal of Asian and African Studies*, 44 (2): 199–214.

Andersson, L.-G. and Janson, T. (1997) *Languages in Botswana. Language Ecology in Southern Africa*, Gaborone: Longman Botswana.

Arua, E.A. and Magocha, K. (2000) 'Attitudes of parents to their children's use of English in Botswana', *Language, Culture and Curriculum*, 13 (3): 279–90.

——(2002) 'Patterns of language use and language preference of some children and their parents in Botswana', *Journal of Multilingual and Multicultural Development*, 23 (6): 449–61.

Bagwasi, M.M. (2004) 'The functional distribution of Setswana and English in Botswana', in M.J. Muthwii and A.N. Kioko (eds) *New Language Bearings in Africa: A Fresh Quest*, Clevedon: Multilingual Matters.

——(2006) 'A developing model of Botswana English', in A.E. Arua, M.M. Bagwasi, T. Sebina and B. Seboni (eds) *The Study and Use of English in Africa*, Newcastle, UK: Cambridge Scholars Press.

Baker, C. (1993) *Foundations of Bilingual Education and Bilingualism*, Clevedon: Multilingual Matters.

Batibo, H.M. (1992) 'The fate of ethnic languages in Tanzania', in M. Brenzinger (ed.) *Language Death. Factual and Theoretical Explorations with Special Reference to East Africa*, New York: Mouton de Gruyter.

——(1996) 'Patterns of language shift and maintenance in Botswana: the critical dilemma', paper presented at the International Conference on Endangered Languages, Environments and Knowledge, University of California, Berkeley, October.

——(1997) 'The fate of the minority languages in Botswana', in B. Smieja and M. Tasch (eds) *Human Contact through Language and Linguistics*, Frankfurt am Main: Peter Lang.

——(2004) 'Setswana: an under-exploited national resource?' in K. Bromber and B. Smieja (eds) *Globalisation and African Languages: Risks and Benefits*, Berlin: Mouton de Gruyter.

Batibo, H.M. and Mosaka, N. (2000) 'Linguistic barriers as a hindrance to information flow. The case of Botswana', in H.M. Batibo and B. Smieja (eds) *Botswana: The Future of the Minority Languages*, Frankfurt am Main: Peter Lang.

Batibo, H.M. and Smieja, B. (eds) (2000) *Botswana: The Future of the Minority Languages*, Frankfurt am Main: Peter Lang.

——(2006) 'Language attitudes among young minority language speakers in Botswana', *PULA, Botswana Journal of African Studies*, 20: 66–74.

Batibo, H.M., Mathangwane, J.T. and Tsonope, J. (2003) *A Study of the Third Language Teaching in the Botswana: Preliminary Report*, Gaborone: Department of Curriculum Development, Ministry of Education.

Botswana Government (1977) 'Education for Kagisano: Report of the National Commission of Education', Gaborone.

Central Statistics Office/Republic of Botswana (1997a) *Report of the First National Survey on Literacy in Botswana 1993*, Gaborone: Government Printer.

——(1997b) *Education Statistics 1995*, Gaborone: Government Printer.

Chebanne, A.M. and Nyati-Ramahobo, L. (2003) 'Language use and language knowledge in Botswana', paper delivered at the 2001 Population and Housing Census Dissemination Seminar, Gaborone, September.

Crystal, D. (2004) *English as a Global Language* (2nd edition), Cambridge: Cambridge University Press.

Cummins, J. (1981) 'The role of primary language development in promoting educational success for language minority students', in California State Department of Education (ed.) *Schooling and Language Minority Students. A Theoretical Framework*, Los Angeles: California State Department of Education.

Dirven, R. and Pütz, M. (1993) *Sprachkonflikte: Versuch einer Typologie* (Series B 242) Duisburg: LAUD.

Fasold, R.W. (1984) *The Sociolinguistics of Society*, Oxford: Blackwell.

Ferguson, C. (1959) 'Diglossia', *Word*, 15: 325–40.

——(1964) 'Diglossia', in D. Hymes (ed.), *Language in Culture and Society*, New York: Harper & Row.

——(1967) 'National sociolinguistic profile formulas', in W. Bright (ed.) *Proceedings of the UCLA Sociolinguistic Conference*, The Hague: Mouton.

Fishman, J.A. (1965) 'Who speaks what language to whom and when?' *Linguistics*, 2: 67–88.

——(1966) *Language Loyalty in the United States: The Maintenance and Perpetuation of Non-English Mother Tongues by American Ethnic and Religious Groups*, The Hague: Mouton.

——(1972) *Sociolinguistics. A Brief Introduction*, Rowley, MA: Newbury House.

——(1975) *Soziologie der Sprache. Eine interdisziplinäre sozialwissenschaftliche Betrachtung der Sprache in der Gesellschaft*, Munich: Max Hueber.

——(1980) 'Bilingualism and biculturalism as individual and as societal phenomena', *Journal of Multilingual and Multicultural Development*, 1: 3–15.

Gordon, R.G., Jr (ed.) (2005) *Ethnologue: Languages of the World* (15th edition), Dallas, TX: SIL International.

Grimes, B.F. (1996) *Ethnologue: Languages of the World* (13th edition), Dallas, TX: SIL International.

Hasselbring, S. (1996) *A Sociolinguistic Survey of the Languages of Gantsi District*, Gaborone: Bible Translation Society of Botswana, Botswana Language Use Project.

——(2000a) 'Where are the Khoesan of Botswana?' in H.M. Batibo and B. Smieja (eds) *Botswana: The Future of the Minority Languages*, Frankfurt am Main: Peter Lang.

——(2000b) *A Sociolinguistic Survey of the Languages of Botswana, Vol. 1* (Sociolinguistic Studies of Botswana Language Series), Gaborone: Basarwa Language Project, University of Botswana.

——(2001) *A Sociolinguistic Survey of the Languages of Botswana, Vol. 2*, Gaborone: Basarwa Languages Project, University of Botswana.

Janson, T. and Tsonope, J. (1991) *Birth of a National Language. The History of Setswana*, Gaborone: Heinemann Botswana and NIR (National Institute of Development Research and Documentation of the University of Botswana).

Kachru, B.B. (1985) 'Standards, codification and sociolinguistic realism', in R. Quirk and H.G. Widdowson (eds) *English in the World: Teaching and Learning the Language and Literatures*, Cambridge: Cambridge University Press for the British Council.

Lukusa, S.T.M. (2000) 'The Shekgalagadi struggle for survival: aspects of language maintenance and shift', in H.M. Batibo and B. Smieja (eds) *Botswana: The Future of the Minority Languages*, Frankfurt am Main: Peter Lang.

Mathangwane, J.T. (2008) 'English in Botswana: a blessing or a curse?' in M.M. Bagwasi, M.M. Alimi and P.J. Ebewo (eds) *English Language and Literature: Cross Cultural Currents*, Newcastle upon Tyne, UK: Cambridge Scholars Publishing.

Mathangwane, J.T. and Gardner, S.F. (1997) 'Language attitudes as portrayed by the use of English and African names in Botswana', paper presented at the LICCA conference in Kenya, July.

——(1999) 'Ambivalent attitudes to English and African names in Botswana', in *Language, Literature and Society: A Conference in Honour of Bessie Head Proceedings*, special issue of *Marang*.

Ministry of Labour and Home Affairs (2001) *Report of the National Commission on Education*, Gaborone: Government Printer.

National Commission on Education (1993) *Report of the National Commission on Education*, Gaborone: Government Printer.

Nyati-Ramahobo, L. (1991) 'Language planning and education policy in Botswana', unpublished PhD thesis, University of Botswana.

——(1999) *The National Language – A Resource or a Problem?* Gaborone: Pula Press.

Phillipson, P. (1992) *Linguistic Imperialism*, Oxford: Oxford University Press.

Raditladi, M. (2001) 'Keynote address at the National Conference on Botswana's National Heritage and the Culture of Peace', in E. Biakolo and T.T. Mogobe (eds) *Botswana's National Conference on Botswana's National Heritage and the Culture of Peace*, Gaborone: Printing and Publishing Company.

Republic of Botswana (1994) *Government Paper No. 2 of 1994: The Revised National Policy on Education*, Gaborone: Government Printer.

Smieja, B. (2003) *Language Pluralism in Botswana – Hope or Hurdle?* Frankfurt am Main: Peter Lang.

Smieja, B. and Batibo, H.M. (2007) 'The effect of language policy on language attitudes: a case study of young Khoesan language speakers in Botswana', in C. Van der Walt (ed.) *Living through Languages: An African Tribute to René Dirven*, Stellenbosch: SUN Press.

Sommer, G. (1992) 'A survey on language death in Africa', in M. Brenzinger (ed.) *Language Death. Factual and Theoretical Explorations with Special Reference to East Africa*, New York: Mouton de Gruyter.

The Cambridge Encyclopaedia of the English Language (1995) Melbourne: Cambridge University Press.

Tlou, T. and Campbell, A. (1984) *History of Botswana*, Gaborone: Macmillan Botswana.

University of Botswana (2007) *UB-Calendar 2007–2008*.

Wald, B. (1994) 'Sub Saharan Africa', in C. Moseley and R.E. Asher (eds) *Atlas of the World's Languages*, London: Routledge.

Williams, G. (1992) *Sociolinguistics. A Sociolinguistic Critique*, London: Routledge.

13

English in Singapore and Malaysia

Differences and similarities

Low Ee Ling

Introduction

Early scholars (Tongue 1974; Tongue 1979; Platt and Weber 1980) working on describing the English spoken in Singapore and Malaysia have classified both varieties as a single entity known as Singapore and Malaysian English (SME). Platt and Weber (1980: 21) suggest that the birth of SME may date back to the formation of the Straits Settlements in 1826 when Singapore, Malacca and Penang were ruled administratively as one by the British. It is therefore interesting to explore when and how SME became two separate entities and varieties of English which we presently term as Singapore English (SgE) and Malaysian English (MalE) respectively. Today, according to the classical Kachruvian model of the three circles of English (Kachru 1992), both varieties are described as being part of the outer circle where, broadly speaking, English is classified as having been institutionalized and described as being 'norm-developing', meaning that it is developing its own norms and standards and where English is generally spoken as a second language (ESL). The language policies adopted by each country post-independence (1965) when Malaysia and Singapore were totally independent from the British and each other have undoubtedly had an impact on the development of English in both countries. The purpose of this chapter is to briefly trace the historical development of English in Singapore and Malaysia, from its birth to the point where they were considered as distinct varieties. The different language policies adopted by each country post-independence will be surveyed as an attempt to understand when and how the different varieties emerged. Variation in present-day English in Singapore and Malaysia will be examined. The chapter will then summarize the main linguistic features of each variety of English, highlighting similarities and differences where relevant. Finally, directions for further research will be suggested, which will increase our understanding of the development of both varieties of English.

Development of English in Singapore and Malaysia (SME)

A shared history

While the advent of English in both Singapore and Malaysia is obviously linked to the arrival of the British in both countries, the dates of arrival differ. Penang, which was originally part of the Malay sultanate of Kedah, was ceded to the British in 1786, specifically the British East India Company, in exchange for British protection from the Siamese and Burmese troops (Baker 2008), while Singapore was founded by Sir Stamford Raffles in 1819, some 33 years later. Linking the birth of SME to the formation of the Straits Settlements in 1826, it is important to know the different ethnic groups living in Singapore and the different languages spoken by these ethnic groups, since they are likely to have had an impact on the variety of English spoken in Singapore and Malaysia in the nineteenth century. Table 13.1 summarizes the languages and dialects spoken by these main ethnic groups.

The British government set up English-medium schools in the early nineteenth century in order to produce a local English-educated elite group to fulfil the occupational positions previously staffed by the British themselves. The English-medium schools were of two main types: free schools and mission schools (Platt and Weber 1980: 34–41). Free schools admitted students regardless of race, creed or colour. The first free school in Singapore was Raffles Institution, established in 1823 (originally called the Singapore Free School), while in Penang, the Penang Free School was established in 1816 and the Malacca Free School was founded in 1826. The mission schools, as the name suggested, were established and maintained by the missions of different religious orders like the Sisters of the Infant Jesus (IJ) and the Anglican Mission, to name but two. When the English-medium schools were first set up in the nineteenth century, much of the instruction was in Malay rather than English (Gupta 1994). The establishment of these English-medium schools meant that a local English-speaking population was beginning to emerge, and it is important to ask which variety of English was spoken by this group. Gupta (1998: 125) hypothesizes about the main substratum languages that may have contributed to the development of a colloquial variety of English spoken in Singapore and Malaysia. She identifies the superstrate as Standard English, a main substrate comprising Baba Malay (Malay spoken by Straits-born Chinese of mixed Malay and Chinese parentage) and Bazaar

Table 13.1 Languages and dialects spoken by main ethnic groups in the Straits Settlements

Ethnic group	*Main languages*
Malays	Formal Malay, local dialects according to region, native dialects of immigrants
Chinese	Host of Chinese dialects: Hokkien, Teochew, Cantonese, Hakka
Indians	Southern Indian: mainly Tamil, Malayalam and Telugu
	Northern Indian: mainly Punjabi and Bengali etc.
Eurasians	Languages according to ethnic background
Europeans	British upper-class English
	English, Scottish, Welsh and Irish regional dialects
	Other languages spoken by minority groups

Source: From Low and Brown 2005: 17, adapted from Platt and Weber 1980: 5.

Note: Note that the definition of dialect here refers to a regional variation of a particular language.

Malay (a pidgin variety of Malay often used as the lingua franca for communication across the different ethnic groups), and a secondary substrate comprising the various southern varieties of Chinese, especially Hokkien, Teochew and Cantonese.

In 1957, Malay was declared the national language of Malaya (known as Bahasa Melayu). The purpose of this policy was to ensure that all ethnic groups living in Malaya could identify with and establish an emotional attachment to the language (Azirah 2009). Both Malay and English were assigned equal prominence from 1957 to 1967. This was largely a result of the Barnes Commission of 1951, which had advocated Malay–English bilingualism. Under British rule, Malay, Chinese and Tamil were the main media of instruction in the national, vernacular schools (Azirah 2009), while English was used in some English-medium schools, as earlier described. As a result of the 1956 Razak Report, two types of primary schools were established, the *national schools*, which used Malay as the medium of instruction, and the *national-type schools*, which could use either English, Chinese or Tamil as the media of instruction. The only secondary schools were national schools, although Chinese schools were allowed to function as long as they adhered to the national curriculum and examinations.

In 1957, Malaysia gained independence from the British, while Singapore attained self-government in 1959. From 1963 to 1965, Singapore and Malaysia were part of the Federation of Malaysia. The merger between the two countries broke down in 1965, with Singapore becoming a fully independent nation on 9 August 1965. The next section will review key language policy differences that are likely to have shaped the development of English in both countries in the post-independent era.

Language policy in Singapore and Malaysia: post-1965

Post-independent language policies in Singapore

The post-independent language policies in Singapore may be characterized by two main concerns: the attempt to address the issue of parity in the language policy adopted for a multilingual, multi-ethnic population; and the growing concern over the falling standards of English, which still dominates the agenda today. With regard to the first concern, Kuo and Jernudd (1994, as cited in Lim 2009) term such a policy as 'pragmatic multilingualism' where the mother tongues and English are positioned in a way where English and the officially designated mother tongues – Malay, Tamil and Mandarin – are functionally allocated such that English is the language of international trade, science and technology, while the official mother tongues serve to provide a cultural pivot for the preservation of Asian values amongst the different ethnic groups. In 1956, an all-party committee was designated to look specifically into the issue of linguistic diversity in multilingual Malaya and to address the disputes and demonstrations that took place as a protest against Chinese-medium education. The result was a report which outlined several main language policy directions. To signal the fact that all ethnic groups received equality in treatment, four co-official languages were declared, namely English, Mandarin, Malay and Tamil. Malay was maintained as the national language so as not to estrange Singapore from its neighbours, but it was used mainly for ceremonial purposes. From 1960, the learning of a second language became compulsory, sowing the seeds of the bilingual education policy. Alongside these official policies, however, the role of English continued to rise in prominence, as it was not just ethnically neutral but allowed one to communicate with the rest of the world.

The bilingual education policy (see Gopinathan *et al.* 1998 and Low and Brown 2005 for more details) was introduced as a means to anchor pupils in their ethnic and cultural traditions by allowing them to learn an ascribed mother tongue (Mandarin, Malay and Tamil). This policy allowed for schools of different language media to be retained, and for those in English-medium schools the mother tongue was taught as a second language. English was offered as a second language in non-English-medium schools, while civics and history classes were taught using Mandarin, Malay or Tamil. This policy gave rise to what Pakir (1991: 174) termed the 'English-knowing bilingual in Singapore', defined as someone who is bilingual in English and their ethnically ascribed mother tongue. The main milestone in the bilingual policy was the introduction of English as the medium of instruction in Nanyang University, which originally only had Mandarin Chinese as the medium of instruction. In 1978, when Nanyang University merged with the University of Singapore, English was used as the medium of instruction, and in 1979, English was made the primary medium of instruction in pre-university classes, even in the non-English-medium schools.

In the late 1970s to 1990s, several landmark language policies were introduced. The first was the implementation of the Speak Mandarin Campaign in 1979. This aimed to simplify the Chinese language situation by attempting to create a Mandarin-speaking environment, which it was felt would help students better their chances of becoming bilingual. Other key policies included the introduction, in 1980, of streaming at the Primary Three level, whereby academically weaker students were channelled into the monolingual English stream and exempted from passing a second language. Students were streamed again at Primary Six level, according to their Primary School Leaving Examination (PSLE) results. The top 10 per cent took two 'first' languages and had the option of taking a third. The majority, comprising about 70 per cent of the cohort, took a first and a second language, while the bottom 20 per cent also took two languages, but at a more basic level. These students were also given an additional year to complete their secondary education. In 1985, a pass in both English and a second language was the minimum language requirement set for entry into the local university. In 1987, English became the main medium of instruction for all schools. This policy led to the increased dominance and prominence of the English language in Singapore.

Alongside the policies outlined above, by the late 1970s another language problem arose, and this had to do with the perceived falling standards of English. In 1977, both the British Council and the Regional Language Centre (RELC) were appointed to look into the issue of the teaching and learning of English in Singapore. By 1982, two varieties of English were clearly in existence: a standard variety used mainly for formal purposes of communication, and an informal colloquial variety, termed by linguists as Singapore Colloquial English (SCE) or Singlish. The concern over the proliferation of Singlish led to the national broadcasting station, then known as the Singapore Broadcasting Corporation (SBC), to stipulate that Singlish was no longer allowed to be aired freely over national television. The Singlish–Standard English debate continues to plague the language scene in Singapore to the present. On 26 July 1999, the Ministry of Education announced an initiative to re-train 8,000 primary school teachers in traditional grammar. This move was a clear recognition by the Ministry that those who had undergone primary school in the 1980s were products of the Communicative Language Teaching approach that emphasized fluency at the expense of accuracy, and where traditional grammar rules were not taught. In 2000, the government launched the Speak Good English Movement (SGEM) which aims to encourage Singaporeans to speak grammatically correct English that can be internationally understood. The movement has run for almost a decade now and has, in recent years, decided to target different groups of Singaporeans (for example, retailers, teachers, youth and parents) so that each year's activities are organized along themes that appeal to the target group selected and with annual taglines that characterize the year's focal activities. The movement's work has met with much scepticism, especially among linguists who have criticized it mainly for failing to recognize that different varieties of English can, in fact, co-exist and be used for different speech situations (Rubdy 2001; Chng 2003; Lim 2009). The concern over falling standards of English perennially resurfaces, and in 2009, at the Ministry of Education's annual workplan seminar, the Minister for Education, Dr Ng Eng Hen, announced plans to establish the English Language Institute of Singapore (ELIS). This would 'build deeper capabilities in EL proficiency training for teachers' and help students to become articulate speakers of English. The present concern, therefore, is targeted at raising Singaporeans' mastery of the English language such that Singapore will not lose its competitive edge as an English-speaking nation over its neighbours in an age where excellent communication skills are very much a prerequisite of functioning effectively in the global marketplace.

Post-independent language policies in Malaysia

The language concerns in post-independent Malaysia were quite different and had to do mainly with the predominance of the role of Malay against the other languages spoken in Malaysia (Azirah 2009). In 1956, the Institute of National Language, the Dewan Bahasa dan Pustaka, was established in order to develop the language capacities and use of the Malay language. The 1957 Reid Commission adopted the main recommendations of the Razak Report (1956) and introduced Malay-medium national schools and non-Malay-medium national-type schools where English, Chinese and Tamil were used as media of instruction, but where Malay was taught as a compulsory subject. Article 152 of the Constitution stated clearly that Malay was to be the sole national and official language, while English was given the *status* of an official language. The privileged status of English was removed via the Language Act of 1967, however, and English was relegated to the position of a second language.

In 1961, the Education Act passed a bill which made Malay the only medium of instruction in secondary schools. Further, the National Language Act of 1967 ruled that English-medium primary schools had to become Malay-medium schools by 1976, and the secondary schools by 1982. In 1971, the use of Malay as a medium of instruction was imposed at tertiary institutes as well. English continued to be preserved as a compulsory subject at the national schools. Alongside the national schools, however, the Chinese- and Tamil-medium schools continued to exist.

The policy of Malay as the sole medium of instruction continued until 2002, when English was introduced as the medium of instruction for the teaching of mathematics and science from Primary One. This policy was motivated by science and mathematics graduates being unable to function in English, thus being denied access to the latest research and publications about science and mathematics on the one hand, and employment opportunities on the other. The tertiary institutes also followed suit, so English became the medium of instruction in the science faculties, while in the arts faculties the percentage of courses using English as the medium of instruction increased.

In July 2009, however, the Ministry of Education announced a reversal of this policy, with the teaching of mathematics and science to revert back to Malay in primary and

233

secondary schools in 2012. At the pre-university and tertiary levels, mathematics and science will continue to be taught in English. There were two major reasons for this reversal: first, many children from poorer and rural areas were failing; and second, there were insufficient qualified teachers who could teach these subjects through the medium of English. Increasing pressure mounted by the parents of students in the vernacular (Chinese- and Tamil-medium) schools also played a role (*The Malaysian Insider*, 11 July 2009; www.themalaysianinsider.com).

Variation in present-day English in Singapore and Malaysia

The previous section has highlighted the main differences in language policies that both countries have adopted in the post-independence era. Such an understanding is crucial in explaining how and why the varieties of English language spoken in Singapore and Malaysia have become distinct.

Any attempt to describe English in either Singapore or Malaysia needs to take into account the variation that exists. It is important to understand the demographics of each country if we wish to understand the substratum influences that speakers of English in each country are exposed to. According to the latest figures released by the Department of Statistics (Singapore Department of Statistics 2009), in June 2009 Singapore's population was 4,987,600, made up of 3.73 million residents and 1.25 million non-residents. In terms of the ethnic make-up of the resident population, the Chinese formed 74 per cent of the population, the Malays 13 per cent and the Indians 9.2 per cent. Malaysia has a much larger population, totalling 26 million, comprising 60 per cent Malays, 25 per cent Chinese and 7 per cent Indians (Statistics Singapore 2000). What is immediately apparent in comparing the demographic profile of the two countries is that the Chinese make up the majority of Singapore's population, while the Malays make up the majority of Malaysia's population, although the main ethnic groups residing in both countries are similar (Chinese, Malays and Indians).

Several models have been put forward to account for variation in Singapore English (Platt 1977; Platt and Weber 1980; Gupta 1986; Pakir 1991; Deterding and Poedjosoedarmo 2000; Alsagoff 2007). Platt (1977) and Platt and Weber (1980) described language variation according to the educational levels of the speakers and came up with the lectal continuum. Gupta (1986) talked about a diglossic language situation with the high (H) and low (L) varieties each having a distinct function. Deterding and Poedjosoedarmo (2000) discuss ethnic variation that arises, especially during informal discourse.

One of the most influential models of language variation in Singapore is Pakir's (1991) expanding 'triangles of English expression'. She describes English in Singapore as varying along the clines of proficiency and formality and shows that these determine the type of variety spoken, i.e. Singapore Colloquial English (SCE) or Standard Singapore English (SSE). Pakir postulates that the speaker with the highest proficiency in English has the largest triangle of expression, being able to move effortlessly between the colloquial and standard varieties of English depending on the formality of the communicative domain. Conversely, the lowest educated have the smallest triangle of expression since they are constrained, by virtue of their proficiency level, from moving upwards to speak Standard Singapore English, even when the discourse situation calls for it.

Alsagoff (2007) postulated a new model known as the Cultural Orientation Model (COM) to explain language variation in Singapore. Her model is premised on the fact

234

that English in Singapore has to fulfil two functions: as a global language and as a means of intra-ethnic communication and social networking. She states that 'Speakers of Singapore English vary their style of speaking by negotiating fluidly within a multidimensional space framed by bipolar cultural perspectives' (Alsagoff 2007: 44), one global and the other local. The use of International Singapore English (ISE) is associated with formality, distance and authority, and symbolizes educational attainment and economic value. Conversely, the use of Local Singapore English (LSE) has associations with informality, camaraderie, equality and membership within a community, and has value as sociocultural capital. The use of ISE or LSE is determined both by speakers' competence in the language and by whether they choose to use English for global or local purposes.

To turn to Malaysia, according to Baskaran (2004), as reported in Tan and Low (forthcoming), there are two categories of Malay speakers: the Austronesians and the Austroasiatics. The migrant population comprises Chinese, Indians, Arabs, Eurasians, Thais and Europeans, who each speak a host of different languages. Table 13.2 summarizes the languages spoken by the different ethnic groups residing in Malaysia.

Baskaran (1987) and Morais (2000) talk about three sub-varieties of Malaysian English. The acrolectal variety of Malaysian English is similar to Standard English, while the mesolectal variety tends to have more colloquial elements and is usually spoken rather than written. An educated speaker of Malaysian English will use the acrolectal variety of Malaysian English for formal speech situations or when communicating with speakers from other countries and may switch to the mesolectal variety for communication in less formal situations. The third category, the basilect, is considered the uneducated style of speech communication. Baskaran (2004, 2005) has suggested new names for the different varieties of Malaysian English as Official Malaysian English (previously the acrolect), Unofficial Malaysian English (previously the mesolect) and Broken Malaysian English (previously the basilect).

In terms of categorizing the developmental phases of English in Singapore and Malaysia, Schneider (2007: 148, 155) has suggested that Malaysia is in Phase 3 (nativization), while Singapore has moved on to Phase 4 (endonormative stabilization), as articulated in his Dynamic Model of Postcolonial Englishes (see also this volume).

Table 13.2 Languages spoken by the different ethnic groups

Ethnic group	Languages spoken
Austronesians: Malays in West Malaysia, Kadazans and Dayaks of Sarawak	Bahasa Melayu Kadazan Iban
Austroasiatics: Malays in West Malaysia	Bahasa Melayu Temiar
Settler population: Chinese, Indians, Arabs, Eurasians, Thais, Europeans	Hokkien, Cantonese, Hakka, Teochew, Hainanese, Mandarin Tamil, Malayalam, Telugu, Punjabi, Bengali, Gujerati, Singhalese Arab Thai Bahasa Melayu

Source: cf. Baskaran 2004.

Schneider's model is influenced by scholarship on language contact and the idea of linguistic ecologies (Mufwene 2001). He theorizes that, in the evolution of a variety of language, there is a constant process of competition and selection of features available to the speakers from a 'feature pool of possible linguistic choices' (Schneider 2007: 21). As speakers select from this pool, they redefine the expression of their social and linguistic identities, and accommodate their speech patterns depending on whom they wish to associate with. Varieties of English classified as being in Phase 3 tend to show a marked local accent with great variability in terms of the range of the sociolinguistic accent (Schneider 2007: 44), while varieties of English classified as being in Phase 4 tend to demonstrate more linguistic homogeneity in their language, as some linguistic stabilization has occurred (Schneider 2007: 51).

In what follows, the description of the features of English in Singapore and Malaysia will focus on the standard varieties. Standard Singapore English (henceforth SgE) refers to the variety of English used by educated speakers for formal speech occasions, while Standard Malaysian English (MalE) will be used to refer to the variety that has been described as the acrolect or Official Malaysian English.

Linguistic features of Standard Singapore and Malaysian English

Lexis

Most of the lexical items that have been documented in previous scholarship tend to be about the colloquial variety of Singapore English (Lim and Wee 2001; Wee 2004a, 2004b). However, there are also studies that have focused on features of lexical items that appear in both Standard and Colloquial Singapore English and some of these studies also provide a comparison with MalE or focus solely on MalE (Lowenberg 1984; Wee 1998; G. Lim 2001; Ooi 2001; Tan 2001; Tan and Azirah 2007).

Several categories can be used to describe the lexical innovations that occur in both SgE and MalE and a few key ones will be highlighted here. Note that in many of the examples given below, when they do appear in Standard SgE and MalE, even in the local newspapers or in speeches, these lexical innovations are used when no Standard English equivalents can fully express the intended meaning.

   1 Lexical borrowings: this is the most commonly described lexical word-formation process described in both varieties. Borrowings occur widely in Standard British or American English, and when these loanwords from other languages become so commonly used they are accepted as part of the English language. Examples of such loanwords into Standard English are: *acronym* (from Greek), *data* (from Latin), *garage* (from French), *ketchup* (from French), *noodle* (from German), to name a few (see Leong *et al.* 2006: 51 for more examples). Tan and Azirah (2007) identify the following categories of borrowings for MalE and, as a native speaker of SgE, I would consider these to occur in Singapore as well. The bulk of the borrowings into MalE are from Malay, while in the case of SgE, borrowings from Hokkien and Tamil are also common.

     (a) Linked to food: *durian* (tropical thorny fruit), *mee goreng* (fried noodles normally spicy), *rojak* (mixed salad in prawn paste sauce), *teh tarik* (from Malay:

sweetened milk tea which is tossed from a jug to a cup to create froth). One obvious area of difference occurs when Singaporeans do not have the equivalent food items. For example, *pesembur* (from Tamil), a spicy salad dish is found only in Malaysian English.

(b) Linked to culture and religious practices: *kampong* (from Malay, meaning 'village' or 'home town'), *bomoh* (from Malay meaning 'medicine man with supernatural powers'), *surau* (place of prayer for Muslims). Words more closely associated with MalE include *penghulu* (from Malay to refer to the headman of the village) and *bumiputra* (from Malay meaning 'the original inhabitants of the land').

(c) Linked to daily life, description of character traits: for this category, MalE and SgE are quite distinct, which clearly shows different concerns about daily life and character traits. In MalE for example, *lepak* is used to refer to someone who is idle and likes to waste time and *lesen terbang* refers to a driving licence that is obtained illegally. Exclusive to SgE, we have *kiasu* (a Hokkien borrowing referring to the fear of losing out which motivates behaviour such as rushing for good deals, hoarding library books, all in an effort to get ahead), *cheem* (from Hokkien to describe something as being deep and profound) and *siong* (from Hokkien, literally meaning 'injured', but more often to describe the immensity of a task assigned).

2   Compounding: this process refers to two words being joined together to form a new word. In SgE, compound words include: *shophouse* (a shop where the owners live upstairs), *outstation* (referring to being overseas), *neighbourhood school* (to refer to schools around the neighbourhood where one lives and which do not usually enjoy high prestige compared to the *independent schools* which are partially privately funded and which attract the best students academically). Note that while *shophouse* and *outstation* are found in both varieties, MalE does not have the equivalent compounds for schools because of the differences in the school system.

3   Blending: this refers to a process where parts of two different words are combined together to form a new word. In SgE, a *distripark* is a distribution park or a warehouse complex.

4   Clipping: this refers to the process of shortening a word without changing its word class. In SgE, some examples of clipping include: *air-con* (for *air conditioner*), *Taka* (to refer to the shopping chain called *Takashimaya*).

5   Back-formation: this refers to a process where a word is shortened but, in the process of shortening, its word class has also changed. An example of back-formation in SgE and MalE is the verb *stinge*, formed from the adjective 'stingy' to refer to someone who is overly careful with finances to the extent of being miserly.

6   Conversion: this refers to a process where the word class changes. An example from SgE and MalE is *arrow*, as in 'The boss likes to *arrow* the difficult tasks to me'.

7   Acronyms abound in SgE and MalE. In SgE, many acronyms are formed which refer to the infrastructure of the country, such as major expressways as *BKE* for Bukit Timah Expressway, *CTE* for Central Expressway and the underground transport system *MRT* for Mass Rapid Transit, for example. An example of an acronym used in both varieties is *MC* for medical certificate.

8   Derivation: this refers to adding suffixes to root words. In SgE, some borrowings undergo derivational processes. For example, *kiasuism* is the noun form of *kiasu*,

237

defined earlier. A MalE example is *lepaking*, which is the verb form of the adjective *lepak*, defined earlier.

9 Lexical innovations (coinages): there is also a whole category of words which are either completely new words in SgE and MalE, or which are created to describe particular things or phenomena that are unique to each country. Lim (2001) studied lexical borrowings used in the local newspapers *The Straits Times*, *The Singapore Times* and *The New Straits Times* (Malaysia) from 1993 to 1995 and lists clearly differentiated uniquely Singaporean and uniquely Malaysian lexical items. The uniquely Singaporean items refer to things or phenomena pertaining to lifestyle. For example, *killer litter* refers to rubbish discarded from high-rises and which may end up killing someone by accident. Examples from urban transport include *ez-link card*, a stored-value cashcard which can be used for all forms of public transport. Examples from education include *TLLM*, meaning Teach Less Learn More, *PERI*, meaning Primary Education Review and Implementation committee, and *allied educators* (teaching assistants who do not possess a teaching certification but assist teachers in classrooms).

Ooi (2001) groups the lexical items found in Standard SgE and MalE into different categories, namely: Group A (words used and known globally, such as *durian*, *lychee*, *samfoo*); Group B (words accepted in formal situations, such as *love letters* (a delicacy served during the new year season); and Group C (words widely accepted and used, such as *bumiputra*, earlier defined). The other two groups pertain to informal, colloquial SgE and MalE, which are not the focus of this chapter.

Syntax

Most of the syntactic features described in previous work on SgE tend to focus on colloquial Singapore English (Ho and Platt 1993; Ho 1995; Alsagoff and Ho 1998; Alsagoff 2001; Lim and Wee 2001; Wee 2004a, 2004b; Low and Brown 2005). As this chapter focuses on features of Standard SgE and MalE, only features of the standard varieties will be highlighted. They are rather few, since the syntax of Standard SgE and MalE generally resembles that of Standard English.

1 Noun phrase structure: article deletion is common in Standard SgE and MalE, especially when referring to a particular designation of a person, usually of senior rank, even in cases of formal communication. For example, *Director/Boss has asked for the admission numbers for all initial teacher preparation programmes for the July 2009 intake.*

2 Verb phrase structure:

   (a) A notable occurrence in both SgE and MalE even in formal writing, is the tendency for agreement to take place with the nearest noun rather than the head of the noun phrase; for example, *The criteria for assessing the student needs to be spelt out clearer* (where Standard English would prefer 'need', since 'criteria' is in the plural form).

   (b) Another feature is use of 'would' to indicate politeness, tentativeness and as a marker of the irrealis aspect (Alsagoff and Ho 1998:141). Thus 'would' is often used when 'will' would be used in Standard English. An example is, *It is likely that the implementation of the recommendations of the programme review effort would take place by 2012.*

(c) The habitual aspect is expressed using the adverb 'always'. An example of this is, *I always see her leaving at 7 p.m. every day.* The perfective aspect is commonly expressed using the adverb 'already', as in *I have already given her the slides for the meeting.* In Standard English, the use of 'already' is not necessary.

3 Adverb phrase structure: there is a preference for certain adverbs. For example, 'actually' and 'basically' are mainly used as hedges. For example, *I basically want to let you know about the rules and regulations* and *There is actually a need to hold a meeting next week.*

The discourse/pragmatic particles which have been the focus of much previous research will not be described here, since they are unequivocally linked with colloquial, informal usage in both varieties (e.g. Wee 1998, 2002, 2003; Low and Brown 2005: 175–80; and Lim 2007).

Table 13.3 Phonemic vowel inventory of SgE and MalE

BrE (Lim 2004)	SSE (Lim 2004)	Standard SgE and MalE	Keywords
ɪ	ɪ	ɪ	KIT
ɛ	ɛ	ɛ	DRESS
æ	æ	ɛ	TRAP
ʊ	ɒ	ɔ	LOT
ʌ	ʌ	ʌ	STRUT
ʊ	ʊ	ʊ	FOOT
ɑː	ɑː	—	BATH
ɒ	ɒ	—	CLOTH
ɜː	ɜː	ə	NURSE
iː	iː	ɪ	FLEECE
eɪ	eɪ	ɛ	FACE
ɑː	ɑː	ʌ	PALM
ɔː	ɔː	ɔ	THOUGHT
oʊ	oʊ	oʊ	GOAT
uː	uː	ʊ	GOOSE
aɪ	aɪ	aɪ	PRICE
ɔɪ	ɔɪ	ɔi	CHOICE
aʊ	aʊ	ɑu	MOUTH
ɪə	ɪə	iə	NEAR
ɛə	ɛ	ɛ	SQUARE
ɑː	ɑː	—	START
ɔː	ɔː	—	NORTH
ɔː	ɔː	—	FORCE
ʊə	ʊə	uə	POOR
Similar to 'poor'	Similar to 'poor'	—	CURE
ɪ	i	—	HAPPY
ə	ə	ə	LETTER
ə	ə	ə	COMMA

239

Phonology

The description of the phonology of Standard SgE and MalE will focus on the seg-mental inventory of vowels and consonants as documented in previous research and then sketch briefly the supra-segmental features of lexical stress placement and rhythm.

Vowels

Wells' (1982) standard lexical sets will be used for the description of the vowel phonemic inventory of SgE and MalE. This was also used by Kortmann and Schneider (2004) in their description of the vowels of varieties of English around the world. The phonemic vowel inventory (Table 13.3) mirrors the one provided by Low (forthcoming), Low and Brown (2005) for SgE and the description provided by Tan and Azirah (2007). British English (BrE) as described by Lim (2004) will be used as a convenient reference point.

The conflation of the long/short vowel pairs and the /e/ and /æ/ vowels for MalE were observed by Tan and Azirah (2007). Tan and Low (forthcoming) did an acoustic measurement of the vowels produced by ten speakers each of SgE and MalE, com-prising five females and five males from each variety. The results are summarized below and confirm that, as far as the vowel qualities of all vowel pairs are concerned, there is substantial overlap and they therefore can be consider conflated in both vari-eties. However, in terms of durational differences, it is clear that only /ɒ, ɔː/ was con-flated in MalE. For all other vowel pairs, however, there was a significant difference between the long and short vowel pairs.

Vowel pairs	SgE	MalE
/iː, ɪ/	Males: conflated Females: conflated Difference in vowel length	Males: conflated Females: conflated Difference in vowel length
/e, æ/	Males: some overlap, both vowels at about same height, /æ/ slightly more fronted than /e/ Females: overlap	Males: some overlap, /æ/ appears slightly more fronted and lower than /e/ Females: overlap
/v, ɑː/	Males: conflation Females: overlap Difference in vowel length	Males: some overlap, /v/ generally higher Females: overlap Difference in vowel length
/ɒ, ɔː/	Males: /ɔː/ more back, generally a little higher Females: some differentiation, /ɔː/ more back, generally a little higher Difference in vowel length	Males: vowel quality not differentiated Females: vowel quality not differentiated No difference in vowel length
/ʊ, uː/	Males: vowel pair not differentiated Females: not differentiated Difference in vowel length	Males: vowel pair not differentiated Females: not differentiated Difference in vowel length

Monophthongization of the BrE diphthongs are described in both varieties. For example /eɪ/ is realized as long monophthong /ɛː/ (with a quality between /e/ and /æ/), while /əʊ/ is realized as the long monophthong /oː/. This supports findings by Deterding (2000) and Lee and Lim (2000).

Impressionistic observations of SgE indicate that Singaporeans treat words which contain triphthongs in BrE as two syllables with a glide insertion. For example, [aɪ.jə] instead of [aɪə] and [aʊ.wə] instead of [aʊə] and this confirmed Lim and Low's (2005) acoustic and perceptual study.

Consonants

In terms of the consonantal features of SgE and MalE, Low and Brown (2005) agree with Bao's (1998) analysis that, at the acrolectal level, the consonantal inventory hardly differs from BrE. However, in quick speech, even in formal circumstances, several consonantal features have been observed.

1 Consonant cluster simplification. Both varieties note this phenomenon (Lim, 2004; Wee 2004a; Deterding 2007; and Tan and Azirah 2007).
2 Replacement of dental fricatives with alveolar plosives. This is noted by Tan and Azirah (2007) for MalE and studied acoustically by Moorthy and Deterding (2000), who investigated the use of dental fricatives in Singapore English but found it very difficult to establish the exact acoustic correlates of the realization of [t] compared to [ŧ].
3 Lack of aspiration of initial /p, t, k/. Tan (forthcoming) did an acoustic study on whether word-initial voiceless plosives were unaspirated in SgE and MalE and found that there was a significant difference between the duration of the aspiration for SgE compared to MalE.
4 The replacement of final consonants with glottal stops appears to be most common with voiceless final plosives, as also noted by Brown and Deterding (2005) for SgE and for MalE by Tan and Azirah (2007). Gut (2005) conducted a detailed acoustic study and confirmed that word-final plosives are either unreleased or replaced by glottal stops.
5 The vocalization of [l] was investigated by Tan (2005) for Singapore English. His perceptual test confirmed that Singaporeans do vocalize dark /l/.

Stress

In terms of word or lexical stress placement, SgE and MalE both have a tendency to lengthen the final syllables of polysyllabic words that occur at the end of sentences, to the extent that stress is perceived on these syllables. However, stress returns to the initial position, as found in BrE, when the polysyllabic word is placed in sentence-medial position. Examples are:

She did it carefulLY (final position)
She CAREfully removed his stitches (medial position)

In BrE, compounds are generally stressed on the first item but noun phrases are stressed on the second item (the noun). Thus, stress on 'eng' in *ENGlish teacher* refers to the compound noun meaning 'someone who teaches English', while stress on 'teach' in *English TEACHer* refers to the noun phrase meaning 'a teacher from England'. SgE and MalE speakers tend to stress the final syllable 'er' in both the compound and the noun phrases above.

In BrE, some words are stressed differently according to the grammatical category they belong to. For example, when 'convert' is used as a noun, stress is on the first syllable, as in *CONvert*, but when it is used as a verb, stress moves to the second syllable, as in *conVERT*. In SgE and MalE, however, both words, whether used as a noun or as a verb, are stressed on the second syllable.

Finally, stress can occur later in some words when compared to BrE, as:

BrE (nouns)	*COLleague*		*CALendar*	
SgE/MalE		*colLEAGUE*		*caLENdar*
BrE (verb)	*INculcate*			
SgE/MalE		*inCULcate*		
BrE (adjective)		COMpetent		
SgE/MalE		comPEtent		

Rhythm

Research documenting the rhythmic differences between SgE and BrE has been extensive (Low *et al.* 2000; Deterding 2001; Low 2006). Tan and Low (forthcoming) and Tan (forthcoming) have compared acoustically the rhythmic patterning of SgE and MalE. All studies point to the fact that SgE and MalE are more syllable-based (where syllables receive more or less equal timing) than stress-based (where stresses are more nearly equal in timing). The absence of reduced vowels for unstressed function words, absence of linking between words, the replacement of final voiceless plosives with glottal stops and the absence of a distinction between long and short vowels all appear to contribute to the syllable-based characteristics of SgE and MalE.

Conclusion and directions for further research

This chapter has described the main differences in language policies adopted by Singapore and Malaysia in the post-independent years and outlined key linguistic features of both varieties of English. What is noteworthy is that, while clear differences do exist, there are still many similarities between the two varieties. Another point worthy of mention is that many recent lexical and syntactic studies have been based on large corpora, while phonological research has been helped tremendously by acoustic analysis. These findings have helped to provide clear empirical evidence to either validate or refute earlier impressionistic observations.

As stated at the beginning of this chapter, Schneider suggests that MalE is in Phase 3 of the Dynamic Model of Postcolonial Englishes where there is more variation (Schneider 2007: 56), while SgE is in Phase 4 where there is deemed to be greater linguistic homogeneity. This survey of linguistic features has shown that, while there are differences between SgE and MalE, these are still not yet compelling enough to show clearly that MalE is indeed in Phase 3 and SgE in Phase 4 of the Dynamic Model of Postcolonial Englishes. Perhaps what can be surmised from the present chapter, however, is that these varieties of English are diverging. In the light of the Malaysian government's recent decision to revert to teaching mathematics and science in Bahasa Malaysia in place of English, it is possible that this divergence will gradually increase. Further research is needed which can help shed further light on the evolution and developmental cycles of these two neighbouring varieties of English.

Suggestions for further reading

Deterding, D. (2007) *Dialects of English: Singapore English*, Edinburgh: Edinburgh University Press. (Covers the background, phonetics and phonology, morphosyntax, lexis and history of Singapore English and also includes an annotated bibliography.)

Lim, L. (ed.) (2004) *Singapore English: A Grammatical Description*, Amsterdam: John Benjamins. (A thorough account of contemporary Singapore English with detailed coverage of the phonology, lexis and syntax of this variety and predictions about its future evolution.)

Low, E.L. and Brown, A. (2005) *English in Singapore: An Introduction*, Singapore: McGraw-Hill (Education) Asia. (A readable introductory pack to beginning scholars in the field which contains key references and an annotated bibliography to guide future research.)

Ooi, V. (ed.) (2001) *Evolving Identities: The English Language in Singapore and Malaysia*, Singapore: Times Academic Press. (A useful collection that is the first comparing both varieties of English.)

Tan, S.K. and Low, E.L. (forthcoming) 'How different are the monophthongs of Malay speakers of Malaysian and Singapore English?' *English World-wide*. (A useful acoustic comparison between the two varieties that extends our understanding of these two varieties.)

References

Alsagoff, L. (2001) 'Tense and aspect in Singapore English', in V. Ooi (ed.) *Evolving Identities: The English Language in Singapore and Malaysia*, Singapore: Times Academic Press, pp. 79–88.

——(2007) 'Singlish,' in V. Vaish, S. Gopinathan and Y. Liu (eds) *Language, Culture, Capital*, Rotterdam: Sense Publishers, pp. 25–46.

Alsagoff, L. and Ho, C.L. (1998) 'The grammar of Singapore English', in J.A. Foley, T. Kandiah, Z.M. Bao, A.F. Gupta, L. Alsagoff, C.L. Ho, L. Wee, I. Talib and W. Bokhorst-Heng (eds) *English in New Cultural Contexts: Reflections from Singapore*, Singapore: Oxford University Press, pp. 127–51.

Azirah, H. (2009) 'Not plain sailing: Malaysia's language choice in policy and education', *AILA Review*, 22: 36–51.

Baker, J. (2008) *A Popular History of Malaysia and Singapore*, Singapore: Marshall Cavendish.

Bao, Z.M. (1998) 'The sounds of Singapore English', in J.A. Foley, T. Kandiah, Z.M. Bao, A.F. Gupta, L. Alsagoff, C.L. Ho, L. Wee, I. Talib and W. Bokhorst-Heng (eds.) *English in New Cultural Contexts: Reflections from Singapore*, Singapore: Oxford University Press, pp. 152–74.

Baskaran, L. (1987) 'Aspects of Malaysian English Syntax', unpublished PhD dissertation, University of London.

——(2004) 'Malaysian English: morphology and syntax', in B. Kortmann and E. Schneider (eds) *A Handbook of Varieties of English*, New York: Mouton de Gruyter, pp. 1072–85.

——(2005) *A Malaysian English Primer*, Kuala Lumpur: University of Malaya Press.

Brown, A. and Deterding, D. (2005) 'A checklist of Singapore English pronunciation features', in D. Deterding, A. Brown and E.L. Low (eds) *English in Singapore: Phonetic Research on a Corpus*, Singapore: McGraw-Hill (Education) Asia, pp. 7–13.

Chng, H.H. (2003) 'You see me no up: is Singlish a problem?' *Language Problems and Language Planning*, 27 (1): 45–62.

Deterding, D. (2000) 'Measurements of /eɪ / and /əʊ/ vowels of young English speakers in Singapore', in A. Brown, D. Deterding and E.L. Low (eds.) *The English Language in Singapore: Research on Pronunciation*, Singapore: Singapore Association for Applied Linguistics, pp. 93–9.

——(2001) 'The measurement of rhythm: a comparison of Singapore and British English', *Journal of Phonetics*, 29: 217–30.

——(2007) *Dialects of English: Singapore English*, Edinburgh: Edinburgh University Press.

Deterding, D. and Poedjosoedarmo, G. (2000) 'To what extent can the ethnic groups of young Singaporeans be identified from their speech?' in A. Brown, D. Deterding and E.L. Low (eds) *The*

English Language in Singapore: Research on Pronunciation, Singapore: Singapore Association for Applied Linguistics, pp. 1–9.

Gopinathan, S. Pakir, A., Ho, W.K. and Saravanan, V. (eds) (1998) *Language, Society and Education in Singapore: Issues and Trends*, Singapore: Times Academic Press.

Gupta, A.F. (1986) 'A standard for written Singapore English?' *English World-wide*, 7 (1): 75–99.

——(1994) *The Step-tongue: Children's English in Singapore*, Clevedon: Multilingual Matters.

——(1998) 'The situation of English in Singapore', in J.A. Foley, T. Kandiah, Z.M. Bao, A.F. Gupta, L. Alsagoff, C.L. Ho, L. Wee, I. Talib and W. Bokhorst-Heng (eds) *English in New Cultural Contexts: Reflections from Singapore*, Singapore: Oxford University Press, pp. 106–26.

Gut, U. (2005) 'The realisation of final plosives in Singapore English: phonological rules and ethnic differences', in D. Deterding, A. Brown and E.L. Low (eds) *English in Singapore: Phonetic Research on a Corpus*, Singapore: McGraw-Hill (Education) Asia, pp. 14–25.

Ho, M.L. (1995) 'The acquisition of a linguistic variable', in S.C. Teng and M.L. Ho (eds) *The English Language in Singapore: Implications for Teaching*, Singapore: Singapore Association for Applied Linguistics, pp. 88–106.

Ho, M.L. and Platt, J. (1993) *Dynamics of a Contact Continuum: Singaporean English*, Oxford: Clarendon Press.

Kachru, B. (1992) *The Other Tongue: English Across Cultures*, Illinois: University of Illinois Press.

Kortmann, B. and Schneider, E. (eds) (2004) *A Handbook of Varieties of English*, Berlin: Mouton de Gruyter

Kuo, E. and Jernudd, B.H. (1994) 'Balancing macro- and micro-sociolinguistic perspectives in language management: the case of Singapore', in S. Gopinathan, A. Pakir, W.K. Ho and V. Saravanan (eds) *Language, Society and Education in Singapore: Issues and Trends*, Singapore: Times Academic Press, pp. 25–46.

Lee, E.M. and Lim, L. (2000) 'Diphthongs in Singaporean English: their realisations across different formality levels and attitudes of some learners towards them', in A. Brown, D. Deterding and E.L. Low (eds) *The English Language in Singapore: Research on Pronunciation*, Singapore: Singapore Association for Applied Linguistics, pp. 100–11.

Leong, A., Deterding, D. and Low, E.L. (2006) *An Introduction to Linguistics*, Singapore: McGraw-Hill (Education) Asia.

Lim, C.Y. and Wee, L. (2001) 'Reduplication in colloquial Singapore English', in V. Ooi (ed.) *Evolving Identities: The English Language in Singapore and Malaysia*, Singapore: Times Academic Press, pp. 89–102.

Lim, G. (2001) 'Till divorce do us part: the case of Singaporean and Malaysian English', in V. Ooi (ed.) *Evolving Identities: The English Language in Singapore and Malaysia*, Singapore: Times Academic Press, pp. 125–39.

Lim, L. (ed.) (2004) *Singapore English: A Grammatical Description*, Amsterdam: John Benjamins.

——(2007) 'Mergers and acquisitions: on the ages and origins of Singapore English particles', *World Englishes*, 27 (4): 446–73.

——(2009) 'Beyond fear and loathing in Singapore: the real mother tongues and language policies in multilingual Singapore', *AILA Review*, 22: 52–71.

Lim, S.S. and Low, E.L. (2005) 'Triphthongs in Singapore English', in D. Deterding, A. Brown and E.L. Low (eds) *English in Singapore: Phonetic Research on a Corpus*, Singapore: McGraw-Hill (Education) Asia, pp. 64–73.

Low, E.L. (2006) 'A review of recent research on speech rhythm: some insights for language acquisition, language disorders and language teaching', in R. Hughes (ed.) *Spoken English, Applied Linguistics and TESOL: Challenges for Theory and Practice*, London: Palgrave Macmillan, pp. 99–125.

——(forthcoming) 'Sounding local and going global: current research and implications for pronunciation teaching', in L. Lim., A. Pakir and L. Wee (eds) *English in Singapore: Unity and Utility*, Hong Kong: Hong Kong University Press.

Low, E.L. and Brown, A. (2005) *English in Singapore: An Introduction*, Singapore: McGraw-Hill (Education) Asia.

Low, E.L., Grabe, E. and Nolan, F. (2000) 'Quantitative characterisations of speech rhythm: syllable-timing in Singapore English', *Language and Speech*, 43 (4): 377–401.

Lowenberg, P. (1984) 'English in the Malay archipelago: nativisation and its functions in a sociolinguistic area', unpublished PhD dissertation, University of Illinois.

Moorthy, S. and Deterding, D. (2000) 'Three or tree? Dental fricatives in the speech of educated Singaporeans,' in A. Brown, D. Deterding and E.L. Low (eds) *The English Language in Singapore: Research on Pronunciation*, Singapore: Singapore Association for Applied Linguistics, pp. 76–83.

Morais, E. (2000) 'Talking in English but thinking like a Malaysian: insights from a car assembly plant,' in M.S. Halima and K.S. Ng (eds) *English as an Asian Language: The Malaysian Context*, Kuala Lumpur: Macquarie Library and Persatuan Bahasa Modern Malaysia, pp. 90–106.

Mufwene, S. (2001) *The Ecology of Language Evolution*, Cambridge: Cambridge University Press.

Ooi, V. (2001) *Evolving Identities: The English Language in Singapore and Malaysia*, Singapore: Times Academic Press.

Pakir, A. (1991) 'The range and depth of English-knowing bilinguals in Singapore', *World Englishes*, 10 (2): 167–79.

Platt, J. (1977) 'The sub-varieties of Singapore English: their sociolectal and functional status', in W. Crewe (ed.) *The English Language in Singapore*, Singapore: Eastern Universities Press.

Platt, J. and Weber, H. (1980) *English in Singapore and Malaysia: Status, Features and Functions*, Oxford: Oxford University Press.

Rubdy, R. (2001) 'Creative destruction: Singapore's Speak Good English Movement', *World Englishes*, 20: 341–55.

Schneider, E. (2004) 'Evolutionary patterns of new Englishes and the special case of Malaysian English', *Asian Englishes*, 6: 44–63.

——(2007) *Postcolonial English Varieties Around the World*, Cambridge: Cambridge University Press.

Singapore Department of Statistics (2009) *Population Trends 2009*, Singapore: Singapore Department of Statistics, Ministry of Trade and Industry.

Statistics Singapore (2000) *Census of Population 2000*. Online. Available www.singstat.gov.sg/pubn/popn/c2000sr4.html (accessed 18 February 2010).

Tan, P. (2001) 'Melaka or Malacca, Kallang or Care-Lang: lexical innovation and nativisation in Malaysian and Singaporean English', in V. Ooi (ed.) *Evolving Identities: The English Language in Singapore and Malaysia*, Singapore: Times Academic Press, pp. 140–67.

Tan, S.K. (forthcoming) 'An acoustic investigation of segmental and suprasegmentals in Malaysian English', unpublished PhD dissertation, Nanyang Technological University, Singapore.

Tan, S.K. and Azirah, H. (2007) 'Malaysian English', in M. Nakano (ed.) *World Englishes and Miscommunications*, Japan: Waseda University International.

Tan, S.K. and Low, E.L. (forthcoming) 'How different are the monophthongs of Malay speakers of Malaysian and Singapore English?' *English World-wide*.

Tan, Y.Y. (2005) 'Observations on British and Singaporean perceptions of prominence,' in D. Deterding, A. Brown and E.L. Low (eds) *English in Singapore: Phonetic Research on a Corpus*, Singapore: McGraw-Hill (Education) Asia, pp. 95–103.

Tongue, R.K. (1974) *The English of Singapore and Malaysia*, Singapore: Eastern Universities Press.

——(1979) *The English of Singapore and Malaysia* (2nd edition), Singapore: Eastern Universities Press.

Wee, L. (1998) 'The lexicon of Singapore English', in J.A. Foley, T. Kandiah, Z.M. Bao, A.F. Gupta, L. Alsagoff, C.L. Ho, L. Wee, I. Talib and W. Bokhorst-Heng (eds) *English in New Cultural Contexts: Reflections from Singapore*, Singapore: Oxford University Press, 175–200.

——(2002) 'Lor in colloquial Singapore English', *Journal of Pragmatics* 34: 711–25.

——(2003) 'The birth of the particle know in colloquial Singapore English', *World Englishes*, 22: 5–13.

——(2004a) 'Singapore English: morphology and syntax', in B. Kortmann and E. Schneider (eds) *A Handbook of Varieties of English*, Berlin: Mouton de Gruyter, pp. 1058–72.

——(2004b) 'Reduplication and discourse particles', in L. Lim (ed.) *Singapore English: A Grammatical Description*, Amsterdam: John Benjamins, pp. 105–26.

Wells, J. (1982) *Accents of English*, Cambridge: Cambridge University Press.

Online resources

Speech by the Minister of Education, Dr Ng Eng Hen, at the MOE Workplan seminar held on 17 September 2009. Online. Available www.moe.gov.sg/media/speeches/2009/09/17/work-plan-seminar.php

14

Periphery ELT

The politics and practice of teaching English in the Philippines[1]

Isabel Pefianco Martin

Introduction

The sociolinguistic profile of English reveals that ownership of the language is shared across continents and cultures. Following the World Englishes paradigm, the language is approached as having a multiplicity of meanings and a plurality of centres. Such a phenomenon doesn't come without myths and fallacies. In the Philippines, this is especially true in the 'periphery' – in English language and literature education in the public schools.

This chapter presents illustrative data that reveal four myths about English in the Philippines. The chapter begins by describing ELT during the American colonial period when canon and pedagogy merged to produce a public education system that marginalized Philippine literature in English and propagated present-day myths about the English language. The chapter ends by exploring possibilities for resistance in Philippine ELT.

Filipino poet Amador T. Daguio, in the poem 'Man of Earth' (1932), speaks eloquently about the proverbial Filipino resilience. The Filipino is likened to the pliant bamboo. He may have been forced to stoop and bend, but he persists in rising despite the 'wind [that] passes by'. Like the persona in the poem, who tries to 'measure fully [his] flexibility', the Filipino teacher of English rises above the challenges of ELT in the Philippines.

The history of English in the Philippines cannot be mapped out without having scrutinized the agenda of ELT in the country. English was first introduced to the Filipinos through the American public school system. For half a century, the language was systematically promoted as a civilizing tool. Today, beliefs and attitudes about English, as well as the various ways in which the language is used, are products of the Filipino experience of American colonial education.

In this chapter, I shall present English in the Philippines from the perspective of ELT. In particular, I take the perspective of the periphery in describing the politics and practice of teaching English in the Philippines. Canagarajah uses the term 'periphery' to refer to 'communities where English is of post-colonial currency' (1999: 4). Such is the situation of the ELT community in the Philippines, especially where the public school system is concerned.

Taking the public school perspective in describing Philippine ELT is taking a perspective that is doubly peripheral. The basic education sector is a largely neglected and vertically structured monolith. When everything – from policy to budget to curriculum to teacher training – is decided from the distant political centre, one cannot expect the system to be efficient and productive. By sheer size, it is impossible to overlook the extent of the impact of basic education on Philippine society. In 2007, the Department of Education (DepEd) reported the enrolment figures shown in Tables 14.1 and 14.2 (Department of Education 2008d).

That same year, the DepEd reported the figures shown in Tables 14.3 and 14.4 for number of teachers in the public and private elementary and high schools. The figures reveal that, of the total school enrolment in 2007, 92 per cent of Filipino students study in a public elementary school, while 79 per cent study in a public high school. The proportion of private school teachers to public school teachers is 1:7 in the elementary level and 1:3 in the high schools. Clearly, public basic education, by sheer size compared to the private sector, cannot be overlooked.

Every year, the DepEd administers the National Achievement Test (NAT), a national assessment of the competencies of students in the elementary and high school levels. The NAT was administered to fourth graders in 2003, to sixth graders from 2004 to 2008, to second-year high school students from 2006 to 2008 and to fourth-year high school students from 2003 to 2006, with disappointing results in maths, science and English (Department of Education 2008d). Tables 14.5 and 14.6 illustrate this point.

The NAT results for the elementary and high school levels reveal that the highest average percentage scores in maths, science and English since 2003 have not exceeded 65 per cent in the elementary level and 54 per cent in the high school level. The DepEd identifies the 'mastery' level as having received 75 per cent and above. Following this criterion, one may conclude that many Filipino students have not come close to achieving mastery of maths, science and English (National Statistical Coordination Board 2007).

In the 2008 Education for All Global Monitoring Report, UNESCO describes the Philippines as having 'performed dismally' in the 2003 Trends in International Mathematics and Science Study, when Grade 4 students came out third to the last in both maths and science tests. In addition, the Philippines ranked 41st in maths and 42nd in science (out of 46 participating countries) in the second-year high school level (Caoli-Rodriguez 2007: 13). It was noted in this report that the low scores in maths and science 'prompted

Table 14.1 Elementary school enrolment 2007

Public	12,304,207
Private	1,092,781
Total	13,396,988

Table 14.2 High school enrolment 2007

Public	5,126,459
Private	1,332,846
Total	6,459,305

Table 14.3 Elementary school teachers 2007

Public	348,028
Private	49,440
Total	397,468

Table 14.4 High school teachers 2007

Public	131,865
Private	53,018
Total	184,883

Table 14.5 NAT Elementary school results (percentage scores)

School year	Maths	Science	English
SY 2003–4	59.45	52.59	49.92
SY 2004–5	59.10	54.12	59.15
SY 2005–6	53.66	46.77	54.05
SY 2006–7	60.29	51.58	60.78
SY 2007–8	63.89	57.90	61.62

Table 14.6 NAT High school results

School year	Maths	Science	English
SY 2003–4	46.20	36.80	50.08
SY 2004–5	50.70	39.50	51.30
SY 2005–6	47.82	37.98	47.73
SY 2006–7	39.00	41.99	51.78
SY 2007–8	42.85	46.71	53.46

the government to re-evaluate science and math education in the country and implement remedial actions such as intensified teacher training' (Caoli-Rodriguez 2007: 13).

The peripheral position of Philippine public education, especially where English language and literature teaching (ELT) is concerned, may be traced to the public education system introduced by the Americans more than a hundred years ago.

Longfellow's legacy: what Filipino students *do not* read

> Our sense … of our country is a sustained act of imagination. From that vantage, it can be said that *our writers and artists, who are men and women of imagination, create our country* … We are our own best interpreters of our history and culture because it is we who have lived through that history and created our own values by which we live.
>
> (Abad 2003, italics mine)

Filipino poet Gemino Abad captures in elegant language the importance of national literature. That writers and artists 'create our country' is a statement of faith in the role Philippine literature plays in the formation of national consciousness and identity. Literature is not simply inscribed, written, encoded. It is read. And what better place for literature to unleash its power to create a country than the literature classroom?

When the Americans arrived in the Philippines in 1898, they took pains to untie the knots that the Spanish colonizers left in the country after occupying it for 300 years. On 13 August 1898, a few months before American forces officially occupied Manila, American soldiers had already begun to teach in Corregidor (Estioko 1994: 186). It is assumed that their first lesson was English. The Americans introduced public education as an essential component of political strategy. Thus, it was no accident that the first teachers of English in the Philippines were American soldiers.

Throughout the American colonial period, English was systematically promoted as the language that would 'civilize' the Filipinos. It was educational policy to confine the native languages outside the territories of formal schooling. The policy was institutionalized through the heavy use of instructional materials of Anglo-American origin for language instruction. Throughout four decades of American public education, Filipino students were exposed to a canon of literature that included works of Henry Wadsworth Longfellow, Washington Irving, Ralph Waldo Emerson, as well as those of Shakespeare, George Elliott, Matthew Arnold and the romantic poets (Martin 2008). Meanwhile, Filipinos were using their own languages outside the schools.

The 1925 Monroe Report noted that Filipino students had no opportunity to study in their native language. The report recommended that the native language be used as an auxiliary medium of instruction in courses such as character education, and good manners and right conduct (Board of Educational Survey 1925: 40). In spite of this, American education officials insisted on the exclusive use of English in the public schools until 1940.

Other than language, a more compelling reason for barring Philippine literature from the literary canon was that Anglo-American literature best served the interests of the colonizers. A detailed analysis of the texts in this canon, as well as the way they were taught to Filipino children, reveals the combined power of curriculum, canon and pedagogy in promoting myths about colonial realities. In the early 1900s, Filipino students were already being asked to read the works of Longfellow. Beginning 1904, *Evangeline* was read by all Filipino high school students. In 1911, *The Song of Hiawatha* was a required reading in all public elementary schools in the country. A closer inspection of *Evangeline* and *The Song of Hiawatha* reveals themes that directly promote American colonialism. In these texts one can almost find prescriptions for good behaviour in a colonized society (Martin 2008).

The canon, curriculum and pedagogical practices that prevailed during the American colonial period in the Philippines are widely believed to have had a lasting impact on Philippine education today, especially where language and literature education are concerned. When asked what literary texts were required by their high school teachers, 1,077 male and female freshman university students reported titles that did not include a single work by a Filipino writer (Martin 2007). In the list of top ten required readings, five texts are works of Shakespeare, two are translations from languages other than English, and the rest are works of American or British writers. In fact, the list of top twenty required readings reveals that *all* literary texts are of American or European origin. When asked what literary texts they read on their own, the same university students also reported a list of texts of Anglo-European origin.

Many questions arise out of the results of the survey. One question that comes to mind is why, after more than five decades since the Americans officially ended colonial rule over the Philippines, the list of required and personal readings continues to be dominated by American and European literature.

Estrellita Y. Evangelista, Director III of the DepEd's Bureau of Secondary Education (BSE), asserts that literature education in the Philippines 'can serve as an avenue in terms of understanding diverse culture and in discovering universal values contained in the varied literary selections or masterpieces' (personal communication, 27 December 2007). The statement suggests that Philippine literature education today aims for students to have access to cultures of the world through works of literature. This approach to teaching literature is reinforced through the specific learning competencies that are the end goals of high school literature courses in the Philippines. The concern for teaching literature in Philippine high schools is primarily to impart knowledge and wisdom that literary texts contain. Thus, literature education in the Philippines approaches literature as a storehouse of culture, implying the transparency of texts as these accurately mirror realities. Such lofty aims of literature education are, of course, desirable for teachers whose interests mainly lie in the formation of positive values among their students (also known as 'values education' among Filipino basic education teachers). However, there is also a danger in a literature education that approaches the act of reading as simply the act of decoding meaning. For one, such an approach may encourage an uncritical stance to reading literature, which consequently treats works of literature as decontextualized and necessarily universal.

The perceived deterioration in English language proficiency has pushed the DepEd officials to take what Evangelista describes as a 'more integrated approach' to teaching literature in Philippine high schools. The integration referred to is the teaching of language through literature. Following this approach, it is argued that literature provides not only a wealth of knowledge about other cultures, but also an exposure to excellent English. Thus, literary texts are presented as models after which students must pattern their language.

The absence of Philippine literature in English in the list of required and personal readings, despite the excellence of Philippine writing in English, as well as the tendency for a decontextualized, universalist approach to teaching literature in Philippine high schools today, may be an indication of what Braj Kachru refers to as the myths that propagate Anglophone Asia. Kachru writes:

> The power of mythology is immense; it is like a linguistic albatross around the necks of the users of the [English] language. The result is that innovative and creative initiatives are paralyzed and these result in *self-doubt* when there is a conflict with the paradigms of authority.
>
> (Kachru 2005: 16–17, italics mine)

That both Filipino teachers and students of literature privilege texts of American and European origins may be symptomatic of the self-doubt that Kachru describes above. Such doubt about one's own literature, as well as the elevated status of American and European texts in Philippine literature education today, is disconcerting. Not only is it reminiscent of the century-old American colonial education, it is also a preview of the future shape of Filipino consciousness and identity.

Myths about English in the Philippines

During the early years of colonial public education, memory work became a popular method of teaching. In 1911, this was described by one school principal as the only way by which Filipino students could learn English:

> We must insist that every day in his first three years of school life, the Filipino child has a dialogue lesson, and we must make him commit that lesson absolutely to memory. For instance suppose his first lesson is as brief as this:

> Good morning, Pedro.
> Good morning, Jose.

251

How are you this morning, Pedro?
Thank you, I am very well.

It would not be cruelty to animals to insist on any second grade pupil's committing that lesson to memory.

(Fee 1911: 114)

The quote above illustrates a belief among American teachers of English that the language was so easy to learn that even animals could memorize simple dialogues. This school principal believed that, like American students, Filipinos would best learn the language, not by reading, but by memorizing dialogues, the same dialogues American children memorized in American schools. This teaching practice and other mechanical methods of teaching the English language manifested itself in different pedagogical practices in the colonial public schools: stressing eye movements in reading, asking students to read aloud, making them perform grammar drills, and expecting them to recite memorized passages. The practice became so widespread that in 1925 the Board of Educational Survey, which conducted a comprehensive study of the Philippine public school system, reported the following:

> Children in upper grades seem to have a 'reciting' knowledge of more technical English grammar than most children in corresponding grades in the American schools. To what degree this helps them in speaking and writing English no one really knows.

(Board of Educational Survey 1925: 239)

Such teaching practice – the mechanical, grammar-oriented approach – stems from linguistics which is perceived to be a more objective and rigorous study of language. Thus, with the authority of science, American teachers presented the English language to the Filipino students. One effect of such practice was the tendency of students to mimic the Anglo-American writings they read in class. This mimicking was also evident in Philippine writing in English, which was described in 1928 as manifesting a 'slavish imitation' of Anglo-American texts (cited in Martin 2008: 254).

The Filipinos' propensity for slavish imitation of the American model persists to this day. It comes in the form of one of four myths about English that prevail.

Myth 1: American English is the only correct English

Because the Americans brought English to the Philippines, it seems logical for Filipinos to look up to American English as their model. However, a century after English was first introduced in the country, the language had begun to take on new features. These new features come in many forms, among them grammatical deviations and lexical innovations.

Maria Lourdes S. Bautista (2000: 146–58) investigated the grammatical features of educated Philippine English and found deviations in subject–verb agreement, articles, prepositions and tenses. Some examples follow:

> Liquidity *problems* of rural banks on a massive scale *is* [are] being experienced for the first time.

[A] Majority of the public school teachers do not want to serve as poll officials in the May elections.

This *results to* [in] a better quality of life.

But it was only in 1510 that a more authentic epidemic *has been* [was] described.

Other than grammatical deviations, lexical innovations also exist in the Philippine variety of English. Kingsley Bolton and Susan Butler have documented the following 'localized vocabularies of English usage' in Philippine dailies:

Politicians are found guilty of *economic plunder* ('large-scale embezzlement of public funds') or challenged by the press in *ambush interviews* ('surprise interviews'); corrupt cops are accused of *coddling* criminals ('treating leniently'), or *mulcting* ('extorting money from') motorists. Hapless citizens borrow money from *five-six* money lenders ('borrowing at high rates of interest', i.e. borrowing five thousand and returning six …). Meanwhile, motorists stuck in traffic get *high blood* ('enraged') in frustration, and the affairs of various *topnotchers* ('high achievers') fill the gossip columns.

(Bolton and Butler 2008: 182–3)

The existence of a Philippine variety of English does not necessarily translate into acceptance of that variety. In a survey of 185 public elementary and high school teachers of English, 47 per cent reported that their target model for ELT is American English. This, despite their admission that they considered English to be a Philippine language (72 per cent) and that they spoke Philippine, not American, English (54 per cent).

The 'albatross of mythology', as Kachru (2005: 16) puts it, weighs heavy around the necks of Filipino teachers of English. This myth is evident in the reasons cited for identifying American English as the target model of Philippine ELT:

1 It is a global language.
2 American English is the universal language.
3 American English is the standard international language.
4 They [Filipino students] have to learn the basics first.
5 American English is universally accepted.
6 Knowing American English can avoid arguments and debates about the correct spelling and pronunciation.
7 The pronunciation of some words is conventional.
8 An approximately correct English – understandable and acceptable internationally.
9 Since it is the most accepted English.
10 It's the ideal, the standard in terms of language usage.
11 American English is applicable nationwide.
12 Because the expressions used are familiar to us having being under the American regime/way of education.
13 Because the Americans were the first to teach English to the Filipinos.
14 So that pupils will become more eloquent, smart in talking, and can communicate the language not only in speaking but in writing as well.
15 You could use American movies as patterns for [teaching] speaking skills.
16 It's widely used in communicative learning.

The list betrays what Kachru (1995) refers to as the Model Dependency Myth, which hinges on the belief that the exocentric models of American and British English are standard and must therefore be taught. Such dependence on the American model is further reinforced by the fact that the language was brought to the Philippines as a colonial tool (evident in reasons 12 and 13).

One also finds in the list a strong dependence on the unique correctness of American English, so much so that even the strategies for teaching the language have become dependent on American texts (reason 15). This dependence on the correctness of inner circle varieties is described in a colourful fashion by a teacher who identified British English as her target model for ELT:

> I was hired as an English teacher in mainland China and one Chinese student on my first day of teaching corrected my spelling of COLOR (COLOUR with a U!!!!). My basal metabolism rate shot up and the sweat in my armpits and temples cascaded with stench! I told myself (as an advocacy) that when I return to the Philippines, I would expose students, my nieces, and others to British English!!! Such an interesting and truthfully, more correct set of English!

Textbooks in the public schools also betray this dependence on American models. In *E-way to Better Communication 4*, issued in Marikina City, Lesson 1 begins with a dialogue between Mr John Coleman and some students (Alabastro and Sandagan 2003: 2– 4). It is assumed that Mr Coleman is an American expert. The use of an American character in the opening lesson may be an attempt to observe communicative language teaching (CLT), a popular approach in Philippine ELT. As CLT aims to develop language fluency and accuracy using authentic tasks and texts, one wonders how it is possible to achieve authenticity when English-speaking communities using the correct American variety are few and far between for the average public school student.

Further evidence of dependence on American English is revealed by the popularity of guidebooks to correct English, such as *American English for Filipinos* (2005) written by Terry Bennett. Bennett describes himself as an American 'who has been visiting the Philippines regularly for more than twenty years with his wife, a native of Iloilo City'. In the introduction, Bennett writes:

> Much has been made of racism in the American populace over the last fifty years, and 90 percent of it is hogwash. The fact is, most Americans have a favorable impression of Asians, and are accepting to the point that they find it desirable to marry one (as I have myself done). Yes, there are a handful of professional racists in the US, who promote the usual silly ideas about white supremacy, but the typical American will not judge you on the basis of your skin color. *Instead, they will judge you by your speech* … Americans will open up to you only to the degree that you can speak our language: English, the way we speak it.
>
> (Bennett 2005: 8)

A corollary to the myth that American English is the only correct English is the belief that the language is learned primarily to communicate with native speakers. This is evident in the following reasons for identifying American English as the target for ELT:

1 [It is] easier for us to speak and apply [for a job abroad].
2 It's clearer, more widely used and a lot of Filipinos go to the USA to work.
3 This is preferred by companies with networks abroad.
4 For wherever [my students] may go, they will be able to survive.
5 So we can cope up [in communicating] with other countries.
6 To make the children more globally competitive.

The reasons cited do point to the illusion that Filipinos not only need English to communicate with native speakers, but also to communicate with the native speakers *because* they employ Filipinos. This leads to another set of myths about English in the Philippines – the myth that the language cures all economic ailments.

Myth 2: English is the only cure to all economic ailments

From the cover of the high school textbook *E-Way to Better Communication 1* (Alabastro and Panelo 2003), one may conclude that there is a prevalent belief that English is the only key to achieving economic success. The textbook cover presents an attractive call-centre agent in a business suit. As early as the first year of high school, when Filipino students are still in their early teens, the image of call-centre agents earning US dollars is already being ingrained into their minds. In fact, schools have increasingly become targets of call-centre head-hunters.

American businessman Russ Sandlin, in a letter to a national daily, writes about his experience of managing call centres:

> I closed my call center here. Filipinos have much worse English than their Indian counterparts. Not even three percent of the students who graduate college are employable in call centers. Trust me; all of us are leaving for China.
> … The Philippines has a terrible talent shortage, and the government and the press are in denial … English is the only thing that can save the country, and no one here cares or even understands that the Filipinos have a crisis … God save the Philippines. I hate to see the country falling ever deeper into an English-deprived abyss.
> (Sandlin 2008)

This English-deprived abyss is indeed what the Philippine government is desperately attempting to prevent, sadly at the expense of more basic needs of the education sector. On 17 May 2003, President Gloria Macapagal Arroyo issued Executive Order No. 210, which aimed to establish a policy to strengthen the use of English as medium of instruction because of the 'need to develop the aptitude, competence and proficiency of our students in the English language to maintain and improve their competitive edge in emerging and fast-growing local and international industries, particularly in the area of Information and Communications Technology [ICT]' (Arroyo 2003).

The Philippine government's formula for economic success may be summarized as follows: improve English in schools to produce more English-proficient graduates in order to supply the ICT sector with skilled human resources so that they may earn US dollars for the Philippine economy. The formula is painfully simplistic: English equals money. Whether these graduates are capable of critical and creative thinking, or have acquired basic life skills other than language, is not a concern. The policies seem to be fixated on English alone.

Soon after Arroyo assumed the presidency, she called for structural reforms, which included the creation of telecommunications infrastructure to attract more ICT investments. In her 2001 State of the Nation Address (SONA), Arroyo, an economist by profession, promised the following: 'We will promote fast-growing industries where high-value jobs are most plentiful. One of them is information and communications technology, or ICT, our English literacy, our aptitude and skills give us a competitive edge in ICT' (Arroyo 2001).

In her 2006 SONA, Arroyo claimed success in the structural reforms her government implemented. She described having coffee with a call-centre agent as a touching experience:

> I had coffee with some call center agents last Labor Day. Lyn, a new college graduate, told me, 'Now I don't have to leave the country in order for me to help my family. *Salamat po*. (Thank you.)' I was so touched, Lyn, by your comments. With structural reforms, we not only found jobs, but kept families intact.
>
> (Arroyo 2006)

Arroyo's 2007 SONA had a more boastful tone when she declared that the Philippines 'ranks among top off-shoring hubs in the world because of cost competitiveness and more importantly our highly trainable, English proficient, IT-enabled management and manpower' (Arroyo 2007).

Like Russ Sandlin who closed his call centre in the Philippines, those who manage call centres paint a less optimistic picture of the industry. Robert S. Keitel, Regional Employment Advisor of the United States Embassy in Manila, reports that an average of 4 per cent of applicants are hired by call centres because of the applicants' 'substandard English skills' (Keitel 2008). This, despite 400,000 graduates being produced every year. Keitel notes the 'mismatch between the call centers' expectations of applicants and the preparedness of graduates from Philippine HEIs', thus forcing call centres to collaborate with schools. Keitel writes:

> It has been an evolution for academe to recognize that call center employment is an appropriate career opportunity for their graduates. Such recognition has necessitated changes in the curriculum. Initially, one reaction was, 'we speak English already ... are we not one of the largest English speaking countries in the world?' Yes, Filipinos speak English but it is a variety called Filipino English, and it is not the international (global) English required for call center employment.
>
> (Keitel 2008)

Other than the ICT industry, the overseas Filipino workers (OFW) are also exposed to the myth that English cures all economic ailments. This is evident in the following employer's guide posting about the advantage of hiring Filipino nurses: 'The facility in expressing himself/herself in English gives the Filipino nurse the extra advantage. With a good command of the language, he/she is able to communicate effectively with his/her employer, co-workers, and most importantly, with his/her patient or ward' (POEA 2005).

To be sure, a good command of English is beneficial in employment situations where the language is used. However, language proficiency alone may not ensure economic success. As the language is not equally accessible to the Filipinos, an over-emphasis on English proficiency because of the proliferation of call centres and medical transcription agencies in the Philippines, as well as increasing demands for Filipino workers abroad, pushes ELT further to the periphery by propagating the illusion that only proficiency in American English guarantees economic success.

Myth 3: English and Filipino are languages in opposition

In 2003, at the 75th founding anniversary of a Manila university, Arroyo made the following statement that set off a series of reactions among language stakeholders:

> Our English literacy, our aptitude and skills give us a competitive edge in ICT (information and communications technology) ... Therefore, until Congress enacts a law mandating Filipino as the language of instruction, I am directing the Department of Education to return English as the primary medium of instruction, provided some subjects will still be taught in Filipino.
>
> (Pazzibugan 2003)

Although the statement did not depart from the Bilingual Education Policy (BEP) of the DepEd, language stakeholders regarded it as an affront to the promotion of Filipino, the national language. A few months later, Executive Order No. 210, entitled 'Establishing the Policy to Strengthen the Use of the English Language as a Medium of Instruction in the Educational System', was issued, followed by DepEd Order No. 36, which detailed the implementing rules and regulations for EO 210. A group of language stakeholders, WIKA, challenged EO 210 and DepEd Order 36 by petitioning the Supreme Court to declare the orders unconstitutional. In its petition, WIKA claims that EO 210 'subverts the present status of Filipino in non-Tagalog areas, and violates the constitutional injunction that the regional languages shall serve as auxiliary media of instruction' (WIKA vs Arroyo 2007).

The petition betrays another myth about English in the Philippines – that the language is in direct opposition with other Philippine languages, especially the national language. Often, when stakeholders of the national language are confronted with attempts to institutionalize English in the education domain, they cite nationalism, or the lack of it, as a reason for resisting English.

The belief that English and Filipino have mutually exclusive domains in basic education is evident in the BEP itself, which was first introduced in 1974. In 1987, the BEP was revised with 'minor modifications' (Gonzalez 1999: 11). This policy has been in place for more than thirty years and assigns the maths and science subjects to instruction in English only; instruction in Filipino is allotted to social studies, music and the arts (Sibayan 1996).

The BEP has been widely criticized for many reasons, one being the perception that it does not contribute to upgrading the students' mastery of language and content areas. Legislators have persistently attempted to pass laws to revise the BEP. Of these, the most persistent is Cebu Representative Eduardo Gullas, who was successful in getting 205 co-authors for House Bill 305 (the Gullas Bill), or 'An Act to Strengthen and Enhance the Use of English as the Medium of Instruction in Philippine Schools' (*Sunstar Cebu* 2008). Gullas claims that the bill 'aims to correct the defects of the current bilingual education program of the Department of Education. Its ultimate objective is the improvement of the learning process in schools to ensure quality outputs' (*Manila Times* 2007).

Another bill filed was House Bill 1138, authored by Gabriela Representative Liza Maza, which provides for the use of Filipino as the only language of instruction. HB 1138 is premised on the position that any bilingual education policy violates Article 13 of the 1987 Philippine Constitution, which explicitly identifies Filipino as the national language. This bill also claims to correct the flaws of the BEP, especially in the area of strengthening the national language. In addition, it is believed that using Filipino as the sole medium of instruction would contribute to upgrading knowledge because the language is the student's own (14th Congress of the Republic of the Philippines 2007a).

The two bills pending in Congress betray conflicting perspectives about languages. On the one hand, there is the position that English offers more access to knowledge and is therefore the cure to all educational and (eventually) economic ailments. On the other hand, Filipino, being the national language, is more familiar to the students, and therefore offers more support for mastering content. Both positions take the perspective of language purity, or the notion that the two languages have mutually exclusive domains and should therefore be separated from each other. It is commonly believed that mixing the two would result in some form of contamination of one language, consequently producing low proficiency among the students.

Myth 4: English is the only language of knowledge

In 2008, Education Secretary Jesli Lapus launched the DepEd's flagship programme, known as Project TURN. Lapus explains that the project recognizes 'the importance of English proficiency as an important building block in learning' (Department of Education 2008a). Lapus notes that 'English proficiency is critical in learning as other key subjects such as Science and Mathematics use English in textbooks and other reference materials' (Department of Education 2008a).

Project TURN was launched through DepEd Order 7, which required all teachers of English, maths and science in low-performing elementary and high schools to take an English proficiency test and be trained in oral and written communication in English. Congressman Gullas himself announced that Php 500 million (roughly US$ 11 million) had been earmarked for the 'in-service English retooling of public school teachers' (Martel 2008).

These interventions illustrate the prevalence of the myth that, in the Philippines, if you don't know English, you simply don't know. English in the Philippines is believed to be the *only* language through which knowledge can be accessed, especially maths and science. School administrators who insist that only English be spoken in schools further reinforce this myth.

Another piece of evidence of the myth that only English provides access to knowledge is found in strong opposition to House Bill 3719, filed by Valenzuela Representative Magtanggol Gunigundo during the 14th Congress. This bill was filed in an attempt to thwart the passing of the Gullas Bill (discussed in Myth 3), which sought to make English the sole medium of instruction.

Known as the Multilingual and Literacy Act of 2008, the Gunigundo Bill aims to 'upgrade the literacy program of the government by making the native tongue as the medium of instruction for the formative years of basic education' (14th Congress of the Republic of the Philippines 2008). Socioeconomic Planning Secretary Ralph Recto, in a letter to Executive Secretary Eduardo Ermita, endorsed HB 3719 and explains that it is:

> consistent with the goals of the Philippine Education for All (EFA) 2015 Plan and the Updated Medium-Term Philippine Development Plan (MTPDP) 2004–10,

which supports the utilization of the mother tongue as a fundamental tool to enhance the learning process itself and improve the relevance of basic education.

(Personal communication, 12 August 2008)

Despite this endorsement, as well as the endorsement of Secretary Jesli Lapus, Arroyo remained cold to HB 3719 by not making it a priority for her administration.

Seeds of resistance in Philippine ELT

In his study of ELT in Sri Lanka, Canagarajah takes the resistance perspective, which approaches English as not necessarily evil, despite its colonial and postcolonial faces. Canagarajah explains, 'The intention is not to *reject* English, but to *reconstitute* it in more inclusive, ethical, and democratic terms, and so to bring out the creative resolutions to their linguistic conflicts' (1999: 2). However, formulating creative resolutions to linguistic conflicts is easier said than done, especially in public school ELT, a sector that is doubly peripheral in the Philippines. Still, there are signs in ELT that point to the beginnings of resistance to myths about English in the Philippines.

In the 1990s, linguist Brother Andrew Gonzalez, who later became Secretary of Education, reflected on the BEP and wrote about his 'obsession ... to make Filipinos linguistically competent to be able to think deeply and critically in any language' (Gonzalez 1999: 13). Gonzalez appeals for:

a maximum of flexibility in the media of instruction ... Not everything in Philippine education has to be uniform; in fact, even if we have policies towards uniformity, we never accomplish enough to be able to attain uniformity of results. So why not recognize this limitation and exploit it so that we can move faster towards development?

(Gonzalez 1999: 13)

Two research studies that support resistance to English-only in education are Allan Bernardo's cognitive science experiments about the effects of language on mathematical learning and performance and my own study of code-switching among teachers and students in science courses.

Bernardo (2000) investigated the effect of using the Filipino students' first or second language on his or her mathematical problem-solving ability. He concludes that there is no single effect of language on mathematical ability. Instead, the language effects are 'multifarious and specific to the different components of mathematic problem solving' (Bernardo 2000: 310). Bernardo notes that those who insist that maths be taught in English assume 'some kind of structural-fit effect between English and mathematics learning and performance' (2000: 311) which doesn't exist.

It is in this spirit of flexibility and resistance to uniformity that Filipino teachers reject the language purity imposition of the BEP and try to promote code-switching in the classrooms. Code-switching, despite the policy of English-only in maths and science, may be a form of resistance to prevailing myths about languages in the Philippines.

Studies on code-switching in the Philippines reveal that it is practised in various domains, by different groups, for different reasons (Martin 2006). Still, that code-switching is natural, inevitable and perhaps necessary in Philippine education remains a touchy issue, especially where content learning is concerned.

My own study of code-switching in college science analysed two cases which found that the practice does in fact support the goals of delivering content knowledge. Code-switching was used by science teachers as a pedagogical tool for motivating student response and action, ensuring rapport and solidarity, promoting shared meaning, checking student understanding, and maintaining the teaching narrative (Martin 2006).

English teachers in the public schools also report that they code-switch when they teach. Dionisia B. Fernandez writes about how the English-only policy did not work:

> One rule I have in my classroom is fairly simple: Speak only English! It was agreed that whoever broke this rule would pay a fine of one peso for each non-English word. For two days my students tried very hard to speak English only …
>
> A week after imposing the Speak English Only campaign, I felt frustrated not because the students' carabao English worsened, or that the class treasurer did not collect a single peso, but because most of my pupils chose to keep their mouths shut. The campaign was a failure!
>
> (Fernandez in press)

Teachers do not just resist the English-only practice, they also try hard to eliminate their students' fear of the language – a fear that makes it difficult for teachers to teach. Marilyn C. Braganza writes about resisting the image of an English-speaking monster:

> I was assigned to a school where students had a mix of tongues. Some spoke with a heavy Bagobo accent, while others spoke in the more dominant dialects of the South. Those with heavy Bagobo accents usually lack the confidence to perform in my classes. One such student was a boy in my Bridge Class who refused to participate during oral drills. Because his written output was really not bad, I often wondered why he would not speak in my class. In my frustration, I found myself threatening to move him to another class. He then confessed that he spoke to only three students in school who were his relatives; he was afraid of being ridiculed by his classmates.
>
> At that moment, I realized that I only had two options available to me: fail him or teach him. I decided on the second option. Every week I spent one hour with Jovanni to build his self-confidence and make him realize that it was okay to be different. It was not easy talking to a 13-year-old boy who saw me as an English-speaking monster.
>
> (Braganza in press)

Another public school teacher, Desiree C. Hidalgo, writes about the creative ways of teaching English to her low-performing students:

> In one lesson about gender, I asked the students what the English term was for female pig or male pig. *Takal. Takong.* A roar of laughter ensued as the students offered the Ilocano terms instead. One student mentioned that her father was nicknamed 'Takal' or boar. Such a nickname was customary in the barrios to refer to womanizing men with many children. 'Takong' was the nickname appended to the female counterparts. The students then shared other monikers …

I seized that moment to intensify the students' attention to zoomorphism by intro-ducing English words that point to animal-like characteristics ... The students went home with new set of words. I was amused to hear one boy say to one girl, 'Your voice is so lovingly feline,' to which the girl promptly replied, 'And you have a canine smile.' The students were learning new words by actually using them in their own creative ways. And they were enjoying the humor each new word evoked.

(Hidalgo in press)

Among the public school teachers of English who reported that American English was their target for ELT, we also find seeds of resistance. When asked why they considered English to be a Philippine language, some stated the following:

1 We have adapted it for our own use and so I believe we own it in a certain sense.
2 Like the Filipino language, English is spoken and understood by Filipinos.
3 We Filipinos have many languages and we consider English as our Philippine language.
4 It is a means of communication inside and outside the country.
5 Many Filipinos use English in daily language and they speak good English, too.
6 Most Filipinos do speak the language; therefore it is a Philippine language.
7 We use it everyday, wherever we go or [whatever we] do.

The First Quarter 2008 Social Weather Survey reported a slight improvement in the Filipinos' self-assessment of English proficiency from the previous 2006 survey. The number of Filipinos who believe that they were not competent in English has decreased (Social Weather Stations: 2008). One wonders if this is an indication of a growing accep-tance of or confidence in the language. Whatever it may be, the present-day myths about English in the Philippines, if these persist, will continue to push ELT further to the margins and prevent the Filipinos from embracing the English language as their own. English *is* a Philippine language. Poet Amador T. Daguio captured this well when he wrote the following poem (Daguio 1941):

Though I may speak the English language,
Let me tell you: I am a Filipino,
I stand for that which make my nation,
The virtues of the country where I was born.
I may have traces of the American,
Be deceived not: Spain has, too, her traces in me,
But my songs are those of my race.

('To those of other lands', Amador T. Daguio 1941)

Suggestions for further reading

Bautista, Ma. L.S. (ed.) (1996) *Readings in Philippine Sociolinguistics*, Manila: DLSU Press.
Bernardo, Allan B.I. (ed.) (2008) *The Paradox of Philippine Education and Education Reform: Social Science Perspectives*, Quezon City: Philippine Social Science Council.
Tupas, T. Ruanni (ed.) (2007) *Re-making Society: The Politics of Language, Discourse, and Identity in the Philippines*, Quezon City: University of the Philippines Press.

References

14th Congress of the Republic of the Philippines (2007a) *An Act that Provides for Filipino as the Official Medium of Instruction in All Schools* (House Bill 1138).

——(2007b) *An Act to Strengthen and Enhance the Use of English as the Medium of Instruction in Philippine Schools* (House Bill 305).

——(2008) *An Act Establishing a Multi-lingual Education and Literacy Program* (House Bill 3719).

Abad, Gemino H. (2003) 'Amador T. Daguio: a turning-point in Filipino poetry from English', National Commission for Culture and the Arts. Online. Available www.ncca.gov.ph/about_cultarts/articles.php?artcl_Id=29 (accessed 16 January 2007).

Alabastro, S. and Panelo, T. (2003) *E-Way to Better Communication I*, Marikina City: J.C. Palabay Enterprises.

Alabastro, T. and Sandagan, L. (2003) *E-Way to Better Communication IV*, Marikina City: J.C. Palabay Enterprises.

Arroyo, G. (2001) State of the Nation Address at the Opening of Congress, Batasang Pambansa, Quezon City, 23 July.

——(2003) Executive Order No. 210 Establishing the Policy to Strengthen the Use of the English Language as a Medium of Instruction in the Educational System.

——(2006) State of the Nation Address at the Opening of Congress, Batasang Pambansa, Quezon City, 24 July.

——(2007) State of the Nation Address at the Opening of Congress, Batasang Pambansa, Quezon City, 23 July.

Bautista, Ma. L.S. (2000) 'The grammatical features of educated Philippine English', in Ma. L.S. Bautista, T. Llamzon and B. Sibayan (eds) *Parangal Cang Brother Andrew: Festschrift for Andrew Gonzalez on His Sixtieth Birthday,* Manila: Linguistic Society of the Philippines, pp. 146–58.

Bennett, T. (2005) *American English for Filipinos*, Pasig City: Anvil Publishing.

Bernardo, Allan B.I. (2000) 'The multifarious effects of language on mathematical learning and performance among bilinguals: a cognitive science perspective', in Ma. L.S. Bautista, T. Llamzon and B. Sibayan (eds) *Parangal Cang Brother Andrew: Festschrift for Andrew Gonzalez on His Sixtieth Birthday*, Manila: Linguistic Society of the Philippines, pp. 303–16.

Board of Educational Survey (1925) *A Survey of the Educational System of the Philippine Islands*, Manila: Bureau of Printing.

Bolton, K. and Butler, S. (2008) 'Lexicography and the description of Philippine English vocabulary', in Ma. L.S. Bautista and K. Bolton (eds) *Philippine English: Linguistic and Literary Perspectives*, Hong Kong: Hong Kong University Press, pp. 175–200.

Braganza, M. (in press) 'The Tough Get Going', in I.P. Martin (ed.) *How, How the Carabao: Tales of Teaching English in the Philippines*, Quezon City: Ateneo de Manila University.

Bureau of Secondary Education (2004) *Learning Competencies for High School Literature*, Pasig City: Department of Education.

Canagarajah, A.S. (1999) *Resisting Linguistic Imperialism in English Teaching*, Oxford: Oxford University Press.

Caoli-Rodriguez, R. (2007) 'The Philippines country case study', in UNESCO *Country Profile Commissioned for the EFA Global Monitoring Report 2008, Education for All by 2015: Will We Make It?* Online. Available http://unesdoc.unesco.org (accessed 4 July 2008).

Daguio, A. (1932) 'Man of Earth', in G. Abad (2003) *Amador T. Daguio: A Turning-point in Filipino Poetry from English*, Manila: National Commission on Culture and the Arts. Online. Available www.ncca.gov.ph/about_cultarts/articles.php?artcl_Id=29 (accessed 16 January 2007).

——(1941) 'To those of other lands', in G. Abad, G. (2003) *Amador T. Daguio: A Turning-point in Filipino Poetry from English*, Manila: National Commission on Culture and the Arts. Online. Available www.ncca.gov.ph/about_cultarts/articles.php?artcl_Id=29 (accessed 16 January 2007).

Department of Education (2008a) 'English proficiency: DepEd's flagship program in 2008', Office of the Secretary, 15 January. Online. Available www.deped.gov.ph (accessed 4 July 2008).

——(2008b) 'DepEd: 2008 NAT results very encouraging', Office of the Secretary, 25 June. Online. Available www.deped.gov.ph (accessed 4 July 2008).

——(2008c) 'Turning around low performance in English: a priority program for 2008', DepEd Order No. 7, Series 2008, 29 January. Online. Available www.deped.gov.ph (accessed 4 July 2008).

——(2008d) 'Basic Education Statistics [data file]', 11 September. Online. Available www.deped.gov.ph/factsandfigures/default.asp (accessed 17 November 2008).

Estioko, L. (1994) *History of Education: A Filipino Perspective*, Manila: Society of Divine Word.

Fee, M.H. (1911) 'A Learning English: A plea for new methods', *The Teachers' Assembly Herald*, 9 May: 113–15.

Fernandez, D. (in press) 'The Red Carabao', in I.P. Martin (ed.) *How, How the Carabao: Tales of Teaching English in the Philippines*, Quezon City: Ateneo de Manila University.

Gonzalez, A. (1999) 'Philippine bilingual education revisited', in Ma. L.S. Bautista and G. Tan (eds) *The Filipino Bilingual: A Multidisciplinary Perspective [Festschrift in Honor of Emy M. Pascasio]*, Manila: Linguistic Society of the Philippines, pp. 11–15.

Gonzalez, P., Guzmán, J.C., Partelow, L., Pahlke, E., Jocelyn, L., Kastberg, D. and Williams, T. (2004) *Highlights From the Trends in International Mathematics and Science Study (TIMMS) 2003*, National Center for Education Statistics, US Department of Education, Washington, DC: US Government Printing Office.

Hidalgo, D. (in press) 'Please excuse me for my absent yesterday because my mother is born again', in I.P. Martin (ed.) *How, How the Carabao: Tales of Teaching English in the Philippines*, Quezon City: Ateneo de Manila University.

Kachru, B. (1995) 'The intercultural nature of modern English', in Department of Immigration and Citizenship, *1995 Global Cultural Diversity Conference Proceedings*, Sydney, Australia. Online. Available www.immi.gov.au/media/publications/multicultural/confer/04/speech19a.htm (accessed 17 November 2008).

——(2005) *Asian Englishes: Beyond the Canon*, Hong Kong: Hong Kong University Press.

Keitel, R. (2008) 'Academe-call center partnerships', *Manila Bulletin Online*, 20 January. Online. Available www.mb.com.ph/issues/2008/01/20/OPED20080120114885.html (accessed 27 November 2008).

Manila Times (2007) 'Lawmaker sees need for English', 22 December. Online. Available www.manilatimes.net (accessed 11 July 2008).

Martel, R. (2008) 'Spreading English as opposed to "Taglish"', *Manila Times*, 10 June. Online. Available www.manilatimes.net (accessed 4 July 2008).

Martin, I.P. (2006) 'Language in Philippine classrooms: enabling or enfeebling?' *Asian Englishes Journal*, 9 (2): 48–66.

——(2007) 'The literature Filipino students DO NOT read', in D. Prescott, A. Kirkpatrick, I.P. Martin and A. Hashim (eds) *English in Southeast Asia: Literacies, literatures and varieties*, Newcastle: Cambridge Scholars Publishing.

——(2008) 'Colonial education and the shaping of Philippine literature in English', in Ma. L.S. Bautista and K. Bolton (eds) *Philippine English: Linguistic and Literary Perspectives*, Hong Kong: Hong Kong University Press, pp. 245–60.

National Statistical Coordination Board (2007) 'Factsheet: students' scores in achievement tests deteriorating'. Online. Available www.ncsb.gov.ph/factsheet/pdf07/FS-200705-SS2–01.asp (accessed 22 November 2008).

Pazzibugan, D. (2003) 'President wants English back; Estrada objects', INQ7.NET, 29 January. Online. Available www.inq7.net/nat/2003/jan/30/text/nat_6–1-p.html (accessed 22 October 2003).

Philippine Overseas Employment Administration (POEA) (2005) 'Filipino workers: moving the world today (employer's guide). Online. Available www.poea.gov.ph/about/moving.htm (accessed 25 November 2008).

Recto, R. (2008) Personal communication to Executive Secretary Eduardo Ermita, 12 August.

Sandlin, R. (2008) 'English remains the only hope of the Philippines' (letter to the editor), *Philippine Daily Inquirer*, 1 March.

Sibayan, B. (1996) 'Bilingual education in the Philippines: strategy and structure', in Ma. L.S. Bautista (ed.) *Readings in Philippine Sociolinguistics*, Manila: DLSU Press, pp. 287–307.

Social Weather Stations (2008) 'National proficiency in English recovers', 16 May. Online. Available www.sws.org.ph (accessed 24 November 2008).

Sunstar Cebu (2008) 'House to pass English bill: Gullas', 11 February. Online. Available www.sunstar. com.ph/static/ceb/2008/02/11/news/ house.to.pass.english.bill.gullas.html (accessed 28 November 2008).

WIKA vs Arroyo (Wika ng Kultura at Agham, Inc. (WIKA) vs President Gloria Arroyo, *et al.*) (2007) 27 April. Online. Available www.sawikaan.net/petition.pdf (accessed 11 November 2008).

15

East Asian Englishes

Japan and Korea

Yuko Takeshita

Introduction

Japan realized the need for English in response to threats from outside. In 1808, when the government strictly controlled and limited foreign diplomacy and trade, the *Phaeton*, an English ship flying a Dutch flag, arrived in the southern part of Japan. The government had given Holland permission to trade with Japan, and Dutch was used by government officials as a language for international communication. This made the government order Dutch–Japanese interpreters and translators to learn English. With the Convention of Kanagawa in 1854, through which US Commodore Mathew Perry forced Japan to open up to the West, the English language increased its presence in Japan. The start of English teaching in schools did not begin until 1872, however.

In Korea, English education officially started in 1883, when the government established an English language school to train interpreters (Matsumoto 2003; E. Kim 2008). In the 1880s, other schools, both governmental and private, also opened and English was taught by English and American teachers who were invited or came to Korea for missionary work. One school, established in 1886, taught not only English but all subjects in English. The reason behind the introduction of English language teaching was the Korean awareness of the need for modernization, and the fact that such awareness existed before the Japanese colonization, is emphasized in studies of Korean modern history (Matsumoto 2003).

In both countries English has been taught as a foreign language. The two countries, therefore, belong in the expanding circle. However, the desire for and roles of English are increasing to a remarkable degree, as both countries try to increase their international presence by developing better English proficiency. This chapter will describe some of the social and cultural phenomena concerning English learning and attempt to describe where the two countries are heading in terms of English and English education.

Both Korea and Japan place strong emphasis on English education, as well as on education as a whole. The high percentage of children enrolled in schools bear testimony to this. For example, in Korea almost 100 per cent of primary school students go on to middle and junior secondary schools, and the percentage of junior high school students going on to senior secondary school is almost as high. The percentage of senior high school students continuing their studies at the tertiary level, i.e. universities, junior colleges and teachers' colleges, slightly decreased from a high of 90.2 per cent to 87.1 per cent in 2007 (Korean Ministry of Education, Science and Technology Development, hereafter referred to as Korean MEST 2009).

In Japan, the percentage of junior high school students going on to senior high school reached 90 per cent around 1975, since when it has steadily increased, reaching as high as 97.6 per cent in 2005. Upon graduating from senior high school, 51.5 per cent (49.8 per cent for female students) went on to four-year and two-year colleges and universities. If we include those taking correspondence courses, those studying in vocational schools and those enrolled in the Open University of Japan, which offers higher distance education mainly for high school graduates, 76.2 per cent (76.5 per cent for female students) continued on to higher education (Japanese Ministry of Education, Culture, Sports, Science and Technology, hereafter referred to as Japanese MEXT 2006).

English is an integral part of the curricula in both Korea and Japan, especially in this age of globalization. Whether or not one can access the abundant information provided in English and has the ability to respond and act upon the information appropriately can determine how capable and efficient one may be. Such high percentages of school enrolment suggest that graduates should acquire high proficiency in English, as long as the process involves well-motivated students receiving good education in English over several years in schools with appropriate curricula, qualified teachers, effective teaching and learning materials and equipment. Neither Korea nor Japan, however, has found her nation's English programmes successful enough to provide her students with adequate communication skills. Curriculum revisions, suggestions for better teacher training programmes and development of more effective teaching methods and learning materials, and the dependence on non-Japanese or non-Korean teachers of English indicate that the two countries are still searching for a way to help their citizens acquire a better proficiency in the English language.

English education naturally attracts much attention. In Korea, where people's English ability is considered to be the key to the country's economic success and international competitiveness, English learning concerns the prestige of the country. Shim and Baik argue that such international events as the 1986 Seoul Asian Games, the 1988 Seoul Olympics and the 2002 World Cup made Koreans realize that English is 'a crucial element in achieving success in a global world' (Shim and Baik 2004: 241). Since Japan saw that English ability is a must for increasing its international presence, the government has revised the national curriculum. Although English is not used much for intra-national communication in either Japan or Korea, we shall see that this use is increasing and this, together with its international importance, is making English highly sought after in both countries.

Controversies over a proposal to make English an official language in Korea and Japan

English, however enthusiastically people try to master it, remains a 'foreign' language, or rather, a language for international communication. Thus, proposals to give the language official status provoked heated debate in both countries.

The debate started in Korea in July 1998 with the publication of *Ethnic Language in the Age of a Global Language* (Bok), and a subsequent review of the book in the *Chosun Ilbo* newspaper (Yoo 2005). According to Yoo:

> Bok's main argument is that ethnic languages will die out soon because people have realized the power and prestige of English as the present global language, and therefore, that the South Korean government should take the initiative to adopt English as a co-official language with Korean for the time being and, in the long run, establish English as the one and only official language in South Korea.
>
> (Yoo 2005: 7)

In December of the following year, the president of the Korean Novelists Association suggested at a Novelist Forum that Koreans should learn from the bilingual policy in Singapore.

The issue caught Japanese people's attention in January 2000, when the proposal to make English an official language was included in *The Frontier Within: Individual Empowerment and Better Governance in the New Millennium*, a report published by an advisory panel to then Prime Minister Obuchi. The report reads:

> It is necessary to set the concrete objective of all citizens acquiring a working knowledge of English by the time they take their place in society as adults. In addition, the central government, local governments, and other public institutions must be required to produce their publications, home pages, and so on in both Japanese and English. In the long term, national debate on whether to make English a second official language will be needed.
>
> (Honna and Takeshita 2004: 212)

The debates are like waves rolling and falling between Korea and Japan, two traditionally monolingual countries, and they continue to capture public attention.

The Korean government and English education

The Korean MEST is responsible for the nation's education by stipulating the national curriculum and authorizing textbooks compiled in accordance with the curriculum. The government's education policy is crucial because the national curriculum controls the teaching procedure and the content. The government has revised the national curriculum every five to ten years since its first revision in 1954. The seventh and current national curriculum was introduced in December 1997, but first took effect in 2000 at the primary level and gradually expanded to senior high level in 2004. It is aimed at educating students into becoming individual and creative citizens in the globalized world with access to new knowledge and values:

> To prepare students for the 21st century, the era of globalization and knowledge-based society, the Seventh Curriculum attempts to break away from the spoon-fed and short-sighted approach to education of the past towards a new approach

in the classroom to produce human resources capable of facing new challenges. Study loads for each subject have been reduced to an appropriate level, while curricula that accommodate different needs of individual students have also been introduced. Independent learning activities to enhance self-directed learning required in the knowledge-based society have either been introduced or expanded.

(Korean MEST 2009)

Research institutes such as KEDI (the Korean Educational Development Institute), KERIS (the Korea Education and Research Information Service), KRIVET (the Korea Research Institute for Vocational Education and Training), and KICE (the Korea Institute for Curriculum and Evaluation) play important roles in the development and assessment of the national curriculum. KICE, for example, established in 1998 as a government-funded educational research institution, operates two offices and several divisions and bureaus, namely the Office for Planning and Innovation, the Office for College Scholastic Ability Test, the Division of Curriculum-textbook Research, the Division of Teaching and Learning Research, the Division of Educational Evaluation Research, the Division of National Tests Administration, the Bureau of Administration, Computing and Information, and the English Education Policy and Research Centre.

The Korean president's great authority makes it possible for a curriculum to be drastically revised once an education reform plan is incorporated in the national policy (Honna *et al.* 2008). As the nation's English ability is considered to be an important factor in Korea's international competitiveness, English education remains at the centre of the government's policy to build up the country's strength. The introduction of English as a required subject at the primary level is a good example of education reform driven by the government's strong leadership. This has not proved possible in Japan, as will be mentioned below.

A recent example of the government's influence and initiative is President Lee Myung-bak's English education reform plans, which include an English immersion programme aimed at improving teachers' and students' English proficiency. President Lee, who took office in February 2008, had announced, as President-elect, that he would implement such a programme in schools throughout the country. Objections to this programme eventually forced Lee to withdraw it. At present, although there remain concerns and objections about the immersion programme, the government is trying to strengthen English-medium education at all education levels, with the possibility of English becoming the medium of instruction for some subjects in certain districts. Some administrative districts are more supportive than others of the President's educational policy. For instance, Gyeonggi Province, at the centre of which the capital city of Seoul is located, has decided that English language classes should be conducted only in English starting in 2011, that some schools will start teaching other subjects in English, and that native speakers of English should be assigned to all schools in the province as assistant teachers by 2010. According to the education office, the plan aims 'at teaching students to be comfortable speaking with English-speaking foreigners without taking extra classes at private institutions' (*Chosun Ilbo* 2008), and that the 'ratio of English teachers, who can conduct classes only in the language, will increase by 15 percentage points every year from the current 56.3 per cent to the full 100 per cent by 2010' (*Chosun Ilbo* 2008). Some subjects other than English should also have English-medium instruction.

The Japanese government and English Education

The Japanese Ministry of Education, Culture, Sports, Science and Technology (MEXT) presents itself as the agent and promoter of education reforms. On 1 March 2003, MEXT published the document, 'Regarding the establishment of an action plan to cultivate "Japanese with English abilities"'. Its main purpose was to reiterate that Japanese people should acquire better English communication skills. In her statement, an excerpt of which is presented below, then Education Minister Atsuko Toyama analysed the environment in which Japan faced globalization, encouraged her citizens to meet various international challenges, emphasized the importance of the English language, and then pointed out the fact that Japanese people are not equipped with enough language skills to significantly function in the international community:

> In such a situation, English has played a central role as the common international language in linking people who have different mother tongues. For children living in the 21st century, it is essential for them to acquire communication abilities in English as a common international language. In addition, English abilities are important in terms of linking our country with the rest of the world, obtaining the world's understanding and trust, enhancing our international presence and further developing our nation. At present, though, due to the lack of sufficient ability, many Japanese are restricted in their exchanges with foreigners and their ideas or opinions are not evaluated appropriately. It is also necessary for Japanese to develop their ability to clearly express their own opinions in Japanese first in order to learn English.

> (Japanese MEXT 2003)

'A strategic plan to cultivate "Japanese with English abilities"' was formulated in July 2001 by MEXT in its effort to reform Japan's English teaching and learning towards higher levels of proficiency. The features of this highly ambitious plan included a set of quantitative goals to be achieved by the end of 2008. For example, the plan indicated that English teachers' English proficiency should be at least STEP pre-first level,[1] TOEFL 550, TOEIC 730. Specific levels for junior and senior high school graduates as well as university graduates are also listed.

The action plan sees the introduction of English in the primary school as a formal subject. Although English has been taught as a formal subject at the secondary and tertiary levels, this has not previously been the case at the primary level. English has been part of a lesson called a 'Period of Integrated Study', in which pupils could have educational activities using/concerning English, rather than formal language lessons, for international understanding. The action plan is aimed at formalizing these English activities.

The annual MEXT reports show that such English activities at the primary level have greatly increased. Figure 15.1 indicates the rising percentages of public primary schools that conduct activities through English. These used to take place during the Period of Integrated Study or as extracurricular activities. But, by April 2011, all public elementary schools will have introduced English as a required subject for the fifth and sixth grades.

In spite of the Ministry's energy, effort and careful attempt to obtain consensus among teachers, parents and other stakeholders, the schools still have mixed feelings about the formal introduction of English as a subject at the primary level. A study conducted in August and September 2008 by Obunsha Co. Ltd, a leading publishing

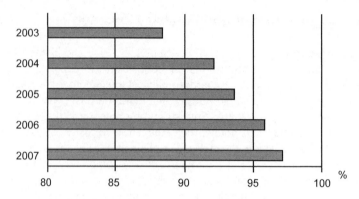

Figure 15.1 Percentages of primary schools with English activities.

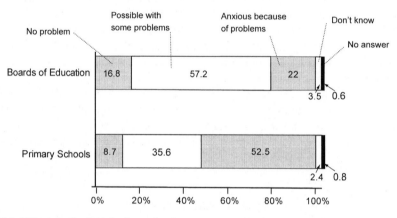

Figure 15.2 Attitude to English at primary level.

company that publishes education-related materials, reported that 52.5 per cent of the nation's public elementary schools expressed concerns for English teaching, although the percentage of Boards of Education nationwide so doing was only 22.0 per cent (Obunsha 2009). The discrepancy in the degree of confidence and preparedness between schools and boards of education probably means that many teachers feel that there are problems yet to be solved in offering compulsory English classes. Many elementary school teachers who have not been trained in teaching English as a subject have expressed, during lectures, seminars and workshops, great anxiety about their new challenges (Figure 15.2).

Japanese and Korean English proficiencies and the Test of English as a Foreign Language (TOEFL)

Despite all the changes, Korean and Japanese proficiency in English remains relatively low, if the results from the international TOEFL test are reliable. According to the 'TOEFL Test and Score Data Summary 2004–05: Test Year Data', a total of 86,348 Japanese sat the Computer-Based TOEFL Test and the Paper-Based TOEFL Test and

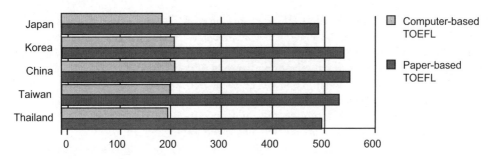

Figure 15.3 TOEFL scores 2004–5.

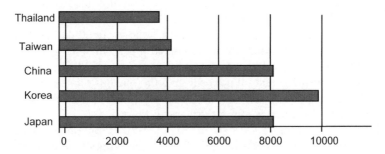

Figure 15.4 Numbers of TOEFL takers.

their average scores were 191 and 495 respectively. In comparison the 103,225 Koreans who sat the tests scored 215 and 545 respectively. (See Figures 15.3 and 15.4, with data from China, Taiwan and Thailand for comparison.) Koreans scored better than Japanese in both versions of the test. The percentage of the population taking the tests is low, however, with only 0.07 per cent of Japanese and 0.21 per cent of Koreans taking them.

An accurate number of South Korean TOEFL takers is difficult to obtain. As the demand for taking TOEFL is much bigger than the supply, more and more Koreans are taking TOEFL outside their country. One test-preparation school estimates that approximately 500 Koreans a month travel to such places as Japan, South East Asia and even Australia to take the tests. In addition to the purpose of studying in educational institutions overseas, they need the scores at home: teenagers need the score to apply to prestigious secondary schools, many universities require TOEFL for graduation, and adults are also required to submit the score to apply for jobs 'with no obvious need for fluency in English' (Lee 2007: 1). Koreans call this phenomenon the 'TOEFL crisis,' creating special TOEFL tours to other countries.

The contribution and involvement of native speakers of English in educational environments

The Japanese MEXT's strategic plan mentioned above includes a policy to increase the number of native speakers of English as assistant teachers in government schools. These assistant teachers, or ALTs (assistant language teachers), come from a variety of countries and are invited to Japan on a renewable one-year contract as participants in the Japan Exchange and Teaching (JET) Programme. ALTs in the JET Programme are dispatched to public schools throughout the archipelago to team-teach with Japanese teachers in order to improve students' practical communication skills in English. At the same time, ALTs are called upon to play the important role of developing the English proficiency of Japanese teachers of English. This can be expanded to large-scale in-house training for Japanese teachers (Honna and Takeshita 2004: 212).

Although the programme today recruits not only native speakers, they nonetheless constitute the great majority of its participants. (See Table 15.1.)

The JET programme started in 1987 with 813 ALTs for the English programme, 'all coming from English-speaking countries (570 from the USA, 149 from Britain, 72 from Australia and 22 from New Zealand)' (Honna and Takeshita 2000: 63). With the demand for ALTs increasing, the programme has continued to expand, and in 1995 there were 4,243 ALTs, 2,248 coming from the US, 790 from the UK and 692 from Canada (Honna and Takeshita 2000). As Table 15.1 shows, in 2008, 2,571 ALTs, or 60 per cent of the total number, came from the United States. In spite of trying to encourage ALTs with diverse cultural backgrounds, the percentage of Americans, 70 per cent in 1987, 53 per cent in 1995 and 60 per cent in 2008, remains remarkably high. This is evidence of Japan's proclivity for native-speaker English (Honna and Takeshita 2000: 53–64; Honna 2008: 146), especially for American English.

The Korean version of the JET Programme is the EPIK Programme, or EPIK Korea. Established in 1995 and sponsored by the Ministry, the programme aims at improving the English-speaking abilities of students and teachers in Korea, to develop cultural exchanges, and to reform English teaching methodologies in Korea (National Institute for International Education, hereafter cited as NIIED 2008). Just as ALTs in Japan are employed as team-teachers or co-teachers with their Japanese counterparts, team-teaching

Table 15.1 Number of participants in the JET Programme by country, 2008–9

Country	ALTs (Assistant language teachers)
Total participants from all countries	4,288
United States	2,571
United Kingdom	428
Australia	249
New Zealand	194
Canada	498
Ireland	76
France	9
Germany	2
China	10
Korea	3
Russia	1
Brazil	0
South Africa	99
India	17
Singapore	48
Jamaica	46
Italy	0
21 other countries	11

Source: JET Programme 2008b

in the Korean primary- and secondary-level English classrooms has been made possible with the establishment of the EPIK Programme.

The programme started with 51 native speakers of English as English Language Instructors or ELIs (Choi 1996 as cited in J.-K. Park 2008) from six designated countries, namely Australia, Canada, Ireland, New Zealand, the UK and the USA. The number of participants in the programme increased to 632 in 1996, but decreased to 348 in 1998 due to the economic crisis in the previous year, and it is increasing again owing to the government's decision that, in order to systematically establish an English education infrastructure in Korea, native speakers of English will be placed in all Korean middle schools by 2010 (Kim and Ko 2008).

Some researchers have questioned the dependence of English language teaching upon ELIs. J.-K. Park (2008) queries the 'eligibility' of the native speakers who apply to the programme: those who are eligible should be a citizen of one of the six countries listed above; have lived in one of these countries for at least ten years; have studied in one of these countries from the seventh grade; and hold at least a bachelor's degree (NIIED 2008; Park 2008). She sees a serious problem in equating English teachers with somebody from the inner circle and who does not require ELT expertise and experience. She calls this 'native-speakerism', and suggests a thorough examination of what is expected from English teachers, 'regardless of their ethnicity or nationality' (J.-K. Park 2008: 150).

J.-K. Park (2008) also advises inviting 'more diverse groups of proficient English-speaking ELT professionals' (p. 150) to teach in Korean schools. She argues for 'the probable enhancement of the Korean public's understanding and awareness of World Englishes' and states that 'the Korean public no longer considers American English the sole model for English education' (Shim and Baik 2004: 253). Nevertheless, the prejudice for native speakers' English(es) remains remarkably strong, as will be illustrated below.

English learning and using situations in Korea and Japan

English villages in Korea: an 'authentic' environment for learning English

English learning costs money, and this creates a gap between the rich and the poor. English villages were first conceived to serve as 'an attempt to provide residents of this country with an opportunity for an English language immersion experience without the need to travel abroad' (Kim 2006). Today, despite arguments about the pros and cons about such 'authentic' English-speaking environments, 'about 55 English villages are either in operation or planned to be established in Korea by 2008' (Song 2006, cited in Kim 2006).

An example is Seoul English Village, an English language immersion camp established by the Seoul Metropolitan Government to provide students between 5 and 19 years of age the opportunity to live in a simulated English-speaking environment. Children can visit and stay at the camp. There is a choice of five different programmes: One-Week Programme; One-Day Programme; Two-Days-One-Night-Weekend Programme; a Summer/Winter Immersion Camp; and School Excursion Programmes for non-Korean students. Teachers and parents can also stay at the camp for the Teacher Training and Family Programmes respectively.

Students at the camp purportedly experience the culture and daily lives of English-speaking countries. To make children's experience successful, native speakers of English 'from North America, UK, New Zealand, Ireland, Australia and South Africa with a minimum of BA/BSC degree in any major with a keen interest in acting, role-playing and interactive teaching' (Seoul English Village, http://suyu.sev.go.kr/main/main.asp) can apply for teaching positions. While some admire the environment the village can offer, others frown upon a situation which leads to the degradation of Korean teachers of English caused by the prejudice and proclivity for native speakers. What culture students can learn by living in the village with American, English, New Zealand, Irish, Australian and South African teachers is a question one may want to ask. What kind of English Korean learners of English are expected to produce is another.

Wild geese

Park defines English as 'a major key to success in society' because it 'has enabled people to raise their social status' (2009: 62). She also explains the important relationship between English and Korean women, especially mothers, who were prohibited in the old Confucian society to pursue and fulfil their own educational goals. English has become a tool for today's Korean mothers 'to accomplish their dreams and desires through their children's success' (2009: 62).

Disappointed with the English education available at the nation's public schools and with great expectations of better results elsewhere, Korean mothers take their children abroad, leaving their husbands behind. This is known as the 'wild geese' phenomenon, in which the wife and the child(ren) live in English-speaking countries and the husband stays home to earn a living and school expenses, occasionally flying abroad for a family reunion. As the remarkable figures in Table 15.2 indicate, this is getting more and more popular (Onishi 2008).

Currently, more than 40,000 Korean children are living overseas with their mothers. In addition a total of 29,511 primary and secondary students are said to have left Korea in 2006 alone for study abroad, nearly double the number who left in 2004. There are more than 103,000 Korean children living in the United States and they make up the largest group of foreign students. In 2007, 6,579 Korean children were in primary and secondary schools in New Zealand, constituting 38 per cent of all foreign students in the country (Onishi 2008).

This lifestyle has deformed 'marriages and the Confucian ideal of the traditional Korean family' (Onishi 2008: 1). English education fever has created a serious psychological burden and sacrifice, not to mention the enormous amount of money needed for living and studying abroad.

Table 15.2 Korean students studying abroad by school level by year

Classification	1995	2000	2005	2006	2007
Elementary school students	235	705	8,148	13,814	12,341
Junior high school students	1,200	1,799	6,670	9,246	9,201
Senior high school students	824	1,893	5,582	6,451	6,126

Source: Kim, C.-H., 2008, simplified by author.

Note: Students who went abroad to accompany their parents stationed in foreign countries and those who have emigrated to foreign countries are excluded.

Lingual frenectomy

The length to which some Koreans will go to ensure successful language learning even extends to medical intervention. Ambitious parents take their children, including toddlers, to clinics for an operation known as lingual frenectomy. This severs the frenulum and is believed to make the tongue more flexible and adept at producing the sounds of English (Demick 2008). While there are no statistics about how many Korean children have undergone such operations, doctors have attributed the popularity of the tongue surgery to the boom in English instruction (Demick 2008).

The National Human Rights Commission of Korea produced a film to warn parents of the danger and ineffectiveness of the operation. The film contains a disturbing scene at the paediatrician's office where a boy is undergoing surgery on the tongue in order to be able to pronounce the 'r' in English better. The belief that children's English skills would improve with the surgery does not seem to have died away, however: 'in the wealthy neighborhoods of Seoul, the procedure has become widespread' (*Chosun Ilbo* 2004).

The diversification of Japanese society: more demand for English communication skills

Japan has recently been undergoing various social, cultural and linguistic changes. Notable phenomena concerning Japan's internationalization drive include a tourism promotion project called the 'Visit Japan Campaign', which started in 2003 in a bid to balance the number of incoming with outgoing tourists. The number of Japanese tourists overseas exceeded 16 million in 2002, while the number of tourists visiting Japan was only 5.24 million. Therefore, the government of then Prime Minister Koizumi aimed at doubling the number of foreign visitors to 10 million by 2010.

The Ministry of Land, Infrastructure, Transport and Tourism has been cooperating with the public and private sectors to promote Japan's attractiveness as a tourist destination. The headquarters at the Japan National Tourism Organization currently carries information about Japan on its website in nine languages: English, three dialects of Chinese, Korean, French, German, Thai and Russian (Japan National Tourism Organization 2008). The selection of these languages seems to have been in accordance with the locations of their overseas offices. Once foreign tourists arrive in Japan, actual contact with Japanese citizens will require communication in English more than in any other language. Opportunities for Japanese people to use at home the English which they have learned for at least six years are steadily on the increase. This in turn is a motivating factor for Japanese learners of English.

Receiving incoming information and people from overseas is one thing, but processing information about Japan in such a way that people in the world may have a better understanding of the country, which has been criticized for its insufficient visibility, is another. One attempt to improve the situation has been the establishment of Japan International Broadcasting Inc. (JIBtv), a company launched in April 2008 by the Japanese public broadcaster NHK. JIBtv started transmitting 24-hour programming in English through the internet and satellite within a year of its establishment, and now reaches 110 million households in North America, Europe, the Middle East, North Africa, South East Asia and other regions around the world. President and CEO Hatsuhisa Takashima says, 'why should people around the world need to depend on

American and European media for information on Japan? It's clear that Japan needs to make a bigger effort to tell the world about itself' (Japan International Broadcasting 2009). Their service is the first of its kind in Japan, and the expectation behind its launch is to increase Japan's international presence, and international knowledge and awareness of Japan.

Korean and Japanese Englishes for international communication

Despite all the strenuous attempts to teach a native-speaker variety of English and the Japanese proclivity for American English (Honna and Takeshita 1998, 2000), Korean English and Japanese English are two different varieties of English, influenced phonetically, semantically, grammatically and culturally by the native languages and cultures of their speakers. Here I list a small selection of examples.

The phonetic characteristics of Korean and Japanese may often make it difficult for Korean and Japanese speakers of English to pronounce certain words in the same way as Anglo native speakers. Sounds that do not exist in the Korean and Japanese languages are difficult to pronounce and therefore difficult to discern for Korea and Japanese users of English.

As neither Korean nor Japanese have the 'friction' sounds that exist in English such as /f/, /v/, /z/, TH, a Korean may pronounce 'film' as '*p*ilm', 'coffee' as 'co*p*ee', 'philosophy' as '*p*iloso*p*y' and 'fine' as '*p*ine,' whereas a Japanese may pronounce 'film' as '*hu*ilm', 'coffee' as 'co*h*ee', 'size' as 'si*s*e' and 'cosy' as 'co*j*ee'.

Korean and Japanese are languages whose lexical structure is consonant followed by vowel. Consonant clusters are therefore often difficult for Koreans and Japanese to pronounce. Each consonant may be accompanied by a vowel so that words such as 'disks', 'tasks' and 'asks' may be pronounced as 'dis*u*kusu', 'tas*u*kusu' and 'as*u*kus.'

Probably the most iconic feature of Japanese and Korean Englishes is that the difference between /l/ and /r/ is not sounded. These sounds are not distinctive in either Korean or Japanese. An English word containing both /l/ and /r/ such as 'liberal' and 'world' can thus be difficult to pronounce. 'Right' and 'light' and 'rice' and 'lice' may be sounded the same. Other sets of words Koreans and Japanese find difficult to differentiate include the pairs of long and short vowels, which are distinctive in Standard British English. As in many new varieties of English, these can be merged so that, for example, the sounds in 'live' and 'leave' may be pronounced the same.

As far as lexicon is concerned, divergences in meaning may occur when English words become part of the Korean and Japanese language as loan words and then reappear in the local variety of English, or when the definition of an English word does not coincide with that of its equivalent. A Korean speaker of English might say, 'We had a lot of audience at home', meaning they had many guests; the Korean equivalent of 'guest' can also mean 'customer' and 'audience'. Likewise, the Korean word for 'house' can also mean 'family', 'family members' and even 'family line', and therefore a Korean speaker of English might naturally say, 'Our house is rich' instead of 'We are a rich family.' An example from Japanese English may be 'He sent a happy life' instead of 'He spent a happy life', as the Japanese language has a word that can mean both 'send' and 'spend'.

Many 'foreign' words have become part of 'standard' Englishes and Japanese has contributed to such evolution. Here are but a few examples, whose spellings and definitions are based upon those in Merriam-Webster Online or in Dictionary.com.

1 Food: *daikon* (a large long hard white radish used especially in Asian cuisine), *mirin* (a sweet Japanese cooking wine made from fermented rice), *sake* (a Japanese alcoholic beverage of fermented rice often served hot), *satsuma* (any of several cultivated cold-tolerant mandarin trees that bear medium-sized largely seedless fruits with thin smooth skin), *shoyu* (a brown liquid sauce made by subjecting beans (as soybeans) to long fermentation and to digestion in brine), *sushi* (cold rice dressed with vinegar, formed into any of various shapes and garnished especially with bits of raw seafood or vegetables), *tofu* (a soft food product prepared by treating soybean milk with coagulants), *udon* (a thick Japanese noodle made from wheat flour and usually served in a soup).

2 People: *geisha* (a Japanese girl or woman who is trained to provide entertaining and light-hearted company especially for a man or a group of men), *honcho* (a group leader), *issei* (a Japanese immigrant especially to the United States), *nisei* (a son or daughter of Japanese immigrants who is born and educated in America and especially in the United States), *sansei* (a son or daughter of *nisei* parents who is born and educated in America and especially in the United States), *kamikaze* (a member of a Japanese air attack corps in World War II assigned to make a suicidal crash on a target), *otaku* (an avid collector or enthusiast, especially one who is obsessed by *anime*, video games, or computers and rarely leaves home), *samurai* (a military retainer of a Japanese daimyo practising the code of conduct of Bushido), *shogun* (one of a line of military governors ruling Japan until the revolution of 1867–8), *yakuza* (a Japanese gangster).

3 Clothing: *kimono* (a long robe with wide sleeves traditionally worn with a broad sash as an outer garment by the Japanese), *obi* (a broad sash worn especially with a Japanese kimono), *zori* (a flat thonged sandal usually made of straw, cloth, leather or rubber).

4 Martial arts: *dojo* (a school for training in various arts of self-defence), *judo* (a sport developed from *jujitsu* that emphasizes the use of quick movement and leverage to throw an opponent), *karate* (a Japanese art of self-defence employing hand strikes and kicks to disable or subdue an opponent).

5 Social phenomena and culture: *kaizen* (Japanese 'change for the better'), *karoshi* (death due to overwork or exhaustion from one's work), *keiretsu* (a powerful alliance of Japanese businesses often linked by cross-shareholding), *manga* (a Japanese comic book or graphic novel).

6 Miscellaneous: *harakiri* (ritual suicide by disembowelment practised by the Japanese *samurai* or formerly decreed by a court in lieu of the death penalty), *hibachi* (a charcoal brazier), *karaoke* (a device that plays instrumental accompaniments for a selection of songs to which the user sings along and that records the user's singing with the music), *origami* (the Japanese art or process of folding squares of paper into representational shapes), *tsunami* (a great sea wave produced especially by submarine earth movement or volcanic eruption).

The grammatical differences between English and Korean/Japanese produce certain features in Korean and Japanese Englishes. The lack of inflections in both Japanese and Koreans may be the reason why Japanese and Korean speakers of English overlook distinctions between singular and plural nouns. The same may be true with definite and indefinite articles. Another example in which the mother tongues could influence

Korean and Japanese speakers of English is the yes/no response. A conversation between a Korean and a Japanese speaker of English could turn out as follows:

Korean: Can you speak Chinese?
Japanese: No.
Korean: Oh, you can't speak Chinese?
Japanese: Yes. (meaning, 'Yes, what you've just said is correct. I can't speak Chinese.')

To what extent Korean and Japanese Englishes assume Korean-ness and Japanese-ness may depend not only on the experience of the speakers in using English in international communication, but the speakers' preference for sounding like Koreans or Japanese. While it is true that many may want to sound like a native speaker of English, others might wish to remain speakers of their own varieties of English. For example, the international scholar of Asian Englishes, Nobuyuki Honna, prefers to use idioms derived from Japanese, such as 'I can do it before breakfast,' to show something is easily done. Korean speakers of English might say 'we' when 'I' would do, which reflects the typical Korean respect for the family system.

Either intentionally or unintentionally, Korean and Japanese users of English will continue to use English in their own ways, adapting their language to accommodate to various audiences. Some international users of English may insist that the 'wrong' pronunciation should be corrected to sound more native-speaker-like, while others may wish to become familiar with varieties of English different from their own to enjoy, for example, successful communication with Korean and Japanese speakers of English. The chapters in this Handbook show how the English language has developed in, and spread to, different parts of the world. Korean and Japanese English can contribute to its growth. Speakers of different varieties of English will see more Korean-ness and Japanese-ness expressed in international situations as Korean and Japanese speakers of English continue to use English in their own ways as members of the international community and interchange ideas with English speakers from all over the world.

Conclusion

Both Korea and Japan have experienced heated debates triggered by proposals to give the English language official status (Hatta 2002; Honna and Takeshita 2004; Yoo 2005). The controversy continues over the status of the English language – for example, whether or not to make it official, whether or not to rely on native speakers or whether or not to encourage a more multilingual English language teaching approach are just some questions for which a solution acceptable to most has yet to be found.

Further debates will no doubt develop, and more social phenomena will arise out of people's remarkable enthusiasm to master 'good' English. Cultural, financial and personal sacrifices will inevitably continue to be made in this search for 'better' English. Many Koreans and Japanese have clearly seen that the English language continues to increase its importance as an international language and as a language that enables Koreans and Japanese to communicate with each other.

As young children learn English in schools, efforts should be made to help them become aware of the many different varieties of World Englishes and show that these function as useful tools for inter-regional and international communication. Raising people's awareness about the roles and functions of English, in particular, the roles of one's own variety of English, is the key to a more effective and productive use of English for Korean and Japanese people.

Note

1 STEP (the Society for Testing English Proficiency), a non-profit foundation established in 1963, is Japan's largest testing body that administers the Test in Practical English Proficiency, widely known in Japan as EIKEN. STEP pre-first level is said to be equivalent of TOEFL 550 (http://stepeiken.org/benefits/comparison-toefl.shtml).

Suggestions for further reading

Honna, N. and Takeshita, Y. (2005) 'English language teaching in Japan: policy plans and their implementations', *RELC Journal*, 36 (3): 363–83.
Park, J.-K. (2002) 'Teaching English as a global language in Korea: curriculum rhetoric and reality', *Asian Englishes*, 12 (1): 124–9.
Park, J.S. (2009) *The Local Construction of a Global Language: Ideologies of English in South Korea* (Language, Power and Social Process), Berlin: Mouton de Gruyter.
Smith, D. (2006) 'English in disguise: Japanese renditions of words lifted from English', *Asian Englishes*, 9 (2): 68–79.

References

Choi, S.-H. (1996) *Wenemin yenge kyosa sukup cheykyey kaypal yenku [A Study on Employing the EPIK teachers]*, Korean Educational Development Institute.
Chosun Ilbo (2004) 'Tongue operations popular in Korea for English education', 2 January. Online. Available http://english.chosun.com/w21data/html/news/200401/200401020031.html (accessed 20 November 2008).
——(2008) 'Gyeonggi province embraces English immersion', 28 March 2008. Online. Available http://english.chosun.com/w21data/html/news/200803/200803280014.html (accessed 4 December 2008).
Demick, B. (2008) 'A snip of the tongue and English is yours!' *Los Angeles Times*, 8 April. Online. Available www.tomcoyner.com/a_snip_of_the_tongue_and_english.htm (accessed 30 December 2008).
Educational Testing Service (2004–5) 'TOEFL Test and Score Data Summary 2004–05: Test Year Data'. Online. Available www.ets.org/Media/Research/pdf/TOEFL-SUM-0405-DATA.pdf (accessed 30 December 2008).
EIKEN (2005) 'Test in Practical English Proficiency'. Online. Available http://stepeiken.org/benefits/comparison-toefl.shtml (accessed 9 December 2008).
Hatta, Y. (2002) 'The issues of making English an official language and English education in Japan', *Bulletin of Faculty of Literature and Linguistics, Bunkyo University*, (*16*) 2. Online. Available www.bunkyo.ac.jp/faculty/lib/klib/kiyo/lit/l1602/l160205.pdf (accessed 15 November 2008).
Honna, N. (ed.) (2006) *Eigo wa ajia wo musubu [English Connects Asia]*, Tokyo: Tamagawa University Press.
——(2008) *English as a Multicultural Language in Asian Contexts: Issues and Ideas*, Tokyo: Kuroshio Publishers.

Honna, N. and Takeshita, Y. (1998) 'On Japan's propensity for native speaker English: a change in site', *Asian Englishes*, 1 (1): 117–37.

——(2000) 'English language teaching for international understanding in Japan', *EA Journal*, 18 (1): 60–78.

——(2004) 'English education in Japan today: the impact of changing policies', in H.W. Kam and R.Y.L. Wong (eds) *English Language Teaching in East Asia Today: Changing Policies and Practices* (2nd edition), Singapore: Eastern Universities Press, pp. 195–220.

Honna, N., Takeshita, Y., Higuchi, K. and Saruhashi, J. (2008) *Kokusai hikaku-de miru '"eigo-ga tsukaeru nihonjin" no ikuseinotameno kodo keikaku' no seika ni kansuru chosa kenkyu* [An International Comparative Study of the Outcome of 'Action Plan to Cultivate "Japanese with English Abilities"'], Tokyo: Aoyama Gakuin University.

Japan International Broadcasting (2009) 'About the company'. Online. Available http://jibtv.com/info/first_j.html (accessed 5 February 2009).

Japan National Tourism Organization (2008) 'Yokoso! Japan'. Online. Available www.visitjapan.jp/ (accessed 10 December 2008).

Japanese Ministry of Education, Culture, Sports, Science and Technology (Japanese MEXT) (2003) 'Regarding the establishment of an action plan to cultivate "Japanese with English abilities"'. Online. Available www.mext.go.jp/english/topics/03072801.htm (accessed 9 December 2008).

——(2006) 'School education'. Online. Available www.mext.go.jp/b_menu/shuppan/toukei/06122122 /001.pdf (accessed 3 January 2008).

——(2008) 'Shogakkou gakushu shidou yoryo kaisetsu: gaikokugo katsudo hen [Notes to the course of study: Foreign Language Activities]'.

Japanese Ministry of Foreign Affairs (2002) 'Comprehensive measures to accelerate reforms'. Online. Available www.mofa.go.jp/policy/economy/japan/measure0210-f.html (accessed 18 December 2008).

JET Programme (2008a) Home page. Online. Available www.jetprogramme.org/index.html

——(2008b) 'JET Programme participant numbers'. Online. Available www.jetprogramme.org/e/ introduction/statistics.html (accessed 3 January 2008).

Kim, C.-H. (2008) 'Brief statistics on Korean education, Korean Educational Development Institute'. Online. Available http://eng.kedi.re.kr/ (accessed 20 January 2008).

Kim, E.-G. (2008) 'History of English education in Korea', *The Korea Times*, 2 April. Online. Available www.koreatimes.co.kr/www/news/special/2009/02/181_21843.html (accessed 18 March 2009).

Kim, H. and Ko, K. (2008) 'Issues in hiring native English teachers in the elementary school: focused on Gyeonggi Province', *Primary English Education*, 14 (2): 23–43.

Kim, M.-Y. (2006) '"English villages" in South Korea: what do they really promote?' *NNEST Newsletter,* 8 (2). Online. Available www.tesol.org/s_tesol/article.asp?vid=151&DID=7118&sid=1&cid=718&iid =7112&nid=2982 (accessed 30 March 2009).

Korean Ministry of Education, Science and Technology (Korean MEST) (2009) 'Education system'. Online. Available http://english.mest.go.kr/main.jsp?idx=0201040101 (accessed 5 January 2009).

Lee, Su-Hyun (2007) 'High demand causes "Toefl crisis" in South Korea', *International Herald Tribune*, 14 May 2007. Online. Available www.iht.com/articles/2007/05/14/asia/english.php?page=1 (accessed 22 November 2008).

Matsumoto, S. (2003) 'Kankoku no sekaika to daigaku kyoiku: kankoku gaikokugo daigakkou no jirei wo toshite (Globalization and university education in South Korea: through the case of Hankuk University of Foreign Studies), *Toyo Daigaku Shakaigakubu Kiyo*, 41 (2): 147–80.

National Human Rights Commission of Korea (2003) *If You Were Me (Japan Version)*, Seoul: SPO.

National Institute for International Education (NIIED) (2008) 'English program in Korea'. Online. Available http://epik.go.kr/1 (accessed 20 December 2008).

Obunsha (2009) 'Shogakko no eigo katsudou ni kansuru anketo (Questionnaires on English activities in primary schools)'. Online. Available www.obunsha.co.jp/files/document/090127.pdf (accessed 29 January 2009).

Onishi, N. (2008) 'For English studies, Koreans say goodbye to Dad', *New York Times*, 8 June. Online. Available www.nytimes.com/2008/06/08/world/asia/08geese.html?ex=1370664000&en=7ccbc38c430d5 b35&ei=5124&partner=permalink&exprod=permalink (accessed 12 November 2008).

Park, J.-K. (2008) 'EPIK and NEST-NNEST collaboration in Korea revisited', *English Language and Literature Teaching*, 14 (4): 141–60.

——(2009) 'Education in Korea: the key to success', in N. Honna and Y. Takeshita (eds) *Understanding Asia*, Tokyo: Cengage Learning, pp. 62–3.

Park, S. (2008) 'On college-entrance exam day, all of South Korea is put to the test', *Wall Street Journal*, 12 November 2008. Online. Available http://online.wsj.com/article/SB122644964013219173.html?mod=todays_us_page_one (accessed 12 January 2009).

Seoul English Village in Suyu (n.d.) 'Information, recruiting'. Online. Available http://suyu.sev.go.kr/eng/notice/recruiting.asp (accessed 31 December 2008).

Shim, R.J. and Baik, M.J. (2004) 'English education in South Korea', in H.W. Kam and R.Y.L.Wong (eds) *English Language Teaching in East Asia Today: Changing Policies and Practices* (2nd edition), Singapore: Eastern Universities Press, pp. 241–61.

Song, D. (2006) 'English village: a successful model for innovation of public education', *Hankuk kyung-jae* (Korean Economy), 16 May 2006. Online. Available www.hankyung.com (accessed 5 September 2006).

Takeshita, Yuko (2002) 'Nihon [Japan]', in N. Honna (ed.) *Jiten: Ajia no saishin eigo jijyo [The Encyclopedia of the English Language Situation in Asia]*, Tokyo: Taishukanshoten, pp. 141–56.

Teach English in Asia (2008) 'English program in Korea'. Online. Available www.teachenglishinasia.net/english-program-in-korea-epik (accessed 20 January 2009).

The Economic Times (2008) 'Speak English, child! This is Korea'. Online. Available http://economictimes.indiatimes.com/ET_Cetera/Speak_English_child_This_is_Korea/articleshow/3077907.cms (accessed 30 December 2008).

Yoo, O.K. (2005) 'Discourses of English as an official language in a monolingual society: the case of South Korea', *Second Language Studies*, 23 (2): 1–44.

Yoshikawa, H. (2002) 'Kankoku [Republic of Korea]', in N. Honna (ed.) *Jiten: Ajia no saishin eigo jijyo [The Encyclopedia of the English Language Situation in Asia]*, Tokyo: Taishukanshoten, pp. 38–52.

16

Chinese English

A future power?

Xu Zhichang

Introduction

English has become 'the world's default mode' for communication (McArthur 2002: 13). As a *de facto* lingua franca, English and its associated cultures are increasingly pluralistic. According to Kachru (1996: 135), 'the term "Englishes" is indicative of distinct identities of the language and literature. "Englishes" symbolizes variation in form and function, used in linguistically and culturally distinct contexts, and a range of variety in literary creativity.'

As far as Chinese English (CE) is concerned, Kirkpatrick and Xu (2002: 278) suggest that since the great majority of the estimated 350 million Chinese who are currently learning English are far more likely to use it with other non-native speakers, the development of a variety of English 'with Chinese characteristics' may be an inevitable result. Kirkpatrick and Xu also predict that such a variety of English will be characterized by a number of linguistic and cultural norms derived from Chinese.

This chapter will review the definitions of CE, and then identify a selection of lexical, syntactic, discourse and pragmatic features of CE based on an analysis of a variety of CE data including interviews, newspaper articles and literary works. The chapter will conclude by considering the likelihood of CE becoming an established and powerful variety of English.

Background

Since the late 1970s, a number of Chinese scholars (Ge 1980; Huang 1988; Sun 1989; Cheng 1992; Li 1993; Wang 1994; Xie 1995; Jia and Xiang 1997; Du and Jiang 2001; Jiang 2002; Hu 2004, 2005; Poon 2006; Xu 2006) have been looking into the regional features of English in China, and distinguishing 'Chinglish' with what they call 'Sinicized English', 'Chinese-coloured English', 'China English' or 'Chinese English' to refer to a developing Chinese variety of English. In making such a distinction, Jiang (1995: 51) proposes that 'Chinglish', as the blend itself suggests, is something of a pidgin, or an 'interlanguage', a term used by Selinker to emphasize the structurally and phonologically intermediate status of a learner's language system between mother tongue and target language.

One of the first Chinese scholars to exemplify the distinction is Ge (1980). He refers to those English expressions that are uniquely Chinese as China English in contrast with Chinglish, e.g. *Four Books, Five Classics, eight-legged essay, May Fourth Movement, baihua wen* or *baihua*, and *four modernizations*. Ge's pioneering distinction is of significance not only because it has been frequently referred to in the studies of CE and has therefore started a debate over the issue of Chinglish versus China English (cf. Kirkpatrick and Xu 2002), but also because it has laid the groundwork for theories of World Englishes to be introduced into China (cf. Sun 1989).

Looking at 'Chinese varieties of English' from an overseas perspective, Cheng (1992: 162) claims that 'the varieties of English spoken by native Chinese around the world presumably share certain features because of common language background'. Cheng further claims that 'there appears to be a kind of English peculiar to the Chinese culture: one might call it Sinicized English' (1992: 163). Cheng's 'Sinicized English' resembles Ge's 'China English' in that it refers primarily to lexical items and phrases that are unique to Chinese contexts.

Another Chinese scholar, Huang (1988), has reiterated the distinction between Chinglish and China English, but his term for China English is 'Chinese-coloured English'. He defines the term as 'the English that has been adapted to Chinese ideology and civilization, and also enriched by this adaptation' (1988: 47). He also stresses that 'it is, first of all, correct, and secondly Chinese coloured' (1988: 47).

In the meantime, Gui (1988) has proposed the existence of a 'Chinese-style English', stating that

> there does exist a kind of Chinese-style English in China, but it comprises a continuum. On the one end is the learner's English used by Chinese students ... On the other end are the well-educated users of English ... In between the two ends, there exist variations.
>
> (Gui 1988: 13–14)

Wang (1994: 7) discussed 'China English' in the sense of a variety of English and he defined it as 'the English used by the Chinese people in China, being based on standard English and having Chinese characteristics'. Wang's definition of China English has been questioned by Li (1993), especially with regard to the first two elements in the definition. Li (1993: 19) argues that 'it is nonetheless Westerners who unavoidably use vocabulary of China English when they talk about China, and therefore China English has exceeded the confines of its native land'. Li has also questioned the existence of 'Standard English', on which Wang's definition is based. Instead, Li uses the term 'Normative English' (1993: 19), and therefore revises the definition of China English as

> the lexis, sentence structure and discourse that have Chinese characteristics. It takes Normative English as a core, and it expresses things that are uniquely Chinese. It bears no mother tongue (Chinese) interference, and it is involved in English communications by means of transliterations, loan translations and semantic shifts.
>
> (Li 1993: 19)

Li's definition of China English, especially the insistence that it contains no influence from Chinese, has itself been challenged by Xie, who thus argues that China English is 'an interference variety' (1995: 7). Xie defines China English as 'an interference variety used by Chinese in cross-cultural communication. The interference is expressed at varying levels of language, including language itself as well as schema and culture' (Xie 1995: 10).

Jia and Xiang (1997: 11) have reviewed the notion of 'China English' and they define China English as 'a variety of English used by speakers of Chinese, based on standard English, and with inevitable Chinese characteristics or characteristics that help disseminate Chinese culture'. They have also positively commented on the 'feasibility' and 'significance' of the existence of 'Chinese English', saying that

> only if we admit the existence of Chinese English, can we decide, on the basis of identifying and analyzing features of English nativization in China, what features are unavoidable by Chinese speakers so that in English language teaching the students are not forced to overcome what they should and could not overcome.
>
> (Jia and Xiang 1997: 12)

Jiang (1995: 51–2) considers 'China English' to be a member of the big family of World Englishes with Chinese characteristics. Yan (2002: 218) also takes a World Englishes approach to the study of CE, defining CE as 'the spread, use and variation of English in China'. In addition, Du and Jiang (2001) and Jiang (2002) have provided an overview of the ongoing research on CE. What the Chinese scholars have in common is their intention to distinguish Chinglish from their versions of CE.

Based on the research of CE in the past three decades, a number of researchers (Pang 2002; Jiang 2003; Hu 2004) argue that CE has become a member of World Englishes. Pang (2002: 24) suggests that 'as a member of World Englishes, Chinese English should be researched from varying perspectives, including sociolinguistics, cross-cultural communication, pragmatics, stylistics and translatology'. Jiang (2003: 3–7) argues that 'English is indeed becoming a Chinese language', and that 'the Chinese variety of English will become more and more distinctive as an independent member of the family of world Englishes'.

For the operational purpose of this chapter, CE is defined as

> a developing variety of English, which is subject to ongoing codification and normalization processes. It is based largely on the two major varieties of English, namely British and American English. It is characterized by the transfer of Chinese linguistic and cultural norms at varying levels of language, and it is used primarily by Chinese for intra- and international communication.
>
> (Xu 2006: 287)

Based on this operational definition, speakers of Chinese English comprise a huge number of Chinese learners, users and professionals of English. According to Kirkpatrick (2007: 146), 'this number of people learning and speaking English will lead to a distinctive Chinese variety of English'.

Linguistic features of CE

As far as the linguistic features of regional varieties of English are concerned, Bolton (2003: 46) argues that

> the identification of sets of distinctive linguistic items typically associated with a new variety is a central feature of the discussion of such Englishes as Indian English, Malaysian English, Singapore English and Philippine English, as well as other varieties around the world.

This indicates that systematic research on the linguistic features of CE is central to the discussion of CE as a variety of English. This chapter describes lexical, syntactic, discourse and pragmatic features of CE, while acknowledging that phonological features of CE are also distinctive (cf. Hung 2002; Deterding 2006; Schneider 2009). According to Deterding (2006: 176), many different languages and dialects are spoken in China, so there is substantial variation in the English of speakers from different regions. However, 'there are also some features in common, and these mark the English of speakers from China as distinct from other varieties of English'.

The data used to investigate the lexical, syntactic, discourse and pragmatic features of CE include 36 interviews (referred to as the ID data) with Chinese university and postgraduate students. They include science and engineering students, who have passed their national College English Test Band 4, and English and linguistics major postgraduate students. The features of their English represent the features used by expert learners and competent speakers of CE. The data also include 20 newspaper articles (referred to as the ND data) from the *China Daily*; and 12 short stories (referred to as the SD data) from Ha Jin's collection of short stories *The Bridegroom* (Jin 2000). The ID data represent spoken CE, whereas the ND and SD data represent written CE.

Lexical features of CE

Knowlton (1970) and Cannon (1988) have extensively documented Chinese borrowings in English, the number of which has been increasing. 'When Chinese speakers of English refer to things Chinese, they naturally have to use certain expressions that may not have existed in other varieties of English' (Kirkpatrick and Xu 2002: 270–1).

The ID, ND and SD data for this chapter have provided ample lexical evidence of words and expressions that are specific to Chinese language and culture. For example,

1   In his keynote speech addressing the conference, Hu Jintao, general-secretary of the CPC Central Committee, pointed out that 'if the benefits of *xiaokang* cannot be attained by rural people, China will fail to live up to its dream of a *xiaokang* society.'

(ND data)

Xiaokang society was a concept put forward at the 16th National Congress of the Communist Party of China (CPC) (8–14 November 2002). *Xiaokang* literally means 'a comfortable level of living; a better-off life; moderate prosperity'.

2   'Your name?' the chief asked, apparently reading out the question from a form.
      'Chiu Maguang.'
      'Age?'
      'Thirty-four.'
      'Profession?'
      'Lecturer.'
      '*Work unit*?'
      'Harbin University.'
      '*Political status*?'
      'Communist Party member.'

                                                                         (SD data)

Work unit refers to a working and living place (a factory or a school, etc.) where most urban residents have lived and worked since 1950 and where many still do. A *work unit* would usually provide housing, schooling, health care, food ration coupons and other basic goods and services to its staff and their family members. *Political status* is another concept with Chinese characteristics. The *political status* can be a Communist Party member, a Youth League Member, a Young Pioneer, or simply 'the masses'.

3   R (Researcher): Interesting. You mean the farmers are busier during the spring and autumn. Now, what do they usually do in winter or in the hot summer?
      P1 (postgraduate student 1): Take a rest. And do some … how to say …
      P2 (postgraduate student 2): *Fuye*.
      P1: Yeah. *Fuye*.
      R: *Fuye*. That's an interesting word. Now how do you explain it in English, the *fuye*?
      P1: It's kind of work they do in their spare time.

                                                                         (ID data)

The nearest equivalent of *fuye* in English is sideline or side occupation. It refers to an activity pursued in addition to one's regular occupation. What makes *fuye* a characteristic Chinese concept is that *fuye* was once officially forbidden or discouraged in the days of people's communes. Those who undertook *fuye* had to keep it quiet. However, since China's opening up and reforms, when 'getting rich is glorious', people have been encouraged to practice *fuye*.

The distinctiveness of such words and expressions as *xiaokang, work unit, political status* and *fuye* lies not only in the fact that they are characteristic of the English spoken or written by users and learners of English in China, but also in the fact that readers or listeners have to call upon knowledge of China in order to fully understand these words. Benson (2002: 162) proposes that words unique to certain regional varieties of English should generally have 'some degree of currency and stability' and should 'originate in the region concerned or be formally, semantically or collocationally distinctive from usage elsewhere in the world'.

The CE words comprise three distinct categories, namely Chinese loanwords in English, nativized English words and common English words. To adopt Kachru's (1982) analogy of the three circles, the Chinese loanwords in English form the inner circle CE lexis, while the nativized English words form the outer circle CE lexis, and the expanding circle CE lexis consists of the common English words, shared by users of the majority of English varieties.

Inner circle CE lexis refers to Chinese loanwords in English, which come primarily from two sources: Cantonese and Putonghua. As Britain had an early trading-base in Canton (the current Guangdong province), many early Chinese loanwords in English were based on the Cantonese pronunciation, such as *bok choy*, *chow mein*, *dimsum* and *kwai-lo*. However, Putonghua has now become the major source for Chinese loanwords in English. Examples of Chinese loanwords based on Putonghua include *fengshui*, *pipa*, *guanxi* and the word *Putonghua* itself. In addition to the transliterated loanwords, loan translations also form part of the inner circle CE lexis. Examples include *barefoot doctor*, *the Cultural Revolution*, *Great Leap Forward*, *Red Guard*, *the reform and opening up* and *a well-off society*.

Some loanwords (such as *Taichi*, *tofu*, *fengshui*, *Red Guard* and *the Cultural Revolution*) have existed in English for some time. These words can be referred to as the 'standing' Chinese loanwords in English. In contrast, there are also *ad hoc* loanwords, which arise to ensure effective communication involving Chineseness. Such loanwords are usually used among speakers of Chinese communicating in English when certain terms or concepts involving Chineseness do not seem to have any explicit or 'standing' equivalents in English. These *ad hoc* Chinese loanwords are mostly transliterated from Chinese into English as communication takes place. Examples of *ad hoc* loanwords found in the ID data include *fuye* (a part-time job that provides additional income), *ganqing* (emotional involvement or attachment), *qinqing* (emotional attachment among family members) and *maodun* (a contradiction or a dilemma).

Outer circle CE lexis consists of nativized English words, whose original meanings in English have shifted to a greater or lesser extent in Chinese contexts. For example, CE speakers tend to equate *face* in English with *miànzi* in Putonghua, therefore, *face* in CE can be associated with self-image, pride, honour and sometimes embarrassment.

The key feature of the outer circle CE lexis is semantic change based on Chinese contexts. Such semantic change takes place in either the denotation or the connotation of a word. The former involves semantic broadening or narrowing, while the latter involves amelioration or pejoration. In semantic broadening, 'the word takes on a wider, more general meaning than it had previously' (Radford *et al.* 1999: 261). Take, for example, the word *cadre* in example (4) below,

4   As the city will host the 2008 Olympics Games, *cadres* at all government levels in Beijing should grasp the valuable chance to make better success at their jobs under the guidance of the important thought of 'Three Represents', Hu said.

(ND data)

Cadre is used both in CE and in British English. According to the *Cambridge Advanced Learner's Dictionary* (CALD), it means 'a small group of trained people who form the basic unit of a military, political or business organization' or 'a member of such a group'. However, *cadre* in CE can be used to refer to anyone who is in charge of a group of people in an organization. Thus, its meaning in CE is broadened to a sense that is close to the English word *leader*.

'The opposite of semantic broadening is semantic narrowing, with the word taking on a more restricted meaning than before' (Radford *et al.* 1999: 262). The term *migrant workers* is an example of semantic narrowing in CE.

5   Such *migrant workers* could find employment in township enterprises or the rapidly growing service sectors of cities.

(ND data)

Migrant workers refer to those who have temporarily migrated from rural areas to the major cities in China. The number of these *migrant workers* has been increasing since the 1980s, and the reasons for this 'tidal wave of peasant workers', as it is called in Chinese, are mostly economic.

'Pejorations involve the development of a less favourable meaning or connotation for a particular word', while ameliorations are the opposite to pejorations (Radford *et al.* 1999: 262). Take for example *comrade* and *individualism* in CE and English. Gao (1993) conducted surveys in 1988 and 1991 on the semantic change of the two expressions in China with groups of students and staff including both Chinese and native speakers of English. She found that the native speakers of English group view *individualism* positively, in that it embodies self-actualization with an emphasis on individual freedom and rights, while they associate *comrade* with autocracy and the former Soviet KGB members. However, the Chinese group associate *comrade* with 'equality' and 'friendship', and *individualism* with 'selfishness' or 'personalism'. Therefore, it can be argued that *comrade* and *individualism*, when used by CE speakers, bear more or less ameliorative and pejorative connotations respectively. However, Gao (1993) also discovered that the meanings of *individualism* and *comrade* change over time, with the meaning of *individualism* shifting from 'selfishness' to 'sense of independence and competition', and *comrade* from 'equality' to 'social distance'. *Individualism* in CE, pejorative as it was, has been ameliorated from its very pejorative sense over the past few decades in China, while *comrade* in CE has been steadily gaining a pejorative sense. Dramatic semantic shifts can take place also over time. For example, 'comrade' (*tóngzhì*) has taken on a new meaning of a gay or a homosexual if used in China (cf. Zhou 2004).

An interesting feature of the ID data is the high frequency of *ad hoc* loanwords. Examples include *Beida* (Beijing University), *Qinghua* (Tsinghua University), *huoguo* (hot pot), *malatang* (a specific hot and spicy food in Sichuan), *dandan mian* (a type of noodles in Sichuan) and *jiajiao* (private tutoring).

An interesting feature of the ND data, on the other hand, is that most transliterated Chinese borrowings in their *pinyin* forms are followed by either loan translations or explanations. This pattern is relatively common when discussing things or concepts that are uniquely Chinese. For example, 'addressing the meeting, Hu Jintao, general-secretary of the CPC Central Committee, said these goals will help China attain its cherished dream of building a *xiaokang* society, which means well-off in the broadest of senses, not only materially, but socially'.

In contrast to the ID data and the ND data, the SD data is distinctive in its more frequent use of loan translations. In the SD data, instances of loan translations outnumber other types of inner circle CE words. Similar to the loan translations in the ID and ND data, the loan translations in the SD data are also of apparent Chinese reference, e.g. *national food coupons*, *Street Committee*, *residence card* and *grain rations*.

A second distinctive feature of the SD data is the use of Chinese idioms and pro-verbs. Examples of these idioms and proverbs include *a flowered pillowcase* (someone who is beautiful/handsome in appearance, but not capable of doing anything), *since you are already in here, you may as well stay and make the best of it* (a saying by Chair-man Mao), and *when a scholar runs into soldiers, the more he argues, the muddier his point becomes* (a Chinese proverb). These expressions reflect local culture and display linguistic creativity.

Syntactic features of CE

Compared with the well-edited written ND and SD data, the unedited spoken ID data contain a number of features that are unique to spoken CE, as well as some features of Chinese learners' English. According to Givón (2002: 75), 'the grammar of oral lan-guage is replete with features that are unique to face-to-face communication'. Second, one of the potential issues with the ID data is that it is difficult to determine the sys-tematization of the identified syntactic features. Although the ID data was collected from expert learners and competent users of CE, some features could still be develop-mental errors. However, the codification and normalization processes of CE are ongo-ing, so it is worth exploring these syntactic features, and considering to what extent they may develop into systematic features of CE.

In analysing the ID data, I primarily looked for syntactic expressions that are seemingly deviant from those in native varieties of English, with Quirk *et al.* (1985) as a major reference. The major deviant syntactic expressions observed from the ID data include adjacent default tense (ADT), null-subject/object utterances (NS/O), co-occurrence of connective pairs (CCP), subject pronoun copying (SPC), yes–no response (Y/NR), topic comment (TC), unmarked OSV (OSV) and inversion in subordinate finite wh- clauses (ISC). Examples of these are illustrated below.

Adjacent default tense (ADT) means that if the overall tense of an utterance is marked in the context of the utterance, then the 'adjacent' finite verbs in the utterance can (but may not necessarily) be set in their 'default' forms. For example:

6   When I was a 7 years old, I first came here and lived with my relatives.
    So, maybe at that time, I think Beijing is a good city as a child.

In comparison, instances of ADT in most native varieties of English are 'virtually ungrammatical' (Quirk *et al.* 1985: 183–4).

Null-subject/object (NS/O) means that in an utterance or a sentence, there are null subject or object pronouns in the positions where they can be expected. This syntactic feature occurs in Chinese, and it is known as 'zero pronouns' (Li and Thompson 1981: 657–8). This feature is also partly known as 'pro-drop' or 'null subject parameter'. In the ID data, examples of NS/O occurrences include:

7(a) 'Okay, yes. What do you do in your spare time, usually?'
     'Sometimes – just play basketball, and sometimes – go to the Beijing Library, and sometimes – just play some games on computer.'
7(b) We can see movies, and other activities about English. Yes, I like – very much.

Co-occurrence of connective pairs (CCP) means that in an utterance or a sentence where there are subordinate and main clauses, for example indicating cause or concession, the connective pairs *because* and *so*, and *although/though* and *but* are both used. For example,

> 8(a) Yes, *although* it's not as big as Beijing, *but* I like it, because I was born in it. I have some special feeling about my home town.
>
> 8(b) 'When you first got on to the Great Wall, how did you feel?'
> 'Some stranger feelings, *because* I couldn't get the same feeling as others, *because* others always feel powerful, and happy or others, *because* I didn't have some special feeling, *so* I think it's very strange.'

Subject pronoun copying (SPC) is a feature of spoken CE. It is also a feature that is used in native varieties of English for 'stylistic effect', and it can be a useful device when the subject is very long. However, in the ID data, the use of SPC is unmarked. For example:

> 9 I'm the youngest one in my family, so I think *my parents, they* have no interest in … on … in … me.

As far as the feature of yes–no response (Y/NR) is concerned, in most native varieties of English, 'since the *yes–no* question typically asks for a response on the truth value of the corresponding statement, the responses coincide with an assertion (*yes*) or a denial (*no*) of its truth value' (Quirk *et al.* 1985: 793). Similarly the selection of *yes* or *no* is determined by whether it asserts or negates the implied or given statement. The use of *yes* or *no* is not determined by the speaker's agreement or disagreement with a previous speaker's statement. In the ID data, this Y/NR syntactic feature occurs frequently. Examples include:

> 10(a) 'You do not want to make a living by playing guitar on the street.'
> '*Yes*. Of course not.'
>
> 10(b) 'So, have you been to many different places in Beijing, or around China?'
> 'No.'
> 'Okay, now. You haven't been to many places.'
> '*Yes*.'

The feature of Topic Comment (TC) occurs in most native varieties of English. In Radford *et al.*'s (1999: 248) example, *Cigars, the president never smokes them in front of his wife*, the word *cigars* functions as the 'topic' of the sentence. TC is also a CE syntactic feature, and it is closely related to the 'topic prominence' of Chinese. According to Li and Thompson (1981: 15),

> one of the most striking features of Mandarin sentence structure, and one that sets Mandarin apart from many other languages, is that in addition to the grammatical relations of 'subject' and 'direct object', the description of Mandarin must also include the element 'topic'.

Examples of TC from the ID data include:

11(a) And the second is I think *Beijing* … there are many old buildings.

11(b) You know, I think *this society*, the people get more and more practical.

Another syntactic feature of spoken CE is unmarked OSV. English, according to Quirk *et al.* (1985: 51), is commonly described as a 'fixed-word-order language'. For instance, 'in English the positions of subject, verb, and object are relatively fixed.' In contrast, Chinese is not an easy language to classify in terms of word order, according to Li and Thompson (1981: 19–21). The following examples from the ID data show that it is common for speakers of CE to pre-pose the object in a sentence, thus making the order of OSV.

12(a) Yes, I think *many many easy words we have forgotten.*

12(b) Probably *some other kind of jobs I* also *want to try.*

Inversion in subordinate finite wh- clauses (ISC) refers to the inverted subject-operator in subordinate finite wh- clauses, as if it were in an independent wh- question. For example,

13(a) I really don't know *what is* International English.

13(b) It's actually … um … it is made in the kind of … I don't know *what is … how should I put it*, but it is made of bamboo.

ISC may also occur in native varieties of English. For example, Quirk *et al.* (1985: 1051–2) state that 'although the subordinate clause usually does not have subject-operator inversion, such inversion may occur, particularly when the clause functions as complement and the superordinate verb is BE or when it functions as appositive'.

As far as the ND data is concerned, the major identified syntactic features include 'nominalization', 'coordination of clause constituents' and 'modifier-modified sequencing'.

Quirk *et al.* (1985: 1288–9) define 'nominalization' as a noun phrase which has 'a systematic correspondence with a clause structure'. Based on this definition, I have identified a large number of nominalized noun phrases (NNPs) in the ND data. Table 16.1 shows the number of nominalized noun phrases and their average number per sentence in four of the news articles in the ND data.

Examples of nominalizations in the ND data include:

14(a) The Central Committee of the Communist Party of China (CPC) and the State Council decided to increase *investment in the sectors of education, health and culture in rural areas.*

Table 16.1 Distribution of nominalized noun phrases (NNPs) in four articles in the ND data

	Number of NNPs	*Number of sentences*	*Average number of NNPs per sentence*
ND-4	18	13	1.4
ND-7	24	17	1.4
ND-13	12	9	1.3
ND-20	24	18	1.3
Subtotal	78	57	1.4

14(b) *A just concluded two-day rural work conference* has ushered in a new development stage for work in the three issues.

14(c) Therefore, it is *a fair judgement as well as timely recognition* that agricultural development has made huge contributions to and laid a solid foundation for the country's present-day accomplishments.

According to Li and Thompson (1981: 575), different languages may employ different strategies for nominalization, and in Chinese, 'nominalization involves placing the particle *de* after a verb, a verb phrase, a sentence, or a portion of a sentence including the verb'.

Another feature, coordination of clause constituents, refers to the parallel structure of two or more conjoins within a sentence. According to Quirk *et al.* (1985: 941–2), 'a conjoin may be any constituent such as a predicate, a predication, a phrase, or a word'. They also state that the important point for a coordinate construction is that 'the conjoins of each construction are parallel to one another in meaning, function, and also (generally) in form'. Examples of coordinate construction in the ND data include (with the conjoins being marked by square brackets):

15(a) To close the economic gap, top officials agreed yesterday to [deepen the ongoing reforms on the grain distribution system], [further restructure the agricultural sector] and [regulate agricultural business, by making it more efficient and structured].

15(b) The main focus of the work over the coming weeks will be [improving the reliability of the craft], [completing the manned operating system which will act as a back up to mission control] and also [adding the finishing touches to the space capsule, to provide a comparatively comfortable environment for the astronauts].

While coordination of clause constituents is also common in native varieties of English, what makes the construction unique in CE is that the construction, when being used, is always coupled with Chinese pragmatic motivations. For example, when it comes to non-finite verbs, predicates, predications and nominal *-ing* participle clauses, or in a more general term, verb-related phrases or clauses, chances are that they come in threes. The figure 3, in particular, is likely to be used when verb-related phrases or clauses are expressed in China.

Another syntactic feature of CE is the modifying–modified sequence. Kirkpatrick (1996: 107) argues that

while topic-comment is an important sentence type in Modern Standard Chinese and is significant in determining ways of sequencing information at sentence level, it is not the only sentence type. In addition, the modifying–modified sequence, which is expressed by the subordinate clause to main clause sequence in complex sentences, is also an important information sequencing principle in MSC.

In describing the positions of subordinate clauses, Quirk *et al.* (1985: 1037) propose that the subordinate clause can be in an initial, medial or final position. They also point out that 'one of the factors which determine the order in which the constituent clauses of a sentence are arranged is the principle of RESOLUTION, the principle that states that the final clause should be the point of maximum emphasis' and that in English 'it is, in fact, a dominant tendency of syntactic structure that the greatest depth of subordination is reached in the final part of the sentence' (Quirk *et al.* 1985: 1037–9).

In my investigation of the positions of subordinate clauses in the ND data, I take four subordinators for finite clauses into consideration. They are *although (though)*, *because*, *if* and *when*. The concordancing throughout the ND data shows a tendency for written CE to prefer to place subordinate clauses in sentence initial position. This is especially true with *although/though-*, *if-* and *when-* clauses. To account for the phenomenon, I have looked into how Chinese speakers normally place the subordinate clauses initiated by the Chinese equivalents of *although/though*, *if*, *when* and *because*. According to Li and Thompson (1981: 633–55), in many sentences composed of two linked clauses, 'each of the two constituent clauses contains a linking element, the first clause having a forward-linking element and the second one a backward-linking element'. Examples of forward-linking elements in Chinese include *de shíhòu* (when, while), *yǐhòu* (after), *yǐqián* (before), *de huà / rúguǒ / jiǎrú / jiǎshǐ / yàoshi* (if), *chúfēi* (unless), *jíshǐ / jiùshì* (even if), *suīrán* (although/though), *yīnwèi / yóuyú* (because) and *zhǐyào* (if only, as long as). Examples of backward-linking elements include *kěshi / dànshi / búguò / ránér* (but, nevertheless, however), *wèideshì* (in order to), *suǒyǐ* (so) and *yīnwèi* (because).

It can be noted that the Chinese equivalents of *although/though*, *if* and *when* all belong to the forward-linking elements. That means the subordinate clauses preceded by these equivalents tend to be placed in sentence initial position. Therefore, it can be predicted that speakers of CE prefer to place the *although/though-*, *if-* and *when-* subordinate clauses in the sentence initial position, functioning as modifying clauses, whereas the main clauses are placed in the final position, functioning as the modified clauses. Thus, we have the modifying–modified sequence.

Discourse and pragmatic features of CE

'Cultural expectations' about how texts are spoken or written are as important as vocabulary and grammar (Kirkpatrick 2000: 86). This dimension of research is largely in line with discourse analysis and cross-cultural pragmatics. Speakers of CE by definition possess competing sets of discourse and pragmatic knowledge of both Chinese and English. When communicating with other speakers in English, they inevitably carry out not only lexical and syntactic transfers from Chinese into English, but also discourse and pragmatic transfers.

In the analysis of the ID data, the use of what I have termed 'ancestral home-town discourse' is of particular interest. CE speakers talk about their ancestral home towns when they first meet, because their home towns constitute part of their identity. Topics covered include historical events, food, weather, architecture, dialect and typical cultural activities. In addition, CE interlocutors also readily enquire about the speaker's home town. This supports Scollon and Scollon's (2001: 100) position that 'a spoken discourse represents the joint product of all of the participants in the situation'. This 'joint product' can be culturally specific. The social bonds among people from the same ancestral home town can often play a part in formulating a social *guanxi* network. Table 16.2 illustrates the 'schema' of CE 'ancestral home town' discourse as identified in the data.

It is noteworthy that the topics concerning location, size, special food and dialect(s) of the home town always occur, while other topics are optional depending on the contexts of communication.

293

Table 16.2 'Ancestral home town' discourse of CE speakers

ancestral home town	location size special food dialect(s) historical significance typical festival activity weather architecture speaker's feeling for it ('I love it') positive remarks ('It's beautiful')

The SD data also displays a number of discourse and pragmatic features of CE. Zhang (2002: 311) argues that throughout Ha Jin's works, 'elements of Chinese discourse patterns are interwoven in the text in almost seamless fashion'. These socio-pragmatic discourses are often reflections of the cultural norms and social values of Chinese society throughout the last quarter of the twentieth century. The variety of discourse in the SD data includes (1) discourse of 'political status' and 'political life', implying that Communist Party membership and the Youth League Party membership are key indicators of political status; (2) discourse of 'law' and 'social order', implying that the power of law can sometimes be overridden by social hierarchical power; (3) discourse of 'power' and 'hierarchy', implying that power is a symbol of privileges, and that power can be taken advantage of; (4) discourse of '*guānxi*' and 'backdoor practice', implying that people involved in *guānxi* or a *guānxi* network are generally expected to exchange favours in terms of goal-directed interpersonal or inter-organizational strategic interactions; (5) discourse of 'work unit (or *dānwèi*)' and 'welfare', implying that a work unit is closely associated with the welfare of its employees, and that the interpersonal relationships among employees within a work unit are affected by their share of welfare, often resulting in the sense of inequality, unfairness and injustice among the employees; and (6) discourse of 'face', and 'name and honour', implying that such concepts as face, name and honour are paramount in Chinese society.

The discourse types and features of CE that are reflected in the SD data are interwoven with the pragmatic features of CE. The study of CE in pragmatic terms is essentially about the assumptions, purposes and the kinds of speech acts CE speakers perform when they communicate in English. Much of what CE speakers say and communicate is determined by the social relationships shaped by Chinese cultural values and pragmatic norms. In terms of English nativization, Li (1998: 39) argues that 'there is no reason to see systematic deviations from Anglo-American norms at the pragmatic and discourse levels as errors'. In order to make sense of Ha Jin's short stories data, readers are expected to understand that the Chinese discourse and pragmatic features reflect Chinese cultural values and pragmatic norms.

The pragmatic features of the SD data typically involve assumptions that are generally shared by speakers of Chinese, and the expectations based on Chinese cultural discourses and schemata. For example, the use of Chairman Mao's quotes can convey meanings far beyond what the quotations literally mean. Li (1998: 37) has expressed the same argument about the Chinese quoting the words of authorities by saying that echoing the voice of some established authority, past or present, is one way of showing shared cultural values and, in so doing, helps preserve group harmony, which is collectively prized much more than the individual's display of personal whims or bright ideas.

For example, in the SD data, when Mr Chiu was mistakenly arrested and put in detention, he reminded himself that he should have taken the detention in his stride. He recalled Mao's writing to a hospitalized friend 'since you are already in here, you may as well stay and make the best of it'. The intended meanings associated with the quote from Chairman Mao include: (1) Mr Chiu's respect for social hierarchy, which indirectly indicated that he was a good law-abiding citizen; (2) Mr Chiu's learnedness and good education, as being compatible with his social status as a university lecturer; and (3) Mr Chiu's belief in the power of an unchallengeable truism as embedded in the quote.

The use of Chairman Mao's quotes is only one of the pragmatic features of the SD data. Other pragmatic features of the SD data are partly encoded in the use of curse words, proverbs and address terms. 'The use of curse words and obscenities in literature often reflects the underlying cultural values of a particular society' (Zhang 2002: 307). In the SD data, for example, the loan translation curse words such as 'egg of a tortoise' and 'an arrogant son of a rabbit' occur.

Address terms are also of pragmatic significance in Chinese society. The SD data is full of examples in which address terms bear pragmatic meanings. People in the short stories sometimes extract social meanings out of the address terms. For example,

16 The man cleared his throat and said, '**Miss Chen**, we appreciate your interest in the job.' She was taken aback by his way of addressing her, not as a '**Comrade**,' as though she were a foreigner or a Taiwanese.

(SD data)

CE: a rising expanding circle variety and a future power?

Much research has been conducted on South and South East Asian Englishes. In China, however, whether the 'WE-ness' of World Englishes includes CE and Chinese speakers of English is still debatable. However, increasing evidence shows that CE has developed into a stage which makes it worthy of serious linguistic analysis.

It is, in the view of the author, likely that CE will become a variety of English, and a powerful one at that. First, the guestimated 350 million Chinese who are currently learning English will speed up the development of CE and make it powerful. Second, as a result of China's economic and sociopolitical reforms and the 'open-door' policies, rapid changes have taken place in China over the past half century. These changes are enhancing and increasing the communication between China and the rest of the world, and therefore helping the global spread of English in China. Bolton and Tong (2002: 180) predict that 'with China's emergence as a world power, with its increasing integration into the world system, China will need English to project its own presence on the regional and the international scene'. The identification and analyses of the linguistic features of CE suggest that this English will become a variety of English and it will be important for the international English-speaking community to become familiar with it.

Research on CE as a variety of English in the expanding circle will make a valuable contribution to the studies of World Englishes. Berns (2005: 92) has pointed out that:

> As more research is conducted and more studies made of the sociolinguistic reality of English across Expanding Circle contexts, it becomes increasingly difficult to take seriously the charge that the Englishes of this circle are products of poor teaching and learning. In fact, current activity among the users of Expanding Circle Englishes in language policy and planning and in language teaching pedagogy and practice evidence the irrelevance of purist and clitist positions.

This is indeed the dawning of the age of expanding circle Englishes in general and of CE in particular. With ongoing codification and normalization, CE shall become a major variety of English, and a powerful member of the World Englishes family.

Suggestions for further reading

Bolton, Kingsley (2003) *Chinese Englishes: A Sociolinguistic History*, Cambridge: Cambridge University Press.

Kirkpatrick, Andy and Xu, Zhichang (2002) 'Chinese pragmatic norms and "China English"', *World Englishes*, 21 (2): 269–79.

Kirkpatrick, Andy (2007) 'World Englishes: implications for international communication and English language teaching', Cambridge: Cambridge University Press, pp. 137–52.

Xu, Zhichang (2008) 'Analysis of syntactic features of Chinese English', *Asian Englishes*, 11 (2): 4–31.

References

Benson, P. (2002) 'Hong Kong words: variation and context', in K. Bolton (ed.) *Hong Kong English: Autonomy and Creativity*, Hong Kong: Hong Kong University Press.

Berns, M. (2005) 'Expanding on the Expanding Circle: where do WE go from here?' *World Englishes*, 24: 85–93.

Bolton, K. (2003) *Chinese Englishes: A Sociolinguistic History*, Cambridge: Cambridge University Press.

Bolton, K. and Tong, Q.S. (2002) 'English in China: interdisciplinary perspectives', *World Englishes*, 21: 177–80.

Cannon, G. (1988) 'Chinese borrowings in English', *American Speech*, 63: 3–33.

Cheng, C.C. (1992) 'Chinese varieties of English', in B.B. Kachru (ed.) *The Other Tongue: English Across Cultures* (2nd edition), Chicago: University of Illinois Press.

Deterding, D. (2006) 'The pronunciation of English by speakers from China', *English World-Wide*, 27: 175–98.

Du, R. and Jiang, Y. (2001) 'Jin ershi nian "Zhongguo yingyu" yanjiu shuping ["China English" in the past 20 Years]', *Waiyu jiaoxue yu yanjiu [Foreign Language Teaching and Research]*, 33: 37–41.

Gao, Y. (1993) 'Dui "tongzhi" he "geren zhuyi" de butong lijie: ciyi de wenhua chayi yu yanbian diaocha [The different understandings towards "comrade" and "individualism": looking into the cultural difference and shift of word meanings]', in R. Li (ed.) *Ying han yuyan wenhua duibi yanjiu [Comparative Research on English–Chinese Languages and Cultures]*, Shanghai: Shanghai Foreign Language Education Press, pp. 131–41.

Ge, C. (1980) 'Mantan you han yi ying wenti [Talking about some problems in Chinese–English translation]', *Fanyi Tongxun [Translator's Notes]*, 2: 1–8.

Givón, T. (2002) *Bio-linguistics: The Santa Barbara Lectures*, Amsterdam, John Benjamins.

Gui, S. (1988) *Yingyong yingyu yu Zhongguo yingyu jiaoxue [Applied English and English Language Teaching in China]*, Jinan: Shandong jiaoyu chubanshe [Shandong Education Press].

Hu, X. (2004) 'Why China English should stand alongside British, American, and the other "World Englishes"', *English Today*, 78 (20): 26–33.

——(2005) 'China English, at home and in the world', *English Today*, 83 (21): 27–38.

Huang, J. (1988) 'Yingdang kending "xi yi han hua" xianxiang de jiji mian [The positive role of "Sinicism" in the English-translated version]', *Zhongguo fanyi [Chinese Translators Journal]*, 1: 39–47.

Hung, T.T.N. (2002) 'The phonology of Chinese varieties of English', paper presented at Beijing Normal University Centenary International Conference on English Teacher Education and Development, 26–28 August.

Jia, G. and Xiang, M. (1997) 'Wei Zhongguo Yingyu yibian [In defence of China English]', *Waiyu yu waiyu jiaoxue [Foreign Languages and Foreign Languages Teaching]*, 105: 11–12.

Jiang, Y. (1995) 'Chinglish and China English', *English Today*, 11: 51–3.

——(2002) 'China English: issues, studies and features', *Asian Englishes*, 5: 4–23.

——(2003) 'English as a Chinese language', *English Today*, 18: 3–8.

Jin, H. (2000) *The Bridegroom: Stories*, New York: Vintage International.

Kachru, B.B. (1982) *The Other Tongue: English Across Cultures*, Urbana: University of Illinois Press.

——(1996) 'World Englishes: agony and ecstasy', *Journal of Aesthetic Education*, 30: 135–55.

Kirkpatrick, A. (1996) 'Topic-comment or modifier-modified? Information structure in Modern Standard Chinese', *Studies in Language*, 20: 93–113.

——(2000) 'Contrastive rhetoric and the teaching of writing: seven principles', in A. Liddicoat and C. Crozet (eds) *Teaching Languages, Teaching Cultures*, Melbourne: Applied Linguistics Association of Australia, pp. 79–88.

——(2007) *World Englishes: Implications for International Communication and English Language Teaching*, Cambridge: Cambridge University Press.

Kirkpatrick, A. and Xu, Z. (2002) 'Chinese pragmatic norms and "China English"', *World Englishes*, 21: 269–79.

Knowlton, J. (1970) 'Chinese, Japanese, and Korean loanwords in Webster's Third', *American Speech*, 45: 8–29.

Li, C.N. and Thompson, S.A. (1981) *Mandarin Chinese: A Functional Reference Grammar*, Berkeley: University of California Press.

Li, D.C.S. (1998) 'Incorporating L1 pragmatic norms and cultural values in L2: developing English language curriculum for EIL in the Asia-Pacific region', *Asian Englishes*, 1: 31–50.

Li, W. (1993) 'Zhongguo yingyu yu zhongguo shi yingyu [China English and Chinese English]', *Waiyu jiaoxue yu yanjiu [Foreign Language Teaching and Research]*, 96: 18–24.

McArthur, T. (2002) *The Oxford Guide to World English*, Oxford: Oxford University Press.

Pang, Z. (2002) 'Zhongguo Yingyu bianti de yanjiu: huigu yu zhanwang [Research on Chinese variety of English: retrospect and prospect]', *Waiyu yanjiu [Foreign Languages Research]*, 76: 24–7.

Poon, F.K.-C. (2006) 'Hong Kong English, China English and World English', *English Today*, 86: 22–8.

Quirk, R., Greenbaum, S., Leech, G. and Svartvik, J. (1985) *A Comprehensive Grammar of the English Language*, London: Longman.

Radford, A., Atkinson, M., Britain, D., Bailey, R.W., Clahsen, H. and Spencer, A. (1999) *Linguistics: An Introduction*, Cambridge: Cambridge University Press.

Schneider, E.W. (2009) 'English into Asia: from Singaporean ubiquity to Chinese learners' features', in A. Curzan and M. Adams (eds) *Contours of English and English Language Studies: In Honor of Richard W. Bailey*, Ann Arbor: University of Michigan Press.

Scollon, R. and Scollon, S.W. (2001) *Intercultural Communication: A Discourse Approach*, Oxford: Blackwell.

Sun, L. (1989) 'Yingyu guobie bianti de yanjiu he yingyu zai Zhongguo [Research on English varieties and English in China]', *Waiguo yu [Foreign Languages]*, 60: 17–23.

Wang, R. (1994) 'Zhongguo Yingyu shi keguan cunzai [China English is real]', in *Shuo dong dao xi hua yingyu [Talking about English]*, Beijing: Waiyu jiaoxue yu yanjiu chubanshe [Foreign Language Teaching and Research Press].

Xie, Z. (1995) 'Zhongguo yingyu: kua wenhua yuyan jiaoji zhong de ganrao xing bianti [China English: an interference variety in cross-cultural communication]', *Xiandai waiyu [Modern Languages]*, 70: 7–11.

Xu, Z. (2006) 'Rectifying "Chinese English"', in A. Hashim and N. Hassan (eds) *Varieties of English in Southeast Asia and Beyond*, Kuala Lumpur: University of Malaya Press.

Yan, Z. (2002) *World Englishes*, Beijing: Foreign Language Teaching and Research Press.

Zhang, H. (2002) 'Bilingual creativity in Chinese English. Ha Jin's *In the Pond*', *World Englishes*, 21: 305–15.

Zhou, L. (2004) 'Those addresses, they keep on changing', *China Daily* (Beijing), 7 January.

17

Slavic Englishes

Education or culture?

Zoya Proshina

A brief history of Slavic and English language contacts

Various Slavic languages came into contact with the English language at different times. For the Russian language, the recorded history of its interaction with English dates back to the mid sixteenth century when British sailors and merchants, the first British to have arrived in Russia, were granted an audience with the Russian Czar, Ivan the Terrible, and were allowed to trade with Russians (Aristova 1978; Proshina and Ettkin 2005). However, it was not until the eighteenth century, the epoch of Peter the Great followed by the epoch of the so-called 'enlightened sovereign' Catherine the Great, that we can speak of increasing Russian–British contacts that resulted in a number of borrowings into both languages (Beliaeva 1984). Though she did not speak English herself, Catherine the Great encouraged the spread of English literature in Russia, which is why she was called an anglophile (Labutina 2002). In the nineteenth century, Russia had diplomatic and other types of contact with both Great Britain and the USA. Nevertheless, at that time English as a foreign language was only second in popularity, with French the most popular, being regarded as a domestic language of the nobility.

Like Russian–British contacts, Czech (Bohemian) and British contacts, later strengthened by dynastic marriages, have been known since the Middle Ages (Evans 2008). In Poland, Polish–English language interactions, marked primarily in education and publishing, have been traced to the late eighteenth and nineteenth centuries (Reichelt 2005).

More recently, and as Jeffrey Griffin (2001) notes, the increased profile of English in all Slavic countries has been common since 1989. Since the collapse of the Warsaw Treaty in 1991, contacts between Western and Eastern countries have further intensified.

The Slavic family of languages includes three groups of related languages: East Slavic (Russian, Ukrainian and Belarusian), West Slavic (Polish, Czech, Slovak, Sorbian), and South Slavic (Bulgarian, Slovene, Macedonian, Serbian, Croatian, Montenegrin, Bosnian). East Slavic cultures, having adopted Orthodox religion, were originally under strong Greek influence, while West Slavic cultures, being closely linked to the Roman Catholic Church, have experienced greater influence from Western Europe. These influences account for the differences in script in Slavic cultures – Cyrillic letters are used by Eastern Slavs and Roman letters by Western and to some extent by Southern Slavs.

Current sociolinguistic situation and functions of English

Nearly all Slavic languages have spoken dialects and a standard literary norm strongly supported by educational institutions and mass media. In the twentieth century, Slavic countries made up a political and economic block, included in or allied to the Warsaw Pact. Thus, their languages were significantly influenced by Russian, which played a great role as a lingua franca (Pavlenko 2006; Prendergast 2008) and was predominantly studied as a foreign language at East European educational institutions.

Before the 1990s, English was of minor importance in these countries. It started to play the role of a language for intercultural communication only in the late twentieth to early twenty-first centuries. When English is used by Slavs, its functions largely match those ascribed to expanding circle varieties (Kachru 1985), i.e. it functions as a lingua franca more for outreaching to other cultures than for domestic reasons, and is learned (not acquired) as a foreign language through education. Since the functions of English are similar in all Slavic cultures, I will primarily discuss its position in Russia, whose situation I know best.

Despite the fact that Russia is multilingual (with over 150 languages) and multiglossic, with a great number of regional and social dialects, it is hard to speak about Russian Englishes in the plural (Ter-Minasova 2007: 268). Standardization in the education system is so rigid that it is difficult to believe that several varieties of the learnt language can exist in one country, especially when its functions are restricted. It is important to stress, however, that this needs further research.

In Russia, like all other Slavic countries, English is used mostly for intercultural, outercultural (Kabakchi 1998) and international communication across various domains, namely business, politics, research, tourism and mass media (Eddy 2007). In business and the economy, English is used for correspondence and negotiations with both native and non-native speakers of the language. In order to conduct successful negotiations, Russians thus need to be familiar with those non-native speakers' varieties of English with which we deal and to 'be alerted to which linguistic features cause particular problems of mutual intelligibility' (Kirkpatrick 2007: 193). This practical need has motivated the research into mutual intelligibility of Asian Englishes, their features (Proshina 2001; Bondarenko 2007) and their so-called 'intermediary transla-tion' (Proshina 2005: 521) into English as a lingua franca (Jenkins 2004, 2007) as opposed to direct translation from Asian languages into Russian.

English is used as a working language in transnational companies, such as Mars, Coca-Cola, Proctor & Gamble, Toyota, Samsung, Levi's and many others which do business in Russia and other Slavic countries. In 2001, three large Russian companies, LukOil, FESCO (Far Eastern Shipping Company) and PRISCO (Primorsk Shipping Company), were included in the UNCTAD list of transnational corporations (Vladimirova 2001). In transnational companies, cases of language-mixing and code-switching are not infre-quent. Russian companies cooperating with international partners conduct correspon-dence in English, and many companies even take English names to show that they are internationally-oriented: e.g. *JapanStart* (a car auction company in Vladivostok), *SunRay* (a jam producer in Krasnodar), *RUSTEEL* (a metal company), *VladSoft* (a computer company), *URALTRANS* (a shipment company) and many others. Especially prolific in this respect are commercial establishments – stores, shops and boutiques (*Red-Mart, Digital Hall, Stock*, etc.), travel agencies (*Lucky Tour, Discovery Tours, Ariadne Business Travel*, etc.), restaurants and fast-food cafés (*Royal Burger, King, PizzaLand*, etc.), entertainment establishments (*Lips, Infinity, New Wave*, etc.), beauty salons (*Studio Beauty, Lady Boss, City Style*, etc.) and others (Proshina *et al.* 2008). Advertising is another vast field for English use in all Slavic cultures (Griffin 2001; Schlick 2003; Reichelt 2005; Šabec 2005; Ustinova and Bhatia 2005; Ustinova 2006, 2008; Dimova 2008).

The frequency and depth of English use is proportionate to the economic significance of the region to international companies. The autonomous Republic of Sakha-Yakutia, rich in diamonds and gold, attracts a lot of foreign investment and, because of its close contacts with other countries, the Sakha authorities declared English as a working language of the republic. Sakha is already richly multilingual with two national languages (Russian and Yakut) and five official languages (Even, Evenk, Yukagir, Chukchi and Dolgan) (Samsonov 2003). The development of oil deposits on Sakhalin Island attracted British, Japanese, American and other capital investments, which has now stimulated an English language boom in the region.

In the early twenty-first century, the number of tourists has grown considerably. According to the Rosturism governmental agency, the number of tourists increased by 11 per cent in 2006 (Otdykh v Rossii 2006). The number of travel agencies has doubled over the last two years, a phenomenon which is partly explained by the improvement of people's standard of living and their financial position in post-Soviet Russia (Konsaltingovaya Kompaniya AMICO 2008). For tourists English has become the language for interpersonal communication and for cultural enrichment. A new type of tourism has emerged – educational tourism. While going abroad, people try to combine recreation with the study of a foreign language. In 2006, 45,000 Russians received student visas, about twice as many as in 2005. In 2006, about 60 per cent of the students chose Great Britain as a place to study English (Obrazovatel'nyi turizm 2007). In 2008 the USA and Canada became the leading countries admitting 'language tourists' (S Sh A i Kanada 2008). And it is not just the traditional native-speaking countries that are attracting these education tourists. For example, in 2006, Russian students were the second most numerous among those students who went to Malta to study English (Obrazovatel'nyi turizm 2007). About 70 per cent of such education tourists are high and middle school children, sometimes accompanied by their parents; 25 per cent are college students and only 5 per cent are adult professionals (StarTravel 2008).

English is supported, to some extent, by the mass media. Before *perestroika*, Russia had only one English language newspaper, *The Moscow News*, which was intended for foreigners and at the same time served as educational material for students learning English. Today, the number of English language papers has increased, and includes *The St Petersburg Times, The Nizhny-Novgorod Times, The Vladivostok News, The Vladivostok Times, The Sakhalin Times* and *The Sakhalin Independent*, to name only a few. At least 20 newspapers also issue English-translation online editions. News can be read on blog sites (www.russiaprofile.org; www.siberianlight.net and others), as well as on main Russian web service sites: www.mail.ru; www.rambler.ru; www.yandex.ru. Other Slavic countries also have online newspapers featuring both local and international news: Ukraine's *Kiev Post* and *Ukrainian Observer* magazine; the Polish *Warsaw Voice* and *Daily News*; the Czech *Prague Daily Monitor, Prague Post* weekly and the *Transitions*

Online international magazine. *The Slovak Spectator*, Bulgaria's *Sofia Echo* and *The Bulgarian Post* and Croatia's *Nacional* are further examples. The Belarusian Telegraph Agency site provides updates in English on the republic.

English language channels like CNN, BBC, MTV, Discovery, Disney, History, Deutsche Welle and Korean Arirang are available in homes thanks to satellite and cable television. However, movies which are aired on TV and shown in cinemas are usually dubbed. In December 2005, the first informational government-sponsored English language TV channel, Russia Today, was launched. Its programmes include news, Alexander Gurnov's talk-show *Spotlight*, Peter Lavelle's analytical programme *In Context*, documentary movies about Russian history and culture, and sightseeing programmes.

Many scientists and academicians are aware that English is a powerful research instrument. To be published in English abroad means to receive international recognition. However, very few domestic journals – mostly scientific ones (Eddy 2007) – publish full-text research articles in English, limiting themselves to English abstracts. The country's publishing houses prefer publishing books in Russian rather than in English (except for guide-books and books for foreigners). They thus conform to official government policy to enhance Russian language and culture.

English in education

Background

In Russia, foreign languages have always been looked upon as a window to a new world (Pavlovskaya 2003). The more languages you know, the wider the vistas which will open before you. That is why the families that could afford to study foreign languages invited native speakers (usually as governesses) or proficient non-native speakers as tutors for their children. In the nineteenth century, it was common for educated people to be bilingual. This was, in the main, a French–Russian bilingualism, but with French as the dominant language (Zemskaya 2001a). While English was not as popular as French, it was respected by the Russian intelligentsia for its literature and culture. The ability to read English authors in the original was regarded as a mark of good breeding and education. English playwrights, especially Shakespeare and later Bernard Shaw and Oscar Wilde, were very popular and their work was often staged.

By the twentieth century, French–Russian bilingualism gave way to Russian–English bilingualism. While the French–Russian bilingualism of the nineteenth century was developed in the home, today the languages are learned in different settings, with the foreign language, usually English but sometimes French or German, being learned in school.

Nowadays, the secondary school curriculum mandates a foreign language. It can be English, French or German, but, in reality, English is the language of first choice. According to the Ministry of Education and Research figures for 2007, 12,500,000 Russian schoolchildren studied English, 3,500,000 students learnt German, and 756,800 studied French (Kruglyi stol 2007). With Russia's adoption of the European policy of school multilingualism (following the Bologna protocol, which requires that two foreign languages be included in school curricula), the chance of further expanding the number of English learners is tremendous – English will almost certainly be chosen as the second foreign language because it is the global lingua franca.

Issues

There are several problems currently facing educators with regard to English learning: first, when should students begin to study the language; second, how long should they study it; third, how should they study it; fourth, where should they study it; and fifth, which model should they study?

An average Russian child starts primary school at the age of six or seven. The school period includes 11 years, comprising four grades of primary education, five years of compulsory middle school, and two years of high school. In most Russian schools students begin to learn English in the fifth grade and study it for seven years until they leave high school. The middle school (grades 5–9) curricula provide 525 academic hours (three hours a week) and high school (grades 10–11) provides a total of 210 hours of English. There is now a trend to start learning English earlier. The Department of Education encourages schools to launch ELT at primary school, in the second or even first grade. Many preschools (for children younger than seven) have introduced English classes in response to parents' demand for an early start in English for their children.

There are also state-run and private schools offering intensive English programmes. At these intensive English schools, students start English in the second grade and can reach an advanced level by the time they leave school.

Life-long learning is promoted. On leaving secondary school, the person will continue English learning when admitted to a tertiary educational institution. Although English is not mandatory for university entrance, some disciplines (including the humanities) require it. English majors have up to 14 hours of language classes a week, plus linguistics, literature, culture and history courses which can also be delivered in English. Non-English majors continue studying the language for two more years (two or four hours a week). However, we are witnessing a new drive for more intensive and ongoing English and some universities offer additional programmes of ESP and translation (for two or three more years). Evening English classes for professionals (medical doctors, engineers, economists, for example) have become very popular at universities.

Speciality subjects (usually economics and business) are taught in English to students in joint Russian–American departments, the first of which opened in the 1990s. Despite the high price of tuition, these joint departments attract students by awarding two diplomas (degrees), Russian and American. One of the first joint Russian–American departments, involving the University of Maryland University College, the Far Eastern National University (Vladivostok) and the Irkutsk State University, opened in 1991. It was followed by the Ulyanovsk State University–Oklahoma City University programme and the Far Eastern State Transportation University–Alaska State University programmes. Moscow University Touro opened in 2004 and in 2006 the Russian–American Economic and Business Institute at the Ural State University was established.

Students are aware that English is a tool for international education and necessary if they want to receive education overseas, even in non-English-speaking countries. For example, humanities students can receive Immanuel Kant and Michail Lomonosov stipends to study in English at a German university. In 2008, four types of competitive graduate scholarships were announced for Russian students wishing to obtain a Master's degree through English at German universities.

American foundations (for instance, a number of Fulbright programmes, the Fulbright–Kennan Institute Research Scholarship Programme, the Global Undergraduate

303

Exchange Programme, the Edmund S. Muskie Graduate Fellowship Programme and the Hubert H. Humphrey Programme) also motivate Russian students and scholars to improve and develop their English.

The question of where to study English raises other questions – how to study it and which model of English to study. Traditionally, Russian schools paid great attention to knowledge about the language structure and to students' ability to translate into their native language; this is why the Grammar–Translation method was prevalent for such a long time (Lovtsevich 2001; Ter-Minasova 2005). Today, a primary goal of school curricula is developing communicative competence, which requires classes in listening and speaking, reading and writing. Among the four skills, writing is the skill that usually is the least developed, since emphasis is placed on reading and speaking. Translation, the so-called fifth skill, is still the teachers' favourite objective – it is no accident that translation departments have been established within almost every university.

Traditionally, Russian schools adopted the model of British English. British (or Queen's) English is still considered to be pure, classical, aristocratic and the most intelligible variety (McCaughey 2005). Most textbooks are based on British English norms. Indeed the adjective 'English' is itself associated with 'British', so when asking about the origin of a word, students might say, 'Is this word English or American?' However, the importance of American English has become greater as the contacts with the US have become closer. The American English model has thus begun to prosper, with the opening of the joint Russian–American departments referred to above. This is true even in places like Bulgaria and other Slavic countries, where British and American Englishes have become 'sibling rivals' (O'Reilly 1998: 71), with the former regarded as an 'elite language of refined literature' (p. 82) and the latter as an 'engineer of change' in business and technology (p. 75).

While Russia was closed off from English-speaking countries by the Iron Curtain, English in Russia was taught by non-native English-speaking teachers. Today these teachers are still prevalent, though there are now far more native English speakers at students' and teachers' disposal. The English Language Office (ELO) of the US Embassy, the British Council and British and American publishers are major providers of resources.

The ELO, established in Moscow in 1993, provides resources throughout the Russian Federation. It cooperates on a wide variety of ELT projects with the Ministry of Education and local professional associations such as the National Association of Teachers of English (NATE), the Far Eastern English Language Teachers' Association (FEELTA), the St Petersburg English Language Teachers' Association (SPELTA), and with associations from Voronezh, Samara, Saratov and many others. The office supports the work of senior English Language Fellows at universities and teacher training institutions, and provides upgrades for local ELT professionals, thereby raising the standard of English instruction. The US Embassy has facilitated the creation of 30 'American Corners' in public libraries around Russia, making information about the United States available to visitors and spreading American English.

Also of great help to local schools in recent years were the Peace Corps volunteers who worked in Russia in 1992–2002.

The British Council, whose offices are in Moscow, St Petersburg and Yekaterinburg, has promoted the spread of British English language teaching materials, sponsored English lecturers and spread information about the availability of scholarships to study in Britain.

Though today's market is inundated with British and American ELT materials, many schools still use textbooks compiled by Russian authors, finding that their materials better suit their teaching goals as they take into consideration both new and traditional methods, understand the specific difficulties facing Russian students, and are better aligned with Russian culture.

However, the help provided by the ELO and the British Council is highly valued by local educationalists, and English teachers in the many cities that have no permanent representatives from these institutions feel envious of those which do.

Similar ELT resources are now available in other Slavic countries (O'Reilly 1998; Dimova 2003; Reichelt 2005).

English in culture

Pop culture provides a good medium for people, especially the younger generation, to study English. From jazz, the first American musical genre to be imported to Russia, to the most recent rap and pop music, English easily found its way to young people's hearts as it 'was associated with freedom, expression of sexuality, rebellion against the staleness of the system, and individual creativity' (Eddy 2008: 20). The influence of pop music has been felt for some time and at least three generations have grown up on the songs of such British groups as the Beatles, the Rolling Stones and Deep Purple. Today pop culture continues to be associated with English.

In music, English influence can be seen in learning and performing English songs, composing music in the framework of a certain borrowed genre, writing lyrics in English, and inventing English names for bands and groups (Eddy 2007).

There are several reasons, both social and artistic, to explain this. For social reasons musicians connect with the wider public, making their songs more marketable. Many of them have aspirations to become known outside Russia. Besides, 'English represents the "otherness", the desire of the participants to estrange themselves from the rest' (Eddy 2008: 21) of their community. Artistic reasons include the performers' claim that English helps songs sound authentic on the one hand, and that Russian does not suit the melodic structure of the song on the other. When composing lyrics in English, musicians have to think more about the combined effect of sound and music (Willard and Shchepetova 2003). Code-mixing and code-switching are also common features of the lyrics.

One-fourth of about 200 names of Russian rock-groups presented at wikipedia.ru have been influenced by English. This is seen in:

- English names in English script (*Mechanical Poet*; *Aftermath*; *Blind Vandal*; *Gorky Park*; *Neversmile*; *Everything Is Made In China*);
- English names in Cyrillic script (Тайм Аут = *Time Out*; Томас = *Thomas*; Моби Дик = *Moby Dick*);
- script-mixing (Безумные Усилия; *Animal* ДжаZ; Мультфильмы; Dёргать!);
- other creative techniques: using homophones (*Jane Air*), specific division of words (Пеп-Си = *Pep-Si*), allusion and play upon words (Бони НЕМ = *Bony NEM,* lit. *Bony is dumb*, allusion to *Bony M*), as well as mixing stems (РОСКМЕХАНИКА = *ROCKMECHANICS*, Башня Rowan = *Tower Rowan*).

English also allows fiction writers to explore their creativity. For example, English comprises some of the material for 'an English–Russian language play' (Rivlina 2008: 98), i.e. play upon words, and its influence is seen clearly in book titles such as Духless

305

('Soulless') by Sergey Minayev; Sex в большой политике ('Sex in big politics') by Irina Khakamada; МультиMILLIONAIRES ('MultiMillionaires') by Lena Lenina; Про люб off/on ('About Love+off/on') by Oksana Robsky; Брачный коNтракт или *Who is ?* ... ('Marriage coNtract, or Who is who ... ') by Tatyana Ogorodnikova. Hybridization attracts the reader's attention.

The marriage of English and indigenous cultures results in so-called contact literature (Spooner 1987), a term which has received recent criticism (Thumboo 2006). Many felt that there was no Russian literature in English except for that written by coordinate bilinguals, like V. Nabokov who wrote in both English and Russian.

The current situation is different. New emigration from Russia (and other Slavic countries) has produced new émigré writers such as Olga Grushin, Anya Ulinich, Lara Vapnyar and Gary Shteyngart.

Most of these emigrant writers appear to have left Russia for good. Gary Shteyngart belongs to the 1.5 generation of Americans. Having left Russia as a seven-year-old boy, he was raised in the culture of the United States. O. Grushin, A. Ulinich and L. Vapnyar also emigrated in their youth. No wonder that the English novels of Russian authors, which appeared at the turning points of Russia's history, convey the most pressing issues facing society, including relations between the officialdom and common people, socialist art and its dependence on the ruling ideology, the betrayal of talent, friends and principles for the comforts of high-ranking Soviet privilegentsia, attitudes to Jews, new entrepreneurship, deceitful pyramid schemes, the oil oligarchy and mafia, and many others. As could be expected from emigrant literature, the work tends to be critical, ironic, darkly funny and wickedly whimsical. Some works show Russian (Soviet) life as black and white. However, they also follow the fantastic and realistic traditions of Russian literature, convey Russian sensibility, reveal Russian concepts like 'spirit' and 'soul', and interpret culture-loaded phenomena.

The international media speak highly of the authors' perfect English, although it is their second language. Though, indeed, their English is excellent, we can easily trace Russianness in their writing. The works are abundant in Russian culture-loaded words used to describe Russian life and easily recognized by any Russian. For example, A. Ulinich describes a typical New Year celebration in a Russian school: 'She needed to discuss the upcoming Winter Pageant. The first-grade girls, the teacher explained, would play Snowflake Fairies ... twirling tutus, flying blond braids, and flushed pink faces, against which Grandfather Frost and Snegurochka were to display their benevolence' (Ulinich 2007: 13).

I now turn to considering some distinctive linguistic features of Russian English.

Russian English linguistic features

Despite the recent history of its development discussed above, Russian English has yet to win social acceptance and few Russians will acknowledge they are speaking Russia English or Russian English (Proshina 2006). However, many English-speaking Russians understand that their English is a mixture of British norms, Standard American and elements formed under the influence of their native Russian (and other) indigenous languages and cultures. The concept of Russia (or Russian) English has not been recognized yet, even though local teachers 'have no option but to teach the model they themselves have learned' (Kirkpatrick 2007: 192). Some linguists reject point blank the idea of a local variety of English in Russia (Safonova 2000). The attitude towards Russian English is mainly negative, as it is associated with broken and bad English rather than being seen as a variety able to convey Russian culture and Russian ways of thinking to others. We need an 'attitudinal readjustment' (Kachru 1983: 85) about Russian English.

Although the status of the English language used in Russia is still a subject of domestic debate, the variety of English spoken and written by educated Russians can be identified by the use of certain distinctive features. These distinctive features are typical of mesolectal speech and sometimes occur in acrolectal speech. They are noticeable at all language levels: phonetic, morphological, syntactic and pragmatic.

Phonological features include the distinctive pronunciation of some English sounds, positional and combinatorial changes of sounds, and specific supra-segmental characteristics:

- lack of aspiration in pronouncing initial [p, t, k];
- replacing the interdental *th* by [z/s/d/t/f] as in 'Hepy bursday to you!' (Ulinich 2007: 144);
- replacing [w] by [v] or [u]: 'William' becomes 'Villiam' or 'Uilliam';
- shortening of vowels ('seat' becomes 'sit');
- devoicing of final consonants and regressive assimilation of middle consonants ('bag' ~ 'back'; 'absorption' becomes [apso:pshn]);
- specific intonation;
- rising tone of special and alternative questions (Why did you ⁄say that? Is his name Mike or ⁄Andrew?).

At the morphological and syntactic levels, the following features can be explained by the difference between Russian and English grammar:

- substituting the past simple or present simple for the present perfect: 'From a historical point of view, Vladivostok is young – a little bit over 140 years old. But like a magnet, it always **attracted** people.'
- use of articles (Russian has no articles): '**The** unusual quiet reigned in Sukhanov's heart.' (Grushin 2005: 343); 'This fabulous emerald-turquoise necklace is **incomparable decoration** of Vladivostok';
- avoiding attributive clusters ('the form of the nineteenth century') and pre-positioning ('the problem *generation gap*'). Russian is a right-branching language, unlike English, which is left-branching;
- distinctive use of gerunds: 'on a text analysing', 'bursting-at-the-seams suitcase' (Vapnyar 2003: 12). There is no gerund in Russian;
- lack of the copula 'be', especially in the present tense form: 'At the moment the main subject I'm responsible for American Culture'. Russian sentences of this type do not require the copula;
- topicalization of the object and its inversion: '**Mornings** we usually spent at the beach' (Vapnyar 2003: 52).

Lexical features of Russian English include distinctive usages and innovations. Distinctive usages are systemic traits typical of educated speakers and differ from the standard because of influence from Russian. Innovations result from nativization and acculturation when English needs to express Russian culture. Examples include:

- Russian culture-loaded loans: *dacha*, *Duma*, *kvass*; some of them being Sovietisms (Yuzefovich 2005): *Socialist realism*, *kolkhoz*, *nomenklatura*;
- calques: 'foreign passport' (for Russian citizens going abroad), 'heroine mother' (a mother with many children), 'New Russians' (rich Russians); 'social work' (volunteering/unpaid work);
- calqued Russian idioms: 'to keep the wolves full and the sheep whole' (Grushin 2005: 174), 'A comrade in trouble should never be afraid to ask for help ... it's **from each according to his abilities**, to each according to his incompetence' (Ulinich 2007: 9);
- words borrowed from other languages with a different meaning in Russian and/or Russian English: 'hostess' (geisha + waitress), 'Chechen warlord' (rebel leader);
- new coinages: 'shop-tour' (trip abroad for shopping), 'groupmate' (at the university, member of the same study group) (Lovtsevich 2005).

Distinctive discourse-level features can be found at both pragmatic and semantic levels. Use of Russian norms can give listeners the wrong impression about the Russian speaker. Examples include:

- masculine-oriented language: 'The lexical units involved in our study concern **man** as social being, his activities.' There is still no movement in Russia for so-called 'politically correct' gender language;
- preference for the imperative mood structures: 'Open the door', 'Sit down, please.' Since Russian use of polite positive interrogative structures expressing request is very restricted and negative forms of the type 'Will you not open the door?' have a different meaning in English, these forms are apt to be substituted by imperative structures that sound in Russian far less categorical than in English;
- the Russian language does not use understatements, so typical of English. Many Russians do not feel that the positive form of a sentence, preferred by Russians, sounds far more categorical than the one with two negations: cf. 'His dream came true only in 1900' vs 'His dream did not come true until 1900'. So a Russian will more typically say, 'I believe you' than 'I do not disbelieve you.'

These distinctive features are characteristic of mesolectal Russian English. Basilectal English (Ruslish/Russlish) is typical of uneducated speakers and is represented by the code-mixed speech of Russian immigrants in the United States. Zhukova's examples (2001) illustrate the pidginized character of such code-mixing of Russian grammar and English lexis, a sort of 'Russian in foreign clothes' (Zemskaya 2001b: 160). Some features of Ruslish include:

- adding Russian suffixes and endings to nouns: 'girlfrienda' (girlfriend); 'dishvoshka' (dishwasher);
- double plural endings: 'shoesy'; 'childrenyata';
- adding suffixes and prefixes to verbs 'zainshuryu' (I'll ensure).

The formation and description of lectal varieties of Russian immigrants' English can make a subject of further investigation.

English influence on Russian

The Russian language of immigrants to English-speaking countries has been described by several linguists (Benson 1957, 1960; Kouzmin 1973; Olmsted 1986; Andrews 1990, 1997; Polinsky 1995, 1998; Glovinskaya 2001; Zemskaya 2001a, 2001b). These descriptions reveal Englishization of Russian in the new (mostly American) linguistic environment. Some of the processes are parallel to those taking place in Russia where English influence on the vernacular is so great that it is causing heated disputes in various media. Prof. V. Kostomarov (1999), the Director of the Institute of the Russian Language, considers borrowings from American English to be the most salient feature in this linguistic development. The flood of American loans is so powerful that English borrowings have been replacing old French and German loans: e.g. макияж (*maquillage*) is giving way to мэйкап (*make-up*); and бутерброд (*Butterbrod*) is being substituted by сэндвич (*sandwich*). We are also witnessing the change of word stress in similar-sounding words that were borrowed from different languages at different periods of time. For example, the word дискурс (*diskurs* < *discourse*) originated from French and English, with the stress on the last and first syllables correspondingly. However the French-influenced pronunciation is being replaced by an English one. English influence is also observed in borrowings from East Asian languages – for example, in Russian, Japanese loans often have a form that corresponds to Romanized English: суши [sushi] instead of суси [susi], as it would be if the word had been borrowed directly from Japanese; тамагочи [tamagochi] instead of тамаготи [tamagoti], for example.

English loans can be seen everywhere but most commonly in computer and information technology domains (*site, interface, display, monitor, chat, email*), business and economics (*promotion, head-hunter, merchandizing*), politics (*electorate, consensus, pluralism, summit*), sports (*freestyle, armwrestling, overtime, kickboxing*), and pop-culture (*DJ, hip-hop, single, re-make, thriller*). Using romanized versions of transplanted loans represents a new trend for early twenty-first-century Russian (Kabakchi 2005).

In Russian, English loans are used not only for imported ideas (Krysin 2000), but also provide an exotic flavour. Cross-linguistic puns are common. Several years ago TV commercials encouraged customers to keep money in the bank named *Russkiy Dom Selenga* ('Russian House *Selenga*'). In Russian, the word *Selenga* brings to mind a river or lake, while in reality the name is derived from the word *selling* with a slight change of a vowel (Kostomarov 1999: 122). English can confer prestige in advertisements and in product and company names. *Charmzone, Outhall, Pacific Tourservice*, are examples. Language play based on loans creates a humorous effect, attracts attention and is often employed in book titles. For example, Рублевка. *Live*. 'Rublyovka. Live'. Sometimes loans produce the impression of a dearth of actual information (Romanov 2000). This occurs in certain academic works whose authors conceal trivial ideas behind pseudo-scientific words, termed 'agnonyms' (Morkovkin and Morkovkina 1997), i.e. words of foreign origin, whose meanings are unclear and incomprehensible. Examples of Englishized words being used instead of Russian ones to sound more academic, but actually virtually meaningless, include: 'динамика … фундирована … связями' (the dynamic is founded on links); 'коммуцирует знания' (communicates knowledge).

Hybridization of stems is a productive way of creating neologisms. English stems are used as affixes: for example, by analogy with *peacemaker*, we have имидж-мейкер (*imagemaker*), слухмейкер (*rumour-maker*), ньюсмейкер (*newsmaker*), маркетмейкер (*marketmaker*) and the like. The suffix -*shop* has given a number of derivatives: мини-шопы (*minishops*), кофе-шопы (*coffee-shops*), секс-шопы (*sex-shops*), принт-шопы (*print-shops*).

Hybridization is facilitated by Russian affixation: affixes are easily added to English roots to make the word flexible for borrowing and using in speech: беспрайсовый (*bespraisovyi* – 'having no **price**'), отъемелить (ot**yemel**it 'send an **email** message'), сидишка (*sidishka* < CD). The English abbreviation *PR* (*public relations*) has become a basis for the Russian word family, as in пиар (the noun, meaning PR), пиарить (the verb), пиарщик (a noun, meaning a person in PR) and пиаровый (the adjective).

Russian linguists (Kostomarov 1999; Zemskaya 2001a; Rivlina 2005) have noted a new trend in Russian grammar. With the increase of loan words, the number of non-inflected words has also increased, leading to typological change. Second, the use of English noun + noun phrases, when borrowed, brings changes to the word order in Russian attributive clusters, where a borrowed noun is used instead of an adjective: интернет-кафе (*internet-café*), офис-менеджер (*office-manager*), офис-применение (*office employment*) (Aitmukhametova 2000).

Englishization is also found in calquing collocations, as in these examples: делать бизнес (*delat' biznes* 'to do business'; взять курс лекций (*vziat' kurs lektsiy* 'to take a course of lectures'), etc.

Borrowed words frequently experience a shift in meaning. Usually, the meaning is narrowed as the word is used in a specific field: киллер (killer) becomes a special type of killer, a hired killer), органайзер (an organizer) becomes an electronic device, шейпинг (shaping) comes to mean fitness.

A loan word may also have a Russian equivalent. However, gradually their meanings get differentiated and thus both forms survive without forcing one another out of the lexicon. For instance, the English loan *image* is applied to official business situations, as in: имидж работника (image of an employee), имидж нашего банка (image of our bank), while the Russian equivalent образ (obraz) is used in more personal settings: образ Татьяны (*obraz Tatyany* 'the image of Tatyana'), образ учителя (*obraz uchitelia* 'the image of the teacher'). Thus Russian and English interact, with Russian often influencing and shaping the English (Rivlina 2005).

Attitudes: purification vs enrichment

The attitudes of the Russian community to the flood of English loans is ambivalent. On the one hand, there are those who want to purify the Russian language, to develop linguo-ecology as a branch of applied linguistics, and to toughen state laws protecting the Russian language and culture. These people compare the excessive use of English loans with 'a tumour in the vocabulary body' (Kostomarov 1999: 144). The Russian government has also been taking steps to preserve and promote the Russian language and culture. In 1995, President Putin decreed the setting up of the Russian Language Council. Its aim was to develop language policy to protect the ecology of the Russian language. However, the work of the Council was not effective. In June 2005, the Russian Parliament passed the National Language Law, which was later criticized by the media and public as unrealistic. Under this law, the official use of foreign words where suitable Russian words exist was forbidden (www.rg.ru/). However, no particular restrictive or punishing measures were proposed; moreover, the text of the law itself comprised quite a number of loans, which proves that the Russian language is rich with foreign words that Russians have adapted and consider their own. In June 2007, President Putin signed a decree establishing the Russkiy Mir Foundation, for the purpose of 'promoting the Russian language, as Russia's national heritage and a significant aspect of Russian and world culture, and supporting Russian language teaching programs abroad' (http://russkiymir.org). Thus, the linguo-ecological position has received official support. This would appear to be popular, as a sociolinguistic survey conducted by A. Romanov in St Petersburg in the late 1990s revealed that 76 per cent of the respondents believe that a massive number of foreign loans in Russian are unjustified; 72 per cent of the respondents said that they viewed English loans negatively (Romanov 2000: 63).

With the increase in the number of English-speaking bilinguals in Russia, however, Anglicisms are considered a guide to a person's level of education. The more English words a person knows, the more educated s/he is assumed to be. Thus English words characterize and rank a person socially. Generally speaking, foreign borrowings are natural in any language; they enrich the language and open windows to other cultures' worldviews. They can facilitate international communication. So borrowing is a positive phenomenon unless it threatens ethnic identity, ethnic culture and ethnic languages. We cannot dictate to a living language how it may develop.

Conclusion: intercultural approach and prospects of research

The idea of Russia(n) English is gradually gaining sociolinguistic support, as the language is strengthening in range and depth (Kachru 1985: 243) along the 'identity–communication continuum' (Kirkpatrick 2007). With regard to identity, for example, English is being used more and more for conveying messages about Russia and its culture to people across the world. Russia(n) English is our means of expressing our identity to the global world. Transculturizing information about Russia, English implements the very important role of an envoy, providing information, withdrawing barriers of intercultural misunderstanding and promoting interest in the nation.

Sociolinguistic studies of Englishes, when taking an intercultural approach, have a significant practical application (Honna 2008). Slavic Englishes are developing members of the World Englishes club, thus their description is not as complete as those of other varieties. The prescriptive approach to English which has prevailed in East European educational institutions for so many years should now, to a certain degree, give way to descriptive and intercultural approaches. This does not mean substituting one for another. The appropriate ratio of description and prescription in the pursuit of intercultural intelligibility, comprehensibility and interpretability (Smith 1992) should be a subject for investigation and joint research among of educationalists and linguists.

Finally, it is likely that Slavic Englishes will continue to develop, and a comparison between them and their use in different settings – in their indigenous Slavic settings and in English-speaking environments as in immigrant diasporas – needs to be part of a future research agenda.

Suggestions for further reading

Alexandrova, O. and Konurbayev, M. (eds) (1998) *World Englishes: A Festschift for Olga S. Akhmanova from her Disciples, Friends and Colleagues*, Moscow: Moscow State University Press.

311

Eddy, A. (2007) 'English in the Russian context: a macrosociolinguistic study', PhD dissertation, Wayne State University, Michigan (publication no. AAT 3288961). Online. Available http://digitalcommons. wayne.edu/dissertations/AAI3288961/ (accessed 15 July 2009).

Prendergast C. (2008) *Buying into English: Language and Investment in the New Capitalist World*, Pittsburgh: University of Pittsburgh Press.

Proshina, Z.G. (ed.) (2005) 'Russian Englishes', special issue of *World Englishes*, 24 (4).

——(2007) 'The ABC and controversies of World Englishes' Хабаровск: ДВИИЯ. Available at www.ffl.msu.ru/ru/personalpages/proshina_zg/2/

Ward, D. (1986) 'The English contribution to Russian', in W. Viereck and W. Bald (eds) *English in Contact with Other Languages*, Budapest: Academiai Kiado, pp. 307–31.

References

Aitmukhametova, D.I. (2000) 'Leksicheskaya sintagmatika kak obyekt zaimstvovaniya [Lexical syntagmatics as a target of borrowing]', unpublished thesis, Moscow State University.

Andrews, D.R. (1990) 'A semantic categorization of some borrowings from English in third-wave émigré Russian', in M.H. Mills (ed.) *Topics in Colloquial Russian* (American University Studies, Series XII, Slavic Languages and Literature 11), New York: Peter Lang, pp. 157–74.

——(1997) 'Piat' podkhodov k lingvisticheskomu analizu yazyka russkikh emigrantov v S Sh A [Five approaches to the linguistic analysis of the language of Russian emigrants in the USA]', *Slavianovedeniye* [Slavic Studies], 2: 18–30.

Aristova, V.M. (1978) *Anglo-Russkie Yazykovye Kontakty: (Anglizmy v Russkom iazyke) [English and Russian Language Contacts: Anglisms in the Russian Language]*, Leningrad: Leningrad University Publishers.

Beliaeva, S.A. (1984) *Angliiskie Slova v Russkom Iazyke XVI-XX vv [English Words in the Russian Language of the 16–20th Centuries]*, Vladivostok: Far Eastern University Publishers.

Benson, M. (1957) 'American influence on the immigrant Russian press', *American Speech*, 32 (4): 257–63.

——(1960) 'American–Russian speech', *American Speech,* 35 (3): 163–74.

Bondarenko, L. (ed.) (2007) *Slog i Ritm Angliiskoi Rechi v Stranakh Vostochnoi i Yugo-Vostochnoi Azii [Syllable and Rhythm of English Speech in East and South-East Asia]* (in Russian), Vladivostok: Far Eastern University Publishers.

Dimova, S. (2003) 'Teaching and learning English in Macedonia', *English Today*, 76 (19/4): 16–22.

——(2005) 'English in Macedonia', *World Englishes*, 24 (2): 187–201.

——(2008) 'English in Macedonian commercial nomenclature', *World Englishes*, 27 (1): 83–100.

Eddy, A. (2007) 'English in the Russian context: a macrosociolinguistic study', unpublished dissertation, Wayne State University. Detroit, Michigan.

——(2008) 'English in the Russian musical subculture: current trends and attitudes', in Z. Poshina (ed.) *Kul'turno-yazykovye kontacty [Culture and Language Contacts]* (Issue 10), Vladivostok: Far Eastern University Publishers.

Evans, R.J.W. (2008) 'Britons, Czechs and Slovaks: some historical links'. British–Czech-Slovak historians'. Forum. Online. Available http://users.ox.ac.uk/~bcsforum/rjwe.html (accessed 23 July 2008).

Glovinskaya, M.Ya. (2001) 'Yazyk emigratsii kak svidetel'stvo o neustoichivykh uchastkakh yazyka metropolii [The language of emigration as a proof of unstable parts of the language of the mother country]', in S.M. Kuz'mina (ed.) *Zhizn' yazyka. [Life of a Language]*, Moscow: Yazyki slavianskoi kultury.

Griffin, J.L. (2001) 'Global English infiltrates Bulgaria', *English Today*, 68 (17/4): 54–60.

Grushin, O. (2005) *The Dream Life of Sukhanov*, New York: G.P. Putnam's Sons.

Honna, N. (2008) *English as a Multicultural Language in Asian Contexts: Issues and Ideas*, Tokyo: Kurosio.

Jenkins, J. (2004) 'The ABC of ELT ... "ELF"', *IATEFL Issues*, 182 (December 2004–January 2005): 9.
——(2007) *English as a Lingua Franca: Attitude and Identity*, Oxford: Oxford University Press.
Kabakchi, V.V. (1998) *Osnovy angloyazychnoi mezhkul'turnoi kommunikatsii [Fundamentals of the English Crosscultural Communication]*, St Petersburg: Russian State Pedagogical University Press.
——(2005) 'Funktsional'nyi dualism yazyka I yazykovaya konvergentsiya (opyt modeliriovaniya yazykovoi kartiny zemnoi tsivilizatsii) [Language functional dualism and language convergence (Modelling a linguistic picture of the world civilisation)]', in N.A.Abiyeva and E.A. Belichenko (eds) *Kognitivnaya lingvistika: Mental'nye osnovy i yazykovaya realizatsia [Cognitive Linguistics: Mental Bases and Language Actualization]*. Part 2, St Petersburg: Trigon.
Kachru, B.B. (1983) 'Models for non-native Englishes', in L.E. Smith (ed.) *Readings in English as an International Language*, Oxford: Pergamon Press.
——(1985) 'Standards, codification and sociolinguistic realism. The English language in the outer circle', in R. Quirk and H.G. Widdowson (eds) *English in the World: Teaching and Learning the Language and Literatures*, Cambridge: Cambridge University Press; reprinted in K. Bolton and B.B. Kachru (eds) (2006) *World Englishes: Critical Concepts in Linguistics, Vol. 3*, London and New York: Routledge.
Kirkpatrick, A. (2007) *World Englishes: Implications for International Communication and English Language Teaching*, Cambridge: Cambridge University Press.
Konsaltingovaya kompaniya AMICO [AMICO Consulting Co.] (2008) Online. Available www.bsplan.ru/marketing.phtml?a=print&id=130 (accessed 27 July 2008).
Kostomarov, V.G. (1999) *Yazykovoi vkus epokhi [Language Taste of the Epoch]*, St Petersburg: Zlatoust.
Kouzmin, L. (1973) 'The morphological integration of English lexical items in the Russian speech of bilingual migrants living in Australia', *Melbourne Slavonic Studies*, 8: 5–9.
Kruglyi stol (2007) 'Problemy mnogoyazychiya v prepodavanii inostrannykh yazykov v obrazova-tel'nykh uchrezhdeniyakh goroda Moskvy' [Round table 'Multilingual issues in teaching foreign languages in Moscow educational institutions'], paper presented at Moscow Pedagogical Institute of the Humanities, 2007. Online. Available www.mhpi.ru/institute/events/table/ (accessed 29 July 2008).
Krysin, L.P. (2000) 'Inoyazychnoe slovo v kontekste sovremennoi obschestvennoi zhizni [A foreign word in the context of life of the modern community]', in E.A. Zemskaya (ed.) *Russkiy yazyk kontsa XX stoletiya (1985–1995) [The Russian Language of the Late 20th century (1985–1995)]*, Moscow: Yazyki russkoi kul'tury.
Labutina, T.L. (2002) 'Vliyanie angliiskoi kul'tury v vek prosvescheniya [The influence of English culture in the Enlightenment period]'. Online. Available http://ideashistory.org.ru/pdfs/08lab.pdf (accessed 25 July 2007).
Lovtsevich, G. (2001) 'Teaching English in the Russian Far East', paper presented at 'People, Languages and Cultures in the Third Millenium', FEELTA 2000 International Conference. Vladivostok, June.
——(2005) 'Language teachers through the looking glass: Expanding Circle teachers' discourse', *World Englishes*, 24 (4): 461–70.
McCaughey, K. (2005) 'The *kasha* syndrome: English language teaching in Russia', *World Englishes*, 24 (4): 455–9.
Morkovkin, V.V. and Morkovkina, A.V. (1997) *Russkiye agnonimy. Slova, kotorye my ne znayem [Russian Agnonyms. Words that We Don't Know]*, Moscow: A.S. Pushkin Institute of the Russian Language and Russian Academy of Sciences V.V. Vinogradov Institute of the Russian Language.
'Obrazovatel'nyi turizm nuzhdayetsia v dopolnitel'nykh zakonakh [Educational tourism needs addi-tional laws]' (2007) 'Travel.ru. Vsyo o turizme I puteshestviyakh [Everything about travel and journeys]', 27 July. Online. Available www.travel.ru/news/2007/07/27/112242.html (accessed 27 July 2008).
Olmsted, H.M. (1986) 'American interference in the Russian language of the third-wave emigration: Preliminary notes', *Folia Slavica*, 8: 91–127.
O'Reilly, L.M. (1998) 'English language cultures in Bulgaria: a linguistic sibling rivalry?' *World Englishes*, 17 (1): 71–84.

313

'Otdykh v Rossii i stranakh blizhnego zarubezhya [Recreation in Russia and nearby abroad]' (2006) 22 June. Online. Available www.rustur.ru/news/news1450.html (accessed 27 July 2008).

Pavlenko, A. (2006) 'Russian as a lingua franca', *Annual Review of Applied Linguistics*, 26: 78–99.

Pavlovskaya, A.V. (2003) *Obrazovanie v Rossii: istoria i traditsii [Education in Russia: History and Traditions]*, Moscow: Olma-Press.

Polinsky, M.S. (1995) 'Russian in the US: an endangered language', in E. Golovko (ed.) *Russian in Contact with Other Languages*, Oxford: Oxford University Press.

——(1998) 'American Russian: a new pidgin', *Moskovskiy lingvisticheskiy zhurnal* [Moscow Linguistic Journal] 4: 78–138.

Prendergast, C. (2008) *Buying into English. Language and Investment in the New Capitalist World*, Pittsburg: University of Pittsburg Press.

Proshina, Z.G. (2001) *Angliiskiy yazyk i kul'tura Vostochnoi Azii [The English Language and Culture of East Asian People]*, Vladivostok: Far Eastern University Press.

——(2005) 'Intermediary translation from English as a lingua franca', *World Englishes*, 24 (4): 517–22.

——(2006) 'Russian English: status, attitudes, problems', *The Journal of Asia TEFL*, 3 (2): 79–102.

Proshina, Z.G. and Ettkin, B.P. (2005) 'English-Russian language contacts', *World Englishes*, 24 (4): 439–44.

Proshina, Z., Kubritskaya, A. and Sergeyeva, K. (2008) 'Angliiskii yazyk v reklamnoi deyatel'nosti Vladivostoka i Nakhodki [English in Vladivostok's and Nakhodka's advertising]', in Z. Proshina (ed.) *Kul'turno-yazykovyie kontakty [Culture and Language Contacts]* (Issue 11). Online. Available http://ifl.wl.dvgu.ru/download/sborn.doc#_Toc194219876 (accessed 1 June 2008).

Reichelt, M. (2005) 'English in Poland', *World Englishes*, 24 (2): 217–25.

Rivlina, A.A. (2005) ' "Threats and challenges": English–Russian interaction today', *World Englishes*, 24 (4): 477–86.

——(2008) 'ELF creativity and English–Russian language play', in Z. Proshina (ed.) *Kul'turno-yazykovye kontacty [Culture and Language Contacts]* (Issue 10). Vladivostok: Far Eastern University Press.

Romanov, A. Yu. (2000) *Anglitsizmy i amerikanizmy v russkom yazyke i otnoshenie k nim* [Anglicisms and Americanisms in Russian and Attitudes to them], St Petersburg: St. Petersburg University Press.

Russian Federation (2005) 'Russian Federation Federal Law of 1 June no. 53-FZ, On the National Language of the Russian Federation' (in Russian). Online. Available www.rg.ru/2005/06/07/yazyk-dok.html (accessed 1 August 2008).

Russkiy Mir Foundation (2007) 'Creation'. Online. Available http://russkiymir.org/en/about/creation (accessed 1 August 2008).

Šabec, N. (2005) 'Element globalizacije u slovenskim reklamama u medijima [The globalization element in Slovene media advertising]', paper presented at 'Jezik i mediji: jedan jezik: više svjetova: knjižica sažetaka: One Language: Many Worlds', Zagreb, May.

Safonova, O.E. (2000) 'Angliiskii lingvisticheskii komponent v yazykovoi situatsii sovremennoi Rossii [English language component in the linguistic situation in current Russia]', in *Teoreticheskaya i prikladnaya lingvistika. Yazyk i sotsial'naya sreda. [Theoretical and Applied Linguistics. Language and Social Environment]* (Issue 2), Voronezh: Voronezh State Technical University Press. Online. Available www.philology.ru/linguistics3/safonova-00.htm (accessed 15 December 2005).

Samsonov, N.G. (2003) '*O funktsionirovanii russkogo yazyka kak gosudarstvennogo yazyka Rossiiskoi Federatsii v Respublike Sakha (Yakutia) [On the Russian language functioning as the Russian Federation national language in Sakha (Yakutia) Republic]*', report for the Russian Language Council, RF Government, 5 January 2003. Online. Available www.learning-russian.gramota.ru/journals.html?m=mirrs&n=2003–02&id=496 (accessed 16 March 2006).

Schlick, M. (2003) 'The English of shop signs in Europe', *English Today*, 73 (19/1): 3–17.

'S Sh A i Kanada stanoviatsia veduschimi stranami dlia "yazykovykh" turistov [The USA and Canada are the leading countries for "language" tourists]' (2008) *Travel.ru. Vsyo o turizme i puteshestviyakh* [Everything about travel and journeys], 21 July. Online. Available www.travel.ru/news/2008/07/21/125200.html (accessed 8 August 2008).

Smith, L.E. (1992) 'Spread of English and issues of intelligibility', in B. Kachru (ed.) *The Other Tongue. English Across Cultures* (2nd edition), Chicago: University of Illinois Press.

Spooner, M. (1987) 'Foreign affairs: contact literature in English', *The English Journal*, 76 (7): 45–8.

StarTravel Studencheskoye turisticheskoye agenstvo [*StarTravel* Student Travel Agency] (2008) Online. Available www.startravel.ru/ru/langcourses/info/partnership/ (accessed 27 July 2008).

Ter-Minasova, S.G. (2005) 'Traditions and innovations: English language teaching in Russia', *World Englishes*, 24 (4): 445–54.

——(2007) *Voina i mir yazykov i kul'tur [War and Peace of Languages and Cultures]*, Moscow: AST-Astrel-Khranitel.

Thumboo, E. (2006) 'Literary creativity in World Englishes', in B.B. Kachru, Y. Kachru and C.L. Nelson (eds) *The Handbook of World Englishes*, Oxford: Blackwell.

Ulinich, A. (2007) *Petropolis*, New York: Viking.

Ustinova, I.P. (2005) 'English in Russia', *World Englishes*, 24 (2): 239–51.

——(2006) 'English and emerging advertising in Russia', *World Englishes*, 25 (2): 267–77.

——(2008) 'English and American culture appeal in Russian advertising', *Journal of Creative Communications*, 3 (1): 77–98.

Ustinova, I.P. and Bhatia, T.K. (2005) 'Convergence of English in Russian TV commercials', *World Englishes*, 24 (4): 495–508.

Vapnyar, L. (2003) *There are Jews in my House*, New York: Anchor Books.

Vladimirova, I.G. (2001) 'Issledovaniye urovnia transnatsional'nykh kompaniy [Survey of transnational companies' level]', *Menedzhment v Rossii i za rubezhom* [Management in Russia and Abroad], 6. Online. Available www.cfin.ru/press/management/2001–6/12.shtml (accessed 27 July 2008).

Willard, G. and Shchepetova, A. (2003) 'Avenue. A rock group', *The Ukrainian Observer*, 206. Online. Available www.ukraine-observer.com/articles/206/631 (accessed 30 July 2008).

Yuzefovich, N. (2005) 'English in Russian cultural contexts', *World Englishes*, 24 (4): 509–16.

Zemskaya, E.N. (2001a) 'Rech emigrantov kak svidetel'stvo rosta analitizma v russkom yazyke [Emigrant speech as a proof of the increase of analytic trends in Russian]', in S.M. Kuz'mina (ed.) *Zhizn' yazyka. [Life of a Language]*, Moscow: Yazyki slavianskoi kultury.

——(ed.) (2001b) *Yazyk russkogo zarubezhya: Obschiye voprosy i rechevye portrety [The Language of Russians Abroad: General Issues and Speech Portraits]*, Moscow: Yazyki slavianskoy kul'tury.

Zhukova, I. (2001) 'Russlish: the language of Russian-speaking immigrants in the United States', paper presented at 'People, Languages and Cultures in the Third Millenium' FEELTA 2000 International Conference. Vladivostok, June 2001.

18

West Indian Englishes

An introduction to literature written in selected varieties

Hazel Simmons-McDonald

Introduction and background

In recent years, I have heard the term 'Caribbeans' used in some contexts to refer to the peoples of the region. This would rarely be used by Caribbean people to refer to themselves, although the term 'Caribbean' is accepted in the context of wider reference to the people from Anglophone, Francophone and Hispanophone countries in this region. One is more likely to say 'I am from the Caribbean' or 'I am from the West Indies/I am West Indian' rather than *I am a Caribbean/we are Caribbeans*. The term 'West Indies' is used generally to refer to all the countries of the region, but Roberts notes that the term 'does not always refer to the very same islands or territories', and there is some uncertainty as to whether some specific islands 'are included under that designation' (Roberts 1988: 1).

Within the Anglophone countries of the West Indies distinguishable varieties of English are used. Differences in accent between a Trinidadian, a Barbadian and a Jamaican can be easily identified because of the differing phonological and supra-segmental features that mark the English varieties spoken in these countries. West Indian English, or Caribbean English, is broadly used to refer to the English spoken in the region. It is included among varieties of 'international' or 'World' English used across the globe, such as Australian, Canadian and British English, and is mutually intelligible with them, although there are differences in features such as accent and vocabulary. These varieties are considered dialects of English, and, within a given country, there is further variation based on geographical and other factors. As Roberts (1988: 16) puts it, 'West Indian English ... shares features with all other dialects of English but at the same time has features found only in the West Indies.' In Allsopp's words, 'Caribbean English is a collection of sub-varieties of English distributed ... over a large number of non-contiguous territories' (1996: xli).

While dialects of English are not homogeneous, there are accepted norms for grammaticality and correctness in their use for international discourse. Similarly, West Indian English is not homogeneous, as there are variations in countries in the region in which the language is spoken. Thus one can refer to Jamaican (Standard) English, St. Lucian and so on. The differences are less marked in the areas of grammaticality and correctness of usage than in lexicon, phonology and supra-segmental features.

One might contend that if this is so, why use the term 'Englishes' at all? This question raises the issue as to whether one might extend the designation 'English' to other sub-varieties of English spoken in the West Indies. Some authors, for example Ashcroft *et al.* (1989: 8), make a distinction between 'standard' English, which they use to refer to the 'British English' that was spread throughout the Empire, and 'english' spelt with a lower case e, to refer to what they perceive the language to have become in postcolonial countries. They argue thus:

> Though British imperialism resulted in the spread of a language, English, across the globe, the english of Jamaicans is not the english of Canadians, Maoris, or Kenyans. We need to distinguish what is proposed as a standard code, English (the language of the erstwhile imperial centre), and the linguistic code, english, which has been transformed and subverted into several distinctive varieties throughout the world.
>
> (1989: 8)

The authors seem to include in the variety 'english' all sub-varieties that are not 'British English', and one needs to question whether it is even the case that 'British English' itself has not undergone change and variation as a consequence of its contact with speakers from other communities. If one excludes phonological features such as accent, intonation, some nouns and other lexical entries that are incorporated in the so-called 'sub-varieties', one would note that there is less variation at the level of what the authors call the 'standard' in the area of grammar and syntax. This is why one can make reference to 'World English' or Internationally Accepted English (IAE), as there is a high level of mutual intelligibility in varieties that are included in this group. While there are differences between the varieties spoken in different countries, these do not hinder communication among speakers from various countries who use their Standard English variety that is incorporated into the IAE group.

The Concise Oxford Dictionary of Linguistics defines a standard as a variety 'which is learned and accepted as correct across a community or set of communities in which others are also used (e.g. Standard English, as used especially in writing,) vs regional dialects, creoles based on English' (1997: 352). Quirk (1962: 100) makes the qualification that Standard English 'is particularly associated with English in its written form'. Standard English varieties have common core features of grammar and word order, but will exhibit some differences of expression and vocabulary which do not render them mutually unintelligible. Allsopp (1996: lv) provides clarification with respect to West Indian English; he explains that this variety 'has contributed to the lexicon of the core IAE while having a very large body of regionalisms which have not entered that core'. He goes on to say that:

> These regionalisms have the unique status of belonging to a conglomerate of several Standard Englishes, those of the nations and states of the former British West Indian colonies – of Barbadian SE, Jamaican SE, Guyanese SE, Trinidadian SE, etc. That conglomerate is Caribbean Standard English.

He defines Caribbean Standard English as:

the literate English of educated nationals of Caribbean territories and their spoken English such as is considered natural in formal contexts ... Caribbean Standard English would be the total body of regional lexicon and usage bound to a common core of syntax and morphology shared with Internationally Accepted English, but aurally distinguished as a discrete type by certain phonological features such as a marked levelling of British English diphthongs and a characteristic disconnection of pitch from stress as compared with British and American sound patterns.

(Allsopp (1996: lvi)

The foregoing provides a framework for understanding variation in English – with the uppercase E – in the distinction proposed by Ashcroft *et al*. However, there is a broader sense in which the reference to english (lower case e) and what they call the 'linguistic code' requires a more detailed explanation; I will return to this later.

Roberts (1988: 17 ff.) discusses another dimension of variation in English existent in the Anglophone Caribbean. The range is from what he refers to as 'Foreign English' to 'Profane English' with types such as 'Radio and Television English', 'Erudite English', 'Colloquial English', 'Creole English', 'Rasta English' and 'Profane English' occurring as recognizable varieties along this spectrum. For purposes of this discussion, I would categorize Foreign English, Radio and Television English and Erudite English within the English group (uppercase E – IAE and World English) as these varieties more often than not are used formally and are standard, although on radio and television one does hear colloquial and dialect usage depending on the programme and intended audience.

The emergence of creoles

The transformation into several distinct varieties of which Ashcroft *et al*. speak seems to be less of an issue with regard to standard varieties than to other sub-varieties that have emerged as a result of the contact between English and other languages which were spoken by those with whom the British interacted from the earliest times of colonization. I would include among these the creole English varieties spoken in the countries of the West Indies, for example Jamaican Creole and Guyanese Creole. In the case of Barbados, the dialect Bajan is considered by some linguists to be a variety that is 'less creolized' than others such as Jamaican, although others (e.g. Burrowes 1983; Fields 1995; Rickford 1992) have identified creole features in Bajan. The status of Bajan as a creole continues to be discussed. The St Lucian English Vernacular (SLEV) now widely spoken in St Lucia in addition to English and French Creole (Kwéyòl) is another special case which developed in recent times, and discussion has already begun in the literature as to whether it can be referred to as a creole (Garrett 2003). It is important to determine how the creole English varieties emerged and how creole in general has been defined.

Mühlhäusler (1986: 6) reduces the definitions of creole in the literature to the following 'three major types':

1　Creoles are regarded as mixed languages typically associated with cultural and often racial mixture.
2　Creoles are defined as pidgin languages (second languages) that have become the first language of a new generation of speakers.

3 Creoles are reflections of a natural bioprogramme for human language which is activated in cases of imperfect language transmission (cf. Bickerton 1981).

Bickerton (1981) explores the process of creolization in the context of language acquisition in situations in which the input language has been restricted. Roberts (1988) acknowledges as a 'controversial element' theories about the development of languages in the West Indies, the role attributed to the child versus the role of the adult. He indicates:

> The traditional and most tenacious interpretations of the word 'Creole' itself accord a crucial role to the child ... However, most theories explicitly or implicitly regard the initial formative period of West Indian language as second-language learning by West African speakers with then a second stage which involved first-language learning by children born into a slave society.
>
> (1988: 110)

Todd suggests that the creoles in the Caribbean evolved in one of two ways, one of which is, 'Speakers of a pidgin may be put in a position where they can no longer communicate by using their mother tongues. This happened on a large scale in the Caribbean during the course of the slave trade' (1974: 3). Hymes (1971: 3) presents a terse definition of both varieties: 'Pidgins arise as makeshift adaptations, reduced in structure and use, no one's first language; creoles are pidgins become primary languages.'

Leith (1996: 206) points out that the slave trade, which gave rise to what he generally calls 'Black English in the USA and the Caribbean' has been an influence on the speech of 'young English speakers world wide' and it has also 'provided the extraordinary context of language contact which led to the formation of English pidgins and creoles'. In an earlier paper I indicated that in the countries in which 'the creole derived its lexicon from English and co-existed with a standard form of English there was progressive decreolization which resulted in the formation of a post-creole continuum with a range of varieties between the creole and the standard' (Simmons-McDonald 2003: 182). It is important to note also that, while it is accepted that pidgins and creoles emerged as a result of the contact between slaves and the colonizers who occupied the countries of the West Indies, the nature of the contact situation dictates that both groups would have been instrumental in the development of the pidgin for meaningful communication to take place at all. So the stigma of inferiority, which historically has been attributed to pidgins and creoles because of the notion that they were spoken by slaves, merits revision since these varieties were spoken by both colonizer and colonized. However, while the colonizers could communicate among themselves, the Africans who spoke different languages, for the most part, could not use their native languages to communicate among themselves. The pidgin and the creole were used for communication where a common language did not exist.

The construct of a post-creole continuum provides a general explanation of the existence of lectal variability, but the ways in which these lects came into being can be explained by the social structure which existed on the plantations in the West Indies during the period of slavery. Alleyne's (1976) explanation is worth considering in some detail. Alleyne views the development of Caribbean languages as

> normal developments in a certain kind of contact situation that does not allow ... close social integration between the two communities in contact; one that does

319

not allow a great deal of social mobility, but rather keeps people in the social station in which they were born and from which they can never move out.

(Alleyne 1976: 40)

He claims that in this kind of contact situation 'you will find that the initial changes that are introduced by a group or people who are undergoing language shift will be eliminated only very slowly' (ibid.). Alleyne explains how the social fabric on the plantation would have yielded the variability evident in the lects along a post-creole continuum, and observes that 'slaves were differentiated in terms of occupation' which seemed to correspond 'with degrees of social interaction with the European sector of the population'. He continues:

This division of slaves into field, artisan, and domestic provided the domestic slaves with much more contact, much more interaction with European languages. On the other hand, it afforded the field slaves little or none ... Linguistically, this meant that the field slaves developed a certain form of speech consistent with the kind of social interaction they were involved in, and consistent with the kind of communication needs that they had ... On the other hand, the domestics had to develop a rather varied range of linguistic ability because their communication needs were varied ... The kind of linguistic differentiation that emerged at that time can be seen as existing in present-day Caribbean socio-linguistic structure.

(Alleyne 1976: 40–1)

One can therefore conclude that the variety spoken by the field slaves would have been further removed from the variety spoken by the colonizers (the imported standard) than that spoken by domestics, and that this variety would correspond to what linguists refer to as the *basilect*; it would thus be positioned at the opposite end of the continuum from the *acrolect*, the variety which corresponds closely to the standard variety or that which has most prestige. The intervening varieties are referred to as *mesolects*.

Many speakers in the West Indies, particularly educated speakers, have multilectal competence and can switch codes easily within a communication interaction, depending on the appropriateness for the situation and audience. This is frequently demonstrated in the literature, particularly prose, in which writers often use the range of dialects available to them in their writing to portray authenticity in characterization. This is also evident in the work of poets. Chamberlin (1993: 124–5) comments on the two inheritances of language available to the Caribbean writer. He notes:

The most radical division for West Indian poets is that which separates their African and European inheritances. Whether descendants of slaves or not, West Indian poets all share that sense of division, and it distinguishes them from their sometime European masters.

In his introduction to the second volume of *Caribbean Voices: The Blue Horizons*, Figueroa (1970: 7) identifies similar concerns addressed by poets, referring to them as 'the experience of conflict of heritages'. These issues emerge from the major concern of the day to discard the trappings of colonialism and find an authentic West Indian voice. Figueroa asks the question 'Should our poets, then, set out to be different?' And he provides the following answer:

The question of what makes one a West Indian writer is difficult, and is fraught with all kinds of emotional problems. When 'West Indianismus', as Slade Hopkinson calls it, started, it was in many ways a healthy reaction to the attitude which had nothing but blind eyes for 'burnished beauty nearer home'; which always looked (and looks) abroad, and only to certain countries abroad, for approval and for standards. It was also a healthy reaction against the kind of second-hand experience by which some West Indian writers would fool themselves into believing that they were writing about Spring when they had not ever experienced, in any sense, Spring.

(Figueroa 1970: 10)

The poems written in the period to which Figueroa refers were couched primarily in Standard English, Ashcroft *et al.*'s English with upper case E. The acceptance of English with lower case e liberated poets from the trappings of the colonial experience. As I observe elsewhere (Simmons-McDonald 2003: 195),

The use of the various lects by Caribbean writers asserts the cultural realities of the region while contributing to the liberation and transformation from a colonised mentality ... The creation of successful counter-discourses stems from the expert manipulation of the range of varieties which results from multidialectal/ (multilingual) competence. This competence also involves the communicative dimension of an understanding of the cultural contexts or place in which these varieties are used.

Chamberlin (1993: 112) notes that 'a sense of divided or dual allegiance ... is a fact of life' for West Indian poets and 'a feature of their languages'. However, it is also a source of power as they have used both the European and African influences on their culture and language to express an identity that is uniquely West Indian. As Chamberlin indicates,

West Indian poets have found ways to break free from the spell of a debilitating schizophrenia by recognizing that it is precisely this sense of divided allegiance that unites [West Indian poets] with other poets, and that the language of poetry in all its traditions, African as well as European, routinely includes both high and low varieties of language, as well as elements of both artifice and naturalness.

Chamberlin (1993: 112)

The work of Jamaican poet Edward Baugh exemplifies that naturalness in the use of English and 'english' that evokes the sense of comfort with identity and mastery over the lects from the inheritances of the forebears.

When the final carry-down artist lock down   1
this town and scorch the earth till not
even lizard don't crawl, those who still living
next morning will see me surviving still
wood of life, salvation tree   5
I renew my phases of lilac-blue
and gold and always green, I am

a shady place for those who have lost
their way to the house of the man who gave
them stones for bread.   10
I don't want to sound
like I boasting, but too many small men in this two-
by-four place is giant, and you only have to open
your mouth and you can hang up a shingle outside
your gate with 'expert' behind your name.   15
And to think, so many people born
and grow and dead and never feel
the rainbreeze blowing cool across
Cinchona from Catherine's Peak at middle
day. Sometimes I feel my heart   20
harden, but I not going nowhere, my root
sink too deep, and when the 8 o'clock sun
wake up the generations of stale pee and puke
that stain the sidewalk by Parade, I weep
I bloom choirs of small butterflies.   25

> (Edward Baugh (2000) 'Lignum vitae',
> in *It was the Singing*, Kingston: Sandberry Press, p. 97)

In this poem, Baugh moves effortlessly between Jamaican Creole English and Standard Jamaican. In lines 1 through 4, the poet uses the idiom of a mesolectal variety of Jamaican Creole, evident in the terms *carry-down artist* (line 1); *not even lizard don't crawl* (lines 2–3) and *lock down*. A more commonly attested feature in creoles is where the morphology eliminates redundancy by omitting the s, as in *lock*. The second example – a double negative – provides the rhetorical emphasis the poet requires in the line. The standard equivalent *till not even lizards crawl* seems weak in comparison. The double negative as used by Baugh is logical because it not only carries the rhythm of the lect, but it also provides the force of emphasis that the standard could not carry in such a context.

The term *carry-down artist* is culturally relevant in the Jamaican context. A collea-gue (Velma Pollard, personal communication) presented me with the following as a literal meaning for the term as 'someone who in some way subverts your intention. Usually it is someone you don't expect to carry you down.' In this case, the poet uses the image of the 'carry-down artist' figuratively to represent a force of nature that brings deprivation and death to the town, and the barrenness of the landscape is con-trasted with the life of the lignum vitae tree, which represents hope, renewal and regen-eration. The use of Creole in lines 1–3 evokes the starkness and dryness of the earth as well as the absence of life (not even lizard don't crawl) crisply, and with economy of expression. It also evokes the softness of nature 'never feel the rainbreeze ... at middle day'.

In line 4, Baugh moves seamlessly into the idiom of the standard by using the full standard verb form 'will see me surviving still' (line 4) and the grammar and idiom of the standard are carried over into the following five lines. The use of 'rainbreeze' (line 13) which is not, as far as I am aware, a common Creole word, but which operates similarly to the process of juxtaposition of nouns that often occurs in the Creole, initiates the shift from Creole to Standard Jamaican in that stanza, but this is not sustained, as the insertion of the non-standard double negative in line 16 introduces the (other) Creole voice 'my root sink too deep', which then becomes almost undecipherable from the use of the standard in the last two lines of the poem. The voice of the lignum vitae is the Creole voice and its identity is that of the people, rooted in the earth and deriving the sustenance that allows it to 'renew its phases' cyclically, without succumbing to death.

Status and roles of Englishes in Caribbean communities

The language situations in countries in the Caribbean in which the 'mass' language (usually a creole) is different from the official language vary according to the socio-political history of the countries, with attitudes towards the languages being influenced by the status and prestige of the languages. Alleyne observes that 'two or three types of language situations' can be observed in the Caribbean (1976: 42). He distinguishes between bilingual situations in which there is no relationship between the creole language spoken by the masses and the official language. He lists as examples Surinam or the Dutch Antilles, St Lucia and Dominica. In St Lucia, for example, English is the official language, while French Creole, the language spoken by the masses, is not mutually intelligible with English. Continued contact between the French Creole and English resulted in the emergence of an English lexicon vernacular which is now widely spoken on the island. '[T]he continued contact between the French Creole and English has resulted in the emergence of a "new" English' (Simmons-McDonald 2003: 183) with 'features that are common to other English-lexicon creoles in the Caribbean' (Le Page and Tabouret-Keller 1985: 147) and 'strongly influenced by Creole phonetic, semantic and syntactic patterns' (Alleyne 1961: 5–6). This St Lucian English Lexicon Vernacular (SLEV) may constitute a 'third' type of 'new English' or 'an alternative English variety' which is distinguished from a variety like Jamaican, for example, because it emerged out of 'a more recent and ongoing contact situation' (Simmons-McDonald 2003: 195).

Other suggestions have been made in the literature about the emergence and spread of SLEV. One such is that it developed in the school context as a result of the attempts of French Creole speakers to learn English (e.g. Christie 1983, referring to Dominica, which has a similar sociolinguistic situation to that of St. Lucia). Another is that it developed and spread from casual contact in communities between speakers of English and Kwéyòl (e.g. Garrett 2003). I argue that both of these explanations are plausible, with the school providing the catalyst for emergence early on, and spread occurring as a result of continuous and increasing contact between speakers in communities (Simmons-McDonald 2009).

Le Page and Tabouret-Keller reported that the emerging varieties of English in use in St Lucia seemed to represent a 'multidimensional continuum' (1985: 140), which involves the co-existence of Kwéyòl features commonly found in Barbadian dialect and features common to other English-based creoles in the Caribbean. Carrington speculated that 'highest concentrations of competence in English would be in the area of Castries, with concentrations of competence in [Kwéyòl] being the privilege of rural districts' (1984: 184). More recent observation (Simmons-McDonald, ongoing study on attitudes to language in St Lucia) suggests that there is more widespread use of English, even in rural communities. Trends indicate that there has been considerable language shift in St Lucia, from a predominantly Kwéyòl-speaking community in the late 1940s, with a relatively high percentage of exclusive Kwéyòl speakers (43 per cent), to a predominantly bilingual community, in which varieties of English are becoming increasingly dominant, and in which the percentage of exclusive Kwéyòl speakers is probably small.

Garrett (2000: 73) states that although the vernacular is 'acknowledged to exist in recent scholarly literature ... it is not acknowledged by most St Lucians'. He goes on to say that:

> St Lucians are certainly attentive to the fact that some persons speak English better than others – that is, that some speak more in accordance with pedagogical standards ... But for everyday purposes of most St Lucians, English is English, and no further distinctions need be made.
>
> Garrett (2000: 73)

Before scholars ever discussed or studied the variation that exists in the varieties of English used on the island, one found nuanced instances of SLEV in the work of writers such as Roderick and Derek Walcott, and Garth St Omer.

Garrett's comment cited above points to the fact that most St Lucians do not recognize a difference between the official variety and SLEV, which is now being acquired as a first language by children in areas where formerly Kwéyòl would have been more likely to have been the first language. St Lucian Standard English, the official language, is ascribed a higher status than either Kwéyòl or SLEV. The emergence of SLEV and its recognition as a lect that is different from the official variety is fairly recent, and the few early empirical studies that were done on attitudes to language in St Lucia did not include it as a variable for analysis. Early studies on the language situation in St Lucia compared St Lucian Standard and Kwéyòl. For the most part, the views expressed about Kwéyòl were mostly negative. The following comments reflect the attitudes towards the French Creole that existed on the island in earlier times.

- 'Patois [Kwéyòl] is inferior to English; it is not a language; it has no grammar; it is only broken French ... ' (Vérin 1958: 164, writing about language use in the school system and commenting on the 'postulates ... pumped into the scholar's head').
- 'Patois is making [St Lucians] backwards; it is nothing but palawala and it is merely a ploy to keep us back' (Yarde 1989).

Despite these negative sentiments some studies reported that St Lucians were ambivalent about Kwéyòl but may have a higher regard for it than for English, as they rated Kwéyòl versions of a story in a matched guise test 'more confident' and 'more wise' than English (Liebermann 1975: 487). Attitudes towards Kwéyòl in the teaching profession have changed for the better, since 81 per cent of principals reported that they allowed teachers to use Kwéyòl to children in class when necessary and 92 per cent of primary school teachers reported that they use Kwéyòl with children for a range of purposes (Simmons-McDonald 1988: 30). This was encouraging, as earlier studies had reported that students would sometimes be punished for using French Creole on the school compound.

More recent studies have commented on the increased use and recognition of SLEV as another English variety, and it has been the subject of study in the last decade (e.g. Garrett 2003; Simmons-McDonald 2006). The latter study reported that SLEV was valued less highly than either Standard St Lucian or Kwéyòl, whereas there was greater similarity in valuation of Standard St Lucian and Kwéyòl on all attitude traits included in the study. This was interpreted to indicate that Kwéyòl is valued as highly as Standard

St Lucian, whereas SLEV is less highly valued than either of the two former varieties. An interesting finding from that study was that teachers were more likely to allow the use of Kwéyòl in the classroom for purposes of providing explanations to students, but they were less tolerant of the use of SLEV, which they characterized as 'broken or bad English'. Yet SLEV is used increasingly with Kwéyòl and Standard St Lucian in the work of writers to portray the language and culture of St Lucians in a realistic way.

Attitudes to creoles where these have co-existed with a standard variety have been similar to those described in the case of St Lucia. Across the Caribbean and even further afield, creoles have been described in such disparaging terms that even the speakers of these language varieties have accepted the lower status ascribed to creoles and many have discouraged their use by children in the expectation that learning the standard will lead to success in education. For example, one Leopold is reported to have said: 'The Sierra Leone patois is ... a standing menace and a disgrace hindering not only educational development but also the growth of civilization in the colony' (Spitzer 1966: 41).

Such sentiments and the attachment of creoles to slavery have historically influenced the status of these languages, and countries like Jamaica and Guyana in which the creoles are lexically related to the standard variety have been no exception. Jamaica had a long history of colonization by the British and, consequently, English has been the official language in that country for decades. It has higher status than Jamaican Creole, although the latter is widely used in the literature and lyrics of reggae and exported via these media to the rest of the world. The language situation in Jamaica is also one that is described as a continuum, with a basilect variety that is widely spoken by the masses and with mesolectal varieties that approximate to Jamaican Standard English. Alleyne describes the situation in Jamaica as follows:

> [T]he mass language ... referred to as 'dialect', arose out of a contact situation with English, and ... English remains the language official, the language of the elite, and the language of the colonial or former colonial power ... [I]n the case of someone speaking the mass language of Jamaica and an Englishman, there is a great deal of communication difficulty, there is some breakdown, and some disruption of communication, but it is said that it is not total.
>
> (Alleyne 1976: 43)

Comparing the situations in Barbados and Jamaica, Roberts makes a similar point, noting that in both countries there is 'a spectrum of varieties related to the English Language', but in the case of Jamaica there are 'more varieties distant from English' (1988: 6). Yet, De Camp (1971) cited in Rickford (1987: 18) observed that many Jamaicans do not recognize the heterogeneous situation that exists in that context since

> Many Jamaicans persist in the myth that there are only two varieties: the patois and the standard. But one speaker's attempt at the broad patois may be closer to the standard end of the continuum than is another's attempt at the standard.
>
> (De Camp, cited in Rickford 1987: 18)

Jamaican Creole is used widely in the country and it is highly valued by its speakers. The current situation in Jamaica is one in which decreolization towards Jamaica Standard is unlikely, as more widespread use of the mass language is becoming the norm. This has led academics like Cooper (2003) and Devonish (1983) to advocate the use of

Jamaican Creole in education. Cooper made the point about the adequacy of Jamaican Creole for functions like addressing educational subjects and doing critical literary analysis in Jamaican Creole by presenting her professorial inaugural lecture in that variety.

> Wen mi riid *Lionheart Gal* an si se di hai op uman dem a rait fii dem stouri–
> (When I read *Lionheart Gal* and saw what these cultured women were writing in their stories)
> Dem no ina no tiepin bizniz; and dem a rait ina pyuur Ingglish
> (They aren't in any tiepin business, and they write in pure English)
> An mi si se dem ada wan dem, a taak fii dem stuori, ina Jamiekan, mi se,
> (And I saw these other ones talking about their stories in Jamaican, I said)
> 'Hmnn. Jakaas se di worl no levl.' An den mi si se if me no main shaap,)
> ('Hmm, Jackass says the world is not level.' And then I figured that if I did not pay attention)
> mi a go en op a pop stail ina Ingglish pon di uman dem uu a tel fe dem stuori ina Jamiekan.
> (I would end up showing off in English to the women who told their stories in Jamaican.)
> So mi se 'naa.' Mi a go chrai a ting.
> (So I said 'No.' I will try something.)
> Mi a go shuo unu se wi kyan yuuz Jamiekan fi taak bout aal kain a big sobjek.
> (I will show you that we can use Jamaican to talk about all kinds of lofty subjects.)
>
> (Cooper 2003: 4)

Her reference in this excerpt to the literary collection of short fiction titled *Lionheart Gal* by the group Sistren, and her critique of their rendering of their stories in Jamaican Creole, served to validate the richness of the Creole for literary purposes and its use as a tool for critiquing literary works. But the validation of Jamaican Creole for literary purposes is something that writers had been working on for a long time. They, like writers across the Caribbean, used the creoles and creole-influenced vernaculars (CIVs) in their writing 'to express the cultural realities of the people' (Simmons-McDonald 2003: 190), and in so doing have elevated the status of the creoles and contributed to their increased valuation in recent times.

Some considerations related to culture and identity

Just as language played an important role in the lives of slaves on the plantations in circumscribing notions of personal and collective freedom, it plays an even bigger role in determining and defining notions such as identity and equality and perhaps more importantly in shaping the destinies of speakers of creole language varieties. Kramsch (1998: 8) makes the point that:

> Language is not a culture-free code, distinct from the way people think and behave, but rather, it plays a major role in the perpetuation of culture, particularly in its printed form ... Language is intimately linked not only to the culture that is and the culture that was, but also to the culture of the imagination that governs people's decisions and actions far more than we may think.

326

Kramsch goes on to suggest that 'national cultures resonate with the voices of the powerful, and are filled with the silences of the powerless' (1998: 9).

The imposition of English as the official language during colonization was a decision of the colonizer. It was the means by which English was established as the voice that would articulate a particular course of development for the people of the Anglophone Caribbean. It was a reality in which the creoles would be rendered powerless. However, some writers subvert that very notion of the powerlessness of the dialect/creoles/'english' by using processes in writing that Ashcroft *et al.* refer to as 'abrogation' and 'appropriation' (i.e. use of the 'english' varieties) as 'a medium of power' (1989: 38). The power stems from the capability of writers to manipulate the range of varieties expertly to assert the cultural realities of the Caribbean while at the same time 'contributing to the liberation and transformation of a colonized mentality' (Simmons-McDonald 2003: 195). Condé says '[the creole] was a means of communication to be understood by both masters and slaves'. As such, 'it can be seen as the first example of the Caribbean syncretic culture'. She continues, 'when Creole became widespread in each island, at its outset, it was not perceived as a unique linguistic creation, but rather as a distortion, a perversion of the model of the European colonizer's language' (Condé 1998: 102). The validation of alternative varieties of English, 'english'/creoles and creole-influenced vernaculars through their use in literature is one of the ways by which writers assert their culture and identity that are bound up in the concept of 'creolization' or *créolité*, the French equivalent used by Pépin and Confiant (1998: 97), and which involves the assumption of a rich linguistic heritage that allows for the adoption of what they perceive to be 'an identity of co-existence'.

Rickford asserts that the transplantation of English around the world has dramatically transformed it, particularly in Commonwealth and Third World countries in which English exists with pidgins and creoles (Rickford 1998: 58). The examples presented thus far serve to demonstrate this clearly, but perhaps the contribution to world literature by the work of writers from the Caribbean cannot be more strongly demonstrated than in the work of Nobel Laureates for Literature, Vidia Naipaul and Derek Walcott. The following extract from Walcott's play *The Sea at Dauphin* uses SLEV for authentic presentation of character.

> Malice! Compassion! What it have in this morning before sun even wipe his eye, that I must take this dirty tongue from you, eh? When I did working your age with Bolo, you think I could show my teeth in disrespect? And this new thing, compassion? Where is compassion? Is I does make poor people poor, or this sea vex? Is I that put rocks where should dirt by Dauphin side, man cannot make garden grow? Is I that swell little children belly with bad worm, and woman to wear clothes white people use to wipe their foot? In my head is stone, and my heart is another, and without stone, my eyes would burst for that, would look for compassion on woman belly. I born and deading in this coast that have no compassion to grow food for children, no fish enough to buy new sail, no twine. Every day sweat, sun, and salt, and night is salt and sleep, and all the dead days pack away and stink, is Dauphin life. Not I who make it!
>
> (Derek Walcott (1970) *Dream on Monkey Mountain and Other Plays*,
> New York: Farrar, Straus and Giroux, p. 53)

Perhaps what is most striking about this extract is that it represents, for the most part, a direct translation from Kwéyòl. Isaac (1986) reports the existence of a continuum in the

St Lucian context with a variety of English similar to Kwéyòl, in syntactic structure which consists of 'calqued forms' that represent direct translation from Kwéyòl. She presents the continuum as a pyramid, with Kwéyòl at the base, leading sharply into the English Lexicon Variety with phrases and sentence patterns mirroring those of Kwéyòl and forming what she referred to as the basilect. Mesolectal varieties containing fewer similarities to Kwéyòl but having features similar to some Caribbean Creole English varieties occur above the basilect and taper to St Lucian Standard English at the apex of the pyramid. Garrett (2000) discusses a continuum which, if graphically presented, would be similar to that of Isaac's.

Examples of calques on the French Creole constructions in the excerpt include the following: *What it have*; *Is I does make poor people poor* ... ; *Is I that put rocks* ... ; *I born and deading in this coast* ... ; *that have no compassion* ... ; *Not I who make it*! and Walcott captures a variety closest to what Isaac and Garret would consider Basilect SLEV, while including phrases from other mesolectal forms: *'you think I could show my teeth in disrespect?' 'and woman to wear clothes white people use to wipe their foot?' 'Man cannot make garden grow?'* The interweaving of these varieties captures the rich texture of the fabric of St Lucian English while hinting, through the primary use of the basilect, at the underlying Kwéyòl nuances in the phrasing of the text.

The character chides Bolo for showing disrespect by speaking rudely – 'dirty tongue' – and disclaims responsibility for the hardships endured by fishermen, eking out an existence on the Dauphin coast. The images are of nature, the dawn 'before sun even wipe his eye' and of abject poverty and a life of deprivation conveyed by the image of children with extended tummies, suffering from worms, and women wearing the hand-me-down rags cast away by white people. The experience of the fisherman speaker is given authenticity and presented with realism through the use of the vernacular and the weaving of the different varieties that represent the voice of St Lucian folk.

The selections have illustrated some of the ways in which writers make variable use of the 'englishes' spoken in the region to convey message and enrich meaning through the evocation of the authentic language to portray the life experience and culture of a people. The literature, like the music, has international reach and has achieved wide acceptance, recognition and validation as a significant part of world literature. It is not that English has been 'subverted' and new lects created based on its lexicon; it is rather that English itself has been enriched by its interaction with speakers of other lects and languages. As Rickford notes, 'English is enriched too, by its new geographical and social contexts, and by the new content of the millions who use it ... and it is gifted with ideas and perspectives, rhythms and metaphors which it would not otherwise have had' (1998: 58).

Creoles in the future

Language change is a dynamic process and languages go through this process of change over time in a gradual way. This is no different with the 'english' varieties that are creoles and creole-influenced vernaculars and dialects. These varieties are vehicles of communication used by masses of people for a variety of everyday purposes and, as such, they continue to be studied by linguists, who not only engage in the description of their grammars but also chronicle the process of change in these varieties. This of itself indicates that, if these activities can be undertaken with the varieties under consideration, they are languages that can be studied in the same ways and subjected to the same types of analysis. It is therefore important to note as a most basic fact that there is nothing inherent in a given language to lead one to conclude that some languages are inferior.

Languages have different systems for conveying meaning and it is the study of these systems that leads to an understanding of how the languages work. The circumscription and restriction of creoles to functions that exclude those of education and other official areas have resulted, not from an understanding of the systems of the languages or how they can be used in a wider range of functions for the benefit of people, but from the perception of a dominant group who made value judgements about language and determined that certain languages did not have the capacity for dealing with abstraction or serious thought or for literary criticism.

However, the creoles are the varieties with which the masses identify and they are important to their identity as a people, an identity of 'creoleness'. Wilson Harris observes that the term 'creoleness' is peculiar as it may sustain 'a conservative, if not reactionary purist logic' (Harris 1998: 26). Yet he asserts that creoleness 'signifies ... a cross-cultural nemesis capable of becoming a saving nemesis', the latter implying 'recuperative powers and vision'. Embracing the notion of 'creoleness' is seen as a force for forging a particular identity and for achieving liberation from the hegemony of the colonial language. This has already been manifested in the literature written by West Indians, in which they use the full range of lectal varieties available to them to explore issues of identity and to assert the realities of a creole culture that is part and parcel of West Indian life. As Ashcroft *et al.* have shown (1989), writers have used that mastery to 'deconstruct' the colonial language of power through the use of vernacular languages, either minimally or extensively in their texts. Condé (1998: 102–3) lists many specific examples of texts that attempt such deconstruction. She argues that by using the strategy of embedding creole in texts writers 'injected the marginalized and despised culture into the heart of the dominant one and in so doing, destroyed the latter's hegemony' (103). She notes:

> The control of language is one of the primary aspects of colonial oppression – the dependency of the periphery upon the center. Language is a site of power: who names controls. The politically and economically alienated colonized are first colonized linguistically. In their attempt to gain freedom and self-determination, the colonized must put an end to the pre-eminence of the colonial language.
>
> (Condé 1998: 103)

The power for achieving such freedom and self-determination is realized in the use of the 'englishes' of the region in the literature, the lyrics of songs to express the experience and culture of a people. Through these forms of expression 'creoleness' can become the 'saving nemesis' to which Harris refers. The significant contribution of West Indian writers to the international recognition and acceptance of creoles and creole-influenced vernaculars as 'alternative English varieties' presents a compelling medium through which the full potential of these languages can be appreciated.

Suggestions for further reading

Aceto, M. and Williams, J. (eds) (2003) *Contact Englishes of the Eastern Caribbean*, Amsterdam: John Benjamins.

Chamberlin, J. Edward (1993) *Come Back to Me My Language: Poetry and the West Indies*, Urbana: University of Illinois Press.

Roberts, Peter (1988) *West Indians and their Language*, Cambridge: Cambridge University Press.

Simmons-McDonald, Hazel (2003) 'Decolonizing English: the Caribbean counter-thrust', in Christian Mair (ed.) *The Politics of English as a World Language: New Horizons in Postcolonial Cultural Studies* (Cross/Cultures 65, ASNEL Papers 7), Amsterdam: Rodopi, pp. 179–201.

References

Alleyne, Mervyn (1961) 'Language and society in St Lucia', *Caribbean Studies*, 1 (1): 1–10.

——(1976) 'Linguistic aspects of communication in the West Indies', in Marlene Cuthbert and Michael Pidgeon (eds) *Language and Communication in the Caribbean* (3rd edition), Bridgetown, Barbados: CEDAR Press, pp. 35–48.

Allsopp, Richard (1996) *Dictionary of Caribbean English Usage*, Oxford: Oxford University Press.

Ashcroft, Bill, Griffiths, Gareth and Tiffin, Helen (1989) *The Empire Writes Back: Theory and Practice in Post-colonial Literatures*, London: Routledge.

Bickerton, Derek (1981) *Roots of Language*, Ann Arbor: Karoma.

Burrowes, Audrey (in collaboration with Allsopp, Richard) (1983) 'Barbadian Creole: a note on its social history and structure', in Lawrence Carrington (ed.) with Denis Craig and Todd Dandare, *Studies in Caribbean Language*, St Augustine, Trinidad: Society for Caribbean Linguistics, pp. 38–45.

Carrington, Lawrence (1984) *St Lucian Creole: A Descriptive Analysis of its Phonology and Morpho-Syntax*, Hamburg: Helmut Buske Verlag.

Chamberlin, J. Edward (1993) *Come Back to Me My Language: Poetry and the West Indies*, Urbana: University of Illinois Press.

Christie, Pauline (1983) 'In search of the boundaries of Caribbean Creoles', in Lawrence Carrington (ed.) with Denis Craig and Todd Dandare, *Studies in Caribbean Language*, St Augustine, Trinidad: Society for Caribbean Linguistics.

Condé, Maryse (1998) 'Créolité without the Creole language', in K. Balutansky and M. Sourieau (eds) *Caribbean Creolization*, Gainsville: University of Florida Press; Kingston: University Press of the West Indies, pp. 101–9.

Cooper, Carolyn (2003) 'Professing slackness: language, authority and power within the academy and without', inaugural professorial lecture presented at the UWI, Mona, 25 September.

Devonish, Hubert (1983) 'Towards the establishment of an institute for Creole language standardization and development in the Caribbean', in L. Carrington (ed.) with Denis Craig and Todd Dandare, *Studies in Caribbean Language*, St Augustine, Trinidad: Society for Caribbean Linguistics, pp. 300–16.

Fields, Linda (1995) 'Early Bajan: Creole or non-Creole?' in Jacques Arends (ed.) *The Early Stages of Creolization*, Amsterdam: John Benjamins, pp. 89–112.

Figueroa, John (ed.) (1970) *Caribbean Voices: An Anthology of West Indian Poetry. Vol. 2: The Blue Horizons*, London: William Clowes and Sons.

Garrett, Paul (2000) '"High" Kwéyòl: the emergence of a formal Creole register in St Lucia', in John McWhorter (ed.) *Language Change and Language Contact in Pidgins and Creoles*, Amsterdam: John Benjamins, pp. 64–101.

——(2003) 'An "English Creole" that isn't', in Michael Aceto and Jeffrey Williams (eds) *Contact Englishes of the Eastern Caribbean*, Amsterdam: John Benjamins.

Harris, Wilson (1998) 'Creolness', in Kathleen Balutansky and Marie-Agnès Sourieau (eds) *Caribbean Creolization*, Barbados: University of West Indies Press, pp. 23–35.

Hymes, Dell (1971) 'Introduction, Part III – General conceptions of process', in Dell Hymes (ed.) *Pidginization and Creolization of Languages*, Cambridge: Cambridge University Press, pp. 230–41.

Isaac, Martha (1986) 'French Creole interference in the written English of St Lucian secondary school students', MPhil thesis, UWI Cave Hill.

Kramsch, Claire (1998) *Language and Culture*, Oxford: Oxford University Press.

Le Page, Robert and Tabouret-Keller, Andrée (1985) *Acts of Identity: Creole-based Approaches to Language and Identity*, Cambridge: Cambridge University Press.

Leith, Dick (1996) 'English – colonial to postcolonial', in David Graddol and John Swann (eds) *English: History Diversity and Change*, London: Routledge.

Liebermann, Dena (1975) 'Language attitudes in St. Lucia', *Journal of Cross Cultural Psychology*, 6: 471–81.1.

Matthews, P.H. (1997) *The Concise Oxford Dictionary of Linguistics*, New York: Oxford University Press.

Mühlhäusler, Peter (1986) *Pidgin and Creole Linguistics*, Oxford: Blackwell.

Pépin, Ernest and Confiant, Raphaël (1998) 'The stakes of créolité', in Kathleen M. Balutansky and Marie-Agnès Sourieau (eds) *Caribbean Creolization*, Gainesville: University of Florida Press; Kingston: University of the West Indies Press, pp. 96–100.

Quirk, Randolph (1962) *The Use of English*, New York: Longman.

Rickford, John (1987) *Dimensions of a Creole Continuum: History, Texts, and Linguistic Analysis of Guyanese Creole*, Stanford, California: Stanford University Press.

——(1992) 'The Creole residue in Barbados', in Joan H. Hall, Nick Doane and Dick Ringler (eds) *Old English and New: Studies in Language and Linguistics in Honor of Frederic G. Cassidy*, New York: Garland.

——(1998) 'English transplanted, English transformed!' *Kyk-Over-Al*, 48 (April): 45–60.

Roberts, Peter (1988) *West Indians and Their Language*, Cambridge: Cambridge University Press.

Simmons-McDonald, Hazel (1988) 'The learning of English negatives by speakers of St Lucian French Creole', unpublished PhD dissertation, Stanford University.

——(1996) 'Language education policy: the case for Creole in formal education in St Lucia', in Pauline Christie (ed.) *Caribbean Language Issues Old and New*, Kingston: University of the West Indies Press, pp. 120–42.

——(2003) 'Decolonizing English: the Caribbean counter-thrust', in Christian Mair (ed.) *The Politics of English as a World Language: New Horizons in Postcolonial Cultural Studies*, (Cross/Cultures 65, ASNEL Papers 7), Amsterdam: Rodopi, pp. 179–201.

——(2006) 'Attitudes of teachers to St Lucian language varieties', *Caribbean Journal of Education*, 28 (1): 51–84.

——(2009) 'Review of *Contact Englishes of the Eastern Caribbean* (M. Aceto and J. Williams (eds), John Benjamins)', *Journal of Pidgin and Creole Languages*, 24 (1): 159–67.

Spitzer, Leo (1966) 'Creole attitudes toward Krio: an historical survey', *Sierra Leone Language Review*, 5: 41.

Todd, Loreto (1974) *Pidgins and Creoles*, London: Routledge and Kegan Paul.

Vérin, Pierre M. (1958) 'The rivalry of French Creole and English in the British West Indies', *De West Indische Gids*, 38: 163–7.

Yarde, Clive (1989) 'Patois making us backward', *The Voice*, 26 August.

19

English and English teaching in Colombia

Tensions and possibilities in the expanding circle

Adriana González

Introduction

This chapter presents a general picture of the current status of English in Colombia. Along with many expanding circle nations, Colombia is experiencing a growth in terms of the presence and roles of English. The interest from the population to learn it, the need to have teachers prepared to teach it, the establishment of language education policies to regulate its practices, and the academic debates around all these issues reflect the new relationships between language and society.

I attempt to contribute to the field of World Englishes from the Colombian perspective in my various roles as a non-native-speaker teacher-educator who was once a learner and a teacher of English. I would like to re-evaluate the traditional views of English in our country with a view to transforming Colombian ELT and teacher education.

Two main issues will guide the analysis: the tensions and the possibilities concerning the status of English in our nation, analysed from the perspective of its current teaching endeavours. First, however, I will present some background information about Colombia and the history of English in the country. Regarding the tensions and possibilities, I will explore the new language policies that the national government issued to improve the quality of education and English Language Teaching (ELT). Finally, I will summarize the main points presented in the chapter.

Some background information about Colombia and English in Colombia

Colombia is a country in north-western South America. Ethnically diverse, it has a population of 44,000,000 inhabitants, according to the 2008 national census. Traditionally considered as a monolingual Spanish-speaking country, Colombia's rich linguistic diversity surprises both locals and outsiders. Besides Spanish, the language used by the majority of the population, there are 64 indigenous languages (González and Rodríguez 1999; Landaburu 1999; Spolsky 2004) and two creoles: a Caribbean English-based creole, called Islander (Bartens 2003) and Palenquero (Patiño Roselli 1992; Dieck 1998). In 1991, the Constitution promulgated a new status for minority languages making them the official languages of the communities which use them. However, the notion of bilingualism is often associated with the mastery of Spanish and another Western language, mainly English. Bilingualism seen as English–Spanish is particularly obvious in the government initiatives to promote the teaching and learning of English (De Mejía 2004, 2006a). Native bilingual and multilingual communities are often marginalized and impoverished in many countries in the Third World (Grosjean 1987). These communities experience in Colombia serious social and economic problems and often suffer ethnic discrimination (Behrman *et al.* 2003). The use of two or more languages from these peoples and the sign language of the deaf are forms of 'invisible bilingualism' in the country (De Mejía 2006b: 382).

The Caribbean islands of San Andrés, Providencia and Santa Catalina have the highest presence of English in the country. Spanish, Islander and English co-exist in a diglossic and often triglossic situation for the native inhabitants: 'Spanish is the language of business, banking, the government, and education. Creole is the language of informal and everyday situations; and English is restricted mainly to religious services' (Sanmiguel 2007: 29–30, own translation). English is also used in communications with foreign tourists.

> Caribbean forms of English and Creole English remain the language and dominant culture of the native islanders. This is due in great part to the distance from the Colombian mainland, and its socio-historical, commercial and economic relations with Jamaica, the United States and the English-speaking coast of Central America.
>
> (Dittman forthcoming: 29)

Nero (2006: 502) reports that 'among Caribbean and other linguists, there is still a debate about whether to consider English-based Creoles dialects of English or separate languages'. I will refer to them in this paper as different languages.

Vollmer (1997: 56), as cited by Morren (2001), reports that in San Andrés 'by the end of the 19th century 95 per cent of the Island population were Baptists, and more than 90 per cent of these were able to read and write in English'. Before 1953, almost all the population of the islands was of African origin and spoke English in church and schools, while Islander was used for other domains. In that year, the Colombian government declared San Andrés a duty-free port and built the airport. These actions changed dramatically the sociolinguistic situation as people with diverse languages and cultural backgrounds, including a large influx of Spanish speakers from continental Colombia, moved there (Botero 2007).

Islander: our English-based creole

Edwards (1974: 1) says that 'San Andrés Creole is similar in many aspects to rural Jamaican Creole, and it is in part descendent from it'. Decker and Keener (2001) report linguistic similarity with other related English Creole varieties in Belize and Central American communities.

Islander is a language of a strong oral tradition with a recent standardized orthography developed by a group of local academic and religious leaders. This standardization responded to the need to use Islander as a means of instruction in elementary schools (Morren 2001). Initially using the Rule-based Phonemic Model used in Belize,

Islander-speaking teachers and the spelling committee decided later that a more pho-nemic orthography would be better for pedagogical purposes (Morren 2001). Even if some of the spelling conventions do not seem the ideal, for example using [-y] for /i/ and [-ow] for /-ou/, 'these solutions were agreed upon in order to make (or actually maintain) the spelling of Islander visually elegant' (Bartens 2003: 17). The Islander orthography is more phonematic, something recommended by linguists because it aspires at 'one-to-one correspondence between grapheme and sound which is the most economic and logical solution on linguistic terms' (Bartens 2003: 17).

Attitudes towards Islander are quite diverse. Decker and Keener highlight that for the population of San Andrés the language 'seems to be the most important symbol of their identity as Native Islanders' (Decker and Keener 2001: 12) and a source of pride. Patiño Roselli (1992) found this linguistic pride mainly among young people. Nero (1997) reports this pride towards creole use among speakers of other Caribbean Englishes, but only in the domains of private and domestic life. Many of the speakers feel discouraged, and often discriminated against, to use their creole in other sociolinguistic scenarios because it is often seen as bad English. She says that for many speakers their creole and colonial identities compete because even if they 'actually speak some variety of English-based Creole, they continue to label their language as English, at least in the public domains, for Creole is associated with low racial, social, political and economic status' (Nero 1997: 587). This favouritism towards English is also found on the islands of San Andrés and Providencia. Most political leaders see Islander as a form of substandard English, and, as the islands belong to a Spanish-speaking country, they believe that the second language to be taught should be Standard English, and not Islander (Morren 2001).

Nero (2000: 486) says that Caribbean varieties of English 'comprise a combination of the phonology, morphology, and syntax of West African and other ethnic languages, with the largest contribution to the lexicon coming from British English – hence the term *Creole English*'. This resemblance to Standard English has perpetuated the idea that Caribbean English is a deviant version of English. Kachru (1992: 362) finds it difficult to place Caribbean Englishes within the concentric circles, saying that 'the functions of English in their situations are rather complex'. Nero (2000) questions this assumption and claims that Anglophone Caribbean speakers are often discriminated against in American universities that place them in ESL courses because they do not seem to have the competence to perform academically.

Islander tends to have an analytical organization with markers of tense, modality and aspect used before the verb (Dieck 1998). Regarding its morphology, the majority of words have one single morpheme and very little variation. The presence of various homophone words with different syntactical categories is particular to the language (O'Flynn de Chaves 1990):

Im **de de** ded
Third-person, singular, animated–copula verb (time/space)–adverbial location–durative
He/she is dying there
Di monki **de de**
Article–noun–copula verb–adverbial location
The monkey is there

Nominal plural may be unmarked and person and number are not marked on verbs, therefore, subject–verb concord does not apply. Bartens (2003) presents the nominal plurals as formed by postposing or preposing the third-person plural pronoun *dem* to the noun:

Di bwai
The boy
Di bwai **dem**
The boys
Dem bwai go skuul
The boys go to school

O'Flynn de Chaves (1990: 123) says that for dynamic (action) verbs '[t]here is no formal change to make the distinction between present and past tenses. Generally, the context provides the extra-verbal information required for the correct interpretation' (own translation):

Im kom evri die
He/she comes/came everyday
Im kom las nait
He/she came last night

Wen/wehn functions as an auxiliary for tense and aspect, but some inflected English verbs have been adopted such as *nju* 'knew', *went*, *had* in Providencia (Bartens 2003: 76).

Im gat lanch
He/she has a motorboat
Im **wen** gat lanch
He/she had a motorboat

(O'Flynn de Chaves 1993: 126)

Regarding the syntactical organization, Bartens (2003) says that an affirmative sentence in Islander has a similar pattern to English: subject–verb–object–complement. Adverbials are placed more freely, depending on the length of the sentence as shown below:

Iina flesh kain–yu–kyan put iin–pig teil, kongs, krab, fish
Adverbial–subject–verb–direct object
For the meat kind of ingredients–you–can put in–pig tail, conch, crabs, fish

(Bartens 2003: 113)

Absence of possessive marker -s is another characteristic of the language: 'my brother's book' corresponds to 'mai breda buk'.

The lexicon of Islander is mainly composed of English words and Africanisms, the latter being preferred in the domestic and private domains (Bartens 2003). The examples of Africanisms below the three English-derived terms come from O'Flynn de Chaves (1990, 2003), Dittman (1992) and Edwards (1974):

Uman   'woman'
Shaak   'shark'
Chorch   'church'

Ishili	'a black lizard'
Wola/woula	'boa, large snake'
Pinda	'peanut'
Dorí	'canoe'

The phonological system contains almost the same consonant system of English, with the exception of interdental fricatives /θ/ and /ð/, a main characteristic of some other creoles and varieties of English. These sounds may be used by people that have studied English formally and use them when they talk to native-speaker foreigners (Dittman 1992: 58). Islander speakers pronounce them as alveolar stops /t/ and /d/: 'thin' [dɪn] and 'that' [dat]. Consonant clusters /-sk/ turn into /-ks/: 'ask' becomes 'aks'. Consonant clusters that include CCC after the vocalic nucleus such as 'world' or 'first' are simplified becoming 'worl' and 'fos'. The combinations /-ar/ and /-or/ become /aa/ with 'start' and 'morning' becoming 'staat' and 'maanin'.

In the Islander vowel system, English /æ/ may be pronounced as /e/ or /a/ as in 'thanks' /tengki/ and 'hat' /hat/. Mid central vowels /ə/ and /ɚ/ are pronounced as /o/: 'ugly' [ogli], 'bird' [bod] (Bartens 2003). Dittman (1992) found that English diphthongs /ei/ and /ou/ are pronounced respectively as /ye/ and /wo/ as in 'say' [sie] and 'boat' [bwot].

The stressed-time nature is preferred to the syllable-timed nature of American and British English. Crystal (1995: 344) remarks that 'a consequence of this "syllable-timed" rhythm is that vowels which would be unstressed in most other English accents are here spoken with prominence, and schwa /ə/ is little used'.

Dittman (forthcoming) provides a story written in the standardized version of Islander with the corresponding English version:

Di Guos we Kuda Plie Gitar

Di likl gyal wehn glad bikaaz evry June wen vakieshan kom, him and ihn big breda go dong da dehn granfaada an granmada. Wan Saturday maanin, wen dehn gaan vizit dehn granpierans, dehn gaan grong wid dehn grandaada. Dehn gaan luk fi mango an guava. Wail dehn wehn gwain lang de waak, di grandaada tel dem wan stuory bout wan big wait guos. Di siem taim dehn hier wan gitar de plie iina di bush. So dehn granfaada gaan si da wat. Wen ihn get iina di bush, ihn uonly fain di gitar an nonbady neva de plie ih. Den ihn se da mos wan guos wende plie ih. Di two pikniny wehn so fraitn dehn staat ron an hala, an neva stap til dehn get bak huom we dehn granmada de!

The Ghost that Could Play a Guitar

[Once there was] a little girl who was glad because every June when vacation came, she and her big brother would go down to their grandmother and grandfather's place. One Saturday morning, when they had gone to visit their grandparents, they decided to accompany their grandfather to his field. They went to look for guavas and mangos. So, while they were walking along with their grandpa, he began to tell them a story about a big white ghost. At the same time, they began to hear the strumming of a guitar in the woods. So, their grandpa went to investigate. When he got into the woods, he found the guitar and no one was playing it! He told his grandchildren that it was probably the ghost who had been playing the guitar. The two children were so frightened that they started to run and holler, and didn't stop until they got home where their grandma was waiting for them!

English in San Andrés and Providencia islands

English spoken in San Andrés and Providencia belongs to the subset of Caribbean Englishes (Roberts 1988). It shares many features with Islander Creole, therefore many people believe they are one single language. Several authors and local academics from the islands say that English had a stronger presence in the life of the community before the 1950s when the island was not a free port. Native islanders feel an inadequacy with their general proficiency in English and report attrition among younger generations (Bartens 2003). The decrease in the use of English is a consequence of the Colombianization policy promulgated by the government in the 1950s promoting the use of Spanish and the presence of the Catholic Church. O'Flynn de Chaves (1990) states that not having English as a means of instruction in schools and the fact that fewer young people go to church have affected the use of English in the community. She says that the Baptist Church 'is the institution that has contributed the most to the maintenance of English' (1990: 23, own translation).

As English is a prestigious language, many islanders 'claim that their native language is only and exclusively English. It is very offensive to them to imply that there is another native language on the island ... They do not care if it is called "broken English", as long as it is clear that it is English' (O'Flynn de Chaves 1990: 24, own translation). Although many islanders believe that the main bilingualism of the islands is English–Spanish, different studies show that Islander–Spanish is the most common bilingual situation for the indigenous population (Sanmiguel 2006; Andrade 2006).

English in San Andrés has many of the features presented above for Islander. The preference for unmarked verbs and nouns and the flexibility in the use of markers of time, mode and aspect are salient features. Bartens (2003: 114) provides two examples of San Andrés English that represent this feature: '**The three** from civil society that **was** selected was Dr Juvencio Gallardo, Mr Felix Mitchell Modem who represent the youth and this host, Juan Ramírez Dawkins' and '**It read** as follow: ... '

The phonological differences may confuse many listeners (Nero 2006), mainly if they have little contact with other varieties of English. Many Colombians consider this variety of English as substandard and call it 'patois'. This prejudice seems to reach some islanders who pursue university studies in continental Colombia. They avoid using English because they are aware that their English is different from the English spoken by educated professionals (O'Flynn de Chaves 1990).

English in continental Colombia

Regarding users of English outside the islands of San Andrés and Providencia, Colombia belongs to the expanding circle (Kachru 1992). This classification is 'due to the pedagogical status of English as a foreign language, its lack of official status, its restricted uses, and the increasing number of learners' (Vélez-Rendón 2003: 188). As in many countries, the inner circle varieties are preferred for teaching purposes in the different school settings (Matsuda 2003). Colombian people have mixed attitudes about the preference of American or British English, but there is a stronger preference for the American variety of spelling and pronunciation. There seems to be little knowledge about outer circle varieties of English, which are commonly believed to be of lower prestige and linguistically impure.

English in Colombia is mandatory in high school and, since a few years ago, in elementary schools. A typical Colombian citizen may say that English instruction in government schools is quite poor, and that actual learning of the language takes place in private schools, language centres or in higher education. Depending on the socioeconomic status of the population, proficiency in English may vary considerably. Vélez-Rendón (2003), citing a web page of the British Council from 1999, states that 3 per cent of the Colombian population can use English, mainly in major urban cities such as Bogotá, Medellín and Cali. She also reports that there is an increase in the number of universities that use English as a means of instruction in English teacher preparation programmes.

The requirements for teaching English in Colombia are diverse. Although employers prefer a candidate who holds a teacher university degree, a native speaker, someone who grew up or lived in an English-speaking country or has a good score in an international proficiency test may be a teacher. In fact, the new recruitment policies for public education do not include an education degree as a requirement. Professionals from other academic fields may become English teachers if they pass the content examinations and obtain high scores in the language component.

Local researchers have found that there is a gap in the teaching of English in public and private schools regarding the teachers' language proficiency and use of English in English classes (González 1995), the access to professional development programmes (González et al. 2002), teaching resources (González 2006a), and formal teacher education. This is particularly so in elementary schools (Cadavid et al. 2004; McNulty and Quinchía 2007). Additionally, Ordóñez (2004: 450) describes the presence of elite bilingualism among some Colombian high school students, saying that it is 'an urban, middle-class, private school phenomenon'.

English in Colombia: landmarks of a growing demand

It is hard to explain the rapid expansion of English in Colombia solely as the result of either linguistic imperialism or from the perspective of the econocultural model, because they are not mutually exclusive (Bhatt 2001). With regard to linguistic imperialism, the British Council, publishing companies and TESOL (Teaching English to Speakers of Other Languages) participate using power and colonial discourses that perpetuate the dominant status of the culture and speakers of English (Phillipson 1992; Pennycook 1994, 1997, 1998; Canagarajah 1999; Wilson 2005). The second view analyses English growth as a consequence of the development of the world market where English is a lingua franca in commerce and trade (Quirk 1988; Brutt-Griffler 1998 cited by Bhatt 2001). Local scholars identified with either the imperialistic or econocultural view feel they explain the various reasons for the expansion of the language (Cárdenas 2006; Cely 2006, 2007; González 2007; Hernández 2007; Salamanca 2007; Sánchez and Obando 2008; Usma 2009).

It is clear that English is spreading in Colombia as a major component of the globalization movement and its discourses (Fairclough 2006). Fairclough states that in the understanding of language in the process of globalization it is important to distinguish five main agencies or sets of agents, 'academic analysis, governmental agencies, non-governmental agencies, the media, and people in everyday life' (2006: 5). The participation of these five agencies in Colombia is clear, mainly in the ways that they all construct discourses about bilingualism and English in globalization.

The introduction of English as part of language policy (Spolsky 2004; Shohamy 2006) began in Colombia in the 1940s through cooperation with the American and British governments (García et al. 2007). The Binational Colombo–American centres were founded in 1942 in Bogotá and in 1947 in Medellín. The Colombian–British

Cultural Centre was founded in Medellín in 1941 (García *et al.* 2007). Both institutions had, as a major aim, cultural and economic support for the development of the country and the promotion of the English language and culture.

The presence of English in Colombia became more evident after the 1980s. Attempts to reform ELT included the 1982 *Programa de Inglés* (English Syllabus), the 1994 *Ley General de Education* (General Law of Education), the 1997 *Proyecto Educativo Institucional* (Institutional Educational Project), the 1999 *Indicadores de Logros* (Attainment Targets) and the 2000 *Revolución Educativa* (Educational Revolution) (Valencia 2006: 13). Although Valencia (2006: 13) concludes that these policies 'have not produced the changes expected', the growing interest of the government to improve the teaching of English is clear.

One important national attempt at a collaborative approach to the teaching of English took place in the 1990s when a group of Colombian universities, sponsored by the Colombian and British governments, designed the COFE (Colombian Framework for English). This project 'was the result of a complementary arrangement ... concerning technical cooperation for the improvement in the teaching of English' (Rubiano *et al.* 2000: 38). A major orientation of the project was the development of EFL teachers' autonomy to generate personal commitment in the consolidation of better professional standards (Frodden and Picón 2005; Usma 2007).

Among the main achievements of the project, the authors highlight the increase of hours of English instruction devoted to develop language proficiency, the introduction of curricular changes regarding the inclusion of practicum semesters and the emphasis on research in teacher preparation programmes and the organization of resource centres in major cities. It is clear that the project had an impact on the quality of teacher education in the country because it set up the bases for local research. Professors involved in the COFE project included some of the first Colombian authors to publish their work in the field of ELT.

The use of English in higher education is growing dramatically. Since the 1990s, English has become increasingly important for undergraduate students in the majority of Colombian universities, especially those which are keen to promote internationalization. The initiatives to study English include access to scholarships for graduate programmes abroad. The number of universities, particularly the research universities, which demand reading skills in English from all their undergraduates and promote the acquisition of communication skills has increased in the last five years. Major research universities demand candidates for professorships with the ability to communicate in a foreign language, English being preferred. Although this requirement has provoked various reactions both in favour and against, there seems to be an agreement on the importance for professors and graduate students to have competence in English. Publications in international refereed journals are an academic requirement and this also motivates the learning of the language.

There is very little research on the status of English learning in non-formal education in the country, but the growth of programmes, the market demand for EFL teachers and the number of new language institutes are increasing.

Current English language education policies

Colombia has set an educational agenda for 2004–19 called *Revolución Educativa* (Educational Revolution). It seeks to increase the educational coverage, the quality and the efficiency of education to make citizens competitive in a globalized world (Ministerio de Educación Nacional 2002, 2008). One of the main features of that competitiveness is the aim of making the population bilingual through the mastery of English and the acquisition of skills in the use of information and communication technologies (ICTs). Typical citizens identify English–Spanish bilingualism and technological skills as a *sine qua non* in the education of any Colombian student. Although access to technology and connectivity may be a major challenge in our nation, Clavijo (2008) concluded that EFL teachers and students may obtain significant gains if English and ICTs are combined in areas such as content learning and the development of literacy skills.

The National Programme for Bilingualism (NPB) set the levels of English proficiency expected. The programme aims to 'have citizens qualified to communicate in English with standards comparable internationally so that they may be able to involve the country in the processes of international communication, global economy and cultural opening' (Ministerio de Educación Nacional 2006a: 2). Several projects have been established within the framework of the NPB, including: the creation of national standards for English learning; the search for better standards in the professional development of English teachers; and the assessment of English language proficiency. The Ministry of Education designed the national standards according to the Common European Framework of Reference for Languages (CEFR) (Council of Europe 2001) (see further discussion below). The national agenda sees as targets for the year 2019 the following minimum levels of proficiency within the CEFR: B1 level for high school graduates; B2 for EFL teachers and graduates from university programmes; and C1 for graduates from English teacher preparation programmes (Ministerio de Educación Nacional 2006a).

Tensions and possibilities in the expanding circle

The growth in the use of English in the country has brought new tensions and possibilities that I address below.

Tensions

The current status of English in Colombia reveals tensions between different actors that participate in ELT as decision-makers or implementers of the language policies. These tensions are evident in the interpretation and implementation of policy and have become central to academic debates in conferences and publications. The main tensions are:

Use of the CEFR as the model to set the standards and levels of proficiency

While the Ministry of Education states that CEFR was chosen because it promotes language competences, has proven its international efficiency and is supported by substantial academic research (Hernández 2007), other voices criticize its adoption. Ayala and Alvarez (2005), Cárdenas (2006), Sánchez and Obando (2008) and Usma (2009) state that the educational, social, linguistic and economic reality of Colombia may not be compared to Europe in the achievement of language goals. Therefore the CEFR should not be the main benchmark. Cárdenas (2006) also questions the pertinence of the CEFR as the referent for English standards for students and teachers. She argues that the reality established in the CEFR would have to be contrasted with the conditions of Colombian educational institutions, namely, infrastructure, curriculum organization, use of foreign languages in the academic and cultural domains of the country, working hours and competences of language teachers.

(p. 3)

The notion of bilingualism

Policy-makers and some scholars see English–Spanish bilingualism as a desirable goal because it raises the competitiveness of the citizens in the job market and promotes interaction with the world (Ministerio de Educación Nacional 2002, 2008; Salamanca 2007). Others question the reduction of the concept of bilingualism to these two languages and argue for the inclusion of other foreign languages and the indigenous languages in the policy (De Mejía 2006a, 2006b; Guerrero 2008).

EFL teachers' responsibility in the attainment of the goals

Ministry of Education representatives argue that the levels of proficiency identified will raise the quality of education and improve ELT (Ministerio de Educación Nacional 2006b). In the National Standards booklet, they highlight the importance of EFL teachers' commitment for the success of this project. However, critical reviews say that the real major problems of schools are not solved and warn about the risks of making teachers responsible for the success of the achievement of the proficiency goals (Sánchez and Obando 2008). 'Investment in the social and political environment outside as well as in the schools themselves (infrastructure, resources, reduction of the number of students in classrooms, etc.) are necessary conditions for changing the face of education' (Libman 2009: 5). Sánchez and Obando (2008: 192) also question the country's readiness to attain a 'bilingual status'. They think that 'the goal of bilingualism looks more like a utopia than a feasible plan' because there are many factors that intervene in successful teaching and the plan has not considered them.

The role of the British Council

Although many people and scholars see the British Council as helpful in guaranteeing quality in ELT (Cely 2006; Hernández 2007), other voices express their concern about its role in Colombia. González (2007) raises questions of academic colonialism and the businessification of ELT that may come from the adoption of the tests, the teacher development courses, teaching materials and experts related to the British publishing companies. Usma (2009: 12) warns that only a minority obtains the benefits of the 'consolidation of a lucrative market around language teaching, learning, and certification in Colombia'.

The promotion of standards in teaching and learning

The Ministry of Education values these highly as they promote quality in education, create a coherent common language and guarantee accountability. Standards are 'means for improving all components of the educational system, from standards for student achievement, standards for teacher preparation programs, and standards for teacher induction

341

through standards for advanced professional certification' (Yinger and Hendricks-Lee 2000: 94). Apple (2001) warns about the dangers of standardization in education, saying that its hidden agendas and the powers in which they operate may represent harm rather than a benefit for education because of the risks of marketization of a public good. Regarding English teaching and learning, Guerrero (2008) questions the definition of a bilingual person implied in the Colombian standards based on the CEFR. She challenges the fact that the writers of these standards 'set up the goals of the PNB as a packed whole, implying that the proficiency level must be the same for everybody regardless of the needs, resources, context, socio-economic situation, and/or motivation of students' (pp. 40–1). Additionally, she highlights the inadequacy of the standards' conception of 'an ideal group of students who differ greatly from the real students who attend schools' (p. 42). Cárdenas (2006) questions the expectations generated by the policy, mainly in the language levels to be attained by 2019. She argues that the actual conditions for teaching English in Colombia do not correspond to the aims of the policy because they are not realistic. These levels are unattainable for many schools located in underprivileged or conflicted areas where the major concern of the population is surviving, not becoming bilingual.

The use of international professional development models for EFL teachers

The use of the ICELT (In-service Certificate in English Language Teaching) and the TKT (Teaching Knowledge Test) represents the main instruments that the Ministry of Education promotes as part of the search for quality in ELT. Hernández (2007: 33, own translation) claims the validity of the ICELT is based on three arguments: one, the solid knowledge of the field of teaching from 'theories formulated by widely known specialists' gained during the course; two, the connection between the content addressed, the teaching practice and the ability to evaluate the teaching and learning processes; and three, the prestige and seriousness of a programme implemented in many other countries. González (2008, 2009) questioned the uses of the ICELT and the TKT as alternative certifications (Salyer 2003; Zeichner 2006; Libman 2009) and shows how they can become instruments of exclusion, inequality, standardization, and businessification in teacher education. Additionally, Usma (2009) criticizes the marketization of teachers' development as these two models are very expensive and remain out of the reach of the majority of Colombian teachers.

One of the main justifications of the inclusion of a professional development programme for the country was the low level of language proficiency found among EFL teachers. According to Cely (2006, 2007) the massive testing of teachers that took place in 2003 and 2004 showed that the majority of teachers only had an A2 level of proficiency in the CEFR. Therefore, English instruction and methodology should be part of the solution to the problem and the models proposed by the British Council addressed both.

Possibilities

English in Colombia represents a potentially interesting case study within the framework of the parameter of possibility defined in Kumaravadivelu's post-method pedagogy (1994, 2003, 2006). The place and roles of English in 'our' expanding circle may 'tap the socio-political consciousness that participants bring with them to the classroom so that it can also function as a catalyst for a continual quest for identity formation and social transformation' (2003: 37). The following possibilities thus emerge:

More opportunities to learn English

Even if the Colombian government has not addressed some of the fundamental problems that require urgent attention in education, there is more expenditure in ELT initiatives than before. Through the NPB, more regular citizens may have access to English instruction. Strategies such as *Idiomas sin Fronteras* (Languages with No Barriers) have obtained financial support from private language institutes, and universities have joined the project through massive discounts in foreign language courses as a contribution to the consolidation of bilingualism. Although this may reduce the government's responsibility for providing good education and emphasize general competitiveness (Giroux 1992), nobody can deny the positive effect on motivation for the general population to learn English.

More professional development opportunities for EFL teachers

Some local governments see the need to sponsor their teachers' development in language proficiency and methodology. To achieve that goal, they search for academic alternatives in the in-service programmes offered by universities (González *et al.* 2002). Although some schools may prefer international certifications endorsed by American and British bi-national centres, Jerez (2008), Clavijo *et al.* (2004) and Torres and Monguí (2008) report some of the successful learning experiences in professional development programmes carried out by Colombian universities.

Inclusion of a Colombian English variety in the repertoire of language immersion for EFL teachers

An English immersion programme for Colombian teachers on the island of San Andrés gives them the opportunity to use and value a variety of English which is neither American nor British. Exposing EFL teachers to the variety spoken in the islands represents a major step towards the construction of pedagogies that include World Englishes and English as a lingua franca (ELF) (Jenkins 2006) in Colombia. As stated by Bartens (2004: 1),

> there is no such a thing as a language which is superior because of some *structural* features it possesses. Languages which are nowadays widely spoken are basically just varieties at some point diffused by nations with powerful armies and/or a commercial fleet.

Although some language purists reject the value of this immersion experience and call for 'good and accurate native speaker models of English', the experience is definitely a way to enrich the sociolinguistic and pedagogical repertoire of participating teachers (Colombia Aprende n.d.b).

If English in Colombia includes a more pluralistic approach that goes beyond the British and American traditions, the 'five sacred cows' – namely the acquisitional, sociolinguistic, pedagogical, theoretical and ideological views of English as being part of the European and American cultural and linguistic heritage – may be challenged, if not sacrificed (Kachru 1988; Bhatt 2001). The acquisitional sacred cow relates to 'the relevance of concepts such as interference, error, interlanguage, and fossilization to the users and

343

uses of English in the outer circle' (Bhatt 2001: 539). I argue that we in the expanding circle are also creating new forms of English. Sacrificing the sociolinguistic sacred cow transmits the idea of constructing pluralistic identities that English has developed in contexts outside the inner circle. The presence of new forms and linguistic structures challenges the pedagogical sacred cow. This is where post-method pedagogy (Kumaravadivelu 1994, 2003) provides the parameters of possibility, particularity and practicality of finding ways of teaching consonant with local contextual realities. The theoretical sacred cow deals with three key concepts: the speech community, the native speaker, and the ideal speaker–hearer. Under the new paradigm that emerges from World Englishes, I view non-native speakers as valid interlocutors and owners of the language (Graddol 1999). This is particularly important in seeing non-native-speaker teachers of English (Liu 1999; Llurda 2005a, 2005b) as valid models of language input (Brutt-Griffler and Samimy 2001; Chacón *et al.* 2003). Questioning the ideological sacred cow, Bhatt (2001: 451) sees the teaching of English as a means to inculcate the culture, ideologies and social relations 'to promote and sustain the status quo'. This is relevant also for the varieties of English in the expanding circle, even if the use of English is not as frequent as in the outer circle contexts.

In addition to exposure to the forms of Caribbean English from the island of San Andrés, Colombian people have access to texts produced by Colombian non-native speakers of English. These texts include news articles published in local papers. They contribute to the creation of richer input for students and are materials easily available for teachers. As an example, I quote an item of news published in the electronic version of a local newspaper, *El Colombiano* (The Colombian), in a blog called Global Newsroom (Villa 2009):

Libraries will remain open

January 5, 2009 Education

During vacation the books in the libraries of Medellín branch of the Universidad Nacional will still be available. The administration decided to keep the Efe Gomez Library and the library in the Mining Department, in Robledo, open for the season.

The goal is that the 150,000 books in the catalogue remain accessible to researchers and professors who don't stop working when students are on vacation. The hours will be weekdays from 8:00 a.m. until 4:30 p.m. and will only close on weekends.

On Sundays *El Colombiano* has a special section in English with short summaries of the main news of the week. Language purists see this publication as a repertory of deficient English because the sentence structure and the use of specific regional Spanish vocabulary make the texts look unnatural to native-English-speaking readers, yet these texts appear appropriate to Colombian speakers of English, mainly to EFL teachers, who use them as materials for their classes.

The construction of local knowledge

The possibility of creating peripheral knowledge (Canagarajah 2005b) on ELT, teacher education and teacher development and counter discourses in these fields has given voice to local scholars (González 2007). Publications by Colombian teachers and teacher educators have gained a respected space in national curricula in teacher education (Pineda and Clavijo 2003), displacing some traditional voices of world-renowned scholars from the United States and the United Kingdom. Soon they will make a stronger contribution to the analysis of World Englishes in the expanding circle. This represents one of the main assets of the epistemological debate around English in Colombia. Clavijo (2009: 16) sees our process of 'becoming more independent intellectually … from the imposed dominant ideologies and being able to value and support local knowledge' as a priority in our country.

The need to search for new pedagogies to teach English varieties

The current situation of English in Colombia within the framework of the NBP requires the expansion of ELT to recognize the English variety in San Andrés and Providencia and, consequently, explore new ways to teach the language. A growing interest on the part of the islanders and the educational authorities to develop models of bilingual education which assign equal status to the three languages has become evident in the last decade (Abouchaar *et al.* 2002). Initiatives such as the trilingual curriculum model presented by Morren (2001, 2004) for San Andrés require support from the Colombian government. Teachers and teacher educators need effective professional development and resources to preserve Islander, develop more curricula and design new materials to teach it (Moya 2006; Dittman forthcoming). The traditional approach to teaching EFL is not sufficient to provide the multilingual education that islanders need. Granting Islander and the variety of English spoken in San Andrés the linguistic status they deserve will strengthen diversity and further democratic relationships among Colombian people.

The collaborative construction of ELT agendas between policy-makers and scholars

This possibility represents a challenge in itself as divergent voices are often stigmatized (Cárdenas 2006; González 2007). Salamanca (2007) calls for more analyses that defend the bilingualism policy and expresses surprise about some of the positions that question issues such as our identity and the choice of English. In any discussion, participation is a must, even if this generates new disagreements and discussions. González (2006b) portrays in Figure 19.1 the different actors in the policy decision-making. In the lowest levels we can find the greater number of people, while at the top we find the very few in charge of policy-making. A communication gap appears between researchers and policy-makers. This gap deserves a closer look on the part of all those Colombian English users, from students to policy-makers.

De Mejía (2007: 38) concludes that it is necessary to adopt a broader view of bilingualism and bilingual education in Colombia. To achieve this

> there is need for an open and constructive dialogue among the available sources of expertise and knowledge: the Ministry of Education, the institutes located in minority bilingual and multilingual communities, universities, private bilingual schools, and local secretaries of education to work together in the search for development of excellence in bilingual programmes in the country.

> (own translation)

345

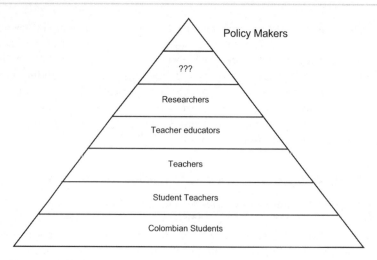

Figure 19.1 The pyramid of Colombian ELT policy.
Source: González 2006b.

As a final remark, I would like to argue for the need of more critical applied linguistics approaches to teaching ELT in the expanding circle (Pennycook 2001 and this volume). Teachers and teacher educators should embrace 'linguistics with an attitude' as academia is not neutral and depoliticized and we are the academics involved in teaching.

Conclusion

This chapter addresses the situation of English in Colombia, an expanding circle country. Before dealing with the sociolinguistic status of the language, I described the linguistic diversity of the nation, focusing on Islander and the Caribbean English variety spoken in the islands of San Andrés and Providencia. I also analysed language-education policies, showing how they have transformed the teaching and learning of English as well as the professional development of EFL teachers. I focused my analysis on the tensions and possibilities that English brings to the academic and everyday life spheres attempting to contribute to the transformation of EFL teaching and teacher education in Colombia.

Suggestions for further reading

Bartens, A. (forthcoming) *Life-lines. Spanish and (Creole) English in San Andrés Isla*, Colombia, Helsinki: Finnish Academy of Science and Letters.
De Mejía, A.M. (2002) *Power, Prestige and Bilingualism: International Perspectives on Elite Bilingual Education*, Clevedon: Multilingual Matters.
——(ed.) (2005) *Bilingual Education in South America*, Clevedon: Multilingual Matters.
Pennycook, A. (2007) *Global Englishes and Transcultural Flows*, New York: Routledge.
Ricento, T. (ed.) (2006) *An Introduction to Language Policy*, Malden, MA. Blackwell.
Tatto, M.T. (2005) *Reforming Teaching Globally*, Oxford: Symposium Books.
Tollefson, J.W. (1991) *Planning Language, Planning Inequality*, New York: Longman.

References

Abouchaar, A., Hooker, Y. and Robinson, B. (2002) 'Estudio Lingüístico para la implementación del programa de educación bilingüe en el Municipio de providencia y Santa Catalina', *Cuadernos del Caribe*, 3: 66–101.

Andrade, J. (2006) 'Estudio sociolingüístico de San Andrés isla: un aporte a la cultura sanandresana', *Cuadernos del Caribe*, 8: 42–53.

Apple, M. (2001) 'Markets, standards, teaching, and teacher education', *Journal of Teacher Education*, 52 (3): 182–96.

Ayala, J. and Alvarez, J.A. (2005) 'A perspective of the implications of the common European framework: implementation in the Colombian socio-cultural context', *Colombian Applied Linguistics Journal*, 7: 7–26.

Bartens, A. (2003) *A Contrastive Grammar Islander – Caribbean Standard English – Spanish*, Helsinki: Academia Scientiarum Fennica.

——(2004) 'The rocky road to education in Creole', paper presented at the Society for Caribbean Linguistics' Curacao Creole Conference, World Trade Centre, Curacao, Netherlands Antilles. 11–14 August.

Behrman, J.R., Gaviria, A. and Székely, M. (eds) (2003) *Who's In and Who's Out: Social Exclusion in Latin America*, Washington, DC: Johns Hopkins University Press.

Bhatt, R. (2001) 'World Englishes', *Annual Review of Anthropology*, 30: 527–50

Botero, J. (2007) 'Oralidad y escritura en la Isla de San Andrés', *Universitas Humanisticas*, 64: 275–89.

Brutt-Griffler, J. (1998) 'The development of English as an international language: a theory of world language', unpublished PhD thesis, Ohio State University Columbus, Ohio.

Brutt-Griffler, J. and Samimy, K. (2001) 'Transcending the nativeness paradigm', *World Englishes*, 20 (1): 99–106.

Cadavid, I., McNulty, M. and Quinchía, D. (2004) 'Elementary English language instruction: Colombian teachers' classroom practices', *Profile*, 5: 37–55.

Canagarajah, A.S. (1999) *Resisting Linguistic Imperialism in English Teaching*, Oxford: Oxford University Press.

——(ed.) (2005a) *Reclaiming the Local in Language Policy and Practice*, Mahwah, NJ: Lawrence Erlbaum Associates.

——(2005b) 'Reconstructing local knowledge, reconfiguring language studies', in S. Canagarajah (ed.) *Reclaiming the Local in Language Policy and Practice*, Mahwah, NJ: Lawrence Erlbaum Associates.

Cárdenas, M.L. (2006) 'Bilingual Colombia: are we ready for it? What is needed?' Proceedings of the 19th Annual English Australia Education Conference. Online. Available www.englishaustralia.com.au/ea_conference2006/proceedings/ (accessed on 20 March 2007).

Cely, R.M. (2006) 'The National Bilingual Programme: recent developments and the years ahead', paper presented at the 41st ASOCOPI Congress, Ibagué, 11–13 October.

——(2007) 'Programa Nacional de Bilingüismo: En Búsqueda de la Calidad en Educación', *Revista Internacional Magisterio*, 25: 20–3.

Chacón, C., Alvarez, L.C., Brutt-Griffler, J. and Samimy, K. (2003) 'Dialogues around "revisiting the colonial in the post-colonial: critical praxis for nonnative-English-speaking teachers in a TESOL program"', in J. Sharkey, and K. Jonson (eds) *The TESOL Quarterly Dialogs: Rethinking Issues of Language, Culture, and Power*, Alexandria, VA: Teachers of English to Speakers of Other Languages, pp. 141–50.

Clavijo, A. (2008) 'Challenges in the implementation of ICT national policies', plenary speech at the II International Seminar on the Professional Development of Foreign Language Teachers, Universidad de Antioquia, Medellín. 13–15 August.

——2009) 'New perspectives on language teacher education and social transformation', in Proceedings of the II Latin American Conference in Language Teacher Education, Rio de Janeiro: Pontifical Catholic University of Rio de Janeiro.

Clavijo, A., Guerrero, C.H., Torres, C., Ramírez, L.M. and Torres, N.E. (2004) 'Teacher acting critically upon the curriculum: innovations that transform teaching', *IKALA, Revista de Language y Cultura*, 9 (15): 11–41.

Colombia Aprende (n.d.a) La Red del Conocimiento. Colombia Bilingüe. Online. Available www.colombiaaprende.edu.co/html/directivos/1598/article-76053.html (accessed 20 March 2007).

——(n.d.b) 'La Red del Conocimiento. Programa de inmersión en inglés estándar-San Andrés'. Online. Available from Colombia Aprende: La Red del Conocimiento, www.colombiaaprende.edu.co/html/productos/1685/article-159310.html (accessed 16 February 2009).

Council of Europe (2001) *Common European Framework of Reference for Languages: Learning, Teaching and Assessment*, Cambridge: Cambridge University Press.

Crystal, D. (1995) *The Cambridge Encyclopedia of the English Language*, Cambridge: Cambridge University Press.

De Mejía, A.M. (2004) 'Bilingual education in Colombia: towards an integrated perspective', *Bilingual Education and Bilingualism*, 7 (4): 381–97.

——(2006a) 'Bilingual education in Colombia: towards a recognition of languages, cultures, and identities', *Colombian Applied Linguistics Journal*, 8: 152–68.

——(2006b) 'Realidades de la Educación Bilingüe en Colombia', Memorias del Segundo Simposio Internacional de Bilingüismo y Educación Bilingüe en América Latina, Bogotá, 5, 6, 7 Octubre, pp. 3–28.

——(2007) 'Visiones del bilingüismo y de la educación bilingüe en Colombia', *Revista Internacional Magisterio*, 25: 36–39.

Decker, K. and Keener, A. (2001) 'A report on the English-based Creole of San Andrés and Providence Islands, Colombia', *SIL Electronic Survey Reports 2001–10*. Online. Available www.sil.org/silesr/2001/010/ (accessed 27 November 2008).

Dieck, M. (1998) *Criollística Afrocolombiana. In Geografía Humana de Colombia: Los Afrocolombianos. Tomo VI*, Santafé de Bogotá: Instituto Colombiano de Cultura Hispánica, pp. 305–38.

Dittman, M. (1992) *El criollo sanandresano: lengua y cultura*, Cali: Universidad del Valle.

——(forthcoming) 'English in the Colombian archipelago of San Andres', in T. Hopkins, K. Decker and J. McKenny (eds) *World Englishes, Vol. 3: Central American English*, London: Continuum.

Edwards, J. (1974) 'African influences on the English of San Andrés island, Colombia', in D. Decamp and I.F. Hancock (eds) *Pidgins and Creoles: Current Trends and Prospects*, Washington DC: Georgetown University Press, pp. 1–26

Fairclough, N. (2006) *Language and Globalization*, New York: Routledge.

Frodden, C. and Picón, E. (2005) 'El desarrollo de la autonomía del profesor: un estudio de caso', *Boletín de Investigación Educacional*, 20 (1): 285–300.

García, R., Alvarez, V., López, A., Patiño, B. and Saldarriaga, R. (2007) *Legado de una Amistad*, Centro Colombo Americano: Medellín.

Giroux, H. (1992) 'Educational leadership and the crisis of democratic government', *Educational Researcher*, 21 (4): 4–11.

González, A. (1995) 'Language attrition and retention among non native speaker EFL teachers', unpublished PhD dissertation, State University of New York at Stony Brook.

——(2003) 'Who is educating EFL teachers: a qualitative study of in-service in Colombia', *IKALA, Revista de Lenguaje y Cultura*, 8 (14): 153–72.

——(2006a) 'On materials use training in EFL teacher education and professional development', *Profile*, 7: 101–15.

——(2006b) 'Professional development: the key to policy success', plenary presented at the 40th ASOCOPI Conference, Ibagué, 15 October.

——(2007) 'The professional development of Colombian EFL teachers: between local and colonial practices', *IKALA, Revista de Lenguaje y Cultura*, 12 (18): 309–32.

——(2008) 'On becoming a bilingual country: reflections of a teacher educator-administrator', paper presented at the Second International Seminar on the Professional Development of foreign language teachers, Universidad de Antioquia, Medellín, Colombia, 13–15 August.

——(2009) 'On alternative and additional certifications in English language teaching: The case of Colombian EFL teachers' professional development', *IKALA, Revista de Lenguaje y Cultura*, 14 (22): 183–209.

González, A., Montoya, C. and Sierra, N. (2002) 'What do EFL teachers seek in professional development programs? Voices from the teachers', *IKALA, Revista de Lenguaje y Cultura*, 7: 29–50.

González, M.S. and Rodríguez, M.L. (1999) *Lenguas Indígenas de Colombia*, Bogotá: Instituto Caro y Cuervo.

Graddol, D. (1999) 'The decline of the native speaker', *AILA Review*, 13: 57–68.

Grosjean, F. (1987) *Life with Two Languages*, Cambridge: Harvard University Press.

Guerrero, C.H. (2008) 'Bilingual Colombia: What does it mean to be bilingual within the framework of the National Plan of Bilingualism?' *Profile*, 10: 27–45

Hernández, L.J. (2007) 'Pertinencia de un modelo de metodología del Inglés Certificado Internacionalmente', *Revista Internacional Magisterio*, 25: 32–5.

Jenkins, J. (2006) 'Current perspectives on teaching World Englishes and English as a lingua franca', *TESOL Quarterly*, 40 (1): 157–81.

Jerez, S. (2008) 'Teachers' attitudes towards reflective teaching: evidences in a professional development program (PDP)', *Profile*, 10: 91–111.

Kachru, B.B. (1988) 'The spread of English and sacred linguistic cows', in P.H. Lowenberg (ed.) *Georgetown Round Table on Language and Linguistics*, Washington, DC: Georgetown University Press.

——(1992) (ed.) *The Other Tongue: English Across Cultures*, Urbana: University of Illinois Press.

Kumaravadivelu, B. (1994) 'The postmethod condition: (e)merging strategies for second/foreign language teaching', *TESOL Quarterly*, 28: 27–48.

——(2003) *Beyond Methods: Macrostrategies for Language Teaching*, New Haven, CT: Yale University Press.

——(2006) 'TESOL methods: changing traces, challenging trends', *TESOL Quarterly*, 40 (1): 59–81.

Landaburo, J. (1999) *Clasificación de las lenguas indígenas de Colombia*, Universidad de los Andes: Centro colombiano de estudio de lenguas aborígenes.

Libman, Z. (2009) Teacher licensing examinations – true progress or an illusion? *Studies in Educational Evaluation*, 35 (1): 7–15

Liu, J. (1999) 'Nonnative-English-speaking professionals in TESOL', *TESOL Quarterly*, 33 (1): 85–102.

Llurda, E. (ed.) (2005a) *Non-native Language Teachers: Perceptions, Challenges, and Contributions to the Profession*, New York: Springer.

——(2005b) 'Looking at the perceptions, challenges, and contributions. … Or on the importance of being a non-native teacher', in E. Llurda (ed.) *Non-Native Language Teachers: Perceptions, Challenges, and Contributions to the Profession*, New York: Springer, pp. 1–9.

McNulty, M. and Quinchía, D. (2007) 'Designing a holistic professional development program for elementary school English teachers in Colombia', *Profile*, 8: 131–43.

Matsuda, A. (2003) 'Incorporating World Englishes in teaching English as an international language', *TESOL Quarterly*, 37 (4): 719–29.

Ministerio de Educación Nacional (2002) 'La Revolución Educativa: Plan Sectorial 2002–6'. Online. Available www.mineducacion.gov.co/1621/articles-85273_archivo_pdf (accessed 20 March 2008).

——(2006a) 'Estándares Básicos de Competencias en Lengua Extranjera: Inglés. Formar en lenguas extranjeras: El reto'. Online. Available www.colombiaaprende.edu.co/html/mediateca/1607/articles-115375_archivo.pdf (accessed 8 May 2008).

——(2006b) 'Visión 2019 Educación: Propuesta para discusión'. Online. Available www.mineducacion. gov.co/cvn/1665/articles-110603_archivo_pdf.pdf (accessed 8 May 2008).

——(2007) 'Se inicia la consolidación de la enseñanza del inglés', press release. Online. Available www.mineducacion.gov.co/cvn (accessed 8 May 2008).

——(2008) 'Revolución educativa: Plan sectorial 2006–2010'. Online. Available www.mineducacion. gov.co (accessed 8 May 2008).

Morren, R. (2001) 'Creole-based trilingual education in the Caribbean Archipelago of San Andres, Providence and Santa Catalina', *Journal of Multilingual and Multicultural Development*, 22 (3): 227–41.

——(2004) 'Results of a Creole reading inventory. Paper presented at the Society for Caribbean Linguistics', Curacao Creole Conference, World Trade Centre, Curacao, Netherlands Antilles, 11–15 August.

Moya, S. (2006) 'Fi Wii news: a creole writing experience', *Cuadernos del Caribe*, 8: 89–95.

Nero, S. (1997) 'English is my native language ... or so I believe', *TESOL Quarterly*, 31 (3): 585–93.

——(2000) 'The changing faces of English: a Caribbean perspective', *TESOL Quarterly*, 34 (3): 483–510.

——(2006) 'Language, identity, and education of Caribbean English speakers', *World Englishes*, 25 (3/4): 501–11.

O'Flynn de Chaves, C. (1990) *Tiempo, Aspecto y Modalidad en el Criollo Sanandresano*, Bogotá: Colciencias-Universidad de los Andes.

——(2002) 'Una descripción lingüística del crillo de San Andrés', *Cuadernos del Caribe*, 3: 19–22.

Ordóñez, C.L. (2004) 'EFL and native Spanish in elite bilingual schools in Colombia: a first look at bilingual adolescent frog stories', *International Journal of Bilingual Education and Bilingualism*, 7 (5): 449–74.

Patiño Roselli, C. (1992) 'La Criollística y las lenguas criollas de Colombia', *Thesaurus*, XLVII (2): 233–64.

Pennycook, A. (1994) *The Cultural Politics of English as an International Language*, London: Longman.

——(1997) 'English and capital: some thoughts', *The Language Teacher*, 21: 10. Online. Available http://jalt-publications.org/tlt/files/97/oct/ur.html (accessed 3 April 2007).

——(1998) *English and the Discourses of Colonialism*, London: Routledge.

——(2001) *Critical Applied Linguistics: A Critical Introduction*, Mahwah, NJ: Lawrence Erlbaum Associates.

Phillipson, R. (1992) *Linguistic Imperialism*, Oxford: Oxford University Press.

Pineda, C. and Clavijo, O. (2003) 'Growing together as teacher researchers', *Colombian Applied Linguistics Journal*, 5: 65–85.

Quirk, R. (1988) 'The question of standards in the international use of English', in P.H. Lowenberg (ed.) *Language Spread and Language Policy*, Washington, DC: Georgetown University Press, pp. 229–41.

Roberts, P. (1988) *West Indians and their Language*, Cambridge: Cambridge University Press.

Rubiano, C.I., Frodden, C. and Cardona, G. (2000) 'The impact of the Colombian framework for English (COFE) project: an insiders' perspective', *IKALA, Revista de Lenguaje y Cultura*, 5 (9–10): 37–55.

Salamanca, A. (2007) 'Reflexiones sobre el lugar del inglés en tiempos de globalización', *Revista Internacional Magisterio*, 25: 68–70

Salyer, B.A. (2003) 'Alternatively and traditionally certified teachers: the same but different', *NASSP Bulletin*, 87 (636): 16–27.

Sánchez, A.C. and Obando, G. (2008) 'Is Colombia ready for bilingualism?' *Profile*, 9: 181–95

Sanmiguel, R. (2006) 'Mitos, hechos y retos actuales del bilingüismo en el Archipiélago de San Andrés, Providencia y Santa Catalina', *Cuadernos del Caribe*, 8: 110–22.

——(2007) 'El bilingüismo en el Archipiélago de San Andrés, Providencia y Santa Catalina', *Revista Internacional Magisterio*, 25: 28–31.

Shohamy, E. (2006) *Language Policy: Hidden Agendas and New Approaches*, London: Routledge.

Spolsky, B. (2004) *Language Policy*, Cambridge: Cambridge University Press.

Torres, C. and Monguí, R. (2008) 'Professional development schools: establishing alliances to bridge the gap between universities and schools', *Profile*, 10: 181–94.

Usma, J. (2007) 'Teacher autonomy: a critical review of the research and concept beyond applied linguistics', *IKALA, Revista de Lenguaje y Cultura*, 12 (18): 245–75.

——(2009) 'Education and language policy in Colombia: exploring processes of inclusion, exclusion, and stratification in times of global reform', *Profile*, 11: 123–41

Valencia, S. (2006) 'Literacy practices, texts, and talk around texts: English language teaching developments in Colombia', *Colombian Applied Linguistics Journal*, 8: 7–37.

Vélez-Rendón, G. (2003) 'English in Colombia: a sociolinguistic profile', *World Englishes*, 22 (2): 185–92.

Villa, B. (2009) 'Libraries will remain open', *El Colombiano*, 5 January. Online. Available www. elcolombiano.com/portada.asp?NM=Inicio (accessed 7 January 2009).

Wilson, R. (2005) 'Imposition or adoption? The globalisation of ELT practices', unpublished MA assignment, University of Essex. Online. Available www.winjeel.com/Documents/wilson%202005a. pdf (accessed 23 December 2008).

Yinger, R.J. and Hendricks-Lee, M.S. (2000) 'The language of standards and teacher education reform', *Educational Policy*, 14 (1): 94–106.

Zeichner, K. (2006) 'Reflections of a university-based teacher educator on the future of college- and university-based teacher education', *Journal of Teacher Education*, 57 (3): 326–40.

Section III

Emerging trends and themes

20

Lingua franca English

The European context

Barbara Seidlhofer

Introduction

The sociolinguistic situation in continental Europe is very different from most other contexts discussed in this volume, and the place of English is not adequately accounted for by reference to the Kachruvian circles. It is worth remembering that when Kachru first proposed his concentric model he did so 'tentatively' and recognized that demarcations between the circles were not always easy to make (Kachru 1985: 12, 13–14). Developments in global English over the past 25 years have made such demarcations even more difficult and confirm how right he was to be tentative. As Modiano points out, 'the complexities of European society, which differ radically from postcolonial speech communities, challenge established sociolinguistic precepts' (Modiano 2006: 234). Continental Europe is usually assigned expanding circle status and one can, of course, see that there are obvious differences in the role and status of the language here as compared with the inner circle, where English is a first language, and the postcolonial settings of the outer circle. But there are considerable differences too in comparison with other expanding circle contexts such as China, Japan and Korea, which are three separate nation-states and are the subjects of chapters in this book. Although Slavic Englishes are also thought to warrant separate treatment, Europe is, for the purposes of this book, considered to be one geo-political entity, but it is obvious that linguaculturally it is an extremely diverse area, a whole continent, in which English plays a distinctive and unique role.

Unlike the other continents (except Antarctica), Europe is home to a relatively small number of languages: *Ethnologue* (Lewis 2009) quotes 234 for Europe as a whole. The European Union (EU), with some 450 million inhabitants in currently 27 member states, recognizes 23 official languages, and about 60 other indigenous and non-indigenous languages are spoken in its geographical area. The role of English as such is similar within the EU and outside it in countries such as Iceland, Norway, Switzerland and Croatia, but for the treatment of some key issues this chapter will focus on the European Union (except the UK and Ireland) and its language policy.

For all kinds of reasons, English has become the *de facto* 'extraterritorial' lingua franca throughout Europe. This has, however, brought about resistance and controversy, due to the continued symbolic significance of national languages that European policy-makers still seem to insist on. In contrast with English as an (intra)national language like the other (national) languages of Europe (where of course regional lingua francas also exist), the role of English as a lingua franca (henceforth ELF) is not a national one; it fulfils different roles from national languages. And since 'language is as it is because of what it has to do' (Halliday 2003: 309), ELF is also developing its own, supranational forms.

All this seems familiar enough. However, English as a lingua franca is quite literally an emerging theme in the European context in that there is a marked discrepancy between the European Union's discourse about language and communication on the one hand, and the reality on the ground on the other. The forceful and enforced promotion of multilingualism as an official policy is in stark contrast with the actual practice of European citizens and institutions alike increasingly converging towards one lingua franca. This discrepancy has been stubbornly ignored by both policy-makers and the academic mainstream, and only very recently have there been signs of any serious debate on this important issue.

The European legacy: territory, people, language, culture

It may be difficult to see why policy-makers hesitate to prepare the way for what is obviously needed: a common means of communication, both in the institutions of the European Union and in Europe at large. So why do we, after more than forty years of a political movement towards integrating Europe, still have a top-down policy that is in stark contradiction with bottom-up practice? Why is there no vigorous public debate of the pros and cons of different language options? Why is there such resistance to openly acknowledging the pragmatic solution that apparently most people are actually subscribing to? Why are official communications and websites suggesting that there is a fully functional multilingualism in EU institutions, while, unofficially, one learns from the people involved that this is simply not the case?

As I see it, a large part of the explanation for this puzzling state of affairs is the difficulty Europeans experience in reconciling their relatively recent past reality with current ideals and aspirations for the future. The proclaimed ideals of integration, harmonization and transcultural understanding are radically at odds with what most Europeans have been brought up with: an education in and socialization into what Florian Coulmas once called 'the ideological dead weight of the nineteenth century' (Coulmas 1991: 27), characterized by a conflating of political loyalties with linguistic loyalties, and of language with culture. This means that the unification and formation of nation-states in the nineteenth century with its close association of nationhood and language still shapes the mindsets of many of today's Europeans. And this sense of independent national lingua-cultural identity has, of course, been strengthened by a long history of conflict, with the changing fates and roles of dominating and dominated countries distributed over the continent in relatively close geographical proximity. It is no wonder that the question as to 'who has to learn whose language' is inextricably linked in people's minds to issues of power.

With most of the member states having joined the EU in the 1990s and after 2000, the majority of today's decision-makers were still socialized into mindsets characterized by a strong sense of personal identification with nationhood, bred by long tradition, and reinforced by two world wars and their aftermath. And this identification with a nation has been supported and symbolized very strongly by national languages. Linguistic standardization played an important role in forming and confirming nations, and the monolingual individual came to be seen as the unmarked case. Strangely though, the very processes that supported nation-building, such as convergence on a shared means of communication, were not carried over on to the supranational EU level, although the principle of giving up emblems of individual identity for the greater good of shared community values and visions for the future should obviously be the same at both levels.

Instead, the thinking that prevailed was that as a logical consequence of the intricate relationship between nationhood and linguistic belonging, a great deal is at stake when it comes to the relative importance and power of individual languages: in this line of reasoning, if a language is dominant, the nation that 'owns' it is bound to be dominant, too. So insistence on the (theoretical) equality of all languages is mandatory for a union in which all the member states are claimed to be equal partners.

An optimistic reading of this situation would be that it may be a generational problem that will resolve itself when today's young people get to the age at which they may be involved in the formulation of policies. For they have grown up in an increasingly globalized world in which many physical boundaries are easily overcome: electronic means afford them access to often virtual communities, and they habitually switch between their local and non-local networks that they value as distinct but equally important, with each having their own linguistic ground rules (Seidlhofer 2007; Dewey 2009). In this view, the hope is that a more relaxed and flexible attitude towards the use of linguistic repertoires will gradually assert itself enough to make it possible for top-down policies to be realigned with reality, to the extent that anachronistic ideas of language loyalties cease to obstruct the direct intercultural communication that may well be necessary for enhancing mutual understanding and further integration within the larger community.

ELF as the *de facto* lingua franca of Europe

On the ground, English in Europe is firmly established as a language of wider communication, enabling people to link up about common interests, needs and concerns across languages and communities. It has entered the continent broadly speaking in two ways, by fulfilling functions in various professional domains and, simultaneously, by being encountered and used by speakers from all levels of society in practically all walks of life. Where the impact of English in Europe is probably most obvious is in the domains of the media, the internet, advertising, popular youth culture and entertainment (Preisler 1999: 242ff.; Truchot 2002: 18f.; Phillipson 2003: 72f.; Berns *et al.* 2007; Pennycook 2007). It is in these domains that English has evidently been spreading beyond the elites. In addition, the (striving for) increased European integration has led to the creation of various informal communication networks and contact situations among 'ordinary Europeans' (Labrie and Quell 1997: 23). In these situations, English often functions 'as a direct mediator between participants in a discourse who would otherwise have to rely on translation or a third party' (Breidbach 2003: 20).

English impinges on the lives of all European citizens, in many different ways: academics, business executives and hip-hoppers use English in their everyday activities; people listen to English pop lyrics, encounter advertising slogans such as 'I'm lovin' it', 'Just do it'; watch CNN and MTV; and so on. And English is not only a continual presence in their daily environment. Thanks to the internationalization of the economies of European countries, English also forms an integral part of the professional lives of a growing number of Europeans. A significant number of multinational, but also national, companies have adopted English as their company language, no matter whether they have subsidiaries in English-speaking countries or not (Melchers and Shaw 2003: 184). The companies do this in order to downplay their national affiliations and position themselves as transnational companies (Truchot 2003: 306).

In European education systems, English is the most important foreign language taught in its own right from the primary level onwards, and it is increasingly employed in 'content-and-language-integrated learning' (CLIL) mainly at the secondary level (see e.g. Dalton-Puffer 2007) – where, more often than not, CLIL equals CEIL ('content-and-English-integrated learning') in geography, biology and many other subjects. The predominance of English as a language for learning also has come to be acknowledged by European institutions themselves. For example, the 2008 edition of the Eurydice network's *Key Data on Teaching Languages at School in Europe* reports that, in the vast majority of EU member states, over 90 per cent of pupils in secondary schools study English, either as a compulsory subject or as an elective. This tendency is on the rise, and since 2002 the numbers of pupils learning English have been growing, especially in the states of Central and Eastern Europe (particularly in Bulgaria, the Czech Republic, Hungary, Slovakia), but also in Portugal. Generally speaking children start learning English at an ever younger age. The Eurydice report summarizes the situation thus: 'The teaching of English is constantly expanding and predominates almost everywhere' (Eurydice 2008: 12).

The strong presence of English in school curricula is continued in the tertiary sector, where one of the most significant trends is the teaching of courses and degrees exclusively in English (Truchot 1997: 71; Murray and Dingwall 2001: 86; Ammon and McConnel 2002: 171). This process is stimulated (somewhat paradoxically) by policy efforts to create a common European higher education area (cf. the Bologna Process, see http://ec.europa.eu/education/higher-education/doc1290_en.htm), where student and staff mobility results in a strengthening of the most readily available common language.

This trend in tertiary education goes hand in hand with language choice in scientific research, where English is perceived as a *sine qua non* for accessing information and communicating with fellow academics internationally (Viereck 1996; Ammon 2001; Truchot 2002). Accordingly, the majority of European scientific associations embrace English as the dominant, or indeed sole, language for the exchange of ideas (Crystal 2003: 88f.). In order to secure an international audience, the use of English in scientific conferences and publications is similarly unquestioned (Ammon 1994: 5; Truchot 2002: 11). As a consequence, scientists seem to 'function more as members of an international community having one common language than as members of national communities, both in their writing and in their selection of background readings' (Truchot 1997: 67; see also Widdowson 2003: Chapter 5).

Even though the EU eagerly presents itself as a multilingual area, the supremacy of English is being established step by step in European politics and various European and international organizations in Europe, e.g. the European Commission, UN, NATO (Dollerup 1996: 27f.). Official multilingual policies are often abandoned in practice in order to facilitate the working process. For example, van Els (2005) reports that all internal and external communication in the European Central Bank (ECB) in Frankfurt is conducted only in English. This restriction to English 'amounts to a tacit agreement within the ECB which everyone adheres to, but it is in no sense a matter of official policy. This characterizes the manner in which the EU deals with the problems of internal communication' (van Els 2005: 269).

Generally speaking, the situation between Reykjavik and Heraklion is that individuals usually have one first language (sometimes more), and are often exposed to other languages spoken locally, but most of them also have contact with English – which can be extensive or minimal – in their professional and private lives. Since the end of World War II, English has continually gained importance in Europe (Hoffmann 2000; Truchot 2002: 7), so that in the early twenty-first century, the significance of a certain command of English is closely comparable to that of reading and writing at the time of industrialization in Europe (Carmichael 2000: 285f.). Accordingly, proficiency in English is becoming something like a taken-for-granted cultural technique (Grin 1999; Neuner 2002: 7; Breidbach 2003: 20) like literacy or computer skills, with the consequence that, on a global scale, 'the competitive advantage which English has historically provided its acquirers (personally, organisationally, and nationally) will ebb away as English becomes a near-universal basic skill' (Graddol 2006: 15).

'Having English' in Europe has thus become a bit like having a driving licence: nothing special, something that most people have, and without which you do not get very far.

The contradictions of EU language policy

As the EU Commission's 'Europa languages portal' explains,

> Each Member State, when it joins the Union, stipulates which language or languages it wants to have declared official languages of the EU.
>
> So the Union uses the languages chosen by its citizens' own national governments, not a single language or a few languages chosen by itself and which many people in the Union might not understand.
>
> Our policy of official multilingualism as a deliberate tool of government is unique in the world. The EU sees the use of its citizens' languages as one of the factors which make it more transparent, more legitimate and more efficient.
>
> The European Union has recognised the importance of its special language policy by appointing a top official to champion the cause at the highest level. The portfolio of Leonard Orban includes responsibility for multilingualism.
>
> (http://europa.eu/languages/en/home)

The tendency for policy to be informed by ideology rather than logic is particularly clear from the assumption that allowing national governments to stipulate their own languages as 'official' somehow guarantees that these will be understood by other citizens in the Union. Whether it makes sense or not, this is intended as a declaration of the EU's commitment to furthering 'unity in diversity', for which various policy measures have been undertaken, culminating, in 2007, in the creation of a new Commission for Multilingualism.

'Unity in diversity' is, of course, an appealing slogan, but as a realistic proposition it presents formidable challenges, for, as I have already indicated, the present quest for it is beset with the counter-influence of past history. Europe is 'a continent where the tradition of "one language, one state, one people" is … deeply entrenched' (Wright

2000: 1), where national languages have great symbolic importance, with long traditions and close ties with their speakers' sociocultural identities. Linguistic diversity within the state has in the past been deliberately suppressed by standardization in countries like France in the interests of national unity and sociocultural cohesion. The independent status of European national languages, often hard won, is therefore highly prized, and it is not surprising that it should be jealously guarded.

The ever-growing demand for learning English described above is thus at odds with the forceful promotion of Europe's multilingual image, in which the notion of linguistic diversity figures like a mantra. Thus on the website of the European Commission for Multilingualism we can read: 'In its new Communication, entitled "Multilingualism: an asset for Europe and a shared commitment", the Commission gives an overview of what needs to be done *to turn linguistic diversity into an asset for solidarity and prosperity*' (http://ec.europa.eu/education/languages/news/news2853_en.htm, emphasis added).

'Turning' linguistic diversity into a social and economic advantage is an ambitious objective indeed, especially when this linguistic diversity appears not to be high on the list of priorities of the citizens themselves, who predominantly go for English if given a choice, plus a few other 'big' languages. That this trend is not what the policy-makers would ideally want to report can be seen from a certain reluctance to confront the real issues, as becomes evident in EU commentaries. The above-quoted Eurydice document reports:

> The sometimes very broad range of possible foreign languages included in the curricula of several countries ... may reflect the determination of educational policy-makers to diversify school provision for foreign language learning. However, statistical data on this provision indicate that in secondary education, English, French, German, Spanish and Russian represent over 95 per cent of all languages learnt in the majority of countries ... Pupils thus essentially appear to opt for learning more widely used languages. *This may be attributable either to pressure from families or a lack of qualified teachers in other languages.*
> (Eurydice 2008: 11, emphasis added)

The last sentence highlighted above comes across as an attempt to 'explain away' precisely what seems to be at issue here: surely the questions that need to be asked in this context are just why there should be 'pressure from families' and 'a lack of qualified teachers in other languages'. When 90 per cent of learners opt for the most widely used language, English, then exhortations to choose other languages will be to no avail as long as English is conceptualized as just one out of several 'foreign languages' on offer, and treated accordingly in school curricula and syllabuses.

A case in point: EU interpreting

That English is a special case that calls for a reconsideration of our 'inner linguistic landscapes' is evident not only in the area of education, but also in the professional sphere, especially in the EU institutions themselves. As explained on the website of the EU Directorate-General for Translation,

> The EU policy of communicating in 23 official languages (multilingualism policy) is unique in the world. All official languages enjoy *equal status*. EU citizens in

the 27 member countries can use any of them to communicate with the European institutions, which helps to make the Union more open and more effective.

It is clear from the quotation given earlier about the educational provision for the teaching of foreign languages and the preferences of families that all official languages do not, in fact, enjoy equal (social) status. What the EU seeks to do is to designate them as equal by making them official by legislation, and this can only be done by the process of intervention by translation. The quotation continues:

> A multilingual organisation like the EU needs high quality translation and relies on professional linguists to keep it running smoothly. The role of the language services in the various EU institutions and bodies is to support and strengthen multilingual communication in Europe.
>
> (http://ec.europa.eu/dgs/translation/translating/index_en.htm)

It will be obvious that, especially with the recent enlargements of the EU, providing adequate translation and interpreting services has become a complex and costly undertaking. Furthermore, there will obviously be occasions when it is simply not practicable or convenient to call on these services, and the multilingual ideal will be of less pressing concern than people's immediate communicative needs. It is therefore not surprising to find that alongside policy statements such as the one quoted above, we also have reports from within the EU institutions, which reveal that legal provisions protecting citizens' linguistic rights and pronouncements of principle in support of multilingualism co-exist with actual practices, especially on less public occasions such as informal talk and study groups, of converging on one lingua franca, which increasingly is English (Schlossmacher 1994; Melander 2001).

The growth of English in EU institutions has been accelerated by the substantial rise in the number of member states and this has resulted in an even more complex linguistic situation. This can be illustrated in a particularly interesting way by looking at how conference interpreting works, for instance in European institutions. While it had been feasible to provide interpretation out of and into all official EU languages in the early years of the European Union, the addition of many 'smaller' languages such as Czech, Finnish, Estonian, Hungarian, Latvian, and so on, in recent years has brought with it quite radical changes in the interpreting process. An important principle of interpreting services has always been that all interpreting should be into the interpreter's first language. This would now mean that large numbers of interpreters would be required to allow for all language combinations – for instance, from Finnish into Czech, from Estonian into Hungarian and vice versa, and so on. Since it has turned out to be impossible to find native-speaker interpreters who could interpret into all these languages and from all these languages, more and more use is now being made of so-called 'relay interpreting'. This involves the use of a 'larger' pivot language, now more often than not English, into which the speaker's speech (in, for example, Latvian) is interpreted. As a second step, the English translation is then rendered in the required other languages by the respective native speakers. Interpreters also work out of their own languages into the pivot language, thus breaking the principle of only interpreting into their first language. That is to say, 'small' languages are often dealt with by their native speakers working from and into two languages, interpreting into English and vice versa, in a process called 'bi-active'. Their (non-native) English speech is then rendered into various other languages by their native speakers. Melchers and Shaw (2003) give a succinct description of this intricate process and offer the following intriguing comment:

> Three interesting and symptomatic points arise from these changes in interpreting practice. One is that since the pivot will often be English, the position of English will be strengthened – all information will have 'passed through' the language. The second is that combining relay and bi-active interpreting means that no native speakers of English will be involved: an expansion of English appears to result in a reduction of the significance of native speakers. Consequently, the third observation is that the English that occupies such an important position will be an 'offshore' variety not controlled by native speakers.
>
> (Melchers and Shaw 2003: 182)

The massive presence of a non-native language is a situation that many professional translators and interpreters experience as a potential threat both to the demand for their services and to their self-image, which sets great store by a special expertise in rendering fine nuances of meaning in their first language. Others, however, recognize this new situation as a welcome opportunity: 'ELF brings a refreshing – if unexpected – dose of reality to translation theory, and can help contribute to its renewal' (Hewson 2009: 119; see also Tosi 2005 and several contributions in Anderman and Rogers 2005).

The way forward and the ELF alternative

The developments described here are due to a very new phenomenon that requires quite some conceptual adjustment because the notion of 'a language' and its native speakers have traditionally, over millennia, been inextricably linked in our minds, perhaps especially so in the post-nineteenth-century Europe of nation-states. What interests us here are the sociolinguistic consequences of this unprecedented state of affairs. One important implication that ELF researchers and (some other) applied linguists recognize is that the lingua franca – especially if it is used on a daily basis as is now the case for increasing numbers of Europeans – ceases to be perceived as the property of the ancestral speakers in whose territories it originated. Instead, ELF gets appropriated by its non-native users, who – like hitherto just native speakers of a language – become acknowledged as agents in the processes that determine how the language spreads, develops, varies and changes (Brumfit 2001; Brutt-Griffler 2002; Widdowson 2003: Chapter 5).

This switch of mindset is of great relevance for European language policy. One case in point is the issue of combating the proliferation of official languages and contested proposals for settling on one, two or three working language(s) – English, plus French, plus German. Van Els (2005) discusses various options that have been suggested and leaves no doubt as to which solution he favours:

> There is a [further] modality that perhaps has a better prospect of success. This one, however, does impose a very drastic restriction, i.e. to only a single working language. It may seem surprising, but in this modality the language handicap for non-natives, as opposed to the variant with a number of working languages, is significantly reduced. In the first place, they only need to develop competence in one foreign language. Secondly, and this is very important, this one foreign language

will also become – and to an increasing extent – the property of the non-natives. If they constitute a large majority, as in the EU, they will, without doubt, use the working language as their language and share in the fashioning of this language to meet their own needs. Native speakers will notice – sometimes to their great annoyance – that their language is frequently being changed in unorthodox ways.

(van Els 2005: 276)

A crucial advantage of opting for one working language is that this scenario would offer a way of avoiding the danger of what has been termed 'hegemonic multi-lingualism' (Krzyzanowski 2009), namely the use of two or three 'big' working languages at the cost of many 'small' languages – for that scenario would allow the native speakers of those languages to retain 'ownership' of their respective language while at the same time requiring speakers of all the other languages to develop high proficiency not just in one but in two or even three languages.

The one working language van Els is talking about in the above quote is English: '*Without any doubt, English will be the working language*' (2005: 278, original emphasis), and from what the author says about the role of non-native users' share 'in the fashioning of this language to meet their own needs' it is clear that by 'English' he means ELF.

This is also the view that Wright (2009) presents in a comprehensive and highly enlightening consideration of the role of language issues in the European Union, especially the role of English, 'the elephant in the room' in her title. Her article presents similar arguments as van Els' but is much more detailed in its argumentation. Thus she also presents the case for the acceptability of ELF as the lingua franca of the EU rather than perpetuating 'the unresolved clash between top-down policy and bottom-up practice, and the unacknowledged language problems this causes in both the European institutions and the wider world' (Wright 2009: 97). She observes:

At present, the linguistic side effect of current social phenomena is linguistic convergence towards a single lingua franca. Language policy cannot work against these social currents and impose multilingualism from the top down. It alone will not reverse the trend to use English as a lingua franca. If the move to English is halted, it will be because of other, external factors that we cannot yet foresee. We can do little to influence this and the lesson that we should take from the nation-state experience is not that language policy can be imposed from the top down but that this only works when it is in harmony with other social, political and economic developments.

(Wright 2009: 107)

Crucial to the acceptability and functionality of English as the common means of communication is, of course, its explicit conceptualization as ELF rather than the native language of the British and the Irish. This is what van Els is referring to in his proposal, and what Wright emphasizes too. Importantly, she argues that while it is understandable that the predominance of English has often been discussed in terms of Gramscian hegemony, this approach cannot simply be mapped from colonial situations on to Europe:

in the European setting, there is no elemental link between centre, power and English. The majority of those in positions of authority using English within elite

363

networks are not native English speakers. They have acquired English as a second language and use it as a lingua franca.

(Wright 2009: 105)

So in Europe today, it is simply not the case that English emanates from the native-speaker 'centre' in a way that is designed to benefit its native speakers. It may be true that these do have some advantage in that they are the only ones that do not need to learn the most widespread European lingua franca from scratch, but it does not follow that they are therefore more adept in its actual communicative use, and there are now studies becoming available that show that native speakers of English may actually be at a disadvantage because – probably for that very reason – they tend not to be very effective communicators in intercultural encounters (Jenkins 2007; Wright 2008): 'They may not have understood the new rules of engagement, or even grasped that there are such new rules', as Wright (2009: 105) aptly puts it.

It is precisely these rules of engagement that ELF research into intercultural interactions is seeking to understand more deeply. Over recent years, an energetic area of enquiry has developed, with corpora of spoken ELF discourse being compiled in order to make detailed descriptions possible. VOICE, the Vienna–Oxford International Corpus of English, comprises data from a range of domains of use, and provides free online access to ELF researchers (www.univie.ac.at/voice/). ELFA, a corpus of ELF interactions in academic settings, has also been completed (www.uta.fi/laitokset/kielet/engf/research/elfa/corpus.htm).

While many corpora offer samples or extracts of longer texts, both VOICE and ELFA contain complete speech events, i.e. from the beginning of an interaction to the end. This decision was taken in order to allow for qualitative analyses of the corpus texts, in the sense that corpus users would not be limited to sampling the corpus in essentially context-deprived fashion, homing in on individual words and word clusters via the usual corpus tools. Instead, it should be possible to read and make sense of entire speech events, both as a frame for what the participants experience and as an analytic construct for the observer/researcher. VOICE Online 1.0 has a European focus, but also includes speakers of non-European languages.

A further important asset of VOICE is that it offers users ample contextual information about the speakers, the location, the purpose of the interaction, etc., so that researchers can understand 'what is going on', thus again enhancing support for conducting qualitative descriptive work.

The insights emerging from such empirical ELF studies help us perceive and understand how people from diverse linguacultural backgrounds appropriate and adapt English for their own needs. ELF speakers make use of their multifaceted plurilingual repertoires in a fashion motivated by the communicative purpose and the interpersonal dynamics of the interaction. They draw on the underlying resources of the language, not just the conventional encodings of English as a native language, and adjust and calibrate their own language use for their interlocutors' benefit. Thus they exploit the potential of the language while fully focused on the purpose of the talk and on their interlocutors as people rather than on the linguistic code itself. Most of these studies, then, take an emic perspective and observe people absorbed in the *ad hoc*, situated negotiation of meaning. And now that we are able to investigate these naturally occurring ELF interactions closely, the general picture that is emerging is certainly not one of inarticulate, linguistically handicapped non-native speakers incapable of holding their own in interactions with both other non-native as well as native speakers of English, but of an agreed-upon lingua franca employed in a fashion that is appropriate to the occasion – and appropriated, negotiated and shaped by all its users.

For instance, some studies have focused on the crucial role of accommodation in ELF talk (e.g. Jenkins 2000; Cogo 2009; Seidlhofer 2009a). Others explore how speakers signal their cultural identities in various ways, e.g. by making code-switching an intrinsic part of many interactions (Klimpfinger 2009), by creating their own online idioms (Seidlhofer and Widdowson 2007; Pitzl 2009), new words (Pitzl *et al.* 2008) and, more generally, their own inter-culture (Pölzl and Seidlhofer 2006; Thompson 2006). The interdependence of form(s) and function(s) is at the centre of studies looking at various aspects of lexicogrammar, such as Breiteneder (2009), Ranta (2006), Dewey (2007), Hülmbauer (2007, 2009) and Seidlhofer (2009b). Other studies show ELF users successfully resolving instances of miscommunication when they occur (Pitzl 2005; Watterson 2008), establishing rapport (Kordon 2006), and employing communicative strategies such as repetition (Lichtkoppler 2007), silences (Böhringer 2009) and considerate and mutually supportive communicative behaviour overall (e.g. Kaur 2009; Pullin-Stark 2009). There are also ethnographic, even longitudinal studies investigating the use of ELF in various settings, such as Björkman (2008), Schaller-Schwaner (2008), Smit (2010) in higher education and Ehrenreich (2009) in multinational corporations.

These descriptive findings, in turn, bring us back to the theoretical challenges mentioned above since they raise important issues about what 'English' is and how it can be described. They reveal that the widespread assumption that one cannot communicate effectively without adhering to the norms of native English is a myth. So, even at this relatively early stage of analysis, it is evident that ELF users appropriate and exploit linguistic resources in complex and creative ways to achieve their communicative purposes. They use the language at their disposal to negotiate meaning and personal relationships and so co-construct mutual understanding and establish the common conceptual and affective ground of a 'third space'. They get high-stake jobs done, they shape policies and they negotiate business contracts; they engage in banter and troubles-telling/problem-swapping and language play. The very linguistic 'abnormalities' of ELF talk in reference to the norms of native English draw attention to the essentially normal functions they realize as a natural and actually occurring use of language.

What needs to be stressed is that this *natural* English is not the *national* English of its native speakers. It cannot be if it is to serve its essential function as a means for making the concept of unity an operational reality rather than an ideological illusion. As a lingua franca, English is necessarily complementary to other languages in Europe and not in competition with them. And since this is the way English is used, it would seem to make sense to make provision for this in the way it is taught.

Implications for language education

There is no doubt, then, that 'English' has a special status among European languages and that it is high time to act on this insight, also – indeed, especially – as far as language education policy is concerned. The more widely English is used, the greater the demand for it in European education systems: 'The more people learn a language, the more useful it becomes, and the more useful it is, the more people want to learn it' (Myers-Scotton 2002: 280). This well-nigh universal demand for English is obviously not

365

motivated by an overwhelming desire of European citizens to communicate or identify with native-speaking neighbours in Britain or Ireland. As we have seen, English has therefore ceased to be a 'foreign language' in the sense that other European languages are. Of course, there are still people that want to learn English because they want to, say, study in Britain, communicate with their friends in the USA or emigrate to New Zealand, and for whom therefore 'English as a native language' would constitute an appropriate target. But given the differences between various native varieties of English it would be impossible to prepare those learners for effortless communication with their chosen group of native speakers, and anyway, they will pick up the variety they are aiming for as and when the situation requires it. From the point of view of language education policy, what needs to be recognized and acted upon is that by far the majority of all European citizens need English primarily as a lingua franca for communication with all sorts of people in different domains, more often than not non-native speakers of English.

It would therefore seem obvious that if educational policy is to take account of reality, English – conceived of as a lingua franca – needs to be taken out of the canon of 'real' foreign languages and recognized as a co-existent and non-competitive addition to the learner/user's linguistic repertoire. Thus English is removed from contention with other languages and thereby, far from reducing diversity in language choice in educational institutions, actually enhances it. It is only when English is conceived of as belonging to its native speakers and as a foreign language like any other that it constitutes a threat.

And yet in the documents put out by the Language Policy Division of the Council of Europe that **is** how English is persistently represented – just like other foreign languages, defined by its native speakers. The focus has so far remained very much on 'cumulative' proficiency (becoming better at speaking and writing English as native speakers do) and on the goal of successful communication with native speakers (and for some levels, approximating native-like command of the language). It is true that a general shift in curricular guidelines has taken place from 'correctness' to 'appropriateness' and 'intelligibility', but by and large 'intelligibility' is taken to mean being intelligible to native speakers, and being able to understand native speakers. This orientation is clearly discernible in some of the specifications of the European Language Portfolio (www.coe.int/portfolio).

> I can interact with a degree of fluency and spontaneity that makes regular interaction with native speakers quite possible. I can take an active part in discussion in familiar contexts, accounting for and sustaining my views. (Spoken Interaction / B2)
>
> I have no difficulty in understanding any kind of spoken language, whether live or broadcast, even when delivered at fast native speed, provided I have some time to get familiar with the accent. (Listening / C2)
>
> (www.coe.int/portfolio)

In a similar vein, Hoffman (2000: 19) describes the English of European learners as spanning 'the whole range from non-fluent to native-like', as though fluency in English were not a possibility for those whose speech does not mimic that of a native speaker.

In accordance with such views, the focus in curricula, textbooks and reference materials is still largely on Anglo-American culture(s), plus sometimes 'exotic optional extras' such as postcolonial literature and New Englishes, but again through a predominantly British 'lens'. In policy statements and curriculum specifications, Standard British English or American English norms are taken for granted as the only valid measures of proficiency.

The advocacy of 'authentic' materials constitutes a kind of pedagogic mantra, and teachers are expected to help their learners cope with 'real English', which is taken to be the English used by native speakers in their speech communities in, say, the UK or the US. This 'real English' can now be described with unprecedented accuracy thanks to the availability of huge corpora of native English. The effect of this, of course, has been to further consolidate the position of native-speaker English as the only English that counts, and in so doing to necessarily ensure the continuation of its conflict with other competing languages and provide further confirmation of fears that it will prevail and dominate.

When the only descriptions of English available were those of the native-speaker language, it is understandable that they should be deferred to, but, as I have pointed out earlier, descriptions of ELF are now underway and what they show is that the English of Europe is in reality very different in form and function from the English that has been promoted by European educational policy. This, at the very least, should lead us to a critical reconsideration of how far the taken-for-granted assumptions that have informed the teaching of English in the past still remain relevant in the present.

Suggestions for further reading

Ahrens, R. (ed.) (2003) *Europäische Sprachenpolitik. European Language Policy*, Heidelberg: Universitätsverlag Winter. (This volume is a collection of papers considering the role of English as the recognized lingua franca in Europe and the impact of English on professional domains, national contexts as well as language teaching and learning.)

Mauranen, A. and Ranta, E. (eds) (2009) *English as a Lingua Franca: Studies and Findings*, Newcastle upon Tyne: Cambridge Scholars Publishing. (This is the first substantial collection of research articles reporting on conceptual issues and empirical studies of English as a lingua franca, with a distinct European focus.)

Phillipson, R. (2003) *English-Only Europe?* London: Routledge. (This book criticizes the predominant position of English within Europe and presents a fervent argument for a strong EU language policy to protect and ensure equal linguistic rights for all European citizens.)

Seidlhofer, B. (2010) *Understanding English as a Lingua Franca*, Oxford: Oxford University Press. (This book provides a detailed account of the nature of English as a lingua franca, in Europe and elsewhere, and discusses the implications of this unprecedented sociolinguistic development for educational policy and practice.)

References

Ammon, U. (1994) 'The present dominance of English in Europe. With an outlook on possible solutions to the European language problems', in U. Ammon, K. Mattheier and P. Nelde (eds) *English Only? In Europa / In Europe / En Europe* (Sociolinguistica 8), Tübingen: Niemeyer, pp. 1–14.

——(ed.) (2001) *The Dominance of English as a Language of Science. Effects on Other Languages and Language Communities*, Berlin: Mouton de Gruyter.

Ammon, U. and McConnel, G. (2002) *English as an Academic Language in Europe: A Survey of its Use in Teaching*, Frankfurt am Main: Peter Lang.

Anderman, G. and Rogers, M. (eds) (2005) *In and Out of English: For Better, for Worse?* Clevedon: Multilingual Matters.

Berns, M., de Bot, K. and Hasebrink, U. (eds) (2007) *In the Presence of English: The Media and European Youth*, New York: Springer.

367

Björkman, B. (2008) '"So where we are?" Spoken lingua franca English at a technical university in Sweden', *English Today*, 94: 35–41.

Böhringer, H. (2009) *The Sound of Silence: Silent and Filled Pauses in English as a Lingua Franca Business Interaction*, Saarbrücken: VDM Verlag.

Breidbach, S. (2003) *Plurilingualism, Democratic Citizenship and the Role of English*, Strasbourg: Council of Europe. Online. Available www.coe.int/t/dg4/linguistic/Source/BreidbachEN.pdf (accessed 20 February 2010).

Breiteneder, A. (2009) 'English as a lingua franca in Europe: an empirical perspective', *World Englishes*, 28 (2): 256–69.

——(2010) *English as a Lingua Franca in Europe: A Natural Development*, Saarbrücken: VDM Verlag.

Brumfit, C.J. (2001) *Individual Freedom in Language Teaching: Helping Learners to Develop a Dialect of their Own*, Oxford: Oxford University Press.

Brutt-Griffler, J. (2002) *World English. A Study of its Development*, Clevedon: Multilingual Matters.

Carmichael, C. (2000) 'Conclusions: Language and national identify in Europe', in S. Barbour and C. Carmichael (eds) *Language and Nationalism in Europe*, Oxford: Oxford University Press, pp. 280–9.

Cogo, A. (2009) 'Accommodating difference in ELF conversations: a study of pragmatic strategies', in A. Mauranen and E. Ranta (eds) *English as a Lingua Franca: Studies and Findings*, Newcastle upon Tyne: Cambridge Scholars Publishing, pp. 254–73.

Coulmas, F. (1991) 'European integration and the idea of the national language', in F. Coulmas (ed.) *A Language Policy for the European Community. Prospects and Quandaries*, Berlin: Mouton de Gruyter.

Crystal, D. (2003) *English as a Global Language* (2nd edition), Cambridge: Cambridge University Press.

Dalton-Puffer, C. (2007) *Discourse in CLIL Classrooms*, Amsterdam: John Benjamins.

Dewey, M. (2007) 'English as a lingua franca and globalization: an interconnected perspective', *International Journal of Applied Linguistics*, 17 (3): 332–54.

——(2009) 'English as a lingua franca: heightened variability and theoretical implications', in A. Mauranen and E. Ranta (eds) *English as a Lingua Franca: Studies and Findings*, Newcastle upon Tyne: Cambridge Scholars Publishing, pp. 60–83.

Dollerup, C. (1996) 'English in the European Union', in R. Hartmann (ed.) *The English Language in Europe*, Oxford: Intellect, pp. 24–36.

Ehrenreich, S. (2009) 'English as a lingua franca in multinational corporations – exploring business communities of practice', in A. Mauranen and E. Ranta (eds) *English as a Lingua Franca: Studies and Findings*, Newcastle upon Tyne: Cambridge Scholars Publishing, pp. 126–51.

Eurydice (2008) 'Key data on teaching languages at school in Europe'. Online. Available http://eacea. ec.europa.eu/education/eurydice/documents/key_data_series/095EN.pdf (accessed 22 February 2010).

Graddol, D. (2006) *English Next: Why Global English May Mean the End of 'English as a Foreign Language'*, London: British Council.

Grin, F. (1999) 'Language spread and linguistic diversity', in M. Kontra, R. Phillipson, T. Skutnabb-Kangas and T. Varady (eds) *Language – A Right and a Resource*, Budapest: Central European University Press.

Halliday, M.A.K. (2003) 'On language and linguistics', in J. Webster (ed.) *The Collected Works of M.A.K. Halliday, Vol. 3*, London: Continuum.

Hewson, L. (2009) 'Brave new globalized world? Translation studies and English as a lingua franca', *Revue Française de Linguistique Appliquée*, XIV: 109–20.

Hoffman, C. (2000) 'The spread of English and the growth of multilingualism with English in Europe', in J. Cenoz and U. Jessner (eds) *English in Europe: The Acquisition of a Third Language*, Clevedon: Multilingual Matters, pp. 1–21.

House, J. (2003) 'English as a lingua franca: a threat to multilingualism?' *Journal of Sociolinguistics*, 7 (4): 556–78.

Hülmbauer, C. (2007) '"You moved, aren't?" – the relationship between lexicogrammatical correctness and communicative effectiveness in English as a lingua franca', *Vienna English Working*

PaperS, 16 (2): 3–35. Online. Available http://anglistik.univie.ac.at/fileadmin/user_upload/ dep_anglist/weitere_Uploads/Views/Views_0702.pdf (accessed 22 February 2010).

——(2009) '"We don't take the right way. We just take the way that we think you will understand" – the shifting relationship between correctness and effectiveness in ELF', in A. Mauranen and E. Ranta (eds) *English as a Lingua Franca: Studies and Findings*, Newcastle upon Tyne: Cambridge Scholars Publishing, pp. 323–47.

Jenkins, J. (2000) *The Phonology of English as an International Language. New Models, New Norms, New Goals*, Oxford: Oxford University Press.

——(2007) *English as a Lingua Franca: Attitude and Identity*, Oxford: Oxford University Press.

Kachru, B.B. (1985) 'Standards, codification and sociolinguistic realism: the English language in the outer circle', in R. Quirk and H.G. Widdowson (eds) *English in the World: Teaching and Learning the Languages and Literatures*, Cambridge: Cambridge University Press, pp. 11–30.

Kaur, J. (2009) 'Pre-empting problems of understanding in English as a lingua franca', in A. Mauranen and E. Ranta (eds) *English as a Lingua Franca: Studies and Findings*, Newcastle upon Tyne: Cambridge Scholars Publishing, pp. 107–23.

Klimpfinger, T. (2009) '"She's mixing the two languages together" – forms and functions of code-switching in English as a lingua franca', in A. Mauranen and E. Ranta (eds) *English as a Lingua Franca: Studies and Findings*, Newcastle upon Tyne: Cambridge Scholars Publishing, pp. 348–71.

Kordon, K. (2006) '"You are very good" – establishing rapport in English as a lingua franca: the case of agreement tokens', *Vienna English Working PaperS*, 15 (2): 58–82. Online. Available www.univie.ac.at/Anglistik/views0602.pdf (accessed 22 February 2010).

Krzyzanowski, M. (2009) 'Discourses about enlarged and multilingual Europe: perspectives from German and Polish national public spheres', in P. Stevenson and J. Carl (eds) *Language, Discourse and Identity in Central Europe*, Basingstoke: Palgrave Macmillan, pp. 23–47.

Labrie, N. and Quell, C. (1997) 'Your language, my language or English? The potential language choice in communication among nationals of the European Union', *World Englishes*, 16: 3–26.

Lewis, M. (ed.) (2009) *Ethnologue: Languages of the World* (16th edition), Dallas, TX: SIL International. Online. Available www.ethnologue.com/ (accessed 22 February 2010).

Lichtkoppler, J. (2007) '"Male. Male." – "Male?" – "The sex is male." The role of repetition in English as a lingua franca conversations', *Vienna English Working PaperS*, 16 (1): 39–65. Online. Available http://anglistik.univie.ac.at/fileadmin/user_upload/dep_anglist/weitere_Uploads/Views/views_0701.pdf (accessed 22 February 2010).

Melander, B. (2001) 'Swedish, English, and the European Union', in S. Boyd and L. Huss (eds) *Managing Multilingualism in a European Nation-State*, Clevedon: Multilingual Matters.

Melchers, G. and Shaw, P. (2003) *World Englishes*, London: Arnold.

Modiano, M. (2006) 'Euro-Englishes', in B. Kachru, Y. Kachru and C. Nelson, *Handbook of World Englishes*, Oxford: Blackwell. pp. 223–39.

Murray, H. and Dingwall, S. (2001) 'The dominance of English at European universities: Switzerland and Sweden compared', in U. Ammon (ed.) *The Dominance of English as a Language of Science. Effects on Other Languages and Language Communities*, Berlin: Mouton de Gruyter, pp. 85–112.

Myers-Scotton, C. (2002) *Contact Linguistics. Bilingual Encounters and Grammatical Outcomes*, Oxford: Oxford University Press.

Neuner, G. (2002) *Policy Approaches to English*, Strasbourg: Council of Europe. Online. Available www.coe.int/t/dg4/linguistic/Source/NeunerEN.pdf (accessed 20 February 2010).

Pennycook, A. (2007) *Global Englishes and Transcultural Flows*, London: Routledge.

Phillipson, R. (2003) *English-Only Europe?* London: Routledge.

Pitzl, M.-L. (2005) 'Non-understanding in English as a lingua franca: examples from a business context', *Vienna English Working PaperS*, 14 (2): 50–71. Online. Available www.univie.ac.at/Anglistik/Views0502mlp.pdf (accessed 22 February 2010).

——(2009) '"We should not wake up any dogs": idiom and metaphor in ELF', in A. Mauranen and E. Ranta (eds) *English as a Lingua Franca: Studies and Findings*, Newcastle upon Tyne: Cambridge Scholars Publishing, pp. 298–322.

Pitzl, M.-L., Breiteneder, A. and Klimpfinger, T. (2008) 'A world of words: processes of lexical innovation in VOICE', *Vienna English Working PaperS*, 17 (2): 21–46. Online. Available http://anglistik.univie.ac.at/fileadmin/user_upload/dep_anglist/weitere_Uploads/Views/views_0802.pdf (accessed 22 February 2010).

Pölzl, U. and Seidlhofer, B. (2006) 'In and on their own terms: the "habitat factor" in English as a lingua franca interactions', *International Journal of the Sociology of Language*, 177: 151–76.

Preisler, B. (1999) 'Functions and forms of English in a European ELF country', in T. Bex and R.J. Watts (eds) *Standard English. The Widening Debate*, London: Routledge, pp. 239–67.

Pullin-Stark, P. (2009) 'No joke – this is serious! Power, solidarity and humour in Business English as a Lingua Franca (BELF)', in A. Mauranen and E. Ranta (eds) *English as a Lingua Franca: Studies and Findings*, Newcastle upon Tyne: Cambridge Scholars Publishing, pp. 152–77.

Ranta, E. (2006) 'The "attractive" progressive – why use the -ing form in English as a lingua franca?' *Nordic Journal of English Studies*, 5: 95–116.

——(2009) 'Syntactic features in spoken ELF – learner language or spoken grammar?' in A. Mauranen and E. Ranta (eds) *English as a Lingua Franca: Studies and Findings*, Newcastle upon Tyne: Cambridge Scholars Publishing, pp. 84–106.

Schaller-Schwaner, I. (2008) 'ELF in academic settings: working language and edulect, prestige and solidarity', paper presented at the ELF Forum 'The First International Conference of English as a Lingua Franca', Helsinki University, March.

Schlossmacher, M. (1994) 'Die Arbeitssprachen in den Organen der Europäischen Gemeinschaft. Methoden und Ergebnisse einer empirischen Untersuchung', in U. Ammon, K. Mattheier and P. Nelde (eds) *English Only? In Europa/in Europe/en Europe* (Sociolinguistica 8), Tübingen: Niemeyer, pp. 101–22.

Seidlhofer, B. (2003) *A Concept of 'International English' and Related Issues: From 'Real English' to 'Realistic English'?* Strasbourg: Council of Europe. Online. Available www.coe.int/t/dg4/linguistic/Source/SeidlhoferEN.pdf (accessed 20 February 2010).

——(2007) 'English as a lingua franca and communities of practice', in S. Volk-Birke and J. Lippert (eds) *Anglistentag 2006 Halle Proceedings*, Trier: Wissenschaftlicher Verlag Trier, pp. 307–18. (Reprinted in abridged form in J. Jenkins (2009) (ed.) *World Englishes* (2nd edition), London: Routledge, pp. 206–14.)

——(2009a) 'Accommodation and the idiom principle in English as a lingua franca', *Intercultural Pragmatics*, 6 (2): 195–215.

——(2009b) 'Orientations in ELF research: form and function', in A. Mauranen and E. Ranta (eds) *English as a Lingua Franca: Studies and Findings*, Newcastle upon Tyne: Cambridge Scholars Publishing, pp. 37–59.

Seidlhofer, B. and Widdowson, H.G. (2007) 'Idiomatic variation and change in English. The idiom principle and its realizations', in U. Smit, S. Dollinger, J. Hüttner, G. Kaltenböck and U. Lutzky (eds) *Tracing English through Time. Explorations in Language Variation*, Wien: Braumüller, pp. 359–74.

Smit, U. (2010) *English as a Lingua Franca in Higher Education. A Longitudinal Study of Classroom Discourse*, Berlin: Mouton de Gruyter.

Thompson, A. (2006) 'English in context in an East Asian intercultural workplace', PhD thesis, Ontario Institute for Studies in Education, University of Toronto.

Tosi, A. (2005) 'EU translation problems and the danger of linguistic devaluation', *International Journal of Applied Linguistics*, 15 (3): 384–8.

Truchot, C. (1997) 'The spread of English: from France to a more general perspective', *World Englishes*, 16: 65–76.

——(2002) *Key Aspects of the Use of English in Europe*, Strasbourg: Council of Europe. Online. Available www.coe.int/t/dg4/linguistic/Source/TruchotEN.pdf (accessed 20 February 2010).

——(2003) 'Some facts and some questions on the use of English in the workplace', in R. Ahrens (ed.) *Europäische Sprachenpolitik. European Language Policy*, Heidelberg: Universitätsverlag Winter, pp. 303–10.

van Els, T. (2005) 'Multilingualism in the European Union', *International Journal of Applied Linguistics*, 15 (3): 263–81.

Viereck, W. (1996) 'English in Europe: its nativisation and use as a lingua franca, with special reference to German-speaking countries', in R. Hartmann (ed.) *The English Language in Europe*, Oxford: Intellect, pp. 16–23.

Watterson, M. (2008) 'Repair of non-understanding in English in international communication', *World Englishes*, 27: 378–406.

Widdowson, H.G. (2003) *Defining Issues in English Language Teaching*, Oxford: Oxford University Press.

Wright, S. (2000) *Community and Communication. The Role of Language in Nation State Building and European Integration*, Clevedon: Multilingual Matters.

——(2008) 'The case of the crucial and problematic lingua franca', paper given at AILA, Duisburg-Essen. August.

——(2009) 'The elephant in the room', *European Journal of Language Policy*, 1 (2): 93–120.

21

Developmental patterns of English

Similar or different?

Edgar W. Schneider

Introduction

World Englishes are spoken today on practically all continents and in a wide range of different social and cultural contexts, with many different contact languages involved. This diversity of input factors quite naturally should make us expect widely different outcomes of the individual evolutionary processes. Contrary to this expectation, however, surprising similarities between many World Englishes have been observed, with respect to both their sociolinguistic settings and their linguistic properties. For example, on the social side we can observe the emergence of a 'complaint tradition' (discussed further later), of local varieties of English adopting the role of local identity carriers, and of processes towards codification in a wide range of different countries. In a similar vein, linguistically speaking, phenomena like plural uses of noncount nouns, progressive forms of stative verbs, the formation of hybrid compounds, or the occurrence of innovative (but basically similar) verb complementation patterns have also been found to transcend regional and linguistic boundaries. Of course, this is not to deny the diversity that is also there, naturally and unavoidably. For example, certain regional pronunciation phenomena of English in Nigeria reveal transfer from Yoruba, and some rules of the grammar of colloquial Singaporean English can be accounted for as substrate phenomena from Chinese and other local languages. So an interesting question to ask is, therefore: how can differences or similarities between World Englishes be accounted for by their developmental patterns?

To some extent an answer to these questions also depends on definitions and delimitations. The older term 'New Englishes', as coined by Platt *et al.* (1984) and others, focused on second-language varieties of the outer circle only, thus circumscribing a relatively more homogeneous and consistent category of language varieties. 'Postcolonial Englishes', in contrast, the term preferred by Schneider (2007), also includes native-speaker colonial settler varieties like American or Australian English and emphasizes the common origins of inner and outer circle varieties in shared processes of colonial history and similar postcolonial developmental trajectories. Kachru's term 'World Englishes', the broadest of all, includes all inner circle varieties, has a special interest in outer circle (typically second language or 'L2') varieties, and recognizes a fuzzy boundary in the expanding circle, encompassing countries where English did not have colonial foundations, but is nevertheless spreading rapidly these days as a 'foreign' or an 'international language'. The question of how similar or different these varieties are also needs to consider these categorial distinctions. Basically, however, a broad understanding of 'World Englishes' is adopted here.

Similarities and differences: a broad survey

In the first main section, a general survey of similarities and differences is given, essentially by listing and exemplifying pertinent observations from a range of different countries and contexts. Indirectly, this is meant to give some substance to later, more abstract discussions of the topic. I look at extralinguistic and intralinguistic observations in turn. Readers who are interested in more extensive documentation and discussions of these and other similar phenomena are referred to Schneider (2007), where the subject is dealt with in greater detail, and with an eye on an even wider range of relevant observations.

Sociolinguistic settings

First, we need to look at extralinguistic contexts, i.e. the historical processes by which English came to be spoken in new lands, and the sociolinguistic settings which determine its uses today. The similarities which can be observed across many locations ultimately result from constants in sociological group interaction, as it were, deeply rooted patterns of group interaction, delimitation, segregation and integration. The core idea of all of this is that in all postcolonial Englishes (in the narrow sense, i.e. excluding both ancestral English countries and those where English has no colonial background) a gradual diminishing in the social distance between English-speaking settler populations and indigenous populations emerges, due to the recognized need to share territory and life resources, and this process is reflected in language use, the symbolic use of forms of English.

The first similarity is trivial: English was transported to new locations, introduced into regions where other indigenous languages had been spoken, by English-speaking traders, missionaries and settlers. World Englishes have been shaped by the contact between English-speaking migrants and local, resident populations who, initially in any event, had no choice in the matter.

Importantly, though perhaps not quite as naturally, the burden of linguistic adjustment typically fell upon the indigenous populations. Why shouldn't the English immigrants have worked towards acquiring the established local languages? Some actually did, especially missionaries. Much more commonly, however, sooner or later we find a growing number of the indigenous population working towards acquiring English, and we find the gradual growth of bilingualism amongst them. The reason is simple, if unsettling: the unequal distribution of power and wealth in colonial settings. The representatives of the British Empire were the carriers of political power, explicitly or implicitly, and dealing and trading with the Europeans meant new opportunities, so from the early days of colonial history, a knowledge of English promised a share in these attractions for indigenous people.

Consequently, contact forms of English can be observed emerging. Indigenous speakers of English transfer their own pronunciation habits, lexical expressions and also patterns of sentence composition from their respective native languages into their way of speaking

English. When this happens with many indigenous speakers increasingly using English for communicating amongst themselves, and when English is taught by local teachers who themselves have adopted it through such processes, then the shape of the language as spoken in a given location is gradually appropriated and transformed. English undergoes a process of nativization. The outcome of this is a distinctly local, new dialect of English, with sound patterns, word choices and syntactic habits which are characteristic of speakers from that locale, not necessarily transparent to an outsider. A 'New English' has been born.

Another shared feature to be found in the majority of countries in which such indigenous varieties have developed is the occurrence of what has come to be known as the 'complaint tradition' (Milroy and Milroy 1985), where educated, typically high-status speakers, deplore the quality of local linguistic performance and linguistic usage, and perceive the local English as becoming increasingly deficient. Typically this is done in public, as in the 'Letters to the Editor' sections of quality papers. Teaching authorities and gatekeepers typically defend old norms. For example, British norms of pronunciation or usage are upheld as the only correct ones, and are imposed upon the educational system, even if this turns out to be unrealistic as a goal. If we take Nigeria or Hong Kong as examples, British English norms and an RP-like pronunciation are linguistic targets in the school system, even though the vast majority of not only students but also most educated speakers do not speak this model. At the same time, you typically also find linguists and others who suggest that the educated local variety of English should be accepted as correct and as a model for others. Thus, discussions about what are appropriate norms are widespread in many countries which are at a certain developmental stage, as we can see in Africa and Asia at present.

Typically, such a public struggle for what is and what is not correct in matters linguistic is followed by an increasing tendency towards the acceptance of a new, local variety of English as appropriate even in formal contexts. It is adopted by some first, then spreads gradually in a society until even policy-makers accept it. It seems that, at present, many societies where 'New Englishes' in the narrow sense are spoken are not yet quite ready for this step of an endonormative orientation, while postcolonial inner circle countries have passed through it. For Australians and New Zealanders the local variety is nowadays accepted, even required in certain public domains and in the media, while this is clearly not yet the case in, say, Cameroon or Hong Kong. In Singapore, one can hear educated speakers saying that they are proud of their accents and that they can recognize other Singaporeans by the way they speak in international contexts, but this definitely does not reflect the government's official position.

Accepting a new variety as adequate in formal situations and as a norm in education naturally requires the codification of the variety. Typically, this happens first in the form of dictionaries and then grammars. An important example is the *Macquarie Dictionary* in Australia, which recorded and established a newly respected local variety of English, at least at the lexical level. In Singapore and Malaysia, the *Times-Chambers International Dictionary* of 1997 was the first to include a wide range of indigenous words alongside its core vocabulary. In other countries, preliminary word collections have been published, and similar dictionary projects (some spearheaded by Macquarie Press) are in preparation.

Of course, a variety that is being codified and is on the point of being accepted locally cannot be too diverse. For it to be a national icon, only limited internal variation is permissible. In the process of nation-building, which frequently emphasizes the unity of a nation which has grown out of multicultural roots, there is an emphasis on homogeneity in public discourse. Perhaps this is more a matter of perception than real. Differences between social and ethnic groups do not fade away and usually persist, but they tend to be down-played, at least at the beginning where slogans such as 'unity in diversity' are common.

Another sign of the newly established self-confidence that comes with new nationhood and the cultural acceptance of indigenous language forms and cultural habits is the appearance of literary productivity in a New English variety. In many countries of Africa and Asia, indigenous writers have produced highly influential and acclaimed artistic products which employ and reflect local language habits and thus testify to the cultural appropriation of English in these contexts. Chinua Achebe, Wole Soyinka, Amy Tan and Salman Rushdie are internationally recognized examples.

It is noteworthy that this pull towards English in the postcolonial period has occurred even in the absence of a substantial number of English 'native speakers'. It is not individual speakers who are modelled, it is the language and the promises of personal growth, improvement and prosperity that come with it that give it its impetus. That also means that English in many of these countries spreads via indigenous models, rather than through the adoption of so-called 'native-speaker' models. English speakers in Asia primarily use the language to communicate with other Asians, so they use a form which is successful in such contexts, intelligible to other Asians. They do not need automatically to strive for, say, British models.

Finally, a shared trait that can be observed in many postcolonial Englishes after the stage of endonormative stabilization, described above, is the emergence of increasing internal differentiation. Regional, social and ethnic differences are again allowed to develop, backed by the shared process of successful nation-building and the creation of a national variety. This results from the fact that, after a period of emphasis on the development of national unity, the members of a young nation re-focus on their individual group alignments. This is what we find in Australia and New Zealand now, where, for example, the emergence of new regional speech differences is reported.

While the similarities are striking, given the global range of contexts under discussion, it would be unwise to downplay the differences between countries, languages and contexts where English has been and is being appropriated. Here are some points worth noting.

Demography, the purely numerical relationship between settlers and indigenous people, clearly plays a central role: the more English speakers there are, the stronger their power base (and, hence, the importance of English) is likely to be, and the more readily exposure to English is available. This facilitates the acquisition of English and decreases the likelihood of strong contact effects. Obviously, when English immigrants constitute the majority of the population, as was the case in settler colonies such as Australia or New Zealand, the situation is quite different from one where only a handful of missionaries were around, as in the early phase of the English outreach to Tanzania.

However, communicative patterns and language diffusion are not only shaped by purely numerical relations. Another important aspect is the social relationship between English-speaking newcomers and local people, and here, again, quite a wide range of different patterns occurred. Clearly, this has to do with the amount of respect paid to indigenous cultures, and correspondingly with the form of dominance or involvement practised. Traders were interested in exchanging commodities, a process which required communication on a restricted range of topics and between partners of roughly equal standing. Missionaries tended to live together fairly closely with indigenous populations, and thus provided linguistic models. Settlers usually built their own communities, largely separate from indigenous populations, and the relations between them soon tended to be marked more by competition than collaboration – which implied distancing, seclusion and even outright hostility. Political dominance of a region by the Empire, supported by military presence or occupation, created a mixture of alignments ranging from close collaboration with those natives who served the occupants' interests and purposes, to more distanced attitudes with many others, who had less immediate contact with the rulers and felt subjugated. In British colonial history this specifically took the form of Lord Lugard's principle of 'indirect rule', which implied that, to a certain extent, indigenous power structures were recognized, but exploited by the British: a stratum of local leaders were educated in British institutions with the intention of making them friendly to British interests. These people were 'sandwiched' between the Europeans and the local masses, who would thus be ruled by their traditional leaders, but these leaders, to some extent, served the interests of the foreign occupants. All these differences were reflected in the relative amount of language contact and language acquisition.

Both the numerical and the social relationship between the parties involved in a colonization process were determined by the primary motivation for expanding to some other territory. Accordingly, a number of different colonization types have been distinguished, notably by Mufwene (2001), who distinguished between 'trade', 'exploitation' and 'settlement' colonies. Yet, even within these types of colony, a range of different social structures exists, causing different contact situations and linguistic outcomes.

Consequently, the social and political setting to some extent also determined the form(s) of English introduced, varying from standard to non-standard. A classic example of a formal institution would be the Malay College Kuala Kangsar (MCKK). This was set up in Malaysia as an elitist institution which transmitted standard forms of English, thus sowing the seeds of the prescriptive attitudes to be found to the present day in neighbouring Singapore's 'Speak Good English Movement'. Conversely, lower-class people like rural settlers, prisoners or soldiers introduced vernacular forms of English to settler colonies such as New Zealand and Australia, but also to the exploitation colonies of Africa and Asia.

Certainly the time frame and historical setting of contact with and the re-rooting of English plays a major role. In America and the Caribbean the history of English goes back almost four centuries. Even in India, English has been present for three centuries. Australia and South Africa have been shaped by a little more than two hundred years of English, while Singapore, Hong Kong and New Zealand have had a little less than that. Kenya experienced large-scale English settlement only about a hundred years ago. However, interestingly enough, in many contexts the evolution and indigenous appropriation of English has become more vibrant after independence.

An interesting and important sideline of the demographic aspect mentioned above is the question of how many people of British descent remained in a country after independence (typically around the 1960s). When in countries such as Singapore, Nigeria or Hong Kong the British pulled out, many of the English-speaking resident population returned home, thus making access to genuinely British speech models more scarce and modifying the conditions for the further use and spread of English. One major difference resulting from this situation is the fact that language-teaching duties and the role as linguistic models fell more strongly upon local speakers of English.

Linguistic processes and features

In this section we look more closely at linguistic processes and features. That there are linguistic differences between varieties is fairly obvious. It comes as no surprise that, for example, Indian speakers of English sound different from Nigerians, or that different loan words can be found in English texts from Pakistan and Botswana, and so on. There are also differences of a purely syntactic nature – for example, Singaporean Colloquial English features a relative pronoun use of *one* (e.g. *That boy pinch my sister one very naughty*) or a passive with *kena* (*The thief kena caught by the police*) both of which are unique and distinctive to that variety. Most New Englishes feature similar examples which can normally be accounted for by some kind of contact effect and local language transfer. More interestingly, and perhaps surprisingly, many similarities have also emerged from all these contact processes, despite all the differences in input languages and varieties, and in their respective historical and social settings.

The processes and the broader typological effects to be observed in such situations of language contact include the following:

Koinéization

Both in the dialect contact between speakers of different regional and social dialects of British English and in the evolution of new lingua franca forms for interethnic use, there is a tendency for an intermediate, 'middle-of-the-road' variety of English to emerge, i.e. a form which encompasses many forms and patterns which are widely shared and from which strongly dialectal forms disappear.

Emergent bilingualism

When two groups who speak different languages are in continuous contact with each other it will be necessary for them to communicate with each other, and so some speakers will gradually acquire (elements of) the other group's language. While this may go both ways, typically the lower-status group adjusts to the politically dominant one, so in most of the cases under discussion here, the consequence is that first some, and then more and more, speakers of indigenous languages acquire English. In extreme cases, this process may lead to complete language shift.

Substrate transfer

Both on an individual and on a communal basis the growth of bilingualism implies processes of second language acquisition. Characteristically, in such situations second language usage is marked by the transfer of some first-language phenomena on all linguistic levels (sounds, words, structures, pragmatic habits), either because these are persistent and deeply rooted in one's language behaviour (like motoric articulatory movements in sound production), or because they are employed to fill gaps in one's expressive potential in the target language. These gaps can be caused by the target language, English, having no words for indigenous concepts, a situation which frequently results in the lexical transfer of indigenous cultural terms into English.

Sequence of contact effects

The sequence of such transfer phenomena appearing in a new variety of English is not haphazard; quite to the contrary, there are strong similarities across regions and varieties. Characteristically, the earliest traces of English being influenced by indigenous languages are to be found in the lexicon: words travel easily. And here it is also typical

377

to have certain semantically defined groups of words appearing in a regular sequence: The oldest loans which English adopts from indigenous contexts are typically place-names, soon to be followed by designations and plants and animals, and then by words labelling local customs and cultural objects and relations in general. Phonological transfer tends to be next; grammatical influences come last, and most reluctantly.

Contact effects in line with cline of contact intensity

Thomason and Kaufman (1988) were the first to point out that there is a characteristic sequence of such transfer effects which correlates strongly with the intensity of social contact between two groups. Light and superficial contact results in lexical borrowing. More intensive mutual involvement produces morphological transfer (e.g. appending the inflectional morphemes of one language to words of another) and structural transfer. An example of this is the combination of English words by employing syntactic rules internalized from one's knowledge of indigenous language. This is illustrated in the sub-jectless clause patterns of Singapore English as in *Can or not?*, which employ the Chinese syntactic option of omitting a subject noun phrase. In the case of extremely strong dominance or intertwining of two social groups, creolization or language alternation may result (cf. Thomason 2001; McLellan, this volume).

Structural nativization

All of these processes together result in the evolution of a 'New English', the gradual growth of a new dialect of English which has been 'nativized' or 'indigenized'. This means it is marked by a distinctive set of lexical, phonological and grammatical properties which can be theoretically accounted for by looking into the history and development of the variety of English concerned and the effect of contact processes.

Adoption of indigenous forms

It was stated above that these innovative forms appear originally through acquisition processes, and thus in the speech of indigenous users of English. However, in the course of time they also spread to the resident population of British descent, in parti-cular to lower-class immigrants, who tend to have more intimate contacts with the indigenous population. Again, this applies more immediately and widely to lexis than to grammar. Indigenous words are used in English texts by just about everyone, and also in formal contexts. Grammatical patterns used by members of an indigenous ethnic group are adopted much more reluctantly by British immigrants or their descendants, but it also happens: we have reports of white overseers and plantation owners' wives in the Caribbean speaking forms of local creoles, and of so-called 'white babus' in India who sound like Indians speaking English.

Appropriation of innovative linguistic forms for social purposes

In the course of time, these innovative linguistic features (words and sound patterns more so than grammatical details) tend to be accommodated for social purposes. Using them becomes a symbolic expression of some attitude or group membership. Like in many other societies, in Malaysia, using distinctively local mesolectal forms of English signals a desire for social solidarity. In general, 'New Englishes' are deliberate expressions of local identities, and symbols expressing a strong sense of identification and belonging.

All of this tends to result in structural outcomes which are surprisingly similar at times. For more details, the reader is referred to the *Varieties of English* handbook volumes (Kortmann *et al*. 2004, see 'Suggestions for further reading') and to Deterding (this volume) and Kortmann (this volume).

Explanations and models

Various frameworks have been proposed to account for these similarities and differences, and to categorize World Englishes into groups of related varieties. Below, I distinguish between models which are static ('Categorial models') and those which recognize internal evolutionary trends ('Cyclic models').

Categorial models

Kachru's three circles

Braj Kachru, one of the main founding fathers of the field of World Englishes as a scholarly discipline, is probably best known for his conceptualization of these varieties as belonging to one of three circles, the 'inner', 'outer' and 'expanding' circles (typically represented graphically as concentric circles or overlapping ovals). Inner circle countries, such as the UK, the USA, Canada or Australia, are those where English is spoken natively by the vast majority of the population. In outer circle countries such as Ghana, Zambia, Pakistan, Sri Lanka or the Philippines, English fulfils important internal roles (typically as the language of administration and education, often explicitly as an 'official' language); usually these cases are the product of an earlier colonial phase. The expanding circle comprises countries without such a colonial history, but in which English is used and is now spreading as a foreign language. Egypt, Indonesia, Thailand, Korea, China, Japan and Saudi Arabia are examples. While this categorization is clearly useful and has been highly influential, it essentially builds upon a metaphor and is thus inherently fuzzy. Some multilingual countries in which English is spoken widely, but not predominantly, as a native language, such as South Africa and Canada, fail to fall clearly into any of the categories. It also seems that some twenty-plus years after its inception the model has become somewhat dated in that it ignores the strong proportion of first-language English speakers in countries such as Singapore, Malaysia, the Philippines and others. Such difficulties notwithstanding, however, the impact of Kachru's model primarily stems from his emphasis on the important and essentially independent status of the outer circle, a position that implies that inner circle countries have no longer any privilege as to the 'ownership' of English. In terms of international communication and visibility, outer circle countries thus have a right to establish norms of their own. This position was voiced most articulately in Kachru (1992), and has influenced many scholars from such countries.

ENL–ESL–EFL

This framework, described, for instance, in McArthur (1998: 42), is actually a little older than Kachru's, and in its terminology it is a little more descriptive: the language situations portrayed by Kachru as 'circles' are simply labelled 'English as a Native Language (ENL)', 'English as a Second Language (ESL)' and 'English as a Foreign Language (EFL)' countries. Apart from the political implications of Kachru's proposal the two schemes are quite similar; the limitations noted above apply here in much the same fashion. However, this scheme implies a hierarchy, because in a sense ESL and EFL are judged against the ENL model, while Kachru's line of thinking emphasizes the plurality of Englishes without attributing a superior status to any of these classes.

Cyclic models

Moag, Llamzon, Schmied

Some cyclic models have also been proposed. These regard emerging new varieties as going through characteristic developmental processes. Among earlier proposals along these lines, those by Moag, Llamzon and Schmied focused on specific countries or regions rather than similarities or differences between countries. All of them are suggestive more than descriptive, and not worked out in great detail.

Moag (1992; originally published in 1982) suggested that Fiji English has gone through four different phases, which he called (with the labels being largely self-explanatory) 'transportation', 'indigenization', 'expansion in use and function' and 'institutionalization'. As a possible fifth phase he expects a 'restriction of use and function', thus giving expression to the view that in the long run English will lose ground and fall back to foreign language status. However, he believes another developmental track is also possible, with 'English inexorably becoming a native language in some societies' (Moag 1992: 247).

Llamzon (1986), adapting this line of thinking to the Philippines, perceived a decline in English there and thus focused upon the 'restriction phase'. It remains to be seen, however, whether he didn't give undue weight to the disappearance of native-speaker models and, as I suspect, underestimated the dynamic effect of indigenous uses of English.

Schmied (1991) applied Moag's idea to the growth of English in Africa. He suggests that after the first three stages (which he calls 'contact', 'institutionalization' and 'expansion') two alternative paths of further development are possible. In some countries, such as in Nigeria, 'recognition' leads to 'adoption', while in others, most notably in Tanzania, 'repression' of English results in 'deinstitutionalization' (194–7). In a similar vein, Chumbow and Simo Bobda (1996) explicitly adopted a lifecycle perspective and viewed the history of English in Cameroon as a sequence of three stages up to 'expansion', which was strongest in the mid twentieth century but is still going on; they believe that the future of English in the country will depend upon the government's decision, pending at the time of writing, on whether to adopt or to repress it (1996: 410).

Schneider's 'Dynamic Model'

Inspired by these developmental frameworks, Schneider (2003, 2007) developed a 'Dynamic Model', which claims to identify an underlying, fundamentally uniform evolutionary process that has been effective in all instances of the postcolonial diffusion of English. Since its publication this model has been applied by other scholars and to other contexts.

The model builds on similarities in the social dynamics between the two parties involved in a colonization process, and ultimately upon theories of sociolinguistic accommodation and identity symbolization. In colonization, settlers move into a territory inhabited by people with different cultural roots and a different linguistic background. In the beginning, both groups perceive each other as distinct from each other. In the long run, these boundaries get increasingly blurred. Typically, after having shared the land for many decades or even centuries, both groups recognize that this need to co-exist will continue for good, and they move more closely towards each other, both socially and linguistically. Frequently this happens after political independence from the erstwhile mother country (in our case mostly Great Britain), and it also typically involves a stage of nation-building intended to diminish ethnic boundaries and to develop a pan-ethnic feeling of nationhood. The model assumes that the political history of a country is reflected in the identity re-writings of the groups involved in these processes, which, in turn, determine the sociolinguistic conditions of language contact, linguistic usage and language attitudes; and these affect the linguistic developments and structural changes in the varieties concerned.

Schneider posits that evolving World Englishes typically proceed through five characteristic stages, with the aforementioned political, sociolinguistic and structural patterns observable in each:

- During the 'foundation' phase, English is brought to a new territory, which leads to incipient bilingualism, the borrowing of toponyms, and other minor processes.
- 'Exonormative stabilization': during a stable colonial situation, the politically dominant 'mother country' determines the norms of linguistic behaviour, and elite bilingualism spreads amongst some representatives of the indigenous population, with lexical borrowing continuing.
- 'Nativization' is the most vibrant and interesting of all the phases. With ties with the settlers' country of origin weakening, and interethnic contacts increasing, bilingual speakers forge a new variety of English, shaped strongly by phonological and structural transfer – though conservative speakers resent such innovative usage.
- 'Endonormative stabilization' implies that, after independence and inspired by a process of nation-building, a new linguistic norm is increasingly observed to exist (as remarkably homogeneous in many cases). The new norm is beginning to be codified and to be accepted in society, and is employed culturally in literary representations.
- 'Differentiation' may conclude the process. In a stable young nation, internal social group identities become more important and get reflected in increasing dialectal differences.

Certainly this is a very rough sketch (for more details see Schneider 2003, 2007); and certainly, like any model, this one abstracts strongly from complex realities (so that in many real contexts subsequent phases overlap and not all constituent phenomena can be observed), but the basic pattern seems well established and is based upon observations drawn from a wide range of different countries.

Discussion: further issues

Let us now consider some additional issues which are relevant in this context and in the evaluation of these models.

Of 'native speakers' and 'first languages' – or for what it's worth

One of the most interesting aspects of the 'Dynamic Model' is its claim of validity for both postcolonial ENL countries and ESL nations. Is it really possible and realistic to treat first-language and second-language English-speaking countries jointly, under one and the same framework? Conversely, is there still sufficient reason to insist on the difference between 'native' and 'second' language usage as a primary criterion; isn't the difference between first and second languages (and first and second language English countries, in some contexts) getting increasingly blurred? The concept of native speakers, typically applied to English speakers from Great Britain or the US, has been consistently challenged over the last few decades on several fronts. Aren't children who grow up speaking English as their first language in, say, Singapore or Lagos, also 'native speakers' of English? So surely their language competence and usage can be provided with the same degree of authority. In highly multilingual contexts even notions such as 'native' or 'first' language seem difficult to pin down accurately, given that many children grow up speaking several languages from early childhood, each restricted to different context situations or interlocutors. In many such countries, some speakers tend to switch to using English almost exclusively in their professional and even private lives at a certain age, so that English becomes their 'primary' or 'first' language, even if it may not have been the first one acquired. The notion of 'native speaker' stems from nineteenth-century British nationalism, and it still tends to be highly politicized: in Singapore the Asian national languages are 'ethnic mother tongues' by definition, irrespective of usage realities (so, for instance, differences between Chinese dialects spoken by parent generations and Putonghua are disregarded; and Eurasians, who speak English 'natively', are denied an official mother tongue because by definition English must not occupy that culturally loaded role). In Cameroon, I have come across cases where children are instructed to view their grandparents' ancestral African languages as their own 'mother tongues' even if they do not speak them at all. So – the 'native speaker' concept does not seem helpful and sufficient to adequately describe complex realities.

Are the categorical models, which were certainly most useful and influential in the 1980s, still adequate, given the rapidly changing contexts of the use of English in recent decades in many countries? We can conclude that distinctions such as the one between the inner circle and the outer circle were perfectly appropriate for the twentieth century, but may no longer be so for the twenty-first, in the face of radically changing situations.

Adstrates and global patterns of ethnic diffusion

A few more complicating factors need to be considered when looking at present-day similarities and differences between World Englishes and their causes, only a few of which can be addressed here. An interesting phenomenon which has contributed both to the complexity of language situations in individual countries and to similarities between otherwise unrelated locales are 'adstrate' communities – groups of immigrants other than (and usually coming later than) the British-descendant settlers. Throughout history, there have been certain strands of migrants who originate from the same source or region and who then move to many different countries. For example, the Chinese now live all over Asia, and South East Asia in particular, so one interesting question is whether any features of an ethnically marked Chinese influence can be observed in the

Englishes of various regions. Indians are perhaps the most interesting and obvious case in point. During the nineteenth and early twentieth centuries, Indian labourers migrated to various countries where there was a need for cheap manual labour, and so we find strong Indian population groups in countries as diverse as in South Africa, Trinidad, Guyana or Fiji. Again, there are both similarities between these global 'Indian Englishes' on account of their 'Indian-ness' and differences between them caused by local adjustments and linguistic adoptions. Similarities or differences caused by these migratory processes are worthwhile topics for future research.

Conclusion

In conclusion, the outcome of the task of establishing similarities and differences between World Englishes in terms of their evolutionary patterns and properties needs to be critically assessed. Essentially, this is a categorization process, an attempt at pattern recognition or of finding order in what appears to be chaos. As such it represents a fundamental trait of human beings: seeking patterns to help us cope with complex realities. Insights gained from such a comparative approach can be useful, for example by transferring successful strategies (say, in language teaching or of language policy) from one context to another. But we should also recognize the inherent limitations of such a comparison. For one thing, categorization means establishing prototypes; boundaries between such categories typically are fuzzy and overlapping, rather than sharp and clearly delimited. They are based upon the observation of properties which themselves are always changing, so we are talking about network-like family resemblances here, rather than about a mosaic structure. Second, the results of such an undertaking always depend on one's purpose, for instance with respect to the level of specificity aimed at. We can be looking at the forest, establishing broad, non-specific categories, or at the trees, introducing finely graded distinctions and thus positing many and precisely defined categories, but thereby weakening the comparative perspective.

Finally, in the realm of World Englishes, the recognition of similarities or differences also depends on the stylistic level that is being focused on. The notion of a 'glocal' (both global and local) development, of there being both centrifugal and centripetal forces in the evolution of Englishes, is helpful here, but these two sides of the coin are not equally represented in all contexts. In writing and in transnational or global usage contexts, more similarities are likely to be found. On the other hand, differences from one variety to another will probably surface more strongly in speech and in local contexts, emphasizing friendliness, proximity and identity through the use of local idioms, including indigenized varieties of English.

Suggestions for further reading

Kachru, B., Kachru, Y. and Nelson, C. (eds) (2006) *The Handbook of World Englishes*, Malden, MA: Blackwell. (A voluminous collection of articles which together provide a systematic survey of the major issues in the field.)

Kirkpatrick, Andy (2007) *World Englishes: Implications for International Communication and English Language Teaching*, Cambridge: Cambridge University Press. (A very accessible survey of the topic, strongly considering the applied perspective and consequences for language teaching.)

Kortmann, Bernd and Upton, Clive (eds) (2008) *Varieties of English 1: The British Isles*, New York: Mouton de Gruyter.

Schneider, Edgar W. (ed.) (2008) *Varieties of English 2: The Americas and the Caribbean*, New York: Mouton de Gruyter.

Burridge, Kate and Kortmann, Bernd (eds) (2008) *Varieties of English 3: The Pacific and Australasia*, New York: Mouton de Gruyter.

Mesthrie, Rajend (ed.) (2008) *Varieties of English 4: Africa, South and Southeast Asia*, New York: Mouton de Gruyter.

(These four accessibly priced paperback volumes, each one on a major world region, consist of a large number of articles which in some detail describe the historical origins and the phonological and morphosyntactic characteristics of almost all the major World Englishes.)

Mesthrie, R. and Bhatt, R. (2008) *World Englishes*, Cambridge: Cambridge University Press. (A recent introduction to the field which emphasizes structural properties of World Englishes.)

Schneider, E.W. (2007) *Postcolonial English. Varieties Around the World*, Cambridge: Cambridge University Press. (A systematic discussion of the 'Dynamic Model' outlined above, with a chapter on the linguistic processes involved and a historical survey of the evolution of English in 17 countries around the globe.)

References

Chumbow, B.S. and Simo Bobda, A. (1996) 'The life cycle of post-imperial English in Cameroon', in J.A. Fishman, A.W. Conrad and A. Rubal-Lopez (eds) *Post-Imperial English: Status Change in Former British and American Colonies 1940–1990*, Berlin: Mouton de Gruyter, pp. 401–29.

Kachru, B.B. (ed.) (1992) *The Other Tongue: English Across Cultures*, Chicago: University of Illinois Press.

Llamzon, T.A. (1986) 'Life cycle of New Englishes: restriction phase of Filipino English', *English World-Wide*, 7: 101–25.

McArthur, T. (1998) *The English Languages*, Cambridge: Cambridge University Press.

Milroy, J. and Milroy, L. (1985) *Authority in Language*, London: Routledge.

Moag, R.F. (1992) 'The life cycle of non-native Englishes: a case study', in B.B. Kachru (ed.) *The Other Tongue: English Across Cultures*, Chicago: University of Illinois Press, pp. 233–52.

Mufwene, S.S. (2001) *The Ecology of Language Evolution*, Cambridge: Cambridge University Press.

Platt, J., Weber, H. and Ho, M.L. (1984) *The New Englishes*, London: Routledge and Kegan Paul.

Schmied, J.J. (1991) *English in Africa: An Introduction*, London: Longman.

Schneider, E.W. (2003) 'The dynamics of New Englishes: from identity construction to dialect birth', *Language*, 79: 233–81.

——(2007) *Postcolonial English. Varieties Around the World*, Cambridge: Cambridge University Press.

Thomason, S.G. (2001) *Language Contact: An Introduction*, Washington, DC: Georgetown University Press.

Thomason, S.G. and Kaufman, T. (1988) *Language Contact, Creolization and Genetic Linguistics*, Berkeley: University of California Press.

22

Variation across Englishes

Phonology

David Deterding

Introduction

The spread of English around the world can be described in terms of four 'diaspora' (Kachru *et al.* 2006): the first was to Scotland, Wales and Ireland; the second was to the USA, Canada, Australia, New Zealand and South Africa; the third was during the colonial era to places such as India, Singapore, Nigeria and the Caribbean; and the most recent has been to the rest of the world, such as Brazil, Japan, China and throughout continental Europe.

The pronunciation that is found in each of the places in the second diaspora can to a certain extent be predicted on the basis of two factors: when the settlers left Britain; and where they came from. Therefore, for example, most speakers in the USA have a rhotic accent (so [r] is pronounced wherever 'r' occurs in the spelling, including in words such as *four* and *cart*) because the original settlers left England at a time when rhoticity was the norm throughout most of the country, and furthermore, many of the early immigrants came from the west of England, Scotland and Ireland, which by and large have rhotic accents. In contrast, migration to Australia and New Zealand took place later, mostly in the nineteenth century, by which time the standard pronunciation in England was non-rhotic (Mugglestone 2003: 87), and furthermore the bulk of the settlers were from the south-east of England, especially London, where rhoticity is not generally found.

We may note that the indigenous languages in the countries of the second diaspora had little impact on the pronunciation of English that evolved in these places, and the most salient permanent influences from the original local languages were on place-names and also terms used for fauna and flora (Schneider 2007). The only exceptions in this respect are the English of South Africa, which shows substantial influences both from the Afrikaans spoken by the settlers of Dutch descent and also from the indigenous African languages such as Xhosa and Zulu, and New Zealand English, which is, to a certain extent, influenced by Maori (Bauer and Warren 2004: 581).

In contrast, for varieties of English from the third diaspora, in places that mostly shook off their colonial status during the second half of the twentieth century, there generally are quite substantial influences from the indigenous languages spoken in each place. As a result, there are huge differences between the Englishes of these countries, varieties that are often described as belonging to the outer circle (Kachru 2005: 14). Nevertheless, despite such large differences between them, some patterns seem to recur in the various outer circle Englishes. For example: the dental fricatives [θ, ð] are often missing, which is hardly surprising given that they are fairly rare sounds in the languages of the world and also because many speakers find them hard to produce; and it is furthermore common to find full vowels in function words such as *that* and *of* and in the first syllable of words such as *concern*.

This chapter will discuss in some detail the pronunciation of three outer circle Englishes, those of Singapore, India and Nigeria, and the analysis will consider the features that make each of these varieties unique as well as those that are shared between them. It will then look at the extent to which the shared features are also found in other outer circle Englishes, and finally it will consider implications for intelligibility.

Data

The primary data described here involve recordings of three male university lecturers in various disciplines (but not English Language or Linguistics) at the University of Brunei Darussalam. All three have excellent competence in English, as English is the medium of instruction in the subjects they teach. Brief biographical details of each speaker will be given when his recording is discussed.

Of course, the data of just three speakers is quite insufficient to allow us to draw wide-ranging conclusions about speech patterns, especially as there is substantial variation in each of the countries discussed. However, the data analysed here is merely intended to provide an illustration of some of the features that have previously been reported for speakers from Singapore, India and Nigeria, and thereby to allow us to consider shared characteristics which may be found in these varieties and which might serve to set them apart from inner circle varieties of English.

The recordings involved a reading of the Wolf passage, a text that has been specially designed to facilitate the description of all the consonants and vowels of English (Deterding 2006a). The Wolf passage is as follows:

The Boy who Cried Wolf
There was once a poor shepherd boy who used to watch his flocks in the fields next to a dark forest near the foot of a mountain. One hot afternoon, he thought up a good plan to get some company for himself and also have a little fun. Raising his fist in the air, he ran down to the village shouting 'Wolf, Wolf.' As soon as they heard him, the villagers all rushed from their homes, full of concern for his safety, and two of his cousins even stayed with him for a short while. This gave the boy so much pleasure that a few days later he tried exactly the same trick again, and once more he was successful. However, not long after, a wolf that had just escaped from the zoo was looking for a change from its usual diet of chicken and duck. So, overcoming its fear of being shot, it actually did come out from the forest and began to threaten the sheep. Racing down to the village, the boy of course cried out even louder than before. Unfortunately, as all the villagers were convinced that he was trying to fool them a third time, they told him, 'Go away and don't bother us again.' And so the wolf had a feast.

The intention of the analysis offered here is to focus on outer circle varieties of English, without always making comparison with inner circle varieties such as those of Britain or the United States. However, some of the acoustic measurements that are made are inherently comparative, including that for diphthongal change in vowel quality and also the index used as an indication of rhythm, and this means that we need something to compare with. Here, when necessary, comparison will be made with the reading of the Wolf passage by the three male speakers of RP British English whose monophthong vowels are described in Deterding (2006a). At the time when they were recorded, they were aged 47, 48 and 57, and all were university lecturers at the National Institute of Education in Singapore. Here they will be referred to as B1, B2 and B3.

Analysis

The pronunciation of each of the three outer circle speakers will be described in a separate section. In each case, the analysis will include a plot of the monophthongs based on measurements made using Praat software (Boersma and Weenink 2007). In these figures, the first two formants are plotted on inverted scales so that the front vowels are shown on the left and the open vowels are at the bottom, as is standard practice in the acoustic description of vowels (Ladefoged 2006: 188). For these plots, an auditory Bark scale is used (rather than a physical Hertz scale), so that the spacing approximates how humans hear sounds (Hayward 2000: 141). The measurements were made adopting the methodology discussed in Deterding (2006a), using the tokens listed in Table 22.1. The phoneme categories are shown using the keywords suggested by Wells (1982: xviii). As all three speakers have non-rhotic accents with RP British English as the superstrate, it is assumed that THOUGHT is merged with FORCE and NORTH, PALM is merged with START and BATH, and LOT is merged with CLOTH; so in each case, only one of these keywords will be used.

In some cases, one or more tokens cannot be used. For example, the Singapore speaker has FACE rather than DRESS in *next*, so this token cannot be included in the measurements for DRESS; and the Nigerian has LOT in the first syllable of *cousins* and *company*, so these tokens cannot be included in the data for STRUT. Although judgements like this introduce an unfortunate element of subjectivity, as decisions must be

Table 22.1 Tokens used in the measurement of the monophthongs

Vowel	Tokens
FLEECE	sheep, even, feast
KIT	lit(tle), fist, this, chic(ken), did, (con)vinced
DRESS	shep(herd), next, get, pleas(ure), (suc)cess(ful)
TRAP	plan, (ex)act(ly), ac(tually), (be)gan, had
STRUT	up, com(pany), fun, cous(ins), much, duck, come
PALM	dark, af(ternoon), af(ter)
LOT	flocks, hot, not, shot, bo(ther)
THOUGHT	thought, short, more, course, (be)fore, (un)for(tunately)
FOOT	foot, good, look(ing)
GOOSE	(after)noon, soon, two, zoo
NURSE	heard, (con)cern, third

made about what can and cannot be included, such choices are inevitable. For example, for speakers whose pronunciation is influenced by an American accent, a decision would have to be made whether to include the first syllables of *after* and *afternoon* (from the BATH lexical set) with TRAP or with PALM.

Singapore English

The speaker from Singapore is 49 years old and he is ethnically Chinese. He listed his first languages as 'Peranakan Patois' (a colloquial form of Malay) and Hokkien, both of which he still speaks fairly well. However, with his wife, his children, his colleagues and all his friends, he speaks English, a language he started learning at the age of six, so although English is not his first language, it is now almost certainly his best language.

Measurements of his monophthong vowels (with the exception of FACE and GOAT) are shown in Figure 22.1. From this, we can see that FLEECE and KIT are almost merged, with the result that, in the reading of the passage, *feast* and *fist* are homophones. Similarly, THOUGHT and LOT are close together, so there is no distinction between *short* and *shot*; and GOOSE and FOOT are also in a similar position, so *fool* and *full* sound the same. In addition, TRAP and DRESS are merged, so *band* and *bend* would probably be homophones (though the Wolf passage does not have a minimal pair for these two vowels). These measurements all confirm the measurements reported in Deterding (2003) and also overviews of Singapore English such as Bao (1998) and Wee (2004).

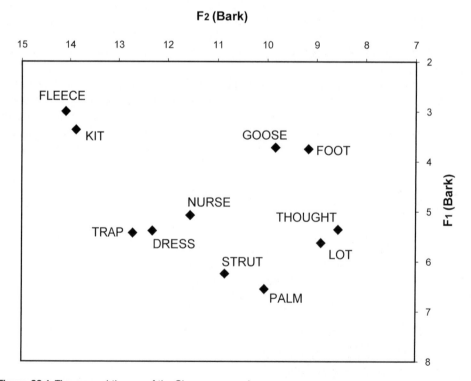

Figure 22.1 The monophthongs of the Singapore speaker.

In addition, we find the following features in the pronunciation of this Singaporean speaker:

- [t] occurs at the start of *thought*, *threaten* and *third*;
- [d] occurs at the start of *there* and *this*;
- the consonant in the middle of *racing* is voiced, so this word is a homophone with *raising*;
- there is very little aspiration for the [t] in *two* and *time* (so they sound rather like *do* and *dime*);
- the final [t] in *fist* and *feast* is omitted;
- both FACE and GOAT are monophthongal;
- the vowel in *next* is FACE (instead of DRESS);
- the vowel in the second syllable of *began* is FACE (instead of TRAP);
- a full vowel (instead of [ə]) occurs in the first syllable of *concern* and *convinced*;
- there are no weak forms for the function words *as*, *of*, *for*, *that* and the auxiliary *had*, so each of these has a full vowel (instead of [ə]);
- there is syllable-based rhythm;
- the pronoun *he* is stressed in 'were convinced that he was trying to fool them again'.

The use of [t] and [d] for voiced and voiceless TH respectively has been widely reported for Singapore English (Moorthy and Deterding 2000). Neutralization of the voicing of fricatives at the end of a morpheme is common (Deterding 2005), so *raising* and *racing* as homophones is not unexpected. Lack of aspiration for initial plosives is not found with the majority of speakers in Singapore, but it does sometimes occur (Deterding 2007a: 20). Simplification of word-final consonant clusters is extremely frequent in Singapore English (Gut 2005).

Monophthongal FACE and GOAT in Singapore is widely reported, and it has been confirmed by measurements of the movement of the formants (to be discussed further below) (Deterding, 2000; Lee and Lim 2000).

The occurrence of the FACE vowel in *next* confirms a similar observation in Deterding (2007b), where it was shown that two ethnically Chinese Singaporean undergraduates did not have the same vowel in *next* and *text*. Similarly, Deterding (2007b) showed that about half of his Singaporean subjects have a closer vowel in *began* than in *plan*, and further recordings showed that *began* sometimes rhymes with *regain*.

The use of full vowels in function words and the unstressed syllables of polysyllabic words is very common (Heng and Deterding 2005), and syllable-based rhythm is widely reported for Singapore English (Brown 1988; Low *et al.* 2000).

Stressing of pronouns is found throughout South East Asia, and it may constitute a feature of the English lingua franca that seems to be emerging in the region (Deterding and Kirkpatrick 2006).

Nigerian English

The speaker from Nigeria is 51 years old, and his first language is Idoma, a language spoken by about 250,000 people in central Nigeria (though the speaker himself maintains that there are at least a million speakers of Idoma). He speaks to his wife and children in Idoma. He also speaks Hausa fairly well, though he did not learn it till he was 24 and he only uses it with people from northern Nigeria. Currently, English is the language he speaks most widely, and he uses it with friends, colleagues and nearly everyone other than his family. He started learning English at the age of ten.

Figure 22.2 shows the monophthong vowels for the Nigerian speaker. This reveals that FLEECE and KIT are merged, so *feast* and *fist* are homophones, and also that TRAP and PALM are merged, so presumably *match* and *march* would sound the same, though Gut (2004) observes that these two words tend to be differentiated by speakers of Hausa in northern Nigeria.

Some features of pronunciation found in this recording are:

- [d] occurs at the start of *this* and some tokens of *the*, though [ð] occurs in *there*, *their* and *than*;
- the final [t] is omitted in *fist* and *just*;
- [g] occurs at the end of *long*;
- both FACE and GOAT are monophthongal, especially the vowel in *go*;
- LOT occurs in the first syllable of *cousins* and *company*;
- there is a full vowel in the first syllable of *concern* and *convinced*;
- there are no weak forms for the function words *as*, *of*, *for*, *that* and the auxiliary *had*, so each of these has a full vowel (instead of [ə]);
- there is syllable-based rhythm.

The existence of a variety that might be labelled 'Nigerian English' has been disputed, because of the substantial variation throughout the country, especially between

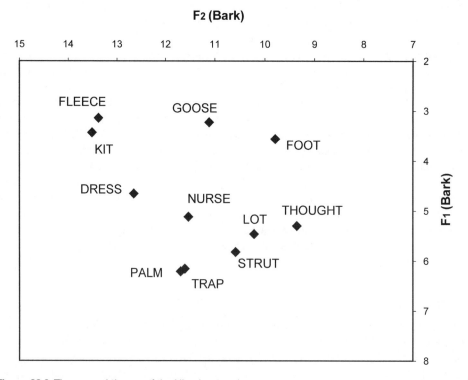

Figure 22.2 The monophthongs of the Nigerian speaker.

the three main ethnic groups, the Hausa, Yoruba and Igbo (Kirkpatrick 2007: 102). In some cases, Gut (2004) lists different realizations of features of pronunciation for each of these groups. However, there are also many shared features.

Among the features that Gut (2004) lists in the pronunciation of Nigerian English are: avoidance of dental fricatives, omission of plosives from word-final consonant clusters (such as *hand* and *post*), [g] at the end of words such as *sing* and *hang*, a monophthongal vowel in FACE and GOAT, and use of full vowels in unstressed syllables of polysyllabic words. Trudgill and Hannah (1985: 103) also note the omission of final [t] in *last* and [g] occurring at the end of words such as *ring* and *long*.

Measurements of rhythm (Gut 2006) confirm that Nigerian English has a substantially more syllable-based rhythm than British English.

Indian English

The speaker from India is 45 years old and he comes from Kerala in the south of India. His first language is Malayalam, a Dravidian language, and he still speaks that to all his family members. He started learning English at the age of ten, and he uses English when talking to friends and colleagues. He also learned Hindi from the age of 13, but he rates his ability in it as just 'OK', and he only uses it with Indians from other states.

Figure 22.3 shows a formant plot of the monophthong vowels of the Indian speaker. It seems that THOUGHT and LOT are merged, so *short* and *shot* sound the same, but all the other vowel phonemes in this classification are kept distinct.

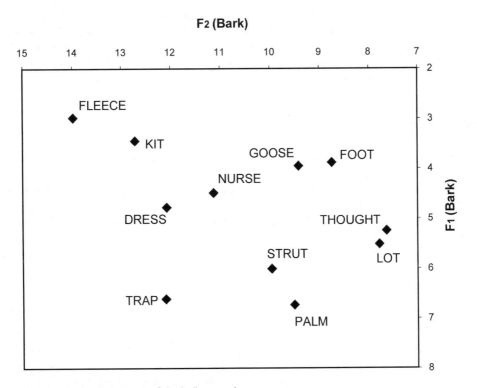

Figure 22.3 The monophthongs of the Indian speaker.

Some features of the pronunciation found in this recording are:

- [t] occurs at the start of *thought, threaten* and *third*;
- [d] occurs at the start of *this* and *than*;
- a retroflex consonant occurs at the end of *hot* and in the middle of *louder* (though the consonant at the start of words such as *two* or *down* is not retroflex);
- a sound intermediate between [v] and [w] occurs at the start of *once*;
- both FACE and GOAT are monophthongal;
- LOT occurs in *wolf* (so this word would presumably rhyme with *golf*);
- the second syllable of *village* has FACE (so the end of the word would be homophonous with *age*);
- a full vowel occurs in the first syllable of *concern* and *convinced*;
- there are no weak forms for the function words *as, of, for, that* and auxiliary *had*, so each of these has a full vowel (instead of [ə]);
- there is syllable-based rhythm.

Many of these features are widely reported for Indian English. Gargesh (2004), Kachru (2005: 44–6), Wells (1982: 626–31) and Trudgill and Hannah (1985: 106) all list the use of plosives for the TH sounds, a retroflex quality for [t] and [d], the sporadic merger of [v] and [w], a monophthongal quality in FACE and GOAT, the occurrence of full vowels instead of [ə] in function words, and syllable-based rhythm as typical of the English spoken in India.

One feature that is reported by all these sources is the occurrence of [j] or [w] before words that start with a vowel, so *every* may have initial [j] (Gargesh 2004) and *open* may have initial [w] (Kachru 2005: 45). However, the speaker considered here seems not to exhibit this feature of pronunciation, at least in this short recording, so for example neither *escaped* nor *even* begin with [j]. It is not clear if this feature would emerge with a longer stretch of speech or in more casual, conversational data.

Shared features

Each of the varieties that has been described has its own unique features, with for example the speaker from Singapore showing a merger of DRESS and TRAP and also no distinction between *raising* and *racing*, the Nigerian having a merger between TRAP and PALM and also a final [g] in *long*, and the Indian using retroflex [t] and [d] and also occasionally conflating [v] and [w]. However, there are also a number of features that are shared by these different varieties, and these may even constitute some common elements of an emergent 'outer circle World English'. Shared features include: avoidance of dental fricatives; monophthongal FACE and GOAT; the relative absence of reduced vowels; and syllable-based rhythm. Each of these shared features will now be considered in turn.

The TH sounds

The avoidance of the dental fricatives [θ, ð] is widespread in Englishes throughout the world, not just in outer circle varieties, but also in some inner circle styles of pronunciation, such as those of London, Ireland and New York (Wells 1982: 328, 428, 515). The avoidance of dental fricatives in outer circle varieties is not surprising given that most other languages do not have these sounds and many speakers find them difficult. In the data considered here, both the Singaporean and the Indian use [t] for initial voiceless TH, and although the Nigerian speaker uses [θ], he has [d] for voiced TH at the start of *this*; and furthermore Gut (2004) notes that avoidance of [θ] is common in Nigeria, with Yoruba and Igbo speakers in the south tending to use [t] instead and Hausa speakers in the north preferring to use [s].

The sound that is adopted for voiceless TH in new varieties of English differs, with [s] being used by speakers from places such as China (Deterding 2006b), Taiwan (Chung 2005), Germany (Swan 1987) and Russia (Monk and Burak 1987), [f] occurring in Hong Kong (Hung 2000; Deterding *et al.* 2008), and [t] being found not just in Singapore, India and with some speakers from Nigeria, but also in the Caribbean (Gramley and Pätzold 2004: 270), Brunei (Mossop 1996) and throughout South East Asia (Deterding and Kirkpatrick 2006). We might note that although [s] as a replacement occurs in many regions which, in their use of English, belong to the fourth diaspora (the expanding circle countries), [t] is the replacement which seems to predominate in outer circle countries, with Hausa speakers in Nigeria and also speakers from Hong Kong being notable exceptions. One wonders if [t] might one day become established and accepted as the norm for voiceless TH in outer circle World English.

The vowels in FACE and GOAT

The peak of the imperial expansion by Britain into the new colonies in Asia and Africa occurred in the late nineteenth century, and this was also the time when there was substantial immigration to Australia and New Zealand. On this basis, one might expect similar features of pronunciation for these outer circle and inner circle Englishes. However, for FACE and GOAT this does not seem to be the case. While both Australia and New Zealand have wide diphthongal movement for FACE and GOAT (Trudgill and Hannah 1985: 17–18), probably as an influence of the pronunciation of these vowels among speakers from London (Wells 1982: 307–8), there is very little such movement for them in the Englishes of Singapore, Nigeria and India, so we might regard these two vowels in such outer circle Englishes as monophthongs. In fact, measurements can confirm this auditory impression.

When FACE and GOAT are realized as diphthongs, as for example as [eɪ] and [əʊ] in many varieties of British English, they are generally closing diphthongs, and acoustically for a closing diphthong one would expect the first formant to fall during the course of the vowel. We can therefore obtain a simple but effective estimate of the

Table 22.2 Rate of change (ROC) for FACE and GOAT

	FACE		GOAT	
	ROC (Hz/sec)	Average	ROC (Hz/sec)	Average
Singapore	−100		−241	
Nigeria	−102		95	
India	−226	−143	−233	−126
B1	−1495		−1640	
B2	−1065		−763	
B3	−874	−970	−714	−1039

393

degree to which these vowels exhibit diphthongal movement by measuring the slope of the first formant over the duration of the vowel. The resulting value is usually termed Rate of Change (ROC), with units in Hertz per second (Deterding 2000). A large negative value for ROC indicates substantial diphthongal movement, while a small negative or even positive value suggests little or no change in vowel quality. For our data, for FACE, measurements were made of the ROC of the vowels in *stayed*, *change*, the first syllable of *safety* and *later*, and the second syllable of *escaped*, and for GOAT, the vowel in *homes*, *so*, *go* and the first syllable of *overcoming* was measured, and Table 22.2 shows the results for our three outer circle speakers and also the three British speakers, B1 to B3.

Clearly, there is less diphthongal movement for both FACE and GOAT for all three outer circle speakers than there is for all three British speakers, and the difference is highly significant for FACE (t = 5.32, df = 4, two-tailed, p < 0.01) and marginally significant for GOAT (t = 2.85, df = 4, two-tailed, p < 0.05). (The greater significance for FACE is because of the larger variation among the speakers for the GOAT measurements, partly arising out of the difficulties involved in measuring the formants of back vowels.)

FACE and GOAT are also monophthongal in some inner circle varieties of English, including those of Wales and Scotland (Wells 1982: 382, 407). It is not clear if emigrants from places such as these might have had an influence on the outer circle varieties, perhaps because of a large number of expatriate teachers. However, whatever the reason, monophthongal FACE and GOAT seems to be very common in most outer circle varieties of English (Kachru and Nelson 2006: 38), not just those we have considered, but also those of places such as Jamaica (Gramley and Pätzold 2004: 270), Brunei (Salbrina 2006), and much of the rest of South East Asia (Deterding and Kirkpatrick 2006), though a few other outer circle Englishes seem to be an exception to this rule, such as that of Hong Kong (Deterding *et al.* 2008) and also Indian South African English as well as Pakistan English (Mesthrie and Bhatt 2008: 123–4).

Reduced vowels

There is a shared tendency among outer circle Englishes for the use of full vowels rather than reduced vowels, not just in the unstressed syllables of content words such as the first syllable of *concern* and *convinced*, but also in some function words such as *of*, *for*, the subordinator *that* and the auxiliary verb *had*. Table 22.3 shows the quality of some of the vowels for our three outer circle speakers in two phrases: 'full of concern for his safety' and 'that had just escaped from the zoo'.

We can see from Table 22.3 that *of*, *for*, *that*, *had* and the first syllable of *concern* have a full vowel for all three speakers, though *from* has a reduced vowel for two of

Table 22.3 Vowel quality in function words and the first syllable of *concern*

	of	*con(cern)*	*for*	*that*	*had*	*from*	*the*
Singapore	1	1	1	1	1	0	0
Nigeria	1	1	1	1	1	1	0
India	1	1	1	1	1	0	0

Note: 1 = full vowel, 0 = reduced vowel.

them. We should note, however, that the schwa is never completely absent for any speaker, as the definite article *the* has [ə] for all three speakers.

Vowel reduction has a direct effect on the perception of rhythm, so we will consider these two issues together.

Rhythm

One of the consequences of the relative absence of reduced vowels in many outer circle varieties of English is that the rhythm is perceived to be syllable-based.

Nowadays, it is generally accepted that there are no absolutes in rhythm, but that the rhythm of speech exists along a continuum of stress/syllable timing (Miller 1984), so it is necessary to compare any measurements with something else. Here we will compare the measurements of rhythm of the three outer circle speakers for two utterances, 'full of concern for his safety' and 'that had just escaped from the zoo', with similar measurements for the data of the three British speakers, B1 to B3.

Estimates of the rhythm of these utterances were derived using the PVI (the Pairwise Variability Index) suggested by Low *et al.* (2000), which is based on a comparison of the duration of vowels in neighbouring syllables. Two minor modifications were introduced to the PVI as suggested by Low *et al.*: the final syllable was excluded from the calculations, to eliminate the effects of final-syllable lengthening; and the minimum value for the duration of a vowel was set at 30 ms, to limit the effects on the calculations of extremely short vowels, some of which can be so short that they actually become absorbed by surrounding consonants (Shockey 2003: 22). Large values for the PVI indicate substantial variation in the duration of neighbouring vowels, so they suggest greater stress-based rhythm. The average PVI for the two utterances analysed for each of the six speakers is shown in Table 22.4.

Clearly, the three outer circle speakers have a substantially more syllable-based rhythm than the British ones, a difference that is statistically highly significant (6.39, df = 4, two-tailed, p < 0.01).

Syllable-based rhythm is extremely common in outer circle varieties of English. In addition to the three varieties described here, it is reported for a wide range of other Englishes, including those of East Africa (Gramley and Pätzold 2004: 323), Jamaica (Trudgill and Hannah 1985: 98), the Philippines (Wells 1982: 647) and Hawaiian Creole (Wells 1982: 651).

Crystal (1995) notes that inner circle Englishes also sometimes exhibit syllable-based rhythm, for example in baby talk, sarcastic utterances or those carrying a note of irritation, many types of popular music and some television commercials, and he further wonders

Table 22.4 Rhythm measured using the PVI

	PVI	*Average*
Singapore	29.9	
Nigeria	34.2	
India	25.0	29.7
B1	58.6	
B2	64.0	
B3	51.7	58.1

whether syllable-based rhythm might one day become the norm even in Britain and America (Crystal 2003: 171).

One issue that arises with regard to the relative absence of reduced vowels in styles of English that have a syllable-based rhythm is the effect it might have on psychological processes involved in perception. It has been suggested that speakers with reduced vowels in their function words tend to process these words differently from content words, so that for inner circle Englishes the function words constitute the 'mortar' that holds together the 'bricks' of the content words (Field 2008). If syllable-based rhythm becomes the norm for English, it is not clear what effect this will have on the processing of English sentences; quite possibly, there might be substantial knock-on effects on the structure of English.

Discussion

It has been shown that, although there are substantial differences between the Englishes found in the various outer circle countries, some features seem to be shared, particularly the avoidance of the dental fricatives, a monophthongal quality for FACE and GOAT, the use of full vowels in function words and the unstressed syllables of poly-syllabic words, and syllable-based rhythm. We might note that all these features fit in perfectly with the Lingua Franca Core (LFC), the set of pronunciation features which Jenkins (2007) suggests are essential for successful international communication, as she proposes that the dental fricatives, the precise quality of vowels, use of reduced vowels, and stress-timed rhythm should all be excluded from the LFC and should only be taught to students who choose to try and approximate an inner circle norm.

We might here consider what effects these features have on intelligibility, especially since it has long been established that inner circle varieties of English are not always the most intelligible for listeners around the world (Smith and Nelson 2006). Of course, intelligibility is hard to measure, and so it is not straightforward to determine if any particular feature of pronunciation might improve or degrade the chances of being understood by a range of listeners; but it is interesting to note that the language of air traffic ('Airspeak') is one of the domains that Crystal (1995) identifies as exhibiting syllable-based rhythm 'because of the need to articulate with extra clarity' (p. 175). And it does indeed seem likely that use of full vowels instead of reduced vowels in unstressed syllables can help in improving intelligibility, at least for the kind of short, critically important utterances that characterize the language of air-traffic control.

Given that there are now almost certainly more outer circle than inner circle speakers of English around the world (Crystal 2003: 61), one might further speculate on the possible impact on the future development of English of the features that are shared among outer circle speakers. It seems likely that patterns of pronunciation found in a wide range of outer circle Englishes will have a substantial influence on the way that the language evolves in the future, so even if these patterns do not constitute a world standard that is adopted by everyone, they will at least become increasingly accepted as one possible standard. When that happens, English teachers around the world will no longer have to continue with the confidence-sapping practice of constantly making reference to the inner circle for their norms of pronunciation (Kirkpatrick 2007: 189), and furthermore they can truly come to believe that English belongs to them as much as to anyone else.

Suggestions for further reading

Jenkins, J. (2007) *English as a Lingua Franca: Attitude and Identity*, Oxford: Oxford University Press. (An important discussion of which features of pronunciation are important for maintaining intelligibility in World Englishes.)

Kirkpatrick, A. (2007) *World Englishes: Implications for International Communication and English Language Teaching*, Cambridge: Cambridge University Press. (A survey of World Englishes that shows that the evolution of English is a process of regularization as well as language contact, so outer circle varieties can contribute just as easily as inner circle ones.)

Mesthrie, R. and Bhatt, R.M. (2008) *World Englishes: The Study of New Linguistic Varieties*, Cambridge: Cambridge University Press. (An overview of World Englishes that focuses especially on features that are shared by different outer circle varieties.)

Schneider, E.W., Burridge, K., Kortmann, B., Mesthrie, R. and Upton, C. (eds) (2004) *A Handbook of Varieties of English. Volume 1: Phonology*, Berlin: Mouton de Gruyter. (An invaluable compendium of detailed descriptions of the pronunciation of a wide range of different varieties of English.)

Wells, J.C. (1982) *Accents of English*, Cambridge: Cambridge University Press. (The classic, authoritative description of varieties of English around the world which still makes sense after all these years.)

References

Bao, Z. (1998) 'The sounds of Singapore English', in J. Foley, T. Kandiah, Bao Zhiming, A.F. Gupta, L. Alsagoff, Ho Chee Lick, L. Wee, I.S. Talib and W. Bokhorst-Heng (eds) *English in New Cultural Contexts: Reflections from Singapore*, Singapore: Oxford University Press, pp. 152–74.

Bauer, L. and Warren, P. (2004) 'New Zealand English: phonology', in E.W. Schneider, K. Burridge, B. Kortmann, R. Mesthrie and C. Upton (eds) *A Handbook of Varieties of English. Volume 1: Phonology*, Berlin: Mouton de Gruyter, pp. 580–602.

Boersma, P. and Weenink, D. (2007) 'Praat: doing phonetics by computer'. Online. Available www.fon.hum.uva.nl/praat/ (accessed 6 September 2007).

Brown, A. (1988) 'The staccato effect in the pronunciation of English in Malaysia and Singapore', in J. Joley (ed.) *New Englishes: The Case of Singapore*, Singapore: Singapore University Press, pp. 115–28.

Chung, K. (2005) 'The sounds and allophones of Taiwan English III'. Online. Available http://ccms.ntu.edu.tw/~karchung/intro%20page%2029.htm (accessed 26 October 2008).

Crystal, D. (1995) 'Documenting rhythmical change', in J. Windsor Lewis (ed.) *Studies in General and English Phonetics: Essays in Honour of Professor J.D. O'Connor*, London: Routledge, pp. 174–9.

——(2003) *English as a Global Language* (2nd edition), Cambridge: Cambridge University Press.

Deterding, D. (2000) 'Measurements of the /eɪ/ and /əʊ/ vowels of young English speakers in Singapore', in A. Brown, D. Deterding and E.L. Low (eds) *The English Language in Singapore: Research on Pronunciation*, Singapore: Singapore Association for Applied Linguistics, pp. 93–9.

——(2003) 'An instrumental study of the monophthong vowels of Singapore English', *English World-Wide*, 24 (1): 1–16.

——(2005) 'Emergent patterns in the vowels of Singapore English', *English World-Wide*, 26 (2): 179–97.

——(2006a) '"The North Wind versus a Wolf": short texts for the description and measurement of English pronunciation', *Journal of the International Phonetic Association*, 36: 187–196.

——(2006b) 'The pronunciation of English by speakers from China', *English World-Wide*, 27 (2): 175–98.

——(2007a) *Singapore English*, Edinburgh: Edinburgh University Press.

——(2007b) 'The vowels of the different groups in Singapore', in D. Prescott, A. Kirkpatrick, A. Hashim and I. Martin (eds) *English in Southeast Asia: Varieties, Literacies and Literatures*, Newcastle, UK: Cambridge Scholars Publishing, pp. 2–29.

Deterding, D. and Kirkpatrick, A. (2006) 'Emerging South-East Asian Englishes and intelligibility', *World-Englishes*, 25 (3/4): 391–409.

Deterding, D., Wong, J. and Kirkpatrick, A. (2008) 'The pronunciation of Hong Kong English', *English World-Wide*, 29 (2): 148–75.

Field, J. (2008) 'Bricks or mortar: which parts of the input does a second language listener rely on?' *TESOL Quarterly*, 42: 411–32.

Gargesh, R. (2004) 'Indian English: phonology', in E.W. Schneider, K. Burridge, B. Kortmann, R. Mesthrie and C. Upton (eds) *A Handbook of Varieties of English. Volume 1: Phonology*, Berlin: Mouton de Gruyter, pp. 815–29.

Gramley, S. and Pätzold, K.-M. (2004) *A Survey of Modern English* (2nd edition), London: Routledge.

Gut, U. (2004) 'Nigerian English: phonology', in E.W. Schneider, K. Burridge, B. Kortmann, R. Mesthrie and C. Upton (eds) *A Handbook of Varieties of English. Volume 1: Phonology*, Berlin: Mouton de Gruyter, pp. 992–1002.

——(2005) 'The realization of final plosives: phonological rules and ethnic differences', in D. Deterding, A. Brown and E.L. Low (eds) *English in Singapore: Phonetic Research on a Corpus*, Singapore: McGraw-Hill, pp. 14–25.

——(2006) 'Nigerian English prosody', *English World-Wide*, 26 (2): 153–77.

Hayward, K. (2000) *Experimental Phonetics*, Harlow: Longman.

Heng, M.G. and Deterding, D. (2005) 'Reduced vowels in conversational Singapore English', in D. Deterding, A. Brown and E.L. Low (eds) *English in Singapore: Phonetic Research on a Corpus*, Singapore: McGraw-Hill, pp. 54–63.

Hung, T. (2000) 'Towards a phonology of Hong Kong English', *World Englishes*, 19: 337–56.

Jenkins, J. (2007) *English as a Lingua Franca: Attitude and Identity*, Oxford: Oxford University Press.

Kachru, B.B. (2005) *Asian Englishes: Beyond the Canon*, Hong Kong: Hong Kong University Press.

Kachru, B.B., Kachru, Y. and Nelson, C.L. (2006) *The Handbook of World Englishes*, Malden, MA: Blackwell.

Kachru, Y. and Nelson, C.L. (2006) *World Englishes in Asian Contexts*, Hong Kong: Hong Kong University Press.

Kirkpatrick, A. (2007) *World Englishes: Implications for International Communication and English Language Teaching*, Cambridge: Cambridge University Press.

Ladefoged, P. (2006) *A Course in Phonetics* (5th edition), Boston, MA: Thomson Wadsworth.

Lee, E.M. and Lim, L. (2000) 'Diphthongs in Singapore English: their realisations across different formality levels, and some attitudes of listeners towards them', in A. Brown, D. Deterding and E.L. Low (eds) *The English Language in Singapore: Research on Pronunciation*, Singapore: Singapore Association for Applied Linguistics, pp. 100–11.

Low, E.L., Grabe, E. and Nolan, F. (2000) 'Quantitative characterizations of speech rhythm: syllable-timing in Singapore English', *Language and Speech*, 43: 377–401.

Mesthrie, R. and Bhatt, R.M. (2008) *World Englishes: The Study of New Linguistic Varieties*, Cambridge: Cambridge University Press.

Miller, M. (1984) 'On the perception of rhythm', *Journal of Phonetics*, 12: 75–83.

Monk, B. and Burak, A. (1987) 'Russian speakers', in M. Swan and B. Smith (eds) *Learner English: A Teacher's Guide to Interference and Other Problems*, Cambridge: Cambridge University Press, pp. 117–28.

Moorthy, S.M. and Deterding, D. (2000) 'Three or tree: dental fricatives in the speech of educated Singaporeans', in A. Brown, D. Deterding and E.L. Low (eds) *The English Language in Singapore: Research on Pronunciation*, Singapore: Singapore Association for Applied Linguistics, pp. 76–83.

Mossop, J. (1996) 'Some phonological features of Brunei English', in P.W. Martins, C. Ożóg and G. Poedjosoedarmo (eds) *Language Use and Language Change in Brunei Darussalam*, Athens, OH: Ohio University Center for International Studies, pp. 189–208.

Mugglestone, L. (2003) *Talking Proper: The Rise of Accent as a Social Symbol* (2nd edition), Oxford: Oxford University Press.

Salbrina, H.S. (2006) 'The vowels of Brunei English: an acoustic investigation', *English World-Wide*, 27 (3): 247–64.

Schneider, E.W. (2007) *Postcolonial Englishes: Varieties around the World*, Cambridge: Cambridge University Press.

Shockey, L. (2003) *Sound Patterns of Spoken English*, Malden, MA: Blackwell.

Smith, L.E. and Nelson, C.L. (2006) 'World Englishes and issues of intelligibility', in B.B. Kachru, Y. Kachru and C.L. Nelson (eds) *The Handbook of World Englishes*, Malden, MA: Blackwell, pp. 428–45.

Swan, M. (1987) 'German speakers', in M. Swan and B. Smith (eds) *Learner English: A Teacher's Guide to Interference and Other Problems*, Cambridge: Cambridge University Press, pp. 30–41.

Trudgill, P. and Hannah, J. (1985) *International English: A Guide to Varieties of Standard English* (2nd edition), London: Edward Arnold.

Wee, L. (2004) 'Singapore English: Phonology', in E.W. Schneider, K. Burridge, B. Kortmann, R. Mesthrie and C. Upton (eds) *A Handbook of Varieties of English. Volume 1: Phonology*, Berlin: Mouton de Gruyter, pp. 1017–33.

Wells, J.C. (1982) *Accents of English*, Cambridge: Cambridge University Press.

23

Variation across Englishes

Syntax

Bernd Kortmann

Introduction

This chapter will offer a qualitative and quantitative survey of morphosyntactic variation based on the major findings of recent and ongoing research. The backbone of this chapter will be the author's own research and research agenda (see especially the publications co-authored with Szmrecsanyi), which boils down to a typologist's interest in cataloguing and trying to account for the observable variation across varieties of English world-wide. The ultimate aim of such an endeavour is to identify correlations, clusters and overall patterns of variation among the morphological and syntactic properties within and across the individual varieties and variety types, and to suggest interpretations and possible explanations, in an attempt at uncovering the wood behind the trees, as it were. Thus questions like the following will be addressed in this chapter:

- Which varieties are most alike concerning morphosyntactic properties they either display or do not display?
- Are the observable similarities and differences across varieties of English around the world best accounted for in terms of geography, i.e. where they are spoken, or in terms of the type of variety they constitute, i.e. the sociohistorical conditions in which they developed and are currently used?
- Is it possible to identify large-scale areal patterns, e.g. morphosyntactic properties exclusively shared by, or at least distinctive of, varieties spoken in the British Isles as opposed to varieties spoken in North America, Africa or Asia?
- Is it possible to identify morphosyntactic features found in all or at least a vast majority of the Englishes around the world? In other words: can we postulate something like universals in the realm of morphosyntax for all the non-standard varieties of English?
- Do varieties of English exhibit different complexity profiles, such that different (sets of) varieties tend to exhibit higher or lower degrees of morphosyntactic complexity, and how can such structural complexity be measured in the first place?

These and related questions discussed in the recent research literature will be answered primarily on the basis of a rich set of survey data of 46 varieties of English and naturalistic corpus data for more than a dozen varieties of English. Wherever feasible, information on morphosyntactic features in additional varieties described in the research literature will be included. With its focus on large-scale patterns, coding strategies and complexity profiles, this chapter complements Kortmann (2006), which has a more descriptive orientation and provides in the first place a catalogue of the most widespread morphological and syntactic features of non-standard Englishes.

The chapter will be structured as follows. First, an account will be given of the data primarily used and the varieties from which they have been taken, including a brief discussion of the way in which the varieties have been grouped into different types. This will be followed by a look at the current state of the vernacular universals debate. The most distinctive features of each of the major variety types across different domains of morphosyntax will be sketched in the fourth section. In the fifth section we will engage with a current debate in the World Englishes community, concerning the impact of language contact on morphosyntactic structure: does a high degree of contact with another language or dialect trigger simplification processes so that, for example, pidgins and creoles tend to have the simplest (or least complex) grammars, whereas traditional dialects, which typically qualify as low-contact varieties, tend to retain many complex features in their morphosyntax? This section will present metrics which can be used for comparing grammars (across varieties of a language) with regard to complexity, take a stand on the 'high contact leads to simplified grammars' position, and discuss different kinds of generalizations which have been offered in the literature concerning which (types of) varieties tend to exhibit which (patterns of) morphosyntactic features. The major line of argument in the fifth section, and indeed in this chapter, will be that variety type, i.e. whether a given variety is a (high- or low-contact) L1 variety, an indigenized non-native L2 variety, a pidgin or a creole, is a better predictor of what kind of morphosyntactic profile this variety will exhibit, than the part of the English-speaking world where this variety is spoken. Geography does matter, too, but only at a secondary level, as will be shown in the sixth section, where large-scale areal patterns for different Anglophone world regions will be addressed. The chapter will close with a brief summary and outlook on the most promising next steps to be taken in the study of morphosyntactic variation in English on a global scale.

Data

The data on which this chapter is based have been drawn from a wide range of sources, especially surveys such as Kortmann *et al.* (2004), Holm and Patrick (2007), Schneider (2007) and Mesthrie and Bhatt (2008), with the first of these, the *Handbook of Varieties of English* (HVE) clearly figuring as the main source. Of the more than 60 varieties of English from seven Anglophone world regions covered there (British Isles, North America, Caribbean, Australasia, Pacific, Africa, South and South East Asia), it is for a subset of 46 varieties that, together with the HVE, the *World Atlas of Morphosyntactic Variation in English* (WAMVE) was compiled as an interactive electronic tool to provide information on a set of 76 morphosyntactic features. These survey data form the backbone of the qualitative and especially quantitative generalizations offered in the second half of the chapter (for details see 'Survey data' and the Appendix). For the section asking 'Do grammars of varieties differ in degrees of complexity?', the WAMVE data will be complemented by corpus data from selected L1 and L2 varieties (see 'Corpus data').

This chapter draws on data from all types of spontaneous spoken varieties of English classified as the *English Language Complex*, a cover term for each and every variety of English (McArthur 2003: 56). Space considerations forbid a detailed discussion of which types of varieties could, in principle, be distinguished (see Mesthrie and Bhatt 2008: 3–12) and which considerations were responsible for grouping a given variety with a given type. Suffice it to say that the major variety types which will be distinguished in this chapter are the following: L1 (or ENL) varieties, non-native indigenized L2 (or ESL) varieties and (English-based) pidgins and creoles. In assigning individual varieties to a specific variety type, we largely followed standard practice in the research literature, and especially the decision of the relevant HVE author and/or WAMVE specialist (and often native-speaker) informant. Alternative classifications, such as 'New Englishes', (high- or low-) contact varieties or shift varieties, will be used only occasionally, and defined where relevant.

Survey data

For the WAMVE survey and its close analysis in Kortmann and Szmrecsanyi (2004), material was collected from (often native-speaker) experts on 76 non-standard morphosyntactic features from 46 (exclusively spoken) non-standard varieties from all seven Anglophone world regions (see Table 23.1 below). The features in the survey (see the Appendix) cover 11 broad areas of morphosyntax: pronouns, the noun phrase, tense and aspect, modal verbs, verb morphology, adverbs, negation, agreement, relativization, complementation, discourse organization and word order. For each of these 76 features the informants were asked to specify into which of the following three categories the relevant feature in the relevant variety (or set of closely related varieties, e.g. the dialects of the north of England) falls:

A   pervasive (possibly obligatory) or at least very frequent;
B   exists but is a (possibly receding) feature used only rarely, at least not frequently;
C   definitely does not exist/informant does not know/inapplicable.

Generally speaking, especially for all quantitative analyses, only those features which are present in a given variety or set of varieties (regardless whether they are classified as 'A' or 'B') will be considered relevant. The latter distinction will only come in when pointing out which morphosyntactic features are particularly pervasive in (and thus distinctive of) one or the other of the major variety types and Anglophone world regions.

Table 23.1 provides a breakdown of the 46 varieties by Anglophone world region (British Isles, America, Caribbean, Australia, Pacific, South/South East Asia, Africa) and variety type (20 L1 varieties, 11 L2 varieties, 15 English-based pidgins and creoles). The asterisk for some L1 varieties indicates traditional dialects, and is motivated by Trudgill's (2009a) division of L1 varieties of English into low-contact varieties (in the WAMVE sample, eight out of 20 L1 varieties) and high-contact varieties (12 out of 20); more on the high- vs low-contact distinction below.

What emerges from Table 23.1 is a division of the seven Anglophone world regions into homogeneous and heterogeneous regions, depending on whether they display varieties

Table **23.1** WAMVE: distribution of 46 non-standard varieties across world regions and variety types

World region	Varieties for which feature classifications are available in WAMVE			Total L1	Total L2	Total P/C
	L1	L2	P/C			
British Isles	Orkney and Shetland*, ScE, IrE, WelE, North*, East Anglia*, Southwest*, Southeast*			8	0	0
America	NfldE*, CollAmE, AppE*, OzE, IsSEUS*, Urban AAVE, Earlier AAVE	ChcE	Gullah	7	1	1
Caribbean			BahE, JamC, Tob/TrnC, SurCs, BelC	0	0	5
Australia	CollAusE, AusVE (Tasmania)		AusCs, AbE	2	0	2
Pacific	Norfolk, regional NZE	FijE	Bislama, TP, SolP, HawC	2	1	4
Asia		ButlE, PakE, SgE, MalE		0	4	0
Africa	WhSAfE	GhE, CamE, EAfE, InSAfE, BISAfE	NigP, GhP, CamP	1	5	3

Source: Adapted from Kortmann and Szmrecsanyi (2004: 1145).

of English belonging exclusively or predominantly to one variety type, or whether there is a fair mix of variety types (of course, always within the limits of the WAMVE sample). The following qualify as homogeneous world regions: the British Isles and North America for L1 varieties, (South and South East) Asia for L2 varieties, and the Caribbean for pidgins and creoles. Heterogeneous world regions are Australia (L1 and P/C) and the two dominantly non-L1 world regions Pacific (with a majority of pidgins and creoles) and Africa (with a majority of L2 varieties). The division into homogeneous and heterogeneous world regions will become relevant later when addressing the question whether geography or variety type is the better predictor for the morphosyntactic profile of varieties of English around the world.

Corpus data

For the quantitative study of different degrees of morphosyntactic complexity and overall coding strategies such as analyticity vs syntheticity (see below 'Do grammars of varieties differ in degrees of complexity?'), naturalistic digitized corpus data from 15 spontaneous spoken L1 and L2 varieties of English (13 non-standard, two standard) have been used in a range of studies by Kortmann and Szmrecsanyi (forthcoming) and Szmrecsanyi and Kortmann (2009a, 2009b). The data for the 13 non-standard varieties have predominantly been extracted from the Freiburg Corpus of English Dialects (FRED; cf. Kortmann and Wagner 2005; Hernández 2006; Anderwald and Wagner 2007) and the International Corpus of English (ICE; cf. Greenbaum 1996). From these, two high-contact L1s, five low-contact L1s and five L2s were sampled. The Northern Ireland Transcribed Corpus of Speech (NITCS) was used as an additional source of a high-contact L1 (cf. Kirk 1992). Included for purely benchmarking purposes were spoken data from two high-contact standard varieties of British English (from the ICE-GB) and American English (from the Corpus of Spoken American English; cf. Du Bois *et al.* 2000). Table 23.2 provides the total picture of the 15 samples drawn from digitized speech corpora.

As mentioned above, the distinction between high- and low-contact varieties of English goes back to Peter Trudgill (2009a). In a nutshell, Trudgill's idea is that high- and low-contact varieties exhibit different complexity profiles. His basic assumption is that contact implicates adult language learning, which in turn implicates simplification of grammars, especially by the reduction of inflectional morphology. He claims that high-contact varieties (which in his view include all varieties of English, whether non-standard or standard, except for the traditional dialects of England and North America) are characterized by simplification processes, whereas low-contact varieties, i.e. those classified as traditional dialects in Tables 23.1 and 23.2, retain morphosyntactic complexity or may even undergo complexification processes (see also 'Do grammars of varieties differ in degrees of complexity?'). Unfortunately, Trudgill does not provide hard-and-fast criteria for classifying a given L1 variety of English as either high or low contact. The classification of the L1 varieties in Table 23.2 (and accordingly for those in Table 23.1) is based on the following reasoning. There are three kinds of high-contact L1 varieties (cf. Kortmann and Szmrecsanyi forthcoming):

(i) *Transplanted L1 Englishes* or *colonial standards* (cf. Mesthrie 2006: 382; Mesthrie and Bhatt 2008: 4), i.e. varieties whose genesis is such that, through settlement colonization in the course of the past 400 years, settlers with diverse linguistic and/or dialectal backgrounds – with all the dialect and language contact

Table 23.2 Speech corpora and varieties of English investigated

Corpus	Subcorpus	Variety/varieties	Variety type
Freiburg Corpus of English Dialects (FRED)	FRED-SE	English Southeast + East Anglia (SE+EA)	traditional L1
	FRED-SW	English Southwest (SW)	traditional L1
	FRED-MID	English Midlands (Mid)	traditional L1
	FRED-N	English North (N)	traditional L1
	FRED-SCH	Scottish Highlands (ScH)	traditional L1
	FRED-WAL	Welsh English (WelE)	high-contact L1
International Corpus of English (ICE)	ICE-NZ-S1A	New Zealand E (NZE)	high-contact L1
	ICE-HK-S1A	Hong Kong E (HKE)	L2
	ICE-JA-S1A	Jamaican E (JamE)	L2
	ICE-PHI-S1A	Philippines E (PhilE)	L2
	ICE-SIN-S1A	Singapore E (SgE)	L2
	ICE-IND-S1A	Indian E (IndE)	L2
	ICE-GB-S1A	colloquial British E (collBrE)	high-contact L1
Northern Ireland Transcribed Corpus of Speech (NITCS)		Northern Irish E (NIrE)	high-contact L1
Corpus of Spoken American English (CSAE)		colloquial American E (collAmE)	high-contact L1

that this implies – formed new indigenized English dialects that have had native speakers from early on. Examples include New Zealand English and Australian English.

(ii) *Language-shift Englishes*, i.e. varieties 'that develop when English replaces the erstwhile primary language(s) of a community' and that have 'adult and child L1 and L2 speakers forming one speech community' (Mesthrie and Bhatt 2008: 6). This group also includes varieties that used to be genuine language-shift varieties within the past 400 years but which do not now have significant numbers of L2 speakers. A prime example of such a *shifted variety* is Irish English.

(iii) *Standard varieties*, such as Standard British English, the genesis of which, according to Trudgill (2009a), always implies a high degree of dialect contact.

In sum, the set of high-contact L1 varieties can be defined by the following mathematical term: 'New Englishes' (cf. Pride 1982; Platt *et al.* 1984) *minus* non-native, indigenized L2 varieties *minus* English-based pidgins and creoles *plus* standard varieties. All other varieties are considered *low-contact L1 dialects of English*, i.e. traditional (typically) non-transplanted regional dialects which are 'long-established mother tongue varieties' (Trudgill 2009a: 320).

From vernacular universals to vernacular angloversals

In recent comparative studies of morphosyntactic variation in Englishes around the world, Chambers' sociodialectological notion of vernacular universals (VU) (2000, 2001, 2003, 2004) has given rise to controversy (cf. Filppula *et al.* 2009a). According to Chambers, these universals comprise 'a small number of phonological and grammatical processes [that] recur in vernaculars wherever they are spoken ... not only in working class and rural vernaculars, but also in ... pidgins, creoles and interlanguage varieties' (2004: 128). Moreover, he makes a strong case for these universals to be 'primitive features of vernacular dialects' (2003: 243) in any language, i.e. unlearned and thus innate features which are 'the outgrowths of ... rules and representations in the bioprogram' (2004: 129). Chambers (2004: 129) lists the following four candidates for VUs in the domain of morphosyntax:

1 conjugation regularization, or levelling of irregular verb forms: e.g. *John seen the eclipse*, *Mary heared the good news*;
2 default singulars, or subject–verb nonconcord: e.g. *They was the last ones*;
3 multiple negation, or negative concord: e.g. *I don't/ain't know nothing*;
4 copula absence, or copula deletion: e.g. *She smart, We going as soon as possible*.

This is not the place for an exhaustive survey of the arguments which figure most prominently in the controversial VU debate documented in Filppula *et al.* (2009a; for an overview cf. Filppula *et al.* 2009b). In short, the cons seem to outnumber the pros so that, ultimately, the notion of specifically *vernacular* universals – as opposed to universals as formulated in language typology – cannot seriously be upheld. Nevertheless, provided the notion VU is used with caution and considerably downsized, the concept contains some interesting ideas (for details cf. Kortmann and Szmrecsanyi forthcoming). The most important overall argument in defence of the notion is that, even if Chambers may have overshot the mark, it has motivated dialectologists, sociolinguists, creolists and typologists to look for generalizations in the morphosyntactic behaviour of non-standard varieties of English (and, in future, no doubt in other languages). Broadly, at least three kinds of such generalizations concerning features which tend to recur can be distinguished (cf. Szmrecsanyi and Kortmann 2009a: 33). Features may recur:

(i) in vernacular varieties of a specific language, e.g. *angloversals* in the case of English vernaculars or *francoversals* for French vernaculars;
(ii) in variety types (within a specific language, but most likely also across languages) with a similar sociohistory, historical depth and mode of acquisition (e.g. L1 or L2 or creole *varioversals*);
(iii) in varieties restricted to a given world region or smaller geographic area (e.g. *areoversals* for the British Isles or North America).

Adopting standard typological practice, generalizations of all three types can and should be formulated, not just in absolute, but also in relative terms (i.e. as statistical tendencies), and moreover, not just in non-implicational, but also in implicational terms (cf. Szmrecsanyi and Kortmann 2009a: 39–44). For example, the following biconditional implication holds for 94 per cent of the 46 varieties in WAMVE and is thus a candidate for an implicational angloversal: if a variety has *ain't* as the negated form of *be*, it also has *ain't* as the negated form of *have*, and vice versa (and a variety that doesn't have *ain't* as the negated form of *be* neither has *ain't* as the negated form of *have*, and vice versa).

Varioversals will be addressed in the sections headed 'Distinctive morphosyntactic features of individual variety types' and 'Do grammars of varieties differ in degrees of complexity?', areoversals in the section on large-scale areal patterns. However, the

Table 23.3 Top candidates for morphosyntactic angloversals

	WAMVE feature	No. of varieties where feature is attested
74	lack of inversion in main clause *yes/no* questions	41
10	*me* instead of *I* in coordinate subjects	40
49	*never* as preverbal past tense negator	40
42	adverbs same form as adjectives	39
14	absence of plural marking after measure nouns	37
73	lack of inversion/lack of auxiliaries in *wh*-questions	36
44	multiple negation/negative concord	35
43	degree modifier adverbs lack *-ly*	35
3	special forms or phrases for the second person plural pronoun	34
25	levelling of difference between present perfect and simple past	34
19	double comparatives and superlatives	34

WAMVE survey clearly shows that none of Chambers' candidates for VU can lay claim even to being angloversals, since those WAMVE features most closely corresponding to Chambers' VU candidates are found in no more than 67–78 per cent of the 46 varieties investigated. However, all of them clearly qualify as American areoversals since it is only for North America that 100 per cent of all varieties in an Anglophone world region exhibit the relevant features (cf. Szmrecsanyi and Kortmann 2009a: 36ff.). Those morphosyntactic features which are found in the largest number of WAMVE varieties, i.e. in at least 75 per cent, are listed in Table 23.3 (Kortmann and Szmrecsanyi 2004: 1154). So these then are the top candidates for vernacular angloversals, with Chambers' VU candidates forming a subset, but none of them (not even multiple negation) figures at the very top.

The top four of the 11 angloversals in Table 23.3 are top for every single major variety type, i.e. are found in at least 75 per cent of all L1 varieties, of all L2 varieties, and of all pidgins and creoles covered in WAMVE. The distinctive morphosyntactic profiles of each of the major variety types (L1, L2, pidgins and creoles) will be outlined in the next two sections.

Distinctive morphosyntactic features of individual variety types

The focus of this section will be on features and (heterogeneous, non-correlated) feature sets covered in WAMVE which are particularly prominent for the individual variety types (Kortmann and Szmrecsanyi 2004: 1183–93). Prominence will mean either or both: (a) the relevant feature is observable in at least 75 per cent of the varieties of the variety type under consideration *and* is at the same time found in fewer (often far fewer) varieties belonging to the other two variety types; (b) the relevant feature is pervasive in each or at least in the vast majority of the varieties of the given variety type (i.e. this feature received an 'A' ranking as outlined above). In the discussion of 'Do grammars of varieties differ in degrees of complexity?' the focus will be on clusters of features that allow us to characterize the major variety types in terms of their distinct profiles of morphosyntactic complexity. Recall Table 23.1 for the assignment of the 46 WAMVE varieties to the major variety types (20 L1s, 11 L2s, 15 P/Cs).

L1 varieties

The following seven features qualify as highly distinctive L1 features since they are among the top features of neither L2 varieties nor pidgins or creoles. They are ordered according to the (decreasing) number of L1 varieties in which they are found:

> 'existential/presentational *there's, there is, there was* with plural subjects' (19 varieties);
> '*them* instead of demonstrative *those*' (18 varieties);
> 'levelling of preterite and past participle verb forms' (via a past form replacing the participle or unmarked forms) and '*as what/than what* in comparative clauses' (17 varieties);
> 'a regularized reflexives-paradigm' and 'regularized comparison strategies' (16 varieties).

Three L1 features are rated 'A', i.e. as pervasive features, as they occur in at least 15 of the 20 L1 varieties:

> '*them* instead of demonstrative *those*';
> 'existential/presentational *there's, there is, there was* with plural subjects';
> the angloversal '*me* instead of *I* in coordinate subjects'.

From an areal point of view, which will take centre-stage at the end of the chapter, it should be pointed out that of those 21 features which are found in a minimum of 75 per cent of all L1 varieties (i.e. in at least 15 out of 20), every single one is also among the top features of North America, and still about three-quarters of the top L1 features (15 out of 21) are among the top features in the British Isles. This correlation was to be expected, given what was pointed out earlier concerning the relative homogeneity (in the WAMVE sample) of the British Isles and North America as the two L1 regions of the Anglophone world.

Indigenized, non-native L2 varieties

Four (out of the altogether 19) features found in 75 per cent or more of the 11 L2 varieties investigated qualify as features which are exclusively top in L2s and in none of the other variety types. These are:

> 'resumptive/shadow pronouns' (documented in ten varieties);
> 'zero past tense forms of regular verbs' (ten varieties);
> 'invariant non-concord tags' (nine varieties);
> 'invariant *don't* for all persons in the present tense' (eight varieties).

The following features have exclusively or overwhelmingly been rated 'pervasive':

> 'lack of inversion in main clause *yes/no* questions' (ten varieties);
> 'irregular use of articles' (nine varieties)

and the following four in eight L2 varieties:

'wider range of uses of the Progressive';
'*never* as preverbal past tense negator';
'inverted word order in indirect questions';
'lack of inversion/lack of auxiliaries in *wh*-questions'.

Pidgins and creoles

Morphosyntactic features which are top (>75 per cent) exclusively in the mesolects of 15 pidgins and creoles in the WAMVE are the following four:

'deletion of *be*' and 'invariant present tense forms due to zero marking for the third-person singular' (found in 14 varieties each);
'*no* as preverbal negator' as well as 'serial verbs' (13 varieties).

All of the following features have been rated 'pervasive' in at least 80 per cent of the pidgins and creoles in the sample.

- Pervasive in all 15 P/Cs are 'lack of inversion/lack of auxiliaries in *wh*-questions' and 'lack of inversion in main clause *yes/no* questions'.
- Pervasive in 12 to 14 P/Cs are 'special forms or phrases for the second-person plural pronoun' and 'deletion of *be*' (14 P/Cs); 'serial verbs', 'absence of plural marking after measure nouns', and 'zero past tense forms of regular verbs' (13 P/Cs) '*me* instead of *I* in coordinate subjects', '*past* tense/anterior marker *been*', '*no* as preverbal negator' and 'invariant present tense forms due to zero marking for the third-person singular' (12 P/Cs).

The features listed in this and the previous section are prime candidates for what Mair (2003) calls *angloversals*. Mair employs this term for general tendencies frequently found in the morphosyntax of both L2 varieties and P/Cs, some of which he considers to be the result of the learning strategies of non-native speakers. At the very least, three groups of relevant features can be identified on the basis of the WAMVE:

 (i) those features which are top (>75 per cent) both among L2 varieties and among pidgins and creoles, but *not* in L1 varieties of English. These include 'the lack of inversion/auxiliaries in *wh*-questions', 'zero past tense forms of regular verbs' and 'the lack of number distinction in reflexives';
 (ii) features which are exclusively top in L2 varieties: 'the use of resumptive pronouns in relative clauses', 'the loosening of the sequence of tenses rule', 'invariant non-concord tags' and 'invariant *don't* for all persons in the present tense';
 (iii) features which are exclusively top in pidgins and creoles: 'the deletion of *be*', 'invariant present tense forms due to zero marking for the third-person singular', 'serial verbs' and '*no* as a preverbal negator'.

As regards Mair's (2003) quest for 'angloversals', Sand (2005, 2008) offers a corpus-based investigation of some central morphosyntactic domains (notably article usage, tense and aspect, subject–verb concord, inversion in direct and indirect questions) in the relevant ICE-corpora of Irish English, Indian English, Jamaican English, Kenyan English and Singapore English. She, too, arrives at the conclusion that 'the non-standard forms and constructions are very similar across the corpora under analysis, regardless of the substrate languages involved in the formation of the individual varieties', thus weakening 'claims in favour of substrate evidence' (2008: 200) and strengthening the argument of the present chapter, namely that variety type outperforms geography as a predictor of the morphosyntactic profiles of Englishes around the world. In-depth knowledge about processes of early second-language acquisition helps interpret the recurrently observable feature clusters exhibited by the morphosyntax of pidgins and creoles. This point has been forcefully made in the recent literature (cf., for example, Siegel 2006 on the long history of this argument and its revival, and especially on the role of simplification and transfer in SLA and the genesis of pidgins and creoles). Similarly, Plag (2008a, 2008b) convincingly argues in favour of the so-called interlanguage hypothesis, i.e. the hypothesis that 'Creoles are conventionalized interlanguages of an early stage' (2008a: 2). Plag deplores, however, 'that there are no general metrics available according to which we can classify languages holistically as "more simple" or "less complex"' (2008a: 21). A possible solution to this problem will be outlined below and in the following section.

The morphosyntactic profiles of the major variety types

In the previous sections we have gone some way towards identifying vernacular angloversals as well as candidates for universals (or rather varioversals) of non-L1 World Englishes and, more specifically, particularly prominent features of the major variety types. In this section it will be shown that each of the major variety types (L1, L2, pidgins and creoles) have clearly identifiable morphosyntactic profiles which emerge when applying refined statistical tools to the data set in WAMVE (cf. Szmrecsanyi and Kortmann 2009a, 2009b). The relevant tool in this case is Principal Component Analysis. Using this tool for exploring the distribution of the 76 morphosyntactic features across the 46 varieties of English allows us to identify patterns of co-presence and co-absence pointing to two highly explanatory dimensions. As can be seen in Figure 23.1, the 46 varieties cluster very nicely according to whether they are L1 varieties (represented by squares), L2 varieties (represented by triangles) or English-based pidgins and creoles (represented by circles). Detailed analysis shows that this clustering according to variety type clearly explains a higher degree of the observable variance (and has to account for fewer outliers) than geography (cf. Szmrecsanyi and Kortmann 2009c). In other words, variety type turns out to be the better predictor of overall morphosyntactic similarity or distance between individual varieties than where they are spoken.

The importance of variety type in trying to account for similarities and differences in the morphosyntax of non-standard varieties of English and, thus, ultimately of the sociohistorical conditions in which the grammars of varieties have emerged and developed, should be confirmed in large-scale comparative studies of the morphosyntax of vernaculars of other languages. Moreover, there is good reason to postulate that each variety type, regardless which vernaculars of which languages we are looking at, will exhibit a characteristic morphosyntactic profile, with certain types and clusters of morphosyntactic features being present and others conspicuously absent. These overall morphosyntactic profiles, or coding strategies, can be seen to be instantiated by the two dimensions (components 1 and 2) that Principal Component Analysis (PCA) has yielded in Figure 23.1. In light of the research presented in the following section, these two

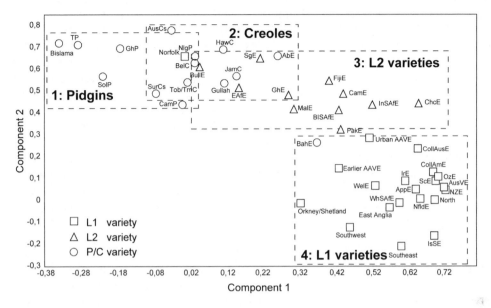

Figure 23.1 Visualization of principal components of variance in the 76 × 46 WAMVE database.
Note: Dotted boxes indicate statistically significant group membership.

components can most meaningfully be interpreted in terms of two central types of complexity, as displayed by the morphosyntax of languages and varieties thereof. These two types of complexity are, first, L2 acquisition difficulty (component 1, increasing degrees along the horizontal axis) and, second, regularity and semantic transparency for synthetic markers of grammatical information (component 2, increasing degrees along the vertical axis). Thus L1 varieties cluster in the bottom-right corner of Figure 23.1, exhibiting those (bundles) of the 76 WAMVE-features which display a low degree of transparency and are known to create most problems for (adult) learners of a language. Pidgins, on the other hand, cluster in the top-left corner: their morphosyntactic profile is characterized by a high degree of transparency and low degree of L2 acquisition complexity (cf. Szmrecsanyi and Kortmann 2009c).

In a different set of large-scale cross-varietal studies by Kortmann and Szmrecsanyi, various types or facets of structural complexity (including the degree to which grammatical information is coded analytically or synthetically) are explored on the basis of naturalistic corpus data for a smaller set of spontaneous spoken varieties (all L1 or L2). Once again, variety type turns out to be the best predictor for a given variety's morphosyntactic profile. A brief sketch of the design and major results of these studies will be provided in the following section.

Do grammars of varieties differ in degrees of complexity?

Scholars have answered yes to this question. John McWhorter (2001, 2007) made a strong case for the grammars of creoles being considerably simpler than those of much

411

older varieties and languages. Peter Trudgill (2001, 2009a, 2009b) not only sides with McWhorter as regards the low degree of complexity in creole grammars, but also claims that the grammars of high-contact varieties of English are, in general, characterized by simplification processes, whereas the grammars of low-contact varieties, i.e. essentially traditional L1 dialects, exhibit a high(er) degree of structural complexity, or even undergo complexification processes. For Trudgill, high-contact varieties range from non-standard urban varieties via non-native, indigenized L2 varieties and English-based pidgins and creoles to Standard English(es) (see 'Survey data' and especially 'Corpus data' above). Simplification relates to levelling processes and/or processes which have the cumulative effect of making life easier for adult learners of the L1 target variety, especially of the standard variety. Despite these views, the complexity debate is far from settled (cf. Sampson *et al.* 2009). To start with, the notion of 'grammatical complexity' needs to be defined and operationalized to make it the basis for cross-varietal or cross-linguistic comparison. In other words, complexity metrics are needed. It is against this background that the studies reported in Kortmann and Szmrecsanyi (forthcoming) and Szmrecsanyi and Kortmann (2009b) need to be seen.

In these studies four types of metrics of (overt, 'surfacy') morphosyntactic complexity have been explored: (i) *Ornamental rule/feature complexity*, i.e. the number of 'ornamentally complex' features (cf. McWhorter 2001) attested in a given variety's morphosyntactic inventory; (ii) *L2 acquisition difficulty*, i.e. the number of features known from SLA research to make life difficult for adults acquiring the grammar of a second language (outside the classroom); (iii) *grammaticity*, i.e. the token frequency of grammatical markers, synthetic or analytic, in naturalistic discourse; and (iv) complexity deriving from *irregularities*, or a lack of *transparency*.

The first two complexity types, *ornamental rule/feature complexity* and *L2 acquisition difficulty*, were investigated on the basis of the WAMVE survey data. The 76 morphosyntactic WAMVE features were classified as to whether they qualify as ornamental (i.e. as complicating the system of Standard English without any added communicative bonus, such as having a *be*-perfect on top of a *have*-perfect) or, in view of state-of-the-art SLA research, as L2 simplifying, such as zero past tense markers or the use of resumptive pronouns in relative clauses. On the whole, seven out of the 76 WAMVE features qualify as ornamental, and 24 as L2 simple (see the Appendix). In a second step, it was determined how many of the ornamental and the L2 simple features form part of the morphosyntax of each of the 46 varieties. In a third step, based on the assignment of the 46 varieties to one of the variety types (see Table 23.1), the averages were calculated for each of the variety types and compared. Three major results are worth noting:

(i) traditional L1 varieties clearly turn out to have more than twice as many ornamental features as all other variety types;

(ii) equally clearly, pidgins and creoles exhibit more than twice as many L2 simple features as all other variety types;

(iii) on average, L2 varieties of English have less than half of these L2 simplifying features compared with pidgins and creoles and thus behave exactly like L1 varieties in this respect.

The third and fourth type of complexity, i.e. *grammaticity* and *transparency*, were investigated using naturalistic corpus data for the 13 non-standard L1 and L2 varieties sketched in 'Corpus data', above. In connection with *grammaticity*, the token frequency was determined for *synthetic* and *analytic grammatical markers*, i.e. the number of bound grammatical markers vis-à-vis function words, in each of the varieties of English under consideration. On the basis of 1,000 random, decontextualized tokens (i.e. orthographically transcribed words) per variety and corpus giving a total of 13,000 words for these 13 non-standard varieties, the following frequency indices were calculated for each sample: (i) a *grammaticity index*, i.e. the total frequency of grammatical markers (regardless whether bound or free, thus the total frequency of both inflectional affixes and function words); (ii) an *analyticity index*, i.e. the total frequency of free grammatical morphemes (or function words); (iii) a *syntheticity index*, i.e. the total frequency of bound grammatical morphemes; and (iv) a *transparency index*, i.e. the total frequency of regular bound markers (see Szmrecsanyi and Kortmann 2009b).

Four important results can be reported:

(i) Traditional L1 varieties exhibit the highest degree of grammaticity, L2 varieties the lowest degree, and high-contact L1 varieties cover the middle ground. This can be represented by way of the following hierarchy governing grammaticity levels: traditional L1 vernaculars > high-contact L1 vernaculars > L2 varieties. This is taken as evidence in favour of claims by McWhorter and Trudgill concerning simplification, mentioned above (cf. Siegel 2004, 2008). Varieties with a

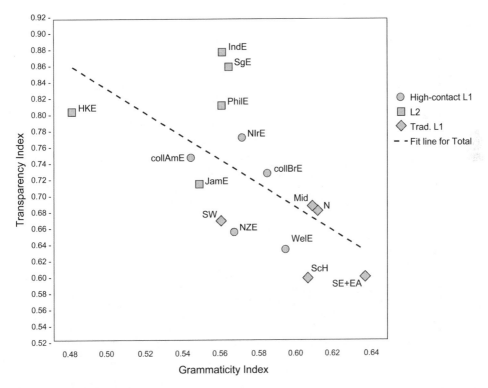

Figure 23.2 Transparency by grammaticity.
Note: Dotted trend line represents linear estimate of the relationship.

history of contact and adult language learning tend to do away with certain types of redundancy, especially those found in grammatical marking. This strategy seems to be followed most radically by L2 varieties: the corpus data suggest that L2 speakers appear to prefer zero marking over explicit marking, i.e. zero marking is even preferred over grammatical marking by means of L2 easy features.

(ii)   Traditional L1s are most synthetic and least transparent, while L2s are least synthetic and most transparent.

(iii) Transparency correlates negatively with grammaticity, i.e. the more frequently a variety makes use of (bound or free) grammatical markers, the lower is the number of transparent (i.e. regular, bound) grammatical markers, and vice versa. As shown in Figure 23.2, variety type can once again be shown to matter: traditional (or low-contact) L1 varieties clearly exhibit most grammaticity and least transparency, while L2 varieties exhibit least grammaticity and most transparency.

(iv)   In cross-variety perspective, there is no trade-off between syntheticity and analyticity. Instead, analyticity and syntheticity correlate positively such that a variety

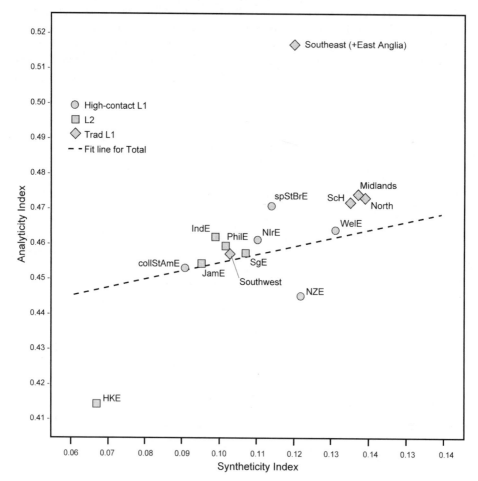

Figure 23.3 Analyticity by simplicity.
Note: Dotted trend line represents linear estimate of the relationship.

that is comparatively analytic will also be comparatively synthetic, and vice versa (see Figure 23.3). Once again, in terms of L2 varieties this is another way of saying that these tend to opt for a coding strategy of less overt marking rather than trading off synthetic marking for analytic marking, which is generally taken to be L2 easy (for an extreme example cf. Hong Kong English in the bottom-left corner).

It should be noted, though, that the astonishing absence of a trade-off between syntheticity and analyticity holds only for spontaneous spoken varieties of English; subjecting the written registers of the varieties represented in Figure 23.3 to the same method does yield the expected trade-off (cf. Kortmann and Szmrecsanyi forthcoming).

Large-scale areal patterns: a comparison of Anglophone world regions

Geography matters too

Compared with variety type, geography is only of secondary importance – this has been argued throughout this chapter. When looking at the overall morphosyntactic and complexity profiles of varieties of English around the world, there are no geographical patterns which could explain more than the dominant variety type(s) in the relevant Anglophone world region. Yet despite the higher explanatory and prognostic value of variety type, once it comes to holistic characterizations of grammars, large-scale areal patterns are also worth looking at. Geography starts to matter as soon as we explore the individual features in each variety. At least three relevant scenarios can be distinguished in which we can expect area-specific patterns and geographical differences between varieties of the same variety type to emerge on a larger scale. Such patterns on a larger scale contrast with small-scale differences, like specific features occurring exclusively in a few varieties of English spoken in one world region or special local constraints obtaining concerning otherwise widely found morphosyntactic features. A nice example of a highly regionally restricted feature is the progressive *was sat/was stood*, which is exclusively found in the British Isles (in Welsh English, Irish English and the dialects of northern England). Local constraints on otherwise widely found features may include specific syntactic contexts (including specific constructions), in which a given feature is exclusively found, special discourse types (as investigated, for example, in the new research area of variational pragmatics) or a special semantics that goes with the relevant features in a given variety or set of varieties in a given Anglophone world region (cf. e.g. Sharma 2009).

The first scenario in which we can expect large-scale areal patterns to emerge concerns the degree to which a certain aspect of the overall morphosyntactic profile is borne out in the individual varieties (e.g. the degree of grammaticity, the degree of inflectional marking or its loss, the degree of L2 simplicity). Thus South East Asian varieties of English, for example, seem to be far more radical in getting rid of inflectional endings and grammaticity, in general, than L2 varieties in other parts of the world (cf. Hong Kong English in Figure 23.3). Mesthrie and Bhatt (2008: 90–2) suggest a broad dichotomy among World Englishes of 'deleters' vs 'preservers'. Varieties qualifying as 'deleters' 'favour deletion of elements' found in Standard (L1) English

415

(e.g. deletion of (pronominal) subjects or objects in Singapore English). 'Preservers', by contrast, are varieties like Black South African English which 'disfavour the deletion of elements' like infinitive *to* (e.g. *He made me to do it*), dummy *it* after verbs like *make clear* (e.g. *As I made it clear before ...*), or complementizer *that* after *as you know, as I said* (e.g. *As you know that I am from Ciskei*).

Mesthrie and Bhatt (2008) consider Asian varieties to be typically of the deleting type and African varieties of the preserving type. This contrast is considered to be motivated by the Chinese substrate in Asia and the substrate of African languages in Africa. Thus, as soon as we say that geography starts to matter, we are saying that substrate influences matter. However, the broad dichotomy suggested by Mesthrie and Bhatt soon runs into trouble. First, compare Singapore English and Hong Kong English in Figure 23.3, where Hong Kong English is the clear outlier (i.e. an extreme case in terms of very low degrees of syntheticity as well as analyticity, amounting to a very low overall degree of grammaticity). Second, counterexamples to the Asia vs Africa generalization can easily be found, sometimes even in the same domains of grammar that Mesthrie and Bhatt (2008) considered. For example, deletion of subject pronouns and/or dummy *it* is attested for both Indian and Black South African English as well as, for example, East African English; dummy *it* deletion and object pronoun deletion are attested even for an African L1 variety, namely White South African English. The 'deletion' vs 'preservation' criterion promises to be more fruitful when capturing differences between variety types, especially between pidgins and creoles (as 'deleters') and L1 varieties ('preservers').

Geography typically translates into substrate effects leaving their imprint on the morphosyntax of varieties of English, as can be clearly seen in the second scenario: world region and specific substrate language(s) do matter once it comes to the choice of specific constructions and, in particular, lexical material used for coding a given grammatical function (e.g. the choice of tense and aspect markers, of pronouns, or of prepositions and conjunctions). A classic example is the *after*-perfect in Irish English (as in *She's after selling the boat*) which is clearly modelled on an Irish construction using the preposition *tréis* 'after' (cf. Siegel 2006: 36–7). This example from Irish English, a variety that shifted from an L2 to an L1 variety, is an example where substrate effects will be strongest and most visible in L2 varieties and in pidgins and creoles. The general story behind that is what Heine and Kuteva (2006) have labelled grammatical replication, i.e. structural change due to language contact, with restructuring and, above all, contact-induced grammaticalization as its two major types.

The third scenario where geography can be shown to matter concerns the degree of pervasiveness to which a given (set of) morphosyntactic features is represented in the different world regions. It is this third scenario which will concern the remainder of this section.

Prominent features in the individual world regions

The Anglophone world regions explored in this section are those seven investigated in the *Handbook of Varieties of English* (Kortmann *et al.* 2004), i.e. the British Isles, North America, the Caribbean, Australia, Pacific, Africa and (South and South East) Asia (recall Table 23.1). Speaking of prominent features here means either or both of two things (cf. Kortmann and Szmrecsanyi 2004: 1160–83): (a) the relevant WAMVE feature is observable in at least 75 per cent of the varieties of the relevant world region (and is thus called a top feature) and is a top feature in no other world region ('Type (a) pervasive-ness'); (b) the relevant feature is pervasive (i.e. this feature received an 'A' ranking) in every one of the varieties of the given world region ('Type (b) pervasiveness').

As for Type (a) pervasiveness, only the following morphosyntactic features are exclusively top in one and only one Anglophone world region:

North America: '*ain't* as the negated form of *be* and *have*';
Caribbean: 'completive/perfective *done*';
Australia: 'object pronoun forms serving as base for reflexives', '*that/what* as relativizers in non-restrictive contexts';
Pacific: 'the use of non-standard habitual markers other than *be* and *do*'.

For Africa, the British Isles, and South and South East Asia no such exclusively top features could be identified. The toughest criterion for Type (b) pervasiveness is an 'A' rating for every single variety of a given Anglophone world region. This is attested for the following features and world regions (the figure in brackets gives the total number of the WAMVE varieties for the relevant region):

- British Isles (8): '*there's, there is, there was* with plural subjects';
- Caribbean creoles (5): 'special forms or phrases for the second-person plural pronoun'; '*me* instead of *I* in coordinate subjects'; 'absence of plural marking after measure nouns'; 'multiple negation/negative concord'; 'lack of inversion/lack of auxiliaries in *wh*-questions'; 'lack of inversion in main clause *yes/no* questions';
- Australia (4): 'special forms or phrases for the second-person plural pronoun'; 'lack of inversion/lack of auxiliaries in *wh*-questions'; and 'lack of inversion in main clause *yes/no* questions';
- Pacific (7): 'special forms or phrases for the second-person plural pronoun' and 'lack of inversion in main clause *yes/no* questions';
- Africa (9): 'adverbs having the same form as adjectives';
- Asia (4): 'irregular use of articles'; 'inverted word order in indirect questions'; 'lack of inversion in *wh*-questions and *yes/no* questions'.

Note that the Asian varieties of English exhibit a much lower number of non-standard features compared with all other world regions. For North America not a single morphosyntactic feature received an 'A'-rating for every single of the altogether nine varieties documented in WAMVE. However, the two features listed among Type (a) pervasiveness for North America, i.e. *ain't* as the negated form of *be* and *have*, are also Type (b) pervasive in eight of the North American WAMVE varieties. This confirms that these two features are clearly the two most prominent features of this world region.

In sum, judging at the level of large-scale morphosyntactic profiles, it can be firmly stated that geographical patterns largely fall out from variety type, i.e. varioversals largely determine or at least predict areoversals. For example, the British Isles and North America are the two homogeneous L1 regions in the Anglophone world and they share almost all of the most widely documented morphosyntactic features. Similarly, the two major L2 Anglophone world regions (South and South East) Asia, a homogeneous L2 region, and Africa, a heterogeneous L2 world region, share many of the most prominent of their top features; with no other world region do they share so many top features as with each other.

417

Conclusion

A handbook chapter, like any state-of-the-art survey, can never be more than an interim report. This is true especially for such a dynamic field as the study of morphosyntactic variation in varieties of English around the world. As in so many other fields of linguistic research, English linguistics is at the forefront of research here, too. What it is now that we need in the study of morphosyntactic variation in Englishes is the following:

- more detailed descriptions of the grammars of individual varieties, not just of the forms and structures available, but also of their use;
- to study more phenomena from a comparative point of view, ideally using a more fine-grained feature classification system such as the one used in WAMVE. In a significantly larger set of morphosyntactic features (minimum size of 200 features), properties of L2 varieties and P/Cs should be more strongly represented. This project is currently under way in Freiburg;
- to interpret the large patterns presented in this chapter against other, potentially more fine-grained classifications of varieties of English. Is there, for example, a distinctive morphological and syntactic profile of shift varieties? What can we say about L2 varieties in comparison with (both early and advanced) learner varieties of English?
- to interpret the large-scale patterns and morphosyntactic profiles presented here from a historical perspective, for example against Schneider's (2007) five-stage cycle for the evolution of postcolonial Englishes and Holm's (2007) partial restructuring model.
- to explore the varioversals identified for English for the same variety types in other languages. For pidgins and creoles an important first step in this direction will be the Leipzig APiCS project (Michaelis *et al.*, *The Atlas of Pidgin and Creole Language Structures*), which is currently underway.

There is reason to be optimistic that the main argument presented in this chapter will largely be confirmed. That is to say, variety type – and not geography – is of primary importance, at least when we look at large-scale patterns, profiles and coding strategies in morphosyntax. It is to be expected that the impact of geography is stronger in phonology, in the lexicon and in phraseology.

Appendix: The WAMVE Feature Catalogue

Pronouns, pronoun exchange, pronominal gender

1   *them* instead of demonstrative *those* (e.g. *in them days*, *one of them things*);
2   *me* instead of possessive *my* (e.g. *He's me brother*, *I've lost me bike*);
3   special forms or phrases for the second-person plural pronoun (e.g. *youse, y'all, aay', yufela, you ... together, all of you, you ones/'uns, you guys, you people*);
4   regularized reflexives-paradigm (e.g. *hisself, theirselves/theirself*);
5   object pronoun forms serving as base for reflexives (e.g. *meself*);
6°   lack of number distinction in reflexives (e.g. plural *-self*);
7*   *she/her* used for inanimate referents (e.g. *She was burning good* [about a house]);
8°   generic *he/his* for all genders (e.g. *My car, he's broken*);

9   *myself/meself* in a non-reflexive function (e.g. *my/me husband and myself*);
10   *me* instead of *I* in coordinate subjects (e.g. *Me and my brother/My brother and me*);
11   non-standard use of *us* (e.g. *Us George was a nice one, We like us town, Show us 'me' them boots, Us kids used to pinch the sweets like hell, Us'll do it*);
12* non-coordinated subject pronoun forms in object function (e.g. *You did get he out of bed in the middle of the night*);
13* non-coordinated object pronoun forms in subject function (e.g. *Us say 'er's dry*).

Noun phrase

14° absence of plural marking after measure nouns (e.g. *four pound, five year*);
15   group plurals (e.g. *That President has two Secretary of States*);
16   group genitives (e.g. *The man I met's girlfriend is a real beauty*);
17   irregular use of articles (e.g. *Take them to market, I had nice garden, about a three fields, I had the toothache*);
18   postnominal *for*-phrases to express possession (e.g. *The house for me*);
19   double comparatives and superlatives (e.g. *That is so much more easier to follow*);
20   regularized comparison strategies (e.g. in *He is the regularest kind a guy I know, in one of the most pretty sunsets*).

Verb phrase: tense and aspect

21   wider range of uses of the progressive (e.g. *I'm liking this, What are you wanting?*);
22   habitual *be* (e.g. *He be sick*);
23   habitual *do* (e.g. *He does catch fish pretty*);
24   non-standard habitual markers other than *be* and *do*;
25   levelling of difference between present perfect and simple past (e.g. *Were you ever in London? Some of us have been to New York years ago*);
26* *be* as perfect auxiliary (e.g. *They're not left school yet*);
27° *do* as a tense and aspect marker (e.g. *This man what do own this*);
28° completive/perfect *done* (e.g. *He done go fishing, You don ate what I has sent you?*);
29° past tense/anterior marker *been* (e.g. *I been cut the bread*);
30   loosening of sequence of tense rule (e.g. *I noticed the van I came in*);
31° *would* in *if*-clauses (e.g. *If I'd be you, ...*);
32* *was sat/stood* with progressive meaning (e.g. *when you're stood 'are standing' there you can see the flames*);
33   *after*-perfect (e.g. *She's after selling the boat*).

Verb phrase: modal verbs

34   double modals (e.g. *I tell you what we might should do*);
35   epistemic *mustn't* ('can't, it is concluded that ... not'; e.g. *This mustn't be true*).

Verb phrase: verb morphology

36° levelling of preterite and past participle verb forms: regularization of irregular verb paradigms (e.g. *catch–catched–catched*);

419

37°   levelling of preterite and past participle verb forms: unmarked forms (frequent with e.g. *give* and *run*);

38   levelling of preterite and past participle verb forms: past form replacing the participle (e.g. *He had went*);

39   levelling of preterite and past participle verb forms: participle replacing the past form (e.g. *He gone to Mary*);

40°   zero past tense forms of regular verbs (e.g. *I walk* for *I walked*);

41*   *a*-prefixing on *ing*-forms (e.g. *They wasn't a-doin' nothin' wrong*).

Adverbs

42   adverbs (other than degree modifiers) have same form as adjectives (e.g. *Come quick!*);

43   degree modifier adverbs lack *-ly* (e.g. *That's real good*).

Negation

44   multiple negation/negative concord (e.g. *He won't do no harm*);

45°   *ain't* as the negated form of *be* (e.g. *They're all in there, ain't they?*);

46°   *ain't* as the negated form of *have* (e.g. *I ain't had a look at them yet*);

47°   *ain't* as generic negator before a main verb (e.g. *Something I ain't know about*);

48°   invariant *don't* for all persons in the present tense (e.g. *He don't like me*);

49   *never* as preverbal past tense negator (e.g. *He never came* (= he didn't come));

50°   *no* as preverbal negator (e.g. *me no iit brekfus*);

51   *was–weren't* split (e.g. *The boys was interested, but Mary weren't*);

52°   invariant non-concord tags, (e.g. *innit/in't it/isn't* in *They had them in their hair, innit?*).

Agreement

53°   invariant present tense forms due to zero marking for the third-person singular (e.g. *So he show up and say, What's up?*);

54   invariant present tense forms due to generalization of third-person *-s* to all persons (e.g. *I sees the house*);

55°   existential/presentational *there's, there is, there was* with plural subjects (e.g. *There's two men waiting in the hall*);

56   variant forms of dummy subjects in existential clauses (e.g. *they, it*, or zero for *there*);

57°   deletion of *be* (e.g. *She – smart*);

58   deletion of auxiliary *have* (e.g. *I – eaten my lunch*);

59   *was/were* generalization (e.g. *You were hungry but he were thirsty*, or: *You was hungry but he was thirsty*);

60*   Northern Subject Rule (e.g. *I sing* [vs **I sings*], *Birds sings, I sing and dances*).

Relativization

61   relative particle *what* (e.g. *This is the man what painted my house*).

62   relative particle *that* or *what* in non-restrictive contexts (e.g. *My daughter, that/ what lives in London* …).

63   relative particle *as* (e.g. *He was a chap as got a living anyhow*).
64   relative particle *at* (e.g. *This is the man at painted my house*).
65°   use of analytic *that his/that's, what his/what's, at's, as'* instead of *whose* (e.g. *The man what's wife has died*).
66   gapping or zero-relativization in subject position (e.g. *The man – lives there is a nice chap*).
67°   resumptive/shadow pronouns (e.g. *This is the house which I painted it yesterday*).

Complementation

68   *say*-based complementizers (e.g. *Him all swear seh him was going to tell me*);
69   inverted word order in indirect questions (e.g. *I'm wondering what are you gonna do*);
70   unsplit *for to* in infinitival purpose clauses (e.g. *We always had gutters in the winter time for to drain the water away*);
71   *as what/than what* in comparative clauses (e.g. *It's harder than what you think it is*);
72°   serial verbs (e.g. *give* meaning 'to, for', as in *Karibuk giv mi*, 'Give the book to me').

Discourse organization and word order

73°   lack of inversion/lack of auxiliaries in *wh*-questions (e.g. *What you doing?*);
74°   lack of inversion in main clause *yes/no* questions (e.g. *You get the point?*);
75   *like* as a focusing device (e.g. *How did you get away with that like? Like for one round five quid, that was like three quid, like two-fifty each*);
76   *like* as a quotative particle (e.g. *And she was like 'What do you mean?'*).

Notes

* 'ornamental' features
° L2 simple features

Suggestions for further reading

Filppula, M., Klemola, J. and Paulasto, H. (eds) (2009) *Vernacular Universals and Language Contacts: Evidence from Varieties of English and Beyond*, London/New York: Routledge. (Captures the vernacular universals controversy very nicely, tackling it from a sociolinguistic, typological, historical and, overall, contact perspective.)

Kortmann, B. (2006) 'Syntactic variation in English: a global perspective', in B. Aarts and A. McMahon (eds) *Handbook of English Linguistics*, Oxford: Blackwell, pp. 603–24. (Offers a survey of the most widespread features of non-standard Englishes in different domains of morphology and syntax.)

Kortmann, B., Schneider, E., Burridge, K., Mesthrie, R. and Upton, C. (eds) (2004) *A Handbook of Varieties of English, Vol. 2: Morphosyntax*, Berlin: Mouton de Gruyter. (Comprehensive collection of descriptions of the grammars of more than 60 varieties of English (L1s, L2s, P/Cs), with an interactive CD-ROM featuring, among other things, audio samples and WAMVE, the *World Atlas of Morphosyntactic Variation*.)

Mesthrie, R. and Bhatt, R.M. (2008) *World Englishes: The Study of New Linguistic Varieties*, Cambridge: Cambridge University Press. (Highly readable state-of-the-art survey addressing structural aspects of World Englishes along with pragmatics and discourse, language acquisition and language contact issues in current research on World Englishes.)

Trudgill, P. and Chambers, J. (eds) (1991) *Dialects of English: Studies in Grammatical Variation*, London: Longman. (Classic collection of early dialectological and sociolinguistic studies on morphosyntactic variation in English.)

References

Anderwald, L. and Wagner, S. (2007) 'The Freiburg English Dialect Corpus (FRED): Applying corpus-linguistic research tools to the analysis of dialect data', in J. Beal, K. Corrigan and H. Moisl (eds) *Using Unconventional Digital Language Corpora, Vol. I: Synchronic Corpora*, Basingstoke: Palgrave Macmillan, pp. 35–53.

Chambers, J.K. (2000) 'Universal sources of the vernacular', in U. Ammon, K.J. Mattheier and P.H. Nelde (eds) *The Future of European Sociolinguistics*, special issue of *Sociolinguistica: International Yearbook of European Sociolinguistics*, 14: 11–15.

——(2001) 'Vernacular universals', in J.M. Fontana, L. McNally, M.T. Turell and E. Vallduví (eds) *ICLaVE 1: Proceedings of the First International Conference on Language Variation in Europe*, Barcelona: Universitat Pompeu Fabra, pp. 52–60.

——(2003) *Sociolinguistic Theory: Linguistic Variation and Its Social Implications*, Oxford: Blackwell.

——(2004) 'Dynamic typology and vernacular universals', in B. Kortmann (ed.) *Dialectology Meets Typology*, Berlin: Mouton de Gruyter, pp. 127–45.

Du Bois, J.W., Chafe, W.L., Meyer, C. and Thompson, S.A. (2000) *Santa Barbara Corpus of Spoken American English, Part 1*, Philadelphia: Linguistic Data Consortium.

Filppula, M., Klemola, J. and Paulasto, H. (eds) (2009a) *Vernacular Universals and Language Contacts: Evidence from Varieties of English and Beyond*, London: Routledge.

——(2009b) 'Vernacular universals and language contacts: an overview', in M. Filppula, J. Klemola and H. Paulasto (eds) *Vernacular Universals and Language Contacts: Evidence from Varieties of English and Beyond*, London: Routledge, pp. 1–18.

Greenbaum, S. (1996) *Comparing English Worldwide: The International Corpus of English*, Oxford/ New York: Clarendon Press/Oxford University Press.

Greenberg, J.H. (1960) 'A quantitative approach to the morphological typology of language', *International Journal of American Linguistics*, 26: 178–94.

Heine, B. and Kuteva, T. (2006) *The Changing Languages of Europe*, Oxford: Oxford University Press.

Hernández, N. (2006) 'User's guide to FRED'. Online. Available www.freidok.uni-freiburg.de/volltexte/ 2489 (accessed 18 February 2010).

Holm, J. (2004) *Languages in Contact. The Partial Restructuring of Vernaculars*, Cambridge: Cambridge University Press.

Holm, J. and Patrick, P.L. (eds) (2007) *Comparative Creole Syntax. Parallel Outlines of 18 Creole Grammars* (Westminster Creolistics Series), London: Battlebridge.

Kirk, J. (1992) 'The Northern Ireland Transcribed Corpus of Speech', in G. Leitner (ed.) *New Directions in English Language Corpora*, Berlin: Mouton de Gruyter, pp. 65–73.

Kortmann, B. (ed.) (2004) *Dialectology Meets Typology*, Berlin: Mouton de Gruyter.

——(2006) 'Syntactic variation in English: a global perspective', in B. Aarts and A. McMahon (eds), *Handbook of English Linguistics*, Oxford: Blackwell, pp. 603–24.

——(2009) 'World Englishes between simplification and complexification', in L. Siebers and T. Hoffmann (eds) *World Englishes: Problems–Properties–Prospects*, Amsterdam: John Benjamins, pp. 265–85.

Kortmann, B. and Szmrecsanyi, B. (2004) 'Global synopsis: morphological and syntactic variation in English', in B. Kortmann, E.W. Schneider, K. Burridge, R. Mesthrie and C. Upton (eds) *A Handbook of Varieties of English, Vol. 2: Morphosyntax*, Berlin: Mouton de Gruyter, pp. 1142–202.

——(forthcoming) 'Parameters of Morphosyntactic Variation in World Englishes: Prospects and limitations of searching for universals', in P. Siemund (ed.) *Linguistic Universals and Language Variation*, Berlin: Mouton de Gruyter.

Kortmann, B. and Wagner, S. (2005) 'The Freiburg English Dialect Project and Corpus', in B. Kortmann, T. Herrmann, L. Pietsch and S. Wagner (eds) *A Comparative Grammar of British English Dialects: Agreement, Gender, Relative Clauses*, Berlin: Mouton de Gruyter, pp. 1–20.

Kortmann, B., Schneider, E.W., Burridge, K., Mesthrie, R. and Upton, C. (eds) (2004) *A Handbook of Varieties of English, Vol. 2: Morphosyntax*, Berlin: Mouton de Gruyter.

Kortmann, B., Herrmann, T., Pietsch, L. and Wagner, S. (2005) *A Comparative Grammar of British English Dialects: Agreement, Gender, Relative Clauses*, Berlin: Mouton de Gruyter.

Mair, C. (2003) 'Kreolismen und verbales Identitätsmanagement im geschriebenen jamaikanischen Englisch', in E. Vogel, A. Napp and W. Lutterer (eds) *Zwischen Ausgrenzung und Hybridisierung*, Würzburg: Ergon, pp. 79–96.

McArthur, T. (1987) 'The English languages?' *English Today*, 11: 9–11.

——(2003) 'World English, Euro English, Nordic English?' *English Today*, 19: 54–8.

McWhorter, J. (2001) 'The world's simplest grammars are creole grammars', *Linguistic Typology*, 5: 125–66.

——(2007) *Language Interrupted: Signs of Non-Native Acquisition in Standard Language Grammars*, Oxford: Oxford University Press.

Mesthrie, R. (2006) 'World Englishes and the multilingual history of English', *World Englishes*, 25: 381–90.

Mesthrie, R. and Bhatt, R.M. (2008) *World Englishes: The Study of New Linguistic Varieties*, Cambridge: Cambridge University Press.

Michaelis, S., Maurer, P., Huber, M. and Haspelmath, M. (eds) (n.d.) *Atlas of Pidgin and Creole Language Structures* (APiCS) website. Online. Available http://lingweb.eva.mpg.de/apics/ index. php/The_Atlas_of_Pidgin_and_Creole_Language_Structures. Pages used here: 'Questionnaire' and feature pages. Online. Available http://lingweb.eva.mpg.de/apics/index.php/ APiCS_Questionnaire (accessed 14 January 2009).

Plag, I. (2008a) 'Creoles as interlanguages: inflectional morphology', *Journal of Pidgin and Creole Languages*, 23: 109–30.

——(2008b) 'Creoles as interlanguages: syntactic structures', *Journal of Pidgin and Creole Languages*, 23: 307–28.

Platt, J., Weber, H. and Ho, M.L. (1984) *The New Englishes*, London: Routledge and Kegan Paul.

Pride, J.B. (ed.) (1982) *New Englishes*, Rowley, MA: Newbury House.

Sampson, G., Gil, D. and Trudgill, P. (eds) (2009) *Language Complexity as a Variable Concept*, Oxford: Oxford University Press.

Sand, A. (2005) 'Angloversals? Shared morpho-syntactic features in contact varieties of English', postdoctoral thesis, Freiburg; in preparation for Amsterdam: John Benjamins.

——(2008) 'Angloversals? Concord and interrogatives in contact varieties of English', in T. Nevalainen, I. Taavitsainen, P. Pahta and M. Korhonen (eds) *The Dynamics of Linguistic Variation. Corpus Evidence on English Past and Present*, Amsterdam: John Benjamins, pp. 183–2002.

Schneider, E.W. (2007) *Postcolonial English. Varieties around the World*, Cambridge: Cambridge University Press.

Sharma, D. (2009) 'Typological diversity in New Englishes', *English Word-Wide*, 30: 170–95.

Siegel, J. (2004) 'Morphological simplicity in pidgins and creoles', *Journal of Pidgin and Creole Languages*, 19: 139–62.

——(2006) 'Links between SLA and creole studies', in C. Lefebvre, L. White, and C. Jourdan (eds) *L2 Acquisition and Creole Genesis. Dialogues*, Amsterdam: John Benjamins, pp. 15–46.

——(2008) *The Emergence of Pidgin and Creole Languages*, Oxford: Oxford University Press.

Siemund, P. (2009) 'Linguistic universals and vernacular data', in M. Filppula, J. Klemola and H. Paulasto (eds) *Vernacular Universals and Language Contacts: Evidence from Varieties of English and Beyond*, London: Routledge, 323–48.

Szmrecsanyi, B. and Kortmann, B. (2009a) 'Vernacular universals and angloversals in a typological perspective', in M. Filppula, J. Klemola and H. Paulasto (eds) *Vernacular Universals and Language Contacts: Evidence from Varieties of English and Beyond*, London: Routledge, pp. 33–53.

——(2009b) 'Between simplification and complexification: non-standard varieties of English around the world', in G. Sampson, D. Gil and P. Trudgill (eds) *Language Complexity as a Variable Concept*, Oxford: Oxford University Press, pp. 64–79.

——(2009c) 'The morphosyntax of varieties of English worldwide: a quantitative perspective', *Lingua*, 119 (11): 1643–63.

Thomason, S.G. (2009) 'Why universals versus contact-induced change?', in M. Filppula, J. Klemola and H. Paulasto (eds), *Vernacular Universals and Language Contacts: Evidence from Varieties of English and Beyond*, London: Routledge, pp. 349–64.

Trudgill, P. (2001) 'Contact and simplification: historical baggage and directionality in linguistic change', *Linguistic Typology*, 5: 371–4.

——(2009a) 'Vernacular universals and the sociolinguistic typology of English dialects', in M. Filppula, J. Klemola and H. Paulasto (eds) *Vernacular Universals and Language Contacts: Evidence from Varieties of English and Beyond*, London/New York: Routledge, pp. 304–22.

——(2009b) 'Sociolinguistic typology and complexification', G. Sampson, D. Gil and P. Trudgill (eds) *Language Complexity as a Variable Concept*, Oxford: Oxford University Press, pp. 98–109.

Trudgill, P. and Chambers, J. (eds) (1991) *Dialects of English: Studies in Grammatical Variation*, London: Longman.

24

Mixed codes or varieties of English?

James McLellan

Introduction

This chapter is based on the premise (truism) that speakers and writers of World Englishes have access to other languages in the linguistic ecosystem of their national or local community. These languages contribute to the variety of English used for their intranational communication. They include languages learned as a first language in the home, and those acquired informally through social interaction in the community and formally within the educational domain.

In these contexts English can be considered as an overlay, as the other languages are not usually replaced by English but are retained, and they function as communicative resources for the construction of varieties of English. Fijian, Malaysian, Bruneian, Indian, Kenyan and Nigerian Englishes provide excellent examples.

This chapter investigates the consequences of this pattern of multilingual overlaying, and the hypothesis that World Englishes are by definition code-mixed varieties, mainly from a linguistic perspective, but with some reference to sociolinguistic issues.

The linguistic analysis draws mainly on a corpus of Brunei online discussion forum texts, and highlights single Malay nouns and nominal groups inserted into English main-language texts. In so doing they exert an influence on the main language, English.

Sociolinguistics, being 'the study of speakers' choices' (Coulmas 2005: 1), leads us to pursue a line of enquiry which suggests a threefold choice, between

- using the local language(s) monolingually,
- using an exonormative variety of English monolingually,
- using a mixed code which can be regarded as a separate variety which is unmarked in some multilingual contexts.

Background and frame of reference

Much of the scholarship in World Englishes (WEs) has understandably sought to relate these Englishes to the L1 or inner circle varieties spoken in the United States of America, the United Kingdom, Canada, Australia and New Zealand. This tendency also applies in related fields such as English as an International Language (EIL), and in the more recent impassioned debates over English as a lingua franca (ELF). In seeking to make these linkages between WEs and the Centre varieties, we may fail to take full account of the intranational roles and functions that are central to the definition of the institutionalized, norm-developing Englishes found in parts of West and East Africa, the Caribbean, and in South and South East Asia.

An alternative framework is proposed here, influenced by the pioneering work of Mufwene (2001, 2004) and drawing on theories of language contact (Thomason and Kaufman 1988; Thomason 2001). This takes the institutionalized varieties as autonomous, and describes them in terms of their contact with other languages in the contexts in which they developed. For example, Singapore English (whether 'standard' or 'colloquial') can usefully be described with reference to other languages in the Singaporean linguistic ecosystem (e.g. Bao 2005). Singapore English can thus be distinguished from neighbouring South East Asian Englishes in Malaysia, Brunei and Indonesia, by virtue of the unique patterns and processes of contact which have brought about its development in the local context, in parallel to Singapore's development from colony to independent nation-state. Likewise Malaysian and Brunei English have been found to differ, partly as a result of the different roles of English in these neighbouring multilingual polities, but in part also through the mediation of the distinct varieties of Malay which distinguish Brunei from Malaysia.

One criterion for determining the existence of these varieties is that they have intranational, as distinct from international, functions (Platt *et al.* 1984: 2–3). They are used between inhabitants of the country concerned, and have a tendency to become identity markers and even objects of pride for their users. The archetypal example of this is the oft-cited remark of T.T.B. Koh about Singapore English (e.g. Tongue 1979: 4):

> when one is abroad in a bus or train or aeroplane and when one overhears someone speaking, one can immediately say that this is someone from Malaysia or Singapore. And I should hope that when I'm speaking abroad my countrymen will have no problem recognizing me as a Singaporean.

There is nothing new or original in this autonomous approach to the analysis of World Englishes. It is in some respects a regression towards older Contrastive Analysis paradigms, which sought to account for 'interference' and 'transfer' features, but then became entangled in arguments over behaviourist approaches to second-language acquisition.

The languages in the linguistic ecosystem of each national or local community contribute to the variety of English used for their intranational communication. These may comprise languages learned as a first language in the home, as well as those acquired informally through social interaction in the community, or learnt formally within the educational domain. This aspect of language contact has been more thoroughly researched in the field of Pidgin and Creole Linguistics. One model of pidgin and subsequent creole language development posits one or more local vernacular 'base' languages which supply grammatical features, and a 'lexifier' language which is usually a colonial language of wider communication (Todd 1974: 1–11; Holmes 2001: 83; Mufwene 2001: 3–4; Thomason 2001: 159–62). The base language, for example Motu in Papua New Guinea, may be referred to as 'substrate', and the lexifier, for example English for Tok Pisin, as 'superstrate'.

Investigation of varieties of English from this 'substrate' perspective will naturally tend to foreground differences, rather than commonalities, but it will also portray the indigenized Englishes as autonomous and dynamic, and as part of a multilingual ecosystem.

This chapter thus investigates both the linguistic and the sociolinguistic consequences of this pattern of multilingual overlaying, and the hypothesis that World Englishes are by definition code-mixed varieties.

Review of relevant literature: 'substratum' perspectives

Two relevant frameworks for such an investigation are Mufwene's (2001: 3–6, 106–25) theory of the feature pool, and Kachru's (1994) dual notions of 'Englishization' of local languages and 'nativization' of English. These both point towards a conceptualization of World Englishes as code-mixed varieties, which develop in contexts where speakers and writers have other code choices as well as English available to them. Chitravelu (2007: 236–7) has recently labelled these paradigmatic choices as a research priority within multilingual South East Asian societies.

Mufwene's feature pool theory seeks to explain processes of language contact: creolization and koinéization. Features from both the superstrate languages of the colonizing powers and those languages spoken in the colonized territories are available for selection for the creation and development of new varieties. One example, discussed by Mufwene (2001: 52) with reference to Melanesian English pidgins, is the inclusive/exclusive first-person distinction, which derives from local vernacular languages: 'yumi': inclusive, 'mipela': exclusive. Both of these would be expressed by 'we/us' in English.

A modified version of Kachru's nativization/Englishization model was used by Rosnah et al. (2002) to investigate both processes in the context of Brunei: Englishization of the Brunei variety of Malay, alongside nativization of English. For the purposes of this chapter the main focus will be unidirectional, investigating the influence of Malay, especially Brunei Malay, on English texts. Exemplification is principally from Negara Brunei Darussalam (Brunei), where Bahasa Melayu (Malay) is the national and official language, and where the Brunei variety of Malay is an important marker of national and ethnic identity and the main lingua franca (Martin 1996; Jaludin Haji Chuchu 2003). Although high levels of multilingualism can be found in Brunei, the salience of Brunei Malay makes it easier to identify its influence in English texts produced by Bruneians. Ożóg's (1987, 1993) pioneering studies provide initial descriptions of features of Brunei English as a code-mixed variety, emphasizing the influence of both the standard and the Brunei varieties of Malay (see also Chitravelu and Rosnah 2007).

In common with other research into aspects of language contact, the question can be approached from both linguistic and sociolinguistic perspectives. The challenge, as pointed out by Gardner-Chloros and Edwards (2004) with specific reference to code-switching research, is to merge these two strands. In pidgin and creole linguistic research an earlier focus on the lexifier or 'superstrate' languages has been counterbalanced by greater attention to the roles played by the 'substrate' languages (e.g. Migge and Smith 2007; Lim and Gisborne 2009: 125–31).

A focus on the 'substratum' thus serves to counterbalance the bias in research towards the 'English' in World Englishes, and may shed more light on the contribution of the local languages. 'Substratum' is, however, a contested term, as the substrate/ superstrate model might be seen as implying superiority of the colonizers' languages over local indigenous languages. Hence it is used with reservations, for want of a better term, and appears in inverted commas.

Brunei English examples

The data examples discussed here are from McLellan (2005), with some reworking of the categories used in that study. They are taken from two Brunei online discussion forums, thus they are examples of computer-mediated, as opposed to spoken or written, communication. Computer-mediated communication (CMC) is defined by Herring (1996: 1) as 'communication that takes place between human beings via the instrumentality of computers'. Data from such a source does not of course allow for analysis of phonological influence deriving from 'substrate' languages, hence the focus is on lexis and syntax.

A corpus of 211 texts, with a total word count of 31,513, was initially categorized according to five language classifications as shown in Table 24.1.

Appendix A contains texts or extracts from texts in all these five categories. Categories (2), (3) and (4) are those in which some measure of language alternation (code-switching) occurs. These categories apply to the whole text, calculated by means of a word count and a count of the syntactic groups. Table 24.1 shows that 49.8 per cent of the texts show some measure of language alternation, whilst 50.2 per cent are monolingual English or monolingual Malay. For this chapter the major interest lies in category (2), main-language English (i.e. with some Malay insertions) and category (3), equal language alternation.[1]

1

Auction stuff: *Frankly speaking,* /[1] baiktah   jangan   dibali   barang[2]
                         good-DM NEG-IMP PASS-buy RDP-thing

yg   kena \\[2] *auction* /[3] atu   bukannya   apa \\[4], *if we buy them, in a way, we*
REL PASS   DEM, NEG-3s-POSS what

are helping those who have used /[5]   duit   ketani \\[6] *for their personal interest, to*
                              money 1pi-POSS

pay for their debts. /[7] Mana tia yang dulu \\[8]*the famous* /[9]7 org   atu?
                  Where DM REL before   ABBR-person DEM

Inda kedengaran \\[10] *Has the trial started? It's so sad, isn't it, how our beloved*
NEG hearing

country /[11]   jadi   cemani.
              become like-DEM

Table 24.1 Presence/absence of language alternation in corpus of 211 postings

	Language classification	Number of postings	% of total
1	English only (E-)	83	39.3
2	Main-language English (ML-E)	36	17.1
3	= Language Alternation (= LA)	12	5.7
4	Main-language Malay (ML-M)	57	27.0
5	Malay only (M-)	23	10.9

Auction stuff: Frankly speaking, it's better not to buy the things that are being auctioned, isn't it right, that if we buy them, in a way, we are helping those who have used our money for their personal interest, to pay for their debts. Wherever are the famous seven people from before? We don't hear of them anymore. Has the trial started? It's so sad, isn't it, how our beloved country has come to this.

(Data source: Brudirect HYS, posting 2.58)

In this text English is predominant by the word-count criterion: 43 words as against only 21 Malay words. It has eleven English-only syntactic groups, three mixed groups and nine Malay-only groups, and is thus classified = LA. As indicated by the forward and back slashes, there are eleven switching points within this short text, demonstrating a high level of bilingual proficiency on the part of the anonymous producer, and a comparable expectation of equivalent bilingual proficiency on the part of the reader. Texts with complex switching of this type challenge the asymmetric matrix–language–frame model of code-switching (Myers Scotton 1993, 2002, 2006), which claims that the matrix language supplies the syntactic frame whilst the embedded language supplies only lexical items.

Text (1) is also notable for mixing Brunei Malay with a formal standard and grammatically accurate variety of English. Outside of the Malay sections, the English shows no 'substratum' influence. The use of the Brunei Malay noun phrase 'duit ketani' ('money our' = 'our money'), inserted into a stretch of English, illustrates that code choice is deliberate and strategic here, since the writer could equally well have used the English noun phrase 'our money'. The Malay phrase is chosen for its emotive and rhetorical effect.

The following examples of nouns and noun phrases from the 'substratum' language, Malay, show a variety of patterns of alternation, for which different motives are suggested.

Single or 'bare' nouns

This is the simplest category, where a single Malay noun is inserted into a stretch of main-language English text, as in example set (2). Apart from proper nouns (including local place-names and references, and pseudonyms of previous message posters), these are the only examples of single Malay nouns found in ML-E environments in the online discussion forum corpus.

2   Bare/single Malay nouns in ML-E environments:

(a) *Jones can give all he's* '<u>alasan</u>' *to the public like 2 players are still schooling* lah

reason   DM

Jones can give all his reasons to the public, such as that two players are still at school (2.28)

(b) *maybe after all I live under* <u>tempurung</u>

coconut shell

maybe after all I live under a coconut shell (3.28)

(c) JPM *for this matter should be thankful that they have avenue to look at* <u>rakyat</u> *argument*

PM's Department   people

The Prime Minister's Department should be thankful that they have an avenue to look at the people's arguments (3.40)

(d) *So* <u>rakyat</u> *could make formal complain*

people

So the people could make formal complaints (3.40)

(e) *There are ample parking spaces in most* <u>masjid</u>

mosques

There are ample parking spaces in most mosques (4.1)

In each case, as shown by the free translations, morphological markers required by English syntax do not occur, suggesting that the insertion of the single Malay nouns influences the syntax of the sentence. In (2a) and (2e) the context shows that the Malay nouns are to be interpreted as plural (reasons, mosques): Malay nouns can reduplicate to show plurality, but reduplication only occurs when plurality is not retrievable from the surrounding context. In (2a) the Malay noun 'alasan' is flagged by inverted commas: the message topic is the national soccer team coach giving explanations to the local media for the poor performance of the team. Example (2b) is a reference to the Malay idiom 'katak dibawah tempurung' (frog under a coconut shell), which describes someone with limited horizons and little knowledge of the wider world. The use of the Malay noun causes deletion of the required English indefinite article. The lexeme 'rakyat' ('people') would require the definite article in both (2c) and (2d) to conform to standard English syntax. In (2b) the mixed noun phrase 'rakyat *argument*' follows the modifier-head word order of English, but the possessive ('s) is not attached to the Malay noun. In (2e) the reference is clearly plural: in this posting the writer is complaining about Bruneians' tendency to double-park outside mosques at the Friday prayers.

As with 'duit ketani' in (1) above, there may be cultural or emotive reasons for the switch to the Malay single nouns 'rakyat' and 'masjid': the writers may feel that the English terms 'people' and 'mosques' do not carry the same emotional and rhetorical weight.

Many similar examples of Malay lexemes have been found to occur in the English language print media in Brunei and in Malaysia, both in news report texts and in headlines (Lowenberg 1991; David and McLellan 2007; David *et al.* 2009).

Noun phrases

In example set (3) all the examples contain more than one word of Malay, and the Malay head-modifier nominal group structure is maintained. There are no examples of Malay nouns and their modifiers following the English modifier-head structure: forms such as *'malam pasar' or *'melayu bangsa' do not occur.

3 Malay nominal groups in main-language English environments:

(a) *BAN*   pasar malam
           market night
    Ban the night market (1.26)

(b) *As for the men out there who resort to* 'pujuk   rayu' *or coercion to demand sex...*
                                             persuade coax
    As for the men out there who resort to coercion to demand sex (2.12)

(c) *the Concept* MIB *had suppressed certain group of individual especially*   puak2 lain
                                                                            RDP-group other
    the MIB concept has suppressed a certain group of individuals, especially other ethnic groups (3.39)

(d) *... and there is no more* bangsa   melayu
                               race   Malay
    and there is no more Malay race (3.41)

(e) *Are we still*   berkonsepkan MIB? *I wonder*
                    concept

Are we still following the MIB concept? I wonder (3.41)

(f) *when I went for*   jalan-jalan
                              RDP-walk
    when I went for a walk around (3.45)

These are all set phrases in Malay which collocate closely. 'Pasar malam' occurs frequently in English speech among expatriates resident in Brunei, in preference to the English equivalent 'night market'. 'Puak2 lain' shows the use of the numerical abbreviation for the plural reduplication: in more formal written text this would appear as 'puak-puak lain'. In example (3b) there is flagging of the Malay phrase, and this is a rare case of a parallel English translation being provided. Example (3c) shows the Malay head-modifier order applied to the mixed nominal group 'Concept MIB', even though it occurs in an English syntactic frame with the definite article present. The absence of the indefinite article, also omitted in (3f), and the absence of plural marking on 'individual' are further evidence that the grammatical systems of both English and Malay are operative here, signifying a further challenge to the matrix-embedded language distinction.

Malay influence in English-only texts

Even in texts which are English-only with no Malay insertions, there is evidence of 'substrate' influence from Malay. These are among the characteristic features of Brunei English, which may also be found in neighbouring South East Asian Englishes where Malay or related Austronesian languages form part of the linguistic ecosystem. They have also been analysed as shifts between formal and informal varieties of English, or between acrolects, mesolects and basilects, where the basilectal varieties – Manglish in Malaysia, Singlish in Singapore, Taglish in the Philippines, and Brulish or Brunglish in Brunei – show the greatest amount of 'substrate' influence.

Features discussed by other researchers include the absence of plural marking. Example set (4) shows instances of absent plural marking from English-only texts in the online discussion forum corpus.

4

(a) *I hope the management would train their staff properly so that next time incident like this wouldn't happen again* (2.11)

(b) *the Concept MIB had suppressed certain group of individual* (3.39)

(c) *But I guess the effort will be futile because as the BB* said the customer would just shop outside the border* (3.42)
    * = abbreviation for Borneo Bulletin newspaper

Variation between count and non-count nouns is another frequent feature of South East Asian Englishes (Platt *et al.* 1984: 46–52). In set (5) there are two examples from the corpus which show 'advice' used as a countable noun, as also noted by Cane (1994: 354) with specific reference to Brunei English.

5

(a) *Just a simple comment and advice to all out there. We all know how 'upset' we are with the current situation in Brunei* (1.15)

(b) *An advice to THOR*, lift the veil from your inner eye* (1.57)
    * = pseudonym of previous message poster

In verb phrases the past conditional 'would' occurs in place of 'standard' English 'will' as a future tense auxiliary (Svalberg 1998: 336–7). The examples in set (6) from the discussion forum corpus support Svalberg's analysis.

6

(a) *I would make sure that those who applied have the means to service the loan. Otherwise, I would be accused in the future of generating bad loans and also mismanagement* (2.3)

(b) *I hope the management would train their staff properly so that next time incident like this wouldn't happen again* (2.11)

(c) *They intent to monopolise the market using the copyright act as an excuse. So they are the one initiating all the raids because they <u>would</u> end up making lots of money* (3.42)

(d) *But I guess the effort will be futile because as the BB* said the customer <u>would</u> just shop outside the border* (3.42)
   * = abbreviation for Borneo Bulletin newspaper

(e) *I am going on leave now and <u>would</u> be back in January 2002 to share my views, advice, proposals (all constructive of course)* (3.20)

Svalberg (1998: 338–9) also discusses instances of the past perfect found in non-past contexts. Examples (7a) and (7b) show this occurring:

7

(a) *But let us be rational that the Concept MIB <u>had</u> suppressed certain group of individual* (3.39)

(b) *My father <u>had</u> just retired from Government service and has limited funds to do a few vital renovation to his house at Kampong Rimba* (4.32)

For similar examples to (7b) from her corpus, Svalberg (1998: 339) offers the plausible explanation that in Brunei English the past perfect has a 'stage-setting' function when used in discourse contexts where the time reference has yet to be established. An alternative analysis, proposed by Noor Azam and McLellan (2000: 9–10), is that in Brunei English both have/had and will/would occur in free variation. Examples (6d) and (7b), above, offer support for this view.

Parallel studies by Deterding (2000) and by Poedjosoedarmo (2000) of Mandarin and Malay influence on Singapore English show that it is not always easy to determine whether distinctive constructions in World Englishes arise from 'substratum' influence. Nor in the case of Singapore can one be certain whether the influence is from Mandarin, other Chinese languages or from Malay. In Brunei, however, where Malay is the predominant 'substrate' language, the lack of inflectional morphology for signalling tense and aspect in Malay may be a contributory factor to the variability found in Brunei English.

Rich intrasentential alternation

Moving outside the original corpus, similar patterns of language alternation continue to occur in the Brudirect HYS forum, even though the website has now been restructured in order to separate postings and discussion in English and Malay.

Example text (8) is taken from a recent posting on the site, and can be compared with text (1):

8
Breaking News in Brunei – '(airline) pilot stab filipino dance instructor'
/[1] Hari bulan kurang lebih 27-Nov-08: Ada satu \\[2]*(airline) pilot caught*/[3]
    Day month less more   have one

ia punya \\$^4$*Wife in bed (in her 40s)* /^{5} sama \\$^6$*married Filipino* /^{7}(iatu \\$^8$
3s POSS   with   3s-DEM

supposedly her dancing instructor /^{9} lah) dan \\$^{10}$*stabbed him* /^{11} dgn
                                                              DM and   ABBR-with

pisau,   \\$^{12}$ *subsequently pilot* /^{13} ni pun terus \\$^{14}$*reported himself* /^{15} ke \\$^{16}$
knife   DEM DM straightaway   to

police, /^{17} dan *Filipino* ni \\$^{18}$ *was admitted* /^{19} ke RIPAS \\$^{20}$ ICU! / ^{21} Ia \\$^{22}$*Wife*
                and   DEM   to (hospital)   3s

/^{23} ni \\$^{24}$ has *been well-known* /^{25} d \\$^{26}$ *local community as well as* /^{27}d
     DEM   ABBR-in   ABBR-in

Belait \\$^{28}$ *District*/^{29} jua \\$^{30}$, *for 'man-izing'. Despite* /^{32} banyak
                                       also   many

berapa \\$^{33}$ *occasions* /^{34} udah \\$^{35}$ *indecent affairs being caught,* /^{36}
how many   already

unfortunately /^{37} tak \\$^{38}$ *taken as lessons learnt* /^{39} lah.\\$^{40}$ *Wife* /^{41} ni \\$^{42}$
                                NEG   DM   DEM

was previously a (airline) air stewardess /^{43} jua, \\$^{44}$ *renowned for*
                                                                    also

such hyper-activities with crews /^{45} ya, ia pun \\$^{46}$ *own few game shops in town* …
                                                           yes 3s DM

(Data source: www.bruneiclassified.com/newhys/category/english-postings)

This short extract contains a total of 46 switches, and demonstrates a remarkable level of interplay between the Brunei Malay and English grammatical systems. At various points the constraints of Myers Scotton's (1993) matrix-language frame theory are challenged:

> 'satu (airline) pilot', 'Ia punya wife' and 'pilot ni' are mixed noun phrases with
>   English heads and Malay modifiers
> 'sama married Filipino', 'ke police' and 'despite banyak berapa occasions'
>   show switches between the prepositions and noun phrases they govern

Text (8) also shows how CMC texts are akin to informal spoken interaction, as this extract mirrors the way bilingual Bruneians alternate in speech. The use of 'man-ize' as a logical counterpart to 'womanize', and 'hyper-activities' are illustrations of bilinguals' creativity in the coining and use of original but logical lexical items, akin to the Indian English lexeme 'prepone'.

Two further examples of = LA texts, showing rich mixing of English and Malay, are provided in Appendix B for readers who may like to conduct their own analysis. Those with no knowledge of Malay can follow the suggestion made by Jacobson (2001: 69) and determine whether the overall sense of the text can be understood from the English alone. If this is not possible, then it would suggest that both languages are contributing jointly to both the grammar and the meaning.

Discussion: a separate code-mixed variety?

In all the examples drawn from the Brunei online discussion forum corpus there is no suggestion that the 'substrate' Malay insertions impede the intelligibility of the texts for the targeted readership. In fact the converse is more likely: texts producers draw on lexical resources of both languages in order to achieve message clarity, aware that their readers, who are fellow members of this online discourse community, have a comparable level of bilingual proficiency in English and Malay.

Code-switching research literature (e.g. Myers Scotton 1993: 8), has raised the important argument as to whether code-mixed texts constitute a separate 'third code', distinct from both the languages which contribute to the mix. This issue has also been discussed recently in the context of World Englishes by Kirkpatrick (2007: 127–8). Clearly example texts (1) and (8) can be classified neither as pure Malay, nor as pure English. McLellan's (2005) study concludes that the Brunei CMC context is unlike the research contexts out of which the separate third code hypothesis has evolved, e.g. the Philippines (Marasigan 1983), the Puerto Rican community in New York (Poplack 1988) and the former Zaire, now Congo (Meeuwis and Blommaert 1998; Blommaert 1999). These researchers argue that the mixed code has become the normal, unmarked choice for interaction, and that monolingual communication is a marked choice. In Brunei CMC discourse, on the contrary, monolingual English and monolingual Malay postings are unproblematic, as shown by the frequency of their occurrence (Table 24.1). The variable language choices within the threads of postings on the same topic also demonstrate this clearly. Those who choose English-only or Malay-only are not necessarily making a marked choice, as they know that their texts will be fully accessible to their intended readership, as are the texts showing intricate patterns of language alternation.

Hence a more valid model, based on the evidence presented here, would be a continuum of code choices, as presented earlier in Table 24.1, available to members of the Brunei online discourse community, with categories (1) (English-only), (2) (main-language English) and (3) (equal language alternation) all qualifying as sub-varieties of Brunei English.

Conclusion

One major focus of World Englishes research has been the search for features in common between the varieties, a tradition which goes back at least as far as Platt *et al.* (1984), for which the underlying rationale is the investigation of issues of mutual intelligibility. It is hoped that the approach taken in this chapter will demonstrate the potential for further research into all the languages that co-exist in local and national linguistic ecosystems. Researchers and users may then come to realize that World Englishes are by definition code-mixed varieties, deriving their features from a diverse pool, as described by Mufwene (2001).

Appendix A

Example texts for each category listed in Table 24.1

1 English only (E-)
I am proud of Brunei. Everybody here is treated the same irrespective of race, religion and colour. When one fills in forms, there is no need for one to differentiate between race nor religion. You see, we trust each other. I am proud of that. We preach for moderation and tolerance and harmony and respect. We are proud of our richness in culture, our country is the more richer because we tolerate diversities. I am proud that we can live together in harmony despite our differences and diversities. We are proud of ourselves because through the teaching of our elders, we are trusted to distinguish ourself between right and wrong. (1.39)

2 Main-language English (ML-E)
Nop, you're wrong Dear. I think you miss my point as well as   C-Daun's *point*
                                              (name)

All the cases such as /[1] 'dadah belabih-labih, kes rogol,\[2] *domestic abuse*/[3], rasuah etc.
                   drug   RDP-more   case rape   corruption

have nothing to do with /[5]MIB. MIB\[6] *is the concept that our gov't is and is going to be*
                       (Malay Islamic monarchy*)

     Free translation:
     No, you're wrong dear, I think you miss my point as well as C-Daun's point. All the cases such as more and more drugs, rape cases, domestic abuse, corruption, etc., have nothing to do with MIB. MIB is the concept that our government is and is going to be.

    Note = Melayu Islam Beraja, Bruneian national ideology

3 Equal language alternation (= LA)
For your info ah, as a teacher, I come across so many different students with so many

different backgrounds, /[1] baik anak pehin atau org2   biasa,   betukar
                    good child (title) or   person-RDP ordinary AV-change

sudah \[2] *attitude* /[3] kanak2   sekarang ani,\[4] *and also the parents, they work hard*
already   child-RDP now   DEM

to achieve good results and parents /[5] nya   pun \[6] *very* /[7] bertanggung jawab \[8]
                     3pPOSS DM   support   answer

and /[9] berfikiran terbuka\[10] *and educated* …
     thinking open

Free translation:
For your info, ah, as a teacher I come across so many different students with so many different backgrounds, both the children of Pehins* and of ordinary people, now the children's attitudes have changed, and also the parents, they work hard to achieve good results and their parents are very responsible, open-minded and educated people.
* Pehin: title conferred by the Sultan on those of non-royal and non-noble birth for distinguished service, corresponding to a UK knighthood.

4   Main-language Malay (ML-M)
   As for me, Bruclass /¹ ani \²*my mind opener* /³ walaupun ada   masanya \⁴ *idea* /⁵
                          DEM   although   have time 3s-POSS

   atu   inda sehati   dengan \⁶*contributors. I have also been proud* /⁷ meliat \⁸
   DEM NEG one-heart with   AV-see

   idea-idea /⁹ yang diusulkan   menunjukkan anak2   Berunai ani   pintar
   RDP   REL PASS-originate AV-show   RDP-child Brunei DEM smart

   dan befikiran. Mungkin cara penyampaian seseorang atu   berbeda\¹⁰ *and* /¹¹
   and thoughtful Maybe   way presentation one-person DEM AV-differ

   ada masanya   tunggang tebalik panjang \¹² (*like me*) *and* /¹³ payah   kan
   have time-3s-POSS topsy-turvey   long   difficult FUT

   di \¹⁴ *comprehend, but at the end of the day it's one opportunity* /¹⁵untuk diorang
   PASS-   for   3p

   meluahkan isihati   demi. kepentingan negara. Samada   diterima
   AV-reveal contents-heart for   interest   nation same-have PASS-receive

   atau inda atu   terserahlah ...
   or   NEG DEM   PASS-offer-DM

Free translation:
As for me, Bruclass has opened my mind, although at times my ideas are not in line with those of the contributors. I have also been proud to see original ideas showing that Bruneians are smart and thoughtful. Maybe their manner of presentation is different and at times topsy-turvy, lengthy (like me) and hard to comprehend but at the end of the day it's one opportunity for people to open up their hearts in the national interest. Whether they're accepted or not, they're freely offered. (3.26)

5   Malay only (M-)
   Selama ani   aku perhatikan RBA inda ada   peningkatan apalagi
   During DEM 1s   AV-observe RBA NEG have improvement what-again

   kemajuan, apalagi   sekarang ani dengan pentadbiran   yang diambil   alih
   progress   what-again now   DEM with administration REL PASS-take move

daripada shike   Jamal, banyak perkara yang diselindungi dan ada   perkara yang
from   Sheikh (name) many   matter REL PASS-hide and have matter REL

inda perlu dibuat   jadi   dibuat   tampa, memikirkan akibatnya
NEG should PASS-do happen PASS-do without AV-think   outcome-3s-POSS

contohnya   penerbangan keHongkong   untuk apa? lisen   untuk berjual
example-3s-POSS flight   to-Hong Kong for   what licence for   AV-sell

tiket juga belum dapat sudah   membuat penarbangan kesana dan kesurabaya,
ticket also not yet get   already AV-make flight   to-there and to-Suarabaya

penerbangan permulaannya   waktu petang tapi kenapa sekarang dirubah
flight   inaugural3s-POSS time   evening but why   now PASS-change

kepagi,   apakah   sudah   difikirkan   sebelum ianya   dijalankan,
to-morning what-INT already PASS-think before 3s-3s-POSS PASS-operate

dan berapa banyak sembutan penumpang yang mengunakan jadual
and how   many   receive   passenger REL   AV-use   schedule

penambahan ini.
addition   DEM

Free translation:
Recently I have observed that Royal Brunei Airlines has neither improved nor pro-
gressed, especially now that the administration has been taken away from Sheikh
Jamal. There are many matters which have been covered up, and some things that
should not have happened have been done without thinking of the consequences, for
example, why the flight to Hong Kong? The licence to sell tickets has not yet been
obtained but already they are flying there and also to Surabaya, the inaugural flight
was in the evening but why has it now been changed to the morning, has this all
been thought through before being implemented, and what has been the response of
those passengers using these additional scheduled flights? (4.31)

Appendix B

Additional = LA texts for readers' own analysis (see p. 434 main text)

1   *After reading* /[1] komen-komen di laman ini \[2] *I wonder what happened to our*/[3]
     bahasa jiwa bangsa \[4] *has it become so* /[5] rojak \[6] *– is the language we are
     using called* /[7] dwibahasa \[8] *now – hey c'mon you all* /[9] kalau Pengarah Dewan
     Bahasa membaca laman ani \[10] *he will surely FREAK OUT! I remember his call
     to keep* /[11] Bahasa Melayu \[12] *pure when using your SMS and this column is
     hardly an SMS! C'mon* /[13] dwibahasa \[14] *does not mean* /[15] rojak \[16] *– you learn
     another language (English in our case) as a second language* /[17] untuk

menambah ilmu – \\[18] *sorry, beg your pardon, I know, I know* /[19] aku pun sama juga – cakap inda serupa bikin!\\[20] *Case closed!*

(Brudirect HYS Forum 2002)

2   *So if JP Management* /[1] betul-betul \\[2] *thinking of profits and service, then they should open the park during* /[3] Hari Raya \\[4] (*worst to worst, close only one day* /[5] Hari Raya \\[6]). *JP Playground is our only source of good family entertainment.* /[7] Sudah tah banyak \\[8] *rides* /[9] yang rosak, kan ditutop tia lagi \\[10]. *Crazy management.* /[11] Mudah-mudahan \\[12] *GE will come back and take over the whole complex like in the good old days.* (4.34)

Note

1 Transcription and glossing conventions used in this paper (and see 'Abbreviations, p. xx'):
      Citation from the online discussion forum postings is verbatim; English text is in *italics*.
      '-2', in the top line of text following nouns, signals reduplication of the noun (e.g. barang2 = barang-barang, 'things').
      Numbers following the free translation indicate the posting in the corpus from which the example is taken.
      / \\ : slash and backslash marks denote English > Malay and Malay > English switches, numbered within full-text extracts.

Suggestions for further reading

Readers wishing to read more on World Englishes as mixed codes, and on 'substratum' influences, may like to refer to these:

The articles in the special Issue of *English World-Wide* 30 (2), edited by Lisa Lim and Umberto Ansaldo.
Siegel, J. (2008) *The Emergence of Pidgin and Creole Languages*, Oxford: Oxford University Press.

References

Bao, Ximing (2005) 'The aspectual system of Singapore English and the systemic substrate explanation', *Journal of Linguistics*, 41: 237–67.
Blommaert, J. (1999) 'Reconstructing the sociolinguistic image of Africa: grassroots writing in Shaba (Congo)', *Text*, 19 (2): 175–200.
Cane, G. (1994) 'The English language in Brunei Darussalam', *World Englishes*, 13 (3): 351–60.
Chitravelu, N. (2007) 'Multilingualism in Southeast Asia: a tentative research agenda' in D.L. Prescott (ed.) *English in Southeast Asia: Literacies and Literatures*, Newcastle-upon-Tyne: Cambridge Scholars Publishing, pp. 224–45.
Chitravelu, N. and Rosnah, Haji Ramly (2007) 'English–Malay border crossings: a study of code-switching in Brunei Darussalam' in Lee Su Kim, Thang Siew Ming and Lee King Siong (eds) *Border Crossings*, Kuala Lumpur: Pelanduk Publications, pp. 5–19.
Coulmas, F. (2005) *Sociolinguistics: The Study of Speakers' Choices*, New York: Cambridge University Press.
David, M.K. and McLellan, J. (2007) 'Nativised varieties of English in news reports in Malaysia and Brunei Darussalam', in D.L. Prescott, T.A. Kirkpatrick, I.P. Martin and Azirah Hashim (eds) *English*

in Southeast Asia: Literacies and Literatures, Newcastle-upon-Tyne: Cambridge Scholars Publishing, pp. 94–119.

David, M.K., Kuang Ching Hei, McLellan, J. and Ain Nadzimah, Abdullah (2009) 'Code-switching practices in newspaper headlines in Malaysia: a 50-year comparative study and lexical analysis', in M.K David, J. McLellan, S. Rafik-Galea and Abdullah Ain Nadzimah (eds) *Code Switching in Malaysia*, Frankfurt am Main: Peter Lang, pp. 179–201).

Deterding, D. (2000) 'Potential influences of Chinese on the written English of Singapore', in A.A. Brown (ed.) *English in Southeast Asia '99*, Singapore: Division of English Language and Applied Linguistics, NIE, Nanyang Technological University, pp. 201–9.

Gardner-Chloros, P. and Edwards, M. (2004) 'Assumptions behind grammatical code-switching: when the blueprint is a red herring', *Transactions of the Philological Society*, 102 (1): 103–29.

Herring, S. (1996) *Computer-mediated Communication: Linguistic, Social and Cross-cultural Perspectives*, Amsterdam: John Benjamins.

Holmes, J. (2001 [1992]) *An Introduction to Sociolinguistics*, Harlow: Pearson Education.

Jacobson, R. (2001) 'Language alternation: the third kind of codeswitching mechanism', in R. Jacobson (ed.) *Codeswitching Worldwide II*, Berlin: Mouton de Gruyter, pp. 59–76.

Jaludin Haji Chuchu, Haji (2003) *Dialek Melayu Brunei dalam Salasilah Bahasa Melayu Purba*, Bangi, Malaysia: Penerbit Universiti Kebangsaan Malaysia.

Kachru, B.B. (1994) 'Englishization and contact linguistics', *World Englishes*, 13 (2): 135–54.

Kirkpatrick, T.A. (2007) *World Englishes: Implications for International Communication and English Language Teaching*, Cambridge: Cambridge University Press.

Lim, L. and Gisborne, N. (2009) 'The typology of Asian Englishes: setting the agenda', *English World-Wide* 30 (2): 123–32.

Lowenberg, P. (1991) 'Variation in Malaysian English: the pragmatics of languages in contact', in J. Cheshire (ed.) *English around the World: Sociolinguistic Perspectives*, Cambridge: Cambridge University Press, pp. 364–75.

McLellan, J. (2005) 'Malay–English language alternation in two Brunei Darussalam online discussion forums', unpublished PhD thesis, Curtin University of Technology, Australia.

Marasigan, E. (1983) *Code-switching and Code-mixing in Multilingual Societies*, Singapore: RELC.

Martin, P.W. (1996) 'Brunei Malay and Bahasa Melayu: a sociolinguistic perspective', in P.W. Martin, A.C.K. Ożóg and G.R. Poedjosoedarmo (eds) *Language Use and Language Change in Brunei Darussalam*, Athens, OH: Ohio University Center for International Studies, pp. 27–36.

Meeuwis, M. and Blommaert, J. (1998) 'A monolectal view of code-switching: layered code-switching among Zairians in Belgium', in J.P. Auer (ed.) *Code-switching in Conversation*, London: Routledge, pp. 76–97.

Migge, B. and Smith, N. (2007) 'Substrate influence in creole formation', *Journal of Pidgin and Creole Languages*, 22 (1): 1–15.

Mufwene, S. (2001) *The Ecology of Language Evolution*, Cambridge: Cambridge University Press.

——(2004) 'Language birth and death', *Annual Review of Anthropology*, 33: 201–44.

Myers Scotton, C. (1993) *Duelling Languages: Grammatical Structure in Codeswitching*, Oxford: Clarendon Press.

——(2002) *Contact Linguistics: Bilingual Encounters and Grammatical Outcomes*, Oxford: Oxford University Press.

——(2006) *Multiple Voices: An Introduction to Bilingualism*, Malden, MA: Blackwell.

Noor Azam, Haji Othman and McLellan, J. (2000) 'Brunei culture, English language: textual reflections of an Asian culture located in the English-language output of Bruneians', *Asian Englishes*, 3 (1): 5–19.

Ożóg, A.C.K. (1987) 'The syntax of the mixed language of Malay-English Bilinguals', *RELC Journal*, 18 (1): 72–90.

——(1993) 'Brunei English: a new variety?' in J.T. Collins (ed.) *Language and Oral Traditions in Borneo: Selected Papers from the First Extraordinary Conference of the Borneo Research Council, Kuching Sarawak, Malaysia*, Williamsburg, VA: Borneo Research Council, pp. 54–68.

Platt, J., Weber, H. and Ho, M.L. (1984) *The New Englishes*, London: Routledge.

Poedjosoedarmo, G. (2000) 'Influences of Malay on the written English of university students in Singapore', in A.A. Brown (ed.) *English in Southeast Asia '99*, Singapore: Division of English Language and Applied Linguistics, NIE, Nanyang Technological University, pp. 211–19.

Poplack, S. (1988) 'Contrasting patterns of codeswitching in two communities', in M. Heller (ed.) *Codeswitching: Anthropological and Sociolinguistic Perspectives*, Berlin: Mouton de Gruyter, pp. 215–43.

Rosnah, Haji Ramly, Noor Azam, Haji Othman and McLellan, J. (2002) 'Englishization and nativization processes in the context of Brunei Darussalam: evidence for and against' in T.A. Kirkpatrick (ed.) *Englishes in Asia: Communication, Identity, Power and Education*, Melbourne, VIC: Language Australia, pp. 95–112.

Svalberg, A.M.-L. (1998) 'Nativization in Brunei English: deviation vs standard', *World Englishes*, 17 (3): 325–44.

Thomason, S.G. (2001) *Language Contact: An Introduction*, Edinburgh: Edinburgh University Press.

Thomason, S.G. and Kaufman, T. (1988) *Language Contact, Creolization and Genetic Linguistics*, Berkeley: University of California Press.

Todd, L. (1974) *Pidgins and Creoles*, London: Routledge and Kegan Paul.

Tongue, R.K. (1979 [1974]) *The English of Singapore and Malaysia*, Singapore: Eastern Universities Press.

25

Semantic and pragmatic conceptualizations within an emerging variety

Persian English

Farzad Sharifian

Introduction

This chapter presents a semantic–pragmatic account of Persian English, an emerging variety of English among Persian speakers, from the perspective of *cultural conceptualizations.* Cultural conceptualizations are conceptual structures such as *schemas*, *categories*, and *metaphors* that emerge from the interactions between members of a cultural group. The chapter elaborates on a number of significant Persian cultural schemas, such as *âberu* and *târof*, and explores how they underlie the semantic and pragmatic aspects of certain words and expressions in Persian English, in contexts both of intercultural and intracultural communication. The study calls for similar explorations of cultural conceptualizations in other varieties of English, to provide a basis for improving people's *metacultural competence,* a competence which is needed for successful communication in those contexts in which English functions as an international language.

Numerous books and journal articles have been published dealing with the linguistic, sociolinguistic and sociopolitical aspects of the spread of English world-wide. However, there is a place for approaching World Englishes from the point of view of other recent advances in the study of language, such as cognitive linguistics and cultural linguistics (Sharifian 2006; Polzenhagen and Wolf 2007; Wolf, this volume). This chapter explores the study of World Englishes from the emerging perspective of cultural conceptualizations (Sharifian, 2003, 2008a). As a preamble, the following section elaborates on the notion of cultural conceptualizations, followed by examples of the application of this framework to the study of Aboriginal English and African English. The remaining sections of the chapter will discuss how the semantic and pragmatic aspects of Persian English may be characterized in terms of Persian cultural conceptualizations.

Cultural conceptualizations

Rather than describing an objective reality, languages are largely used to communicate the ways in which their speakers *conceptualize* experiences of different kinds. Even the very basic notions of 'time' and 'space' are the product of human conceptualization and are not, as sometimes thought, concrete structures that exist independently of a particular conceptual system. Moreover, the resources that we use in our conceptualization of experience are not limited to our cognitive life. We use our bodies as well as objects and entities around us in making sense of the world. Our conceptual system interacts with culture at a further level, in the sense that we constantly negotiate and renegotiate our conceptualizations with other members of our cultural group. What emerges from our constant interactions is a system of conceptual structures such as *schemas* (or the more complex ones called *models*), *categories* and *metaphors* between the members of a cultural group across time and space. I refer to such conceptualizations collectively as *cultural conceptualizations* (Sharifian 2003, 2008a). Languages embody the cultural conceptualizations of their speakers and also often act as archives for the sociohistorical developments of the conceptualizations of their speakers.

Cultural conceptualizations have a collective life. This level is technically referred to as *emergent level* (Johnson 2001), but the discussion of this falls beyond the scope of this chapter. Furthermore, cultural conceptualizations are *heterogeneously distributed* across the minds in a cultural group in the sense that they are not equally imprinted in the mind of every individual member of the cultural group. Without wishing to enter too much into theory here, I maintain that World Englishes should be differentiated and explored in terms of not just their phonological and syntactic dimensions, but also in terms of the cultural conceptualizations that underpin their semantic and pragmatic levels. The following section provides examples of this approach to World Englishes from the studies that have been conducted so far.

Cultural conceptualizations in World Englishes

Thus far, the framework of cultural conceptualizations has mainly been used to explore two varieties of World Englishes: Australian Aboriginal English and African Englishes. Recent research on Aboriginal English has shown that various features of this indigenized variety of English are associated with Aboriginal cultural conceptualizations. Even everyday words such as 'family' and 'home' evoke cultural schemas and categories among Aboriginal English speakers that largely characterize Aboriginal cultural experiences (e.g. Sharifian 2005, 2006, 2007). The word 'family', for instance, is associated with categories in Aboriginal English that move far beyond the usual referent of the 'nuclear' family in Anglo-Australian culture. A person who comes into frequent contact with an Aboriginal person may be referred to using a kin term such as 'brother' or 'cousin' or 'cousin brother' (Malcolm and Sharifian 2007: 381). The word 'mum' may also be used to refer to people who are referred to as 'aunt' in Anglo-Australian culture. Such usage of kinship terms does not stop at the level of categorization, but usually evokes schemas associated with certain rights and obligations between those involved. The word 'home' in Aboriginal English usually evokes categories that are based on family relationships and not so much the building occupied by a nuclear family. For instance, an Aboriginal English speaker may refer to their grandparents' place as 'home'.

Polzenhagen and Wolf (2007) investigate cultural conceptualizations in African English by analysing linguistic expressions from the domains of political leadership, wealth and corruption. They observe that the African cultural model of 'community' is characterized by conceptualizations of kinship, such as COMMUNITY MEMBERS ARE KIN and LEADERS ARE FATHERS. Polzenhagen and Wolf also observe that the African models of 'leadership and wealth' are both largely metaphorically conceptualized in terms of EATING. This is reflected in sentences such as *They have given him plenty to eat*, which is used in Cameroon when a new government official is appointed (see also Wolf and Polzenhagen 2009). Against this background, the following section focuses on the case of the emerging variety of Persian English from the perspective of cultural conceptualizations.

English in Iran and the emerging variety of Persian English

There has been an unprecedented growth in the use and learning of English in Iran in the last decade. New language schools are opening across the country on a daily basis and the number of Iranians attending English classes is increasing exponentially. The motivation for this heightened interest in learning English varies from individual to individual; some pursue this as part of their attempt to travel or migrate to other countries and others have educational or occupational motivations. There are also people who learn English because of the 'prestige' associated with it.

English is also increasingly being used on the internet and in electronic communications, even between Persian-speaking people themselves (see, for example, www.xzamin. com/forum/). Several years ago the Iranian government launched a satellite transmitting three channels. Most programmes carry an English translation in the form of either subtitles or an optional dubbed voice. All of this appears to be leading to the emergence of a variety of English that I would call 'Persian English'. A thorough treatment of the linguistic structures of Persian English falls beyond the scope of this chapter, as the main aim here is to provide examples of cultural conceptualizations in this variety, as detailed in the following section.

Cultural conceptualizations in Persian English

I maintain that many lexical items and phrasal expressions in Persian English instantiate Persian cultural conceptualizations. These include everyday words from various domains such as greetings. In this section, I elaborate on this theme by providing several examples.

Âberu

Aryanpur Persian–English Dictionary (1984) defines *âberu* as 'respect, credit, prestige, honour'. Some other bilingual dictionaries also give 'reputation' as an English equivalent of *âberu*. I maintain that *âberu* captures a complex cultural schema that overlaps with the concepts given by the bilingual dictionaries but also includes elements that are not covered by them. The closest concept to *âberu* in other cultures is that of 'face' (e.g. Leech 1983; Hill *et al.* 1986; Brown and Levinson 1987; Matsumoto 1988; Ide 1989; Spencer-Oatey 2000) and in fact *âberu* literally means 'the water of the face' (*âb* = water, *ru* = face). Originally 'face' was a metonym for how a person as a whole would appear to others: that is, their social image. The inclusion of *âb* in the concept is associated with its connotative meanings that include 'healthy appearance' and 'sweat'. In the first sense, 'water of the face' could be interpreted as the healthy appearance of one's face, which is reflective of things such as wealth. In the second sense, 'the sweat of the face' is a metonym for cases where one is sweating due to losing face.

Âberu in contemporary Persian captures conceptualizations of the social image and status of a person and/or their family, both nuclear and extended, and their associates and friends. This social image and face is tied to a large number of social norms in relation to financial status, behaviour, both linguistic and non-linguistic, and social relationships and networks. It is hard to find something that one does or has that would not have any implications for or impact on one's *âberu*. Thanks to the significance of this schema in the life of Persian speakers, the word is used very frequently (the interested reader can Google 'aberoo' to see the number of websites that contain the word) and in many different forms of expression in conversation. The following are some examples of its usage:

Âberu rizi kardan (pouring *âberu*) '~to disgrace'
Âberu bordan (taking *âberu*) '~to disgrace'
Âberu kharidan (buying *âberu*) '~saving face'
Âberu dâri kardan (maintaining *âberu*) '~maintaining face'
Bi âberu (without *âberu*) '~disgraced'
Âberu-dâr (*âberu*-POSS) '~respectable, decent'

As a Westerner who has lived in Iran, O'Shea (2000: 101) maintains that for Iranians '*Aberu*, or honour, is a powerful social force. All Iranians measure themselves to a great extent by the honour they accumulate through their actions and social interrelations'. This accumulated *âberu*, or the lack of it, determines who one would expect to marry, the kind of career one is expected to pursue and, in general, what sort of behaviour is expected from a person from a particular family background. In a sense, a family's *âberu* acts as a pointer for social classification and stratification.

The cultural schema of *âberu* is expressed through words such as 'honour', 'reputation', 'pride' and 'dignity' in Persian English. The following examples written by Persian-speaking expatriates are from various web pages:

I think the problem is more giving too much value to your social picture. We have even an important word for it in Farsi, Aberoo, that I don't know of a good English equivalent for it. So maybe we should pay less attention about how people think about us, and try to be the way, that we would like ourselves to be. Back in Iran, I was always frustrated by arguments like 'We should not do this, since our "Aberoo" would be compromised'.

(http://freethoughts.org/cgi-bin/mt-comments.cgi?entry_id=594)

Some of us eyeranians [Iranians] have this weird concept of *Aberoo* or honor of our outside persona we try to protect so dearly at any cost.

(www.eyeranian.net/?p=992)

Thank you for your valuable insights. First of all: The Nuclear Energy issue is a matter of national pride for each and every Iranian. If Iran stops now it will be a shame for the entire country. In Persian there is a saying 'Aberoo e ma miree'. It means our dignity and respect will be gone.

(http://muslimunity.blogspot.com/2006/03/impact-of-sanctions-on-iran.html)

It is clear from the first two quotes above that some Iranians have developed a conscious awareness of, and some even a negative attitude towards, this cultural schema. This is more common among the Persian speakers who live outside Iran and is likely to be a consequence of exposure to cultures in which 'face' does not play a significant role in people's lives.

As mentioned above, Persian English is also increasingly being used among Persian speakers to communicate with each other, partly through its convenience, English being the main language of the internet. In cases of intra-cultural communication, the word *âberu* is often used without an attempt to render it in English, such as in the following cases:

good idea, we only have our aberoo left in that game and putting in the subs is a good way to blow it and become the Saudi Arabias of 06.

(from an archive of www.irankicks.com/ikboard/)

Many important concepts in our culture, one's ABEROO, for example, is placed above almost anything else.

(http://freethoughts.org/archives/000318.php)

Please tell Reza that I hope some other Reza will be found to do some 'Aberoo Rizi' for his Concert. Exactly the same as what he did for 'AmAn''s one.

(www.haloscan.com/comments/nazlik/111660745918695958/)

While clearly showing that English is now being used for intra-cultural communication between speakers of Persian, these examples also suggest that the speakers are aware of the lack of an exact equivalence for the concept of *âberu* in English but fully recognize its importance in Persian culture.

Târof

Several authors have noted the significance of the notion of *târof* in Persian as a communicative strategy (Hodge 1957; Assadi 1980; Hillman 1981; Asdjodi 2001; Koutlaki 2002; Eslami Rasekh 2005). *Târof* is a cultural schema that underlies a significant part of everyday social interactions in Persian. Its realization in conversations may be in the form of 'ostensible' invitations, repeated rejection of offers, insisting on making offers, hesitation in making requests, giving frequent compliments, hesitation in making complaints, etc. Often, a combination of these occurs, in varying degrees, within one conversation, with all parties involved. It is often not easy to tease out genuine attempts from *târof*, and that is why speakers constantly ask each other not to engage in *târof*, but to ensure that the communicative act is a genuine one. The following excerpt, from the author's personal data, reveals the instantiation of this cultural schema in Persian conversations:

1 *L:*   *Miveh   befarmâyin*
        fruit   eat:polite.form
        'Please have some fruit.'

    S: *Merci   sarf   shodeh*
         thanks   I   have.had
         'Thanks, I have had some.'

L: *Khâhesh mikonam   befarmâyin,   ghâbel-e   shomâ   ro   nadâreh*
      please   eat:polite.form   worthy-of you DO-marker it.is.not
      'Please have some, they are not worthy of you'

S: *Sâhâbesh ghabel-eh, dast-e-toon   dard   nakoneh,*
      its.owner worthy-is hand-of-your pain   doesn't
      'You are worthy, thanks'

L: *Torokhodâ   befarmâyin,   namak   nadâreh*
      for.God's.sake   eat:polite.form   salt   doesn't.have
      'For God's sake please have some, it has no salt'

S: *Târof   nemikon-am, tâzeh   shâm   khord-im*
      târof   don't-I   just   dinner had-we
      'I don't do *târof*, we just had dinner'

L: *Ye   dooneh portaghâl be oonjâhâ nemikhoreh*
      one orange   is   not that   much
      'One orange wouldn't be that much'

S: *Chashm, dast-e-toon   o   kootâh nemikon-am*
      okay   hand-of-your DO.marker short   will.not-I
      'Okay, I won't turn down your offer'

The general aim of the cultural schema of *târof* is to create a form of social space for speakers to exercise face work, and also to provide communicative tools to negotiate and lubricate social relationships. It also provides a chance for interlocutors to construct certain identities and images of themselves, for example to portray themselves as very hospitable. Persian society traditionally revolves around social relations. Almost all forms of social institution in Iran, from marriage to employment and business, hinge upon social relations. Usually a person's ability to exercise and respond to *târof* appropriately has a significant bearing on their social relationships. Beeman (1986) compares personal relations in Iran to an art that requires sophisticated verbal skills.

Several authors have noted the absence of the Persian concept of *târof* in English and have used various labels to describe it, including 'ritual courtesy' (Beeman 1986: 56), 'communicative routine' (Koutlaki 2002: 1741), 'ritual politeness' (Koutlaki 2002: 1740) and 'polite verbal wrestling' (Rafiee 1992: 96, cited in Koutlaki 2002). Koutlaki observes that *târof* 'is a very complex concept, carrying different meanings in the minds of native speakers [of Persian] and baffling anyone endeavouring to describe it'. Beeman (1986: 196) maintains that:

> tæ'arof is the active, ritualized realization of differential perceptions of superiority and inferiority in interaction. It underscores and preserves the integrity of cultu-rally defined roles as they are carried out in the life of every Iranian, every day, in thousands of different ways.

Some non-Iranian writers have naively described *târof* as 'insincerity' or even 'hypocrisy'. For example, de Bellaigue (2004: 14) states that

You should know about *ta'aruf*. In Arabic *ta'aruf* means behaviour that is appropriate and customary; in Iran, it has been corrupted and denotes ceremonial insincerity. Not in a pejorative sense; Iran is the only country I know where hypocrisy is prized as a social and commercial skill.

The root of the cultural schema of *târof* dates back to pre-Islamic Persia, especially to the teachings of Prophet Zartosht (Zarathushtra) (Beeman 1986; Asdjodi 2001), although the word itself is Arabic in origin. The core principles of Zoroastrian religion are 'good words', 'good thoughts' and 'good deeds', known in English as three Gs. The use of kind words in Zoroastrian religion is not merely a virtue but a kind of prayer (www3.sympatico.ca/zoroastrian/Avesta.htm). It is also a pivotal part of one's identity as a Zoroastrian. It should be emphasized that this use of kind words is not just a matter of verbal display, but should be backed by good thoughts, and that is why I refer to the whole system as a cultural schema rather than just a set of linguistic strategies. In other words, *târof* is a conceptual system, which feeds into not only speech but also behaviour, as 'good deeds'. O'Shea (2000: 122) observes that *târof* in Persian has both physical and verbal manifestations. She notes that 'the former consist of activities such as jostling to be the last through the door, seeking a humble seating location, or standing to attention on the arrival or departure of other guests'. Assadi (1980: 221) also observes that 'Ta'arof is a generic term which denotes a myriad of verbal and *non-verbal* deferential behaviours in Persian' [emphasis added].

Two websites have discussed *târof* metaphorically in terms of 'war', 'dance' and 'game'. Taghavi (www.iranian.com/HamidTaghavi/Oct98/Tarof/index.html) likens *târof* to war because of the repeated exchanges that take place between interlocutors, during which they constantly make offers, reject offers, give compliments, etc. The Persian Mirror web page views *târof* as 'a verbal dance between an offerer and an acceptor until one of them agrees' (www.persianmirror.com/culture/distinct/distinct.cfm#art). On the same web page, *târof* is considered as an art that 'in the end becomes a ritual or a game that both participants are aware of playing'.

Since the inner circle varieties of English do not have an identical cultural schema for *târof*, speakers of Persian English may use words such as 'compliment' or 'courtesy' to refer to it. They may also use the original Persian word in their use of English for intra-cultural communication with other speakers of Persian. A glance at some Persian chat rooms revealed examples such as the following:

A: *What do you do that is very Persian?*
B: *Me ... I tarof a lot*
C: *I always like watching americans accept the offer and the immediate look of slight shock on the Iranians face before recomposing themselves. Hahaha.*
(www.xzamin.com/forum/read.php?forumid=4619& forumind = forum)

Interestingly, the website of the Iranian Singles Network (www.iraniansingles.com/) has a section under every person's profile with the title 'having etiquette/tarof kardan', where the members need to specify the extent to which they like or exercise *târof*. As can be seen, *târof* here is translated as 'etiquette'. Other words that may be used in Persian English to capture the concept of *târof* are 'formal' and 'formality'. Consider the following example from a movie which was broadcast on Jam-e-Jam Satellite Channel (speaker A is talking to speaker B at the door of B's house):

A: *Biâ too* (meaning 'Come in').
   Subtitle: 'Come in.'
B: *Mozâhem nemisham* (meaning 'I won't bother you').
   Subtitle: 'I won't trouble you.'
A: *Târof nakon* (meaning 'don't do *târof*').
   Subtitle: 'Stop being formal.'
B: *Na jooneh to, bâyad beram* (meaning 'no, really I have to go').
   Subtitle: 'Thanks, I have to go.'

In light of the observations made so far in this chapter about *târof*, it is clear that it is not intrinsically a display of formality. In fact, the above exchange does not reflect a formal conversation. Both speakers are using singular forms to address each other, which is one characteristic of a familiar style. If the conversation had been formal, they would have used plural forms: *biâyin* 'come:PL' instead of *biâ* 'come:SG', *nakonin* 'don't do:PL' instead of *nakon* 'don't do:SG', and *shomâ* 'you:PL' instead of *to* 'you:SG'.

Shakhsiat

Târof is closely tied to the concept of *shakhsiat*, which has been translated into English variously as 'character', 'personality', 'pride' (Koutlaki 2002) and 'integrity' (Eslami Rasekh 2005). Koutlaki (2002: 1742) observes that *shakhsiat* 'is a complex concept which could be rendered as "personality", "character", "honour", "self-respect", "social standing"'. She relates *shakhsiat* to politeness and the expected codes of behaviour, in the sense that those who observe 'politeness' are considered as having *shakhsiat*. Thus, it is conceptualized as an attribute that one can have developed to various degrees, depending on variables such as family background, level of education, etc. *Shakhsiat* is at least partly tied to *târof* in the sense that one's ability to exercise appropriate *târof* is an indication of heightened *shakhsiat*.

An important point about the concept of *shakhsiat* is that it is a multifaceted notion and a polysemous word. It can refer to one's character if used in contexts such as (2) below:

2 Shakhsiat-e ajib   o   gharibi   dâreh.
   personality-a strange and   peculiar   has-he/she
   'He/she has a strange personality'

However, it is predominantly a concept that is defined in relation to the way one's outward, including verbal, behaviour, is perceived by society. Unlike *âberu*, which is very much tied to social stratification and social groupings, such as family status in the Iranian society, *shakhshiat* is primarily construed as the result of an individual's concerted efforts in constructing a socially acceptable image of *shakhs* 'person' in the eyes of others. It is, however, a dynamic concept in the sense that people can gain or lose *shakhshiat*, for example by not exercising appropriate *târof*.

Concepts such as 'character' and 'personality', and more so 'individuality', which are often viewed as the equivalent of *shakhsiat*, primarily capture the qualities that make up a person as an individual rather than a member of a social group. Koutlaki (2002: 1743) recognizes that giving *shakhsiat* 'to an addressee has to do with society's

449

injunctions about paying face, and also with group face wants'. As can be seen in the quote, *shakhsiat* is conceptualized as something that a speaker can give to an addressee, for example by somehow saving their face in communication. Koutlaki compares *shakhsiat* to Brown and Levinson's (1987) notion of 'positive face' and observes that, although the two notions are similar, there are also important differences between them. As indicated above, *shakhsiat* is a person's concern with societal face, whereas 'positive face' reflects 'a person's individual want to be desired, respected, and liked, and to have her wants shared by others' (Koutlaki 2002: 1743). It may be said that in English, your 'personality' is defined by what you do when no one is watching you, but your *shakhsiat* is the result of what you do and say when people are watching you.

In Persian English, the cultural schema of *shakhsiat* is usually instantiated through the use of words such as 'with/without character or high/low character' (for *bi/bâ shakhsiat*), 'honour' (for giving *shakhsiat*). Someone who is *bâ shakhsiat* 'with *shakhsiat*' is often referred to as 'gentle', or 'polite'. However, it should now be clear that the conceptualizations that are associated with such words in Persian English may not be exactly the same as those which characterize other varieties of English.

The cultural schema of *târof* also underlies the ways in which words such as *zahmat* 'trouble' are interpreted. The cultural schema profiles a request or a favour in terms of what must be gone through by the person who fulfils the request rather than the speech act initiated by the person who makes the request. Consider the following example.

3 Yek zahmat barât   dâr-am,   misheh   in   nâmaro barâm post koni?
   One trouble for.you have-I   is.it.possible this letter   for.me post do-you
   'I have a request, could you post this letter for me?'

Here the act of posting a letter may be construed in different ways depending on whether it is the intention of the speaker that is highlighted, or the effect that it will have on the hearer. In cases such as the above, if it is the intention of the speaker which is highlighted, then the act is construed as a 'request' but if its *effect*, or potential effect, on the hearer is foregrounded, then it may be construed as 'trouble'. In Persian, most often the latter holds – that is, speakers construe their requests and whatever has been done for them as *zahmat,* 'trouble', for the person addressed. Note that sentence (3) could have been formulated as *yek taghâza azat dâram* 'I have a request for you', rather than *yek zahmat barât dâaram* 'I have a trouble for you', but this option is rare in Persian. The following examples (4–6) reveal other contexts in which a service, a favour, is construed as *zahmat*.

4 (An excerpt from a leave-taking conversation between a visitor and the host)
   (a) Bebahkhshin zahmat dâd-im
        Forgive (us) trouble gave-we
        'Sorry for giving you the trouble'
   (b) Khâhesh mikonam, khooneyeh   khodetoon-e
        Please   house   yours-is
        'Please, it is your house'

5 Merci bâbateh   zahmat-i ke   keshid-i,   lebâsa-m o otoo kard-i
   thanks for trouble-the that   went through-you dress-mine DO marker iron did-you
   'Thanks for ironing my dress'

6 Zahmat   bekesh   yek   châyi   barâm   biâr
  trouble   take   one   tea   for me   bring-you
  'Please bring me a cup of tea'

In Persian English, the use of the word *trouble*, in the above sense, is very common in the context of requests, services and favours. It is also frequently used to express gratitude. A sentence such as *sorry to give you the trouble* is not so much an act of apology but an expression of gratitude. Other words that may be used in such circumstances are *bother* and *inconvenience*. Thus again, *so sorry to bother you* and *so sorry for the inconvenience* may be simple acts of thanking a person for favours such as making someone a cup of tea. They could also be used as part of ending a telephone conversation, to foreground and acknowledge the time that the hearer has spent talking to the speaker on the phone. In the following section I discuss the locus of *târof* in the act of greetings in Persian English.

Greeting in Persian English

Greeting in Persian English often follows the patterns of greeting in Persian. In Persian, greetings usually go far beyond the act of acknowledging the other person. The phrases that are used to refer to greeting in Persian include *salâm va ahvâlporsi* 'greeting and asking about health' and *sâlam va adab* 'greeting and expressing politeness', and *salâm o târof*. This is due to the fact that the Persian cultural schema of greeting overlaps with other schemas such as *adab* (Sharifian 2004) and *târof*. The schema usually encourages enacting several, often repeated, communicative acts that reveal the speaker's care about not only the interlocutor but also his/her extended family (see Beeman 1986: 181; Taleghani-Nikazm 2002: 1811). In viewing *târof* as the Iranian style of war, Taghavi observes that in Persian conversations 'greetings start with the inevitable exchange of an array of compliments and the ensuing battle to convince the other party of their relative high status. This is similar to diplomatic efforts preceding a war' (www.iranian. com/HamidTaghavi/Oct98/Tarof/index.html). O'Shea (2000: 79) observes that '[g]reetings take up a lot of time in Iran. Not only does one usually inquire about someone's health, but also about the health of any of that person's friends and relatives with whom one is acquainted.' The author of this chapter noted that in a language school in Iran, some teachers made the following exchange part of every greeting they made:

Speaker A: How's your folks?
Speaker B's response: Everyone says hello to you.

A very frequent part of greeting in Persian is sending greetings to family members, even if the speaker does not know the interlocutor's family. Often, the speaker just says *salâm beresoonid*, 'give my regards'.

The Persian cultural schema of *salâm o ahvâlporsi* also involves 'ostensible' invitations. Eslami Rasekh (2005: 473) observes that in Persian culture, ostensible invitations 'are primarily used as opening or closing telephone conversations or in face-to-face encounters, which may function as a leave-taking act and an expression of good will on the part of the inviter'. She notes that 'by using invitation in leave-taking, the host not only shows respect (*ehterâm*) to the guest, but also enhances his/her own face by offering hospitality'. Eslami Rasekh rightly argues that such invitations are manifestations of *târof*, discussed above. She maintains that 'offering such invitations are [sic] part of the art of knowing how to make *ta'arof* (ritual politeness), in order to be *bâ šæxsiat* (polite) and not to incur bad reputation: that is, to live up to the society's expectations' (2005: 479).

The fact that such aspects of the Persian cultural schema of greeting may surface in Persian English is reflected in Eslami Rasekh's (2005: 453) remark on her own experience that

> Over the years of my intercultural experiences in the United States and observation of other Iranian/American interactions, I have witnessed that Iranians sometimes take Americans' genuine invitations as ostensible (not to be taken seriously) and therefore reject them, while Americans may take Iranian ostensible invitations as genuine and accept them.

This is, of course, not to imply that all invitations that are offered as part of greeting and leave-taking among Persian speakers are ostensible. Usually the sincerity of invitations hinges upon how far the invitation is extended in the exchange, who is inviting who, and in what context.

Terms of address

Persian has a rather elaborate system of honorifics and address terms which are largely associated with cultural conceptualizations that speakers of Persian learn as part of their socialization into the language (Keshavarz 2001). For example, the concepts of *âghâ* and *khânom*, which are usually rendered as *Mr* and *Mrs* in Persian English, are associated with a cultural schema that not only encodes gender but also expresses a certain degree of respect. Thus a speaker of Persian English may use *Mr X* or *Mrs X* to express some form of respect, and not just to highlight the person's gender. In the above frame, X could be a person's first name or surname. The latter involves a higher degree of formality and distance between the addressor and the addressee. If a person has a title such as Doctor, the formal form of address for him/her would then be *âghâyeh* or *khânomeh Doctor (surname)*, which may be expressed in Persian English as *Mr/Mrs Dr (surname)*. It should be mentioned that the surname is often dropped in conversations. This is reflected in Persian English sentences such as (7), which was part of an email to the author.

7 Hello Mr Dr

Conceptualizations of emotions in Persian English

A major part of human life is the experience of emotions. However, the ways in which people conceptualize their emotional experience and the ways in which they express their emotions may vary across different cultures (e.g. Wierzbicka 1999). For example, people across different languages and cultures may attribute their emotional experience to different body parts; for some the heart is the seat of emotions, for others it is the liver, the belly or even the throat (see Sharifian *et al.* 2008). Moreover, different cultures may attach different meanings to emotional experiences of different kinds and may also value and express emotions differently.

As for the case of conceptualizations of emotions in Persian English, it appears that there are similarities and differences with other varieties of English. Inner circle varieties of English abound with expressions that reflect the heart as the seat of emotions (e.g. *she broke my heart*). Persian also has many expressions that reflect a similar conceptualization, such as *delbâkhtan* (lit. 'losing heart') 'falling in love'. However, there are differences in terms of what the heart signifies in particular expressions (see further in Sharifian 2008b). For example, in Persian *del* (fig. 'heart', lit. 'stomach') is also the seat of courage, as in *deldâr* (lit. *del* + possess) 'brave', contrasting with inner circle varieties of English, where courage is mainly associated with 'guts'.

A significant emotional experience among Persian speakers is 'grief', which has an important symbolic place in the religious and everyday life of many Iranians (see also de Bellaigue 2004). Many religious and cultural ceremonies provide a chance for Iranians to discharge their 'grief' in a space in which this emotional experience is construed as positive, as a sign of piety, loyalty, etc. Good and Delvecchio Good (1988: 46) observe that:

> 'Sadness and grief' – *gham o ghoseh* – pose special problems of understanding for the psychological anthropologists or for the student of Iranian society and culture. They have dramatically different meanings and forms of expression in Iranian culture than in our own. A rich vocabulary of Persian and Azeri terms of grief and sadness translate uneasily into English language and American culture. 'Dysphoria' in Iranian culture is hardly the lack of happiness or pleasure of the individual, to be overcome by therapy or medical treatment – though it may be the focus of both. It is rather a core effect – the central emotion of religious ritual, an important element of the definition of selfhood, a key quality of a developed and profound understanding of the social order, and most recently a symbol of political loyalty.

Part of the complexity of *gham o ghoseh* comes from the dual role that it has for Iranians. On the one hand, it has religious significance, but it is also conceptualized in the everyday non-religious experiences of Iranian people, and the two influence each other in dynamic ways. In everyday experiences, *gham o ghoseh* captures a whole range of emotional states that one goes through from being hurt by what someone has said, to being away from relatives or even having financial difficulties. Very frequently people exchange these emotional experiences during speech events that are known as *dard-e del* (lit. 'pain of the heart'), which provide people with emotional spaces where they can find relief in communicating their *gham o ghoseh*. In this sense, it is a virtue to listen to and share others' *gham o ghoseh*. The person who does this is referred to as *gham-khâr* (lit. '*gham* eater'). A mother may refer to her caring daughter as *ghamkhâr.*

Conceptually, *gham o ghoseh* does not refer to a state of being, as *sadness* does, but rather to a 'thing' that one can have, or throw away. The verb for *gham o ghoseh* is *ghoseh khordan* (lit. 'to eat *ghoseh*') 'to grieve', which reflects the conceptualization of grief as an entity. A thorough treatment of this complicated emotional experience falls beyond the scope of this chapter, but thus far it should be clear that the emotional experiences that may be expressed as *sorrow, grief* and *sadness* in Persian English may not exactly match what is captured by the use of these words in other varieties of English. Beeman (1988: 20) realizes this when he makes the following remarks:

> I am hampered in my own description of emotional expression in Iranian society by lack of terms sufficiently neutral to avoid the overtones that adhere to English

words for expressing emotions. *Affection, anger, sadness, disappointment*, etc. are all words that carry a cultural load, but they are all we have at present.

As Behzadi (1994: 321) puts it, 'emotionally based cultural practices are an ecologically meaningful domain to study how people make sense of their emotional life events, the meanings of these emotional experiences, and how they are expressed'. He notes the use of two culture-specific emotion terms in Persian *ghahr* (not to be on speaking terms with someone) and *âshti* (to make up) and observes that they 'represent a complex culture-specific fusion of emotional dynamics, cognitive evaluations, and behavioral tendencies, which both codes negative and "distancing" emotions and initiates a set of social actions and gestures that lead to amelioration of that emotional state' (Behzadi 1994: 321; see also Beeman 1988: 25). These terms are very frequent in conversations among Persian speakers and are associated with their affectionate interpersonal relationships. Often when one's expectations in relation to interpersonal relationships with someone else are not met, the person enters the state of *ghahr*, which involves avoidance and distancing between the parties involved. *Âshti* is when this state of affairs ends and the two make up and reconcile, often with someone acting as a mediator.

Behzadi (1994: 322) notes the difficulty in translating *ghahr* and *âshti* into English and maintains that

> The difficulty is not limited to the absence of synonyms in the English lexicon; it is rooted in the cultural meaning of the terms, the associated behaviors, the culturally appropriate sequence of actions, the rituals and ceremonies involved, and their implications for the self and others.

English subtitles that are used in Persian movies mostly translate *ghahr* as 'sulk', as in the following examples:

Mina ghahr kard o raft 'lit. Mina *ghahr* did and left'
Subtitle: Mina sulked and left.
To nabâyad ghahr mikardi 'lit. you shouldn't have done *ghahr*'
Subtitle: You shouldn't have sulked.

This usage appears to be very prevalent and these two notions often constitute major themes in Persian movies and in Persian literature.

Conclusion

The analyses presented in this chapter provide further emerging evidence that different varieties of English express and embody cultural conceptualizations of their speakers. They also reveal how speakers may struggle to find accurate equivalents in English for these conceptualizations. In traditional SLA paradigms, some of the features that I have analysed in this chapter would be identified as 'negative transfer', a term that depends for its force on taking a so-called 'native' variety as a norm. However, I argue that, first of all, the norms of Persian English should be examined in the light of Persian cultural conceptualizations, not in terms of another variety such as American English. The use of these features and communicative strategies is, for many speakers, tied to their cultural and psychological interiority, and they may find it hard not to express cultural conceptualizations that they have internalized into their *cultural cognition* (Sharifian 2008a) throughout their life. It would be naive to expect a speaker to become a culturally and emotionally totally different person when speaking a second language. Of course, learning a second language in many cases expands speakers' horizons towards new cultural, social and cognitive experiences, but expecting learners to abandon old and adopt totally new sets of norms for their cultural and emotional experiences would in many cases be unreasonable and unfeasible.

Further, many speakers who share, or speak culturally overlapping 'non-native' varieties will find that they hold similar conceptualizations, and therefore find the expression of their cultural conceptualizations when communicating in English, completely appropriate (that is transparent) during intercultural/international communication. In fact, it would not be hard to imagine situations where, for example, speakers of Persian English would offend speakers of a variety such as Pakistani English by following the norms of a so-called 'native' variety such as American English. If more than 80 per cent of communication in English is now taking place between non-native speakers, it is high time to further research the cultural conceptualizations that these speakers draw on to negotiate their intercultural communication. The findings of such studies would then need to be included in ELT materials for awareness-raising and to develop learners' *metacultural competence*, an absolute requirement for successful and effective international communication. But, of course, what needs to come first is attitude change among educators and learners about whose norms to follow in international/intercultural communication in English. In short, the 'colonial' assumptions that have been dominant in the traditional SLA paradigm should be abandoned.

This chapter makes another case for the study of World Englishes from the perspective of cultural conceptualizations by providing examples from the variety of English that is emerging among speakers of Persian. It shows that the analytical notions that I have covered by the term 'cultural conceptualizations', such as 'cultural schema', provide helpful tools for understanding culturally constructed levels of semantic and pragmatic meaning in World Englishes. The nature of the examples that have been chosen for investigation in this chapter suggests a methodological approach: researchers could begin to systematically construct comparative cultural maps showing how deeply rooted cultural concepts, which have no equivalent in inner circle varieties, are nevertheless instantiated in English, if only through borrowings. I hope this study also sets another precedent for similar explorations of cultural conceptualizations in other varieties of English elsewhere in the world. Finally, it is acknowledged that a thorough investigation of the emerging variety of Persian English requires much more systematic collection and description of data. However, the data presented in this chapter should suffice to support the argument made about the strength and the necessity of the study of World English from the perspective of cultural conceptualizations.

Suggestions for further reading

Sharifian, F. and Palmer, G.B. (eds) (2007) *Applied Cultural Linguistics: Implications for Second Language Learning and Intercultural Communication*, Amsterdam: John Benjamins. (A collection of essays that adopt a cultural-conceptual approach.)

Wolf, H. and Polzenhagen, F. (2009) *World Englishes: A Cognitive Sociolinguistic Approach*, Berlin: Mouton de Gruyter. (An in-depth study of African English following a cultural conceptual approach.)

References

Aryanpur Persian–English Dictionary (1984) Tehran: Amir-Kabir Publications.

Asdjodi, M. (2001) 'A comparison between *ta'arof* in Persian and *limao* in Chinese', *International Journal of the Sociology of Language*, 148 (1): 71–92.

Assadi, R. (1980) 'Deference: Persian style', *Anthropological Linguistics*, 22: 221–4.

Beeman, W.O. (1986) *Language, Status, and Power in Iran*, Bloomington: Indiana University Press.

——(1988) 'Affectivity in Persian language use', *Culture, Medicine and Psychiatry*, 12: 9–30.

Behzadi, K.G. (1994) 'Interpersonal conflict and emotions in an Iranian cultural practice: *qahr* and *ashti*', *Culture, Medicine, and Psychiatry*, 18: 321–59.

Brown, P. and Levinson, S. (1987) *Politeness: Some Universals in Language Usage*, Cambridge: Cambridge University Press.

de Bellaigue, C. (2004) *In the Rose Garden of the Martyrs: A Memoir of Iran*, London: HarperCollins.

Eslami Rasekh, Z. (2005) 'Invitations in Persian and English: ostensible or genuine?' *Intercultural Pragmatics*, 2 (4): 453–80.

Good, J.B. and Delvecchio Good, M. (1988) 'Ritual, the state, and the transformation of emotional discourse in Iranian society', *Culture, Medicine and Psychiatry*, 12: 43–63.

Hill, B., Ide, S., Kawasaki, A., Ikuta, S. and Ogino, T. (1986) 'Universals of linguistic politeness. quantitative evidence from Japanese and American English', *Journal of Pragmatics*, 10: 347–71.

Hillmann, M.C. (1981) 'Language and social distinctions', in B. Michael and N.R. Keddie (eds) *Modern Iran: The Dialectics of Continuity and Change*, Albany: State University of New York Press, pp. 327–40.

Hodge, C. (1957) 'Some aspects of Persian style', *Language*, 33: 355–69.

Ide, S. (1989) 'Formal forms and discernment: two neglected aspects of universals of linguistic politeness', *Multilingua*, 8: 223–48.

Johnson, S. (2001) *Emergence: The Connected Lives of Ants, Brains, Cities and Software*, New York: Scribner.

Keshavarz, M.H. (2001) 'The role of social context, intimacy, and distance in the choice of forms of address', *International Journal of the Sociology of Language*, 148: 5–18.

Koutlaki, S.A. (2002) 'Offers and expressions of thanks as face enhancing acts: *tae'arof* in Persian', *Journal of Pragmatics*, 34 (12): 1733–56.

Leech, G. (1983) *Principles of Pragmatics*, London: Longman.

Malcolm, I.G. and Sharifian, F. (2007) 'Multiwords in Aboriginal English', in P. Skandera (ed.) *Phraseology and Culture in English*, Berlin: Mouton de Gruyter.

Matsumoto, Y. (1988) 'Reexamination of the universality of face: politeness phenomena in Japanese', *Journal of Pragmatics*, 12: 403–26.

O'Shea, M. (2000) *Cultural Shock: Iran*, Portland, OR: Graphic Arts Publishing.

Polzenhagen, F. and Wolf, H. (2007) 'Culture-specific conceptualisations of corruption in African English', in F. Sharifian and G.B. Palmer (eds) *Applied Cultural Linguistics: Implications for Second Language Learning and Intercultural Communication*, Amsterdam: John Benjamins.

Rafiee, A. (1992) 'Variables of communicative incompetence in the performance of Iranian learners of English and English learners of Persian', unpublished PhD thesis, University of London.

Sharifian, F. (2003) 'On cultural conceptualisations', *Journal of Cognition and Culture*, 3 (3): 187–207.

——(2004) 'Cultural schemas and intercultural communication: a study of Persian', in J. Leigh and E. Loo (eds) *Outer Limits: A Reader in Communication across Cultures*, Melbourne: Language Australia, pp. 119–30.

——(2005) 'Cultural conceptualisations in English words: a study of Aboriginal children in Perth', *Language and Education*, 19 (1): 74–88.

——(2006) 'A cultural–conceptual approach to the study of World Englishes: the case of Aboriginal English', *World Englishes*, 25 (1): 11–22.

——(2007) 'Aboriginal language habitat and cultural continuity', in G. Leitner, and I.G. Malcolm (eds) *The Language Habitat of Aboriginal Australia*, Berlin: Mouton de Gruyter, pp. 181–96.

——(2008a) 'Distributed, emergent cognition, conceptualisation, and language', in R.M. Frank, R. Dirven, T. Ziemke and E. Bernárdez (eds) *Body, Language, and Mind, Vol. 2: Sociocultural Situatedness*, Berlin: Mouton de Gruyter.

——(2008b) 'Conceptualizations of *del* "heart-stomach" in Persian', in F. Sharifian, R. Dirven, N. Yu and S. Niemeier (eds) *Body, Culture, and Language: Conceptualisations of Heart and Other Internal Body Organs across Cultures and Languages*, Berlin: Mouton de Gruyter, pp. 247–65.

Sharifian, F., Dirven, R., Yu, N. and Neiemier, S. (eds) (2008) *Culture, Body, and Language: Conceptualisations of Heart and Other Internal Body Organs across Cultures and Languages*, Berlin: Mouton de Gruyter.

Spencer-Oatey, H. (2000) *Culturally Speaking: Managing Rapport through Talk across Cultures*, London: Continuum.

Taleghani-Nikazm, C. (2002) 'A conversation analytical study of telephone conversation openings between native and nonnative speakers', *Journal of Pragmatics*, 34 (12): 1807–32.

Wierzbicka, A. (1999) *Emotions across Languages and Cultures: Diversity and Universals*, Cambridge: Cambridge University Press.

Wolf, H. and Polzenhagen, F. (2009) *World Englishes: A Cognitive Sociolinguistic Approach*, Berlin: Mouton de Gruyter.

Section IV
Contemporary contexts and functions

In defence of foreignness[1]

Ha Jin

One unique glory English has is a body of literature created by writers to whom English is not a given but an acquisition. These migrant writers arrived at this language individually, unlike writers in or from formerly colonized countries, such as India and Nigeria, where English is an official language and where national literature is written in English. These non-native writers' struggles, survivals and achievements in this language are mostly personal affairs – their creative efforts mean little to collectives in the short run. Yet this is not to deny that there are similarities and overlapping interests between writers who acquired English and writers who inherited English.

It is safe to say that Joseph Conrad is the founding figure of this literary tradition, whereas Nabokov embodies its acme. Conrad's struggle in his adopted language is a commonly known fact; even in his later fiction we still encounter slips occasionally in spite of his linguistic prowess and the stark beauty of his prose. In contrast, Nabokov has been revered as a verbal adventurer and a virtuoso stylist. He is also known to have learned to read English before he could read Russian and to have grown up trilingual. The halo around this master's head tends to eclipse the fact that, like Conrad, Nabokov also had to strive to acquire English after he stopped writing fiction in Russian. Nabokov himself was quite candid about his struggle, as he states in his famous essay, 'On a Book Entitled *Lolita*': 'I had to abandon my natural idiom, my untrammeled, rich, and infinitely docile Russian tongue for a second-rate brand of English' (1977: 288). On another occasion, he confessed that 'the absence of a natural vocabulary' was his 'secret flaw as a writer' in English (1973: 106). Even so, few of us seem willing to reflect on the harrowing experience that this great magician of words went through.

His biographer Brian Boyd (1991), however, recorded his linguistic struggle in his initial years of writing in this language. Nabokov wrote his best English poem, 'A Discovery', two years after arriving in the United States. The poem was inspired by his stumbling on one of his own butterflies, a Grand Canyon, displayed as a standard specimen of the species in New York's American Museum of Natural History. Despite the confident poetic voice and the speaker's buoyant spirit, his biographer cannot help but remark: 'But the fair copy of the poem … showed all too painfully the occasional thinness of his English' (1991: 53). The 'thinness' can be discerned in these lines:

461

'I found it and named it, being versed / in taxonomic Latin; thus became / godfather to an insect and its first / describer – and I want no other fame.' Boyd also mentioned the early exchanges between Nabokov and Edmund Wilson over Nabokov's English. Wilson chided his friend for his bold way of using his adopted language. The American man of letters had misgivings about the ability of the Russian new arrival who had just begun making his way in English, and Wilson never stopped carping about Nabokov's puns and mistakes. Their frictions eventually developed into the full-blown argument in 1965, when Wilson published his lengthy article 'The Strange Case of Pushkin and Nabokov', pointing out some 'solecisms' in Nabokov's translation of *Eugene Onegin*; in response, Nabokov wrote his well-known essay 'Reply to My Critics'. By then, twenty-five years after emigrating to the United States, Nabokov was already a master of this language, completely competent to engage his former friend polemically. He outshone Wilson in the debate.

However, in their early private exchanges over Nabokov's use of English, Wilson always got the upper hand, especially during Nabokov's beginning years in America. To Nabokov, the switch from Russian to English was excruciatingly painful; in his own words, it felt 'like learning anew to handle things after losing seven or eight fingers in an explosion'(1973: 54). He started writing his first English novel, *The Real Life of Sebastian Knight*, when he was still in Paris. Soon after arriving in the United States, he resumed working on it. At the time he was diffident about his English, although the signature of his gorgeous and elaborate style was already manifest in the prose. Wilson read the proofs of the novel, was full of praise, and even provided a positive blurb. Yet, as usual, he did not refrain from quibbling about some verbal slips and quirks in the book. In his letter to Nabokov of 20 October 1941, he wrote: 'I hope you will get someone at Wellesley to read your proofs – because there are a few, though not many, mistakes in English.' He went on to point out several. In his reply, Nabokov lamented that he had returned the proofs to the press, unable to make the corrections any more, but he also argued that the narrator is supposed to 'write English with difficulty' (Karlinsky 2001: 56–7). In other words, the verbal defects are characterized and can be somewhat justified. In fact the narrator of the novel admits this weakness, too: 'The dreary tussle with a foreign idiom and a complete lack of literary experience do not predispose one to feeling overconfident' (Nabokov 1941: 101). Despite the technical justification, Nabokov later did correct those slips Wilson had mentioned. Clearly, Nabokov was apprehensive about his ability in English and still had a long way to go before becoming a master of English prose. In retrospect, it is hard to imagine the amount of labour he undertook to develop from the relatively simple prose in *The Real Life of Sebastian Knight* to the rich, subtle style of *Lolita*, and to the confident playfulness based on deliberate distortion and misuse of English in *Pnin*.

In spite of Wilson's extraordinary generosity to his friend, he was also a pain in Nabokov's neck. He would not stop, privately and publicly, admonishing Nabokov to avoid using puns. Fortunately Nabokov ignored his chiding and continued with his word games, which gradually became a hallmark of his genius. Wilson gave a mixed review of Nabokov's *Nikolay Gogol* (1944) in *The New Yorker*, saying, '[Nabokov's] puns are particularly awful' (Wilson 1950: 78). From the very beginning of their friendship, Wilson compared Nabokov to Conrad, as he wrote in the same letter of 20 October 1941, 'You and Conrad must be the only examples of foreigners succeeding in English and in this field.' Nabokov was displeased with such a comparison, though we do not know in what wording and format he objected to it initially. Wilson certainly knew how to nettle his friend. Years later, when abbreviating the original *New Yorker* review into the essay 'Vladimir Nabokov on Gogol' for his book *Classics and Commercials* (1950), Wilson added this sentence as the conclusion of the piece: 'in spite of some errors, Mr Nabokov's mastery of English almost rivals Joseph Conrad's'. Affronted, Nabokov wrote back: 'I protest against the last line. Conrad knew how to handle *readymade* English better than I; but I know better the other kind. He never sinks to the depths of my solecisms, but neither does he scale my verbal peaks' (Karlinsky 2001: 282–3). By 'readymade' Nabokov meant conventional. In an interview in 1964, he was more explicit about this: 'I cannot abide Conrad's souvenir-shop style, bottled ships and shell necklaces of romanticist clichés' (1973: 42).

I have cited Nabokov's negative view of Conrad's English only to illustrate the two masters' opposite approaches to their adopted language. In Conrad's fiction, we can sense a linguistic boundary demarcated by the English dictionary – he would not invent words and expressions that might sound alien to the English ear. Except in a handful of sea stories, such as *The Nigger of the 'Narcissus'* and *Lord Jim*, where some seamen's dialogues are occasionally put in substandard English, Conrad on the whole stayed within the boundary of Standard English. By saying that, I do not mean to depreciate Conrad's accomplishment. Even within such a boundary, he managed to do monumental work, and besides, he brought a clear foreign sensibility to his sinewy and elegant prose. It was no secret that he viewed himself as a foreigner taking refuge in England. The word 'refuge', referring to his own situation, almost became a catchword in his correspondence. He even claimed that English literature was not his tradition when he declined a knighthood from the British government and honorary degrees offered by a number of universities, including Cambridge and Yale. In his later years he always longed to return to Poland, though his sudden death prevented him from fulfilling this wish (Najder 1983: 489). We can surmise that the combination of Conrad's strict approach to English and his sense of being a foreigner in England, a country he loved, must have been a source of his anguish.

Like Conrad, Nabokov also depended heavily on dictionaries. His English got more artistically bookish and mannered as he grew as a stylist. However, he never confined himself to Standard English, and often pushed the limits of the language. Leland de la Durantaye summarizes the rationale of Nabokov's approach as follows:

> Nabokov prefers the obscure to the invented epithet. To invent words was, for him, only permissible in cases where there really was no word to name the thing – and he went to considerable length to verify this. But this conservatism knew limits. Inasmuch as the vocabulary existed, Nabokov respected it – but as to the company he placed it in and the contortions he put it through, he was far from conservative … Nabokov clearly shared Sebastian's [distrust of easy expressions] … and, like Sebastian, 'had no use for ready-made phrases because the things he wanted to say were of an exceptional build and he knew moreover that no real idea can be said to exist without the words made to measure'. Nabokov's verbal clothes were made from the fabric of the language as he found it – but special tailoring was always required.
>
> (de la Durantaye 2007: 142)

The second point in the above passage means 'to find new combinations of words'. It was a principle Nabokov practised throughout his career, in both Russian and English, whereas to invent new words, a much more cautious move, is predicated on acquaintance with the entire English vocabulary. Nabokov, known as 'a lexicomaniac', an epithet he might happily have accepted, was proud of his scholarship, gained from studying dictionaries. The famous photograph of him with his well-thumbed elephantine *Webster* bears witness to the pains he had taken to master English (Boyd 1991: 562–3). In fact, even the *Webster* did not establish a boundary for him but was more like a map, since he would make up words and new expressions without hesitation if they were unavailable in the dictionary. For example, in his novel *Pnin* we come across words like 'radiophile', 'psychoasinine' and 'footnote-drugged maniac'. Even his first English novel contains invented words, such as 'love-embers', 'a sexophone note', 'tipwards' and 'thought-image'. In addition to verbal inventions, there is also the occasional interplay between English and French and Russian, which takes place beyond the borders of English. At some places the narrator of *Pnin* simply speaks Russian, and Pnin's former wife Liza's maudlin poems are given in Russian and then transcribed in English (1981: 56 and 181). Evidently, unlike Conrad, Nabokov worked in the periphery of the English language, whose frontiers stretch into foreign terrains.

Pnin is an important immigrant novel. Probably because its protagonist is a white Russian exile, readers might forget that Pnin is also an immigrant, and that, like millions of immigrants, he faces the same challenge of finding home in this country. At the end of the story, he flees Waindell College and vanishes into the American wilderness, where there seems to remain some hope, as this beautiful sentence suggests:

> [Pnin's] little sedan boldly swung up the shining road, which one could make out narrowing to a thread of gold in the soft mist where hill after hill made beauty of distance, and where there was simply no saying what miracle might happen.
>
> (Nabokov 1981: 191)

The American promise, though almost shattered by the sadness and the ironies in the story, still lingers in the free space of the distant land. Indeed, unlike the fiction written by writers of minority groups, *Pnin* does not touch on one of the major American themes, race; but, like the fiction written by European immigrants, it depicts the torment and the frustrations that a new arrival in this country went through. In addition, the novel tackles a fundamental issue in the immigrant experience, namely language. No matter how hard Pnin worked at it, his flawed English could not improve once he had reached the stage where he could toss out expressions like 'wishful thinking', 'okey-dokey' and 'to make a long story short'. In his adopted language, he appeared so silly and flaky that some of his colleagues thought that he should not be entitled to wander within the vicinity of the campus; but when speaking Russian and mixing with Russian expatriates, he was an entirely different man, erudite, articulate and even athletic. His is a typical predicament of an immigrant whose first language is not English.

Technically, Nabokov faced two challenges that most writers of the immigrant experience have to confront. The first is how to present non-native speakers' Englishes, and the second is how to render their mother tongues in English. In practice, the first challenge usually has an empirical basis, since most of the time the author can imitate a character's accent and ungrammatical speech. This Nabokov handled masterfully. Pnin invites Professor Thomas Wynn to his housewarming party, giving him directions this way: 'It is nine hundred ninety nine, Todd Rodd, very simple! At the very very end of the rodd, where it unites with Cleef Ahvnue. A leetle breek house and a beeg blahk cleef' (Nabokov 1981: 151). Grammatically his speech is impeccable, which is congruous with Pnin's pedantic personality, but it is heavily accented because he has trouble with some vowels. He speaks differently from most immigrants, who have grammatical problems as well, and some of whom can hardly come up with a complex sentence. In fiction writing, the rendition of non-native characters' English speeches, despite the empirical bases, cannot but be somewhat artificial, created by the author, though the creations must be done well enough to give the impression of authenticity. If a man, as Vadim in *A Feather on the Breath of God*, says to his beloved, 'When you put your head on my breast, my heart runs out of me' (Nunez 1995: 147), we can tell that he is a foreigner, as his peculiar idiom authenticates his identity. This technical demand precludes Standard English, which is inadequate for presenting so many Englishes used by non-native speakers.

The second technical challenge – how to render foreign languages in English – is more complicated. First, once put in English, the rendition has little empirical basis, because English cannot possibly resemble the original sound. Second, there is a difference between the narrative language and the dialogue language; the former, theoretically, can be confined to Standard English as in translation. In essence, what the writer faces here is an interplay between English and a foreign language, and ideally speaking, English in this context should reflect the other language to some extent. As far as dialogue goes, I believe that few fiction writers object to this principle. Therefore, if a recent widow in *Christ in Concrete* laments, 'Whom shall my children seek? Who will now put food into the open mouths of my little birds? – for they must live and blossom as tall-tall pillars in this land that swallowed their father – I must live so that they shall live!' (Donato 1993: 42), we know she speaks Italian. The unusual idioms and the contorted syntax are meant to defamiliarize English a little to fit the character and the drama. Practically speaking, this approach is to force English to be closer to another foreign language so as to make the dialogue more characterized. As a result, the English cannot but become somewhat alien. In US immigrant fiction, this, however, is a conventional technique. It is the narrative language that complicates the issue of the interplay between languages.

As I stated above, theoretically it is possible to confine the narrative language to Standard English, but in practice many non-native writers don't do so. This is mainly for two reasons: first, the writer's mother tongue and foreign sensibility affect their English, making it peculiar to the native ear; second, Standard English is insufficient in presenting the experiences and ideas that the author describes. Nabokov knew these setbacks, but used them to his advantage. In *Pnin* the narrator cracks jokes and twists English words and idioms, calling 'a curriculum vitae' in a nutshell 'a coconut shell' and following the adverbial phrase 'on the other hand' with 'on the third hand'. By so doing, the narrator virtually highlights his foreignness, since foreigners, with their childlike gaze at English, are more likely to come up with that kind of fascination with the most common features of their adopted language. In American fiction, even some non-characterized narrators, in the third-person point of view, cannot but preserve some foreignness in the narrative language. For example, the narrative language in *Christ in Concrete* heavily depends on the passive voice, which must be meant to reflect the way the Italian immigrants speak. The narrator describes the noise from a bathroom this way: 'The toilet above flushed with watery roar, pish-thrash-gargled down the exposed pipe and trick-trickled away in its hollow metal throat' (Donato 1993: 42). We can tell that he is a non-native speaker.

When my novel *A Free Life* came out last winter, John Updike reviewed it in *The New Yorker* and cited some expressions as 'small solecisms' (2007: 101). The Chinese-language media reported the review widely, because Updike is revered in China as an eminent man of American letters. On the internet there were discussions about the examples Updike gave, and yet the Chinese who knew English could not see what was wrong with them. People offered different explanations, none of which, however, was convincing. Indeed, how can you say it is inappropriate to use the word 'emplomaniac' if, everywhere you turn, you encounter someone obsessed with his official position and career? Etymologically, *emplo* in the French origin means 'employment and public office', and an obsession with public office is of course a mania. A word like 'emplomaniac' may sound alien to the English ear, but in the Chinese context it is the only suitable word. A mild expression is 'office seeker', but it does not convey the madness and perversion.

Once we enter a foreign terrain in our fiction, Standard English may have to be stretched to cover the new territory. Ultimately this is a way to expand the capacity of the language, a kind of enrichment.

Among the Chinese, there are some misperceptions of my way of using English. People often say I directly translate Chinese idioms. That is not true. I did use a good number of Chinese idioms because most of my characters speak Mandarin, but in most cases I altered the idioms some, at times drastically, to suit the context, the drama and the narrative flow. The Chinese idiom referring to a man dreaming of a beautiful woman beyond his reach is 'a toad that wants to eat a swan's flesh'; I used this idiom at least twice in my fiction, but I rendered it as 'a toad dreaming of nabbing a swan'. 'To hit a dog with a pork bun' is a Chinese idiom referring to a bad venture that will not pay off, and I put it into English as 'to hit a dog with a meatball'. Most times I tailored the idioms for the needs of the story.

At times Chinese idioms serve only as leads to something more colourful and more interesting. For instance, a Chinese expression describing a bald crown is *di zhong hai*, a sea within a landscape, which sounds funny mainly because it is a homonym of 'the Mediterranean' in Mandarin. In English there is no way to reproduce the humour if we simply transcribe the idiom, so the narrator of my story 'A Pension Plan' describes her boss's crown this way: 'with a shiny bald spot like a lake in the mouth of an extinct volcano'. Clearly, the expression may sound Chinese to the English ear, but it has actually shed its Chineseness. Sometimes even a common Chinese idiom would change meaning once it is put into English. 'Rice barrel' originally means a nuisance or a good-for-nothing, but in the story 'Children like Enemies' the narrator thinks about his son this way: 'I wanted to yell at him that he was just a rice barrel thinking of nothing but food.' Actually, the son, an accomplished bridge engineer, is not a nuisance, and his father takes him as a 'rice barrel' mainly because he keeps eating without interfering with his children's changing their last name, Xi, which is unpronounceable to most Americans. In other words, despite the literal rendition, the meaning of the original idiom has changed in English, shaped by the dramatic situation. This kind of 'stretching' is to utilize the space between two languages to create something fresh and different in one language.

Another criticism of my way of using English is that my English is too poor and too simple. 'The fourth-grade', in an English professor's words. That means high-school level. In this case, the Chinese hold Standard English, or dictionary English, as the yardstick – the more $50 words you can put down on paper, the better your English is.

They have failed to understand that writers of my kind do not work within the boundary of dictionaries. We work in the border areas of English, in the space between languages, and therefore our ability and accomplishments cannot be measured only by the mastery of Standard English.

Besides the technical need for a particularized English, there is also the concern about one's identity. I often emphasize that a writer's identity should be something earned. In truth, a part of one's identity may also be something given, beyond the writer's control. Just a few years ago, there was a consensus among Chinese literary scholars that those writers in the diaspora writing in Chinese produced Chinese literature, whereas those writing in other languages belonged to foreign literatures. They ignored the fact that, in world literature, some writers have dual citizenship. Conrad belonged to Polish literature as well as to English letters, although he never wrote in his mother tongue. Nabokov is also a Russian writer in spite of his insistence on being an American writer. Recently, however, Chinese scholars have begun talking about how to include in the Chinese literary canon those writers in the diaspora who write in adopted languages. To the individual writer, the categorization may not be that important – at most, it is like having an extra room in another building, since in world literary history, no significant writer does not have some kind of home. Yet it is the fate of most migrant writers who have written significant works to be claimed by more than one nation, because they exist in the space in between countries, a region where languages and cultures mingle and penetrate each other. Any valuable work that appears in this peripheral area is likely to be claimed by more than one country as something that can enhance their national soft power.

Most writers existing on the margin are aware of this duality in their identity. Even Maxine Hong Kingston, American born and having English as her first language, believes that her work is an extension of Chinese literature, as the heroine of *The Woman Warrior* celebrates at the end of the book:

[Ts'ai Yen] brought her songs back from the savage lands, and one of the three that has been passed down to us is 'Eighteen Stanzas for a Barbarian Reed Pipe', a song that Chinese sing to their own instruments. It translated well.

(Kingston 1976: 209)

In an interview, Kingston told the poet Marilyn Chin about her meeting with some writers in China:

Here I was in America, where I had free speech and free press. And I spent this lifetime working on roots. So what they [Chinese writers] were saying was that I was their continuity. And they wanted help in figuring out where to go … God, I felt so terrific. Because they were telling me I was part of Chinese canon. And here I was writing in English.

(Skenzay and Martin 1998: 94)

Although negligent about the Chinese writers' diplomatic and political savvy, Kingston did express her genuine elation at being embraced by the people of her ancestral land. The aspiration to cross the borders of languages and return to one's origin is commonplace among writers of minority groups in the United States, though there is probably no way to return. If we are rational about this, we can see that most writers working in the in-between space have been defined more or less by alienation and exclusion. One thing they can do is make the best use of their disadvantages and marginality, and they should not be possessed by the dream of return. They should rely on nothing but valuable work that can give one a solid identity. Then, the very notion of identity may become meaningless, if one has produced significant work.

To migrant writers, the periphery is their working space, much more essential for their existence than the other areas. They should not strive to join the mainstream or to attain a place in the cultural centre of a nation. They must hold on to their in-betweenness, tapping various sources, including the foreign, and making the best of their losses. They should accept their marginality, which shapes their ambitions differently from native writers.

T.S. Eliot in his poem *Little Gidding* defines the task for poets this way: 'Since our concern was speech, and speech impelled us / To purify the dialect of the tribe' (1944: ll.126–7). That is a task, however, for native poets, who can stay at the centre of English, as Eliot lived in London, and strive to refine the language. But such a vision is unreasonable to non-native writers, nor is it applicable to many other kinds of writers. Despite using English as their national language, most people in former British colonies use their local dialects in their daily life. Most US immigrants have to speak foreign languages or corrupted versions of English at home. Therefore, it is infeasible for non-native writers to have the kind of ambition annunciated by T.S. Eliot. In fact, too much purification can sterilize and enervate a language. It is commonly known that the vitality and the prevalence of English are largely due to its impurity and its messiness.

Like migrant writers, writers of the former British colonies and writers of the US immigrant experience are all keenly aware of the issue of how to use English differently from native writers. Salman Rushdie in his essay 'Imaginary Homelands' speaks at length about Indian writers' struggle with the language:

> Those of us who do use English do so in spite of our ambiguity towards it, or perhaps because of that, perhaps because we can find in that linguistic struggle a reflection of other struggles within ourselves and the influences at work upon our societies. To conquer English may be to complete the process of making ourselves free.
>
> (Rushdie 1991: 17)

Rushdie describes the use of English as a struggle both within and without, the victory of which will liberate the writers from the confinement of the colonial heritage. Evidently, he envisions an English that is not the conventional idiom, but an English capable of expressing the experiences of the colonized, the local and the peculiarities of the Indian life. Therefore, such a language has yet to be invented.

Among writers of the US immigrant experience, the search for a new English seems to be an individual effort associated with self-discovery and personal identity, perhaps because there are so many ethnic groups of immigrants that it would be impossible to form a united effort. David Mura's remarks about this matter exemplify a stand often taken by these writers:

> The trick, then, was to learn to write out of my sense of duality, or that plurality, to write not in slavish imitation of the European tradition but to use it and combine it with other elements of my background, trying to achieve a difficult balance. In

order to understand who I was and who I would become, I would have to listen to voices that my father, or T.S. Eliot or Robert Lowell, did not dream of. Voices of my family, or Japan, or my own wayward and unassimilated past. In the world of the tradition, I was unimagined. I would have to imagine myself.

(Mura 1991: 77)

That is an individual approach to English, though it may also represent a vision shared by many others, especially by writers of colour who were born in this country and who write about the Americanizing experience, having to look for a language different from the English they learned at school.

Personally, I believe that Chinua Achebe's position on this issue is wiser and more feasible. In the early 1960s, after the publication of *Things Fall Apart*, there was an intense debate among African writers over the use of English. Achebe was a key participant in the debate and wrote about the issue in a few essays. The following paragraph summarizes his position:

For an African, writing in English is not without its serious setbacks. He often finds himself describing situations or modes of thought which have no direct equivalent in the English way of life. Caught in the situation he can do one of two things. He can try and contain what he wants to say within the limits of conventional English or he can try to push back those limits to accommodate his ideas. The first method produces competent, uninspired and rather flat work. The second method produces something new and valuable to the English language as well as to the new material he is trying to put over. But it can also get out of hand. It can lead to bad English being accepted and defended as African or Nigerian. I submit that those who can do the work of extending the frontier of English so as to accommodate African thought-patterns must do it through their mastery of English and not out of innocence.

(Ogbaa 1999: 193).

What Achebe said is vital not only to African writers but also to migrant writers who came to this language individually and to writers of the US immigrant experience who look for idioms that can capture the emotions and thoughts of their characters. Essentially, the first method Achebe describes is similar to Conrad's approach, whereas the second method he suggests is close to Nabokov's approach. Achebe's phrases – 'extending the frontier of English' and 'through their mastery of English' – point out the peripheral territory where we work and the boundaries we must be aware of so as to push and expand the limits of English. As a matter of fact, he also advocates a sense of responsibility, namely to enrich the language we share and use.

Indeed, the frontiers of English verge on foreign territories, and therefore we cannot help but sound foreign to native ears, but the frontiers are the only proper places where we can claim our existence and make our contributions to this language.

Note

1 This essay was a keynote address at Brown University for the Conference 'Reassessing the Foreign Language Curriculum in the Age of Globalization', on 4 April 2008.

References

Boyd, R. (1991) *Vladimir Nabokov: The American Years*, Princeton: Princeton University Press.

de la Durantaye, L. (2007) *Style is Matter*, Ithaca: Cornell University Press.

Donato, Pietro di (1993) *Christ in Concrete*, New York: Signet Classic.

Eliot, T.S. (1944) 'Little Gidding', in *Four Quartets*, London: Faber & Faber.

Karlinsky, S. (2001) (ed.) *Dear Bunny, Dear Volodya: The Nabokov–Wilson Letters (1940–1971)*, Berkeley: University of California Press.

Kingston, M. Hong (1976) *The Woman Warrior*, New York: Vintage.

Mura, D. (1991) *Turning Japanese: Memoirs of a Sansei*, New York: Atlantic Monthly.

Nabokov, V. (1941) *The Real Life of Sebastian Knight*, New York: New Directions.

——(1973) *Strong Opinions*, New York: McGraw-Hill.

——(1977) *Lolita*, New York: Berkley Books.

——(1981) *Pnin*, New York: Vintage Books.

Najder, Z. (1983) *Joseph Conrad: A Chronicle*, New Brunswick, NJ: Rutgers University Press.

Nunez, S. (1995) *A Feather on the Breath of God*, New York: HarperCollins.

Ogbaa, K. (1999) *Understanding 'Things Fall Apart'*, Westport, CT: Greenwood.

Rushdie, S. (1991) *Imaginary Homelands*, London: Granta Books.

Skenzay, P. and Martin, T. (1998) (eds) *Conversations with Maxine Hong Kingston*, Jackson: University Press of Mississippi.

Updike, J. (2007) 'Review: *A Free Life* by Ha Jin', *New Yorker*, 3 December 2007.

Wilson, E. (1950) *Classics and Commercials: A Literary Chronicle of the Forties*, New York: Wolff.

27

Writing in English(es)

Tope Omoniyi

Many thousands of [British] men and women ... have sloughed off their native dialects and acquired a new tongue.

George Bernard Shaw (Pygmalion)

Introduction

In this chapter, my objective is to determine what variation between different writing spaces and moments brings to the World Englishes (WE) debate. In other words, if we shift the focus from the actors to the spaces of action, then we can appreciate the skills with which writers converge with or diverge from different varieties to invest their writing with particular effects. As cultural producers, like actors, writers can and do get into character(s) and it is up to their readers to discern these characters in order to grasp the full meaning of a story. The spaces and moments of narration are instigators for these, as I shall illustrate from my own writing later. I shall discuss the ideological complexity of the two categories *Writing in English* and *Writing in Englishes* within the framework of a sociolinguistics of globalization (Blommaert 2010) and the practice of writing in diasporic contexts. I shall explore notions of linguistic capital (Bourdieu 1991), heteroglossia (Bakhtin 1981) and Kamau Brathwaite's 'Nation language' (1984, 1995) to proffer explanations for a postcolonial writer's code choice.

I contend that the normative categorization of writers by reference to geographical or regional identity is problematic in our contemporary world in which writers engage in unceasing dialogues with worlds beyond their own. Consequently, they find themselves in the cross-currents of global 'transcultural flows' (Pennycook 2008, and this volume), facilitated by ease of travel, the information superhighway and its virtual communities and networks, and other textual contact experiences. Using reflexivity as part of an (auto) ethnographic regime, I shall interrogate the varieties of English in my own writing and explore the tensions that are the consequence of my multiple cultural locations and third space experiences (Bhabha 1994; Bhatt 2008), both in real time and in virtual reality. The third space is a construct rather than a territorial reference *per se* and, as such, it is a useful frame within which a writer's voice can be examined. It is the idea of performance related to a perception of contact. So, for a writer, invoking such in-between realities results from a perceived audience or readership for whom contacts, pidgins and creoles have a meaning.

It is important to declare that I have multiple subjectivities in this task. I am a sociolinguist (I-Sociolinguist) trying to deploy sociolinguistic tools in looking at the I-Poet author of the poetry I have written and published. This I is further complexified by the contrasting and peculiar spaces of identity within which my poems have come to life and the roles I had in those spaces and the manner in which those roles inflected my perception of Self and therefore my use of language. My relationship with English, the language in which I write, varies between all of those spaces. By this I am implying that my linguistic resources, particularly at a register level, encode the space(s) of birth in the poems such that my trajectory up to the birth moment is discernible. These experiences resonate with those conveyed by Wimal Dissayanake who notes that, in the works of postcolonial writers, old and new,

> the complex relationship between self, narrative, and language becomes evident. These writers are seeking to gain entrance to their multifaceted subjectivities by 'decolonizing' the English language and the sedimented consciousness that goes with it. Many of them regard the English language as the repressive instrument of a hegemonic colonial discourse. They wish to emancipate themselves from its clutches by probing deeper and deeper into their historical pasts, cultural heritages, and the intricacies of the present moment. Through these means they seek to confront their protean selfhoods. What is interesting is that these writers are striving to accomplish this liberation through the very language that has in the past shackled them to what can be characterized as an ambiguous colonial legacy.
>
> (Dissayanake 2006: 559)

Writing in Englishes is a departure from the literary canon that takes Western epistemology as default. The former represents a counter-voice to the icons of the literary tradition of the 'mother country' in postcolonial critique. It is rooted in the idea of multiple epistemologies from which new canons have emerged. Thus, depending on perspective, writing in Englishes could be perceived as an indicator of language and culture shift, culture maintenance and hybridization. For the latter, the alternative is multilingualism and multiple voices, dialects and accents, the raw materials from which Englishes are formed and achieved through cultural hybridity and crossing.

When I first became interested in World Englishes (WE) research in the mid 1980s, it was within the framework of understanding the rural–urban dichotomy in the proficiency of Nigerian students preparing for and writing the West African School Certificate Examination in English Language (an equivalent of the GCSE Ordinary Level examination). I was a teacher in the school system and an examiner for the West African Examinations Council. At that time, my approach to WE and the issue of Mother Tongue in education had been to regard them uncritically as 'neutral' topics. Only later did this scholarship become a forum for ideology-laden responses to my postcolonial realities, both from the province as well as from within the metropolis as a diasporic writer. As an advocate of mother tongue education inspired by the UNESCO-funded Ife Six Year Primary Project (see Bamgbose 1976) ironically my published advocacy is all in the 'other' language – English. Second, as a writer, my subjectivity started out already heavily ideologized. My public writing experience began within the genre of 'letters to the editor' in the Nigerian weekly *Sunday Times* as a teenage social critic. The published letters went through several stages of redrafting, determined as I was to reduce to the barest minimum the chances of rejection on the basis of mechanics. These pieces reflected a conformist Self playing by the prescribed rules of the Standard language as I knew them at the time though only as a means to the end of being published. In other words, error-consciousness was part of the art of writing for me because I realized that grammar played a role in deciding to publish or not to publish my letters. I remember that even then my letters tended to have a level of prosody to them, but I have no way of empirically determining what role that had in the more than average success I had with getting the letters into print. I was aware I had access to some kind of capital which I can only now in hindsight critically analyse.

Bourdieu's linguistic capital

I have argued elsewhere (Omoniyi 2003, and forthcoming) that the notion of the linguistic capital applies intra-systemically and refers to the relative statuses of varieties of the same language. In contrast, language capital is a phenomenon of multilingual societies where various indigenous languages co-exist with former colonial languages and very often have a subordinate status where the latter are instituted as official languages. This distinction raises a number of questions for the postcolonial African writer. First, if s/he writes in English, does the product join other English literary products and become subject to Bourdieu's linguistic capital? If the variety of English used is perceived and rated in relation to an exogenous standard, i.e. Standard British English, then linguistic capital applies, and writing in Englishes is arguably a neo-colonial activity and heritage and must, as a consequence, orientate towards to the metropolitan standards and values. However, if as Achebe and others claim African writers have successfully indigenized the English language and are able to make it say what they want it to say, then these Englishes are not the Other in relation to English elsewhere, but, by right, they qualify as separate languages only in relation to the other languages in their ecological environment. In this latter paradigm language capital applies and they are evaluated on the same scales as the local African languages. However, linguistic capital applies to variation between educated and uneducated varieties of an indigenized variety of English as competing items in 'a market of accents' or dialects (cf. Blommaert 2009: 243). We must note, though, that sometimes, for effect, writers may in their code choices move between the language and linguistic capital frameworks, especially in their role as social critics. These instances must be differentiated from those efforts at writing which are framed by limitation or lack of access to a more elaborate register.

We are a product of our environment. We are constructed by our history as much as we are producers of that history. The distinction I seek to establish between 'writing in English' and 'writing in Englishes' is not new. It is the same distinction that we find between English Literature and Literature in English in the syllabi of many postcolonial institutions, where the former includes the Western canons (William Shakespeare, T.S. Eliot, Edmund Spenser, Ezra Pound, Ernest Hemingway and so on) and the latter writings of many creative writers in the English-using world or the English Language Commonwealth, including mine. This focus is a slight departure from the English Language Teaching one that the scholarship on globalization has hitherto promoted, albeit writing is as much a vehicle of the spread of English as teaching has been. Books and blogs and the migrant teachers and curriculum of ELT programmes are partners in the perpetuation of what Pennycook (1994) describes as the cultural politics of English as an international language. As I noted earlier, a language–place association, that is, the identification of writers by reference to their home region, is flawed in an era of unbridled transcultural flows. If we distinguish between the languages of, for instance, writing in the UK and writing in Jamaica or Nigeria, we do not factor into the equation membership in exterritorial networks which may be drawn upon during the writing process. With language–people association the distinction is between individuals (or groups of them) practising in different language and linguistic ecologies, as we find in Blommaert's (2008) literacy regimes in his grassroots literacy research in Central Africa. The latter option challenges the three circles analytical framework and accommodates realities of intensified movement and hybridization in the era of globalization (Omoniyi and Saxena in press).

As writers, we write for an audience in (a) language that we assume they understand, otherwise our effort is wasted. But this decision results from a debate internally that a writer has with him/herself as part of an identity regime. By identity regime I refer to the range of possibilities from which a writer may choose. So, for example, there is a difference between being identified as a dramatist and a poet from the point of view of English usage. These are genre differences and such distinction is different from that made earlier between the UK, Nigeria and Jamaica. It is in the latter distinction that the hegemony of Anglo-American Western culture that Brutt-Griffler refers to (2002: vii) resides. I hurry to add, though, that Brutt-Griffler strikes at the very heart of that hegemony by recognizing not only one 'World English' but also 'many English writers from Africa and Asia' (2002: viii), a position which washes against the tide of the customary distinction between native and nativized varieties of English which Kirkpatrick (2007: 5) says 'can be questioned'.

Voice and Englishes

Riding on the back of Blommaert's (2009) recent economic analysis of accents of English within his globalization thesis, I shall begin this section on 'voice' by presenting an extended extract from a New York City speech given by the British writer Zadie Smith in December 2008. She reveals that her public speaker voice as a famous writer is not the voice of her youth and home. She has indeed appropriated across class lines, a permanent crossing if we allude to Ben Rampton's (1995) notion of language crossing, in this case linguistic crossing, since we are dealing with intralingual shift.

> Hello. This voice I speak with these days, this English voice with its rounded vowels and consonants in more or less the right place – this is not the voice of my childhood. I picked it up in college, along with the unabridged *Clarissa* and a taste for port. Maybe this fact is only what it seems to be – a case of bald social climbing – but at the time I genuinely thought *this* was the voice of lettered people, and that if I didn't have the voice of lettered people I would never truly be lettered …
>
> My own childhood had been the story of this and that combined, of the synthesis of disparate things. It never occurred to me that I was leaving the London district of Willesden for Cambridge. I thought I was *adding* Cambridge to Willesden, this

new way of talking to that old way. Adding a new kind of knowledge to a different kind I already had. And for a while, that's how it was: at home, during the holidays, I spoke with my old voice, and in the old voice seemed to feel and speak things that I couldn't express in college, and vice versa. I felt a sort of wonder at the flexibility of the thing. Like being alive twice.

But flexibility is something that requires work if it is to be maintained. Recently my double voice has deserted me for a single one, reflecting the smaller world into which my work has led me. Willesden was a big, colourful, working-class sea; Cambridge was a smaller, posher pond, and almost univocal; the literary world is a puddle. This voice I picked up along the way is no longer an exotic garment I put on like a college gown whenever I choose – now it is my only voice, whether I want it or not. I regret it; I should have kept both voices alive in my mouth. They were both a part of me. But how the culture warns against it! As George Bernard Shaw delicately put it in his preface to the play *Pygmalion*, 'many thousands of [British] men and women … have sloughed off their native dialects and acquired a new tongue'.

Whoever changes their voice takes on, in Britain, a queerly tragic dimension. They have betrayed that puzzling dictum 'To thine own self be true', so often quoted approvingly as if it represented the wisdom of Shakespeare rather than the hot air of Polonius. '*What's to become of me? What's to become of me?*' wails Eliza Doolittle, realizing her middling dilemma. With a voice too posh for the flower girls and yet too redolent of the gutter for the ladies in Mrs Higgins's drawing room.

Two issues stare us starkly in the face in this extract. First is the immigrants' attitude to the language of their domination, and second, the relationship to their own language. Agency has shifted from the colonizer because the postcolonial writer is armed with an all-powerful tool. This is the spirit that drives the whole positioning in 'the empire writes back' in literary critique. Against this backdrop, we are unable to reconcile Zadie's seeming romance with the higher currency accent of lettered or snooty English society. We do not detect any indications of her multilingual identity. She is multidialectal certainly. Thus the reality that confronts English language-using writers is a case of shifts at two levels, and responses vary from writer to writer: a shift between dialects, which is seen as an upgrade strategy and achieved in the context of education right inside the core of the erstwhile colonizer's sanctuary. This may also be a form of subversion.

The second kind of shift is tragic if we look at it within the paradigm of scholars like Skutnabb-Kangas who theorize language issues as a component of the larger environmental agenda of biodiversity and protection. It is one in which people born into an environment of multiple languages grow up monolingual rather than multilingual because there are insufficient social resources to maintain multilingualism. Immigrants' mother tongues and traces of those in their second-language performances of English are socially marked, stigmatized, and employed as markers of ethnosocial borders and stereotypes. Unless diversity is an established institutional policy, people are confronted by a social reality in which they are constantly being othered by being ascribed the membership of a social outgroup, especially adolescents. In the winter of 1991, I made a conscious decision to go six months without writing a single poem unless it came to me in Yoruba, my mother tongue. It never did and I sought closure.

What is not clear from Zadie's lament above is, whether beyond the more obvious dialect and accent swap, she had also swapped an immigrant 'language' or patois for

English, or whether the swap had already occurred in her family by the time she was born. The fact that the voice she speaks with 'these days' is one that assigns to her the lettered identity raises a question about the perceived status of writers like me who do not permanently cross from a provincial to a metropolitan variety.

In relation to writers, writing in English and writing in Englishes draw on different sets of resources, including linguistic ones, although these are not mutually exclusive. Blommaert's (2009) idea of the market of accents applies here and resonates with my reference to the claim of accent choice and de-selection by Zadie Smith. The hierarchy of accents exists in much the same way as the hierarchy of languages. Writing in English and writing in Englishes are assigned social capital differently depending on the ideological affiliation of those conducting evaluation. Although I see the daring in Brutt-Griffler's position, as a product of the (post)colonial experience, I have greater faith and trust in the capacity of *Englishes* to resist hegemony – we see that in the decentring that has taken place in English language testing, even if there is still more work to be done. By decentring, I refer to the examination councils that have either replaced or now co-exist with the Cambridge Examinations Syndicate in, for instance, former colonies. One such is the West African Examinations Council to which I referred earlier.

In extolling Kamau Brathwaite's art on the occasion of winning the Neustadt Prize in 1997, Ngugi wa Thiong'o, who himself had, in an ideological twist, ditched his Western/Christian/English name, *James* Ngugi, and Literature in English for Gikuyu Literature, notes that its distinctive quality is in his orature. He writes, 'The voice: we were being mesmerized by the voice of orature, we were captives of a heritage we knew so well but from which our education had been alienating us' (1997: 134). The interrogation arising from this is whether one can have a voice in a language other than their mother tongue, that is, in a second or foreign language. This question is at the core of the native versus non-native speaker debate (see, for instance, Myhill 2003; Davies 2006). It pertains to rights in this usage. Literary theorists have argued that Bakhtin (1981) ties voice and its authenticity to identity. Every writer has a voice and a community of writers comprises individuals who share certain similarities of voice – parallel to the sociolinguistic notion of speech community. This is traditional thinking. This is how we are able to compartmentalize literary texts into categories such as Commonwealth, Balkan, British, Japanese, Caribbean and so on. In relation to literature in English, each variety bears the weight of a history of engagement between peoples, either within the framework of empire and colonial encounters or, more recently, with globalization. In the contemporary global dispensation, however, we function as members of numerous networks, all of which have varying influences on perceptions and narrations of our worlds. Voice is no longer monolithic and human, and material mobility means that the local bears traces of the global.

The interconnectedness of local and global in relation to English can be traced to empire structures and is covered in the sociolinguistics of colonization (Omoniyi in press). Again, the rebirth of English in non-native climes included its infusion with the localizing agents of those climes. Kamau Brathwaite (1984) remarks that

> We in the Caribbean have a … kind of plurality: we have English, which is the imposed language on much of the archipelago. It is an imperial language, as are French, Dutch and Spanish. We also have what we call creole English, which is a mixture of English and an adaptation that English took in the new environment of the Caribbean when it became mixed with the other imported languages. We have

also what is called *nation language*, which is the kind of English spoken by the people who were brought to the Caribbean, not the official English now, but the language of slaves and labourers, the servants who were brought in.

(Brathwaite 1984: 5–6)

The Nairobi Declaration had called for a reconstitution of the English Department to replace the centrality of English Literature in the syllabus with one that emphasized the centrality of the African experience (wa Thiong'o 1997: 132). But in June 1979, a whole decade after the declaration, I had just completed my first year of a Bachelor of Arts degree at the University of Lagos and both my Philosophy and English Literature modules had been no less Western. At the end of what became dubbed in some Nigerian universities as the Rain Semester (spring and summer terms) and the commencement of the long vacation (summer vacation), I attempted to capture the emotions of temporary loss of friendship over the holidays in a poem. A friend and critic Dare Babarinsa commented on the poem thus: 'There is no snow in Nigeria. Why are you writing about Winter and Summer?' I do not remember what became of the poem nor do I recall the details of its content now, but Babarinsa's comment stayed with me and impacted my perception of authenticity in writing. This experience parallels Brathwaite's (1984) critique of Caribbean writing in which he notes,

And in terms of what we write, our perceptual models, we are more conscious (in terms of sensibility) of the falling snow, for instance … than of the force of the hurricanes which take place every year. In other words, we haven't got the syllables, the syllabic intelligence, to describe the hurricane, which is our own experience, whereas we can describe the imported alien experience of the snowfall.

(Brathwaite 1984: 8–9;
www.courses.vcu.edu/ENG-snh/Caribbean/Barbados/Caribbean/language.htm)

According to him, Nation Language is the strategy for reclaiming and asserting Caribbean identity. This includes the use of conversation, call and response, and a break from the rhythmic patterns of Western canon poetry such as the iambic pentameter. As a final year undergraduate, I published a poem in *The Shuttle*, the departmental journal, which I titled 'The Crawl'. It was a critical commentary on the chaotic traffic of Lagos City. In that poem I remember describing cars as metallic horses, obvious evidence that I had come under the tutelage of colonial writers like Chinua Achebe who had to interpret and translate the colonizer's foreign culture within the framework of indigenous language systems. Horses and metal horses served indigenous and expatriate mobility needs respectively. I set up and presided over *Ijiomi* ('The Whirlpool' in Yoruba) a university-wide poetry group with an annual poetry festival on May Day. In our writings, we fulfilled the meshed roles of artists and social critics for which African writers of the day were renowned. Failed governments, corruption, decay, struggles elsewhere in Africa and postcolonial angst about happenings in the independent nations were themes that we constantly explored. My poem 'Season of Tribulation' which won the runner-up prize in the 1985 National Anti-Apartheid Poetry Competition (Nigeria) and appeared in my volume *Farting Presidents and Other Poems* (2001: 95) ended with Zimbabwe's ZANU-PF's rallying call to action during the struggle for independence: '*Pamberi nachirimenga, pamberi!*' It is glossed 'Forward with the revolution, forward!' Codeswitching English and Shona which I explore to convey a pan-Africanist stance also undermined

477

my claim, as I found out years later that I had wrongly transcribed the Shona noun phrase *neChimurenga* as 'nachirimenga' – a flaw in my auditory perception of soundwaves of what was then an 'alien' phonological system from my radio broadcast source.

Akin Euba (2001: 119) reminiscing about his early experience as a composer after training in English at Trinity College of Music in London in 1957 noted that he

> wanted to write African songs in English, but because that language is such a potent signifier of English traditions, it was not immediately clear to me how my English language songs could be infused with an African identity. I decided that one solution to this problem was to reject British poets for Africans writing in the English language. Consequently, I began a search of the literature of modern African poetry in English (or English translation) and not only found that the existing material was copious but also made a number of discoveries about what African poets were doing. I was particularly fascinated by what they were doing and because their creativity inspired mine from both the stylistic and ideological points of view.

The sentiment or dilemma articulated by Euba here is a diasporic one which one shares as a writer with African sensibilities. What this means is that there is a particular way of seeing and knowing that is heavily influenced by the realities of the African continent. This was captured by Wole Soyinka in his presentation to the Festival of Black Arts and Culture (FESTAC) Colloquium in January 1977 titled 'The Scholar in African Society', in which he lamented that:

> neither of us has yet found a definition, so woefully trapped are we in their languages, and their alphabets.
>
> This Union finds it regrettable that twenty years have been wasted since the Second Congress of African writers in Rome recommended the adoption of one language for African peoples. Resolved to end this state of inertia, hesitancy and defeatism, we have, after much serious consideration, and in the conviction that all technical problems can and will be overcome, unanimously adopted Swahili as the logical language for this purpose.
>
> We exhort all writers to apply every strategy individually and collectively on both national and continental levels to promote the use and the enrichment of Swahili for the present and future needs of the continent. In this connection, we have resolved that the proposed African Co-operative Publishing House shall adopt the policy of translating every work it publishes into Swahili. We exhort all schools to accelerate this process by substituting the study of Swahili for the least viable subject on their curriculum such as European ballet, la Civilisation Française, English Social History, etc., etc.

The lament over twenty years has turned by now into the lament of half a century, including a decade since the 2000 Asmara Declaration on African Languages and Literatures. I capture these laments in my own poem below:

Language death

We choke in the languages we desire
To speak but can't

And die in those we know
But refuse to speak
When the last of us falls
A language lies in state
Waits in vain for post-mortem
Undertakers and final rites
But there's none to attend it.
A language dies in our choice
Not to give it voice
And with it, parts of us.

(From H. Killingray (ed.) (2004)
A Picture in Words: An Anthology of Poetry,
Peterborough: Anchor Books, p. 50)

Of course, this has also raised debates about the agency which structuralists argue is not down to the postcolonial 'us', but to those who manage hegemony globally and create environments in which speakers of African languages are forced to accept that their languages lack cultural capital and a mobile capacity.

However, literature in Englishes has become well established at the Centre with writers from the former literary margins ensconced in the heart of the Centre through the many Booker Prize nominations and awards, the Commonwealth Prize for Literature nominations and Awards and, of course, the Nobel Prize for Literature that have been won by those erstwhile marginal voices (Wole Soyinka and Derek Walcott). There are also prominent inscriptions of that arrival at the Centre. First, Ben Okri's text embossed into one of the pillars on Constitution Road on the approach to Buckingham Palace which reads, 'Our future is greater than our past.' The second instance is Derek Walcott's consideration as the Oxford Poet Laureate in 2008. Both of these instances complement the institutionalization of WE voices within the Centre through cultural ceremonies such as the conferment of national honours on some who have settled permanently in the United Kingdom – broadcaster Sir Trevor Macdonald comes to mind, as does poet–musician and activist Benjamin Zephaniah, who rejected his nomination for the Queen's New Year's Honours List as Officer of the British Empire on ideological principles (www.guardian.co.uk/books/2003/nov/27/poetry.monarchy).

The features of these voices in the main include the transfiguration of the language in ways that necessitate the discovery of the cultural terrain of their creation in order to access the art in them. Ben Okri's Booker-winning 1992 book, *The Famished Road*, is a testimony to that. Beyond the call and response and conversations that Brathwaite had already identified as condiments of Caribbean and African Literature in English, that is, Englishes, the lexical borrowings and wholesale metaphor infusion are also means by which such transfiguration is achieved.

In an interview with African-Writing Online, Emma Dawson (2008) remarked that she would:

like to create a forum for people to come and have a debate around what I have called *World Englishes Literature* – however I am interested to redefine and rename it as whatever it may be – but essentially to talk about whatever this 'new wave' is, this thing that is not Achebe, that is not Desai, which is new in terms of people publishing who have not known the moment of independence of their

479

country, whatever this thing is, that we have spent an hour talking about, that is what I want people from different countries to come and tell each other about. This is a symposium in that sense: let's assemble and talk to each other. Let's see if the writers from Kenya have some kind of trends at whatever level with the writers from India. Let's have a debate about that. That's really what I'd like to happen, instead of pretending to know it already.

[my emphasis]

The concerns addressed in Dawson's statement encompasses the interface between literary and sociolinguistics scholarship. The cultural themes that interested the Achebe and Desai generation and which they explored in new Englishes are different from those that younger generation writers like Zadie Smith, Arundathi Roy and Chimamanda Ngozi Adichie engage with in new mixed Englishes codes, fashioned or facilitated by globalization. I shall use two pieces of my own work to illustrate this point. The first of these is:

Gone with the Eagle

A thousand jingles to clear
the eardrums of angel witnesses
this dawn of fresh starts

I have found the right wings
so if my mother asks,
comrades in plumage
tell her I have left the parrot
and gone with the Eagle
on wings that glide in the wind
smoothly in peace

tell my mother
when I nested with the parrot
I had no name
because it brought me shame
its household called me
all but what I craved

gossip knew no bounds
and quarrels devoured my soul
dusts of deceit and pebbles
of gracelessness weighed me down
as we raced for ground

tell my mother another tale
that now I have a name
one that gives me pride
when I pick a worm for lunch
my household hails my victory

believing tomorrow
I'll net enough for a barbecue.

when I nested with the parrot
a rabbit in my trap was no sport
whilst the lion roamed free
denying our pot and ego
those additional trips

tell my mother I got tired
of namelessness and greed
tell her the parrot's nest was
too hot for me
tell my mother I have gone with the Eagle
to print my name on the moon.

(Forthcoming in my volume of poems Intimate Notes)

In the poem above we have an illustration of the process of the nativization of English through metaphor transfer from the cultural frame of an indigenous African language into that of English. In this metaphor, the speaker tells the story of a relationship gone awry and explains why they traded the 'parrot's nest' for the 'eagle's nest', and namelessness for a name on the wind. Is there any obvious disconnect as a result of the switch between language and cultural frame? There should not be if the nativization of English is conclusive. The non-native speaker status in the Kachruvian sense, or a non-mother tongue speaker of English in more general parlance, is often invoked to explain a failing or inadequacy expressed in the following poem:

Absentee words

Some times
Absentee words run around caverns
In my head, slippery
Like a truant school kid
Avoiding the teacher
I can't catch them
When I need them most
To plug a hole
In something I'm saying
To an unfortunate someone
Who then has to rack their brain
To figure me out
Absentee words hang me
Like an incomplete sentence.

(©topeomoniyi)

But the question is, can we legitimately claim that this 'condition' is peculiar or unique to non-native or non-mother tongue speakers of English language? Memory lapse may affect speech, but that experience is not restricted to non-native speakers of languages; after all, native speakers of English may be non-native speakers of other languages.

The torment of difference

I was a member of the Thin Raft Poetics, in Reading, Berkshire (south-east England) in the early 1990s. We met Tuesday evenings (7 p.m.–9 p.m.) in the town's main public library. The general philosophy of the group was to constitute a critical audience or readership for members. I was the only 'outsider' non-white member of the group, so, out of a desire to shed the difference and claim belonging, I wrote a poem with the same kinds of metaphor and cadence as my British colleagues. My literary compatriots tore into me. 'The beauty of your work is in your unique voice which makes you stand out and compel people to listen. Surely, you don't want to be lost in a crowd?' Thus autoethnography becomes a theoretical exposé of the self. As a methodological approach it is the ethnography of self, a self that is subject to constant change and negotiation. It is the subjection of oneself and personal experiences over a period to scrutiny and critical analysis through self-reflexivity, self-generated as well as colla-borative textual endeavours. The former are a product of creativity in moments of extraction from the social and/or communal core to a critical space or distance that facilitates, as it were, a process of objectification of the otherwise subjective. In con-trast, collaboration may result from harmonious or conflictual encounters between individual and public bodies. I shall return to elaborate on this later. The poem below won runner-up in the 1999 Society for Humanistic Anthropology's poetry competition. It is my voice in two tones in an attempt to unify the cultural aesthetics of my home-home, Yorubaland (and Sub-Saharan Africa more generally) and the cultural aesthetics of my diasporic home in the West, the United Kingdom. *Gbomo gbomo* means 'child snatcher/abductor' in Yoruba. Eight-year-old Sarah Payne was snatched close to her grandmother's home in July 2000 and found dead and naked in a field 12 days later, obvious victim of a paedophile on the prowl.

Gbomo gbomo
(for Sarah Payne)

You spawn shivers and send every soul
Into a terrifying tremble *gbomo gbomo*
You're the kind stranger from whom
Children must not accept cookies
In case they're laced with spells
That make them vanish or turn into goats
To be led away at the end of a tether
Seen by many but unknown to any

When you strike at home
Everyone brow-beaten thinks
Of a newly carved calabash
Waiting to sit on the hot palms
Of a tot cut down to feed avarice

We all think of windowless rooms
Or dungeons, some attic spaces
Their labyrinths known and walked
By you and your ilk alone
We think of the lava
Of hot currency that flows
From the spirit world or hell
When you summon a mummified kid
Yours is a factory of blood-money

Now away from home
I see you in a different garb
Old wine in new bottle
But I recognize your bad breath
In the air, I'm not deceived.
You rode the crest of gusty winds
To assume a European face
One painted in paedophilic strains
Of red, maiden blood from hymeneal
Rupture of the children whose Barbie dolls
You chopped up and flung in the fields
Or those whose sand castles you leave
On the beach as vital clue for detectives
Reconstructing the final moments
Of a life that hardly begun.

But there's a difference between you now
And you I used to know
For the tots you snatched at home
Fuelled a myth for you and them
Through the mystery of their permanent exit
You were invincible, unseen and unknown
Because the gone stayed gone and silent

But here you strewn them in the fields
Bared of all dignities, empty shells
Left to the elements to further defile
Angered spirits disembodied haunt you down
So you leave your trails of guilt on security
Cameras and DNA-ed garments and shoes
For a profiler to piece together a face
And endorse a warrant for your arraignment
Unveiling the horrid directory of your tribe
On pages of The News of the World

Folks say a dead child is better than a missing one
For then the mourning is done and grief is mastered
Which-ever way, there's a hollow of sorrow

Gorged into the souls of your harrowed victims
So when I think of the two faces of you
I have genocidal feats and embrace your tribe

(*Anthropology and Humanism*, 26 (1) (June 2001): 90)

I shall comment briefly on features in this poem that are not essentially Western even if the topic event is. Consider the following extracts from the poem:

(i) Folks say a dead child is better than a missing one
(ii) You were invincible, unseen and unknown/ Because the gone stayed gone and silent
(iii) maiden blood from hymeneal/ Rupture of the children whose Barbie dolls/ You chopped up and flung in the fields

In (i), I convey a Yoruba worldview which holds that the closure of the death experience is preferable to the open-ended emotional turmoil of a missing child. Interestingly, (ii) is simply a play on the title of a novel I read as a teenager, *The Dead Stay Dumb* (James Hadley Chase, 1971). My journeying between cultural terrains is again evident in 'whose Barbie dolls you chopped up'. The commentary on paedophilia speaks to the moral fibre of societies within which my poems have been birthed. In the next poem, I report my tourist impression of a visit to Berlin. Here I mix not just cultural references that derive from different global localities, but also codeswitching between English and German.

Berlin 1997

I came
thinking of the wall
that halved you long ago
I came unprepared
for what you've become

East to West
Coca-Cola and McDonalds
Spaghetti and Tandoori
light global candles
on concrete mantles and glass screens
your days filter into lit nights
gently scouring the blot
from an old and evil desire

At Zoologischer Garten
the World congregated to engage
the past and savour your present
one full length poster spoke
for silenced children:
'*Geschlossen wegen Einsamkeit*'
Mehr Zeit für Kinder.

Endorsements on your billboards
were of humour and happier times;
of Chasing Amy one philosophised:
'Sex ist einfach – Liebe ist schwer'
greeted by a long queue of lovers
seeking to learn a lesson or two
in the darkness of cinema halls

It is six decades since Jesse Owens
his testimony and your new wisdom
warm U-Bahn seats for my tribe
spread beyond Afrikanische Straße
but your grapevine is full
of the scourge of Istanbul's children
a new rage for a new age?

Whilst I hum millennium chants
of harmony among men
open up Berlin, open more
for that which is to come
that knows no borders!

©topeomoniyi Berlin, August 1997
(Forthcoming in my volume of poems *Word-o-graphs*)

The political sensibility expressed above addresses specific diaspora realities such as Jesse Owens' reception in Berlin on the eve of the Third Reich and the impact of his performance on ideology. My exploration of this topic arguably is the consequence of relocation and a personal response to a presumed metropolitan construction of 'I'. The 'I' matures into the voice-over commentator in the poem below. The voice owes any claim of authenticity to an implicit endorsement by Englishes and the ideological binary 'Us/Them' invoked by the pronominals 'they' and 'their' as the poet, and I play spokesperson for asylum seekers awaiting deportation.

Removal Centre

They say it's The Removal Centre
But they intend a euphemism
For late modernity's House of Horror
Presided over by a pack of dogs
On hind-legs playing gods
In Gosport

At Haslar
Nothing is removed
Only man's dignity
Without which he returns
To beast. Apes in grandeur
Prepped for their Circus

©topeomoniyi

485

There is nothing obviously provincial in the language variety used in these final poems. The significance of this observation is that Writing in English and Writing in Englishes could be options between which one moves as a writer depending on the target readership. I shall conclude this discussion with an observation about native-like structures with non-native spirits coursing through them. By this I refer to the use in creative writing of forms that by the rules of grammar are flawless and could in fact pass for native, but become problematic or 'different' within a semiotic framework of analysis, as in the extracts from 'Exile songs' and 'Tempe, Arizona' below:

Exile songs

> every day now I hear a music
> different from all around me,
> one fit for my exile ears
> I ride the buses on Dublin roads
> but the tar runs past Ojota
> in the direction of home
>
> in the silent cruise of the trans-island
> coach, I hear the motor boys of home
> screaming *'one more passenger, one more passenger!'*
> low-tones coaxes in gaelicised English
> settle like pidgin upon my senses
>
> when the Angelus sounds
> I hear it as music in the voice
> of a distant Imam summoning Faithfuls
> to the 4 o' clock
> yet I see no gourds and no ablutions
> and no spotlessly clean robes fit
> for the presence of God.
>
> even the billboards
> are in on this giant conspiracy
> hoisting pictures of Herzegova spotting
> the Wonderbra and a quizzical smile
> teasing 'are you game lads?'
> yet I behold not her splendour
> splashed upon the billboards
> but familiar bosoms
> with a different statistics
> rolling to the rhythm of girdles and beads
> imagination and recollections explode
> to billboard size.

©topeomoniyi1998

Tempe, Arizona

Tearducts of a burdened river
sirens for a distressed eco-system
as the Colorado feeds sprinklers
for a carpet of green vanity
on the luscious lawns of Tempe

Visions of the Nature Brigade
behind diswatered mermaids
and other homeless amphibians
in a protest march down Apache Boulevard
past the Holiday Inn

I joined them at the corner
of Adam South's run
after I tanked up on doritos,
no one should go to war
running on empty.

But the spring in the steps
of those who marched with me,
the excitable faces of the 4WD damsels
flashing false hooters from coconut shells
alongside us in Freeway traffic

Got me thinking about the hero
who labelled women lubricants of the revolution,
and how a nation in synchronized
orgasm defines the axis of evil
I was lost on the moment.

©topeomoniyi2003

In both of these poems I indulge in multivariety Englishes which is a reflection of my trajectories, as well as of my locations at the moment of writing. 'One more passenger, one more passenger' and 'rolling to the rhythm of girdles and beads' are not part of the commuter experience in Dublin City. As a social practice they are a developing world phenomenon. Passengers board buses at designated bus stations and are pre-ticketed. In Lagos, passengers are harvested en route. Gaelicized English and Pidgin English belong to different sociolinguistic scales depending on who and where evaluation is taking place. Yet in a creative moment the two worlds merged bringing their discourses along with them. Similarly in the poem 'Tempe, Arizona', 'I tanked up' (ate/filled my stomach) in Nigerian colloquialism but was affronted by American 'false hooters', bringing about once again, a union of discursive worlds. It is for this reason that I suggested at the beginning that it may be unwise to attempt to identify writers using nation-state tags when the reality they live and express in contemporary times is a global one.

Suggestions for further reading

Alim, H.S., Ibrahim, A. and Pennycook, A. (eds) (2009) *Global Linguistic Flows: Hip Hop Cultures, Youth Identities, and the Politics of Language*, London: Routledge.
Higgins, Christina (2009) *English as a Local Language: Post-colonial Identities and Multilingual Practices*, Bristol: Multilingual Matters.
Omoniyi, Tope (2006) 'Hip-hop through the World Englishes lens: a response to globalization', in J. Kachru and J. Lee (eds) *World Englishes in Global Popular Cultures*, Oxford: Blackwell.
Saxena, Mukul and Omoniyi, Tope (eds) (in press) *Contending with Globalisation in World Englishes*, Bristol, Multilingual Matters.

List of poems

'Language death' from *A Picture in Words: An Anthology of Poetry*, edited by Heather Killingray (2004), Peterborough: Anchor Books, p. 50.
'Gone with the eagle' forthcoming in my volume of poems *Intimate Notes*.
'Gbomo gbomo', *Anthropology and Humanism* (June 2001), 26 (1): 90.
'Berlin' forthcoming in my volume of poems *Word-o-graphs*.
'Removal Centre' forthcoming in *Word-o-graphs*.
'Exile songs' from my *Farting Presidents and Other Poems* (2001), Ibadan: Kraft Books, p. 87.
'Tempe Arizona' forthcoming in *Word-o-graphs*.

References

Bakhtin, Mikhail (1981) *The Dialogic Imagination: Four Essays*, ed. Michael Holquist, trans. Caryl Emerson and Michael Holquist, Austin: University of Texas Press.
Bamgbose, Ayo (ed.) (1976) *Mother Tongue Education: The West African Experience*, London: Hodder and Stoughton.
Bhabha, Homi (1994) *The Location of Culture*, London: Routledge.
Bhatt, Rakesh M. (2008) 'In other words: language mixing, identity representations, and third space', *Journal of Sociolinguistics*, 12 (2): 177–220.
Blommaert, J. (2008) *Grassroots Literacy: Writing, Identity and Voice in Central Africa*, London: Routledge.
——(2009) 'A market of accents', *Language Policy*, 8 (3): 243–59.
——(2010) *The Sociolinguistics of Globalisation*, Cambridge: Cambridge University Press.
Bourdieu, P. (1991) *Language and Symbolic Power*, Cambridge, MA: Harvard University Press.
Brathwaite, Edward Kamau (1984) *History of the Voice: The Development of Nation Language in Anglophone Caribbean Poetry*, London: New Beacon Books.
——(1995) 'Nation language', in Bill Ashcroft, Gareth Griffiths and Helen Tiffin (eds) *The Postcolonial Studies Reader*, London: Routledge, pp. 309–13.
Brutt-Griffler, J. (2002) *World English: A Study of Its Development* (Bilingual Education and Bilingualism 34), Clevedon: Multilingual Matters.
Chase, James H. (1971) *The Dead Stay Dumb*, Panther Books.
Davies, Alan (2006) *The Myth of the Native Speaker*, Clevedon: Multilingual Matters.
Dawson, Emma (2007) 'Outside the inner circle', English, Drama, Media NATE 9 (October): 30–4.
——(2008) 'Post-colonial versus World Englishes literature: an interview', *African Writing Online: Many Literatures, One Voice*, 4 (April 2008), at www.african-writing.com/four/emmadawson.htm (accessed 14 November 2009).
Dissayanake, Wismal (2006) 'Cultural studies and discursive constructions of World Englishes', in Braj B. Kachru, Yamuna Kachru and Cecil L. Nelson (eds) *The Handbook of World Englishes*, Oxford: Blackwell, pp. 545–66.

Euba, Akin (2001) 'Text Setting in African Composition', *Research in African Literatures*, 32 (2): 119–32.

Kirkpatrick, Andy (2007) *World Englishes: Implications for International Communication and English Language Teaching*, Cambridge: Cambridge University Press.

Lippi-Green, Rosina (1997) *English with an Accent: Language, Ideology, and Discrimination in the United States*, London and New York: Routledge.

Myhill, John (2003) 'The native speaker, identity and the authenticity hierarchy', *Language Sciences*, 25: 77–97.

Omoniyi, Tope (2003) 'Indigenous language capital and development in Sub-Saharan Africa', BAAL/ CUP seminar, 12–14 December 2003, Gregynog.

——(2008) '"So I choose to do am Naija style": hip-hop and postcolonial identities', in H. Samy Alim, Ibrahim Awad and Alastair Pennycook (eds) *Global Linguistic Flows: Hip-Hop Cultures, Identities and the Politics of Language*, London: Routledge, pp. 113–35.

——(in press) 'The sociolinguistics of colonization: a perspective of language shift', in Herbert Igboanusi (ed.) *Language Shift in Sub-Saharan Africa*, special edition of *Sociolinguistic Studies* 3 (3).

——(forthcoming) 'Introduction', in Tope Omoniyi (ed.) *Language Capital in the Development Process in Sub-Saharan Africa*, special issue of *International Journal of the Sociology of Language*.

Omoniyi, Tope and Saxena, Mukul (in press) 'Introduction', in M. Saxena and T. Omoniyi (eds) *Contending with Globalization in World Englishes*, Clevedon: Multilingual Matters.

Pennycook, Alastair (1994) *The Cultural Politics of English as an International Language*, London: Longman.

——(2008) *Global Englishes and Transcultural Flows*, London: Routledge.

Phillipson, R. and Skutnabb-Kangas, T. (1986) 'English: the language of wider colonisation', paper presented at the 11th World Congress of Sociology, New Delhi.

Smith, Z. (2009) 'Speaking in tongues', *New York Review of Books*, 56 (3) (26 February), at www. nybooks.com/articles/22334.

Spivak, Ghayatri (1988) 'Can the subaltern speak?' in Cary Nelson and Lawrence Grossberg (eds) *Marxism and the Interpretation of Culture*, Chicago: University of Illinois Press, pp. 271–313.

Wa Thiong'o, N. (1997) *Writers in Politics: A Re-engagement with Issues of Literature and Society*, Nairobi: East African Educational Publishers/Heinemann

28

Online Englishes

Mark Warschauer, Rebecca Black and Yen-Lin Chou

Introduction

The last few decades have witnessed some of the most rapid changes in human communication in world history. Though the internet was barely known a quarter of a century ago, today some 1.5 billion people around the world read, write and communicate online (Miniwatts Marketing Research 2008). An estimated 55 billion emails are sent every day, not including spam (Grossman 2008), and the blogging search engine Technorati is tracking some 133 million blogs around the world (Technorati 2008). From knowledge workers to office staff to teenage youth, large numbers of people around the world rely extensively on computer-mediated communication.

A disproportionate amount of this global communication is conducted in English. More than half of the .com and .net internet sites in the world are hosted in the US (Paolillo 2005), and the nine most heavily visited websites in the world are all in English (Alexa 2008). An estimated 29.4 per cent of world internet users are native speakers of English (Miniwatts Marketing Group 2008), and English has become the dominant lingua franca for cross-language communication online (Crystal 2001; Paolillo 2005).

Online communication is different than previous forms of interaction in many important ways. Online, large numbers of people from around the world can interact at the same time in a single forum. While interacting at a fast pace, they can still maintain a written archive of their communication. People can quickly encounter and get to know large numbers of strangers, and they can stay in constant close communication with friends at almost all hours of the day. They can publish their reports or multimedia documents for virtually free, and they can hotlink parts of their texts to link to the words of others.

For all of these reasons, online communication is engendering its own styles, genres and forms of English. Some people contend that it is resulting in the bastardization of English, the ruining of standards, and the misinformation of the public, while others contend that it is democratizing English by extending new forms of low-cost interaction, collaboration, and publishing to native and non-native English speakers around the world. While there are certainly elements of truth in both arguments, there is no doubt that online Englishes are challenging prior notions of who the language belongs to, whose voices are heard, and who contributes to knowledge formation and dissemination.

Whose language?

Anatoly Voronov, then the director of a pioneering telecommunications network in Russia, spoke for many around the world when in 1996 he called the English-dominant World Wide Web 'the ultimate act of intellectual colonialism' (Specter 1996: 1). In France, Russia, China, the Middle East and elsewhere, government officials, language rights activists and others were up in arms about the fact that upwards of 80 per cent of the web's content was in a single colonial language (Warschauer 2000a).

Since then, these concerns have subsided, as the internet has become much more multi-lingual. The percentage of English online has fallen by about half, with the amount of online content growing rapidly in both major languages and minor languages (Pimienta 2005). For example, Wikipedia alone has versions in 262 languages, 163 of which include 1,000 or more articles, and a number of which are endangered (Cohen 2006; Wikipedia 2009a).

The growth of multiple languages online undermines neither the internet's use as a medium for communication *across* language groups nor the role of English as domi-nant lingua franca in such cross-linguistic contact. This lingua franca role both corre-sponds to, and has accelerated, the already prominent role of English in international media, political and business communication at the advent of the internet (Crystal 2003). At first glance, the pre-eminence of English as the *de facto* global lingua franca would seem to privilege native English speakers, who can participate effortlessly in international online fora. However, by simultaneously facilitating daily communication in English by hundreds of millions of non-native speakers around the world, this trend also calls into question who controls English and sets its standards. There is thus a growing movement around the world to teach a denationalized version of English based on local and regional standards of pronunciation, syntax and usage, rather than US or British English (Warschauer 2000b), and to use a simplified global English rather than US or British English in international business correspondence (McAlpine 2006). At the same time, the US- and British-dominated English language teaching (ELT) pub-lishing industry is being increasingly challenged by competitors from *outer* or *expand-ing circle* (Kachru 1990) countries such as Singapore, Israel, Greece and Spain (Francis 2000). This internationalization of English was brought home to the first author of this chapter when I worked on a large ELT project in Cairo, and my Egyptian colleagues revised my English language correspondence to ensure that it met the standards of pragmatics and politeness of English language communication in Egypt, even when that communication was directed from one American to another (see discussion in Warschauer 2000b).

Stultified norms of what constitutes English are also being challenged by the wide-spread use of highly colloquial, informal and hybrid forms of interaction referred to as *Netspeak* (Crystal 2004). These new forms are especially prominent in highly interactive forms of computer communication, such as electronic mailing (emailing), instant messa-ging (IMing), internet-relay chat (IRC or chatting) and short-messaging service (SMS, also known as texting). A great deal of public rhetoric is grounded in what Crystal (2001: 1) calls a 'genre of worry' that focuses on the potentially corruptive nature of online registers and the idea that non-standard linguistic conventions associated with electronic media are spilling over into offline writing and conversation. Scholarly research surrounding these forms of computer-mediated communication (CMC) has tended to fall into two distinct camps: studies celebrating the unique nature of online registers; and studies disavowing any significant difference between on- and offline communication, save for the medium. Of late, such scholarship has turned towards a more holistic approach to understanding online discourse, emphasizing the interplay of technical and contextual factors.

Electronic mail

Email, which predates the internet, is an asynchronous form of online communication that allows users to write, send, save and sort electronic messages. When it came into common use in the 1990s, email was heralded as a revolutionary medium that would change the face of communication. Early examinations of the linguistic features of email suggested that users' language tended to be less formal, less lexically sophisticated, and less grammatically and orthographically correct than paper-based prose (Baron 1998; Crystal 2001). Scholarly analysis of email and similar forms of CMC also gave rise to preliminary discussions about electronic text as a new hybrid communicative mode that blurred the distinction between spoken and written language (Ferrara *et al.* 1991; Werry 1996; Yates 1996).

In spite of this auspicious beginning, in terms of transformative linguistic and generic potential, email has continued, in Herring's (2004: 27) words, 'slouching toward the ordinary'. No longer on the cutting edge of information and communication technologies (ICTs), email is viewed as passé by youth, and is often used by adults in lieu of paper letters, announcements and memos. The English language forms and grammatical conventions for personal and business interactions conducted via email have come to mimic their print-based counterparts to a great degree (Crystal 2001). Some exceptions include the aforementioned informality that often manifests in a lack of salutations, an extended range of punctuation (e.g. '!!!!!!'), and a reduced use of capitalization (Crystal 2001).

Instant messaging and chatting

IMing and chatting are real-time or synchronous forms of online communication that came into popular use in the 1990s. The primary difference between IMing and chatting is that IMing only allows dyadic communication while chatting allows multiple users to exchange messages at the same time in what is known as a *chat room*. According to Pew Internet and American Life surveys, around 53 million online adults (Shiu and Lenhart 2004) and around 13 million online teens (Leinhart *et al.* 2001) use IM on a daily basis, with around 41 per cent of working internet users using IM in the workplace (Madden and Jones 2008). Recent studies have shown that IM is more than just a communicative medium; it also serves as a way for youth to strengthen and expand social networks (Lewis and Fabos 2005), and as a means of self-expression via customized user profiles, buddy icons and away messages (Shiu and Lenhart 2004).

Due to their synchronous nature, IM and chat interactions, more so than email, tend to take on a highly informal, conversational format and have been catalysts for a great deal of public concern surrounding the possible deleterious effects of online communication on the English language. For example, in a *New York Times* article, a teacher expressed concern over abbreviations such as 'u, r, ur, b4, wuz, cuz, 2', appearing of late in student writing. According to the article, such abbreviations are part of an 'online lingua franca: English adapted for the spitfire conversational style of internet instant messaging' (Lee 2002: eighth paragraph). However, the media also have described this 'online lingua franca' as 'the bastardization of language' (O'Connor 2005, cited in Tagliamonte and Denis 2008: 4) and 'the linguistic ruin' (Axtman 2002, cited in Tagliamonte and Denis 2008: 4) of modern times.

Public concern about language change seems to stem from several discourse features that are commonly used in IM and other forms of online communication. One such feature is the tendency towards the aforementioned abbreviations. Other common features include acronyms and initialisms, which are abbreviations formed using the initial letters or syllables of a phrase. Abbreviations typically associated with IM and chat are *lol* (laugh out loud), *brb* (be right back), *afk* (away from keyboard), *asl* (age, sex, location). America Online, provider of AIM, the first widely used IM program, hosts a website with a list of AIM acronyms (America Online 2008). Another discourse feature commonly associated with online communication is the emoticon. The word 'emoticon' comes from a portmanteau of the words *emote* (or *emotion*) and *icon* and it describes graphic or keyboard representations of facial and bodily expressions or emotional content. Common emoticons include :) (smiling face), ^_^ (Asian smiling face), ;_; (face with tears), @_@ (surprised face), and XD (mischievous face). Rebus forms of writing are also commonly associated with IM and, as will be discussed in the next section, SMS. Common rebuses include *aar8* (at any rate), *b4n* (by for now) and *cul8r* (see you later).

Linguists, on the other hand, have proposed that IM language use is much less radical than the press suggests. For example, Baron's (2004) study, based on a corpus of US college students' instant messages, found that only 0.3 per cent of words were common IM abbreviations, less than 0.8 per cent were common IM acronyms, only 0.4 per cent were emoticons, and that only 65.3 per cent of contracted word forms were used. A study based on a corpus of Canadian teens' IM use findings yielded similar statistical results (Tagliamonte and Denis 2008). This latter study also examined 'the extent to which IM language mirrors everyday language' by comparing the use of discourse features such as personal pronouns, quotatives and intensifiers in written text, IM and spoken youth language. According to the authors, the analysis revealed that 'IM language is characterized by a robust mix of features from both informal spoken registers and more formal written registers – in essence it is a hybrid register' (Tagliamonte and Denis 2008: 5).

In a qualitative study of CMC, Lam (2004) investigated youths' use of language in a Chinese–English bilingual chat room. According to Lam, youth in this chat room code-switched between English and Chinese in order to express modality, convey humour and emotion, and mark social roles and relationships in their conversations. Much like the previous study, Lam's findings suggest that IM language is a hybrid register in several respects. First, the IM language of youth in the bilingual chat room incorporated features of spoken Chinese, as well as written English text. Moreover, Lam points out that use of Chinese discourse markers 'could be a simple yet pervasive way in which a Cantonese conversational tone is introduced into an otherwise English dialogue' (2004: 54), thus representing the global forms of English being used by adolescents in online spaces that attract interlocutors from around the world. She concludes that use of such hybrid forms serves to help create a 'collective ethnic identity' (2004: 45) for Chinese immigrants.

Finally, though research in this area has just begun, initial studies indicate that messaging on youth-oriented social network sites, such as MySpace and Facebook, features the same kind of informal elements found in instant messaging and chat rooms, such as written description of non-linguistic cues (e.g. 'hug,' 'wink'), use of non-linguistic symbols to display emotions (e.g. ♥), shortened forms (e.g. *bday, pic, luv*) and extensive code-switching between multiple dialects and languages (Chou 2008).

Short-messaging service

Another electronic form of communication that is rapidly growing in popularity among youth and adults alike is short-messaging service (SMS), otherwise known as *texting*. Text messages are asynchronous and are constrained by a protocol that allows a maximum of 160 characters per message. This constraint on the number of characters has prompted widespread use of abbreviated forms of language often referred to as 'textese'. Much like the language associated with IM and chat, textese consists of abbreviation, logographic spelling and rebus forms of writing. In recent years, there have been linguistic analyses of texting in several languages, including Swedish (Hård af Segerstad 2002), Norwegian (Ling 2005) and German (Döring 2002, cited in Ling and Baron 2007). Save for one study on British English (Thurlow 2003), there have been relatively few studies of the language forms associated with English-based texting. This can in part be attributed to the ubiquity of mobile phones and thus texting in Europe and Asia, versus the high percentage of personal computers and thus IM and chat in the US (see Ling and Baron 2007).

As the one exception, Thurlow (2003) examined the linguistic forms and communicative functions of youth's text message use. Findings revealed that the primary linguistic changes that youth made (abbreviations, contractions, acronyms, misspellings and non-conventional spellings) were 'serving the sociolinguistic "maxims" of (a) brevity and speed, (b) paralinguistic restitution and (c) phonological approximation' (Thurlow 2003: section 4). According to the authors, these changes were linguistically 'unremarkable' and 'would not be out of place on a scribbled note left on the fridge door' (2003: section 4). Thurlow's discussion highlights a theme that runs through much of the academic research and commentary on the potential linguistic changes associated with new ICTs – that technologies such as email, IM, chat and SMS do not, for the most part, bring about changes in language forms, but rather amplify trends already underway. Studies consistently show that levels of informality and the use of non-standard linguistic forms vary according to context and purpose. As Crystal (2008) points out in the following passage, rebuses and other abbreviated forms of writing have been around for centuries:

> Similarly, the use of initial letters for whole words (*n* for 'no', *gf* for 'girlfriend', *cmb* 'call me back') is not at all new. People have been initialising common phrases for ages. IOU is known from 1618. There is no difference, apart from the medium of communication, between a modern kid's *lol* ('laughing out loud') and an earlier generation's *Swalk* ('sealed with a loving kiss').
>
> (Crystal 2008: 14th paragraph)

In summary, electronic interaction today features many of the same types of abbreviations and colloquialisms as those that occurred previously when conversational English was put into writing. However, thanks to the sheer size and volume of the internet, and the amount of time many people spend chatting or texting online, such forms have become more widespread and controversial. Overall, they represent an expansion of the written use of colloquial English vs formal or academic English. As such, they enable many people on the margins of power, including youth and immigrants, to communicate in a form that better expresses their sense of identity and community.

Whose voice?

The principal inventor of the web, Timothy Berners-Lee, intended it to be a read–write medium in which it was as easy to create and publish material as it was to read and browse (Berners-Lee 1999). However, the web that emerged frustrated that vision, as online publishing in the web's early days necessitated mastery of complex coding processes. The development of specialized web design software partially solved this problem, but it was the development and diffusion of free blogging software and host sites that truly allowed web-based publishing to become a mass phenomenon.

Blogs fall within a range of categories, each with its own antecedents in other media (for an overview, see Miller and Shepherd 2004). As Chesher (2005) notes, the majority appear to fall within two general types. First, there are personal journals, which fall within the pre-internet tradition of diaries and personal letters. They largely describe people's personal thoughts, feelings and day-to-day experiences, and serve the dual purpose for the writer of keeping friends or family informed and reflecting on one's identity through writing. A second type of blog falls within the tradition of the newspaper column or pamphlet. It seeks to inform, agitate and persuade, most frequently on political topics.

Herring and colleagues carried out content and genre analysis of several hundred randomly selected blogs in a series of studies published in 2004–6 (Herring, Kouper, Scheidt and Wright 2004; Herring, Scheidt, Bonus and Wright 2004; Herring *et al.* 2005; Herring and Paolillo 2006; Herring *et al.* 2006). They found that personal journals constituted 70.4 per cent of their sample (Herring *et al.* 2005). The next largest group, constituting 12.6 per cent of the sample, was what they called *filter blogs*, because they often filtered news and information from the broader web (see Blood 2002 for original use of the term). These filter blogs primarily contained observations and were of external, typically public, events and tended to correspond to the informational/agitational purpose described above. A third type of blog was identified that seeks to provide information and observations on a topic, project or product; this category, referred to as k-log (knowledge log), constituted 4.5 per cent of the blogs they examined.

Though Herring and her colleagues did not match blog purpose with blog topic in their analyses, the sample blogs they chose as illustrations for each of the three main purpose categories match exactly with the topical categorization suggested by Stone (2004), with personal journal blogs typified by personal experience topics, filter blogs typified by political topics, and knowledge blogs typified by technology topics.

There is wide variation in blog structure, from single-author blogs with few links to external sites, few if any comments and infrequent updates, to complex multi-author blogs with extensive linking and tagging, constant updates and voluminous commenting. The majority of blogs analysed by Herring's group fell on the simple side. A total of 90.8 per cent of the randomly selected blogs they analysed were single-authored, and blogs in their sample were updated on an average of every 2.2 days. The typical blog entry contained 0.65 links to other material, and only 43 per cent of blogs allowed comments by others. A total of 9.2 per cent of blog entries contained images (Herring *et al.* 2005).

However, what is typical in a random sample of blogs is quite different than what is typical in people's experiences with blogs. That is because the majority of blogs are rarely visited, while a small number of *a-list* blogs dominate the traffic on the blogosphere (Shirky 2003; Herring *et al.* 2005). Many of these high-traffic blogs feature complex networking features that enable highly innovative forms of communication and advocacy. For example, Daily Kos, a left-of-centre activist political blog, has a main editor and 15 contributing editors who write front-page postings known as stories; hundreds of people who write additional postings linked from the front page known as diaries; thousands of people that write threaded comments on stories and diaries; extensive linking to other blogs and websites from within comments, stories, diaries and user signature lines; tagging of all diaries and stories to create a folksonomy (i.e. user-generated taxonomy) of blog topics; a search mechanism to find stories, diaries or comments by tag, content or author; an elaborate user recommendation system so that the most highly recommended diaries rise to the top of the list while the most negatively rated comments disappear; a hierarchical system of participants so that those who receive the most positive comments achieve greater privileges to negatively rate others; a main blogroll linking to other link-minded blogs on the front page and distinct blogrolls on other pages created by users; and a collaboratively edited political encyclopedia (Kos Media 2009). Launched by a Salvadoran immigrant in 1982, Daily Kos now has more than 175,000 registered users (Kos Media 2009), receives nearly a million daily visits (The Truth Laid Bear 2009), and has established itself as a major force in US politics (Chait 2007).

Examining the overall blogosphere, Herring and her colleagues suggest that blogs fill an intermediary role within online genres, about midway between standard HTML documents, such as personal home pages, and asynchronous computer-mediated communication (CMC), such as newsgroups, bulletin boards or email discussion lists (see Figure 28.1; Herring *et al.* 2005). They are more frequently updated and include more exchange among people and a higher percentage of text (as opposed to multimedia) than standard web pages. But the exchanges on them tend to be more asymmetric (i.e. dominated by main authors) and less frequently updated (with sites such as Daily Kos an exception) than CMC sites such as newsgroups.

Herring and her colleagues have also begun to examine whether gender differences exist in the language used on weblogs, as they do in other written texts. Their initial research suggests that *within* particular blog genres, little differences exist between males' and females' use of language, with *both* men and women using more formal

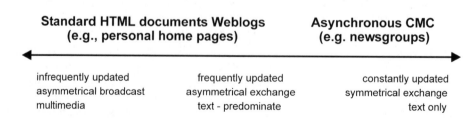

Figure 28.1 The overall blogosphere.

typically 'male' language on filter blogs and more typically 'female' language on personal journal blogs (Herring and Paolillo 2006). However, since filter blogs are mostly written by men and personal journal blogs are mostly written by women (Herring, Kouper, Scheidt and Wright 2004; Herring and Paolillo 2006), the overall use of language in the blogosphere is still gendered.

Scholars have just begun to explore authorship and social participation in the blogosphere (for a discussion of some research questions, see Lankshear and Knobel 2006). A number of initial reports have examined the motivations and personal experiences of bloggers, either from a third-person (e.g. Nardi *et al.* 2004) or first-person perspective (e.g. Krause 2004; Davies and Merchant 2007).

Chesher (2005) analysed authorship on blogs, comparing the conventions of authorship in the blogosphere to those in other electronic or print genres. Authorship in blogs tends to be strongly identified to a real or pseudonymous person through a username or display name for each blog and blog entry, or through an about or profile section that gives more information about the writer. In contrast, older web documents, such as standard web pages, often lack this information. The visual consistency of a blog, compared to a typical HTML web page, also highlights personal ownership and authorship, and the reverse chronological order and specific time stamp on postings create a temporal link between author and reader. Blogs that are most successful, whether in reaching out to a few readers or hundreds of thousands, tend to have a strong authorial voice. In most cases, this personal voice is more easily achieved in blogs than in print journalism, such as newspapers, since blogging encourages an informal, idiosyncratic style and content. In addition, the sheer ease of publishing a blog, as compared, for example, to either setting up and maintaining a frequently revised standard website or becoming a writer for a print newspaper or magazine, makes authorship accessible to a greatly expanded number of people. Chesher concludes that the 'death of the author', which was originally predicted by post-structuralists (Barthes 1977), and which was supposedly going to be hastened by the decentred and collaborative nature of hypertext (Poster 1990; Landow 1992), is greatly exaggerated. As he states, 'the author is alive and well, and has a blog' (2005: first paragraph).

Beyond giving tens of millions of people new opportunities for authorship, the blogosphere also offers a political voice to those on the margins of power. This is due in part to its structural features discussed earlier. By occupying an intermediary format between the highly interactive form of computer-mediated communication and the more permanent forms of traditional online publishing, blogs can simultaneously replace both institutions pointed to by political theorist Tocqueville as vital for citizen participation: the meeting hall and the newspaper (Tocqueville 1937; Warschauer 2003). Thus, in authoritarian countries such as Iran, blogging has emerged as an important, if risky, form of citizen advocacy to challenge both the censored media and the restricted space for traditional organizing (see, e.g., Hendelman-Baavur 2007). In the United States, the grassroots left, which was relatively dormant from the 1970s to 1990s, has found the blogosphere to be a particularly potent organizing tool, using it more successfully than the right to mobilize funds and support for its favoured candidates and causes, and thus counterbalancing the right's dominance over talk radio (Chait 2007). In 2008, online mobilizing and fundraising campaigns played a critical role in the election of the first African-American president, helping Obama first overcome a heavily favoured Democratic competitor for the nomination, and then defeat a popular Republican war hero (Lister 2008).

Of course, blogging is not a silver bullet for achieving social change. The success of the US Democratic Party in the 2006 and 2008 elections was due to many factors beyond successful online mobilization. Also, authoritarian regimes have the power to censor or block blogs and arrest bloggers (see, e.g., Gray 2008), or publish their own misinformation on blogs. The blogosphere is a complex and competitive social and political environment, with those seeking to spark, resist or co-opt social reform movements all fighting for influence, together with millions of others without political agendas (for mappings of the Iranian and US blogospheres, see Kelly and Etling 2008; linkfluence 2008).

Whose knowledge?

If blogs create new opportunities for expressing voice, then wikis create new opportunities for sharing and producing knowledge. Wikis are simply websites that any visitor can contribute to or edit (Richardson 2006). Though there is no authoritative listing or account of the number of wikis, they are surely far fewer than blogs. They have been principally established so that groups of people can contribute their knowledge and writing skills to collaboratively create informational documents. For example, some of the largest wikis (based on statistics from S23 2007) include Richdex (an open source directory on a wide range of topics), WowWiki (an information source about the World of Warcraft online game), and wikiHow (a collaborative how-to manual).

By far the largest wiki, and one of the ten most visited websites in the world (for listing, see Alexa 2008), is Wikipedia. Its English version alone includes more than 2,600,000 articles totalling some 1 billion words, more than 25 times as many as are in the next largest English language encyclopedia, the *Encyclopædia Britannica* (Wikipedia 2009c). Most remarkably, there have been some 236 million edits to Wikipedia since its inception in 2001 made by 5.77 million contributors (Wilkinson and Huberman 2007).

Most of the textual analysis of wikis has been directed at Wikipedia, with much of the research focus on its accuracy. Its breadth of content, ease of access, free cost and links to external material make Wikipedia potentially highly useful to a vast online audience. The foremost question for casual users and researchers alike has been whether a collaborative process that welcomes the participation of novices as well as experts can produce satisfactorily accurate results. In a widely cited study on this topic, *Nature* (Giles 2005) had a panel of experts compare content from 42 entries of approximately the same length on scientific topics from Wikipedia and the *Encyclopædia Britannica*. The experts identified 162 errors in the Wikipedia content (four of which were serious) and 123 in the *Encyclopædia Britannica* content (four of which were serious), thus suggesting that neither encyclopedia is infallible, and that the six-year-old open-source Wikipedia is only slightly less accurate than the 238-year-old professionally edited *Britannica*. In a related study, Chesney (2006) had 258 research staff judge the credibility of two Wikipedia articles, one in their area of expertise and one chosen randomly. In general, the researchers found the articles to be credible, and even more so in their own area of expertise.

Though anyone can accidentally or purposely introduce errors into Wikipedia, they are usually found and corrected quickly by the site's large number of volunteer editors. In one experiment, a professor of communication intentionally introduced 13 errors, some obvious and some subtle, in a range of Wikipedia articles. He checked back on the articles three hours later and all 13 had been corrected (Read 2006).

Focusing on linguistic features rather than accuracy, Bell (2007) compared articles in Wikipedia and the online version of *Encyclopædia Britannica* on three measures: readability, syntax (specifically nominal vs verbal nature) and use of fact statements vs value statements. He found the two encyclopaedias roughly comparable on all three measures. A similar study by Elia, focusing on lexical density, use of formal nouns and impersonal pronouns, and average word length, concurred that the language in Wikipedia 'shows a formal and standardized style similar to that found in *Britannica*' (2007: 18), even though its articles were twice as long on average and had far more hypertextual links.

If blogs served to suggest that the author is well and alive, wikis fulfil the prophecy of authorship fading away. In essence, the distance between the author and audience is eliminated when the audience can directly edit the author's work. In many Wikipedia articles, it is difficult to discern a principal author. For example, a review of the history (posted with each article) for the Wikipedia entry on the innocuous topic of *asparagus* indicates it has been edited hundreds of times by dozens of people over the last five years.

Wikipedia provides a fruitful source for researching the nature of collaborative authorship and editing. A study by Wilkinson and Huberman (2007) analysed the impact of cooperation among editors on Wikipedia on article quality. Specifically, when controlling for age and visibility of articles, they found that both the numbers of edits and the numbers of editors were strongly correlated with article quality. On the one hand, this seems intuitive, in that more attention should result in higher quality. However, the authors point out that in other areas, such as software development, industrial design and cooperative problem-solving, large collaborative efforts are known to produce ambiguous results.

In a study on the Hebrew version of Wikipedia, Ravid (2007, cited in Warschauer and Grimes 2007) analysed how this collaboration worked, and how it differed between featured articles (which are generally recognized as being higher quality) and non-featured articles. Using a variety of social network analyses, he compared structures of dominance and heterogeneity among contributors in 432 featured articles and 410 non-featured articles. In general, he found a greater degree of inequality of participation in the featured articles. In other words both featured and non-featured articles had large numbers of contributors, but a smaller circle of presumably more expert authors contributed a larger portion of the articles selected for their high quality.

One controversy surrounding Wikipedia has focused on it as a source for student research. The founder of Wikipedia, Jim Wales, provides the most commonsense answer to this, suggesting that although Wikipedia can help provide an overview of issues and a starting point for identifying primary sources, students are better off using primary sources as definitive sources in their research. 'For God's sake, you're in college; don't cite the encyclopedia,' Wales told one college student (Young 2006: second paragraph.)

A more interesting question is how writing for wikis can affect the learning process. The potential of wikis for teaching and learning is hinted at by Ward Cunningham, inventor of the wiki, who commented that 'The blogosphere is a community that might produce a work, whereas a wiki is a work that might produce a community' (Warschauer and Grimes 2007: 12). Cunningham's statement illuminates a central contradiction of CMC since its inception: it has served as a powerful medium for exploring identity, expressing one's voice, airing diverse views and developing community, yet has proven a very unsuitable medium for accomplishing many kinds of collaborative work through the inherent difficulty of arriving at decisions in groups dispersed by space and time (see meta-analysis comparing face-to-face and computer-mediated decision-making by Baltes *et al.* 2002).

Wikis turn traditional CMC activity around in several respects. Whereas email and chat, the most traditional CMC genres, facilitate informal, author-centric, personal exchange, writing on a wiki facilitates more formal, topic-centric, depersonalized exchange. Each edit makes a concrete contribution to a collaborative written product, with authorships relegated to a separate page that only the most serious of readers are likely to notice. Wikis are thus an especially powerful digital tool for knowledge development, and thus for education (for examples, see Mader 2007; Wikipedia 2009b).

Finally, the existence of a 'simple English Wikipedia' – with more basic vocabulary and grammatical structures, fewer idioms and jargon, and shorter articles – further democratizes this knowledge tool, as it makes the process of accessing and dis-seminating information more accessible to learners of English, people with learning difficulties, and children (Simple English Wikipedia 2009).

Wikis, and Wikipedia, are just one way that control of the knowledge production process is being challenged. For example, in the area of scholarly and scientific research, online research databases and journals are also threatening academic publishers' control of knowledge dissemination (Willinsky 2006).

Conclusion

When the internet first emerged, there were simplistic notions of a single online Eng-lish, which contrasted with both spoken and written English. In fact, there are many varieties and genres of online English, just as such diversity exists in the spoken and written realms. However, there are some commonalities across this diversity, and one important common trend involves the challenge to traditional gatekeepers of English language use, as exemplified by Wikipedia challenging the *Encyclopædia Britannica*, the blogosphere challenging the mainstream media, or tens of millions of youth challenging notions of correct English.

None of these challenges are, in and of themselves, revolutionary. Non-standard varieties and usages of English have existed for centuries, and new media have continually emerged to either complement or replace the old. The significance of these changes in language and communication will in the future, as in the past, depend on the broader social circumstances in which they unfold. Kaplan's comments on the matter, first made in the early days of the World Wide Web and published in a then-new online magazine, still ring true today:

> The proclivities of electronic texts – at least to the extent that we can determine what they are – manifest themselves only as fully as human beings and their institutions allow, that they are in fact sites of struggle among competing interests and ideological forces.
>
> (Kaplan 1995: 28)

Youth, immigrants and others may seize on new hybrid forms of online Englishes to express their identity, but they will require mastery of sanctioned varieties of English for social or economic advancement. Bloggers can challenge state authority, and can be thrown in jail for doing so. And the viability of new sources of online knowledge, whether in Wikipedia or non-commercial journals, will be called into question by traditional gatekeepers.

Finally, we have only scratched the surface in this chapter of the ways that Englishes are evolving online. Multiplayer games, podcasting and video publishing will all have their own impact on the evolution and use of English. And, in these audiovisual domains, as in the textual domains discussed in this chapter, the proclivities of new Englishes will manifest themselves as human beings and their institutions allow. However, that discussion will have to await another chapter, perhaps to be published on YouTube.

Acknowledgments

This paper draws in part on the first author's previous discussion of blogs and wikis in 'Audience, authorship, and artifact: the emergent semiotics of Web 2.0' (Warschauer and Grimes 2007).

Suggestions for further reading

Baron, N. (2008) *Always On: Language in an Online and Mobile World*, New York: Oxford University Press.

Coiro, J., Knobel, M., Lankshear, C. and Leu, D.J. (eds) (2008) *Handbook of Research on New Literacies*, New York: Lawrence Erlbaum.

Crystal, D. (2006) *Language and the Internet* (2nd edition), Cambridge: Cambridge University Press.

Danet, B. and Herring, S.C. (eds) (2007) *The Multilingual Internet: Language, Culture, and Communication Online*, New York: Oxford University Press.

References

Alexa (2008) 'Global top sites'. Online. Available www.alexa.com/site/ds/top_sites (accessed 23 December 2008).

America Online (2008) *Acronym Dictionary*. Online. Available www.aim.com/acronyms.adp (accessed 8 November 2008).

Baltes, B.B., Dickson, M.W., Sherman, M.P., Bauer, C.C. and LaGanke, J.S. (2002) 'Computer-mediated communication and group decision making', *Organizational Behavior and Human Decision Processes*, 87 (1): 156–79.

Baron, N. (1998) 'Letters by phone or speech by other means: the linguistics of email', *Language and Communication*, 18: 133–70.

——(2004) 'See you online: gender issues in college student use of instant messaging', *Journal of Language and Social Psychology*, 23: 397–423.

Barthes, R. (1977) *Images, Music, Text*, New York: Hill and Wang. Online. Available www.ubu.com/aspen/aspen5and6/threeEssays.html#barthes (accessed 12 June 2007).

Bell, M. (2007) 'The transformation of the encyclopedia: a textual analysis and comparison of the Encyclopædia Britannica and Wikipedia', MA thesis, Ball State University, Muncie, IN. Online. Available www.storygeek.com/?page_id=85> (accessed 9 June 2007).

Berners-Lee, T. (1999) *Weaving the Web: The Original Design and Ultimate Destiny of the World Wide Web by its Inventor*, New York: HarperCollins.

Blood, R. (2002) 'Introduction', in J. Rodzvilla (ed.) *We've Got Blog: How Weblogs are Changing our Culture*, Cambridge, MA: Perseus Publishing, pp. ix–xiii.

Chait, J. (2007) 'The left's new machine', *The New Republic*, 7 May. Online. Available www.tnr.com/politics/story.html?id=9de6735c-9904-4cb4-9fb4-e7305fb3c4a7 (accessed 25 February 2009).

Chesher, C. (2005) 'Blogs and the crisis of authorship', paper presented at the Blogtalk Downunder conference in Sydney, Australia, 19–22 May. Online. Available http://incsub.org/blogtalk/?page_id=40 (accessed 7 June 2007).

Chesney, T. (2006) 'An empirical examination of Wikipedia's credibility', *First Monday*, 11(11). Online. Available http://outreach.lib.uic.edu/www/issues/issue11_11/chesney/ (accessed 25 February 2009).

Chou, Y.-L. (2008) 'Facebook: immigrant students' semiotic production and identity representation in the digital sphere', paper presented at the Future of Writing conference, University of California, Irvine, November.

Cohen, N. (2006) 'African languages grow as a Wikipedia presence', *The New York Times*. Online. Available www.nytimes.com/2006/08/26/arts/26wiki.html> (accessed 24 December 2008).

Crystal, D. (2001) *Language and the Internet*, Cambridge: Cambridge University Press.

——(2003) *English as a Global Language* (2nd edition), Cambridge: Cambridge University Press.

——(2004) *A Glossary of Netspeak and Textspeak*, Edinburgh: Edinburgh University Press.

——(2008) '2b or not 2b?' *Guardian* (online edition), 5 July 2008. Online. Available www.guardian.co.uk/books/2008/jul/05/saturdayreviewsfeatres.guardianreview (accessed 29 September 2008).

Davies, J. and Merchant, G. (2007) 'Looking from the inside out: academic blogging as a new literacy', in M. Knobel and C. Lankshear (eds) *A New Literacies Sampler*, New York: Peter Lang, pp. 167–97.

Elia, A. (2007) 'An analysis of Wikipedia digital writing', proceedings of the 11th Conference of the European Chapter of the Association for Computational Linguistics, pp. 16–21. Online. Available www.aclweb.org/anthology-new/W/W06/W06-2804.pdf (accessed 10 February 2009).

Ferrara, K., Brunner, H. and Whittemore, G. (1991) 'Interactive written discourse as an emergent register', *Written Communication*, 8 (1): 8–34.

Francis, R. (2000) 'Youngsters drive ELT growth'. Online. Available www.allbusiness.com/retail-trade/miscellaneous-retail-miscellaneous/4665137-1.html (accessed 24 December 2008).

Giles, J. (2005) 'Internet encyclopaedias go head to head', *Nature*, 438: 900–1. Online. Available www.nature.com/nature/journal/v438/n7070/full/438900a.html (accessed 25 February 2009).

Gray, S. (2008) 'Iranian blogger arrested "as Israeli spy"', *Guardian* (online edition), 19 November. Online. Available www.guardian.co.uk/world/2008/nov/19/iran-middleeast (accessed 24 December 2008).

Grossman, A.J. (2008) 'Experts reveal e-mail nightmares, safety tips', *CNN.com/living*. Online. Available www.cnn.com/2008/LIVING/worklife/10/20/lw.recovering.email.mistakes/index.html (accessed 23 December 2008).

Hård af Segerstad, Y. (2002) 'Use and adaptation of written language to the conditions of computer-mediated communication', unpublished PhD dissertation, Department of Linguistics, Göteborg University. Online. Available www.ling.gu.se/~ylvah/dokument/ylva_diss.pdf (accessed 31 December 2008).

Hendelman-Baavur, L. (2007) 'Promises and perils of Weblogistan: online personal journals and the Islamic Republic of Iran', *Middle Eastern Review of International Affairs*, 11 (2). Online. Available http://meria.idc.ac.il/journal/2007/issue2/jv11no2a6.html (accessed 24 December 2008).

Herring, S.C. (2004) 'Slouching toward the ordinary: current trends in computer mediated communication', *New Media and Society*, 6 (1): 26–36.

Herring, S.C. and Paolillo, J.C. (2006) 'Gender and genre variation in weblogs', *Journal of Sociolinguistics*, 10 (4): 439–59. Online. Available www.blackwell-synergy.com/doi/abs/10.1111/j.1467-9841.2006.00287.x (accessed 14 June 2007).

Herring, S.C., Kouper, I., Scheidt, L.A. and Wright, E. (2004) 'Women and children last: The discursive construction of weblogs', in L. Gurak, S. Antonijevic, L. Johnson, C. Ratliff and J. Reyman (eds) *Into the Blogosphere: Rhetoric, Community, and Culture of Weblogs*. Online. Available www.blogninja.com/women.children.pdf (accessed 25 February 2009).

Herring, S.C., Scheidt, L.A., Bonus, S. and Wright, E. (2004) 'Bridging the gap: a genre analysis of weblogs', *Proceedings of the 37th Hawai'i International Conference on System Sciences*, IEEE Press: Los Alamitos, pp. 1–9. Online. Available http://ieeexplore.ieee.org/xpls/abs_all.jsp?arnumber=1265271 (accessed 14 June 2007).

Herring, S.C., Kouper, I., Paolillo, J.C., Scheidt, L.A., Tyworth, M. and Welsch, P. (2005) 'Conversations in the blogosphere: an analysis "from the bottom up"', *Proceedings of the 38th Hawai'i International Conference on System Sciences*, Los Alamitos: IEEE Press, pp. 1–11. Online. Available www.blogninja.com/hicss05.blogconv.pdf (accessed 25 February 2009).

Herring, S.C., Scheidt, L.A., Kouper, I. and Wright, E. (2006) 'A longitudinal content analysis of weblogs: 2003–4', in M. Tremayne (ed.) *Blogging, Citizenship, and the Future of Media*, London: Routledge, pp. 3–20.

Holloway, T., Božicevic, M. and Börner, K. (2007) 'Analyzing and visualizing the semantic coverage of Wikipedia and its authors', *Complexity*, 12 (3): 30–40. Online. Available http://arxiv.org/abs/cs/0512085 (accessed 14 June 2007).

Kachru, B. (1990) *The Alchemy of English: The Spread, Functions, and Models of Non-native Englishes*, Urbana, IL: University of Illinois Press.

Kaplan, N. (1995) 'E-literacies: politexts, hypertexts, and other cultural formations in the late age of print', *Computer-Mediated Communication Magazine*, 2 (3): 3–35. Online. Available www.december.com/cmc/mag/1995/mar/kaplan.html (accessed 31 December 2008).

Kelly, John J. and Etling, B. (2008) 'Mapping Iran's online public: politics and culture in the Persian blogosphere', Berkman Center for Internet and Society at Harvard University. Online. Available http://cyber.law.harvard.edu/publications/2008/Mapping_Irans_Online_Public (accessed 24 December 2008).

Kos Media (2009) 'Daily Kos: state of the nation', *Daily Kos*. Online. Available www.dailykos.com/ (accessed 21 May 2007).

Krause, S.D. (2004) 'When blogging goes bad: a cautionary tale about blogs, email lists, discussion, and interaction', *Kairos Online Journal*, 9.1. Online. Available http://english.ttu.edu/kairos/9.1/praxis/krause/ (accessed 12 June 2007).

Lam, W.S.E. (2004) 'Second language socialization in a bilingual chat room: global and local considerations', *Language Learning and Technology*, 8: 44–65. Online. Available http://llt.msu.edu/vol8num3/lam/default.html (accessed 16 August 2006).

Landow, G.P. (1992) *Hypertext: The Convergence of Contemporary Critical Theory and Technology*, Baltimore: Johns Hopkins University Press.

Lankshear, C. and Knobel, M. (2006) 'Blogging as participation: the active sociality of a new literacy', paper presented at the American Educational Research Association, San Francisco, April. Online. Available www.geocities.com/c.lankshear/bloggingparticipation.pdf (accessed 10 June 2007).

Lee, J. (2002) 'I think, therefore IM', *New York Times* (online edition), 19 September 2002. Online. Available http://query.nytimes.com/gst/fullpage.html?res=9F06E5D71230F93AA2575AC0A9649C8B63 (accessed 1 January 2009).

Lenhart, A., Rainie, L. and Lewis, O. (2001) 'Teenage life online: the rise of the instant-message generation and the internet's impact on friendships and family relationships', Washington, DC: Pew Internet and American Life Project. Online. Available www.pewinternet.org/report_display.asp?r=36 (accessed 25 February 2009).

Lewis, C. and Fabos, B. (2005) 'Instant messaging, literacies, and social identities', *Reading Research Quarterly*, 40 (4): 470–501.

Ling, R. (2005) 'The socio-linguistics of SMS: an analysis of SMS use by a random sample of Norwegians', in R. Ling and P. Pedersen (eds) *Mobile Communications: Renegotiation of the Social Sphere*, London: Springer, pp. 335–49.

Ling, R. and Baron, N. (2007) 'Text messaging and IM: linguistic comparison of American college data', *Journal of Language and Social Psychology*, 26 (3): 291–8.

linkfluence (2008) 'Map of the political blogosphere – June 2008'. Online. Available http://presidentialwatch08.com/index.php/map/ (accessed 24 December 2008).

503

Lister, R. (2008) 'Why Barack Obama won', *BBC News* (online edition), 5 November. Online. Available http://news.bbc.co.uk/2/hi/americas/us_elections_2008/7704360.stm (accessed 24 December 2008).

McAlpine, R. (2006) 'From plain English to global English', *Quality Web Content.* Online. Available www.webpagecontent.com/arc_archive/139/5/ (accessed 2 October 2008).

Madden, M. and Jones, S. (2008) 'Networked workers', Washington, DC: Pew Internet and American Life Project. Online. Available www.pewinternet.org/pdfs/PIP_Networked_Workers_FINAL.pdf (accessed 8 November 2008).

Mader, S. (2007) 'Using wiki in education'. Online. Available www.wikiineducation.com (accessed 25 February 2009).

Miller, C.R. and Shepherd, D. (2004) 'Blogging as social action: a genre analysis of the weblog', in L. Gurak, S. Antonijevic, L. Johnson, C. Ratliff and J. Reyman (eds) *Into the Blogosphere.* Online. Available http://blog.lib.umn.edu/blogosphere/blogging_as_social_action_a_genre_analysis_of_the_weblog.html (accessed 8 June 2007).

Miniwatts Marketing Group (2008) 'Internet world users by language', *Internet World Stats.* Online. Available www.internetworldstats.com/stats7.htm (accessed 21 May 2007).

Miniwatts Marketing Research (2008) 'Internet usage statistics', *Internet World Stats.* Online. Available www.internetworldstats.com/stats.htm (accessed 23 December 2008).

Nardi, B.A., Schiano, D.J., Gumbrecht, M. and Swartz, L. (2004) 'Why we blog', *Communications of the ACM*, 47 (12): 41–6. Online. Available http://portal.acm.org/citation.cfm?id=1035134.1035163 (accessed 25 February 2009).

Paolillo, J. (2005) 'Language diversity on the internet', in UNESCO Institute for Statistics (ed.) *Measuring Linguistic Diversity on the Internet*, Paris: UNESCO, pp. 43–89.

Pimienta, D. (2005) 'Linguistic diversity in cyberspace: models for development and measurement', in UNESCO Institute for Statistics (ed.) *Measuring Linguistic Diversity on the Internet*, Paris: UNESCO, pp. 12–34

Poster, M. (1990) *The Mode of Information: Poststructuralism and Social Context*, Chicago: University of Chicago Press.

Read, B. (2006) 'Can Wikipedia ever make the grade?' *Chronicle of Higher Education*, 53 (10): A31. Online. Available http://chronicle.com/weekly/v53/i10/10a03101.htm (accessed 14 June 2007).

Richardson, W. (2006) *Blogs, Wikis, Podcasts, and Other Powerful Web Tools for Classrooms*, Thousand Oaks: Corwin Press.

S23 (2007) 'List of largest (media) wikis'. Online. Available http://s23.org/wikistats/largest_html (accessed 8 June 2007).

Shirky, C. (2003) 'Power laws, web logs, and inequality'. Online. Available www.shirky.com/writings/powerlaw_weblog.html (accessed 7 June 2007).

Shiu, E. and Lenhart, A. (2004) 'How Americans use instant messaging', Washington, DC: *Pew Internet and American Life Project.* Online. Available www.pewinternet.org/report_display.asp?r=133 (accessed 1 January 2009).

Simple English Wikipedia (2009) 'Simple English Wikipedia', *the free encyclopedia.* Online. Available http://simple.wikipedia.org/wiki/Wikipedia:Simple_English_Wikipedia (accessed 1 January 2009).

Specter, M. (1996) 'Computer speak; world, wide, web: 3 English words', *New York Times* (online edition), 14 April 1996. Online. Available http://query.nytimes.com/gst/fullpage.html?res=9E0DE2DA1139F937A25757C0A960958260 (accessed 24 December 2008).

Stone, B. (2004) *Who Let the Blogs Out? A Hyperconnected Peek at the World of Weblogs*, New York: St Martin's Griffin.

Tagliamonte, S. and Denis, D. (2008) 'Linguistic ruin? LOL! Instant messaging and teen language', *American Speech*, 83 (1): 3–34.

Technorati (2008) 'State of the blogosphere 2008'. Online. Available http://technorati.com/blogging/state-of-the-blogosphere/ (accessed 23 December 2008).

The Truth Laid Bear (2009) 'The TTLB blogosphere ecosystem ranking by traffic'. Online. Available http://truthlaidbear.com/TrafficRanking.php (accessed 1 January 2009).

Thurlow, C. (2003) 'Generation Txt? The sociolinguistics of young people's text-messaging', *Discourse Analysis Online*, 1 (1). Online. Available http://extra.shu.ac.uk/daol/articles/v1/n1/a3/thurlow2002003. html (accessed 1 January 2009).

Tocqueville, A. de (1937) *Democracy in America, Vol. 1*, New York: Vintage Books.

Warschauer, M. (2000a) 'Language, identity, and the internet', in B. Kolko, L. Nakamura and G. Rodman (eds) *Race in Cyberspace*, New York: Routledge, pp. 151–70.

——(2000b) 'The changing global economy and the future of English teaching', *TESOL Quarterly*, 34: 511–35.

——(2003) *Technology and Social Inclusion: Rethinking the Digital Divide*, Cambridge: MIT Press.

Warschauer, M. and Grimes, D. (2007) 'Audience, authorship, and artifact: the emergent semiotics of Web 2.0', *Annual Review of Applied Linguistics*, 27: 1–23.

Werry, C.C. (1996) 'Linguistic and interactional features of internet relay chat', in Herring, S. (ed.) *Computer-mediated Communication: Linguistic, Social and Cross-cultural Perspectives*, Amsterdam: John Benjamins, pp. 47–63.

Wikipedia (2009a) 'List of Wikipedias'. Online. Available http://meta.wikimedia.org/wiki/List_of_Wiki pedias (accessed 24 December 2008).

——(2009b) 'Wikipedia: school and university projects'. Online. Available http://en.wikipedia.org/wiki/Schools_and_universities_project (accessed 1 January 2009).

——(2009c) 'Wikipedia: size comparisons'. Online. Available http://en.wikipedia.org/wiki/Wikipedia: Size_comparisons (accessed 1 January 2009).

Wilkinson, D.M. and Huberman, B.A. (2007) 'Assessing the value of cooperation in Wikipedia', *First Monday*, 12 (4). Online. Available http://firstmonday.org/htbin/cgiwrap/bin/ojs/index.php/fm/article/view/1763/1643 (accessed 18 February 2010).

Willinsky, J. (2006) *The Access Principle: The Case for Open Access to Research and Scholarship*, Cambridge, MA: MIT Press.

Yates, S.J. (1996) 'Oral and written linguistic aspects of computer conferencing: a corpus based study', in S. Herring (ed.) *Computer-mediated Communication: Linguistic, Social and Cross-cultural Perspectives*, Amsterdam: John Benjamins, pp. 29–46.

Young, J. (2006) 'Wikipedia founder discourages academic use of his creation', *Chronicle of Higher Education* (online edition), 12 June 2006. Online. Available http://chronicle.com/wiredcampus/article/1328/wikipedia-founder-discourages-academic-use-of-his-creation (accessed 1 January 2009).

29

The Englishes of business

Catherine Nickerson

Introduction

Braj Kachru's classic work on World Englishes distinguishes three groups of speakers of English: speakers of English as a first language (e.g. the UK, USA); speakers of English as a second language (e.g. Singapore, India), who have developed their own norms for using English; and speakers of English as a foreign language (e.g. China, Italy) in which norm referencing is made to an Anglo-Saxon variety of English, e.g. American or British English (Kachru 1985). In this seminal work, Kachru presents three concentric circles, each of which contains a different set of nations depending on the status that English has within those nations and the way in which English is used. The *inner* circle is composed of the Anglo-Saxon countries, where English is used across all domains, although it may increasingly co-exist with other languages. The *outer* circle consists of those countries that were colonized (by Britain), where English was adopted in some domains as a result of this colonization, and where it is still widely used for institutional, legal and educational purposes. And the *expanding* circle consists of the remaining countries in the world, where there are no linguistic or historical ties to any of the English-speaking countries, but where English may now be widely used for business, educational or technological reasons, alongside the individual nations' first languages. Researchers interested in the use of English in business have also focused on these three different sets of countries and the groups of speakers associated with them, and have shown that for at least the last two decades, English has been the dominant language of business. In this chapter, I will give an overview of the existing research, focusing on the use of English as a first language, second language and foreign language in business organizations, and the different situations in which it is used. In doing so, I will also attempt to place the Englishes of business within the existing World Englishes framework.

The Englishes of business in the inner circle

Research has shown that English is used as a first language by numerous speakers involved in business interactions, using a variety of different business genres and in order to accomplish a variety of different tasks e.g. in meetings, negotiations, email communication, etc. The speakers that have been investigated belong primarily to the Anglo-Saxon countries, such as the United States, Australia and the United Kingdom, which are in turn often seen as holding a hegemonic position in the way in which they determine the business norms that are followed by the rest of the world. Scollon and Wong Scollon (1995), for instance, refer to this way of doing business as being characterized by the Utilitarian discourse system, a style of discourse that dominates written business communication that prides itself on the use of clarity, brevity and sincerity. In this section I will first give a brief outline of what research has told us about the Englishes of business in the inner circle. I will then discuss three areas of relevance to the presence of first-language speakers in the business world, namely: the initial dominance of research and research methods in the investigation of Business English (BE) that were a reflection of first-language contexts; the first-language dominance of the textbook market designed to teach or train people in BE; and the recent research that has contributed information on the attitudes towards first-language (BE) speakers held by second- or foreign-language (BE) speakers from the outer and expanding circles.

Despite the obvious dominance of the United States as a business power, few studies in applied linguistics have looked at American English as one of the major inner circle Englishes of business. This is probably a reflection of the North American context where researchers interested in business communication who are also applied linguists or teachers of English for Specific Business Purposes are few in number. Clearly a great deal of the work done in Conversational Analysis (CA) focused on American English encounters, but I will not refer to that here unless CA was applied purposefully to business meetings as a way of saying something useful about those meetings as a specific type of spoken business genre rather than as a form of spoken interaction (see Bhatia 1993 for further discussion on models such as CA and their applicability or otherwise to business genres). Early studies, such as that by Jenkins and Hinds (1987) and by Yli-Jokipii (1994) provide information about the characteristics of American English business letters (compared to other types of business letters). For annual general reports and mission statements in the US, the studies by Thomas (1997) and by Swales and Rogers (1995) respectively, are language-based accounts. In addition, Graves provides a rare account of the differences between US and Canadian business culture as viewed through the genre of direct marketing letters in English (Graves 1997). For spoken language, the edited collection on negotiations by Ehlich and Wagner (1995) includes American English, as does a study which compares point-making styles in US business negotiations with those in Brazil (de Moraes Garcez 1993). Also in the 1990s, Haru Yamada's work on the differences between Japanese and US meetings is a landmark publication that reveals a great deal about the US business meeting and the language used within it. For example, the Americans use a meeting to come to a decision, whereas the Japanese use a meeting to exchange opinions (Yamada 1990, 1992). Finally, the 1994 publication by Deidre Boden, is a definitive account of the role played by meetings in the US in shaping business organizations (Boden 1994).

Elsewhere in the inner circle, the strong tradition of English for Specific Purposes (ESP) research in the UK has produced several studies focusing on British Business

English, particularly in the work of Francesca Bargiela-Chiappini. These include Bargiela-Chiappini and Harris' investigation of British (and Italian) business meetings (Bargiela-Chiappini and Harris 1997), Bargiela-Chiappini's account of human resource management magazines in Britain (and Italy) (Bargiela-Chiappini 1999) and her recent discussion of a British banking website (Bargiela-Chiappini 2005). Work by other researchers, such as Lampi (1986; see further discussion below) on business negotiations, Nickerson (2000) on email in a multinational corporation and de Groot (2008) on annual general reports, focuses on different aspects of the English produced by British inner circle speakers in business settings.

For Australia, in addition to the seminal study by Clyne (1996), the studies by Yeung (2000, 2003, 2004a, 2004b) on Australian (and Chinese) management discourse, and by Willing (1992) on white-collar multicultural workplaces, provide some insights into the language and discourse used in business meetings by Australian inner circle speakers, although, as I will discuss below, these are often involved in interactions with speakers from both the outer and expanding circles who are resident in Australia. Both studies are based on real-life data, and they focus on not only the language produced, but also the underlying discourse strategies that underpin the interaction. Similar work exists for New Zealand, where the Language in the Workplace project (LWP) based at Wellington University has sought to fulfil the following three aims: (i) to identify characteristics of effective communication between people; (ii) to diagnose possible causes of miscommunication; and (iii) to explore possible applications of the findings for New Zealand workplaces. Over the past 12 years, approximately 2,000 interactions involving a total of 420 people in 14 different workplaces have been recorded, and the project team have investigated a diverse range of topics, including the use of humour, the discourse skills needed to run an effective meeting, and the use of small talk (Holmes 2001, 2005; Holmes and Stubbe 2003; Holmes and Marra 2004). As in the case of the Australian studies, the participants involved are not only inner circle speakers of English from New Zealand, but they also represent a range of other cultures and language backgrounds – all now located in New Zealand – from both the outer and expanding circles. The profile that emerges is of business contexts in which many different Englishes now co-exist side by side in a physical location that was traditionally part of the inner circle. I will discuss the consequences of this in more detail below.

Many of the researchers who are interested in BE are applied linguists, or teachers of English for Specific Business Purposes, or very often both. As a result, the field has been dominated by discourse analysis (in particular the Birmingham School), the application of conversational analysis to business meetings, and genre analysis (especially Swalesian genre analysis, particularly its extension by Bhatia), i.e. the types of analysis that characterize the field of (English) applied linguistics. In addition, research into business discourse in general has been dominated by the study of the use of English as a business language, either on its own in first-language contexts, or frequently in comparison with other languages used in business. The pioneering 1986 study of the discourse of negotiations by Mirjaliisa Lampi (now Charles), for instance, is a micro-analytical discourse analysis (following the Birmingham School) of British business negotiations and, similarly, Haru Yamada's work on business meetings (1990) uses an ethnomethodological approach and is a contrastive study of US speakers of BE and Japanese speakers of BE. For written business discourse, early studies such as that by Jenkins and Hinds (1987) contrast US, French and Japanese business letters. English continued to dominate in the 1990s. Maier's (1992) study contrasts the politeness strategies used in business letters written by native and non-native speakers of English. The discussion of application letters by James *et al.* (1994) takes the perceptions of inner circle application letters by expanding circle speakers as its central theme. In most cases in the early work in the analysis of business discourse, inner circle varieties of English are something of a default option, whether the researcher is contrasting other varieties of English with (first-language) English, or whether the researcher is contrasting (first-language) English with other business languages (e.g. French, German, Dutch, etc.). Although, as I will discuss in the later sections of this chapter, native-speaker English has lost some of its influence on BE research in the intervening years, several recent studies still refer to it for contrastive purposes. For example, Nickerson (2000) contrasts the email in English in a multinational setting written by Dutch and British writers respectively, and van Mulken and van der Meer (2005) compare US (English) and Dutch (English) company replies to customer enquiries. In studies such as these, the focus is on the English produced by second- or foreign-language users of BE located in the outer and expanding circles, rather than on the UK or US varieties of BE produced by native speakers or writers. In the rest of this section I will review two important studies, which, in very different ways, have produced findings about the BE produced by first-language speakers.

The corpus-based study by Nelson is a comparative study of general English and British and US Business English, using sources such as company brochures, emails, annual reports, meetings and negotiations (Nelson 2000, 2006). Nelson shows that Business English is quite distinct from General English, at least on the basis of the inner circle sources he refers to. In addition, he found that, when he surveyed textbooks that were intended to teach Business English, these were in fact presenting language that had little to do with the reality of his BE corpus. In other words, learners were not being presented with relevant and appropriate language if their target was to understand and reproduce UK or US Business English. Nelson's work suggests, therefore, that there is no guarantee that the BE being presented in BE textbooks is actually representative of real (native-speaker) BE. A second, related, point is that such textbooks may not always usefully represent the BE that second or foreign language users need in many, or perhaps most of the contexts in which they operate (see also Nair-Venugopal 2001 and Nickerson 2008, for further discussion on this point within the Malaysian and Indian contexts respectively). The realities of global business would suggest, for example, that numerous business interactions take place on a daily basis between business people representing all three of the WE concentric circles, such that for most of those people, striving for a native-like proficiency in BE may be of little relevance. I will return to this discussion at a later stage in this chapter.

The 2002 study by Charles and Marschan-Piekkari is an extensive survey and interview investigation of middle management at a major multinational corporation, Kone Elevators, which provides a fascinating insight into the interaction between the inner circle speakers of English at Kone and the BE speakers of other languages. The study shows that, although Kone had adopted English as its company language 30 years before the study took place, there was a shadow structure in existence at the corporation which did not always run parallel to the formal organizational structure, but which was based on those individuals who were most able to function effectively in English. One top manager the authors interviewed went so far as to say, 'There is actually no other practical barrier than language when we have co-operation and meetings with each other' (Charles and Marschan-Piekkari 2002: 19). Charles and Marschan-Piekkari conducted interviews with 110 staff, representing 25 corporate units in ten different countries in Europe, Mexico and the Far East, about the role played by language in all forms of horizontal communication at the corporation. They report that the majority of the transactions that take place are between non-native speakers of English, and that communication problems were caused by the insufficient language skills of one or more of the interactants. The interviewees identified translation and telephone conversations as the most problematic areas, together with the fact that there were so many different kinds of English spoken within the company. One of their most interesting findings was that the non-native English-speaking employees had much more difficulty understanding the Inner speakers of English within the corporation, than they did the speakers of other varieties of English. As a result of this, Marschan-Piekkari and Charles recommend that staff at Kone are encouraged 'to understand and negotiate global Englishes to ensure that they are exposed to the communication strategies, expressions and accents they will be dealing with at their particular organization' and also that native English speakers are included 'in communication training to help them understand how to communicate effectively with non-native speakers' (2002: 23–6).

Perhaps the most important finding in the Charles and Marschan-Piekkari study was that some of the employees at Kone were disempowered as a result of the corporation's opting for English as the main corporate language. This supports findings by both Gimenez (2002) and Chew (2005) for the Argentinean and Hong Kong contexts discussed later in the chapter, where there was also evidence of an imbalance in power for the outer circle speakers of English in Hong Kong and the expanding circle speakers of English in Argentina. Likewise, the recent studies by Rogerson-Revell of meetings at the European Commission (2007, 2008), also suggest that the presence of native speakers of English has a tendency to hinder rather than facilitate the effectiveness of the communication that takes place.

In this section, I have looked at some of the ways in which research has shed light on to the Englishes of business in the inner circle, including both the influence that native-speaker varieties of English continue to have in textbooks in particular, and the interactions between inner circle English speakers and outer and expanding circle speakers, which are now an everyday occurrence in the world of international business. There also seems to be some evidence that inner circle speakers may benefit just as much as their outer and expanding circle colleagues from language and communication training. The WE framework is clearly still of relevance in understanding the role played by inner circle varieties of BE, especially as, at least in the global business arena, other forms of BE may be considerably more prevalent and perhaps of increasingly more influence. In the next section, I will discuss English in business contexts in those countries where it is used as a second language in outer circle countries such as India, Malaysia, Singapore and the Philippines.

The Englishes of business in the outer circle

Speakers of English as a second language are those speakers who, according to the WE framework, have developed their own norms for using English. In India alone, 90 million people claim to speak English as a second (or third) language. One of the areas in which English is in widespread use in outer circle countries is in business, where it is frequently used not only for international communication in interactions with business people from outside of a particular country, but also in intra-national communication. In the Indian context, for instance, Gargesh has commented that, despite official language policies to the contrary designed to promote the use of regional languages, 'Careers in business and commerce, government positions of high rank (regardless of stated policy), and science and technology (attracting many of the brightest) continue to require fluency in English' (Gargesh 2006). It seems plausible that many business people, regardless of their position, in countries such as India, Malaysia and Singapore, use English at least part of the time. Indeed, many will find themselves in situations where they are using English almost all of the time in interactions, either with other colleagues or customers with whom they do not share another language.

An area where there has been a great deal of research focusing on the use of English by outer circle speakers in the business context is Hong Kong. For example, Hong Kong's City University and the Hong Kong Polytechnic University are actively involved in research into professional communication, and this has resulted in a wealth of information. The Teaching English to Meet the Needs of Business Education in Hong Kong project, for instance, was a comprehensive survey carried out over a number of years at the end of the 1990s to collect information from several key stakeholder groups, including management professors, business students and banking employees. Nineteen researchers from five different universities worked on the project, and a range of different methodologies and information from specialist informants was included (Bhatia and Candlin 2001; Chew 2005; Jackson 2005). Chew's study investigated the English language skills used by new employees of four banks and focused on the communicative tasks they needed to undertake. The study revealed a complex situation, where Cantonese co-existed with English, and where the respondents reported difficulties with the language demands posed by the tasks they required to complete. As in the case of the Charles and Marschan-Piekkari study at Kone Elevators discussed above, the Hong Kong bank employees also reported that they had the most difficulties when they needed to interact with inner circle speakers of English as a first language.

Numerous other studies have also revealed the complex situation in Hong Kong. For example, Baxter et al. (2002) describe a management communication project that they designed for the Training Department of the Hong Kong Jockey Club, which revealed that 'most of the participants were highly competent in the use of spoken and written English as their second language' (2002: 117–18), and that the writing they did in English in the form of committee papers was a crucial way through which decisions were made within the organization. Similarly, the 2000 study of the English language needs of textile and clothing merchandisers in Hong Kong, by Li So-mui and Mead (2000), confirmed that English was used extensively at work. In addition, Li So-mui and Mead's respondents reported that, not only did they have to move between Cantonese and English on a momentary basis as a result of their international contacts (US, Japan, Korea, Canada, Italy, UK, etc.) and local Cantonese-speaking contacts, they also needed to be proficient in Putonghua, in order to do business with Mainland China, Macau and Taiwan. As in Chew's study, the interviewees reported that they frequently felt the need to improve on their English skills, and also that proficiency in English was seen as a determining factor in career advancement. Outer circle speakers of English in Hong Kong, therefore, use English very frequently in the course of their work, and they were also communicating with speakers of English from both of the other circles, in this case the inner and expanding circles.

In other countries where English is commonly used as a second (or third) language in the business context, studies like Briguglio's study of the use of English in Malaysian

511

business (Briguglio 2005) as well as Nair-Venugopal's study of language choice and communication in Malaysian business (Nair-Venugopal 2001), also discuss the complex situations that can arise when English co-exists with regional languages, or with other languages spoken as a second language by all those involved in the interaction. In Briguglio's study for instance, Malaysian English dominated both spoken and written communication in the multinational corporation she studied, and a similar situation is reported in Singapore in the call-centre sector, where Clark *et al.* (2008) show that customer representatives need to be able to code-switch between Singaporean English and a more standard variety of English on a moment-to-moment basis. This may prove to be a characteristic of call-centre communication in outer circle locations, such as customer service representatives in countries like India, Singapore and the Philippines (see Bolton this volume). In other words, call-centre operators may have to be proficient at switching between inner and outer circle varieties of business English when dealing with their customers. Nair-Venugopal has summarized the realities and expectations within outer circle countries, as follows:

> The language of local team work interactions and negotiations on the shop floor tends to be the dominant local language (which may well be English as a loca-lized community norm or lingua franca) especially in sites of outsourced operations (with the exclusion of call centres). However, many business organizations in postcolonial sites continue to expect their middle and top management to be proficient, if not fluent, in English and aspire towards the use of idealized norms i.e. 'good', 'proper' or 'quality' English, which remain abstractions.
> (Shanta Nair-Venugopal, in interview, in Bargiela-Chiappini *et al.*, 2007: 37)

In this section I have discussed the Englishes of business as they exist in the countries in the outer circle. I have suggested that speakers located in these countries may use their own norms for English in interaction with business people from their own country with whom they may not share a common language, but that they may also need to be proficient in the varieties of English associated with the inner circle countries if their job requires them to interact with people from the Inner or expanding circles. In the next section I will go on to discuss the Englishes of business used in the expanding circle.

The Englishes of business in the expanding circle

For the time being at least, English is the undisputed choice as the language of inter-national business in the countries within the expanding circle. Although the predictions are that languages such as Chinese, Hindi or Arabic may come to play a more promi-nent role (Graddol 2004), this seems unlikely to occur in the near future, especially with the exponential rise in the importance of the internet and the transfer of knowledge across different business organizations (see Porter 1990; Friedman 2005, for a discus-sion on these issues and how they impact the business world). Numerous studies have also investigated the nature, use and attitudes towards English when it is used as an International Business Language (IBE) or as a Business English Lingua Franca (BELF). Work on BELF has generally referred to situations in which there are no native speakers of English present in the interaction, i.e. English is being used as a lingua franca and it is a second or foreign language for all those involved. BELF interactions therefore include interactions between EFL speakers of two different European languages (e.g. Swedes and Finns), between EFL speakers of two different Asian languages (e.g. Japanese business people and Chinese business people), and indeed between ESL speakers of different languages (e.g. Hindi speakers and Kannada speakers in India). IBE, on the other hand, has been used to refer to all interactions within the business arena which involve speakers who are not using the same variety of English, regardless of whether they are first-, second- or foreign-language speakers, e.g. a business meeting that involves Dutch (EFL) speakers, Canadian (native) speakers of English and Indian (ESL) speakers would be conducted in IBE. BELF may therefore be seen as a specific type of BE, that does not involve native speakers of English, whereas IBE refers to BE encounters that include native speakers as well as ESL and/or EFL speakers.

Figure 29.1 shows a categorization of BE according to the speakers involved in each type of interaction. The innermost circle includes native speakers of the same variety of BE (NS1 + NS1). The second circle includes ESL speakers of the same variety of BE (ESL1 + ESL1) where English is being used as a BELF. The third circle includes native speakers of different varieties of BE (NS1 + NS2) and the fourth circle includes ESL and/or EFL speakers who do not share the same variety of BE, where English is again being used as a BELF. The fifth and final circle refers to interactions between NS, ESL and/or EFL speakers, where English is being used as an IBE. In Kachru's terminology, the first and third BE circles involve only *inner* circle speakers, the second BE circle involves speakers from the same *outer* circle country, the fourth circle involves speakers from different countries in the *outer* and/or *expanding* circles, and the fifth BE circle involves speakers from *inner* circle countries in interaction with speakers from the *outer* and/or *expanding* circles. I have ordered them in this way to try to capture the

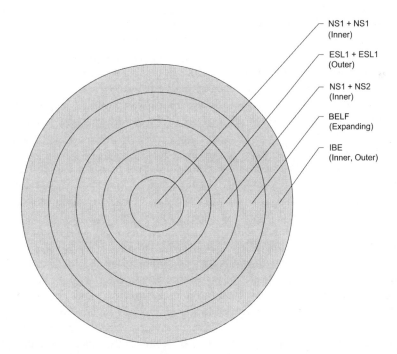

Figure 29.1 A categorization of BE interactions in global business.

increase in complexity in the interaction from the inside to the outside of the five BE circles, as a consequence of the increase in number of the different varieties of BE that are being used, as well as the increase in the number of the different national cultures that each group of speakers represents. In the rest of this section I will selectively review a number of studies from around the world that represent some of the work that has been done recently on IBE and BELF, with particular reference to the countries in the expanding circle.

One of the most interesting studies in recent years is the study of Business English as a Lingua Franca (BELF) in the Scandinavian context (Louhiala-Salminen *et al.* 2005). The study focuses on two cross-border mergers dating from the late 1990s, involving Finnish and Swedish partners and their corporate language policies. The central aim of the study was to identify the cultural and linguistic challenges that were faced by Finnish- and Swedish-speaking employees at Paper Giant and PankkiBanken/Scandi Bank, as a result of the decision to use English as a Business English Lingua Franca (BELF) (2005: 403). Louhiala-Salminen *et al.* looked at the communicative practices in both organizations, the perceptions held by Finnish and Swedish employees about each other, and the discourse produced in spoken and written BELF interactions within the corporations in meetings and in emails. The study used a questionnaire survey and a series of interviews. Conversational analysis (CA) was used to analyse the meetings, and genre analysis was used to analyse the emails. The findings revealed that for both organizations and both nationalities, IBE was used about 20 per cent of the time, with many of those interviewed reporting difficulties on the telephone and in meetings where they needed to respond in English quickly. The other findings in the study suggest that BELF was not associated by those who used it with the culture of any of the inner circle countries, 'Rather, it can be seen to be a conduit of its speaker's communication culture' (2005: 417). In other words, a Finnish or Swedish cultural identity and associated discourse strategies characterized the Finnish-BELF and Swedish-BELF.

Other studies within the countries of the European Union have revealed English being used as an IBE or BELF, with or without the presence of inner circle speakers. Poncini's (2004) longitudinal study of an Italian company is an account of a multilingual encounter, where English is only one of the languages used. The study focuses on several meetings which took place at the company, involving 36 participants (the majority from expanding circle countries), 14 different cultures and several different languages. Although the meetings were officially held in English, Poncini reports that the meetings were successful because the participants used a combination of code-switching, where necessary, to explain a point, judicious pronoun choice (e.g. the use of inclusive 'we' to include everyone at the meeting), specialized terminology and strategic evaluation strategies. This all helped to create a positive atmosphere. Rogerson-Revell (2007, 2008) also reports on multicultural meetings held in the European context, where both inner and expanding circle speakers were present. In her studies, she discusses the challenges perceived by the non-native speakers of English and the strategies they used to meet them. Although she reports that the inner circle speakers did not dominate the proceedings in terms of actual talk time, she also found that the expanding circle speakers were less likely to participate. On a more positive note, with specific reference to the performance of the speakers of English from the expanding circle, Rogerson-Revell comments that, 'despite concerns from some participants that communication in English can be problematic, the analysis illustrates the overall positive linguistic performance of speakers in the meetings themselves' (2008: 338). Studies such as these reveal that English is used for pragmatic reasons by speakers from the expanding circle, simply as a means of achieving a business transaction. There seems to be little or no need to use or mimic inner circle varieties of English. In other words, speakers use English as a means to communicate. They do not attempt to replicate the English produced by their inner circle colleagues.

A 2007 study (Gerritsen *et al.*) also focuses on the use of English in part of the European Union. They analysed the use of language in glossy advertising in Belgium, France, the Netherlands, Germany and Spain. A detailed discussion of this study is beyond the scope of this chapter (see Hashim, this volume, for a discussion on the Englishes of advertisements), but one of the aims in the study was to investigate whether the English used in advertising in glossy magazines in these five expanding circle countries had any of the characteristics of the English used in outer circle countries, i.e. where English is a second language. The study surveyed more than 2,000 advertising texts across the five countries, and found that two out of every three texts contained English. However, the amount of English was very small. Only 13 per cent of the total number of words in the advertisements were in English, i.e. in advertisements where the text was a combination of English, together with Dutch, French, German or Spanish respectively. Only 7 per cent of the total number of English words showed any evidence of the development of a nativized variety of English. The study found little evidence of expanding circle English developing nativized norms.

The use of English as a business language has recently begun to attract more attention in the Asia-Pacific region. For example, the English as the Language of Asian Business (ELAB) group is a group of researchers and practitioners located in the region with a special interest in English. The group aims to conduct empirical research into the use of English in business contexts in the Asian-Pacific region, with a view to understanding its nature and use, and the attitudes held towards it. The work of the group thus far would seem to indicate that English is on the increase as an international business language throughout the region, not only in outer circle countries like India and Hong Kong with their traditional historical links to English, but also in expanding circle countries like Japan and Thailand, where the need for English has dramatically increased in the last decade. The findings of the group would also suggest that much of the communication that takes place in English in the region is between speakers from countries located within the Asia-Pacific region rather than from outside. Thompson (2006) provides an excellent example of the use of English in Japanese business. The study focuses on the use of English in a multinationally staffed international cooperation agency. It investigates the interactions that take place within the workplace and the influence that this has on the use of English, in an attempt to understand when English is used as a regional (or international) lingua franca. The study drew on ethnographic observations, on interviews, and on the grammar, discourse analytic and CA-based analysis of workplace interactions. Thompson found that, whereas Japanese was preferred for interpersonal interactions, English was selected for ideational discussions because it was associated with directness and status-neutral grammar. As in the case of the Scandinavian joint ventures discussed earlier in this chapter, English was viewed as a complement to the interactants' first languages. It did not impact their culture, and they used it for pragmatic reasons, as practisers, to accomplish their work, rather than as learners, making overt reference to the English associated with the inner circle. Unlike the Finnish and Swedish speakers, however, the Japanese speakers in Thompson's study purposefully did not use their own cultural and discourse patterns when they chose to speak English. Rather, they viewed and used English as a language that would allow them to deselect the indirectness and observance of status that would generally characterize their use of Japanese.

The final two studies I will review investigate the Business English used in Turkey and Argentina respectively. Akar (2002) gives an overview of the written business texts produced by Turkish business practitioners, and Gimenez (2002) the consequences of using English between an Argentinean subsidiary and its European head office. Although the studies focus on the English communication that takes place in two very different locations, the researchers are both concerned with the impact of the surrounding context on the nature and effectiveness of the communication. In Akar's study, the focus is on the macro-contextual factors that influence the English that is produced. She identifies Turkish national culture and the bureaucratic tradition prevalent in Turkey as having a particular influence on the politeness strategies used in Business English. In addition, the type of company affected the communication style used, as did the access that the writers had to communication technology (e.g. access to fax communication). As in many of the studies I have reviewed above, Akar concludes that the English reflected the local business language and culture more than an inner circle variety of English.

Gimenez's Argentinean study investigated the conflicts in communication (in English) between the subsidiary company and its head office, as a result of organizational factors. The study reveals an ethnocentric language policy on the part of the head office which imposed the use of IBE in all internal communication. This caused problems for some managers in Argentina as their English was not good enough to read the necessary texts (unless a Spanish translation was also provided, but this was against corporate rules). As in the case of the 2002 study by Charles and Marschan-Piekkari (2002) discussed above, senior managers were aware of the fact that they did not have the necessary language skills to cope with the demands of their job. Gimenez reports that the managers at the Argentinean subsidiary depended on their assistants to provide them with English language support. He ends his study with the main conclusion that 'communication conflicts do not result from the language (English) misunderstandings but from the two realities operating in the corporation' (2002: 323), i.e. the ethnocentric attitudes to language use imposed by head office and the day-to-day realities of coping with such attitudes at the subsidiary.

In this section I have given a brief overview of some of the research studies that have focused on the use of English by speakers originating in the countries within the expanding circle. I have shown that English is in widespread use as an international business language across the globe and that its use is not normally associated with an inner circle variety of English. I have attempted to categorize the different types of BE that are in use in global business, depending on the speakers who are involved in each case.

Conclusion

The studies I have reviewed in this chapter would seem to suggest that, in business in particular, English transcends national and cultural barriers. It is used as a first language for some speakers in business, but for millions, perhaps billions, more, it is used either as a business lingua franca or as an international business language. As I have attempted to show in this chapter, situations of all three types have been well documented and discussed as separate entities by researchers. In reality, however, particularly in multinational corporations with an increasingly global workforce, all three situations may well occur simultaneously, and in many cases, because of the constant changes in the business world and the exponential rise in knowledge transfer over the past decade, the boundaries between these three situations have become blurred. Inner circle countries are increasingly multicultural in nature, many outer circle countries have recently become an economic force to be reckoned with, and English has become a fact of corporate life for most of the countries located in the expanding circle. Across the World Englishes framework, Business English can no longer be seen as the preserve of inner circle users. For the vast majority of those business people who use it on a daily basis, BE is simply a neutral and shared communication code which allows them to get their work done (Louhiala-Salminen *et al.* 2005; Bargiela-Chiappini *et al.* 2007); they neither associate it with the inner circle varieties of English, nor do they try to reproduce them. As the world continues to look to the BRIC countries and to the other emerging economies around the world for new and innovative economic solutions, it seems plausible that BELF and IBE will continue to take centre-stage, posing a new set of challenges for all those involved with teaching, researching and writing about the Englishes of business.

Suggestions for further reading

Bargiela-Chiappini, F., Nickerson, C. and Planken, B. (2007) *Business Discourse*, Basingstoke: Palgrave Macmillan. (An overview of the field of business discourse.)

Bhatia, V.K. (2004) *Worlds of Written Discourse. A Genre-based View*, London: Continuum. (A definitive account of the role played by writing in professional communication.)

LWP Project. Online. Available www.vuw.ac.nz/lals/research/lwp/index.aspx (A large project on the use of spoken language in the workplace.)

References

Akar, D. (2002) 'The macro contextual factors shaping business discourse: the Turkish case'. *International Review of Applied Linguistics in Language Teaching*, 40: 305–22.

Bargiela-Chiappini, F. (1999) 'Meaning creation and genre across cultures: human resource management magazines in Britain and Italy', in F. Bargiela-Chiappini and C. Nickerson (eds) *Writing Business: Genres, Media and Discourses*, London and New York: Longman.

——(2005) 'In memory of the business letter: multimedia, genres and social action in a banking website', in P. Gillaerts and M. Gotti (eds) *Genre Variation in Business Letters*, Bern: Peter Lang.

Bargiela-Chiappini, F. and Harris, S. (1997) *Managing Language: The Discourse of Corporate Meetings*, Amsterdam: John Benjamins.

Bargiela-Chiappini, F., Nickerson, C. and Planken, B. (2007) *Business Discourse*, Basingstoke: Palgrave Macmillan.

Baxter, R., Boswood, T. and Peirson-Smith, A. (2002) 'An ESP program for management in the horse-racing business', in T. Orr (ed.) *English for Specific Purposes*, Alexandria, VA: TESOL.

Bhatia, V.K. (1993) *Analysing Genre: Language in Professional Settings*, London: Longman.

Bhatia, V.K. and Candlin, C.N. (eds) (2001) *Teaching English to Meet the Needs of Business Education in Hong Kong*, Hong Kong: City University of Hong Kong.

Boden, D. (1994) *The Business of Talk. Organizations in Action*, London: Polity Press.

Briguglio, C. (2005) 'Developing an understanding of English as a global language for business settings', in F. Bargiela-Chiappini and M. Gotti (eds) *Asian Business Discourse*, Bern: Peter Lang.

517

Charles, M. and Marschan-Piekkari, R. (2002) 'Language training for enhanced horizontal communication: a challenge for MNCs', *Business Communication Quarterly*, 65: 9–29.

Chew, S.K. (2005) 'An investigation of the English language skills used by new entrants in banks in Hong Kong', *English for Specific Purposes*, 24: 423–35.

Clark, C., Rogers, P., Murfett, U.M. and Ang, S. (2008) 'Is courtesy enough? "Solidarity" in call center interactions' (Ross School of Business Paper No. 1103). Online. Available http://ssrn.com/abstract=1128246 (accessed 11 November 2008).

Clyne, M. (1996) *Inter-cultural Communication at Work*, Cambridge: Cambridge University Press.

de Groot, E.B. (2008) *English Annual Reports in Europe: A Study on the Identification and Reception of Genre Characteristics in Multimodal Annual Reports Originating in the Netherlands and in the United Kingdom*, Utrecht: Netherlands Graduate School of Linguistics.

de Moraes Garcez, P. (1993) 'Point-making styles in cross-cultural business negotiation: a micro-ethnographic study', *English for Specific Purposes*, 12: 103–20.

Ehlich, K. and Wagner, J. (eds) (1995) *The Discourse of International Negotiations*, Berlin: Mouton de Gruyter.

Friedman, T.L. (2005) *The World is Flat*, New York: Farrar Straus and Giroux.

Gargesh, R. (2006) 'Language issues in the context of higher education in India', paper presentation given during the symposium 'Language Issues in English-medium Universities across Asia', University of Hong Kong, Hong Kong. Online. Available www.hku.hk/clear/doc/DAY%201/Ravinder%20Gargesh.PPT (accessed 11 November 2008).

Gerritsen, M., Nickerson, C., van Hooft, A., van Meurs, F., Nederstigt, U., Starren, M. and Crijns, R. (2007) 'Selling their wares: English in product advertisements in Belgium, France, Germany, the Netherlands and Spain', *World Englishes*, 26: 291–315.

Gimenez, J. (2002) 'New media and conflicting realities in multinational corporate communication: a case study', *International Review of Applied Linguistics in Language Teaching*, 40: 323–44.

Graddol, D. (2004) 'The future of language', *Science Magazine*, 303: 1329–31.

Graves, R. (1997) '"Dear friend" (?): culture and genre in American and Canadian direct marketing letters', *Journal of Business Communication*, 34: 235–52.

Holmes, J. (2000) 'Victoria University's Language in the Workplace Project: an overview', Language in the Workplace Occasional Papers 1. Online. Available www.victoria.ac.nz/lals/resources/Publications/op1.pdf (accessed 17 February 2010).

——(2005) 'Leadership talk: how do leaders "do mentoring", and is gender relevant?', *Journal of Pragmatics*, 37: 1779–800.

Holmes, J. and Marra, M. (2004) 'Relational practice in the workplace: women's talk or gendered discourse?' *Language in Society*, 33: 377–98.

Holmes, J. and Stubbe, M. (2003) *Power and Politeness in the Workplace*, Upper Saddle River, NJ: Pearson Education.

Jackson, J. (2005) 'An inter-university, cross-disciplinary analysis of business education: perceptions of business faculty in Hong Kong', *English for Specific Purposes*, 24: 293–306.

James, C., Scholfield, J.C.P. and Ypsiladis, G. (1994) 'Cross-cultural correspondence', *World Englishes*, 13: 325–34.

Jenkins, S. and Hinds, J. (1987) 'Business letter writing: English, French and Japanese', *TESOL Quarterly*, 21: 327–49.

Kachru, B.B. (1985) 'Standards, codification and sociolinguistic Realism: the English language in the Outer Circle', in R. Quirk and H. Widdowson (eds) *English in the World: Teaching and Learning the Language and Literatures*, Cambridge: Cambridge University Press.

Lampi, M. (1986) *Linguistic Components of Strategy in Business Negotiations* (Helsinki School of Economics, Studies B-85), Helsinki: Helsinki School of Economics.

Li So-mui, F. and Mead, K. (2000) 'An analysis of English in the workplace: the communication needs of textile and clothing merchandisers', *English for Specific Purposes*, 19: 351–68.

Louhiala-Salminen, L., Charles, M. and Kankaanranta, A. (2005) 'English as a lingua franca in Nordic corporate mergers: two case companies', *English for Specific Purposes*, 24: 401–21.

Maier, P. (1992) 'Politeness strategies in business letters by native and non-native English speakers', *English for Specific Purposes*, 11: 189–205.

Nair-Venugopal, S. (2001) 'The sociolinguistics of choice in Malaysian business settings', *International Journal of the Sociology of Language*, 152: 21–52.

Nelson, M. (2000) 'The Business English Lexis Site'. Online. Available http://users.utu.fi/micnel/business_english_lexis_site.htm (accessed 8 April 2006).

——(2006) 'Semantic associations in business English: a corpus-based analysis', *English for Specific Purposes Journal*, 25: 217–34.

Nickerson, C. (2000) *Playing the Corporate Language Game: An Investigation of the Genres and Discourse Strategies in English Used by Dutch Writers Working in Multinational Corporations*, Amsterdam: Rodopi.

——(2008) 'Towards the creation of appropriate teaching materials for high proficiency ESL learners: the case of Indian management students', *TESL-EJ*, 12. Online. Available http://tesl-ej.org/ej47/a3.html (accessed 24 February 2009).

Poncini, G. (2004) *Discursive Strategies in Multicultural Business Meetings*, Bern: Peter Lang.

Porter, M. (1990) *The Competitive Advantage of Nations*, New York: Free Press.

Rogerson-Revell, P. (2007) 'Using English for international business: a European case study', *English for Specific Purposes*, 26: 103–20.

——(2008) 'Participation and performance in international business meetings', *English for Specific Purposes*, 27: 338–60.

Scollon, R. and Wong Scollon, S. (1995) *Intercultural Communication*, Oxford: Blackwell.

Swales, J.M. and Rogers, P.S. (1995) 'Discourse and the projection of corporate culture: the mission statement', *Discourse and Society*, 6: 223–42.

Thomas, J. (1997) 'Discourse in the marketplace: the making of meaning in annual general reports', *Journal of Business Communication*, 34: 47–66.

Thompson, A. (2006) 'English in context in an East-Asian intercultural workplace', unpublished PhD thesis, University of Toronto.

Van Mulken, M. and van der Meer, W. (2005) 'Are you being served? A genre analysis of American and Dutch company replies to customer enquiries', *English for Specific Purposes*, 24: 93–109.

Willing, K. (1992) *Talking it Through: Clarification and Problem-Solving in Professional Work*, Sydney: National Centre for English Language Teaching and Research.

Yamada, H. (1990) 'Topic management and turn distribution in business meetings: American versus Japanese strategies', *TEXT*, 10: 271–95.

——(1992) *American and Japanese Business Discourse: A Comparison of Interactional Styles*, Norwood, NJ: Ablex.

Yeung, L. (2000) 'The question of Chinese indirectness: a comparison of Chinese and English participative decision-making discourse', *Multilingua*, 19: 221–64.

——(2003) 'Management discourse in Australian banking contexts: in search of an Australian model of participation as compared with that of Hong Kong Chinese', *Journal of Intercultural Studies*, 24: 47–63.

——(2004a) 'The paradox of control in participative decision-making: gatekeeping discourse in banks', *International Journal of the Sociology of Language*, 166: 83–104.

——(2004b) 'The paradox of control in participative decision-making: facilitative discourse in banks', *TEXT*, 24: 113–46.

Yli-Jokipii, H. (1994) *Requests in Professional Discourse: A Cross-cultural Study of British, American and Finnish Business Writing* (Annales Academiae Scientiarum Finnicae Dissertationes Humnarum Litterarum 71), Helsinki: Suomalainen tiedeadatemia.

30

Englishes in advertising

Azirah Hashim

Introduction

This chapter begins with an introduction to English in advertising and an overview of relevant literature in the field. Research on advertisements from different parts of the world focusing on language choice, code-switching and the role of English is then surveyed. Examples of print and radio advertisements from a specific country – Malaysia – are provided and the linguistic features discussed. Finally, a summary of the chapter is provided.

Advertising in English began with an advertising supplement appearing in the *London Gazette* as far back as 1666 and over a period of a hundred years the number and style of advertisements grew. Slogans and trade names then became famous in the nineteenth century (Graddol 1997). Advertising grew increasingly popular at the end of the nineteenth century owing to social and economic factors in the more industrialized countries. Mass production led to an increase in competition as companies vied for consumers and started using printing techniques to get the extra edge. Publishers in the United States realized that income from advertising would lead to lower selling prices for their publications, a realization that soon spread. More and more publications allocated pages of a magazine and newspaper to advertising, and today, 'two thirds of a modern newspaper, especially in the USA, may be devoted to advertising' (Graddol 1997: 85).

In an increasingly globalized world, issues regarding advertising are becoming more and more important. Companies that wish to reach out to potential consumers have to expand to other countries and need to use strategies that are successful for any one market. The effectiveness of advertisements has led to the spread of advertising all over the world and a significant amount of this advertising uses English in some form. Indeed, advertising in just about every city and town can be considered 'one of the most noticeable global manifestations of English language use' (Graddol 1997: 86). As language is often used to sell products along with the visuals used to support the words, the choice of words, phrases or sentences is therefore crucial. Language is used to capture the attention of the readers/listeners and persuade them to purchase a product. Phonology, lexis and grammar can all play a role. In countries where English is not the first language, English use in advertising is still very noticeable. According to Duncan and Ramaprasad (1995: 55), 'advertising for multinational products uses standardisation most often in strategy (the creative selling proposition), less often in execution (actual elements and their structure in an ad), and least often in language.' Since advertising offers insights into the cultures that make up a country or a region, a study of the types of languages used can be extremely informative.

Unlike naturally occurring data, advertising data responds to market forces or aims to influence attitudes and perceptions. In outer circle countries, local varieties of English and the vitality of localized forms are often emphasized in advertisements. Standard English is also commonly used in radio advertisements, often representing the 'master's voice'. Given the current multiplicity of English, researchers are interested in finding a coherent picture of English in the world today. Approaches to English have included: the World Englishes approach, which looks at different national varieties of English; the lingua franca approach, which argues that English is a language that is primarily used between non-native speakers and is thus one which no one owns; the dynamic approach, which explores the historical, social and ecological factors that have shaped Englishes; and the habitat approach, which sees English embedded inside complex language habitats within which its form, functions and status vis-à-vis other languages are determined (Kachru 1982/1992; Leitner 1992, 2004; Schneider 2003, 2007; Jenkins 2007; Kirkpatrick 2007).

Many countries have bilingual or multilingual populations creating additional complexity when it comes to advertising in these countries. Advertisers have to take into account the languages that are spoken by the people in any particular country and the choice of language or languages for advertising. Many of these advertisements opt for either one of the main languages spoken or use a mixture of two languages, and in some cases three or more. Advertisers use the 'think and act both global and local at the same time approach' (Bhatia 2000: 161), and integrate languages in advertisements for various reasons. English is commonly used to suggest sophistication and modernity and a cosmopolitan identity, as will be shown in the review of literature below.

In Asia, English is widely used in the mass media, in print, radio and television. Many Asian countries also see a high amount of code-switching and code-mixing, especially in informal domains. The role of English in advertising is extremely common, especially in the countries which can be considered outer circle countries, but increasingly so in expanding circle countries. For example, outer circle countries like Malaysia and Singapore have many advertisements in English and they often mix standard and localized varieties of English with the local languages. Expanding circle countries like Japan and Thailand now increasingly use English as an additional language in advertising. The growth of the consumer culture (and also other parts of the world) has had a great impact on the development of advertising strategies and language. According to Graddol (2006), much of the development of an urban, middle-class population throughout the world has made English an important symbol of its growth.

Research on advertisements

A review of the literature shows how English and other languages co-exist in advertisements in bilingual and multilingual contexts, where English is used as a second or other language. How different languages convey certain meanings about a product is exploited by advertisers. For example, a number of studies on the use of different

European languages such as English, French, German (e.g. Haarmann 1984, 1989) in Japanese advertisements show:

> how French, given its ethno-cultural associations with 'high elegance, refined taste, attractiveness, sophisticated life style, fascination and charm' is used to market items such as perfume, watches, food and fashion. English, on the other hand, is seen as a marker of 'international appreciation, reliability, high quality, confidence, practical use, practical lifestyle' and so on, and is used to associate products such as television, sportswear, alcohol and cars with these qualities.
>
> (cited in Bishop *et al.* 2005: 347)

In another study of advertisements in the European Union, Kelly-Holmes (2000) found that French is used 'as a marker of refinement, fashion and haute cuisine, while German is used to signify reliability, precision, and superior technology' (cited in Bishop *et al.* 2005: 347). Piller (2001) found, in a corpus of German advertisements, that in German and English bilingual advertisements, English is used to encourage the association of the product with transnational cosmopolitan values implying that the buyer would become a member of the elite community if he/she were to purchase the item.

In print advertisements, English has supplanted French, and Romance languages more generally as the languages which traditionally connote *joie de vivre* for Germans. In TV commercials, on the other hand, French and Italian continue to be vested with these functions, mainly through the use of setting and accents. French is the language of love and carries erotic connotations whenever it occurs; Italian is the language of the good life as expressed through food (Piller 2001: 169).

Bilingualism in English and German is seen to indicate successful middle-class Germans while other languages like Italian, Russian and Spanish are presented as languages of the Other. Stereotypical views about English would then be linked to the product. As Piller (2003: 173) points out, language choice within advertising becomes a powerful 'tool in the construction of social identity, be it national, racial or class identity' (cited in Bishop *et al.* 2005). Similar findings have been found by Bishop *et al.* (2005) who looked at functional specificity of Welsh and English in advertisements and concluded that each language is used to achieve a 'specific voice or mode of address ... English articulates the institutional identities of an organisation or a service provider. Welsh, on the other hand, performs more relationally oriented functions' (p. 359).

Callow and Mcdonald (2005) compared advertisements in monolingual Spanish and bilingual Spanish–English magazines in the USA and observed that many of the bilingual advertisements use English for slogans or brand names and Spanish for the copy. There is also extensive use of 'Spanglish' and code-switching in these bilingual advertisements. The Hispanic market is important because of the size of the Hispanic population. It is therefore important for advertisers to know if choice of language plays a role in determining the decision to buy a product. The research indicates that Hispanics are not a homogeneous group and that 'highly acculturated Hispanics prefer more standardized (i.e. English language) advertising campaigns, whereas less acculturated Hispanics prefer more customized (i.e. Spanish language) advertising campaigns' (Callow and Mcdonald 2005: 284).

Research by Luna *et al.* (2005) suggests that code-switching may be used as a tool for highlighting certain words or phrases in advertisements. They referred to the markedness model (Myers-Scotton 1999) to show that code-switching would attract readers' attention to the code-switched word or phrase, as this becomes marked or noticed when it appears in another language. They provide this example of an advertisement targeted at Hispanics:

Twenty million hijas are covered by AFLAC. Is yours?

The Spanish word *hijas* means daughters. The use of the Spanish word emphasizes the importance of family in this community and its use here is aimed at drawing the attention of the Spanish-speaking community and making them view the advertised product favourably.

In another study which examined advertisements for a Hispanic audience, Luna and Peracchio (2005) proposed that inserting a Spanish word into a predominantly English sentence would draw attention to the Spanish word that is used or the 'minority' language, and that the Spanish-speaking audience would then evaluate the product more favourably. By adopting this code-switching, the advertiser is able to highlight parts of the message in the advertisement and at the same time acknowledge the audience's Hispanic heritage and identity. Similarly, Ahn and La Ferle (2008) explore how the use of foreign and local elements of an advertisement influences young Koreans in their recall and recognition of the brand name and the main message. An advertisement that presents a brand name in the foreign language with the main message in the local language constitutes an effective strategy for enhancing recall and recognition of the brand name and the overall message. Another study (Noriega and Blair 2008) examined how the choice of language influenced bilingual consumers in their response to an advertisement. They suggest that a native-language advertisement is more likely to elicit thoughts about family, friends, home or homeland and this in turn would lead to a more positive attitude towards a product. Similar findings have been obtained by Krishna and Ahluwalia (2008), who examined advertisements in India and found that English is more effective in promoting luxury goods, but that Hindi or the use of code-mixing is more effective in selling basic necessities.

In a study of advertising in Japan, Takashi (1990) analysed English borrowings that were phonologically, morphologically and syntactically integrated into Japanese advertising texts. From a total of 5,556 loanwords from television commercials and print advertising, he drew up a list of five functional categories in the following order of occurrence: special effect giver, brand name, lexical gap filler, technical term and euphemism. Examples of each are given below:

Special effects givers:	*sukin-kea* (skincare), *puresutiiji-na* (prestigious), *herushii* (healthy)
Brand names:	name of a product, service and company: Xerox, Vicks, Kent, Regein (Regain), Supaaku (Spark).
Lexical gap:	*Amerika* (America), *Furansu* (France) and *Madoriddo* (Madrid), James Dean.
Technical terms:	*konpyuutaa* (computer), *fakushimiri* (facsimile)
Euphemism:	Mai hoomu (my home), mai kaa (my car) (these words are used to avoid directness)

(Takashi, 1990: 331)

In contrast, monolingual Japanese advertisements promote traditional Japanese and Chinese items. Takashi therefore concluded that English is used to signal the modernity

523

and the sophistication of a product. His findings support Bhatia (1987), who found that, in India, English is associated with being modern, Western and scientific, while Sanskrit is associated with high quality and reliability. For this reason, Sanskrit terms are preferred over English in advertising traditional Indian products. These findings are similar to those of Masavisut (1986), who observed that English is used in Thai advertisements for products which wish to be seen as Western.

Russian TV commercials have also seen an increasingly abundant use of English in advertisements. English is present in brand names, in the names of companies, in logos, wrappers and attention-getters (see also Proshina, this volume). English and Russian mixing takes place both inter- and intrasententially. Ustinova and Bhatia (2005) give two reasons for the use of English, one functional and the other social.

> When Western firms promote the brand name in English and a familiar graphic form in Roman script, the product name stands for company identity, then functional and pragmatic reasons are exploited. When English symbolizes the language of novelty, prestige and modernization social reasons are employed.
>
> (Ustinova and Bhatia 2005: 504)

They found that the majority of the persuasive devices used contain English–Russian code-mixing. English also plays an important role in literary devices and figures of speech. As has been found by other researchers, the use of English serves as an indicator of a product's prestige and costliness. They conclude that English in advertisements functions to get the attention of the potential customers, as well as being 'a marker of Westernization, internationalism, modernization, innovation and prestige' (Ustinova and Bhatia 2005: 505).

In their study of a global magazine published in different countries, Machin and van Leeuwen (2008) showed that trendiness and youth culture is often associated with English. Examples of localized English words taken from the Indian version of the magazine are: *vamp varnish* (nail polish), *mane* (hair), *babes and chicks* (girls) and *pouters* (lips). Examples from the Dutch and Chinese versions are provided below:

> Saaie novembermaaden vragen om een lekker opvallende make-up, die niet. Ophoudt bij een beetje mascara en gekleurde lippen. Smoky eyes, roze wangen en lippen, en vooral: glamorous glans!
> [Dull November months call for a nice eye-catching make-up which doesn't stop. Add a little mascara and coloured lips. Smoky eyes, pink cheeks and lips and above all: glamorous gloss!]

> Ni de mei li Must-Have shi shen me?
> [What is your beauty Must-Have?]
>
> (Machin and van Leeuwen 2008: 596)

In his study of advertisements in six languages (Hindi, Chinese, Japanese, French, Italian and Spanish) Bhatia (1992) found that language-mixing is universal and that English is commonly the 'mixed' language. English is often code-mixed with local languages to fulfil the advertising industry's needs of having creativity and innovation in advertisements.

In the next section I turn to look at advertisements from one specific country, Malaysia.

English in Malaysian advertisements

Before language use in advertisements in Malaysia is discussed, some background infor-mation about the ethnic composition and languages in the country is provided.

There are three main ethnic groups in the country: Malays, Chinese and Indians. The Malays normally use Malay in intragroup communication, although it is also common for Malays to code-switch with English, or speak mostly English to one another, espe-cially in urban areas. Colloquial Malay is the form that is used at home or with friends to indicate intimacy or solidarity. Thus, a Malay who has been living in Kuala Lumpur will probably speak a lot of English to his/her workmates, but switch to the mother tongue when speaking to family members. There are a number of reasons for code-switching, such as to establish rapport or for intimacy.

The Chinese dialects used are largely determined by locality, although in the past their use was differentiated through occupation as well. In certain parts of Malaysia, for instance in Penang, the majority are Hokkien speakers, whilst in Kuala Lumpur the majority are Cantonese speakers. Mandarin is the language used in mass media and education. Chinese dialects and Mandarin are used in intragroup communication, while Malay or English is often used in intergroup communication. Increasingly, homes where the parents have been educated in Chinese schools, use Mandarin as the home language. English-speaking Chinese families are also common in urban areas, although often these families also speak a local dialect. The less educated use bazaar (colloquial) Malay in intergroup communication.

The Indians use one of the Indian languages or English in intragroup communication. In intergroup communication, Malay or English is used, with English the preferred lan-guage among the more educated Indians and Malay among the less educated Indians. A minority of the Indians are Muslims who generally practise the Malay way of life and speak Malay as their first language.

Apart from the three main languages, English is widely used especially in urban areas. Malaysian English is a distinct variety of English that contains linguistic features of nativization comprising features of other local languages and dialects and accepted as a marker of national identity. It contains words borrowed and assimilated from local lan-guages and dialects. A speaker may also switch from the standard version of the language to a dialect, or from a more formal standard variety of English to a colloquial variety for certain reasons. When the situation is formal, speakers usually monitor themselves and speak a variety that is fairly standard. However, in informal situations, there is often a shift down the lectal scale with speakers using basilectal features in their speech.

While some research has been conducted into advertisements in Malaysia, only a few studies have focused on the language used in them. Hashim (2006) for example, looked at advertisements using a framework derived from systemic functional linguistics to determine how the messages, expressed both linguistically and visually, are integrated to form a composite whole. The advertisements were chosen to illustrate the ethnic and cultural diversity that exists in the country. In the example given, a telephone card adver-tisement is shown. This product is advertised using different images and texts showing different values and beliefs to two different ethnic groups, but a common background represented by the Malaysian batik material is chosen. Fauziah and Khatijah (2006) selected advertisements from corporate companies in Malaysia and found that the dis-course of the advertisements is aimed at fostering unity between the ethnic groups in the country and to promote Malaysian identity.

Radio advertisements have been studied, but only on a small scale. Leong (2004) investigated the extent to which Malaysian English is used in radio ads and described the salient lexical and syntactic features. She found that 53 per cent of the 60 advertisements analysed used a local, colloquial English, as well as standard Malaysian English. Amongst the reasons she gives for this colloquial use are that the advertisers want to attract the listeners by establishing a closer rapport with them and making the dialogue more natural or realistic, as the ultimate aim is to persuade the listeners to want to purchase the product.

Radio advertisements have also been studied to see how their use of English attempts to influence and change the behaviour of the target group of customers (Hashim 2007). It was observed that there is a need to be interactive to capture the attention of the listeners. The use of performative features serves to minimize the experience of distance. The use of a lively style is also employed to persuade listeners (Tolson 2006). The use of conversational style in public communication is commonly deliberately used to give a sense of equality to communication, in fact a false sense, as one-way communication of this type does not allow feedback from the listeners. A similar strategy was also discovered in Scannell and Cardiff's (1991) study of the BBC during the 1920s, that of 'a conversational style for radio speakers, complete with fully scripted hesitations and errors, so as to sound more "natural", and to soften the new intrusion of public speech into private living rooms' (cited in Machin and van Leeuwen 2008: 596).

Both standard Malaysian English (SME) and colloquial Malaysian English (CME) are routinely employed in many of radio advertisements in Malaysia. A few examples of radio advertisements are given below.

Example 1.1: Automax, Mix.fm, 2008
Abah (Father): Listen, *abah's* got a save-petrol plan for our *balik kampung* (going back to the home town/village) trip. First, you can only take one small bag each.
Wife: That's impossible
Abah: Well, less weight saves petrol. Next, air-con will be off.
Son: *Abah,* I'll sweat to death.
Abah: No air-con saves more petrol.
Announcer: Don't worry. Now with Automax Nano Tech, you can save on petrol and enjoy your journey home. Automax saves you up to 28 per cent and boosts engine power up to 20 per cent. Automax Nano Tech is made in the USA. Available at Cosway and 7–11. Enjoy a special discount today.

Example 1.2: Tesco Extra, Mix.fm, 2008
Chinese man: Egg, *ah* ... everything extra *lah.*
Indian man: Eh, extra this, extra that! Wait for Tesco Extra to open first *lah dey* [mate/brother]!
Chinese man: Huh? When?
Announcer: Tesco Extra Seberang Jaya Prai is opening soon. Over 200 food varieties to tantalize your taste buds, and more than 40 shops and kiosks for your extra shopping convenience. Everything is extra. Tesco Extra Seberang Jaya for you and your family.

Example 1.3: TM I Talk, Hitz.fm, 2006
Employee: *Ah,* boss! 'I Talk' *ah* ...

Employer: Talk *lah!*

Employee: No, no, no. 'I Talk.'

Employer: Okay, talk.

Employee: 'I Talk.'

Employer: *I also can talk!* But, what are you talking about?

Employee: *Aiya!* I want 'I Talk.'

(Music)

Announcer: Keeping talking on 'I Talk'. Enjoy low, low rates for longer talks on IDD and long-distance calls. Easily available at Maybank2u.com, most petrol marts and more than 10 000 other outlets nationwide. Get yours today. 'I Talk', only from TM.

Employer: Oh, 'I Talk', *ah?*

Employee: Ha, talk more, pay less. 'I Talk' *lah!*

(Closing music)

Example 1.4: Support Local Tourism PSA, Mix.fm, 2008

Man 1: *Eh, brother!* I just got back from my holiday *lah*. We went to Rome, Milan *(laughs)*.

Man 2: Oh, really, *ah?* I just got back from my holiday too. I went to Taman Negara with my wife. We saw so many types of animals.

Man 1: Animals? I'm going to South Africa and *they got* more animals there *(laughs)*.

Man 2: Last year, I went to Pulau Redang. It's beautiful.

Man 1: *Eh, eh,* is that like in somewhere in Sabah or … ?

Man 2: No, no, it's off in Terengganu *lah, dude.*

Man 1: *Eh,* if I want an island, I'm going to Maldives, *y'all.*

Man 2: Before you get to know other people's countries, get to know your own first.

Man 1: Mix FM in support of seeing all of beautiful Malaysia.

Man 2: *Malaysia boleh* (can)!

Example 1.5: TM Let's Talk – Puas-puas

(Song)

> Let's talk *puas-puas* (until satisfied)
> Now you don't have to talk fast, fast
> Call nationwide for free
> From just 68 monthly
> Let's talk *puas-puas* (until satisfied)
> If you love to talk, don't miss it
> Call nationwide for free
> From just 68 monthly

(Background music)

Announcer: From only 68 ringgit monthly, you can enjoy free calls nationwide. Hurry, call 100 and sign up before 31st October.

(Music continues)

Hello, hello!

(Source: www.lets-talk.com.my/radio_commercials.html)

In all five radio advertisements above, there is the interplay between colloquial Malaysian English and standard Malaysian English. There is what might be called a 'direct' address when the message of the advertiser is directed at the consumer, usually by the commentator, and there is what we might call 'indirect' address, when the message is presented in the form of a dialogue. The 'direct' address is usually in Standard English and the indirect address in colloquial English.

An example of direct address can be seen in Example 1.5.

> For only 68 ringgit monthly, you can enjoy free calls nationwide. Hurry, call 100 and sign up before 31st October.

As Cook has pointed out, a hegemonic, authoritative voice occurs or recurs at the end of advertisements: 'There is in advertisements a reluctance to leave matters open, which results, even in the most heteroglossic advertisements, in the assertion of a single mono-logic and authoritative voice at the end' (1992: 190). The purpose of the consumer's voice seems to be to make explicit what is found in the monologues or the dialogues. From the advertisements we can perceive a sense of pride and affinity with the localized variety of English. While this cannot be determined from the transcripts alone, there is an exaggeration of the Malaysian accent to assert identity and show membership in a local speech community. Interplay between standard and colloquial English can be observed in the skilful switching between the two, as well as ethnically marked pronunciation, to portray the stereotypical characteristics of the three main ethnic groups, Malays, Chinese and Indians, in an attempt to ensure the success of the advertisement.

The influence of substrate languages can be seen and heard in the lexical borrowing, simplified syntax and distinctive phonology used in the radio advertisements. Exaggerated use is often meant to inject humour and to identify the speaker as being from a particular ethnic group. As Coupland (2001: 351) has argued, 'broadcast talk is a natural environment for stylization' and that 'radio talk involves overtly motivated selections from pre-existing stylistic repertoires, addressed to enculturated audiences'. His study reveals how radio presenters creatively choose from a repertoire of culturally significant Welsh dialect forms of English to project shifting social personas and stances.

Features of Malaysian English (see also Low, this volume) can be identified in the radio advertisements. The speaker's ethnic group can usually be identified as being Malay, Chinese or Indian from his or her pronunciation. Common to all the speakers is a lack of distinction between short and long vowels in colloquial speech, and little vowel reduction. Consonant cluster reduction is also common and there is a tendency to devoice fricatives in the final position. The dental fricatives are often realized as dentals and word final plosives are often unreleased or glotalized when preceded by a vowel.

There are a number of lexical borrowings in the radio advertisements for terms of address (e.g. 1.1 *abah (father)*), names of places (e.g. 1.4 *Pulau Redang*) and for certain adjectives (e.g. 1.5 *puas (satisfied)*).

Grammar simplification can also be observed, as in the use of reduction, omission and restructuring, as shown in the following examples.

> Next, air con will be *off*. (e.g. 1.1)
> … everything extra *lah*. (e.g. 1.2)
> I *also can* talk. (e.g. 1.3)
> I'm going to South Africa and they *got* more animals there. (e.g. 1.4)

Adjectives play an important role in advertisements as 'many adjectives can apply to both the advertised product (the signifier) and to the values it signifies' (Machin and van Leeuwen 2008: 590). Reduplication of an adjective can be seen in Example 1.5 above:

'*puas puas*' (until satisfied), '*fast fast*'.

Adjectival reduplication is often used to intensify the meaning of the adjective or to place emphasis on the word.

Discourse particles from the three main different languages in the country, Malay, Chinese and Tamil, are frequently employed by the speakers in the radio advertisements:

Egg, *ah* … everything extra *lah*.
Eh, extra this, extra that! Wait for Tesco Extra to open first day *lah dey*! (1.5)

Ah, boss 'I Talk' *ah* ...
Talk *lah!* (1.3)

Oh really *ah?*
No, no, it's off in Terengganu *lah* dude. (1.4)

Particles in Malaysian English perform certain functions fulfilled by grammatical functions and intonational variation in Standard English. They can be used to affirm a statement, to soften a remark, to emphasize a certain word/phrase and, when placed at the end of a sentence, to form a question. '*Lah*' is often used to convey emotive or affective attitudes of the speaker. It can be used as a softener, and even to change a command to a request. '*Lah*' can also place emphasis on the statement in which it is found or on the word that comes before the particle. For example, in 1.2 above, '*lah*' is used to place emphasis on the word 'extra'. '*Eh*' is a form of address used among friends and often to get someone's attention. '*Ah*' is often used with questions when there is no subject inversion.

In Malaysian print advertisements, English is commonly used either on its own or together with another language or languages. The following advertisements illustrate this use of more than one language.

Example 2.1: Pizza Hut

As can be seen in the above advertisements, code-switching is commonly found in Malaysian advertisements. This can be explained by the somewhat complex interplay of language use in Malaysia. Among the reasons a speaker may switch from a more formal variety to a colloquial variety which contains local words is when there is an absence of an equivalent word in English for a culinary or cultural item, for example. Local words may also be preferred if the use of the English words would result in the loss of an important cultural association: for example, the use of a term of address such as '*abah*' (father).

Some examples of this from the data are:

Pizza Hut *Sensasi* (sensational) Delight (2.1)
The adjective in the phrase that highlights the product is in a Malay borrowed word *'sensasi'*.

Coffee, *kopi* (coffee) or cafe? (2.2)
The Malay word for coffee *kopi* is used here to indicate the different types of coffee outlets in a mall.

Her eyes rolled heavenwards as a soft, tender sigh escaped her clenched lips: '*Kirukku payale* (mad fellow) ... *Katrika* (Brinjal)! Just take one little one, a strand.' (2.3)

A Tamil phrase *kirukku payale* and word *katrika* are used here to remind Indians of family ties during the festive period of Deepavali.

In some cases, the advertisements can be bilingual, as exemplified below:

Pilih reka bentuk kegemaran anda.
Select your favourite design.

Hantarkan gambar kegemaran anda.
Submit your favourite photo.

Penuhkan borang pesanan.
Complete order form.

Reka bentuk untuk dipilih.
Designs to choose from.

Further examples are shown in Tables 30.1, 30.2, 30.3 and 30.4.

Visuals

Visuals play an important role in advertisements and need some mention here. They often support the text that appears in the advertisement and in some cases play a bigger role than the text itself. The advertisements from which the visuals in Tables 30.5 and 30.6 are found appeared during festive occasions such as Hari Raya (Eid), celebrated by the Muslims, and Deepavali, celebrated by the Hindus.

Table 30.1 Culture

Muslim	*Selamat Hari Raya, Hari Raya, Raya* (Happy Festive Day)
	Duit Raya (festive money)
	Aidilfitri, Salam Aidilfitri (Happy Festive Day)
	Ramadhan (month of fasting)
	Balikkampung (return to the village)
	Kenduri (feast)
	Sahur (meal before dawn during the fasting month)
	Selamat Berpuasa (Happy fasting)
Hindu	*Deepavali* (Indian festival)
	Henna (plant dye)

Table 30.2 Food

Indian	Murukku
	Oomapodhi
	Roti Canai
	Briyani
	Roti Naan
	Tandoori
Malay	Kurma
	Sup Soto Ayam
	Ayam Percik
	Gandum
	Rendang
	Ketupat
	Lemang
	Satay
Chinese	Longan

Table 30.3 Forms of address

Language	Form of address	Meaning
Malay	Abah	Father
Indian dialect	Ammama	Grandmother

Table 30.4 Events/celebrations

Events/celebrations	Significance
Merdeka	Malaysian Independence Day
Hari Raya Aidil Fitri	Celebration which marks the end of Ramadhan, the holy month of fasting
Deepavali/Diwali	Hindu Festival of Lights

Table 30.5 Raya advertisements

Visual	Meaning/example
Ketupat	Traditional food served during Aidil Fitri
Minaret	Muslim architecture
Crescent	Symbol of Islamic faith
Traditional costumes	Baju Melayu, Baju Kurung
Green	Islam venerates this colour as paradise is expected to be full of lush greenery

Conclusion

This chapter has illustrated and discussed the respective roles of standard and local Englishes as well as other languages in advertisements from different parts of the world and especially in Malaysia, and how they are used to appeal to a wide range of ethnic, national and regional audiences. In bilingual and multilingual populations, the choice of language or variety can be a complex issue. Innovations in the form of code-switching and choice of language for different functions indicate that the choice of language plays

531

Table 30.6 Deepavali/Diwali advertisements

Visual	Meaning/example
Murukku	Popular Indian savoury snack
Oil lamps	The Hindus thank the Goddess Lakshmi for the joy, knowledge, peace and wealth that they have received by lighting the oil lamps
Kolam	To bestow prosperity upon homes
Henna	Regarded as having blessings, and is applied for luck, joy and beauty
Peacock (feathers)	Sacred bird of India
	In Hinduism, the image of the God of Thunder, Rain and War, Indra, was depicted in the form of a peacock.
	In south India (where most Malaysian Indians are from), peacock is considered as a *vahana* or vehicle of Lord Muruga.
Traditional costumes	Saree, dothi, accessories (bangles, bindhi)

a crucial role in the advertising industry. The illustrations in this chapter show that a mixture of two or more languages is commonly used in advertisements, as advertisers try to reach out to potential clients using both global and local strategies. In the Malaysian advertisements illustrated here, the use of standard and local varieties of English, alongside one or more of the 'local' languages such as Malay, Chinese or Tamil, can be seen. The study of English in advertisements shows that English can be said to be embedded inside complex language habitats that determine its form, functions and status vis-à-vis other languages.

More research on the use of language in advertisements is needed to determine the roles played by varieties of English and other languages in various parts of the world in order to identify which features of linguistic advertising are unique to certain markets and which can be considered universal. This will also help to identify the respective roles of local and global cultures in advertising. This is crucial in today's globalized world, where issues pertaining to advertising are becoming increasingly important.

Suggestions for further reading

Brutt-Griffler, J. (2002) *World English: A Study of its Development*, Clevedon: Multilingual Matters.
Crystal, D. (2003) *English as a Global Language*, Cambridge: Cambridge University Press.
McArthur, T. (1998) *The English Languages*, Cambridge: Cambridge University Press.

References

Ahn, J. and La Ferle, C. (2008) 'Enhancing recall and recognition for brand names and body copy: a mixed-language approach', *Journal of Advertising*, 37 (3): 107–17.
Bhatia, T.K. (1987) 'English in advertising: multiple mixing and media', *World Englishes*, 6: 33–48.
——(1992) 'Discourse functions and pragmatics of mixing: advertising across cultures', *World Englishes*, 6 (1): 33–48.
——(2000) *Advertising in Rural India: Language, Marketing Communication and Consumerism*, Tokyo University of Foreign Studies: Tokyo, Japan.
Bishop, H., Coupland, N. and Garrett, P. (2005) 'Globalisation, advertising and language choice: shifting values for Welsh and Welshness in Y Drych, 1851–2001', *Multilingua*, 24: 342–78.

Callow, M. and Mcdonald, C.G. (2005) 'The "spanglification" of advertising campaigns in Hispanic media? A comparison of approaches in Spanish-only and dual language magazines', *Journal of Marketing Communications*, 11 (4): 283–95.

Cook, G. (1992) *The Discourse of Advertising*, London: Routledge.

Coupland, N. (2001) 'Dialect stylization in radio talk', *Language in Society*, 30: 345–75.

Duncan, T. and Ramaprasad, J. (1995) 'Standardized multinational advertising: the influencing factors', *Journal of Advertising*, XXIV (3): 55–68.

Fauziah, Kamaruddinn and Khatijah, Shamsuddin (2006) 'Interculturalism and language in Malaysian corporate advertisements', in Zuraidah Mohd. Don (ed.) *English in a Globalised Environment*, Kuala Lumpur: University of Malaya Press.

Graddol, D. (1997) *The Future of English?* London: The British Council.

——(2006) *English Next*, London: The British Council.

Haarman, H. (1984) 'The role of ethnocultural stereotypes and foreign languages in Japanese commercials', *Journal of the Sociology of Language*, 50: 101–21.

——(1989) *Symbolic Values of Foreign Language Use: From the Japanese Case to a General Sociolinguistic Perspective*, Berlin: Mouton de Gruyter.

Hashim, Azirah (2006) 'A multimodal analysis of cultural identity construction in Malaysian advertisements', in Zuraidah Mohd. Don (ed.) *English in a Globalised Environment*, Kuala Lumpur: University of Malaya Press.

——(2007) 'Radio advertisements in English in Malaysia: unity and diversity', paper presented at the 10th English in Southeast Asia Conference, Perth, Australia, December.

Jenkins, J. (2007) *English as a Lingua Franca: Attitude and Identity*, Oxford: Oxford University Press.

Kachru, B. (1982/1992) *The Other Tongue*, Chicago: Illinois University Press.

Kelly-Holmes, H. (2000) 'Bier, parfum, kaas: language fetish in European advertising', *European Journal of Cultural Studies*, 3: 67–82.

Kirkpatrick, A. (2007) *World Englishes: Implications for International Communication and English Language Teaching*, Cambridge: Cambridge University Press.

Krishna, A. and Ahluwalia, R. (2008) 'Language choice in advertising to bilinguals: asymmetric effects for multinationals versus local firms', *Journal of Consumer Research*, 35: 1–14.

Leitner, G. (1992) 'Pluricentric English', in M. Clyne (ed.) *Pluricentric Languages*, Berlin: Mouton de Gruyter, pp. 185–200.

——(2004) *Australia's Many Voices. Australian English-The National Language*, Berlin: Mouton de Gruyter.

Leong, Y.L. (2004) 'The use of Malaysian English in radio advertisements', unpublished MA research project, Kuala Lumpur, University of Malaya.

Luna, D. and Peracchio, L.A. (2005) 'Advertising to bilingual consumers: the impact of code-switching on persuasion', *Journal of Consumer Research*, 31: 760–5.

Luna, D., Lerman, D. and Peracchio, L.A. (2005) 'Structural constraints in code-switched advertising', *Journal of Consumer Research*, 32: 416–23.

Machin, D. and van Leeuwen, T. (2005) 'Language style and lifestyle: the case of a global magazine', *Media, Culture and Society*, 27: 577–600.

Masavisut, N. (1986) 'The power of the English language in Thai media', *World Englishes*, 5(2/3): 197–207.

Myers-Scotton, C. (1999) 'Explaining the role of norms and rationality in codeswitching', *Journal of Pragmatics*, 32 (9): 1259–71.

Noriega, J. and Blair, E. (2008) 'Advertising to bilinguals: does the language of advertising influence the nature of thoughts?', *Journal of Marketing*, 72: 69–83.

Piller, I. (2001) 'Identity constructions in multilingual advertising', *Language and Society*, 30: 153–86.

——(2003) 'Advertising as a site of language contact', *Annual Review of Applied Linguistics*, 23: 170–83.

Scannel, P. and Cardiff, D. (1991) *Serving the Nation: A Social History of British Broadcasting, Vol. 1*, Oxford: Blackwell.

Schneider, E. (2003) 'The dynamics of new Englishes: from identity construction to dialect birth', *Language*, 79 (2): 233–81.

——(2007) *Postcolonial English*, Cambridge: Cambridge University Press.

Takashi, K. (1990) 'A sociolinguistic analysis of English borrowings in Japanese advertising texts', *World Englishes*, 9: 327–41.

Tolson, A. (2006) *Media Talk: Spoken Discourse on TV and Radio*, Edinburgh: Edinburgh University Press.

Ustinova, I.P. and Bhatia, T.K. (2005) 'Convergence of English in Russian TV commercials', *World Englishes*, 24: 495–508.

31

The Englishes of popular cultures

Andrew Moody

Introduction

One of the longstanding and rarely challenged conventions of sociolinguistic research is that linguistic data should be both 'spontaneous' and 'naturally occurring'.

This convention was probably derived in early sociolinguistic work from traditions in dialectology, an approach that was careful to exclude speakers who are not authentically representative of the speech of the particular region. Within sociolinguistic work, however, the notion of authenticity was extended to the collection of speech styles. Not only were speakers to be deemed as authentic speakers of the regional variety, but the authenticity of the speech style (i.e. 'casual style' representing 'vernacular speech' versus 'careful style' representing 'standard speech') should also be validated. In his early work on the stratification of /r/ in New York, Labov (1972: 61) addresses the problem of authenticity in what he calls the 'Observer's Paradox' by noting that 'our goal is to observe the way people use language when they are not being observed'. In the same volume he suggests a way to overcome the observer's paradox:

> We can also involve the subject in questions and topics which recreate strong emotions he has felt in the past, or involve him in other contexts. One of the most successful questions of this type is the one dealing with the 'Danger of Death': 'Have you ever been in a situation where you were in serious danger of being killed?' Narratives given in answer to this question almost always show a shift of style away from careful speech towards the vernacular.
>
> (Labov 1972: 209–10)

With this methodology Labov argues that the sociolinguist may be able to confirm results of data from less 'spontaneously' occurring speech styles by showing a consistent trend in the way that sociolinguistic features appear in different speech styles. Although the principled privileging of spontaneous and naturally occurring data has been a very important feature of the examination of language use within traditionally defined speech communities, it has also facilitated a sustained neglect of linguistic data from popular culture, a neglect that has only recently begun to be reversed.

It is both appropriate and significant that the sociolinguistic importance of data from popular culture be examined in a handbook of World Englishes. In the same way that World Englishes represent the interaction between local norms of divergence and global norms of convergence, the development of multiple popular cultures that are inevitably related to one another, yet, at the same time, distinct from one another, is a feature frequently attributed to popular cultures. In Edward Said's (1993) description of the whole of American identity and culture as 'a complex but not reductively unified one', he continues to note that 'partly because of empire, all cultures are involved in one another; none is single and pure, all are hybrid, heterogenous [sic], extraordinarily differentiated, and unmonolithic' (1993: xxv). In much the way that World Englishes theorists celebrate the plurality of English varieties, Storey argues for the plurality – what we might think of as 'world cultures' – as the goal of globalization of culture, 'to build a world culture that is not a monoculture, marked only by hierarchical distinctions, but a world culture which values plurality, in which diversity and difference exist in horizontal relations' (Storey 2003: 120). Relevant to the study of World Englishes, therefore, is the spread of popular culture by many of the same mechanisms that have produced globalization within linguistic varieties.

But what is meant by the term 'popular culture' and how is it related to notions such as globalization? In his textbook introduction to the study of popular culture, Storey (2006) outlines six distinct definitions of 'popular culture'. The series of definitions begin with a possible definition that popular culture – in opposition to so-called 'high culture' – is 'simply culture which is widely favoured or well liked by many people' (2006: 4). The sixth definition finally rejects this opposition and instead relies upon a 'claim that postmodern culture is a culture which no longer recognizes the distinction between high and popular culture' (2006: 9). Across the six definitions, however, several common features of popular culture are noteworthy in understanding the role of English in popular cultures. First, Storey (2006) notes that popular culture is usually associated with mass media, and especially media that are free, or at least very inexpensive, for public consumption. These media may include television, film, newspapers, magazines and music. Second, Storey (1999, 2006) discusses the important role of consumer culture in the development of popular culture and stresses that popular culture is intended for consumption, and therefore may include artefacts like advertising, branding and activities associated with becoming a 'fan' of certain pop culture (e.g. blogging, collecting, 'fanzines', etc.). Finally, to the degree that the development of consumer cultures largely results from what we identify as economic 'globalization', there is a natural dialogue between global and local expressions, identities and products within popular culture:

> The process [of globalization] is much more contradictory and complex, involving the ebb and flow of both homogenizing and heterogenizing forces and the meeting and mingling of the 'local' and 'global' in new forms of hybrid cultures. Roland Robertson (1995) uses the term 'glocalization' (a term borrowed from Japanese business) to describe globalization as the simultaneous interpenetration of the global and the local. In other words, what is exported always finds itself in the context of what already exists; that is, exports always become imports as they are incorporated into an indigenous culture.
>
> (Storey 2003: 112)

Therefore, to examine English within popular culture is to examine both the global spread of English *and* the global spread of popular culture. To the degree that English is indigenized according to local norms and values, so is popular culture. But is the global spread of English and popular culture merely coincidental, or are these two phenomena somehow related to one another? This chapter will review much of the literature about English in popular culture and suggest a methodological approach that will capture the glocalization of both language and culture as related phenomena. To this extent it will be argued that English can and should be examined as a language *of* popular culture.

The Englishes *of* popular culture and English *in* popular culture

One of the purposes of this chapter is to develop a theoretical and methodological framework that will justify the examination of Englishes *of* popular culture. To date, most work on English used in popular culture genres has instead focused on English *in* popular culture. The distinction between the two terms – *of* and *in* – determines the ownership of the language. Those studies that examine language *in* popular culture do not attempt to account for the variability of language in pop culture. Instead, these studies treat language phenomena within pop culture data the same way that sociolinguistics treat phenomena in naturally occurring or spontaneous genres or speech styles. The use of English in a popular culture, therefore, is not substantially different from the English of the popular culture's broader speech community, and there is no attempt within these approaches to take into account the possible effect that a pop culture genre may have on particular instances of language use. For example, an examination of Malaysian English on the radio may choose to treat the data as generally representative of that English variety and, without taking into account the influence of the pop culture genre, this approach would constitute an example of English *in* popular culture.

On the other hand, studies that examine the language *of* popular culture choose to see the language variety as a specialized genre-specific variety that belongs to the pop culture. In these types of studies, the language variety is owned and regulated by the popular culture apart from the larger speech community. Attempts to understand and explain the use of language do not usually attempt to generalize conclusions to the entire speech community. For example, an examination of spelling conventions used in computer-mediated communication (CMC) may choose to treat the conventions solely as a feature of the communication medium and without antecedent within the larger speech community. In that case we would call this approach one that studies the English *of* popular culture. Review of previous studies of the English and popular culture, therefore, will attempt to make clear the distinction between the two types of research strategies.

Sociolinguistic studies can also generally be divided into two large categories: those that study variation and those that study interaction. To the degree that sociolinguistics has recently begun to focus on language use in popular culture, these two types of sociolinguistic studies are closely related to the tendency to focus either on the Englishes *of* popular culture or English *in* popular culture. The examination of linguistic variation focuses on differences between formal features of language used by various speakers, or within variable contexts. In the case of pop culture, variationist approaches to sociolinguistics suggest that there are varieties of English that may be thought of as pop Englishes. These Englishes *of* popular culture tend to say something unique about the variety of language used specifically within pop culture genres. Alternatively, the examination of linguistic interaction within popular culture attempts to use data from popular culture to generalize about interactions or attitudes within a speech community. These studies do not tend to find varieties that are unique to popular culture, but instead look for interactional patterns that may be indicative of more general patterns of linguistic usage in the speech community. Although the distinction between English *of* popular culture and English *in* popular culture does not allow for an entirely neat mechanism of distinguishing all studies about language and popular culture, it does allow us two ways to see how traditional oppositions to pop culture data have recently been questioned within sociolinguistic work on English varieties. Therefore, despite the fact that the *of*/*in* distinction does not form perfectly neat compartments with which to classify studies of English and popular culture, the distinction is nevertheless useful in organizing the two broadly complementary approaches.

The Englishes of popular culture

Adams (2000) argues that 'ephemeral language', which includes forms that are derived from or influenced by popular culture media, should be examined as possible sources of innovation in American English. Although many of the forms or innovations of 'ephemeral language', by definition, do not retain long-term currency within the language, they can serve to illustrate larger trends of language change, and they can be used to illustrate the language of a particular moment. Similarly, Eble (2003) argues that the study of lexis from slang is an area that is typically marginalized in mainstream linguistics and sociolinguistics, despite that fact that slang maintains important links to popular culture and has had a special degree of influence in the global spread of American English. These studies point out the special nature of English in popular culture as a language that is distinct from the forms of language used in other segments of society. In the same way, examination of specific popular cultural registers, such as Reaser's (2003) examination of sports announcer talk, suggests that the English of popular culture can be examined without reference to larger linguistic issues in a society.

There are, however, few studies that attempt to study the features of English across multiple genres or media of popular culture. Instead, the majority of studies that examine the English *of* popular culture instead look at the distinctive features of a particular media format or a pop culture genre. For example, the kinds of communicative activities that Bhimji (2001) describes in her analysis of 'talk radio' are exclusively found in the genre, but the unique combination of activities – and the linguistic form of those activities – is highly characteristic of 'talk radio' discourse. Other generic approaches to the English *of* popular culture include analyses of advertising (see Faulkner 2000; Mika 2004; Hashim, this volume), computer-mediated communication (see Ooi 2002; Herring 2004; Warschauer *et al.*, this volume) and short-messaging services (i.e. SMS). In particular, Thurlow (2003) challenges claims that SMS is a site of linguistic innovation that is distinctly different from other types of face-to-face or computer-mediated communication. Similarly, Rojo-Laurilla (2002) argues that SMS messages do not demonstrate gendered differences that are usually found in the speech community.

Examinations of the English *of* popular culture incorporate various types of linguistic approaches, but one approach, critical discourse analysis, has afforded especially good insights into how language functions differently within popular culture than in other segments of society. For example, Godeo (2006) examines the role of language in the construction of identity in the problem pages of British men's magazines. Warner (2005: 293) examines the discourses of institutions as they are 'reproduced, resisted, or modified' in the medium of 'talkback radio'. Finally, Gaudio (2003) argues that the commercialization of conversation is one effect of the spread of Starbucks™ within popular culture. Within these approaches to English and popular culture, there is no need to reference linguistic forms outside the popular culture genres or media in which they are examined. These approaches treat the English *of* popular culture as a linguistic entity that does not need to represent other linguistic forms or social relations.

English in popular culture

By examining English in popular culture, however, researchers examine varieties of English as they exist within the society at large and are not necessarily exclusively representative of pop culture or of a pop culture media. Instead, these studies attempt to examine language in society by using data that have been drawn from popular culture genres. Perhaps the most obvious way to do this has been to collect data from genres that are 'unscripted' and, therefore, presumably closer to naturally occurring data. For example, Brownlow *et al.* (2003) compare and contrast the linguistic behaviours of men and women in unscripted televised interviews to speculate on the types of messages that are sent with various sociolinguistic features. Thornborrow and Morris (2004) examine unscripted interaction from the reality TV show *Big Brother* in order to understand the social functions of gossip. However, Thornborrow and Morris also question the naturalness of the reality game show setting, which 'has been designed to provide entertainment and elicit "performance" in a context which is highly constrained in terms of its enforced sociability and heightened competitiveness between participants' (2004: 268). Nevertheless, gossip in the game show does illustrate many of the authentic features and evaluations of gossip in other segments of society.

The search for authenticity within data drawn from pop culture, and especially that drawn from movies, highlights many of the arguments in favour of adopting such data for linguistic description, but it also illustrates the problems. In his examination of compliments and compliment responses in film, Rose (2001) notes that, in terms of the frequency use of syntactic formulae, compliment topics and compliment responses, data from film are very similar to data drawn from a corpus of naturally occurring speech. However, the gender distribution of compliments and the gender association with specific compliment response strategies were quite different when comparing film and natural data, and it is suggested that the usefulness of film data is limited and cannot be relied on *a priori*. Similarly, Taylor (2004) examines the script of the film *Notting Hill* and the actual language that is used in the movie to conclude that the performance of a script may make the language more authentic, rather than less.

A number of other scholars have begun to look at the language of popular culture without any reference to the authenticity of the language. For example, Weatherall (1996: 59) examines potentially sexist language in the British soap opera *Coronation Street* to conclude that there is no quantitative evidence of 'a pervasive bias against women in language'. Similarly, Richardson (2006) looks at the imaginative portrayal of a 'spin doctor' on the US television show *The West Wing*. Examination of the character is noteworthy in the way that this kind of character portrays a sociolinguistically sophisticated performance and because it elicits an audience reaction about 'spin' as a type of workplace talk. With reference to sociolinguistic portrayal of phonological variants of speech, Elliott (2000) observes the decade-on-decade decrease in the occurrence of non-rhotic speech (i.e. r-less speech) in American film speech from the 1930s to the 1970s to conclude that the decrease results from a shift away from a prestige norm of r-less speech towards a prestige norm of rhotic speech. While this analysis primarily treats the changing norms of rhoticity as a language phenomenon that is not artistically manipulated, it does examine some of the effects of:

> sociolinguistic accommodation to the pronunciation of a co-star, pronunciation modification towards the prestige norm by male speakers when addressing female co-stars, and the use of different pronunciations to portray a character's status, moral qualities, and, in a few cases, regional origin.
>
> (Elliott 2000: v)

Elliott's analysis charts the change of prestige norm in the movies against the development of a rhoticized prestige variety of 'General American' speech at the same time in the US. While there is reference to the way that language in the movies reflects a change in language attitudes within the general culture, there is also some attention given to the way that language variety can be used to portray attitudes towards the character.

The use of language variety to portray stereotypical features of characterization is the goal of Lippi-Green's (1997) examination of dialect in Disney animated feature films. In addition to using characterizations that are easily identifiable as 'good guys', 'bad guys' and 'bad guys who transform to good', the movies tend to link language varieties with 'specific national origins, ethnicities, and races with social norms and character-istics in non-factual and sometimes overtly discriminatory ways' (1997: 101). Hence, Lippi-Green observes that 40 per cent of characters who speak a non-native variety of English are evil (i.e. 'bad guys'), while only about 20 per cent of the speakers of US English are 'bad guys'. Similarly, Mesthrie (2002) examines the text of a popular radio series in Natal from the 1940s to compare distinctive grammatical constructions that do occur in Indian South African English at that time period, but whose grammatical functions are greatly distorted in association with stereotypes about the ethnic group. As such, Mesthrie claims that the language portrayed in the radio programme is a type of 'mock language' that amplifies linguistic and social stereotypes about the ethnic speakers portrayed. While the attention brought to ethnically or racially biased portrayals of speakers in popular culture may be somewhat recent, the discriminatory practices are not new. Porter (1999) examines the portrayal of Lowland Scots in popular street bal-lads from seventeenth-century London to conclude that the misrepresentation of Low-land Scots speech echoes derogatory designations of the speakers and reinforces a language ideology that marginalized the speakers. Using the framework of language ideology Shuttlesworth (2004: v) examines the way that 'dialogue of twentieth century novels and plays written by [United States] Southerners is transformed into film dialo-gue'. In many cases the transformation of dialogue reflects language ideologies and prejudices about Southern speakers that operate within North American society.

Trudgill (1983) was one of the earliest studies to examine the attitudes towards regional dialect in popular culture to conclude that identities may be performed in the appropriation of other varieties. In particular, Trudgill examined the occurrence of features of American pronunciation in British popular music in the 1960s, 1970s and 1980s to conclude that the influence of American pronunciations weakened over time and that expression of an 'English' identity in British pop music simultaneously developed. As an early sociolinguistic approach to language variation in popular music, Trudgill (1983) is certainly important, but it is also important in bringing to the forefront the study of performed identity. These performed identities not only reflect stereotypes and attitudes within the larger culture towards the varieties (and, of course, their speakers), but they also allow for the expression of multiple identities both within a popular culture and over time. Simpson (1999) extends Trudgill's original analytical framework to examine the pronunciation of English in pop music over a longitudinal selection of recordings. Changes in pronunciation, according to Simpson, parallel 'broader cultural, cross-cultural and sociopolitical changes' (343) that can be observed in British society. For example, Speicher and McMahon (1992) examine attitudes towards African-American English and note that the language variety is closely associated with the commercialization of rap music and widely perceived as a recognizable variety. These examinations of language attitudes are important indices about the general evaluation of language varieties within specific sociolinguistic contexts, but they are also informative about issues of ethnic and national identity formation. Rajadurai (2004) examines attitudes towards two varieties of Malaysian English – what she calls Standard Malaysian English and Colloquial Malaysian English – in classroom exchanges and on commercial radio advertising. While Standard Malaysian English may be used in most functional domains in Malaysian society, shifts into Colloquial Malaysian English may be used to signify different generic needs. Specifically, Rajadurai argues that Colloquial Malaysian English is used in a 'defiant celebratory manner' (2004: 57) to denote a Malaysian national identity. Shankar (2004) examines the appropriation of film dialogue from 'Bollywood' films into the conversational exchanges of South Asian-American (Desi) teenagers, who use the dialogue to 'enact their own dynamics of humor, flirting, conflict, and other types of talk' (2004: 317) in ways that reinforce their Desi identity.

One theoretical approach that has been particularly useful in understanding the performance of identity in popular culture is 'language crossing' as described in Rampton (1995). 'Language crossing' is the use of stereotypical features of a dialect belonging to a group that the user does not belong to. Cutler (1999) describes that appropriation of African-American English by a white upper-middle-class New York City teenager and his identification with popular culture genres association with hip-hop music. Following the global phenomenon of hip-hop music world-wide, described in Mitchell (2001), Pennycook (2003) argues that the appropriation of forms of speech from other groups represents an important area of research about the development of World Englishes and global media. Similarly, Lee (2005) examines various types of crossing in Korean and Japanese pop music to describe the creative force of English within those popular cultures.

Finally, a number of sociolinguistic studies of World Englishes like Lee (2006) have used popular culture as a site for language contact that does not usually take place in other media formats around the world. This feature of English in popular culture is especially prevalent within Asian societies (see Lee and Moody forthcoming). Unlike the previous studies that show English in popular culture, the use of English as a contact language of popular culture is often without precedent within the rest of the speech community. In this way, the use of English in pop culture is not clearly representative of how English is used in society, but nevertheless demonstrates the role of a number of ideologies associated with English within the cultures. For example, Omoniyi (2006, and this volume) examines the interaction of language varieties in Nigerian hip-hop song lyrics as a linguistic response and reaction to globalization. In a more general way, Stern (1977) describes the spread of English within Flemish-speaking Belgium as deriving from the widespread American popular culture and as retaining specialized uses, particularly in advertising.

In terms of language-mixing, English is used in a number of pop culture contexts in mixed (i.e. code-switched) form, where code-switching does not generally occur as a widespread phenomenon throughout the society (see discussion in McClellan this volume). Hence, Bhatia (2006) examines the language-mixing – much of which is Englishization – that takes place in Hindi superhero comic books that have recently been introduced in India. Within a society that more clearly does not use English code-switching, Moody and Matsumoto (2003) examine the structure of 'code ambiguation' within the process of Englishization of Japanese pop songs. Finally, Spitulnik (1996) describes the specialized media discourse of mixing English and ChiBemba within Zambian radio broadcasts.

Vertical and horizontal analysis of popular culture

In 2007 Jennifer Hudson won the 2006 Academy Award for Best Actress in a Supporting Role for her performance in the musical movie *Dreamgirls*. Hudson's role in *Dreamgirls* as Effie White was her debut performance on film, and the Oscar win came as a surprise to many cinema fans world-wide who had never before seen her perform. To the US audience, however, Hudson first became familiar on the third season of the audience interactive game/reality television show *American Idol*, where she competed as a contestant until she was eliminated in the sixth round of nationwide votes (from a total of 11 rounds of votes). Since her Academy Award, Hudson continues to perform in movies, but returned to her primary medium of music. As a recording artist, she surprised many in the recording industry in January 2009 when her 2008 debut studio album, *Jennifer Hudson*, won the Grammy award for Best R&B Album. As an award-winning singer, actor and television personality, Jennifer Hudson's career illustrates the diverse popular culture media that individual performers may work in. Starting with music and television, Hudson has moved successfully into movie roles (not limited to movie roles that require singing) and musical recording. This mixing of media is not a new phenomenon within popular culture; it certainly started long before Elvis starred as Clint Reno and sang the theme song in the movie *Love Me Tender*, and it probably started before vaudeville performers built shows around drama, music, dance, magic and trained animals. Media are not static within popular culture and performers are free to move across the different media. Therefore, to understand Jennifer Hudson's – and many other performers' – individual impact in popular culture requires observers to look beyond her performance in any single medium and to consider the full range of media that she performs within.

At the same time, popular cultures are interconnected globally so that a performer or performance style is not limited by national boundary; instead, it may flow transnationally into a different society. Figure 31.1 illustrates these two types of flows as vertical and horizontal flows of performers, content and linguistic forms. The organization of popular culture into 'vertical' and 'horizontal' lines of 'flow' and analysis is largely based upon the organization of corporations vertically and horizontally. While vertical organization aligns the various processes within a production line from raw material to finished consumer good, horizontal organization replicates the vertical organization in different regions or consumer markets. To the degree that popular cultures rely heavily on vertical and horizontal flows, an understanding of the flows will inform studies of English *in* popular cultures as well as justify the study of the Englishes *of* popular culture.

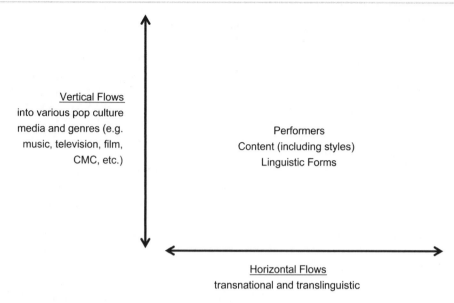

Figure 31.1 Horizontal and vertical flows in popular culture.

Vertical flows in popular culture

In addition to offering celebrities the ability to perform within different media, popular culture also allows for the easy 'flow' of content and even linguistic forms between genres and media. In the same way that the 1994 movie *Quiz Show* is able to tell the true story of a television scandal in the 1950s, television shows like VH1's *Behind the Music* is able to promote the music industry's history and products. Music may also be written or selected to promote movies, TV programmes or advertising, only to find that these media also promote the music. One example of this is Coca-Cola's 1971 'Hilltop' ad, which served as a platform for a new hit pop song. Based on the popularity of the song in the ad, advertisers rerecorded a longer version of the song to produce a US Top Ten hit that was also a number one hit in the UK and Japan: 'I'd love to teach the world to sing (in perfect harmony)' (Coca-Cola Company 2009). What is clear about popular culture is that the content and performers do not belong to a particular medium, but can instead percolate upwards into various types of media. This flow of popular culture performers and content is along the vertical axis of popular culture. Popular culture is, by its nature, a form of expression that is both mass consumable and integrative of different media expressions (Jameson 1991). As such, we see only a very limited range of possible forms of expression if we focus on popular culture in a particular medium, such as film, music or advertising. Instead, these media are inextricably linked, and the expression of language in any medium reverberates within others. This aspect of popular culture is defined by the intertextuality that has come to define what Storey (2003: 70) calls a 'postmodern hyperconsciousness'. Movies may be made as adaptations of books and books may be written as adaptations of a film, but the audiences of these two different media can be the same, and both forms potentially shape the audiences of the two media. Collins (1993) addresses this issue in adaptations of film and fiction and argues that popular culture audiences are intensely aware of the 'genericity' when a pop culture genre borrows and recreates previous forms.

543

While the flow of pop culture content within different genres and media is somewhat obvious and easily illustrated, the flow of linguistic forms is less frequently recognized, but no less easily demonstrated. For example, in 1982 Frank Zappa featured his daughter, Moon Unit Zappa, in the song 'Valley Girl'. The lyrics of the song featured lexicon (e.g. *totally, barf out, I'm sure*, etc.) and pronunciations (e.g. the long [:ndʒriə] of *Andrea* instead of the more usual [æ], or the lowered vowel in [r:li] *really*) that were characteristic of upper-middle-class teenagers in Southern California's San Bernardino County. Although the lexical and phonological characteristics are actual speech forms within the speech community, they were somewhat rare and unfocused as a variety (see LePage and Tabouret-Keller 1985 for discussion of focusing and diffusion in the sense it is used here). The pop song not only associated the speech style with a character, but brought the features of the speech style into focus; after the popularity of the song the speech style came into prominence and became known as 'Valley Girl' speech, or, sometimes, 'Valspeak' (Preston 2003). Once the linguistic forms gained prominence within popular culture, however, the forms began to spread from music into other creative genres: a movie called *Valley Girl*, inspired by the success of the pop song, was made in 1983, and a television spin-off, also entitled *Valley Girls*, from the show *Gossip Girl*, was proposed in early 2009, but never realized. These two other media formats – a movie and a proposed television show – only demonstrate in the most superficial of ways the impact that Frank Zappa's song has had within popular culture. One place to look for the impact of 'Valspeak' and the 'Valley Girl' character is Wikipedia, a self-proclaimed online 'encyclopaedia' that is open to users to revise and update. Although the format of a 'wiki' – a web page that any reader may potentially edit and alter – poses numerous problems when looking for accurate, authoritative and reliable information, the format is also extremely useful in the gathering of information about the vertical spread of popular culture. In a review of Wikipedia's 'Valley girl' page, fans have listed a number of examples that suggest the extent of the vertical flow of this linguistic style and characters who use it: three from pop songs, ten from films, 24 from animated programmes, 42 from television, nine from video games, two from literature and one from an advertising campaign (Wikipedia 2009). Although the linguistic forms of 'Valspeak' have been present within American speech communities for some time, Frank Zappa's song brought those characteristics into focus and into association with a particular social group in popular culture. Because of the vertical nature of popular culture media and products, the linguistic characteristics were able to flow into an unlimited number of popular culture media along with the understanding of the character that was originally developed within the song. In this way, linguistic features may flow vertically within a popular culture, suggesting that language used *in* a particular medium of popular culture can easily flow to become a language *of* popular culture.

Horizontal flows in popular culture

The vertical nature of popular culture explains how performers, content and linguistic forms flow into different media genres and products. Interaction with any product from the popular culture, therefore, potentially entails interactions with other media and products, and consumers may or may not be aware of these products. However, as sociolinguists are intent on the examination of how linguistic forms are representative of linguistic processes within the greater speech community, we should be acutely aware of the interconnectivity of popular culture media and products. At the same time, globalization has enabled the flow of performers, content or linguistic forms of popular culture beyond the society where they were originally produced and into other societies, cultures and speech communities. The example of Jennifer Hudson and *American Idol* above also illustrates the transnational and translinguistic flow along the horizontal axis of popular culture. *American Idol* is an enormously popular television show, but it is also based upon a British show called *Pop Idol* that was adapted to the US entertainment market. Likewise, the show has been adapted into a number of other forms as an international franchise in various countries, including *Australian Idol, Latin American Idol, Idols* (Denmark, Netherlands, Finland, South Africa, Serbia-Montenegro and Macedonia), *Canadian Idol, Idols West Africa, Indian Idol, Indonesian Idol, New Zealand Idol, Hay Superstar* (Armenia), *Idol stjörnuleit* (Iceland), *Nouvelle Star* (France), *Pinoy Idol* (Philippines), *Idol* (Norway), *Idol* (Poland), *Deutschland sucht den Superstar* (Germany), *Singapore Idol, Malaysian Idol, Vietnam Idol, Music Idol* (Bulgaria), *Ídolos* (Brazil and Portugal), *Super Idol* (Greece), *Solo Idol* (Solomon Islands), *Super Star* (Arabic-speaking societies), *Megasztár* (Hungary) and *Looking for You* (Bangladesh). There is little interaction between the various horizontal manifestations of *Pop Idol*, but the vertical format of the programme remains largely unchanged as it is exported from place to place. In each place where the programme has spread it takes with it three basic characteristics: (1) a search (with open auditions) for new and undiscovered talent; (2) a televised competition that incorporates judges' opinions with audience participation and the systematic elimination of contestants; and (3) a recording contract for the winner of the competition. The vertical process that functions to create the products of *Pop Idol*, then, is simply moved horizontally to different locations.

The possibilities for horizontal transnational influences developing between various popular cultures are probably somewhat greater within an age of globalization than they were before, and there is increasing examination of the linguistic content of these horizontal flows (see Fairclough 2006; Pennycook 2007; Alim *et al.* 2009). Trudgill's (1983) examination of language in popular culture is one of the earliest studies of these horizontal flows. When rock 'n' roll style music first began to find popularity in England, the performative pronunciation of the music – i.e. distinctive linguistic features of American English – flowed along with the music into the performance repertoire of many British musicians. This is the historical background to Trudgill's study of eight features of American English in albums recorded by the Beatles and the Rolling Stones. The same kind of borrowing of linguistic features along with musical style can be found in early recordings of Dusty Springfield, an artist who Randall (2009) describes as uniquely postmodern because audiences were frequently unable to classify her as British or American, black or white or even male or female. In each of these cases the language of the popular culture products – specifically, American and African-American linguistic forms found in rock 'n' roll, Gospel and soul music – flowed along the same horizontal path into the performance of those products within a different society.

In no popular culture product is the flow of linguistic features more clearly identifiable than in the horizontal flow of African-American pronunciation with hip-hop music into various cultures and languages. Describing the contents of his edited volume, Alim (2009) alludes to the influence of African-American English (AAE) on other languages within the global spread of hip-hop music:

Hip Hop rhyming practices have altered poetic genres across the globe, with Japan being a particularly intriguing case where Hip Hop artists restructure Japanese in

545

order to rhyme and flow (Tsujimura and Davis 2009), and along with Chinese (Lin 2009), Korean (see Pennycook 2007: 128), and Italian artists (see Androutsopoulos and Scholz 2003: 474–5), have produced similar poetic structures such as the *back-to-back chain rhymes* and *bridge rhymes* described in Black American Hip Hop.

(Alim 2009: 6)

Once the linguistic feature flows horizontally into a different language or popular culture, however, the flow may continue vertically into other media or products within that popular culture. The influence of AAE internationally, therefore, may not be limited to the music that it inspires, but would become recognizable within a range of popular culture media and products internationally influenced by AAE. This influence of AAE in popular culture genres and media world-wide, however, is easy to overlook if the sociolinguist only uses data that are from naturally occurring or spontaneous sources. Likewise, if the vertical nature of popular culture is not sufficiently examined in studies of pop culture linguistic data, the researcher may easily underestimate the extent of a linguistic flow.

Conclusion

Linguistic data from popular culture have traditionally been overlooked within the discipline of sociolinguistics. Although it is not always clear to what degree pop culture data accurately represent linguistic forms and features in a speech community, since 2000, linguists have increasingly turned to media-related and pop culture data for insights into linguistic phenomena. Data can certainly illustrate the role that English may take *in* a popular culture, but a more difficult task is to understand the possible roles that Englishes *of* popular cultures perform. To the degree that popular culture relies upon connections between very different media, a two-dimensional model of popular culture illustrates the manner in which performers, content and linguistic features may flow either horizontally from one language or speech community to another, or vertically from one genre or medium to another. This two-dimensional model, therefore, necessitates that popular culture data are multicultural (forming a kind of intercultural communication) and that they are also usually multimodal. To the extent that English is associated with the global spread of popular culture, English forms and functions can easily travel horizontally across different cultures (i.e. intercultural communication) and vertically within a popular culture (i.e. multimodal communication). In this way, the spread of popular culture not only distributes performers and content, but it also encourages the flow of English and various linguistic forms into a mosaic of Englishes of popular cultures.

Suggestions for further reading

Most of the work on English in popular culture is published in the form of journal articles, but there are several collections of essays that readers would find useful. For discussion of influences specifically in hip hop music see Mitchell (2001) and Alim *et al.* (2009). A volume edited by Lee and Moody (forthcoming) collects essays discussing the influence on English in Asian societies. Although it is not exclusively about popular culture media, essays in Aitchison and Lewis (2003) provide insight and justification for the examination of language in the media. Similarly, Fairclough (2006) examines the global spread of English from the point of view of critical discourse analysis and cultural political economy and offers insights about linguistic flows in the media. Storey (2003 and 2006) are two textbook introductions to the use of cultural theory in the study of popular culture and useful in understanding many of the special issues involved with the study of popular culture. Finally, Pennycook (2007) offers one of the most complete descriptions of the horizontal flow of English into popular culture genres and media.

References

Adams, M. (2000) 'Ephemeral language', *American Speech*, 75 (4): 382–4.

Aitchison, J. and Lewis, D.M. (eds) (2003) *New Media Language*, London: Routledge.

Alim, H.S. (2009) 'Straight outta Compton, straight aus München: global linguistic flows, identities, and the politics of language in a global hip hop nation', in H.S. Alim, A. Ibrahim and A. Pennycook (eds) *Global Linguistic Flows: Hip Hop Cultures, Youth Identities, and the Politics of Language*, New York: Routledge, pp. 1–22.

Alim, H.S., Ibrahim, A. and Pennycook, A. (eds) (2009) *Global Linguistic Flows: Hip Hop Cultures, Youth Identities, and the Politics of Language*, New York: Routledge.

Androutsopoulos, J. and Scholz, A. (2003) 'Spaghetti funk: appropriations of hip-hop culture and music in Europe', *Popular Music and Society*, 26 (4): 463–79.

Bhatia, T.K. (2006) 'Super-heroes to super languages: American popular culture through South Asian language comics', *World Englishes*, 25 (2): 279–97.

Bhimji, F. (2001) 'Retrieving talk from the simple past and the present progressive on alternative radio', *Journal of Pragmatics*, 33 (4): 545–69.

Brownlow, S., Rosamond, J.A. and Parker, J.A. (2003) 'Gender-linked linguistic behavior in television interviews', *Sex Roles: A Journal of Research*, 49 (3/4): 121–32.

Coca-Cola Company (2009) 'The Coca-Cola heritage – Coke lore: "I'd love to buy the world a Coke" – the hilltop story, the Coca-Cola Company'. Online. Available www.thecoca-colacompany.com/heritage/cokelore_hilltop.html (accessed 16 October 2009).

Collins, J. (1993) 'Genericity in the nineties: eclectic irony and new sincerity', in J. Collins, H. Radner and A. Preacher (eds) *Film Theory Goes to the Movies*, London: Routledge, pp. 242–63.

Cutler, C.A. (1999) 'Yorkville crossing: white teens, hip hop and African American English', *Journal of Sociolinguistics*, 3 (4): 428–42.

Eble, C.C. (2003) 'Slang, metaphor, and folk speech', *Publications of the American Dialect Society*, 88: 151–61.

Elliott, N.C. (2000) 'A sociolinguistic study of rhoticity in American film speech from the 1930s to the 1970s', PhD dissertation, University of Indiana, Department of Linguistics.

Fairclough, N. (2006) *Language and Globalization*, London: Routledge.

Faulkner, W. (2000) '"Look how sexist our advert is!" The "postmodernization" of sexism and stereotyped female role portrayals in print advertisements', in F. Ungerer (ed) *English Media Texts – Past and Present: Language and Textual Structure*, Amsterdam: John Benjamins, pp. 111–28.

Gaudio, R.P. (2003) 'Coffeetalk: Starbucks™ and the commercialization of casual conversation', *Language in Society*, 32 (5): 659–91.

Godeo, E.G. (2006) 'Critical discourse analysis as an analytical resource for cultural studies: exploring the discursive construction of subject positions in British men's magazines' problem pages', *Revista Alicantina de Estudios Ingleses*, 19: 83–100.

Herring, S.C. (2004) 'Slouching toward the ordinary: current trends in computer-mediated communication', *New Media and Society*, 6 (1): 26–36.

Jameson, F. (1991) *Postmodernism, or, The Cultural Logic of Late Capitalism*, Durham: Duke University Press.

Labov, W. (1972) *Sociolinguistic Patterns* (Conduct and Communication Series), Philadelphia: University of Pennsylvania Press.

Lee, J.S. (2005) 'Discourse of fusion and crossing: pop culture in Korea and Japan', PhD dissertation, University of Illinois, Department of Linguistics.

Lee, J.S. and Moody, A. (eds) (forthcoming) *English in Asian Pop Culture* (Asian Englishes Today Series), Hong Kong: University of Hong Kong Press.

LePage, R.B. and Tabouret-Keller, A. (1985) *Acts of Identity: Creole-based Approaches to Language and Ethnicity*, Cambridge: Cambridge University Press.

Lin, A. (2009) '"Respect for da Chopstick Hip Hop": the politics, poetics, and pedagogy of Cantonese verbal art in Hong Kong', in H.S. Alim, A. Ibrahim and A. Pennycook (eds) *Global Linguistic Flows: Hip Hop Cultures, Youth Identities, and the Politics of Language*, New York: Routledge, pp. 159–77.

Lippi-Green, R. (1997) *English with an Accent: Language, Ideology, and Discrimination in the United States*, London: Routledge.

Mesthrie, R. (2002) 'Mock languages and symbolic power: the South African radio series *Applesammy and Naidoo*', *World Englishes*, 21 (1): 99–112.

Mika, B. (2004) 'Advertisement/commercial as a text eliminating oppositions', *Semiotica*, 150 (1–4): 491–514.

Mitchell, T. (ed.) (2001) *Global Noise: Rap and Hip-Hop Outside the USA*, Middletown, CT: Wesleyan University Press.

Moody, A. and Matsumoto, Y. (2003) '"Don't touch my moustache": language blending and code ambiguation by two J-pop artists', *Asian Englishes*, 6 (1): 4–33.

Omoniyi, T. (2006) 'Hip-hop through the world Englishes lens: a response to globalization', *World Englishes*, 25 (2): 195–208.

Ooi, V.B.Y. (2002) 'Aspects of computer-mediated communication for research in corpus linguistics', in P. Peters, P. Collins and A. Smith (eds) *New Frontiers of Corpus Research*, Amsterdam: Rodopi, pp. 91–104.

Pennycook, A. (2003) 'Global Englishes, Rip Slyme, and performativity', *Journal of Sociolinguistics*, 7 (4): 513–33.

——(2007) *Global Englishes and Transcultural Flows*, London: Routledge.

Porter, G. (1999) 'The ideology of misrepresentation: Scots in English broadsides', in I. Taavitsainen, G. Melchers and P. Pahta (eds) *Writing in Nonstandard English*, Amsterdam: John Benjamins, pp. 361–74.

Preston, D.R. (2003) 'Presidential address: where are the dialects of American English at anyhow?', *American Speech*, 78 (3), 235–54.

Rajadurai, J. (2004) 'The faces and facets of English in Malaysia', *English Today*, 20 (4): 54–8.

Rampton, B. (1995) *Crossing: Language and Ethnicity Among Adolescents*, London: Longman.

Randall, A.J. (2009) *Dusty! Queen of the Postmods*, New York: Oxford University Press.

Reaser, J. (2003) 'A quantitative approach to (sub)registers: the case of "Sports Announcer Talk"', *Discourse Studies*, 5 (3): 303–21.

Richardson, K. (2006) 'The dark arts of good people: how popular culture negotiates "spin" in NBC's *The West Wing*', *Journal of Sociolinguistics*, 10 (1): 52–69.

Robertson, R. (1995) 'Glocalization: time–space and monogeneity–heterogeneity', in M. Featherstone, S. Lash and R. Robertson (eds) *Global Modernities*, London: Sage, pp. 25–44.

Rojo-Laurilla, M.A. (2002) '"He texts, she texts": gendered conversational styles in Philippine text messaging', *Philippine Journal of Linguistics*, 33 (10): 71–86.

Rose, K.R. (2001) 'Compliments and compliment responses in film: implications for pragmatics research and language teaching', *IRAL: International Review of Applied Linguistics in Language Teaching*, 39 (4): 309–26.

Said, E.W. (1993) *Culture and Imperialism* (Vintage Books edition, 1994), New York: Alfred A Knopf.

Shankar, S. (2004) 'Reel to real: Desi teens' linguistic engagements with Bollywood', *Pragmatics*, 14 (2–3): 317–35.

Shuttlesworth, R.E. (2004) 'Language ideological factors in twentieth century artistic depictions of southern American English', PhD dissertation, University of Alabama, Department of English.

Simpson, P. (1999) 'Language, culture and identity: with (another) look at accents in pop and rock singing', *Multilingua*, 18 (4): 343–67.

Speicher, B.L. and McMahon, S.M. (1992) 'Some African-American perspectives on Black English Vernacular', *Language in Society*, 21 (3): 383–407.

Spitulnik, D. (1996) 'The social circulation of media discourse and the mediation of communities', *Journal of Linguistic Anthropology*, 6 (2): 161–87.

Stern, H.R. (1977) 'English in Flemish Belgium', *American Speech*, 52 (1–2): 128–33.

Storey, J. (1999) *Cultural Consumption and Everyday Life*, London: Arnold.

——(2003) *Inventing Popular Culture*, Malden: Blackwell.

——(2006) *Cultural Theory and Popular Culture: An Introduction* (4th edition), Harlow: Pearson, Prentice Hall.

Taylor, C.J. (2004) 'The language of film: corpora and statistics in the search for authenticity. *Notting Hill* (1998) – a case study', *Miscellanea*, 30: 71–85.

Thornborrow, J. and Morris, D. (2004) 'Gossip as strategy: the management of talk about others on reality TV show Big Brother', *Journal of Sociolinguistics*, 8 (2): 246–71.

Thurlow, C. (2003) 'Generation txt? The sociolinguistics of young people's text-messaging', *Discourse Analysis Online*, 1 (1). Online. Available http://extra.shu.ac.uk/daol/previous/v1_n1.html (accessed 20 December 2008).

Trudgill, P. (1983) 'Acts of conflicting identity: the sociolinguistics of British pop-song pronunciation', in P. Trudgill, *On Dialect: Social and Geographical Perspectives*, Oxford: Blackwell, pp. 141–60.

Tsujimura, N. and Davis, S. (2009) 'Dragon Ash and the reinterpretation of Hip Hop: on the notion of rhyme in Japanese Hip Hop', in H.S. Alim, A. Ibrahim and A. Pennycook (eds) *Global Linguistic Flows: Hip Hop Cultures, Youth Identities, and the Politics of Language*, New York: Routledge, pp. 179–93.

Warner, M.J. (2005) 'Ideology and affect in discourse in institutions', *Journal of Language and Politics*, 4 (2): 293–330.

Weatherall, A. (1996) 'Language about women and men: an example from popular culture', *Journal of Language and Social Psychology*, 15 (1): 59–75.

Wikipedia (2009) 'Valley girl – Wikipedia, the free encyclopedia'. Online. Available http://en.wikipedia.org/wiki/Valley_girl (accessed 21 November 2009).

32

'Thank you for calling'

Asian Englishes and 'native-like' performance in Asian call centres

Kingsley Bolton

Introduction

The use of English as an international language in call centres in India and the Philippines has the potential to illuminate a range of issues relating to World Englishes as well as a number of other questions concerning bilingualism, second-language acquisition, and sociolinguistics. The background to this is that, since the early 2000s, large numbers of clerical, data management and other jobs have been exported from 'native' English-speaking societies, such as the UK and US, to societies such as India and the Philippines, where there are now sufficient numbers of proficient language users able to perform tasks previously reserved for American and British employees. For the last two decades, many linguists have made the claim that English was no longer the sole possession of Britain and America, that it was truly a world language. Now it seems that such a claim is being vindicated, even at the cost of tens of thousands of jobs in the US and UK, as these have been exported to India, the Philippines and elsewhere. In the early 2000s, this development not only caught the attention of the world's press, but it also gave rise to a series of debates in both the developed world and in those developing countries, such as India and the Philippines, where 'linguistic outsourcing' was becoming a key strand in the Business Process Outsourcing (BPO) industries that were being established in such locations as Bangalore, Chennai, Mumbai (in India) and Manila (Philippines).

One influential book that appeared shortly after such news reports began to appear, and was widely cited in business and political circles, was Thomas L. Friedman's *The World is Flat: A Brief History of the Twenty-first Century* (first published in 2005). Both the title and the content of his book were stimulated by a visit Friedman made to the Indian information technology companies Infosys and WiPro in Bangalore, India, in 2004, where he witnessed the work that these companies were doing in writing computer software for US and European businesses and running the back offices of multinational companies, all of which involved such disparate tasks as computer maintenance, high-tech research, answering customer calls from all over the world and dealing with a range of other BPO operations. After its publication, Friedman's bestseller drew a hail of criticism, with the *San Francisco Chronicle* dubbing Friedman the 'High priest of free-trade fundamentalism' (Sirota 2006), and *The Economist* taking Friedman to task for his 'imprecision' and 'sloppiness', and the 'dreary failure' of his book (*The Economist* 2005: 81).

The links between Friedman's analysis and issues related to World Englishes are somewhat indirect, but overall it seems clear that the use of English as a global language is essential to many of the processes Friedman describes. In his account of the workings of an Indian call centre, he provides the following description:

> There are currently about 245,000 Indians answering phones from all over the world or dialling out to solicit people for credit cards or cell phone bargains or overdue bills. These call center jobs are low-wage, low-prestige jobs in America, but when shifted to India they become high-wage, high-prestige jobs. The esprit de corps at 24/7 and other call centers I visited seemed quite high, and the young people were all eager to share some of the bizarre phone conversations they've had with Americans who dialed 1–800-HELP, thinking they would wind up talking to someone around the block, not around the world.
>
> (Friedman 2006: 24)

Friedman goes on to report that the call centre he visited, aptly named 24/7, received about 700 applications a day, but accepted only some 6 per cent of applicants. One major feature of the training of new recruits is the 'accent neutralization class', and Friedman describes how the teacher 'dressed in a traditional Indian sari' conducted the class, and 'moved seamlessly among British, American and Canadian accents' (2006: 27).

The role of English as a world language in assisting globalization is highly contested, and a great deal has previously been written on this topic. It is perhaps important to note, however, that one crucial reason why the role of language in call centres has attracted attention is that in many respects the call-centre and BPO industry provides a testing ground for a range of theories and approaches to language and globalization, which in turn calls into question the relationships between such constructs as 'World Englishes', 'globalization' and 'global English'. The operation of English language call centres in India and the Philippines provides important sites for the investigation of language and globalization, in a region where localized varieties of Asian Englishes (e.g. Indian English, Malaysian English, Singapore English and Philippines English) have become established and have gained recognition, particularly over the last four decades or so (Bolton 2006, 2008). In order to investigate the impact of international call centres on the sociolinguistics of Asian societies, detailed fieldwork was carried out by the author of this chapter in India and the Philippines between 2006 and 2008. The context for this was the participation of the author in a research programme initiated by Stockholm University on 'High-level Proficiency in Second-language Use', in which I was responsible for an individual project entitled 'Linguistic Outsourcing and Native-like Performance in International Call Centres and Business Process Outsourcing (BPO) operations' (funded by the Bank of Sweden Tercentenary Fund, Riksbankens Jubiléumsfond, Dnr M2005–0459, whose generous support is gratefully acknowledged here). In the following discussion, I present a number of initial results drawn from this research (see also Bolton forthcoming).

Researching native-like performance in Philippine call centres

As stated earlier, the broad aim of the project on linguistic outsourcing was to describe the linguistic practices of selected international call centres and BPOs (Business Process Outsourcing), particularly in the Philippines and India, and to investigate the extent to which 'native-like' linguistic behaviour is regularly expected of, and achieved by, call-centre staff (or 'agents') in such locations. More specific research questions included the following: (i) What expectations do employers have of native-like performance from their staff? (ii) How is such performance defined (and judged) by employers? (iii) What is the profile of successful call-centre agents (in terms of language background, education, etc.)? (iv) What strategies do agents use to pass as native users of the language? and (v) What are the characteristics of successful versus unsuccessful communication in such contexts?

The methodology adopted for this study involved a broad-based sociolinguistic research methodology, including extensive interviews with call-centre managers and trainers and call-centre staff; attendance at call-centre industry events; as well as the collection of recorded call-centre conversations. After initial exploratory visits to both India and the Philippines, it was decided to concentrate the initial stage of research on call-centre operations in the Philippines. The main reasons for this were essentially practical and pragmatic. During my two visits to Bangalore, access to call centres in the city was found to be heavily restricted, and despite having colleagues in the city with industry contacts, it was difficult to gain access to call centres during my stays there in 2007 and 2008. This was not the case in Manila, Philippines, where I gained relatively easy access to a number of Manila call centres and call-centre agents, and, eventually, obtained a substantial corpus of actually occurring telephone conversation data.

The linguistic data collected were of two broad types. First, a series of semi-structured interviews were carried out with call-centre agents or 'CSRs' (customer service representatives), as they are most commonly referred to. These interviews surveyed call-centre employees on their personal backgrounds, as well as details of their training and work experience. All interviews were recorded and later transcribed. Second, a corpus of authentic telephone conversations – involving a total of 1,413 telephone conversations in all – was obtained from a major Philippine call centre. These telephone conversations have now been transcribed, and the next stage of research will involve further analysis of this data. A number of initial findings relating to this research are discussed in the following sections of this chapter.

Initial findings of research on the Philippine call-centre industry

In a society where unemployment is endemic and where currently some 10 per cent of the population work abroad as OFWs (Overseas Foreign Workers) in jobs as engineers, technicians or seamen or as nurses, carers and domestic helpers, the growth of the BPO industry has been hailed as a 'sunshine industry'. The Philippine BPO industry has developed very rapidly since the late 1990s, and by 2008 it was estimated that the sector employed some 300,000 workers, placing the Philippines in second place after India as an international outsourcing destination. BPO operations in the country include not only call centres, but also 'back office' work as accounts, engineering design, legal and medical transcription, software development, and animation. Currently, there are ambitious plans to expand the BPO industry from revenues of US$ 3.3 billion in 2008 to 13 billion by 2010–11, and to increase the numbers of employed from 300,000 to 900,000 in the same period (Sañez 2008). Such jobs are low paid compared with their equivalents in North America or the UK, but, in Manila a starting salary of 15,000 pesos (approximately US $320) per month is comparable to that received by a bank clerk or management trainee.

Within the telephone call centres, operations are typically of two kinds. Usually, staff are deployed to handle either *inbound* calls or *outbound* calls. As the name suggests, *inbound* refers to answering incoming inquiries, dealing with various aspects of customer service for a wide variety of products and services, ranging from financial services to various kinds of technical help. In those call centres that were visited by this researcher, the majority of call-centre staff (some 80–90 per cent) were involved in handling inbound calls. By contrast, *outbound* calls essentially involve calling customers or potential customers for sales and telemarketing purposes or even for matters of billing and debt collection. Outbound calls are much less popular among call-centre staff, as handling such calls often involves high levels of stress dealing with rather angry customers.

The English language is relatively well established in the Philippines, where it has a wide range of functions in this outer circle society, including its use as a co-official language of government, law, and education, as well as its extensive use in the business sector, mass media and entertainment (Bautista and Bolton 2008). However, the story of English in the Philippines is one greatly coloured by the effects of colonialism and its aftermath. Indeed, the Philippines experienced almost 400 years of colonial rule, first from Spain from 1565 till 1898, and then from the US from 1898 to 1946. American colonial rule started with a brutal war which was then succeeded by the establishment of the first system of mass education that the Philippine islands had known, with elementary schools established throughout the length and breadth of the country. The medium of instruction in all schools was English, and, remarkably, as early as 1918, some 47 per cent of the population claimed to be able to speak English. In the period following Philippine independence from the US in 1946, English-medium education in the schools gave way to a bilingual system, made official in 1987, which persists to the present. Nevertheless, as noted earlier, a large proportion of Filipinos claim to speak English, with some 76 per cent reporting they understand the spoken language and 75 per cent claiming to read in English.

The linguistic features of Philippine English (PE) have been described in some detail in the research literature, and these include distinctive features at the major levels of language, including phonology, lexis and grammar. Phonological features include the devoicing of sibilant consonants in words like *beige, pleasure, seize, bees*, and *cities*, which are articulated as /s/; the rendering of 'th' sounds as /t, d/, in words such as *this* /dis/, *thin* /tin/. With vowels, other features may occur including a loss of distinction between long and short vowels in such pairs as *sheep/ship, full/fool, boat/bought*, etc.; the /æ/ vowel, in *bat, cat, fat, hat*, etc., may be replaced by the central low vowel /a/; and many speakers deploy a reduced vowel inventory compared with American English. At the supra-segmental level, intonation is typically 'syllable-timed' with distinctive patterns occurring in words such as *elígible, establísh, cerémony*.

At the lexical level, Philippine English has borrowed extensively from Spanish (*asalto* 'surprise party', *bienvenida* 'welcome party', *despedida* 'farewell party', *estafa* 'fraud, scandal', *merienda* 'mid-afternoon tea', *querida* 'mistress'), and Tagalog (*boondock* 'mountain', *kundiman* 'love song', *tao* 'the common man'). Loan translations are also widely used, including *open the light/radio* for 'turn on the light/radio', *joke only* 'I'm teasing you', and *you don't only know* 'you just don't realize'. Local coinages include such items as *to carnap*, *high blood*, *hold-upper* and *topnotcher*, while archaic items derived from late nineteenth-century American English include *comfort room (CR)*, *solon* and *viand* (Bolton and Butler 2008). At the grammatical level, we find variable third-person singular marking, the over-use of the progressive, the variable use of articles, and variation in tense and aspect as in *We have done it yesterday* (versus 'We did it yesterday') and *He lived here since 1996* (compared to 'He has lived here since 1996'). Other features include variation in transitivity and the use of prepositions (Bautista 2008).

However, the frequency and distribution of such features varies greatly according to social class and education, and linguists have long noted the existence of 'edulects' in Philippine society. *Acrolectal Philippine English* is associated with academics, bilinguals from English-speaking homes, and English majors at university level. Thus, acrolectal Philippine English is perceived as approximating to 'near-standard' American English. *Mesolectal Philippine English* is spoken by professionals who are non-English majors and who mostly use English in the workplace, and who display a noticeably Philippine accent. *Basilectal Philippine English* is said to be spoken by such people as janitors and taxi-drivers, and is associated with a broad Philippine accent and a rather low level of education (Tayao 2008).

Typically, in the observations and interviews that were carried out by this researcher, my judgement (and the judgement of Philippine linguists I discussed with) was that call-centre staff typically spoke varieties of English that ranged from mid-level to high-level 'mesolectal' Philippine English, and that the majority of call-centre agents inter-viewed spoke English with what might be perceived as a distinctive Philippine accent, including the characteristic stress timing associated with Philippine English speech. However, despite the existence of the *de facto* norm of educated PE in use by many call-centre agents, a great deal of time and effort was spent in providing new recruits to the industry with courses on 'accent neutralization', which in practice meant instructing new staff in the basics of American English phonology. Other elements in induction training included grammar practice; an introduction to American culture and society; and a course dealing with customer service management.

After training, the performance of individual CSRs within the call centre is continually monitored by their superiors, who are identified by such job titles as 'team leader', 'line manager' and 'supervisor'. The ability to deal with customers on the telephone quickly and efficiently in English is highly valued by the employers and CSRs who score highly in the various metrics applied to their work are often promoted rather quickly to posi-tions of greater authority. In this, a high proficiency of English is a key merit, although it is not the only criterion involved in staff assessment.

Authentic call-centre conversations

As noted above, the types of data collected by this researcher included two varieties of recorded data. The first type of data was collected from interview research with a group of 50 CSRs working for call centres in Manila, the characteristics of which are discussed below. The second type of recorded data was secured in May 2007 from a major telephone company in the Philippines, which comprised recordings of more than 1,400 telephone conversations from a leading call centre. From mid-2007 until early 2009, these telephone conversations were systematically transcribed and a corpus of this material organized.

An examination of the specific characteristics of the dataset indicate that in total there are 1,413 complete interactions in the corpus. The vast majority of these, some 980, are inbound conversations where US customers are dealing with Philippine CSRs with queries regarding such goods and services as cable television subscriptions, cameras, computer parts, computer printers, computer software, credit card charges, digital cameras, hotel reservations and laptop computers. What is noteworthy from the initial investigation of the corpus is that in only very few of the calls are there breakdowns of communication between customers and CSRs. In the vast majority of cases, the linguistic and communicative skills of CSRs are sufficient to deal with customers' inquiries, product orders and service requests. The transcription below of an inbound query about a cable television bill is not untypical of a standard call-centre interaction in this particular call centre. In this interaction, the CSR is a speaker using an educated variety of Philippine English, approximating to that style of speech associated with an upper-range speaker of mesolectal PE. Her caller is someone with a Southern US accent, who is calling to query a billing statement that he has received for a cable television service. The telephone call is quite short, and lasts 5 minutes 30 seconds. The line numbers next to the speaker identifications indicate the line number of the transcript for purposes of reference.

Transcript: incoming call querying a billing statement for cable television

1 CSR: Thank you for calling –. My name is Faye. Can I have your first and last name?

2 Caller: ——.

3 CSR: Thank you. Can I have your telephone number, please?

4 Caller: My phone number is——.

5 CSR: Thank you. And how may we help you today, Mr——?

6 Caller: Well, uh … I … I've got this kind of bill here … and … and … I mean, we … we get this card in the mail and we paid … uh … like … what … 69 dollars or something to start with or whatever. And when I hooked it up and then we ain't had it hooked up two weeks and … uh … anyway we get this rebate we … we just got … we got the mail in here [?] but then, our first two months was supposed to be free. We're supposed to get like 59 dollars back, from that 60 something that we paid to begin with. And we've already got a 31 dollar bill … 31.40 cents.

13 CSR: Okay, I'll be glad to assist you with your concern today, Mr——. So you got a bill for 31 dollars and 47 cents, and this is for two months from April 11th until June 10th. Well, we got a payment from you of 49 dollars and 99 cents and this …

16 Caller: We are supposed … yeah, they said we will get that back.

17 CSR: Yes, it did. On page two of your bill, you will see that you were credited for 49 dollars and 99 cents.

19 Caller: Page two? Page two? I don't …

20 CSR: Yes.

21 Caller: I can't figure … I don't even …

22 CSR: On the back of page one.

23 Caller: Uh … okay, let's see. (sighs). Credit … Uh, where would that be … I don't know …

24 CSR: Do you see … yes.

25 Caller: Uh. ... I see credit adjustment ... 49.99. Okay, and then ... all right. So where's ... all right. So what was it all together ... to start with ... 87 ... what's this 87.95?

27 CSR: Okay, that is if you'll include the 49.99. But your monthly charge is 58.97, but you have to less 12 dollars and 99 cents for this part because this part is free until July 10th, and then you have to less 5 dollars and 99 cents for the home protection plan because this is free for 18 months. So your total monthly rate is 39 dollars and 99 cents, and you mentioned a while ago that you already have the redemption form. And you have 60 days from installation to send it back together with a copy of your first bill and the first 10 dollar credit will kick in after eight to ten weeks after you have submitted the redemption form. So if you'll apply the 10 dollar credit to your account for ten months, your monthly rate will be 29 dollars and 99 cents.

36 Caller: Uh ... 29.99?

37 CSR: Yes, that's right.

38 Caller: Okay, I thought it was ... uh. I thought it was ... according to that ... to that card ... that flyer, the card we got in the mail, it was supposed to be like 19.99 a month or ...

40 CSR: Well you can ... that is only for the America's Top 100. The regular price of the America's Top 100 is 29.99.

42 Caller: Right, but I mean, wouldn't it be 19.99 for the first ten months? With rebate?

43 CSR: Well, you, because you have other charges. So the America's Top 100 with rebate will be 19 dollars and 99 cents, plus 5 dollars for your local channels, plus 5 dollars for the additional receiver fee. So that would be 29 dollars and 99 cents for ten months.

46 Caller: Uh ... okay. Well, we was misled, so ...

47 CSR: I apologize for that.

48 Caller: Uh ... I guess that happens. Uh ... so, so we owe this is for three months, 31.47?

49 CSR: That's correct. So, if you'll pay 31 dollars and 47 cents, then that will make you good until June 10th.

51 Caller: And we won't get a payment for June 10th, right?

52 CSR: That's right. And the next bill will be sent out on May 26th, but that will cover from June 11th until July 10th.

54 Caller: And that'll be 29.99?

55 CSR: That's correct. Uh ... no, it would be 39.99. It will only be 29.99 once the 10 dollar credit will ... begins to appear on your bill. So you have to submit the redemption form for you to have 29.99.

58 Caller: Well, that will be sent out tomorrow morning then.

59 CSR: Okay. So don't forget to include a copy of your first bill. Just a copy, don't include your payment with it.

61 Caller: Don't include your payment with it ... just a copy of the first bill.

62 CSR: That's right and would you like to take care of your bill now, Mr——?

63 Caller: Uh no, not right at this point.

64 CSR: Okay, not a problem.

65 Caller: All right. Well, I just needed to know what was going on.

66 CSR: Okay, is there anything else I can help you with?
67 Caller: No, thank you.
68 CSR: All right, so are we good now?
69 Caller: Yeah, I guess we have to be. Ha, ha! So thank you very much.
70 CSR: You're welcome. Thank you for calling. Have a nice day.
71 Caller: Uh huh.
72 CSR: Bye bye.
73 Caller: Bye.

In analysing this conversation, it is interesting, not least for purposes of exemplification, to apply the discourse-based approach suggested by Forey and Lockwood (2007), who have analysed 'generic' call-centre conversations in terms of such 'stages' as 'opening', 'purpose', 'gathering information', 'establishing purpose', 'servicing the customer', 'summarizing' and 'closing'. An application of their approach to the above conversation then indicates that lines 1–4 comprise the opening stage; lines 5–12 the purpose stage; 13–16 gathering information; 17–25 establishing purpose; 27–53 servicing the customer; 54–61 summarizing; and lines 62–73 closing. In general terms, at least, Forey and Lockwood's generic stages in call-centre communication seem to fit quite well the discourse of this particular conversation. However, if we are concerned to see the extent to which the speech of the CSRs approximates to a 'native-like' command of English, a number of points might be made.

It is interesting to note that although the caller is quite evidently a native speaker of US English, his speech is nevertheless marked by a number of non-standard features at the grammatical level. These include the non-marking of *get* for past tense in line 7, the use of *ain't* in line 9, and *we was* in line 46. By contrast, there is only one comparable deviation from Standard English in the speech of the CSR, which occurs in line 28, when Faye uses *less* as a verb (instead of 'subtract'). Otherwise, at the grammatical level, Faye's speech is generally faultless, although her intonation is syllable-timed throughout.

Otherwise, what is noticeable from this call and many others in the corpus is the skill and professionalism of the call-centre agent in dealing with a rather complex inquiry relating to the bill of the customer. Throughout the conversation, the tone of the CSR is helpful and polite, as she quickly and efficiently navigates a rather bewildered and initially disgruntled customer through the details of a complicated billing procedure. One emblematic exchange here comes in lines 17–22, when Faye directs the caller to page two of his bill, and when he protests at not being able to find the page in question, she gently points out that it is 'On the back of page one'. After having provided a further clarification and dealing with the customer's inquiry, she is able to diplomatically close the conversation by asking 'All right, so are we good now?', which succeeds in evoking a conciliatory 'Yeah, I guess we have to be', and a chuckle from her now-mollified customer.

The corpus of 1,413 call-centre conversations represents an important dataset for the study of international call centres, and it is anticipated that further analysis will help reveal a rather rich set of results, relevant not only to the specifics of business communication in call centres, but also to the investigation of high-level proficiency in second-language use.

Interviews with call-centre agents

In order to discover more about the background and working lives of individual agents, a total of 51 detailed semi-structured interviews were carried out with call-centre employees in Manila, Philippines, between 2007 and 2008. The questions asked in the interviews covered a wide range of topics, including agents' personal histories, on-the-job training, the agents' experience of working in call centres, the use of American (and other native-like) accents, difficulties in handling calls, health issues, attitudes to the call-centre industry, and the perception of gender-related issues.

These interviews yielded a number of very interesting results. In broad terms, it appears that from the data, the 'typical' Philippine call-centre agent is a female graduate in her mid-twenties, who has attended private schools and college or university, and who comes from a lower-middle or middle-class family. Interestingly, many of these call-centre agents reported having started learning English at a relatively early age (i.e. having an early onset time in the learning of English as a second language). Of this group of 51 CSRs, some 38 per cent reported learning English before the age of five, and 82 per cent before the age of seven, with the vast majority reporting having come from bilingual and multilingual homes. A clear majority of those interviewed also expressed positive attitudes to English and also to the industry in which they were working, expressing opinions such as the following:

> I think it's a big help … if you are a graduate of a four-year course and you don't have a job for now it's always an option … just go to a call centre. You apply, for sure you'll have a job. So I think it it's a big help somehow.
>
> (CSR7, female, 24 years)

> It is [positive] because it's a money-making industry … [and] I see right now at least people are getting reacquainted with the English language although some patriotic people or nationalistic people are gonna say that we're not using our language properly any more but then again we just have to be realistic. English is a universal language.
>
> (CSR40, female, 22 years)

> [The] call-centre industry can help our economy uh to boost so that's the impor-tant thing right now, and uh it could provide uh jobs to people … as long as we can speak English, I mean we have we have plus points to have or to ah to enter a call-centre industry. So basic skills, basic computer skills, you know how to speak English then you have a way of a having a work in a call-centre industry so that's it I mean it boosts our economy and then it helps many people here in the Philippines to have a job. A decent one. That's the important thing.
>
> (CSR12, male, 25 years)

> I think uh we contribute a lot to the economy … I think we can contribute and there's a lot of opportunity … I'm just a housewife but I got the position, so there's a lot of opportunity with call centres.
>
> (CSR4, female, 38 years)

Not all comments from CSRs were totally positive, however, and a number of those interviewed discussed the stresses and strains of night work, and the resultant health problems that occur as a result of prolonged employment in the industry. Some of those interviewed also expressed clearly ambivalent views on their work conditions, and cited problems with sleep, health issues and family life. Cameron's (2000) comments concerning the gendered nature of call-centre communication also emerge from such interviews, when female agents discuss the ways in which they often need to placate irritated or 'irate' (a much-used adjective) callers.

The ambivalence of life in a call centre also finds expression in a recent song recorded by the Philippine pop band Cambio, entitled 'The call centre song'. The video of the song shows a scantily-dressed young female walking the streets of Manila on her way home having finished the night shift in the call centre, while the first stanza of the lyrics expresses her less than enthusiastic motivation for having accepted such work, declaiming that:

> Now let's get one thing straight, I don't really want to work this way, but I get paid for my American accent, I got money to pay the rent.

The second stanza notes the importance of speaking good English in order to get such work, but also underlines the strongly material motivation for employment in the industry:

> Now let's get one thing clear, I don't really want to be here, but they pay me for my perfect diction, I got money for my addictions.

This latter reference to addictions is also ambivalent, as there have been some suggestions that work in call centres has also increased drug use by night workers in this industry, who have taken to using various 'pep pills' on occasion. A less sinister interpretation would simply be her 'addictions' would be limited to the consumer goods that money can buy in a society where some 40 per cent of the population live on less than US$ 2 a day. Nevertheless, the song's video has a sultry girl walking the streets under the predatory gaze of male bystanders and it is difficult to escape the implied and partly visual catenation of *call centre, girl,* and *call girl.* Finally, the girl gets home in the early morning, where her boyfriend is waiting, and she tells us, *I party all morning, work all night, get my honey in the broad daylight.*

Some of the most interesting interviews, however, were with neither the female call-centre employees nor the males, but actually with three interviewees who identified themselves as 'gays'. The use of 'gay' here, however, is not uncontested, as, in the Philippines, the term is often used to conflate homosexuality, transvestism and transgenderism. The use of this term here is largely motivated by the fact that the interviewees, two of whom were participants in transvestite (or *bakla* culture), actually referred to themselves using the English word 'gay'. These three CSRs were not only gay, but also visibly, and proudly, so. The first of these, Joey, explained that the call centres provided a space for cross-dressing Philippine gays to gain work and to express themselves in work. And, he asserted, the gay workers in the industry were proving very successful:

> We gays are performing well … I think it's because we are more confident, we are more spontaneous, and we could express ourselves more clearly … if you'll be visiting – you'd see a lot of cross-dressers, gays who are very confident with their sexuality. … we are like natural-born actors and actresses, so it's very easy for us to make a connection or establish rapport with the customers. Unlike with women, or with straight women, or men. That's why if you would really look deeper into our industry, the people who are getting the top posts would be gays.
> (CSR36, Joey, gay, 23 years)

The second gay call-centre CSR interviewed was Chris, who was equally as positive about the abilities of gay call-centre agents, asserting that gays were 'more eloquent' and 'more expressive' than either straight men or straight women. Chris explained this with reference to the trials and tribulations experienced by gays in dealing with the macho prejudices of mainstream Philippines society.

> We've been through a very rough time and we have this motivation and ... call-centre jobs are the cream of the crop ... we've been through a lot of challenges growing up ... and we're up for the workload ... we seek for a place in which we're widely accepted. And we find it very amusing to work in a call centre, because anything goes. We are not prejudiced by being gay. All we have to do is to just meet our metrics. And that's why a lot of gays are doing their best to be in this job that we're currently at. Because we are not threatened ... we can act naturally. We can say our thoughts. We can express. We can talk to people.
>
> (CSR26, Chris, gay, 26 years)

Chris also asserted that gays were emotionally better equipped for call-centre communication:

> Because we have the best of both worlds. We are a man, or we are men. Or we are women trapped in a man's body. So we understand the loopholes or the emotions of both men and women. We have fears of growing old, that's why we can easily adopt with elders, elder customer. We experience being young, and that's why we could connect with younger people who are fun-loving. So we could cater all ... we are able to connect with people of all ages, of all gender, because we are all in one package. Different emotions, like men here, women there. Getting older here, younger experience, being younger there ... we're conversant, we're good. And we're courteous, we're nice.
>
> (CSR26, Chris, gay, 26 years)

The third gay interviewee, James – like Joey and Chris – also came from a provincial town outside Manila, and had also achieved a great deal of success in his call-centre job in Manila. Before joining the call centre, he had worked as a night club performer and in the theatre, explaining that earlier his dream had been 'to become a performer in Japan', but that immigration restrictions in Japan had decided him to pursue a career in call centres. He reported that his experience of performing had helped him in his call-centre work:

> Because when you're in a performance you build discipline, self-confidence, as well as you uhm you become more responsible and in a call centre ... in a call-centre environment you need a lot of values and one of that is self-confidence because you will be talking to a lot of different people. You need a lot of courage and ... as well as confidence to say the things you need to say to the customers.
>
> (CSR37, James, gay, 25 years)

Like the others, James spoke very articulately about his work in the call centre, and the ways in which he had learnt to master the 'emotional labour' (although this was not a term he used) required in call-centre interaction at work:

Well, usually when dealing with irate customers you need a lot of patience. You need to go down to the deepest cause of the problem, you need to pacify them ... You need to put yourself in the shoes of your customers ... you need a lot of patience and a lot of charisma ... when it comes to irate customers I have handled them very positively because I know for sure that I'm also a customer and I say 'Ma'am you're not the only customer, I'm a customer too ... we're here to help you, we're not here to argue with you.'

(CSR37, James)

Another interesting aspect of James' work in the call centre was that he usually used a female name, 'Sunshine', when talking to customers, which he found immensely useful in calming down angry clients, who often assumed that he was a Latina living in the US.

It's 80 per cent sometimes they think that I'm Latina. Which is a good thing that I don't sound like a Filipino, because ... they hate Filipinos. But usually I sound like American 80 per cent, 'cause when in calls my voice sounds soft and modulated and they don't know ... that I'm not a Filipino ... they call me Ma'am. And they don't know that I'm a boy ... sometimes they won't even know that I'm a guy. Sometimes they always call me like B-I-T-C-H!

(CSR37, James)

James was proud of his success, and also proud of the achievements of other gays in the call-centre industry, explaining their success in terms of the special quality that only Philippine gays could bring to the job.

At the bottom line the gays play a very vital role in the call centre because first, you know, their bodies like they're physically able, they're like men, but they have a heart of a woman. They can easily cope up and sympathize and empathize with the customers. They know how to work well with the English language ... and it's only gays and girls who has the capacity as well as the determination to explore more about the language, the English language. Because usually men, straight men, they're not into that.

(CSR37, James)

What is easily retrievable from the discourse of the three call-centre gays quoted here is not only their own atheoretical, individually personalized descriptions of their call-centre experiences, but also the inflections of critical and cultural theory that rise to the surface in their impressively articulate and self-aware reflections. In the extracts above, for example, James directly links his performance in dance and theatre to the performativity of his call-centre work and the abilities of 'Sunshine', his stage self, to 'pass' as female, and to 'cross' linguistic and cultural boundaries. Such discourses thus link not only to Piller's (2002) insights on 'passing' and second-language acquisition, but also to other theorizations of 'crossing' and 'performativity' that have had a major impact on various branches of cultural studies and linguistics in recent years. Thus, for Piller, 'passing is an act, something they do, a performance that may be put on ... a performance that is typical of first encounters, often service interactions, and each new encounter may present a new challenge to test one's performance' (Piller 2002: 191). For Auer, '[c]rossing is a particular kind of code-switching in which speakers "transgress" into a language or variety which … is not generally thought to "belong" to them' (Auer 2006: 490; Rampton 1995). Finally, in her hugely influential work on gender performativity, Butler explains that 'There is no gender identity behind the expressions of gender; … identity is performatively constituted by the very "expressions" that are said to be its results' (Butler 1990: 25).

Commentary and conclusion

In this chapter, I have attempted to provide an overview of a wide range of questions that connect to the sociolinguistic investigation of the use of English in Asian call centres, with particular reference to the Philippines. What emerges, I would argue, from this overview of the research terrain, is the awareness of multilayered possibilities to researching language use in the call-centre context. Thus, it may be argued, research on call-centre communication may provide new insights not only for World Englishes, but also for such other branches of language studies as business communication, intercultural communication and second-language acquisition.

From Thomas L. Friedman's journalistic mapping of global business, knowledge and linguistic outsourcing, we move to the role of English as a language of modernity and economic development in Asia's dramatically developing economies, from the dynamics of Asian Englishes to critical discourse analysis, to the individual lives of young call-centre workers in the capital of the poverty-blighted Philippines. One important insight from the Philippine experience is that in fieldwork, the rhetoric of globalization gives way to a consideration of lives lived locally, as Philippine men and (especially) women adjust their lives to secure what in many Western societies would be regarded as low-paid and low-status work in the global economy. The issue of call-centre work as a gendered occupation is highlighted not only by the numerical predominance of women in this sector, but also, and interestingly, by the liminal, yet highly successful, role of Philippine gays in the Manila call-centre industry.

In 'The call centre song' from the Philippine pop group quoted above, the lines from the girl declaiming that *I get paid for my American accent … they pay me for my perfect diction* resonate with Bhabha's description of mimicry in colonial discourse as twinning not only mimicry with 'mockery', but also, if obliquely, with 'resemblance and menace' (Bhabha 1994). By extension, the Tagalog concept of *gaya* (to imitate or mimic) plays a central role in the culture of a Philippine gay community where transvestism is a dominant strain. As Tolentino (2007) has pointed out:

> The concept of *gaya* (imitate, mimic) foregrounds the transvestite's operation of mediating and transforming high and low. Gaya comes from the word *gagad*, meaning *uliran* (model). The concept points to a copy as gauged through the model; and as mentioned above, the model usually is western or American-based.
>
> (Tolentino 2007: 184–5)

For Tolentino, *gaya* culture is essentially subversive, involving 'performative, portable, transportable, and transgressive attempts at identity formation', although, ironically, while 'copies approximate the model, these can never be the model itself' (Tolentino 2007: 186). In this context, despite the brute power of capitalism in its transnational mode, and the power of English as the international pidgin, sociolinguistic research can serve to uncover individual local experiences and linguistic practices that reveal fresh new insights into World Englishes as well as the locally negotiated dynamics of language and globalization.

Suggestions for further reading

Bautista, Ma. Lourdes S. and Bolton, Kingsley (2008) *Philippine English: Linguistic and Literary Perspectives*, Hong Kong: Hong Kong University Press.

Bolton, Kingsley (2004) 'World Englishes', in Alan Davies and Catherine Elder (eds) *The Handbook of Applied Linguistics*, Oxford: Blackwell, pp. 367–96.

——(2006) 'Varieties of World Englishes', in Braj B. Kachru, Yamuna Kachru and Cecil L. Nelson (eds) *The Handbook of World Englishes*, Oxford: Blackwell, pp. 289–312.

Bolton, Kingsley and Kachru, Braj B. (2006) *World Englishes: Critical Concepts in Linguistics* (six volumes), London: Routledge.

References

Auer, Peter (2006) 'Sociolinguistic crossing', in Keith Brown (ed.) *Encyclopedia of Language and Linguistics* (2nd edition), Oxford: Elsevier, pp. 490–2.

Bautista, Ma. Lourdes S. (2008) 'Investigating the grammatical features of Philippine English', in Ma. Lourdes S. Bautista and Kingsley Bolton (eds) *Philippine English: Linguistic and Literary Perspectives*, Hong Kong: Hong Kong University Press, pp. 201–18.

Bautista, Ma. Lourdes S. and Bolton, Kingsley (2008) *Philippine English: Linguistic and Literary Perspectives*, Hong Kong: Hong Kong University Press.

Bhabha, Homi K. (1994) *The Location of Culture*, London: Routledge.

Bolton, Kingsley (2006) 'World Englishes today', in Braj B. Kachru, Yamuna Kachru, and Cecil L. Nelson (eds) *The Handbook of World Englishes*, Oxford: Blackwell, pp. 240–69.

——(2008) 'English in Asia, Asian Englishes, and the issue of proficiency', *English Today*, 24 (2): 3–12.

——(forthcoming) 'Linguistic outsourcing and native-like performance in international call centres: an overview', in Kenneth Hyltenstam (ed.) *High-level Proficiency in Second Language Use: Linguistic Characteristics and Cognitive and Social Conditions*, Berlin: Mouton de Gruyter.

Bolton, Kingsley, and Butler, Susan (2008) 'Lexicography and the description of Philippine English vocabulary', in Ma. Lourdes S. Bautista, and Kingsley Bolton (eds) *Philippine English: Linguistic and Literary Perspectives*, Hong Kong: Hong Kong University Press, pp. 175–218.

Butler, Judith (1990) *Gender Trouble: Feminism and the Subversion of Identity*, London: Routledge.

Cameron, Deborah (2000) 'Styling the worker: gender and the commodification of language in the globalized service economy', *Journal of Sociolinguistics*, 4 (3): 323–47.

Forey, Gail and Lockwood, Jane (2007) '"I'd love to put someone in jail for this": an initial investigation of English in the business processing outsourcing (BPO) industry', *English for Specific Purposes*, 26: 308–26.

Friedman, Thomas L. (2006) *The World is Flat: A Brief History of the Twenty-first Century* (2nd edition), New York: Farrar, Straus and Giroux.

Piller, Ingrid (2002) 'Passing for a native speaker: identity and success in second language learning', *Journal of Sociolinguistics*, 6 (2): 179–206.

Rampton, Ben (1995) *Crossing: Language and Ethnicity among Adolescents*, London: Longman.

Sañez, Oscar (2008) 'Driving "breakthrough" growth in Philippines O&O: Roadmap 2010'. FUSE General Assembly Meeting, 25 March 2008.

Sirota, David (2006) 'Where economics meets religious fundamentalism', *San Francisco Chronicle*, 11 August 2006. Online. Available www.sfgate.com/cgi-bin/article.cgi?f=/c/a/2006/08/11/EDGOBIQ 0QU1.DTL (accessed 2 September 2008).

Tayao, Ma. Lourdes G. (2008) 'A lectal description of the phonological features of Philippine English', Ma. Lourdes S. Bautista and Kingsley Bolton (eds) *Philippine English: Linguistic and Literary Perspectives*, Hong Kong: Hong Kong University Press, pp. 157–74.

The Economist (2005) 'Confusing Columbus', 31 March: 81.

Tolentino, Rolando B. (2007) 'The cultural idioms of Filipino transvestism', in T. Ruanni F. Tupas (ed.) *(Re)making Society: The Politics of Language, Discourse, and Identity in the Philippines*, Diliman, Quezon City: University of the Philippines Press, pp. 169–88.

Section V

Debates and pedagogical implications

33

Which norms in everyday practice

And why?

T. Ruanni F. Tupas

Introduction

This paper was initially conceptualized around the question, *Which norms – and why?* However, on closer analysis the question itself generates even more fundamental questions and problems. For example, if the question is about choices of norms, then all available models of English in the classroom gravitate towards normative – not descriptive – practice. Whether particular models lean towards, using Halliday's (2003) trajectories, *global* English or *international* Englishes, any choice will inevitably be implicated in ethical and political questions about ideology, power and standardization. Thus, the nature of pedagogical norms must be investigated in the first place in order to find out how they work and why they matter. Only then can we go back to the initial question and attempt to answer it in a more nuanced way.

The following key arguments run through this chapter. First, it argues that pedagogical models are *Standard Englishes* primarily because of their normative nature. Second, it argues that *Standard Englishes*, as viewed from the ground (or real classroom contexts), are rarely taken up, and if they are, we do not know how much the teachers and learners know about the range of options (including their ideological underpinnings) available to them from where they could have made appropriate decisions. Third, it likewise argues that, if teachers indeed have critical awareness of the different choices of pedagogical Englishes, their decisions are much more nuanced than we expect them to be. Last, this chapter contends that norms are both social constructions and constructors of possibilities in the classroom. The question *Which norms – and why?* is and must continue to be a key question in the sociolinguistics of English language teaching around the world. But a major shift in research has to occur – the question must be answered from the perspective of actual classroom practice, and the extent to which this allows autonomous decision-making on the part of the teachers.

Recontextualizing the debate: norms in everyday struggle

Standard Englishes are inner circle Englishes

Any talk about models of English in the classroom involves a normative practice. That is, any preferred model would have to assume a standardized English, no matter what we call it. Most models, whether they be Standard English (Quirk 1990; Gupta 2006), English as a Global Language (Crystal 1998, 2003), English as an International Language (Widdowson 1997; McKay 2002; Tomlinson 2006), English as a Lingua Franca (Jenkins 2000, 2007; Seidlhofer 2001; Seidlhofer and Jenkins 2003), World Englishes (Kachru 1992), are, pedagogically speaking, *Standard Englishes*. This is not only because all models need some form of idealization and codification to make them teachable in the classroom, but also because (speakers of) non-standard Englishes have largely been excluded from any discussion about whether they may or may not be pedagogically appropriate. These 'Standard' Englishes, by their very nature, are, or become, exclusive (Villareal 2002), an ironic twist, as many of the models are presented as attempts to 'empower' learners around the world with the most appropriate norms of English because the current formalized forms are 'disempowering'.

Standard Englishes, therefore, are inner circle Englishes not in the sense of Kachru's concentric circles (see Davies *et al.* 2003), but in the sense of the economic and sociopolitical innerness of *Standard Englishes* within communities of use in any part of the world. There are inner circles and outer circles everywhere (Tupas 2001a, 2006, 2008); for example, speakers of 'Philippine English', as described in the literature, belong to the inner circle of Philippine society, while speakers of other Philippine Englishes who constitute the majority of users of English in the country belong to the outer circle because their sub-standard varieties are not considered legitimate. It is the inner circle English of the Philippines which shares linguistic and discursive affinities with the rest of inner circle Englishes across the globe.

This could explain, for example, why Ranosa-Madrunio (2004) has found that two inner circle Englishes in the Philippines and Singapore (based on data from national newspaper editorials) essentially share the same discourse structure. Rühlemann (2008) argues along the same line, when he notes that 'newspaper texts produced in New Zealand are as intelligible for British readers as academic papers written by a scholar from India are for readers in South Africa' (2008: 674). Inner circle Englishes form the basis of most proposed models today. Although they are deemed to be radically different from each other, they all actually gravitate towards the same norms. As Davies *et al.* (2003) observe in the context of research on the possibility of bias in proficiency tests in English national examinations in China, Singapore, Malaysia and India, including the study of TOEFL and IELTS:

> Now if there is uncertainty about the Old Variety of English (OVE) Standard Englishes, it is hardly surprising that there should be vagueness as to what constitute New Varieties of Standard Englishes. What seems clear is that among the educated, both in OVE and the NVE domains, the differences across Standard Englishes may be small.
>
> (Davies *et al.* 2003: 583)

The models assume respect for diversity, but underscore the need for unity. Although more plural than others, World Englishes' 'unity' is still oriented towards normative practice, but within different (country-based) contexts.

Standard Englishes in everyday struggle

How then do we start answering the question, *Which norms and why?*, if any choice we make necessarily implicates it within the normative practice of standardization or codification? In fact, this problem is made even more complex by two fundamental issues. First, in the literature concerning ELT norms, there is a great imbalance between the powerful sociolinguistic arguments for particular models for teaching English *and* the necessary, but scarce, pedagogic applications of the proposed models. To put this another way, rigorous (socio)linguistic descriptions of English language use across different contexts in the world generally consider the sociolinguistic implications (e.g. see Rajagopalan 2004; Kirkpatrick 2007), but they seldom consider the implications of the actual classroom adoption of specific models of English. One wonders why this is so, when one of the principal targets of sociolinguistic descriptions of English has always been real classroom contexts.

Second, everyone seems to espouse the cause of learners and teachers in advancing their preferred models, usually taking on the discourses of empowerment, democratization or liberation in doing so. For example, Kirkpatrick (2006) prefers the lingua franca model because it 'should be liberating for teachers and learners' (2006: 79), yet his own research (Kirkpatrick and Xu 2002) and that of others (Neufeld 2001; Timmis 2002) has revealed that learners generally want a native-speaker model of English in the classroom. So which norms? Those which have been deemed sociolinguistically and culturally appropriate, or those which teachers and learners want? For Tomlinson (2006), the best teachers of English are those who have experienced learning EIL, but 'how many learners would be happy to pay a lot of money to be taught by teachers whom they do not perceive to be native speakers of the language they are learning?' (2006: 140). There are ideological, political and cultural issues underlying these contradictions.

Standard Englishes, as viewed from the chalkface

In deciding which norms to use in the classroom, we need to first of all step back and enquire into the very nature of norms itself. By doing so, we shall be able to explore possible reasons why strong and sensible sociolinguistic arguments do not automatically translate into workable models of teaching English. We shall consult teachers themselves in elaborating on this disconnect between argumentation and application because, in reality, they, along with students, are 'seldom consulted' (Rubdy and Saraceni 2006: 14) about questions concerning pedagogical standards.

What follows is a discussion of two separate research projects involving two groups of teachers of English in the Philippines (Tupas 2006) and Singapore (Wu *et al.* 2008). These teachers were asked to confront the realities of normative practice, where choices of norms and models of English inevitably involve difficult political, ideological, cultural, socioeconomic and pragmatic considerations. Perhaps the key difference between these projects and many others involving teachers and learners is that these projects investigated the attitudes, beliefs and choices of teachers who clearly have a range of theoretical options concerning pedagogical models of English from both pragmatic and critical perspectives. The problem with promulgating 'what teachers want' or 'what learners want' is that we do not know the range of theoretical and practical options really available to them.

Timmis' (2002) valuable survey of teachers and learners around the world about their views on native-speaker norms is relevant. It presents a 'classroom view' of pedagogical choices in the teaching and learning of English, but it does not privilege the native speaker. Four hundred students from 14 countries and 180 teachers from 45 countries responded to the questionnaire. In brief, the survey found that native-speaker norms were preferred by most students and teachers. But Timmis' work seems to confirm our earlier contention about reported views of learners and teachers: 'What the survey could not show is how far respondents' attitudes are related to their awareness of the socio-linguistic issues involved in the debate about native-speaker norms and international English' (248–9).

Teaching Standard English by resisting it: Philippine examples

The context of the research

Seven Filipino teachers of English took a semester-long module in *Second Language Teaching* (SLT) as part of their postgraduate course with a university in the Philippines. For this particular semester, a textbook on SLT (Tupas 2002) was pilot-tested among these teacher-students (TS). Their teacher was not involved in the writing of the course material. The concept behind the textbook represents a departure from the under-lying principles of many current local and international SLT textbooks. All chapters are framed within critical issues in language teaching. The textbook starts by placing the book within the context of globalization, where SLT is situated within a geopolitical and economic framework, and ends by considering the power of English, especially in the context of the Philippines (Tollefson 1991; Tupas 2001b), within the discourses and practices of resistance and appropriation (Pennycook 1998; Canagarajah 1999). The textbook essentially provides readers with a wide range of options in second-language teaching in order for them to make informed decisions concerning their own work as language teachers.

The TS were required to write five tutor-marked essays (TMEs) in response to critical questions given at different times of the semester. One of these exercises required the TS to conduct classroom observations in their respective localities. These TMEs were analysed to identify the TS' (presumably) changing views on the pedagogical impera-tives of SE and other Englishes. Considering the critical framework of the textbook, the study essentially attempted to capture the TS' views on the teaching of various Eng-lishes. The results were revealing: they affirmed the legitimacy of all Standard Englishes, but refused to be drawn towards any given position.

Resisting Standard English by teaching it

The TS were happy to accept the World Englishes paradigm, noting that the reality of Philippine English (PE) is empowering for both teachers and students. PE to them is now a kind of counter-discourse against linguistic imperialist practices in the country, including the use of exonormative norms culled from Standard American English and the wholesale importation of Western-based pedagogy. However, they stop short of recommending PE as the ideal model in ELT classrooms. They recognize the economic imperative of teaching and learning SE. Students, they say, must learn SE because this too is empowering, especially because English is equated with social mobility and individual achievement.

570

However, whereas this view can be exploited by those whose conservative positions disregard the political and cultural appropriateness of other Englishes, the TS provide a more nuanced position: teach SE as form, but resist it by using PE as content, as can be seen from the two quotes below (quoted in Tupas 2006: 177–8):

1   We should Filipinize our books to portray Phil. Cultures. Writings in English should conform to Filipino standards to instill our identity. Through writing we should infuse great sense of Filipinism that features our desirable traits like hospitality, bayanihan, etc.
2   Integrate through writing about the life aspirations of the Filipino people. Use the language (English) within the context of the Philippines – Filipino setting – the values – and the dreams to be really be independent, not idolizing the principles – the culture of the elite. Use sentences which are within the experiences of the Filipinos.

Cultural strategies in teaching Standard English

They also argue that code-switching is similarly relevant: teach SE through code-switching if this is the best way students will learn the standard variety. In other words, the TS propose indigenous cultural strategies in teaching SE: code-switch and teach local content. The TS believe that these cultural strategies can eventually transform SE in Filipino classrooms, although they do not explain how it can happen. Whether or not (PE) content can indeed be separated from (SE) form, this nuanced position recaptures an ideological space for the teachers, who have had time to consider in-depth questions and issues concerning the teaching of English. This is the TS' way of making sense of the seeming contradictions of their work and in (re)affirming their legitimacy as 'critical' teachers who know what is best for their students.

Their position is both empowering and disempowering, capitulating and resisting, a testament to the conditioned practices of their work as English language teachers. But as the teachers' everyday struggle has been saturated by all sorts of conditioned practices, such conditioning has also been transformed by the teachers' own engagement with such practices. The competing models come from the outside looking in, while the teachers come from the inside looking out. In other words, the teachers have refused to be drawn towards choosing the 'best' or 'most appropriate' model in the market but, instead, have reconfigured the debate.

Codifying errors from the ground: Singapore examples

The context of the research

The Singapore project is of a different nature but it also involves questions about teachers' conditioned choices and beliefs about pedagogical models of English. The project involves creating a corpus of undergraduate and postgraduate writing in order to identify and categorize patterns of written errors made during meaning-focused writing tasks. A random sampling of 1,000 essays of about 1 million words were collected from diverse groups of students, representing different faculties, courses, nationalities and language proficiencies (see initial findings in Wu *et al.* 2008).

571

The project adopts a pedagogical approach which allows teachers themselves to code students' writing and, in the process, identify the dominant types of error specific to these students. The findings are expected to provide an empirically justifiable rationale for designing materials using particular types of error. It is hoped that the use of these materials will lead to more efficient teaching and learning, since teachers can now account for the more frequent errors.

Questions about teachers' beliefs about errors and their practices of identifying or coding them emerge from the manner by which the data were coded. A bottom-up approach to coding data was adopted, instead of relying on available coding systems such as that of Ferris (2002). The rationale was to let the errors 'emerge' from the appraisals of errors by all 12 coders, all of whom were professionally trained English language teachers with at least MA degrees in applied linguistics or related fields. Six coding sessions were conducted over four months before a final coding system was established (Wu *et al.* 2008). In these sessions, the teachers were engaged in animated discussions on the nature of errors and why certain words or sentences were deemed problematic. Just like the Filipino teachers above, most teachers in the Singapore project were aware of the range of sociolinguistic issues surrounding models of English in the classroom. This explains why they sometimes prefaced their assertions with 'my job as an English teacher' and sometimes with 'in sociolinguistics … '

A conflicted discourse on norms

Here, one coder's thoughts (Wee Siang, a pseudonym) are discussed to consider the complex nature of errors in second-language writing. Wee Siang is an ethnic Chinese with a PhD in English Language. He is also a specialist in Singapore English. The interview revolved around sentences which he had coded as errors, even if these errors were believed to have been influenced or shaped by Chinese, the students' first language. For example, he argued that the following sentence is grammatically influenced by Chinese:

The fishes in *the* one of the experimental *group* were kept in large tanks mixed with the solute containing buckyballs so that the overall concentration of fullerenes is 0.5 parts per million.

Wee Siang: To me I think students make this kind of mistake because in Chinese we don't have an article, number one. Number two, we don't have like two different forms for nouns. We always use the same singular forms whether you refer to one of them or many of them.

It may be noted that if 'the' is deleted, then the 'error' may become acceptable to some. However, in the discussion with Wee Siang and the rest of the team, 'one of the experimental group' will still be codified as an error, making codification itself a normative practice. Thus, Wee Siang argues that the sentence is, in his word, 'illegitimate':

It is illegitimate in the sense that again like 'one of the experimental group' I think this is, I don't know, we should do the survey probably to see how many percent of the teachers will accept this. To me I think as a teacher I will take this as an illegitimate sentence, it's wrong. We won't be confused with the meaning, the meaning is clear here. It's just most people will take it as an error and you know when I teach like a non-native speaker we still have the kind of norm in mind. This is the norm and we should try our best to use the correct version.

Wee Siang qualifies his remarks by referring to himself as 'a teacher' and as a 'non-native speaker' who must follow 'the norm' and 'the correct version' because 'most people will take it as an error'. Wee Siang's views on this sentence, in other words, are influenced not by sociolinguistic arguments. He believes, rather, that grammatical correctness is non-negotiable, although this absolutist position is tempered by an earlier statement referring to the acceptability of the sentence from the point of view of most teachers. If most teachers accept it as a legitimate sentence, will he also think the same? In fact, he also thinks that local varieties of English are legitimate, even arguing that these varieties (which are influenced by the speakers' first languages) belong to those who speak them:

> For example, for Singaporeans English is their native language. They have every right to use the language in their own way.

A teacher's duty

So what counts as legitimate and illegitimate depends on whether one describes or prescribes a particular use of English. Thus in the end:

> This is my job and this is my duty. I have to do it to tell the differences. I have to tell them this is wrong in terms of grammar but when I talk to a student from China, for example, of course we don't use grammatical structures all the time. In that sense our purpose is communication: as long as we can communicate with each other, we complete the exchange … But when it comes to the norm, I tell them this is the norm. And this is the structure and we have to follow.

For Wee Siang, it is the teacher's job and duty to let his students know what is 'wrong in terms of grammar' even if English among Singaporeans is 'native' to them as well. Wee Siang is aware of the scholarly debates on 'nativeness' in English language teaching, especially in the context of the emergence of postcolonial Englishes. However, when it comes to prescribing a norm in the classroom, nativeness takes on a much more constricting definition to include only speakers of what he terms (for convenience) as 'old' English, as opposed to 'new Englishes'. In fact, it is here where he advances one of his controversial points:

> To me again whether or not you speak a good English or a bad English I mean, this is prejudice I know, an educated person should speak like the norm. I don't know whether you accept it or not … New Englishes are developing their own norms. But when I look at the new norms, the norms for the new Englishes, for example Singapore English, again in terms of grammar I don't think we have a lot of differences from the original norm. And whenever we describe the features we normally use the term like Colloquial Singapore English so we make it very clear this is not educated Singaporean English or Standard Singapore English. It's more like colloquial Singapore English.

573

Wee Siang is aware of his own prejudice but nevertheless continues to argue that speaking the standard means being educated. He implies that what is referred to as educated Singaporean English or Standard Singapore English is still close to the original norm. To put it in another way, there is an implicit hierarchy in his descriptions of varieties of English in Singapore. What could be uniquely Singaporean because of clear deviations from the 'original norm' are labelled as 'colloquial' in scholarly discourse. In other words, a legitimate localized English in Singapore is codified by linguists as 'educated' or 'standard' Singapore English, whose norms do not radically differ from 'the original norm'.

Form vs content

Just like the Filipino teachers above, however, Wee Siang seems clear about what he is duty bound to teach: SE (form) or Standard English as form. His concession in class as a sociolinguist is to be more tolerant towards localized content which can be realized in local words and metaphors. For him, this is where creative language use is acceptable and justifiable, even if readers not familiar with local culture might struggle with these words and metaphors. Wee Siang's belief in Standard English cannot be interpreted as a mere neo-conservative position ready to be appropriated by proponents of SE, without due regard for the sociolinguistic legitimacy of varieties of English around the world. Rather, his stance is a conditioned position which does not denigrate the status of local varieties, especially those forms which are influenced by the users' first languages, but which is also bound by forces of power and authority largely beyond his control.

Again, it is not clear how form can be separated from content, but for Wee Siang 'non-native' users of English have power over content in the classroom, but not over form, which is stable and non-negotiable. Given the fact that he associates this form with 'educated' English, Wee Siang's position affirms this paper's point articulated earlier: legitimate Englishes remain those which are labelled 'educated', and whose norms do not depart radically from the prescribed standard norms.

Norming and norms

What then do we make of the nature of pedagogical norms of English based on discussions of the two research projects above? There are two important points to note.

Norms are normed

The first point is that norms are normed; that is, they are social constructs generated by a complex of ideological, sociopolitical, socioeconomic and cultural forces. In the case of available pedagogical models, the choices of which norms to legitimize or highlight depend on 'descriptive' or 'prescriptive' practices of linguists and educational researchers themselves. Villareal's (2002) observation is relevant here:

> although much scholarly discussion and literary experimentation have been done on the concepts of hybridity, the appropriation of English, and the development of our varieties of English, it is too facile to speak of equality in language and culture. Note, for instance, the concern to capture the notion of a Filipino variety of English, and the 'standardization of the grammatical features of Filipino English'

or Singlish, or other varieties of English. Languages are documented mainly by the educated and standards set by them.

(Villareal 2002: 33–4)

In other words, pedagogical norms are described and affirmed by the empowered (Milroy and Milroy 1985; Zimmerman 2007); they are promulgated by those whose English(es) have been legitimized as sociopolitically 'inner' or 'standard'. It does not matter whether it is Standard English, English as a Global Language, English as an International Language, English as Lingua Franca or World Englishes, the nature of norms is essentially the same. It is a legitimizing practice; even the most avowedly descriptive work, in order to be true and accurate, must take on some sense of prescriptivism, thus normative work (see Fairclough 1989). This is how codification of errors, as described above, becomes a kind of descriptive work as well; even if the codification of grammar and the description of norms point to two different agendas, both sets of practices are normative in nature.

In the case of the Filipino teachers above, norms are normed in the sense that, whenever they talk about the need for Standard English, they constantly refer to practical realities. Forces larger than individual teachers dictate the norming of norms; these forces are associated with globalist discourses which privilege pragmatist concerns over other sociopolitical questions to do with social access, marginalization, and so on. In recent years, a dangerous ideological narrowing of focus in Philippine education has occurred because of the single-minded promotion of English in the schools to meet the demands of the call-centre industry (see Bolton, this volume). This has led to the reaffirmation of American English as the ideal model for teaching and learning. This is not surprising because American English was never really discarded in the first place. Bautista (2000), the Philippines' foremost scholar in Philippine English, has not endorsed the teaching of the local variety in the classroom because of the presence of what she calls 'a standard of standards' (2000: 17), which dominates the consciousness and practice of ELT in the country.

Norms do norm

A second important point to note about norms is that norms do norm. That is, norms help determine the parameters of practice within which both learners and teachers operate. In the case of the Filipino teachers above, norms of Standard English (whether real or imaginary, see Coupland 2000) militate against the forming of counter-hegemonic Englishes, although they clearly think that they are culturally appropriate and politically correct. These norms have forced the teachers to rethink their biases, but they also have to continue to work within specific boundaries. In the case of teachers of English in Singapore, the same norms help dictate the teachers' coding practices. Coding errors in student writing is guided by perceptions of what norms are relevant and appropriate. Norms help determine the unacceptability of first-language-influenced written forms and sentences. They are not mere pawns of dominant discourses and institutions; they also actively create ways of thinking and a range of classroom practices.

This point should be highlighted because the role of the state in (re)articulating pragmatist ideologies in the service of corporate globalization is undeniable. This is especially so in Singapore where pragmatist thinking, or what Tan (2006) refers to as the state's 'perennial, almost obsessive, concern with economic relevance' (2006: 181), has been the hallmark of social policy-making in the country since it unwillingly became independent in 1966. The nature of norms as being able to determine parameters of practice is paradoxically a liberating moment: the limits they set may not be successfully transcended easily, but they can be stretched and negotiated so that users of norms (like the teachers above) are able to generate creative and fresh ways of thinking and configurations of practice. In other words, the conditioned possibilities of the classroom enable participants to transform their position of weakness into a position of strength: the teachers above have accepted their 'duty' to teach what needs to be taught, as defined by forces larger than them, but their critical awareness of the range of possibilities available has helped them approach their teaching in different, inventive ways. In the choice of a particular pedagogical model, the teachers have engaged in the debate, but have refused to be drawn towards choosing one model at the expense of others.

Conclusion: the way(s) to go

The possibility of change and resistance in the use and teaching of norms in ELT (or what may be referred to as 'agency' in ELT) as articulated above is different in some fundamental ways from other sociolinguistic accounts of the classroom. First, it locates agency within conditioned possibilities: that is, the possibility of change and resistance through 'appropriate' Englishes other than the 'standard' ones is viewed as intricately interwoven into the constraints and structures of real classrooms. The idealization of agency, resistance and appropriation, for example, can be gleaned through Brutt-Griffler's (1998) notion of 'agency in language change' (1998: 381) or Rajagopalan's (1999) valorization of hybridity and appropriation, yet what we also need is research on how these possibilities are actualized or negotiated by teachers and students on the ground. So what we have are celebratory pronouncements on the various Englishes of the world with much less discussion on how these sociolinguistically legitimate Englishes collide with layers of power and control in the classroom.

Second, it does not merely describe or interpret practices of resistance present in the classroom but, more importantly, it tries to find out what teachers actually know about what they do in the classroom. In other words, the focus is not on resistance and agency according to analysts (see Canagarajah 1999; Lin 1999; Martin 2005), but resistance and agency according to classroom participants themselves. And third, this chapter explores the messiness of classroom realities in order to find out what teachers (and potentially students) can do with available models of English. Recent work has explored how 'non-standard' varieties can be exploited in the teaching of Standard English, for example through their use in class as resources for learning (Fong *et al.* 2002; Rubdy 2007; Tan and Tan 2008). These possibilities have been introduced into several curricula, but how they will be appropriated in the classroom by teachers who are critically aware of their choices remains to be seen.

So, is the question, *Which norms, and why?* still worth asking? Certainly. There is no doubt that this question should remain a key issue in the sociolinguistics of English language teaching around the world. However, a major shift is needed: instead of answering the question from a sociolinguistic standpoint (which has been framed by inner circles of Western and Western-influenced academia), we need to consider the question in light of practical classroom realities. This will involve consulting teachers, students and local leaders about what they want to teach and learn; it will require descriptive and evaluative accounts of local and mainstream literacies, the levels of social development, and the relationships between languages in the communities; it will also need to consider the extent globalization has penetrated these specific communities.

Much literacy and development work (see Olson and Torrance 2001; Street 2001) has avoided the homogenizing tendencies of national curricula and the disempowering effects of national educational policies. What emerged were localized, but expanding, curricula which drew on local cultures and which focused on issues directly relevant to the users of language themselves. The specific role of languages in the classroom did not depend on the requirements of national policies, but emerged from the literacy and development needs of the communities in question. These were instances of communities taking control of their own teaching and learning and which critically considered how to engage with and respond to the demands of a globalizing world. Home and community literacies were promoted to develop effective pedagogical models (see Doronila 1996); it was not a case of pedagogical models first then local needs and aspirations next. These did not preclude the inclusion of 'national' and 'global' needs – after all, local education initiatives are usually framed within national curricular frameworks. However these 'external' needs were not addressed at the expense of the more immediate demands of basic literacy and community-based social development.

It goes without saying that, if we want to empower teachers and learners with particular models of English, we must let these models emerge from the communities of teachers and learners themselves, where education is inextricably linked with local cultures, literacies and politics. This is where teacher education is of utmost importance. But instead of training teachers simply in the most current language and pedagogical model, it must work towards addressing the following questions. Do our communities need English in the first place? If yes, in what contexts and for what purpose(s)? How should we (teachers) be empowered to develop our own pedagogies of practice, especially in the use of particular models of English? What does teacher education look like, if the focus is on giving us choices, and not on training us in particular/privileged pedagogical models of English? Can we develop pedagogical models of English from within our communities? Indeed, which norms in *our* everyday practice – and why? With these questions, we shift the burden of empowerment away from choosing the 'appropriate' norms in class to asking why, in the first place, the appropriate norms are not always the right ones, and why the right ones are not always appropriate.

Suggestions for further reading

Jenkins, J. (2007) *English as a Lingua Franca: Attitude and Identity*, Oxford: Oxford University Press.
Kirkpatrick, A. (2007) *World Englishes: Implications for International Communication and English Language Teaching*, Cambridge: Cambridge University Press.
Pennycook, A. (2008) 'Multilithic English(es) and language ideologies', *Language in Society*, 37: 435–44.
Rubdy, R. and Saraceni, M. (eds) (2006) *English in the World: Global Rules, Global Roles*, London: Continuum.

References

Bautista, M.L.S. (2000) *Defining Standard Philippine English: Its Status and Grammatical Features*, Manila, Philippines: De La Salle University Press.

Brutt-Griffler, J. (1998) 'Conceptual questions in English as a world language: taking up an issue', *World Englishes*, 17 (3): 381–92.

Canagarajah, S. (1999) *Resisting Linguistic Imperialism in English Teaching*, Oxford: Oxford University Press.

Coupland, C. (2000) 'Review article: sociolinguistic prevarication about "standard English"', *Journal of Sociolinguistics*, 4 (4): 622–34.

Crystal, D. (1997) *English as a Global Language*, Cambridge: Cambridge University Press.

——(2003) *The Cambridge Encyclopedia of the English Language* (2nd edition), Cambridge: Cambridge University Press.

——(2006) *The Fight for English: How Language Pundits Ate, Shot, and Left*, Oxford: Oxford University Press.

Davies, A., Ham-Lyons, L. and Kemp, C. (2003) 'Whose norms? International proficiency tests in English', *World Englishes*, 22 (4): 571–84.

Doronila, M.L. (1996) *Landscapes of Literacy: An Ethnographic Study of Functional Literacy in Marginal Philippine Communities*, Hamburg: UNESCO Institute for Education.

Fairclough, N. (1989) *Language and Power*, London: Longman.

Farrell, T. and Tan, S. (2007) 'Language policy, language teachers' beliefs, and classroom practices', *Applied Linguistics*, 29 (3): 381–403.

Ferris, D. (2002) *Treatment of Errors in Second Language Students' Writing* (Michigan Series on Teaching Multilingual Writers), Ann Arbor: University of Michigan Press.

Fong, V., Lim, L. and Wee, L. (2002) '"Singlish": used and abused', *Asian Englishes*, 5 (1): 21–39.

Gupta, A.F. (2006) 'Standard English in the world', in R. Rubdy and M. Saraceni (eds) *English in the World: Global Rules, Global Roles*, London: Continuum, pp. 95–109.

Halliday, M.A.K. (2003) 'Written language, standard language, global language', *World Englishes*, 22 (4): 405–18.

Jenkins, J. (2000) *The Phonology of English as an International Language*, Oxford: Oxford University Press.

——(2007) *English as a Lingua Franca: Attitude and Identity*, Oxford: Oxford University Press.

Kachru, B. (1992) 'World Englishes: approaches, issues and resources', *Language Teaching*, 25: 1–14.

Kirkpatrick, A. (2006) 'Which model of English: native-speaker, nativized or lingua franca?' in R. Rubdy and M. Saraceni (eds) *English in the World: Global Rules, Global Roles*, London: Continuum, pp. 71–83.

——(2007) *World Englishes: Implications for International Communication and English Language Teaching*, Cambridge: Cambridge University Press.

Kirkpatrick, A. and Xu Zhichang (2002) 'Chinese pragmatic norms and China English', *World Englishes*, 21 (2): 269–80.

Li, Charles and Thompson, S.A. (1981) *Mandarin Chinese: A Functional Reference Grammar*, Berkeley: University of California Press.

Lin, A.M.Y. (1999) 'Doing-English lessons in the reproduction or transformation of social worlds', *TESOL Quarterly*, 33 (3): 393–412.

McKay, S. (2002) *Teaching English as an International Language*, Oxford: Oxford University Press.

Martin, P.W. (2005) 'Talking knowledge into being in an upriver primary school in Brunei', in A.S. Canagarajah (ed.) *Reclaiming the Local in Language Policy and Practice*, Mahwah, NJ: Lawrence Erlbaum, pp. 225–46.

Milroy, J. and Milroy, L. (1985) *Authority in Language*, London: Routledge and Kegan Paul.

Neufeld, G. (2001) 'Non-foreign-accented speech in adult second language learners: does it exist and what does it signify?' *ITL Review of Applied Linguistics*, 133/134: 185–206.

Olson, D.R. and Torrance, N. (ed.) (2001) *The Making of Literate Societies*, Oxford: Blackwell.

Pennycook, A. (1998) *English and the Discourses of Colonialism*, London: Routledge.

Quirk, R. (1990) 'What is Standard English?' in R. Quirk and G. Stein (eds) *English in Use*, London: Longman, pp. 12–25.

Rajagopalan, K. (1999) 'Reply to Canagarajah', *ELT Journal*, 53 (3): 215–16.

——(2004) 'The concept of "World English" and its implications for ELT', *ELT Journal,* 58 (2): 111–17.

Ranosa-Madrunio, M. (2004) 'The discourse organization of letters of complaint to editors in Philippine English and Singapore English', *Philippine Journal of Linguistics,* 35 (2): 67–97.

Rubdy, R. (2007) 'Singlish in the school: an impediment or a resource?' *Journal of Multilingual and Multicultural Development,* 28 (4): 308–24.

Rubdy, R. and Saraceni, M. (2006) 'Introduction', in R. Rubdy and M. Saraceni (eds) *English in the World: Global Rules, Global Roles,* London: Continuum, pp. 5–6.

Rühlemann, C. (2008) 'A register approach to teaching conversation: farewell to standard English?' *Applied Linguistics,* 29 (4): 672–93.

Seidlhofer, B. (2001) 'Closing a conceptual gap: the case for a description of English as a lingua franca', *International Journal of Applied Linguistics,* 11 (2): 133–58.

Seidlhofer, B. and Jenkins, J. (2003) 'English as a lingua franca and the politics of property', in C. Mair (ed.) *The Politics of English as a World Language* (New Horizons in Postcolonial Cultural Studies, ASNEL Papers 7), Amsterdam: Rodopi, pp. 139–54.

Street, B. (ed.) (2001) *Literacy and Development,* London: Routledge.

Tan, J. (2006) *Singapore. Higher Education in Southeast Asia,* Bangkok: UNESCO Asia and Pacific Regional Bureau for Education.

Tan, P. and Tan, D. (2008) 'Attitudes towards non-standard English in Singapore', *World Englishes,* 27(3/4): 465–79.

Timmis, I (2002) 'Native-speaker norms and International English: a classroom view', *ELT Journal* 56 (2): 240–9.

Tollefson, J. (1991) *Planning Language, Planning Inequality,* New York: Longman.

Tomlinson, B. (2006) 'A multi-dimensional approach to teaching English for the world', in R. Rubdy and M. Saraceni (eds) *English in the World: Global Rules, Global Roles,* London: Continuum, pp. 130–50.

Tupas, T.R.F. (2001a) 'Global politics and the Englishes of the world', in J. Cotterril and A. Ife (eds) *Language across Boundaries: Selected Papers from the Annual Meeting of the British Association for Applied Linguistics,* London and New York: British Association for Applied Linguistics in association with the Continuum Press, pp. 81–98.

——(2001b) 'Linguistic imperialism in the Philippines: reflections of an English language teacher of Filipino overseas workers', *The Asia-Pacific Education Research,* 10 (1): 1–40.

——(2002) *Second Language Teaching,* Philippines: University of the Philippines Open University.

——(2006) 'Standard Englishes, pedagogical paradigms and their conditions of (im)possibility', in R. Rubdy and M. Saraceni (eds) *English in the World: Global Rules, Global Roles,* London: Continuum, pp. 169–85.

——(2008) 'World Englishes or worlds of English? Pitfalls of a postcolonial discourse in Philippine English', in K. Bolton and Ma. L.S. Bautista (eds) *Philippine English: Language and Literature,* Hong Kong: Hong Kong University Press.

Villareal, C.D. (2002) 'Re-searching language teaching', *The ACELT Journal,* 6 (2): 33–7.

Widdowson, H. (1997) 'EIL, ESL, EFL, global issues and local interests', *World Englishes,* 16 (1): 135–46.

Wu, S.M, Tupas, T.R.F. and Zhu, S. (2008) 'Students' written errors: an exploratory study', *Frontiers in Higher Education. Proceedings of the International Conference on Teaching and Learning in Higher Education,* Singapore: Centre for Development of Teaching and Learning, National University of Singapore, pp. 70–2.

Zimmerman, L. (2007) 'Standard English in the EFL classroom', *ELT Journal,* 61 (2): 164–6.

34

Construing meaning in World Englishes

Ahmar Mahboob and Eszter Szenes

Introduction

Research on World Englishes has, beyond any doubt, made a significant contribution to discussions about the politics and status of the English language around the world. It has also raised the awareness of both linguists and non-linguists of how language varies over space and time and how notions of 'standard' English reflect political motives rather than linguistic realities. Nevertheless there are some issues regarding World Englishes that need attention. This paper examines two such issues. The first issue is the practice of using the names of countries in naming varieties of World Englishes; and the second is a focus of World Englishes research on identifying points of structural variation across different varieties of English without considering their semantic functions. This second issue leads to a discussion of how *meanings* are construed in World Englishes. The paper then shares the findings of a study that attempts to do this and discusses the implications of such work to World Englishes.

On naming practices in World Englishes

One of the widespread practices in World Englishes is to name different varieties of English according to the countries in which they are spoken. However, using names of countries as labels to classify language varieties is, arguably, imposing a nationalistic twist to linguistic realities. The result of using these labels is that researchers studying World Englishes draw boundaries between varieties of Englishes across national boundaries when the linguistic evidence may not actually justify such divisions. This is problematic because it leads World Englishes researchers into describing discrete linguistic features that are used to contrast one variety with another and that do not contribute to a theory of language or of how meaning is construed or communicated in and across these varieties.

While one can argue that national boundaries, over time, can lead to language change because of how these boundaries may restrict or permit the flow of people and therefore create different environments for language change, it is hard to argue that national borders in and of themselves can be used to demarcate varieties of English. One could also point out that using geographical labels (for geolects) is a common practice in naming language dialects (e.g. Yorkshire English, Birmingham English, etc.) and that World Englishes follows such practice. However, we argue that an extension of such naming traditions in the context of World Englishes is not appropriate because of at least three reasons.

First, the regional dialects of English were defined traditionally for first-language speakers of English (or other languages) and not speakers who use English as an 'other tongue' (Kachru 1992). One complication that the borrowing of these naming practices into a context of World Englishes raises is that speakers of English as an 'other tongue', unlike those in monolingual settings, are influenced by their first languages. World Englishes are spoken by people who speak a wide range of mother tongues, and these first languages influence the local varieties of English in different ways. Many of these people (speaking different first languages) live in the same country/location. Thus, there may be a large range of Englishes spoken within a single country. For example, there are at least 60 distinct languages in Pakistan and these languages result in variations – most notably phonological variation – in the English that these people use. These differences are a result of a complex language contact situation (in addition to social-, gender-, educational-based variations) and a geographical labelling does not adequately capture or reflect the added levels of complexities involved.

Second, the new varieties of English, especially outer circle Englishes, are spoken by people who live in countries that were strongly influenced by British administrative and colonial policies and these policies have influenced how and what Englishes are used there. For example, during the British colonial period, indentured servants were recruited from India and moved to parts of South and East Africa, the Caribbean Islands, South East Asia (e.g. Malaysia) and the Pacific Islands (e.g. Fiji). The descendants of these people speak a variety of English that is quite distinct from the other Englishes spoken in their countries. So, we find that users of Malaysian English who are of an Indian origin speak a different English from those of Chinese or Malay origin. Similarly, South African Englishes include South African Indian Englishes, South African Black Englishes, and South African White Englishes – and all of these have their own sub-varieties that are influenced by a large variety of first languages. Thus, using country-based names for these Englishes does not do justice to the rich diversity of Englishes used within these countries.

Third, the British, in retreating from their Empire, created a number of new countries that did not necessarily have well-defined natural, historical, cultural or social boundaries. The creation of new nation-states thus did not necessarily reflect linguistic boundaries and therefore cannot be safely used to name language varieties. This can perhaps be exemplified by the following: English spoken in Karachi, Pakistan, is very similar to English spoken in north Indian cities such as Delhi. In contrast to this, English spoken in Delhi is markedly different from that spoken in Chennai or Cochin. However, while Englishes spoken in Karachi and Delhi are seen as dialects of Pakistani English and Indian English respectively, the Englishes spoken in Delhi, Chennai and Cochin are all seen as dialects of the same 'Indian English'. Clearly, linguistic differences between the dialects here are not the leading reason for labelling the varieties in these contexts. The varieties of English are named on the country they are spoken in and do not necessarily reflect the distribution of linguistic features in the context.

Pennycook (2002) also raises a similar concern when he refers to Krishnaswamy and Burde (1998) and states:

> From this point of view, if Quirk represents the imperialistic attitude, Kachru represents … a nationalistic point of view … Indeed, tongue in cheek, they [Krishnaswamy and Burde] ask whether there is not a rather strange parallel between the nationalistic creation of new Englishes and the creation of new airlines: Air India, Singapore Airlines, Malaysian Airlines, etc?
>
> (Pennycook 2002: 7)

Pennycook's observation here highlights the desire of nationalistic movements to project a niche identity for their groups in opposition to others. This is a highly problematic endeavour in terms of linguistic labelling because it imposes ideologically motivated labels on linguistic evidence that do not necessarily reflect the divisions being projected. This process of labelling varieties of English by the country they are used in 'muddies up the possibility of presenting a rational description of what one might call distinct linguistic varieties' (Hasan, personal communication).

One final point, that relates to the nation-based naming practices and nationalistic orientation of World Englishes is that in trying to describe X-country English, researchers use structural features to mark its uniqueness. This focus on structural variation, in the recent years, has come at the cost of looking at how meanings are construed in World Englishes. Such a-semantic descriptions of World Englishes are problematic, as discussed in the following section.

On semantic descriptions of World Englishes

It is well known that discussions on World Englishes attach importance to meaning – as can be seen in early work on World Englishes (e.g. Kachru 1983) which discusses the role of re-semanticization in the evolution of World Englishes. Meanings, of course, are realized in the form of wording and exchanged in social life. The importance given to meaning in Kachru's work is not surprising because Kachru, as a student of M.A.K. Halliday, was well aware of the role context plays in construing meaning in and through language. Meaning was crucial to a discussion of World Englishes to Kachru because, like Halliday, Kachru recognized that language both represents and construes reality and that people, living in different contexts, construe and represent different realities through their language (in this case their variety of English). What this means is that both Kachru and Halliday recognize that language does not simply mirror social structure, but also

> constructs and maintains it: thus every time someone uses language 'appropriate' for a social superior, they are both showing their awareness of their status and simultaneously reinforcing the hierarchical social system. If people begin using less formal language when talking to social superiors (as has happened, for example, with the near disappearance of 'Sir' as a term of respectful address to men in Britain), they are in effect changing the social structure.
>
> (Thompson and Collins 2001: 137)

In the context of World Englishes, this means that linguistic choices made by the speakers of different varieties of Englishes construe and represent meanings that may be different from other varieties of English. Mahboob (2009) provides one example of research demonstrating how English in Pakistan has been *re-semanticized* to construe a local Islamic ideology. It is this kind of expansion of the meaning potential of English in the context of World Englishes that represents distinct linguistic varieties.

Given the importance of the role of meaning in the development of World Englishes, it is surprising that much of the recent work on World Englishes (including some of the first author's work on 'Pakistani' English) describes linguistic variation at or below the clause level (phoneme, phonology, morphology, lexis and syntax) without much discussion of meaning. The research that does look at larger chunks of language in a World Englishes context does so by labelling the work as studies of pragmatics – and thus not 'core' linguistics. Thus, it is not surprising that even the most comprehensive studies of inner and outer circle Englishes (e.g. studies included in Kortmann and Schneider 2004) focus on structural variation in the dialects without giving much consideration to how the choices in the lexicogrammar made by speakers of these varieties of Englishes relate to the meanings being construed.

The critique of World Englishes for lack of attention to meaning in some ways goes back to the classic criticism of variationist sociolinguistics – drawn on by a number of World Englishes researchers to model their own research on structural variation. In her critique of sociolingistics, Beatriz Lavandera (1978) argues that variation studies that deal with 'morphological, syntactic, and lexical alteration suffer from the lack of an articulated theory of meanings' (p. 171). She finds this lack of attention to meaning problematic and argues that different forms mean different things and therefore should be studied as such. Without such consideration, she argues, a study of these variables 'can only be heuristic devices, in no sense part of a theory of language' (p. 179). This is a severe criticism of studies in sociolinguistics that do not consider meaning to be an essential aspect of their study. Regretfully, a substantial body of research on World Englishes falls under this category – paying little attention to the meaning-making aspects of language and, consequently (and as Lavandera predicted), having little influence on theories of language. The structural variation research on World Englishes focusing on country-based Englishes serves as a 'heuristic device' to mark national identities, but does not really contribute to 'a theory of language'.

It needs to be clarified here that we are *not* saying that World Englishes literature has had no impact on the politics of the English language – it has. What we observe is that the influence of World Englishes on linguistic theory has been limited. World Englishes looks at how language is used in diverse global contexts to reflect and construe diverse cultural and human activities and beliefs and therefore has the potential to significantly contribute to a theory of language. However, such a contribution to linguistic theory is not evident at the moment. We posit that this is a consequence of the focus of recent research on World Englishes on only structural variations without much regard to meaning and semantics.

Studying meaning in World Englishes

A study of World Englishes using Hallidayan Systemic Functional Linguistics (SFL) is one way of addressing this criticism because SFL takes meaning and social variation as a starting point for understanding how language functions in different contexts. Thus, in order to explore how individuals using different varieties of Englishes construct meaning, we report on SFL-oriented analyses of texts written by three users of outer circle varieties of English – this analysis will be shared in a later section. One reason for using tools based on SFL is that, as stated earlier, it looks at language as a meaning-making process that

583

is grounded in the context of culture and situation (texts examined here are produced in specific contexts and for specific purposes). A second reason for using SFL is that it considers the whole text as the unit of analysis since '[s]ocial contexts are realized as texts which are realized as sequences of clauses' (Martin and Rose 2005: 4).

Before moving on, it should be pointed out that the criticism against World Englishes in terms of its lack of engagement with meaning and semiotics does not only come from SFL. Lavandera's (1978) criticism of studies focusing on sociolinguistic variables also applies to it. In addition, other linguists in non-Centre countries such as Kandiah (1998) have also raised concerns about research on World Englishes that does not consider semantics and semiotics as a key aspect of their research. For example, Kandiah (1998: 100) argues that World Englishes 'fundamentally involve a radical act of semiotic reconstruction and reconstitution which of itself confers native userhood on the subjects involved in the act' and that this semiotic reconstruction and reconstitution needs to be studied by researchers working in this area.

This paper is one attempt to explore the meaning-making resources used by users of different varieties/dialects of World Englishes. The data used in the study are authentic texts that three students from the outer circle countries wrote as part of their MA coursework at an Australian university. The texts are 'article reviews' – one of the core assignments for the course. In order to complete this assignment, students were asked to read key research articles in their field of study and then to summarize and critique the articles. All article reviews written by the students in the course who agreed to participate in this study were analysed. (There were 28 students enrolled in the course, of whom 20 students participated in this project.) However, for the purposes of this paper (in consideration of space constraints), we will share our analysis of article reviews written by three students only. These three students were selected because they represent different linguistic and national heritages – they were born and grew up in three different outer circle countries. The pseudonyms for the three students whose texts are analysed here are Niloo, Ashwini and Yasmina. Niloo, an Australian citizen of Sri Lankan origin, was educated in English-medium schools in Sri Lanka before migrating to Australia in 2006. Niloo speaks Sinhalese and English at home. Ashwini, a Singaporean student (of Indian heritage), was a first-semester student in the programme and had recently arrived from Singapore, where she was educated in English-medium schools. She speaks English as well as Punjabi at home; however, Ashwini does not consider her Punjabi very proficient and prefers to speak in English. Yasmina, an Australian citizen of Indian origin, received her formative education in India, but attended college in Australia before joining the MA programme. Yasmina speaks English at home, and Tamil, Kannada and Hindi with her extended family. In this paper, we will examine the linguistic resources used by these three individuals to construe specific meanings required in writing article reviews.

In order to proceed, we will provide a broad introduction to SFL theories of genre. We will then briefly describe the analytical tools used in this paper and examine how the three students from the outer circle countries construct their texts and discuss the implications of such an analysis to World Englishes.

Systemic Functional Linguistics and genre studies

Systemic Functional Linguistics views language as a social semiotic system – a resource that people use to accomplish their purposes and to construe and represent meaning in context. This view of language implies that language is a system of choices and that aspects of a given context (e.g. the topics, the users) define the meanings that are to be expressed and the language that can to be used to express those meanings. In SFL theory, language as a social semiotic system is realized on four different levels of abstraction, which have been termed *strata*: phonology–graphology, lexico-grammar, discourse–semantics and context. The most basic resources for meaning-making are basic phonological or graphological units. At the strata of lexico-grammar, the units of phonology and graphology are realized as words and structures and as higher-level abstractions. At the discourse–semantic level, meanings are created across texts as a whole, rather than just within clauses. Context stands at the highest level of abstraction or strata, which can be divided into context of situation (register) and context of culture (genre). Register realizes genre through the metafunctions or variables of *field*, *tenor* and *mode*. Field is concerned with the nature of social action; tenor refers to the relationship among participants, their roles and status; whereas mode refers to the role of language to realize meanings (Martin and Rose 2008).

Genres are defined as 'staged social processes' with particular social roles and functions in society that are goal-oriented, institutionalized forms of discourse (Martin and Rose 2003, 2005). Genres in SFL theory are used to refer to different types of texts, which are created to interact with other people in social contexts by using different social functions. These social functions of language are defined as metafunctions and are used to make *ideational, interpersonal* and *textual* meanings in texts. In brief, within the academic context/texts, ideational meanings (field) are created when technical and specialized discipline areas or discourses are built. Interpersonal meanings (tenor) are constructed in distanced and objectified ways to build relationships between the writer and the reader, as some kind of 'social reality' is constructed. Textual meanings (mode) are used to pack up information and refer to the resources used for the organization of abstract texts (Martin and Rose 2003, 2008; Eggins 2004).

The strata and metafunctions are mapped on to each other in SFL. This mapping is presented in Figure 34.1.

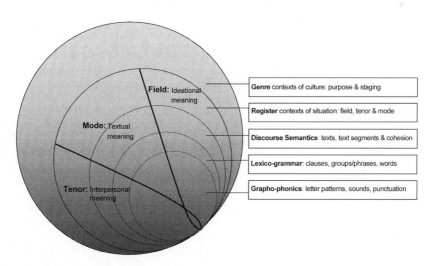

Figure 34.1 Stratification and metafunction in SFL.
Source: www.europa-pages.com

Table 34.1 The 3 × 3 matrix (three metafunctions x three strata)

	1 Genre (at level of whole text)	2 Discourse (across clauses)	3 Grammar and expression (within clause)
A Ideational meanings	▦ Does the text include information which is relevant to the topic and purpose? ▦ Do the Beginning, Middle and End stages of the text achieve the purpose? ▦ Are tables, diagrams, examples and quotes combined with verbal text in logical relationships (e.g. to extend, report, specify or qualify points).	▦ Is field or subject knowledge demonstrated through classifications and generalizations of things and activities (e.g. as a type or part of something)? ▦ Is the information related in logical relationships (e.g. time, cause, consequence, comparison)?	▦ Are activities and things described and classified by expanding noun groups? ▦ Does the text feature technical and formal vocabulary appropriate to the field? ▦ Is explaining and reasoning carried out mainly within the clause (i.e. through nouns, verbs and adverbials)? ▦ Does spelling follow academic conventions?
B Interpersonal meanings	▦ Is the text organized rhetorically to orient reader to a particular position on issue or data (e.g. by accumulating evaluations across the text; by reinforcing thesis within individual arguments)? ▦ Does the text show a critical perspective?	▦ Does the text evaluate phenomena according to institutional rather than personal criteria (e.g. value, benefit, relevance, validity, significance)? ▦ Are assessments and evaluations expressed indirectly? ▦ Are resources of grading used to control the intensity and focus of evaluations? ▦ Does the voice of the student writer control the argument? ▦ Are authoritative sources used to provide evidence? ▦ Are expanding and contracting resources used to control development of arguments and introduce alternate perspectives (e.g. modality, attribution and concession)?	▦ Does clause structure follow recognizable and appropriate patterns of English? ▦ Are subjects and verbs consistent in terms of number? ▦ Are tense and voice choices appropriate and consistent? ▦ Are first- and third-person pronouns used appropriately? ▦ Is grading infused in lexical items rather than expressed as isolated adverbials? ▦ Are sources referenced according to discipline specifications (e.g. MLA)? ▦ Is interpersonal metaphor used to express modality (e.g. probability, obligation)?
C Textual meanings	▦ Do layers of preview and review elements across text predict the information to come and consolidate points made (e.g. Outline, Summary)? ▦ Do global headings, layout conventions and internal conjunctions scaffold generic stages (e.g. in conclusion)?	▦ Are topic sentences used to predict information in paragraphs? ▦ Do choices of given and new information create a logical flow of information across paragraphs? ▦ Are entities tracked through appropriate cohesive resources (e.g. referencing, substitution, repetition and ellipsis)? ▦ Does the text shunt between 'packaged' abstract entity focus in topic sentence and more 'unpacked' concrete activity focus within paragraphs?	▦ Are sentence and clause Themes used to signal topic focus and shifts in meanings? ▦ Is nominalization used to rework processes, qualities and logical relations as abstract things? ▦ Are articles used appropriately? ▦ Does punctuation assist information structure?

In this paper we use the SLF framework in developing our analytical tools for examining student texts. These tools are discussed below.

Analysing the data

The article reviews collected for this study were analysed for their language by using a 3×3 matrix (Humphrey *et al.* 2010). The 3×3 matrix used is based on a systemic functional understanding of language, and maps three levels of strata (genre; discourse; grammar and expression) on the three metafunctions (ideational, interpersonal and textual), discussed in an earlier section. The complete matrix is presented in Table 34.1.

The 3×3 matrix is set up as a set of questions that help identify how and what linguistic resources are used to construct ideational, interpersonal and textual meaning in these texts across the three strata (genre, discourse and grammar). The three strata were conflated within each metafunction for the purposes of this study. By adopting the 3×3 matrix for the purposes of this study, we were able to carry out a detailed linguistic analysis of the students' texts. The following section presents the results of the analysis.

Construing meaning in World Englishes

This section presents the results of the linguistic analysis of the texts written by the three participants chosen for this study. The analyses showed what linguistic resources Niloo, Ashwini and Yasmina used to construct ideational, interpersonal and textual meanings in their texts.

Linguistic resources in Niloo's texts

Niloo, an Australian student of Sri Lankan heritage, received her formative education in Sri Lanka and migrated to Australia about three years ago. In Niloo's essay, ideational meanings at the genre level were constructed through clear functional stages (summary and critical evaluation) to answer the task critically. A range of linguistic resources at the discourse level was used to generalize and classify the field, and points were related logically by addition, extension, exemplification, contrast, cause and time. Examples of these are shown in Table 34.2.

At the grammar and expression level, formal and specialized vocabulary strings and expanded noun groups were chosen as linguistic resources to build discipline-specific field knowledge. Examples of specialized vocabulary within expanded noun groups include 'the lack of student motivation', '29 socially underprivileged Tamil students' and 'grammatical product-based learning indicative of accommodation of the desire for

Table 34.2 Building field and logical relationships: Niloo

Expressions generalizing field	Logical relationships
pedagogical resistance social and linguistic backgrounds oral component in the examination	*exemplification:* in the form of *cause:* [t]herefore, are indicative of *contrast:* while *time:* at the end of the course, before the final examination

587

social mobility'. Recognizable spelling also contributed to the construction of ideational meanings.

Interpersonal meanings at the level of genre created a relatively personal relationship with the reader. Although academic texts usually adopt objectified ways of creating meaning, Niloo's subjective language constructed a convincing and critical evaluation of the article because of her use of authoritative evidence. Examples of this are illustrated in Box 34.1

Box 34.1 Resources used to provide a critical and convincing answer to the task: Niloo

Resources used to introduce a critical perspective

I question [the author]'s credentials and evidential data to pursue such a psychoanalytic argument. Having gone through a compulsory English programme in a Lankan university myself, I argue that 'glosses' is a common phenomenon. Therefore, to link these to unconscious forms of resistance is far fetched. I think a control study of similar glosses in texts used for other subjects might give us more insight to this question.

Niloo's use of evaluative resources on the discourse level contributed to the construction of persuasion. Examples of academically valued ways of assessment (e.g. benefit, relevance, significance, as well as expanding (attribution, modality) and contracting devices (denying, confronting) were widely applied. Excerpts to show examples of these are included in Box 34.2.

Box 34.2 Control of linguistic resources to develop critical stance: Niloo

Resources to develop critical stance

There are some fundamental flaws in his argument. ***The clear message by the students*** that mastery of English is sought primarily for passing the examination, ***is not emphasized***. He also ***overlooks*** the lack of oral component in the examination, which ***if present may have had*** a different response from students. Including a process-based component in the examination ***may have been*** a worthwhile control in this research.

At the grammar and expression level, sentence structure, tense and voice choice, subject/verb agreement and referencing conventions were also used to build the academic status of the writer.

In terms of *textual* meanings, Niloo's text demonstrated an ability to organize the text and signpost meanings. For example, the choices of Themes such as 'The paper examines ... ', '[*The author*] claims ... ', '[*The author*] hypothesizes ... ', 'The analysis finds ... ' and '[*The author*] concludes ... ' keep the focus on the research activity. The construction of a well-organized text on the discourse level was also demonstrated by the use of various cohesive devices, such as topic sentences, Themes, referencing, repetition and shunting to create logical flow throughout the text, as indicated by Box 34.3.

Box 34.3 Cohesive resources: Niloo

A range of cohesive resources/Shunting/Themes

This paper examines how a Sri Lankan Tamil General Purpose English class resists and accommodates **an alien culture, depicted by an American core text** ... **They categorically state** that they enjoyed learning about **American culture. [The author]** concludes that **the students' conscious statements** belie **their** unconscious resistance to **this foreign culture**.

At the level of expression, Niloo used metaphorical expressions of processes and evaluations, such as nominalization, to package information and reasoning through verbal groups. One example of this is given in Box 34.4.

Box 34.4 The use of metaphorical expressions, nominalization and Themes: Niloo

Metaphorical expressions/Nominalization

The lack of student **motivation** is due to an **alien culture** imposed on the students which **result in** student **resistance**.

Therefore, despite a personal focus, Niloo's use of linguistic resources to build technical and abstract meanings at each stratum resulted in the construction of an academically valued genre-specific text.

Linguistic resources in Ashwini's text

Ashwini, a Singaporean student (of Indian origin), was a first-semester student in the programme and had recently arrived from Singapore. At the level of genre, clear functional stages were used to answer the task critically in an objectified way in Ashwini's text. She also demonstrated knowledge of the specialized field through generalizations and built logical relationships (e.g. addition, extension, contrast) throughout the paper. Examples for generalizing the field naming participants, activities and qualities and linguistic resources to create logical relationships in this student's text are shown in Table 34.3. Furthermore, at the grammar and expression level, specialized field knowledge was built by formal and specialized vocabulary, and expanded noun groups, for example:

Table 34.3 Building field and logical relationships (experiential meanings): Ashwini

Expressions generalizing field	Logical relationships
ideological domination	*addition:* also
an empirical study	*extension:* [h]is other findings
the sociopolitics of the language…	*contrast:* although, and yet

'22 Sri Lankan tertiary Tamil students', '[*The author*]'s (1989) definition of ideological domination' and 'the complex range of attitudes of minority students'.

Interpersonal meanings valued in academic writing at the genre level were created by introducing a critical perspective, which means that Ashwini provided an objectified and convincing answer to the task. Examples of these resources can be seen in Box 34.5.

Box 34.5 Resources used to provide a critical and convincing answer to the task: Ashwini

However, this explanation seems tenuous as the threats to cultural alienation are not obvious as the students themselves claim that they enjoy learning about the American culture.

At the level of discourse, regarding the student's control of resources to develop critical stance, there were examples of impersonal and indirect evaluative resources; for instance, assessment of benefit, relevance and significance as well as expanding (attribution and modality) and contracting (denying, confronting) resources as shown in both Box 34.5 and Box 34.6.

Box 34.6 Control of linguistic resources to develop critical stance: Ashwini

Resources to develop critical stance

Undoubtedly, English is seen as a **useful** language that the students **need** to learn and master. Their falling attendance **may simply be due to the fact that** they are not being taught the grammar rules that are **necessary** for them to pass the examinations.

At the expression level, linguistic choices to establish the authority of the text were exemplified by her choice of tense and voice, subject–verb agreement and discipline-specific referencing strategies. Thus, it has been shown that this student's construction of interpersonal meanings was demonstrated by the use of linguistic resources mainly on the discourse and expression levels.

To build textual meanings at the genre level, Themes to signpost and predict stages as well as layers of preview and review were used to organize the text into a coherent piece of academic writing. Some examples of this are: '[*The author*]'s study examines ... ', '[*The author*] examines ... ', '[*The author*] calls for ... ', 'In [*the author*]'s study, he finds ... ', 'His other findings reveal ... ', 'His explanation ... ', 'However, this explanation ... ' and 'Although [*the author*]'s study aims to ... '. At the discourse level, *textual* resources to predict information were found, as Ashwini used a range of cohesive devices such as Theme-as-topic, repetition, referencing and conjunction, as shown in Box 34.7.

Box 34.7 Cohesive resources: Ashwini

Cohesive resources/<u>Themes-as-topic</u>

<u>The opposition</u> to English is seen in **the textbook glosses,** falling attendance and **their resistance** to using English in the classroom.

At the level of grammar and expression, nominalization was one linguistic resource chosen to signal topic focus, examples of which are shown in Box 34.8.

Box 34.8 Nominalization and Themes: Ashwini

Nominalization

Their reasons for learning English are mainly practical as the majority state **educational need** as their first **preference** and suggest more pragmatic reasons in open-ended questions.

All in all, it can be seen that Ashwini used more linguistic resources to build academically valued abstract meanings at the discourse and expression levels than at the genre level to construct an academic text.

Linguistic resources in Yasmina's texts

Yasmina, an Australian citizen of Indian origin, had received her formative education in India before coming to Australia to attend college in 2004. *Specialized field knowledge* at the genre level was constructed in Yasmina's text by clearly marking the stages of summary and critical evaluation. The information provided was easily identified in terms of staging and was relevant to the purpose of the assignment. At the discourse level, specialized field knowledge was built by the use of various linguistic resources, such as generalized vocabulary and logical relationships (addition, cause, comparison, contrast, time, etc.) throughout the text. Some examples of these are included in Table 34.4.

Table 34.4 Building field and logical relationships: Yasmina

Expressions generalizing field	Logical relationships
a longitudinal study	*addition:* [a]dditionally
difference in teaching styles a clash of pedagogical styles and expectations	*cause:* it is because of, the reason for *contrast:* rather than *time:* as the year progressed

At the grammar and expression level, formal and specialized vocabulary strings and the use of expanded noun groups contributed to the construction of technical, discipline-specific meanings. Examples include 'their retaliation in reaction to English language learning', 'Tamil students from Sri Lanka of underprivileged personal backgrounds' and 'a clash of cultural demands in the need for education'.

Interpersonal resources at the level of genre were used in a distanced and objectified way resulting in a convincing and critical answer supported by authoritative evidence. Examples of these are indicated in Box 34.9.

Box 34.9 Resources used to provide a critical and convincing answer to the task: Yasmina

Resources used to introduce a critical perspective

While it is important to understand the way in which resistance in the classroom occurs to language acquisition as a response to cultural threat, perhaps more attention needs to be given towards the notion of English itself.

At the discourse level, the development of critical stance was realized by evaluative examples of attribution, assessment of benefit/relevance, grading, interplay of student voice with authoritative evidence, expanding (attribution, modality) and contracting (denying, confronting) devices, which were widely applied throughout the whole text. Excerpts from the text containing examples of these are shown in Box 34.10.

Box 34.10 Control of linguistic resources to develop critical stance: Yasmina

Resources to develop critical stance

Although he outlines the difference in teaching styles and classroom expectation between his pedagogy and the Tamil pedagogy, there are a few things that ***need to be questioned*** in this study. … By pushing a pedagogical style onto students ***in claim of*** being ***more beneficial*** or ***more appropriate***, it is, ***undoubtedly, placing*** one teaching style ***over*** another ***in value.***

At the grammar and expression level, Yasmina's choices of tense and voice, subject–verb agreement and referencing strategies also contributed to convincing the reader.

To build *textual* meanings on the level of genre, layers of previewing and reviewing were widely used to predict and scaffold stages, examples of which include '[*The author*] attempts to understand … ', '[*The author*] highlights the contrast … ', '[*The author*] suggests … ', 'The predominant suggestion by [*the author*] … ', 'Although [*the author*] spends time … ' and 'The chapter discussed above provides … '. At the discourse level, Yasmina's use of cohesive devices (referencing, repetition, conjunction and shunting) contributed to creating logical flow throughout the text. Some examples of these are included in Box 34.11.

Box 34.11 Cohesive resources: Yasmina

A range of cohesive resources/Shunting/Themes (New)

He aims to analyse … the way in which students react in a way of tackling **a cultural struggle and threat**. Providing students from war-torn, poor backgrounds with **these textbooks** containing images and stories of people from **a culture that can in no way be related to their own**.

At the expression level, metaphorical expressions of processes and evaluations, such as nominalization to package information, reasoning through verbal groups, and topical and marked Themes to signal topic focus, were widely applied in Yasmina's assignment, as shown in Box 34.12.

Box 34.12 The use of metaphorical expressions, nominalization and Themes: Yasmina

Metaphorical expressions/Nominalization/Themes

Most students … did not see English as a language that threatened **their** own culture, and some even believed that it **would provide them with the tools** required **to better their own society** … the reason for student **reaction** … was because of … the complete **lack** of cultural empathy in the material.

The analysis provided above shows that abstract and academically valued meanings were constructed in Yasmina's assignment by using a wide range of linguistic resources across all strata.

In search of patterns

The results of the analysis presented above showed some emerging patterns: the three participants used a number of similar linguistic resources to construct the types of meaning required in the task. In fact, the participants showed more similarities in creating their texts than differences. This is understandable because we had analysed written texts that were written for the same (specific) purpose. Article reviews are a specific genre, and, as discussed earlier, genres tend to share a pool of resources that are used in their construction. While it is possible that people speaking certain varieties of World Englishes use different language resources to create the same text type, the present study did not find any such differences. Had we found such evidence in the present study (and the three participants had used different linguistic resources to create the same text types), there would have been a strong argument to categorize them as different varieties of English – since those varieties would have shown different ways of constructing and representing meaning. However, this was not the case in the present study and for the most part the three participants used similar linguistic resources to create the types of meanings expected in an article review. Thus, in the case of the present study, the three participants – even though they represent three different national, cultural and linguistic backgrounds – can be said to be users of the same variety of English (which may or may not be similar to inner, expanding or other outer circle varieties). In interpreting the results of this study, it does need to be considered that, had the three participants written different types of texts (say, an article review, a research proposal and an exposition), there would have been many more differences in the linguistic resources that they used than similarities. But, these differences would most likely have been a result of the variation in genres rather than in their varieties. Furthermore, given that all three of the participants are students at an Australian university, it is possible that their exposure to the educational system in Australia has influenced their linguistic choices. We need comparable texts from people living in the outer circle countries to examine the similarities/differences in the ways that these text types are produced locally.

While Niloo, Ashwini and Yasmina used a number of similar linguistic resources to create metafunctions across all strata of language, there were a few observable differences in the texts written by the three participants. However, based on the current data, we did not find any strong patterns of differences in their writing. It is possible that the differences observed and discussed below were individual differences and not patterned difference between varieties. To make any claim that the differences are meaningful in terms of identifying varieties of World Englishes, we would need additional data and stronger patterns. Some of the differences observed are discussed below.

When constructing ideational meanings at the discourse level, Ashwini chose to use a narrow range of linguistic resources: addition, extension and contrast were her three choices to relate points logically. In comparison, the other two participants adopted a larger range of linguistic resources to create similar meanings. There were also a few differences in the linguistic choices made to construct interpersonal meanings at the genre level in each text. While Ashwini's and Yasmina's arguments were presented in a distanced and impersonal way, Niloo chose to present her answer in a personal rather than objective manner supported by authoritative evidence. While all the three participants used evaluative resources at the level of discourse to persuade the reader, one difference in their construction was identified once again in Niloo's assignment. While the other two students assessed the original article according to institutional rather than personal criteria along with providing authoritative evidence, some direct value judgements appeared in Niloo's text: for instance, 'there *are* some fundamental flaws' or 'the clear message *is*'. While the differences between Niloo and the other two participants are noteworthy, it needs to be mentioned that Niloo was from Sri Lanka, which was the context in which the study being reviewed was set. Thus, Niloo's choice of adopting a personal tone might be a result of her first-hand understanding of the context being shared – something that the other two participants did not have (and which reflected in their choice of a more objective and distanced stance).

Putting it all together

The results of the linguistic analysis show that these students created meanings using mostly similar linguistic resources when reviewing the same text. The differences between the writers were mostly a result of individual differences and an awareness of the context of the article being reviewed. These findings are consistent with an understanding of genre in that genres are socially determined and shaped by their context and purpose. These findings are also important because they remind us of some important early discussions on language use and users (Halliday *et al.* 1964).

In their 1964 book *Linguistic Sciences and Language Teaching*, Halliday, McIntosh and Strevens outline the linguistic basis for why and how language differs along the dimensions of language use and language users. They point out that, on the one hand language is shaped by the use that it is put to, and on the other hand it carries markers that identify the speakers. This is a key distinction that supports the findings of this study: the three users of English used similar linguistic resources to create a particular type of text in a particular setting, and used different linguistic resources to project their identity and perspective.

An understanding of the linguistic dimension of uses and users has been instrumental in the development of World Englishes. Literature on World Englishes has traditionally focused on the users and looked at linguistic features and structures that can be used to identify them. In doing this, the use of country-based naming practices (critiqued earlier) has worked well for it – the nation-state and the language (structural features) both are used to focus on the 'users' and to mark their identity as unique and different from users of other country-Englishes. Without repeating the problems associated with using such naming practices, the result of such a focus on the users has been a neglect of the 'uses' of English within a World Englishes paradigm. The results of the brief study presented in this paper show that focusing on the 'uses' of English is an equally useful way of studying World Englishes.

A discussion of language uses and users relates closely to some new and interesting discussions of World Englishes in the context of intercultural communication as well. Specifically, the users–uses complementarity in language discussed here corroborates Kirkpatrick's (2006) 'identity–communication continuum'. In describing this model, Kirkpatrick (2007: 11) writes,

> I call one end of the continuum 'communication' because being intelligible and getting your meaning across is the most important aspect of the communicative function. More standard or educated varieties are likely to be better suited for communication. Broad, informal varieties or job- and class-specific registers are likely to be better suited for signifying identity.

This description of 'communication' and 'identity' is compatible with the uses–users continuum: the 'uses' are socially constructed ways of making meaning in specific contexts

595

so that people from different backgrounds can 'communicate' efficiently and effectively; and 'users' mark their personal traits by using 'identity' features. Kirkpatrick further clarifies that the 'communication' function requires a stable common language because

> the more people who are involved and the greater the social distance between them, the greater the intelligibility function of their speech will be in any act of communication ... If they use these [identity] varieties with people outside their group, they can be impossible to understand.
>
> (Kirkpatrick 2007: 11–12)

This discussion of the differences in language and the possible causes behind them is very similar to discussion of genre in SLF. As discussed earlier, genres are 'staged social processes' with particular social roles and functions in society that are goal-oriented, institutionalized forms of discourse (Martin and Rose 2003, 2005). As such, there is a move within World Englishes literature that is starting to consider the uses of language and the linguistic features associated with it as the subject of study.

Although the 'uses' dimension of Englishes has not been researched sufficiently from a World Englishes perspective, educational linguists focusing on the 'uses' of language have shown how an understanding of genres and their linguistic features is important to educational contexts (see, for example, Christie 1992, 1997; Cope and Kalantzis 1993; Martin 1993, 2001; Feez 1998; Macken-Horarik 2002). Critical applied linguists and educational linguists working with genre-based pedagogy have documented that students who come from non-privileged socioeconomic and linguistic backgrounds are not always able to cope with the language needs posed to them in the context of education. They have shown that students from these contexts need to be taught explicitly the social functions, purposes and linguistic features of different discipline-specific genres. They point out that the skills required to produce written academic texts – the genres of power and access – are not equally available to students from minority, immigrant or marginalized groups. However, the aim of genre pedagogy is not simply to teach students genres in an unquestioning manner as in transmission pedagogies, but to also teach them the skills to critically deconstruct texts to avoid creating another assimilationist model of education. We want to clarify here that we do *not* support a prescriptive approach to language teaching/learning. We understand that writers can indeed learn to and be accepted for using alternative ways of making meaning. However, this acceptance comes through a process of learning in which the novice writers first gain access to the community of practice that they want to become members of before posing challenges to it.

The work done by genre pedagogues (Martin and Rose 2008) in Australia is one way of helping students gain access to genres of power. However, there are other options available as well and these need to be considered in order to help students from diverse backgrounds to gain voice in academic contexts. An understanding of how genres work in education and the pedagogical implications of such an understanding of language on education in the context of World Englishes has yet to be fully explored. A discussion of this is beyond the scope of this paper, but this is a debate that does need to take place in a World Englishes context.

Concluding remarks

This paper first problematized two aspects of current World Englishes research: naming practices and the focus on structural (a-semantic) descriptions of World Englishes. It then presents one way in which linguists working on World Englishes can examine ways in which people using different varieties of English construe meaning. The findings of the present study and the similarities in ways in which the three participants created their texts suggest that they are users of the same variety of (World?) English. This is an important finding because it shows how traditional work in World Englishes that uses nation-state based naming systems and focuses on structural variations may have come to a different conclusion. For a start, the three participants would have been labelled as users of Sri Lankan (Niloo), Singaporean (Ashwini) and Indian (Yasmina) Englishes – not of the same English. Furthermore, the texts might have been shown to be different because of minor surface-level morphological and/or syntactic variations. By not focusing on how the texts create meanings in similar ways, the larger function of language – that is to construct and represent meaning – would have been lost. This paper shows the importance of understanding how meanings are construed in World Englishes.

In studying World Englishes from an SFL perspective, it is important to keep the focus on how and what linguistic resources are used to construct and represent specific meanings in context. It is important that focus be kept on language as a meaning making resource and not just as a marker that identifies the country/region that the users of this language belong to. While *user* features are important to consider, the identities of the people using various World Englishes are one aspect of a study of language variation. The *uses* of language significantly contribute to an understanding of language and need to be studied within a World Englishes framework. Studies of World Englishes that focus on meaning and reflect how English functions in different contexts are essential if World Englishes is to develop an appliable[1] dimension and contribute to theorization of language.

Note

1 See Mahboob and Knight (2010) for a detailed introduction to the notion of 'appliable linguistics'.

Suggestions for further reading

Bhatia, V.K. (2003) 'The power and politics of genre', *World Englishes*, 16 (3): 359–71.
Burns, A. and Coffin, C. (eds) (2001) *Analysing English in a Global Context: A Reader*, London: Routledge. (This book successfully brings together systemic-functional and critical applied linguistic theories in discussing the rapid spread of English across the globe. It moves beyond the debate about the statuses of different varieties of Englishes and emphasizes the importance of linguistically informed analyses for describing linguistic variation.)
Humphrey, S., Martin, J., Dreyfus, S. and Mahboob, A. (2010) 'The 3 x 3: setting up a linguistic toolbox for teaching and assessing academic writing', in A. Mahboob and N. Knight (eds) *Appliable Linguistics: Texts, Contexts, and Meanings*, London: Continuum.
Jones, J. (2004) 'Learning to write in the disciplines: the application of systemic functional linguistic theory to the teaching and research of student writing', in L. Ravelli and R.A. Ellis (eds) *Analysing Academic Writing: Contextualised Frameworks*, London: Continuum, pp. 254–73).

References

Christie, F. (1992) 'Literacy in Australia', *ARAL* 12: 142–55.

——(1997) 'Curriculum macrogenres as forms of initiation into a culture', in F. Christie and J.R. Martin (eds) *Genre and Institutions: Social Processes in the Workplace and School*, London: Cassell, pp. 134–60.

Cope, B. and Kalantzis, M. (eds) (1993) *The Powers of Literacy: A Genre Approach to Teaching Writing*, London: Falmer.

Eggins, S. (2004) *An Introduction to Systemic Functional Linguistics*, London: Continuum.

Feez, S. (1998) *Text-based Syllabus Design*, Sydney: NCELTR.

Halliday, M.A.K., McIntosh, A. and Strevens, P. (1964) *Linguistic Sciences and Language Teaching*, Bloomington: Indiana University Press.

Humphrey, S., Martin, J., Dreyfus, S. and Mahboob, A. (2010) 'The 3 x 3: setting up a linguistic toolbox for teaching and assessing academic writing', in A. Mahboob and N. Knight (eds) *Appliable Linguistics: Texts, Contexts, and Meanings*, London: Continuum.

Kachru, B. (1983) *The Indianization of English: The English Language in India*, New Delhi: Oxford University Press.

——(1992) *The Other Tongue* (2nd edition), Urbana: University of Illinois Press.

Kandiah, T. (1998) 'Epiphanies of the deathless native users' manifold *avatars*: a postcolonial perspective on the native-speaker', in R. Singh (ed.) *The Native Speaker: Multilingual Perspectives*, New Delhi: Sage, pp. 79–110.

Kirkpatrick, A. (2006) 'Oral communication and intelligibility among ASEAN speakers of English', in J. Foley (ed.) *New Dimensions in the Teaching of Oral Communication* (Regional Language Centre Anthology Series No. 47), Singapore: SEAMEO Regional Language Centre, pp. 33–52.

——(2007) *World Englishes: Implications for International Communication and English Language Teaching*, Cambridge: Cambridge University Press.

Kortmann, B. and Schneider, E. (2004) *A Handbook of Varieties of English*, Berlin: Mouton de Gruyter.

Krishnaswamy, N., and Burde, A. (1998) *The Politics of Indians' English: Linguistic Colonialism and the Expanding English Empire*, Delhi: Oxford University Press.

Lavandera, B.R. (1978) 'Where does the sociolinguistic variable stop?' *Language in Society*, 7 (2): 171–82.

Macken-Horarik, M. (2002) 'Something to shoot for: a systemic functional approach to teaching genre in secondary school science', in A.M. Johns (ed.) *Genre in the Classroom*, Mahwah, NJ: Erlbaum, pp. 21–46.

Mahboob, A. (2009) 'English as an Islamic language', *World Englishes*, 28 (2): 175–89.

Mahboob, A. and Knight, N. (2010) *Appliable Linguistics: Texts, Contexts, and Meanings*, London: Continuum.

Martin, J.R. (1993) 'Genre and literacy – modeling context in educational linguistics', *Annual Review of Applied Linguistics*, 13: 141–72.

——(2001) 'Giving the game away: explicitness, diversity and genre-based literacy in Australia', in R. de Cilla, H. Krumm and R. Wodak (eds) *Loss of Communication in the Information Age*, Vienna: Verlag der Osterreichischen Akademie der Wissenschaften, pp. 155–74.

Martin, J.R. and Rose, D. (2003) *Working with Discourse: Meaning beyond the Clause*, London: Continuum.

——(2005) 'Designing literacy pedagogy: scaffolding asymmetries', in R. Hasan, C.M.I.M. Matthiessen and J. Webster (eds) *Continuing Discourse on Language*, London: Equinox, pp. 251–80.

——(2008) *Genre Relations: Mapping Culture*, London: Equinox.

Meshtrie, R. and Bhatt, R. (2008) *World Englishes: The Study of New Linguistic Varieties*, Cambridge: Cambridge University Press.

Pennycook, A. (2002) 'Turning English inside out', *Indian Journal of Applied Linguistics*, 28 (2): 25–43.

Thompson, G. and Collins, H. (interviewers) (2001) 'Interview with M.A.K. Halliday, Cardiff, July 1998', *D.E.L.T.A.*, 17 (1): 131–53.

35

Which test of which English and why?

Brian Tomlinson

Introduction

All over the world, learners of English are being tested on a variety of English they do not and never will speak. They are being tested on British English or American English and not on the Singapore English or Brazilian English or the International English that they speak. Based on my experience in over sixty countries, I would say that many of these learners are being tested because administrators, teachers and parents take it for granted that testing is useful and necessary. In many cases the learners are gaining very little from a negative experience and the testers are gaining little more than useful illusions. Many teachers argue that testing is imposed on learners by testers because it benefits the testers more than it does the learners. This view has been captured by British poets. For example, Michael Rosen's 'The Ballad of Roger Ball' (Rosen 2007) in which 'Roger was a lefty' who 'taught slow learners' but one day, when 'resting', saw the future, 'It said: Testing.' Roger uses 'marking, grading, figures, tables, checking, assessing, goals, labels', closes two schools, fires 14 teachers and ends up as an Education Consultant 'as ever useful to the system'. And Brian Patten ends his poem 'The Minister for Exams' (Patten 1996):

Q1. How large is a child's imagination?
Q2. How shallow is the soul of the Minister for Exams?

These are probably emotive reactions based on personal experience and anecdotal evidence. We certainly need to look for the positives in testing, but I am not alone as an academic in claiming that testing can be an unnecessarily painful experience for the learners, and that it can be imposed on them primarily to achieve institutional and political goals. McNamara (2000) for example, whilst acknowledging that testing is becoming more humanistic, describes the suffering that students can go through during oral tests, and Chiba and Morikwa (2006: 289) claim that such 'inhumane' tests still persist. Bachman (1990: 279) claims that tests are 'virtually always intended to serve the needs of an educational system or of society at large' and Spolsky (1995: 1) asserts that testing 'has always been exploited as a method of control and power – as a way to select, to motivate, to punish'. You could certainly apply Spolsky's argument to a situation in which L2 learners from all over the world are judged and punished for their inability to be British or American.

All over the world teachers are administering tests which they have devised in imitation of those discrete point test types which they are familiar with from EFL examinations (e.g. multiple-choice questions, filling in the blanks, sentence transformation, true/false questions, etc.). These tests will almost certainly be inappropriate as classroom tests, will put unnecessary pressure on the learners and will reveal very little useful information to the learners and the teachers. Even learners who are not being tested will suffer washback effects from these tests. They will be spending precious learning time practising doing test-type activities rather than engaging in those many valuable activities which do not correspond to typical test tasks. For a discussion of teacher assessment of learners see Leung (2005), and for discussion of the washback effects of testing see Baker (1989), Hughes (1989) and Bachman (1990). Green (2007) gives a full and systematic account of the washback effect of a particular examination (the International English Language Testing System [IELTS] test of academic or general vocational skills) and, for example, reveals that many essential academic skills are not typically taught in IELTS preparation classes because they are not tested in IELTS.

Many learners are not only being tested on varieties of English which are irrelevant to their present or future, but they are also being tested in ways which have little match with how they need or want to use English. Of course, there will be exceptional classrooms in which useful tests are being enjoyed. As Underhill (1987: 6) says, 'we can make a test challenging, instructive and even an enjoyable experience'. These will be tests based on thoughtful answers to such questions as, 'Why, what, when and how should we test?'

In this chapter I aim to provide answers to the why, what, when and how questions above, based on my fifty years of experience around the world as a test taker, a test setter, an examination setter and an examination marker. I refer to expert opinion on testing but ultimately the views expressed are my own.

Why test?

I have been to countries where L2 learners are tested in the classroom every week and I have worked in countries in which I have had to prepare students for formal examinations every six weeks. Typical justifications for so much testing include:

'We need to keep a record of progress.'
'The parents want to know how their children are doing.'
'The students won't work if you don't test them.'
'We need to make sure that the teachers keep to the syllabus.'
'We need to maintain standards.'

While some of these are understandable reasons in the real world in which learners are learning English, they do not really justify taking up so much learning time with testing, and they do not help teachers to prepare tests which could really help their learners to learn.

Reasons for testing

Accountability

Teachers are accountable to their superiors, who in turn are responsible to their super-iors. The easiest way of demonstrating to your superiors that you are doing your job properly is to publish data. And the easiest way of obtaining such data if you are a teacher or a principal is to submit the learners you are responsible for to frequent tests. If you want to demonstrate how successful you have been, it helps if the classroom tests are easy enough for the learners to score high marks, and if the learners are only entered for those formal examinations which they are likely to pass. On the other hand, you might want to demonstrate how professional your standards are by making sure that a predetermined number of learners fail your tests. A prestigious university required me to fail 10 per cent of my students even though they had satisfied the criteria of a criterion-referenced examination. Many institutions fail learners who communicated effectively, but did not conform to a native-speaker standard variety of English. They were failed in order to 'uphold standards'. For a convincing refutation of the argument that not conforming to native-speaker norms results in reduced standards, see Kirkpatrick (2006).

Another aspect of accountability is the use of tests by governments and other authorities to make selections. Kunnan (2005) reports on various tests with this political objective, for example the New Zealand government's use of the IELTS test as part of the selection procedure for immigrants, and the use of standardized tests of English competence in the USA. The results of such tests include the development of test pre-paration industries and teachers spending disproportionate amounts of classroom time training their students to pass the tests (e.g. 45 hours for teachers preparing students for the Californian High School Exit Examination). And, of course, all such tests assume that L2 learners should be assessed against native-speaker norms. This can result in feelings of inferiority and alienation amongst the less successful, and frustration among the successful who are striving to achieve an impossible goal.

We cannot dismiss accountability as a reason for testing. Teachers, administrators and politicians are human beings who live in a world where their future could depend on the success and failure of their learners. But we should make sure that accountability does not become the prime test objective and that it does not determine the frequency, content and methodology of classroom tests.

Placement

Many institutions test students on entry to determine their level. They do so in order to place them in the class most likely to offer them a successful learning experience. This is a commendable objective as it theoretically helps the learners to receive appropriate tuition and it helps the administrators to select suitable textbooks for each level. However, place-ment tests usually need to be administered and marked quickly and reliably and many institutions therefore resort to objective tests of linguistic knowledge. Obviously a class of students who have obtained 55–60 per cent on such a test are fairly homogeneous in terms of linguistic knowledge; but they are likely to be heterogeneous in terms of needs, wants, communicative competence and preferred learning styles. And one week later, they are unlikely to be homogeneous in terms of linguistic knowledge either.

Ideally a placement test should provide information about:

1 what the students can do in English;
2 what the students cannot do in English;
3 what the students need to do in English;
4 what the students want to do in English;
5 what varieties of English the students use;
6 what varieties of English the students want/need to be able to use;
7 what pedagogical approach the students prefer;
8 who they want to teach them;
9 who they want to learn with.

This information could be obtained through a series of capability tests, questionnaires and interviews, but by the time the information had been collected and analysed the course would probably be over. One quick, valid and reasonably reliable way of obtaining the information is to:

1   collect all the new students in a large room;
2   ask the students to go to one end of the room if they think their English is already effective, to the other end of the room if they think it is not yet effective and to stand in the middle if they think their English is in between effective and ineffective;
3   give the students in groups a short discussion task appropriate to the communicative level of their chosen area;
4   give the students an opportunity to move areas if they find the task too easy or difficult or if they think their fellow group members are at a different level to themselves;
5   give the students a short written task appropriate to the communicative level of their chosen area;
6   encourage the students to show each other their texts;
7   give the students an opportunity to move areas if they find the task too easy or difficult, or if they think the other students are at a different level to themselves;
8   show the students a sample of materials for the level they have opted for;
9   give the students an opportunity to move areas if they found the materials too easy or difficult, or if they thought they were inappropriate for their needs;
10 give the students descriptions of the classes available at their level – including indications of the teaching style, the varieties of English targeted, the objectives of the class and the type of student tasks;
11 invite the students to sample a class at their level for a day;
12 invite the students to either stay in the same class or to sample another one;
13 at the end of the week ask the students to decide which class to join;
14 in the middle of the course invite the students to either continue in the same class or to move to a different one.

This is a placement procedure I once used in a large UK language school. It was very successful in engendering a positive affect (Tomlinson 1998; Arnold 1999) and very popular with the students, who felt that they were learning English in the most comfortable and appropriate environment. It was, however, not very popular with those teachers who found it difficult to accept having students at different linguistic levels in their classes. The institution eventually returned to placing their students according to the results of a one-off placement test of declarative knowledge.

Predicting suitability

One reason for testing learners is to gain information which can contribute to predictions about the learners' suitability for a particular course or career. Ideally such tests should provide information about the learners' ability to perform the type of tasks typical of the course or career. They should also match the learners' preferred learning or working modes against the target course or career and should provide information about the likelihood of the learners being able to gain sufficiently and quickly enough from tuition and experience to be successful. This is obviously a demanding and time-consuming process, and most institutions and companies rely on established examinations to give them enough information to make decisions. For example, most universities in the UK rely on the IELTS test to give them information about L2 speakers' ability to speak, write, read and listen to English in an academic context. IELTS is recognized as an entrance requirement by British, Australian, New Zealand and Canadian universities and jointly run and assessed by the British Council, IDPEA (International Development Program of Education in Australia) and the University of Cambridge ESOL Examinations. In the USA, academic institutions rely on TOEFL (a test which measures the ability of non-native speakers of English to communicate in English in the college or university classroom) to give them similar information. Of course, students might be nervous and perform untypically when taking one of these tests and it could be that topic familiarity influences their scores and makes the tests unreliable as predictors of typical performance. Some overseas students on my UK MA courses with low IELTS scores have eventually improved enough to do well on their courses, while others with high IELTS scores have struggled on their MA courses. A test, regardless of its accuracy, is not enough by itself. It provides insufficient information to make decisions about selection, about placement or about accomplishment. It needs to be supplemented by observation, by continuous assessment and by performance in the real world.

Ideally a predictive 'test' should be ongoing and should make use of performance on actual tasks during a trial period of the course or career. If this is not possible, then it should consist of a number of simulations of typical integrated skills course or career tasks, rather than discrete skill examination questions.

Passing judgement

Unfortunately, one of the main reasons for testing seems to be so that the teacher, institution or government can pass judgement on the learners, and determine 'who gets what' (Bachman 1990: 5). That is what it must seem like to the millions of learners who are told, 'You make too many grammatical mistakes', 'You don't work hard enough', 'You have failed.' One legitimate function of tests and examinations is to provide information about the abilities of the learner. Inevitably this information will be used by institutions and employers to make decisions about the learners. Ideally, though, the information should be about what the learners can do in relation to what they need or want to do; and this information should be available to learners as

603

feedback, which both encourages and helps them to improve. Regrettably, the means of obtaining this information is often a summative examination. No feedback, other than a grade, is provided to the learner. Even more regrettably, the examination often assumes educated native-speaker proficiency as the target, and judges the learner in relation to how close they approximate to this target. This is justified by proclaiming the need to maintain standards. This might make some sense if the learner hopes to enter a university or company in which their performance will be judged against native-speaker norms, but it makes little sense for secondary school learners in Greece, Peru or Indonesia who are going to be mainly using English with other non-native speakers. What matters for them is not the ability to mimic a native speaker of English, but the ability to communicate effectively. If judgements are going to be made about a learner's ability to use English, the learner should be:

1 tested on tasks which replicate the learners' intended uses of English;
2 tested with topics and texts which are relevant to the learners' experience of life;
3 judged against norms of successful users of the varieties of English they need to use (Prodromou 2003);
4 provided with positive feedback which tells them what they can and cannot do well and which helps them to improve.

Improving teaching

To aid improvement should be the main reason for testing. As teachers, we should want to know how to improve our teaching. One way of doing this should be designing tests which give us feedback on the effectiveness of our teaching. Our main goal as teachers is to help each of our learners to improve, and, if a test reveals that very few learners are progressing, we need to ask ourselves what we could do to improve our 'teaching'. It could be, for example, that we have focused too much on grammatical accuracy and have not given our learners enough experience of language in use. Or it could be that we have focused exclusively on developing fluency. In the first scenario, we might decide to replace a grammar lesson with an extensive reading lesson. In the second, we might decide to replace a speaking lesson with a language awareness lesson in which the learners first of all respond personally to a spoken or written text, and then use it to make discoveries about a salient linguistic feature of the text (Tomlinson 1994, 2007; Bolitho et al. 2003).

Improving learning

Teachers need to help learners to improve how they learn. If a test reveals that learners can define the meaning of a set of words, but cannot understand them in texts or use them for communication, then we must try to help them to achieve the deeper processing (Craik and Lockhart 1972) they need for acquisition. One way would be by advising them to read for pleasure and by providing them with the means to do so.

Objectives for testing

Obviously many of the objectives for testing derive from the reasons for testing, but it is very important for the setters of tests and examinations to articulate their objectives prior to setting their tests. These objectives should then inform the setting and marking of the tests and the feedback of information to the learners and other interested parties. For public examinations, the list of objectives should be available so that decisions can be made about which test is the most appropriate. For classroom tests, the objectives should only be made available to the learners at the feedback stage so as to remove pressure and prevent excessive preparation. In fact, my view is that the learners should not even know they are being tested. This is fair to everybody and ensures typical rather than prepared or anxious performance.

Some valid objectives for testing are to provide:

1   information about the most suitable classes, courses, materials, approaches, etc., for the learners;
2   each learner with valuable learning experiences (Tomlinson 2005);
3   each learner with information about their progress;
4   parents or sponsors with information about the progress of their learner(s);
5   each learner with information about what they can do well;
6   each learner with information about what they cannot yet do well;
7   each learner with encouragement;
8   the teacher with information about what their learners can do well;
9   the teacher with information about what their learners cannot do well;
10 the teacher with information about the problems facing their learners;
11 the teacher with information about the effectiveness of their teaching;
12 institutions and potential employers with information about what applicants can do well.

A grade alone cannot provide enough information to achieve any of the above objectives. Much more detailed information is necessary, such as, for example, a statement of the capabilities for which the learner has met the criteria, or a statement of those capabilities which a learner can now perform more effectively than in a previous test. Another important point is that the information provided by a test is only valuable if the test achieves validity (i.e. it actually does test what it intends to test). For detailed discussion of issues relating to validity see Davies and Elder (2005).

What to test?

It is common practice for teachers to test what has been taught, even though we know that each learner will have learned both less and more than they have been taught. It is also common practice for teachers to test what learners know, and yet it is obvious that knowing, for example, about the form and function of the imperative does not necessarily lead to the ability to use it appropriately and effectively. Learners have their own internal syllabus of needs and wants which is much more powerful than the external syllabus of the institution or the course book. This contributes to an efficient learning process in which the teaching of a linguistic feature or skill which is not perceived as salient or relevant by the learner does not lead to learning, while informal encounters with features and skills which are perceived as salient do lead to both learning and use. This suggests that, instead of testing what has been taught, we should be testing what the learners can do; and we should be testing those capabilities that the learner needs and wants to develop. As Norris (2002: 396) says, 'it has also been argued that complex, integrative, open-ended task-specific tasks are necessary for meeting actual inferential demands (e.g. relevant interpretations about what learners know and can do)'.

Public examinations commonly test each of the four skills separately. They also often test grammar and vocabulary separately. Such examinations can quite easily achieve reliability, and they are popular with teachers because they are easy to prepare for. But are they valid? Do they provide information about how effectively their candidates can actually use English in the real world? Is the best way to find out how effectively somebody can read to get them to read a text without any communicative purpose and then to answer multiple-choice questions on it? Or is for an examiner to interrogate learners about their hobbies the best way of finding out if they can communicate effectively in speech? There are some public examinations, however, which do try to replicate authentic communication, for example the UCLES (University of Cambridge) Certificates in Communicative Skills.

Recently both teachers in the classroom and setters of public examinations have been helped by the Common European Framework of Reference for Language (CEFR). This is actually a syllabus consisting of a number of capabilities which learners can be expected to have mastered by specified levels, but it has been used to inform testers about what to test. For example, the Association of Language Testers in Europe (ALTE) have developed a list of 'can do' statements to act as criteria for testing. Table 35.1 shows the ALTE 'can do' statements for general language.

Public and institutional examinations are beginning to be influenced by these capabilities. For example, in Ireland, the Test of Interactive English (TIE) is an EFL exam developed under the aegis of the Advisory Council for English Language Schools (ACELS). The test is task-based, requiring each candidate to carry out a number of pre-specified tasks prior to taking the test. Assessment is given according to the Council of Europe's CEFR (www.acels.ie/acelstie.htm). And the University of Cambridge, in order to inform their examination syndicate (UCLES) and the Cambridge University Press, are conducting research in their English Profile project to find out what language students typically use at each of the capability attainment levels of the CEFR (www.english profile.org).

Which capabilities?

Tests and examinations of English as an L2 should be testing the candidates' ability to use English rather than just their knowledge of it (e.g. Weir 1990; Underhill 1997; McNamara 2000; Tomlinson 2005). The question then remains as to which abilities should be tested. For classroom tests and ESP examinations, the answer is obviously those abilities which the learners will need when they use English outside the classroom. For example, doctors learning medical English to practise in the UK will need to be able to set native-speaker patients at ease, enquire about symptoms, communicate a diagnosis, advise on medication and patient behaviour, and communicate bad news (McCullagh in press). The problem for global examinations is to decide on those core capabilities in which a user of English as an international language needs to develop proficiency. The CEFR has certainly helped testers in deciding which capabilities to test, but consideration also needs to be given to the realities of using English as an international language. Jenner (1997) and Jenkins (2000) argue for the existence of a phonological lingua franca core of English and suggest that a corpus of this core should

Table 35.1 ALTE 'can do' statements: overall general ability

CEFR LEVELS	Listening/speaking	Reading	Writing
C2	CAN advise on or talk about complex or sensitive issues, understanding colloquial references and dealing confidently with hostile questions.	CAN understand documents, correspondence and reports, including the finer points of complex texts.	CAN write letters on any subject and full notes of meetings or seminars with good expression and accuracy.
C1	CAN contribute effectively to meetings and seminars within own area of work or keep up a casual conversation with a good degree of fluency, coping with abstract expressions.	CAN read quickly enough to cope with an academic course, to read the media for information or to understand non-standard correspondence.	CAN prepare/draft professional correspondence, take reasonably accurate notes in meetings or write an essay which shows an ability to communicate.
B2	CAN follow or give a talk on a familiar topic or keep up a conversation on a fairly wide range of topics.	CAN scan texts for relevant information, and understand detailed instructions or advice.	CAN make notes while someone is talking or write a letter including non-standard requests.
B1	CAN express opinions on abstract/cultural matters in a limited way or offer advice within a known area, and understand instructions or public announcements.	CAN understand routine information and articles, and the general meaning of non-routine information within a familiar area.	CAN write letters or make notes on familiar or predictable matters.
A2	CAN express simple opinions or requirements in a familiar context.	CAN understand straightforward information within a known area, such as on products and signs and simple textbooks or reports on familiar matters.	CAN complete forms and write short simple letters or postcards related to personal information.
A1	CAN understand basic instructions or take part in a basic factual conversation on a predictable topic.	CAN understand basic notices, instructions or information.	CAN complete basic forms, and write notes including times, dates and places.

Source: www.cambridge-efl.org.uk

be used to inform L2 testing. Seidlhofer (2001a, 2001b), Cook (2002), Prodromou (2003) and Jenkins (2007) also argue in favour of using corpora of International English to inform L2 teaching and testing. Whilst I would not agree with the many critics who argue that this would lower learners' objectives and achievement, and would agree that corpora of EIL should inform the design and marking of tests, my view is that we have as yet not discovered sufficient commonalities between users of different World Englishes (Rubdy and Saraceni 2006) for us to standardize the linguistic features of English as an International Language. But there are capabilities and abilities which are especially salient when using English as an International Language. For example, the ability to achieve effective accommodation is very important for a Peruvian speaking English with an Indonesian. 'Accommodation' is the ability to vary your language in relation to your interlocutor and to negotiate the interaction in order to achieve effective communication (see Jenkins 2000; Kirkpatrick 2004). In their description of Communication

Accommodation Theory, Giles *et al.* (1991) described how speakers adjust their speech to make it more similar to their interlocutor (convergence) or to make it different (divergence). They defined *convergence* as 'a strategy whereby individuals adapt to each other's communicative behaviors in terms of a wide range of linguistic-prosodic-nonverbal features including speech rate, pausal phenomena and utterance length, phonological variants, smiling, gaze, and so on' (p. 7).

A specification of those capabilities and abilities which are particularly salient to users of EIL, plus a specification of those linguistic features so far demonstrated to be universally and successfully used by educated speakers of EIL would be of great value. These specifications could provide the core syllabus for a global examination in English as an International Language, set by an examination board with an international reputation. This EIL examination could be an additional examination assessing the ability of candidates to achieve intended outcomes when using EIL. It could be at different levels of outcome achievement (rather than at different levels of linguistic difficulty) and it could include tasks requiring the effective achievement of outcomes in typical EIL contexts, as well as tasks requiring understanding of both World and Standard Englishes. There could be a Core Examination of Proficiency in English as an International Language plus supplementary examinations in proficiency in the use of such sub-varieties as EIL for Business Communication, EIL for Media Communication and EIL for Sport. See Tomlinson (2006) for an elaboration of these suggestions.

Which topic content?

A learner in a test or examination is much more likely to communicate effectively if the topics of the texts and tasks are familiar (Alderson 2005). It is important that some learners are not advantaged by dealing with topics with which they are familiar, whilst others are disadvantaged by having to deal with unfamiliar topics. One well-known examination tried to solve this problem by finding a topic which all the candidates in all the countries taking the examination would be familiar with. After considerable research, they discovered that 'the bee' seemed a topic common to all the countries involved. The reading paper therefore used a text on the dance of the bees. The following year a text on bees appeared again. Inevitably, in the third year, candidates all over the world studied bees instead of learning English.

However, a safe approach to global examinations remains to use topics which are universal and to which all candidates can relate – for example, growing up, going to school, making friends, getting married. Tests can be found related to these topics which are both cognitively and emotively engaging. Candidates from all over the world can be stimulated as well as tested fairly.

Which English?

Another question is, 'Which varieties of English should be tested?' My answer is the varieties which the learners are likely to need to communicate in. If Nigerian secondary school learners are going to use English mainly with other Nigerian speakers of English then it follows that it is very important that they are able to communicate in educated Nigerian English. If Nigerian businessmen are going to need English mainly to communicate with other non-native speakers, they will need competence in English as an International Language. If Nigerian university students are going to need to communicate effectively with native speakers of English, then they will need communicative competence in one or more of the standard varieties of English. At the moment, most public examinations (and most classroom tests) evaluate the students' knowledge of and ability to use a standard British or American variety of English. Often, candidates are failed, even though they are communicatively competent in a widely spoken local variety of English or in English as an International Language, but who cannot speak or write like a native speaker. As Jenkins (2006: 45) says, candidates are 'examined for qualifications which claim to have international currency (TOIEC, IELTS and so on), but penalized for using internationally-communicative forms of the language'. Examinations and tests which focus on the use of specified varieties of English, but which also test the candidates' ability to understand other varieties of English and to interact with their users, are needed. In other words, we need tests and examinations which reflect the reality of language use. The major examination bodies are considering moving towards the testing of EIL (e.g. Taylor 2002), but as yet there is little sign that they are taking action.

One objection to the testing of the use of local varieties of English is that it risks lowering standards. Providing, however, that the variety tested is a standardized, educated variety typically used by local professionals, then a high standard is being maintained and learners are not being penalized for not being native speakers.

A major objection to testing English as an International Language (in addition to the accusation of lowering standards) is the claim that it does not exist. It is true that there is, as yet, no conclusive evidence that non-native speakers of different L1s communicate with each other in a universally standard variety of English. However, there are now a number of corpora which have collected data on the language used by non-native speakers of English in international communication (for example, Seidlhofer's Vienna–Oxford International Corpus of English (Seidlhofer 2007), Mauranen's Corpus of Academic English (Mauranen 2003) and Jenkins' Lingua Franca Core (Jenkins 2000)). While there may not yet be enough data to justify basing an examination on, there is enough data to inform the marking of English examinations in ways which do not penalize the use of pronunciation, grammar and lexis which deviate from typical native-speaker norms, but are congruent with typical international use, a point made strongly by Jenkins (2006). There is also enough evidence of what international users of English need to do and how they need to do it to suggest that there are certain specific capabilities (e.g. justification of a position) and general abilities (e.g. accommodation, clarification) which should be assessed in examinations and tests of EIL.

It is worth remembering that the 'standard' varieties of English are idealized and do not exist either (especially in their spoken forms). Effective communication should not be penalized in examinations simply because it breaks a native-speaker rule. Non-native speakers are typically penalized in examinations for making 'mistakes' which native speakers often make too (e.g. using 'some' in interrogative and negative utterances; using 'less' with countable nouns). The English we should test is the variety of English which is appropriate and effective in the contexts in which the candidates are likely to need to use English.

Criteria for testing?

All tests and examinations should be developed, evaluated and revised in relation to principled criteria. The criteria should focus on ways of achieving specified objectives and should be informed by what we know about communication and language acquisition. Universal criteria should apply to any test or examination anywhere. Local criteria apply to a specific test or examination, and should relate to the profile, needs and wants of the learners taking it.

Learner-centred criteria

As tests and examinations should be developed primarily to be useful for the learners who take them, most of the criteria should be focused on learners. Here are some examples of universal and local criteria which have proved useful.

Universal criteria (i.e. those relevant for all ESL tests)

1 Does it provide a useful learning experience? (see Tomlinson 2005, on the importance of learning validity)
2 Is preparing for it a useful learning experience?
3 Does it provide information to the learners (and to their teachers) which will facilitate and/or accelerate learning? (Fradd and McGee 1994; Tomlinson 2005)
4 Does it help the learners to notice the gaps between their actual performance and their desired performance and between their performance and the equivalent performance of more effective users?
5 Does it provide a positive, engaging experience?
6 Does it set achievable challenges?
7 Does it reflect the task conditions which the learners are used to in the classroom?
8 Does it evaluate the learners' ability to communicate accurately, fluently, appropriately and effectively?
9 Does it test typical performance rather than pressurized one-off performance? It is possible to reduce the distance between learning and testing by using samples of typical performances rather than one-off tests as a means of assessment (Alderson 2001).
10 Does it replicate the communicative contexts which the learners are preparing to use English in?
11 Does it reward effective achievement of intended outcomes rather than just correct output?
12 Does it present an equivalent challenge to all its candidates?
13 Is it likely to lead to a positive washback effect in the classroom and/or on the process of learning?

Local criteria (i.e. those relevant to a specific test)

Local criteria will obviously vary from test to test. Here are examples from an end-of-year examination for first-year students at an English-medium university in the Middle East.

1 Does it test capabilities which the students will need to master in order to perform well in their academic subjects in Year Two?
2 Does it test varieties of English which the students will meet in their academic lectures and reading?
3 Does it focus on topics which are familiar to teenage males in the Middle East?

Tester-centred criteria

There are legitimate reasons for also developing tester-centred criteria, both universal and local. Here are some examples:

Universal criteria
1 Is it a valid test of what it claims to be testing?
2 Is it a reliable test which would yield the same results with different markers and with different but equivalent sets of students?
3 Does it provide useful information for teachers?

Local criteria
1 Does it provide valid information about which students are ready to pursue their academic studies through the medium of English?
2 Does it provide reliable information which could help teachers to prepare remedial programmes for those students who are not yet ready to pursue their academic studies through the medium of English?

When to test?

Tests are often set at times which are administratively convenient rather than pedagogically useful. Institutional realities need to be considered, but so too do learners' needs.

Pre-course?

Tests are often set prior to the course in order to place learners in appropriate classes. An even more valuable function of pre-course tests is to record a starting point in relation to which learners can gauge their progress. For example, students can record a conversation and write a story (or a text relevant to their course objectives) before the course starts and then later compare these with their mid- and post-course performance.

Whilst-course?

Most learners are tested at frequent and regular intervals during their English courses. This can be very motivating for successful students and very de-motivating for unsuccessful students. It can also take up valuable learning time and impose a de-energizing marking load on the teacher. A more learner-friendly approach would be to let each student decide every four weeks if they want to take a test or have a lesson. Alternatively a number of classroom tasks can be counted as tests and their marks used for assessment at the end of term. I used the latter approach at Kobe University in Japan, but did not tell the students which tasks would be counted as tests. The students were happy with this approach and gave unstressed, typical performances on the tasks.

One problem with whilst-course tests is they often test something which has just been taught, and they therefore test the teaching and not the learning. One solution to this problem is to test what was learned two weeks previously to see if the learners can still do what they learned to do.

611

Post-course?

Most courses have post-course tests. Many are summative tests, which judge learners without providing them with any useful feedback. Ideally post-course tests should:

1 reveal what the learners can do after the course;
2 provide the learners with feedback designed to help them to do even better;
3 be administered a number of weeks after the end of the course to allow for acquisition and development to take place – though obviously this is not always practical.

Learner-centred decisions

Some important questions to ask about the timing of tests include:

1 Do the students have to be tested?
2 Will the students gain from being tested?

If the answer to these two questions is 'no' then there is no need to test at all and the following questions can be ignored.

3 How often do the students want to be tested?
4 Will the learners get tense if they are tested too often?

Tester-centred decisions

The following are examples of important tester-centred questions:

1 How much time do we need to elapse between teaching and testing?
2 How often do learners need to be tested in order to feed useful information to the teachers about learner progress?
3 Should each learner be tested when they feel ready or with all the other learners at a time determined by the tester(s)?

How to test?

This is a huge question and has been dealt with extensively in the literature on testing. Much of the recent literature deals with how to humanize and how to achieve both validity and reliability for 'classical' tests, that is tests which 'aim to measure to what extent a language learner can perform certain language tasks at a particular moment in time' (Colpin and Gysen 2006: 151). For useful overviews and proposals for such assessment, see Baker (1989), Bachman (1990), Weir (1990), Buck (2001), Read (2001), Chapelle and Brindley (2002) and Fulcher (2003). The recent literature also deals with 'alternative testing', a term which covers such unconventional approaches as observations, portfolios, self-assessment, projects, peer assessment, real-life tasks, individual assessment contracts, shadowing and think-aloud protocols (see, for example, Genesee and Upshur 1996; Brown and Hudson 1998; Van Petegem and Vanhoof 2002; Bultynck

2004). These alternative approaches are to be welcomed: they remove the unfairness and pressure of one-off assessment; they relate to real-world use of language; they are holistic tests of performance rather than discrete tests of knowledge; and they can provide the learners with information which can help them progress.

As indicated earlier, most public examinations have separate papers for reading, writing, speaking and listening skills. For example, the list in Table 35.2 shows how separate papers in the four skills are compulsory for all candidates for UCLES (University of Cambridge) examinations.

Some examinations allow candidates to take different skills papers at different levels and some examinations provide a grade for each skills paper (e.g. IELTS). This separation into skills is understandable as institutions and employers often need information about applicants' performance in particular skills, and institutions often timetable and staff their courses according to the four skills. However, it is my view that it is not possible to set valid and reliable tests of the receptive skills of listening and reading, as learners do not exhibit any observable manifestations of their mental processes whilst performing these skills. Multiple-choice comprehension tests, cloze tests and C tests can be designed so that listening and reading tests are reliable. They are not, however, valid tests of these skills. Reporting on the mental processes during a reading or listening test can provide some indication of the learners' reading or listening skills, as can getting learners to report or summarize what they have read or listened to. However, it is very difficult to achieve reliability for these procedures because of the subjectivity of the marking. It seems that the only valid and reliable response to testing reading and writing is to test the outcomes of the learners' reading and listening by including these receptive skills in pedagogic or real-world tasks which involve integrating both receptive and productive skills. An example of a pedagogic task would be for a learner to listen to a story and then to re-tell it to another student in order to get them interested in the story. An example of a 'real-world task' would be a Malaysian learner, acting as an employee in a Malaysian company, reading a letter of complaint from a Venezuelan and then writing a reply to it. As Colpin and Gysen (2006: 152–3) say, 'assessment tasks ideally should be motivating and authentic tasks that relate to what learners are expected to be able to do with the target language (in real life)'.

Table 35.2 Separate papers required for UCLES examinations

UCLES (University of Cambridge)				
Key English Test	×	×	×	×
Preliminary English Test	×	×	×	×
Business English Certificates Preliminary	×	×	×	×
Certificates in Communicative Skills I	×	×	×	×
First Certificate in English	×	×	×	×
Business English Certificates Vantage	×	×	×	×
Certificates in Communicative Skills II	×	×	×	×
Certificate in Advanced English	×	×	×	×
Business English Certificates Higher	×	×	×	×
Certificates in Communicative Skills III	×	×	×	×
Certificate of Proficiency in English	×	×	×	×
Certificates in Communicative Skills IV	×	×	×	×

Source: English Language Examinations (www.europa-pages.com).

Conclusion

In conclusion, therefore, a good test or examination of English should:

1 have clear objectives about what information it is designed to provide;
2 provide a valuable learning experience for the learners taking it;
3 use the varieties of English and the topic content suitable for the learners taking it;
4 assess the students' typical performance of contextualized communication tasks relevant to their objectives in learning English;
5 be designed so as to provide useful information about the effectiveness of the learners' performance of the tasks;
6 be reliable;
7 be developed and assessed in relation to clear, specific and principled criteria;
8 have a positive washback effect on the teaching of learners of English.

Suggestions for further reading

Green, A. (2007) *IELTS Washback in Context: Preparation for Academic Writing in Higher Education*, Cambridge: Cambridge University Press. (A detailed case study which reveals the negative effects of spending class time preparing students for an examination.)

Jenkins, J. (2007) *English as a Lingua Franca: Attitude and Identity*, Oxford: Oxford University Press. (A provocative view of how ESL teaching and testing should reflect the reality of English as it is used as a lingua franca for international communication.)

McNamara, T. (2000) *Language Testing*, Oxford: Oxford University Press. (A consideration of many of the important issues concerning ELT testing.)

Rubdy, R. and Saraceni, M. (2006) *English in the World: Global Rules, Global Roles*, London: Continuum. (An interesting and provocative presentation of views on what varieties of English should be taught and tested.)

Weir, C. (1990) *Communicative Language Testing*, Hemel Hempstead: Prentice Hall. (A very interesting account of the principles and procedures of testing learners' ability to actually communicate.)

References

Alderson, J.C. (2001) *Assessing Reading*, Cambridge: Cambridge University Press.
——(2005) 'The testing of reading', in C. Nuttall (ed.) *Teaching Reading Skills in a Foreign Language*, Oxford: Macmillan.
Arnold, J. (1999) *Affect in Language Learning*, Cambridge: Cambridge University Press.
Bachman, L.F. (1990) *Fundamental Considerations in Language Testing*, Oxford: Oxford University Press.
Baker, D. (1989) *Language Testing: A Critical Survey and Practical Guide*, London: Edward Arnold.
Bolitho, R., Carter, R., Hughes, R., Ivanic, R., Masuhara, H. and Tomlinson, B. (2003) 'Ten questions about language awareness', *ELT Journal*, 57 (2): 251–9.
Brown, J. and Hudson, T. (1998) 'Alternatives in language assessment', *TESOL Quarterly*, 32: 653–75.
Buck, G. (2001) *Assessing Listening*, Cambridge: Cambridge University Press.
Bultynck, K. (2004) 'Wie A zegt, moet ook B zeggen. Breder evalueren', *Les*, 129: 21–4.
Chapelle, C.A. and Brindley, G. (2002) 'Assessment', in N. Schmitt (ed.) *An Introduction to Applied Linguistics,* London: Arnold.

Chiba, S. and Morikawa, Y. (2006) 'From oral interview test to oral communication test: alleviating students' anxiety', in W.M. Chan, K.N. Chin and T. Suthiwan (eds) *Foreign Language Teaching in Asia and Beyond*, Singapore: Centre for Language Studies, National University of Singapore.

Colpin, M. and Gysen, S. (2006) 'Developing and introducing task-based language tests', in K. Van den Branden (ed.) *Task Based Language Education*, Cambridge: Cambridge University Press.

Cook, V. (2002) *Portraits of the L2 User*, Clevedon: Multilingual Matters.

Craik, F.I.M. and Lockhart, R.S. (1972) 'Levels of processing: a framework for memory research', *Journal of Verbal Learning and Verbal Behaviour*, 11: 671–84.

Davies, A. and Elder, C. (2005) 'Validity and validation in language testing', in E. Hinkel (ed.) *Handbook of Research in Second Language Teaching and Learning*, Mahwah, NJ: Lawrence Erlbaum.

Fradd, S.M. and McGee, P.L. with Wilen, D.K. (1994) *Instructional Assessment: An Integrative Approach to Evaluating Student Performance*, Reading, MA: Addison Wesley.

Fulcher, G. (2003) *Testing Second Language Speaking*, Harlow: Longman/Pearson.

Genesee, F. and Upshur, J. (1996) *Classroom-Based Evaluation in Second Language Education*, Cambridge: Cambridge University Press.

Giles, H., Coupland, N. and Coupland, J. (1991) 'Accommodation theory: communication, context, and consequence', in H. Giles, N. Coupland and J. Coupland (eds) *Contexts of Accommodation. Developments in Applied Sociolinguistics*, Cambridge: Cambridge University Press.

Green, A. (2007) *IELTS Washback in Context: Preparation for Academic Writing in Higher Education*, Cambridge: Cambridge University Press.

Hughes, A. (1989) *Testing for Language Teachers*, Cambridge: Cambridge University Press.

Jenkins, J. (2000) *The Phonology of English as an International Language*, Oxford: Oxford University Press.

——(2006) 'The spread of EIL: a testing time for testers', *ELT Journal*, 60 (1): 42–50.

——(2007) *English as a Lingua Franca: Attitude and Identity*, Oxford: Oxford University Press.

Jenner, B. (1997) 'International English: an alternative view', *Speak Out!* 15: 15–16.

Kirkpatrick, A. (2004) 'English as an ASEAN lingua franca: implications for language teaching', paper presented at IAWE Conference, Syracuse University, 16–18 July.

——(2006) 'Which model of English: native-speaker, nativised or lingua franca?' in R. Rubdy and M. Saraceni (eds) *English in the World: Global Rules, Global Roles*, London: Continuum.

Kunnan, A.J. (2005) 'Language assessment from a wider context', in E. Hinkel (ed.) *Handbook of Research in Second Language Teaching and Learning*, Mahwah, NJ: Lawrence Erlbaum.

Leung, C. (2005) 'Classroom teacher assessment of second language development: construct as practice', in E. Hinkel (ed.) *Handbook of Research in Second Language Teaching and Learning*, Mahwah, NJ: Lawrence Erlbaum.

McCullagh, M. (in press) 'An initial evaluation of the effectiveness of a set of published materials for Medical English', in B. Tomlinson and H. Masuhara (eds) *Research in Materials Development for Language Teaching*, London: Continuum.

McNamara, T. (1996) *Measuring Second Language Performance*, London: Longman.

——(2000) *Language Testing*, Oxford: Oxford University Press.

Mauranen, A. (2003) 'The corpus of English as lingua franca in academic settings', *World Englishes*, 21 (3): 436–40.

Norris, J. (2002) 'Interpretations, intended uses and designs in task-based language assessment', *Language Testing*, 19: 337–46.

Patten, B. (1996) *Armada*, London: Flamingo.

Prodromou, L. (2003) 'In search of the successful user of English; how a corpus of non-native speaker English could impact on EFL teaching', *Modern English Teacher*, 12 (2): 5–14.

Read, J. (2001) *Assessing Vocabulary*, Cambridge: Cambridge University Press.

Rosen, M. (2007) *Fighters for Life*, London: Bookmarks.

Rubdy, R. and Saraceni, M. (2006) *English in the World: Global Rules, Global Roles*, London: Continuum.

Seidlhofer, B. (2001a) 'Towards making Euro-English a linguistic reality', *English Today*, 68: 14–16.

——(2001b) 'Closing a conceptual gap: the case for a description of English as a lingua franca', *International Journal of Applied Linguistics*, 11 (2): 133–58.

——(2007) 'Common property: English as a lingua franca in Europe', in J. Cummins and C. Davison (eds) *The International Handbook of English Language Teaching*, New York: Springer, pp. 137–53.

Spolsky, B. (1995) *Measured Words*, Oxford: Oxford University Press.

Taylor, L. (2002) *Assessing Learners' English: But Whose/Which English(es)?* (Research Notes 10), Cambridge: University of Cambridge ESOL Examinations.

Tomlinson, B. (1994) 'Pragmatic awareness activities', *Language Awareness*, 3 (4): 119–29.

——(1998) 'Affect and the coursebook', *IATEFL Issues*, 145: 20–1.

——(2003) 'Humanising the coursebook', in B. Tomlinson (ed.) *Developing Materials for Language Teaching*, London: Continuum.

——(2005) 'Testing to learn', *ELT Journal*, 59 (1): 39–46.

——(2006) 'A multi-dimensional approach to teaching English for the world', in R. Rubdy and M. Saraceni (eds) *English in the World: Global Rules, Global Roles*, London: Continuum.

——(2007) 'Teachers' responses to form-focused discovery approaches', in S. Fotos and H. Nassaji (eds) *Form Focused Instruction and Teacher Education: Studies in Honour of Rod Ellis*, Oxford: Oxford University Press.

Underhill, N. (1987) *Testing Spoken Language*, Cambridge: Cambridge University Press.

Van Petegem, P. and Vanhoof, J. (2002) *Evaluatie op de testbank: Een handboek voor het ontwikkelen van alternatieve evaluatievormen*, Mechelen: Wolters Plantyn.

Weir, C. (1990) *Communicative Language Testing*, Hemel Hempstead: Prentice Hall.

36

When does an unconventional form become an innovation?

David C.S. Li

Introduction

A lingua franca is needed to facilitate ever-expanding cross-border communication on a global scale. For historical reasons, that role has been and is increasingly assigned to English (McArthur 1998; Crystal 2003; Kirkpatrick 2007), including 'postcolonial English' (Schneider 2007). This has direct implications for language education in countries big and small, rich or poor. For the vast majority of ESL/EFL (hereafter: English-L2) learners who have no choice but to study English, typically as a school subject, the coming of age is hardly complete without developing an acute awareness of how important, and yet how difficult, it is to speak and write 'good English'. English is not at all learner-friendly, especially to learners whose L1 is linguistically unrelated to English (e.g. Altaic languages Korean and Japanese; Sino-Tibetan languages Chinese and Thai). In the learning process, various kinds of cross-linguistic influence from features in the learners' first language(s) have been shown to be major acquisitional problems. Less well-known is the fact that Standard Englishes – the varieties of English being targeted for teaching and learning through education – are fraught with untidiness at different linguistic levels. This is not surprising, given that English, like all natural unplanned languages, evolved over time, rather than being consciously designed for meaning-making purposes – unlike artificial, planned languages such as Esperanto (cf. Li 2003). The untidiness is of two main kinds: (a) inconsistencies in various linguistic subsystems; and (b) considerable variation within each of the standard varieties of English (McArthur 1998; Trudgill and Hannah 2002; Kirkpatrick 2007). These two types of untidiness account for a large number of learner-unfriendly features rooted in standard varieties of English, in particular British English (BrE) and American English (AmE). For practical reasons, we will use 'Standard English' to refer to features which are true of one or more standard varieties of English.

In this chapter, I will first illustrate various kinds of learner-unfriendliness by examining some examples of untidiness in Standard English. Non-standard features will be exemplified using data collected from Hong Kong Chinese English-L2 learners and users. The important distinction between errors and innovations will be discussed.

Sources of learner-unfriendliness

Standard English is inconsistent

As a semiotic, meaning-making system, Standard English is inconsistent at various linguistic levels. This is especially clear with regard to orthography and grammar. Take the case of BrE. One of the best known criticisms of irrational English spelling was made by the British playwright George Bernard Shaw in the 1900s. He argued that 'fish' might well be spelt as GHOTI, where the [f] sound of *gh* is attested in a word like *laugh*, the [i] sound of *o* in *women*, and the syllable-final sibilant [ʃ] of *ti* in *nation*. Another oft-cited example of inconsistent sound-spelling relationship is the various pronunciations (e.g. in RP) associated with *ough*, as in *thought* [ɔː], *though* [ou], *rough* [ʌ], *cough* [ɒ], *drought* [aʊ] and *thorough* [e]. Less eye-catching, nonetheless (or none the less) vexing problems of variation occur across British and American spellings (e.g. *programme* vs *program*; *towards* vs *toward*) and word choices (e.g. *different from* vs *different than*; see, e.g., Trudgill and Hannah 2002: 85–8; cf. Jenkins 2003: 71–2). No wonder 'proper spelling' is sometimes a problem even among English-L1 learners and users.

Paton (2008) reports that 'Standards of spelling among university students [in the UK] are now so bad that lecturers are being urged to turn a blind eye to mistakes'. Among the high-frequency misspellings are *arguement (argument), Febuary (February), Wensday (Wednesday), ignor (ignore), occured (occurred), opertunity (opportunity), que (queue), speach (speech), thier (their), truely (truly)* and *twelth (twelfth)*. A number of principles appear to be at work in these misspellings:

- Silent letters are dropped as spelling reflects pronunciation: *ignor, Febuary, opertunity, twelth, que, Wensday*.
- Regularization or simplification: *truely, arguement, occured*.
- Orthographic analogy: *thier* (cf. the rule of spelling 'i before e, except after c' for the [iː] sound); *speach* after the productive model of *beach, peach, reach, teach*, etc.

At the level of grammar, perhaps no other subsystem is more inconsistent than the choice of singular pronouns for designating indefinite reference, which is more or less equivalent in meaning to 'everyone' or 'anyone'. Traditional grammars allow for the use of the male-gender set of pronouns (*he, him, his* and *himself*) to designate that meaning (e.g. *let everyone make his own choice*). One consequence is that, unlike Buddhists or bird-lovers who can consciously avoid using such unwanted culture-specific idioms as 'killing two birds with one stone', a Hong Kong tycoon-philanthropist like Mr Li Ka-Shing could not help being seen as gender-biased in English: '"While an individual has the duty to reach his highest potential, to be the best that he can be, in his mind, he must not delude himself to think that he is better than who he really is", Li said' (excerpt of speech delivered to all graduates of Shantou University, China; *The Standard*, 27 June 2008: 2).

The original speech was almost certainly delivered in Chinese (Putonghua or the local dialect), which was rendered into Standard English by some bilingual journalist. That journalist should not be blamed for the sexist overtone, however. As Erving Goffman has observed in his celebrated (1981) monograph *Forms of Talk*, unlike other frames of speech such as lecturing or drama performance, the sexist use of male pronouns to express indefinite reference in English (for academic purposes) is a rare sort of frame which is immune from any 'frame break'.

> He who lectures on speech errors and its correction will inevitably make some of the very errors he analyzes … , he who lectures on discourse presuppositions will be utterly tongue-tied unless unself-consciously he makes as many as anyone else … [This] is not to say that other sorts of frame break might be as clearly doomed; for example, a reference at this point to the very questionable procedure of my employing 'he' in the immediately preceding utterances, carefully mingling a sex-biased word for the indefinite nominal pronoun, and an unobjectionable anaphoric term for someone like myself.
>
> (Goffman 1981: 163)

Owing to inconsistencies in the pronominal system in Standard English, the use of *he* and *his* to designate 'anyone', as shown in this revealing quotation, is 'unobjection-able', however 'questionable' it might be in the eyes of gender-conscious users of English, including Goffman himself. He or she who feels unhappy about the status quo may try to get around the problem by adopting one of three options: (a) an 'inclusivist' stance (as in this sentence, i.e. using 'he or she', 'his or her', 'himself or herself'), which sounds clumsy and cumbersome to say the least; (b) a 'pluralist' stance (e.g. saying *those who do it* instead of *he who does it*); and (c) an 'exclusivist' stance, i.e., reversing the discriminatory stance by using the female set of pronouns to designate 'indefinite reference', as Cameron *et al.* have done in their book on critical sociolinguistic research methods, as illustrated in the following example: 'Circumventing the Observer's Para-dox often involves the researcher in concealing *herself* and/or *her* purposes from those *she* is studying' (Cameron *et al.* 1992: 7, emphasis added).

What is interesting is that in some books published in the 1980s, when feminism was on the rise and gendered language use increasingly a concern to sociolinguists, insert-ing a disclaimer in the front matters was considered a necessary and useful strategy to distance the writer(s) from a perceived gender-insensitive stance. For example:

> Finally, whenever I have needed to use a pronoun to refer to the nouns 'learner' and 'teacher', I have used 'he', 'him' or 'his'. This is purely a linguistic con-vention and does not imply that the person is more likely to be male than female.
>
> (Littlewood 1984: 3)

The need for such a disclaimer is itself strong evidence that Standard English is an untidy system that leaks. Grammatically embedded gender bias is not universal. For example, a sexist orientation is also found in Chinese writing by the male-gendered pronoun 他 (Putonghua/Mandarin *tā*), but not in speech, for the third-person singular pronouns are pronounced identically in all Chinese varieties (Chao 1968). In French, the choice of singular possessive pronouns (masculine *son*; feminine *sa*) depends on the grammatical *genre* of the common noun rather than the sex of the possessor. Thus the film *Chacun son cinéma* is rendered into English as 'To Each His Own Cinema', a gender bias not found in the original title.

Another inconsistency is the use of the same form to designate semantically incom-patible meanings. This is clearly the case of using the same morpho-phonological expo-nent '-*s*' (and its allophones and allomorphs) to mark 'third-person singular' present tense verb forms, and the plural forms of regular count nouns. Consequently, young English-L2 learners who are taught simple sentences such as *Tom likes dogs* and *Sue likes cats* have to grapple with rather different reasons why '-*s*' is grammatically indispensable:

suffixed to the verb *like*, it is required for marking the 'third-person singular' meaning 'one and only one'; suffixed to the count nouns *cat* and *dog*, '-s' is needed for signalling the meaning 'necessarily more than one'. Since the two meanings are mutually exclusive, such a semantic discrepancy amounts to logical inconsistency. No wonder in the learning process, the 'third-person singular' and the plural morpheme are among the most slippery grammatical subsystems for English-L2 learners. This is empirically supported by research in ELF communication: detailed analysis of the Vienna Oxford International Corpus of English (VOICE) shows that the 'third-person singular' tops the list of emerging ELF lexico-grammatical features (e.g. *you look very sad, he look very sad*, Seidlhofer 2004, 2005; see also Breiteneder 2005, 2009; Jenkins 2003: 131; for the use of singular noun forms where plural forms are preferred in Standard English, see example 8 below).

Considerable variation in Standard English

Another source of learner-unfriendliness is considerable variation internal to Standard English. Despite being the most highly codified varieties, there continues to be considerable variation within Standard English. Thus the gradual demise of the subjunctive as a verb form (e.g. *we suggest that she go*) has reached a stage where it is generally seen as a stylistic variant of the verb phrase marked with *should* (e.g. *we suggest that she should go*). Guided by the principle of regularization, the explicit marking of this modal function or meaning using 'should' is a welcome development.

Another example of variation in Standard English is the prescriptive rule against 'dangling modifiers'. Accordingly, in a complex sentence made up of two clauses – the first one a dependent (subordinate) clause with no apparent subject, the second one an independent (main) clause – the subject in the independent clause (overt or covert) should also be the antecedent of the missing subject in the dependent clause. This rule is for instance not respected in (1) (source: http://personal.cityu.edu.hk/~encrproj/dangling1.doc):

1 Entering the stadium, the size of the crowd surprised John.

Here the subject ('the size of the crowd') could not be interpreted as the subject in the first clause ('entering the stadium'), thus leaving it 'dangling'. One way to overcome this seemingly illogical sentence structure is to put 'John' in the subject position (e.g. 'Entering the stadium, *John* was surprised by … '). As Huddleston and Pullum (2005: 207–9) have pointed out, however, such a rule is by no means observed by all users of Standard English; some appear to find nothing wrong in a sentence like (2), which was collected from authentic print media data in an ENL country:

2 Jennifer Lopez stars as Marisa, a maid in a fancy New York City Hotel. While *trying on a wealthy woman's dress*, a handsome and rich politician mistakes her for a society woman.

(Huddleston and Pullum 2005: 208)

Other synchronic variations within Standard English are arguably results of more or less recent diachronic changes: witness the neutralization of what used to be a clear functional division of labour between 'compared with' and 'compared to', which was triggered by a gradual shift of the former's functional load to the latter (e.g. *compared to my situation* used to be considered substandard, when *compared with NP* was widely held to be the norm, which was not to be confused with, e.g., *Cio-Cio-San was compared to a butterfly*). Or, consider the collocation between *the amount of* and count nouns like *books*, which used to be seen as substandard about three decades ago when *the number of* was the norm. These examples, barely the tip of the iceberg, are indicative of perennial language change, including in standard varieties of English (Milroy and Milroy 1985).

In the face of the many learner-unfriendly features exemplified above, coupled with cross-linguistic influence at various linguistic levels in the learning process, it is not surprising that deviations from Standard English norms tend to occur at all stages of the English-L2 learning process.

Non-standard lexico-grammatical features

In general, an error is an error if it deviates from the norm. But given that language change takes place all the time, the question arises as to when a deviation may stop being seen as an error and start being considered as (the onset of) an innovation. Before discussing this issue in detail, let us first look at some salient examples of non-standard features which are commonly found among Cantonese-L1 users of English in Hong Kong. Most of the data cited below were collected from undergraduate students' written output, including emails, supplemented by some authentic data from English language print media. Being undergraduate students, their English proficiency level may be characterized as either intermediate or upper-intermediate.

Some deviations from Standard English are clearly due to overgeneralization resulting from the principle of analogy. This is arguably the case with, for example, the use of *widespread* as a noun after the model of the nominal use of *spread*, as in *the widespread of American culture*; *the widespread of Singlish*. Or, consider the use of the *to*-infinitive as the preferred pattern of complementation after the verbs *suggest* and *recommend* (e.g. *He suggested me to do it*; *we recommend you to stop*), which deviates from the normative use of a *that*-clause (i.e., *He suggested that I do it*; *we recommend that you stop*). Given the dominant pattern of complementation required for many other verbs (compare: *She asked/expected/told me to do it*; *they order/persuade/want you to stop*), it is understandable why the *to*-infinitive is regarded by so many English-L2 learners/ users as the preferred pattern of complementation for *suggest* and *recommend*. Indeed, there is some evidence that such a trend has been spread to proficient English-L2 users (3) as well as English-L1 users (4):

3   As a linguist who worked recently on the matter of how spatial notions of *uchi* (inside) and *soto* (outside) relate to language and culture, I would like to *recommend you very strongly to read* Dr James Stanlaw's [2004] book on loanwords as a fascinating case study of interiorization of exterior things and words from English language and culture.

(Seiichi Makino, Princeton University; promotional flyer for a new book, 2004; emphasis added)

4   [Sir Brian Fender] observed that institutions might not have thought sufficiently about the reasons for carrying out knowledge transfer, and as a result might not have accorded sufficient priority to such 'third mission' activities. *He recommended institutions to conduct* more detailed forward planning, and gather comparable and

comprehensive management data with respect to knowledge transfer so that progress can be better monitored.

> (Annex to letter by Mr Michael V. Stone,
> Secretary-General of the University Grants Committee,
> to the President of the Hong Kong Institute of Education:
> 'Proposed Funding & Reporting Mechanism for Strengthening
> "Knowledge Transfer" in UGC-funded Institutions', 6 March 2009, p. 2)

Sometimes variation in Standard English may give rise to disagreement. One such case that happened to me concerns the correct complementation pattern of the verb *report* (*report using* vs *report to use*). In response to my query on the grammaticality of *reported to use* in a draft paper, the author of that paper did a Google search and obtained some interesting results, which are worth quoting at length:

> 5 I couldn't find any hard and fast grammar rules relating to this, but came across two websites:
>
> ▦ www.iei.uiuc.edu/structure/structure1/gerinfvbs.html
> ▦ www.tlumaczenia-angielski.info/angielski/gerund-infinitive.htm
>
> While the first clearly indicates that 'report' can only take a gerund object, the second seems to suggest that it can take both gerund and infinitive complements ... I also did a Google search for '**reported to use**' (where '**reported**' is in active rather than passive voice) and noted that this usage is found in credible texts, such as published journal articles, although the gerund is more often used. Some of the contexts are as follows:
> ' ... respondents' distribution according to how often they **reported to use** different pain control ... ' ...
> ' ... only one in five men and one in ten women **reported to use** no drugs at all'

Of interest here is the indeterminacy of correctness after several rounds of a Google search: while the gerund appears to be the normative pattern of complementation of *report* in active voice (*reported using*), the *to*-infinitive (*reported to use*) is also attested in some credible web pages on grammar and correct usage.

In extreme cases, both sides would contest what the other side regards as *the* correct usage. This is clearly the case of one email request I received in April 2008 from a former student (MD), a novice NET (native English-speaking) teacher of English in a well-known secondary school, who felt there was something wrong in the fill-in-the-blank question 'How well do you know – this little animal?' set by the head of English, with *about* being the intended answer. Below (7) is what MD wrote to me after receiving my affirmative response (6):

> 6 I did a quick Google search using 'How well do you know about ... '; guess what: no websites were returned (from 1–10). I see this as confirmation of our shared intuition: 'about' collocates best with 'How much ... ', not 'How well ... '. I suppose the best way forward is to explain this to your students, and convince them that the so-called 'model answer' is inaccurate ... You could instruct them to do a similar Google search to bring home this message I think.

7 The problem isnt [sic] with my students [sic] the problem is with my panel head [of English]. And she used yahoo … and searched it using inverted commas and came up with a screen full of sites using how well and about. When I explained it to my colleagues they all agreed but my panel head doesn't. She says that it is a common usage. But I disagree. I am not very sure what to do … I am going to search grammar books over the weekend, and collocation books too. I hope I can get some 'evidence' to show her.

Examples (5) to (7) are instructive in that the internet is increasingly resorted to as a means to determine to what extent a particular lexico-grammatical usage is legitimate or acceptable. Given that the ever-expanding internet has emerged as a *de facto* repository or huge English language database, the popular practice of checking for grammatical correctness on the web is thus gradually altering if not revolutionizing our perceptions of what constitutes correct and normative English usage. One crucial point here is that often it is difficult to tell whether the authors of internet texts are English-L2 or English-L1 users.

In the domain of 'grammar proper', one of the most slippery grammatical subsystems in Standard English is the distinction between singular and plural forms of a count noun. It is therefore not surprising that even highly proficient English-L2 users sometimes fail to use the appropriate plural form of a count noun. In the following quarter-page advert placed by a prestigious English-medium secondary school in Hong Kong for 'the post of English teacher', three count nouns – *application*, *requirement*, and *purpose* – are in singular form whereas Standard English usage would have them in plural:

8 XXX College invites **application** from qualified candidates for the post of English teacher (native speaker) as from September 1, 2008.

Requirement
- BA major in English
- Willing to help organizing activities and creating a rich language environment in school
- Salary: negotiable $25,000-$40,000 per month …
[In small print] (All information provided will only be used for recruitment related **purpose**)

(*The Standard*, Careers Page, 13 June 2008: 23)

Keen readers will have noticed that the verb forms after the verb *help* – *organizing* and *creating* – are also non-standard, since verbs that follow *help* should normally be in infinitive rather than *-ing* forms.

At the level of lexis, the correct usage of many verbs and nouns depends on their usual collocational pattern. Owing to a lack of exposure and practice, English-L2 learners tend to have problems acquiring the collocational patterns associated with target verbs and nouns. This is arguably the case with one subset of transitive verbs like *discuss*, *emphasize* and *blame* (9a, 10a, 11a), which do not take a preposition, as opposed to their corresponding nominalization supported by a 'delexical verb' ('*have … discussion about* NP', 9b; '*place … emphasis on* NP', 10b; and '*put … blame on* NP', 11b). Non-standard structures as in 9c, 10c and 11c are arguably the result of the English-L2 learner/user confusing the collocational patterns of the (transitive) verb and the associated nominalization (Li in press).

623

9 (a) They discussed the project for two hours.
   (b) They *had* a long *discussion about* the project.
   (c) ? They *discussed about* the project for two hours.
10 (a) We should emphasize this more.
   (b) We should *place* more *emphasis on* this.
   (c) ? We should *emphasize on* this more.
11 (a) Don't blame her so much!
   (b) Don't *put* so much *blame on* her.
   (c) ? Don't *blame on* her so much.

Plenty of non-standard usage patterns may be accounted for by a similar misanalysis, as shown in the spread of the non-standard complementation pattern of *recommend* to English-L1 speakers (e.g. '*He recommended institutions to conduct* ... ', see examples 3–4 above). Likewise, *in class* is such a high-frequency prepositional phrase that English-L2 learners might take a long time to realize that *in classroom* is inadmissible without the definite article *the*. Other examples in my data include the use of *behind* as a post-nominal modifier as in *the reason behind* (12), the redundant use of *about* in *concerning about X* (13), and the plural form of *room* in the idiom *room for improvement* (14):

12 After finished my associate degree, I chose English as major in my degree. *There were several reasons behind.* Firstly ...
13 May I refer to the following email to Head and Research Degrees Coordinator dated 22 November 2007 *concerning about* the Research Students' Research Output ...
14 Despite the fact that *there are still rooms for improvement* in my English, especially the writing skills, I have never forgotten my own identity as a Chinese even I am able to acquaint myself well with English.

Some of these apparent anomalies are arguably due to idiosyncrasies in Standard English. For example, 'the reason behind', in analogy to 'the day before/after' or 'the point above/below', seems quite reasonable. And it is only relatively recently that *concerning* and *regarding* are formally recognized as prepositions in some dictionaries (see, e.g., *Collins Cobuild Dictionary*), thanks in part to insights obtained in corpus linguistics. This fine detail has yet to trickle down to the English-L2 classroom. There is some evidence that the usage patterns of the verb *concern* and its derivatives are complex and learner-unfriendly. For instance, many English-L2 learners would say/write *father concerns you* or *father concerns about you* (meaning 'father is concerned about you'), partly because they overlook the syntactic constraint of the verb *concern*, partly due to incomplete learning of the periphrastic expression *be concerned about* (e.g. *father is concerned about you*) and the prepositional use of *concerning* (e.g. *concerning your safety*; Li and Chan 2001):

'something *concerns* someone'
'someone *is concerned about* someone/something'

Another group of learner-unfriendly words are adjectives with a meaning related to the degree of difficulty and probability, for example, *difficult, easy, common, convenient, compulsory, necessary, unnecessary, possible, impossible,* etc. One syntactic constraint associated with these adjectives is that in general, the clause should start with the dummy subject *it* rather than a 'human' subject. For example:

15 (a) *I am difficult/not easy to learn English well.
     (b) It is difficult/not easy for me to learn English well.
16 (a) *We are inconvenient to see you now.
     (b) It is inconvenient for us to see you now.

For Chinese EFL learners, however, the normative use of this structure (known as 'postponed carrier' in functional grammar, as in 15b and 16b; see Lock 1995) is learner-unfriendly for two main reasons: the non-existence of a functional equivalent of 'it' in their native language (unlike many European languages in this regard), and the fact that, in Chinese, sentences with such meanings tend to begin with a human subject. This is probably why even highly educated Chinese bilingual users of English are sometimes prone to produce this non-standard structure known as 'pseudo-tough movement' (see Li and Chan 2001). In one seminar given by a Chinese Singaporean lecturer on the impact of the spread of the Chinese language in the world, he said, 'you are difficult to buy non-Chinese products'. (This syntactic constraint is neutralized when the covert object of the verb in the embedded clause is the same as the subject in the matrix clause. Compare: *John is easy to please*; *Liu Xiang is difficult to beat*.)

Learner-unfriendliness is also attested in another salient Standard English structure which is known as 'reduced relative clause' (RRC). When a post-nominal modifier consists of a relative clause in the passive voice (e.g. *I bought that book which was published yesterday*), Standard English allows for a stylistic variant whereby the relative pronoun and the finite auxiliary may be ellipted (e.g. *I bought that book published yesterday*). The RRC structure, however, is blocked if the verb is intransitive (e.g. *I saw the accident which happened yesterday*, but not *I saw the accident happened yesterday*). Such a lexico-syntactic constraint is often overlooked by even advanced English-L2 users. In one quarter-page public notice in a leading English daily in Hong Kong, for example, the verb *appeared* was used in the same RRC structure as *published*:

17 We note from the reports/articles *appeared* at the front page and page 3 of the South China Sunday Morning Post *published* on 27th August 2000 ... that a toy company called 'City Toys Ltd.' ... has employed underage workers.
                                    (*South China Morning Post*, 1 September 2000: 3)

Where the verb in a post-nominal modifier is intransitive (e.g. *appear*), it should either be 'introduced' by a relative pronoun (i.e. ... which appeared ...) or in -*ing* form (i.e. ... appearing ...).

Previous accounts of learner errors in second-language acquisition (SLA) tended to focus on the source of errors, with the primary factor being either cross-linguistic influence from the learners' L1, or incomplete learning of L2, or some combination of these (for a critique of this analytical stance, see Jenkins 2006). While there is some truth in such explanatory accounts, they are incomplete without appreciating the fact that the target language, Standard English, is a system that leaks and, as we have seen, in extreme cases to the extent of logical inconsistency. Another source of difficulty is instability, as shown in various stylistic variants at practically all linguistic levels. Following the emergence of English as a global language, with the result that learners from different L1 backgrounds often have to learn one or more standard varieties of English, a troubling question arises: should English-L2 users' non-standard performance and usage patterns be necessarily dismissed as 'errors'? After more than two decades of

625

research in World Englishes and other related paradigms, few would dispute that at least some of the non-standard features produced by English-L2 users should be regarded as legitimate and recognized as innovations rather than errors. The question is where to draw the line.

Deviations from Standard English: errors or innovations?

Standard varieties of English are products of successive stages of standardization as a direct result of decades (e.g. AusE) or even centuries (e.g. BE and AmE) of codification and/or language planning (Kirkpatrick 2007). To some extent, what standards do is to impose some order on a state of unsystematic variation. For a long time, standards of English were modelled prescriptively on the lexico-grammar in Latin, regardless of how English was actually used by its speakers (Milroy and Milroy 1985). Over time, the prescriptive approach gave way to a descriptive stance among contemporary linguists and grammarians; in the process dogmatic usage patterns (e.g. *it's I*) modelled on Latin gradually succumbed to the collective forces of popular usage and choice (e.g. *it's me*). Before English emerged as the world's *de facto* global language, such collective forces naturally referred to those exerted by the everyday language use patterns of its English-L1 users. Now that English is a required additional language in most non-English-L1 countries in the world, especially in view of the fact that English-L1 users are increasingly outnumbered by English-L2 users, the question arises whether such forces of language change should be attributed to English-L1 users alone. To cite one classic example: why should *prepone*, a well-motivated verb – an antonym for that matter – coined in analogy to *postpone*, be dismissed as a non-English word, even though it has been widely attested among speakers of English on the Indian subcontinent (Widdowson 1994; cf. *discuss about* NP, *emphasize on* NP and *blame on* NP, see examples 9–11)? A Wikipedia entry reads: '"Prepone" is not an English word. It's commonly used in Indian subcontinent to mean the opposite of "post-pone", but the rest of the world is largely unaware of it' (http://wiki.answers.com/Q/Why_the_word_'prepone'_is_not_in_any_dictionary).

Public awareness of a new coinage, however, is far from being the reason why that coinage is not accepted as an innovation in World Englishes (151,000 hits were returned in a Google search in mid-April 2009). Clearly other more potent factors are at stake here. First and foremost, the status of *prepone* is low because its active use to date tends to be limited to the popular parlance of users who are labelled as non-native speakers. Second, more importantly, innovation – including the power to label new coinage as such – was traditionally thought to be the exclusive right of native speakers, notably those residing in UK, USA, Canada, Australia and New Zealand. So what needs to be done before such an ingenious coinage as *prepone* is accepted as part of the lexicon in Standard English?

To my knowledge, Bamgbose (1998) is the most elaborate treatise on the theoretical distinction between English-L2 errors and innovations. Coming from a World Englishes perspective, he asks, 'why should a native-variety-based standard continue to license the norms of non-native Englishes?' (p. 3). As he explains, the current state of affairs favours standard varieties of English, partly because all existing standards are upheld to be correct until otherwise replaced with alternative standards or complemented by stylistic variants, but also because they are the most elaborately codified to date: 'By default, the only codified norms available (which are based on native varieties) will continue to license what is acceptable and what is not, even when there is a desire to encourage and institutionalize non-native English norms' (Bamgbose 1998: 5).

Owing to this prestige factor, English-L2 speakers tend to admire native accents, even though their own pronunciation does not sound native-like, reflecting thereby a kind of 'love–hate relationship' (p. 7). This point has received empirical support in a recent study of Chinese speakers' perceptions of English accents (Li 2009, cf. Jenkins 2007).

To calibrate the status of a local usage as either an error or innovation, Bamgbose (1998) indicates that there are five interrelated internal factors or measures:

- *Demographic:* how many acrolectal speakers use it? Since the language use patterns of basilectal and mesolectal speakers tend to be socially stigmatized, the prospect of the usage being favourably received in the local community is dim if it is not used by acrolectal speakers.
- *Geographical:* how widely has it spread? In principle, the farther it spreads, the higher its acceptance rate.
- *Authoritative:* what is the social status of those who use it? In general, people who are knowledgeable are vested with authority. Thus 'writers, teachers, media practitioners, examination bodies, publishing houses, and influential opinion leaders' (p. 4) tend to be viewed favourably as credible sources of linguistic innovations, for 'the use of unconventional forms may become hallowed, simply because such use has become associated with respected authorities or writers' (p. 4).
- *Codification:* where is the usage sanctioned? One sure way to legitimate a local usage is to have it included in all kinds of written 'authorities', such as dictionaries, course books and reference manuals for teachers.
- *Acceptability:* what are the attitudes of users and non-users towards this usage? In general, compared with linguistic innovations, cultural and pragmatic innovations tend to get accepted more easily and are more likely to be tolerated and nativized.

Of these five internal measures, Bamgbose points out rightly that codification and acceptability are the most important. Beyond any doubt, the key to language change is codification, a point which 'is too important to be belabored' (p. 4). Once a local usage is enshrined in the dictionary or even in a course book, the legitimation process is complete (Dolezal 2006; Butler 2007). This in turn will help tilt the balance, if gradually, in favour of accepting that local usage although, as Bamgbose has observed, English-L2 users, including decision-makers in the education domain, tend to resist making this move (1998).

Internet as catalyst of acceptance: web-enabled innovations in cyberspace

In the decade since Bamgbose's article, the question of grammaticality and acceptability has become considerably more complex following significant breakthroughs in ICT and global advances in bi- or multilingual e-literacy, which invariably includes some English. In the first decade of the new millennium, in some real sense the 'global village' has rendered the world smaller following dramatic improvements in telecommunication mediated by the internet. Physical barriers marked by political and geographical boundaries, real or imagined, are increasingly rendered obsolete relative to people's desire to access information or communicate with others in cyberspace, wherever their internet workstation is located. For about two decades, information on the internet has been and continues to expand at an exponential rate, in more languages than ever, but search engines like Google, Yahoo and Baidu have made this task increasingly manageable for web-surfers (cf. Graddol 2006). Today, whatever the information in the public domain, be it language- or image-dominant, it is rarely more than just a few clicks away. As a result of this development, 'geography' and 'demography' as measures of English users' perception of the correctness of a local usage have become comparatively less significant. Much more pervasive today is what may be termed 'virtual vitality': whatever query about normative English usage one has, a quick check through Google or Yahoo (or any other search engine) can instantiate as many glocal examples as there are in various 'cyber communities', be they English-L2 or English-L1 users (Gupta 2005, 2006, 2007; cf. Pakir 1999).

Gupta (2007), for example, examines the extent of anglophony in official websites of the ten ASEAN nations and found that with few exceptions (notably Myanmar), English is widely used in the key domains of government and education. She also found a 'hierarchy of Anglophony' (p. 366), with English being more commonly used for internal purposes in some ASEAN nations (notably former British colonies) than in others. In terms of the extent of variation, despite minor divergence in spelling and usage patterns, which Gupta regards as 'differences of preference rather than categorical' (p. 357), the formal features of English across ASEAN websites are remarkably similar. This high degree of unity of Standard English is attributed to a loose consensus of elite users, suggesting that 'codification of English follows practice, rather than determining it' (p. 357).

Recent developments on the internet are thus exerting considerable impact on our perceptions of what counts as an error (i.e. the form is an unintended violation of some Standard English norm), as opposed to a linguistic innovation (i.e. the form is intended as a carrier of a new, probably culture-specific meaning with a local or glocal character). We have seen that more and more users of English turn to the internet as an act of licensing or means of legitimation (see examples 5–7): if an English usage is attested by a large enough number of users on the internet, especially if glocal and English-L1 users are included, it is difficult to insist that it is an error. One instructive example is the status of the collocation *advanced booking*, which appears to be non-standard but which is found on a large number of websites, including those of international hotel-booking agencies (see, e.g., www.epoquehotels.com/specials-promotions/promo-info.php/hotel/unahotelcatania/promo/1977) and a journal article on travel research (see Chen and Schwartz 2008). Or consider the spelling of *irresistable* which, while non-standard according to dictionaries in standard varieties of English and Microsoft Word, is no less popular than the normative counterpart *irresistible*, probably because the suffix *-able* is semantically and orthographically more transparent (compare the increasingly popular trend of writing *everyday* to mean 'every day', *can not* [VERB] instead of *cannot* [VERB]). These examples show that the spread of a new usage has the potential to catch on and command a mass following, especially if it is well motivated. When it later spreads to formal communication among educated English users on the internet, the legitimation process is half complete. When that happens, it is the duty of the lexicographer and/or grammarian to have its legitimate status – as an acceptable variant – formally recognized. In short, advances in ICT help explain why our attitudes towards the perceived legitimacy of a new English usage are less bound today by geography or demography than the popular choice of acrolectal English users in cyberspace, who tend to be educated, independent of their first-language background.

Why acrolectal, educated English users? This is related to Bamgbose's third factor or measure: authority. Just as renowned literary figures, writing in any language, enjoy the unquestioned prerogative or poetic licence to deviate from existing lexico-grammatical norms of the language, so educated speakers and writers have the unparalleled privilege to 'bend' the language at times to suit their context-specific needs. Such a move from an 'authority' would rarely raise any eyebrows, for it is generally perceived as a novel way of meaning-making, whatever the communicative purpose (e.g. new concept, imagery or metaphor). The same expression, produced by learners in the classroom or in some language-learning context (e.g. students' assessed class- or homework), would tend to be dismissed as 'interlanguage' in need of correction. For instance, a student of English who feels inspired by the Chinese Premier Wen Jiabao's rendition of *weiji* (危機, 'crisis') in Mandarin as a disyllabic word composed of the morphemes 'crisis' and 'opportunity' (Wen's official visit to London, February 2009), and who is tempted to capture both morphemes by the coinage *crisistunity*, may be praised by the teacher as 'a good attempt', but it would nonetheless be dismissed as 'non-standard' – along with other 'interlanguage' errors. Yet when this coinage appears in a feature article of an English daily, as it does (Gao 2009), complete with sound justification and supportive illustrations, no reader will question its status as a well-conceived innovation. A Google search of *crisistunity* in mid-February 2009 failed to yield any hits. Another Google search two months later (13 April 2009), however, returned over 330 hits, including translations of the original English article into foreign languages such as Italian and Russian, but also in an e-newsletter update of Broome County Peace Action, New York (March 2009, http://bcpeaceaction.org/update.pdf), and a website entitled 'Jump Ultimate Star' featuring air travel, leisure activities and other links (http://crisistunity.com/justp/). Interestingly, the 330 plus hits also include a few other websites containing a similar word 'crisitunity' (with only one 's'), which was apparently coined by Homer Simpson:

> Crisitunity: A Chinese word refered [sic] to by Homer Simpson that means both crisis and oppertunity [sic], just like Ercle.
> (Urban Dictionary, www.urbandictionary.com/define.php?term=Crisitunity)

> Upon being told that the Chinese word for 'crisis' is the same as their word for 'opportunity,' Homer Simpson gave the word 'crisitunity' to the English-speaking world.
> (Crisitunities in Humanist Parenting: The Science Project, http://danceswith
> anxiety.blogspot.com/2008/05/crisitunities-in-humanist-parenting.html)

Crisistunity (coined by a Chinese-L1, English-L2 speaker) and *crisitunity* (coined or adapted by an English-L1 speaker) may sound clumsy to the ear phonologically, but they appear to be catching on. This is a clear example of lexical innovations inspired by Chinese 'equivalents' which are similar in meaning, albeit with subtle semantic nuances. Of further interest is that, after lexical innovations were coined (apparently) independently by an English-L2 and an English-L1 user, the English-L2 coinage (*crisistunity*) appears to be 'crossing' into English-L1 territories, as shown in the above-mentioned New York Broome County Peace Action e-update:

President Obama is a centrist. We don't need a Goldilocks President (not too hot, not 'crisistunity' say [sic] Kevin.

(http://bcpeaceaction.org/update.pdf, p. 2)

In terms of process, the spread of *crisistunity* seems not so different in kind from the popularization of an English-L1 coinage like *nonebrity*, denoting a celebrity who is famous for nothing in particular. There is thus some indication that hybrids and bilingual creativity (Kachru 1995) by English-L2 users have good potential to be appropriated by English-L2 and English-L1 users alike – thanks to forces of globalization mediated and facilitated by the internet.

A second example comes from Phan Le Ha's (2008) book where, in the section 'Ha and English', she writes:

[My parents] did not have the right to choose the language they liked [to study] at that time, Russian or Chinese or French. For historical and political reasons, these languages had high status in Vietnam in those days. It also meant that learning and teaching English then would lead people to an 'insecure' future with almost no chance for further study overseas. And going overseas in the 1970s, 1980s and early 1990s did not just bring about new knowledge but also meant 'changing one's material life' to 'wealthi-ness' or at least 'well-furnituredness'.

(Phan 2008: 15)

The author is unmistakable about her Vietnamese-L1 and English-L2 background. The use of scare quotes in 'well-furnituredness' (and 'wealthi-ness') is a sign of its potentially objectionable status. This is partly confirmed by the result of a Google search (mid-February 2009), which returns no other entry than Phan's (2008) book page itself, suggesting that this usage is idiosyncratic. Be that as it may, the fact that it has survived the copy-editing stage of the book-production process is suggestive of a high level of tolerance of non-standard English usage in works written by acrolectal, educated English-L2 writers.

To sum up, Bamgbose's five internal factors or measures of innovation discussed above should be complemented by a sixth, namely, the popular choice of acrolectal English-L2 users in cyberspace.

Conclusion

One consequence of the emergence of English as the world's *de facto* global language is that, whatever a person's first-language background, he or she will be disadvantaged without learning at least some English. The variety of English which has the greatest currency is Standard English (Li 2007). Despite being standardized and codified for decades (e.g. AusE) or centuries (e.g. BrE and AmE), a standard variety of English is a system that leaks. For millions of English-L2 users, this is one source of learner-unfriendliness. Another source is considerable variation within a standard variety of English. These two sources of learner-unfriendliness, coupled with cross-linguistic influence from the previously acquired language(s), help account for English-L2 learners' propensity to produce all kinds of non-standard features at all stages of the learning process.

For a long time, deviations from Standard English norms were characterized as unsuccessful attempts at imitating the ways native speakers use English, or 'errors' in short. Research in World Englishes and other related paradigms for over two decades, however, has made a very strong case for the legitimacy of non-standard features found in the Englishes of ESL users who use English for intra-ethnic communication. The fine line between errors and innovations has been challenged. It has been shown that many of the seemingly non-standard ESL usage patterns are in fact well-motivated innovations, subject to five factors or measures (Bamgbose 1998): 'demographic' (i.e. percentage of acrolectal users vis-à-vis mesolectal and basilectal users), 'geographical', 'authoritative', 'codification' and 'acceptability' (i.e. attitudes).

A decade after Bamgbose's (1998) landmark article, 'authoritative', 'codification' and 'acceptability' remain important measures of innovation, but 'demographic' and 'geographical' are arguably declining in relative significance following dramatic advances world-wide in ICT (information and communication technologies) – internet communication in particular. Increasingly, English-L2 and English-L1 users alike may turn to the internet to ascertain the 'virtual vitality' of a given coinage or usage pattern with the help of a search engine like Google, Yahoo or Baidu. This practice has significant impact on the degree of its perceived legitimacy and acceptability. Therefore, Bamgbose's five internal factors or measures need to be complemented with a sixth, namely the popular choice of acrolectal, educated users of English on the internet, whatever their first language may be (cf. Gupta 2005, 2006, 2007).

Suggestions for further reading

Bamgbose (1998) is a seminal article covering the key issues in the debate concerning the slippery distinction between errors and innovations.

Breiteneder's (2005) paper provides empirical evidence how the 'third person -s' is systematically flouted by speakers of English as a European lingua franca (cf. Breiteneder 2009).

For a theoretically informed discussion of identity-driven 'user English' as opposed to acquisition-based 'learner English', see Kirkpatrick (2007).

References

Bamgbose, A. (1998) 'Torn between the norms: innovations in World Englishes', *World Englishes*, 17 (1): 1–14.

Breiteneder, A. (2005) 'The naturalness of English as a European lingua franca: the case of the "third person -s"', *Vienna English Working PaperS*, 14 (2): 3–26. Online. Available www.univie.ac.at/Anglistik/Views0502ALL.pdf (accessed 15 February 2009).

——(2009) 'English as a lingua franca in Europe: an empirical perspective', in M. Berns and B. Seidlhofer (eds) Symposium 'Perspectives on Lingua Franca', *World Englishes*, 28 (2): 256–69.

Butler, S. (2007) 'Dictionary publishing in Asia', in D. Prescott (ed.) *English in Southeast Asia. Varieties, Literacies and Literatures*, Newcastle: Cambridge Scholars Publishing, pp. 30–46.

Cameron, D., Frazer, E., Harvey, P., Rampton, M.B.H. and Richardson, K. (1992) *Research Language: Issues of Power and Method*, London: Routledge.

Chao, Y.R. (1968) *A Grammar of Spoken Chinese*, Berkeley: University of California Press.

Chen, C.C. and Schwartz, Z. (2008) 'Timing matters: travelers' advanced-booking expectations and decisions', *Journal of Travel Research*, 47 (1): 35–42. Online. Available www.epoquehotels.com/specials-promotions/promo-info.php/hotel/unahotelcatania/promo/1977 (accessed 15 February 2009).

Crystal, D. (2003) *English as a Global Language*, Cambridge: Cambridge University Press.

Dolezal, F. (2006) 'World Englishes and lexicography', in B.B. Kachru, Y. Kachru and C.L. Nelson (eds) *The Handbook of World Englishes*, Oxford: Blackwell. 'Blackwell Reference Online'. Available www.blackwellreference.com/public/ (accessed 15 February 2009).

Gao, Z. (2009) 'Every crisis offers a golden opportunity', *China Daily (HK edition)*, 7–8 February 2009: 9.

Goffman, E. (1981) *Forms of Talk*, Philadelphia: University of Pennsylvania Press.

Graddol, D. (2006) *English Next?* London: British Council. Online. Available www.britishcouncil.org/learning-research-english-next.pdf (accessed 15 February 2009).

Gupta, A.F. (2005) 'Standard English. Who needs it?', plenary presentation at the Tenth English in Southeast Asia Conference, 'A Decade of Growth', Department of English Language and Applied Linguistics, Faculty of Arts and Social Sciences, Universiti Brunei Darussalam, Brunei, 12–14 December.

——(2006) 'Standard English in the world', in M. Saraceni and R. Rubdy (eds) *English in the World: Global Rules, Global Roles*, London: Continuum, pp. 95–109.

——(2007) 'ASEAN English on the web', in D. Prescott (ed.) *English in Southeast Asia. Varieties, Literacies and Literatures*, Newcastle: Cambridge Scholars Publishing, pp. 353–70.

Huddleston, R. and Pullum, G.K. (2005) *A Student's Introduction to English Grammar*, Cambridge: Cambridge University Press.

Jenkins, J. (2003) *World Englishes. A Resource Book for Students*, London: Routledge.

——(2006) 'Points of view and blind spots: ELF and SLA', *International Journal of Applied Linguistics*, 16 (2): 137–62.

——(2007) *English as a Lingua Franca: Attitude and Identity*, Oxford: Oxford University Press.

Kachru, B.B. (1995) 'Transcreating creativity in World Englishes and literary canons', in G. Cook and B. Seidlhofer (eds) *Principle and Practice in Applied Linguistics*, Oxford: Oxford University Press, pp. 271–88.

Kirkpatrick, A. (2007) *World Englishes: Implications for International Communication and English Language Teaching*, Cambridge: Cambridge University Press.

Li, D.C.S. (2003) 'Between English and Esperanto: What does it take to be a world language?' *International Journal of the Sociology of Language*, 164: 33–63.

——(2007) 'Researching and teaching China and Hong Kong English: issues, problems and prospects', *English Today*, 23 (3 and 4): 11–17.

——(2009) 'Researching NNSs' views toward intelligibility and identity: bridging the gap between moral high grounds and down-to-earth concerns', in F. Sharifian (ed.) *English as an International Language: Perspectives and Pedagogical Issues*, Clevedon: Multilingual Matters, pp. 81–118.

——(in press) 'Improving the standards and promoting the use of English in Hong Kong: issues, problems and prospects', in A.W. Feng (ed.) *English Language Use and Education across Greater China*, Clevedon: Multilingual Matters.

Li, D.C.S. and Chan, A.Y.W. (2001) 'Form-focused negative feedback: correcting three common errors', *TESL Reporter*, 34 (1): 22–34.

Littlewood, W. (1984) *Foreign and Second Language Learning: Language-acquisition Research and its Implications for the Classroom*, Cambridge: Cambridge University Press.

Lock, G. (1995) *Functional English Grammar: An Introduction for Second Language Teachers*, Cambridge: Cambridge University Press.

McArthur, T. (1998) *Concise Oxford Companion to the English Language*, Oxford: Oxford University Press.

Milroy, J. and Milroy, L. (1985) *Authority in Language. Investigating Language Prescription and Standardization* (2nd edition), London: Routledge.

Pakir, A. (1999) 'Bilingual education with English as an official language: sociocultural implications', Digital Georgetown. Online. Available http://digital.georgetown.edu/gurt/1999/gurt_1999_25.pdf (accessed 14 July 2008).

Paton, G. (2008) 'University students cannot spell', *Daily Telegraph*, 6 August. Online. Available www.telegraph.co.uk/news/2510704/University-students-cannot-spell.html (accessed 9 August 2008).

Phan Le Ha (2008) *Teaching English as an International Language: Identity, Resistance and Negotiation*, Clevedon: Multilingual Matters.

Schneider, E. (2007) *Postcolonial English. Varieties around the World*, Cambridge: Cambridge University Press.

Seidlhofer, B. (2004) 'Research perspectives on teaching English as a lingua franca', *Annual Review of Applied Linguistics*, 24: 209–39.

——(2005) 'English as a lingua franca', in A.S. Hornby (ed.) *Oxford Advanced Learner's Dictionary of Current English*, Oxford: Oxford University Press, p. R92.

Trudgill, P. and Hannah, J. (2002) *International English* (4th edition), London: Arnold.

Widdowson, H.G. (1994) 'The ownership of English', *TESOL Quarterly*, 31: 377–89.

37

Academic Englishes

A standardized knowledge?

*Anna Mauranen, Carmen Pérez-Llantada[1]
and John M. Swales*

Some initial considerations

It is a fact universally acknowledged that English has emerged in recent decades as the premier vehicle for the communication of scholarship, research and advanced post-graduate training. The causes of this rise have, however, been the subject of consider-able controversy, with a particularly strenuous debate between Phillipson (e.g. 1999) and Crystal (2000), which is fully reprised and extended in Seidlhofer (2003). What-ever the merits of the various arguments, whether, for example, Crystal's 1997 account is 'triumphalist' or not, there can be no doubt that English has become the principal medium for the transmission and exchange of academic knowledge, just as there can be no doubt that the global number of academic communications, both in English and in other languages, has greatly increased in recent decades. And this applies not simply to the number of research articles and scholarly books published each year, but also to the number of international and more local academic conferences held annually, as well as to other kinds of cross-national academic and research exchange, such as multinational research projects and the growing numbers of students spending study periods outside their home countries (Fortanet-Gómez and Räisänen 2008). In other words, the increasing use of academic English is not confined to the printed word, but equally applies to the spoken utterance.

Aspects of the similarities and differences between written and spoken academic and research speech – in all their uses and varieties – will surface at various points in this chapter. At the outset, however, it is pertinent to consider, and perhaps reconsider, the relationship between these two primary modes. For a number of reasons, the written mode was long privileged by analysts and researchers of academic discourse, as it was by instructors in the applied field of English for Academic Purposes. For one thing, it is written work that is primarily assessed and evaluated, both for students as they journey towards their higher degrees, and for academics as they apply for better jobs or come up for evaluation and potential contract renewal, tenure or promotion. Second, written exemplars have been much easier to get hold of and to get a handle on; they also more readily lend themselves to the traditional methods of linguistic analysis. Third, the recent rise of interest in courses, workshops and manuals designed to develop academic language skills has also been largely focused on the written side. For instance, there is now a considerable body of material designed to help students, both with English as a first language or as an additional language (EAL), in the writing of Master's and PhD theses (e.g. Swales and Feak 2000), but, at present, there is relatively little available to help them with the oral presentation and defence of their work. So, not only has the written side of things been privileged, but, in addition, it has tended to become detached from the various speech events and episodes in which the development of academic text is typically immersed.

Over the last decade, however, there has been something of a change in both perception and outcome with regard to the speech–writing 'divide'. One motivating force is increasing interest on the part of applied linguists and others in ethnographic studies of the academy. An important and influential work in this regard is Prior's *Writing/ Disciplinarity* (Prior 1998). His case studies offer insights into the lived experience of post-graduate seminars in which talk emerges as a crucial element in textualizing processes and also as a negotiated ground that undermines the traditional institutional power imbalance between professors and their post-graduate students. Later work along these lines includes Tardy (2005) and Seloni (2008). Another has been the creation of corpora of spoken academic and research English (e.g. T2K-SWAL), and the more widely available Michigan Corpus in Academic Spoken English (MICASE), and the many publications that have been based on them, such as Biber *et al.* (2002) and Pérez-Llantada and Ferguson (2006). A third development, very much centred on Europe, has been interest by discourse analysts in the conference presentation, over and beyond the traditional research focus on the written research article. A key work here is the outstanding collection edited by Ventola *et al.* (2002).

If the balance of attention between spoken and written genres is now being readjusted, there are other affordances that work for an even greater rapprochement. One requires a recognition of the Bakhtinian notion of 'inner' or 'private' speech. Every time we are faced with a non-trivial speaking or writing task, we run through options in our minds as we prepare to either address an audience (as when preparing to ask a question) or place our fingers on the keyboard (as when composing a conference abstract). We mentally rehearse, as we try to imagine the effects of possible spoken or written offerings. In effect, there are cognitive and rhetorical correspondences here. Another type of affordance derives from the ongoing development of hybrid communicative styles in electronic genres such as emails and blogs, and in those parts of websites that deal with such part-genres as FAQs (Bloch 2008). A third is essentially sociological, or at least socio-academic. A major change in the perception of academia originated in science studies in the 1970s, when sociologists and anthropologists turned their attention to scientific work. Instead of asking scientists what they did and taking their word for it, they observed the activities that scientists actually engaged in. This constituted a major break with the traditional provinces of the philosophy or the history of science. The reorientation in seeing academia coincided with changes in academic practices: while scientists had worked in teams for centuries, scholars in the 'soft' sciences had remained solitary individuals, each on their own projects. Twenty years ago, the concept of the individual scholar toiling away in her solipsistic ivory tower, or of the lonely PhD student immured in her library carrel, has been replaced by a growing speech-writing interconnectedness of those individual members of the academic world, mainly through formal sub-groupings of researchers and research students, as well as via various kinds of informal collectives for study, information or mutual support, not excluding various specialized 'lists' on the web. In consequence of all this, the older models of speaking–writing interaction that tended to consider the oral component as sub-ordinate, preparatory or merely evaluative in a *post hoc* kind of way (as in a thesis defence or a promotion committee) are being replaced. As Rubin and Kang interestingly propose:

> A more apt model might be a double helix with a writing strand and a speaking strand intertwined. At any particular page one strand may be the focal outcome, drawing upon the other. But as a whole, the two strands are reciprocally supportive and leading in the same direction.
>
> (Rubin and Kang 2008: 220)

A third type of initial consideration involves some recognition of the immense phenomenon that academic English has become. There are millions of Anglophone research papers published a year, millions of Anglophone lectures delivered each week, and globally, the number of Anglophone PhD theses completed each year around the world certainly reaches six figures (Swales 2004). Although often well designed, our investigative samples of this vast production are, as a result, necessarily small fractions of the total outputs. In consequence, extrapolations need to be made with some care, partly because of the range of potentially intervening variables.

A further complication arises when we note that drawing a bead on academic Englishes is to focus on a moving target. While this observation also doubtless applies to many objects of study in a wide range of fields, the issue is rather more pressing in our case because getting a useful handle on this type of World English has educational and instrumental ramifications that apply much less to (say) studies of Jamaican English. Although the longer historical view of research English has been traced in the works of Bazerman (1988), Gross *et al.* (2002) and others, contemporary developments may need particular attention. These would include the apparent growing use of promotional elements in research texts as a response to increased pressure to publish and increased time pressure on readers; the increasing proportions of authors and presenters who are speakers of English as a lingua franca; and the growing role of electronic publishing, particularly the consequences of html formats becoming available.

The final accounting needs to reflect the fact that variation in Academic English is multifaceted and extremely complex; indeed, much remains to be teased out, especially in trying to ensure that the sub-corpora used for comparative purposes are appropriately comparable. For example, there is the largely understudied issue of author effects that go beyond the traditional division between native and non-native speakers of English. Are there palpable differences in academic communications between British and American (or Australian for that matter) authors? Are there gender differences? And what about status? Do older, more successful authors and presenters manipulate their discoursal resources differently? Since the work on these issues is relatively scant, we will briefly discuss it in the following section. As already noted, one of the more obvious manifestations of variation in Academic English is that determined by the channel of communication (i.e. speech vs writing). Another well-known kind of variability is that resulting from the differing methodological, research and rhetorical traditions of different disciplines. A third has long been the province of Contrastive Rhetoric or Comparative Rhetoric (Connor 1996) and concerns the putative effects of language and/or culture on academic communications, and how best to account for the variations found (Mauranen 2003). And here there is need to keep in mind, not only broad influences that might derive from national academic traditions, but also more narrowly contextual factors. For instance, one concerns the linguistic consequences of the perceived role of the particular academic communication: is it 'normal science', or is it groundbreaking in some way? Studies here include Paul *et al.* (2001) on the rhetorical manoeuvres undertaken by the first papers launching Chaos Theory, and Helal (2008) on the struggle between the USA and France for priority in early AIDS research. In addition, work by Burgess (2002), among others, suggests that size and nature of the discourse community towards which a piece of academic communication may be directed can also be rhetorically and linguistically significant. In the sections entitled 'Academic English as a lingua franca' and 'Cross-cultural variation in Academic English', respectively, we tackle the broader issues of cross-cultural attitudes and linguistic responses to the exigencies of the contemporary research world. In the final section, we attempt to assess the relative influences of the various differentiating factors we have identified, provide some future trends that may need further exploration and offer a few thoughts on the further likely developments in English as lingua franca in academic contexts (Mauranen 2003, 2006a), and of Academic Englishes, particularly whether we are likely to see growing resistance to its standardization.

Academic Englishes – personal influences

There has been a presumption in the applied linguistics literature that British and North American authors – and less certainly presenters – can be lumped together. However, consider this reconstructed conversation between the co-editors of an ESP journal, which took place about twenty years ago.

> American co-editor: I've got another of those British papers. There are lots of good ideas up front, but the data is small, the methodology is suspect, the results thin, and the so-called discussion is just a summary because all the interesting stuff is in the introduction.

> British co-editor: Well, I've just got another of those American efforts. The intro is just a comprehensive listing of previous research, the methods part is over-detailed and stodgy, and the results are extensive but hard to interpret – only right towards the end of the discussion is there any intellectual spark when the author discusses possibilities for future research.

At that time at least, different traditions seemed to be in play: a British penchant for Oxbridge-type flashiness, and an American one very much in thrall to the *Publication Manual of the American Psychological Association*. More recent experiences and observations would, however, suggest that these differences have become much diminished. One of the few people to have empirically examined this issue is Sanderson (2008) via her corpus of articles drawn from the softer social sciences and the humanities. She found, *inter alia*, that US and UK authors in general did not vary greatly in their use of personal pronouns, certainly in comparison to German scholars writing in German. However, she did find a striking gender difference, as British females used far

637

fewer first and second personal pronouns than any other group. Interestingly, Chang (2004) in her dissertation noted that, of her six informants, the female professor of architecture also used fewer personal pronouns than the others, who remarked in an interview that she preferred a formal style because it was 'more scientific'. Sanderson concludes that more research is needed, observing, 'It would certainly be interesting if academic discourse were to constitute an exception to, or even the disproof of, the widespread stereotype that women's language is more personal than men' (2008: 133). One of the few studies that has explored possible gender differences in academic speech is Poos and Simpson (2002), who investigated the use of the hedges *kind of* and *sort of* in the MICASE corpus – hedges stereotypically associated with female speech. They found that female lecturers did use these more, but then showed that this finding had little to do with gender and much to do with discipline. It turned out that female lecturers were over-represented in the social sciences and the humanities and under-represented in science and engineering, and that the 'softer areas' were intrinsically more prone to this type of modification. Indeed, they suggested that saying something like 'this is sort of a cultural problem' was in fact part of the disciplinary acculturation of students in these softer disciplines, rather than being 'a weak hedge'. Sanderson also explored other possible personal variables in her small corpus, and her preliminary conclusions were that 'higher status academics and male scholars adopt a more explicitly personal academic voice than do more junior and/or female colleagues' (2008: 134). However, as we remarked earlier, the influence, if any, of personal variables such as regional provenance, gender, status and age is as yet largely uncharted. In contrast, we know much more about first-language influences, the topic of the next two sections.

Academic English as a lingua franca

Although English is the global lingua franca of academic discourse, most research in academic English is oriented towards the written language, native speakers of English, and the normative tenets of Standard English as used in academia. As already noted in the preliminaries for this chapter, a number of factors converge towards the emphasis on the written language. Along with the global spread of English as the language of academic publication it was perhaps natural to equate 'good writing' with 'good English', and to call in native speakers of English to act as language revisers of the texts of academics from non-English backgrounds (see, for example, Ventola and Mauranen 1991; Mauranen 1997; Burrough-Boenisch 2004). Language editors saw as their main task the correction of lexicogrammatical errors, but they abstained from tackling the textual organization and pragmatic aspects of the texts they were revising. They said they were doing this on account of not wishing to tamper with the writer's preferred way of presenting themselves, and because they believed the writers knew what they were doing rhetorically (Mauranen 1997). But most studies in contrastive rhetoric showed that it was textual organization and textual preferences beyond lexicogrammatical correctness which showed the strongest influence of different academic writing cultures.

It turned out that our textual practices and preferences develop in our socialization into a particular culture of writing, and since writing cultures vary, there is no universal standard of 'good writing'. Textual aspects of writing are harder to monitor than lexicogrammatical phenomena, since only the latter are really standardized. Writing guides do exist, but until surprisingly recently they were rarely written by linguists, usually relying on the preferences of enthusiastic laymen. As a consequence, their focus was on matters of appropriate 'style' in respect of expressing things like objectivity, simplicity or certainty, often in impressionistic ways that have been easy to question in subsequent linguistic investigations of what real scientific and scholarly texts are like.

In the absence of clear standards of text organization, it has been easy to make a leap in the thought chain and assume that if English is the language of scientific publication, we should not only observe basic grammatical rules of correctness of Standard English, but follow the Anglo-American lead in matters of stylistic and rhetorical preferences as well. Such a leap is mistaken. Clearly, science, as an inherently and traditionally international enterprise, has no natural link to any national culture; its centres have moved from place to place over the centuries. Thus, although we can assume that educated native speakers have a well-entrenched idea of Standard English grammar and lexis, it does not follow that their stylistic or rhetorical preferences are superior to those of scientists who use a second language in their professional lives. When English is written for a world-wide audience, criteria for good rhetoric or effective text organization may be quite different from those required in writing for a British or American audience. In particular, it is important to see that Anglo-American rhetoric is not necessarily the most effective, comprehensible or 'natural' choice for structuring academic texts even if we use English. It goes without saying that it is not more 'scientific'.

The study of academic speaking has developed much later than academic writing as a research area. The field has really taken off since the late 1990s, with the compilation of corpora of contemporary academic speech (MICASE, see http://quod.lib.umich.edu/m/micase; T2K-SWAL, see Biber 2006). The internationalization of university recruitment has raised awareness of speaking, as has the skyrocketing number of international academic conferences. The initial interest in academic speaking was closely tied to the immediate applications of findings in testing and teaching, although scholars were immediately able to see the wider interest value of the data, given the importance and the scarcity of speech data in linguistics. The initial work followed along the lines of written language research in its basic attitude: let us find out how native speakers go about academic speaking and teach the rest of the world to follow suit. Despite the straightforward approach to reaping benefits from native speakers' language to provide a model to non-native speakers, changes had taken place in English for Academic Purposes by the time the first corpora were completed. There was more awareness of cultural variability, and more concern with identities. There was also budding awareness of English as an international lingua franca, rather than as a language exclusively belonging to its native speakers in the 'core' cultures (e.g. Widdowson 1994; Jenkins 2000). These signs of the time found their way to the MICASE corpus, where the proportion of non-native speakers is quite large (12 per cent) as a consequence. Although 'the native speaker bias' was nowhere near as large as in academic writing research, it was nevertheless the dominant mode of thinking, and still is. Nevertheless, there is growing awareness now of the deeply international character of the academic world, not only in publications, but in all its aspects, and at all levels.

The first corpus of academic English spoken as a lingua franca, the ELFA corpus (www.eng.helsinki.fi/elfa/elfacorpus.htm) began its recordings in 2002, close on the heels of the first native corpora. It is interesting to note that in this case the usual progression from written to spoken language has been reversed; although another corpus of English as a lingua franca (ELF), VOICE, is being compiled in Vienna (www.univie.

ac.at/voice/index.php), there is no written database of English as a lingua franca as yet. English is becoming ubiquitous in academic life, as already discussed above, particularly at a moment of increasing international collaborative exchanges across academic institutions. Joint international English-medium degree programmes are also mushrooming in Europe. Although these programmes lean heavily on English especially in their official arrangements, English is not their only language: the programmes and their corollary activities are multicultural and often in practice very multilingual as well (see, e.g., Haberland *et al.* 2008).

It is clear that in order to understand English as an academic language, it needs to be captured in its current contexts. Demands for socially situating the analysis of academic language have been strong since the 1990s, and at present English is deeply embedded in a linguistically complex scene. One crucial aspect of the current situation is the enormous increase in the number of non-native speakers who use English and, more often than not, use it with other non-native speakers. It is estimated that non-native speakers currently outnumber native speakers of English several times, and although there are no direct measurements of the proportions in academic discourse (and the situation changes rapidly as well), we must assume that the situation is roughly the same in academia. Strictly speaking, academic discourses in themselves have no native speakers: they are learned in secondary socialization by all participants in academic communities of practice. Issues of register, specific terminology and phraseology, along with mastery of relevant genres, acceptable modes of argumentation, and ways of presenting a case are all consciously learned skills which are not acquired in the same way as a mother tongue. In this light it is not surprising that guidebooks to academic genres and registers are addressed to both natives and non-natives. More importantly, the internalization of the discourses of science and scholarship does not go hand in hand with the internalization of the minutiae of standard languages. Relations of power and authority in the globalized academic community are therefore far more complex than simply 'natives know best'.

If our purpose is to understand present-day academic speaking in English, we should look at the way English works as a lingua franca (ELF). To capture its nature and features, ELF is a better representative than native English. Conversely, for a linguist interested in ELF, academia offers an excellent vantage point for exploring developments in the language. It is one of the domains that has adopted English as its common language, and it is one where international communication characterizes the domain across the board. With the recent expansion of internationalism, the spread and influence of English used by second-language speakers can be expected to keep growing. Academic language conveys new, often abstract, concepts and thoughts, which participants also co-construct in their discussions and argumentation. Language plays a crucial role in achieving this, without usually being the focus of conscious attention. A good proportion of academic life consists in speech-in-interaction, a primary focus of interest to linguists. Participants have demanding tasks to accomplish with academic speech, often in their second language, which makes it a fascinating source of data for understanding complex language. Some features of academic ELF are sketched out below.

ELF research is a new domain. Although pioneering work was done in the 1990s, and some researchers made very prescient suggestions to take up the issue of English used internationally even before that (Knapp 1987; Haberland 1989), it is really only in the first decade of this millennium that ELF has begun to make its mark on the study of

English at all. Currently it is a widely debated issue in Applied Linguistics, and has begun to appear in the literature in English Studies. Apart from important general empirical work on ELF, notably by Jenkins (2000, 2007) and ground-breaking discussions on the principles and issues (Widdowson 1994; Seidlhofer 2005), most research so far has been based on fairly small-scale analyses, with some exceptions such as Mollin (2006), and perhaps Cogo (2007), Lesznyák (2004). The study of English as a lingua franca in academic contexts has caught on in the Nordic countries in particular: the ELFA corpus, a 1-million-word database of academic speech, has been compiled in Finland (Mauranen 2003, 2006a), and ongoing studies such as Björkman (2009), Shaw *et al.* (2009) and Mortensen (2008) indicate a wider interest in the new field. This is perhaps not so surprising in view of the strong interest in academic discourses in Nordic countries (for recent work, see Shaw and Dahl 2008), and their keenness to participate in international developments of the university world while seeking to maintain equality and plurality in the changing trends. A variety of research methods are being used in these studies, from corpus methods to interviews, questionnaires, storytelling tasks and ethnography and discourse analysis; several studies combine more than one of these in order to understand discourse practices, discourse procedures and disciplinary cultures in academic settings.

On the whole, findings on academic ELF support other observations on English as a lingua franca when similar issues have been investigated. Typical discourse-level findings include the observation that few instances of miscommunication can be observed (Mauranen 2006a; Björkman 2009; Kaur 2009). As a corollary, a number of proactive strategies for ensuring comprehensibility have been found, such as ways of increasing explicitness by frequent rephrasing and repetition, metadiscourse and explicit negotiation of topic (Mauranen 2005a, 2005b, 2006a, 2007). Enhanced cooperation has also been found in many studies, including one concerned with online discussion groups as part of a university course (Karhukorpi 2006). The use of vague expressions is in principle similar in ELF as in native-English academic discourse, as shown by Metsä-Ketelä (2006), with certain differences in the distribution of preferred expressions. Interestingly, a disciplinary domain division is seen in both speaker groups to the effect that vague expressions are more frequent in hard sciences than the social sciences and the humanities (Metsä-Ketelä 2008). It appears that the employment of vague language reflects generic and disciplinary conventions, while explicitness-enhancing discourse strategies arise from situational demands. Lexicogrammatical features bear certain similarities to ELF findings in general; articles and prepositions tend to get used in non-standard ways. Morphological overproductivity is also fairly common, as is the regularization of irregular verbs and the turning of uncountable nouns into countables. Lack of concordance or subject–verb agreement is also often found. The vexed issue of the third-person -s (Breiteneder 2005; Cogo and Dewey 2006) shows that, although ELF speakers tend to drop it, as do many native dialects, they can also produce it and use it when deemed necessary. In the use of multiword phraseological units ELF speakers tend to make new departures from native speakers' conventions and preferences (Mauranen 2004, 2005b, 2006b, 2007; Seidlhofer 2007), although this clearly does not usually disrupt communication or affect comprehensibility. A particularly frequent use of the -*ing* form of the verb has often been seen as a non-native problem, but as Ranta (2006) points out, it can also be seen as a means of making the verb more emphatic or expressive. Interestingly, the -*ing* form is on the increase in native Englishes as well (Leech and Smith 2006; Mair 2006) which may point to intriguing possibilities of parallelism or mutual influences in the development of English (see Kortmann, this volume). A similar point might be made on the tendency of dropping plural marking of nouns after numerals (Björkman 2008), which is an existing feature in older forms of English as well. In all, academic ELF shows many features which can also be discerned in non-academic ELF, learner language (e.g. Granger 2002), vernacular universals (Chambers 2003), native English dialects and even Standard English (Leech and Smith 2006). Its more specifically 'academic' characteristics can be compared to usage in native English, such as the tendency to coin new and *ad hoc* terms by making frequent innovative use of the morphological resources of English (Mauranen 2008). It is clearly an integral part of present-day English, and quite likely to become even more inextricably intertwined with the English used by the native-English speaking minority.

Cross-cultural variation in academic English

If, in the previous section, we noted that a good proportion of academic life consists in speech-in-interaction, it goes without saying that a good proportion of academic life also involves exposure to genres assisting an academic or research career (submission letters, biostatements or job applications) and to genres materializing a research career (theses and dissertations, research articles or grant proposals, for example, cf. Swales and Feak 2000: 8). This fact may explain the current interest in cross-cultural uses of academic written English by non-native speakers of English, as regards the particular textual organization and textual preferences (transferred from their mother languages and their own rhetorical traditions) that they use when transmitting disciplinary knowledge and negotiating textual meanings.

The particular appropriations of the normative tenets of standard academic English by non-native English scholars are becoming more visible in the process of internationalization of universities (cf. Flowerdew 2007: 14). This process has spread the use of English as an Additional Language (EAL) for scholarly exchange across universities and seems to be producing two divergent effects in academic written prose – an increased emphasis on 'Englishization' (Swales 2004: 52) in the world-wide academic arena on the one hand, and a growing attention to the culture-specific textual and rhetorical preferences of Academic English by non-native scholars on the other. While the former effect acts as a centripetal force towards the standardization and hence homogenization of academic writing practices, the latter is a centrifugal force which contributes to heterogeneity and diversity as it brings to the fore the linguistic richness of culture-specific uses of normative Academic English. These multilingual varieties are an integral part of current academic uses of ELF and may somehow contest any standardization trends.

Standardization and homogeneity in academic writing should be intrinsically related to the utility of English as a shared medium for scientific communication, as a 'functional necessity' (Ammon 2006: 25) for monolingualism in academic exchange, not unlike the function of Latin in mediaeval scholarship and science. Standard style guides which, as we mentioned above, are written by non-linguists who take an interest in prescriptive language rules, define standard Academic English as highly lexicalized and conceptually dense *à propos* its propositional meanings, and mainly featured by the passive reporting of research processes with the aim of conveying impartiality, accuracy and objectivity (Barras 1978; Day 1979). However, linguists have broadly argued that academic writing is a socially constructed rhetorical artefact owing to its overlapping communicative goals to transmit new disciplinary knowledge and to persuade the readership of the validity of this new knowledge (see Askehave and Swales 2001). Thus, at some rhetorical 'moments' (e.g. the 'Create a Research Space' moment in research article introductions, or the 'Consolidating Research Findings' move in research article conclusions, cf. Swales 1990), academic writers do not only convey propositional meaning, but also tinge the discourse with evaluative, interpersonal and interaction-oriented meanings. By this means, authors open up a dialogic space within which they can highlight their findings in order to convince their readers of the value of these research outcomes. Echoing what Hunston and Thompson define as 'a local grammar of evaluation' (2001: 74), lexicogrammatical patterns such as evaluative *that*-clauses (Johns 2001), the construction of authorial stance through more or less personal/ impersonal grammaticalizations such as first-person pronouns, active verbs with inanimate subjects and anticipatory *it*-patterns placing heavier constituents at the end of the clause (cf. Hewings 2001; Harwood 2005), as well as stance and engagement resources such as modal and semi-modal verbs, epistemic lexical verbs and hedging mechanisms (Markkanen and Schröder 1997; Hyland 1998) have been reported to help writers construct and negotiate textual meanings in a very standardized way.

Concomitant with these homogeneous practices, heterogeneity in academic writing may be conceived of as a feasible linguistic effect of the pressure that universities worldwide are putting on their researchers to publish in international 'English-only journals' (Belcher 2007). These institutional demands seem to be an immediate response to achieving high quality standards and excellence in higher education and, in the long run, international competition for good students and the desire to support the competitiveness of national economies. As a result, non-native English scholars are encouraged to 'publish in English or perish' since, whether we like it or not, English is to date the language of international knowledge sharing and publishing. Other social reasons are also promoting the gradual homogenization of Academic English. Non-native English scholars are showing interest in achieving higher academic recognition and prestige within their disciplinary communities and, instead of publishing in their own languages, they publish in English 'to be acknowledged by the top scientific community of their discipline' (Hamel 2007: 61). Generally speaking, this seems to be so in most disciplines, although there remain pockets of research with more specific and local interests too.

As noted above, the evidence from Contrastive Rhetoric so far seems to point to notable differences in cultural preferences in academic rhetoric. Whether this will lead to homogenization in time is an open question, but a priori conclusions with regard to its inevitability are not warranted. These institutional and social demands affect the dissemination of scientific knowledge through English-medium communicative channels as diverse as article journals, doctoral theses, grant proposals, lecture talks or research-oriented conferences and seminars, among others. The Contrastive Rhetoric field, for instance, has provided compelling evidence of how non-native scholars adopt the standard rules of academic English, yet transfer some L1 text organization and rhetorical preferences to their texts when publishing internationally.

Linguistic deviation from standard Academic English has been reported on the grounds of different rhetorical features such as text-reflexivity (Mauranen 1993; Dahl 2004), and interpersonal resources or engagement markers (Martín and Burgess 2004; Fløttum 2005; Vold 2006, among others). These rhetorical differences confirm that the native writers use a more reader-oriented style than their non-native counterparts, and that they construct their ideal audiences differently. While the native writers consider their audiences as potentially consenting, the non-natives perceive their readers as potentially dissenting towards authors' points of view and interpretation of the new research findings (Mur 2007; Duszak and Lewkowicz 2008). The ostensible co-existence of standard Academic English discourse and its local uses should perhaps be better conceptualized as a tension between the established conventions for academic writing in the international academic sphere (which have unquestioningly been equated with Anglo-American rhetoric) and the culture-specific uses of those standard practices that ultimately account for the transfer of rhetorical and discoursal preferences of the scholars' L1 to English. This tension inevitably leads – or so it seems – to the hybridization of academic discourse. If we borrow Fairclough's concept of 'interdiscursive hybridity' (2006: 25) to refer to the mixing of 'discourses, genres or styles from different orders of discourse', in the case of academic writing, the mixing of the use of the normative Standard English (pointing towards homogeneity) and the use of the local, culture-specific textual organization and textual preferences of the non-native English scholars (leading to cross-cultural heterogeneity and diversity in Academic English). As depicted in Figure 37.1, this may call for a redefinition of contemporary academic prose in terms of 'interdiscursive hybridity', which could perhaps be seen as a manifestation of the glocalization process (Robertson 1995).

This proposed space for interdiscursive hybridity is indeed far more complex than it seems and is in need of further investigation, as it is difficult to decide whether it is

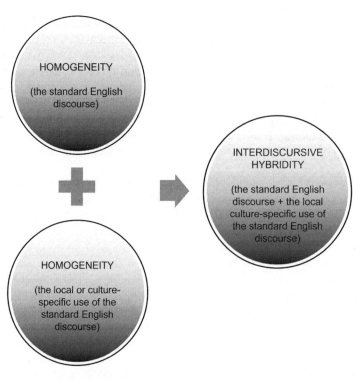

Figure 37.1 A proposed space for interdiscursive hybridity in contemporary academic English.

closer to the standard native discourse or still at a distance from it. To mention one interesting culture-specific phenomenon, Mur (2007) and Pérez-Llantada (2008, 2009) note that, while articles written in English by Spanish scholars in the humanities closely resemble the rhetorical traits of Spanish, medical and business articles written in English by Spanish scholars tend to 'go native' and stick to standardized academic English features. This variability should lead us to assume that the ethos, the nature of the knowledge of the discipline and its social ontology may play a role in the hybridization of academic English, hence substantiating previous claims about the existence of closely tied 'textographies' for academic knowledge production and 'academic tribes and research territories' (Swales 1998; Becher and Trowler 2001).

Leaving aside evident disciplinary variations, it has also been variously shown that the 'hybrid' discoursal features of the texts written in English by the non-native scholars influence the journal referees' opinions on the validity of these contributions, in some way contradicting Belcher's (2007: 11) claims that acceptance of the papers written by non-native English scholars is 'a story of reviewer patience and author persistence'. Using data from questionnaires, Flowerdew (2001) reports that 68 per cent of Cantonese academics feel disadvantaged as non-native writers, and that nearly a third of the respondents show awareness of journal referees' and editors' prejudice towards their contributions. Curry and Lillis's (2004) ethnographic study of academic writing of Hungarian, Slovakian and Spanish academics acknowledges the local scholars' awareness of their difficulty in making new knowledge claims accepted by the global research community. Gosden's (2003: 87) analysis of journal referees' reviews shows that two-thirds of the reviews refer to interactional deficiencies of non-native researchers' manuscripts, and Hewings (2006) observes that referees' reports indicate weak usage of English and information organization as the two main aspects that affect the acceptance of non-Anglophone manuscripts. Interdiscursive hybridity has also been approached from interesting descriptions of the role of native English-speaking language professionals in solving the linguistic, rhetorical and stylistic difficulties of non-Anglophone writers – difficulties ranging from hedging, tense conventions, genre-related principles and suitable development of the argumentation flow, to problems in the expression of authorial voice and its degree of assertiveness. Ventola and Mauranen (1991) explain how changes made by these professionals in revising non-Anglophone scholars' papers relate to grammar, hedging and organization of information. In an interesting case study, Kerans (2002) reports on the retraction of a paper written by a famous Spanish researcher for reasons of inappropriate wording and thematic development, as well as lack of structurally marked introductory and concluding moves. Burrough-Boenisch (2006) provides an account of the procedures followed by native English-speaking language professionals to adapt the scholars' local rhetorical preferences to the standard Academic English conventions of international journals, and Mišak et al.'s (2005) study also bears witness to the fact that non-Anglophone researchers feel disadvantaged by their non-native status and describe their experience as editors of a small Croatian medical journal and their proposals for coping with this linguistic inequality.

Another challenging issue arising from the interdiscursivity phenomenon in current academic writing is concerned with the steady displacement of the national languages in favour of English. Though perhaps not very convincingly, this has been regarded by some scholars as a kind of 'linguistic imperialism' (Canagarajah 1996; Ammon 2006) and a potential 'sociolinguistic conflict model of asymmetric relations' (Hamel 2007:

54) between the native and the non-native speakers of English. Within the EAP domain, attention has been drawn to the extent to which the use of English by non-native English speakers represents a threat for local identities and scholarly traditions and, eventually, a source of linguistic inequities for those non-Anglophone scholars who use English in their research publications (Ferguson 2007). Other examples of contemporary critiques of the displacement of national languages can be also found in Gentil's (2005) and Durand's (2006) objections to the dominant Anglo-American discourse style conventions in international journals gradually displacing French, or in Bennett's (2007) criticism of the predatory effects of English over minority languages, effects which, as she contends, trigger the 'epistemicide' of Portuguese rhetorical conventions. At this point, one may regard interdiscursive hybridity of English in academic settings as a process reaching for the standardization of academic writing, which would confirm that the non-native scholars are gradually losing their L1 rhetorical norms 'at the cost of moulding [their thoughts] in a conventional form' (Coulmas 2007: 6), that is, at the expense of the gradual peripheralization of their national languages and rhetorical traditions. Conversely, one may rather consider this hybridization as a means of reassuring the multicultural forces – or transcultural flows, as Pennycook (2006) more broadly refers to them – that are actively participating in world-wide academic exchange and with current claims on what constitutes acceptable English for academic written and spoken communication.

In recognizing peripheral cultural traits, Ammon (2007: 131, cf. also Ammon 2006: 22–3) advocates 'raising awareness of non-Anglophone difficulties and disadvantages and providing editorial support to those who want or need to publish in English-medium'. Mauranen (2003) stresses the need to conduct theoretical and descriptive studies of culture-specific varieties of ELF, and Seidlhofer (2005) and Seidlhofer *et al.* (2006) advocate awareness of cultural and rhetorical conventions in foreign language educational curricula, and training ELF teachers about linguistic diversity. In a similar vein, Ferguson (2006: 146, cf. also Ferguson 2007) recommends a pedagogical methodology sensitive to national cultures that may find some space for 'alternative models for English language teaching alongside British and American standard English' as a way of coping with the endangerment of minority languages.

Conclusion

If we reflect on the interrogative in this chapter's title ('Academic Englishes: a standardized knowledge?'), we see in this variety, as in some others discussed in this Handbook, a number of opposing tendencies. In other varieties, these tendencies, on the one hand, are likely to include various globalizing impacts such as the internet, US and British media and the universal franchising of products, while, on the other, we can note *inter alia* efforts to revive and maintain 'small cultures', interest in local histories and folkways, and buying and eating locally (the *New American Dictionary* chose 'locavore' as its new word for 2007). In our own case, the tendencies are still opposing but take a somewhat different form. On the globalization–homogenization side, we can recognize the powerful position of the major publication houses for international research (variously American, British, Dutch and German), which strongly privilege the use of English and largely control, through copy-writing mechanisms, the eventual forms of that language. Some of the other factors, as we have already identified, include a growing 'publish in English or perish' syndrome, and ranking and evaluation systems that increasingly operate to privilege publication in ISI Anglophone journals. Against this prescriptivist monolingual onslaught, at least in terms of the written mode, resistance is currently limited. However, there are signs that alternative ELF versions of standard written English may be emerging; for instance, *The Nordic Journal of English Linguistics* has a stated policy of accepting papers written in English without making them go through a process of linguistic cleansing. And here it is worth remembering that so-called local or regional journals (such as the one just cited) are not really local or regional any more once they make their articles globally available on the web in pdf formats. Further, basic physics tells us as volumetric space diminishes, pressure increases, and so it is with alternative academic written Englishes; as the space for them diminishes, so the resistance to their further diminution will only increase.

On the spoken side, as we have shown, ELF is alive and well; indeed, anecdotal evidence of reception histories often reveals that English native-speaker rhetorical habits and linguistic styles do not always travel well. Here is a senior Australian applied linguist, who has been a professor in Spain for many years, discussing the Spanish audience response to a very senior British academic in a recorded conference discussion:

> Sir Randolph Quirk came once to the university to speak, and he spoke much as Trudgill did. He was very funny, very urbane, made jokes about me being Australian and so on and people afterwards were disappointed because of that, because he hadn't been dense and boring enough [*laughter*] so a Spanish audience is expecting this to be difficult, dense.

So, in this mode, there is little expectation that ELF speakers need to approximate to the informality, the slanginess, the culturally specific metaphors and the wide use of examples that are associated with the public speaking styles of many speakers of English as a first language. As Vassileva (2002) and others have noted, a more formal ELF style is normally acceptable, as are all those clarificatory rhetorical strategies noted above, especially when a majority of interlocutors are themselves ELF speakers. In this respect at least, we can (so far) be thankful for *vive la différence.*

Note

1 C. Pérez-Llantada's contribution to this chapter has received the support of the Spanish Ministry of Science and Innovation (research project FFI2009–09792).

Suggestions for further reading

Mauranen, A. (1993) *Cultural Differences in Academic Rhetoric. A Textlinguistic Study*, Frankfurt am Main: Peter Lang. (An in-depth cross-cultural text-linguistic study of textual organization and textual preferences in academic writing.)

Prior, P. (1998) *Writing/Disciplinarity: A Sociohistoric Account of Literate Activity in the Academy*, Mahwah, NJ: Lawrence Erlbaum. (An ethnography-based description of the intersection of writing and disciplinary enculturation.)

Seidlhofer, B. (2005) 'English as a Lingua Franca', *ELT Journal*, 59 (4): 339–41. (An essential reading for the description of the nature of ELF.)

Swales, J.M. (1990) *Genre Analysis. English in Academic and Research Settings*, Cambridge: Cambridge University Press. (Seminal work on the description of genres in academic settings.)

——(1998) *Other Floors, Other Voices: A Textography of a Small University Building*, Mahwah, NJ: Lawrence Erlbaum. (A comprehensive volume on academic discourse across disciplinary domains.)

References

Ammon, U. (2006) 'Language planning for international scientific communication: an overview of questions and potential solutions', *Current Issues in Language Planning*, 7 (1): 1–30.

——(2007) 'Global scientific communication. Open questions and policy suggestions', *AILA Review*, 20: 123–33.

Askehave, I. and Swales, J.M. (2001) 'Genre identification and communicative purpose: a problem and a possible solution', *Applied Linguistics*, 22 (2): 195–212.

Barras, R. (1978) *Scientists Must Write. A Guide to Better Writing for Scientists, Engineers and Students*, London: Chapman and Hall.

Bazerman, C. (1988) *Shaping Written Knowledge: The Genre and Activity of the Research Article in Science*, Madison, WI: The University of Wisconsin Press.

Becher, T. and Trowler, P.R. (2001) *Academic Tribes and Territories. Intellectual Enquiry and the Culture of Disciplines*, Buckingham: The Society for Research into Higher Education and Open University Press.

Belcher, D. (2007) 'Seeking acceptance in an English-only research world', *Journal of Second Language Writing*, 16 (1): 1–22.

Bennett, K. (2007) 'Epistemicide! The tale of a predatory discourse', *The Translator*, 13 (2): 1–19.

Biber, D. (2006) *University Language*, Amsterdam: John Benjamins.

Biber, D., Johansson, S., Leech, G., Conrad, S. and Finegan, E. (2002) *Longman Grammar of Spoken and Written English*, Harlow, UK: Pearson Education.

Björkman, B. (2008) 'English as the lingua franca of engineering: the morphosyntax of academic speech events', *Nordic Journal of English Studies*, 3 (7): 103–22.

——(2009) 'From code to discourse in spoken ELF', in A. Mauranen and E. Ranta (eds) *English as a Lingua Franca: Studies and Findings*, Cambridge: Cambridge Scholars Press.

Bloch, J. (2008) 'Blogging as a bridge between multiple forms of literacy: the use of blogs in an academic writing class', in D. Belcher and A. Hirvela (eds) *The Oral-Literate Connection*, Ann Arbor: University of Michigan Press, pp. 288–309.

Breiteneder, A. (2005) 'The naturalness of English as a European lingua franca: the case of the "third person -s"', *Vienna English Working PaperS*, 14: 13–26.

Burgess, S. (2002) 'Packed houses and intimate gatherings: audience and rhetorical structure', in J. Flowerdew (ed.) *Academic Discourse*, Harlow, UK: Longman, pp. 196–215.

Burrough-Boenisch, J. (2004) *Righting English that's Gone Dutch*, Leidschendam: Kemper Conseil Publishing.

——(2006) 'Negotiable acceptability: reflections on the interactions between language professionals in Europe and NNS scientists wishing to publish in English', *Current Issues in Language Planning*, 7 (1): 31–44.

Canagarajah, A. S. (1996) '"Nondiscursive" requirements in academic publishing, material resources of periphery scholars, and politics of knowledge production', *Written Communication*, 13 (4): 435–73.

Chambers, J.K. (2003) *Sociolinguistic Theory: Linguistic Variation and its Social Significance*, Oxford: Blackwell.

Chang, Y.-Y. (2004) 'Citation and academic careers: six studies from two fields', unpublished thesis, University of Michigan.

Cogo, A. (2007) 'Intercultural communication in English as a Lingua Franca: a case study', unpublished thesis, King's College, University of London.

Cogo, A. and Dewey, M. (2006) 'Efficiency in ELF communication: from pragmatic motives to lexicogrammatical innovation', *Nordic Journal of English Studies*, 5 (2): 59–93.

Connor, U. (1996) *Contrastive Rhetoric*, Cambridge: Cambridge University Press.

Coulmas, F. (2007) 'English monolingualism in scientific communication and progress in science, good or bad?' *AILA Review*, 20: 5–13.

Crystal, D. (1997) *English as a Global Language*, Cambridge: Cambridge University Press.

——(2000) 'On trying to be crystal-clear: a response to Phillipson', *Applied Linguistics*, 21: 415–21.

Curry, J. and Lillis, T. (2004) 'Multilingual scholars and the imperative to publish in English: negotiating interests, demands, and rewards', *TESOL Quarterly*, 38: 666–88.

Dahl, T. (2004) 'Textual metadiscourse in research articles: a marker of national culture or of academic discipline?' *Journal of Pragmatics*, 36 (10): 1807–25.

Day, R. (1979) *How to Write and Publish a Scientific Paper*, Cambridge: Cambridge University Press.

Durand, C.X. (2006) 'If it's not in English, it's not worth reading!', *Current Issues in Language Planning*, 7 (1): 44–60.

Duszak, A. and Lewkowicz, J. (2008) 'Publishing academic texts in English: a Polish perspective', *Journal of English for Academic Purposes*, 7 (2): 108–20.

Fairclough, N. (2006) *Language and Globalisation*, London and New York: Routledge.

Ferguson, G. (2006) *Language Planning and Education*, Edinburgh: Edinburgh University Press.

——(2007) 'The global spread of English, scientific communication and ESP: questions of equity, access and domain loss', *Ibérica*, 13: 7–38.

Flowerdew, J. (2001) 'Attitudes of journal editors to non-native-speaker contributions: an interview study', *TESOL Quarterly*, 35: 121–50.

——(2007) 'Scholarly writers who use English as an additional language: what can Goffman's *Stigma* tell us?' *Journal of English for Academic Purposes*, 7 (2): 77–86.

Fløttum, K. (2005) 'The self and the others – polyphonic visibility in research articles', *International Journal of Applied Linguistics*, 15 (1): 29–44.

Fortanet-Gómez, I. and Räisänen, C. (eds) (2008) *ESP in European Higher Education*, Amsterdam: John Benjamins.

Gentil, G. (2005) 'Does language matter? French biologists publishing in English', paper presented at the 14th World Congress of Applied Linguistics (AILA), Madison, July.

Gosden, H. (2003) 'Why not give us the full story? Functions of referees' comments in peer reviews of scientific research papers', *Journal of English for Academic Purposes*, 2 (2): 87–101.

Granger, S. (2002) 'A bird's–eye view on learner corpus research', in S. Granger, J. Hung and S. Petch-Tyson (eds) *Computer Learner Corpora, Second Language Acquisition and Foreign Language Teaching*, Amsterdam: John Benjamins, pp. 3–36.

Gross, A.J., Harmon, J. and Reidy, M. (2002) *Communicating Science: The Scientific Article from the 17th Century to the Present*, Oxford: Oxford University Press.

Haberland, H. (1989) 'Whose English? Nobody's business', *Journal of Pragmatics*, 13: 927–38.

Haberland, H., Mortensen, J., Fabricius, A., Preisler, B., Risager, K. and Kjaerbeck, S. (eds) (2008) *Higher Education in the Global Village*, Roskilde: Roskilde University.

Hamel, R.E. (2007) 'The dominance of English in the international scientific periodical literature and the future of language use in science', *AILA Review*, 20: 53–71.

Harwood, N. (2005) '*I hoped to counteract the memory problem, but I made no impact whatsoever*: discussing methods in computing science using *I*', *English for Specific Purposes*, 24 (3): 243–67.

Helal, F. (2008) 'Emerging spaces in biomedical science: a historical discourse analysis of AIDS research papers from 1981 to 2001', unpublished thesis, University of Manouba.

Hewings, M. (ed.) (2001) *Academic Writing in Context. Implications and Applications*, Birmingham: University of Birmingham Press.

——(2006) 'English language standards in academic articles: attitudes of peer reviewers', *Revista Canaria de Estudios Ingleses*, 53: 47–62.

Hunston, S. and Thompson, G. (2001) *Evaluation in Text. Authorial Stance and the Construction of Discourses*, Oxford: Oxford University Press.

649

Hyland, K. (1998) 'Persuasion and context. The pragmatics of academic metadiscourse', *Journal of Pragmatics*, 30: 437–55.

Jenkins, J. (2000) *The Phonology of English as an International Language*, Oxford: Oxford University Press.

——(2007) *English as a Lingua Franca: Attitude and Identity*, Oxford: Oxford University Press.

Johns, T. (2001) 'From evidence to conclusion: the case of "indicate that"', in M. Hewings (ed.) *Academic Writing in Context. Implications and Applications*, Birmingham: University of Birmingham Press, pp. 55–92.

Karhukorpi, J. (2006) 'Negotiating opinions in lingua franca e-mail discussion groups, discourse structure, hedges and repair in online communication', unpublished thesis, University of Turku.

Kaur, J. (2009) 'Pre-empting problems of understanding in English as a Lingua Franca', in A. Mauranen and E. Ranta (eds) *English as a Lingua Franca: Studies and Findings*, Cambridge: Cambridge Scholars Press.

Kerans, M.E. (2002) 'Close to home: notes on the post-publication withdrawal of a Spanish research paper', *Ibérica*, 4: 39–54.

Knapp, K. (1987) 'English as an international lingua franca and the teaching of intercultural communication', in W. Lörsche and R. Schulze (eds) *Perspectives on Language in Performance*, Tübingen: Narr, pp. 1022–39.

Leech, G. and Smith, N. (2006) 'Recent grammatical change in written English 1961–92: some preliminary findings of a comparison of American with British English', in A. Renouf, and A. Kehoe (eds) *The Changing Face of Corpus Linguistics*, Amsterdam, New York: Rodopi, pp. 185–204.

Lesznyák, Á. (2004) *Communication in English as an International Lingua Franca. An Exploratory Case Study*, Norderstedt: Books on Demand GmbH.

Mair, C. (2006) *Twentieth Century English*, Cambridge: Cambridge University Press.

Markkanen, R. and Schröder, H. (eds) (1997) *Hedging and Discourse: Approaches to the Analysis of a Pragmatic Phenomenon in Academic Texts*, Berlin: Walter de Gruyter.

Martín, P. and Burgess, S. (2004) 'The rhetorical management of academic criticism in research article abstracts', *Text*, 24 (2): 171–95.

Mauranen, A. (1993) *Cultural Differences in Academic Rhetoric. A Textlinguistic Study*, Frankfurt am Main: Peter Lang.

——(1997) 'Hedging and modality in revisers' hands', in R. Markkanen and H. Schröder (eds) *Hedging and Discourse. Approaches to the Analysis of a Pragmatic Phenomenon*, Berlin: de Gruyter, pp. 115–33.

——(2003) 'The corpus of English as Lingua Franca in academic settings', *TESOL Quarterly*, 37 (3): 513–27.

——(2004) 'Formulaic sequences in Lingua Franca English', paper presented at the ICAME Conference, Verona, Italy, April.

——(2005a) 'English as a Lingua Franca – an unknown language?' in G. Cortese and A. Duszak (eds) *Identity, Community, Discourse: English in Intercultural Settings*, Frankfurt am Main: Peter Lang.

——(2005b) 'Speaking academics', in I. Bäcklund, U. Börestam, U. Melander, U. Marttala and H. Näslund (eds) *Text i Arbete/Text at Work*, Uppsala: ASLA, pp. 330–9.

——(2006a) 'Signalling and preventing misunderstanding in English as lingua franca communication', *International Journal of the Sociology of Language*, 177: 123–50.

——(2006b) 'Speaking the discipline', in K. Hyland and M. Bondi (eds) *Academic Discourse Across Disciplines*, Bern: Peter Lang, pp. 271–94.

——(2007) 'Hybrid voices: English as the lingua franca of academics', in K. Flottum, T. Dahl and T. Kinn (eds) *Language and Discipline Perspectives on Academic Discourse*, Cambridge: Cambridge Scholars Press.

——(2008) 'How do they speak? Evidence from a corpus of academic English as a Lingua Franca', paper presented at the CALPIU Conference, Roskilde, December.

Metsä-Ketelä, M. (2006) '*Words are more or less superfluous*: the case of *more or less* in academic Lingua Franca English', *Nordic Journal of English Studies*, 5 (2): Online. Available https://gupea. ub.gu.se/dspace/handle/2077/204 (accessed 16 January 2009).

——(2008) 'Academic ELF: managing information and interaction with vague language', paper presented at the 1st International Conference of English as a Lingua Franca, Helsinki, March.

Mišak, A., Marušić, M., and Marušić, A. (2005) 'Manuscript editing as a way of teaching academic writing: experience from a small scientific journal', *Journal of Second Language Writing*, 14: 122–31.

Mollin, S. (2006) *Euro-English. Assessing Variety Status*, Tübingen: Narr.

Mortensen, J. (2008) '"Circus English"? Investigating English as an academic lingua franca at BA study group meetings at Roskilde University', in H. Haberland, J. Mortensen, A. Fabricius, B. Preisler, K. Risager and S. Kjaerbeck (eds) *Higher Education in the Global Village*, Department of Culture and Identity, Roskilde University, pp. 85–96.

Mur, P. (2007) '"I/we focus on": a cross-cultural analysis of self-mentions in business management research articles', *Journal of English for Academic Purposes*, 6 (2): 143–62.

Paul, D., Charney, D. and Kendall, A. (2001) 'Moving beyond the moment: reception studies in the rhetoric of science', *Journal of Business and Technical Communication*, 15: 372–99.

Pennycook, A. (2006) *Global Englishes and Transcultural Flows*, London: Routledge.

Pérez-Llantada, C. (2008) 'An exploratory study of interdiscursive hybridity in academic writing', paper presented at the 32nd International Conference of the Spanish Association of Anglo-American Studies, Mallorca, November.

——(2009) 'Shifting identities, textual responses and conflicting demands in knowledge construction processes', in M. Gotti (ed.) *Commonality and Individuality in Academic Discourse*, Bern: Peter Lang.

Pérez-Llantada, C. and Ferguson, G. (eds) (2006) *English as a Glocalisation Phenomenon*, Valencia: Universitat de Valencia.

Phillipson, R. (1999) 'Voice in global English: unheard chords in crystal loud and clear', *Applied Linguistics*, 20: 265–76.

Poos, D. and Simpson, R. (2002) 'Cross-disciplinary comparisons of hedging: some findings from the Michigan Corpus of Academic Spoken English', in R. Reppen, S. Fitzmaurice and D. Biber (eds) *Using Corpora to Explore Linguistic Variation*, Amsterdam: John Benjamins, pp. 3–23.

Prior, P. (1998) *Writing/Disciplinarity: A Sociohistoric Account of Literate Activity in the Academy*, Mahwah, NJ: Lawrence Erlbaum.

Ranta, E. (2006) 'The "attractive" progressive – why use the -ing form in English as a Lingua Franca?' *Nordic Journal of English Studies*, 5 (2). Online. Available https://gupea.ub.gu.se/dspace/handle/ 2077/204 (accessed 16 January 2009).

Robertson, R. (1995) 'Glocalisation: time-space and heterogeneity-homogeneity', in M. Featherstone, S. Lash and R. Robertson (eds) *Global Modernities*, London: Sage, pp. 25–44.

Rubin, D.L. and Kang, O. (2008) 'Writing to speak: what goes on across the two-way street', in D. Belcher and A. Hirvela (eds) *The Oral–Literate Connection*, Ann Arbor: University of Michigan Press, pp. 210–25.

Sanderson, T. (2008) *Corpus-Culture-Discourse*, Tübingen: Gunter Narr Verlag.

Seidlhofer, B. (ed.) (2003) *Controversies in Applied Linguistics*, Oxford: Oxford University Press.

——(2005) 'English as a Lingua Franca', *ELT Journal*, 59 (4): 339–41.

——(2007) 'Accommodation and the idiom principle in English as a Lingua Franca', paper presented at the Tenth International Pragmatics Conference, Göteborg, Sweden, July.

Seidlhofer, B., Breiteneder, A. and Pitzl, M.-L. (2006) 'English as a Lingua Franca in Europe: challenges for applied linguistics', *Annual Review of Applied Linguistics*, 26: 3–34.

Seloni, L. (2008) 'Intertextual connections between spoken and written text: a microanalysis of doctoral students' textual constructions', in D. Belcher and A. Hirvela (eds) *The Oral–Literate Connection*, Ann Arbor, MI: University of Michigan Press, pp. 63–86.

Shaw, P. and Dahl, T. (eds) (2008) Special issue of the *Nordic Journal of English Studies*, 3 (7). Online. Available http://ojs.ub.gu.se/ojs/index.php/njes/issue/current (accessed 11 January 2009).

651

Shaw, P., Caudery, T. and Petersen, M. (2009) 'Students on exchange in Scandinavia: motivation, interaction, ELF development', in A. Mauranen and E. Ranta (eds) *English as a Lingua Franca: Studies and Findings*, Cambridge: Cambridge Scholars Press.

Swales, J.M. (1990) *Genre Analysis. English in Academic and Research Settings*, Cambridge: Cambridge University Press.

——(1998) *Other Floors, Other Voices: A Textography of a Small University Building*, Mahwah, NJ: Lawrence Erlbaum.

——(2004) *Research Genres. Explorations and Applications*, Cambridge: Cambridge University Press.

Swales, J.M. and Feak, C. (2000) *English in Today's Research World: A Writing Guide*, Ann Arbor, MI: University of Michigan Press.

Tardy, C.M. (2005) '"It's like a story": rhetorical knowledge development in advanced academic literacy', *Journal of English for Academic Purposes*, 4: 325–38.

Vassileva, I. (2002) 'Speaker-audience interaction: the case of Bulgarians presenting in English', in E. Ventola, C. Shalom and S. Thompson (eds) *The Language of Conferencing*, Frankfurt am Main: Peter Lang, pp. 255–76.

Ventola, E. and Mauranen, A. (1991) 'Non-native writing and native revising of scientific articles', in E. Ventola (ed.) *Functional and Systemic Linguistics: Approaches and Uses*, Berlin: Mouton de Gruyter, pp. 457–92.

Ventola, E., Shalom, C. and Thompson, S. (eds) (2002) *The Language of Conferencing*, Frankfurt am Main: Peter Lang.

Vold, E.T. (2006) 'Epistemic modality markers in research articles: a cross-linguistic and cross-disciplinary study', *International Journal of Applied Linguistics*, 16 (1): 61–87.

Widdowson, H. (1994) 'The ownership of English', *TESOL Quarterly*, 28: 377–89.

38

Cameroon

Which language, when and why?

Augustin Simo Bobda

Introduction

Cameroon has a uniquely complex sociolinguistic situation, where English co-exists with French, Pidgin English, the indigenous languages and some emerging hybrid idioms such as *Camfranglais*. The country therefore offers a particularly fertile ground for the study of patterns of language use and language choices, and the linguistic, social and educational problems that they generate. This chapter attempts this analysis and offers a comparative overview of the situation on the African continent, with a focus on the choice of language of education.

Background

The contemporary history of Cameroon arguably began in 1884 when Germany took control of the country at the Versailles Treaty. In 1919, Cameroon, hitherto under German colonial rule, was partitioned between Britain and France after Germany's defeat in the First World War. In 1960, French Cameroon became independent. In 1961, the British part of the country was asked to decide, in a plebiscite, whether they wanted to be administered as part of Cameroon or of Nigeria: the northern part of British Cameroon opted to join Nigeria and the southern part joined French Cameroon to form the Federal Republic of Cameroon. In 1972, the two parts of the federal state merged into a unitary state called the United Republic of Cameroon, a name which was changed to Republic of Cameroon in 1984. Cameroon covers an area of 475,000 square kilometres and has a population of about 17 million inhabitants. There are ten regions: eight Francophone regions which cover about 90 per cent of the territory and which contain about 80 per cent of the population, and two Anglophone regions which cover 10 per cent of the territory and which contain about 20 per cent of the population. In addition to English and French, which are the two official languages, and Pidgin English, Cameroon is home to 286 indigenous languages (Gordon 2005).

Language use, language choices and language conflict in Cameroon

Language use

The language policy of Cameroon is notoriously poor. The only provisions laid down by the 1996 Constitution (the latest) are the stipulations that 'the Republic of Cameroon shall adopt English and French as the official languages with equal status' and that the state 'shall guarantee the promotion of bilingualism all over the territory' and shall work towards the protection and promotion of national languages.

Cameroon is also remarkable in that it has no reliable large-scale data on language use. Few population censuses have been conducted since Independence, and these few censuses have addressed language issues only minimally. For example, the 2004 census (Republic of Cameroon 2003), whose results are still awaited has, out of 51 questions, only two on languages. These questions are uninformative about how many people speak which language: the English version of Question 19 is 'Which national languages can each person [sic = each respondent] speak and write?' while that of Question 20 reads: 'Can each person read and write one of the official languages?' Note that Question 19 does not seek to know the first language/mother tongue of the respondents, but the national languages (any national languages) they can speak and write. Further note that most Cameroonian languages do not exist in a written form. And even when they are written, only a handful of people, generally some linguists, can read and write them. Question 19 is therefore of little validity.

With regard to Question 20, it cannot elicit the number of Francophones and Anglophones either, as there is provision for respondents declaring that they are proficient in both English and French, not just in one of the languages.

Since language distribution often indirectly refers to ethnic distribution, the politicians fear that publishing such data might exacerbate ethnic tension, for example, by revealing the numerical importance of some ethnic groups, or by laying bare the mismatch between some political decisions such as the distribution of parliamentary seats and population size. Brock-Utne (2005: 54) reports the same difficulty in obtaining data on the number of speakers of one language in Tanzania where, during the census, the interviewers are not free to enquire about the first language of the respondents.

One sociolinguistic fact is, however, proven: the uniquely rich spectrum of languages used in Cameroon. This kind of landscape explains the wide range of languages to which a Cameroonian is exposed, or speaks daily. A typical Anglophone Cameroonian in the capital, Yaoundé, for example, normally speaks the following languages *daily*: one or more home languages, Pidgin English, English and French. It is this language use and distribution that Tanyi (1978: 10) captures as follows in the response of an Anglophone child to an interview.

> I talk country talk with my mother.
> I talk Pidgin and country talk with my sister and brothers.
> I talk French when I play with my friends.
> I talk English and Pidgin at school.
> [talk = speak; country talk = mother tongue]

As a further illustration of the range of languages a Cameroonian acquires and uses throughout his life, there is an example, not at all uncommon, of a 65-year-old informant in Simo Bobda and Fasse Mbouya (2003) who can speak more than ten languages which she acquired or learnt in turn as an *au pair*, at school, from neighbours, at the marketplace, from peers in school, and so on.

In the absence of a more elaborate and compelling language policy, language use in Cameroon is generally inordinate and, I would say, cacophonic, in the sense that it does not follow any rigid diglossic or multiglossic pattern. Thus, in a government office, for the same issue under discussion, we will hear French, English, Pidgin English and local languages, sometimes simultaneously. It is generally the principle of survival of the fittest that governs the use of languages in the public and private domains. In the public domain, although English and French, *de jure*, have equal status, French overwhelmingly dominates the scene. In general, factors which determine the use and choice of languages in the Cameroonian Tower of Babel include international prestige and usefulness, demographic weight, political dominance and other miscellaneous factors having to do with the prestige of a particular language. International prestige and usefulness accounts for the dominance of English and French over local languages. Demographic weight accounts for the dominance of Fulfulde in the greater north, the Beti language in the southern regions, Bassa in the Littoral and Centre regions, Ghomala in the west, Banyangi in the south west, Mungaka, Ngemba and Lamnso in the north west and Maka in the east. Political dominance accounts for the supremacy of the Beti language, the mother tongue of President Paul Biya, who has been in power since 1982. The high status of Duala is due to the prestige of the Douala ethnic group which, though a minority and of little weight in politics, is deemed in popular opinion to be more 'civilized' because they were the first people to see the Europeans and to travel to Europe in large numbers, and because Douala, the biggest city and economic capital, is located in their region. The popular nature of Douala music and musicians further contributes to the prestige of the Duala language.

Like elsewhere in Africa, local languages are normally associated with ethnic groups. The Bassa will thus normally speak Bassa, the Ewondo language; some ethnic groups, like the Bamileke, have several, sometimes mutually unintelligible, languages. English and French are, obviously, associated, respectively, with the two and eight regions which make up the formerly British and French zones in colonial days, where 'Anglophones' and 'Francophones' live. In popular opinion, the division between Anglophones and Francophones is equated with ethnic division, as people often use these labels the way they do ethnic labels like *Bassa*, *Bulu*, *Maka*, and so on.

The complexity of the language situation brings about a number of unique language phenomena and idioms. In this regard, what Cameroon offers in terms of code-switching, interference and the emergence of Camfranglais is certainly of particular interest. As can be predicted, the large number of languages on the country's landscape suggests frequent switching between several languages. But it has been shown (Simo Bobda and Fasse Mbouya 2003) that the patterns of switching are governed by certain constraints: code-switching mostly takes place between *mate* languages. According to Simo Bobda and Fasse Mbouya (ibid.), languages A and B are *mates* when, for example, one followed the other in the order of acquisition of languages in the speaker's repertoire, and/or one was used to learn the other, they co-exist naturally in the same community, and/or they are used for the same functions. Thus, in the language repertoire of an Anglophone Cameroonian, languages which might be mates are two or more indigenous languages, one or more indigenous languages and Pidgin English, Pidgin English and English, English and French.

The multilingual Cameroonian hardly ever keeps his languages apart. There is a unique network of interference among the languages which affect each other, either directly, or through a third language. In this connection, Tiayon-Lekobou (1990) pertinently discusses the notion of *hidden language* in translated texts between French and English, whereby a local language may be seen *hiding* behind the direct source language under consideration. Thus, Mongo Beti's (1971) *The Poor Christ of Bomba* or Ferdinand Oyono's (1967) *The Old Man and the Medal*, from the original texts *Le Pauvre Christ de Bomba* (1956) or *Le Vieux Nègre et la Médaille* (1956), respectively, can sometimes be fully understood only if placed within the context of the original Beti language and culture of the original setting. (It is the same situation with Chinua Achebe's (1972) *Le Monde s'effondre* translated from English *Things Fall Apart* (1958), with the Igbo language and culture hiding behind it.)

In addition to the above cases of language-mixing, altogether new idioms have emerged on the Cameroonian landscape. The most striking and the most typical of these idioms is Camfranglais, a school/youth slang which combines elements from English, French, Pidgin and the indigenous languages. It has for the past three decades received plenty of scholarly attention, from writers such as Ze Amvela (1983), Tiayon-Lekobou (1985), Chia and Gerbault (n.d.), Essono (1996), Fosso (1996), Biloa (1999), Efoua-Zengue (1999), Kouega (2003a, 2003b) and Ntsobe *et al.* (2008), from whom the following examples of Camfranglais are taken:

> *Ton pater t'a déjà send les dos que tu me speakyait là?*
> (Has your father already sent you the money you were telling me about?)

> *Un day je pout mes freng avec mes tchakass.*
> (One day I put on my clothes and my shoes)

> *Le super 100 qu'il a porté l'autre day-là était sa own ou pour son big?*
> (Was the dress made from the super 100 material that he wore the other day
> his own or his brother's?)

> *Depuis que tu as win ton probat tu ne me mimba plus.*
> (Since you passed your Probatoire, you no longer think of me)

> *Il va win le bacho cette année.*
> (He is going to pass the Baccalauréat this year.)

Language choices

The options resulting from the language situation which prevails in Cameroon include choices, which are not necessarily exclusive, between the following languages or types of languages: between the colonial languages and the indigenous languages; between these colonial languages themselves; between the exonormative forms of the colonial languages and the local norms; and between these colonial languages, especially English, and Pidgin English.

Cameroon is one of the few African countries where the colonial languages still reign supreme, at the expense of the indigenous languages. This phenomenon is amply illustrated by Bitja'a Kody's (2001) study which shows that the frequency of use of French among Francophone parents and children living in Yaoundé at home, in the street, at the market and in the office varies from 42.77 per cent to 90.20 per cent, while that of English among the Anglophones in the same contexts varies from 35.4 per cent to 61.66 per cent. In fact, English and French are fast becoming the first language to many urban youths (see Simo Bobda 2006b), whichever parameter we consider in Skutnab-Kangas' (1981: 13) chart: language first learnt, language in which one expresses oneself best, language one uses most, language one identifies with, and so on.

In contrast to most African countries where local languages are used as medium of instruction at least in the early years of primary school, Cameroonian schools still officially use English and French. The use of local languages as media of instruction is still at the experimental stage, carried out in projects like PROPELCA (Projet Pilote pour l'Expérimentation des Langues Camerounaises) and by associations like NACALCO (National Association of Cameroon's Language Committees) (Simo Bobda 2006c). The government's recent moves towards the official introduction of local languages into the curriculum include the creation of the Department of Cameroonian Languages and Cultures in the Higher Teacher Training College (Ecole Normale Supérieure) of the University of Yaoundé I, at the beginning of the 2008/2009 academic year.

Causes of the supremacy of the colonial languages in Cameroon include the French assimilationist colonial language policy which today affects both the dominant Francophone part of the country and the Anglophone part, the uniquely complex linguistic landscape, and the lack of preparation from the colonial days of a language or some languages for national function (for a more elaborate discussion, see Simo Bobda 2006a).

The stipulation on equality in status between English and French in the 1996 Constitution was an innovation from earlier constitutions, which provided that, if a text was available in English and in French, it was the French version that had legal binding. The *de jure* equality of English and French in the public domain, however, hides a totally different reality on the ground, which is that French overwhelmingly dominates the picture. The real face of Cameroon English–French bilingualism is shown in works such as Chumbow (1980), Simo Bobda and Tiomajou (1995), Chumbow and Simo Bobda (1996), Biloa (1999), Echu (1999), Kouega (1999), Ministry of National Education (2000), Simo Bobda (2001a), Wolf (2001 and this volume), Ministry of Higher Education (2002), which are among the most representative works.

Although English and French have gained considerable ground and, in fact, supplanted the local languages as 'new mother tongues' in urban centres, it is shown (see Simo Bobda 2006b) that they cannot be confused with the traditional mother-tongue varieties. They have significantly divergent forms, which often lead to intelligibility failure. For data on intelligibility between Cameroon English and traditional mother-tongue Englishes, see Atechi (2006). The gap between the two types of English, especially at the phonological level, is such that, during a lecture, the lecturer, in order to be understood, may have to resort to intralanguage translations of the type '[maːtə] *martyr* ... I mean (Cameroon English) [mataja]; [ˈbaɪəst] *biased* ... I mean [baˈjas]; [ʌmˈbrɛlə] *umbrella* ... I mean [ˈɔmbrela]'. The competition, and the need to choose, between the two forms of English or French, is part of an already old debate that has been going on in the world, and there is no specific Cameroonian suggestion, as the English and French spoken and written by students and to a large extent by teachers increasingly violate the traditional exonormative norms.

Pidgin English has been enthusiastically proposed by academics like Alobwede (1998) as the language of consensus to bridge the communication gap between speakers of different linguistic backgrounds. Alobwede (1998: 108) believes that 'it is the language in Cameroon which expresses Cameroon reality without provoking vertical or horizontal hostilities'. He goes on to say (ibid.) that if upon independence Cameroon had 'developed a neutral indigenous language' like Pidgin English, it would have achieved more.

The adoption of Pidgin English as a national language or its empowerment for other functions is, however, hampered by several obstacles. First and foremost, it is not as neutral as it is believed to be. It is mostly restricted to Anglophone and neighbouring Francophone (Littoral and West) regions. The three northern regions (Adamaoua, North and Far North), for example, use Fulfulde as their lingua franca, while the Centre and South use dialects of the Beti language. The second major obstacle is the negative attitude of many Cameroonians towards this language, as it is believed to have a negative influence on performance in Standard English (for more discussion on the history of Pidgin English in Cameroon, its place and attitudes towards it, see Simo Bobda and Wolf 2003; Schroeder 2003a, 2003b).

Language choices in Cameroon, like elsewhere, can be made at state, individual, parental and other levels, and divergences and conflicts may occur between levels. For example, despite the nonchalance of the state in implementing a more coercive English–French bilingual policy reflecting the *de jure* status of these languages, the interest of Cameroonians in learning the other official language has of late been on a steady rise, as shown by the evolution of learner population in language centres. The demand for French among the Anglophone population and more interestingly of English among the Francophone population can be assessed from the number of people who enrol for

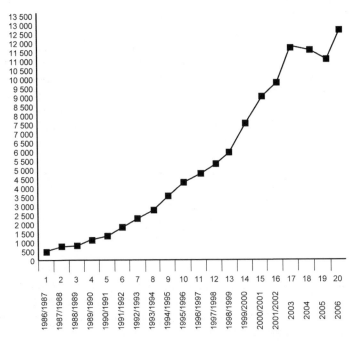

Figure 38.1 Enrolment figures at the Cameroonian Bilingual Training Programme from 1986 to 2006. Source: Bilingual Training Programme, Yaounde

Table 38.1 Adult enrolment for English and French in Cameroon by BTP centre in 2007

BTP centre (region)	French	English	Date of creation
Yaoundé (Centre Region)	395	4994	1986
Douala (Littoral)	175	2794	1989
Buea (South West)	89	119	1990
Bamenda (North West)	58	306	1995
Ebolowa (South)	16	167	1996
Garoua (North)	24	541	2003
Bertoua (East)	31	394	2006
Bafoussam (West)	0	0	Under construction
Maroua (Far North)	0	0	Not yet created
Ngaoundere (Adamaoua)	0	0	Not yet created
TOTAL	788	9335	

Source: Bilingual Training Programme, Yaoundé

these languages at the Bilingual Training Programme (BTP). The BTP is a state-run programme created in 1986 to promote bilingualism through the teaching of English to Francophones and French to Anglophones. The evolution of yearly enrolment figures has been almost exponential, beginning with a meagre 500 registrations in 1986 and hitting an astonishing 13,500 twenty years later, in 2006, as shown in Figure 38.1.

The learner population for English is particularly striking. The figure for adult learner enrolment for English in 2007 was 9,335, as against 788 for French. It should be recalled that the Francophone population in general is much bigger than the Anglophone population; the Francophones are about 80 per cent of the population. But this cannot account for the width of the margin observed here. Details of enrolment per BTP centre can be seen in Table 38.1.

There is a real scramble for English among the Cameroonian Francophone population (Wolf, this volume). More palpable examples of this scramble include the fact that Francophone children are virtually invading English-medium schools, and this constitutes a concern for many Anglophone parents who feel marginalized, as they believe that their children should have priority (see Simo Bobda 2001a). This is a paradox when plotted against the overwhelming dominance of French in society and in state institutions and the consequent marked marginalization of English. But the situation clearly derives from the educational and professional gains that Cameroonians expect from English at the international level.

Cameroon Pidgin English (CPE) offers another example of divergence of choice in Cameroon, between institutional choice and individual choice. From the point of view of school authorities, CPE is very unpopular in many school institutions, where it is actually banned, as in the University of Buea where signboards like the following are found:

No Pidgin on campus, please.
Pidgin is taking a heavy toll on your English; shun it.
L'Anglais, un passeport pour le monde; le pidgin, un ticket pour nulle part.
[English, a passport to the world; Pidgin, a pass for nowhere.]
The medium of studies at UB is English, not Pidgin. (UB = University of Buea)
If you speak Pidgin, you will write pidgin.
English is the password, not Pidgin.

Speak less Pidgin and more English.
The better you speak Pidgin, the worse you will write English.
Speak a language well to write a language well.
Be my friend, speak English.
Succeed at UB by avoiding Pidgin on campus.
Commonwealth speaks English, not Pidgin.

But an investigation into language use at that university by Chia (2009) shows the above prescriptions to have little influence on students' language use. Out of the 1,442 students observed, 904 were found to be using CPE, making 63 per cent, as opposed to 25 per cent who were found to be using English, and 11 per cent who were using French. More detailed results of Chia's study, which includes distribution by gender, can be found in Table 38.2.

Parental language options include the choice between the Francophone and Anglophone sub-systems of education. Anglophone parents almost always keep their children within their own sub-system and send their children to Francophone schools only when compelled by circumstances, like working in an area where no Anglophone school is available. But Francophone parents, as seen above, are increasingly sending their children to Anglophone schools even when they reside in the Francophone part of the country.

Another parental choice is between the colonial languages and the local languages. There seems to be as yet no comprehensive study on this choice. But the unique popularity of the colonial languages in Cameroon shown above is arguably a good clue to the direction of the choice Cameroonians would make.

There is a wide range of motivations behind the language preference of Cameroonians. But they will generally go for languages that yield immediate or future fruit in terms of their competitiveness in the world at large; hence their collective and individual attachment to European languages which indeed they perceive as 'capital' for them (Brock-Utne 2005: 77, after Bruthiaux 2002). This conception of language reflects the rationalist viewpoint discussed by Dirven and Pütz (2008), after Geeraerts (2003) and Dirven and Polzenhagen (2004). It will be recalled that the characteristic features of the rationalist model of language planning include the fact that language is viewed as a medium of communication and a global language as a neutral medium of social participation and emancipation (Dirven and Pütz 2008: 12). It contrasts with the romantic model which views language as a medium of expression, and a global language as a medium of social exclusion and a threat to local identities (ibid.).

Proficiency in the competing languages is also an important factor of language choice. Outside institutional or other types of constraints, and sometimes in violation of

Table 38.2 Distribution of respondents by gender and language use at the University of Buea

	English		French		CPE		Other		Total	
Gender	M	F	M	F	M	F	M	F	M	F
	178	191	62	92	430	474	8	7	678	764
Total	369		154		904		15		1442	
Percentage	18.2	51.7	40.2	59.7	47.5	52.4	53.3	46.6	47	52.9
Total %	25		11		63		1		100	

Source: Emmanuel Chia 2009

these constraints, speakers will use the language in which they are the most comfortable. The growing use of Pidgin English on our school and university campuses, sometimes to discuss topics like Shakespeare or Chomsky, traditionally the preserve of Standard English, aptly illustrates this phenomenon. Although it is often argued that the use of Pidgin English responds to the need of its speakers to assert their identity, it is at least equally true that Cameroonians choose it because they express themselves better in it than, say, in Standard English. It is no news in the literature that there is a dramatically widening gap between the local variety of English and the traditional norms. In fact, pidginized forms are fast fossilizing in this local English, as illustrated by the following syntactic and morphological features, known to associate with pidgins and creoles, which I find quite often in the scripts of my postgraduate English Language majors:

- dropping of plural, possessive, third-person singular and past tense and past participle markers: *different country*; *Jesus friend*; *My gratitude go to* … ; *He is suppose to*;
- dropping of articles: *I have problem*;
- use of a reduced number of conjunctions, very often *that*: *The man that we ate yesterday* (with whom we ate); *The test that the lecturer did not give us the marks* (whose marks/the marks of which the lecturer did not give us); *The girl that you were talking* (the girl you were talking about).

It is understandable that speakers who have such features in their English should feel more comfortable in Pidgin English.

Language conflict

Like elsewhere in Africa (Wardhaugh 1987: 156), language or language choice is generally not a major social concern in Cameroon. Political and other social problems are more regular causes of strife. But the language situation of Cameroon makes it a potential volcano. The nonchalance of the government reported above in coming up with a more elaborate language policy, which would include some choices from among the more than 200 languages, can be interpreted as an avoidance strategy. They want to avoid stirring up a hornet's nest. The example of Malawi, where a broadcasting house was burnt down in protest against the announcement that Chewa was going to replace Yao and Tumbuka as the language of broadcasting and of newspapers (Schmied 1996: 305) is suggestive of what might happen in some places in Cameroon if one language were officially given more status than another. In the face of the state's refusal to commit itself with a top-down policy, there have been a number of bottom-up measures to teach and/or promote some local languages taken by some radio and television stations, educational institutions, research projects like PROPELCA mentioned above and NACALCO, and tribal organizations (see Simo Bobda 2006c). These measures are yielding a lot of fruit, at no cost to social peace.

The use of English and French, however, presents an altogether different picture. The Francophones and Anglophones of Cameroon have been experiencing a rather uneasy co-existence since their reunification in 1961. What is generally known as the *Anglophone problem* has emerged in political and social discourse. The Anglophone problem is made up of a number of political, cultural, educational, and infrastructural grievances which Anglophone Cameroonians level against the dominant Francophone component of the nation. They complain about their insufficient representation in top government positions, held by Francophones since reunification, about the suppression of the cultural values they inherited from the British, which include the legal system, about the absorption by the Francophone system of their educational system, especially at the tertiary level, and not only about the paucity of infrastructure in the Anglophone part of the country, but also about the deterioration or total disappearance of such infrastructure (roads, seaports) from where it once existed in colonial days.

The Anglophone problem also includes sociolinguistic and purely linguistic grievances. The Anglophones complain about the overwhelming dominance of French, especially in the administrative domain. One consequence of this domination is that most administrative documents get to Anglophones only in a translated form; for example, the draft 2009 financial law was submitted to Parliament in December 2008 only in French. In many cases, the translations are poorly done and are unintelligible. Dramatic examples have been found in official examinations where *beton* has turned up in a paper on bricklaying for 'concrete' (as a translation for French *béton*), and *candle* in a paper on motor mechanics for 'plug' (as a translation for French *bougie*) (Chumbow and Simo Bobda 1996). Immigration documents served on aircraft to passengers landing in Cameroon have for long borne *surname* (instead of 'first name, forename, given name') as a translation for French *prénom*. Some official documents of Afriland First Bank, the third biggest bank in Cameroon, bear *device* (instead of 'currency') as a translation for French *devise*. Some time ago, the Yaoundé city dweller would be familiar with the following translation displayed on giant boards at strategic roundabouts:

SWEEP, CLEAN AWAY
TO GATHER DIRTINESS IS GOOD
NOT TO MAKE DIRTY IS BETTER

instead of something like:

SWEEP, REMOVE DIRT
TO CLEAN UP GARBAGE IS GOOD
NOT TO LITTER IS BETTER

as a translation for French

BALAYER, NETTOYER,
RAMASSER LA SALETER C'EST BIEN,
NE PAS SALIR C'EST MIEUX

The literature on the Anglophone problem in Cameroon uses such strong words as *second-class citizen, vassal, slave, beast* to portray the Anglophone condition. This register can be found in articles published in Anglophone newspapers in the last three decades, in widely circulated manuscripts like Dinka (1985) and Maimo (1994), as well as in published creative works like Besong (1990), Ngome (1992) and Nkemngong (2004). The Anglophone problem has manifested itself in a number of ways including street protests, writing (newspaper articles, essays and creative writing as seen in these titles) and diplomatic moves which have included missions to the United Nations to petition for secession). The Anglophone problem has generated a number of fora and organizations such as the AAC (All Anglophone Conference) which was held in 1991 and the secessionist movement known as the SCNC (Southern Cameroon National Council) which for the past few years has posed a serious threat to the unity of the country. A more exhaustive treatment of manifestations of the Anglophone problem in Cameroon can be found in Simo Bobda (2001a).

A comparative overview of the situation in Africa: focus on language of education

One Cameroonian specificity of the language situation painted above is the use of two exoglossic languages as official languages and the official exclusion of the local languages in the public sphere, arguably a unique response to the bewildering number of these local languages hardly paralleled anywhere else in Africa. But, in general, African countries have in common the fact that colonial languages continue to hold sway at the expense of local languages. This is in sharp contrast to the picture in Asian countries where English shares its official function with Hindi in India, with Cantonese in Hong Kong, Chinese, Tamil and Malay in Singapore, Tagalog (also known as Filipino) in the Philippines, Malay in Malaysia, and so on. While Asian countries use colonial languages today mostly as instruments for international communication, Africans have adopted these languages which have supplanted their own local languages in many domains.

The main indigenous languages are taught as subjects in some African countries (e.g. Yoruba, Igbo and Hausa in Nigeria) or taught as media of instruction in the first three years or so of primary education, but the further step to adopt them as media of instruction beyond this level has been, inexplicably, much harder to take. It is difficult to understand, for example, that Yoruba and KiSwahili, which have strong assets for becoming media of instruction across the board in the respective countries in which they are used, are still not allowed to be used beyond the first years of schooling. The assets of Yoruba are documented by Bamgbose (2005). This language is spoken in south-western Nigeria by about 30 million people. It has been a school language for more than one and a half centuries. Quoting Hair (1967: 8), Bamgbose (2005: 233) reports that the teaching of Yoruba in the formal school system began on 29 August 1831, when the first lesson in Yoruba was given at the Charlotte's Girls' School, Freetown, Sierra Leone under the direction of Mrs Hannah Kilham, a Quaker missionary. The lessons Bamgbose (2005: 248–54) reports from the Yoruba experience include the fact that primary education is more meaningful when conducted in the child's first language; that mother-tongue education does not preclude effective education in more than one language; that terminology need not be an obstacle to mother-tongue education; and that mother-tongue education will lead to a reduction of educational failure.

The case of KiSwahili is even more disturbing. It has an even older history than Yoruba. Quoting Whitley (1969) [not mentioned in Brock-Utne's list of references], Brock-Utne (2005: 53) reports that this language spread into the interior of east Africa in the nineteenth century, after some form of pro-standard KiSwahili had been spoken on the coast of East Africa before the tenth century. It was used during the period of German rule as a language of government administration and as the medium of instruction in schools. Brock-Utne (2005: 53) observes that the Germans promoted

KiSwahili 'mainly because they did not think that Tanganyikans (as they were then called) could learn to speak German sufficiently well'. Brock-Utne (2005: 51), after Masato (2004), also reports the 2004 National KiSwahili Council estimate which puts at 99 per cent the proportion of Tanzanians who spoke KiSwahili. Used in Tanzania as a language of instruction through all the seven years of primary and in some teacher colleges, it is also used by the Institute for KiSwahili Research and by the Department of KiSwahili at the University of Dar Es Salaam as the language of instruction in all its courses and meetings, evidence that 'an African language may well be used for the most sophisticated discussions and for research' (Brock-Utne 2005: 51). KiSwahili is spoken by more than 80 million people in 14 nations in East and Central Africa (Brock-Utne 2005: 52, after Masato (2004). It is an official language of the African Union. Yet KiSwahili remains a medium of instruction only at the primary level.

It will continue to be difficult to envisage a large-scale adoption of African languages as media of instruction as long as the factors which have over the years militated for their ban persist. These factors include the negative role of Britain but, to a larger extent, the very attitude of Africans about these languages. Although the British colonial policy was generally more favourable to the use and promotion of African languages than, say, the French policy (Chumbow and Simo Bobda 2000; Simo Bobda 2001b), the postcolonial policy has not always quite followed the same line, being swayed by economic interests. As Sir Richard Francis, Director General of the British Council, was quoted by Makoni (1992: 8) to say, 'Britain's real black gold is not the North Sea oil but the English language', corroborating the view of the Director of the International House in London who declared: 'Once we used to send gunboats and diplomats abroad; now we are sending English teachers' (ibid.). Indeed, the replacement of English by local languages means, for example, less teaching employment for the Brits, fewer English language experts to send to the former colonies and less income for British publishers (Brock-Utne 2005).

Concerning the attitude of the community, a considerable portion of it is still to be convinced about the well-foundedness and virtues of mother-tongue education. Brock-Utne (2005: 68) reports the Tanzanian Minister of Education clearly saying in 2001 at a breakfast meeting that the pressure to change the medium of education from English to KiSwahili in secondary schools is from 'professors', not from the 'community'. The Minister further revealed that he received a large number of groups that want a licence to start English-medium schools, and that he had 'not had a single application from anyone who wants to start a KiSwahili-medium secondary school'. Statistics in the field confirm that English-medium schools attract more parents than KiSwahili-medium ones and charge higher fees (Brock-Utne 2005: 74). The parents who send their children to English-medium schools belong to the higher middle or upper classes (ibid.). Quoting Rubagumya, Brock-Utne (2005: 74) indicates that '[t]he reason most parents give for sending their children to English-medium primary schools … is that KiSwahili cannot help children in the globalised world where they have to be competent in English, especially when it comes to learning of science and technology'. Opinion is largely divided even in the government on the issue of the medium of education in Tanzania, in a debate that involves politicians, intellectuals and the general public, with a considerable representation among the ministers thinking that English should be given top priority (Brock-Utne 2005).

Indeed, as Brock-Utne (2005: 62) rightly notes, '[t]he language in education policy in Tanzania from the 1990s can best be described by words like confusing, contradictory and ambiguous'. It is interesting to learn that even Julius Nyerere, who is overwhelmingly hailed as a great promoter of KiSwahili, was instrumental in opposing the adoption of KiSwahili as a language of instruction in secondary and higher education. He declared that '[w]e cannot allow English to die because English is the KiSwahili of the world' (Brock-Utne 2005: 60, quoting earlier sources).

Nyerere's declaration betrays a major misconception in the minds of those who oppose, or are reluctant to accept, the use of indigenous languages. Many people, even in the elite, see the use of these languages and the use or learning of a European language as mutually exclusive; in other words, they think that the use of local languages in education will prevent the learning of English. This belief is challenged by the Tanzanian Professor Abel Ishumi, at the time head of the Department of Education at the University of Dar es Salaam and 'ardent defender of the continued use of English' in secondary and higher education, quoted by Brock-Utne (2005: 61). The professor declares that he is 'a total convert', having lived in Japan and in Norway and 'seen how youngsters go through their studies in their own languages'. He was impressed by the fact that 'Norwegian university students, who had never had English as language of instruction but had just learnt it as a subject, spoke and wrote it better than Tanzanian university students who had had English as a language of instruction for nine years' (ibid.).

The belief in the colonial language as the only key to the world has as a corollary the belief that emphasis on the use of local languages as media of instruction in some circumstances is a strategy to exclude Africans from the world, and to divide them. It is this interpretation that caused the discontent which followed the 1953 Bantu Education Act in South Africa. This Act sought to increase the use of mother tongue from Grade 4 to Grade 8, but was seen as 'an effort to fragment the African people whose majority status was both a political and social threat to the government' (Makalela 2005, reviewed by Brock-Utne and Hopson 2005b: 17).

Outside the territories of the former British Empire, the fortunes of the colonial languages are even brighter, and the fate of indigenous languages even less enviable, despite their advantages. For example, Wolof, Bambara and Sango are spoken and understood by more than 80 per cent respectively in Senegal, Mali and the Central African Republic, but the school curriculum is still almost exclusively dominated by French. In Guinea Conakry, seen as a pace-setter in the matter in Francophone Africa, the first years of independence saw very successful mother-tongue education. But it suddenly lapsed into an overwhelmingly French-dominated system in the 1983–4 school year after President Sekou Toure's death, as 'the positive aspects of mother tongue education were dismissed and criticized as gimmicks of an oppressive political regime' (Yerendé 2005: 209). In Mozambique, Portuguese continues to go unchallenged as the official language 'and the sole medium of instruction in all aspects of formal education', although 68.7 per cent of the population do not speak Portuguese (Matsinhe 2005: 121–2).

Pidgins and creoles, which could be alternative languages in education, do not fare much better than indigenous languages. The fortunes of Pidgin English recounted above for Cameroon, are shared by other pidgins and creoles across the continent. Seychellois Creole alone has been accorded the status of medium of instruction; it was made the national language together with English and French in 1981, and introduced into the educational system in 1982 (Fleischmann 2008). In 1996, it was, however, downgraded as the dominant language of instruction in favour of English which is a foreign language for 99 per cent of the population and which the Seychellois do not master well enough to receive education in it (Fleischmann 2008: 192). The fortunes of

665

the creole of neighbouring Mauritius are even less bright: it is not an official language there, although it is spoken by 90 per cent of the population (Fleischmann 2008: 24). Sierra Leonean Krio and Cape Verdian Kriolu are further examples of creoles whose roles as lingua francas contrast with their level of marginalization (see Veiga 1999).

The debate over the introduction of indigenous languages – and to a large extent pidgins and creoles in the case of Africa – involves both pros and cons which Chumbow (2005) aptly reviews. The core advantage which Chumbow articulates is that education is the key to development; and this education, which consists in great part in dispensing knowledge, is more successful if carried out in a language with which the children are more familiar, in which they are more competent, and which is more appropriate for the imparting of indigenous knowledge. The arguments against the use of African languages include ones which 'are based on false premises and wrong assumptions' (Chumbow 2005: 173); examples of such arguments are that most African languages have no grammar; that the use of the mother tongue will impede the acquisition of the official languages of the nation (English and French); that the use of African languages will impede national unity; and that children enrolled in a school system where the medium of instruction is an African language will be at a disadvantage vis-à-vis their counterparts who attend schools with English or French as media of instruction from the beginning, a disadvantage which will become more noticeable in higher education and reduce their job possibilities. The arguments based on the practicality of mother-tongue education include the inadequacy of scientific and technical vocabulary, the multiplicity of languages and the lack of resources for the inevitably costly venture.

Chumbow's arguments for mother-tongue education are cogent and persuasive, and echo those of many academics, including those of Bamgbose above in his plea for the introduction of languages such as Yoruba into the educational system. But the persistent supremacy of colonial languages shows that folk beliefs in matters of language are often stronger than scientific truths.

Conclusion

Cameroon is a Tower of Babel, further complicated by the absence of a serious language policy, which sets in competition English and French, the two official languages, the traditional exonormative norms and the local endonormative models for these colonial languages which are gaining more and more ground, Pidgin English, a fast-developing school slang known as Camfranglais, and some 286 languages. Patterns of domination include that of the colonial languages over the indigenous languages in the public domain, that of French over English, and that of Pidgin English over Standard English among Anglophones. Cameroon offers the sociolinguist an impressive array of language phenomena, which result from the co-existence of a wide variety of languages. This co-existence is generally peaceful, except for English and French whose respective Anglophone and Francophone communities do not always live very harmoniously, the former complaining of marginalization. Language choices at state and individual levels are determined by a number of pragmatic and utilitarian considerations. With regard to the preference of the colonial languages to the indigenous languages in education and in the public domain, Cameroonians have adhered to Dirven and Pütz's (2008) rationalist viewpoint which sees language as a medium of communication, not as a tool for the expression of identity, as seen from the romantic viewpoint (ibid.).

Cameroon's overwhelming adoption of the colonial languages and its consequent lukewarm attitude towards the indigenous languages makes her an extreme case in Africa (see Simo Bobda 2006a, 2006b, 2006c for more discussion). However, the country's language choices, to a large extent, reflect those of Africa as a whole. Indeed, compared with Asia, Africa is remarkable for her maintenance of colonial languages, to the detriment of indigenous languages or local pidgins and creoles, even in the many cases where the demographic weight and the educational gains argue for these languages as alternative languages of education and of official transactions. It is true that the adoption of local languages, namely in education, is not unanimous even in Asia. A significant portion of the elite continues to clamour for EMI (English as a medium of instruction), in Hong Kong for example, but they constitute a minority.

Many Africans are yet to be convinced that colonial languages are not undisputed and exclusive assets for global competition and that local languages are not factors of exclusion from this competition. Even the examples of Asian countries like Japan, Korea and Hong Kong which have developed using their local languages do not seem persuasive enough.

A lot of effort is being made at national and continental levels, notably within the framework of the African Union, to reverse the current trend. But it is hard to predict that the colonial languages will concede a significant portion of their ground to the local languages in the near future.

Suggestions for further reading

Anchimbe, Eric A. (ed.) (2007) *Linguistic Identity in Postcolonial Multilingual Spaces*, Newcastle: Cambridge Scholars Publishing.
Echu, George and Grundstrom, Allan W. (eds) (1999) *Official Bilingualism and Communication in Cameroon*, New York: Peter Lang.
Tadadjeu, Maurice (ed.) (1990) *Le Défi de Babel au Cameroon. Yaoundé* (Collection PROPELCA, 53), Yaoundé: PROPELCA.
Wolf, Hans-Georg (2001) *English in Cameroon*, Berlin: Mouton de Gruyter.

References

Achebe, Chinua (1958) *Things Fall Apart*, London: Heinemann.
——(1972) *Le Monde s'effondre*, Paris: Présence Africaine.
Alobwede, Charles d'Epie (1998) 'Banning Pidgin English in Cameroon', *English Today*, 54 (14/1): 54–60.
Atechi, Samuel Ngwa (2006) *The Intelligibility of Native and Non-native English Speech*, Göttingen: Cuvilier.
Bamgbose, Ayo (2005) 'Mother-tongue education. lessons from the Yoruba experience', in Birgit Brock-Utne and Rodney Koffi Hopson (eds) *Languages of Instruction for African Emancipation: Focus on Postcolonial Contexts and Considerations*, Rondebosch: The Centre for Advanced Studies of African Society (CASAS), and Dar es Salaam: Nkuki na Nyota Publishers, pp. 231–57.
Besong, Bate (1990) *Beasts of No Nation*, Limbe: Nooremac Press.
Biloa, E. (1999) 'Structure *Phrastique* du Camfranglais: Etat de la question', in George Echu and A.W. Grundstrom (eds) *Official Bilingualism and Linguistic Communication in Cameroon*, New York: Peter Lang, pp. 147–74.

——(2003) 'Le bilinguisme social au Cameroon est-il un facteur d'integration nationale ou de frag-mentation?' paper presented at the 2003 Day of the *Francophonie*, Yaoundé, 20 March.

Bitja'a Kody, Zachée (2001) 'Attitudes et représentations linguistiques à Yaoundé', *African Journal of Applied Linguistics*, 2: 100–24.

Brock-Utne, Birgit (2005) 'The continued battle over KiSwahili as the language of instruction in Tanzania', in Birgit Brock-Utne and Rodney Koffi Hopson (eds) *Languages of Instruction for African Emancipation: Focus on Postcolonial Contexts and Considerations*, Rondebosch: The Centre for Advanced Studies of African Society (CASAS), and Dar es Salaam: Nkuki na Nyota Publishers, pp. 51–88.

Brock-Utne, Birgit and Hopson, Rodney Koffi (2005a) *Languages of Instruction for African Eman-cipation: Focus on Postcolonial Contexts and Considerations*, Rondebosch: The Centre for Advanced Studies of African Society (CASAS), and Dar es Salaam: Nkuki na Nyota Publishers.

——(2005b) 'Educational language contexts and issues in postcolonial Africa', in Birgit Brock-Utne and Rodney Koffi Hopson (eds) *Languages of Instruction for African Emancipation: Focus on Postcolonial Contexts and Considerations*, Rondebosch: The Centre for Advanced Studies of African Society (CASAS), and Dar es Salaam: Nkuki na Nyota Publishers, pp. 1–21.

Brock-Utne, Birgit, Desai, Zubeida and Qorro, Martha (eds) (2003) *Language of Instruction in Tanzania and South Africa (LOITASA)*, Dar es Salaam: A. & D.

Bruthiaux, P (2002) 'Hold your courses: language education, language choice and economic development', *TESOL Quarterly*, 36 (3): 275–96.

Chia, Emmanuel N. (2009) 'Further developments in Cameroon Pidgin English', *Annals of the Faculty of Arts, Letters and Social Sciences* (University of Yaoundé I), special issue in honour of Professor Paul N. Mbangwana, pp. 39–81.

Chia, Emmanuel and Gerbault, J. (n.d., c. 1990) 'Les nouveaux parlers urbains: le cas de Yaoundé', *Actes du Colloque International des Langues et des Villes* (Marseille): 263–78.

Chumbow, Beban Sammy (1980) 'Language and language policy in Cameroon', in Ndiva Kofele Kale (ed.) *An Experiment in Nation Building: The Bilingual Republic of Cameroon since Reunification*, Boulder, CO: Westview, pp. 22–43.

——(2005) 'The language question and national development in Africa', in Thandika Mkandawire (ed.) *African Intellectuals Rethinking Politics, Language, Gender and Development*, Dakar: CODESRIA Books, pp. 164–92.

Chumbow, Beban Sammy and Bobda, Augustin Simo (1995) 'The functions and status of English in Cameroon', paper presented at the 'English in Africa' Conference, Grahamstown, South Africa, 15 September.

——(1996) 'The life-cycle of post-imperial English in Cameroon', in J.A. Fishman, A.W. Conrad and A. Rubal Lopez (eds) *Post-Imperial English: Status of English after Colonialism*, Berlin: Mouton de Gruyter, pp. 401–29.

——(2000) 'French in West Africa: a sociolinguistic perspective', *International Journal of the Sociology of Language* (special issue), 141: 39–60.

Dinka, George (1985) 'The new social order', unpublished manuscript.

Dirven, René and Polzenhagen, Frank (2004) 'Rationalist or romantic model in language policy and globalisation', paper presented at the 30th LAUD Symposium, University of Koblenz-Landau, Essen, Germany, 19–22 April.

Dirven, René and Pütz, Martin (2008) 'Language conflict seen from the viewpoint of the rationalist and romantic models', in Augustin Simo Bobda (ed.) *Explorations into Language Use in Africa*, Frankfurt am Main: Peter Lang, pp. 12–27.

Echu, George (1999) 'Le bilinguisme officiel au Cameroun: critique et perspective', in George Echu and A.W. Grundstrom (eds), *Official Bilingualism and Linguistic Communication in Cameroon*, New York: Peter Lang, pp. 189–201.

Echu, George and Grundstrom, A.W. (eds) (1999) *Official Bilingualism and Linguistic Communication in Cameroon*, New York: Peter Lang.

Efoua-Zengue, R. (1999) 'L'emprunt: figure néologique recurrente du camfranglais', in G. Mendo Ze (ed.) *Le Français langue africaine*, Paris: Publisud.

Essono, Jean Jacques (1996) 'Le Camfranglais: un code excentrique, une appropriation vernaculaire du français', communication présenté lors du cooloque sur le *Corpus lexicographique: méthode de constitution et gestion*, Yaoundé, Janvier.

Fleischmann, Christina Tamaa (2008) *Pour Mwan Mon Lalang Maternel i Al avec Mwan Partou. A Sociolinguistic Study on Attitudes towards Seychellois Creole*, Bern: Peter Lang.

Fosso (1999) 'Le camfranglais: une praxéogénie complexe et iconoclaste', in G. Mendo Ze (ed) *Le français langue africaine*, Paris: Publisud.

Geeraerts, Dirk (2003) 'Cultural models of linguistic standardization', in René Dirven, Roslyn Frank and Martin Pütz (eds) *Cognitive Models in Language and Thought. Ideology, Metaphors and Meanings* (Cognitive Linguistic Research 24), Berlin; New York: Mouton de Gruyter, pp. 25–68.

Gordon, Raymond G., Jr (ed.) (2005) *Ethnologue: Languages of the World* (15th edition), Dallas: SIL. Online available www.ethnologue.com/ (accessed 19 August 2009).

Hair, Paul E.H. (1967) *The Early Study of Nigerian Languages*, Cambridge: Cambridge University Press.

Kouega, Jean-Paul (1999) 'Forty years of official bilingualism in Cameroon', *English Today*, 60 (I) [15 (4)]: 3843.

——(2003a) 'Camfranglais: a novel slang in Cameroon schools', *English Today*, 74: 23–9.

——(2003b) 'Word formative processes in Camfranglais', *World Englishes*, 22 (4): 511–38.

Jikong, Stephen Yeriwa (2000) 'Official bilingualism in Cameroon: a double-edged sword', *Alizes* (Revue Angliciste de la Reunion): 117–35.

Maimo, Sankie (1994) 'Retributive justice', unpublished manuscript.

Makela, Leketi (2005) 'We speak eleven languages', in Birgit Brock-Utne and Rodney Koffi Hopson (eds) *Languages of Instruction for African Emancipation: Focus on Postcolonial Contexts and Considerations*, Rondebosch: The Centre for Advanced Studies of African Society (CASAS), and Dar es Salaam: Nkuki na Nyota Publishers, pp. 51–88.

Makoni, Sinfree (1992) 'In response to "New Englishes"', *Per Linguam*, 8 (1): 2–13.

Masato, Masato (2004) 'KiSwahili strategies to meet demand for language', *Daily News*, 30 October: 2.

Matsinhe, Sozinho Francisco (2005) 'The language situation in Mozambique: current developments and prospects', in Birgit Brock-Utne and Rodney Koffi Hopson (eds) *Languages of Instruction for African Emancipation: Focus on Postcolonial Contexts and Considerations*, Rondebosch: The Centre for Advanced Studies of African Society (CASAS), and Dar es Salaam: Nkuki na Nyota Publishers, pp. 119–46.

Ministry of Higher Education (2002) 'Comité ad hoc pour la redynamisation du bilinguisme dans les universités d'état: Rapport Final, Yaoundé', unpublished manuscript.

Ministry of National Education (2000) 'Final report on the reinforcement of bilingualism in the Cameroon educational system: Yaoundé', unpublished manuscript.

Mongo Beti (1956) *Le Pauvre Christ de Bomba*, Paris: Robert Laffont.

——(1971) *The Poor Christ of Bomba*, London: Heinemann.

Ngome, Victor Epie (1992) *What God Has Put Asunder*, Yaoundé: Pitcher Books.

Nkemngong, John Nkengasong (2004) *Across the Mongolo*, Ibadan: Spectrum Books.

Ntsobe, André Marie, Biloa, Edmond and Echu, George (2008) *Le Camfranglais: quelle parlure!?* Frankfurt am Main: Peter Lang.

Oyono, Ferdinand (1956) *Le Vieux Nègre et la Médaille*, Paris: Editions Julliard.

——(1967) *The Old Man and the Medal*, London: Heinemann.

Republic of Cameroon (2003) *Third General Population and Housing Census: Household Questionnaire*, Yaoundé, mimeograph.

Schmied, Josef (1996) 'English in Zimbabwe, Zambia and Malawi', in Vivian De Klerk (ed.) *Focus on South Africa*, Amsterdam: John Benjamins, pp. 301–21.

Schroeder, Anne (2003a) *Status, Functions, and Prospects of Pidgin English: An Empirical Approach to Language Dynamics in Cameroon*, Tübingen: Gunter Narr Verlag.

——(2003b) 'Cameroon Pidgin English: a means of bridging the Anglophone–Francophone division in Cameroon?' *AAA – Arbeiten aus Anglistik und Amerikanistik*, 28 (2): 305–27.

Simo Bobda, Augustin (2001a) 'Varying statuses and perceptions of English in Cameroon', *Trans* 11 (December). Online. Available www.inst.at/trans/11Nr/bobda11.htm (accessed 1 October 2009).

——(2001b) 'English in the Sub-Saharan linguistic landscape: beginning of millennium observations', *Anglia*, 119 (4): 579–95.

——(2006a) 'Facing some challenges for language planning for Cameroon', in Kembo-Sure (ed.) *Language Planning for Development in Africa*, Eldoret, Kenya: Moi University Press, pp. 71–96.

——(2006b) 'The emergence of new "mother tongues" in Africa and its implications: the case of Cameroon', in Ch. Van der Valt (ed.) *Living through Languages: An African Tribute to René Dirven*, Stellenbosch: African Sun Media, pp. 5–69.

——(2006c) 'Life in a Tower of Babel without a language policy', in Martin Pütz, J.A. Fishman and J. Neff-van Aertselaer (eds) *Along the Routes to Power: Explorations of the Empowerment through Language*, Berlin: Mouton de Gruyter, pp. 357–72.

——(ed.) (2008) *Explorations into Language Use in Africa*, Frankfurt am Main: Peter Lang.

Simo Bobda, Augustin and Fasse Mbouya, Innocent (2003) 'Revisiting some linguistic concepts and beliefs in the light of the sociolinguistic situation of Cameroon', in J. Cohen, K. McAlister, K. Rolstad and J. MacSwan (eds) *Proceedings of the 4th International Symposium on Bilingualism* (Arizona State University), Somerville, MA: Cascadilla Press, pp. 2122–32.

Simo Bobda, Augustin and Tiomajou, David (1995) 'Integrating ESL and EFL: the Cameroon experience', in the British Council (ed.) *Across the West African Divide: Proceedings of the West Africa English Conference* (Mbour, Senegal, December), Senegal: British Council, pp. 60–83.

Simo Bobda, Augustin and Wolf, Hans-Georg (2003) 'Pidgin English in Cameroon in the new millennium', in Peter Lucko, Peter Lothar and Hans-Georg Wolf (eds) *Studies in African Varieties of English*, Frankfurt am Main: Peter Lang, pp. 101–17.

Skutnabb-Kangas, T. (1981) *Bilingualism or Not: The Education of Minorities*, Clevedon: Multilingual Matters.

Tanyi, Ruth (1978) 'Bilingualism and the young Cameroonian child', unpublished DES dissertation in English Studies, University of Yaoundé.

Tiayon-Lekobou, Charles (1985) *Camspeak: A Speech Reality in Cameroon*, Mémoire de Maitrise, Yaoundé: Université de Yaoundé.

——(1990) 'Exploration in the organisation and management of translational communication', unpublished Master's dissertation, University of Birmingham.

Veiga, M. (1999) 'Language policy in Cape Verde: A proposal for the affirmation of Kriolu', *Cimboa* (Revista Kabuverdianu di Literatura, Arti y Studi), 7 (3): 12–17.

Wardhaugh, Ronald (1987) *Languages in Competition*, Oxford: Blackwell.

Wolf, Hans-Georg (2001) *English in Cameroon*, Berlin: Mouton de Gruyter.

Yerendé, Eva (2005) 'Ideology of language and schooling in Guinea-Conakry. A postcolonial experience', in Birgit Brock-Utne and Rodney Koffi Hopson (eds) *Languages of Instruction for African Emancipation: Focus on Postcolonial Contexts and Considerations*, Rondebosch: The Centre for Advanced Studies of African Society (CASAS), and Dar es Salaam: Nkuki na Nyota Publishers, pp. 199–230.

Ze Amvela, E. (1983) 'The Franglais phenomenon: lexical interference and language mixing in the United Republic of Cameroon', *Bulletin de l'AELIA*, 6: 419–29.

Section VI

The future

39

The future of Englishes

One, many or none?

Alastair Pennycook

Introduction

The question posed here – one, many or no Englishes – can be approached from at least two distinct directions. On the one hand, the answer is dependent on mapping out the possibilities of real-world conditions: language use, demographics, economic change, globalization, and so forth. On the other, the answer is dependent on the epistemological lenses through which we consider these questions. Whether the future of English therefore should be seen in terms of the continuation of English, the plurality of Englishes or the demise of English depends equally on global economic and political changes and theoretical approaches to how we think about language. To talk, for example, of World Englishes, is to focus on the centrifugal forces – from colonialism, to independence and appropriation – that have led to English being changed and adopted in different contexts around the world. Yet it is also to operate with a particular linguistic epistemology based around notions of language spread, continuity and variation. Reviewing global economic and political changes as well as competing theoretical standpoints, this paper will evaluate different positions, from the linguistic imperialism of neo-liberal empire to the ecology of global Englishes, in order to develop ways in which we can think about the futures of English(es).

Language possibilities and ideologies

How we view the potential role of English in the world depends on several key determinants: to the extent that the global spread of English is a product of political and economic forces, its future role will evidently reflect changes to the global economy, as well as other social, political and cultural factors. The realignment of global economic powers, particularly the rise of China and India as the dominant economies of the twenty-first century, has implications for the role of English. So too does the growth of other South East Asian economies and the potential of a new zone of economic cooperation based around ASEAN. The strengthening of the euro in relation to other currencies, the steady increase in the size of the European Union (27 countries at the beginning of 2009), the political realignment of South America, the economic crisis of 2008–9, climate change, and so on, all have implications for the role of English. What exactly these implications are is much harder to determine, but we do know for sure that the waxing and waning of languages is a result of broad economic and political influences.

To show how this may work, it can be useful to speculate on alternative histories and their concomitant linguistic outcomes. While some of these speculations may look implausible, they can shed light on the political processes within which language is embedded. Let us imagine, for example, a different outcome at the end of the Second World War: Germany defeated both the Soviet Union and the UK and established its European German-dominated Reich. Japan did not attack Pearl Harbor and instead successfully established its East Asian economic and political empire. The United States never entered the war, and faced by these two large political entities, turned towards its southern neighbours in a cooperative spirit. By the early twenty-first century, the world is dominated by three major economic, political and linguistic entities: Die Dritte Europäische Gemeinschaft, a powerful bloc including Russia, the UK, North Africa and most of Europe, where German is used as the major language of communication, while other regional languages – English, Spanish, Estonian, Arabic and so on – are used more locally. Japanese, meanwhile, has become the major language, indeed a first language for many, of the Greater East Asia Co-Prosperity Sphere (大東亜共栄圏), which includes the emerging regional power of China. And across the Pacific, Las Americas, a Spanish-dominated (with English a major second language in the north, and a trilingual Canada) conglomeration has become the third major political and economic block. In this alternative world, German, Spanish and Japanese have been recognized as the three major world languages, with Hindi and Arabic forming a second tier, and it is common in other regions of the world to speak, say, Arabic, Spanish and Japanese; or Swahili, German and Spanish. It is important to acknowledge that playing such speculative games also suggests some very serious outcomes. The Japanese and German regimes were not known for their tolerance and encouragement of diversity. In this casual scenario, for example, Hebrew – indeed Israel – would likely never have been revived. Many European and Asian languages might have fared very badly. Clearly a more serious view of these alternative scenarios would have to take into account the destructive language policies that would have likely played out across large parts of the world. Whether these would have been more destructive than the forces of US-dominated capitalism and neo-liberalism is a question for even further speculation.

This simple alternative scenario suggests that the current role of English is obviously a result of a very particular set of historical circumstances, which might have looked very different, and might do so again. While this is based on a fairly straightforward mapping of political, economic and linguistic possibilities, things become more complicated once we bring in different possible language ideologies. It is already, perhaps, a little far-fetched to suggest a bilingual Spanish–English USA (though we may well be heading that way eventually) since this possibility suggests an openness to languages that was not evident in the USA in the mid twentieth century. What if we imagine for Australia, not just the possibility that the French settled the west, and the English the east, so that it became a bilingual, southern hemisphere version of Canada, but rather that the European invaders came with an open-minded interest and capacity to acknowledge and learn indigenous languages, so that many of these languages are not only alive and well today but are also widely spoken by the immigrant populations? Today it would not be uncommon, say, for people in Sydney to speak Chinese, Darug, French and English; in Melbourne, people would commonly use Woiwurrung, Italian, French and English; while in Brest (what we now call Perth in Western Australia), French, Vietnamese and Gardjari are widely used. Along similar lines, Barack Obama's 2009 presidential inauguration would of necessity have been conducted not only in Spanish and English but also in, perhaps, Cherokee. This, I would argue, is somewhat harder to imagine than the scenarios sketched out above, suggesting that while different political outcomes may be imaginable, different language ideologies are harder to conceive. I shall return to this point later when I argue that, in order to think about the futures of English, we need to think not only in terms of the ways languages reflect the political economy, but also in terms of the language ideologies that underpin our ways of thinking about language.

There are several different ways in which we need to consider language ideologies here: first, as linguistic anthropologists (see Blommaert 1999; Kroskrity 2000) have made clear, language ideologies may refer to the ways in which people think about their own languages. How do people understand languages locally? What does a particular language mean to a community? Second, what broader attitudes do people have towards different languages? This is the issue I have been discussing above: what possible different ideologies around multilingualism, indigenous languages and language use might be possible? And third, what particular ways of thinking about language are held by those involved in language studies: in what ways do the particular views of language held by linguists, applied linguists or sociolinguists frame the possible ways we have of thinking about languages in the world? In the second part of this chapter, I shall take up this final question in more detail. While on the one hand we may look to different material conditions to predict different outcomes for English, we may also just as productively consider different ways of thinking about language. To talk of 'new Englishes', for example, may, on the one hand, be an empirical question we can explore through a set of criteria that define the emergence of a language variety; on the other hand, it is also dependent on language ideologies that define languages as separable entities that can spread and diversify.

Seargeant's (2009) analysis of how English is positioned in Japan, both as a linguistic system and as a set of ideologies, for example, shows us how different forms of knowledge about language have an effect upon the way in which language is regulated within society. This focus on language ideology is a significant one for studies of global English. Some critical approaches to the spread of English see ideology only as the necessary reflection of a neo-liberal, English-speaking empire (Phillipson 2008), the means by which the inequitable relations between English and other languages are maintained. Seargeant, by contrast, draws on broader studies of language ideology which, deriving from an anthropological tradition, are interested centrally in the ways in which language is understood locally. This work is of great, and as yet rather untapped, significance for applied linguistics generally and studies of the global spread of English more specifically, since it looks at ideology not as a top-down imposition reflecting only an economic order but rather as a local manifestation of how language is understood. Amongst other things, this focus allows, on the one hand, for a much more complex understanding of language ideology: the ways languages are understood is a product of local cultures, histories, aesthetics, educational orientations, and so on. And, on the other hand, it helps us to question the very solidity that is ascribed to language: if it means different things to different people, then what constitutes English is less clearly defined by recourse to grammar, lexicon or naming practices, and instead is a product of particular conditions of locality.

English amid economic and political forces

The different scenarios suggested above are not, of course, how the world has turned out, but it does suggest that neither the current nor the future role of English is in any way guaranteed or inevitable. Graddol (2006: 14–15) identifies a range of key trends in relation to the global spread of English, including a flattening out in the rise of learners of English once it has reached 2 billion by about 2020, increased competition for ELT services from non-native contexts, and a general decline in the relevance of native speakers – a trend already identified in the 1989 *Economist* report (McCallen 1989) – and the proportional decline of English in the internet. It is often suggested that English is the language of the internet, though evidence does suggest that, although the amount of English use outweighs other languages, and although it is increasing largely as a result of many uses of English as a second language, the overall use of English is decreasing proportionally in relation to other languages. Or put another way, there has been a major increase in the use of other languages on the internet. This is an important observation, since it counters claims that English has become so embedded in domains such as the internet that it will remain so.

While shifts in internet use have been well documented, other communication technology-based possibilities lie more in the realm of speculation. If the internet has revolutionized global communication in the past few decades, new communication technologies might do so again in the near future. Take machine translation, for example. Its untrustworthiness to date has meant that its use still remains somewhat peripheral for most language users. While electronic dictionaries and phrase books have become common, actual translation, and particularly of spoken language, still has many weaknesses. Yet we may get there, and once automatic translation can be built into email and even conversation, the patterns of language use may change again. Imagine, for example, the possibility of translation software on your mobile phone, so that it could also be used as a handheld device for instant translation of spoken language. Of course, this would almost certainly still reflect the basic inequalities between languages – translation software may be installed for major languages but not minor ones, and for many it is already too late – but it would mean that language use and language education could be dramatically changed.

Graddol (2006) points to a decreased advantage from speaking English. There is a basic issue of economic value here, which undermines naive claims that English-learning can be a panacea for global poverty (see Pennycook 2007b): the more people learn English, the less value accrues to this distinction. Graddol also predicts the growth of a polycentric lingua franca global English (with Asia playing a particular role here) and increased competition from certain other languages, particularly Spanish and Chinese (Putonghua). Graddol is particularly interested in the non-competitiveness of monolingual speakers of English, suggesting that they will be at a disadvantage compared to their multilingual colleagues elsewhere. He also suggests that EFL teaching, as it has been understood, is on the way out in favour of the teaching of global English. In sum, he predicts a shift towards a variety of English that is very much a language of global ownership, accompanied by increased value on the capacity to operate multilingually amid the rise of other major languages.

The strength of Graddol's analysis lies in his use of various data sources – global demography (population growth, age trends, movement of people), economic trends (the rise of China, India, Russia and Brazil, shifting patterns of economic exchange, outsourcing) – and reasonable speculations on how these may reinforce or unsettle certain language alliances. All such predictions, of course, are dependent on things continuing along expected pathways. The recent (2008–9) economic crisis, with up to a third of the value of global economies disappearing, major economies in recession, companies that were thought invulnerable collapsing, and large numbers of workers across different sectors being laid off, may have long-term effects on these predictions. By and large, however, these dramatic events look as if they will only hasten the shift towards Asia as the economic power centre of the world, with English – but possibly more Asian English – continuing to play an important role. Predicting the role of English in all this is a speculative business. It is clear, for example, that despite policies favouring the national languages of Europe, language use within the European Union is moving strongly towards English (see Phillipson 2003). Globally we are seeing trends towards greater use of English at primary level in many school systems, as well as a trend towards the use of English as a medium of instruction in secondary science and technology classes. From Chile to Korea, we have seen major proposals for the greater use of English across the educational system. With this comes a shift towards a greater commodification of English (see Tan and Rubdy 2008).

This also means that English is increasingly embedded in education, industry, information technology and other domains in ways that will make it hard to dislodge. The rise of China as the major power of the twenty-first century has implications for English that are not transparent. It will of course strengthen the role of Chinese. Just as Japan's economic potency in the twentieth century led to a large growth in Japanese studies across the world, so this is clearly also the case with Chinese: there has been significant growth world-wide in the learning of Chinese. But this will not necessarily be at the expense of English (we should always be aware that this is not a zero-sum game – more learning of one language does not necessarily mean less of another). Since China has invested so massively in English, it also becomes a purveyor of English. While China does support the learning of other languages, such as Japanese, French and Spanish, its investment in English means that, if business is not to be done in Chinese, English will often be the other option. The parallel rise of India, with its strong pro-English stance in many domains, also continues to consolidate the role of English at a global level. In sum, Graddol is probably right that other languages, notably Chinese and Spanish, may grow in influence, while English will likely remain the most widely used international language. At the same time, there will be a continuing shift away from formerly influential models (UK and US English) towards a more polycentric English, with Asia a major player. As he suggests too, this shift in the locus of English may also be accompanied by a shift in the underlying attitudes towards language, the predominant users of English employing not only a flexible, polycentric English lingua franca, but also using this emergent variety of English from a multilingual perspective.

Models, empires, multitudes

An important question that we need to address, however, is what particular model of the world is being presented in such analyses and how we might, therefore, wish to respond. If, for example, we view the global spread of English in terms always of a reflection of broader economic and political concerns (rather than playing a more dynamic constitutive role), and if we also see those global relations as tied indelibly to the expansion of neo-liberal politics, then the future of English will always be one that follows the shifting relations of global politics. The point here, to be sure, is not to suggest that English is not deeply involved in global political relations, but rather to look at the theoretical position that underpins the understanding of that relationship. Phillipson (2008) has laid out his concerns here most explicitly from what we might call a *neo-realpolitik* view of English, arguing that global English has to be seen as 'the *capitalist neoimperial language* that serves the interests of the corporate world and the governments that it influences so as to consolidate state and empire worldwide' (2008: 33). Drawing on the analyses of neo-liberal empire by Pieterse (2004) and Hardt and Negri (2000), Phillipson argues that this global expansion of English needs to be understood in terms of 'linguistic capital accumulation' (2008: 33).

From Phillipson's (2008) point of view, 'Acceptance of the status of English, and its assumed neutrality implies uncritical adherence to the dominant world disorder, unless policies to counteract neolinguistic imperialism and to resist linguistic capital dispossession are in force' (2008: 38). For Phillipson, the challenge for a macro-sociolinguistics of global English is to understand the relations between English, corporate power and new understandings of neo-liberal empire. He takes Graddol to task for overlooking 'the significance of the corporate world and the role of the guardians of the norms of the standard Anglo-American language' (2008: 36). While it is not so evident that the guardians of Anglo-American Standard English are as powerful as Phillipson believes, this may be an important criticism, since Graddol's analysis, aimed at informing the British Council and other EFL-oriented institutions interested in keeping track of global English trends, is not based on an analysis that aims to critique globalization, but rather tends to accept the political and economic domain, and to focus critique instead on the complacency of the EFL industry and the monolingualism of the Anglo world.

Phillipson's argument draws attention to the need for analysis of the current state of English and speculations about its future to include a focus on inequality and disparity, as well as an awareness of the ideological underpinnings of any of our analyses. I shall return to another aspect of this argument in the next section, suggesting that both Phillipson and those he critiques share assumptions about language that are worth questioning. In relation to the global economy, however, and whether we should take a moral stance in relation to the global spread of English, Phillipson's warning concerning the fundamental inequalities related to global English need to be considered. To take one example discussed by both Phillipson and Graddol, François Grin's (2005) analysis of the advantage that accrues to the UK in terms of the different costs within the European Union linked to the learning of English concludes that the dominance of English resulted in an equivalent annual payment of at least 10 billion euros to the UK. It has even been suggested that perhaps native speakers of English should be taxed to offset their global economic advantage.

At the very least, we need to consider the extent to which English in its possible future roles in the world will continue to play an insidious role in perpetuating inequality. Bruthiaux's (2002: 292–3) warning that, for many of the world's poor, English language education is 'an outlandish irrelevance' is significant. He goes on to argue that 'talk of a role for English language education in facilitating the process of poverty reduction and a major allocation of public resources to that end is likely to prove mis-guided and wasteful'. As English is taught more and more widely, we need to continue to consider its role in relation to poverty, distinguishing very clearly between indivi-dually oriented access arguments about escape from poverty, and class-oriented argu-ments about large-scale poverty reduction. 'For those who already speak English,' suggests Tollefson (2000: 9),

> the economic value of the language translates directly into greater opportunities in education, business, and employment. For those who must learn English, how-ever, particularly those who do not have access to high-quality English language education, the spread of English presents a formidable obstacle to education, employment, and other activities requiring English proficiency.

As Ramanathan's (2005: 112) study of English- and vernacular-medium education in India shows, English is a deeply divisive language, contributing to the denigration of vernacular languages, cultures, and ways of learning and teaching on the one hand, and dovetailing 'with the values and aspirations of the elite Indian middle class' on the other. While English opens doors to some, it is simultaneously a barrier to learning, development and employment for others.

For Phillipson, there are two possible routes to change: on the one hand, changes to the global structures of neo-liberal empire would inevitably change the position of English. Thus since, 'Fundamental changes in the global economy make U.S. dom-inance via the dollar and control of the oil trade precarious', and since there may be growing resistance to US military dominance, it is 'therefore perfectly possible that the global linguistic map may change violently in the coming decades' (2008: 37). Indeed, the changes that befell the global economy soon after Phillipson's comments, with neo-liberalism under concerted attack from a number of quarters, with governments pump-ing vast amounts of money into local economies and buying or propping up private assets, suggest indeed that the relation between English and neo-liberalism may be about to shift. While Phillipson may have a point here, however, the other side of his argument – that it is also possible in the meantime to develop 'explicit language poli-cies based on ethical human rights principles' (2008: 39) – or that this may lead to a major shift in global language ecologies, is less plausible.

Leaving aside the much-discussed problems of overdeterminism in all theories of cultural and linguistic imperialism (humans are much more capable of resistance, appropriation and change than these top-down views suggest), there are other concerns of more interest to the discussion here. The first has to do with the reliance on language policy. On the one hand, large-scale policies are remarkably ineffectual. There is often a confusion here between the pro-English policies of the US and UK, and the global spread of English. The policies would have meant nothing were it not for the political and economic conditions that brought about the global spread of English. Much of what was said about the global spread of English by the British Council, Prince Charles, various American agencies, and so on, would have been laughed at as mere posturing had the economic conditions of the post-war world not produced fertile breeding grounds for English. Of course, there was very clear intent as well as action to spread English, but this was not by and large the cause of the spread. As has become clear in recent years, it is local language policy that is often far more significant than macro policy (Liddicoat and Baldauf 2008).

679

On the other hand, a reliance on language policy based on human rights discourse is surely to propose a bourgeois liberal solution to a neo-Marxist quandary. Hardt and Negri's (2005) follow-up *Multitude* to their work on *Empire* is instructive. Most obviously, if our analysis of the global spread of English ties it critically to studies of neo-liberal politics and economy, in order to be theoretically coherent, the response needs to operate within the same theoretical domain. As Hardt and Negri argue, it is through the action of the Multitude that change may come. Multitude, they explain, can be understood as 'all those who work under the rule of capital and thus potentially as the class of those who refuse the rule of capital' (2005: 106). The concept of multitude, then, is an understanding of class not in the restricted sense of a traditional working class, but in a broader sense that is global and resistant to capital. If we wish to follow a critique of the relation between neo-liberal Empire and English to its conclusion, then opposition needs to be conceived through new forms of global resistance. And such resistance by the multitude, as Hardt and Negri (2005) stress, can be heterogeneous and diverse: it might speak many languages but an analysis of Empire requires an equal analysis of possible resistance, not resistance through the bourgeois workings of humanist language policy.

Finally, this position on English and neo-liberal empire runs into precisely the same problems of all these analyses of English. Not only is it insufficiently explicit about the theories that underlie its analyses of politics and the economy, but it has virtually nothing to say about the language ideologies with which it operates. As Canagarajah (2007) points out such arguments derive

> from the dominant assumptions of linguistics, informed by the modernist philosophical movement and intellectual culture in which they developed. To begin with, the field treats language as a thing in itself, an objective, identifiable product. The field also gives importance to form, treating language as a tightly knit structure, neglecting other processes and practices that always accompany communication.
>
> (Canagarajah 2007: 98)

It is to unravel some of these assumptions in relation to all analyses of English as a global language that I turn in the next section. Whether English remains one thing, a reflection of neo-liberal Empire, diversifies into several languages or disappears altogether, depends not only on the political economy, but also on understandings of language.

Changing English

At the same time that the role of English may change globally in relation to social, economic and political forces, so too does the language change. To date, such changes have been described largely from within the World Englishes and ELF frameworks. And even those, such as Schneider (2007, this volume), who have sought to develop an independent model that can account for commonalities within changing Englishes, operate from many of the same linguistic assumptions. Looking at World Englishes, for example, it is clear that although large amounts of evidence have been brought to bear on the topic of the diversity of new Englishes (see papers this volume), the epistemological questions about what constitutes a variety, or indeed what constitutes English, are left largely untouched. That is to say, once the move has been made to talk about a

THE FUTURE OF ENGLISHES

plurality of Englishes, and to do so along lines that link these varieties of English to different nation-states (Indian, Singaporean, Nigerian English, and so forth), subsequent work only needs to provide evidence of local divergence from core English in order to continue to contribute to the model of World Englishes as divergent language varieties. If we continue along this empirical track, it is likely we will be able to demonstrate the continuing centrifugality of Englishes.

Yet clearly, with an eye on possible future global developments in mind, but also taking into account current global circumstances, such analyses fail to grasp the changing nature of global relations, particularly the changes to nation-states and the role of transcultural media. Along with its focus on hybridity at the expense of a more critical analysis of English in the world, and the descriptive and analytic inconsistencies of the three circles, is the problem that the locus of analysis is on national varieties of English. Overlooking diversity within regions and the scope of change within globalization, therefore, the World Englishes framework has been described as 'a 20th century construct that has outlived its usefulness' (Bruthiaux 2003: 161). Just as a language rights perspective maintains a twentieth-century model of international relations, so a World Englishes perspective maintains a focus on national Englishes. Neither raises the question of whether we need to reconsider what languages are in more fundamental terms.

These approaches to global English – whether linguistic imperialism and language rights, or World Englishes and English as a lingua franca – remain stuck within twentieth-century frameworks of languages and nations. The central concern that the debates between these rival conceptualizations leave uncontested is how we can understand diversity outside those very frameworks that are part of the problem. Neither a defence of national languages and cultures, nor a description of a core of English as a lingua franca, nor even a focus on plural Englishes, adequately addresses questions of diversity under new conditions of globalization. A focus on the worldliness of English (Pennycook 1994; 2007a), however, demands, in Radhakrishnan's (2007) terms, that the very one-ness of English can only be understood on the basis of local perspectives of difference. This is not a question of pluralizing Englishes, but of understanding the way different language ideologies construct English locally. Questioning the ways in which we have come to think about languages within colonialism and modernity, and regarding the grand narratives of imperialism, language rights, linguae francae or World Englishes with suspicion, this perspective looks towards local, situated, contextual and contingent ways of understanding languages and language policies.

We need therefore to reconsider how we think about language. This question can be addressed in several ways. The first has to do with local language ideologies, that is to say with the manner in which language is understood locally. A major problem with studies of global English is that the analysis proceeds from the centre outwards, paralleling the spread of English, and assumes that English means the same thing to different people. If we are interested, however, in the worldliness of English, then we need a more spectival approach that does not assume that English remains the same. This is not a matter of grammatical or lexical variation, but of cultural and ideological difference. At some level, these language ideologies need to be understood in relation to material conditions. Thus, the commodification of English (Tan and Rubdy 2008) and the ways it is connected to economies of desire (Piller and Takahashi 2006) are clearly interlinked with the global role English plays in relation to the global economy. But language ideologies go deeper than this, since they also need to address less clearly determined views on language. A focus on language ideology also needs to ask, not

681

only how people understand English locally, but also how the locality of linguists affects their interpretations of language.

It is all very well to speculate on how changing economic and political circumstances may affect the role of English, or to debate the questions around what constitutes a World English or a lingua franca, but if the notion of language itself remains unexamined, as if English were a clear and identifiable object with countable numbers of speakers, clear borders and uncontested domains of use, we will only have completed part of the task. What this suggests is the need to think about English and globalization outside the nationalist frameworks that gave rise to twentieth-century models of the world. In dealing with English in an uneven world, we do need to understand its historical formation within forms of nationalism and imperialism, and its contemporary roles in the inequitable distribution of resources, in the promotion of certain ideas over others, in the threat it may pose to other languages, cultures and ways of being. And yet we need simultaneously to appreciate not only its appropriation and relocalization by diverse users, but also its reconfiguration as something different. Perhaps it is time to question the very notions that underpin our assumptions about languages (Jacquemet 2005; Makoni and Pennycook 2007), to ask whether the ways we name and describe languages as separate entities, the ways we view bi- and multilingualism, are based on twentieth-century epistemologies that can no longer be used to describe the use of languages in a globalizing world. If it is clear that the ways we think about language are inevitably products of particular historical contexts, then an age of globalization suggests that we need both to reflect on how and why we look at languages as separate, countable, describable entities in the way we do, and to consider that languages may be undergoing such forms of transition as to require new ways of conceptualization in terms of local activities, resources, or practices.

English as local practice

Recent research has started to question whether these old categorizations of language – varieties, code-switching, bilingualism, mother tongue, multilingualism, borrowing – as well as the identities that are assumed along lines of language, location, ethnicity, culture, really work any more. Developed in contexts very different to those in which English now finds itself, many of these concepts simply do not seem to address the forms of hybrid urban multilingualism in which English now partakes. Indeed, there are strong reasons to question the very notion of English, or any language, as discrete entities that are describable in terms of core and variation. On the one hand, then, there are the changing realities of urban life, with enhanced mobility, shifting populations, social upheaval, health and climate crises, and increased access to diverse media, particularly forms of popular culture. On the other hand is the growing concern that we need to rethink the ways in which language has been conceptualized.

Bosire (2006: 192) argues that the

hybrid languages of Africa are contact outcomes that have evolved at a time when African communities are coming to terms with the colonial and postcolonial situation that included rapid urbanization and a bringing together of different ethnic communities and cultures with a concomitant exposure to different ways of being.

At the same time, 'young people are caught up in this transition; they are children of two worlds and want a way to express this duality, this new "ethnicity"'. Out of this mix emerge new language varieties, such as Sheng, a Swahili–English hybrid, which provides urban youth with 'a way to break away from the old fraternities that put particular ethnic communities in particular neighborhoods/estates and give them a global urban ethnicity, the urbanite: sophisticated, street smart, new generation, tough' (Bosire 2006: 192). Higgins' (2009) work on English as a local and multivocal language in East Africa destabilizes some of the dominant conceptualizations of English as a distinct code, as a global language and as an entity bounded by particular domains of use. Instead, she suggests we need to grasp the implications of the hybridity and linguistic bricolage in which English so often participates (see McLellan, this volume).

The next step, therefore, is to move towards an understanding of the relationships among language resources as used by certain communities (the linguistic resources users draw on), local language practices (the use of these language resources in specific contexts), and language users' relationship to language varieties (the social, economic and cultural positioning of the speakers). This is, consequently, an attempt to move away from nation-based models of English and to take on board current understandings of translingual practices across communities other than those defined along national criteria. The interest here is in 'the communicative practices of transnational groups that interact using different languages and communicative codes simultaneously present in a range of communicative channels, both local and distant' (Jacquemet 2005: 265). These transidiomatic practices, Jacquemet explains, 'are the results of the co-presence of multilingual talk (exercised by de/reterritorialized speakers) and electronic media, in contexts heavily structured by social indexicalities and semiotic codes'. For Jacquemet, such practices are dependent on 'transnational environments', the mediation of 'deterritorialized technologies', and interaction 'with both present and distant people' (2005: 265).

The changing cultural and linguistic worlds in which many English users live pose challenges for how we conceive of culture, ethnicity and language. As Maher describes it in the context of Japan, students are rejecting fixed ascriptions of cultural identity and instead playing with notions of metroethnicity: 'Cultural essentialism and ethnic orthodoxy are out. In Japan, metroethnicity is in. Cool rules' (2005: 83). Metroethnicity, he explains, is 'a reconstruction of ethnicity: a hybridised "street" ethnicity deployed by a cross-section of people with ethnic or mainstream backgrounds who are oriented towards cultural hybridity, cultural/ethnic tolerance and a multicultural lifestyle in friendships, music, the arts, eating and dress' (2005: 83). People of different backgrounds now 'play with ethnicity (not necessarily their own) for aesthetic effect. Metroethnicity is skeptical of heroic ethnicity and bored with sentimentalism about ethnic language' (Maher 2005: 83). As language learners move around the world in search of English or other desirable languages, or stay at home but tune in to new digital worlds through screens, mobiles and headphones, the possibilities of being something not yet culturally imagined mobilizes new identity options. And in these popular transcultural flows, languages, cultures and identities are frequently mixed. Code-mixing, sampling of sounds, genres, languages and cultures is the norm (Pennycook 2007a; Alim et al. 2009).

In order to capture how language is used in such contexts, what we might call *metrolingualism*, we need to incorporate the idea of communicative repertoires, as well as a clearer account of linguistic capital and disparity. Lest metrolingualism carry a sense only of urban chic and play, I want to invest the term with a broader understanding of urban multilingualism and social inequality. Language knowledge from this perspective should be defined 'not in terms of abstract system components but as communicative repertoires – conventionalized constellations of semiotic resources for

683

taking action – that are shaped by the particular practices in which individuals engage' (Hall *et al.* 2006: 232). This view insists that language is not so much a system that we draw on in order to communicate but rather a social activity, one of whose outcomes may be communication. To look at language not as a system but as a practice (Pennycook 2010) allows for a view that language knowledge is 'grounded in and emergent from language use in concrete social activity for specific purposes that are tied to specific communities of practice' (Hall *et al.* 2006: 235). Metrolingualism thus locates English use within grounded local practice.

Canagarajah (2007) makes a related point in his discussion of lingua franca English (LFE). This distinction between English as a lingua franca and lingua franca English is an important one, since the former tends towards an understanding of a pre-given language that is then used by different speakers, while the latter suggests that LFE emerges from its contexts of use. According to Canagarajah, 'LFE does not exist as a system out there. It is constantly brought into being in each context of communication' (2007: 91). From this point of view, 'there is no meaning for form, grammar or language ability outside the realm of practice. LFE is not a product located in the mind of the speaker; it is a social process constantly reconstructed in sensitivity to environmental factors' (2007: 94). This is consistent with the argument I have been making for the need to escape the predefinition of a language user by geographical location or variety and instead to deal with the contextual use of language. Put another way, if we adopt a translingual model of language (Pennycook 2007a, 2008) to look at English use, the relationship to be understood is among interlingual resources (what language resources people draw on), colingual relations (who says what to whom where) and ideolingual implications (what gets taken from what language use with what investments, ideologies, discourses and beliefs).

Translingua franca English

While there is clearly something to be gained from trying to map the future of English along the lines of Graddol (2006), it is evident that we also need to rethink language in relation to changing global relations. This is no longer therefore about whether count nouns get pluralized, local language terminology enters English, tag questions become fixed, verb tense and aspect are realized differently or different English users share different pragmatic and cognitive orientations. This is no longer an argument about whether English as a lingua franca implies a static or monolithic concept of English, or about the relative size of varieties of English and English as a lingua franca (is Indian English a variety or a lingua franca?). In looking for ways forward here, we might ask not so much whether we can map out a future of English in relation to global political and economic changes but how we can develop a 'linguistics that treats human agency, contextuality, diversity, indeterminacy, and multimodality as the norm' (Canagarajah 2007: 98). This approach to language no longer treats difference as epiphenomenal variegation, with language users, culture and history peripheral to the similarity at the heart of English; it overcomes 'the inability of linguists to give primacy to language speakers and to the history of a language that remains a fundamental limitation to this day' (Nakata 2007: 39).

I have therefore suggested that any understanding of the future of English needs to move beyond projections – one, many or none – based on twentieth-century linguistic analyses. Instead, we need an understanding of language that seeks neither national nor international framings of English but instead incorporates the local, agency and context in their complex interactions. The crucial question is not one of pluralization – English or Englishes – but rather what language ideologies underlie the visions of plurality. To argue for a monolithic version of English is clearly both an empirical and a political absurdity, but we need to choose carefully between the available models of pluricentric Englishes, avoiding the pitfall of states-centric pluralities that reproduce the very linguistics they need to escape in order to deal with globalized linguascapes. This can help us avoid the national circles and boxes that have so constrained World Englishes and indeed linguistics more generally. In pedagogical terms, this means treating English less as a discrete object – even with its variations – that can be taught only in its own presence, and rather to deal with English as multilingual, as a language always in translation, as a language always under negotiation (Pennycook 2008).

Instead, we can start with an understanding of translingua franca English, which is taken to include *all* uses of English. That is to say TFE is not limited here to expanding circle use or so-called NNS–NNS interactions, but rather is a term to acknowledge the interconnectedness of all English use. In this field, English users all over the world draw on various resources in English. And in this sense, 'in its emerging role as a world language, English has no native speakers' (Rajagopalan 2004: 112). We then need to think not so much in terms of using a language in context (with a pre-given notion of language being deployed in the under-theorized notion of context) but rather as a local practice (Pennycook 2010). Language speakers come with language histories, and means of interpretation – the ideolinguistic dimension where English is one of many languages, a code useful for certain activities, a language connected to certain desires and ideologies. As Canagarajah (2007) reminds us, lingua franca English does not exist outside the realm of practice; it is not a product, but a social process that is constantly being remade from the semiotic resources available to speakers, who are always embedded in localities, and who are always interacting with other speakers.

Suggestions for further reading

Graddol, D. (2006) *English Next: Why Global English May Mean the End of 'English as a Foreign Language'*, London: British Council.
Phillipson, R. (2009) *Linguistic Imperialism Continued*, London: Routledge.
Seargeant, P. (2009) *The Idea of English in Japan: Ideology and the Evolution of a Global Language*, Clevedon: Multilingual Matters.
Tan, P. and Rubdy, R. (eds) (2008) *Language as Commodity: Global Structures, Local Marketplaces*, New York: Continuum.

References

Alim, S., Ibrahim, A. and Pennycook, A. (eds) (2009) *Global Linguistic Flows: Hip Hop Cultures, Youth Identities, and the Politics of Language*, New York: Routledge.
Blommaert, J. (ed.) (1999) *Language Ideological Debates*, Berlin: Mouton.
Bosire, M. (2006) 'Hybrid languages: the case of Sheng', in O.F. Arasanyin, and M.A. Pemberton (eds) *Selected Proceedings of the 36th Annual Conference on African Linguistics*, Somerville, MA: Cascadilla Proceedings Project.
Bruthiaux, P. (2002) 'Hold your courses: language education, language choice, and economic development', *TESOL Quarterly*, 36 (3): 275–96.

——(2003) 'Squaring the circles: issues in modeling English worldwide', *International Journal of Applied Linguistics*, 13 (2): 159–77.

Canagarajah, S. (2007) 'The ecology of global English', *International Multilingual Research Journal*, 1 (2): 89–100.

Graddol, D. (2006) *English Next: Why Global English May Mean the End of 'English as a Foreign Language'*, London: British Council.

Grin, F. (2005) *L'Enseignement des langues étrangères comme politique publique* [*Teaching Foreign Languages as Public Policy*], Paris: Haut Conseil de l'évaluation de l'école.

Hall, J.K., Cheng, A. and Carlson, M. (2006) 'Reconceptualizing multicompetence as a theory of language knowledge', *Applied Linguistics*, 27 (2): 220–40.

Hardt, M. and Negri, A. (2000) *Empire*, Cambridge, MA: Harvard University Press.

——(2005) *Multitude*, London: Penguin.

Higgins, C. (2009) *English as a Local Language: Post-colonial Identities and Multilingual Practices*, Clevedon: Multilingual Matters

Jacquemet, M. (2005) 'Transidiomatic practices, language and power in the age of globalization', *Language and Communication*, 25: 257–77.

Kroskrity, P. (ed.) (2000) *Regimes of Language: Ideologies, Politics and Identities*, Santa Fe, NM: School of American Research Press.

Liddicoat, A. and Baldauf, R. (2008) 'Language planning in local contexts: agents, contexts and interactions', in A. Liddicoat and R. Baldauf (eds) *Language Planning and Policy: Language Planning in Local Contexts*, Clevedon: Multilingual Matters.

Maher, J. (2005) 'Metroethnicity, language, and the principle of cool', *International Journal of the Sociology of Language*, 175/176: 83–102

Makoni, S. and Pennycook, A. (eds) (2007) *Disinventing and Reconstituting Languages*, Clevedon: Multilingual Matters.

McCallen, B. (1989) *English: A World Commodity. The International Market for Training in English as a Foreign Language*, London: The Economist Intelligence Unit.

Nakata, M. (2007) *Disciplining the Savages: Savaging the Disciplines*, Canberra: Aboriginal Studies Press.

Pennycook, A. (1994) *The Cultural Politics of English as International Language*, London: Longman.

——(2007a) *Global Englishes and Transcultural Flows*, London: Routledge.

——(2007b) 'The myth of English as an international language', in S. Makoni and A. Pennycook (eds) *Disinventing and Reconstituting Languages*, Clevedon: Multilingual Matters, pp. 90–115.

——(2008) 'English as a language always in translation', *European Journal of English Studies*, 12 (1): 33–47.

——(2010) *Language as a Local Practice*, London: Routledge.

Phillipson, R. (2003) *English Only Europe? Challenging Language Policy*, London: Routledge.

——(2008) 'The linguistic imperialism of neoliberal empire', *Critical Inquiry in Language Studies*, 5 (1): 1–43.

Pieterse, J. (2004) *Globalization or Empire*, New York: Routledge.

Piller, I. and Takahashi, K. (2006) 'A passion for English: desire and the language market', in A. Pavlenko (ed.) *Bilingual Minds: Emotional Experience, Expression and Representation*, Clevedon: Multilingual Matters, pp. 59–83.

Radhakrishnan, R. (2007) 'Globality is not worldliness', in R Radhakrishnan, K. Nayak, R. Shashidhar, P. Ravishankar Rao and D.R. Shashidhara (eds) *Theory as Variation*, New Delhi: Pencraft International, pp. 313–28.

Rajagopalan, K. (2004) 'The concept of "World English" and its implications for ELT', *ELT Journal*, 58 (2): 111–17.

Ramanathan, V. (2005) *The English–Vernacular Divide: Postcolonial Language Politics and Practice*, Clevedon: Multilingual Matters.

Schneider, E. (2007) *Postcolonial English: Varieties around the World*, Cambridge: Cambridge University Press.

Seargeant, P. (2009) *The Idea of English in Japan: Ideology and the Evolution of a Global Language*, Clevedon: Multilingual Matters.

Tan, P. and Rubdy, R. (2008) *Language as Commodity: Global Structures, Local Marketplaces*, New York: Continuum.

Tollefson, J. (2000) 'Policy and ideology in the spread of English', in J.K. Hall and W. Eggington (eds) *The Sociopolitics of English Language Teaching*, Clevedon: Multilingual Matters, pp. 7–21.

Index